AFRICA 68-69

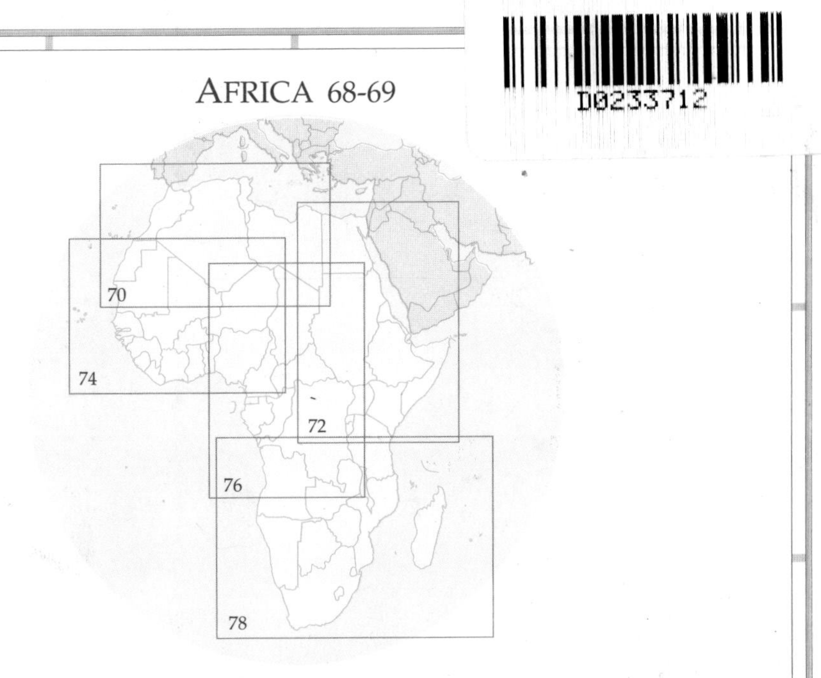

70
74
72
76
78

EUROPE 80-81

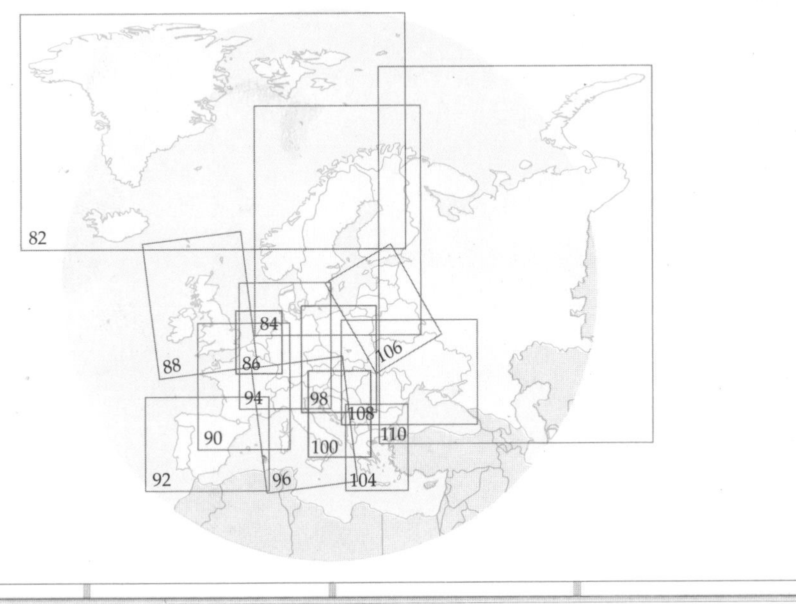

82
84
86
88
90
92
94
96
98
100
104
106
108
110

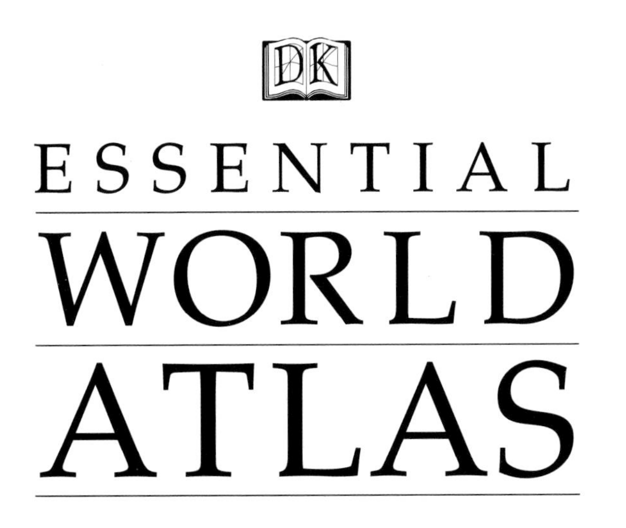

ESSENTIAL
WORLD
ATLAS

ESSENTIAL
WORLD
ATLAS

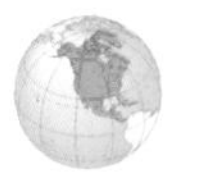

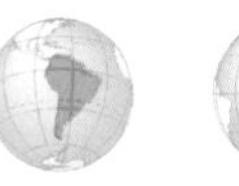

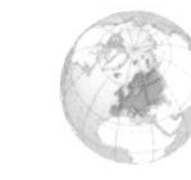

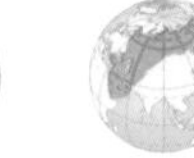

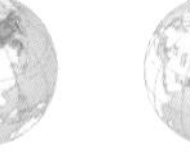

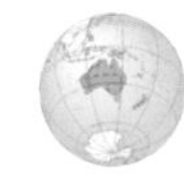

DORLING KINDERSLEY
LONDON • NEW YORK • SYDNEY • MOSCOW

DK

A DORLING KINDERSLEY BOOK

PROJECT CARTOGRAPHY AND DESIGN
Julia Lunn, Julie Turner

CARTOGRAPHERS
James Anderson, Sarah Baker-Ede, Roger Bullen, Bob Croser,
Martin Darlison, Stephen Flanagan, Sally Gable, Dieter Müller,
Simon Mumford, John Plumer, Andrew Thompson,
Scott Wallace, Peter Winfield

DATABASE MANAGER
Simon Lewis

DIGITAL CARTOGRAPHY CREATED IN DK CARTOPIA BY
Tom Coulson, Dan Gardiner, Phil Rowles, Rob Stokes

DESIGN
Katy Wall

INDEX-GAZETTEER
Debra Clapson, Natalie Clarkson, Ruth Duxbury,
Margaret Hynes, Margaret Stevenson

PRODUCTION
Hilary Stephens, David Proffit

CARTOGRAPHIC DIRECTOR
Andrew Heritage

ART DIRECTOR
Chez Picthall

First published in Great Britain as the Concise World Atlas in 1997
Reprinted with revisions 1998
by Dorling Kindersley Limited
9 Henrietta Street, London WC2E 8PS

Copyright © 1997, 1998, 1999 Dorling Kindersley Limited, London
www.dk.com

A CIP catalogue record for this book is available from the British Library

ISBN 0-7513-1118-9

Film output by Colourpath, UK
Printed and bound by Graphicom Srl, Italy

KEY TO MAP SYMBOLS

BOUNDARIES

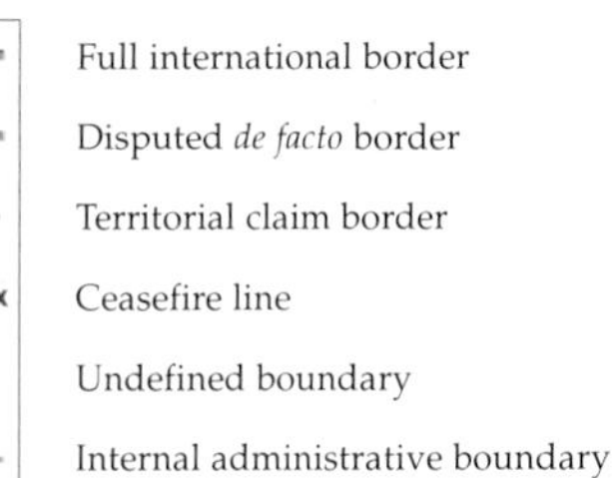

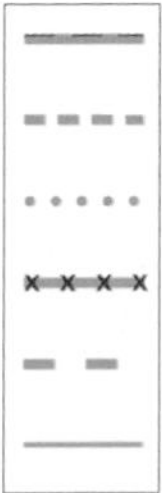

Full international border

Disputed *de facto* border

Territorial claim border

Ceasefire line

Undefined boundary

Internal administrative boundary

COMMUNICATION FEATURES

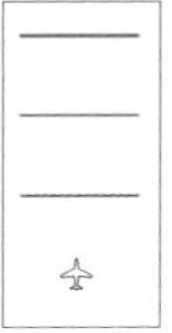

Major road

Minor road

Railway

International airport

DRAINAGE FEATURES

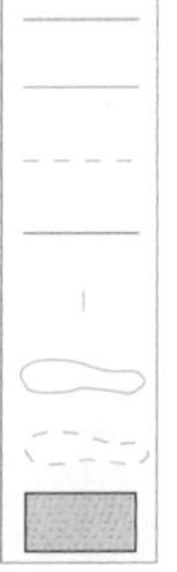

Major perennial river

Minor perennial river

Seasonal river

Canal

Waterfall

Perennial lake

Seasonal lake

Wetland

ICE FEATURES

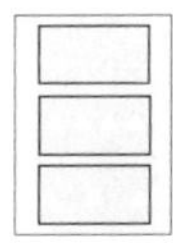

Permanent ice cap/ice shelf

Winter limit of pack ice

Summer limit of pack ice

LANDSCAPE FEATURES

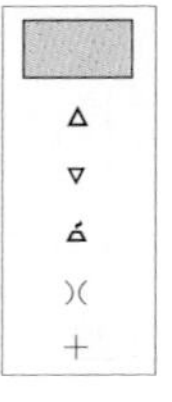

Sandy desert

Spot height

Spot depth

Volcano

Pass/tunnel

Site of interest

POPULATED PLACES

○ Less than 50,000

○ 50,000-100,000

◉ 100,000-500,000

▣ Greater than 500,000

● Capital

⊙ Internal administrative capital

NAMES

TAIWAN Country

JERSEY (to UK) Dependent territory

PARIS Capital

KANSAS Administrative region

Dordogne Cultural region

Sahara Landscape feature

Mont Blanc 4807m Mountain/pass

Blue Nile Drainage feature

Sulu Sea Ocean feature

Chile Rise Underwater feature

INSET MAP SYMBOLS

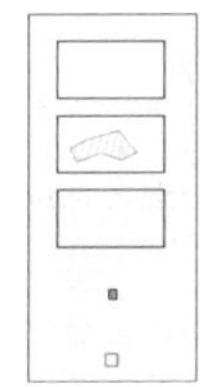

Urban area

City

Park

▪ Place of interest

▫ Suburb/district

CONTENTS

ESSENTIAL WORLD ATLAS

The Political World 8-9
The Physical World 10-11
Time Zones 12-13
Geology & Structure 14-15
World Climate 16-17
Ocean Currents 18-19
Life Zones 20-21
Population 22-23
Languages 24-25
Religion 26-27
The Global Economy 28-29
Global Conflict 30-31

THE WORLD'S REGIONS

NORTH & CENTRAL AMERICA

North & Central America 34-35
Western Canada & Alaska 36-37
Eastern Canada 38-39
USA: The Northeast 40-41
   Bermuda
USA: The Southeast 42-43
USA: Central States 44-45
USA: The West 46-47
   Los Angeles & Hawaii
USA: The Southwest 48-49
Mexico 50-51
Central America 52-53
The Caribbean 54-55
   Jamaica, St Lucia & Barbados

SOUTH AMERICA

South America 56-57
Northern South America 58-59
Western South America 60-61
   Galapagos Islands
Brazil 62-63
Southern South America 64-65
The Atlantic Ocean 66-67

AFRICA

Africa 68-69
Northwest Africa 70-71
Northeast Africa 72-73
West Africa 74-75
Central Africa 76-77
   Sao Tome & Principe
Southern Africa 78-79

EUROPE

Europe 80-81
The North Atlantic 82-83
Scandinavia & Finland 84-85
The Low Countries 86-87
The British Isles 88-89
   London
France, Andorra & Monaco 90-91
   Paris, Andorra & Monaco

continued....

EUROPE *continued*

Spain & Portugal 92-93
 Azores & Gibraltar
Germany & the Alpine States 94-95
 Liechtenstein
Italy 96-97
 San Marino & Vatican City
Central Europe 98-99
The Western Balkans 100-101
 Bosnia & Herzegovina
The Mediterranean 102-103
 Malta & Cyprus
Bulgaria & Greece 104-105
The Baltic States & Belorussia . .106-107
Ukraine, Moldavia & Romania .108-109
European Russia 110-111

NORTH & WEST ASIA

North & West Asia 112-113
Russia & Kazakhstan 114-115
Turkey & the Caucasus 116-117
The Near East 118-119
The Middle East 120-121
 West Bank
Central Asia 122-123

SOUTH & EAST ASIA

South & East Asia 124-125
Western China & Mongolia 126-127

Eastern China & Korea 128-129
 Hong Kong
Japan .130-131
 Tōkyō & Nansei-Shotō
South India & Sri Lanka 132-133
North India, Pakistan &
 Bangladesh 134-135
Mainland Southeast Asia 136-137
Maritime Southeast Asia 138-139
 Singapore
The Indian Ocean 140-141

AUSTRALASIA & OCEANIA

Australasia & Oceania 142-143
The Southwest Pacific 144-145
Western Australia 146-147
Eastern Australia 148-149
 Sydney
New Zealand 150-151
The Pacific Ocean 152-153
Antarctica 154
The Arctic Ocean 155

INDEX – GAZETTEER

Overseas Territories &
 Dependencies 156-159
Glossary of Geographical
 Terms 160-161
Index-Gazetteer of Places &
 Countries 162-256

THE POLITICAL WORLD

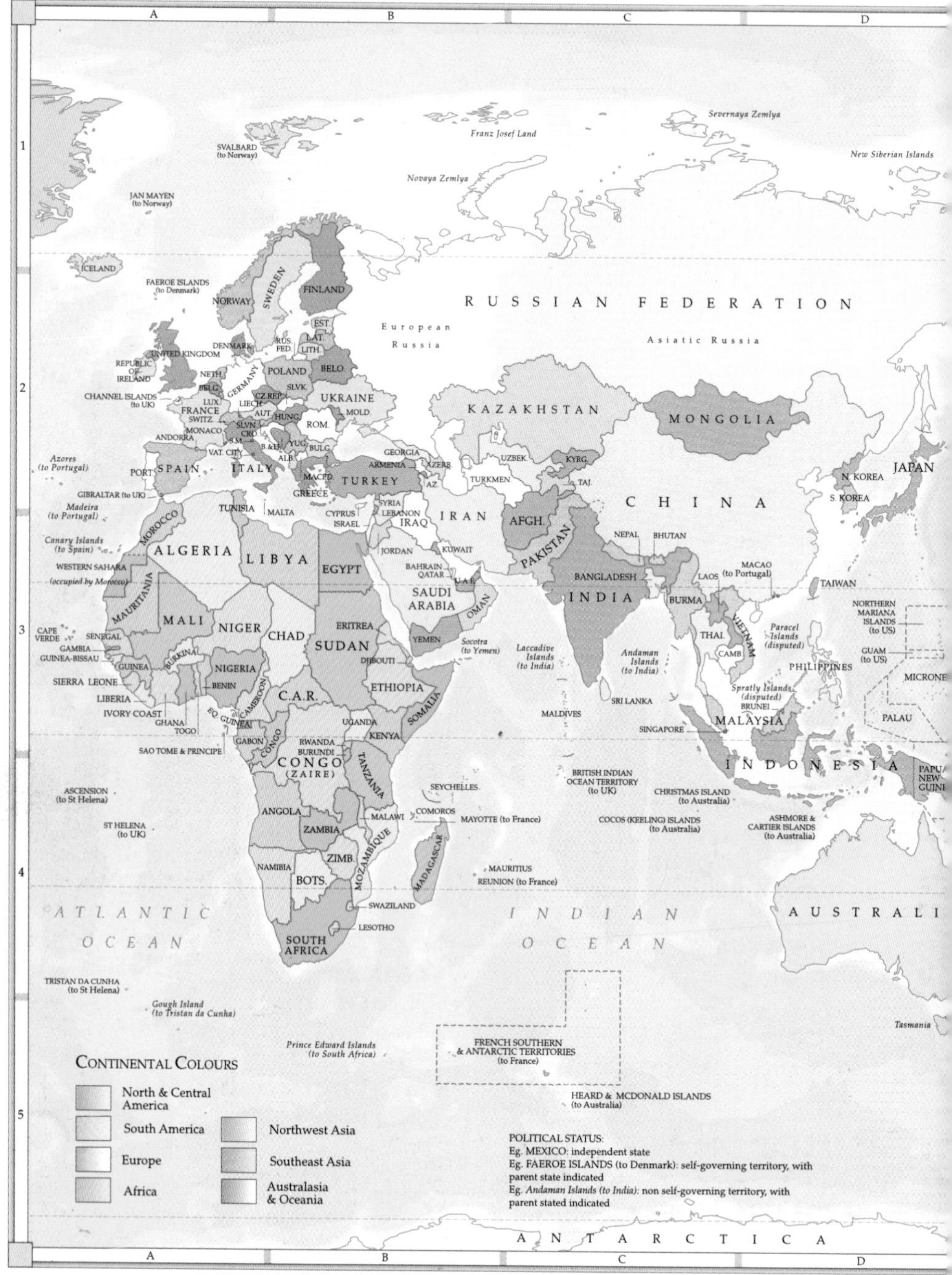

CONTINENTAL COLOURS

North & Central America

South America

Europe

Africa

Northwest Asia

Southeast Asia

Australasia & Oceania

POLITICAL STATUS:
Eg. MEXICO: independent state
Eg. FAEROE ISLANDS (to Denmark): self-governing territory, with parent state indicated
Eg. *Andaman Islands (to India)*: non self-governing territory, with parent stated indicated

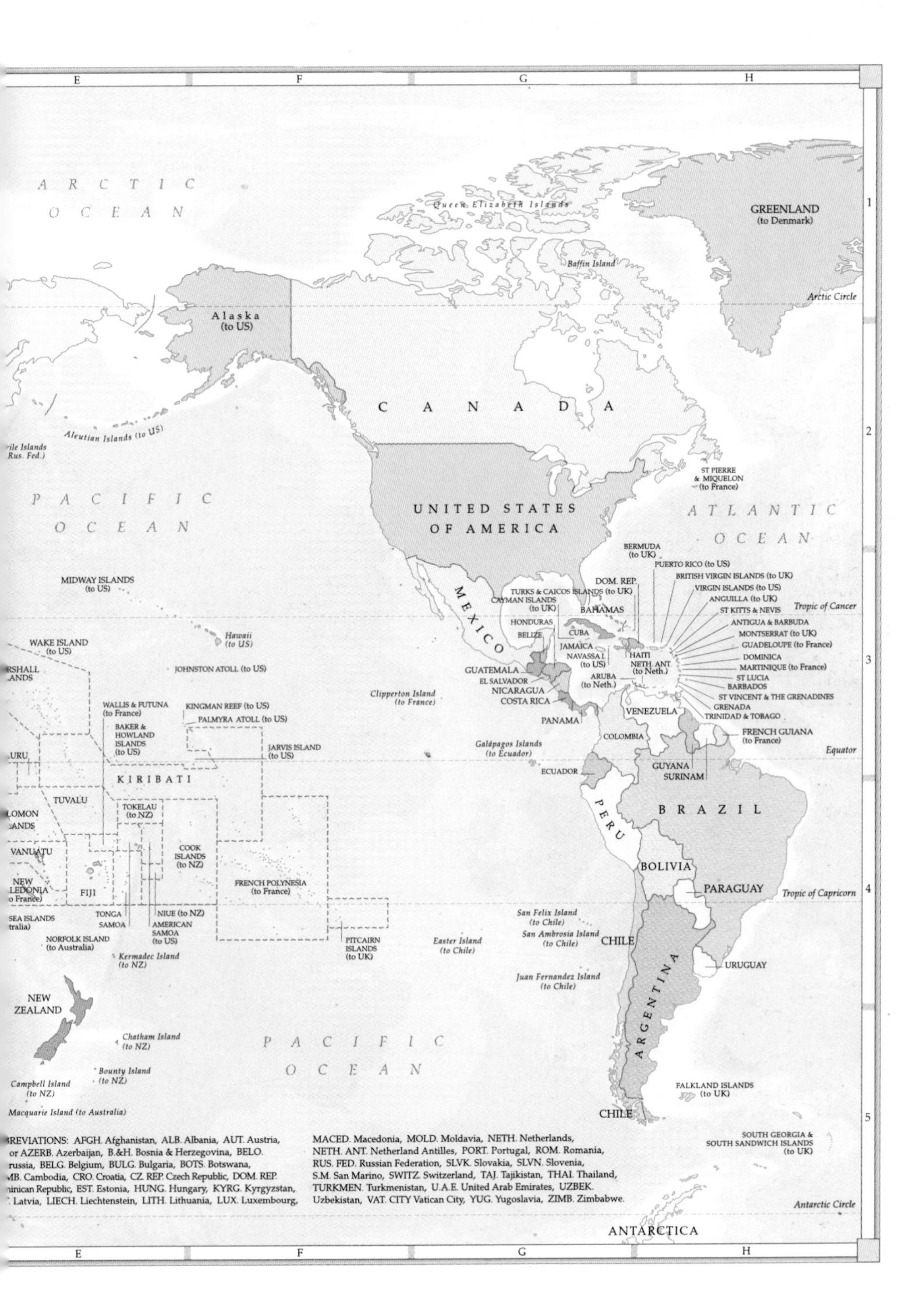
E
F
G
H
1
2
3
4
5
ARCTIC OCEAN
Queen Elizabeth Islands
GREENLAND (to Denmark)
Baffin Island
Arctic Circle
Alaska (to US)
CANADA
Aleutian Islands (to US)
ST PIERRE & MIQUELON (to France)
PACIFIC OCEAN
UNITED STATES OF AMERICA
ATLANTIC OCEAN
BERMUDA (to UK)
PUERTO RICO (to US)
BRITISH VIRGIN ISLANDS (to UK)
VIRGIN ISLANDS (to US)
ANGUILLA (to UK)
ST KITTS & NEVIS
Tropic of Cancer
ANTIGUA & BARBUDA
MONTSERRAT (to UK)
GUADELOUPE (to France)
DOMINICA
MARTINIQUE (to France)
ST LUCIA
BARBADOS
ST VINCENT & THE GRENADINES
GRENADA
TRINIDAD & TOBAGO
DOM. REP.
TURKS & CAICOS ISLANDS (to UK)
CAYMAN ISLANDS (to UK)
BAHAMAS
MEXICO
MIDWAY ISLANDS (to US)
HONDURAS
BELIZE
CUBA
JAMAICA
NAVASSA I. (to US)
HAITI
NETH. ANT. (to Neth.)
ARUBA (to Neth.)
Hawaii (to US)
WAKE ISLAND (to US)
JOHNSTON ATOLL (to US)
GUATEMALA
EL SALVADOR
NICARAGUA
COSTA RICA
PANAMA
Clipperton Island (to France)
VENEZUELA
COLOMBIA
FRENCH GUIANA (to France)
Equator
WALLIS & FUTUNA (to France)
KINGMAN REEF (to US)
PALMYRA ATOLL (to US)
BAKER & HOWLAND ISLANDS (to US)
JARVIS ISLAND (to US)
Galápagos Islands (to Ecuador)
ECUADOR
GUYANA
SURINAM
KIRIBATI
TUVALU
TOKELAU (to NZ)
PERU
BRAZIL
VANUATU
COOK ISLANDS (to NZ)
BOLIVIA
FIJI
FRENCH POLYNESIA (to France)
PARAGUAY
Tropic of Capricorn
TONGA
SAMOA
NIUE (to NZ)
AMERICAN SAMOA (to US)
San Felix Island (to Chile)
San Ambrosia Island (to Chile)
CHILE
NORFOLK ISLAND (to Australia)
PITCAIRN ISLANDS (to UK)
Easter Island (to Chile)
Kermadec Island (to NZ)
URUGUAY
Juan Fernandez Island (to Chile)
ARGENTINA
NEW ZEALAND
Chatham Island (to NZ)
PACIFIC OCEAN
Bounty Island (to NZ)
Campbell Island (to NZ)
FALKLAND ISLANDS (to UK)
Macquarie Island (to Australia)
CHILE
SOUTH GEORGIA & SOUTH SANDWICH ISLANDS (to UK)
Antarctic Circle
ANTARCTICA
BREVIATIONS: AFGH. Afghanistan, ALB. Albania, AUT. Austria,
or AZERB. Azerbaijan, B.&H. Bosnia & Herzegovina, BELO.
russia, BELG. Belgium, BULG. Bulgaria, BOTS. Botswana,
MB. Cambodia, CRO. Croatia, CZ. REP. Czech Republic, DOM. REP.
ninican Republic, EST. Estonia, HUNG. Hungary, KYRG. Kyrgyzstan,
Latvia, LIECH. Liechtenstein, LITH. Lithuania, LUX. Luxembourg,
MACED. Macedonia, MOLD. Moldavia, NETH. Netherlands,
NETH. ANT. Netherland Antilles, PORT. Portugal, ROM. Romania,
RUS. FED. Russian Federation, SLVK. Slovakia, SLVN. Slovenia,
S.M. San Marino, SWITZ. Switzerland, TAJ. Tajikistan, THAI. Thailand,
TURKMEN. Turkmenistan, U.A.E. United Arab Emirates, UZBEK.
Uzbekistan, VAT. CITY Vatican City, YUG. Yugoslavia, ZIMB. Zimbabwe.

THE PHYSICAL WORLD

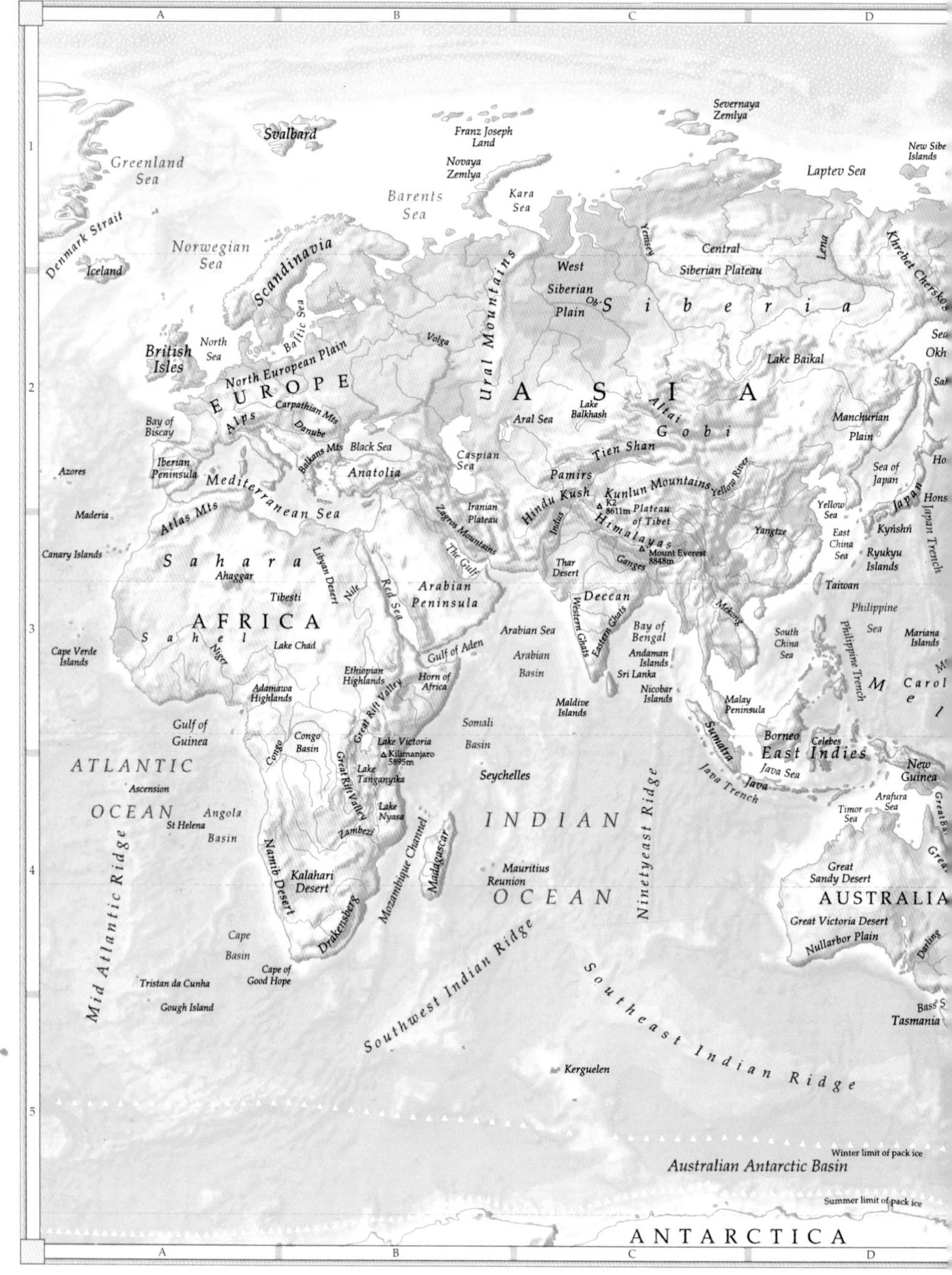

Greenland Sea

Svalbard

Franz Joseph Land

Novaya Zemlya

Severnaya Zemlya

New Sibe Islands

Laptev Sea

Denmark Strait

Iceland

Norwegian Sea

Barents Sea

Kara Sea

Scandinavia

Ural Mountains

West Siberian Plain

Ob

Central Siberian Plateau

Lena

Yenisey

S i b e r i a

Khrebat Cherskoy

Sea Okh

Sa

British Isles

North Sea

North European Plain

Baltic Sea

Volga

EUROPE

Carpathian Mts

Alps

Danube

Balkans Mts

Black Sea

Lake Baikal

A S I A

Manchurian Plain

Altai

Gobi

Bay of Biscay

Azores

Iberian Peninsula

Madeira

Atlas Mts

Mediterranean Sea

Anatolia

Caspian Sea

Aral Sea

Lake Balkhash

Tien Shan

Pamirs

Sea of Japan

Ho

Yellow Sea

East China Sea

Hons

Japan

Japan Trench

Ryukyu Islands

Kyūshū

Canary Islands

S a h a r a

Ahaggar

Libyan Desert

Nile

Zagros Mountains

Iranian Plateau

The Gulf

Hindu Kush

Indus

K2 8611m

Kunlun Mountains

Plateau of Tibet

Himalayas

Mount Everest 8848m

Yellow River

Yangtze

Taiwan

Tibesti

S a h e l

Niger

Lake Chad

Arabian Peninsula

Red Sea

Gulf of Aden

Thar Desert

Ganges

Deccan

Western Ghats

Eastern Ghats

Bay of Bengal

Andaman Islands

Sri Lanka

Mekong

South China Sea

Philippine Sea

Philippine Trench

Mt

Philippine Islands

Mariana Islands

C a r o l

l

Cape Verde Islands

AFRICA

Adamawa Highlands

Ethiopian Highlands

Horn of Africa

Arabian Sea

Arabian Basin

Nicobar Islands

Malay Peninsula

Java Trench

Borneo

Celebes

East Indies

Java

M

Gulf of Guinea

Congo Basin

Congo

Great Rift Valley

Lake Victoria

Kilimanjaro 5895m

Lake Tanganyika

Lake Nyasa

Somali Basin

Maldive Islands

Seychelles

Celebes Sea

New Guinea

Great

ATLANTIC

OCEAN

Ascension

Angola Basin

St Helena

Namib Desert

Zambezi

Mozambique Channel

Madagascar

Kalahari Desert

Drakensberg

Mauritius Reunion

Ninetyeast Ridge

I N D I A N

O C E A N

Sumatra

Java Sea

Timor Sea

Arafura Sea

Great Sandy Desert

Great Victoria Desert

Nullarbor Plain

AUSTRALIA

Darling

Mid Atlantic Ridge

Cape Basin

Tristan da Cunha

Gough Island

Cape of Good Hope

Southwest Indian Ridge

Kerguelen

Southeast Indian Ridge

Bass S

Tasmania

Winter limit of pack ice

Australian Antarctic Basin

Summer limit of pack ice

ANTARCTICA

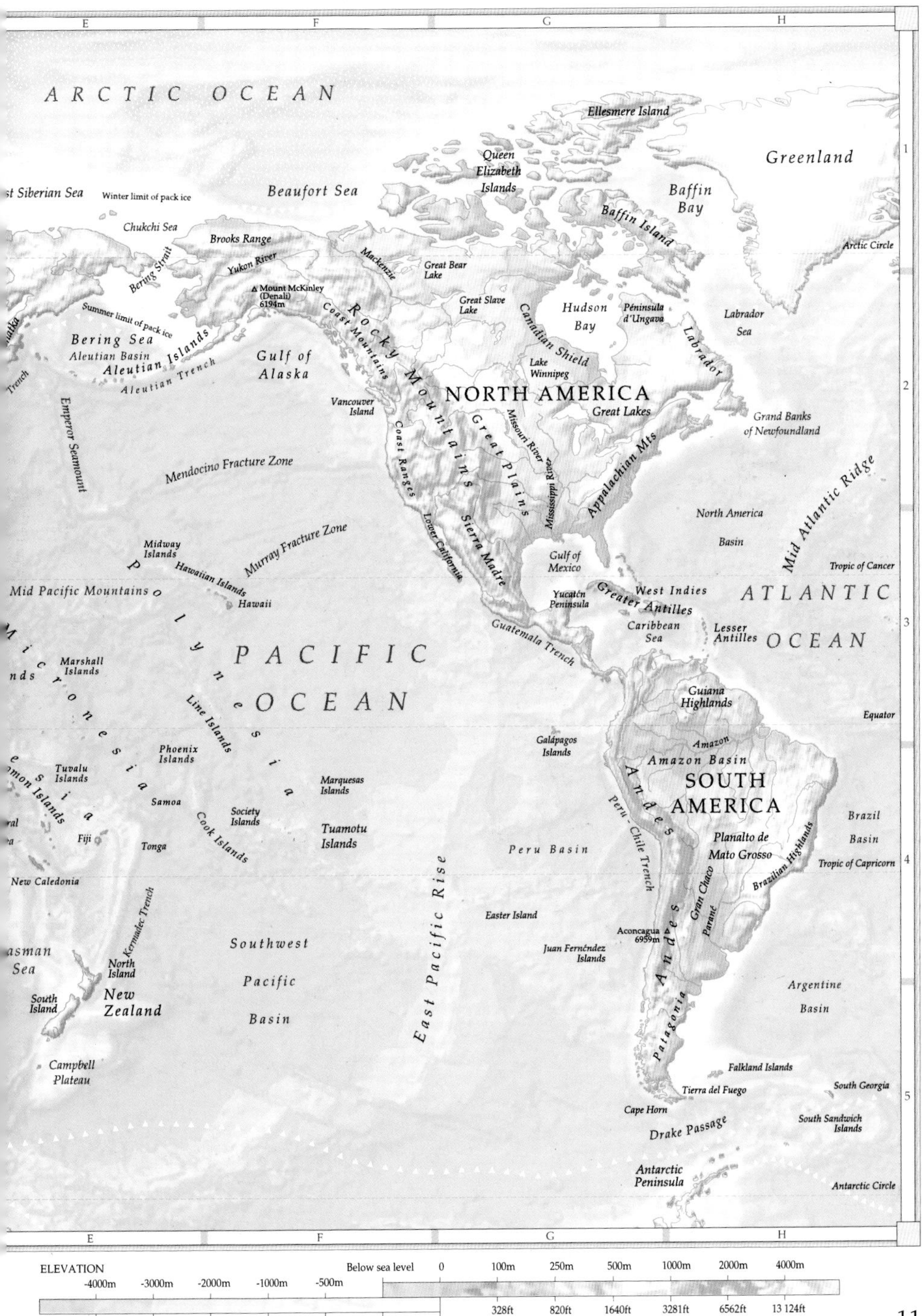
ARCTIC OCEAN
Ellesmere Island
Queen Elizabeth Islands
Greenland
st Siberian Sea
Winter limit of pack ice
Beaufort Sea
Baffin Bay
Baffin Island
Chukchi Sea
Brooks Range
Arctic Circle
Bering Strait
Yukon River
Mackenzie
Great Bear Lake
Mount McKinley (Denali) 6194m
Great Slave Lake
Hudson Bay
Péninsula d'Ungava
Labrador Sea
Summer limit of pack ice
Coast Mountains
Rocky Mountains
Canadian Shield
Labrador
Bering Sea
Aleutian Basin
Aleutian Islands
Aleutian Trench
Gulf of Alaska
Lake Winnipeg
Trench
NORTH AMERICA
Vancouver Island
Great Lakes
Grand Banks of Newfoundland
Emperor Seamount
Missouri River
Great Plains
Coast Ranges
Appalachian Mts
Mendocino Fracture Zone
Mississippi River
Mid Atlantic Ridge
North America Basin
Lower California
Sierra Madre
Murray Fracture Zone
Midway Islands
Gulf of Mexico
Hawaiian Islands
Tropic of Cancer
Mid Pacific Mountains
Yucatán Peninsula
Greater Antilles
West Indies
ATLANTIC OCEAN
Hawaii
Polynesia
Caribbean Sea
Lesser Antilles
Guatemala Trench
Micronesia
PACIFIC OCEAN
Marshall Islands
Guiana Highlands
Line Islands
Equator
Galápagos Islands
Amazon
Amazon Basin
Phoenix Islands
Tuvalu Islands
Solomon Islands
Marquesas Islands
SOUTH AMERICA
Andes
Samoa
Society Islands
Peru-Chile Trench
Brazil Basin
Fiji
Tonga
Cook Islands
Tuamotu Islands
Peru Basin
Planalto de Mato Grosso
Brazilian Highlands
Tropic of Capricorn
New Caledonia
East Pacific Rise
Gran Chaco
Kermadec Trench
Easter Island
Paraná
Aconcagua 6959m
Southwest Pacific Basin
Juan Fernández Islands
Tasman Sea
North Island
Argentine Basin
South Island
New Zealand
Patagonia
Campbell Plateau
Falkland Islands
Tierra del Fuego
South Georgia
Cape Horn
South Sandwich Islands
Drake Passage
Antarctic Peninsula
Antarctic Circle
ELEVATION
Below sea level
-4000m -3000m -2000m -1000m -500m
0 100m 250m 500m 1000m 2000m 4000m
328ft 820ft 1640ft 3281ft 6562ft 13 124ft
-13 124ft -9843ft -6562ft -3281ft -1640ft -820ft/-250m 0

THE WORLD TODAY

TIME ZONES

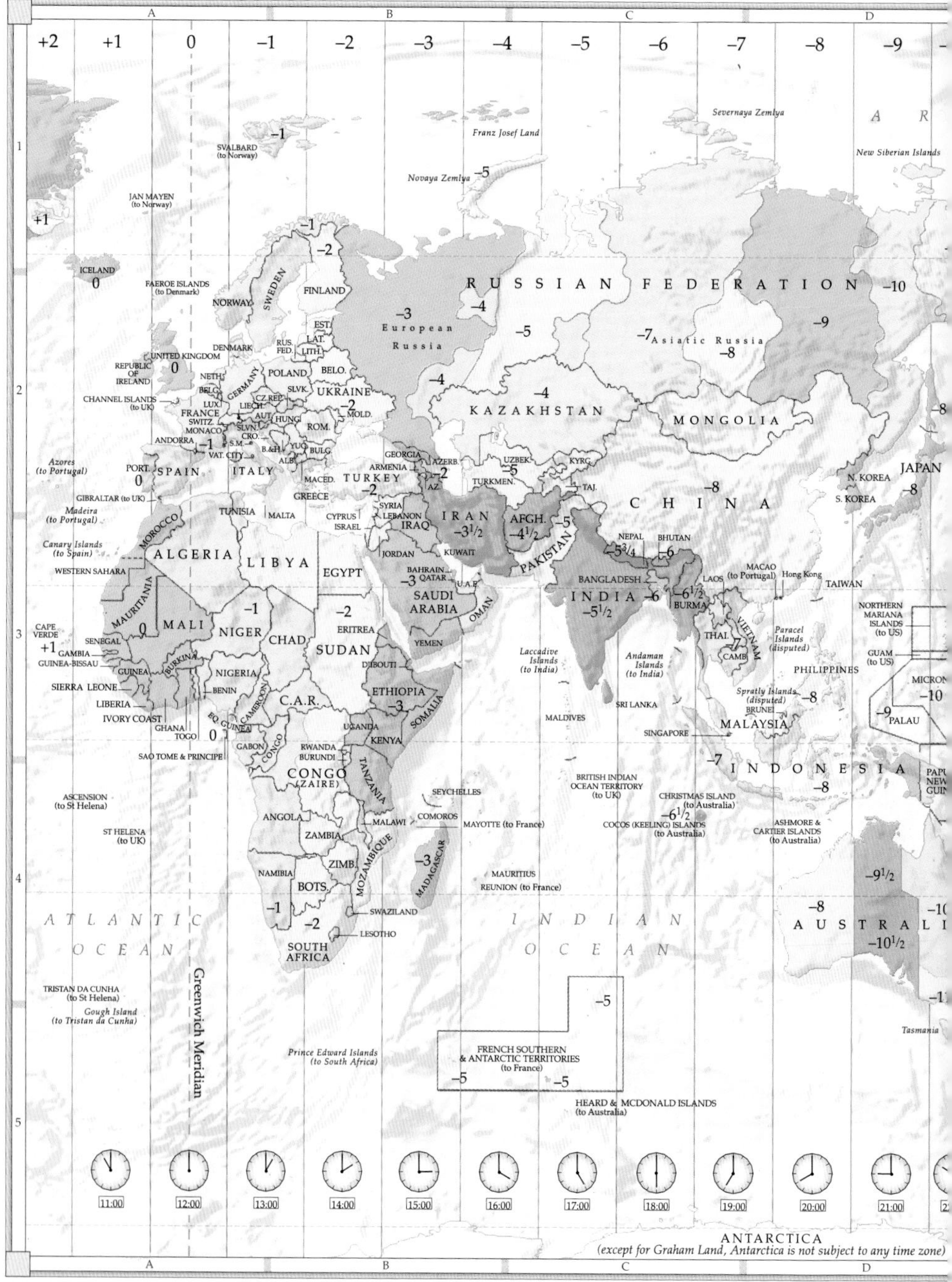

Numbers on the map indicate the number of hours which must be added or subtracted, as appropriate, in that time zone to reach GMT (Greenwich Mean Time).

12

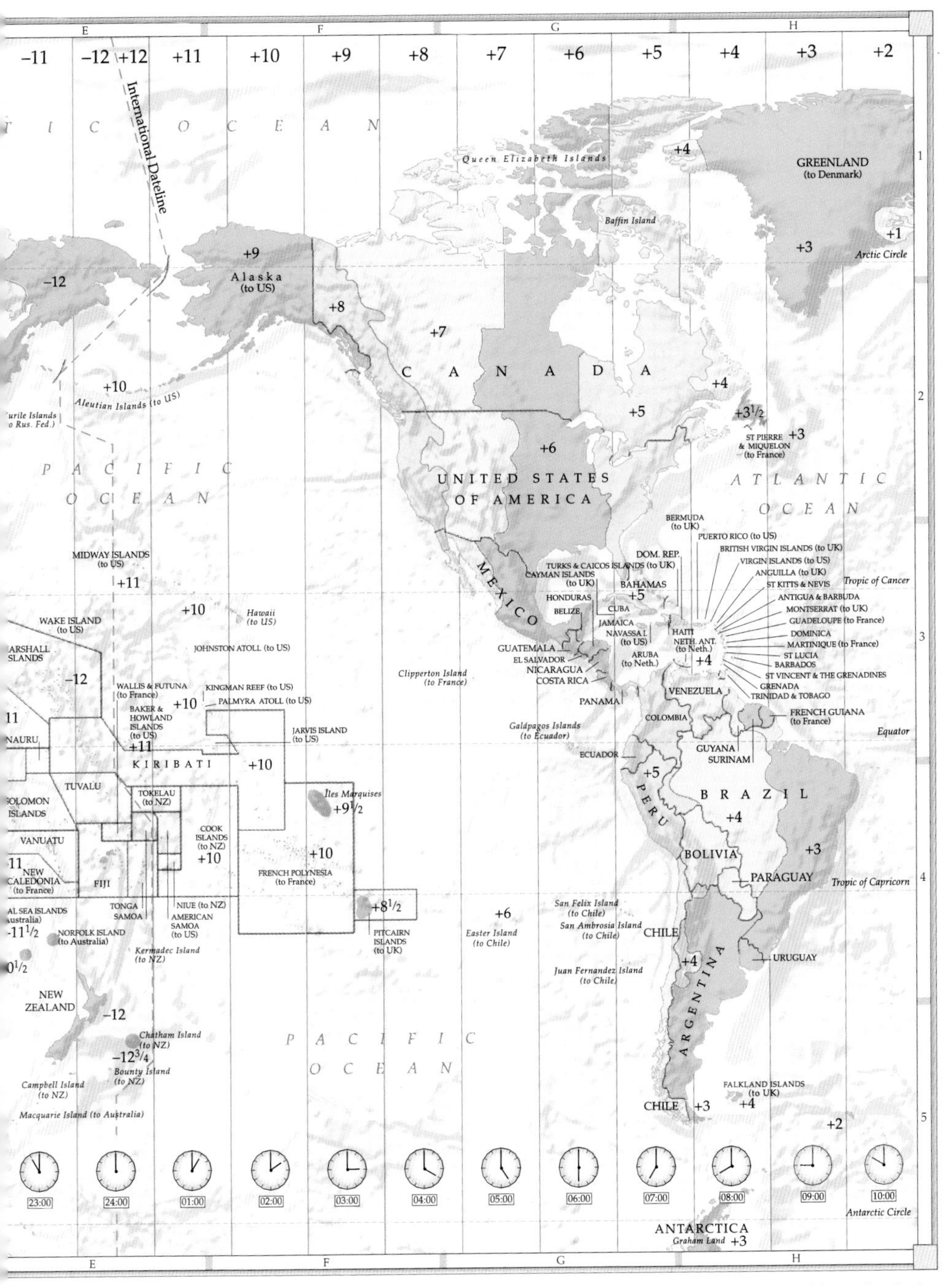

The clocks and 24 hour times given at the bottom of the map show the time in each time zone when it is 12:00 hours, or noon, at GMT.

GEOLOGY & STRUCTURE

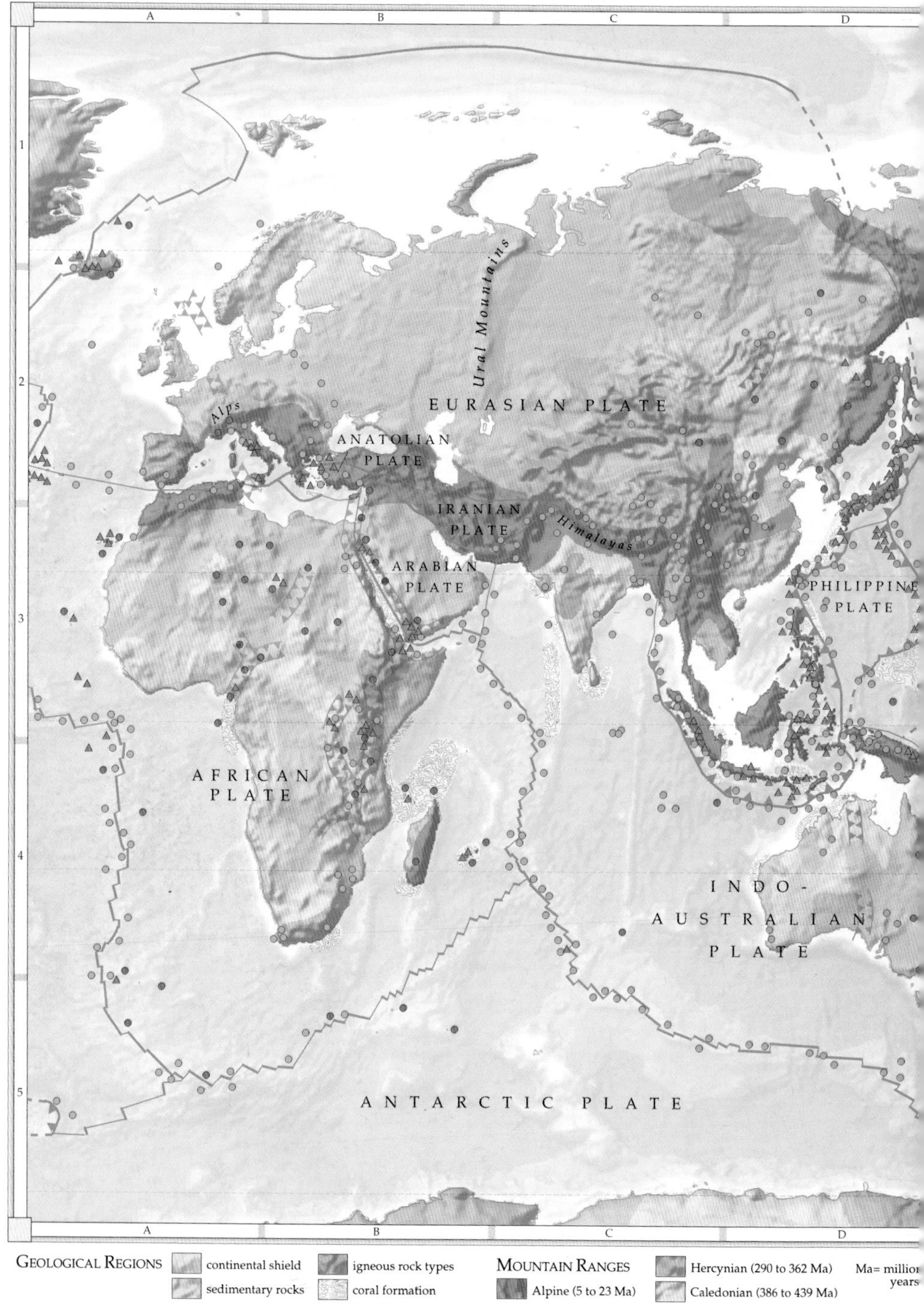

Ural Mountains

Alps

EURASIAN PLATE

ANATOLIAN
PLATE

IRANIAN
PLATE

Himalayas

ARABIAN
PLATE

PHILIPPINE
PLATE

AFRICAN
PLATE

INDO-
AUSTRALIAN
PLATE

ANTARCTIC PLATE

GEOLOGICAL REGIONS			MOUNTAIN RANGES		Ma= million years
	continental shield	igneous rock types		Hercynian (290 to 362 Ma)	
	sedimentary rocks	coral formation	Alpine (5 to 23 Ma)	Caledonian (386 to 439 Ma)	

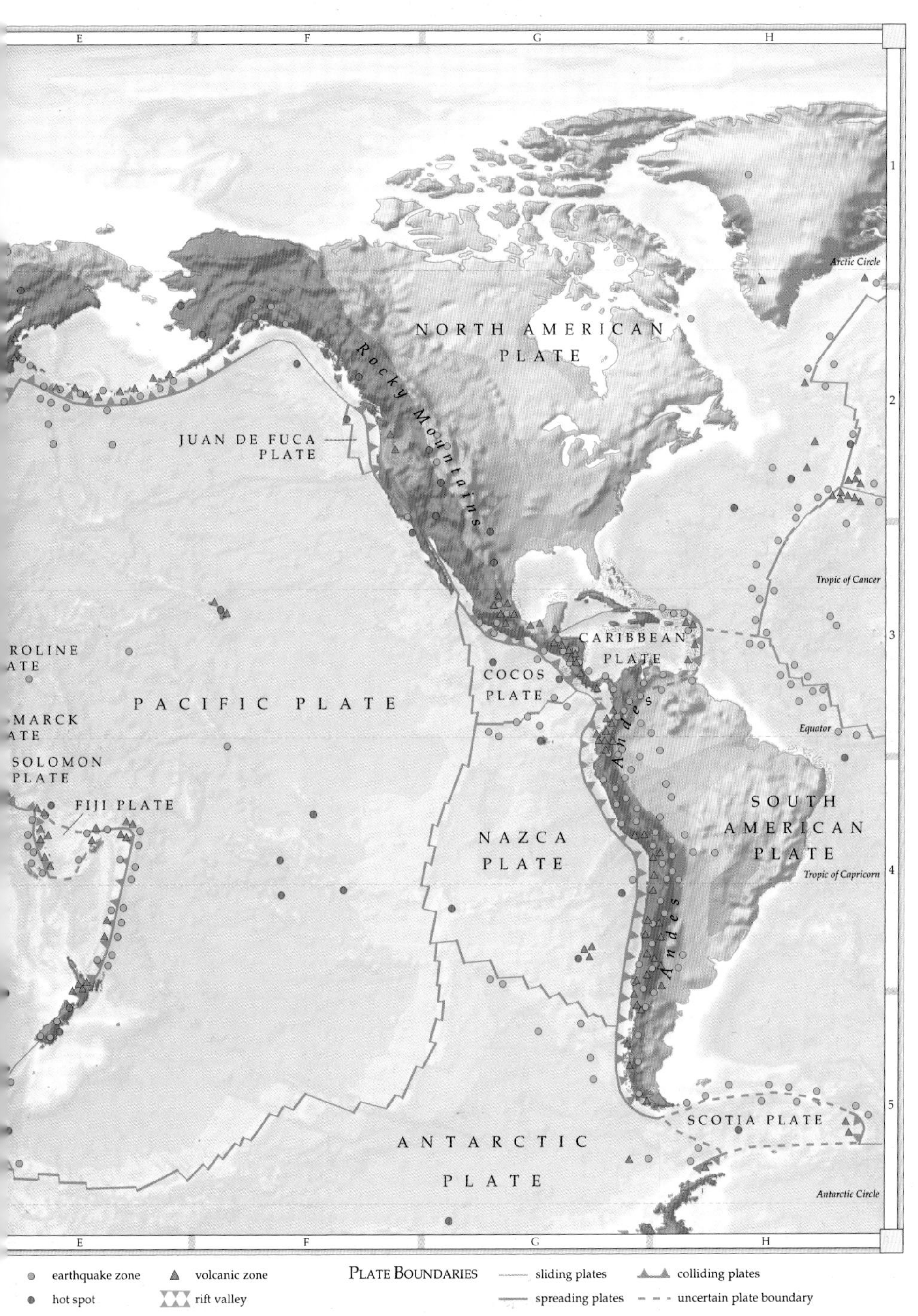

NORTH AMERICAN
PLATE

Rocky Mountains

JUAN DE FUCA
PLATE

Arctic Circle

Tropic of Cancer

CARIBBEAN
PLATE

COCOS
PLATE

ROLINE
ATE

MARCK
ATE

SOLOMON
PLATE

FIJI PLATE

PACIFIC PLATE

Andes

Equator

SOUTH
AMERICAN
PLATE

Tropic of Capricorn

NAZCA
PLATE

Andes

SCOTIA PLATE

ANTARCTIC

PLATE

Antarctic Circle

● earthquake zone	▲ volcanic zone	PLATE BOUNDARIES	—— sliding plates	▲▲ colliding plates
● hot spot	▲▲▲ rift valley		—— spreading plates	- - - uncertain plate boundary

15

WORLD CLIMATE

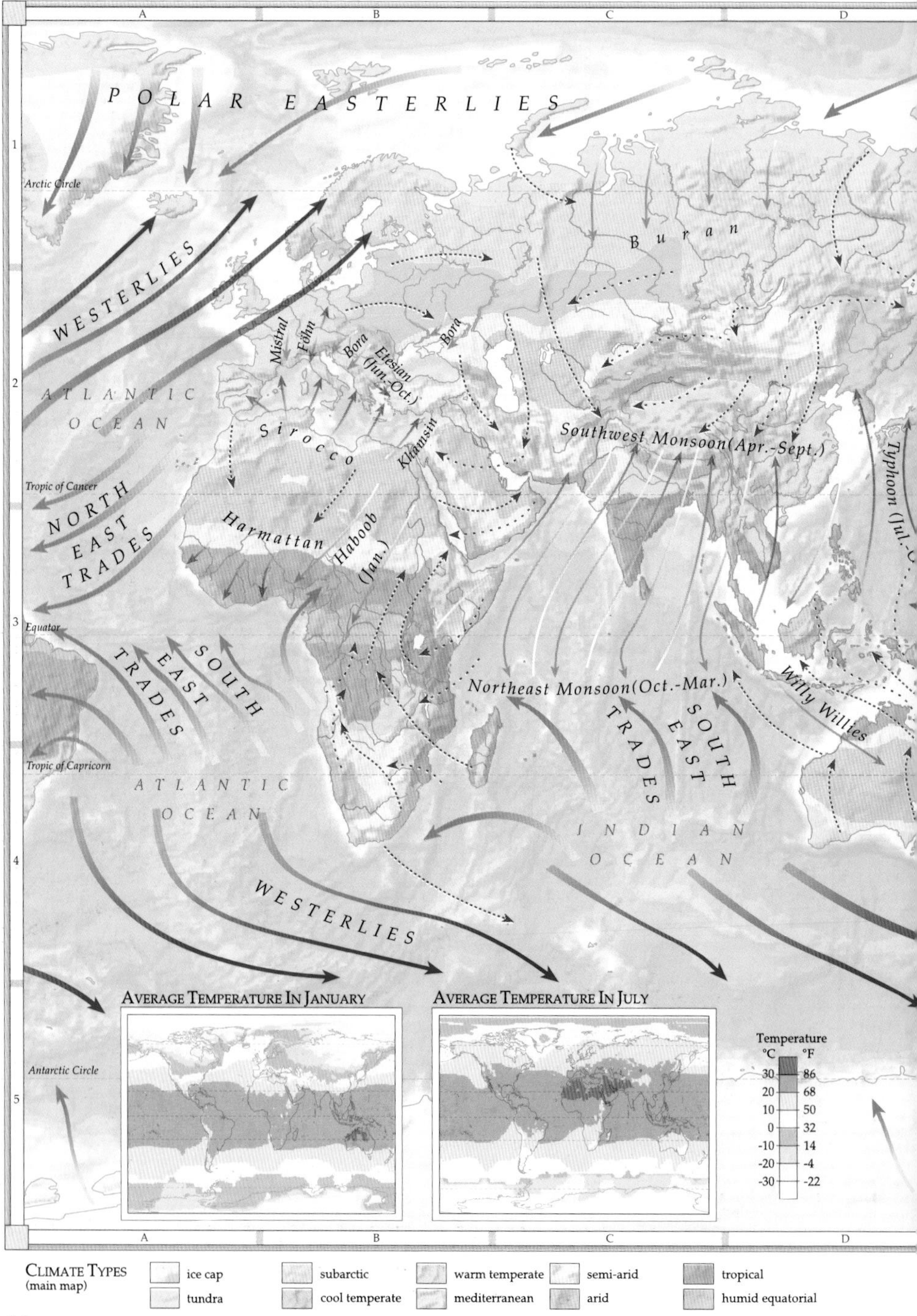

POLAR EASTERLIES

WESTERLIES

ATLANTIC OCEAN

Arctic Circle

Buran

Mistral

Föhn

Bora

Etesian (Jun.-Oct.)

Bora

Southwest Monsoon(Apr.-Sept.)

Sirocco

Tropic of Cancer

NORTH EAST TRADES

Harmattan

Haboob (Jan.)

Khamsin

Typhoon (Jul.-

Equator

SOUTH EAST TRADES

Northeast Monsoon(Oct.-Mar.)

Willy Willies

SOUTH EAST TRADES

Tropic of Capricorn

ATLANTIC OCEAN

INDIAN OCEAN

WESTERLIES

Antarctic Circle

AVERAGE TEMPERATURE IN JANUARY

AVERAGE TEMPERATURE IN JULY

Temperature
°C °F

°C	°F
30	86
20	68
10	50
0	32
-10	14
-20	-4
-30	-22

CLIMATE TYPES (main map)

ice cap

tundra

subarctic

cool temperate

warm temperate

mediterranean

semi-arid

arid

tropical

humid equatorial

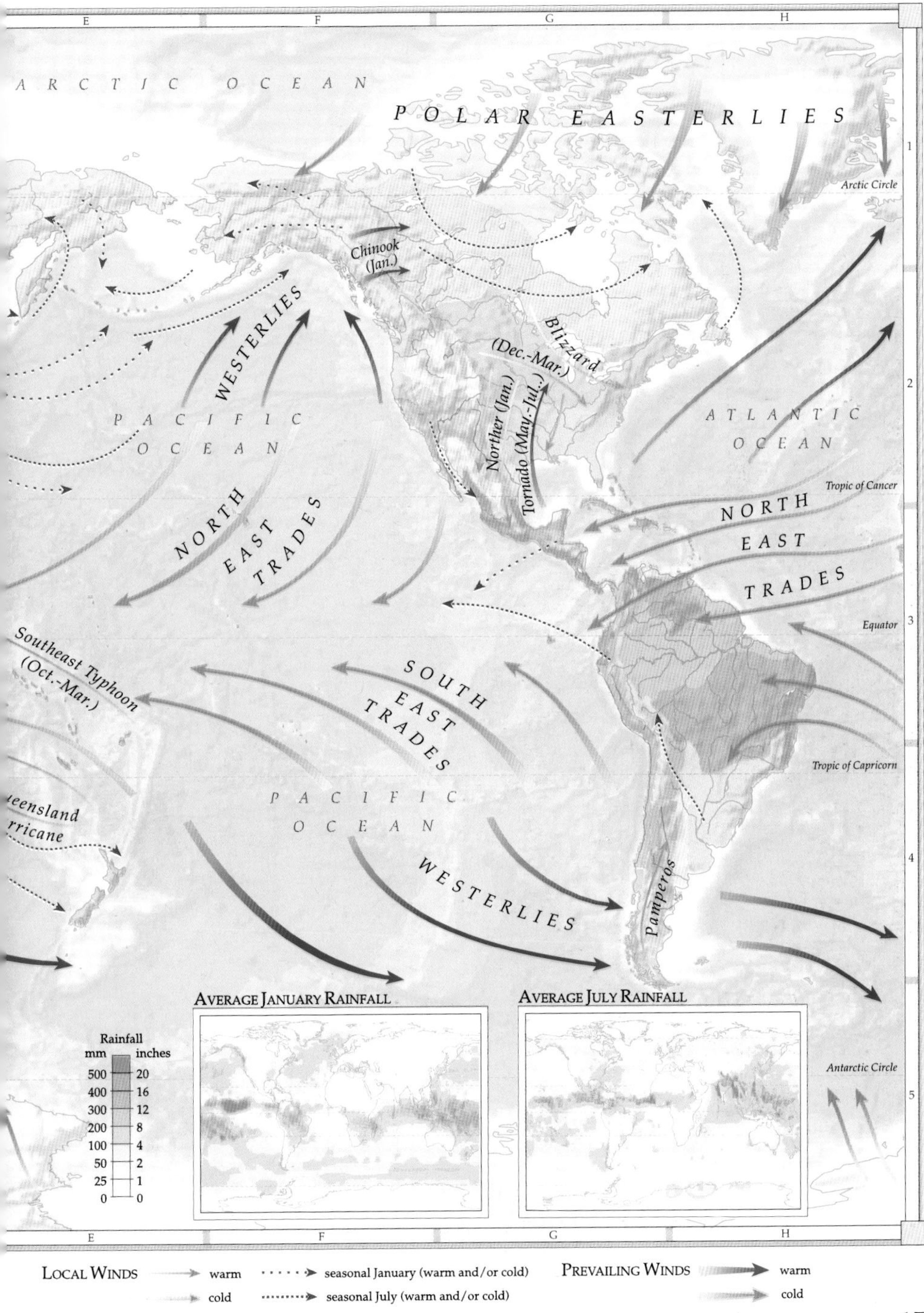

ARCTIC OCEAN

POLAR EASTERLIES

1

Arctic Circle

Chinook
(Jan.)

Blizzard
(Dec.-Mar.)

WESTERLIES

PACIFIC
OCEAN

ATLANTIC
OCEAN

2

Norther (Jan.)

Tornado (May.-Jul.)

NORTH

EAST

NORTH

EAST

TRADES

TRADES

Tropic of Cancer

Southeast Typhoon
(Oct.-Mar.)

SOUTH
EAST
TRADES

Equator

3

Tropic of Capricorn

eensland
rricane

PACIFIC
OCEAN

WESTERLIES

Pamperos

4

AVERAGE JANUARY RAINFALL

AVERAGE JULY RAINFALL

Rainfall
mm | inches
500 — 20
400 — 16
300 — 12
200 — 8
100 — 4
50 — 2
25 — 1
0 — 0

Antarctic Circle

5

LOCAL WINDS	→ warm	· · · ·▸ seasonal January (warm and/or cold)	PREVAILING WINDS	⟹ warm
	→ cold	· · · ·▸ seasonal July (warm and/or cold)		⟹ cold

OCEAN CURRENTS

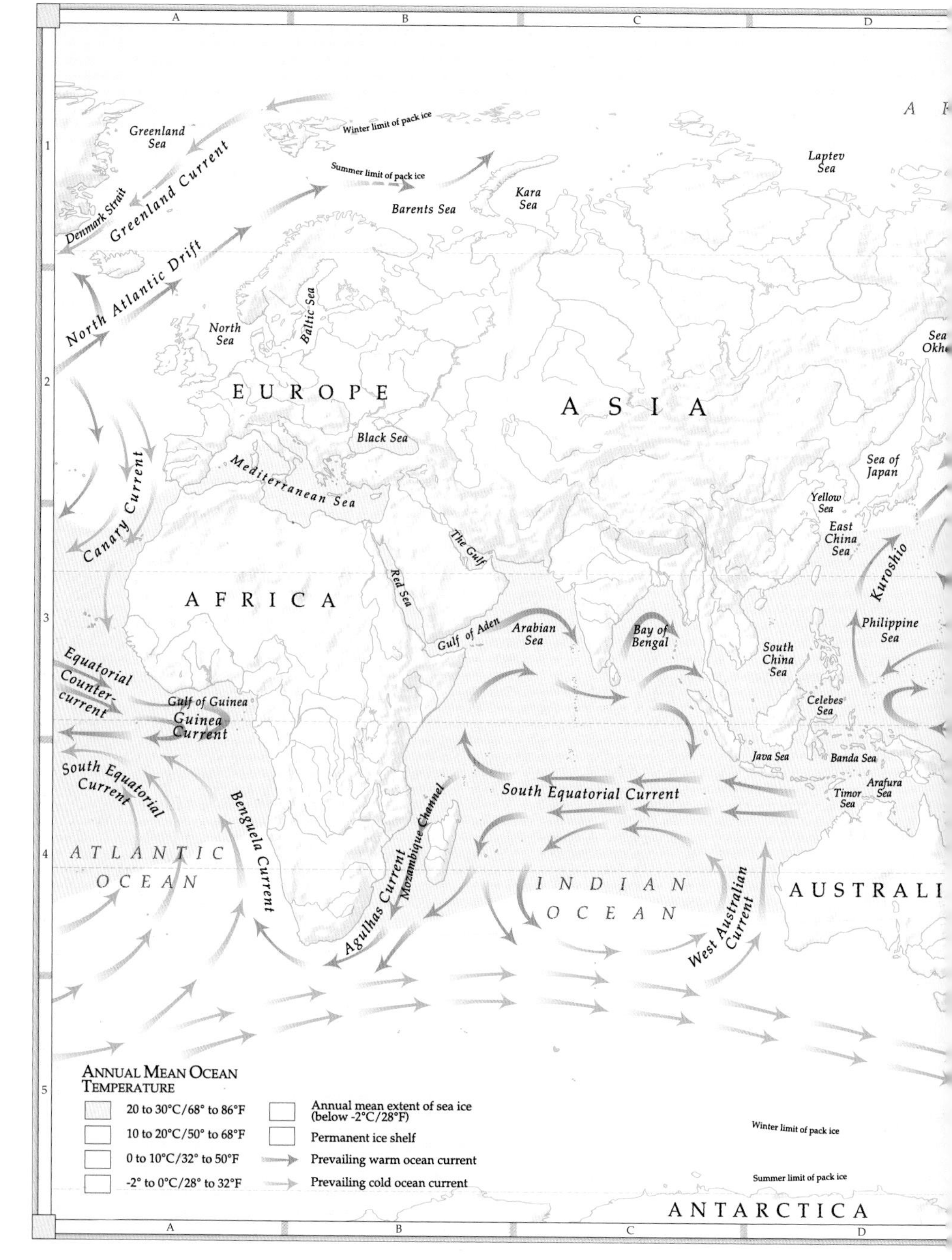

Greenland
Sea

Denmark Strait

Greenland Current

North Atlantic Drift

Winter limit of pack ice

Summer limit of pack ice

Barents Sea

Kara
Sea

Laptev
Sea

A

Sea
Okh

North
Sea

Baltic Sea

EUROPE

ASIA

Canary Current

Black Sea

Mediterranean Sea

Sea of
Japan

Yellow
Sea

East
China
Sea

Kuroshio

AFRICA

Red Sea

The Gulf

Gulf of Aden

Arabian
Sea

Bay of
Bengal

South
China
Sea

Philippine
Sea

Equatorial
Counter-
current

Gulf of Guinea

Guinea
Current

Celebes
Sea

Java Sea

Banda Sea

South Equatorial
Current

Benguela Current

Mozambique Channel

Agulhas Current

South Equatorial Current

Arafura
Sea

Timor
Sea

ATLANTIC
OCEAN

INDIAN
OCEAN

AUSTRALI

West Australian
Current

ANNUAL MEAN OCEAN
TEMPERATURE

	20 to 30°C/68° to 86°F
	10 to 20°C/50° to 68°F
	0 to 10°C/32° to 50°F
	-2° to 0°C/28° to 32°F

	Annual mean extent of sea ice (below -2°C/28°F)
	Permanent ice shelf
→	Prevailing warm ocean current
→	Prevailing cold ocean current

Winter limit of pack ice

Summer limit of pack ice

ANTARCTICA

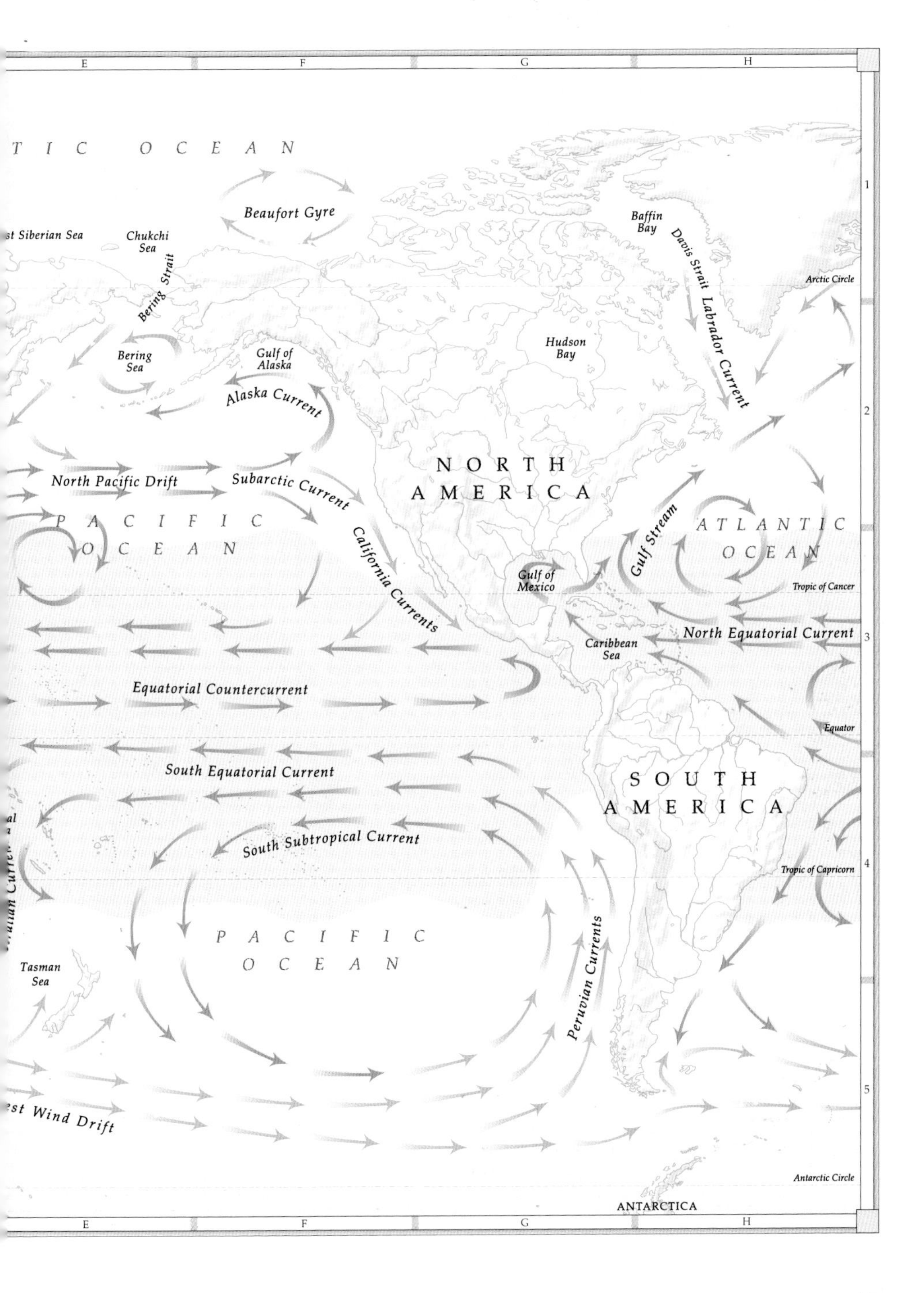

E   F   G   H

TIC OCEAN

Beaufort Gyre

Baffin Bay

1

st Siberian Sea

Chukchi Sea

Davis Strait Labrador Current

Arctic Circle

Bering Strait

Bering Sea

Gulf of Alaska

Hudson Bay

Alaska Current

2

North Pacific Drift

Subarctic Current

NORTH AMERICA

Gulf Stream

ATLANTIC OCEAN

PACIFIC OCEAN

California Currents

Gulf of Mexico

Tropic of Cancer

Caribbean Sea

North Equatorial Current

3

Equatorial Countercurrent

South Equatorial Current

Equator

SOUTH AMERICA

South Subtropical Current

Tropic of Capricorn

4

al

PACIFIC OCEAN

Peruvian Currents

uan Curren

Tasman Sea

5

st Wind Drift

Antarctic Circle

ANTARCTICA

E   F   G   H

LIFE ZONES

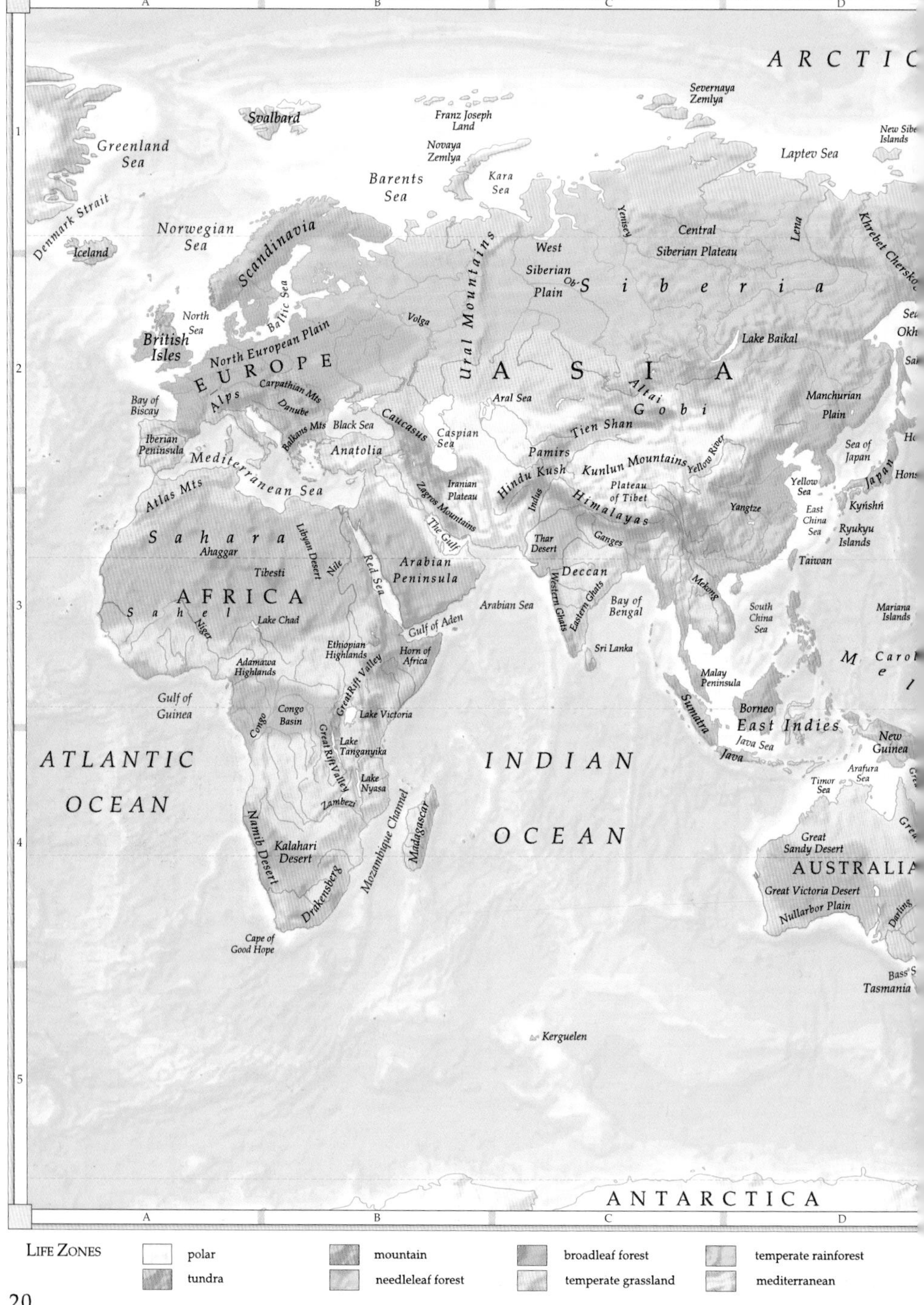

A **B** **C** **D**

ARCTIC

Svalbard

Greenland
Sea

Franz Joseph
Land

Severnaya
Zemlya

New Sib
Islands

Novaya
Zemlya

Laptev Sea

Denmark Strait

Iceland

Norwegian
Sea

Barents
Sea

Kara
Sea

Scandinavia

West
Siberian
Plain

Central
Siberian Plateau

Lena

Khrebet Chersko

Sea
Okh

Yenisey

Siberia

Lake Baikal

Sai

North
Sea

British
Isles

North European Plain

EUROPE

Baltic Sea

Volga

Ural Mountains

ASIA

Altai

Gobi

Manchurian
Plain

Sea of
Japan

Ho

Bay of
Biscay

Alps

Carpathian Mts

Danube

Black Sea

Balkans Mts

Caucasus

Aral Sea

Tien Shan

Hons

Iberian
Peninsula

Mediterranean Sea

Anatolia

Caspian
Sea

Pamirs

Hindu Kush

Kunlun Mountains

Yellow River

Yellow
Sea

Kyūshū

Japa

Atlas Mts

Iranian
Plateau

Indus

Himalayas

Plateau
of Tibet

Yangtze

East
China
Sea

Ryukyu
Islands

Sahara

Libyan Desert

Nile

Zagros Mountains

The Gulf

Thar
Desert

Ganges

Taiwan

Ahaggar

Tibesti

Red Sea

Arabian
Peninsula

Deccan

Mekong

Mariana
Islands

AFRICA

Sahel

Niger

Lake Chad

Gulf of Aden

Arabian Sea

Bay of
Bengal

Western Ghats

Eastern Ghats

South
China
Sea

M

Carol

Ethiopian
Highlands

Horn of
Africa

Sri Lanka

I

Adamawa
Highlands

Malay
Peninsula

Borneo

New
Guinea

Gulf of
Guinea

Congo
Basin

Congo

Great Rift Valley

Lake Victoria

Lake
Tanganyika

INDIAN

Sumatra

East Indies

Java Sea

Java

Arafura
Sea

Gr

ATLANTIC

OCEAN

Lake
Nyasa

Zambezi

OCEAN

Timor
Sea

Grea

Namib Desert

Kalahari
Desert

Mozambique Channel

Madagascar

Great
Sandy Desert

AUSTRALIA

Drakensberg

Great Victoria Desert

Nullarbor Plain

Darling

Cape of
Good Hope

Bass S

Tasmania

Kerguelen

ANTARCTICA

A **B** **C** **D**

LIFE ZONES
- polar
- tundra
- mountain
- needleleaf forest
- broadleaf forest
- temperate grassland
- temperate rainforest
- mediterranean

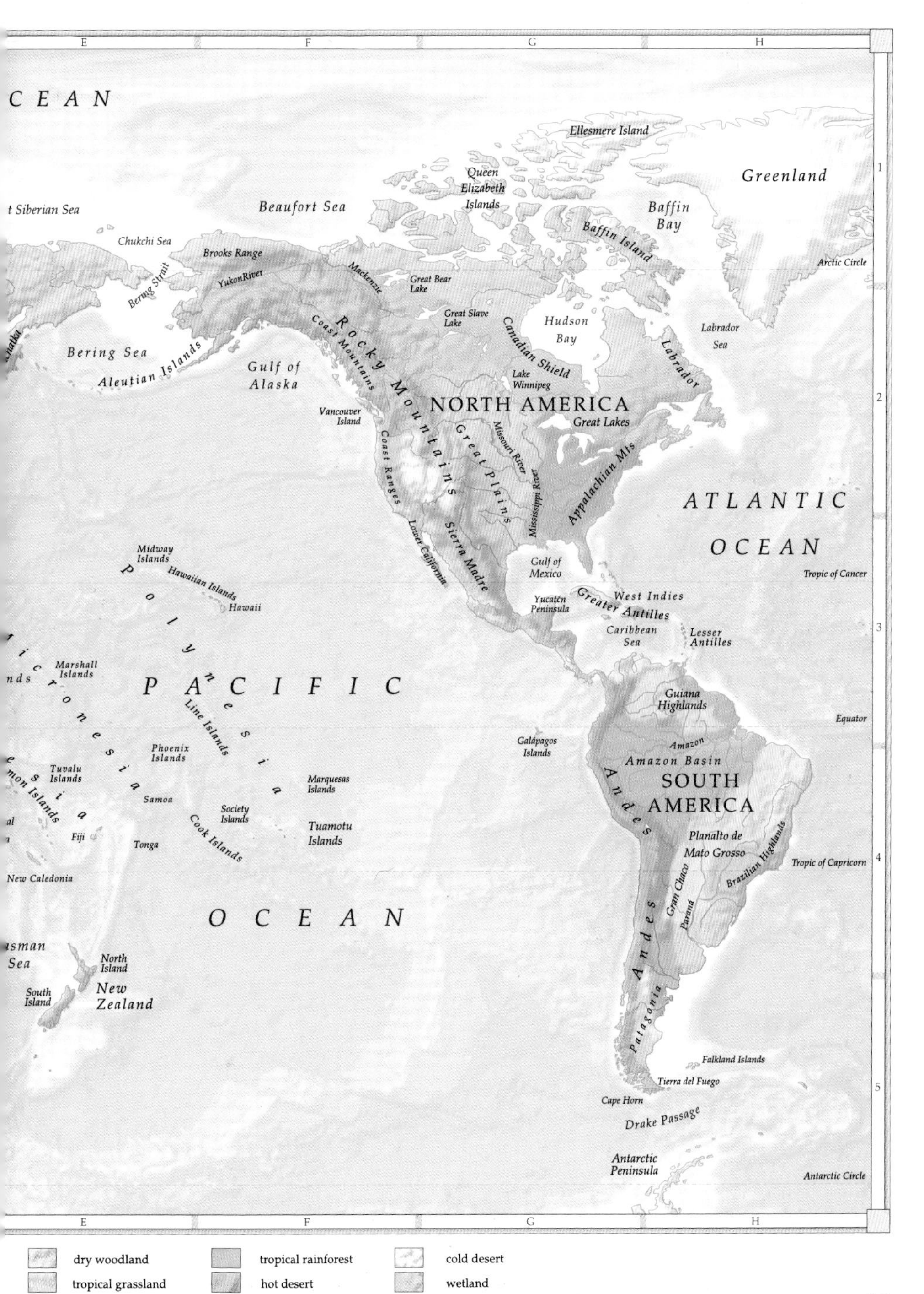

E F G H

1

Ellesmere Island

Greenland

Queen
Elizabeth
Islands

t Siberian Sea

Beaufort Sea

*Baffin
Bay*

Chukchi Sea

Brooks Range

Baffin Island

Arctic Circle

Bering Strait

Yukon River

Mackenzie

Great Bear
Lake

Coast Mountains

Great Slave
Lake

*Hudson
Bay*

*Labrador
Sea*

Bering Sea

Aleutian Islands

*Gulf of
Alaska*

Rocky Mountains

Canadian Shield

Labrador

2

Lake
Winnipeg

NORTH AMERICA

*Vancouver
Island*

Coast Ranges

Great Plains

Missouri River

Great Lakes

Appalachian Mts

ATLANTIC

*Midway
Islands*

Hawaiian Islands

Sierra Madre

Lower California

Mississippi River

OCEAN

Hawaii

Gulf of
Mexico

Greater Antilles

West Indies

Tropic of Cancer

3

P o l y n e s i a

Yucatán
Peninsula

Caribbean
Sea

*Lesser
Antilles*

*Marshall
Islands*

P A C I F I C

Guiana
Highlands

Equator

*Galápagos
Islands*

Amazon

Line Islands

*Phoenix
Islands*

*Tuvalu
Islands*

Amazon Basin

**SOUTH
AMERICA**

Samoa

*Marquesas
Islands*

*Society
Islands*

*Tuamotu
Islands*

Cook Islands

Fiji

Tonga

*Planalto de
Mato Grosso*

Gran Chaco

Brazilian Highlands

Tropic of Capricorn

4

New Caledonia

O C E A N

Andes

Paraná

*asman
Sea*

*North
Island*

*South
Island*

*New
Zealand*

Patagonia

Falkland Islands

5

Tierra del Fuego

Cape Horn

Drake Passage

Antarctic
Peninsula

Antarctic Circle

E F G H

dry woodland

tropical rainforest

cold desert

tropical grassland

hot desert

wetland

POPULATION

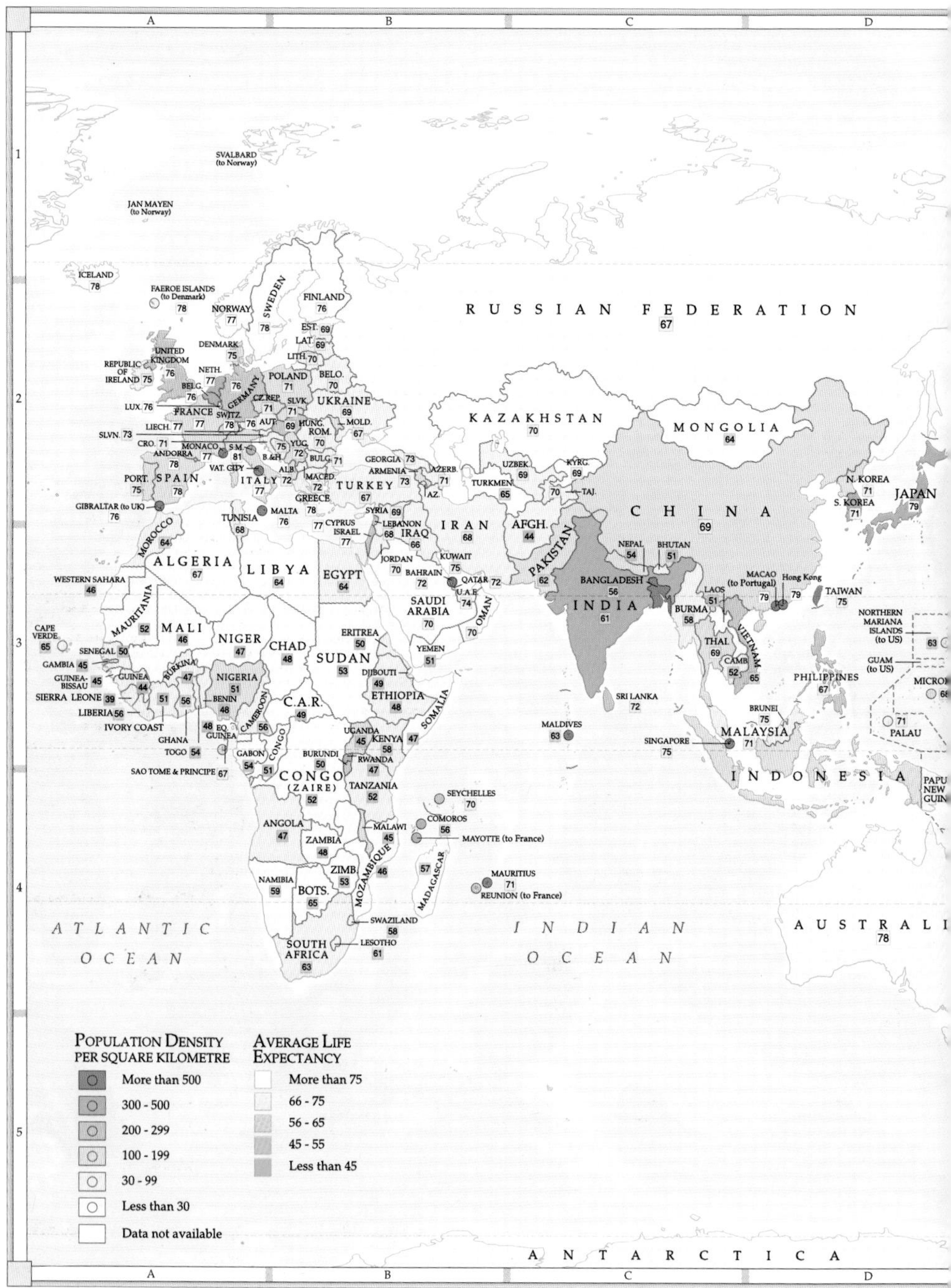

POPULATION DENSITY PER SQUARE KILOMETRE
- More than 500
- 300 - 500
- 200 - 299
- 100 - 199
- 30 - 99
- Less than 30
- Data not available

AVERAGE LIFE EXPECTANCY
- More than 75
- 66 - 75
- 56 - 65
- 45 - 55
- Less than 45

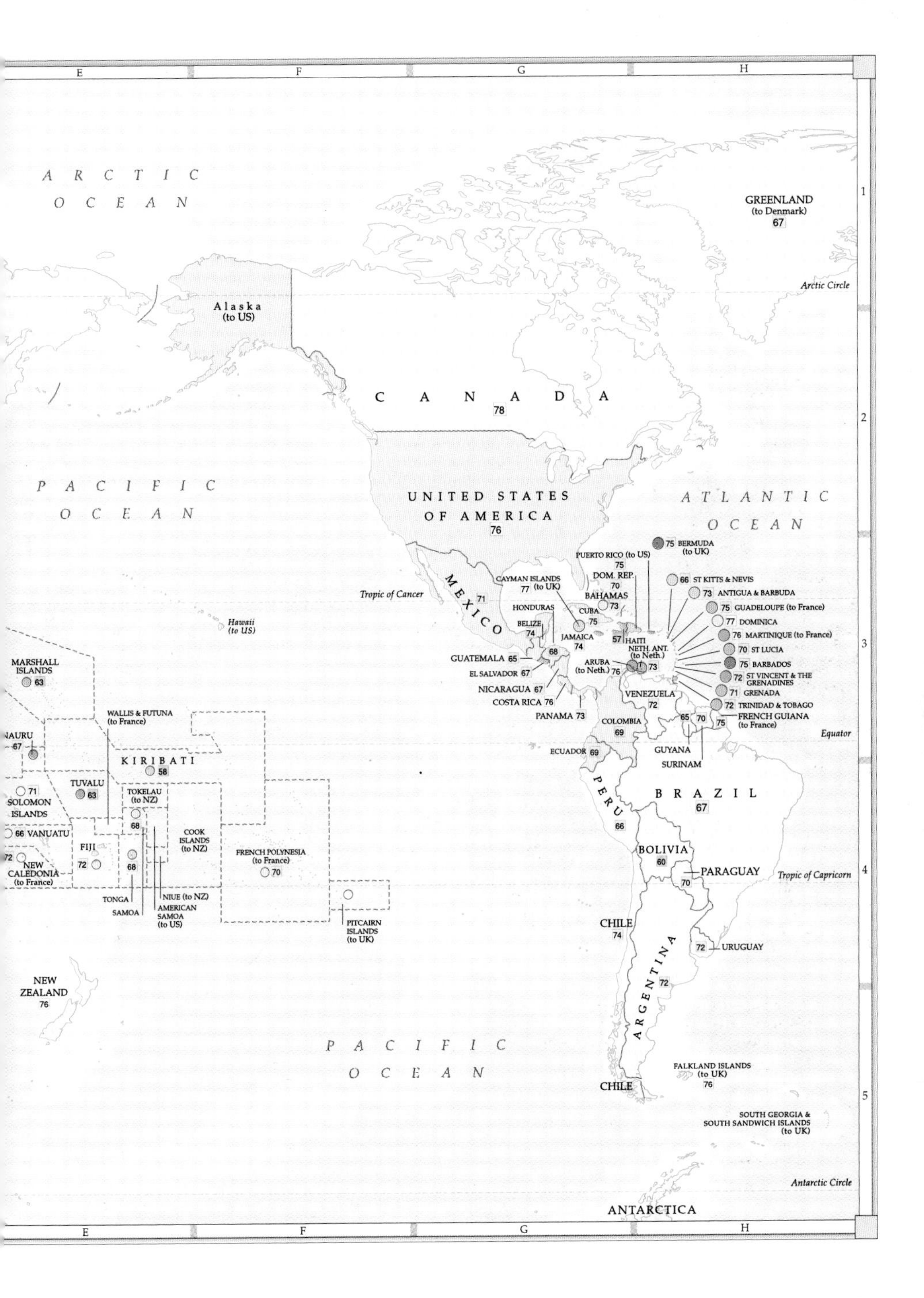
E
F
G
H
ARCTIC OCEAN
GREENLAND (to Denmark) 67
Arctic Circle
Alaska (to US)
CANADA 78
PACIFIC OCEAN
UNITED STATES OF AMERICA 76
ATLANTIC OCEAN
75 BERMUDA (to UK)
PUERTO RICO (to US) 75
DOM. REP. 70
66 ST KITTS & NEVIS
73 ANTIGUA & BARBUDA
75 GUADELOUPE (to France)
77 DOMINICA
76 MARTINIQUE (to France)
70 ST LUCIA
75 BARBADOS
72 ST VINCENT & THE GRENADINES
71 GRENADA
72 TRINIDAD & TOBAGO
FRENCH GUIANA (to France) 75
CAYMAN ISLANDS 77 (to UK)
BAHAMAS 73
Tropic of Cancer
MEXICO 71
HONDURAS 68
CUBA 75
BELIZE 74
JAMAICA 74
HAITI 57
NETH. ANT. (to Neth.) 73
Hawaii (to US)
GUATEMALA 65
ARUBA (to Neth.) 76
EL SALVADOR 67
NICARAGUA 67
COSTA RICA 76
PANAMA 73
VENEZUELA 72
MARSHALL ISLANDS 63
WALLIS & FUTUNA (to France)
COLOMBIA 69
GUYANA 65
SURINAM 70
Equator
NAURU 67
KIRIBATI 58
ECUADOR 69
TUVALU 63
71 SOLOMON ISLANDS
TOKELAU (to NZ)
PERU 66
BRAZIL 67
66 VANUATU
68
COOK ISLANDS (to NZ)
FIJI 72
72 NEW CALEDONIA (to France)
68
FRENCH POLYNESIA (to France) 70
BOLIVIA 60
PARAGUAY 70
Tropic of Capricorn
TONGA
SAMOA
NIUE (to NZ)
AMERICAN SAMOA (to US)
PITCAIRN ISLANDS (to UK)
CHILE 74
72 URUGUAY
ARGENTINA 72
NEW ZEALAND 76
PACIFIC OCEAN
FALKLAND ISLANDS (to UK) 76
CHILE
SOUTH GEORGIA & SOUTH SANDWICH ISLANDS (to UK)
Antarctic Circle
ANTARCTICA
1
2
3
4
5

LANGUAGES

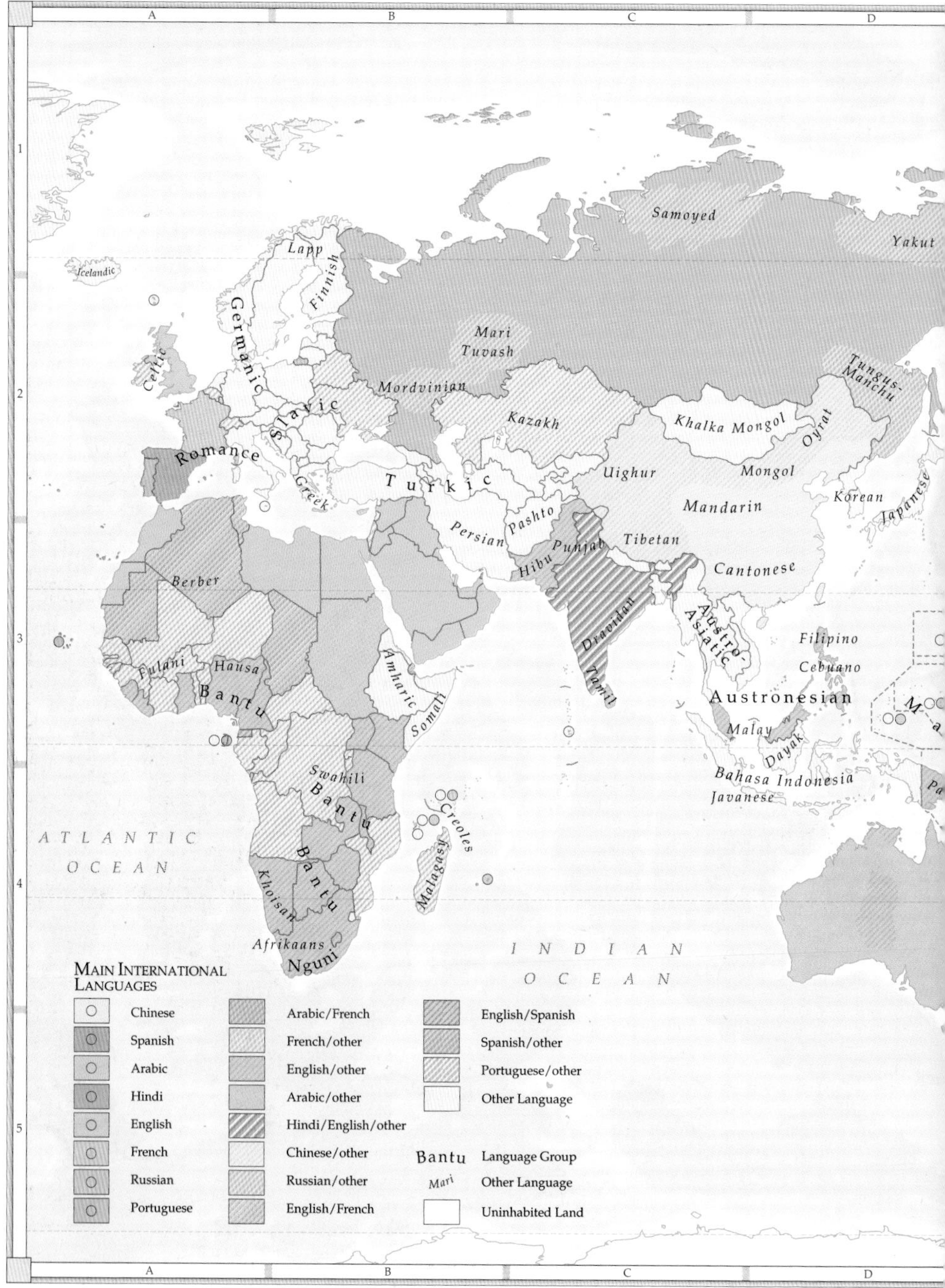

MAIN INTERNATIONAL LANGUAGES

- ○ Chinese
- ○ Spanish
- ○ Arabic
- ○ Hindi
- ○ English
- ○ French
- ○ Russian
- ○ Portuguese

- Arabic/French
- French/other
- English/other
- Arabic/other
- Hindi/English/other
- Chinese/other
- Russian/other
- English/French

- English/Spanish
- Spanish/other
- Portuguese/other
- Other Language

Bantu Language Group
Mari Other Language

Uninhabited Land

Labels on map: Icelandic, Lapp, Finnish, Germanic, Celtic, Slavic, Romance, Greek, Turkic, Mordvinian, Mari, Tuvash, Kazakh, Samoyed, Yakut, Khalka Mongol, Oyrat, Tungus-Manchu, Uighur, Mongol, Korean, Japanese, Mandarin, Cantonese, Persian, Pashto, Punjab, Tibetan, Hibu, Dravidian, Tamil, Austro-Asiatic, Filipino, Cebuano, Austronesian, Malay, Dayak, Bahasa Indonesia, Javanese, Berber, Fulani, Hausa, Bantu, Amharic, Somali, Swahili, Creoles, Malagasy, Khoisan, Afrikaans, Nguni

ATLANTIC OCEAN

INDIAN OCEAN

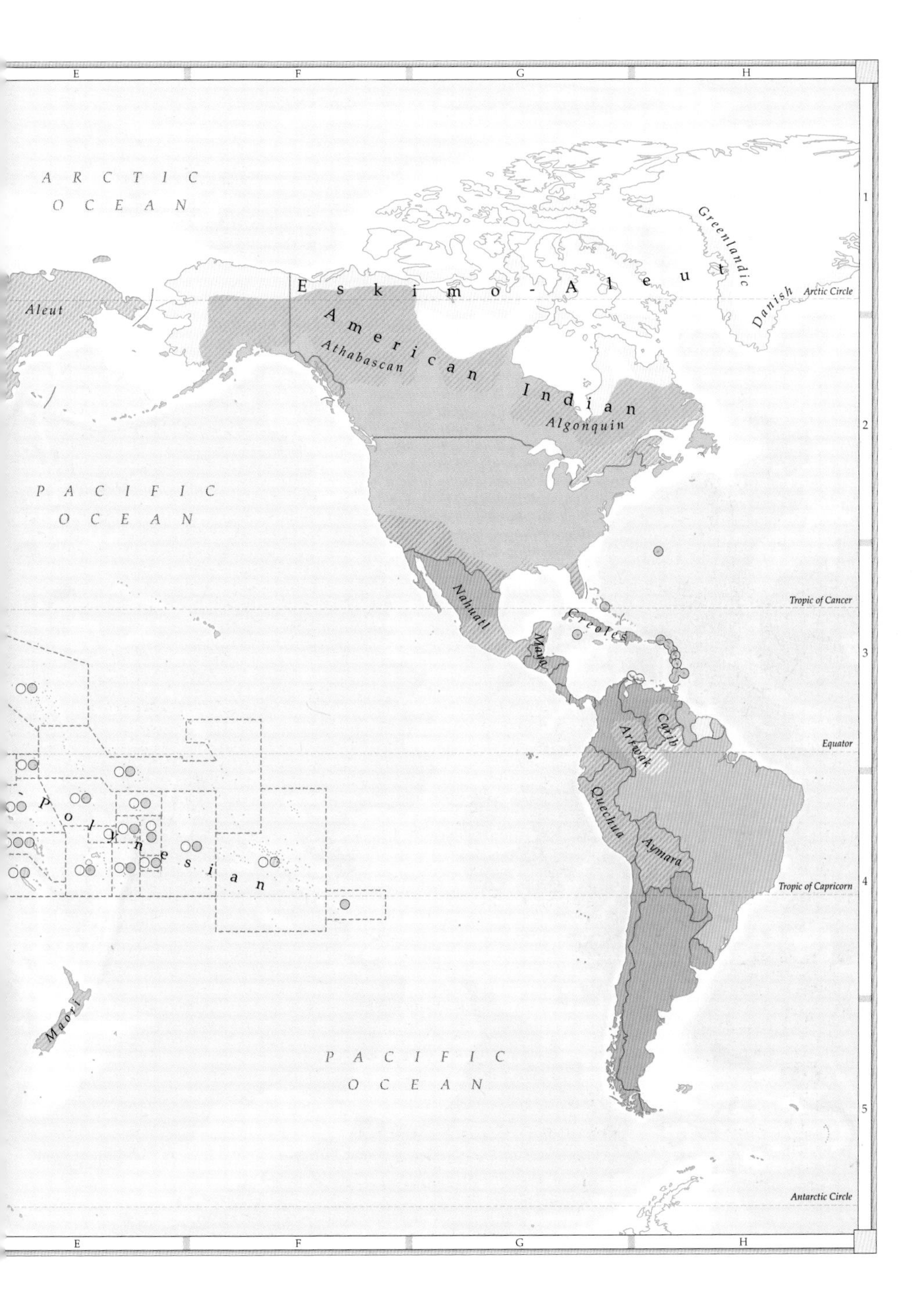

ARCTIC
OCEAN

Greenlandic

Danish   *Arctic Circle*

Eskimo - Aleut

Aleut

American Indian

Athabascan

Algonquin

PACIFIC
OCEAN

Tropic of Cancer

Nahuatl

Creole

Maya

Carib

Arawak

Equator

Quechua

Aymara

Tropic of Capricorn

Polynesian

Maori

PACIFIC

OCEAN

Antarctic Circle

RELIGION

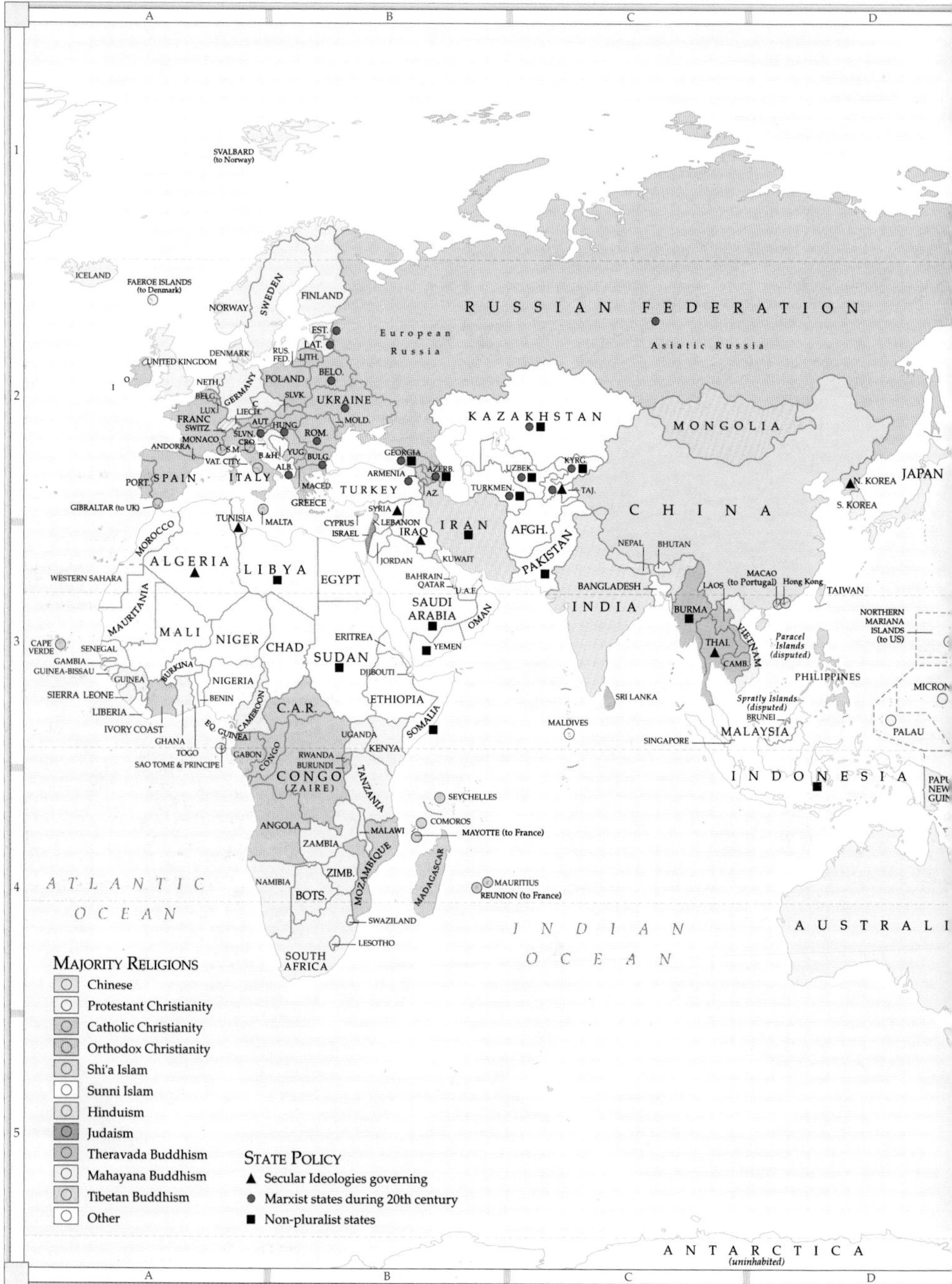

MAJORITY RELIGIONS

- Chinese
- Protestant Christianity
- Catholic Christianity
- Orthodox Christianity
- Shi'a Islam
- Sunni Islam
- Hinduism
- Judaism
- Theravada Buddhism
- Mahayana Buddhism
- Tibetan Buddhism
- Other

STATE POLICY

- ▲ Secular Ideologies governing
- ● Marxist states during 20th century
- ■ Non-pluralist states

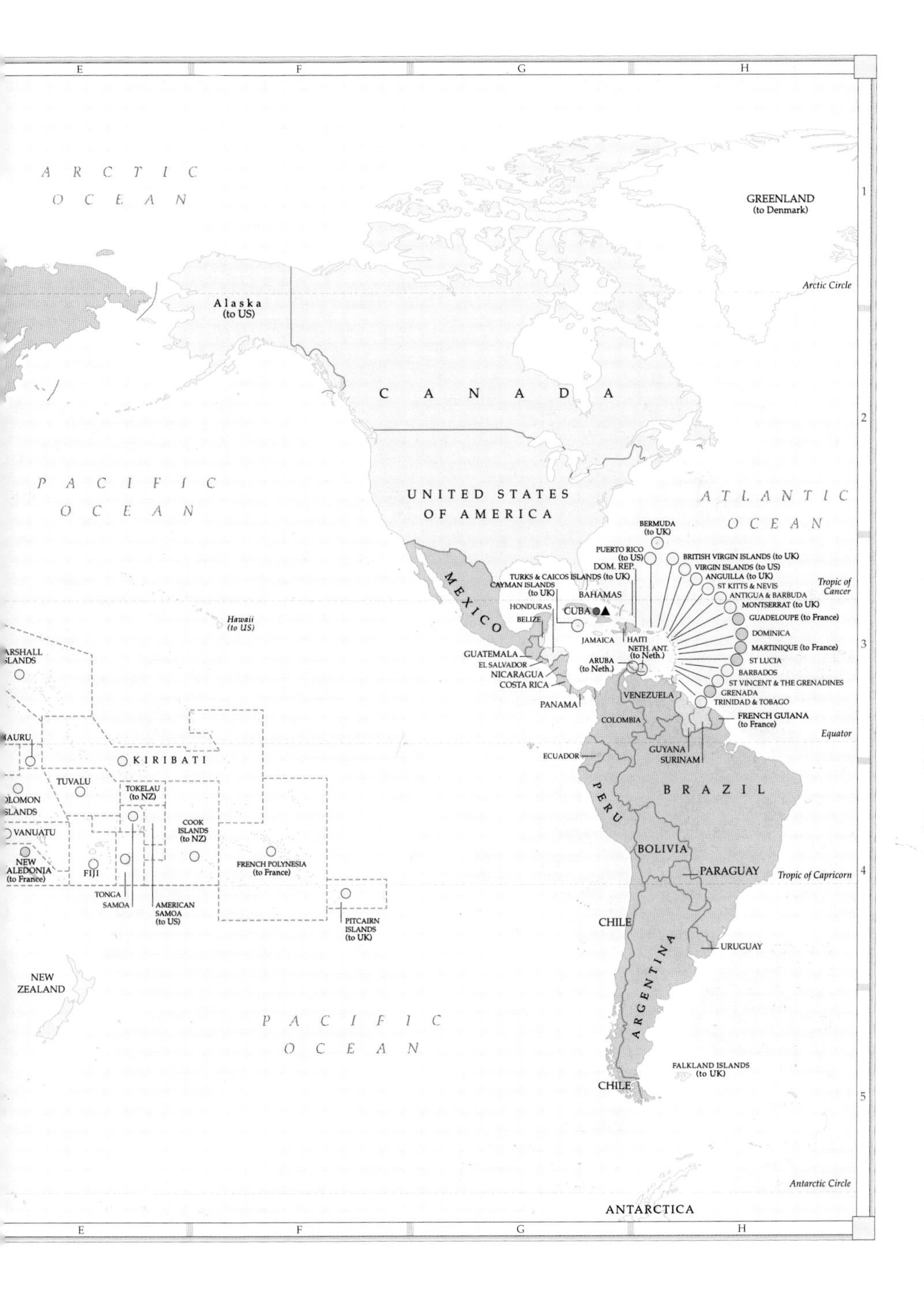

E · F · G · H

THE GLOBAL ECONOMY

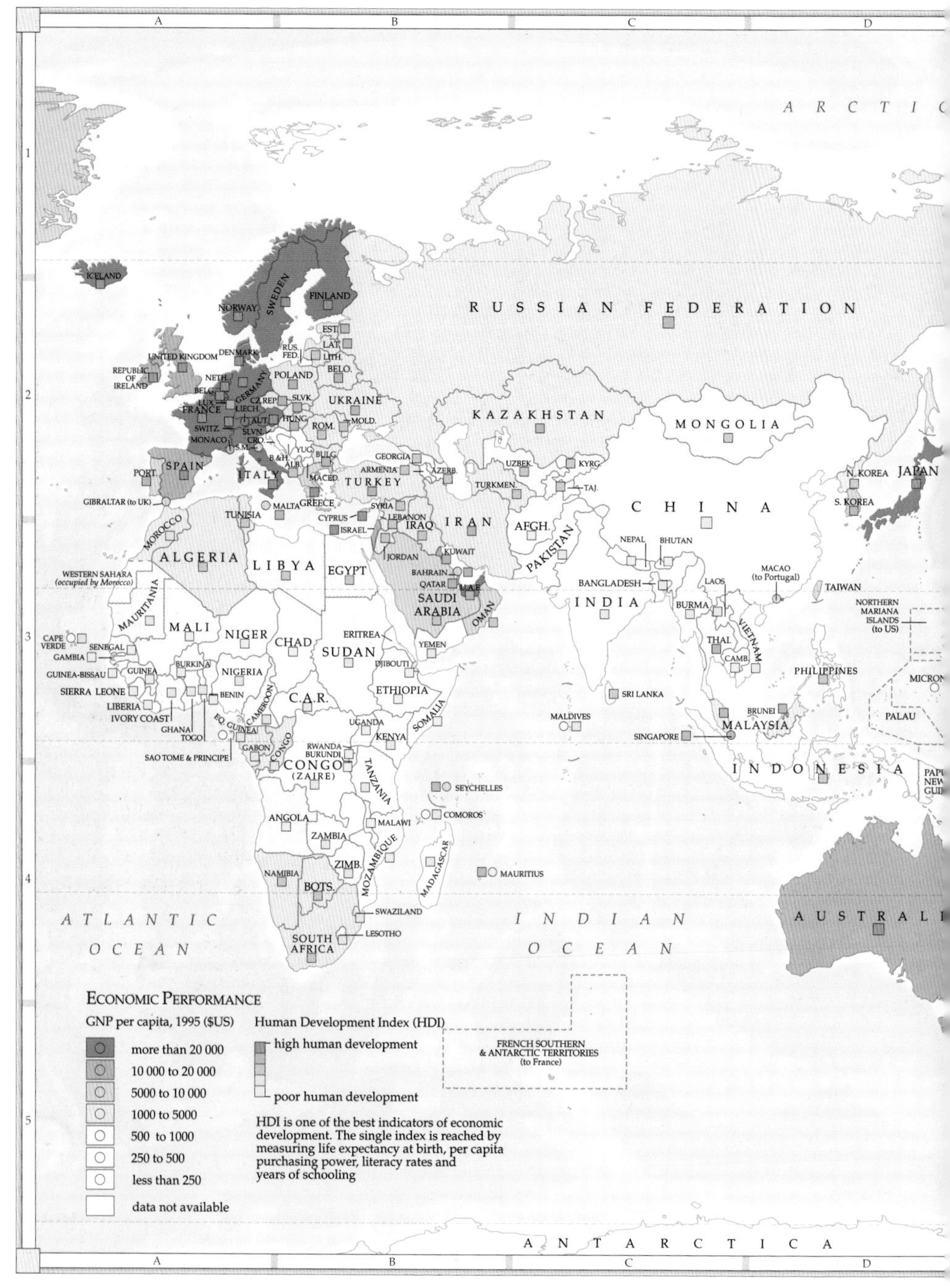

ECONOMIC PERFORMANCE

GNP per capita, 1995 ($US)

- more than 20 000
- 10 000 to 20 000
- 5000 to 10 000
- 1000 to 5000
- 500 to 1000
- 250 to 500
- less than 250
- data not available

Human Development Index (HDI)

- high human development
- poor human development

HDI is one of the best indicators of economic development. The single index is reached by measuring life expectancy at birth, per capita purchasing power, literacy rates and years of schooling

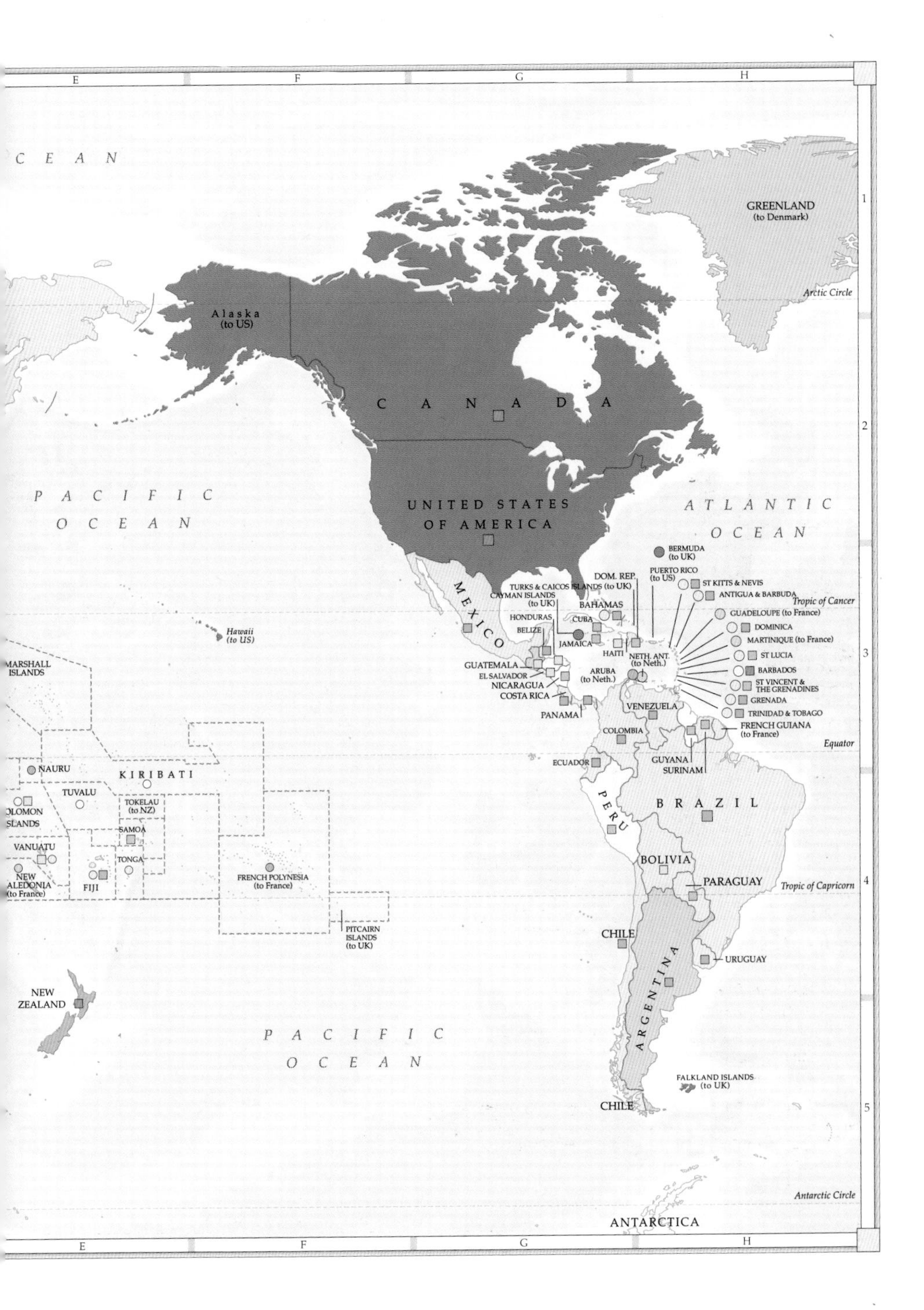

GREENLAND
(to Denmark)

Arctic Circle

Alaska
(to US)

C A N A D A

P A C I F I C
O C E A N

UNITED STATES
OF AMERICA

A T L A N T I C
O C E A N

BERMUDA
(to UK)

PUERTO RICO
(to US)

ST KITTS & NEVIS
ANTIGUA & BARBUDA
Tropic of Cancer
GUADELOUPE (to France)
DOMINICA
MARTINIQUE (to France)
ST LUCIA
BARBADOS
ST VINCENT &
THE GRENADINES
GRENADA
TRINIDAD & TOBAGO

TURKS & CAICOS ISLANDS (to UK)
CAYMAN ISLANDS
(to UK)
BAHAMAS
HONDURAS
BELIZE
CUBA
JAMAICA
HAITI
NETH. ANT.
(to Neth.)
ARUBA
(to Neth.)

DOM. REP.

M E X I C O

Hawaii
(to US)

MARSHALL
ISLANDS

GUATEMALA
EL SALVADOR
NICARAGUA
COSTA RICA
PANAMA

VENEZUELA

COLOMBIA

FRENCH GUIANA
(to France)

Equator

ECUADOR

GUYANA
SURINAM

NAURU
TUVALU

K I R I B A T I

TOKELAU
(to NZ)

SAMOA

P E R U

B R A Z I L

OLOMON
SLANDS

VANUATU
NEW
ALEDONIA
(to France)

TONGA

FIJI

FRENCH POLYNESIA
(to France)

BOLIVIA

PARAGUAY
Tropic of Capricorn

PITCAIRN
ISLANDS
(to UK)

CHILE

ARGENTINA

URUGUAY

NEW
ZEALAND

P A C I F I C
O C E A N

CHILE

FALKLAND ISLANDS
(to UK)

Antarctic Circle

ANTARCTICA

29

GLOBAL CONFLICT

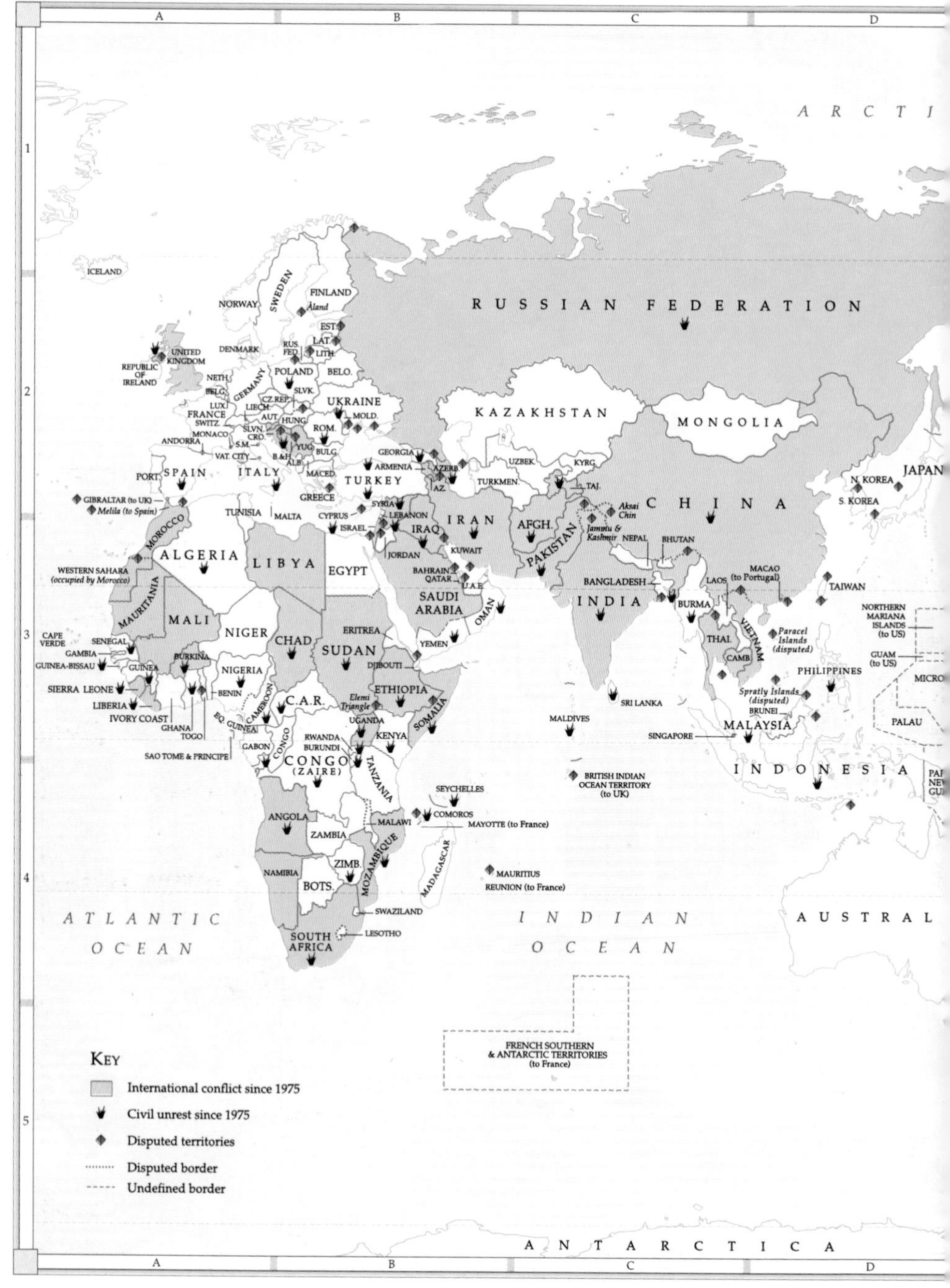

KEY

▨	International conflict since 1975
♆	Civil unrest since 1975
◆	Disputed territories
....	Disputed border
- - - -	Undefined border

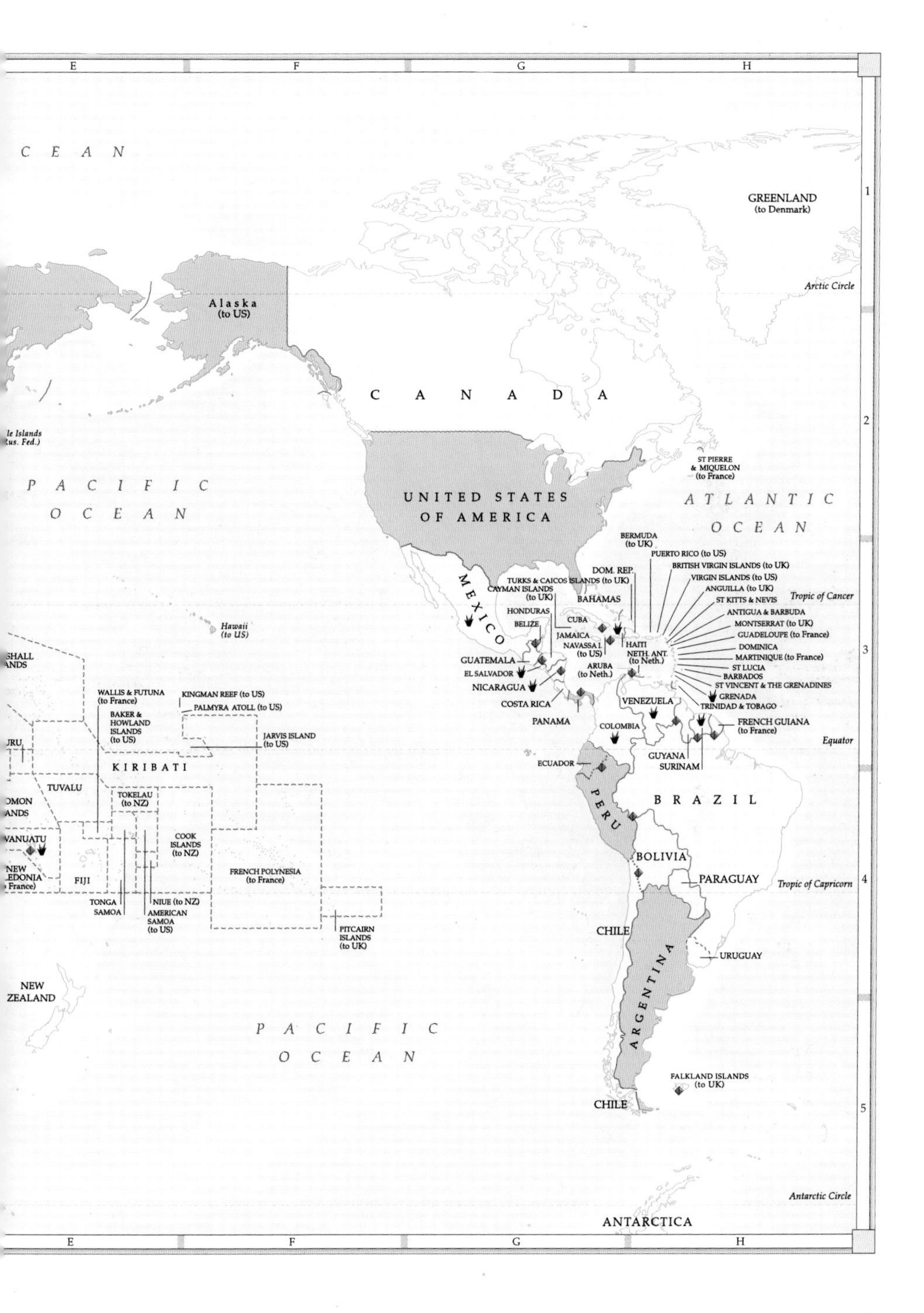

C E A N

GREENLAND
(to Denmark)

1

Arctic Circle

Alaska
(to US)

C A N A D A

2

le Islands
Rus. Fed.)

ST PIERRE
& MIQUELON
(to France)

P A C I F I C
O C E A N

A T L A N T I C
O C E A N

UNITED STATES
OF AMERICA

BERMUDA
(to UK)
PUERTO RICO (to US)
BRITISH VIRGIN ISLANDS (to UK)
VIRGIN ISLANDS (to US)
ANGUILLA (to UK)
ST KITTS & NEVIS
Tropic of Cancer

Hawaii
(to US)

M
E
X
I
C
O

DOM. REP.
TURKS & CAICOS ISLANDS (to UK)
CAYMAN ISLANDS
(to UK)
BAHAMAS

HONDURAS
BELIZE
CUBA
JAMAICA
NAVASSA I
(to US)
HAITI
NETH. ANT.
(to Neth.)

ANTIGUA & BARBUDA
MONTSERRAT (to UK)
GUADELOUPE (to France)
DOMINICA
MARTINIQUE (to France)
ST LUCIA
BARBADOS
ST VINCENT & THE GRENADINES
GRENADA
TRINIDAD & TOBAGO

3

SHALL
ANDS

GUATEMALA
EL SALVADOR
NICARAGUA
COSTA RICA
ARUBA
(to Neth.)
VENEZUELA

FRENCH GUIANA
(to France)

RU

WALLIS & FUTUNA
(to France)
KINGMAN REEF (to US)
PALMYRA ATOLL (to US)

BAKER &
HOWLAND
ISLANDS
(to US)

JARVIS ISLAND
(to US)

K I R I B A T I

PANAMA
COLOMBIA

GUYANA
SURINAM

Equator

ECUADOR

TUVALU

OMON
ANDS

TOKELAU
(to NZ)

P
E
R
U

B R A Z I L

VANUATU

COOK
ISLANDS
(to NZ)

FRENCH POLYNESIA
(to France)

BOLIVIA

NEW
EDONIA
France)

FIJI

NIUE (to NZ)
AMERICAN
SAMOA
(to US)

PARAGUAY

Tropic of Capricorn

4

TONGA
SAMOA

CHILE

URUGUAY

PITCAIRN
ISLANDS
(to UK)

NEW
ZEALAND

A
R
G
E
N
T
I
N
A

P A C I F I C
O C E A N

FALKLAND ISLANDS
(to UK)

CHILE

5

Antarctic Circle

ANTARCTICA

E   F   G   H

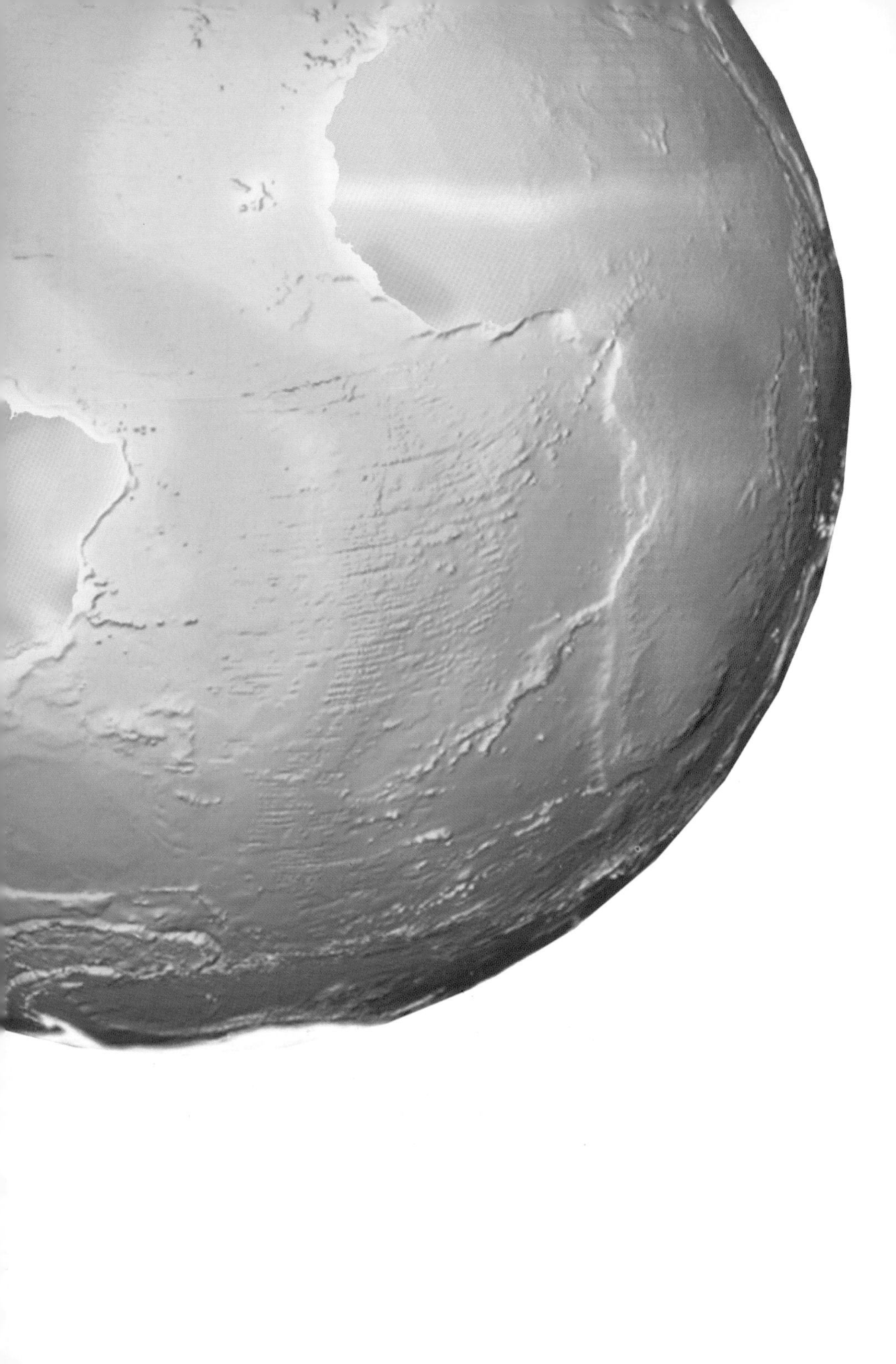

ATLAS *of the* WORLD'S REGIONS

NORTH & CENTRAL AMERICA

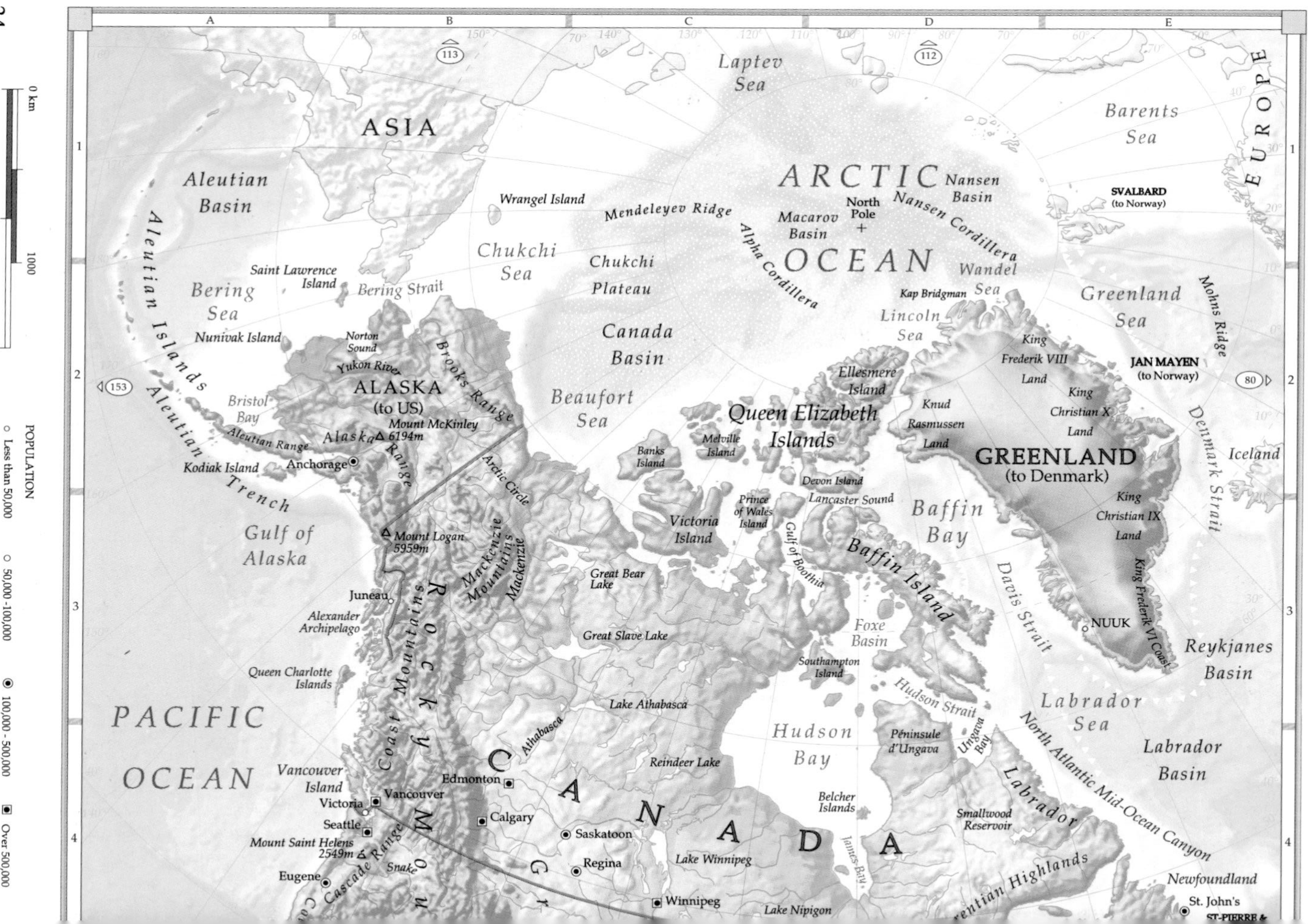

EUROPE

ASIA

Barents Sea

Laptev Sea

Greenland Sea

SVALBARD (to Norway)

Mohns Ridge

JAN MAYEN (to Norway)

Iceland

Reykjanes Basin

Labrador Basin

Newfoundland

St. John's
ST-PIERRE

Denmark Strait

ARCTIC

OCEAN

Nansen Basin

Nansen Cordillera

North Pole

Macarov Basin

Alpha Cordillera

Mendeleyev Ridge

Chukchi Plateau

Canada Basin

Wandel Sea

Kap Bridgman Sea

Lincoln Sea

King Frederik VIII Land

King Christian X Land

GREENLAND (to Denmark)

King Christian IX Land

King Frederik VI Coast

NUUK

Davis Strait

Labrador Sea

Labrador

Torngat Highlands

North Atlantic Mid-Ocean Canyon

Knud Rasmussen Land

Baffin Bay

Smallwood Reservoir

Ungava Bay

Hudson Strait

Peninsule d'Ungava

Ellesmere Island

Baffin Island

Foxe Basin

Lancaster Sound

Devon Island

Queen Elizabeth Islands

Melville Island

Prince of Wales Island

Gulf of Boothia

Southampton Island

Hudson Bay

Belcher Islands

James Bay

Lake Nipigon

Lake Winnipeg

Winnipeg

Banks Island

Victoria Island

Reindeer Lake

Lake Athabasca

Saskatoon

Regina

CANADA

Gr

Beaufort Sea

Great Bear Lake

Great Slave Lake

Athabasca

Calgary

Edmonton

Wrangel Island

Chukchi Sea

Bering Strait

Bering Strait

Brooks Range

Arctic Circle

Mackenzie Mountains

Mackenzie

Arctic Circle

R o c k y   M o u n t a i n s

Coast Mountains

Mou

Saint Lawrence Island

Norton Sound

Yukon River

ALASKA (to US)

Mount McKinley 6194m

Alaska Range

Anchorage

Juneau

Alexander Archipelago

Queen Charlotte Islands

Vancouver

Victoria

Vancouver Island

Seattle

Mount Saint Helens 2549m

Eugene

Cascade Range

Snake

Co

Mount Logan 5959m

Aleutian Basin

Bering Sea

Nunivak Island

Bristol Bay

Aleutian Range

Kodiak Island

Aleutian Trench

Gulf of Alaska

A L E U T I A N   I S L A N D S

PACIFIC OCEAN

80

112

113

153

0 km — 1000

0 miles — 1000

POPULATION

○ Less than 50,000   ◎ 50,000 -100,000   ◉ 100,000 - 500,000   ■ Over 500,000

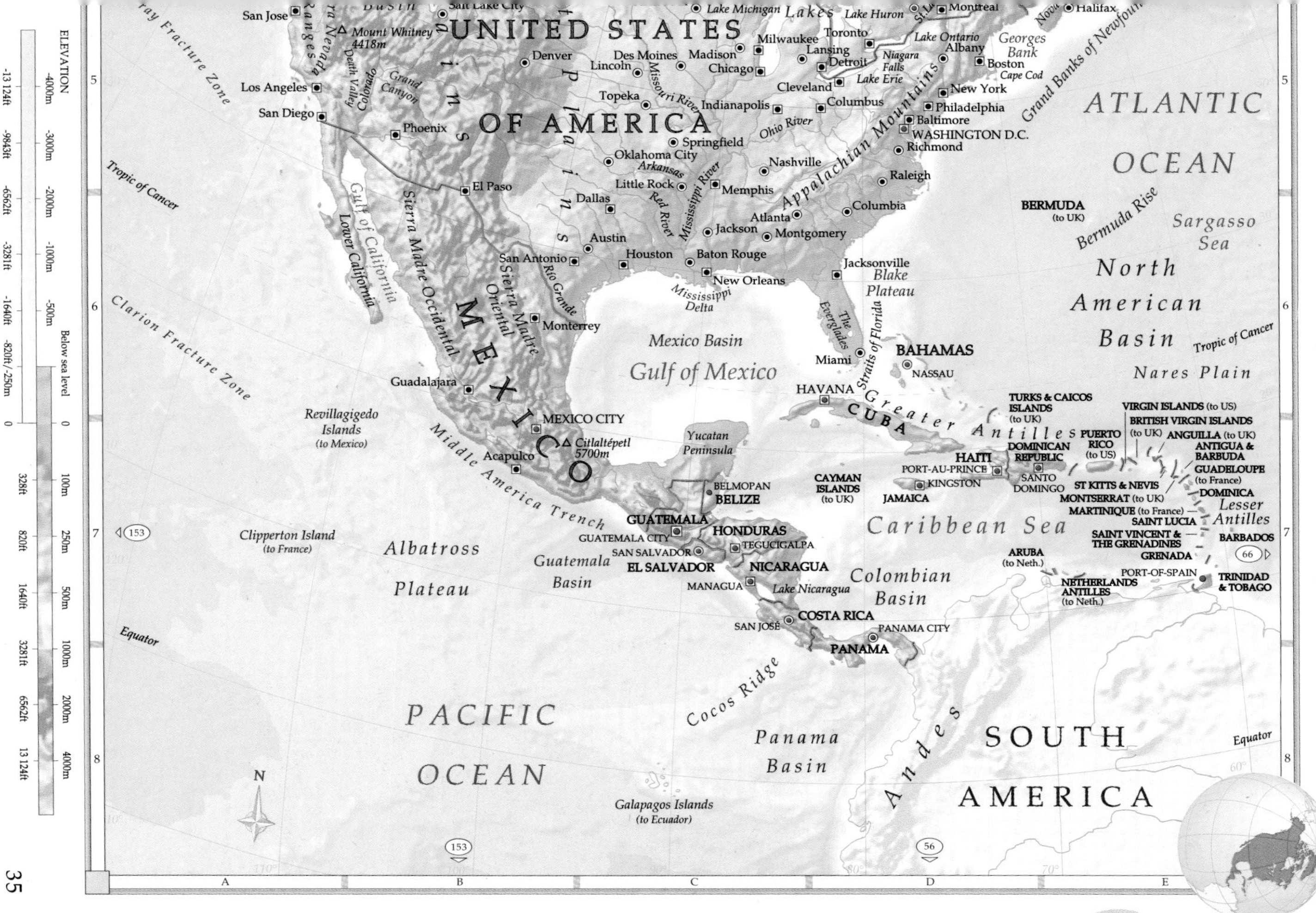

ATLANTIC OCEAN

Sargasso Sea

North American Basin

Nares Plain

Bermuda Rise

Grand Banks of Newfoundland

Flemish Cap

Halifax

Georges Bank

Boston
Cape Cod
New York

Montreal

Lake Ontario
Niagara Falls
Lake Erie

Toronto
Albany

Philadelphia
Baltimore
WASHINGTON D.C.
Richmond

Raleigh

Columbia

BERMUDA (to UK)

BAHAMAS
NASSAU

TURKS & CAICOS ISLANDS (to UK)

VIRGIN ISLANDS (to US)
BRITISH VIRGIN ISLANDS (to UK) ANGUILLA (to UK)
PUERTO RICO (to US) ANTIGUA & BARBUDA
SANTO DOMINGO GUADELOUPE (to France)
DOMINICAN REPUBLIC ST KITTS & NEVIS DOMINICA
HAITI MONTSERRAT (to UK) MARTINIQUE (to France)
PORT-AU-PRINCE SAINT LUCIA
KINGSTON SAINT VINCENT & THE GRENADINES
JAMAICA BARBADOS
GRENADA
NETHERLANDS ANTILLES (to Neth.)
ARUBA (to Neth.)
PORT-OF-SPAIN TRINIDAD & TOBAGO

Greater Antilles
Lesser Antilles

CUBA

HAVANA

Caribbean Sea

Colombian Basin

CAYMAN ISLANDS (to UK)

SOUTH AMERICA

Andes

Tropic of Cancer

Equator

Jacksonville
Blake Plateau
Straits of Florida
The Everglades
Miami

UNITED STATES OF AMERICA

Lake Superior
Lake Michigan
Lake Huron
Milwaukee
Madison
Lansing
Detroit
Chicago
Cleveland
Columbus
Indianapolis
Springfield
Cincinnati
Louisville
Nashville
Memphis
Atlanta
Montgomery
Jackson
Baton Rouge
New Orleans

Appalachian Mountains

Ohio River

Columbia

Des Moines
Lincoln
Topeka
Oklahoma City
Little Rock
Dallas
Austin
San Antonio

Missouri River
Arkansas River
Red River
Mississippi River

Denver

P l a i n s
G r e a t   P l a i n s

El Paso

Phoenix

Grand Canyon

Colorado

Death Valley

Los Angeles
San Diego

Sierra Nevada Ranges

Mount Whitney 4418m

Salt Lake City

San José

Houston

Mississippi Delta

Monterrey
Río Grande
Acapulco
Guadalajara

MEXICO CITY
Citlaltepetl 5700m

M E X I C O

Sierra Madre Oriental

Sierra Madre Occidental

Gulf of California
Lower California

Mexico Basin

Gulf of Mexico

Yucatan Peninsula

BELMOPAN
BELIZE
GUATEMALA CITY
GUATEMALA
SAN SALVADOR
EL SALVADOR
TEGUCIGALPA
HONDURAS
MANAGUA
NICARAGUA
Lake Nicaragua
SAN JOSÉ
COSTA RICA
PANAMA CITY
PANAMA

Guatemala Basin

Middle America Trench

Revillagigedo Islands (to Mexico)

Clipperton Island (to France)

Albatross Plateau

Cocos Ridge

Panama Basin

PACIFIC OCEAN

Galapagos Islands (to Ecuador)

Clarion Fracture Zone

Murray Fracture Zone

Tropic of Cancer

Equator

N

ELEVATION

Below sea level						0	100m	250m	500m	1000m	2000m	4000m
-4000m	-3000m	-2000m	-1000m	-500m		0						
-13 124ft	-9843ft	-6562ft	-3281ft	-1640ft	-820ft/-250m	0	328ft	820ft	1640ft	3281ft	6562ft	13 124ft

35

WESTERN CANADA & ALASKA

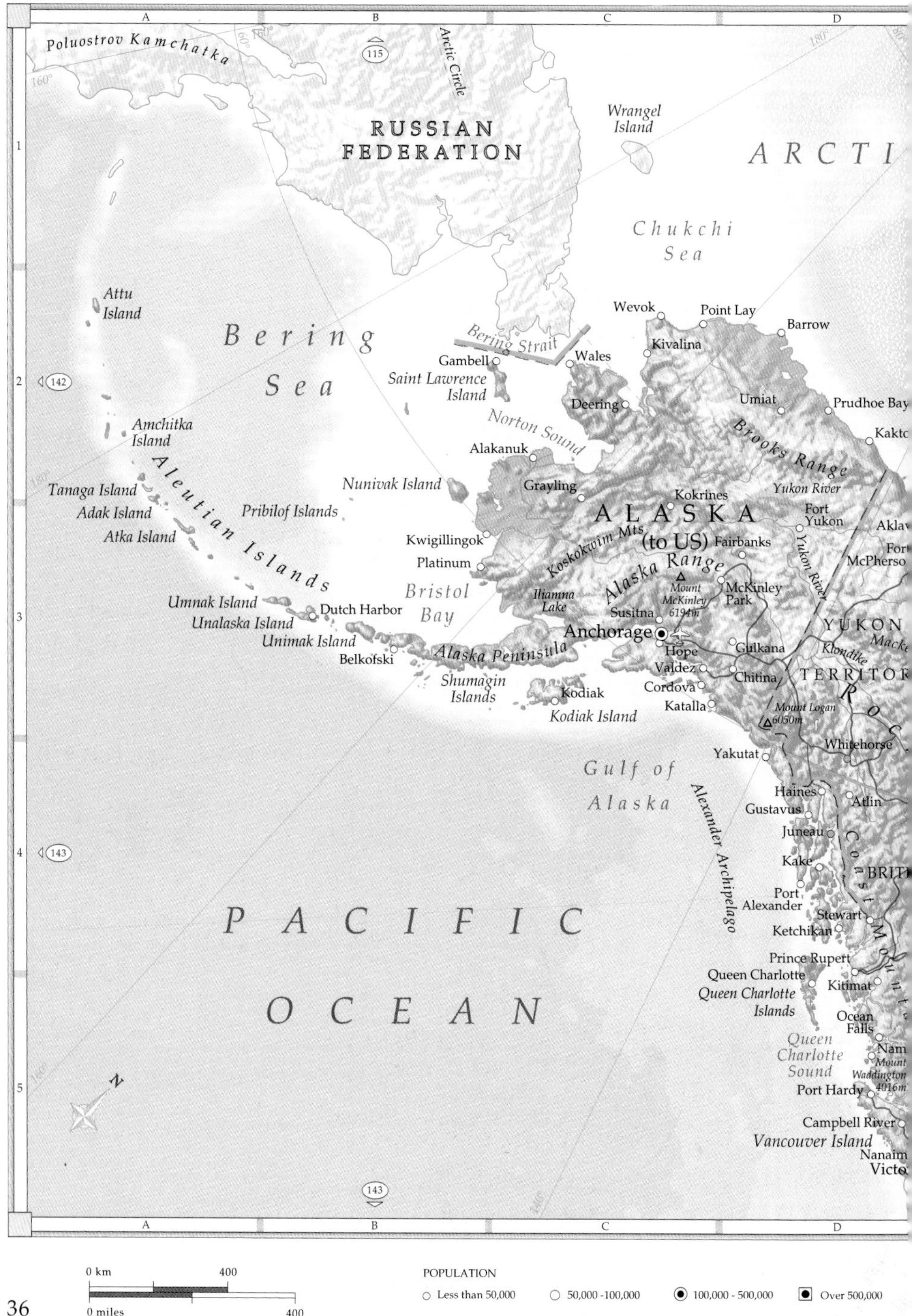

Poluostrov Kamchatka

115

Arctic Circle

RUSSIAN
FEDERATION

Wrangel
Island

ARCTI

Chukchi
Sea

Attu
Island

Bering

Sea

142

Amchitka
Island

Tanaga Island
Adak Island
Atka Island

Aleutian Islands

Pribilof Islands

Umnak Island
Unalaska Island
Unimak Island
Belkofski

Dutch Harbor

Bristol
Bay

Shumagin
Islands

Saint Lawrence
Island

Bering Strait

Gambell

Wales

Norton Sound

Alakanuk

Nunivak Island

Kwigillingok

Platinum

Alaska Peninsula

Kodiak

Kodiak Island

Wevok

Kivalina

Point Lay

Barrow

Deering

Umiat

Prudhoe Bay

Kaktc

Grayling

Kokrines

Yukon River

Kuskokwim Mts

ALASKA
(to US)

Fort
Yukon

Akla

Fairbanks

For
McPherso

Ilianna
Lake

Alaska Range

Mount
McKinley
6194m

McKinley
Park

Susitna

Anchorage

Hope

Gulkana

YUKON

Valdez

Klondike

Macke

Cordova

Chitna

TERRITOR

Katalla

Mount Logan
6050m

Yakutat

Whitehorse

Gulf of
Alaska

Alexander Archipelago

Haines

Gustavus

Atlin

Juneau

Kake

143

Port
Alexander

Stewart

BRI1

Ketchikan

Prince Rupert

Queen Charlotte

Kitimat

Queen Charlotte
Islands

Ocean
Falls

Queen
Charlotte
Sound

Nam
Mount
Waddington
4016m

Port Hardy

Campbell River

Vancouver Island

Nanaim
Victo

PACIFIC

OCEAN

N

143

0 km   400

0 miles   400

POPULATION

○ Less than 50,000   ○ 50,000 -100,000   ◉ 100,000 - 500,000   ■ Over 500,000

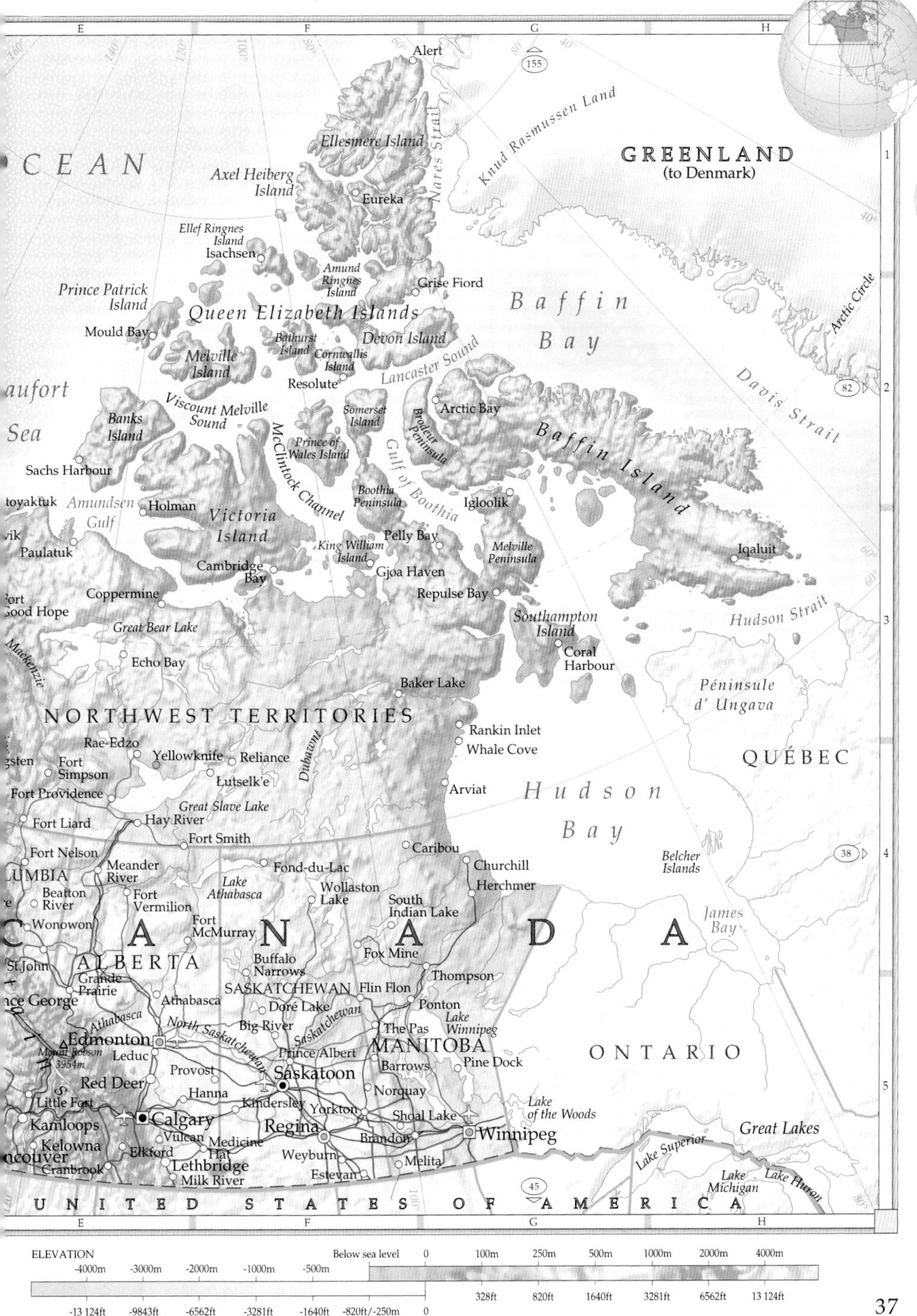

OCEAN

Alert

155

Ellesmere Island

Axel Heiberg
Island

Knud Rasmussen Land

GREENLAND
(to Denmark)

Eureka

Ellef Ringnes
Island
Isachsen

Amund
Ringnes
Island

Grise Fiord

Prince Patrick
Island

Queen Elizabeth Islands

Baffin

Mould Bay

Devon Island

Bay

Melville
Island

Bathurst
Island

Cornwallis
Island

Lancaster Sound

Arctic Bay

aufort

Resolute

McClintock Channel

Banks
Island

Viscount Melville
Sound

Somerset
Island

Prince of
Wales Island

Boothia
Peninsula

Baffin Island

Davis Strait

Sea

Sachs Harbour

Gulf of Boothia

Boothia
Peninsula

Igloolik

toyaktuk

Amundsen
Gulf

Holman

Victoria
Island

King William
Island

Pelly Bay

Melville
Peninsula

Iqaluit

vik

Paulatuk

Cambridge
Bay

Gjoa Haven

ort
ood Hope

Coppermine

Repulse Bay

Southampton
Island

Hudson Strait

Great Bear Lake

Echo Bay

Coral
Harbour

Baker Lake

Péninsule
d' Ungava

NORTHWEST TERRITORIES

Rankin Inlet

Whale Cove

QUÉBEC

Rae-Edzo

Yellowknife

Reliance

Dubawnt

gsten

Fort
Simpson

Łutselk'e

Arviat

Hudson

Fort Providence

Great Slave Lake

38

Fort Liard

Hay River

Bay

Fort Nelson

Fort Smith

Caribou

Belcher
Islands

LUMBIA

Meander
River

Fond-du-Lac

Churchill

James
Bay

Beatton
River

Fort
Vermilion

Lake
Athabasca

Wollaston
Lake

Herchmer

Wonowon

Fort
McMurray

South
Indian Lake

St.John

Buffalo
Narrows

Fox Mine

A

N

A

D

A

Grande
Prairie

ALBERTA

SASKATCHEWAN

Flin Flon

Thompson

ONTARIO

ce George

Athabasca

Doré Lake

Ponton

Athabasca

North Saskatchewan

Big River

Saskatchewan

The Pas

Lake
Winnipeg

Edmonton

MANITOBA

Mount Robson
3954m

Leduc

Prince Albert

Barrows

Pine Dock

Red Deer

Provost

Saskatoon

Norquay

Little Fort

Hanna

Kindersley

Yorkton

Shoal Lake

Lake
of the Woods

Kamloops

Calgary

Regina

Brandon

Winnipeg

Great Lakes

Kelowna

Vulcan

Medicine
Hat

Weyburn

Melita

Lake Superior

ncouver

Ekford

Lethbridge

Estevan

Lake
Michigan

Lake Huron

Cranbrook

Milk River

45

UNITED   STATES   OF   AMERICA

ELEVATION

Below sea level   0   100m   250m   500m   1000m   2000m   4000m

-4000m   -3000m   -2000m   -1000m   -500m

328ft   820ft   1640ft   3281ft   6562ft   13 124ft

-13 124ft   -9843ft   -6562ft   -3281ft   -1640ft   -820ft/-250m   0

EASTERN CANADA

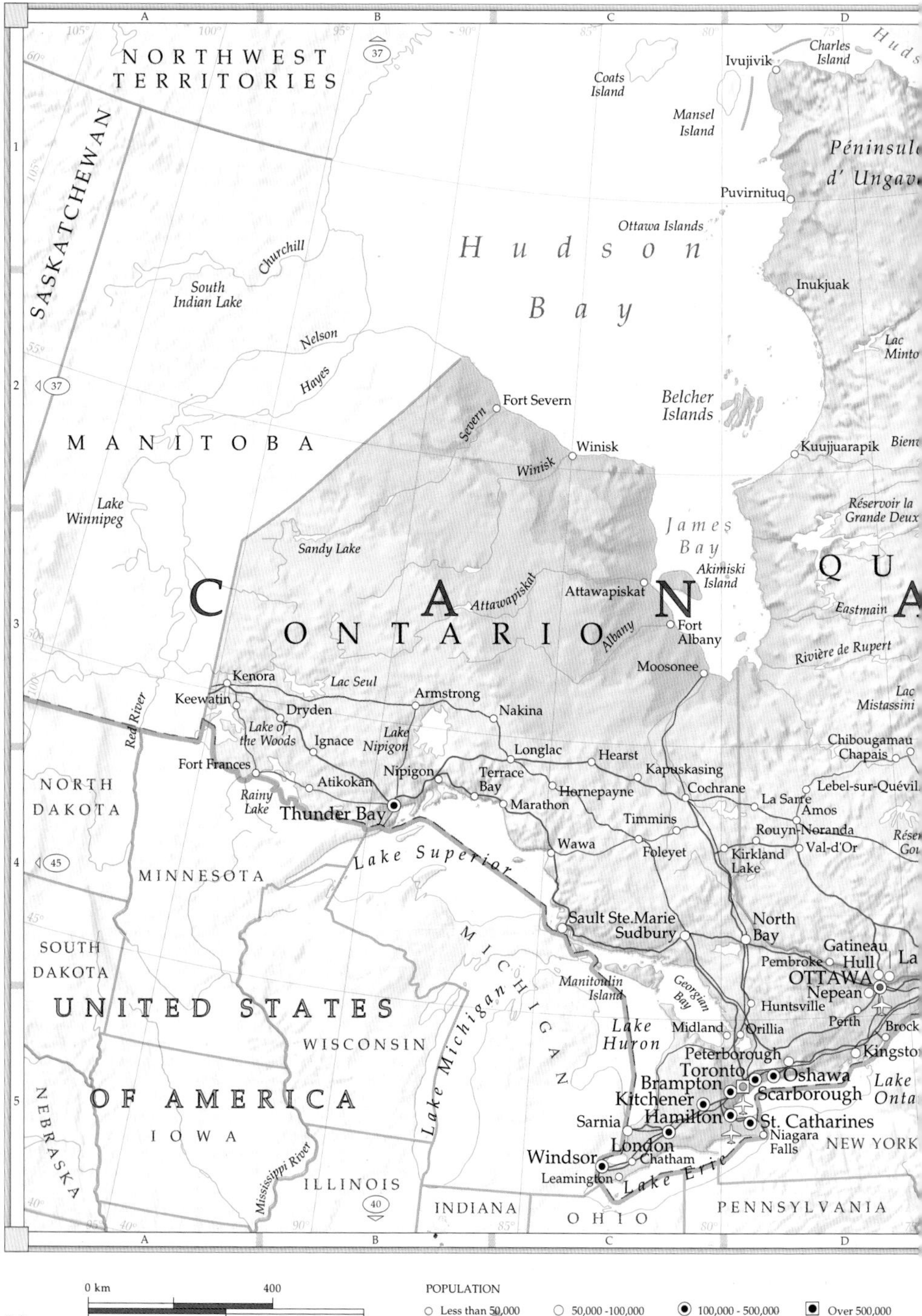
NORTHWEST TERRITORIES
SASKATCHEWAN
MANITOBA
Lake Winnipeg
South Indian Lake
Churchill
Nelson
Hayes
Hudson Bay
Coats Island
Mansel Island
Ivujivik
Charles Island
Péninsule d' Ungava
Puvirnituq
Ottawa Islands
Inukjuak
Lac Minto
Belcher Islands
Fort Severn
Severn
Winisk
Kuujjuarapik
Réservoir la Grande Deux
James Bay
Akimiski Island
Attawapiskat
Fort Albany
Albany
Moosonee
Sandy Lake
CANADA
ONTARIO
QU
Eastmain
Rivière de Rupert
Lac Mistassini
Kenora
Lac Seul
Keewatin
Red River
Dryden
Armstrong
Nakina
Lake of the Woods
Ignace
Lake Nipigon
Longlac
Hearst
Kapuskasing
Chibougamau
Chapais
Fort Frances
Atikokan
Nipigon
Terrace Bay
Hornepayne
Cochrane
Lebel-sur-Quévil
La Sarre
Amos
Rainy Lake
Thunder Bay
Marathon
Timmins
Rouyn-Noranda
Val-d'Or
NORTH DAKOTA
Wawa
Foleyet
Kirkland Lake
Lake Superior
MINNESOTA
Sault Ste.Marie
Sudbury
North Bay
MICHIGAN
SOUTH DAKOTA
Gatineau
Pembroke
Hull
OTTAWA
Nepean
Manitoulin Island
Georgian Bay
Huntsville
UNITED STATES OF AMERICA
Lake Huron
Midland
Orillia
Perth
Brock
WISCONSIN
Peterborough
Kingston
Toronto
Oshawa
Brampton
Scarborough
Lake Ontario
Kitchener
NEBRASKA
IOWA
Lake Michigan
Sarnia
Hamilton
St. Catharines
Niagara Falls
London
NEW YORK
Windsor
Chatham
Mississippi River
Leamington
Lake Erie
ILLINOIS
INDIANA
OHIO
PENNSYLVANIA
37
45
40
POPULATION
Less than 50,000
50,000 -100,000
100,000 - 500,000
Over 500,000
0 km
400
0 miles
400

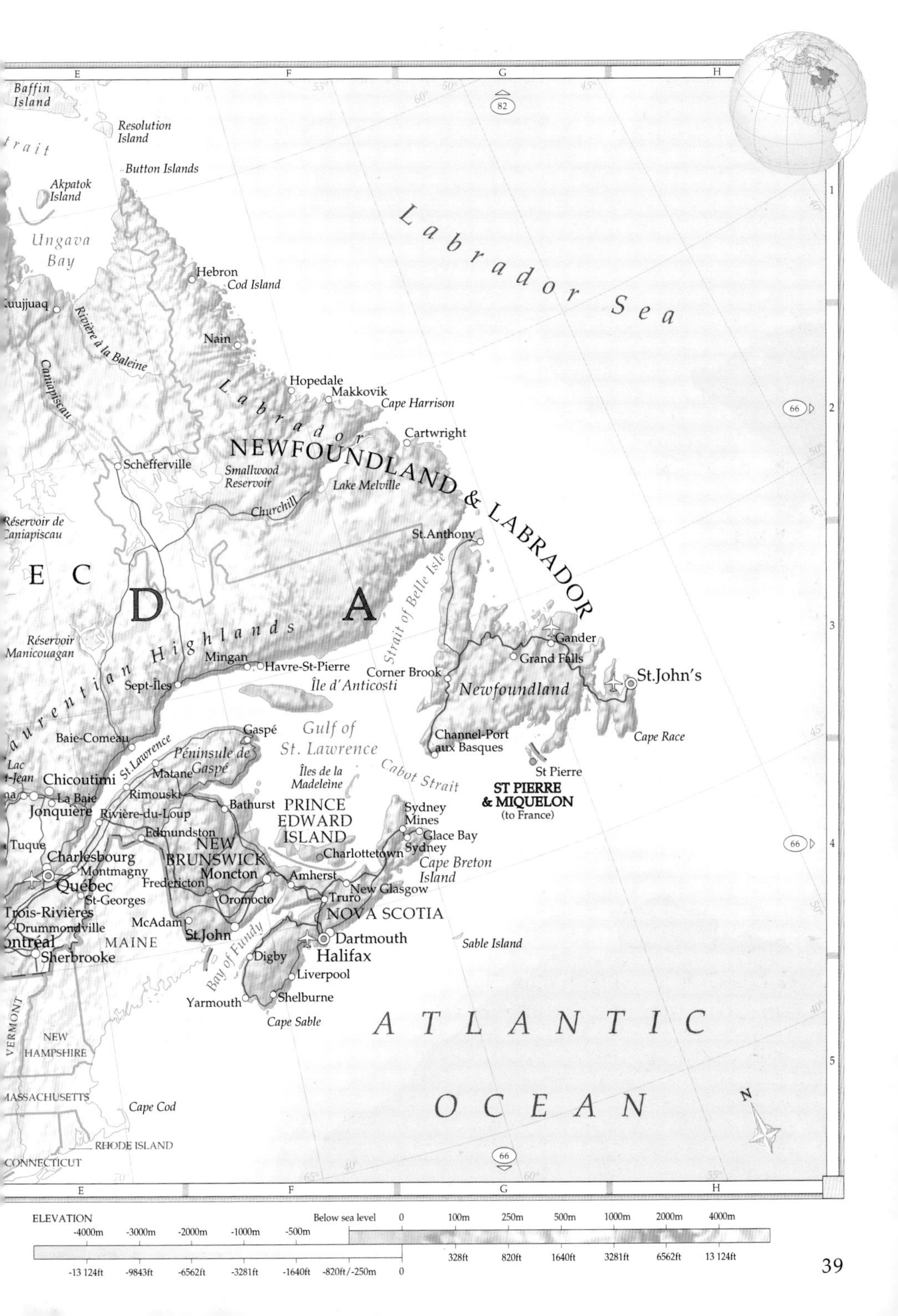

Baffin Island

Resolution Island

Button Islands

Akpatok Island

Ungava Bay

Strait

Kuujjuaq

Rivière à la Baleine

Caniapiscau

Hebron

Cod Island

Nain

Hopedale

Makkovik

Cape Harrison

Cartwright

L a b r a d o r   S e a

Schefferville

NEWFOUNDLAND & LABRADOR

Smallwood Reservoir

Churchill

Lake Melville

L a b r a d o r

Réservoir de Caniapiscau

C A N A D A

Strait of Belle Isle

St.Anthony

E   C

Réservoir Manicouagan

Laurentian Highlands

Mingan

Havre-St-Pierre

Île d'Anticosti

Corner Brook

Gander

Grand Falls

St.John's

Newfoundland

Sept-Îles

Baie-Comeau

St. Lawrence

Matane

Gaspé

Péninsule de Gaspé

Gulf of St. Lawrence

Channel-Port aux Basques

Cape Race

Cabot Strait

Lac t-Jean

Chicoutimi

La Baie

Jonquière

Rimouski

Rivière-du-Loup

Îles de la Madeleine

St Pierre

ST PIERRE & MIQUELON (to France)

Tuque

Charlesbourg

Montmagny

Edmundston

NEW BRUNSWICK

PRINCE EDWARD ISLAND

Bathurst

Sydney Mines

Glace Bay

Sydney

Cape Breton Island

Québec

St-Georges

Fredericton

Moncton

Charlottetown

Trois-Rivières

Drummondville

McAdam

Oromocto

Amherst

New Glasgow

ontréal

Sherbrooke

MAINE

St.John

Truro

NOVA SCOTIA

VERMONT

Bay of Fundy

Digby

Dartmouth

Halifax

Sable Island

Liverpool

NEW HAMPSHIRE

Yarmouth

Shelburne

Cape Sable

A T L A N T I C

MASSACHUSETTS

Cape Cod

O C E A N

RHODE ISLAND

CONNECTICUT

N

ELEVATION

					Below sea level	0	100m	250m	500m	1000m	2000m	4000m
-4000m	-3000m	-2000m	-1000m	-500m								

							328ft	820ft	1640ft	3281ft	6562ft	13 124ft
-13 124ft	-9843ft	-6562ft	-3281ft	-1640ft	-820ft/-250m	0						

39

USA: THE NORTHEAST

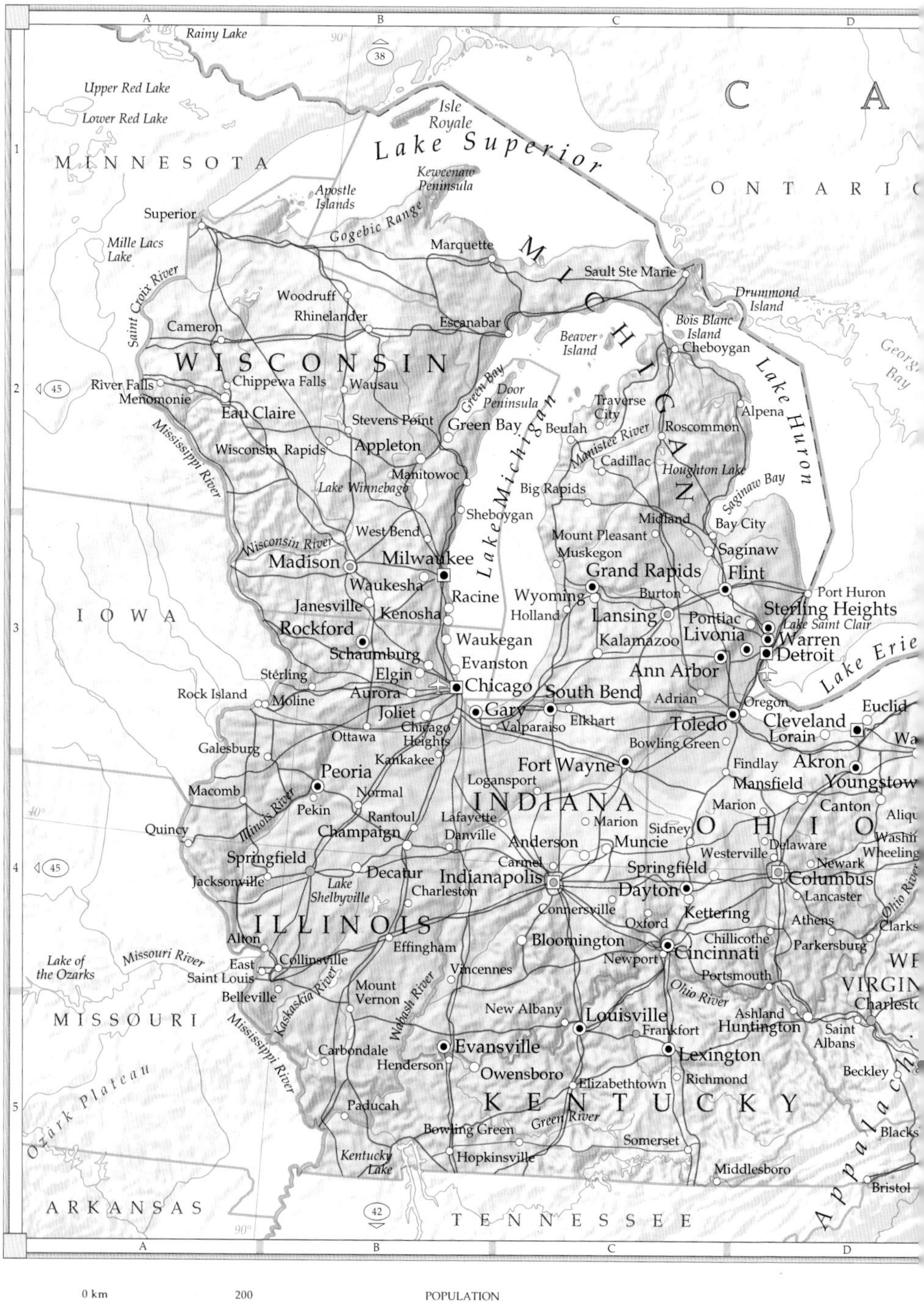

MINNESOTA

Rainy Lake

Upper Red Lake

Lower Red Lake

Isle Royale

Lake Superior

Keweenaw Peninsula

Apostle Islands

Gogebic Range

Marquette

ONTARIO

Superior

Mille Lacs Lake

Saint Croix River

Cameron

Woodruff

Rhinelander

Escanabar

Sault Ste Marie

Drummond Island

Bois Blanc Island

Cheboygan

Beaver Island

Lake Huron

Georgi Bay

WISCONSIN

River Falls

Menomonie

Chippewa Falls

Wausau

Eau Claire

Mississippi River

Wisconsin Rapids

Stevens Point

Appleton

Green Bay

Door Peninsula

Manitowoc

Lake Winnebago

Sheboygan

Traverse City

Beulah

Big Rapids

Cadillac

Manistee River

Roscommon

Alpena

Houghton Lake

MICHIGAN

Saginaw Bay

West Bend

Wisconsin River

Madison

Milwaukee

Waukesha

Janesville

Racine

Kenosha

Mount Pleasant

Muskegon

Grand Rapids

Wyoming

Holland

Lansing

Burton

Kalamazoo

Midland

Bay City

Saginaw

Flint

Pontiac

Livonia

Port Huron

Sterling Heights

Lake Saint Clair

Warren

Detroit

IOWA

Rockford

Schaumburg

Sterling

Rock Island

Moline

Galesburg

Waukegan

Evanston

Elgin

Aurora

Chicago

Joliet

Chicago Heights

Ottawa

Kankakee

South Bend

Gary

Valparaiso

Elkhart

Adrian

Ann Arbor

Oregon

Toledo

Bowling Green

Findlay

Cleveland

Lorain

Euclid

Wa

Lake Erie

Macomb

Quincy

Peoria

Normal

Pekin

Rantoul

Springfield

Jacksonville

Champaign

Danville

Lafayette

Logansport

INDIANA

Marion

Anderson

Muncie

Sidney

Marion

Delaware

Westerville

Canton

Youngstow

Aliqu

Washi

Wheeling

Illinois River

Decatur

Lake Shelbyville

Charleston

Carmel

Indianapolis

Springfield

Dayton

Kettering

OHIO

Newark

Columbus

Lancaster

Athens

Clarks

WE

VIRGIN

Charlest

ILLINOIS

Alton

East Saint Louis

Collinsville

Belleville

Effingham

Mount Vernon

Vincennes

Connersville

Oxford

Bloomington

Newport

Cincinnati

Chillicothe

Portsmouth

Parkersburg

Lake of the Ozarks

MISSOURI

Missouri River

Kaskaskia River

New Albany

Louisville

Frankfort

Ohio River

Ashland

Huntington

Saint Albans

Beckley

Carbondale

Henderson

Evansville

Owensboro

Elizabethtown

Lexington

Richmond

Ozark Plateau

Mississippi River

Paducah

Kentucky Lake

Green River

KENTUCKY

Blacks

Appalachi

Bristol

ARKANSAS

Bowling Green

Hopkinsville

Somerset

Middlesboro

TENNESSEE

0 km   200

0 miles   200

POPULATION

○ Less than 50,000   ○ 50,000 -100,000   ◉ 100,000 - 500,000   ◼ Over 500,000

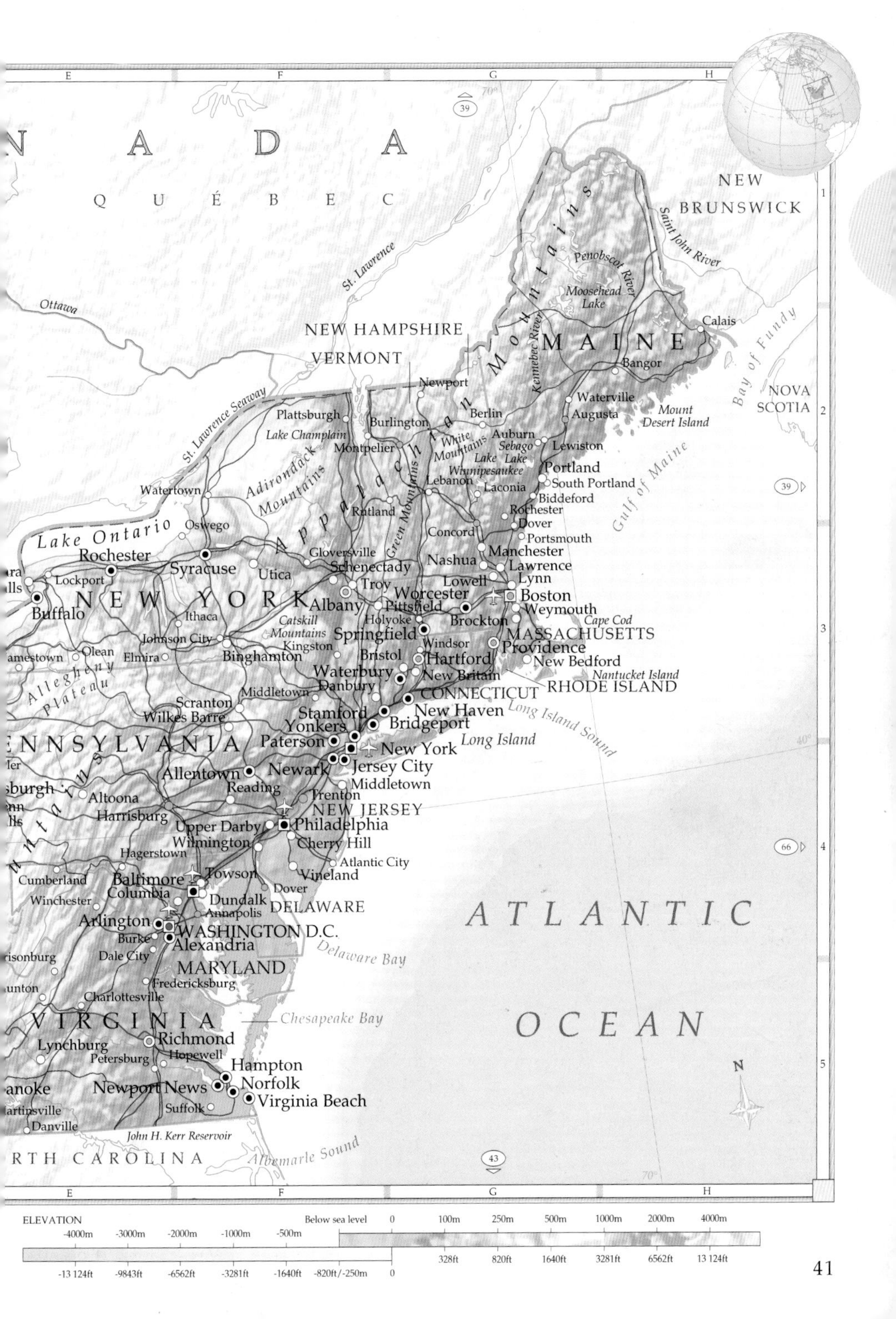

C A N A D A

QUÉBEC

NEW BRUNSWICK

Ottawa

St. Lawrence

St. Lawrence Seaway

Penobscot River

Kennebec River

Moosehead Lake

Saint John River

NEW HAMPSHIRE

VERMONT

MAINE

Calais

Appalachian Mountains

Bangor

Newport

Plattsburgh

Burlington

Berlin

Waterville

Augusta

NOVA SCOTIA

Lake Champlain

Montpelier

White Mountains

Auburn

Lewiston

Mount Desert Island

Watertown

Adirondack Mountains

Lebanon

Laconia

Sebago Lake

Lake Winnipesaukee

Portland

South Portland

Green Mountains

Rutland

Concord

Rochester

Biddeford

Bay of Fundy

Gulf of Maine

Lake Ontario

Oswego

Gloversville

Nashua

Dover

Portsmouth

Rochester

Syracuse

Utica

Schenectady

Troy

Worcester

Manchester

Lawrence

Lynn

Boston

Buffalo

Lockport

NEW YORK

Albany

Pittsfield

Lowell

Weymouth

Ithaca

Catskill Mountains

Holyoke

Springfield

Brockton

MASSACHUSETTS

Cape Cod

Johnson City

Kingston

Windsor

Providence

New Bedford

Olean

Elmira

Binghamton

Bristol

Hartford

RHODE ISLAND

Nantucket Island

Waterbury

New Britain

Danbury

CONNECTICUT

Middletown

New Haven

Allegheny Plateau

Scranton

Wilkes Barre

Stamford

Yonkers

Bridgeport

Long Island Sound

PENNSYLVANIA

Paterson

Newark

New York

Long Island

Allentown

Reading

Jersey City

Middletown

Altoona

Harrisburg

Trenton

NEW JERSEY

Upper Darby

Philadelphia

Hagerstown

Wilmington

Cherry Hill

Cumberland

Towson

Vineland

Atlantic City

Winchester

Columbia

Baltimore

Dundalk

Dover

DELAWARE

Arlington

Annapolis

WASHINGTON D.C.

Burke

Alexandria

Dale City

MARYLAND

Delaware Bay

Fredericksburg

Charlottesville

VIRGINIA

Chesapeake Bay

ATLANTIC

OCEAN

Lynchburg

Richmond

Hopewell

Petersburg

Hampton

Newport News

Norfolk

Virginia Beach

Suffolk

Danville

John H. Kerr Reservoir

NORTH CAROLINA

Albemarle Sound

N

ELEVATION

					Below sea level	0	100m	250m	500m	1000m	2000m	4000m
-4000m	-3000m	-2000m	-1000m	-500m								
-13 124ft	-9843ft	-6562ft	-3281ft	-1640ft	-820ft/-250m	0	328ft	820ft	1640ft	3281ft	6562ft	13 124ft

41

USA: THE SOUTHEAST

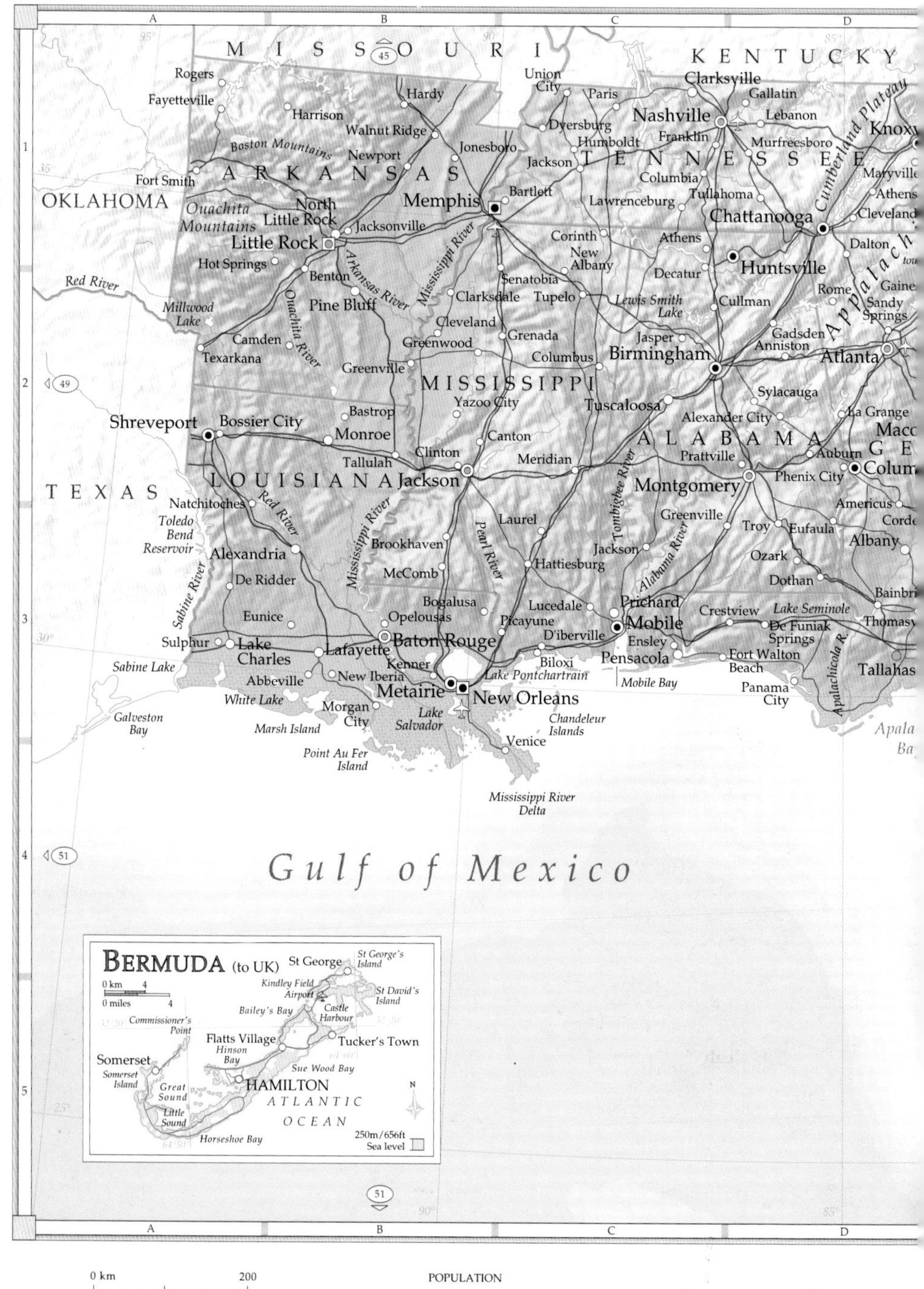

MISSOURI

Rogers
Fayetteville
Harrison
Hardy
Union
City
Paris
Clarksville
Gallatin
Lebanon

KENTUCKY

Walnut Ridge
Newport
Dyersburg
Humboldt
Nashville
Franklin
Murfreesboro
Knox

Fort Smith
Boston Mountains
Jonesboro
Jackson
TENNESSEE
Maryville

OKLAHOMA
ARKANSAS
Memphis
Bartlett
Lawrenceburg
Tullahoma
Chattanooga
Athens
Cleveland

Ouachita
Mountains
North
Little Rock
Jacksonville
Corinth
New
Albany
Athens
Decatur
Huntsville
Dalton
tou

Little Rock
Hot Springs
Benton
Senatobia
Lewis Smith
Lake
Cullman
Gadsden
Anniston
Rome
Gaine
Sandy
Springs

Red River
Millwood
Lake
Pine Bluff
Clarksdale
Tupelo
Jasper
Birmingham
Atlanta

Texarkana
Camden
Greenwood
Grenada
Columbus
Tuscaloosa
Sylacauga

Greenville
MISSISSIPPI
Yazoo City
Alexander City
La Grange
Macc
GE
Colum

Shreveport
Bossier City
Monroe
Bastrop
Canton
ALABAMA

Tallulah
Clinton
Meridian
Prattville
Auburn
Phenix City

TEXAS
LOUISIANA
Jackson
Montgomery
Americus
Corde
Albany

Natchitoches
Toledo
Bend
Reservoir
Alexandria
Laurel
Greenville
Troy
Eufaula
Ozark

De Ridder
Brookhaven
Jackson
Hattiesburg
Dothan

Eunice
Bogalusa
Opelousas
Picayune
Lucedale
D'iberville
Prichard
Mobile
Crestview
De Funiak
Springs
Lake Seminole
Thomasv
Bainbri

Sulphur
Lake
Charles
Lafayette
Baton Rouge
Kenner
Ensley
Pensacola
Fort Walton
Beach
Tallahas

Sabine Lake
Abbeville
New Iberia
Metairie
Biloxi
Lake Pontchartrain
Mobile Bay
Panama
City

Galveston
Bay
White Lake
Morgan
City
New Orleans
Lake
Salvador
Chandeleur
Islands
Apala
Ba

Marsh Island
Point Au Fer
Island
Venice

Mississippi River
Delta

Gulf of Mexico

BERMUDA (to UK)

St George
St George's
Island

0 km   4
0 miles   4

Kindley Field
Airport
St David's
Island

Commissioner's
Point
Bailey's Bay
Castle
Harbour
Tucker's Town

Flatts Village
Hinson
Bay

Somerset
Somerset
Island
Sue Wood Bay

Great
Sound
HAMILTON
ATLANTIC
OCEAN

Little
Sound
N

Horseshoe Bay
250m/656ft
Sea level

0 km   200
0 miles   200

POPULATION

○ Less than 50,000   ○ 50,000 -100,000   ◉ 100,000 - 500,000   ◼ Over 500,000

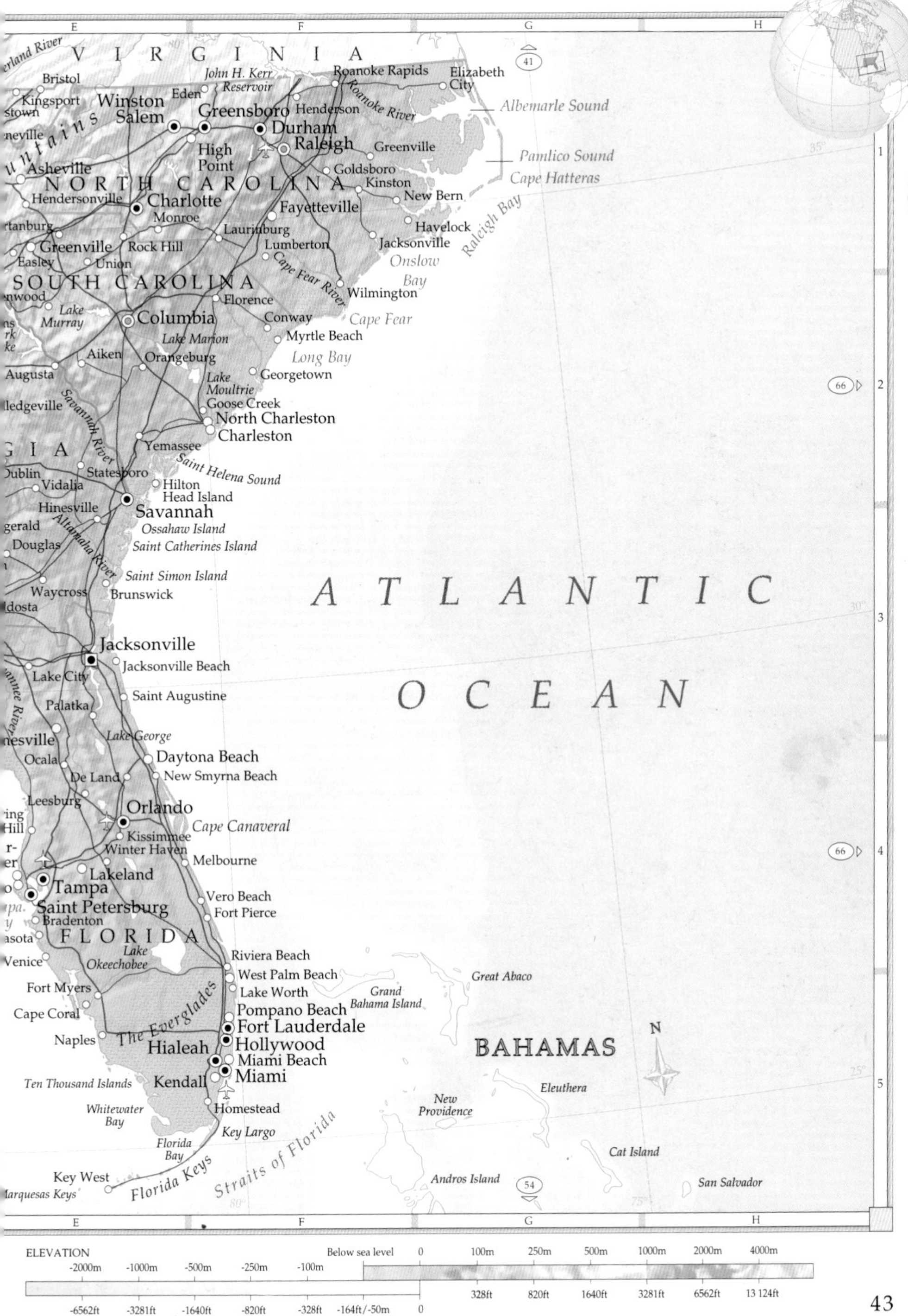

ELEVATION

					Below sea level	0	100m	250m	500m	1000m	2000m	4000m
-2000m	-1000m	-500m	-250m	-100m								
							328ft	820ft	1640ft	3281ft	6562ft	13 124ft
-6562ft	-3281ft	-1640ft	-820ft	-328ft	-164ft/-50m	0						

USA: Central States

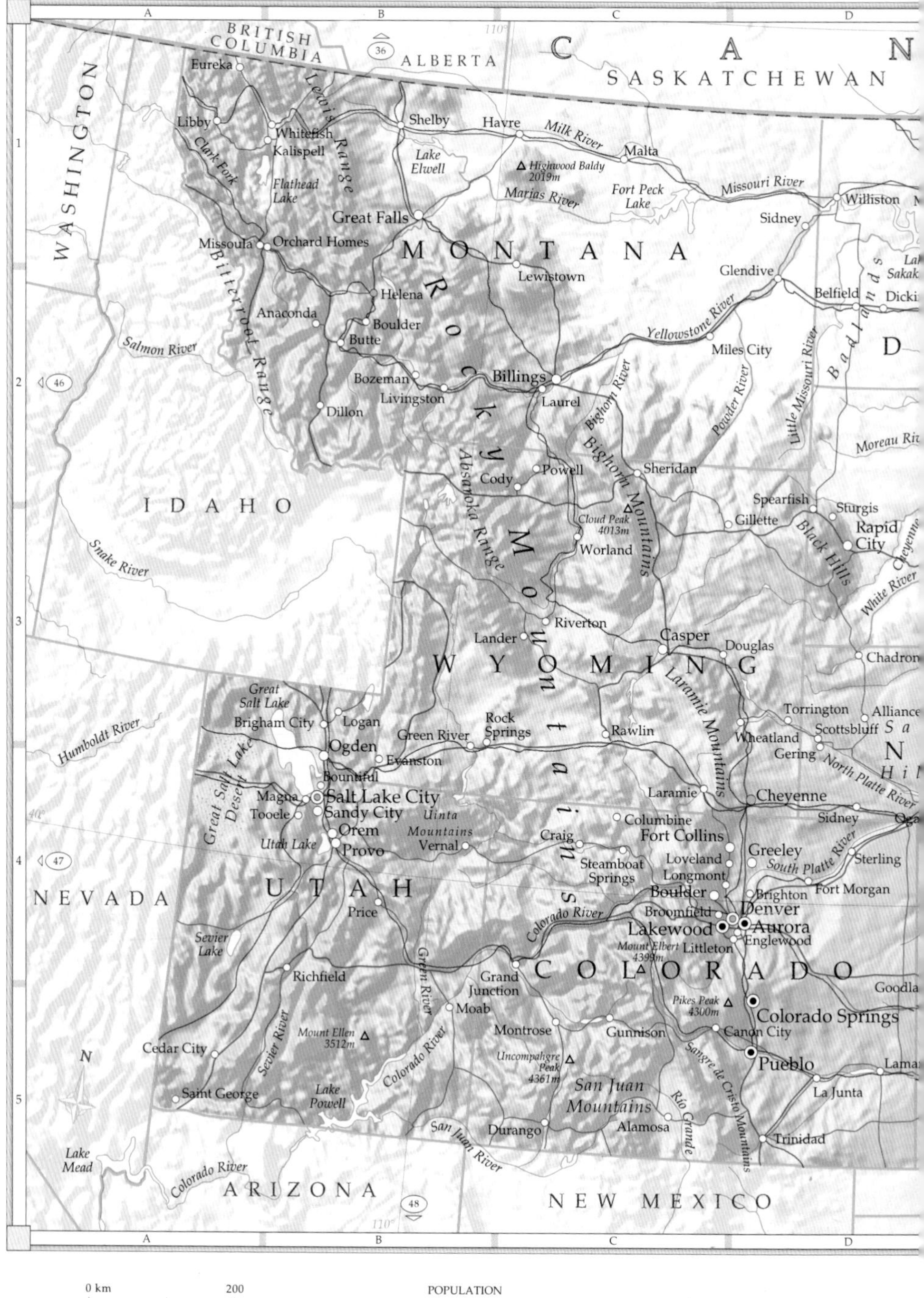

British Columbia
Eureka
Alberta
Saskatchewan
Libby
Whitefish
Kalispell
Shelby
Havre
Milk River
Malta
Lake Elwell
△ Highwood Baldy 2019m
Marias River
Fort Peck Lake
Missouri River
Williston
Flathead Lake
Great Falls
Sidney
Lewistown
Missoula
Orchard Homes
MONTANA
Glendive
Belfield
Dicki
Helena
Sakak
La
Anaconda
Boulder
Butte
Yellowstone River
Miles City
Badlands
D
Salmon River
Bozeman
Livingston
Billings
Laurel
Powder River
Little Missouri River
Dillon
Cody
Powell
Sheridan
Moreau Riv
46
IDAHO
Cloud Peak 4013m
Worland
Spearfish
Gillette
Sturgis
Rapid City
Black Hills
Snake River
Riverton
Cheyenne
White River
Lander
Casper
Douglas
Chadron
WYOMING
Laramie Mountains
Torrington
Alliance
Sa
Great Salt Lake
Brigham City
Logan
Green River
Rock Springs
Rawlin
Wheatland
Scottsbluff
Gering
Hi
N
Humboldt River
Ogden
Evanston
Laramie
Cheyenne
North Platte River
Magna
Salt Lake City
Sandy City
Uinta Mountains
Columbine
Sidney
Tooele
Orem
Craig
Fort Collins
Greeley
Sterling
Utah Lake
Provo
Vernal
Steamboat Springs
Loveland
Longmont
NEVADA
UTAH
Price
Boulder
Brighton
Fort Morgan
Broomfield
Denver
Colorado River
Lakewood
Aurora
Mount Elbert 4399m
Littleton
Englewood
Richfield
Grand Junction
Moab
COLORADO
Pikes Peak 4300m
Goodla
Mount Ellen 3512m
Montrose
Gunnison
Canon City
Colorado Springs
Lama
N
Cedar City
Uncompahgre Peak 4361m
San Juan Mountains
Pueblo
La Junta
Sevier Lake
Green River
Colorado River
Saint George
Lake Powell
San Juan River
Durango
Alamosa
Rio Grande
Trinidad
Lake Mead
Colorado River
ARIZONA
48
NEW MEXICO

0 km   200
0 miles   200

POPULATION
○ Less than 50,000   ○ 50,000 -100,000   ◉ 100,000 - 500,000   ◼ Over 500,000

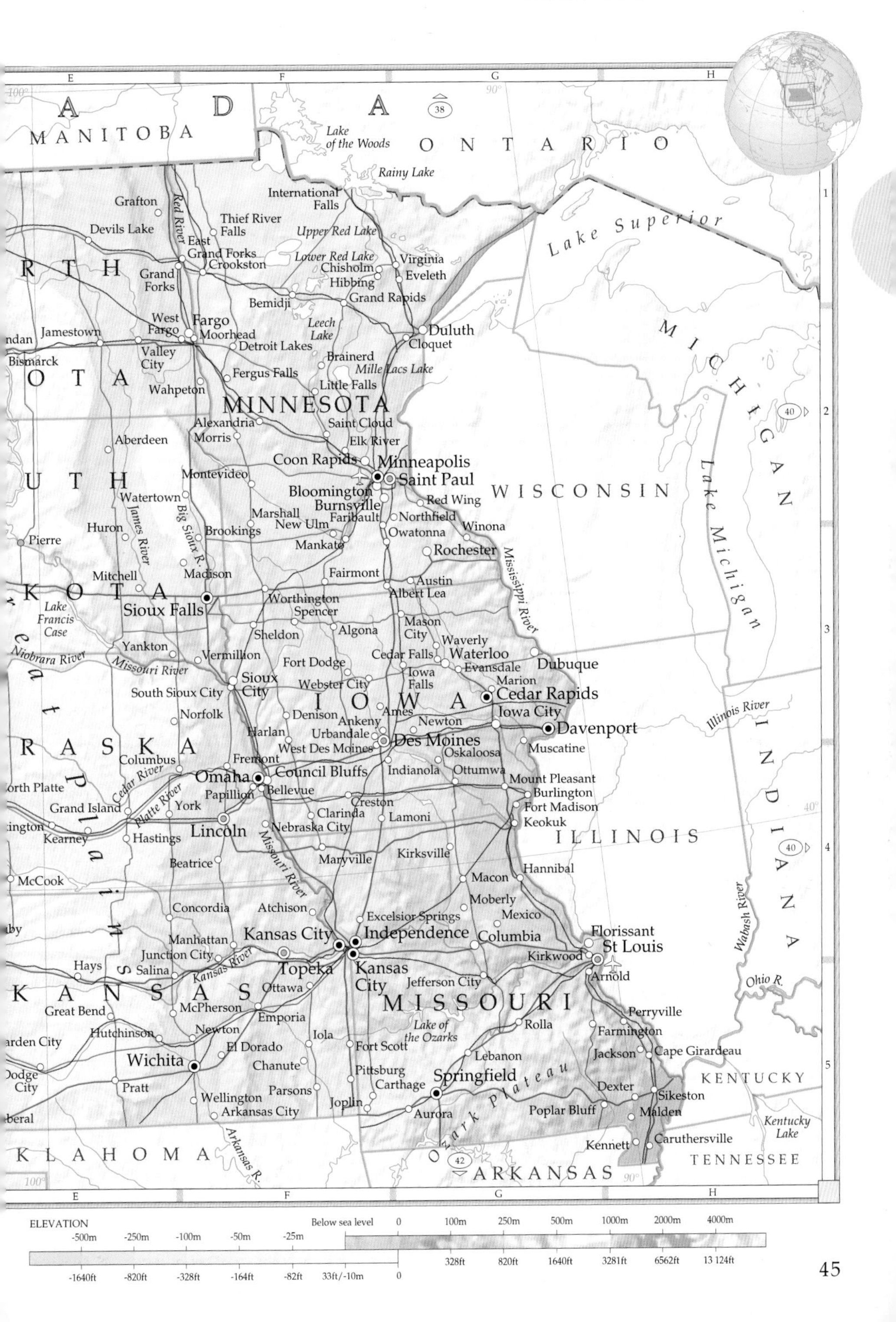

MANITOBA

ONTARIO

Lake of the Woods

Rainy Lake

Lake Superior

MICHIGAN

Grafton
Devils Lake
Thief River Falls
International Falls
East Grand Forks
Upper Red Lake
Crookston
Lower Red Lake
Chisholm
Virginia
Eveleth
Hibbing
Grand Rapids
Bemidji
Grand Forks
West Fargo
Fargo
Moorhead
Leech Lake
Detroit Lakes
Duluth
Cloquet

RTH

Jamestown
ndan
Bismarck
Valley City
Wahpeton
Fergus Falls
Brainerd
Mille Lacs Lake
Little Falls

OTA

Aberdeen

MINNESOTA

Saint Cloud
Elk River
Alexandria
Morris
Montevideo
Coon Rapids
Minneapolis
Saint Paul

WISCONSIN

Lake Michigan

UTH

Watertown
Brookings
Bloomington
Burnsville
Marshall
New Ulm
Faribault
Northfield
Red Wing
Huron
James River
Big Sioux R.
Mankato
Owatonna
Winona
Madison
Fairmont
Rochester

KOTA

Pierre
Mitchell
Lake Francis Case
Sioux Falls
Worthington
Spencer
Sheldon
Algona
Austin
Albert Lea
Mason City
Waverly
Mississippi River

Yankton
Vermillion
Fort Dodge
Cedar Falls
Waterloo
Dubuque
Niobrara River
Sioux City
Webster City
Iowa Falls
Evansdale
Marion
Cedar Rapids
South Sioux City
Missouri River
Norfolk
Denison
Ames
Newton
Iowa City
Davenport
Illinois River

RASKA

Columbus
Cedar River
Harlan
Urbandale
Ankeny
Muscatine
orth Platte
Omaha
West Des Moines
Des Moines
Oskaloosa

IOWA

Grand Island
ington
Kearney
Hastings
Fremont
Papillion
Bellevue
York
Lincoln
Council Bluffs
Indianola
Ottumwa
Mount Pleasant
Burlington
Fort Madison
Keokuk
Platte River
Clarinda
Creston
Lamoni
Nebraska City
Beatrice
Maryville
Kirksville
McCook
Macon
Hannibal

ILLINOIS

INDIANA

Wabash River

Concordia
Atchison
Moberly
Mexico
McCook
by
Manhattan
Excelsior Springs
Columbia
Florissant
Junction City
Salina
Kansas City
Independence
Kirkwood
St Louis
Hays
Topeka
Kansas City
Jefferson City
Arnold
Ohio R.

KANSAS

Ottawa
MISSOURI
Great Bend
McPherson
Emporia
Lake of the Ozarks
Rolla
Perryville
arden City
Hutchinson
Newton
Iola
Lebanon
Farmington
Jackson
Cape Girardeau
Dodge City
El Dorado
Fort Scott
KENTUCKY
Wichita
Chanute
Pittsburg
Springfield
Dexter
Sikeston
Pratt
Carthage
Aurora
Poplar Bluff
Malden
eral
Wellington
Parsons
Joplin
Kansas River
Arkansas City
Kennett
Caruthersville
TENNESSEE
Kentucky Lake

Arkansas R.

KLAHOMA

ARKANSAS

Ozark Plateau

ELEVATION										
-500m	-250m	-100m	-50m	-25m	Below sea level	0	100m	250m	500m	1000m 2000m 4000m
							328ft	820ft	1640ft	3281ft 6562ft 13 124ft
-1640ft	-820ft	-328ft	-164ft	-82ft	33ft/-10m	0				

USA: THE WEST

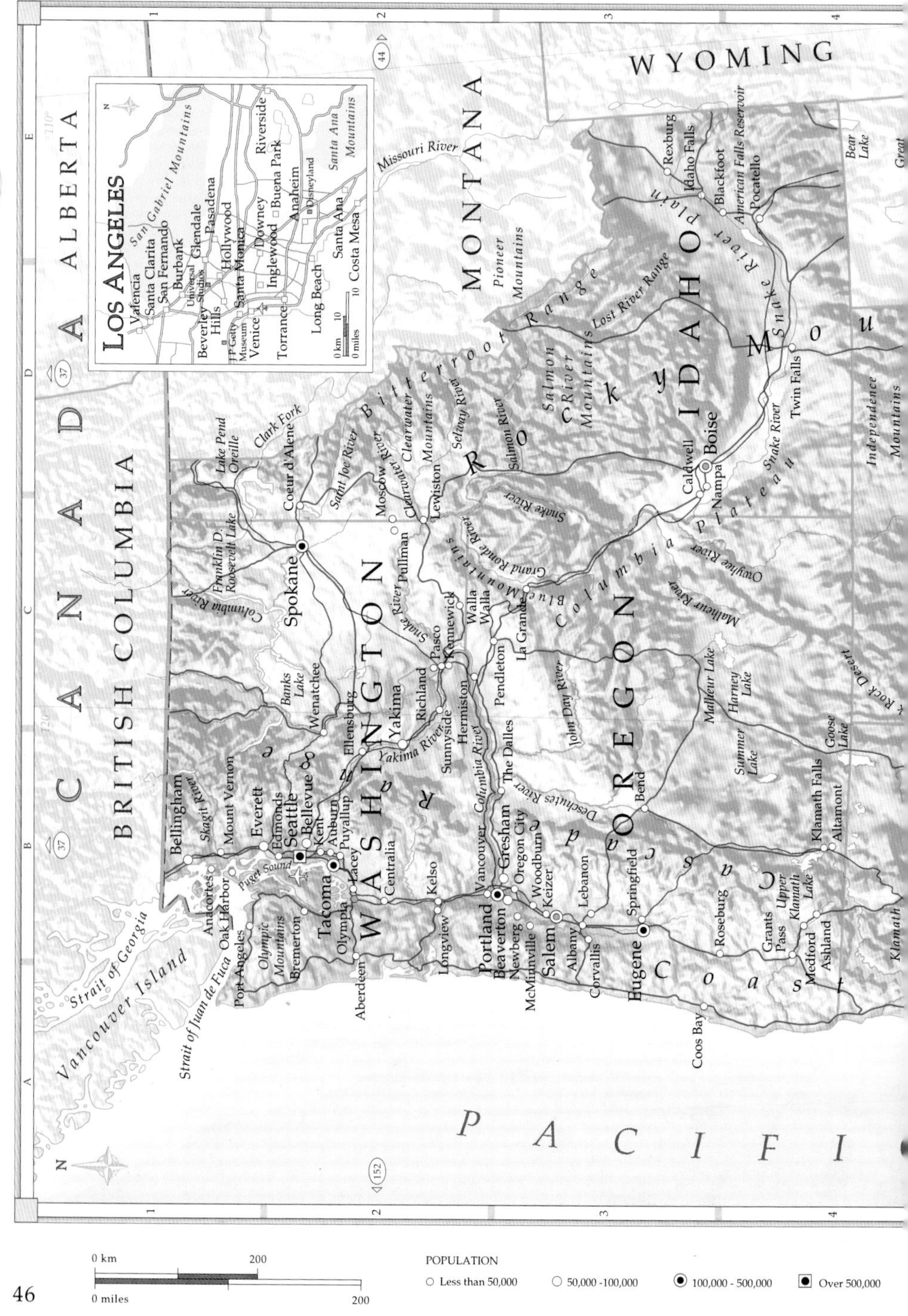

LOS ANGELES

Valencia
Santa Clarita
San Fernando
Burbank
Glendale
Pasadena
Hollywood
Universal
Studios
Santa Monica
Getty
Museum
Venice
Torrance
Inglewood
Downey
Buena Park
Anaheim
Disneyland
Costa Mesa
Santa Ana
Long Beach

San Gabriel Mountains
Beverley Hills
Riverside
Santa Ana Mountains

0 km   10
0 miles   10

CANADA

ALBERTA

BRITISH COLUMBIA

Vancouver Island

Strait of Georgia

Strait of Juan de Fuca   Oak Harbor

Port Angeles
Olympic
Mountains
Bremerton

Bellingham
Anacortes
Mount Vernon
Everett
Edmonds
Seattle
Bellevue
Kent
Auburn
Tacoma
Puyallup
Olympia
Lacey
Aberdeen

WASHINGTON

Skagit River

Franklin D.
Roosevelt Lake

Columbia River

Banks
Lake

Lake Pend
Oreille

Clark Fork

Coeur d'Alene

Spokane

Wenatchee

Ellensburg
Yakima

Puget Sound

Centralia

Kelso

Longview

Yakima River

Sunnyside
Hermiston

Richland
Kennewick
Pasco
Walla
Walla

La Grande

Saint Joe River
Moscow River
Clearwater River
Lewiston
Pullman

Clearwater
Mountains

Snake River
Grand Ronde
Selway River

Bitterroot
Mountains

MONTANA

Missouri River

Pioneer
Mountains

Bitterroot Range

Salmon River
Mountains

Salmon River

Lost River Range

IDAHO

Caldwell
Boise
Nampa

Snake River

Columbia
Plateau

Blue
Mountains

Snake River Plain

Twin Falls

Mou

Independence
Mountains

WYOMING

Rexburg
Idaho Falls
Blackfoot
Pocatello
American Falls Reservoir

Bear
Lake

Great

Vancouver
Portland
Beaverton
Gresham
Oregon City
Newberg
McMinnville
Woodburn
Salem
Keizer
Albany
Corvallis
Lebanon
Springfield
Eugene

OREGON

Columbia River

Deschutes River

The Dalles

Bend

John Day River

Malheur Lake

Harney
Lake

Summer
Lake

Goose
Lake

Klamath Falls
Altamont

Upper
Klamath
Lake

Klamath

Owyhee River

Malheur River

Rock Desert

Coos Bay

Roseburg

Grants
Pass
Medford
Ashland

Coast

Cascade

PACIFI

0 km   200
0 miles   200

POPULATION

○ Less than 50,000   ○ 50,000 -100,000   ◉ 100,000 - 500,000   ◼ Over 500,000

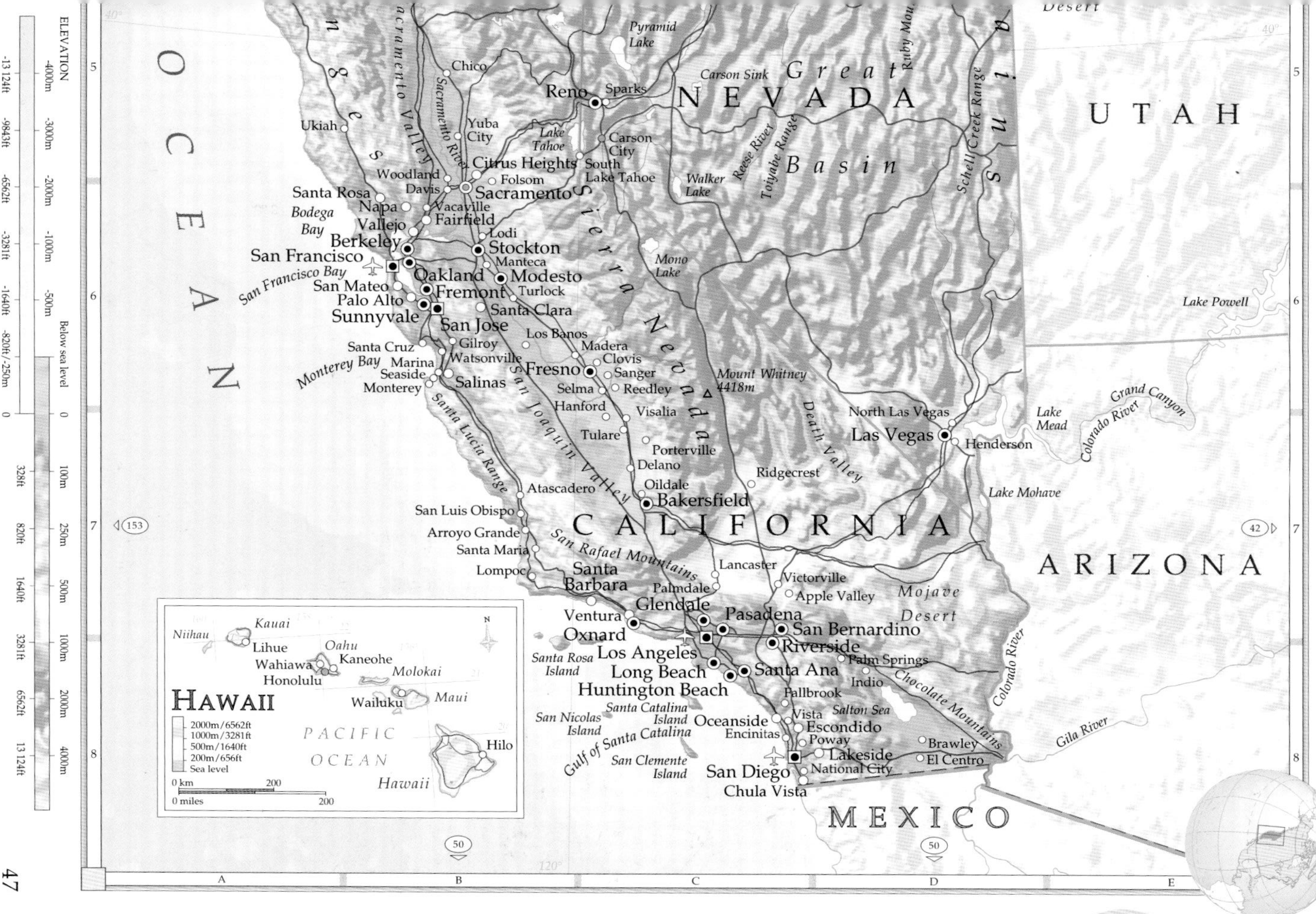

UTAH

Desert

Lake Powell

Grand Canyon

Colorado River

ARIZONA

Lake Mead

Lake Mohave

Henderson

North Las Vegas
Las Vegas

Colorado River

Gila River

MEXICO

El Centro
Brawley

Chocolate Mountains

Fallbrook
Vista Salton Sea
Escondido
Oceanside Encinitas Poway
San Diego
National City
Chula Vista

Lakeside

San Bernardino
Riverside
Santa Ana
Long Beach
Huntington Beach

Palm Springs
Indio

Mojave Desert

Apple Valley
Victorville

Pasadena
Los Angeles
Glendale

Lancaster
Palmdale

San Rafael Mountains

San Gabriel Mountains

Santa Catalina Island

San Clemente Island

San Nicolas Island

Santa Barbara Island

Gulf of Santa Catalina

Santa Barbara
Ventura
Oxnard

Santa Rosa Island
Santa Cruz Island

GREAT BASIN

Scheel Creek Range

Ruby Mou

NEVADA

Great Basin

Reese River

Carson Sink

Toiyabe Range

Walker Lake

Walker Lake

Mono Lake

Pyramid Lake

Reno
Sparks

Carson City
South Lake Tahoe
Lake Tahoe

Carson Heights

Citrus Heights
Sacramento
Folsom

Sierra Nevada

Death Valley

Death Valley

Mount Whitney
4418m

Ridgecrest

Porterville
Oildale
Delano
Visalia
Bakersfield
Tulare
Hanford
Reedley
Selma
Sanger
Clovis
Fresno
Madera
Los Banos

Atascadero
Paso Robles

CALIFORNIA

San Joaquin Valley

Chico
Yuba City

Woodland
Davis

Sacramento River

Sacramento Valley

Vacaville
Fairfield
Lodi
Manteca
Stockton
Modesto
Turlock
Santa Clara
San Jose
Gilroy
Watsonville
Salinas
Seaside
Marina
Monterey

Santa Lucia Range

San Luis Obispo
Arroyo Grande
Santa Maria
Lompoc

Napa
Santa Rosa
Vallejo
Berkeley
Oakland
Fremont
San Mateo
Palo Alto
Sunnyvale
San Francisco
Santa Cruz

San Francisco Bay

Monterey Bay

Bodega Bay

Ukiah

n g e s

a i n s

OCEAN

PACIFIC OCEAN

HAWAII

Niihau
Kauai
Lihue
Oahu
Wahiawa
Honolulu Kaneohe
Molokai
Maui
Hawaii
Hilo
Waihuku

2000m/6562ft
1000m/3281ft
500m/1640ft
200m/656ft
Sea level

0 km   200
0 miles   200

N

50

42

50

153

120

ELEVATION

-4000m	-3000m	-2000m	-1000m	-500m	Below sea level	0	100m	250m	500m	1000m	2000m	4000m
-13 124ft	-9843ft	-6562ft	-3281ft	-1640ft	-820ft/-250m	0	328ft	820ft	1640ft	3281ft	6562ft	13 124ft

USA: THE SOUTHWEST

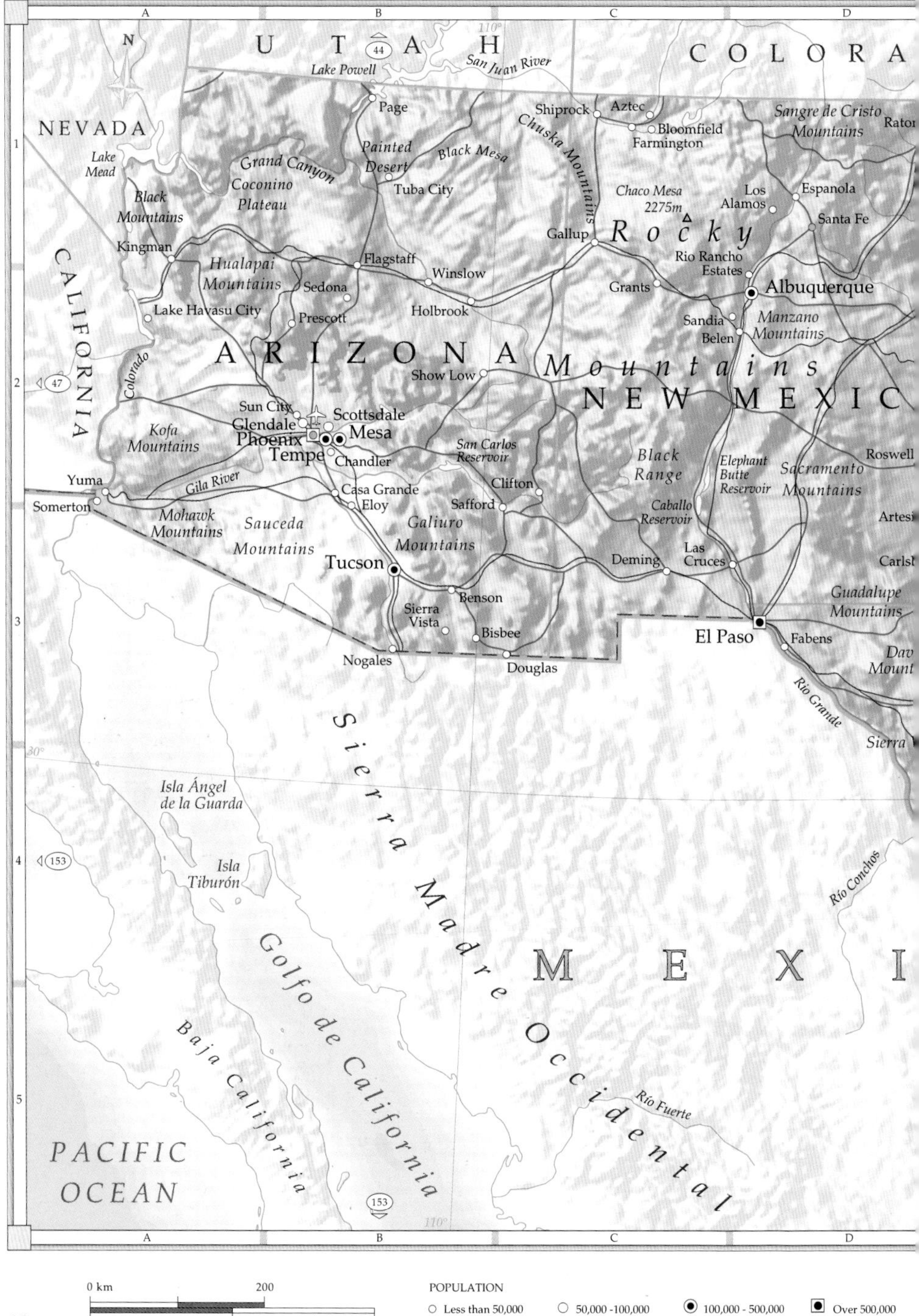

0 km   200

0 miles   200

POPULATION

○ Less than 50,000   ○ 50,000 -100,000   ● 100,000 - 500,000   ■ Over 500,000

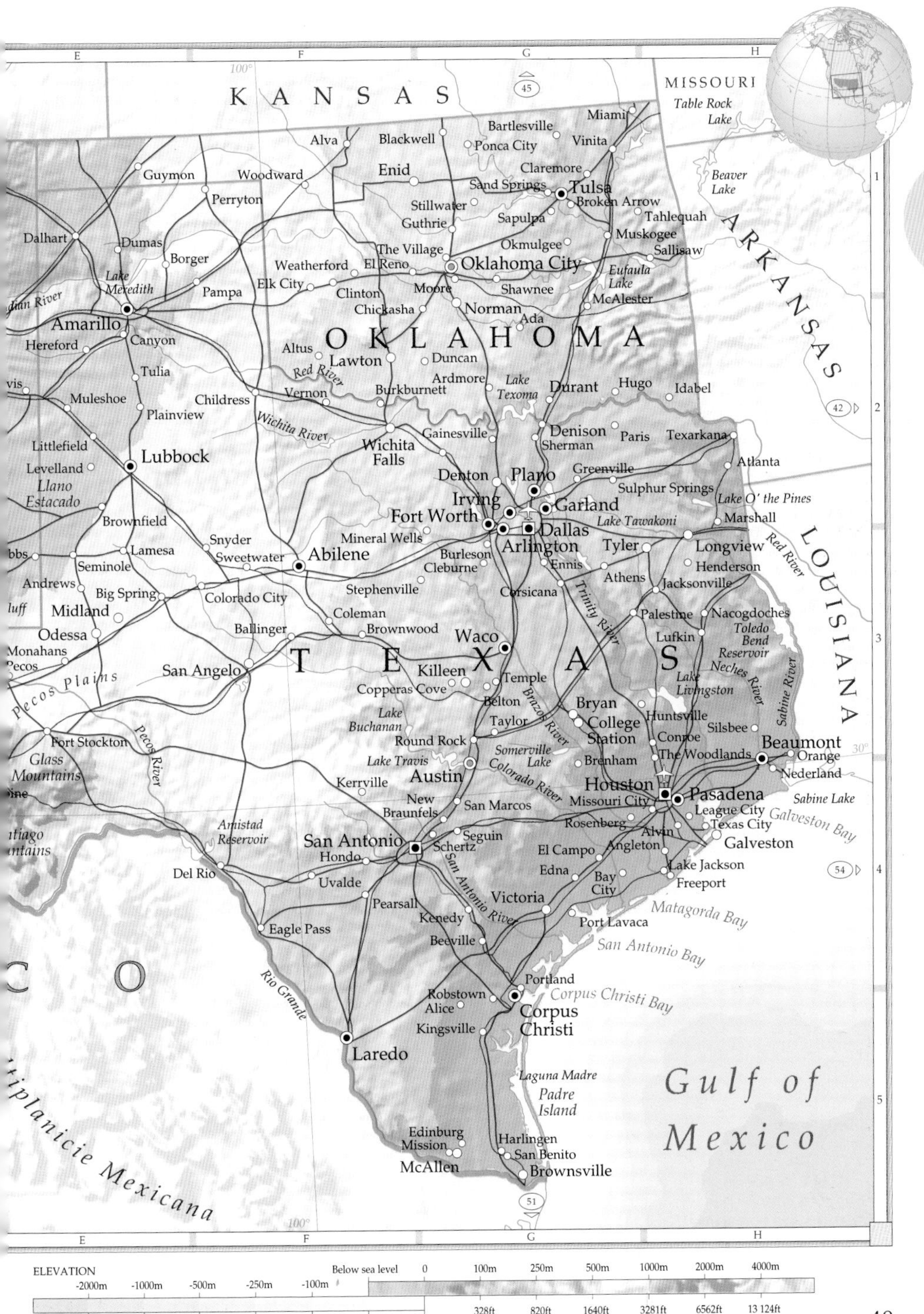

KANSAS

MISSOURI

Table Rock Lake

Guymon
Woodward
Alva
Blackwell
Bartlesville
Miami
Ponca City
Vinita

Perryton
Stillwater
Sand Springs
Tulsa
Broken Arrow

Dalhart
Dumas
Guthrie
Sapulpa
Tahlequah

Beaver Lake

Borger
Weatherford
El Reno
Okmulgee
Muskogee
Sallisaw

Lake Meredith
Pampa
Elk City
Clinton
Moore
Oklahoma City
Eufaula Lake

ARKANSAS

Amarillo
Canyon
OKLAHOMA
Chickasha
Norman
Shawnee
McAlester

Hereford
Altus
Lawton
Ada

Tulia
Duncan

Muleshoe
Childress
Vernon
Burkburnett
Ardmore
Lake Texoma
Durant
Hugo
Idabel

vis.
Plainview
Red River
Wichita River
Gainesville
Denison
Paris
Texarkana

Littlefield
Wichita Falls
Sherman
Atlanta

Levelland
Denton
Plano
Greenville
Sulphur Springs
Lake O' the Pines

Lubbock
Llano Estacado
Irving
Garland
Lake Tawakoni
Marshall

Brownfield
Fort Worth
Dallas
Longview

bbs.
Lamesa
Snyder
Sweetwater
Abilene
Mineral Wells
Arlington
Tyler
Henderson

Andrews
Seminole
Burleson
Cleburne
Ennis
Jacksonville

luff
Big Spring
Colorado City
Stephenville
Corsicana
Athens
Palestine
Nacogdoches

Midland
Coleman
TEXAS
Lufkin
Toledo Bend Reservoir

Odessa
Ballinger
Brownwood
Waco
Neches River

Monahans
San Angelo
Killeen
Temple
Bryan
Lake Livingston
Silsbee

Pecos
Pecos plains
Copperas Cove
Belton
College Station
Huntsville
Conroe
The Woodlands
Beaumont

Fort Stockton
Lake Buchanan
Round Rock
Taylor
Brenham
Orange
Nederland

Glass Mountains
Pecos River
Kerrville
Austin
Lake Travis
Somerville Lake
Colorado River
Houston
Pasadena
Sabine Lake

one
New Braunfels
San Marcos
Missouri City
League City
Texas City
Galveston Bay

Amistad Reservoir
San Antonio
Seguin
Rosenberg
Alvin
Galveston

itago
Del Rio
Hondo
Schertz
El Campo
Angleton
Lake Jackson

ntains
Uvalde
Pearsall
Victoria
Edna
Bay City
Freeport

Eagle Pass
Kenedy
Port Lavaca
Matagorda Bay

Beeville
San Antonio River
San Antonio Bay

CO
Rio Grande
Robstown
Alice
Portland
Corpus Christi
Corpus Christi Bay

Laredo
Kingsville
Corpus Christi

iplanicie Mexicana
Laguna Madre
Padre Island

Gulf of Mexico

Edinburg
Mission
Harlingen
San Benito
McAllen
Brownsville

ELEVATION

					Below sea level	0	100m	250m	500m	1000m	2000m	4000m
-2000m	-1000m	-500m	-250m	-100m								
-6562ft	-3281ft	-1640ft	-820ft	-328ft	-164ft/-50m	0	328ft	820ft	1640ft	3281ft	6562ft	13 124ft

MEXICO

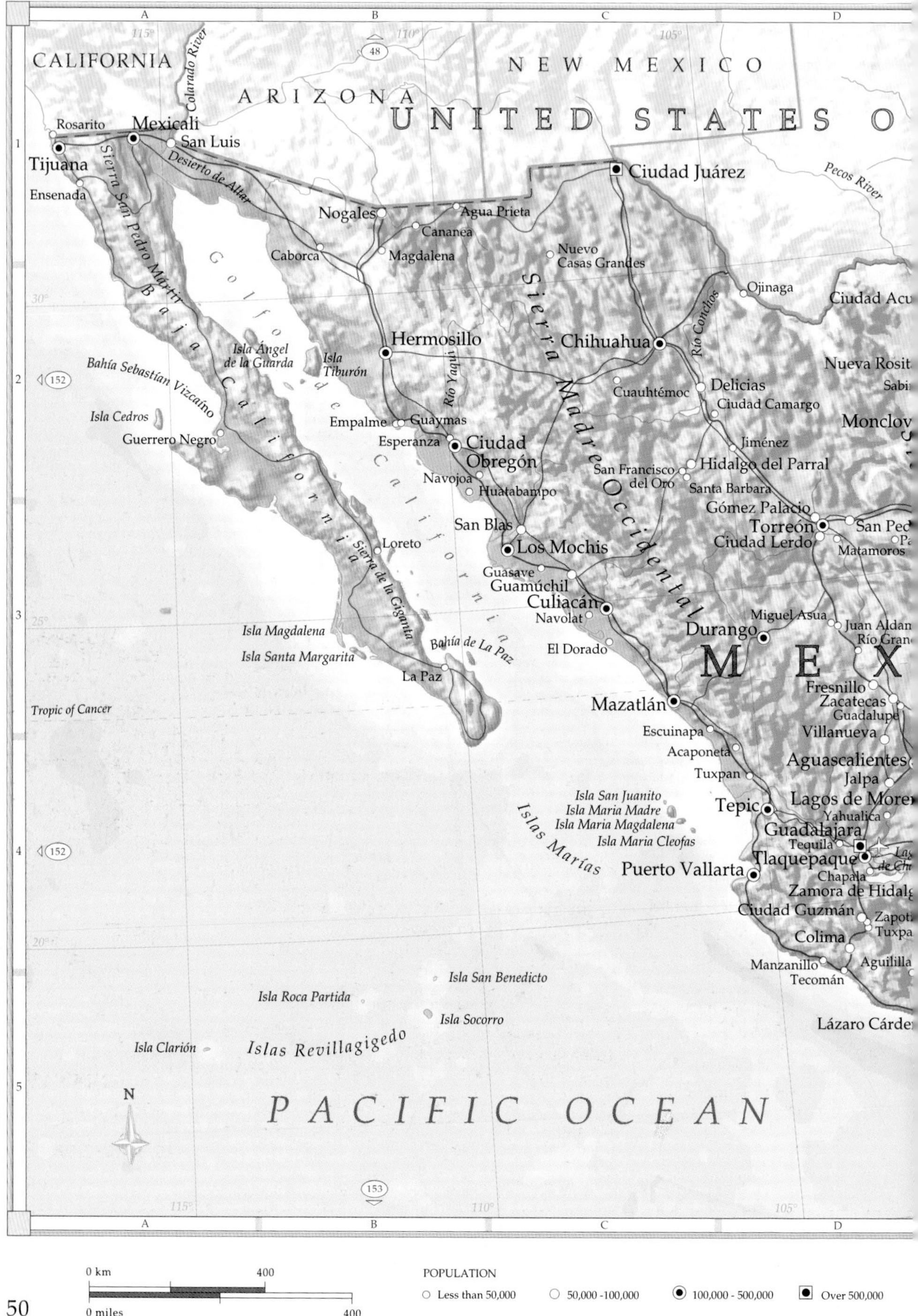

CALIFORNIA

Colorado River

48

NEW MEXICO

ARIZONA

UNITED STATES O

Rosarito

Mexicali

San Luis

Tijuana

Desierto de Altar

Ciudad Juárez

Pecos River

Ensenada

Sierra San Pedro Mártir

Nogales

Agua Prieta

Cananea

Caborca

Magdalena

Nuevo
Casas Grandes

Ojinaga

Ciudad Acu

Bahía Sebastián Vizcaíno

Baja California

Isla Ángel
de la Guarda

Isla
Tiburón

Hermosillo

Chihuahua

Sierra Madre

Río Conchos

Nueva Rosit

152

Cuauhtémoc

Delicias

Sabi

Isla Cedros

Ciudad Camargo

Monclov

Guerrero Negro

Empalme

Guaymas

Río Yaqui

Esperanza

Ciudad
Obregón

San Francisco
del Oro

Jiménez

Hidalgo del Parral

Navojoa

Huatabampo

Santa Barbara

Gómez Palacio

Golfo de California

San Blas

Loreto

Sierra de la Giganta

Los Mochis

Occidental

Torreón

Ciudad Lerdo

San Ped

Pa

Matamoros

Guasave

Guamúchil

Culiacán

Isla Magdalena

Navolat

Miguel Asua

Juan Aldan

Isla Santa Margarita

Bahía de La Paz

El Dorado

Durango

Río Gran

La Paz

MEX

Tropic of Cancer

Mazatlán

Fresnillo

Zacatecas

Guadalupe

Escuinapa

Villanueva

Acaponeta

Aguascalientes

Tuxpan

Jalpa

Isla San Juanito
Isla Maria Madre
Isla Maria Magdalena
Isla Maria Cleofas

Tepic

Lagos de More

Yahualica

Guadalajara

Tequila

Las
de Chi

Islas Marías

Tlaquepaque

Chapala

Puerto Vallarta

Zamora de Hidal

Ciudad Guzmán

Zapot

Colima

Tuxpa

Isla San Benedicto

Manzanillo

Aguililla

Tecomán

Isla Roca Partida

Isla Socorro

Lázaro Cárde

Isla Clarión

Islas Revillagigedo

N

PACIFIC OCEAN

153

0 km 400

0 miles 400

POPULATION

○ Less than 50,000   ○ 50,000 -100,000   ◉ 100,000 - 500,000   ◼ Over 500,000

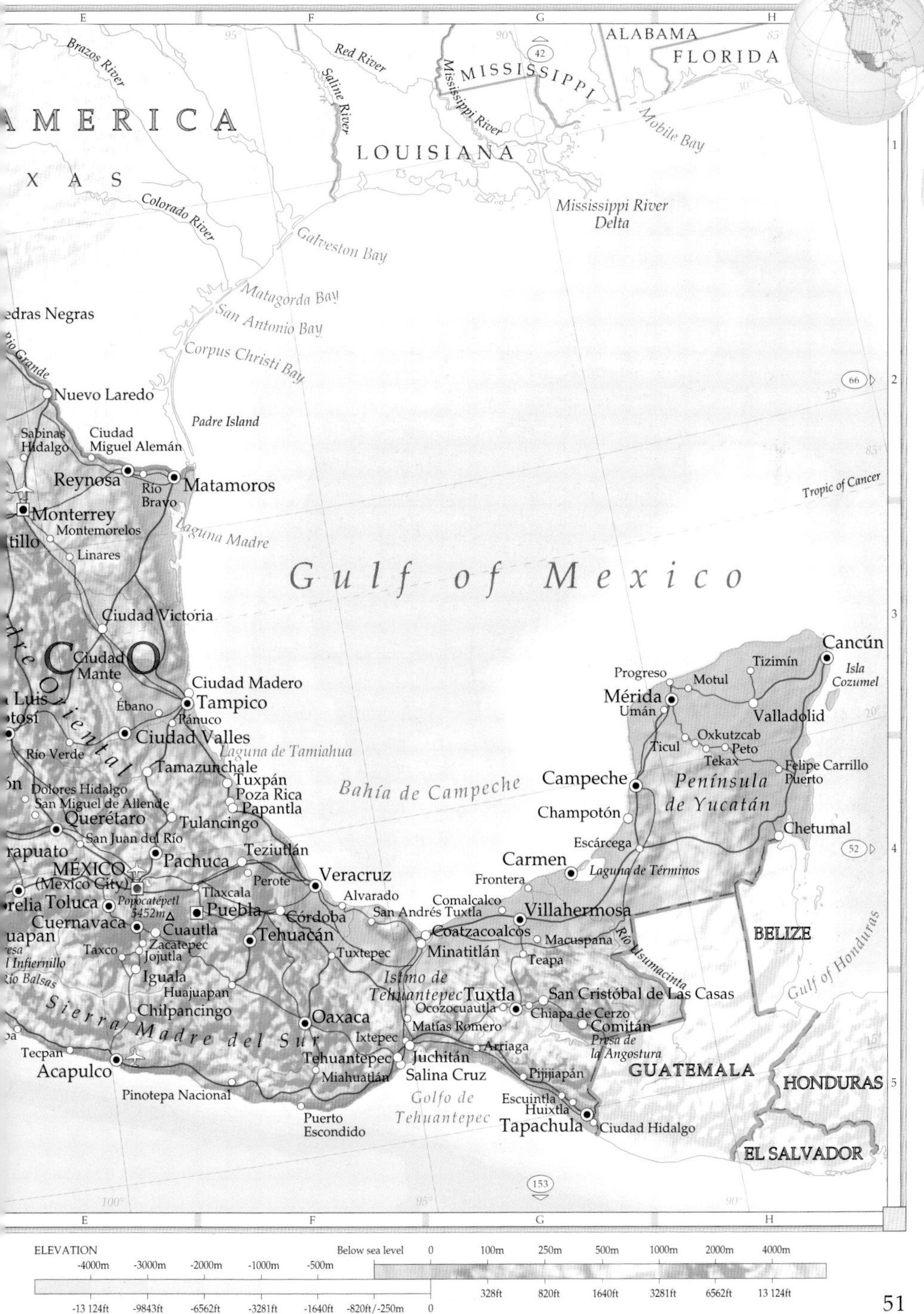

A M E R I C A

T E X A S

edras Negras

Río Grande

Nuevo Laredo

Sabinas Hidalgo

Ciudad Miguel Alemán

Reynosa

Matamoros

Monterrey

Río Bravo

tillo

Montemorelos

Linares

Laguna Madre

Padre Island

Brazos River

Colorado River

Saline River

Red River

MISSISSIPPI

Mississippi River

ALABAMA

FLORIDA

LOUISIANA

Mobile Bay

Galveston Bay

Matagorda Bay

San Antonio Bay

Corpus Christi Bay

Mississippi River Delta

Tropic of Cancer

Gulf of Mexico

Ciudad Victoria

Ciudad Mante

C O

Luis tosí

Ébano

Pánuco

Ciudad Madero

Tampico

Ciudad Valles

Laguna de Tamiahua

Río Verde

Tamazunchale

Dolores Hidalgo

San Miguel de Allende

Querétaro

Tulancingo

Tuxpán

Poza Rica

Papantla

Bahía de Campeche

San Juan del Río

Pachuca

Teziutlán

rapuato

relia

Toluca

Perote

Popocatépetl 5452m

Tlaxcala

Puebla

Veracruz

Alvarado

Cuernavaca

Cuautla

Taxco

Zacatepec

Jojutla

Córdoba

Tehuacán

San Andrés Tuxtla

Iguala

Huajuapan

Tuxtepec

Minatitlán

Coatzacoalcos

Chilpancingo

Oaxaca

Istmo de Tehuantepec

Teapa

esa l Infiernillo

ío Balsas

Sierra Madre del Sur

Ixtepec

Matías Romero

Tecpan

Acapulco

Pinotepa Nacional

Tehuantepec

Miahuatlán

Juchitán

Salina Cruz

Arriaga

Golfo de Tehuantepec

Puerto Escondido

Pijijiapan

Escuintla

Huixtla

Tapachula

Ciudad Hidalgo

Progreso

Mérida

Umán

Motul

Tizimín

Cancún

Isla Cozumel

Valladolid

Ticul

Oxkutzcab

Tekax

Peto

Campeche

Champotón

Península de Yucatán

Felipe Carrillo Puerto

Chetumal

Escárcega

Carmen

Laguna de Términos

Frontera

Comalcalco

Villahermosa

BELIZE

Macuspana

Río Usumacinta

San Cristóbal de Las Casas

Ocozocuautla

Tuxtla

Chiapa de Cerzo

Comitán

Presa de la Angostura

GUATEMALA

Gulf of Honduras

HONDURAS

EL SALVADOR

ELEVATION

					Below sea level	0	100m	250m	500m	1000m	2000m	4000m
-4000m	-3000m	-2000m	-1000m	-500m								
-13 124ft	-9843ft	-6562ft	-3281ft	-1640ft	-820ft/-250m	0	328ft	820ft	1640ft	3281ft	6562ft	13 124ft

CENTRAL AMERICA

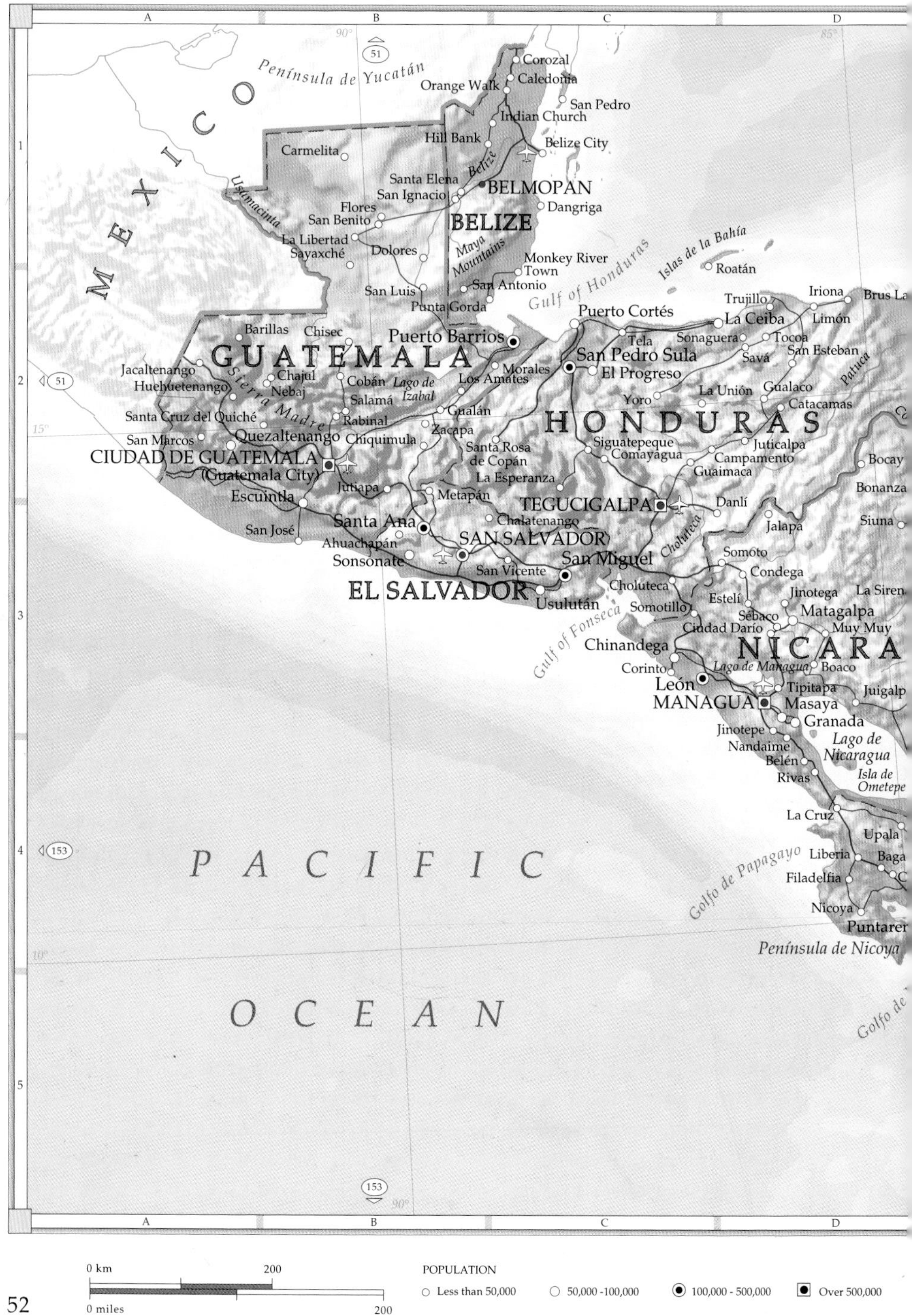

M E X I C O

Península de Yucatán

51

Corozal
Orange Walk
Caledonia
San Pedro
Indian Church
Belize City
Hill Bank
Carmelita
Santa Elena
San Ignacio
BELMOPAN
Flores
San Benito
Dangriga
La Libertad
Sayaxché
Dolores
BELIZE
Maya
Mountains
Monkey River
Town
San Antonio
San Luis
Islas de la Bahía
Roatán
Punta Gorda
Puerto Cortés
Gulf of Honduras
Iriona
Brus La
Trujillo
La Ceiba
Limón

Barillas
Chisec
Puerto Barrios
Tela
Sonaguera
Tocoa
San Esteban
Jacaltenango
Huehuetenango
Chajul
Nebaj
Cobán
Lago de
Izabal
Salamá
Los Amates
Morales
San Pedro Sula
El Progreso
Savá
Gualaco
Catacamas
GUATEMALA
Santa Cruz del Quiché
San Marcos
Quezaltenango
Rabinal
Chiquimula
Gualán
Zacapa
Yoro
La Unión
H O N D U R A S
Juticalpa
Campamento
Bocay
Siguatepeque
Comayagua
Bonanza
CIUDAD DE GUATEMALA
(Guatemala City)
Jutiapa
Santa Rosa
de Copán
La Esperanza
Guaimaca
Escuintla
Metapán
TEGUCIGALPA
Danlí
Siuna
Santa Ana
Chalatenango
SAN SALVADOR
San Miguel
Jalapa
San José
Ahuachapán
Sonsonate
San Vicente
Somoto
Condega
Jinotega
La Siren
EL SALVADOR
Usulután
Choluteca
Somotillo
Estelí
Matagalpa
Chinandega
Ciudad Darío
Sébaco
Muy Muy
Corinto
Lago de Managua
Boaco
León
Tipitapa
Juigalp
MANAGUA
Masaya
NICARA
Jinotepe
Nandaime
Granada
Belén
Lago de
Nicaragua
Rivas
Isla de
Ometepe
La Cruz
Upala
Liberia
Baga
Golfo de Papagayo
Filadelfia
Nicoya
Puntarer
Península de Nicoya
Golfo de

Sierra Madre

Gulf of Fonseca

P A C I F I C

O C E A N

0 km   200
0 miles   200

POPULATION

○ Less than 50,000   ○ 50,000 -100,000   ◉ 100,000 - 500,000   ◼ Over 500,000

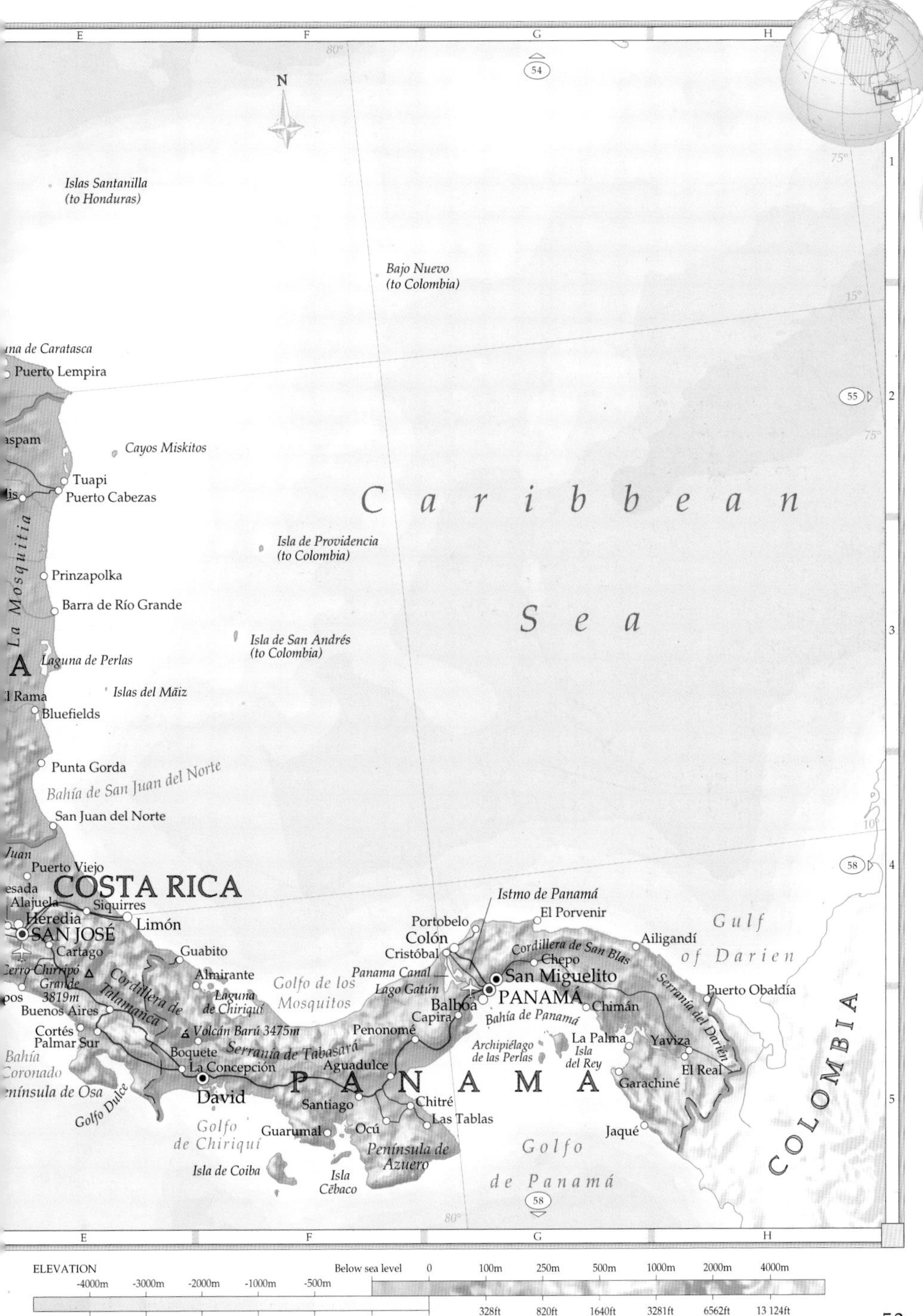

N

Islas Santanilla
(to Honduras)

Bajo Nuevo
(to Colombia)

na de Caratasca

Puerto Lempira

aspam

Cayos Miskitos

Tuapi
Puerto Cabezas

dis

Isla de Providencia
(to Colombia)

Prinzapolka

Barra de Río Grande

La Mosquitia

Isla de San Andrés
(to Colombia)

_A_ Laguna de Perlas

l Rama Islas del Maíz

Bluefields

C a r i b b e a n

S e a

Punta Gorda

Bahía de San Juan del Norte

San Juan del Norte

Juan
Puerto Viejo

esada
Alajuela Siquirres

COSTA RICA

Heredia Limón

SAN JOSÉ

Cartago

Cerro Chirripó △ Guabito

Grande

pos 3819m Almirante

Buenos Aires

Cortés Laguna
de Chiriquí

Palmar Sur

Bahía Boquete Serranía de Tabasará

Coronado La Concepción

nínsula de Osa

David

Golfo Dulce

Golfo
de Chiriquí

Isla de Coiba

Golfo de los
Mosquitos

Istmo de Panamá

El Porvenir

Portobelo
Colón
Cristóbal

Cordillera de San Blas

Ailigandí

Chepo

Panama Canal

Lago Gatún

Balboa

Capira

San Miguelito

PANAMÁ

Bahía de Panamá

Chimán

Puerto Obaldía

Serranía del Darién

Penonomé

P A N A M Á

Aguadulce

Santiago

Guarumal Ocú

Chitré

Las Tablas

Península de
Azuero

Isla
Cébaco

Archipiélago
de las Perlas

La Palma
Isla
del Rey

Garachiné

El Real

Yaviza

Golfo
de Panamá

Jaqué

G u l f

o f D a r i e n

C O L O M B I A

ELEVATION

| Below sea level | 0 | 100m | 250m | 500m | 1000m | 2000m | 4000m |

-4000m -3000m -2000m -1000m -500m

-13 124ft -9843ft -6562ft -3281ft -1640ft -820ft/-250m 0

328ft 820ft 1640ft 3281ft 6562ft 13 124ft

53

THE CARIBBEAN

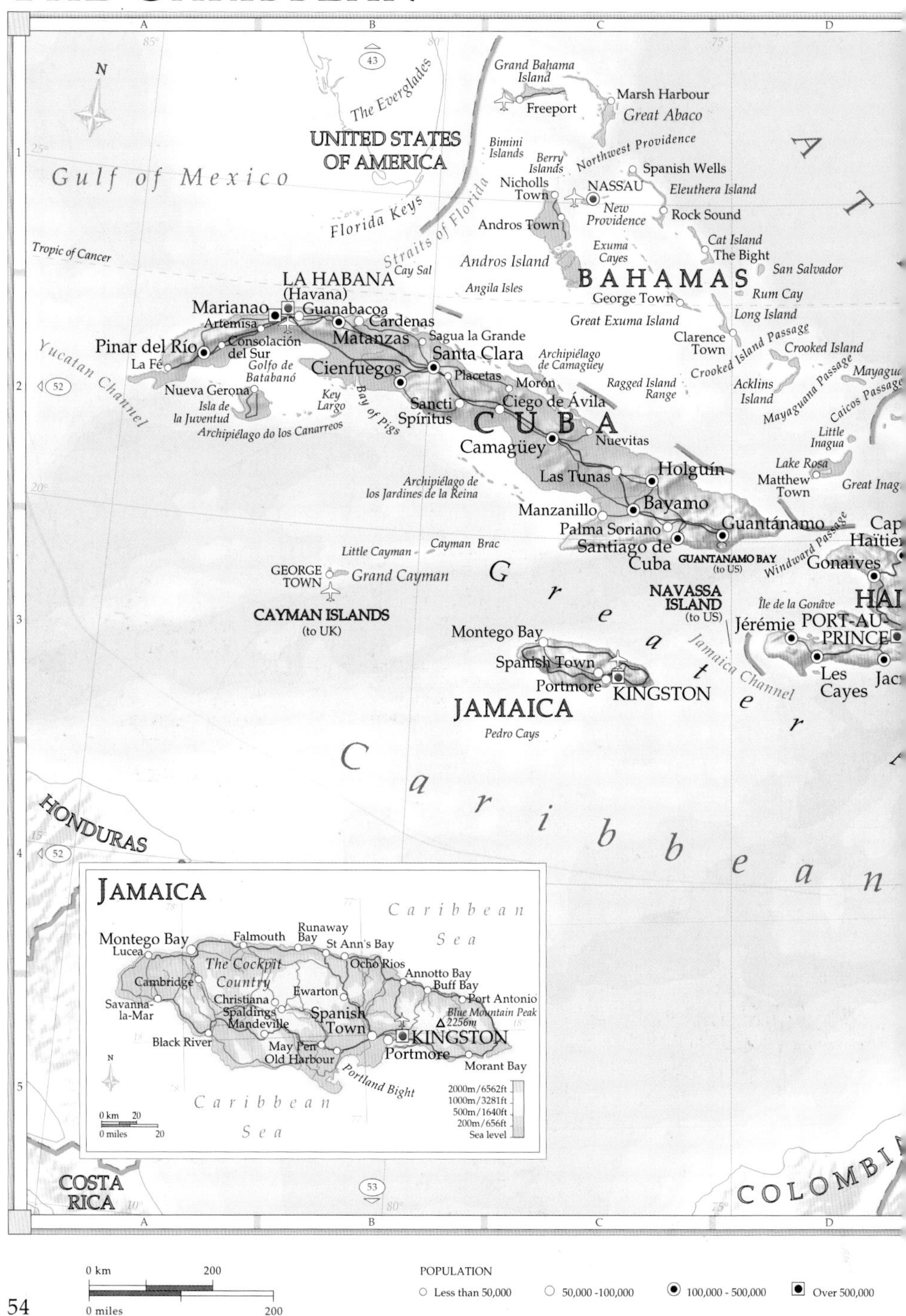

N

UNITED STATES OF AMERICA

Gulf of Mexico

Tropic of Cancer

The Everglades

Florida Keys

Straits of Florida

Grand Bahama Island

Freeport

Marsh Harbour

Great Abaco

Bimini Islands

Berry Islands

Northwest Providence

Nicholls Town

NASSAU

Spanish Wells

Eleuthera Island

Andros Town

New Providence

Rock Sound

Andros Island

Angila Isles

Cay Sal

Exuma Cayes

Cat Island

The Bight

San Salvador

BAHAMAS

George Town

Rum Cay

Long Island

LA HABANA
(Havana)

Marianao

Guanabacoa

Cárdenas

Artemisa

Sagua la Grande

Great Exuma Island

Clarence Town

Crooked Island

Crooked Island Passage

Matanzas

Santa Clara

Placetas

Archipiélago de Camagüey

Acklins Island

Mayaguana Passage

Mayagua

Yucatan Channel

Pinar del Río

Consolación del Sur

La Fé

Golfo de Batabanó

Cienfuegos

Morón

Ragged Island Range

Caicos Passage

Nueva Gerona

Key Largo

Sancti Spíritus

Ciego de Ávila

CUBA

Little Inagua

Isla de la Juventud

Archipiélago do los Canarreos

Bay of Pigs

Camagüey

Nuevitas

Lake Rosa

Matthew Town

Great Inag

Archipiélago de los Jardines de la Reina

Las Tunas

Holguín

Manzanillo

Bayamo

Palma Soriano

Guantánamo

Cap

Haïtie

Little Cayman

Cayman Brac

Santiago de Cuba

GUANTANAMO BAY
(to US)

Gonaïves

Windward Passage

GEORGE TOWN

Grand Cayman

Gr

NAVASSA ISLAND
(to US)

Île de la Gonâve

HAI

CAYMAN ISLANDS
(to UK)

Montego Bay

e

a

Jérémie

PORT-AU-PRINCE

t

Les Cayes

Jac

Spanish Town

Portmore

KINGSTON

Jamaica Channel

e

JAMAICA

Pedro Cays

r

C

a

r

i

b

b

e

a

n

HONDURAS

JAMAICA

Montego Bay

Lucea

Falmouth

Runaway Bay

St Ann's Bay

Caribbean Sea

Cambridge

The Cockpit Country

Ocho Rios

Annotto Bay

Buff Bay

Savanna-la-Mar

Christiana

Ewarton

Port Antonio

Spaldings

Mandeville

Spanish Town

Blue Mountain Peak
△2256m

Black River

May Pen

Old Harbour

KINGSTON

Portmore

Portland Bight

Morant Bay

Caribbean Sea

2000m/6562ft	
1000m/3281ft	
500m/1640ft	
200m/656ft	
Sea level	

0 km 20
0 miles 20

COSTA RICA

COLOMBI

0 km 200
0 miles 200

POPULATION

○ Less than 50,000   ○ 50,000 -100,000   ◉ 100,000 - 500,000   ■ Over 500,000

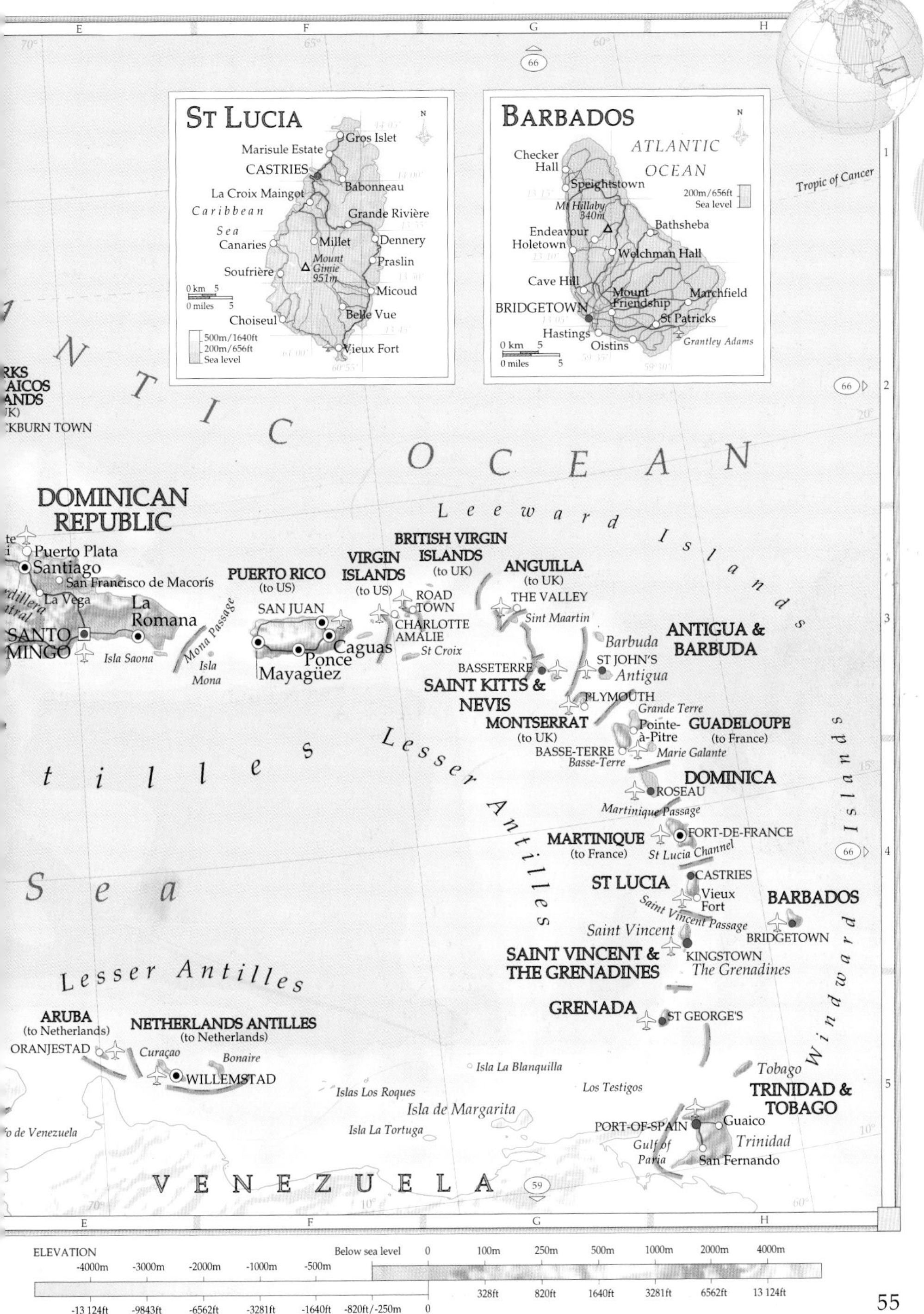

St Lucia

Gros Islet
Marisule Estate
CASTRIES
La Croix Maingot — Babonneau
Grande Rivière
Caribbean
Sea
Canaries — Millet — Dennery
Soufrière — Praslin
△ Mount
Gimie
951m — Micoud
Choiseul — Belle Vue
Vieux Fort

0 km 5
0 miles 5

500m/1640ft
200m/656ft
Sea level

Barbados

ATLANTIC
OCEAN

Checker
Hall
Speightstown
Mt Hillaby
340m — Bathsheba
Endeavour — Welchman Hall
Holetown
Cave Hill
Mount
Friendship — Marchfield
BRIDGETOWN — St Patricks
Hastings
Oistins — Grantley Adams

200m/656ft
Sea level

0 km 5
0 miles 5

Tropic of Cancer

ATLANTIC OCEAN

RKS
AICOS
ANDS
(K)
KBURN TOWN

Leeward Islands

DOMINICAN REPUBLIC

te
1 — Puerto Plata
Santiago
San Francisco de Macorís
La Vega
La Romana
SANTO
DOMINGO
Isla Saona
Isla Mona

PUERTO RICO
(to US)
SAN JUAN
Ponce — Caguas
Mayagüez

Mona Passage

BRITISH VIRGIN ISLANDS
VIRGIN ISLANDS
(to US) — (to UK)
ROAD TOWN
CHARLOTTE AMALIE
St Croix

ANGUILLA
(to UK)
THE VALLEY
Sint Maarten

Barbuda

BASSETERRE
SAINT KITTS & NEVIS
PLYMOUTH
MONTSERRAT
(to UK)
BASSE-TERRE
Basse-Terre

ST JOHN'S
Antigua
ANTIGUA & BARBUDA

Grande Terre
Pointe-à-Pitre
GUADELOUPE
(to France)
Marie Galante

DOMINICA
ROSEAU

Martinique Passage

MARTINIQUE
(to France)
FORT-DE-FRANCE
St Lucia Channel

ST LUCIA
CASTRIES
Vieux Fort
Saint Vincent Passage

Saint Vincent

SAINT VINCENT & THE GRENADINES
KINGSTOWN
The Grenadines

BARBADOS
BRIDGETOWN

GRENADA
ST GEORGE'S

Lesser Antilles

tilles

Sea

Lesser Antilles

Windward Islands

ARUBA
(to Netherlands)
ORANJESTAD
Curaçao
NETHERLANDS ANTILLES
(to Netherlands)
Bonaire
WILLEMSTAD

Islas Los Roques
Isla La Blanquilla
Los Testigos
Tobago

Isla de Margarita
Isla La Tortuga

TRINIDAD & TOBAGO

PORT-OF-SPAIN — Guaico
Gulf of Paria — *Trinidad*
San Fernando

o de Venezuela

V E N E Z U E L A

ELEVATION

| -4000m | -3000m | -2000m | -1000m | -500m | Below sea level 0 | 100m | 250m | 500m | 1000m | 2000m | 4000m |

| -13 124ft | -9843ft | -6562ft | -3281ft | -1640ft | -820ft/-250m 0 | 328ft | 820ft | 1640ft | 3281ft | 6562ft | 13 124ft |

SOUTH AMERICA

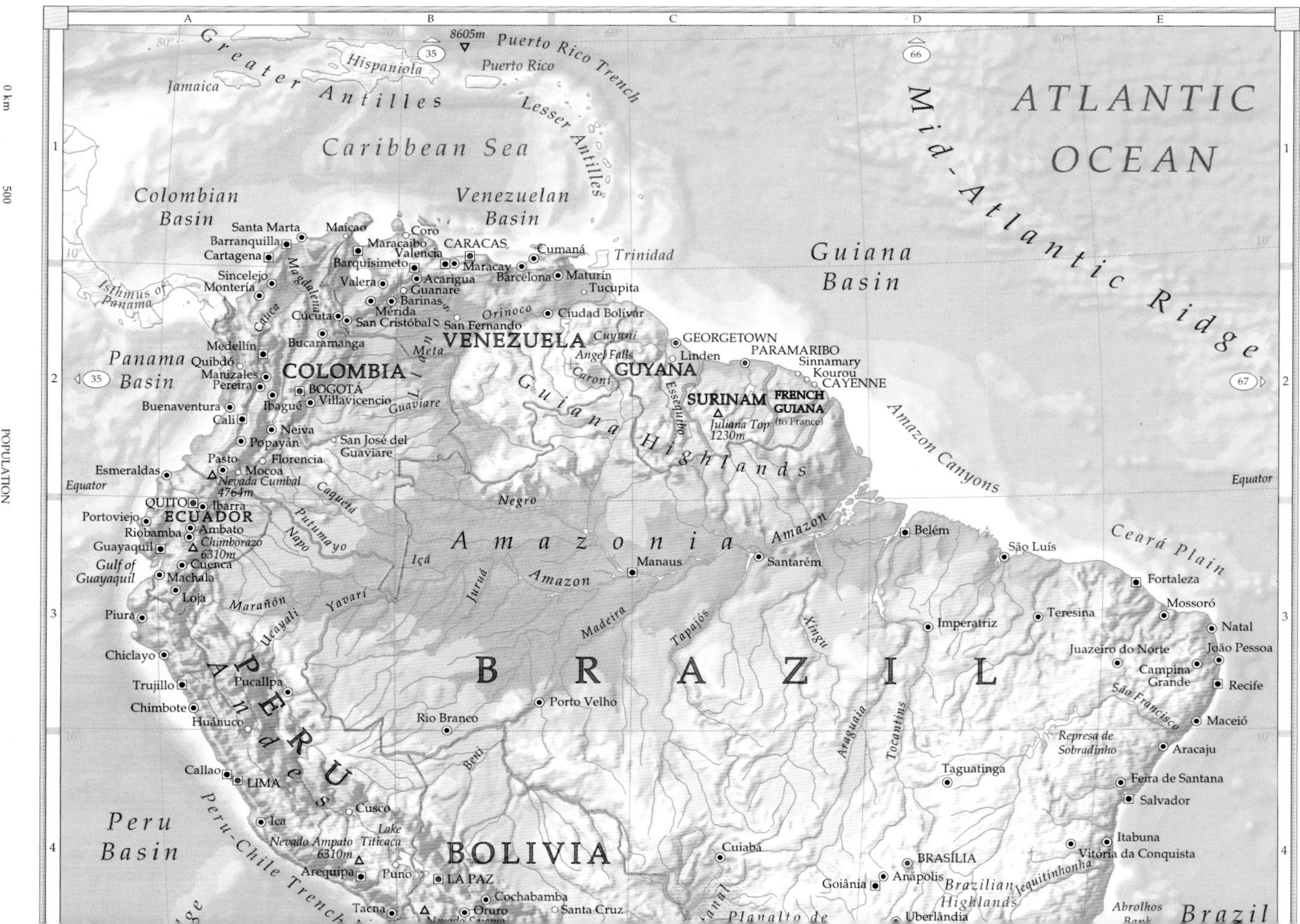

0 km 500
0 miles 500

POPULATION

○ Less than 50,000   ◉ 50,000 -100,000   ◉ 100,000 - 500,000   ◼ Over 500,000

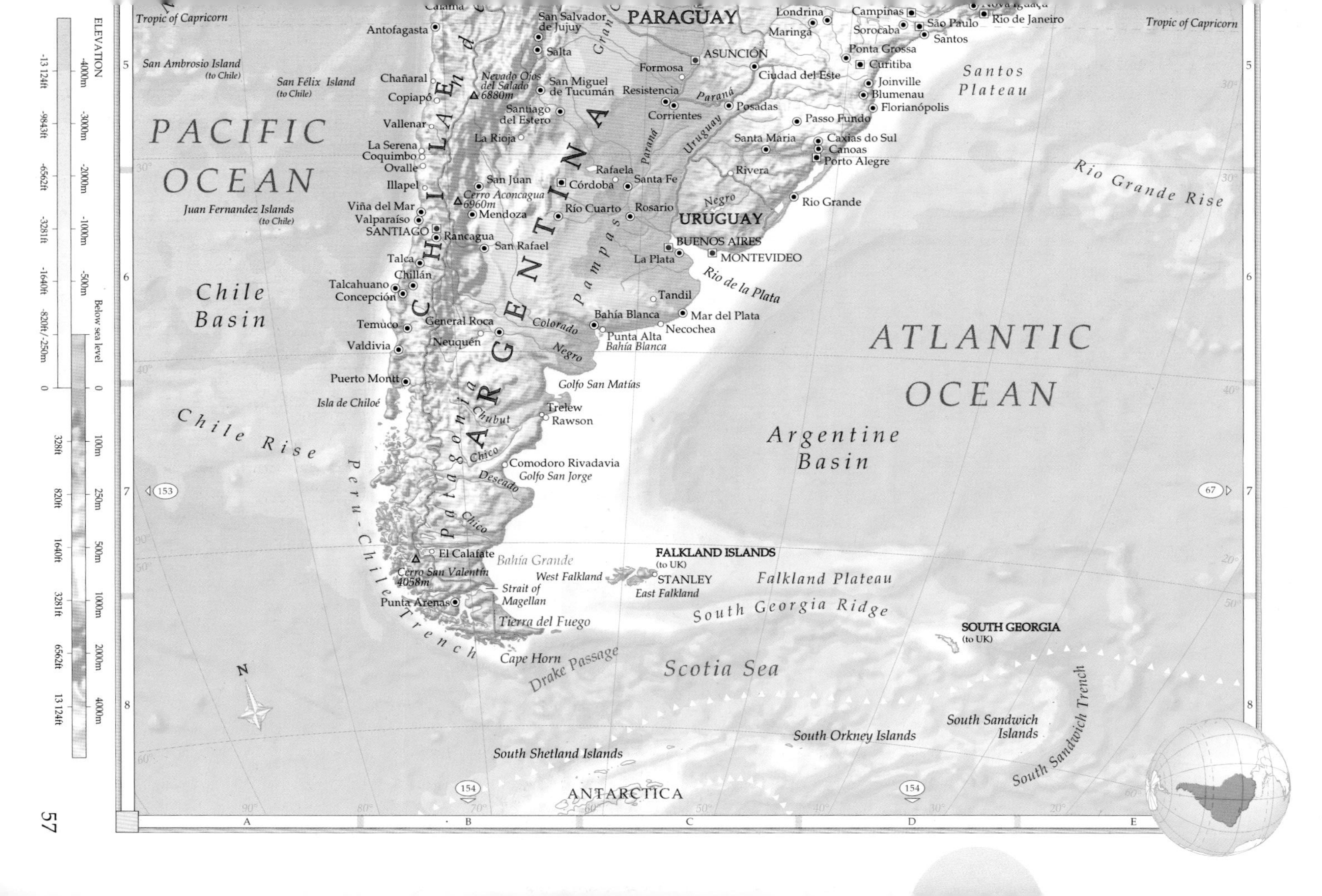

ATLANTIC OCEAN

PACIFIC OCEAN

PARAGUAY

URUGUAY

ARGENTINA

CHILE

ASUNCIÓN

MONTEVIDEO

BUENOS AIRES

SANTIAGO

Tropic of Capricorn

Rio Grande Rise

Santos Plateau

Argentine Basin

Falkland Plateau

South Georgia Ridge

Scotia Sea

South Sandwich Trench

SOUTH GEORGIA
(to UK)

South Sandwich Islands

South Orkney Islands

South Shetland Islands

ANTARCTICA

FALKLAND ISLANDS
(to UK)
STANLEY
West Falkland   East Falkland

Chile Basin

Chile Rise

Peru-Chile Trench

Drake Passage

Cape Horn

Tierra del Fuego

Strait of Magellan

Bahía Grande

Golfo San Jorge

Golfo San Matías

Bahía Blanca

Río de la Plata

Pampas

Patagonia

Gran Chaco

Río de Janeiro
São Paulo
Santos
Campinas
Sorocaba
Ponta Grossa
Curitiba
Joinville
Blumenau
Florianópolis
Londrina
Maringá
Ciudad del Este
Passo Fundo
Caxias do Sul
Canoas
Porto Alegre
Rio Grande
Santa Maria
Rivera
Desidas
Formosa
Resistencia
Corrientes
Santa Fe
Rosario
La Plata
Mar del Plata
Tandil
Necochea
Punta Alta
Bahía Blanca
Córdoba
Río Cuarto
Rafaela
San Salvador de Jujuy
Salta
San Miguel de Tucumán
Santiago del Estero
La Rioja
San Juan
Mendoza
San Rafael
Neuquén
General Roca
Colorado
Negro
Trelew
Rawson
Comodoro Rivadavia
Chubut
Chico
Deseado
El Calafate
Punta Arenas
Río Gallegos
Puerto Montt
Isla de Chiloé
Valdivia
Temuco
Concepción
Talcahuano
Chillán
Rancagua
Viña del Mar
Valparaíso
Illapel
Ovalle
Coquimbo
La Serena
Vallenar
Copiapó
Chañaral
Antofagasta
Calama

San Félix Island
(to Chile)
San Ambrosio Island
(to Chile)
Juan Fernández Islands
(to Chile)

Nevado Ojos del Salado
6880m
Cerro Aconcagua
6960m
Cerro San Valentín
4058m

Paraná
Paraguay
Uruguay

N

ELEVATION

-4000m	-3000m	-2000m	-1000m	-500m	Below sea level 0	100m	250m	500m	1000m	2000m	4000m
-13 124ft	-9843ft	-6562ft	-3281ft	-1640ft	-820ft/-250m	0	328ft	820ft	1640ft	3281ft	6562ft	13 124ft

57

NORTHERN SOUTH AMERICA

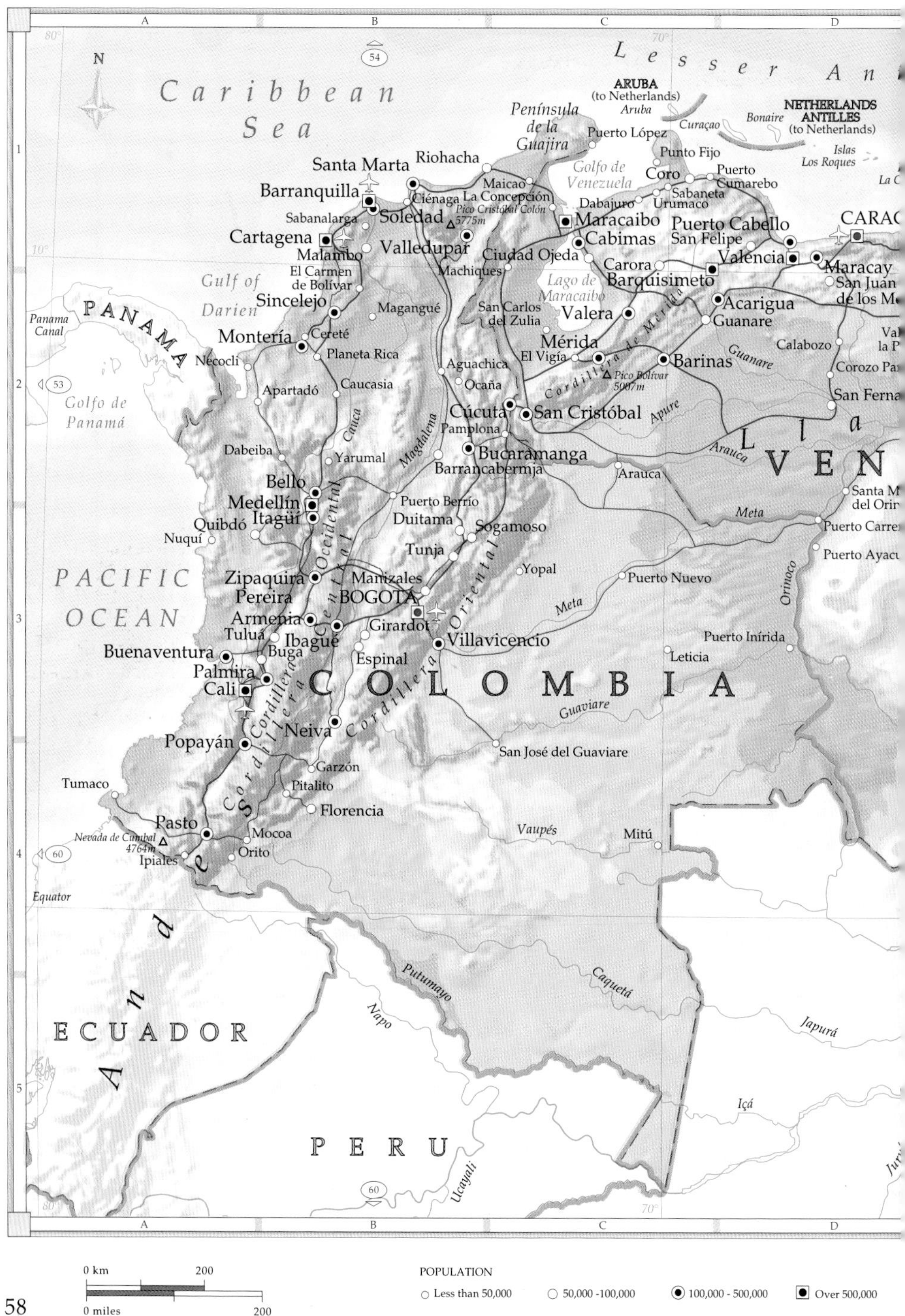

N

C a r i b b e a n
S e a

54

L e s s e r   A n

ARUBA
(to Netherlands)
Aruba

NETHERLANDS
ANTILLES
(to Netherlands)

Curaçao   *Bonaire*

Península
de la
Guajira

Puerto López

Golfo de
Venezuela

Coro

Islas
Los Roques

Punto Fijo

Puerto
Cumarebo

La C

Santa Marta   Riohacha

Maicao

Sabaneta
Urumaco

Barranquilla

Ciénaga   La Concepción

Pico Cristóbal Colón

Dabajuro

Soledad

Pico Cristóbal Colón
△5775m

Maracaibo

Puerto Cabello

CARAC

Cartagena

Sabanalarga

Cabimas

San Felipe

Valencia

Malambo   Valledupar

Ciudad Ojeda

Maracay

El Carmen
de Bolívar

Machiques

Lago de
Maracaibo

Barquisimeto

San Juan
de los M

Gulf of
Darien

Sincelejo

Magangué

San Carlos
del Zulia

Carora

Valera

Acarigua

Guanare

Va
la P

Montería

Cereté

Mérida

Calabozo

Corozo Pa

Panama
Canal

Necoclí

Planeta Rica

El Vigía

Aguachica

△Pico Bolívar
5007m

Barinas

San Fern

Golfo de
Panamá

53

Apartadó   Caucasia

Ocaña

Cúcuta   San Cristóbal

Dabeiba

Pamplona

L   I   a

Yarumal

Bucaramanga

V E N

Bello

Barrancabermeja

Arauca

Santa M
del Orin

Medellín

Puerto Berrío

Itagüí

Duitama

Meta

Puerto Carre

Quibdó

Sogamoso

Puerto Ayacu

Nuquí

Tunja

Zipaquirá   Manizales

Yopal

Puerto Nuevo

PACIFIC

Pereira   BOGOTÁ

Armenia   Girardot

Meta

Puerto Inírida

OCEAN

Tuluá   Ibagué

Villavicencio

Leticia

Buenaventura   Buga

Espinal

Palmira

Cali

C O L O M B I A

Popayán

Neiva

Guaviare

San José del Guaviare

Tumaco

Garzón

Pitalito

Florencia

Vaupés

Mitú

Pasto   Mocoa

Nevada de Cumbal
4764m

Orito

Ipiales

Equator

60

E C U A D O R

Napo

Putumayo

Caquetá

Japurá

Içá

P E R U

Ucayali

Jura

60

0 km   200

0 miles   200

POPULATION

○ Less than 50,000   ○ 50,000 -100,000   ◉ 100,000 - 500,000   ◼ Over 500,000

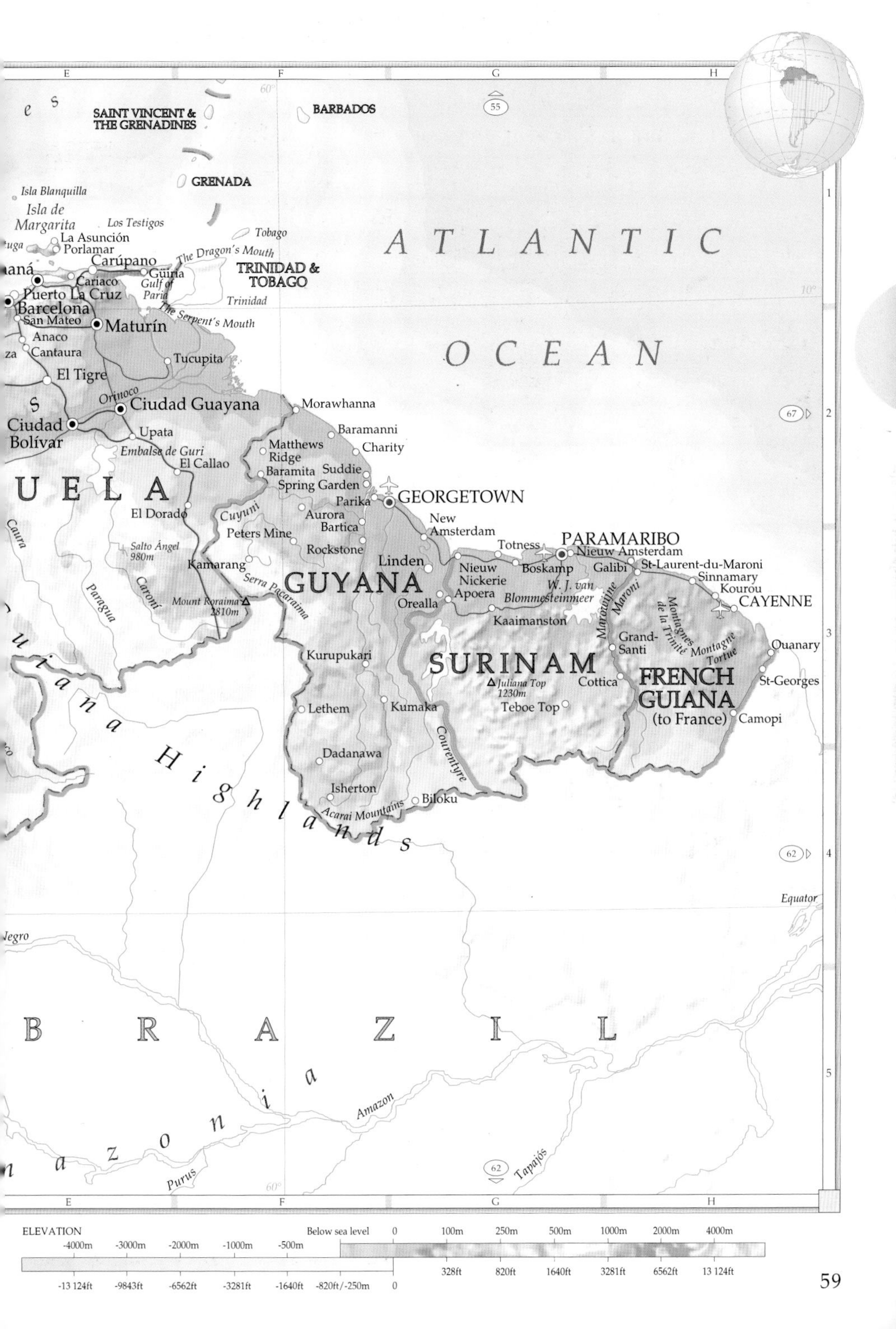

SAINT VINCENT & THE GRENADINES

BARBADOS

Isla Blanquilla
Isla de Margarita
Los Testigos
La Asunción
Porlamar
Tobago

GRENADA

uga
aná
Carúpano
Cariaco
Guiria
Gulf of Paria
Puerto La Cruz
Barcelona
San Mateo
Anaco
za
Cantaura
El Tigre
Maturín

The Dragon's Mouth
TRINIDAD & TOBAGO
Trinidad
The Serpent's Mouth

Tucupita

Orinoco
Ciudad Guayana

Morawhanna

Upata
Embalse de Guri
El Callao

Baramanni
Charity
Matthews Ridge
Baramita
Spring Garden
Suddie

S
Ciudad Bolívar

U E L A

El Dorado

Cuyuni
Peters Mine

Parika
Aurora
Bartica
Rockstone
GEORGETOWN
New Amsterdam
Totness

Caura

Salto Ángel
980m
Kamarang

Caroní
Paragua

GUYANA
Linden
Orealla

Nieuw Nickerie
Apoera

PARAMARIBO
Nieuw Amsterdam
Boskamp
Galibi
St-Laurent-du-Maroni
Sinnamary
Kourou
CAYENNE

Mount Roraima △ 2810m

Serra Pacaraima

Kaaimanston

W. J. van Blommesteinmeer

Marowijne
Maroni
Montagnes de la Trinité
Montagne Tortue

Ouanary

u i a n a

Kurupukari

SURINAM

Grand-Santi

FRENCH GUIANA
(to France)

St-Georges

Lethem
Kumaka
△ Juliana Top
1230m
Teboe Top
Cottica
Camopi

iana
Highlands

Dadanawa

Courantyne

Isherton
Acarai Mountains
Biloku

Equator

Negro

B R A Z I L

A m a z o n i a

Amazon

Purus
Tapajós

A T L A N T I C

O C E A N

WESTERN SOUTH AMERICA

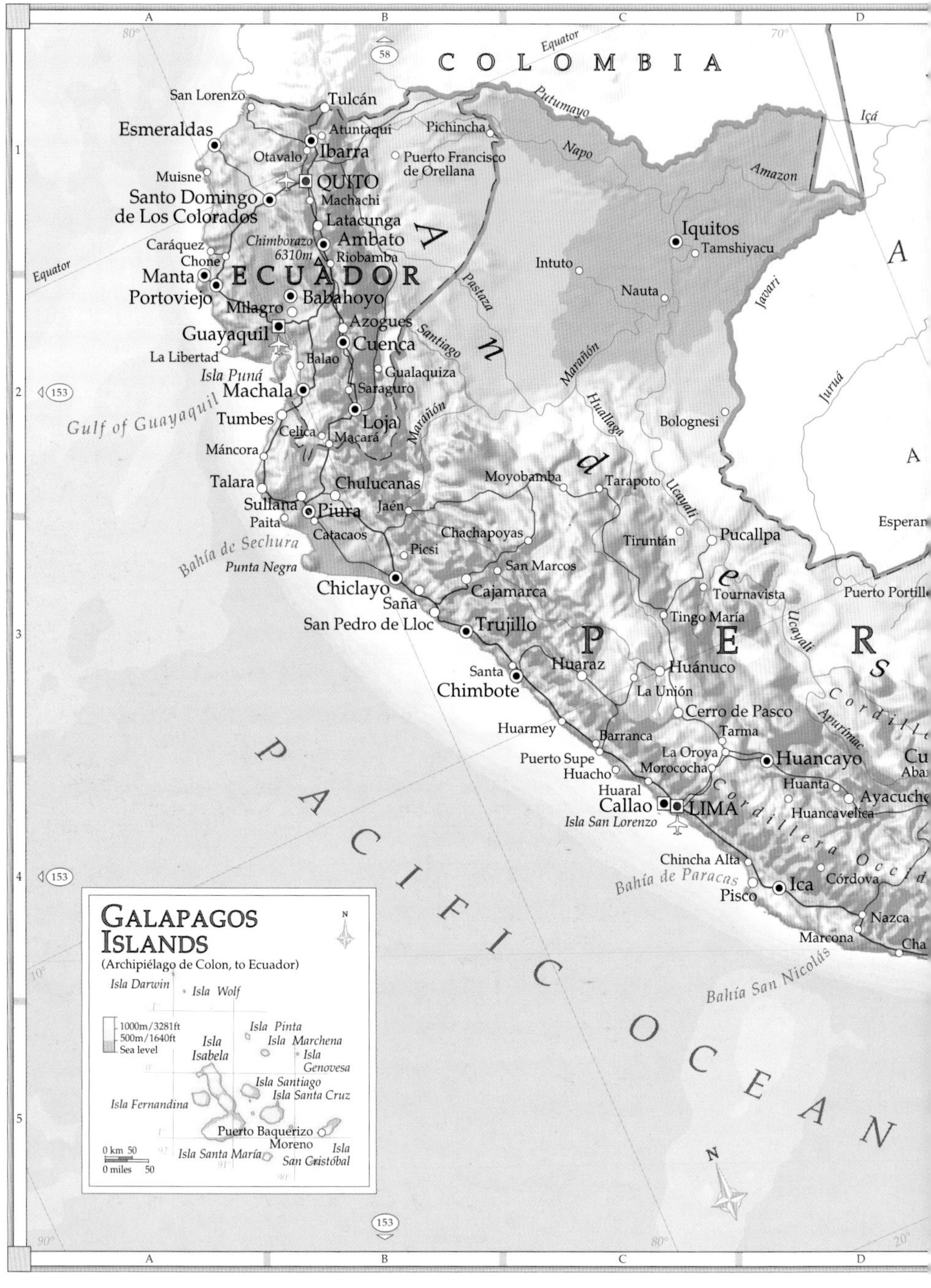

COLOMBIA

Equator

San Lorenzo
Tulcán
Esmeraldas
Atuntaqui   Pichincha
Muisne   Otavalo   Ibarra   Puerto Francisco
de Orellana
Santo Domingo   QUITO
de Los Colorados   Machachi
Latacunga
Caráquez   Chimborazo   Ambato
Chone   6310m   Riobamba
Manta   ECUADOR
Portoviejo   Milagro   Babahoyo
Guayaquil   Azogues
La Libertad   Balao   Cuenca
Isla Puná   Gualaquiza
Machala   Saraguro
Gulf of Guayaquil   Tumbes   Celica   Loja
Mancora   Macará
Talara   Chulucanas
Sullana   Piura   Jaén
Paita   Picsi
Bahía de Sechura   Catacaos
Punta Negra   Chiclayo   San Marcos
Saña   Cajamarca
San Pedro de Lloc   Trujillo   PERÚ
Huaraz   Huánuco
Santa   La Unión
Chimbote   Cerro de Pasco
Huarmey   Barranca   Tarma
Puerto Supe   La Oroya   Huancayo
Huacho   Morococha
Huaral   Huanta   Ayacucho
Callao   LIMA   Huancavelica
Isla San Lorenzo
Chincha Alta
Bahía de Paracas   Ica   Córdova
Pisco
Nazca
Marcona   Cha
Bahía San Nicolás

Putumayo
Içá
Napo
Amazon
Iquitos   Tamshiyacu
Intuto   Nauta
Pastaza   Jacari
Marañón   Jurúa
Huallaga
Moyobamba   Tarapoto
Chachapoyas   Tiruntán   Pucallpa
Tournavista   Puerto Portill
Tingo María   Esperan
Ucayali
Cordille
Apurímac
Cu
Aba
Cordillera Occid

PACIFIC OCEAN

0 km   400
0 miles   400

POPULATION
○ Less than 50,000   ○ 50,000 -100,000   ◉ 100,000 - 500,000   ■ Over 500,000

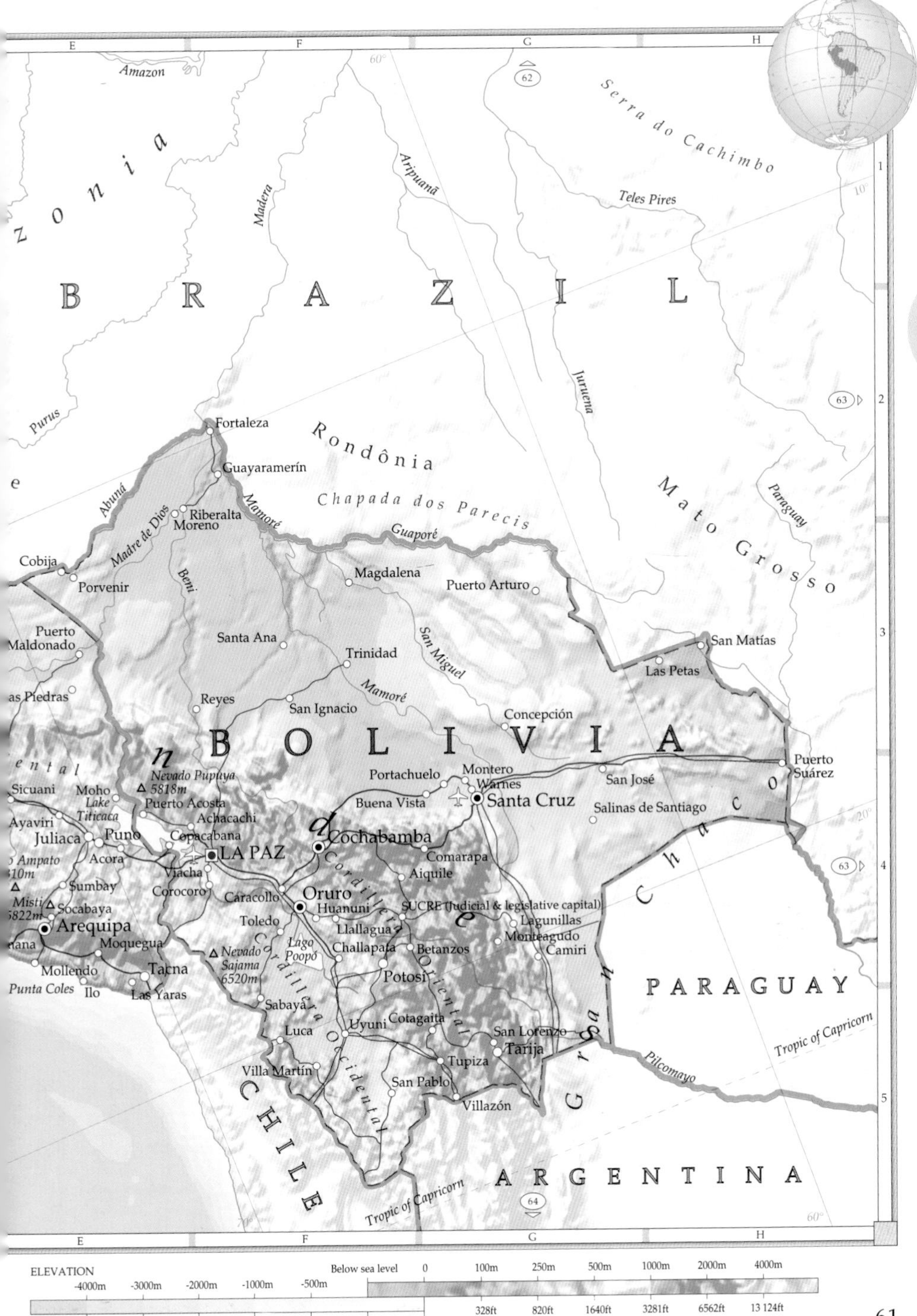

E   F   G   H

Amazon

60°

62

Serra do Cachimbo

Aripuanã

10°

Teles Pires

Madera

1

zonia

Jauriena

B R A Z I L

Purus

2

63

e

Fortaleza

Abunã

Guayaramerín

Rondônia

Paraguay

Madre de Dios

Riberalta
Moreno

Mamoré

Chapada dos parecis

Guaporé

Mato Grosso

Cobija

Porvenir

Beni

Magdalena

Puerto Arturo

Puerto
Maldonado

Santa Ana

Trinidad

San Miguel

San Matías

3

Las Petas

as Piedras

Reyes

San Ignacio

Mamoré

Concepción

ental

B O L I V I A

Puerto
Suárez

n

Portachuelo

Montero

San José

Nevado Pupuya
△ 5818m

Warnes

Sicuani

Moho

Lake
Titicaca

Puerto Acosta

Buena Vista

Salinas de Santiago

Santa Cruz

Ayaviri

Achacachi

Salinas de Santiago

Juliaca

Puno

Copacabana

Cochabamba

C h a c o

4

310m

Acora

Comarapa

△
Ampato

$umbay

Viacha

LA PAZ

Aiquile

63

Misti
5822m

Socabaya

Corocoro

Caracollo

Oruro

Huanuni

SUCRE (judicial & legislative capital)

Lagunillas

Arequipa

Toledo

Llallagua

Betanzos

Monteagudo
Camiri

hana

Moquegua

△ Nevado
Sajama
6520m

Lago
Poopó

Challapata

Potosí

P A R A G U A Y

Mollendo

Tacna

Sabayá

Uyuni

Cotagaita

San Lorenzo

Tropic of Capricorn

Punta Coles

Ilo

Las Yaras

Luca

Tupiza

Tarija

Pilcomayo

Villa Martín

San Pablo

20°

5

Villazón

C H I L E

Gran

A R G E N T I N A

Tropic of Capricorn

64

60°

E   F   G   H

ELEVATION

Below sea level

0   100m   250m   500m   1000m   2000m   4000m

-4000m   -3000m   -2000m   -1000m   -500m

-13 124ft   -9843ft   -6562ft   -3281ft   -1640ft   -820ft /-250m   0   328ft   820ft   1640ft   3281ft   6562ft   13 124ft

BRAZIL

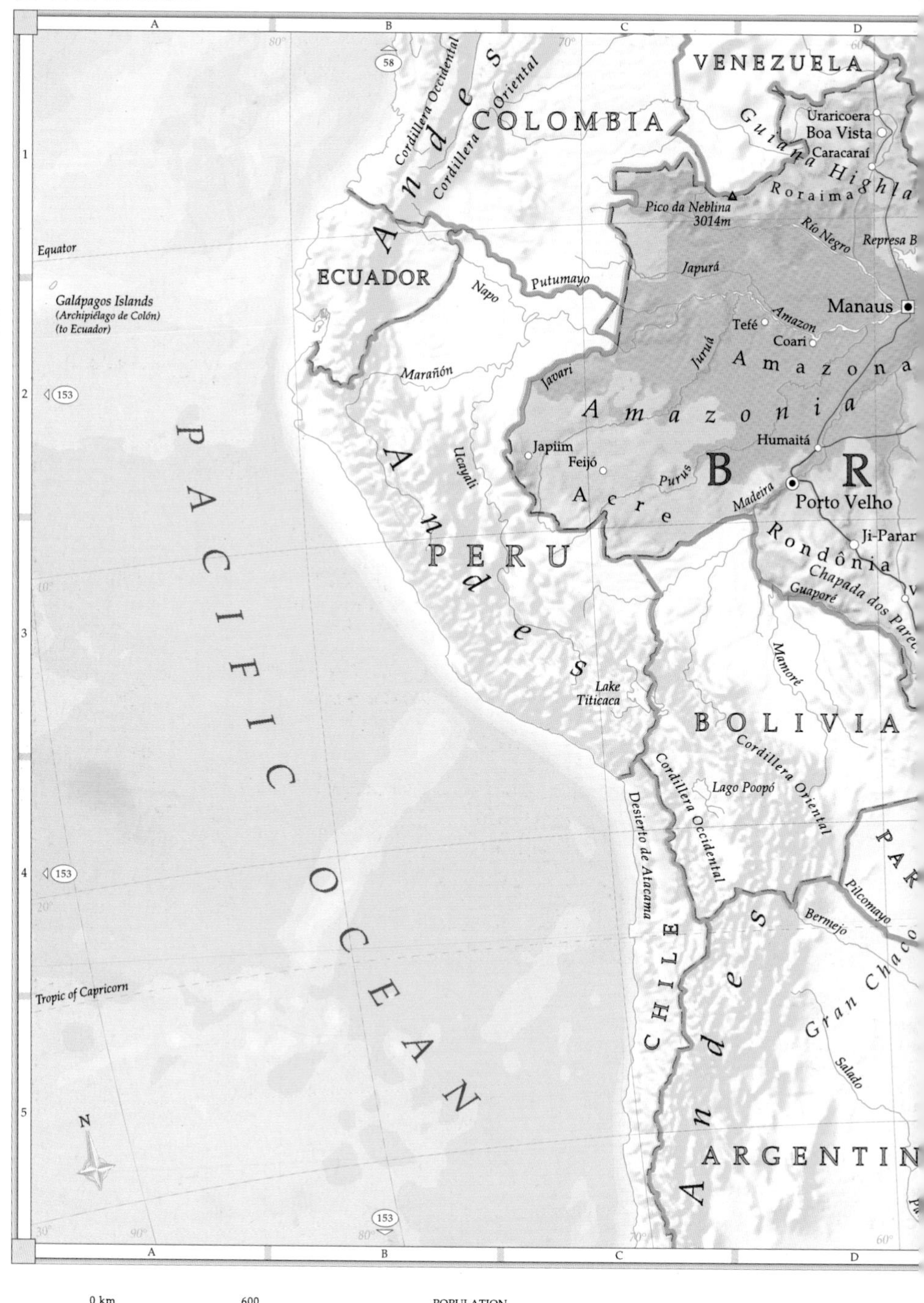

VENEZUELA

Cordillera Occidental

Cordillera Oriental

58

COLOMBIA

Guiana Highla

Uraricoera
Boa Vista
Caracaraí

Pico da Neblina
3014m

Roraima

Río Negro

Represa B

Equator

ECUADOR

Napo

Putumayo

Japurá

Manaus

Galápagos Islands
(Archipiélago de Colón)
(to Ecuador)

Amazon

Tefé

Coari

A m a z o n a

Marañón

Javari

Juruá

153

A m a z o n i a

Jutaí

Ucayali

Japtim
Feijó

Purus

Humaitá

B   R

A
n
d
e
s

PERU

A c r e

Madeira

Porto Velho

Ji-Parar

R o n d ô n i a

Chapada dos Parec.

Guaporé

Lake
Titicaca

Mamoré

B O L I V I A

153

Cordillera Oriental

Lago Poopó

Cordillera Occidental

Desierto de Atacama

Tropic of Capricorn

PA

Pilcomayo

153

Bermejo

P A C I F I C

O C E A N

C H I L E

A
n
d
e
s

Gran Chaco

Salado

N

ARGENTIN

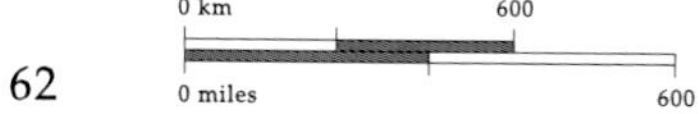

0 km   600
0 miles   600

POPULATION

○ Less than 50,000   ○ 50,000 -100,000   ◉ 100,000 - 500,000   ■ Over 500,000

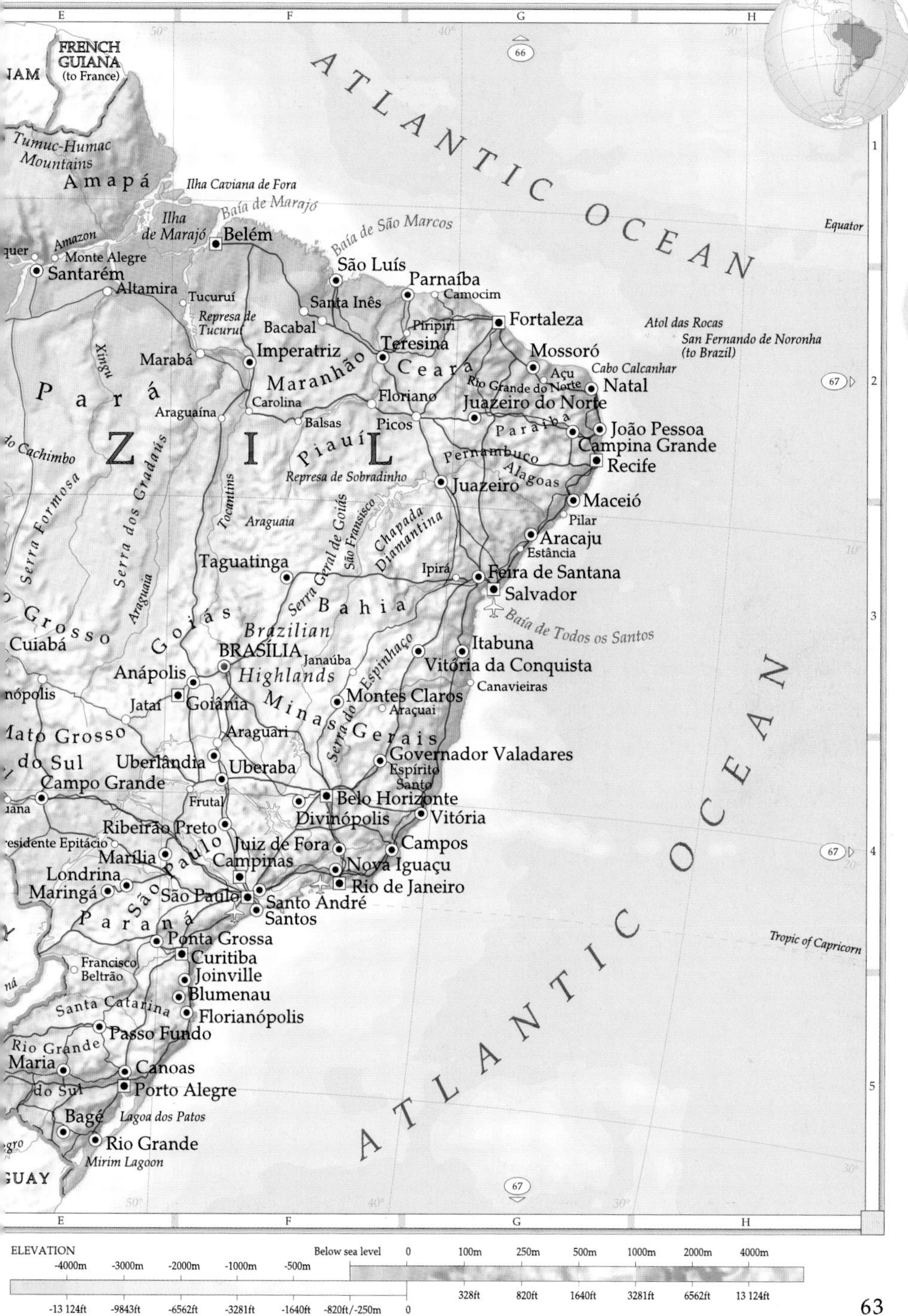

FRENCH
GUIANA
(to France)

IAM

*Tumuc-Humac
Mountains*

A m a p á

Ilha Caviana de Fora

Baía de Marajó

*Ilha
de Marajó*

Amazon

quer

Monte Alegre

Santarém

Altamira

Belém

São Luís

Parnaíba

Baía de São Marcos

ATLANTIC

OCEAN

Equator

Santa Inês

Camocim

Tucuruí

*Represa de
Tucuruí*

Bacabal

Piripiri

Fortaleza

Atol das Rocas

*San Fernando de Noronha
(to Brazil)*

Imperatriz

Teresina

Mossoró

Marabá

Maranhão

C e a r á

Cabo Calcanhar

P a r á

Carolina

Floriano

Rio Grande do Norte

Açu

Natal

66

67

Araguaína

Z

I

L

Picos

Juazeiro do Norte

P a r a í b a

João Pessoa

Balsas

P i a u í

L

Pernambuco

Campina Grande

Recife

Represa de Sobradinho

Juazeiro

Alagoas

Maceió

Araguaia

São Francisco

Ipirá

Pilar

Aracaju

Taguatinga

*Chapada
Diamantina*

Estância

Feira de Santana

Salvador

Serra Geral de Goiás

B a h i a

Baía de Todos os Santos

G r o s s o

Brazilian

BRASÍLIA

Janaúba

Itabuna

Cuiabá

G o i á s

Highlands

Vitória da Conquista

Canavieiras

nópolis

Anápolis

Montes Claros

Jataí

Goiânia

M i n a s

Araçuaí

Serra de Espinhaço

Araguari

G e r a i s

Governador Valadares

Mato Grosso

Uberlândia

Uberaba

*Espírito
Santo*

do Sul

Frutal

Belo Horizonte

Campo Grande

Ribeirão Preto

Divinópolis

Vitória

iana

esidente Epitácio

Marília

Juiz de Fora

Campos

Londrina

Campinas

Nova Iguaçu

Maringá

São Paulo

Santo André

Rio de Janeiro

P a r a n á

Santos

Tropic of Capricorn

Ponta Grossa

Francisco
Beltrão

Curitiba

Joinville

ná

Santa Catarina

Blumenau

Florianópolis

Passo Fundo

Rio Grande

Maria

Canoas

do Sul

Porto Alegre

gro

Bagé

Lagoa dos Patos

Rio Grande

GUAY

Mirim Lagoon

67

ATLANTIC

OCEAN

ELEVATION

				Below sea level	0	100m	250m	500m	1000m	2000m	4000m
-4000m	-3000m	-2000m	-1000m	-500m							
						328ft	820ft	1640ft	3281ft	6562ft	13 124ft
-13 124ft	-9843ft	-6562ft	-3281ft	-1640ft	-820ft/-250m	0					

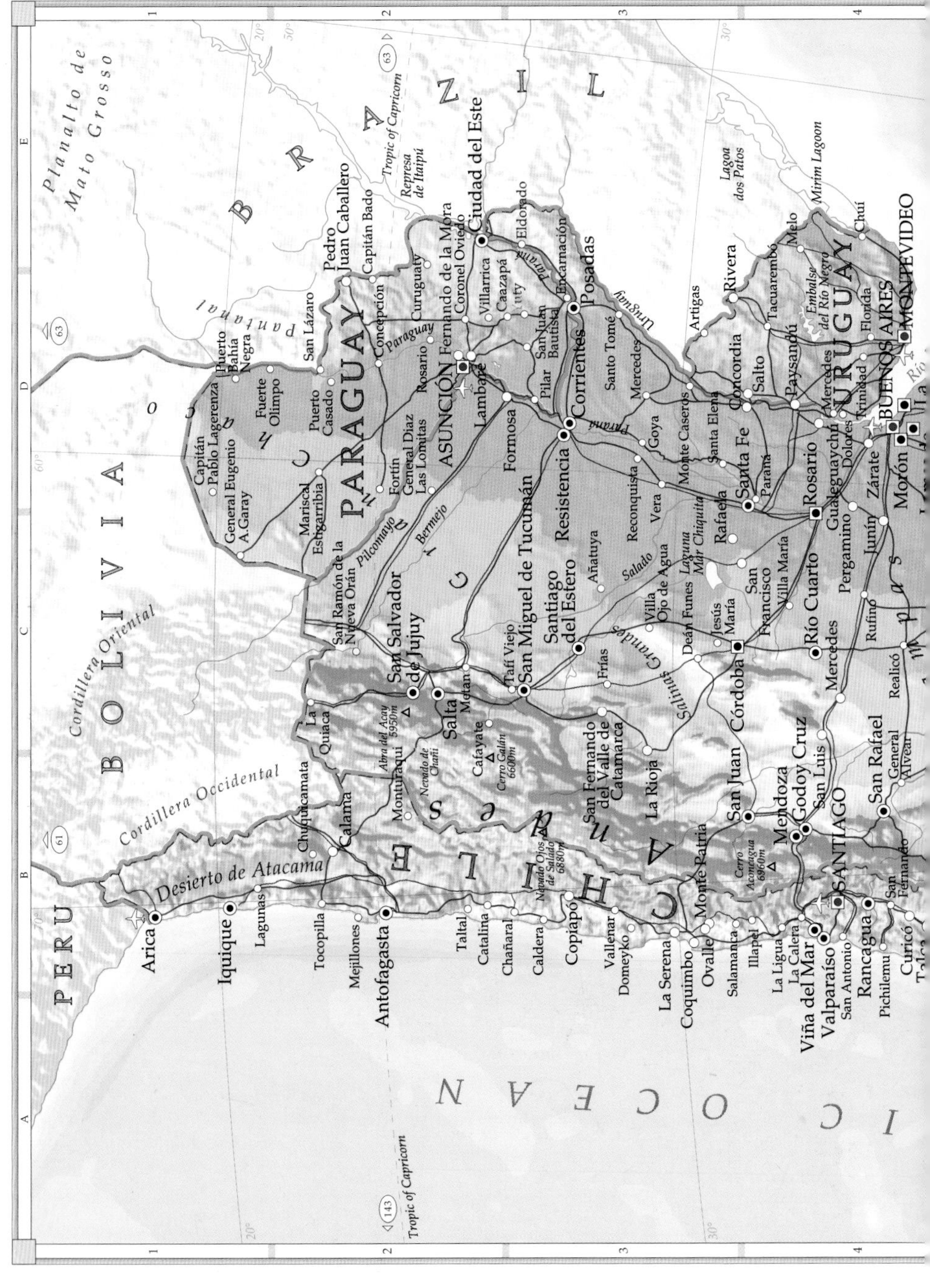

Planalto de Mato Grosso

B R A Z I L

Tropic of Capricorn

Represa de Itaipú

Lagoa dos Patos

Mirim Lagoon

Pantanal

Pedro Juan Caballero
Capitán Bado
Ciudad del Este
Eldorado

San Lázaro

Puerto Bahía Negra

Capitán Pablo Lagerenza
General Eugenio A. Garay

Fuerte Olimpo

Puerto Casado

Mariscal Estigarribia

Concepción

Uruguay
Coronel Oviedo
Villarrica
Caazapá
Ytu
Encarnación
Posadas
Rivera
Tacuarembó
Melo
Embalse del Río Negro
Chuí

Fernando de la Mora

Rafaela

Fortín General Díaz Las Lomitas

ASUNCIÓN
Lambaré
Pilar
San Juan Bautista

Corrientes
Santo Tomé
Mercedes
Artigas
Salto
Paysandú
Mercedes
Florida
MONTEVIDEO

URUGUAY
BUENOS AIRES

San Ramón de la Nueva Orán

Pilcomayo
Bermejo
Formosa
Resistencia
Goya
Monte Caseros
Santa Elena
Concordia
Morón
Zárate

Vera
Reconquista
Santa Fe
Paraná
Rosario
Gualeguaychú
Dolores
Junín

B O L I V I A

Cordillera Oriental

San Salvador de Jujuy

La Quiaca

Chuquicamata

Calama

Cordillera Occidental

Desierto de Atacama

Tilcara
Humahuaca

Salta
Metán
Cafayate
Cerro Galán 6600m

Abra del Acay 5995m

Nevado de Chañi

San Miguel de Tucumán
Tafí Viejo
Frías

Añatuya

Salado
Santiago del Estero

Villa María
Dean Funes

Laguna Mar Chiquita
Jesús María

Córdoba
San Francisco
Villa María

Río Cuarto
Pergamino
Rufino
Realicó

La Rioja

San Fernando del Valle de Catamarca

San Juan

San Luis

Mercedes

Mendoza
Godoy Cruz

San Rafael
General Alvear

Cerro Aconcagua 6960m

Nevado Ojos de Salado 6880m

Monte Patria

SANTIAGO

Salamanca
Illapel
La Ligua
La Calera
Viña del Mar
Valparaíso
San Antonio

Rancagua
San Fernando
Curicó

Pichilemu

C H I L E

P E R U

Arica
Iquique
Lagunas
Tocopilla
Mejillones
Antofagasta

Taltal
Catalina
Chañaral
Caldera
Copiapó
Vallenar
Domeyko
La Serena
Coquimbo
Ovalle

O C E A N

Tropic of Capricorn

0 km   200
0 miles   200

POPULATION

○ Less than 50,000   ◔ 50,000 -100,000   ◉ 100,000 - 500,000   ■ Over 500,000

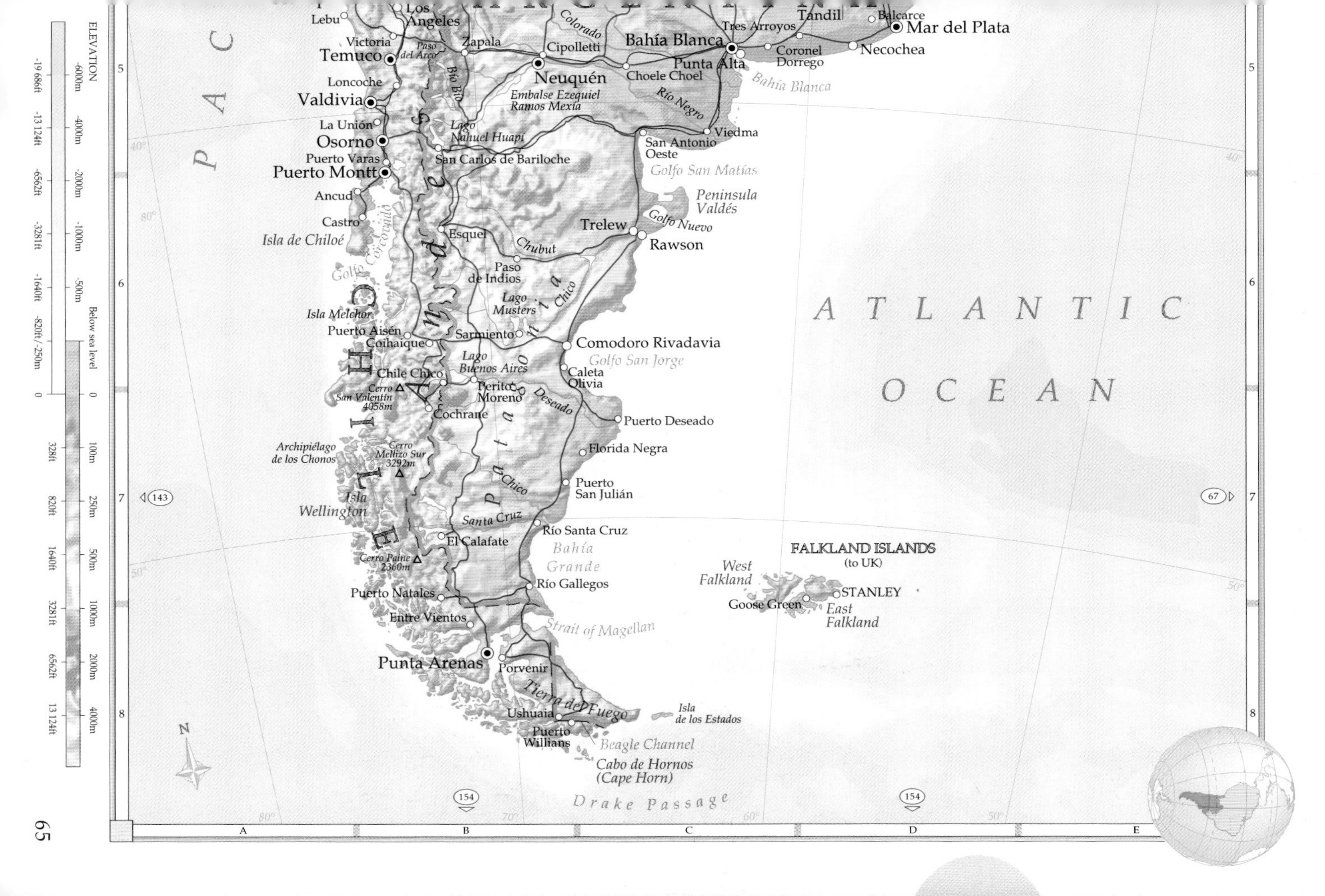

ATLANTIC

OCEAN

PACIFIC

Mar del Plata
Balcarce
Necochea
Tandil
Tres Arroyos
Coronel
Dorrego
Bahía Blanca
Punta Alta
Bahía Blanca
Choele Choel
Viedma
San Antonio
Oeste
Río Negro
Peninsula
Valdés
Golfo San Matías
Golfo Nuevo
Rawson
Colorado
Cipolletti
Neuquén
Zapala
Embalse Ezequiel
Ramos Mexía
Trelew
Comodoro Rivadavia
Golfo San Jorge
Caleta
Olivia
Puerto Deseado
Florida Negra
Puerto
San Julián
Los
Angeles
Victoria
Temuco
Loncoche
La Unión
Valdivia
Osorno
Puerto Varas
Puerto Montt
Ancud
Castro
Isla de Chiloé
Lebu
Bío Bío
Lago
Nahuel Huapí
San Carlos de Bariloche
Esquel
Paso
de Indios
Lago
Musters
Sarmiento
Chubut
Chico
Deseado
Lago
Buenos Aires
Perito
Moreno
Cochrane
Río Santa Cruz
Bahía
Grande
Río Gallegos
Santa Cruz
El Calafate
Chico
Chile Chico
Coihaique
Puerto Aisén
Isla
Melchor
Archipiélago
de los Chonos
Golfo
Corcovado
Cerro
San Valentín
4058m
Cerro
Murallón Sur
2793m
Isla
Wellington
Cerro Paine ▲
2750m
Puerto Natales
Entre Vientos
Punta Arenas
Forvenir
Tierra del Fuego
Ushuaia
Puerto
Williams
Strait of Magellan
Beagle Channel
Cabo de Hornos
(Cape Horn)
Isla
de los Estados
Drake Passage

FALKLAND ISLANDS
(to UK)
STANLEY
East
Falkland
Goose Green
West
Falkland

N

67

154

154

143

65

THE ATLANTIC OCEAN

ARCTIC OCEAN

EUROPE

NORTH AMERICA

ATLANTIC

Summer pack ice limit
Winter pack ice limit
Arctic Circle

Barents Sea

SVALBARD
(to Norway)

Scandinavia

Gulf of Bothnia

Baltic Sea

Caspian Sea

Red Sea

Tropic of Cancer

Mariupol'

Black Sea

Odesa

Port Said

Nile

Suez

Mediterranean Sea

Danube

Hamburg

Venice

Adriatic Sea

Alps

Atlas Mountains

Sahara

Lake Chad

Niger

Sahel

AFRICA

Greenland Sea

Norwegian Sea

Jan Mayen
(to Norway)

Norwegian Basin

FAEROE ISLANDS
(to Denmark)

North Sea

Godthåb

Rotterdam

Antwerp

London

British Isles

Bay of Biscay

Marseille

Algiers

Gibraltar

West European Basin

Iberian Basin

Madeira
(to Portugal)

Canary Basin

Las Palmas

Canary Islands
(to Spain)

CAPE VERDE ISLANDS

Dakar

Freetown

Sierra

Doldrums Fracture Zone

ICELAND

Reykjavík

Denmark Strait

Iceland Basin

Rockall Bank

Reykjanes Basin

Azores
(to Portugal)

Cape Verde Plain

Cape Verde Basin

CAPE VERDE
ISLANDS

GREENLAND
(to Denmark)

Labrador Sea

Labrador Basin

Newfoundland Basin

Mid-Atlantic Ridge

Kane Fracture Zone

Baffin Bay

Baffin Island

Davis Strait

Northwest Atlantic Mid-Ocean Canyon

Newfoundland

Grand Banks of Newfoundland

Bermuda Rise

North American Basin

Sargasso Sea

Puerto Rico Trench

8605m

Guiana Basin

Lincoln Sea

Ellesmere Island

Hudson Bay

Great Lakes

Quebec

St-Lawrence

Montreal

Halifax

New York

BERMUDA
(to UK)

Caribbean Sea

Caracas

Venezuelan Basin

New Orleans

Gulf of Mexico

Mississippi

West Indies

Colombian Basin

Panama

Guatemala

Tropic of Cancer

Arctic Circle

155

155

34

81

60

80

20

0 km   1000

0 miles   1000

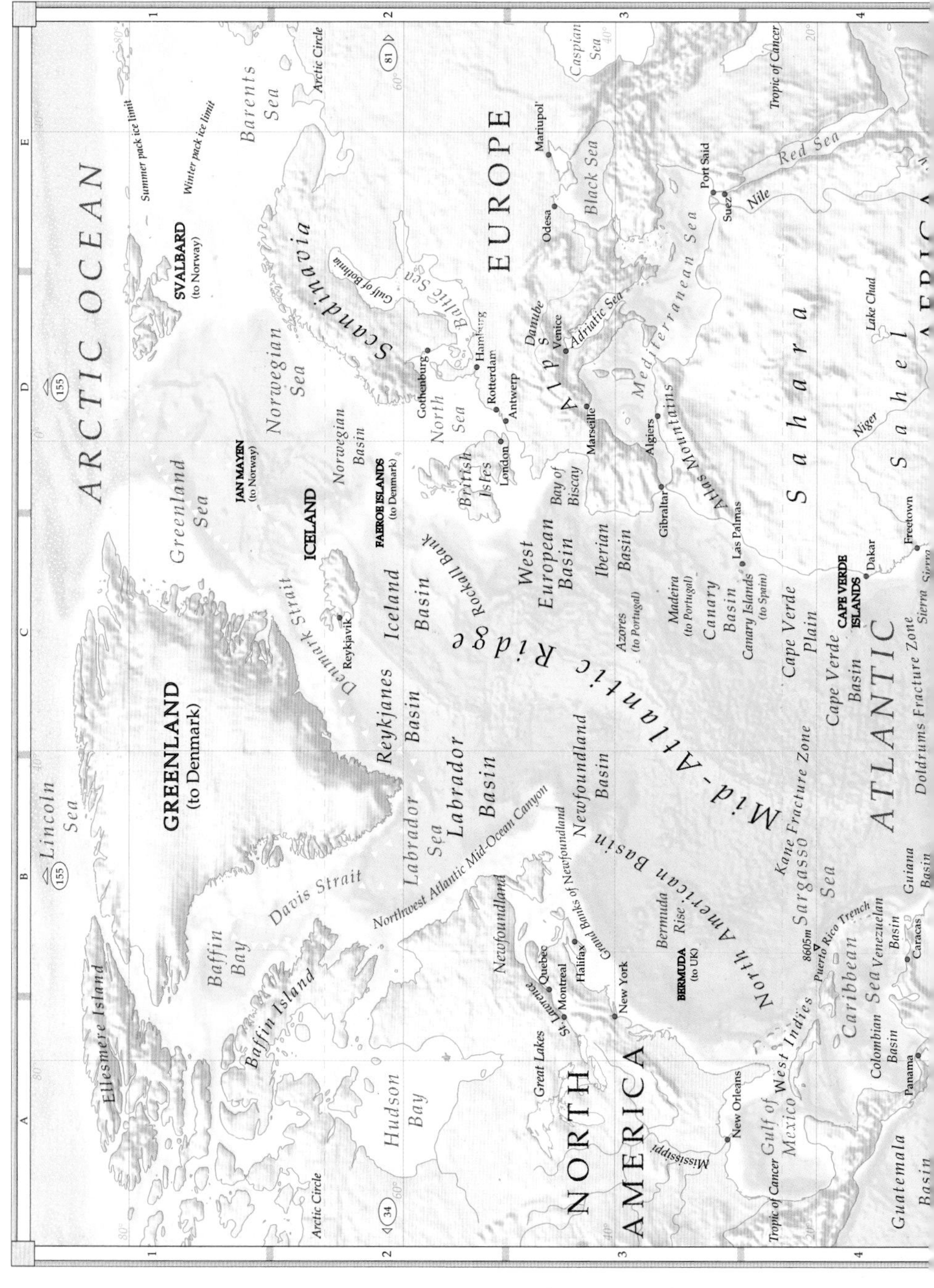

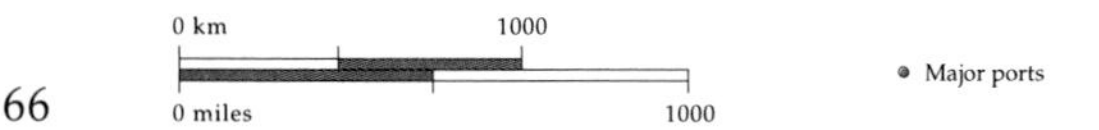

● Major ports

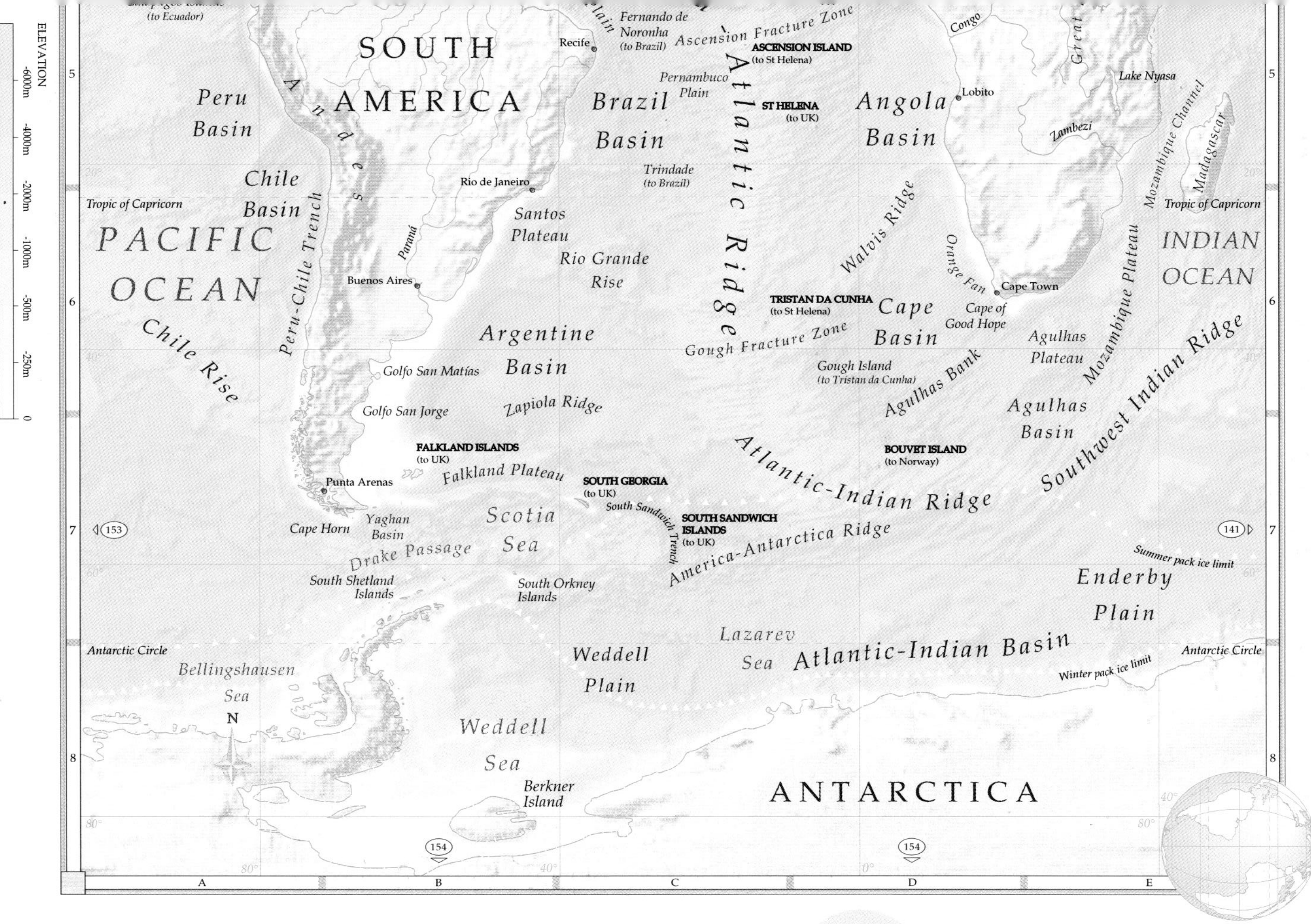

SOUTH AMERICA

PACIFIC OCEAN

ATLANTIC OCEAN

INDIAN OCEAN

ANTARCTICA

Lake Nyasa

Great

Zambezi

Congo

Mozambique Channel

Madagascar

Tropic of Capricorn

Mozambique Plateau

Southwest Indian Ridge

Summer pack ice limit

Antarctic Circle

Winter pack ice limit

Enderby Plain

Atlantic-Indian Basin

Agulhas Plateau

Agulhas Basin

Cape Town

Cape of Good Hope

Orange Fan

Agulhas Bank

Lobito

Angola Basin

Walvis Ridge

Cape Basin

BOUVET ISLAND
(to Norway)

ASCENSION ISLAND
(to UK)

ST HELENA
(to UK)

TRISTAN DA CUNHA
(to St Helena)

Gough Island
(to Tristan da Cunha)

Atlantic-Indian Ridge

Ascension Fracture Zone

Fernando de
Noronha
(to Brazil)

Atlantic Ridge

Pernambuco Plain

Trindade
(to Brazil)

Gough Fracture Zone

America-Antarctica Ridge

Lazarev Sea

Recife

Brazil Basin

Rio Grande Rise

SOUTH GEORGIA
(to UK)

SOUTH SANDWICH
ISLANDS
(to UK)

South Sandwich Trench

Weddell Plain

Rio de Janeiro

Santos Plateau

Argentine Basin

Zapiola Ridge

Scotia Sea

South Orkney Islands

Weddell Sea

Berkner Island

Golfo San Matías

FALKLAND ISLANDS
(to UK)

Falkland Plateau

Paraná

Buenos Aires

Golfo San Jorge

Punta Arenas

Yaghan Basin

Drake Passage

South Shetland Islands

Cape Horn

Andes

Peru-Chile Trench

Chile Basin

Peru Basin

Tropic of Capricorn

(to Ecuador)

Chile Rise

Bellingshausen Sea

Antarctic Circle

N

141

153

154

154

ELEVATION

-6000m	-4000m	-2000m	-1000m	-500m	-250m	0
-19 686ft	-13 124ft	-6562ft	-3281ft	-1640ft	-820ft	0

AFRICA

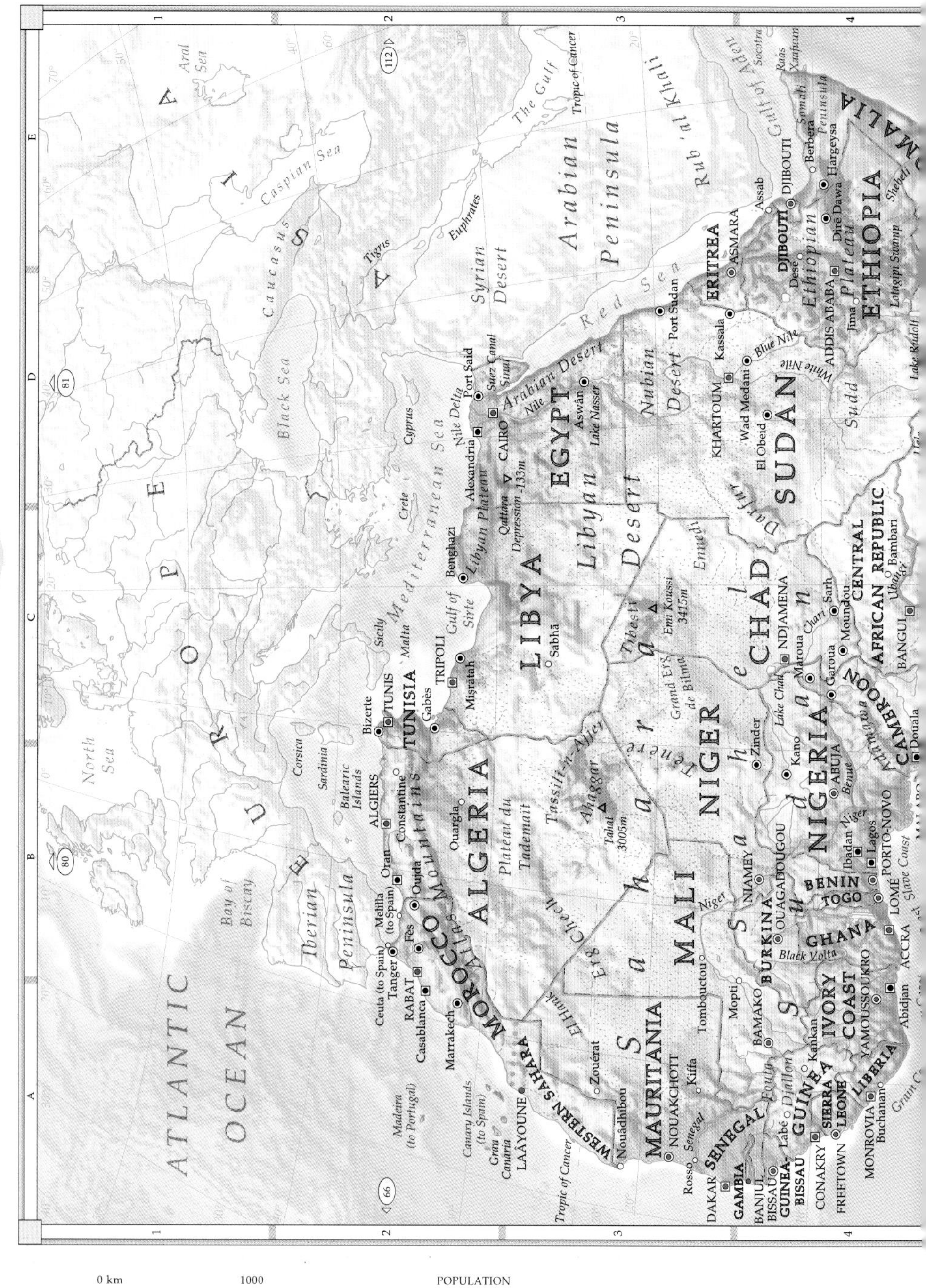

POPULATION

∘ Less than 50,000 ⊙ 50,000 -100,000 ⊙ 100,000 - 500,000 ▣ Over 500,000

0 km 1000

0 miles 1000

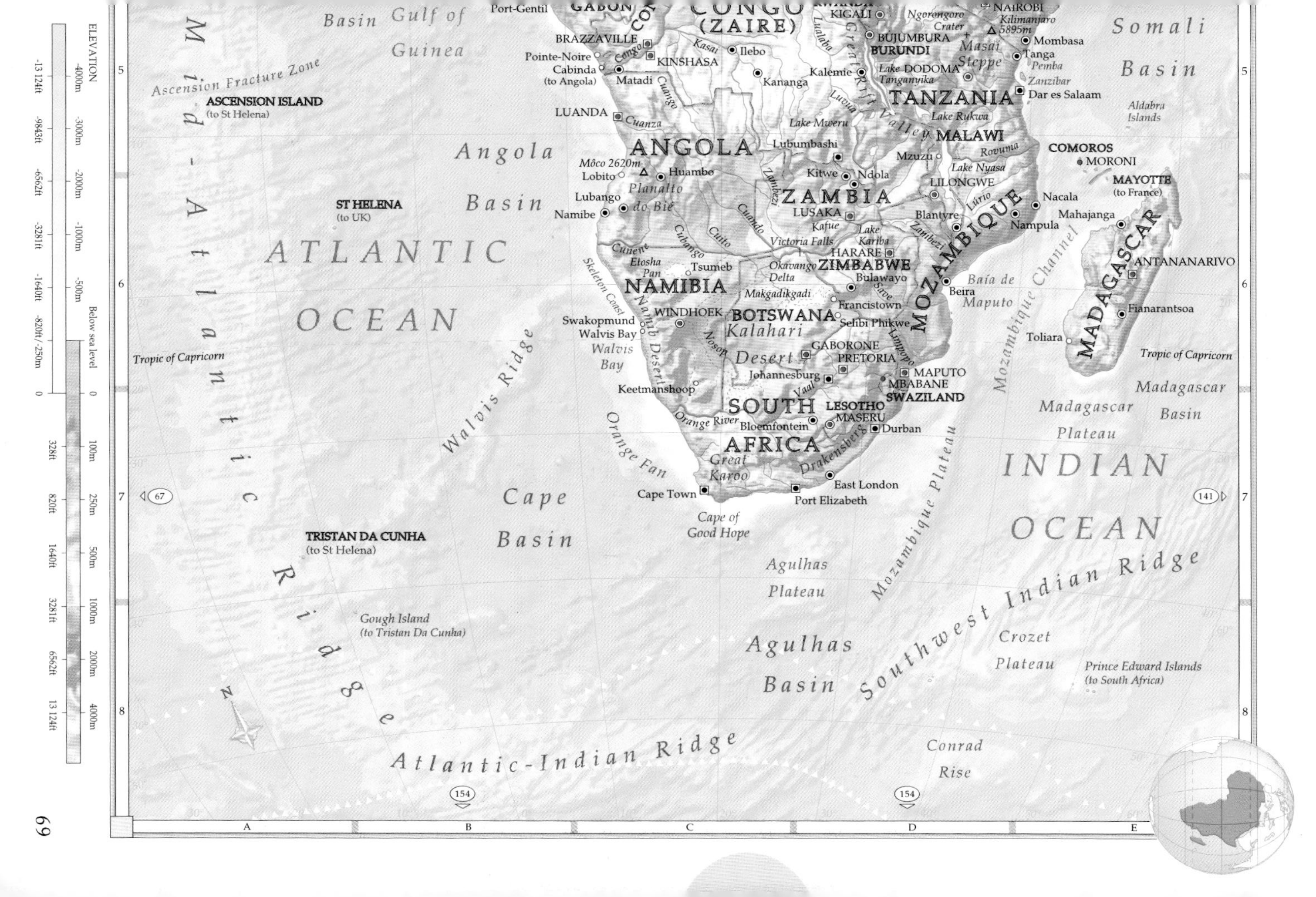

Somali Basin

Allabra Islands

COMOROS
MAYOTTE
(to France)
MORONI

ANTANANARIVO
Fianarantsoa

MADAGASCAR

Madagascar Basin

Madagascar Plateau

INDIAN OCEAN

Prince Edward Islands
(to South Africa)

Southwest Indian Ridge

Crozet Plateau

Conrad Rise

NAIROBI
Mombasa
Kilimanjaro
5895m
Masai Steppe
Tanga
Pemba
Zanzibar
Dar es Salaam

Ngorongoro Crater
KIGALI
BUJUMBURA
BURUNDI

TANZANIA

Great Rift Valley

MALAWI
LILONGWE
DODOMA
Lake Rukwa
Rovuma
Lake Nyasa
Blantyre
Nacala
Nampula
Mahajanga
Toliara

Baía de Beira

Maputo

Mozambique Channel

Mozambique Plateau

CONGO (ZAIRE)
Lualaba
Ilebo
Kasai
KINSHASA
Matadi
Cuango

BRAZZAVILLE
Pointe-Noire
Cabinda
(to Angola)
LUANDA
Port-Gentil
GABON

Gulf of Guinea Basin

Lake Mweru
Karanga
Kalemie
Lake Tanganyika
Mbeya
Lake Rukwa

ZAMBIA
LUSAKA
Kitwe
Ndola
Lufumbashi
Kafue
Victoria Falls
Lake Kariba
Kariba
Zambezi

ANGOLA
Méco 2620m
Lobito
Lubango
Namibe
Cuanza
Planalto
do Bié
Cuito
Cubango
Cunene

HARARE
ZIMBABWE
Bulawayo
Francistown
Seffni Pikwe
Limpopo

MOZAMBIQUE
MAPUTO
MBABANE
SWAZILAND
Durban

BOTSWANA
GABORONE
Makgadikgadi
Kalahari
Odrango Delta
Sua

NAMIBIA
WINDHOEK
Etosha Pan
Tsumeb
Otjiwarongo
Namib Desert
Noso
Nosob

Swakopmund
Walvis Bay
Walvis Bay
Keetmanshoop

Skeleton Coast

Namib Desert

Orange
Orange Fan

SOUTH AFRICA
PRETORIA
Johannesburg
MASERU
LESOTHO
Bloemfontein
Vaal
Great Karoo
Stankerstown
East London
Port Elizabeth
Cape Town
Cape of Good Hope

Agulhas Plateau

Agulhas Basin

Angola Basin

Cape Basin

Walvis Ridge

ST HELENA
(to UK)

ASCENSION ISLAND
(to St Helena)

Ascension Fracture Zone

ATLANTIC OCEAN

TRISTAN DA CUNHA
(to St Helena)

Gough Island
(to Tristan Da Cunha)

Mid-Atlantic Ridge

Tropic of Capricorn

Atlantic-Indian Ridge

154

67

ELEVATION

| -4000m | -3000m | -2000m | -1000m | -500m | Below sea level | 0 | 100m | 250m | 500m | 1000m | 2000m | 4000m |

| -13 124ft | -9843ft | -6562ft | -3281ft | -1640ft | -820ft/-250m | 0 | 328ft | 820ft | 1640ft | 3281ft | 6562ft | 13 124ft |

69

NORTHWEST AFRICA

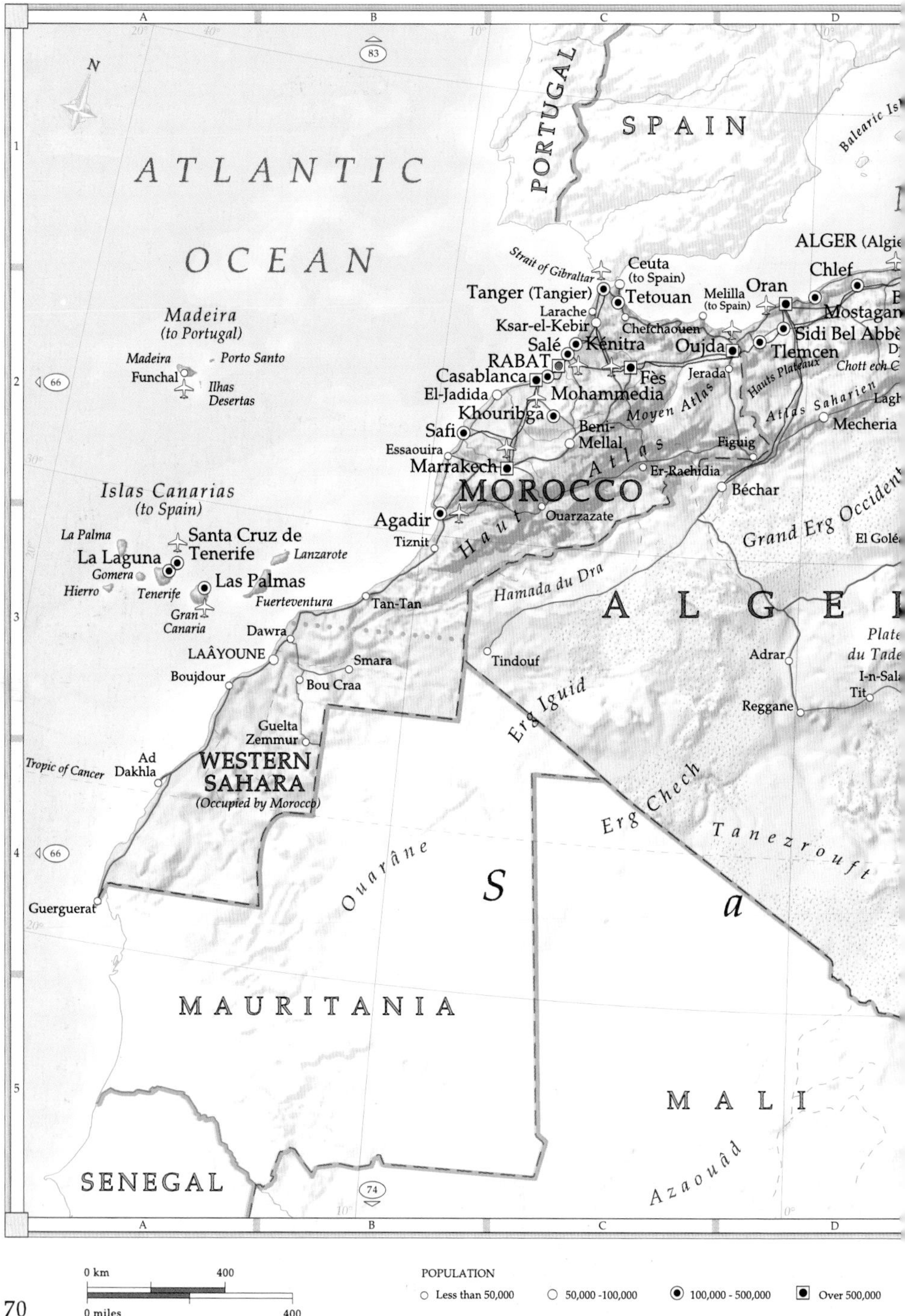

ATLANTIC

OCEAN

PORTUGAL

SPAIN

Balearic Is

Madeira
(to Portugal)
Madeira ◦ *Porto Santo*
Funchal ⌂
Ilhas
Desertas

Strait of Gibraltar
Ceuta
(to Spain)
Tanger (Tangier) ◉ Tetouan
Larache
Ksar-el-Kebir
Salé ◉ Kénitra
RABAT ◉
Casablanca ◉◦
El-Jadida ◦
Khouribga ◦
Safi ◦
Essaouira ◦
Marrakech ◉

Chefchaouen
Melilla
(to Spain)
ALGER (Alger
Chlef
Oran
Mostagan
Sidi Bel Abbè
Tlemcen
Oujda
Jerada
Fès
Mohammedia
Beni-
Mellal
Er-Rachidia
Figuig
Ouarzazate
Béchar

MOROCCO

Haut

Atlas

Moyen Atlas
Hauts Plateaux
Chott ech-C
Atlas Saharien
Lagh
Mecheria

Islas Canarias
(to Spain)
La Palma
La Laguna ◉ Santa Cruz de
Gomera ◦ Tenerife *Lanzarote*
Hierro ◦ *Tenerife* ◉ Las Palmas
Gran
Canaria Dawra ◦
LAÂYOUNE ◉
Boujdour ◦

Agadir ◉
Tiznit ◦
Fuerteventura
Tan-Tan ◦

Hamada du Dra

Tindouf ◦

Grand Erg Occident
El Golé
ALGE
Plate
du Tade
Adrar ◦
I-n-Sala
Reggane ◦
Tit

Smara ◦
Bou Craa ◦

Erg Iguid

Guelta
Zemmur ◦
Tropic of Cancer
Ad
Dakhla ◦
WESTERN
SAHARA
(Occupied by Morocco)

Erg Chech

Tanezrouft

S

a

Guerguerat ◦

Ouarâne

MAURITANIA

MALI

SENEGAL

Azaouâd

0 km 400

0 miles 400

POPULATION
○ Less than 50,000 ○ 50,000 -100,000 ◉ 100,000 - 500,000 ◼ Over 500,000

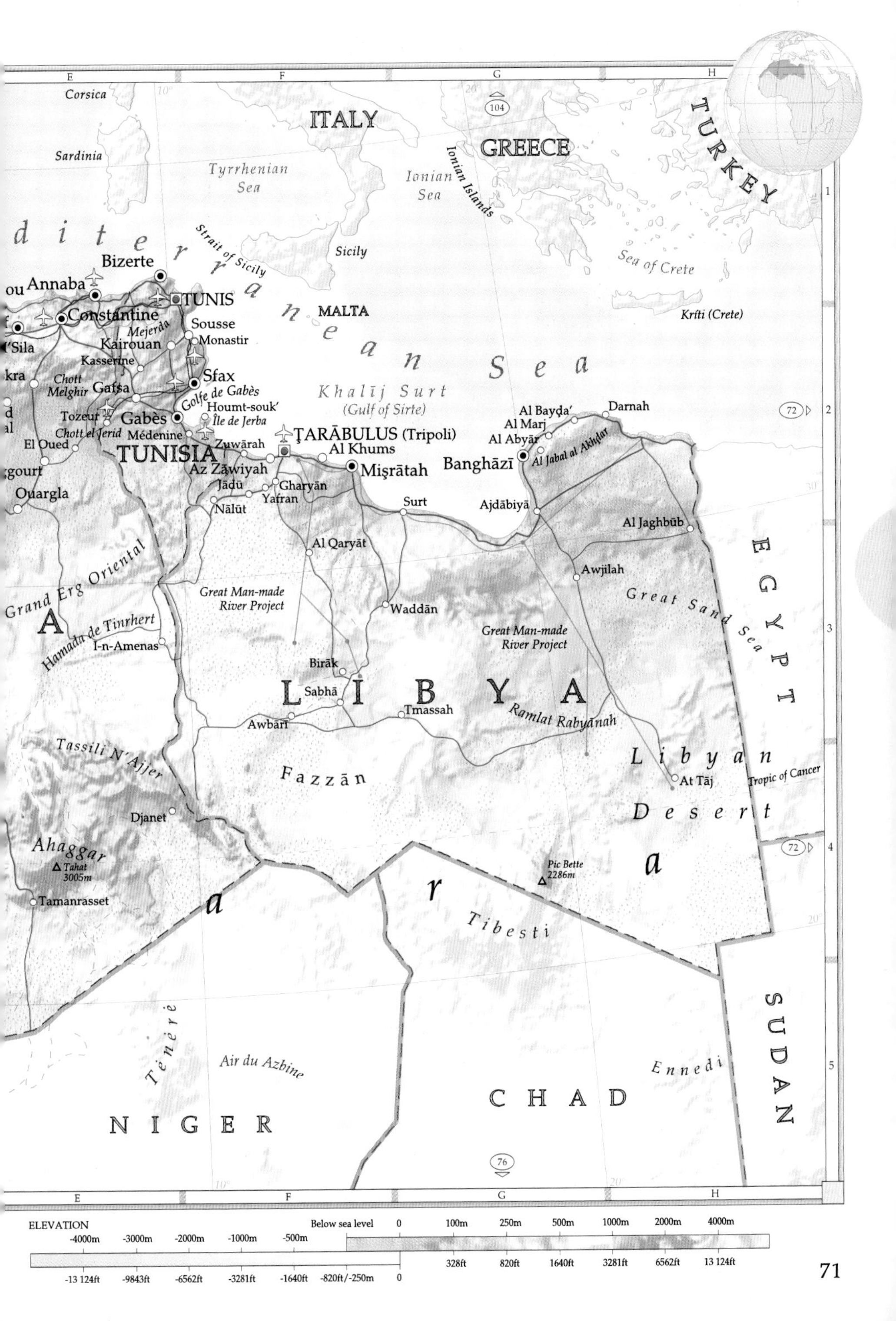

ITALY

GREECE

TURKEY

Corsica

Sardinia

Tyrrhenian Sea

Ionian Sea

Ionian Islands

Sicily

Sea of Crete

Kríti (Crete)

ou Annaba
Bizerte
Constantine
'Sila
Kairouan
Kasserine
kra
Chott
Melghir Gafsa
Tozeur
Gabès
El Oued
Chott el Jerid
gourt
Ouargla

TUNIS
Sousse
Monastir
Sfax
Golfe de Gabès
Houmt-souk'
Île de Jerba
Médenine
Zuwārah
TUNISIA
Az Zāwiyah
Jādū
Nālūt
Yafran
Gharyān

MALTA

Mediterranean Sea

Khalīj Surt
(Gulf of Sirte)

ȚARĀBULUS (Tripoli)
Al Khums
Miṣrātah

Banghāzī

Al Bayḍa'
Al Marj
Al Abyār
Al Jabal al Akhḍar

Darnah

Surt

Ajdābiyā

Al Jaghbūb

Awjilah

Great Man-made
River Project

Waddān

Great Man-made
River Project

Great Sand Sea

EGYPT

Grand Erg Oriental

A

Hamādat de Tinrhert

I-n-Amenas

L I B Y A

Birāk
Sabhā

Tmassah

Ramlat Rabyānah

Al Qaryāt

Tassili N'Ajjer

Awbārī

Fazzān

Libyan

At Tāj

Tropic of Cancer

Desert

Djanet

a

Ahaggar
△ Tahat
3005m

Tamanrasset

a

r

Pic Bette
△ 2286m

Tibesti

SUDAN

Ténéré

Air du Azbine

NIGER

CHAD

Ennedi

ELEVATION

| -4000m | -3000m | -2000m | -1000m | -500m | Below sea level | 0 | 100m | 250m | 500m | 1000m | 2000m | 4000m |

| -13 124ft | -9843ft | -6562ft | -3281ft | -1640ft | -820ft/-250m | 0 | | 328ft | 820ft | 1640ft | 3281ft | 6562ft | 13 124ft |

NORTHEAST AFRICA

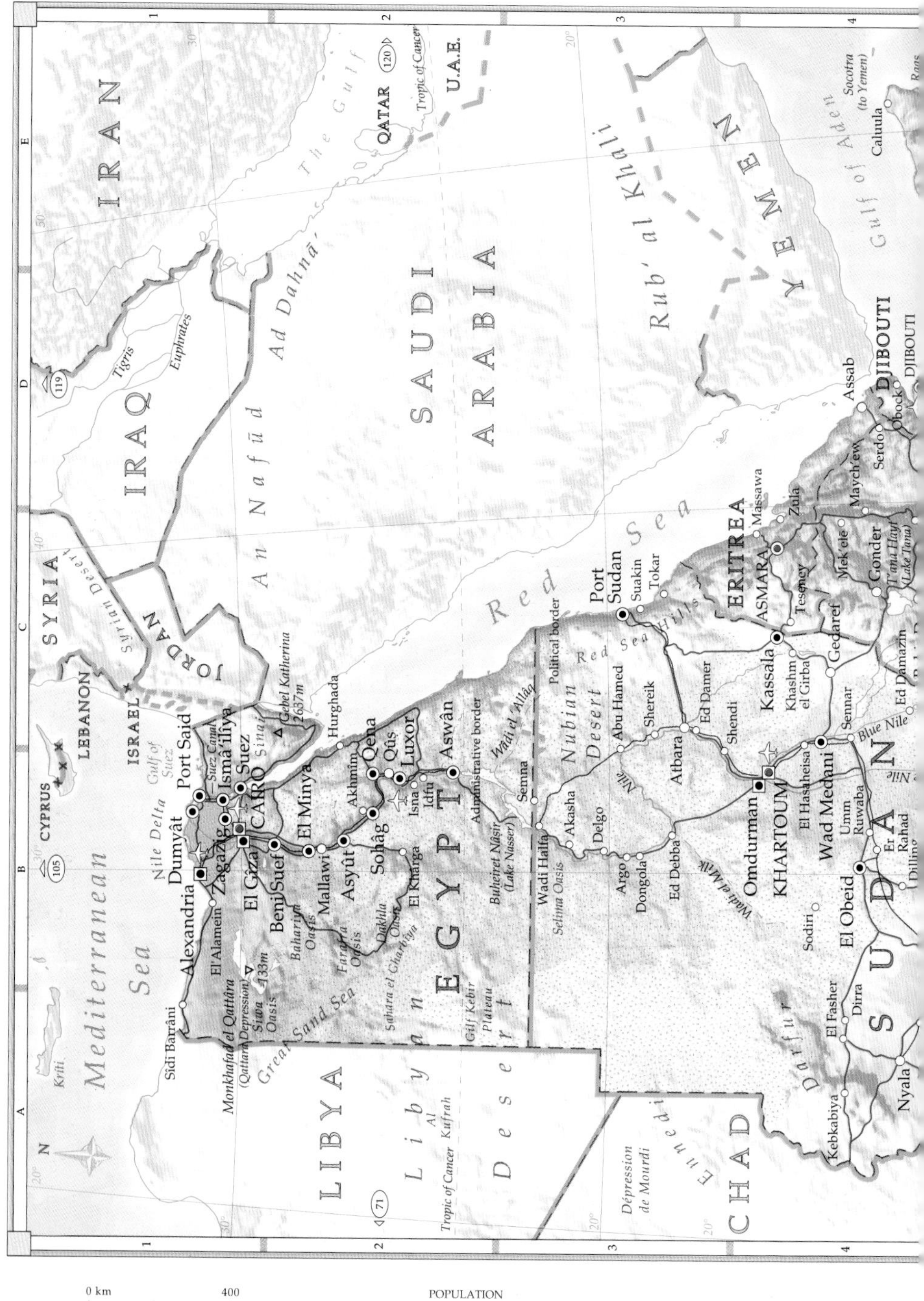

POPULATION

○ Less than 50,000   ○ 50,000 -100,000   ◉ 100,000 - 500,000   ■ Over 500,000

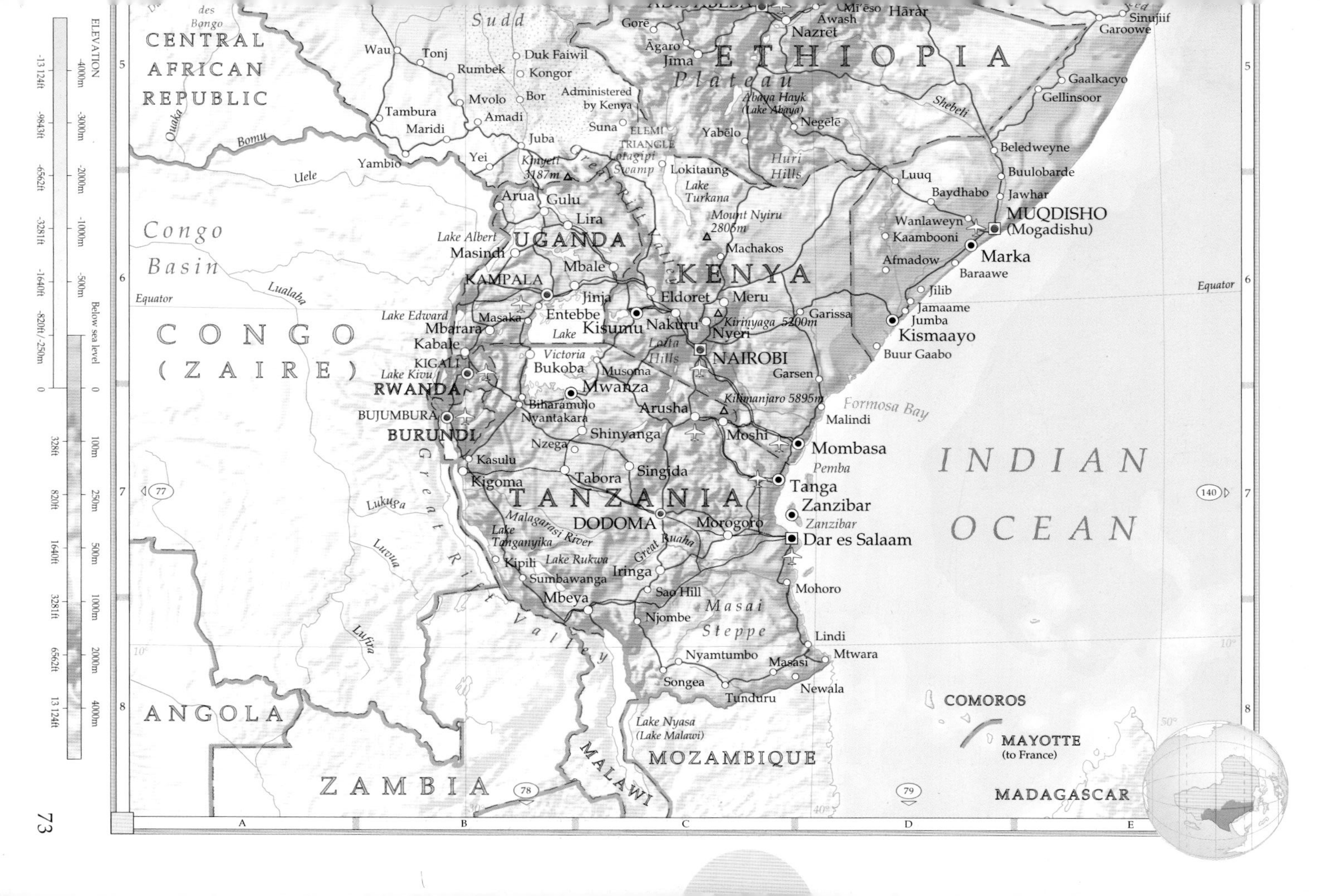
CENTRAL
AFRICAN
REPUBLIC
ETHIOPIA
Plateau
UGANDA
KENYA
TANZANIA
RWANDA
BURUNDI
CONGO
(ZAIRE)
ANGOLA
ZAMBIA
MALAWI
MOZAMBIQUE
COMOROS
MAYOTTE
(to France)
MADAGASCAR
INDIAN
OCEAN
MUQDISHO
(Mogadishu)
NAIROBI
KAMPALA
DODOMA
KIGALI
BUJUMBURA
Sudd
Wau
Tonj
Rumbek
Duk Faiwil
Kongor
Bor
Mvolo
Amadi
Tambura
Maridi
Juba
Yei
Yambio
Administered
by Kenya
Suna
ELEMI
TRIANGLE
Lotagipi
Swamp
Kinyeti
3187m
Gore
Agaro
Jima
Nazret
Awash
Mi'eso
Harar
Abaya Hayk
(Lake Abaya)
Negele
Yabelo
Huri
Hills
Lokitaung
Lake
Turkana
Mount Nyiru
2806m
Machakos
Shebeli
Sinujiif
Garoowe
Gaalkacyo
Gellinsoor
Beledweyne
Buulobarde
Jawhar
Luuq
Baydhabo
Wanlaweyn
Kaambooni
Afmadow
Marka
Baraawe
Jilib
Jamaame
Jumba
Kismaayo
Buur Gaabo
Garissa
Garsen
Formosa Bay
Malindi
Equator
Ouaka
Bomu
Uele
Congo
Basin
Lualaba
Arua
Gulu
Lira
Lake Albert
Masindi
Mbale
Jinja
Entebbe
Eldoret
Meru
Kisumu
Nakuru
Nyeri
Kirinyaga 5200m
Loita
Hills
Lake Edward
Masaka
Mbarara
Kabale
Lake Kivu
Lake
Victoria
Bukoba
Musoma
Mwanza
Biharamulo
Nyantakara
Arusha
Kilimanjaro 5895m
Moshi
Mombasa
Pemba
Shinyanga
Nzega
Kasulu
Kigoma
Tabora
Singida
Tanga
Zanzibar
Zanzibar
Dar es Salaam
Morogoro
Great Ruaha
Malagarasi River
Lake
Tanganyika
Kipili
Lake Rukwa
Sumbawanga
Iringa
Mbeya
Sao Hill
Mohoro
Masai
Steppe
Njombe
Lindi
Mtwara
Nyamtumbo
Masasi
Songea
Tunduru
Newala
Lake Nyasa
(Lake Malawi)
Great Rift Valley
Lukuga
Luvua
Lufira
ELEVATION
-4000m
-3000m
-2000m
-1000m
-500m
Below sea level
0
100m
250m
500m
1000m
2000m
4000m
-13 124ft
-9843ft
-6562ft
-3281ft
-1640ft
-820ft/-250m
0
328ft
820ft
1640ft
3281ft
6562ft
13 124ft

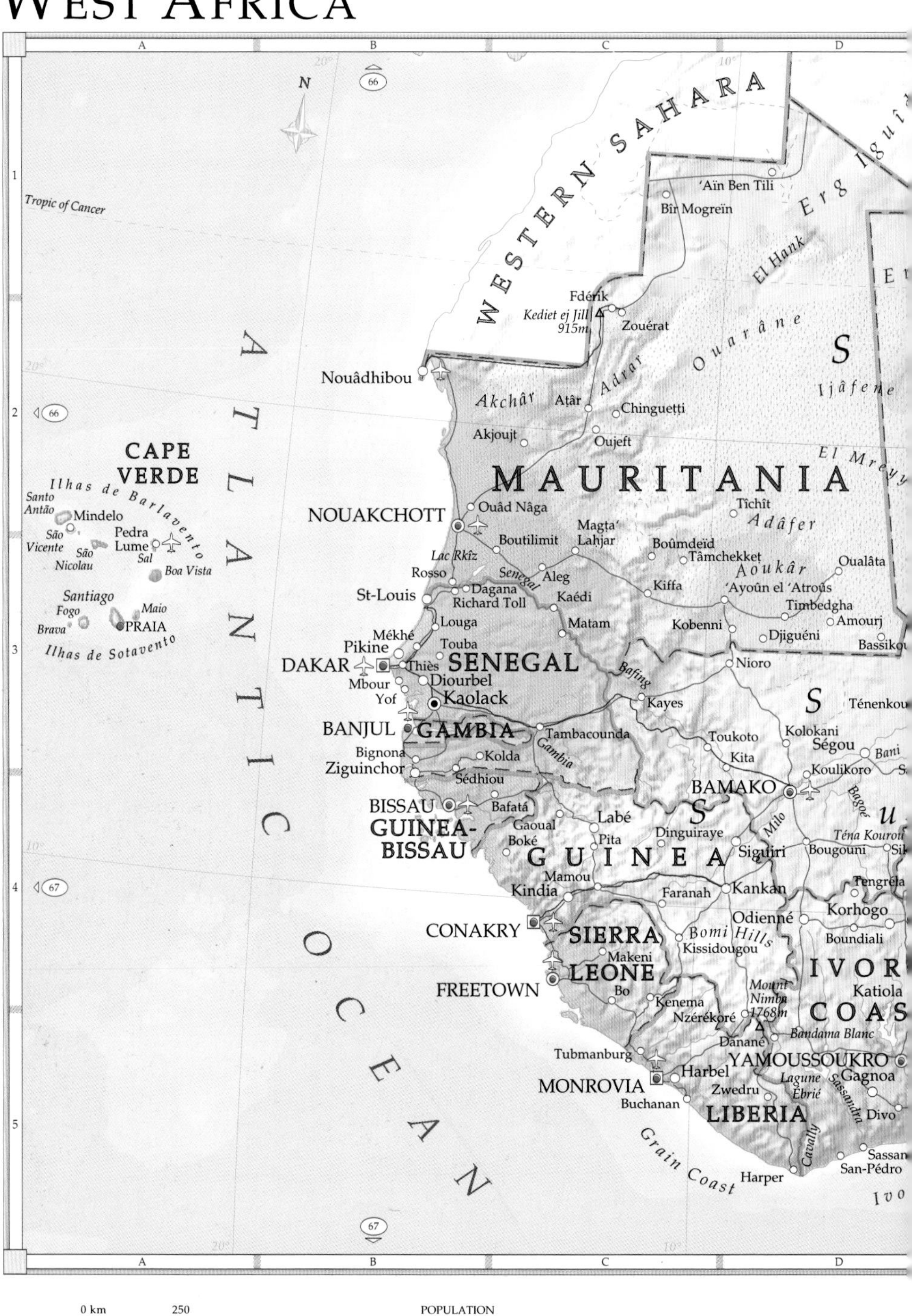

N
66

WESTERN SAHARA

Tropic of Cancer

'Aïn Ben Tili

Bîr Mogreïn

Erg Iguîd

Fdérik
Kediet ej Jill ▲
915m
Zouérat

El Hank

Nouâdhibou

Adrar

Ouarâne

S

Ijâfene

Akchâr
Atâr
Chinguetti

El Mreyy

Akjoujt
Oujeft

CAPE
VERDE

Ilhas de Barlavento
Santo
Antão
Mindelo
São
Vicente
São
Nicolau
Pedra
Lume
Sal
Boa Vista

NOUAKCHOTT

Ouâd Nâga

Tîchît
Adâfer

MAURITANIA

Boutilimit
Magta'
Lahjar
Boûmdeïd
Tâmchekket
Oualâta

Santiago
Fogo
Maio
Brava
PRAIA
Ilhas de Sotavento

Lac Rkîz
Rosso
Dagana
Richard Toll
St-Louis

Senegal
Aleg
Kaédi
Kiffa
'Ayoûn el 'Atroûs
Aoukâr

Louga
Matam
Kobenni
Timbedgha
Amourj

Mékhé
Pikine
Thies
DAKAR
Touba

Nioro
Djiguéni
Bassiko

Senegal

Mbour
Yof
Diourbel
SENEGAL

Bafing

S

Ténenkou

Kayes

Kaolack

BANJUL
GAMBIA
Tambacounda

Kolokani
Ségou

Bani

Bignona
Ziguinchor
Kolda
Cambia
Toukoto
Kita
Koulikoro

Sédhiou

BAMAKO

U

BISSAU
GUINEA-
BISSAU

Bafatá
Gaoual
Boké

Labé

S
Milo

Téna Kourou
Bougouni

Sil

Mamou

Pita
Dinguiraye
Siguiri

Bogou

CONAKRY

Kindia

GUINEA
Faranah

Kankan

Tengréla

Korhogo

Odienné

Boundiali

SIERRA

Makeni

Bomi Hills
Kissidougou

IVOR

FREETOWN

LEONE

Bo

Kenema
Nzérékoré

Mount
Nimba
1768m

Katiola

COAS

Bandama Blanc

Danané

YAMOUSSOUKRO

Tubmanburg

Harbel

Lagune
Ébrié
Gagnoa

MONROVIA

Buchanan

Zwedru

LIBERIA

Divo

Grain Coast

Sassan
Harper
San-Pédro

Ivo

67

0 km   250

0 miles   250

POPULATION

○ Less than 50,000   ○ 50,000 -100,000   ◉ 100,000 - 500,000   ■ Over 500,000

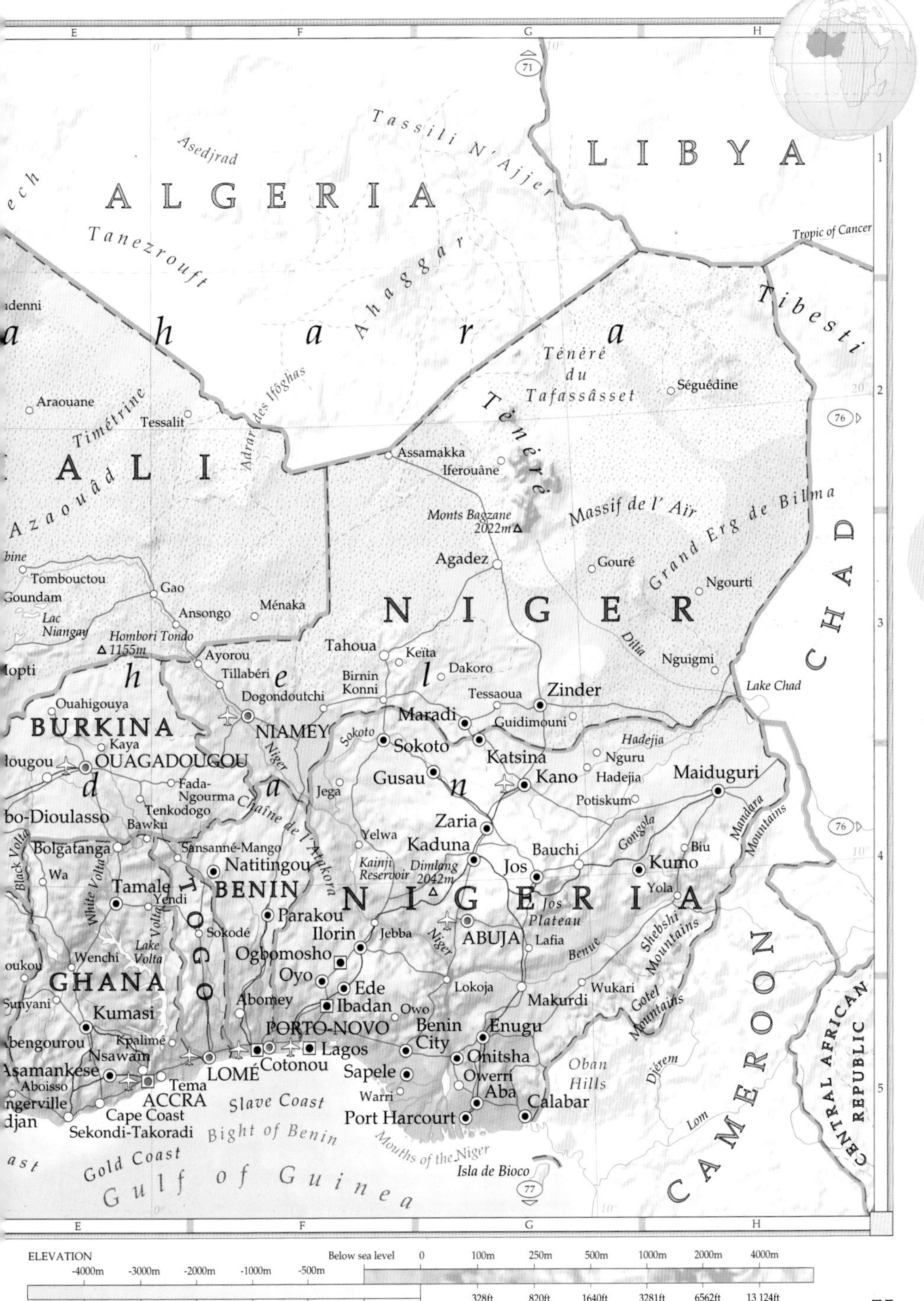

E   F   G   H

71

L I B Y A

A L G E R I A

Tanezrouft

Asedjrad

Tassili N'Ajjer

Tibesti

Tropic of Cancer

Ahaggar

a   *h*   *a*   *r*   *a*

Ténéré
du
Tafassâsset

Séguédine

76

adenni

Araouane

Timétrine

Tessalit

Adrar des Ifoghas

Assamakka
Iferouâne

Massif de l' Aïr

Grand Erg de Bilma

A L I

Azaouâd

bine

Tombouctou

Goundam

Lac
Niangay

Gao

Ansongo

Ménaka

Monts Bagzane
2022m △

Agadez

Gouré

Ngourti

Ténéré

Dilia

Ngouigmi

C H A D

Hombori Tondo
△ 1155m

h

Ayorou

Tillabéri

Dogondoutchi

N I G E R

Tahoua

Keïta

Dakoro

Tessaoua

Zinder

Lake Chad

Mopti

Ouahigouya

e

Birnin
Konni

l

lougou

Kaya

BURKINA

OUAGADOUGOU

d

NIAMEY

Sokoto

Maradi

Sokoto

Guidimouni

Katsina

Hadejia

Nguru

Kano

Hadejia

Maiduguri

Mandara Mountains

76

bo-Dioulasso

Fada-
Ngourma

Tenkodogo

Bawku

Chaîne de l'Atakora

a

Jega

Gusau

n

Zaria

Potiskum

Bolgatanga

Sansanné-Mango

Natitingou

BENIN

Kainji
Reservoir

Kaduna

Dimlang
2042m △

Bauchi

Jos

Gongola

Biu

Kumo

Yola

Shebshi Mountains

Wa

Tamale

Yendi

N I G E R I A

Jos
Plateau

Black Volta

White Volta

Lake
Volta

Sokodé

Parakou

Ilorin

Jebba

ABUJA

Lafia

Benue

Wukari

Gotel Mountains

oukou

Wenchi

Ogbomosho

Oyo

Lokoja

Makurdi

CAMEROON

Djérem

Sunyani

GHANA

Kumasi

Abomey

Ede

Ibadan

Owo

PORTO-NOVO

Benin
City

Enugu

Onitsha

Oban
Hills

engourou

Kpalimé

Nsawam

LOMÉ

Cotonou

Lagos

Sapele

Owerri

Aba

Calabar

Lom

Asamankese

Aboisso

Tema

Warri

ngerville

ACCRA

Slave Coast

Port Harcourt

djan

Cape Coast

Sekondi-Takoradi

Bight of Benin

Mouths of the Niger

CENTRAL AFRICAN REPUBLIC

ast

Gold Coast

Gulf of Guinea

Isla de Bioco

77

Niger

Niger

TOGO

Volta

Niger

ELEVATION

						Below sea level	0	100m	250m	500m	1000m	2000m	4000m
-4000m	-3000m	-2000m	-1000m	-500m									

							328ft	820ft	1640ft	3281ft	6562ft	13 124ft
-13 124ft	-9843ft	-6562ft	-3281ft	-1640ft	-820ft/-250m	0						

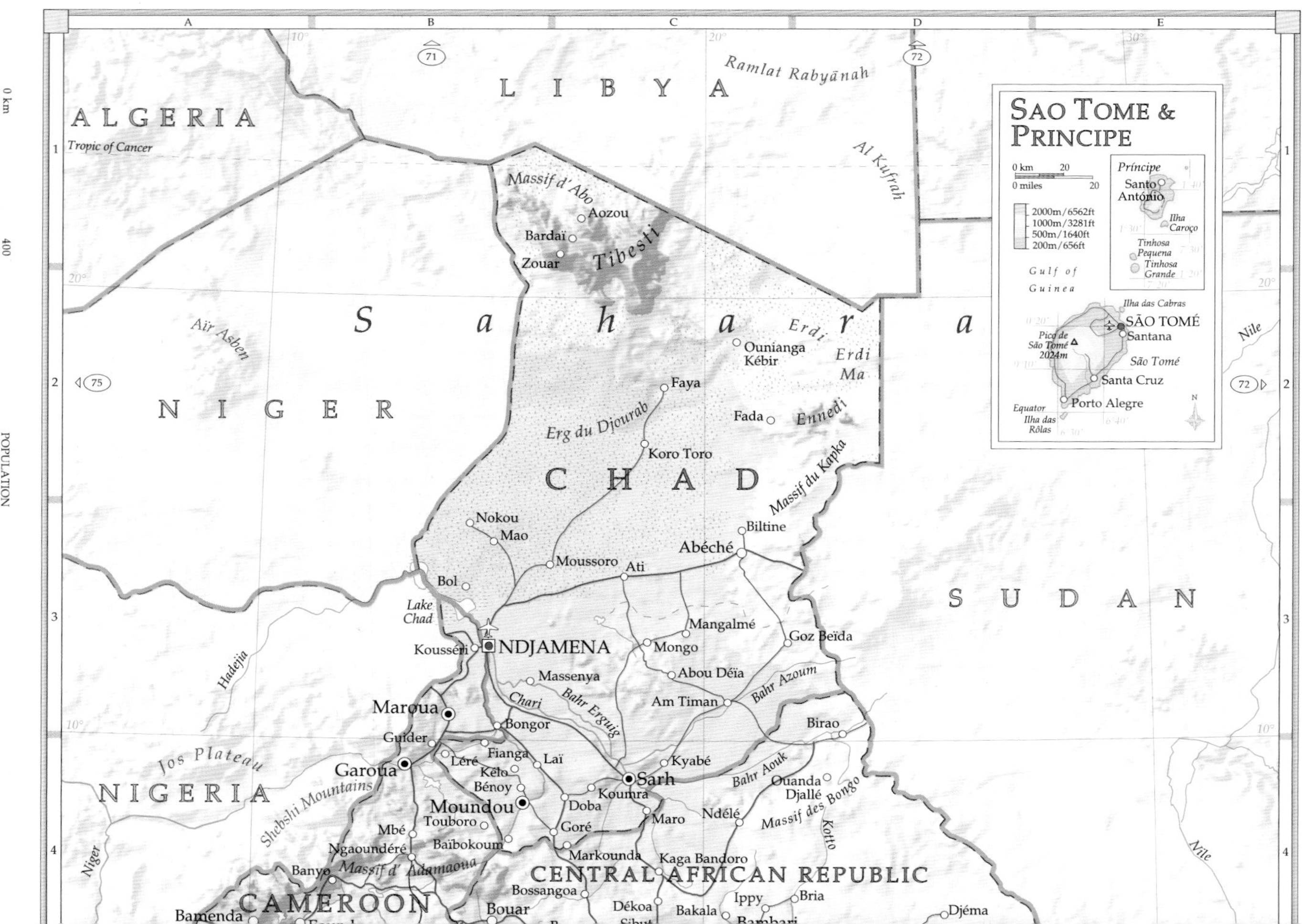

SÃO TOMÉ & PRÍNCIPE

Príncipe
Santo António

Ilha
Caroço

Trinhosa
Pequena
Trinhosa
Grande

SÃO TOMÉ
Santana

São Tomé

Santa Cruz

Pico de
São Tomé
2024m

Porto Alegre

Gulf of Guinea

Equator
Ilha das Rôlas

2000m/6562ft
1000m/3281ft
500m/1640ft
200m/656ft

0 km 20
0 miles 20

Nile

Nile

Djéma

Ramlat Rabyānah

Al Kufrah

SUDAN

LIBYA

Erdi Ma
Erdi
Ennedi
Massif du Kapka

Ouniânga
Kébir
Fada

Biltine

Goz Beida

Birao

Bahr Aouk

Ndélé

Kaga Bandoro

Bria

Ippy

CENTRAL AFRICAN REPUBLIC

Massif d'Abo

Aozou

Tibesti

Bardaï

Zouar

Faya

Koro Toro

Abéché

Mangalmé

Mongo

Am Timan

Abou Déïa

Kyabé

Sarh

Maro

Markounda

Dékoa

Erg du Djourab

Moussoro Ati

CHAD

NDJAMENA

Massenya

Bahr Erguig

Kouhra

Doba

Goré

Bossangoa

Bouar

Sahara

Nokou

Mao

Bol

Lake Chad

Koussêri

Bongor

Chari

Fianga

Lai

Bénoy

Moundou

Touboro

Baibokoum

NIGER

Maroua

Guider

Garoua

Mbé

Ngaoundéré

Mandara Mountains

Banyo

Massif d'Adamaoua

CAMEROON

ALGERIA

Tropic of Cancer

Aïr Asben

Hadejia

Jos Plateau

Shebshi Mountains

NIGERIA

Bamenda

Niger

0 km 400
0 miles 400

POPULATION

○ Less than 50,000   ○ 50,000 -100,000   ◉ 100,000 - 500,000   ◼ Over 500,000

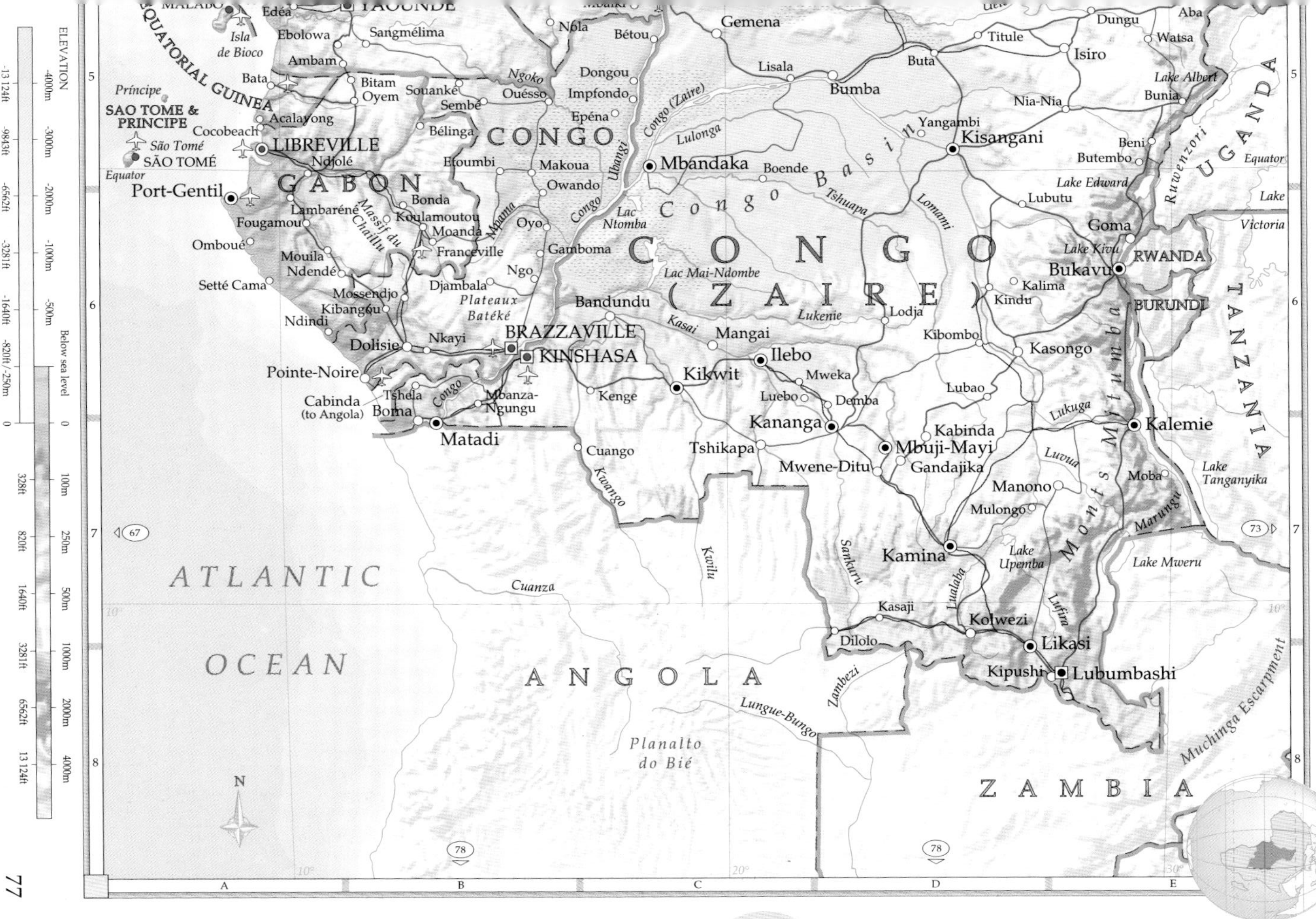

ELEVATION

| | | | | | Below sea level | 0 | 100m | 250m | 500m | 1000m | 2000m | 4000m |

| -4000m | -3000m | -2000m | -1000m | -500m | | | | | | | | |

| -13 124ft | -9843ft | -6562ft | -3281ft | -1640ft | -820ft/-250m | 0 | 328ft | 820ft | 1640ft | 3281ft | 6562ft | 13 124ft |

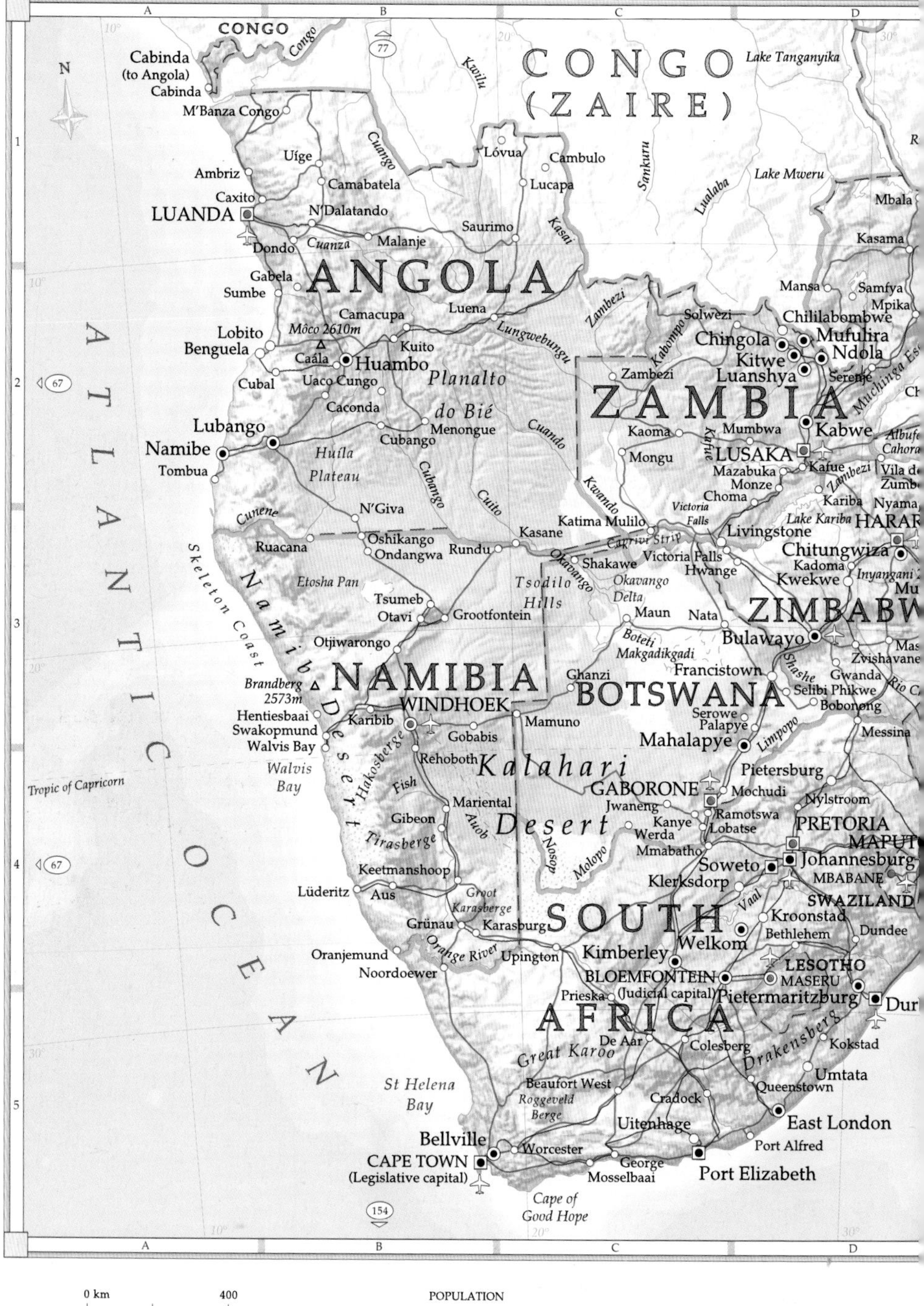

0 km 400
0 miles 400

POPULATION

○ Less than 50,000   ○ 50,000 -100,000   ◉ 100,000 - 500,000   ■ Over 500,000

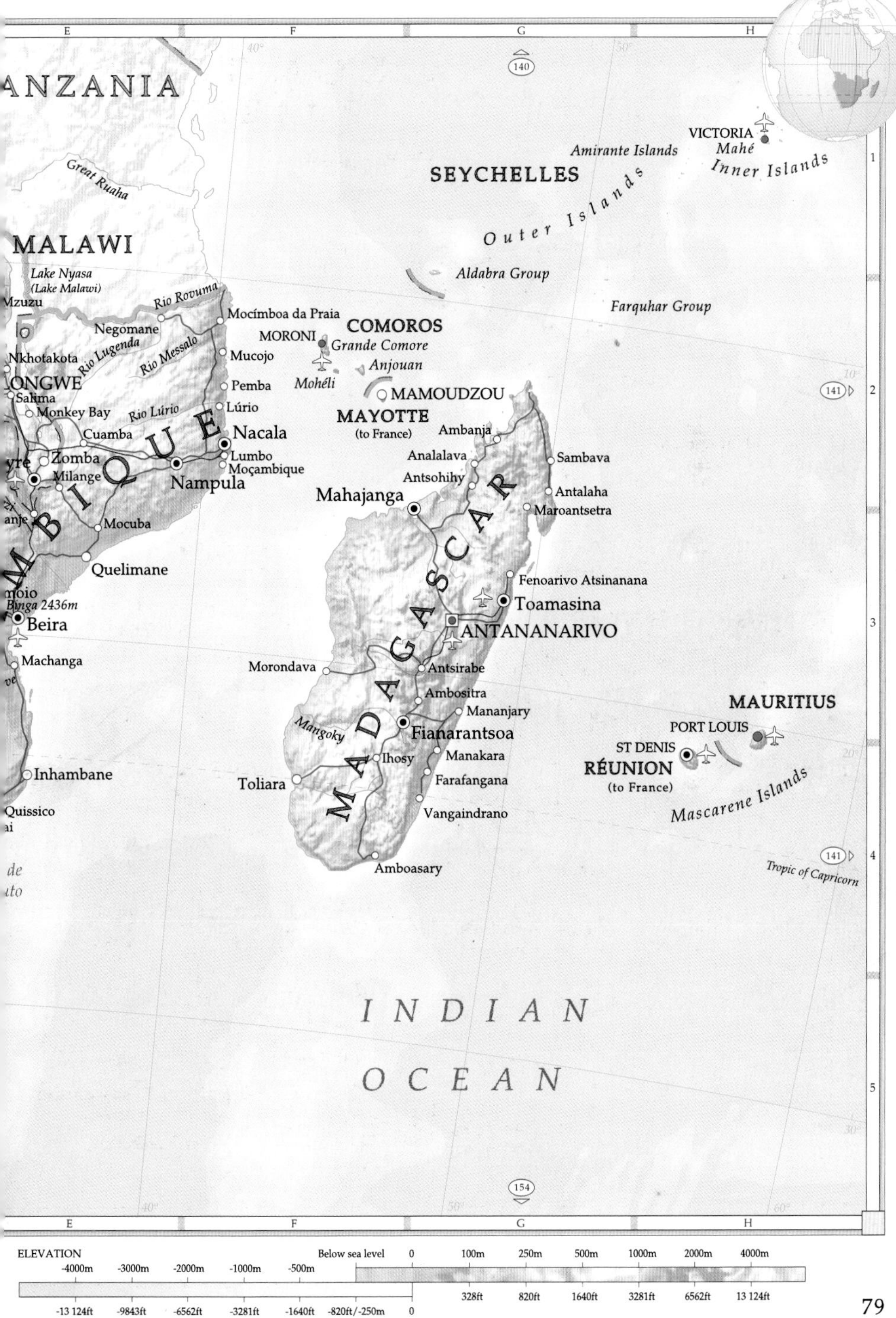

ANZANIA

Great Ruaha

MALAWI

Lake Nyasa
(Lake Malawi)

Mzuzu

Negomane

Nkhotakota

Rio Rovuma

Rio Lugenda

Rio Messalo

Mocímboa da Praia

Mucojo

ONGWE

Salima

Monkey Bay

Pemba

Rio Lúrio

Lúrio

Cuamba

yre

Zomba

Milange

Nampula

Lumbo

Moçambique

Mocuba

Quelimane

oio

Binga 2436m

Beira

Machanga

anje

ve

Inhambane

Quissico

ai

de

uto

MOZAMBIQUE

Nacala

Mahajanga

Morondava

Toliara

Mangoky

MADAGASCAR

SEYCHELLES

Amirante Islands

VICTORIA
Mahé

Inner Islands

Outer Islands

Aldabra Group

Farquhar Group

COMOROS

MORONI

Grande Comore

Anjouan

Mohéli

MAMOUDZOU

MAYOTTE
(to France)

Ambanja

Analalava

Antsohihy

Sambava

Antalaha

Maroantsetra

Fenoarivo Atsinanana

Toamasina

ANTANANARIVO

Antsirabe

Ambositra

Mananjary

Fianarantsoa

Ihosy

Manakara

Farafangana

Vangaindrano

Amboasary

MAURITIUS

PORT LOUIS

ST DENIS

RÉUNION
(to France)

Mascarene Islands

Tropic of Capricorn

I N D I A N

O C E A N

ELEVATION

| -4000m | -3000m | -2000m | -1000m | -500m | Below sea level | 0 | 100m | 250m | 500m | 1000m | 2000m | 4000m |

| -13 124ft | -9843ft | -6562ft | -3281ft | -1640ft | -820ft/-250m | 0 | 328ft | 820ft | 1640ft | 3281ft | 6562ft | 13 124ft |

79

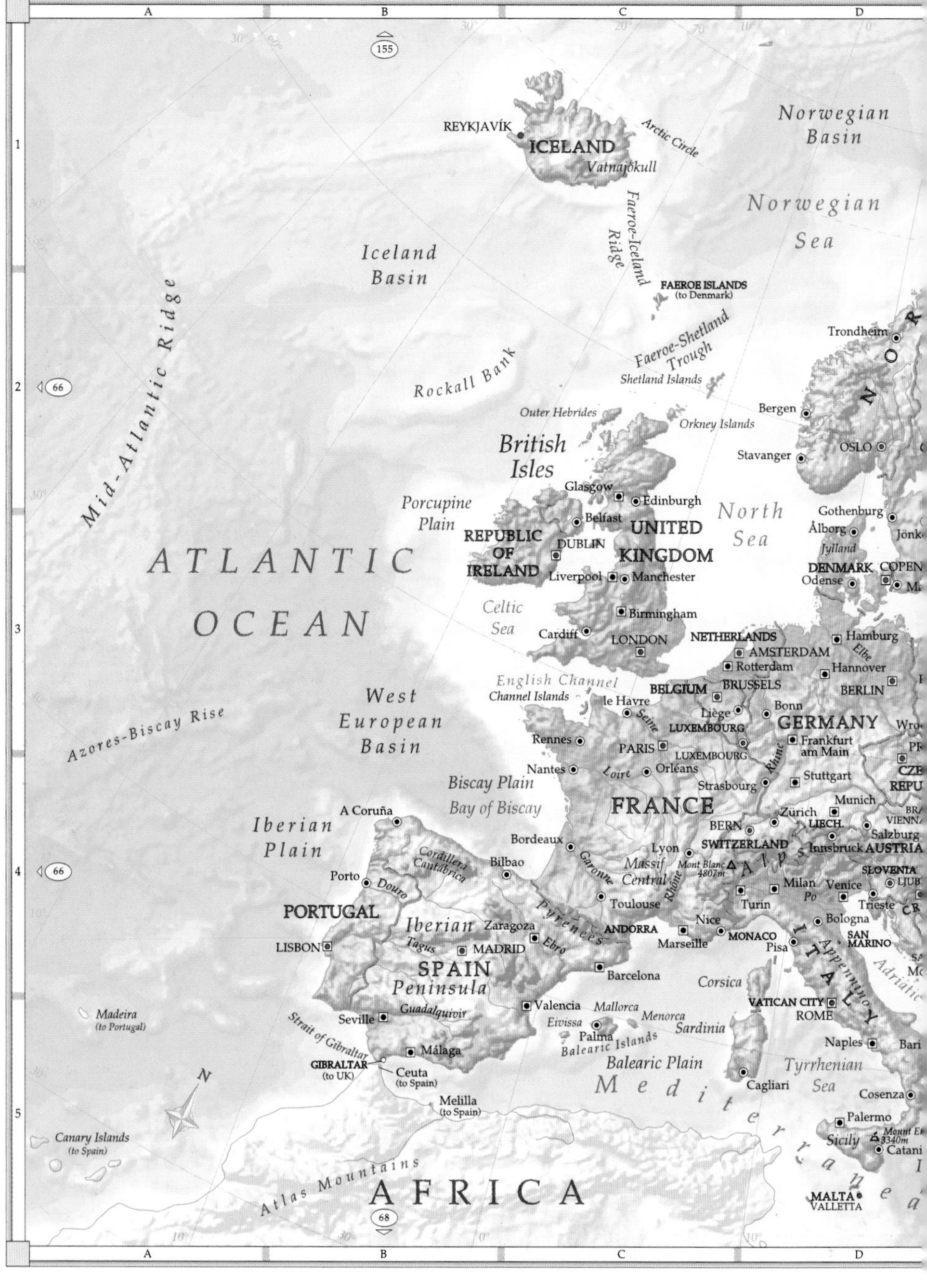

A B C D

155

REYKJAVÍK Arctic Circle
ICELAND *Norwegian*
Vatnajökull *Basin*

Norwegian

Iceland *Sea*
Basin FAEROE ISLANDS
(to Denmark)

Trondheim

66 *Faeroe-Iceland* NOR
Ridge *Faeroe-Shetland*
Rockall Bank *Trough* Bergen
Shetland Islands OSLO
Outer Hebrides Stavanger
Orkney Islands Gothenburg Jönk
British Glasgow Edinburgh *North* Álborg
Porcupine Belfast *Sea* Jylland
Plain **REPUBLIC** UNITED **DENMARK** COPEN
ATLANTIC **OF** DUBLIN **KINGDOM** Odense M
IRELAND Liverpool Manchester
Celtic Birmingham Hamburg
OCEAN *Sea* Cardiff **LONDON** **NETHERLANDS**
AMSTERDAM BERLIN
English Channel **BELGIUM** Rotterdam Hannover
West *Channel Islands* **BRUSSELS** Bonn
Azores-Biscay Rise *European* le Havre Liège **GERMANY** Wro
Basin Rennes **LUXEMBOURG** Frankfurt
PARIS **LUXEMBOURG** am Main
Nantes *Loire* Orléans Stuttgart **CZE**
Biscay Plain Strasbourg **REPU**
A Coruña *Bay of Biscay* **FRANCE** Munich BRA
Zürich VIENN.
Iberian Bordeaux **BERN** **LIECH** Salzburg
Plain *Cordillera* Bilbao Lyon **SWITZERLAND** Innsbruck **AUSTRIA**
66 Porto *Cantábrica* *Massif* Mont Blanc Milan Venice **SLOVENIA**
Douro *Central* 4301m Po Trieste LJUB
Toulouse Turin Bologna CR
PORTUGAL Nice **ANDORRA** **MONACO** **SAN**
Iberian Zaragoza Marseille Pisa **MARINO**
LISBON *Tagus* **MADRID** *Ebro* SA
SPAIN Barcelona Corsica **VATICAN CITY** Mc
Peninsula Valencia Mallorca **ROME** Adriatic
Seville *Guadalquivir* Eivissa Menorca *Sardinia*
Madeira Palma *Balearic Plain* Naples Bari
(to Portugal) *Strait of Gibraltar* Málaga *Balearic Islands* Cagliari *Tyrrhenian*
GIBRALTAR Ceuta *Mediterranean* *Sea* Cosenza
(to UK) (to Spain) Palermo
Melilla Mount Et
N (to Spain) Sicily 3340m
Canary Islands Catani
(to Spain) I
AFRICA *Atlas Mountains* **MALTA**
68 **VALLETTA**

A B C D

0 km	500		POPULATION				
0 miles	500		○ Less than 50,000	○ 50,000 -100,000	◉ 100,000 - 500,000	■ Over 500,000	

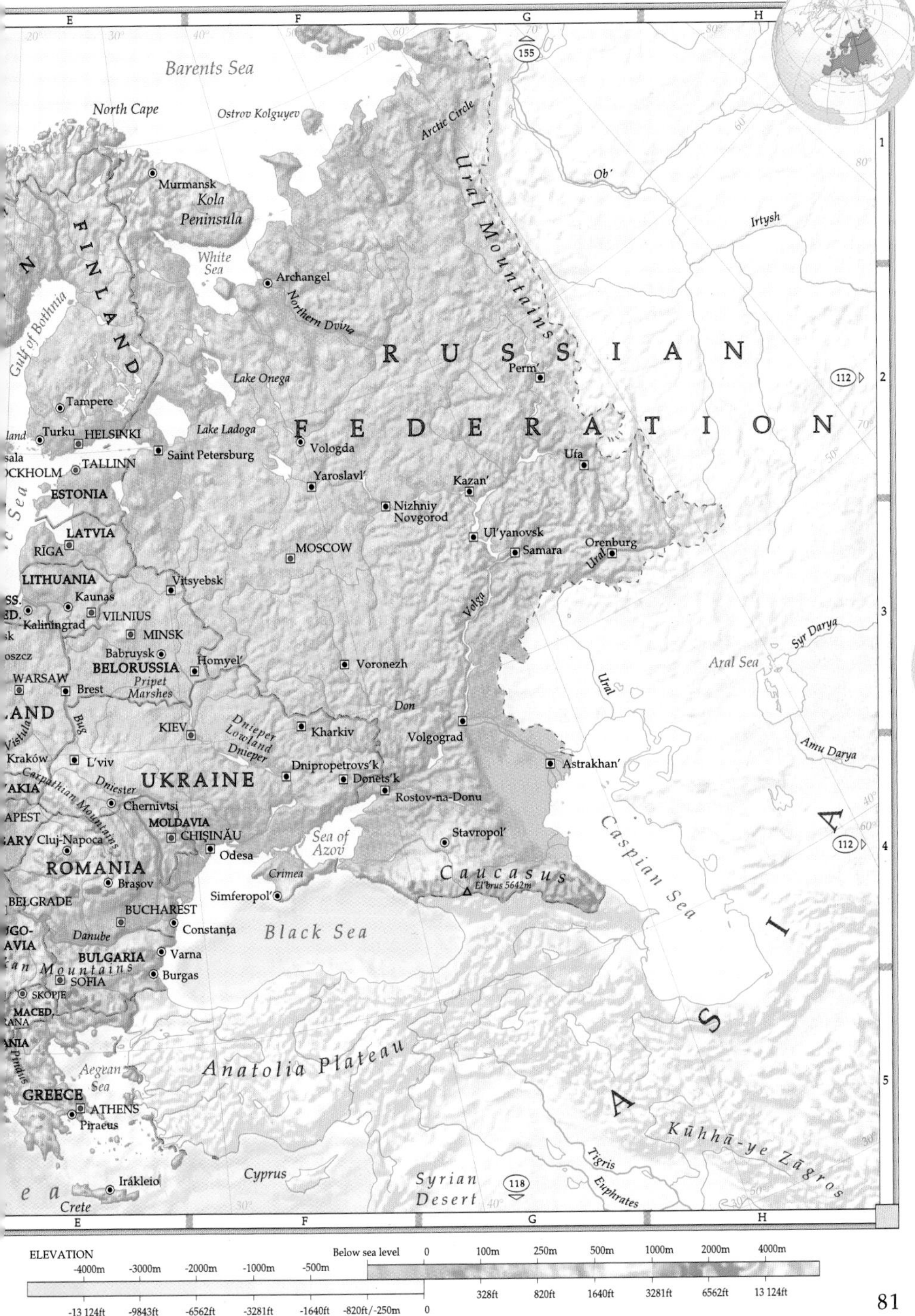

Barents Sea

North Cape
Ostrov Kolguyev
Arctic Circle
Ob'
Ural Mountains
Irtysh

Murmansk
Kola
Peninsula
White
Sea
Archangel
Perm'
R U S S I A N

FINLAND
Northern Dvina
Lake Onega
Vologda
F E D E R A T I O N
Ufa

Tampere
Lake Ladoga
Yaroslavl'
Kazan'
land
Turku HELSINKI
Saint Petersburg
Nizhniy
Novgorod
sala
OCKHOLM TALLINN
Ul'yanovsk
Orenburg
Gulf of Bothnia
ESTONIA
MOSCOW
Samara
Ural
Sea
LATVIA
RĪGA

LITHUANIA
Vitsyebsk
Volga
Syr Darya
SS.
Kaunas
Aral Sea
D.
Kaliningrad VILNIUS
k
MINSK
Ural
oszcz
Babruysk Homyel'
Voronezh
Anu Darya
WARSAW Brest
BELORUSSIA
Pripet
Marshes
Bug
Don
AND
Vistula
KIEV
Dnieper
Lowland
Kharkiv
Volgograd
Kraków L'viv
Dnieper
Dnipropetrovs'k
Astrakhan'
AKIA
Dniester
UKRAINE
Donets'k
Carpathian Mountains
Chernivtsi
Rostov-na-Donu
APEST
MOLDAVIA
Stavropol'
ARY Cluj-Napoca
CHIŞINĂU
Caspian Sea
ROMANIA
Odesa
Sea of
Azov
Braşov
Crimea
Caucasus
BELGRADE
Simferopol'
El'brus 5642m
GO-
BUCHAREST
AVIA
Danube
Constanţa
Black Sea
an Mountains
BULGARIA Varna
SOFIA
Burgas
MACED-
SKOPJE
ANA
NIA
Aegean
Sea
Anatolia Plateau
GREECE
ATHENS
Piraeus
Kūhhā-ye Zāgros
Iráklio
Cyprus
Syrian
Desert
Tigris
Euphrates
Crete
ea

155
112
112
118

A
S
I
A

ELEVATION

	-4000m	-3000m	-2000m	-1000m	-500m	Below sea level	0	100m	250m	500m	1000m	2000m	4000m
	-13 124ft	-9843ft	-6562ft	-3281ft	-1640ft	-820ft/-250m	0	328ft	820ft	1640ft	3281ft	6562ft	13 124ft

THE NORTH ATLANTIC

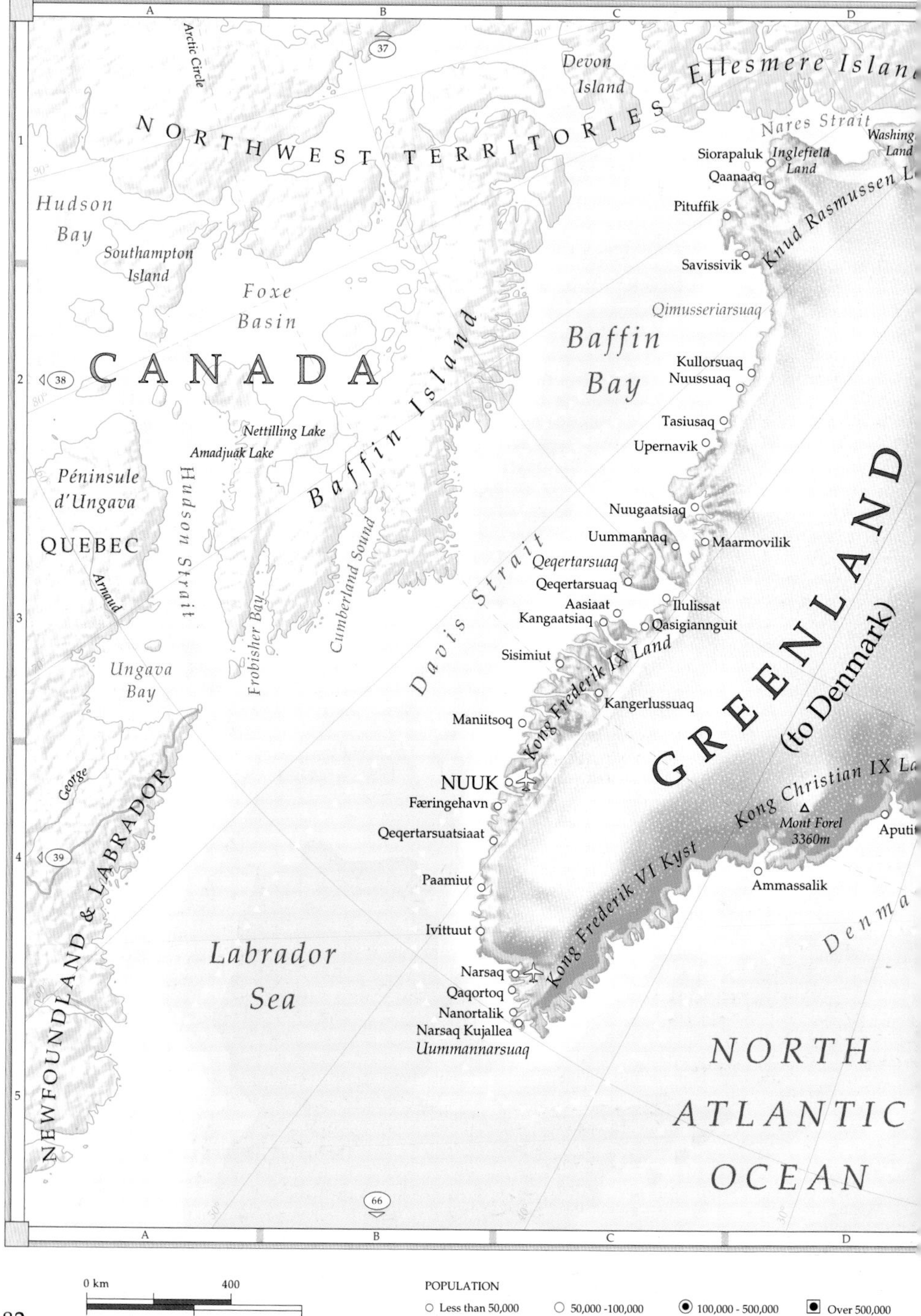

A B C D

Arctic Circle

N O R T H W E S T   T E R R I T O R I E S

Devon
Island

Ellesmere Island

37

Hudson
Bay

Southampton
Island

1

Nares Strait

Siorapaluk   Inglefield   Washing
Land   Land
Qaanaaq

Pituffik

Knud Rasmussen L

Savissivik

Foxe
Basin

C A N A D A

38

Qimusseriarsuaq

Baffin
Bay

Kullorsuaq
Nuussaq

2

Nettilling Lake
Amadjuak Lake

Baffin Island

Hudson Strait

Tasiusaq
Upernavik

Péninsule
d'Ungava

QUEBEC

Arnaud

Davis Strait

Cumberland Sound

Frobisher Bay

Nuugaatsiaq

Uummannaq   Maarmovilik
Qeqertarsuaq
Qeqertarsuaq
Aasiaat   Ilulissat
Kangaatsiaq   Qasigiannguit
Sisimiut

G R E E N L A N D

(to Denmark)

3

Ungava
Bay

George

Kong Frederik IX Land

Kangerlussuaq

Maniitsoq

NUUK

Færingehavn
Qeqertarsuatsiaat

NEWFOUNDLAND & LABRADOR

39

Kong Christian IX La

Mont Forel
3360m   Aputi

4

Paamiut

Ammassalik

Kong Frederik VI Kyst

Ivittuut

Denma

Labrador
Sea

Narsaq
Qaqortoq
Nanortalik
Narsaq Kujallea
Uummannarsuaq

NORTH

5

ATLANTIC

OCEAN

66

A B C D

0 km   400

0 miles   400

POPULATION

○ Less than 50,000   ○ 50,000 -100,000   ◉ 100,000 - 500,000   ◼ Over 500,000

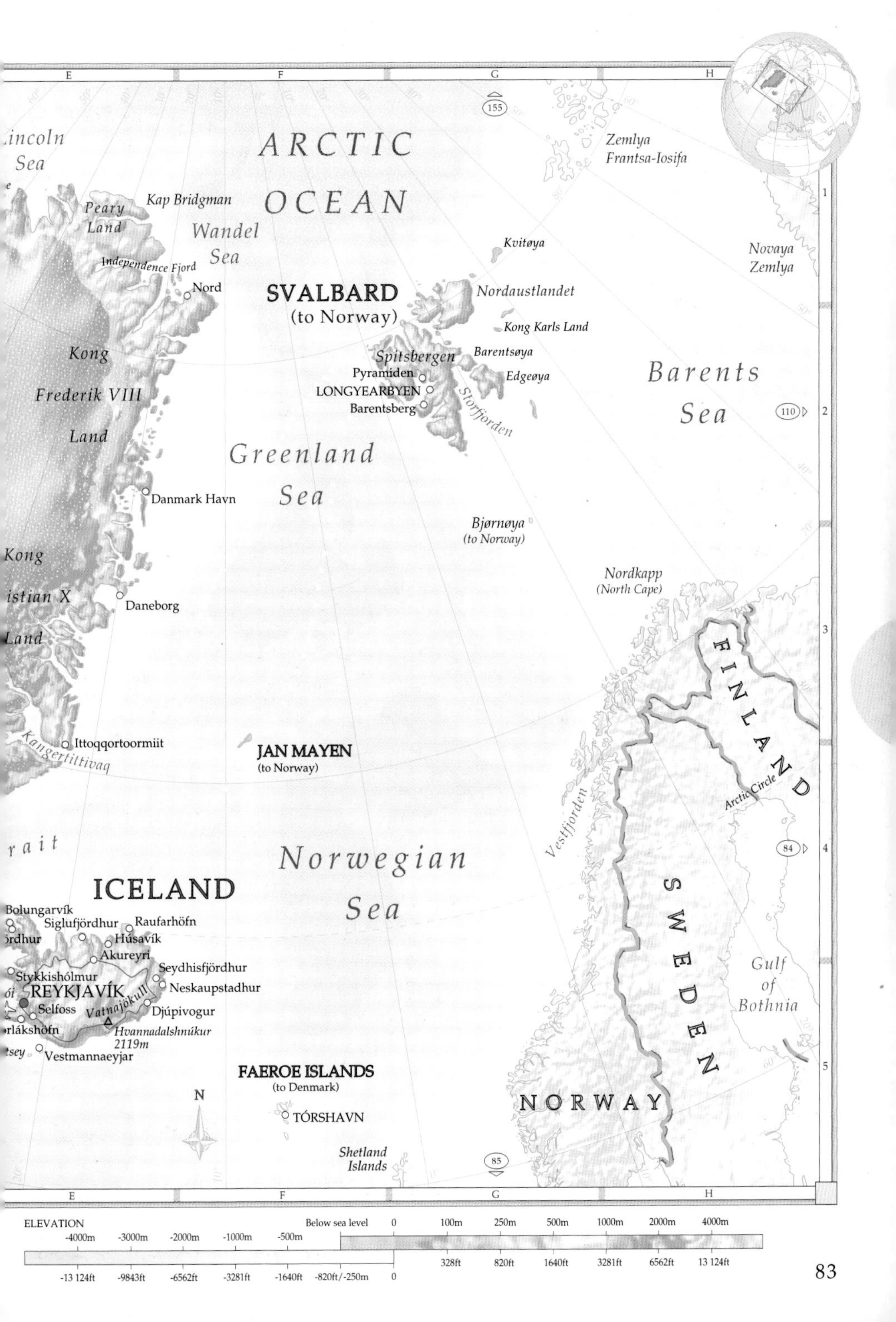

ARCTIC OCEAN

155

Zemlya
Frantsa-Iosifa

Lincoln Sea

Peary Land

Kap Bridgman

Wandel Sea

Kvitøya

Novaya
Zemlya

Independence Fjord

Nord

SVALBARD
(to Norway)

Nordaustlandet

Kong Karls Land

Kong Frederik VIII Land

Spitsbergen

Barentsøya

Barents Sea

Pyramiden
LONGYEARBYEN
Barentsberg

Edgeøya

110

Danmark Havn

Storfjorden

Greenland Sea

Kong istian X Land

Bjørnøya
(to Norway)

Nordkapp
(North Cape)

Daneborg

FINLAND

Kangertittivaq

Ittoqqortoormiit

JAN MAYEN
(to Norway)

Vestfjorden

Arctic Circle

84

Norwegian Sea

ICELAND

Bolungarvík
Siglufjördhur
Raufarhöfn
rdhur
Húsavík
Akureyri
Stykkishólmur
Seydhisfjördhur
REYKJAVÍK
Neskaupstadhur
Selfoss
Vatnajökull
Djúpivogur
rlákshöfn
Hvannadalshnúkur
2119m
sey
Vestmannaeyjar

SWEDEN

Gulf of Bothnia

N

FAEROE ISLANDS
(to Denmark)

TÓRSHAVN

NORWAY

Shetland Islands

85

ELEVATION

| -4000m | -3000m | -2000m | -1000m | -500m | Below sea level 0 | 100m | 250m | 500m | 1000m | 2000m | 4000m |

| 328ft | 820ft | 1640ft | 3281ft | 6562ft | 13 124ft |

| -13 124ft | -9843ft | -6562ft | -3281ft | -1640ft | -820ft/-250m | 0 |

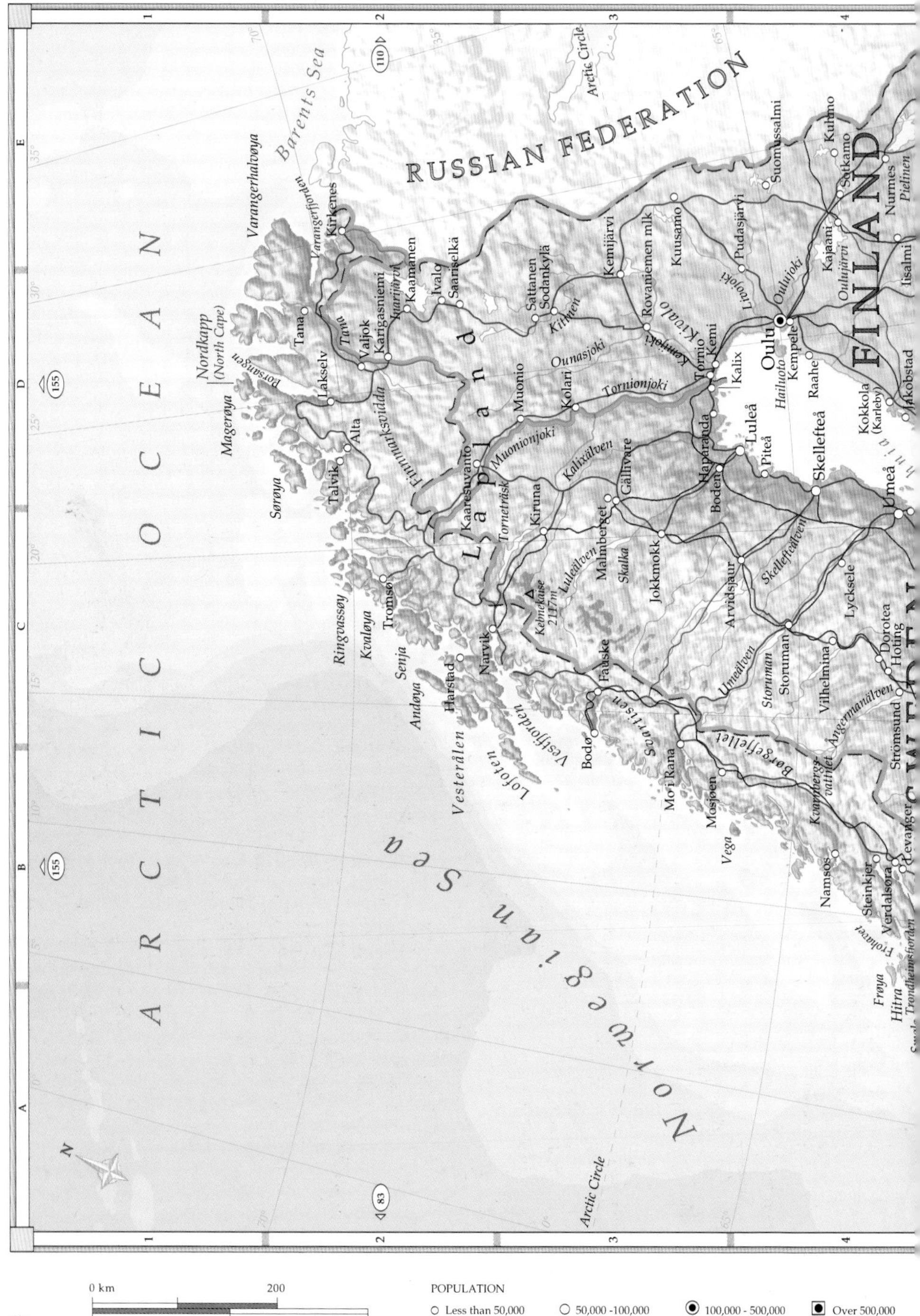

| 0 km | | 200 | |
| 0 miles | | | 200 |

POPULATION

○ Less than 50,000   ○ 50,000 -100,000   ◉ 100,000 - 500,000   ■ Over 500,000

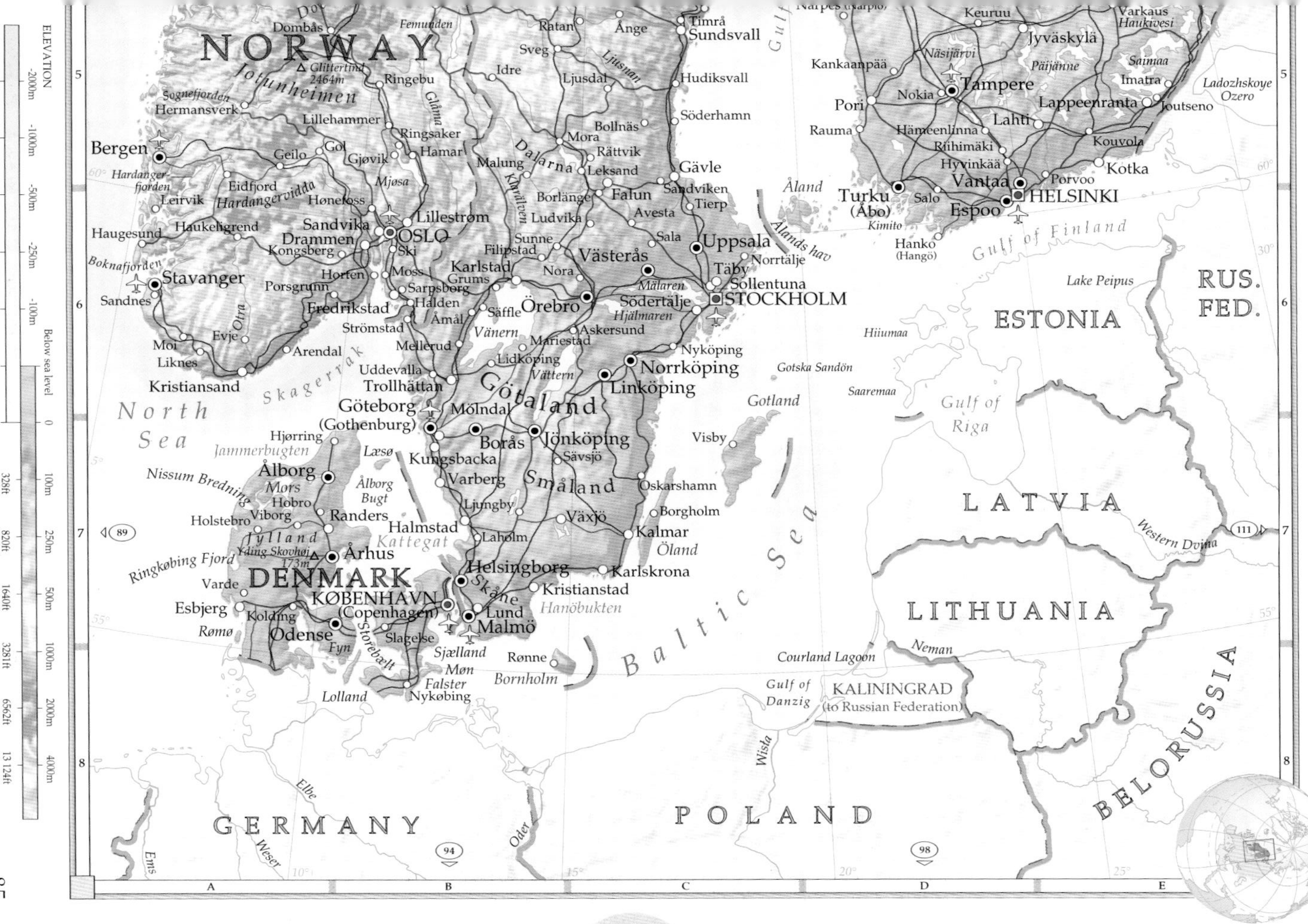

ELEVATION

					Below sea level	0	100m	250m	500m	1000m	2000m	4000m
-2000m	-1000m	-500m	-250m	-100m								
-6562ft	-3281ft	-1640ft	-820ft	-328ft	-164ft/-50m	0	328ft	820ft	1640ft	3281ft	6562ft	13 124ft

85

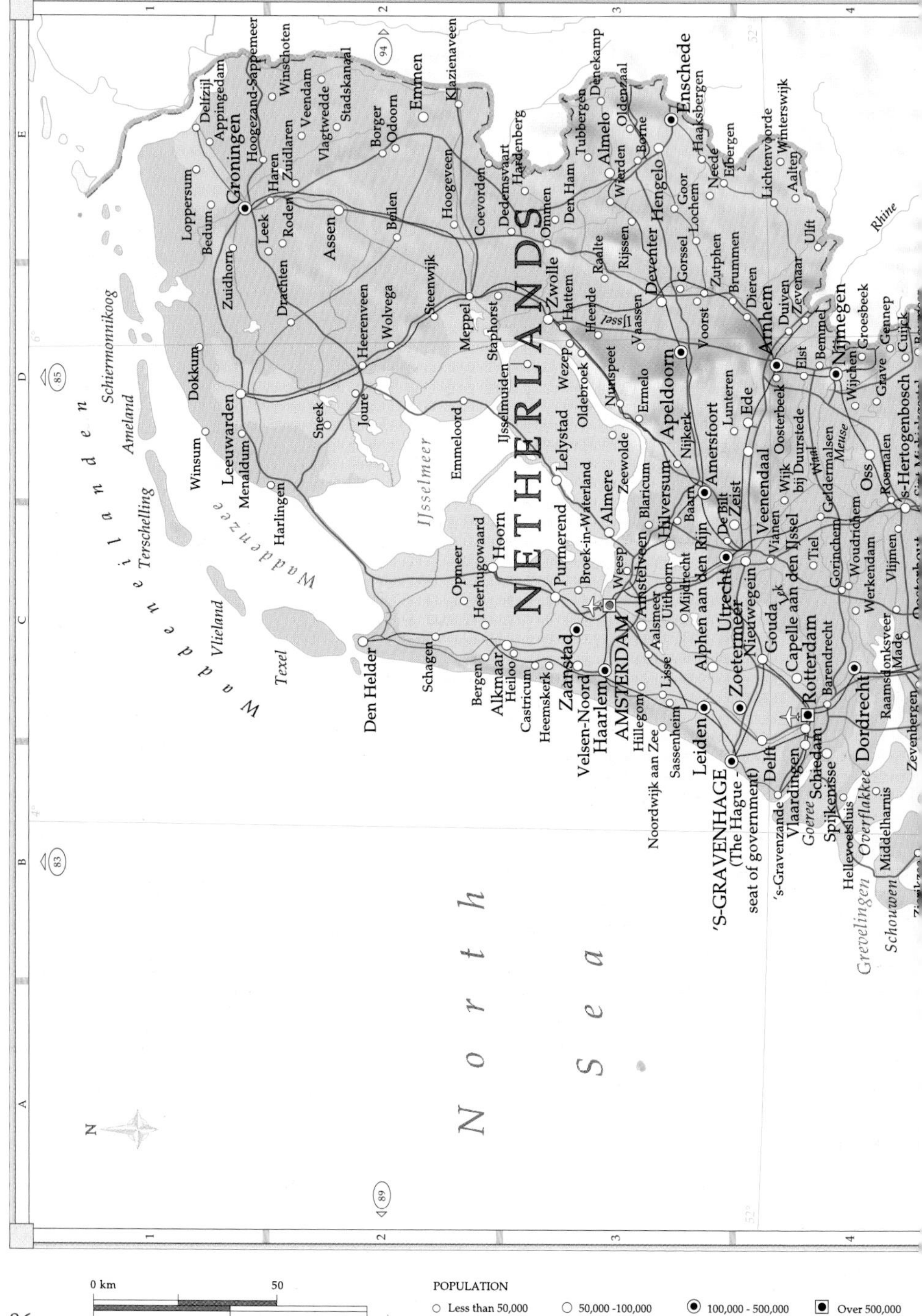

POPULATION

○ Less than 50,000   ○ 50,000 -100,000   ◉ 100,000 - 500,000   ◼ Over 500,000

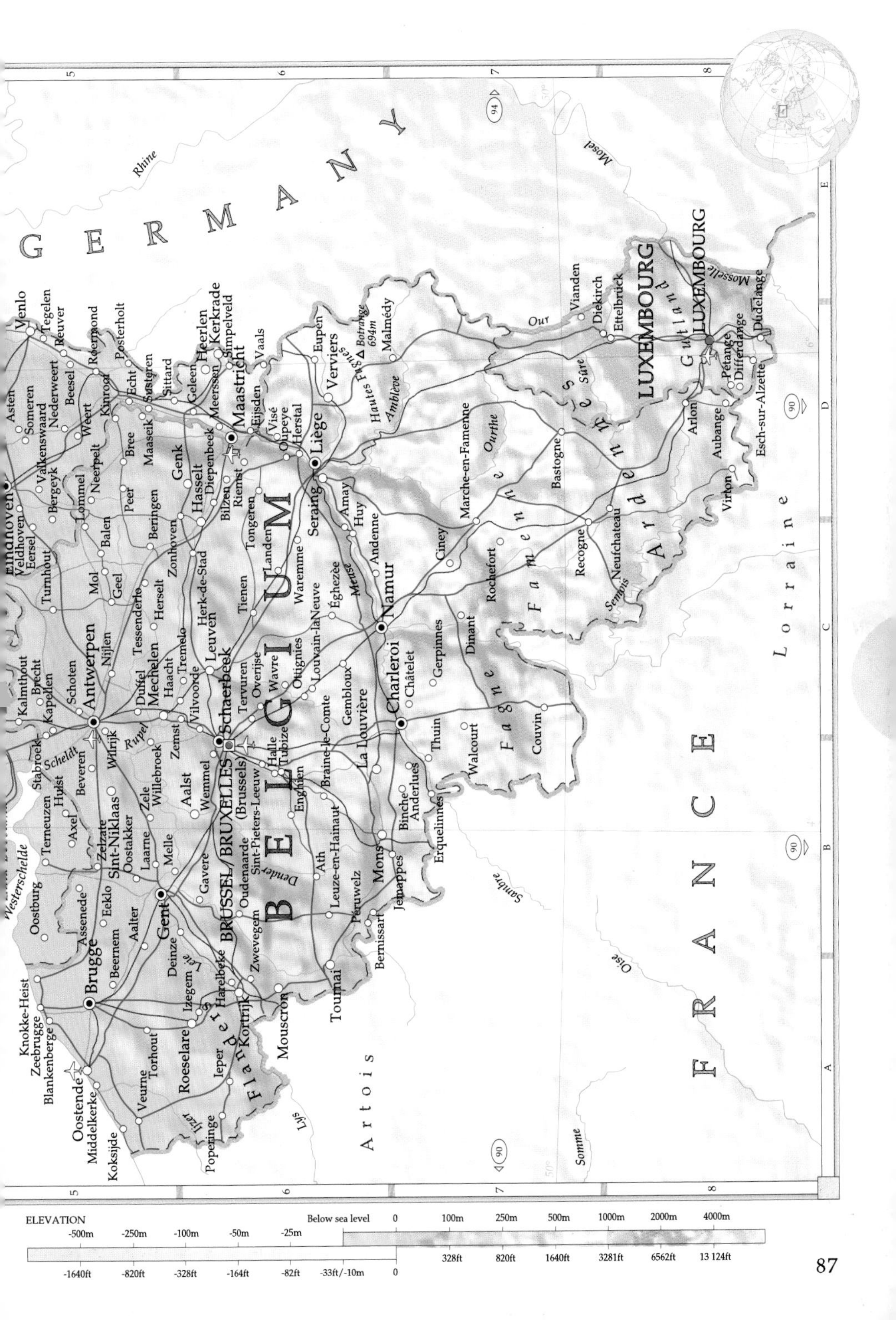

ELEVATION

Below sea level					0	100m	250m	500m	1000m	2000m	4000m
-500m	-250m	-100m	-50m	-25m							
-1640ft	-820ft	-328ft	-164ft	-82ft	-33ft/-10m	0	328ft	820ft	1640ft	3281ft	6562ft	13 124ft

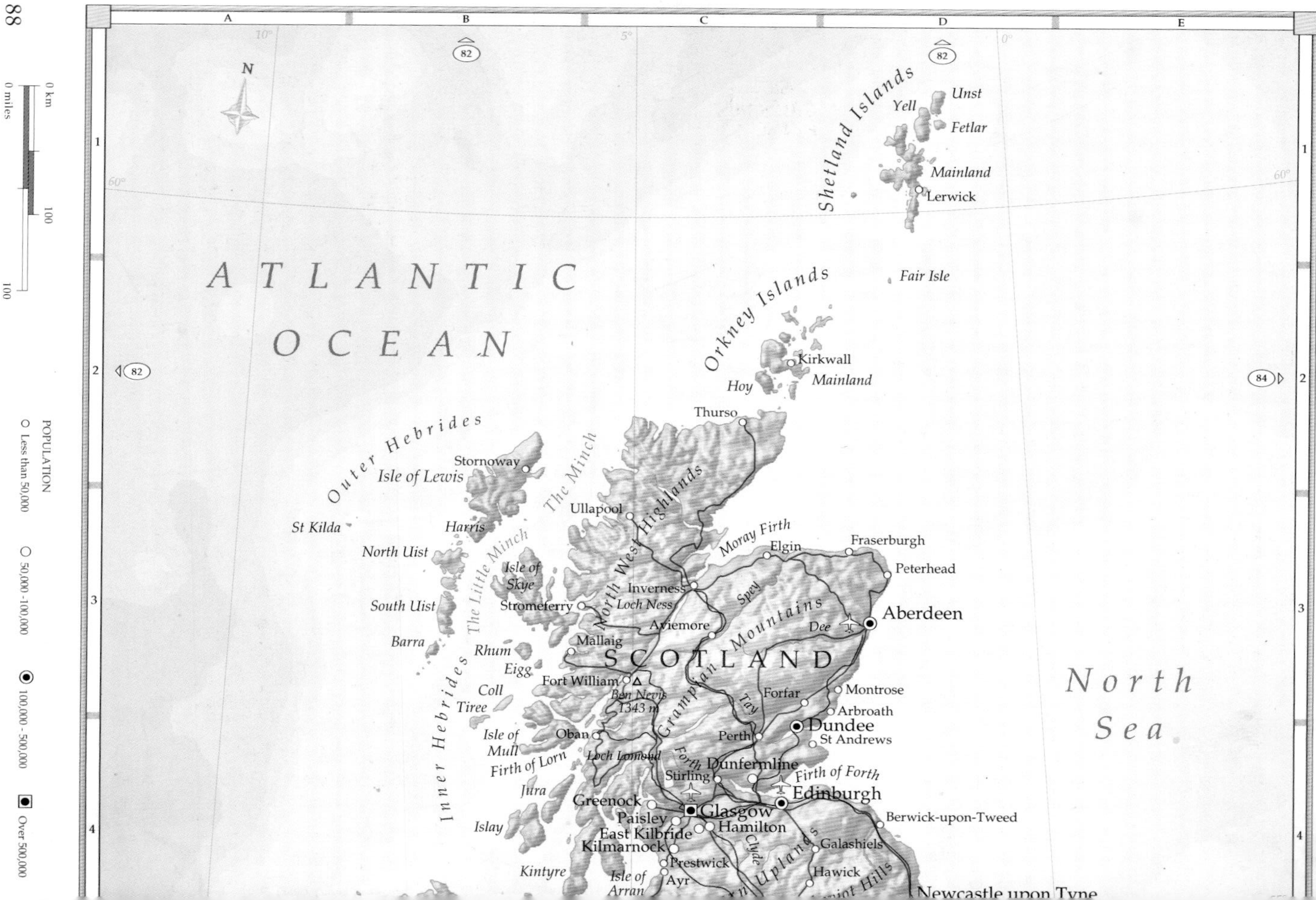

North Sea

ATLANTIC OCEAN

Shetland Islands

Unst
Yell
Fetlar
Mainland
Lerwick

Fair Isle

Orkney Islands

Kirkwall
Mainland
Hoy

Thurso

Moray Firth

Elgin

Peterhead

Fraserburgh

Aberdeen

SCOTLAND

Grampian Mountains

Dee

Montrose
Arbroath
Dundee
St Andrews
Forfar

Firth of Forth

Edinburgh

Berwick-upon-Tweed

Galashiels
Hawick

Newcastle upon Tyne

Perth
Dunfermline
Stirling
Glasgow
Hamilton
Paisley
East Kilbride
Kilmarnock
Prestwick
Ayr
Isle of Arran

Greenock
Oban
Firth of Lorn
Islay
Jura
Kintyre

Inner Hebrides

Isle of Mull
Coll
Tiree

Rhum
Eigg

Fort William
Ben Nevis
1343m
Loch Linnhe
Loch Lomond

Inverness
Loch Ness
Aviemore

Mallaig
Stromeferry
Isle of Skye

Ullapool

North West Highlands

The Minch
The Little Minch

Outer Hebrides

Stornoway
Isle of Lewis
Harris
North Uist
South Uist
Barra
St Kilda

Spey

Tay

Firth of Clyde

North Sea

North

Sea

0 km 100

0 miles 100

POPULATION

○ Less than 50,000   ○ 50,000 -100,000   ◉ 100,000 - 500,000   ◼ Over 500,000

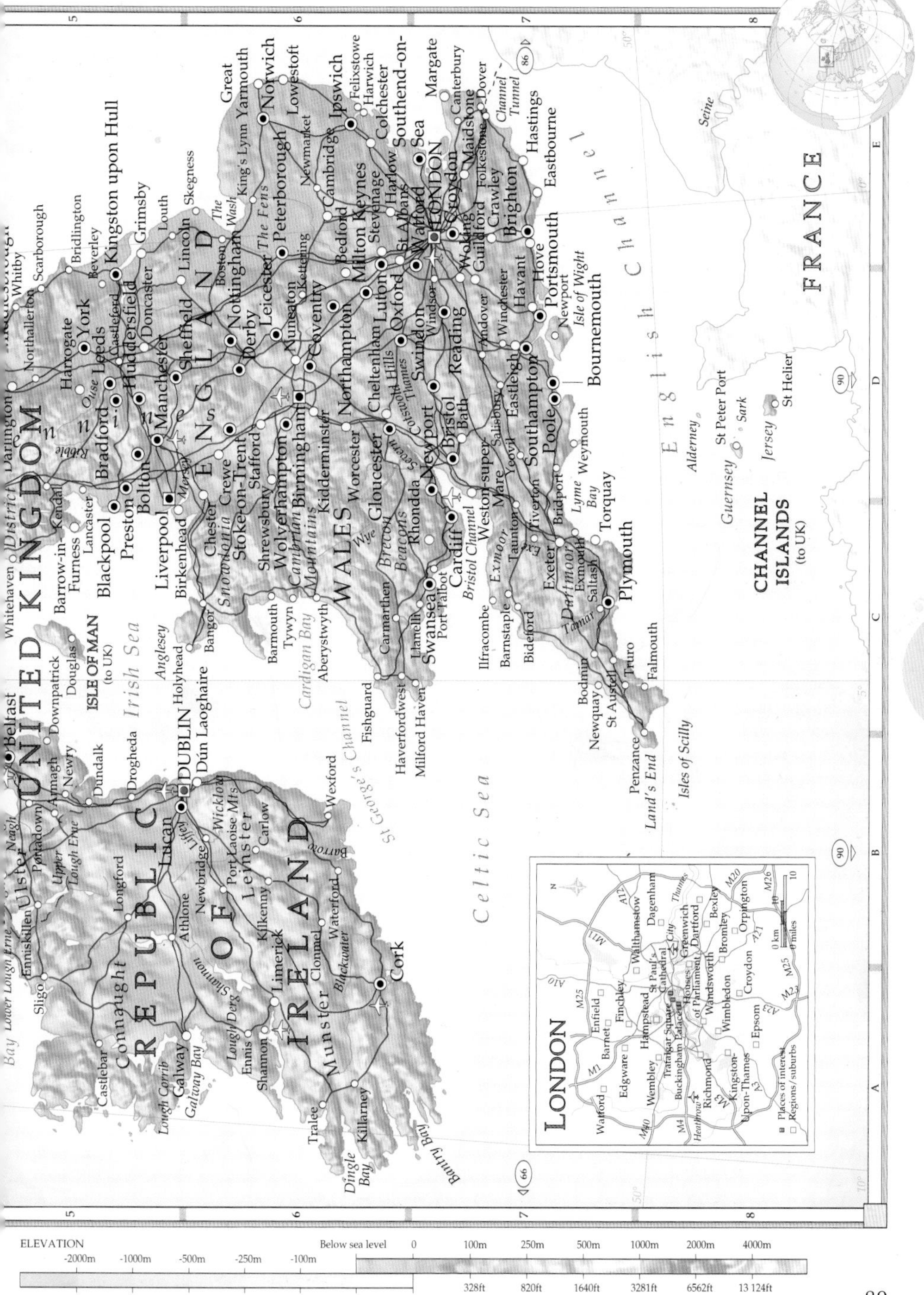
UNITED KINGDOM
REPUBLIC OF IRELAND
ENGLAND
WALES
FRANCE
CHANNEL ISLANDS
(to UK)
ISLE OF MAN
(to UK)
Irish Sea
Celtic Sea
English Channel
St George's Channel
Bristol Channel
Cardigan Bay
Galway Bay
Dingle Bay
Bantry Bay
Lyme Bay
Isles of Scilly
Land's End
Isle of Wight
Anglesey
Alderney
Guernsey
Sark
Jersey
Ulster
Connaught
Leinster
Munster
Lough Corrib
Lough Derg
Lower Lough Erne
Upper Lough Erne
Lough Neagh
Shannon
Liffey
Barrow
Blackwater
Wicklow Mts
Snowdonia
Cambrian Mountains
Brecon Beacons
Exmoor
Dartmoor
Cotswold Hills
The Fens
The Wash
Severn
Thames
Wye
Mersey
Ribble
Ouse
Exe
Tamar
Seine
Channel Tunnel
Belfast
DUBLIN
Dún Laoghaire
Cork
Galway
Limerick
Waterford
Wexford
Kilkenny
Sligo
Tralee
Killarney
Ennis
Shannon
Athlone
Longford
Castlebar
Clonmel
Carlow
Port Laoise
Newbridge
Lucan
Drogheda
Dundalk
Newry
Armagh
Portadown
Downpatrick
Enniskillen
Douglas
Holyhead
Bangor
Barmouth
Tywyn
Aberystwyth
Fishguard
Haverfordwest
Milford Haven
Carmarthen
Llanelli
Swansea
Port Talbot
Rhondda
Cardiff
Newport
Kidderminster
Worcester
Gloucester
Cheltenham
Bristol
Bath
Weston-super-Mare
Taunton
Tiverton
Exeter
Exmouth
Ilfracombe
Barnstaple
Bideford
Bodmin
Newquay
St Austell
Truro
Falmouth
Penzance
Saltash
Plymouth
Torquay
Bridport
Weymouth
Yeovil
Salisbury
Poole
Bournemouth
Southampton
Eastleigh
Winchester
Andover
Portsmouth
Havant
Newport
Hove
Brighton
Eastbourne
Hastings
Crawley
Guildford
Woking
Reading
Swindon
Oxford
Windsor
Watford
LONDON
Croydon
Maidstone
Folkestone
Dover
Canterbury
Margate
Southend-on-Sea
Colchester
Harwich
Felixstowe
Ipswich
Harlow
St Albans
Stevenage
Luton
Milton Keynes
Bedford
Cambridge
Newmarket
Peterborough
Northampton
Kettering
Coventry
Nuneaton
Leicester
Birmingham
Wolverhampton
Shrewsbury
Stafford
Stoke-on-Trent
Crewe
Chester
Birkenhead
Liverpool
Bolton
Preston
Blackpool
Lancaster
Kendal
Barrow-in-Furness
Whitehaven
Manchester
Bradford
Leeds
Huddersfield
Sheffield
Derby
Nottingham
Lincoln
Boston
King's Lynn
Great Yarmouth
Norwich
Lowestoft
Doncaster
Castleford
Harrogate
York
Northallerton
Whitby
Scarborough
Bridlington
Beverley
Kingston upon Hull
Grimsby
Louth
Skegness
St Peter Port
St Helier
LONDON
Watford
Enfield
Barnet
Finchley
Edgware
Wembley
Hampstead
Walthamstow
Dagenham
Greenwich
Dartford
Bexley
Bromley
Orpington
Croydon
Wandsworth
Wimbledon
Richmond
Kingston-Upon-Thames
Epsom
Heathrow
St Paul's Cathedral
City
Houses of Parliament
Trafalgar Square
Buckingham Palace
Places of interest
Regions/suburbs
ELEVATION
Below sea level
0
100m
250m
500m
1000m
2000m
4000m
-2000m
-1000m
-500m
-250m
-100m
328ft
820ft
1640ft
3281ft
6562ft
13 124ft
-6562ft
-3281ft
-1640ft
-820ft
-328ft
-164ft/-50m

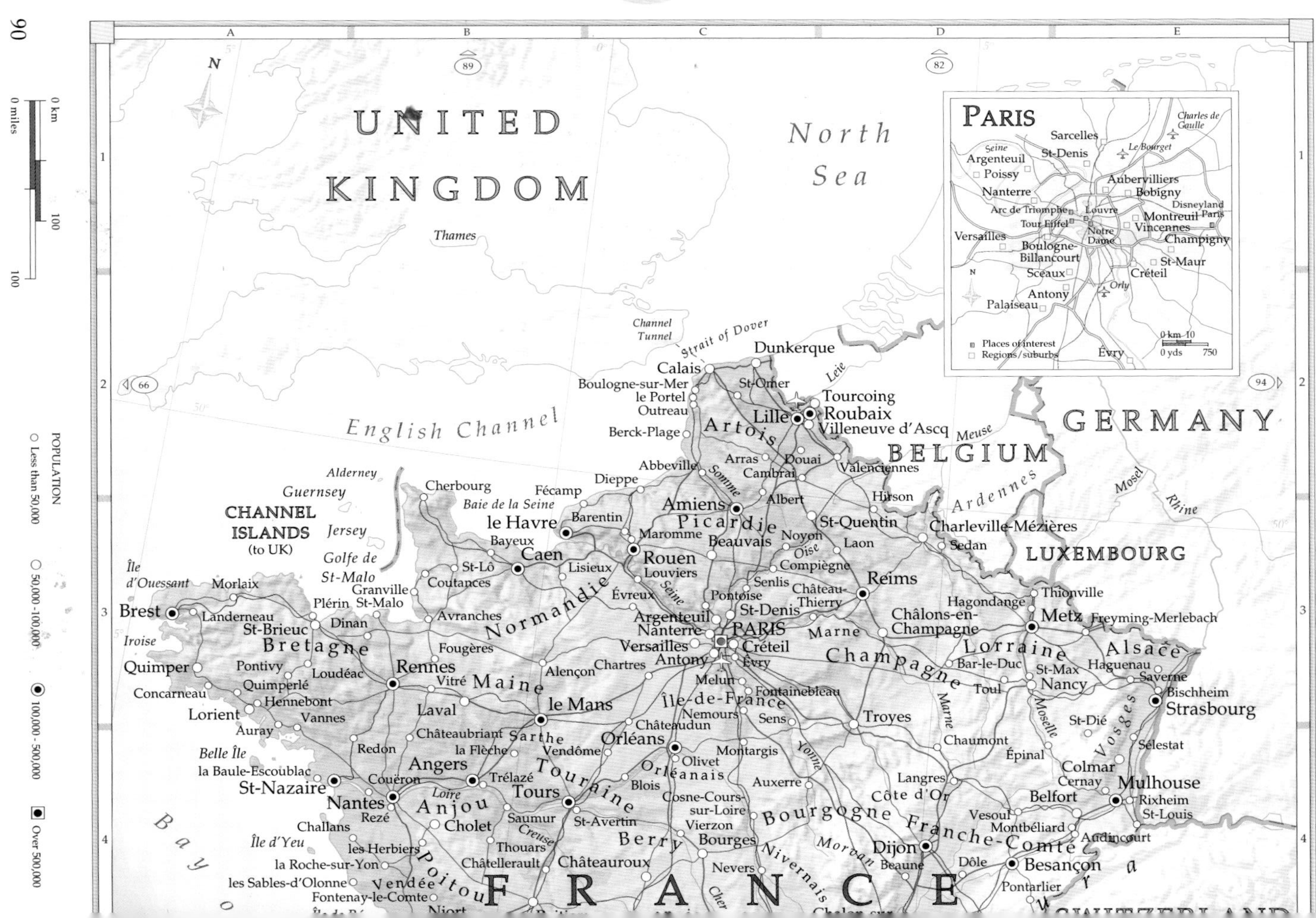

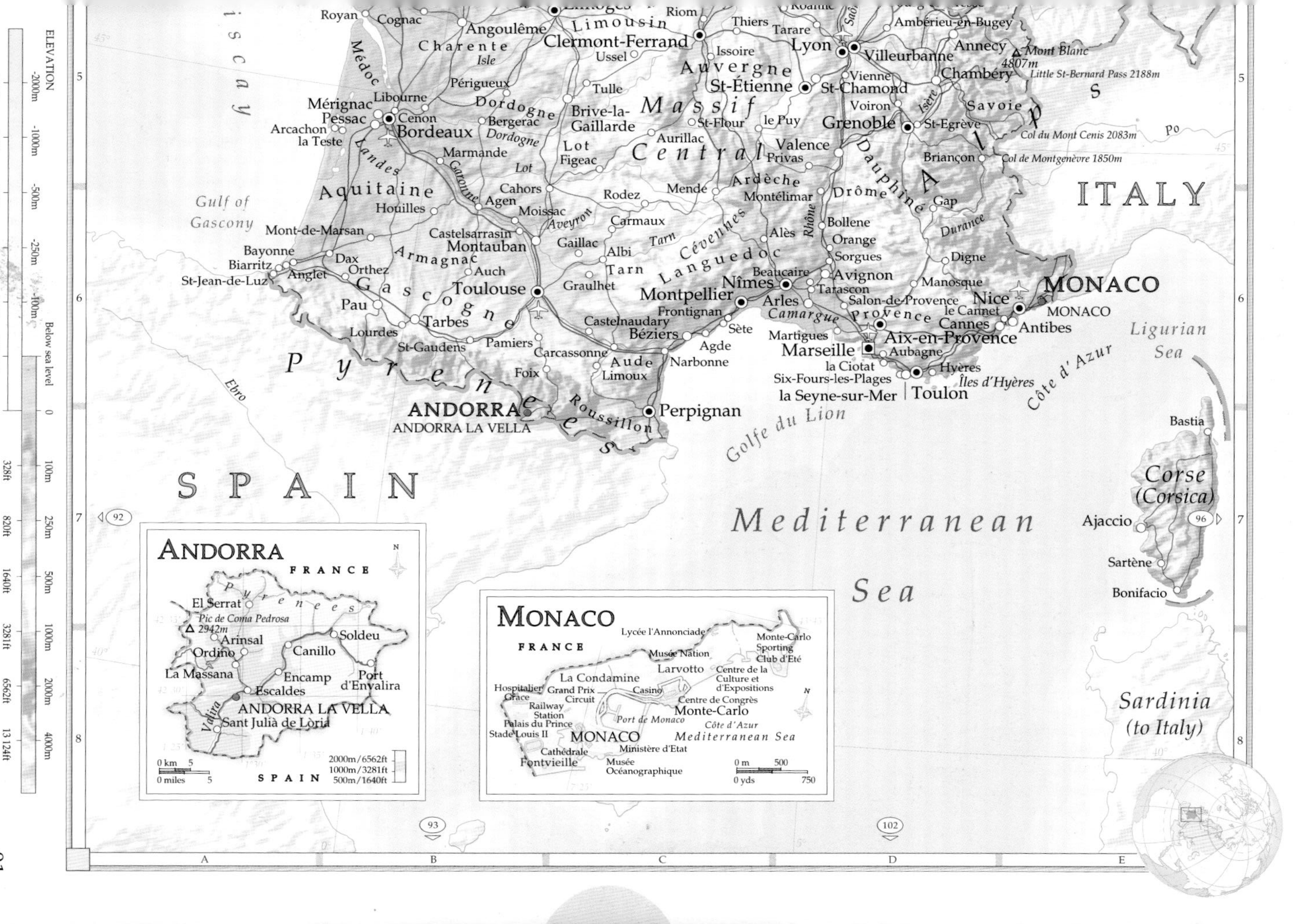
ITALY
SPAIN
Mediterranean Sea
Ligurian Sea
Golfe du Lion
Gulf of Gascony
Corse (Corsica)
Sardinia (to Italy)
Bastia
Ajaccio
Sartène
Bonifacio
MONACO
MONACO
Nice
le Cannet
Cannes
Antibes
Côte d'Azur
Îles d'Hyères
Hyères
Toulon
la Seyne-sur-Mer
Six-Fours-les-Plages
la Ciotat
Aubagne
Marseille
Martigues
Aix-en-Provence
Provence
Salon-de-Provence
Manosque
Digne
Durance
Gap
Briançon
Col de Montgenèvre 1850m
Col du Mont Cenis 2083m
Po
St-Egrève
Grenoble
Voiron
Savoie
Chambéry
Little St-Bernard Pass 2188m
Mont Blanc 4807m
Annecy
Ambérieu-en-Bugey
Villeurbanne
Lyon
Vienne
St-Chamond
St-Étienne
Tarare
Thiers
Riom
Roanne
Clermont-Ferrand
Issoire
Auvergne
Massif Central
Dauphiné
Valence
Privas
Ardèche
Montélimar
Drôme
Bollene
Orange
Sorgues
Avignon
Tarascon
Beaucaire
Arles
Camargue
Nîmes
Montpellier
Frontignan
Sète
Agde
Béziers
Narbonne
Castelnaudary
Carcassonne
Aude
Limoux
Perpignan
Roussillon
Foix
Pamiers
Languedoc
Cévennes
Rhône
Alès
Mende
Le Puy
St-Flour
Aurillac
Rodez
Carmaux
Tarn
Albi
Graulhet
Gaillac
Aveyron
Moissac
Cahors
Lot
Figeac
Brive-la-Gaillarde
Tulle
Ussel
Limousin
Angoulême
Charente
Isle
Périgueux
Dordogne
Bergerac
Cognac
Royan
Médoc
Libourne
Mérignac
Pessac
Cenon
Bordeaux
Arcachon
la Teste
Landes
Marmande
Garonne
Agen
Aquitaine
Houilles
Mont-de-Marsan
Castelsarrasin
Montauban
Armagnac
Auch
Toulouse
Gascogne
Tarbes
Pau
Lourdes
St-Gaudens
Orthez
Dax
Bayonne
Biarritz
Anglet
St-Jean-de-Luz
Pyrenees
Ebro
ANDORRA
ANDORRA LA VELLA
ANDORRA
FRANCE
SPAIN
El Serrat
Pic de Coma Pedrosa
2942m
Arinsal
Ordino
La Massana
Canillo
Soldeu
Encamp
Port d'Envalira
Escaldes
ANDORRA LA VELLA
Sant Julià de Lòria
Valira
0 km 5
0 miles 5
2000m/6562ft
1000m/3281ft
500m/1640ft
MONACO
FRANCE
Lycée l'Annonciade
Musée Nation
Monte-Carlo Sporting Club d'Eté
Larvotto
Centre de la Culture et d'Expositions
La Condamine
Hospitalier Grace
Grand Prix Circuit
Casino
Centre de Congrès
Monte-Carlo
Railway Station
Port de Monaco
Côte d'Azur
Palais du Prince
Stade Louis II
MONACO
Mediterranean Sea
Cathédrale
Ministère d'Etat
Fontvieille
Musée Océanographique
0 m 500
0 yds 750
ELEVATION
Below sea level
-2000m -1000m -500m -250m -100m 0 100m 250m 500m 1000m 2000m 4000m
-6562ft -3281ft -1640ft -820ft -328ft 164ft/-50m 0 328ft 820ft 1640ft 3281ft 6562ft 13 124ft

SPAIN & PORTUGAL

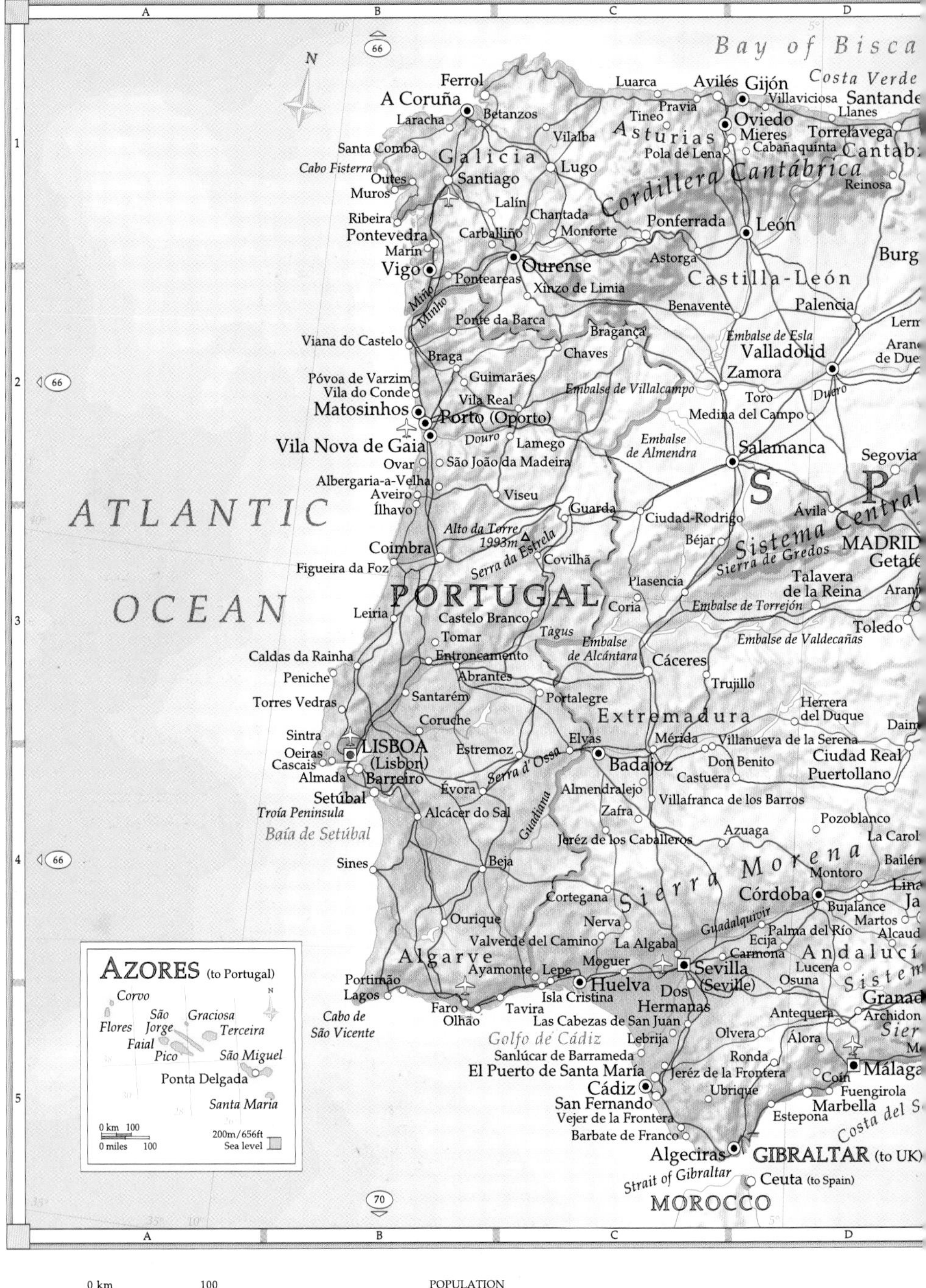

A Coruña
Ferrol
Luarca
Avilés Gijón
Costa Verde
Bay of Biscay
Villaviciosa Santander
Laracha
Betanzos
Pravia
Tineo
Oviedo
Llanes
Santa Comba
Vilalba
Asturias
Mieres
Torrelavega
Cabo Fisterra
Galicia
Lugo
Pola de Lena
Cabañaquinta
Cantáb.
Outes
Santiago
Cordillera Cantábrica
Reinosa
Muros
Lalín
Chantada
Ribeira
Carballiño
Monforte
Ponferrada
León
Pontevedra
Marín
Astorga
Burg
Vigo
Ponteareas
Ourense
Xinzo de Limia
Castilla-León
Ponte da Barca
Benavente
Palencia
Viana do Castelo
Bragança
Embalse de Esla
Lerr
Braga
Chaves
Valladolid
Aran
de Due
Póvoa de Varzim
Guimarães
Embalse de Villalcampo
Zamora
Vila do Conde
Matosinhos
Vila Real
Toro
Due
Porto (Oporto)
Medina del Campo
Vila Nova de Gaia
Douro
Lamego
Embalse
de Almendra
Salamanca
Segovia
Ovar
São João da Madeira
Albergaria-a-Velha
Aveiro
Viseu
Guarda
Ílhavo
Ciudad-Rodrigo
Ávila
ATLANTIC
Alto da Torre
1993m
Béjar
Sistema Central
MADRID
Coimbra
Serra da Estrela
Covilhã
Sierra de Gredos
Getafe
Figueira da Foz
Plasencia
Talavera
de la Reina
Aran
OCEAN
Leiria
PORTUGAL
Coria
Embalse de Torrejón
Toledo
Castelo Branco
Tagus
Embalse de Valdecañas
Caldas da Rainha
Tomar
Peniche
Entroncamento
de Alcántara
Cáceres
Torres Vedras
Abrantes
Santarém
Portalegre
Herrera
del Duque
Sintra
Coruche
Extremadura
Dain
Oeiras
LISBOA
Estremoz
Elvas
Mérida
Villanueva de la Serena
Cascais
(Lisbon)
Don Benito
Ciudad Real
Almada
Barreiro
Badajoz
Castuera
Puertollano
Setúbal
Évora
Serra d'Ossa
Almendralejo
Villafranca de los Barros
Troia Peninsula
Alcácer do Sal
Zafra
Pozoblanco
Baía de Setúbal
Jeréz de los Caballeros
Azuaga
La Carol
Sines
Beja
Sierra Morena
Montoro
Bailén
Córdoba
Lina
Ja
Cortegana
Bujalance
Ourique
Nerva
Guadalquivir
Martos
Alcaud
Valverde del Camino
La Algaba
Ecija
Palma del Río
Algarve
Ayamonte
Lepe
Moguer
Carmona
Andaluc
Portimão
Sevilla
Lucena
Lagos
Huelva
(Seville)
Osuna
Sist
Cabo de
Faro
Tavira
Isla Cristina
Dos
Hermanas
Antequera
Granad
São Vicente
Olhão
Las Cabezas de San Juan
Olvera
Álora
Sier
Golfo de Cádiz
Lebrija
Ronda
M
Sanlúcar de Barrameda
El Puerto de Santa María
Jeréz de la Frontera
Coín
Málaga
Cádiz
Ubrique
Fuengirola
San Fernando
Estepona
Marbella
Vejer de la Frontera
Costa del S
Barbate de Franco
Algeciras
GIBRALTAR (to UK)
Strait of Gibraltar
Ceuta (to Spain)
MOROCCO

POPULATION

○ Less than 50,000   ○ 50,000 -100,000   ◉ 100,000 - 500,000   ◼ Over 500,000

0 km 100
0 miles 100

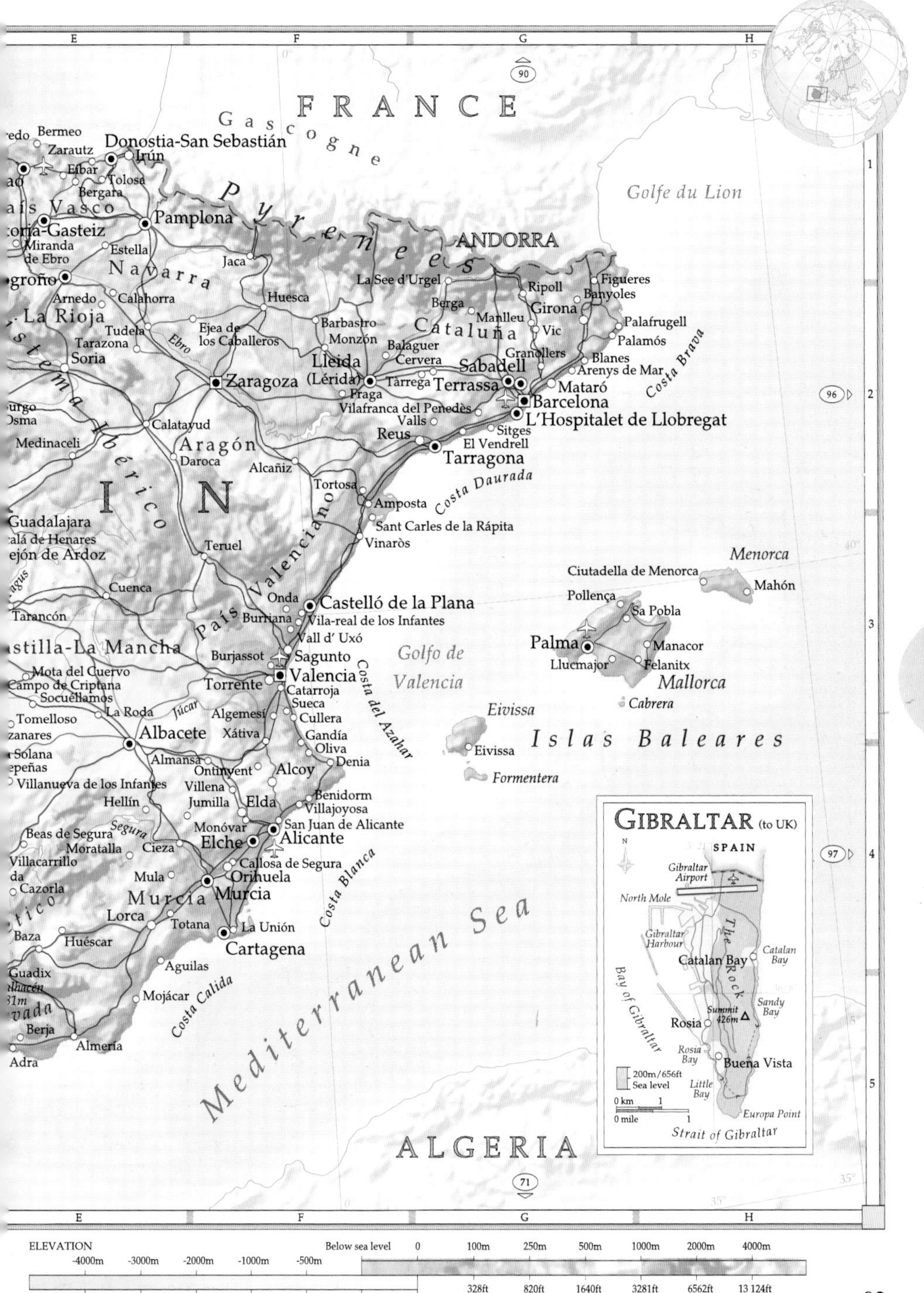

FRANCE

Gascogne

Pyrenees

ANDORRA

Golfe du Lion

edo Bermeo
Zarautz
Donostia-San Sebastián
Irún
ao Eibar Tolosa
als Vasco Bergara
oria-Gasteiz Pamplona
Miranda de Ebro Estella
goño Navarra Jaca
Arnedo Calahorra
La Rioja Tudela
Tarazona
Soria

Huesca
La Seo d'Urgel
Berga
Barbastro
Monzón Manlleu
Balaguer
Cervera
Granollers
Vic
Ripoll
Figueres
Bañoles
Girona
Palafrugell
Palamós
Blanes

Ejea de los Caballeros
Cataluña

Ebro
Lleida
(Lérida)
Praga
Tárrega
Terrassa
Sabadell
Arenys de Mar

Zaragoza

Costa Brava

Vilafranca del Penedès
Valls
Reus

Barcelona
L'Hospitalet de Llobregat
Sitges
El Vendrell

Calatayud
Osma
Medinaceli
Aragón
Daroca
Alcañiz

Tarragona

Guadalajara
alá de Henares
ejón de Ardoz
SISTEMA IBÉRICO

Teruel
Tortosa

Amposta
Costa Daurada
Sant Carles de la Rápita
Vinaròs

Cuenca

Tarancón
Onda
Burriana
País Valenciano
Castelló de la Plana
Vila-real de los Infantes
Vall d' Uxó

Menorca
Ciutadella de Menorca
Pollença
Sa Pola
Mahón

stilla-La Mancha
Mota del Cuervo
Campo de Criptana
Socuéllamos
Tomelloso
zanares
Burjassot
Sagunto
Torrente
Catarroja
Sueca
Valencia
Cullera
Gandía
Oliva
Denia
Golfo de Valencia
Palma
Llucmajor
Manacor
Felanitx
Mallorca
Cabrera

Algemesí
Xátiva
La Roda
Júcar
Albacete
Almansa
Ontinyent
Alcoy
Solana
peñas
Villanueva de los Infantes
Villena
Jumilla
Elda
Benidorm
Villajoyosa

Eivissa
Eivissa
Formentera

Islas Baleares

Beas de Segura
Moratalla
Segura
Cieza
Villacarrillo
da Cazorla
Monóvar
Elche
Alicante
San Juan de Alicante
Callosa de Segura
Mula Orihuela
Murcia Murcia
Lorca
Totana
La Unión
Cartagena

Costa Blanca

Baza
Huéscar
Aguilas
Guadix
llaucín
81m
vada
Berja
Almería
Adra
Mojácar
Costa Calida

Mediterranean Sea

ALGERIA

ELEVATION
-4000m -3000m -2000m -1000m -500m   Below sea level 0 100m 250m 500m 1000m 2000m 4000m

-13 124ft -9843ft -6562ft -3281ft -1640ft -820ft/-250m 0   328ft 820ft 1640ft 3281ft 6562ft 13 124ft

GERMANY & THE ALPINE STATES

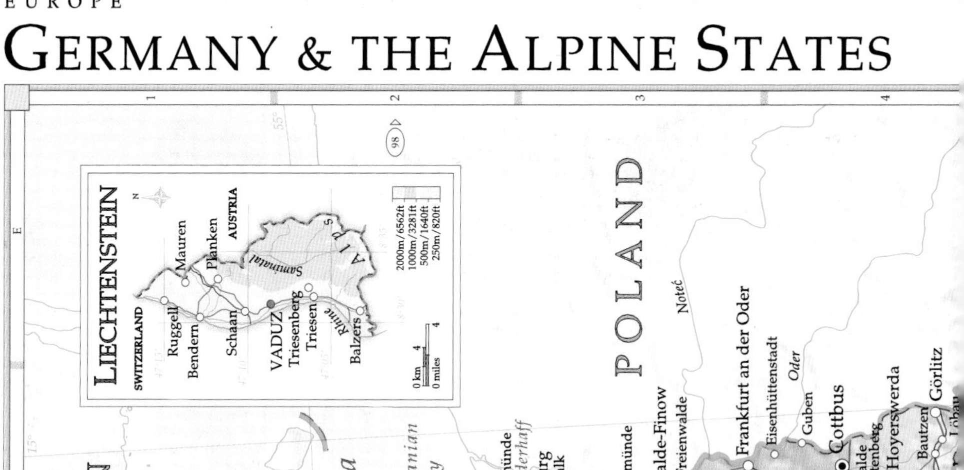

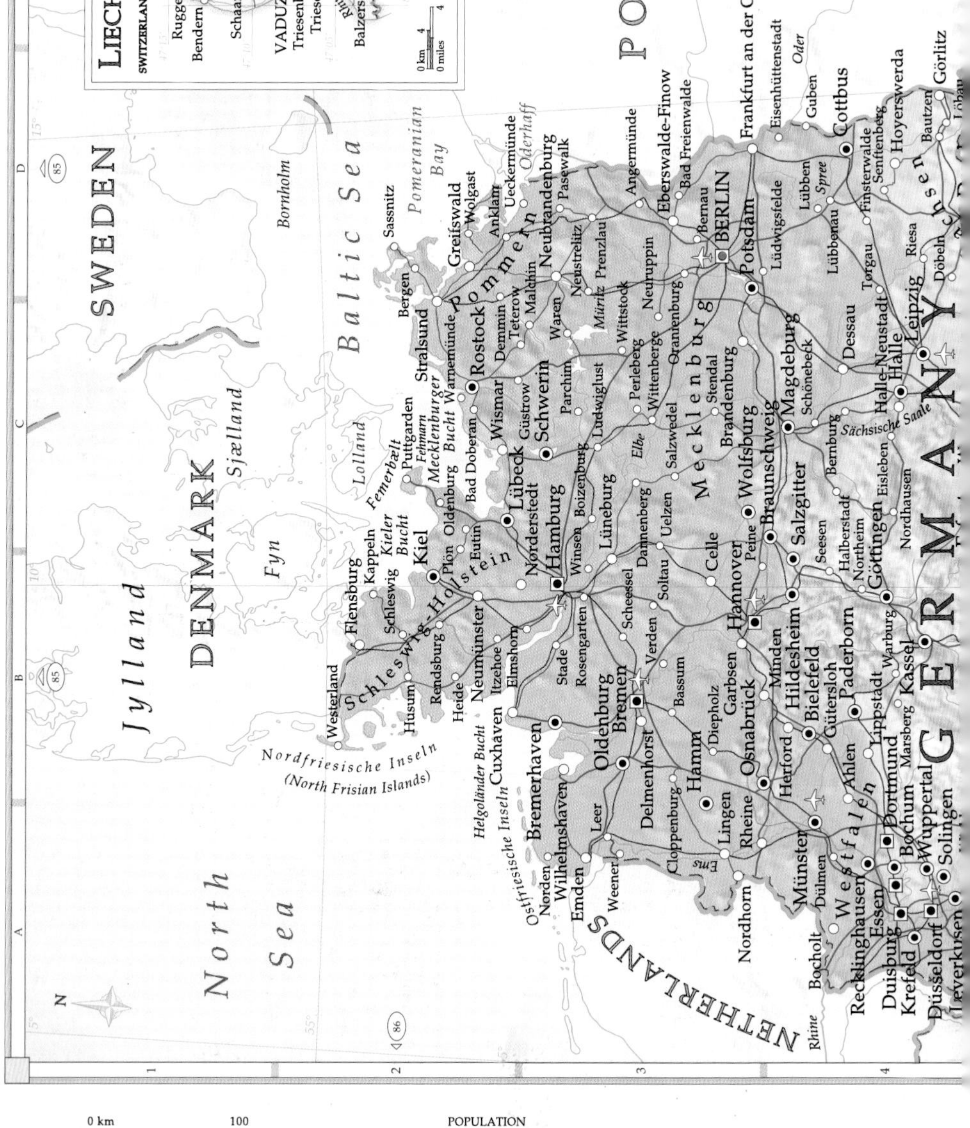

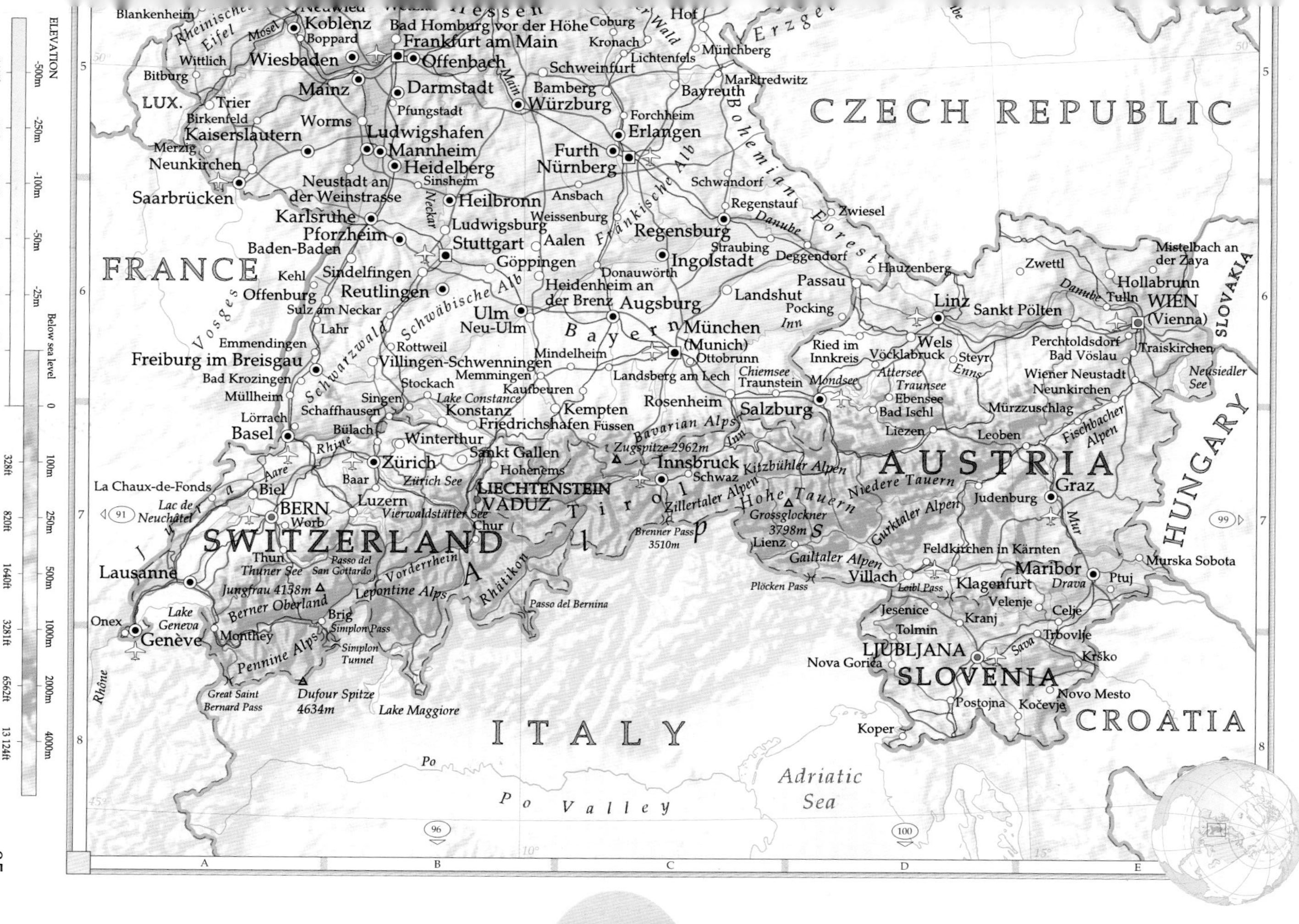

CZECH REPUBLIC

SLOVAKIA

HUNGARY

CROATIA

AUSTRIA

SLOVENIA

ITALY

SWITZERLAND

FRANCE

LUX.

Mistelbach an der Zaya
WIEN (Vienna)
Hollabrunn
Zwettl
Sankt Pölten
Danube
Traiskirchen
Neusiedler See
Perchtoldsdorf
Bad Vöslau
Wiener Neustadt
Neunkirchen
Murzzuschlag
Graz
Mur
Leoben
Leibnitz
Maribor
Ptuj
Drava
Ormož
Krško
Novo Mesto
Kočevje
Celje
Velenje
Kranj
Klagenfurt
Feldkirchen in Kärnten
Judenburg
Linz
Wels
Steyr
Enns
Bad Ischl
Ebensee
Villach
LJUBLJANA
Nova Gorica
Koper
Adriatic Sea
Passau
Ried im Innkreis
Salzburg
Lienz
Plöcken Pass
Hohe Tauern
Niedere Tauern
Kitzbühel Alpen
Villach
Ennstaler Alpen
Gmunden
Traunsee
Attersee
Mondsee
Chiemsee
Traunstein
Rosenheim
München (Munich)
Ottobrunn
Deggendorf
Straubing
Regensburg
Landshut
Pocking
Schwandorf
Zwiesel
Marktredwitz
Münchberg
Bayreuth
Kronach
Lichtenfels
Coburg
Bamberg
Schweinfurt
Würzburg
Erlangen
Fürth
Nürnberg
Ansbach
Forchheim
Ingolstadt
Donauwörth
Augsburg
Heidenheim an der Brenz
Aalen
Göppingen
Ulm
Neu-Ulm
Memmingen
Kaufbeuren
Kempten
Landsberg am Lech
Füssen
Friedrichshafen
Hohenems
Sankt Gallen
Vorarlberg
Rheintal
VADUZ
LIECHTENSTEIN
Innsbruck
Schwaz
Zugspitze 2962m
Brauneck
Brenner Pass
3510m
Ziller taler Alpen
3798m S
Grossglockner
3797m
Tirol
Tauern
Mindelheim
Stockach
Konstanz
Lake Constance
Singen
Schaffhausen
Bülach
Winterthur
Zürich
Zürich See
Baar
Luzern
Rhein
Heilbronn
Ludwigsburg
Stuttgart
Sindelfingen
Reutlingen
Tübingen
Schwäbische Alb
Rottweil
Villingen-Schwenningen
Offenburg
Pforzheim
Karlsruhe
Baden-Baden
Bad Krozingen
Freiburg im Breisgau
Emmendingen
Müllheim
Lörrach
Basel
Kehl
Sulz am Neckar
Neckar
Weissenburg
Sinsheim
Mannheim
Heidelberg
Ludwigshafen
Neustadt an der Weinstrasse
Worms
Mainz
Wiesbaden
Offenbach
Frankfurt am Main
Bad Homburg vor der Höhe
Darmstadt
Pfungstadt
Koblenz
Boppard
Hessen
Rheinland-Pfalz
Mosel
Rhein
Trier
Wittlich
Birkenfeld
Merzig
Neunkirchen
Saarbrücken
Kaiserslautern
Bitburg
Bad Kreuznach
Bingen
Vosges
Schwarzwald
BERN
Worb
Thun
Berner Oberland
Thuner See
Jungfrau 4158m
Pennine Alps
Monthey
Brig
Simplon Pass
Simplon Tunnel
San Gottardo
Passo del San Gottardo
Lepontine Alps
Dufour Spitze 4634m
Great Saint Bernard Pass
Great Saint Bernard Tunnel
Passo del Bernina
Monte Rosa
Lake Maggiore
Po Valley
Po
Lac de Neuchâtel
Biel
Aare
La Chaux-de-Fonds
Lausanne
Lake Geneva
Genève
Onex
Rhône
Erz gebirge
Fichtel gebirge
Bayern (Bavaria)
Bohemian Forest

ELEVATION

					Below sea level	0	100m	250m	500m	1000m	2000m	4000m
-500m	-250m	-100m	-50m	-25m		0						
-1640ft	-820ft	-328ft	-164ft	-82ft	-33ft/-10m	0	328ft	820ft	1640ft	3281ft	6562ft	13 124ft

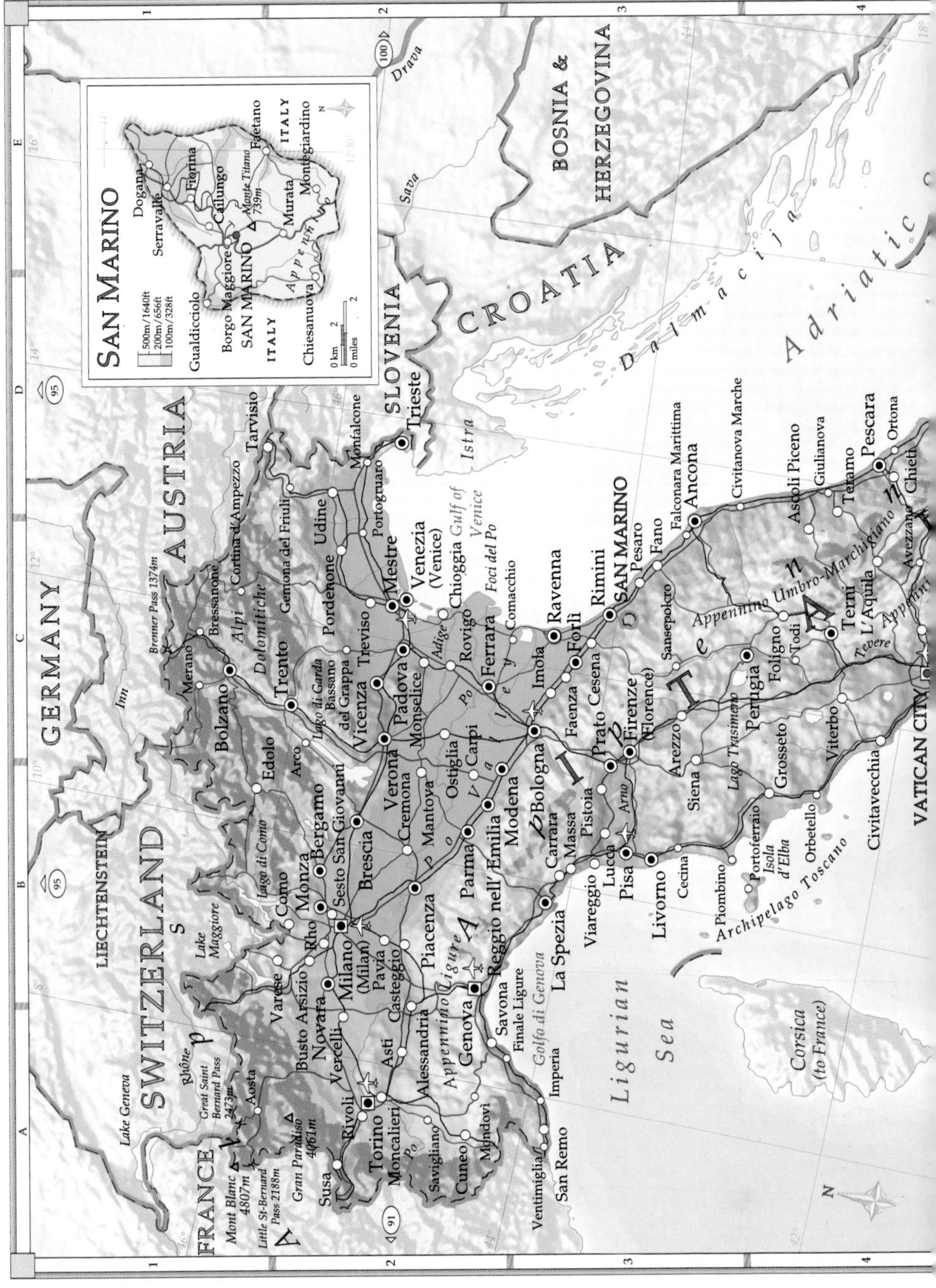

SAN MARINO

Dogana
Serravalle
Fiorina
Gualdicciolo
Borgo Maggiore
Cailungo
Faetano
ITALY
SAN MARINO
Monte Titano
739m
Murata
Montegiardino
ITALY
Chiesanuova

500m/1640ft
200m/656ft
100m/328ft

Appennini

0 km   2
0 miles   2

GERMANY
AUSTRIA
SWITZERLAND
LIECHTENSTEIN
FRANCE

SLOVENIA
CROATIA
BOSNIA & HERZEGOVINA

Drava
Sava
Dalmacija
Adriatic
Istra

Trieste
Monfalcone
Tarvisio
Portogruaro
Udine
Gemona del Friuli
Pordenone
Cortina d'Ampezzo
Bressanone
Brenner Pass 1374m
Merano
Bolzano
Alpi
Dolomitiche
Trento
Edolo
Arco
Lago di Garda
Bassano del Grappa
Treviso
Mestre
Venezia (Venice)
Gulf of Venice
Chioggia
Foci del Po
Comacchio
Ravenna
Forlì
Rimini
SAN MARINO
Fano
Pesaro
Falconara Marittima
Ancona
Civitanova Marche
Ascoli Piceno
Giulianova
Teramo
Pescara
Ortona
Chieti
Avezzano
L'Aquila
Appennino Umbro-Marchigiano
Terni
Todi
Foligno
Perugia
Fiume Tevere
Lago Trasimeno
Arezzo
Siena
Grosseto
Viterbo
Civitavecchia
VATICAN CITY

Vicenza
Verona
Padova
Monselice
Rovigo
Ferrara
Imola
Faenza
Cesena
Prato
Firenze (Florence)
Pistoia
Bologna
Modena
Reggio nell'Emilia
Parma
Piacenza
Carpi
Mantova
Ostiglia
Cremona
Brescia
Bergamo
Monza
Sesto San Giovanni
Rho
Milano (Milan)
Pavia
Casteggio
Como
Lago di Como
Lake Maggiore
Lake Geneva
Varese
Busto Arsizio
Novara
Vercelli
Alessandria
Asti
Rhône
Great Saint Bernard Pass
Little St-Bernard Pass 2188m
Mont Blanc 4807m
Aosta
Gran Paradiso 4061m
Rivoli
Moncalieri
Torino
Susa
Savigliano
Cuneo
Mondovì
Ventimiglia
San Remo
Imperia
Finale Ligure
Savona
Genova
Appennino Ligure
Golfo di Genova
La Spezia
Massa
Carrara
Viareggio
Lucca
Pisa
Livorno
Cecina
Piombino
Portoferraio
Isola d'Elba
Orbetello
Archipelago Toscano
Corsica (to France)

Ligurian Sea

Inn

0 km   100
0 miles   100

POPULATION
○ Less than 50,000
◉ 50,000 -100,000
⬤ 100,000 - 500,000
⬛ Over 500,000

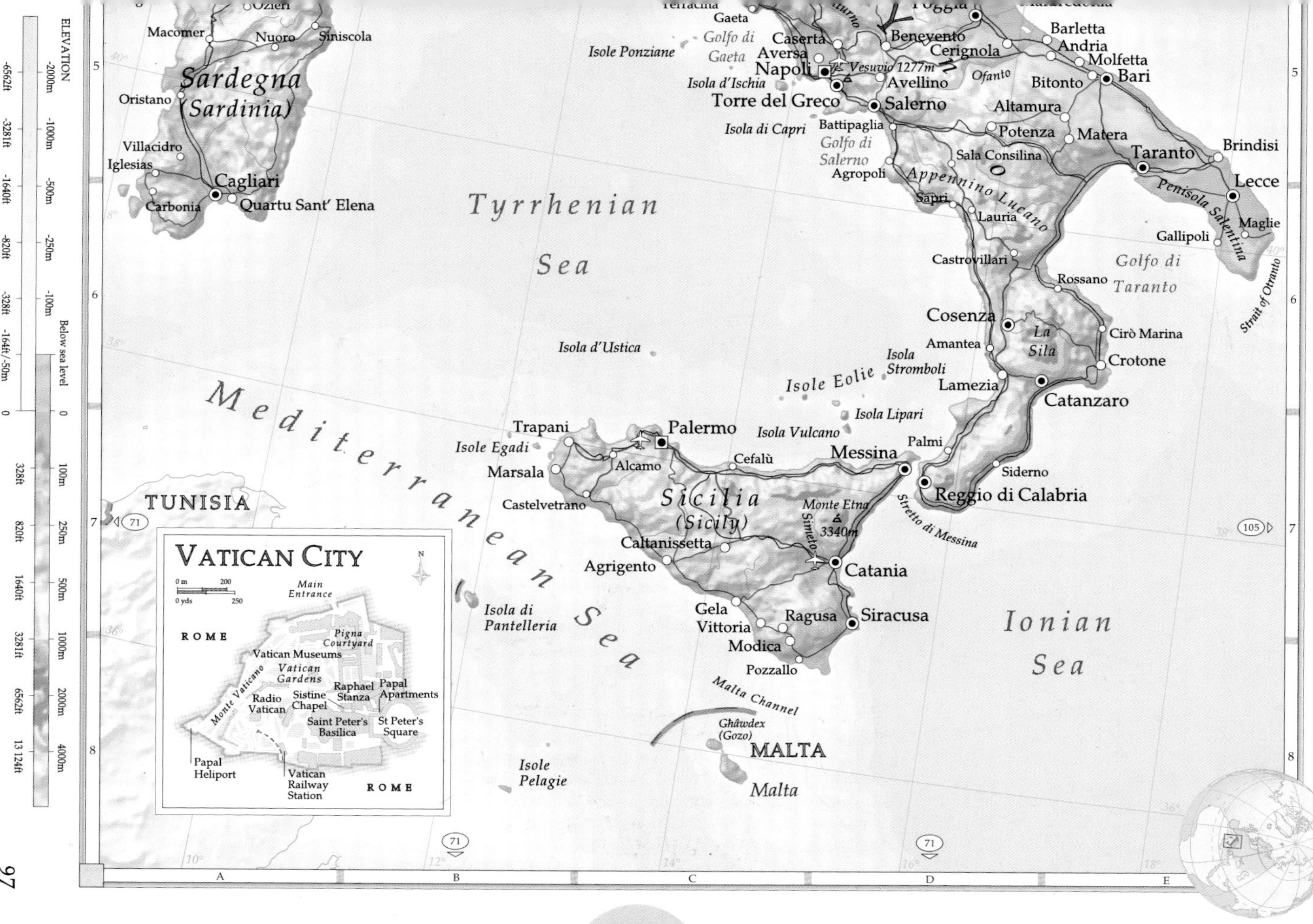

Strait of Otranto

Brindisi
Lecce
Penisola Salentina
Maglie
Gallipoli
Taranto
Golfo di
Taranto
Bari
Molfetta
Andria
Barletta
Ciro Marina
Crotone
Rossano
Catanzaro
Bitonto
Matera
Cerignola
Altamura
Ofanto
Potenza
La
Sila
Reggio di Calabria
Siderno
Benevento
Avellino
Vesuvio 1277m
Salerno
Sala Consilina
Castrovillari
Cosenza
Amantea
Lamezia
Palmi
Stretto di Messina
Caserta
Aversa
Napoli
Battipaglia
Golfo di
Salerno
Agropoli
Lauria
Sapri
Isola
Stromboli
Isola Lipari
Messina
Isole Eolie
Catania
Siracusa
Gaeta
Golfo di
Gaeta
Torre del Greco
Isola di Capri
Isola d'Ischia
Isola Vulcano
Cefalù
Monte Etna
3340m
Simeto
Ragusa
Pozzallo
Modica
Isole Ponziane
Palermo
Sicilia
(Sicily)
Gela
Vittoria
Malta Channel
MALTA
Malta
Isola d'Ustica
Alcamo
Caltanissetta
Agrigento
Ghawdex
(Gozo)
Trapani
Isole Egadi
Marsala
Castelvetrano
Isola di
Pantelleria
Isole
Pelagie

Tyrrhenian
Sea

Ionian
Sea

Mediterranean Sea

Sardegna
(Sardinia)
Siniscola
Nuoro
Macomer
Cagliari
Quartu Sant' Elena
Oristano
Villacidro
Iglesias
Carbonia

Oristano

TUNISIA

Ionian Sea

Appennino Lucano

O

VATICAN CITY

ROME
Pigna
Courtyard
Raphael
Stanza
Papal
Apartments
St Peter's
Square
Vatican
Museums
Vatican
Gardens
Sistine
Chapel
Saint Peter's
Basilica
Vatican
Railway
Station
Main
Entrance
Radio
Vatican
Monte Vaticano
Papal
Heliport
ROME
ROME

ELEVATION

-2000m	-1000m	-500m	-250m	-100m	Below sea level	0	100m	250m	500m	1000m	2000m	4000m
-6562ft	-3281ft	-1640ft	-820ft	-328ft	-164ft/-50m	0	328ft	820ft	1640ft	3281ft	6562ft	13 124ft

97

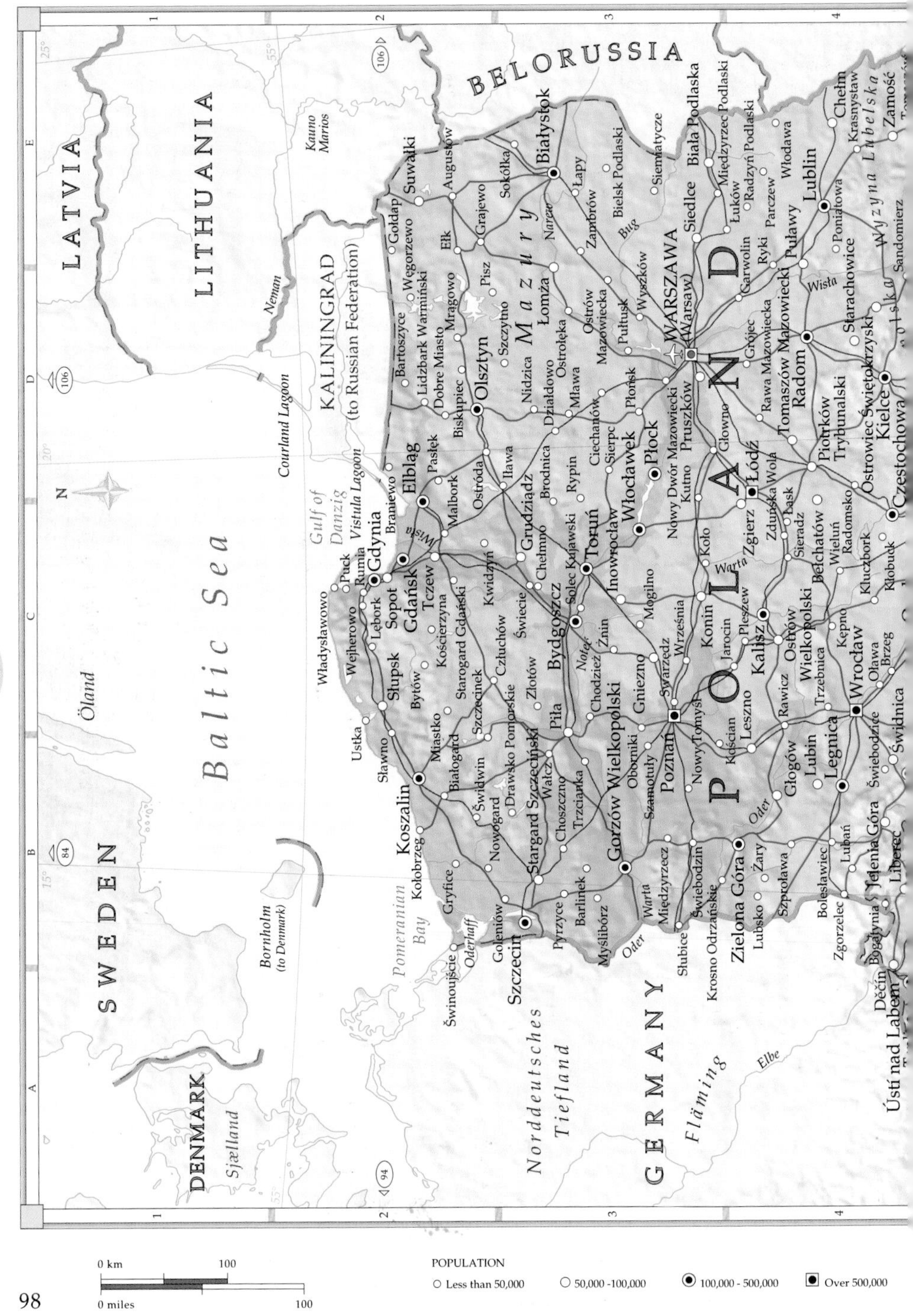

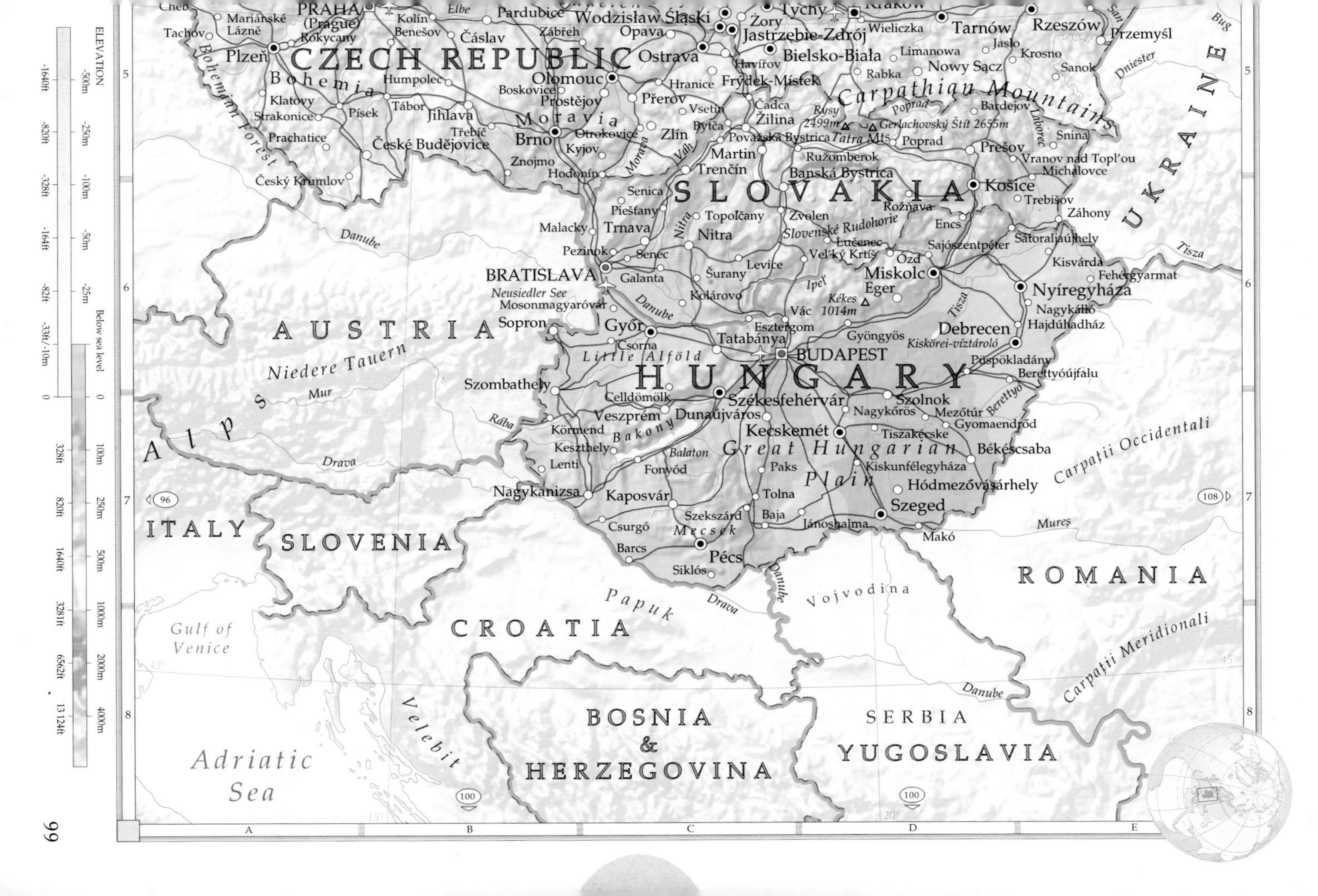

ELEVATION

					Below sea level	0	100m	250m	500m	1000m	2000m	4000m
-500m	-250m	-100m	-50m	-25m								
							328ft	820ft	1640ft	3281ft	6562ft	13 124ft
-1640ft	-820ft	-328ft	-164ft	-82ft	-33ft/-10m	0						

THE WESTERN BALKANS

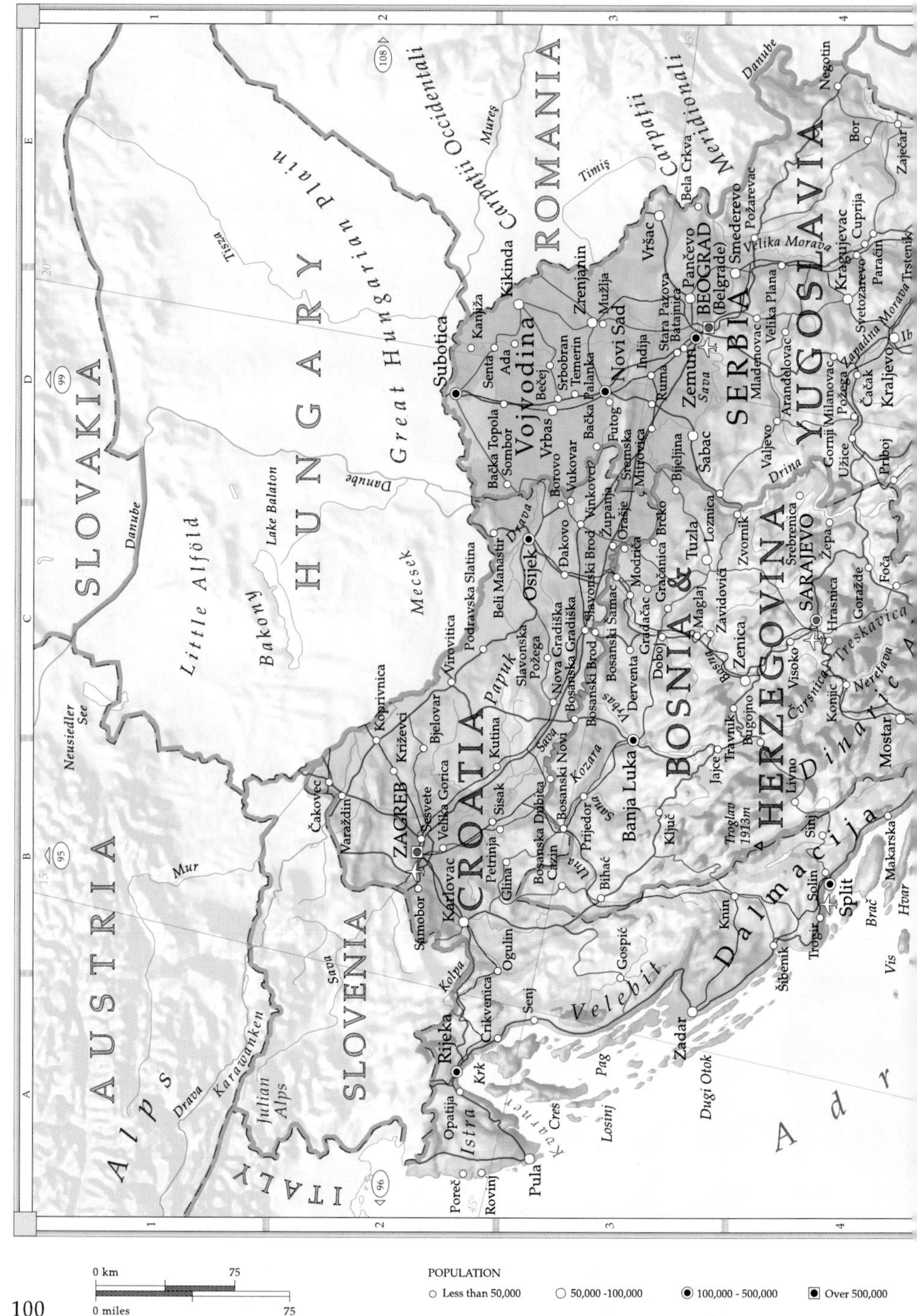

0 km   75

0 miles   75

POPULATION

○ Less than 50,000   ○ 50,000 -100,000   ◉ 100,000 - 500,000   ■ Over 500,000

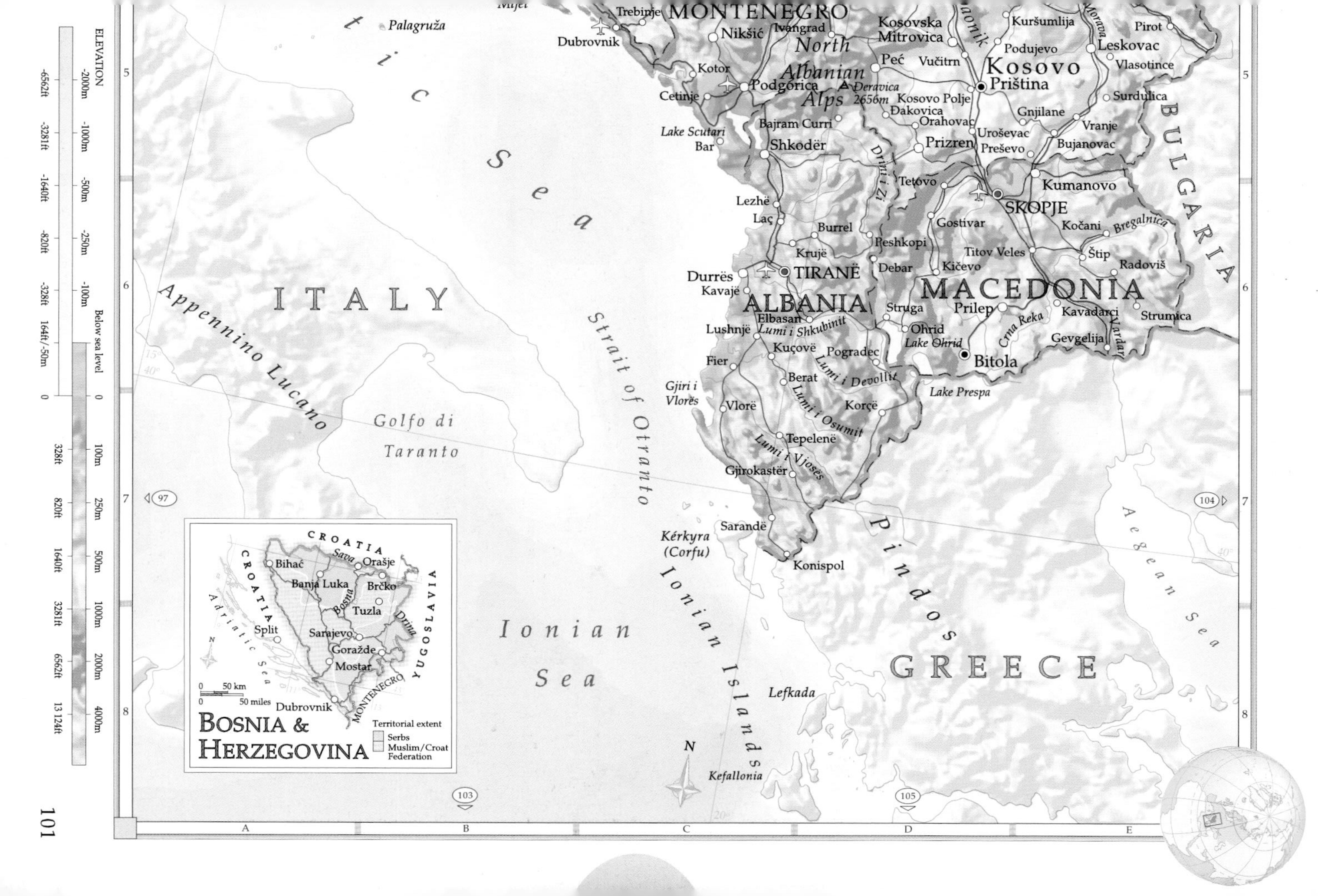

THE WESTERN BALKANS

Aegean Sea

BULGARIA

Pirot
Leskovac
Vlasotince
Surdulica
Morava
Kuršumlija
Podujevo
Kosovo
Priština
Pristina
Kosovska
Mitrovica
Peć
Vučitrn
Vranje
Bujanovac
Preševo
Uroševac
Gnjilane
Kumanovo
SKOPJE
Kočani
Štip
Radoviš
Strumica
Vardar
Kavadarci
Gevgelija
Titov Veles
Prilep
MACEDONIA
Kičevo
Bitola
Lake Prespa
Ohrid
Lake Ohrid
Struga
Debar
Gostivar
Tetovo
Prizren
Orahovac
Đakovica
Kosovo Polje
2656m
Dečani
Drini i Zi
Reshkopi
Pindos
GREECE

MONTENEGRO
North
Albanian
Alps
Podgorica
Nikšić
Ivangrad
Andrijevica
Trebinje
Kotor
Cetinje
Bajram Curri
Shkodër
Lake Scutari
Bar
Burrel
Krujë
Lezhë
Lac
TIRANË
ALBANIA
Elbasan
Lumi Shkumbit
Burrel
Durrës
Kavajë
Lushnjë
Fier
Vlorë
Girri i
Vlorës
Berat
Lumi i Devollit
Kuçovë
Pogradec
Korçë
Lumi Osumit
Tepelenë
Lumi Vjosës
Gjirokastër
Sarandë
Konispol
Lefkada
Lefkada
Kérkyra
(Corfu)
Kefallonia
Ionian Islands

Strait of Otranto

Adriatic Sea

Palagruža

ITALY

Golfo di Taranto

Appennino Lucano

Ionian Sea

104
105
103
97

CROATIA
YUGOSLAVIA
Sava
Orašje
Brčko
Bihać
Banja Luka
Tuzla
Goražde
Bosna
Sarajevo
Mostar
Drina
MONTENEGRO
Split
Dubrovnik
CROATIA
Adriatic Sea
BOSNIA &
HERZEGOVINA

Territorial extent
Serbs
Muslim/Croat
Federation

50 km
50 miles
0

ELEVATION

-2000m	-1000m	-500m	-250m	-100m	Below sea level	0	100m	250m	500m	1000m	2000m	4000m
-6562ft	-3281ft	-1640ft	-820ft	-328ft	164ft/-50m	0	328ft	820ft	1640ft	3281ft	6562ft	13 124ft

101

THE MEDITERRANEAN

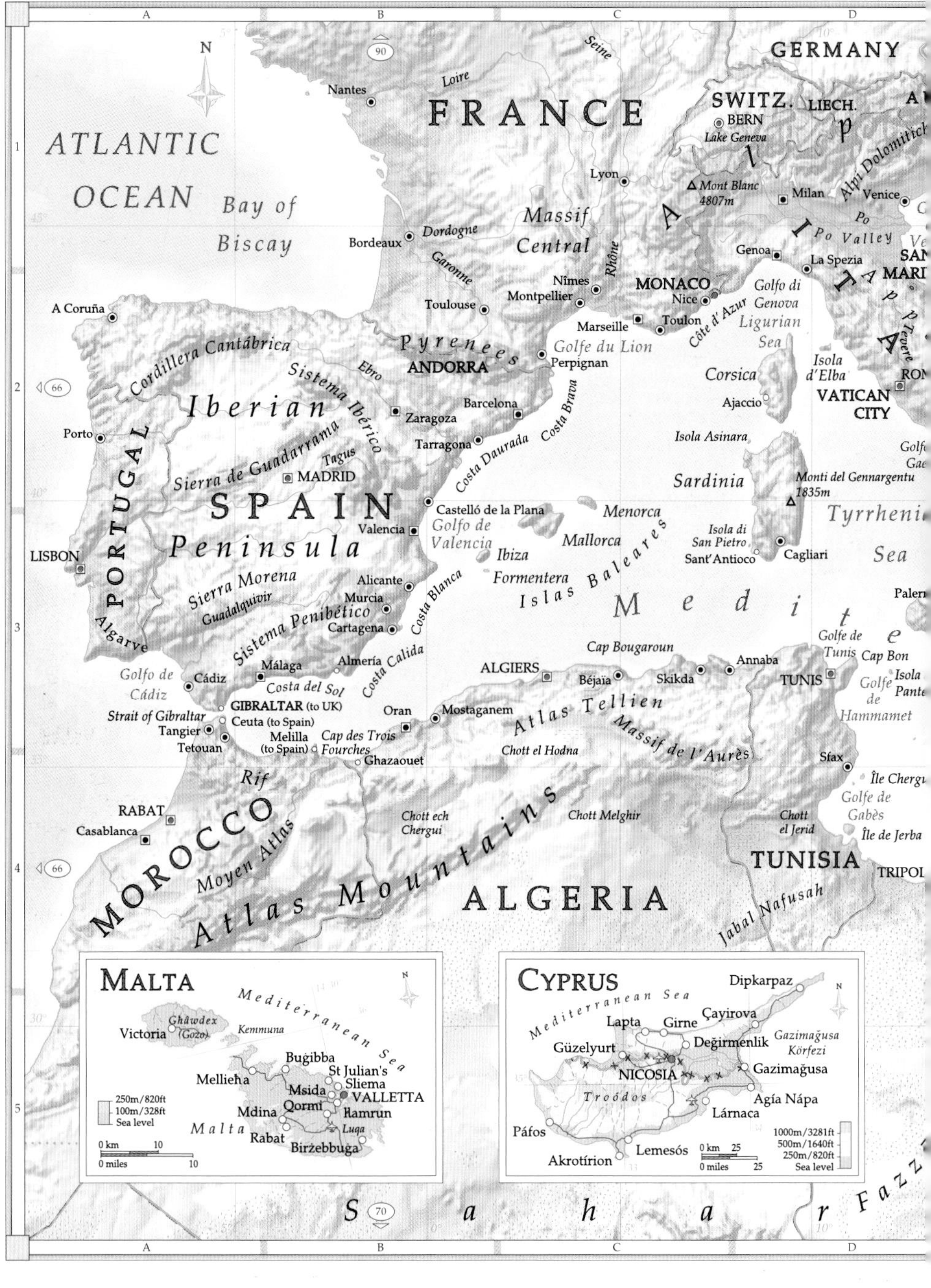

GERMANY

ATLANTIC
OCEAN Bay of
Biscay

N

FRANCE
SWITZ. LIECH. A
BERN
Lake Geneva

Nantes
Loire
Seine
90

Lyon
Mont Blanc
4807m
Milan
Venice
Alpi Dolomitiche
Po Valley
Ve

Bordeaux
Dordogne
Garonne
Massif
Central
Rhône
Genoa
La Spezia
SAN
MARI

Nîmes
Montpellier
MONACO
Nice
Golfo di
Genova
Ligurian
Sea

A Coruña

Toulouse
Marseille
Toulon
Côte d'Azur

Pyrenees
ANDORRA
Perpignan
Golfe du Lion

Corsica
Ajaccio
Isola
d'Elba
RO

VATICAN
CITY

Porto

Cordillera Cantábrica
Sistema Ibérico
Ebro

Barcelona
Zaragoza

Isola Asinara

Golf
Ga

Iberian

Sistema Ibérico

Tarragona
Costa Daurada
Costa Brava

Sardinia
Monti del Gennargentu
1835m

MADRID
Sierra de Guadarrama
Tagus

SPAIN
Peninsula

LISBON

Castelló de la Plana
Valencia
Golfo de
Valencia
Menorca
Mallorca
Isola di
San Pietro
Sant'Antioco
Cagliari

Tyrrheni

Sea

Sierra Morena
Guadalquivir
Sistema Penibético

Alicante
Murcia
Cartagena
Ibiza
Formentera
Islas Baleares

Palen

Algarve

Almería
Costa Cálida
Costa Blanca

Medi
t
e

Golfo de
Cádiz
Cádiz
Málaga
Costa del Sol
ALGIERS
Béjaia
Skikda
Annaba
TUNIS
Golfe de
Tunis
Cap Bon
Isola
Pante

Strait of Gibraltar
Tangier
Tetouan
GIBRALTAR (to UK)
Ceuta (to Spain)
Melilla
(to Spain)
Oran
Mostaganem
Cap des Trois
Fourches
Ghazaouet
Chott el Hodna

Atlas Tellien
Massif de l'Aurès

Golfe
de
Hammamet

Rif
Chott ech
Chergui
Chott Melghir
Chott
el Jerid
Sfax
Île Chergu

RABAT
Casablanca
MOROCCO
Moyen Atlas
Atlas Mountains
ALGERIA
Jabal Nafusah
TUNISIA
TRIPOL
Golfe de
Gabès
Île de Jerba

66

66

MALTA

Mediterranean Sea

N

Ghàwdex
(Gozo)
Victoria
Kemmuna

Mellieha
Bugibba
St Julian's
Sliema
Msida
VALLETTA
Qormi
Mdina
Ramrun
Luqa
Malta
Rabat
Birżebbuga

250m/820ft
100m/328ft
Sea level

0 km   10
0 miles   10

CYPRUS

Dipkarpaz
Çayirova

Mediterranean Sea

N

Lapta
Girne
Güzelyurt
Değirmenlik
Gazimağusa
Körfezi
NICOSIA
Gazimağusa
Troódos
Agía Nápa
Páfos
Lárnaca
Lemesós
Akrotírion

1000m/3281ft
500m/1640ft
250m/820ft
Sea level

0 km   25
0 miles   25

S
70
a
h
a
r
Fazz

0 km   200
0 miles   200

POPULATION
○ Less than 50,000
○ 50,000 -100,000
◉ 100,000 - 500,000
■ Over 500,000

102

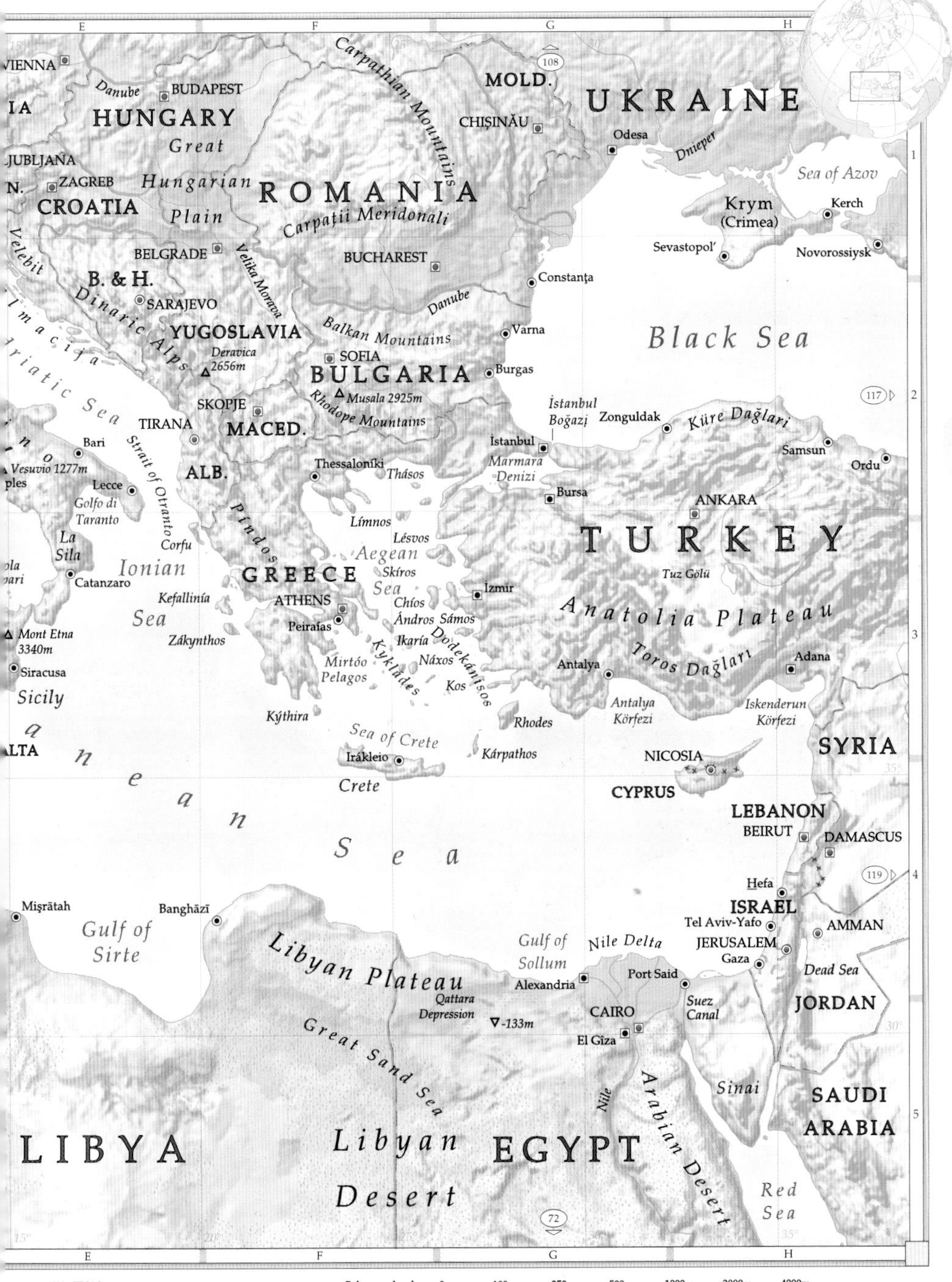

ELEVATION

| | Below sea level | 0 | 100m | 250m | 500m | 1000m | 2000m | 4000m |
| -4000m | -3000m | -2000m | -1000m | -500m | | | | |

| | | | 328ft | 820ft | 1640ft | 3281ft | 6562ft | 13 124ft |
| -13 124ft | -9843ft | -6562ft | -3281ft | -1640ft | -820ft/-250m | 0 | | |

BULGARIA & GREECE

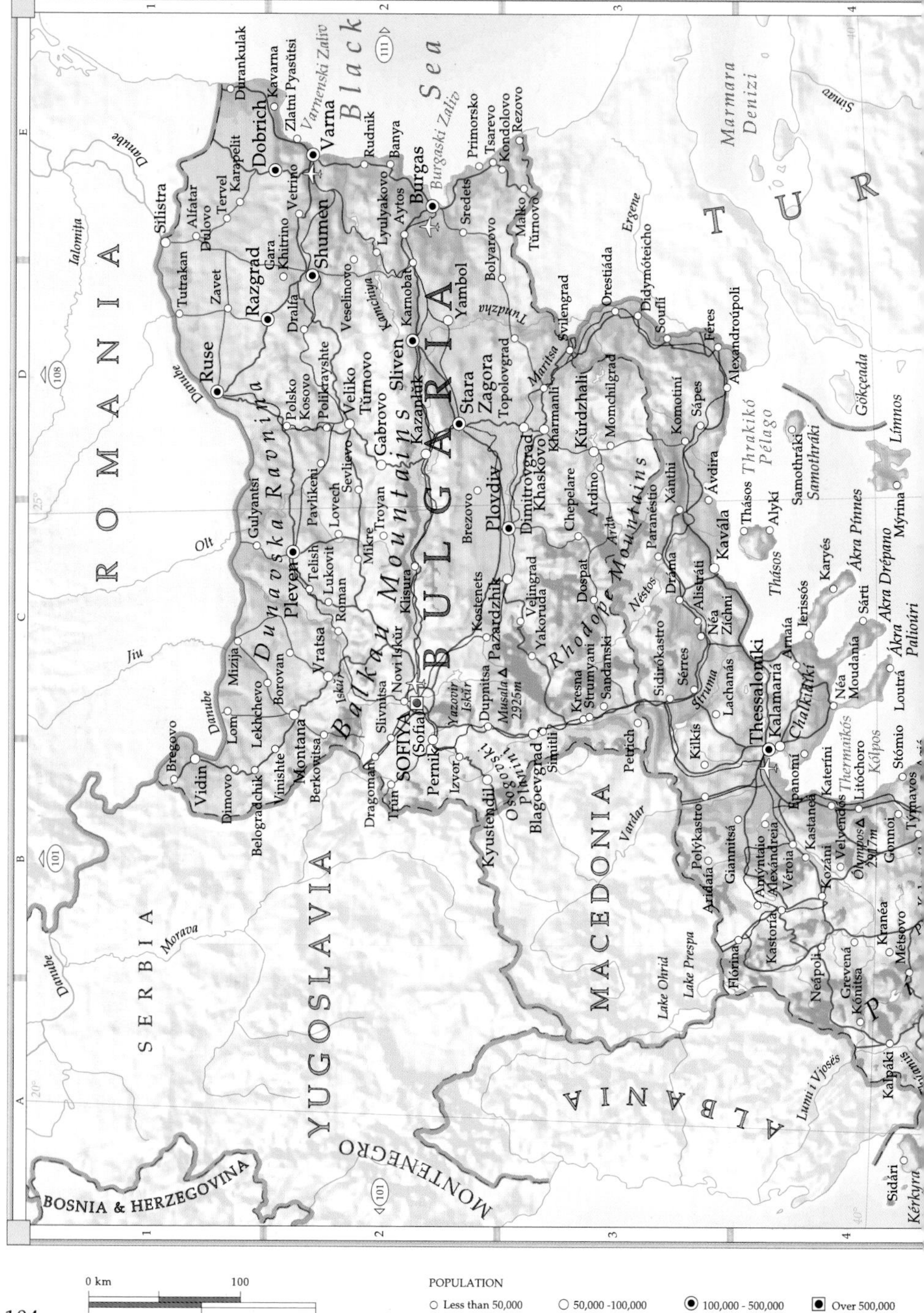

0 km   100

0 miles   100

POPULATION

○ Less than 50,000   ○ 50,000 -100,000   ◉ 100,000 - 500,000   ■ Over 500,000

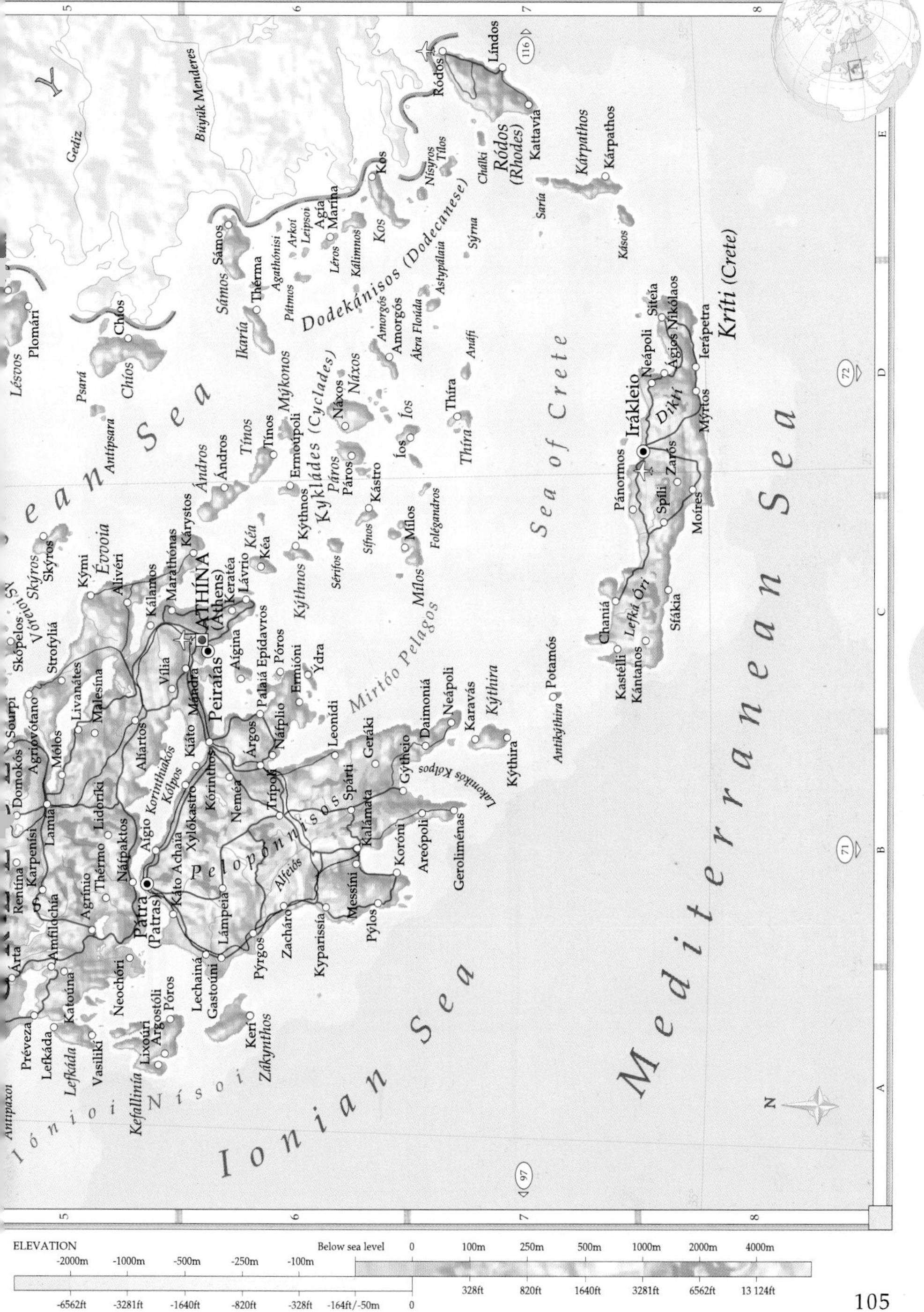

ELEVATION

-2000m	-1000m	-500m	-250m	-100m		Below sea level	0	100m	250m	500m	1000m	2000m	4000m	
-6562ft	-3281ft	-1640ft	-820ft	-328ft	-164ft/-50m	0		328ft	820ft	1640ft	3281ft	6562ft	13 124ft	

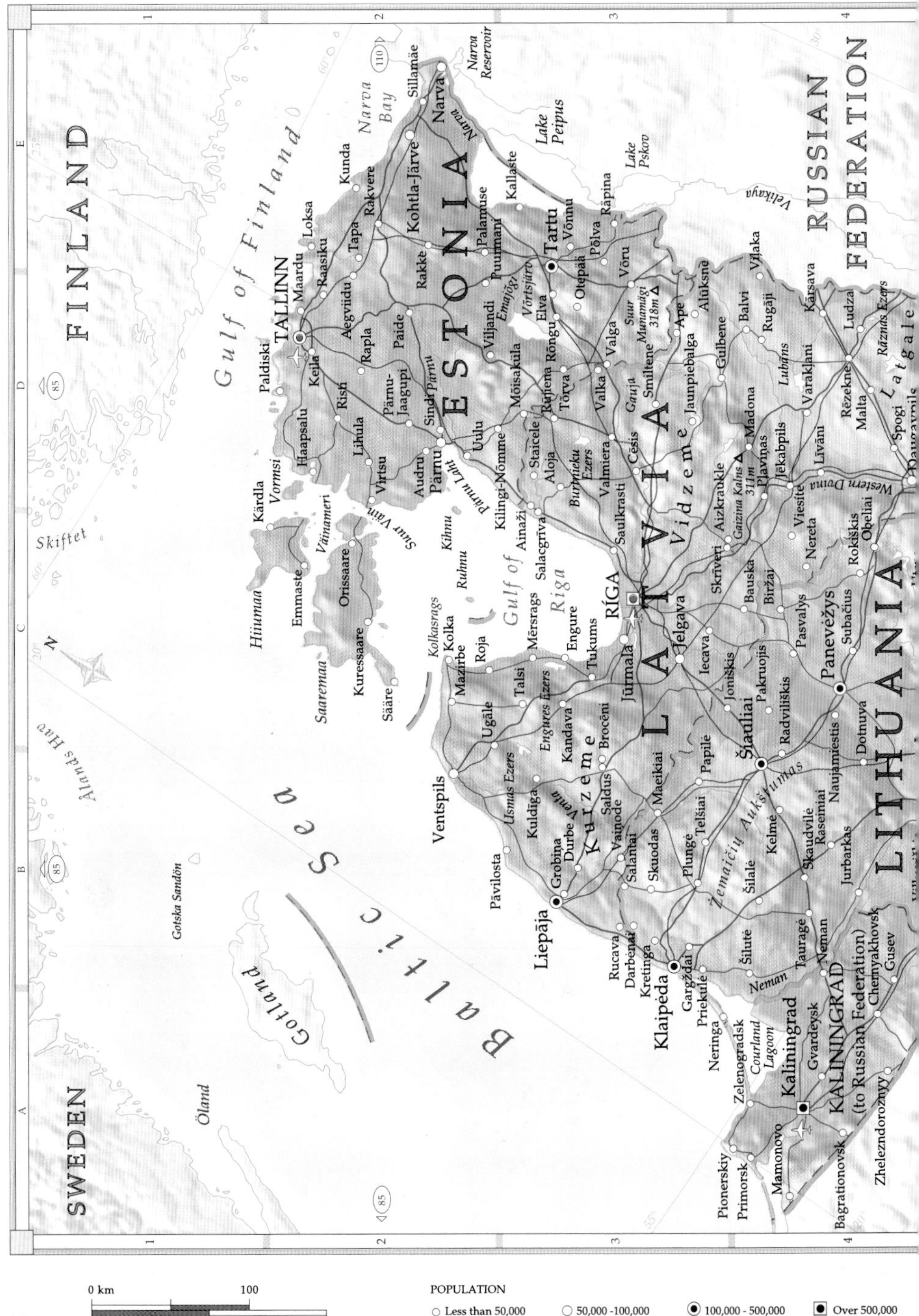

0 km 100

0 miles 100

POPULATION

○ Less than 50,000   ○ 50,000 -100,000   ◉ 100,000 - 500,000   ● Over 500,000

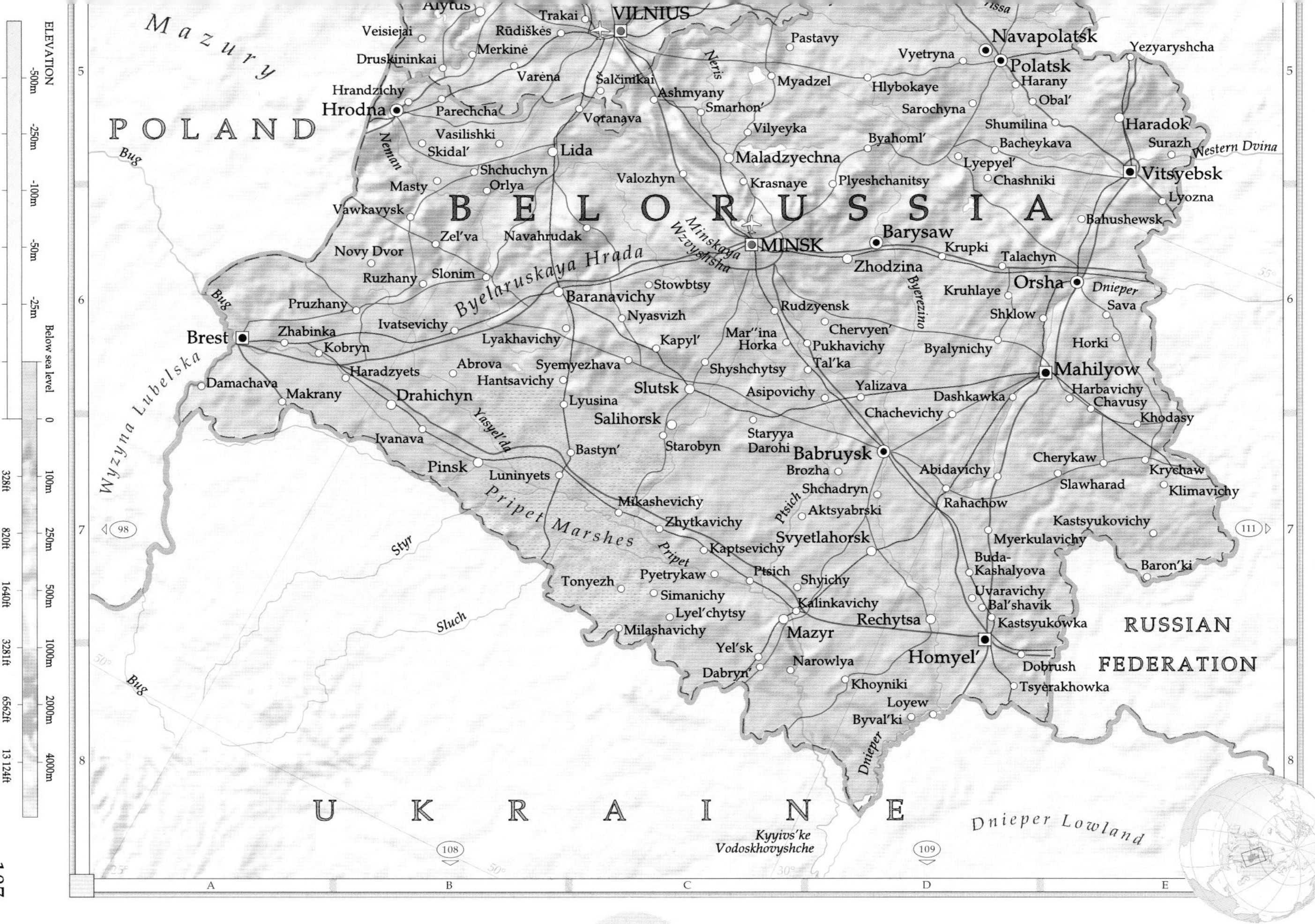

RUSSIAN FEDERATION

Dnieper Lowland

UKRAINE

Yezyaryshcha
Navapolatsk
Polatsk
Harany
Obal'
Shumilina
Bacheykava
Lyepyel'
Chashniki
Harodok
Surazh
Western Dvina
Vitsyebsk
Lyozna
Babushewsk
Dnieper
Sava
Mahilyow
Horki
Chavusy
Khodasy
Kryčaw
Klimavichy
Baron"ki
Navahrudak
Vyetryna
Hlybokaye
Sarodryna
Byahoml'
Plyeshchanitsy
Zhodzina
Byerezino
Barysaw
Krupka
Kruhlaye
Talachyn
Orsha
Shklow
Byalynichy
Dashkawka
Harbavichy
Slawharad
Cherykaw
Kastsyukovichy
Myerkulavichy
Buda-
Kashalyova
Uvaravichy
Bal'shavik
Kastsyukowka
Dobrush
Tsyerakhowka
Homyel'

Pastavy
Myadzel
Vilyeyka
Krasnaye
Smarhon'
Valozhyn
Maladzyechna
Minskaye Wzvyshsha
MINSK
Rudzyensk
Mar"ina Horka
Asipovichy
Babruysk
Brozha
Shchadryn
Aktsyabrski
Svyetlahorsk
Psich
Shyichy
Kalinkavichy
Rechytsa
Mazyr
Khoyniki
Loyew
Byval'ki
Dnieper
Narowlya

VILNIUS
Shchuchyn
Orlya
Lida
Ashmyany
Varanava
Navahrudak
Byelaruskaya Hrada
Stowbtsy
Nyasvizh
Kapyl'
Shyshchytsy
Staryya
Darohi
Starobyn
Slutsk
Salihorsk
Lyusina
Bastyn'
Mikashevichy
Zhytkavichy
Kaptsevichy
Lyel'chytsy
Milashavichy
Tonyezh
Yel'sk
Dabryn'
Pripet Marshes
Pripet

Vasilishki
Skidal'
Hrodna
Masty
Zel'va
Slonim
Ruzhany
Pruzhany
Zhabinka
Damachava
Makrany
Brest
Kobryn
Haradzyets
Drahichyn
Ivanava
Pinsk
Luninyets
Pyetrykaw
Simanichy
Yasyel'da
Styr
Shchara
Kyits"ke Vodoskhovyshche

Alytus
Veisiejai
Druskininkai
Merkine
Rūdiškės
Trakai
Varena
Parechcha
Hrandzichy
Neman
Vawkavysk
Novy Dvor
Ivatsevichy
Lyakhavichy
Abrova
Hantsavichy
Baranavichy
Syemyezhava

POLAND

Mazury
Bug
Wyżyna Lubelska

ELEVATION

	-500m	-250m	-100m	-50m	-25m	Below sea level	0	100m	250m	500m	1000m	2000m	4000m
	-1640ft	-820ft	-328ft	-164ft	-82ft	-33ft/-10m	0	328ft	820ft	1640ft	3281ft	6562ft	13 124ft

107

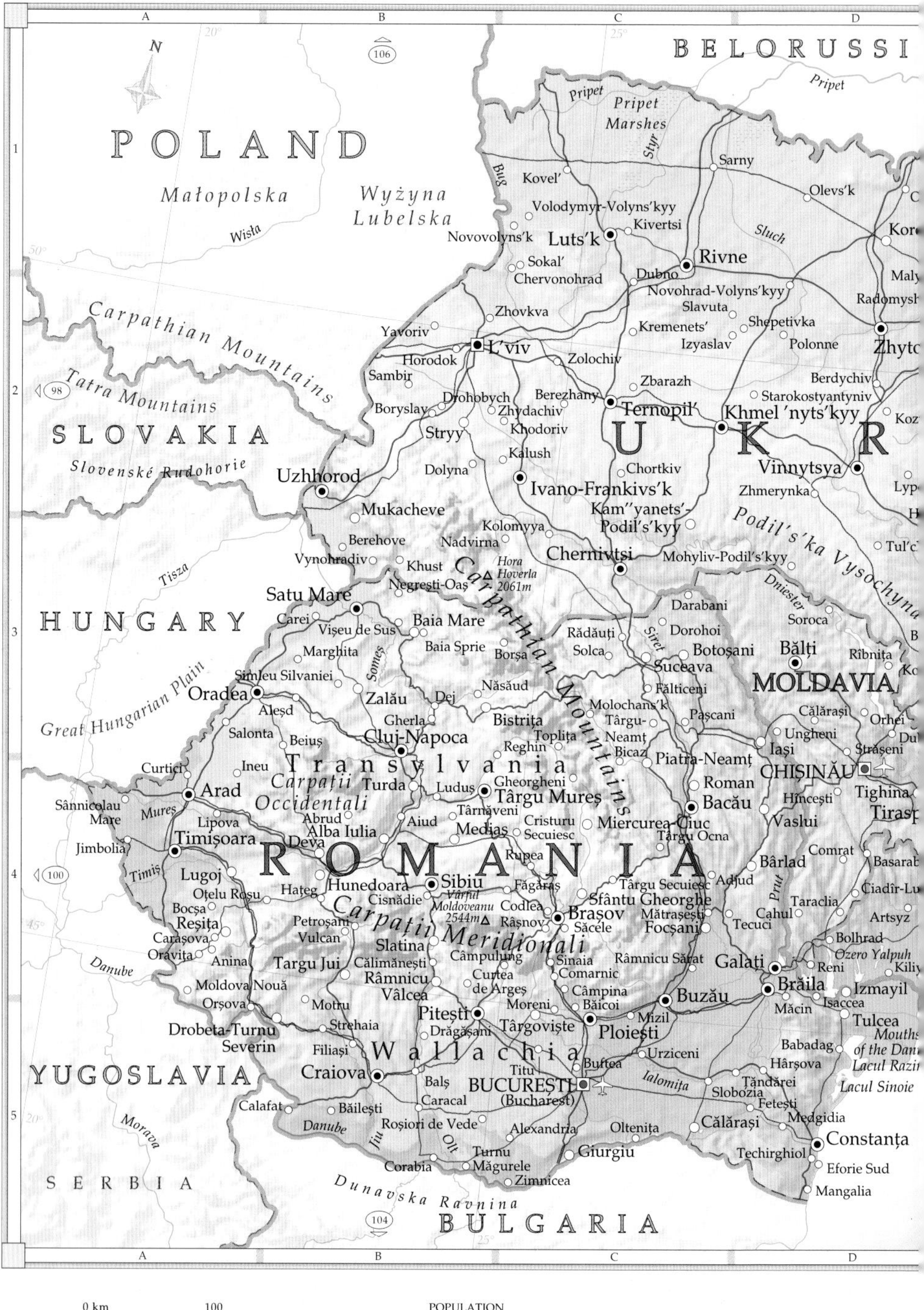

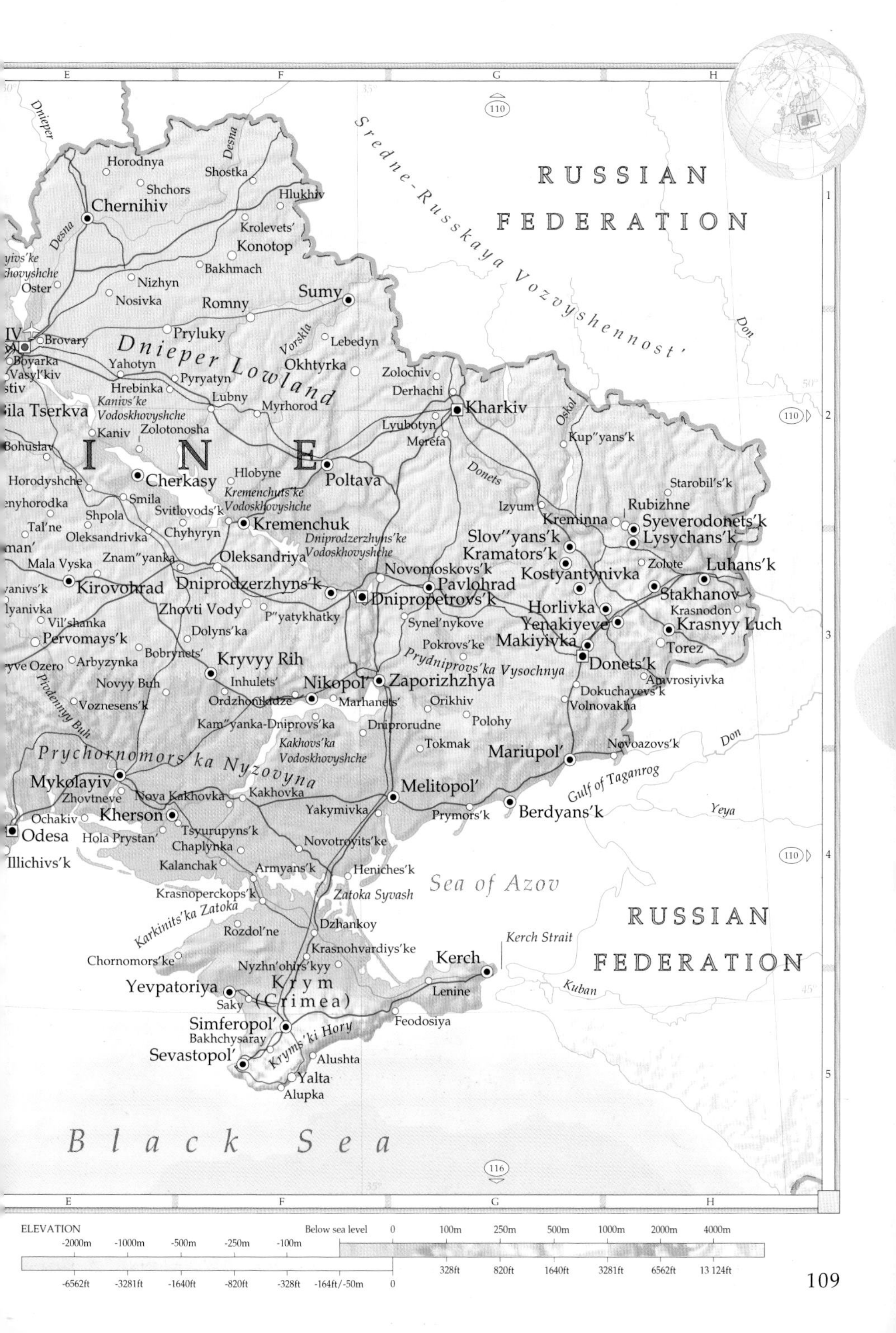

RUSSIAN

FEDERATION

Dnieper

Desna

Srednе-Russkaya Vozvyshennost'

Don

Horodnya
Shostka
Shchors
Hlukhiv
Chernihiv
Krolevets'
Konotop
Bakhmach
yivs'ke
chovyshche
Oster
Nizhyn
Nosivka
Romny
Sumy
Desna

Pryluky
IV
Brovary
Boyarka
Vasyl'kiv
stiv
Yahotyn
Pyryatyn
Hrebinka
Lubny
Kaniv

Pryluky
Vorskla
Lebedyn
Okhtyrka
Zolochiv
Derhachi

Dnieper Lowland

ila Tserkva
Vodoskhovyshche
Kaniv
Zolotonosha
Myrhorod
Kharkiv
Lyubotyn
Merefa
Okol
Kup"yans'k

Bohuslav

I   N   E

Horodyshche
enyhorodka
Shpola
Tal'ne
man'
Mala Vyska
Znam"yanka
yanivs'k
Kirovohrad
lyanivka
Vil'shanka
Pervomays'k
yve Ozero
Arbyzynka
Novyy Buh
Voznesens'k

Cherkasy
Smila
Svitlovods'k
Chyhyryn
Oleksandrivka

Hlobyne
Kremenchuts'ke
Vodoskhovyshche
Kremenchuk
Dniprodzerzhyns'ke
Vodoskhovyshche
Oleksandriya

Poltava

Donets

Starobil's'k

Izyum
Kreminna
Rubizhne
Syeverodonets'k
Lysychans'k
Zolote
Luhans'k

Slov"yans'k
Kramators'k
Novomoskovs'k
Pavlohrad
Kostyantynivka
Stakhanov
Krasnodon
Horlivka
Krasnyy Luch

Dniprodzerzhyns'k
Dnipropetrovs'k
Zhovti Vody
Dolyns'ka
P"yatykhatky
Synel'nykove
Pokrovs'ke
Makiyivka
Yenakiyeve
Torez

Kryvyy Rih
Inhulets'
Bobrynets'
Nikopol'
Zaporizhzhya
Prydniprovs'ka Vysochyna
Donets'k
Amvrosiyivka
Ordzhonikidze
Marhanets'
Orikhiv
Dokuchayevs'k
Volnovakha
Kam"yanka-Dniprovs'ka
Kahovs'ka
Vodoskhovyshche
Dniprorudne
Polohy
Tokmak

Prychornomors'ka Nyzovyna
Prydunnyy Buh

Mykolayiv
Zhovtneve
Nova Kakhovka
Kakhovka
Yakymivka
Melitopol'
Novoazovs'k
Don
Ochakiv
Kherson
Tsyurupyns'k
Chaplynka
Novotroyits'ke
Prymors'k
Berdyans'k
Gulf of Taganrog
Yeya
Odesa
Hola Prystan
Kalanchak
Armyans'k
Henichesk
Illichivs'k
Krasnoperekops'k
Zatoka Syvash
Sea of Azov

RUSSIAN

FEDERATION

Karkinits'ka Zatoka
Rozdol'ne
Dzhankoy
Krasnohvardiys'ke
Kerch
Kerch Strait
Chornomors'ke
Nyzhn'ohirs'kyy
Kerch
Kuban
Yevpatoriya
Saky
Krym
(Crimea)
Lenine
Simferopol'
Bakhchysaray
Feodosiya
Kryms'ki Hory
Sevastopol'
Alushta
Yalta
Alupka

B   l   a   c   k   S   e   a

ELEVATION

-2000m	-1000m	-500m	-250m	-100m	Below sea level	0	100m	250m	500m	1000m	2000m	4000m
-6562ft	-3281ft	-1640ft	-820ft	-328ft	-164ft/-50m	0			328ft	820ft	1640ft	3281ft	6562ft	13 124ft

EUROPEAN RUSSIA

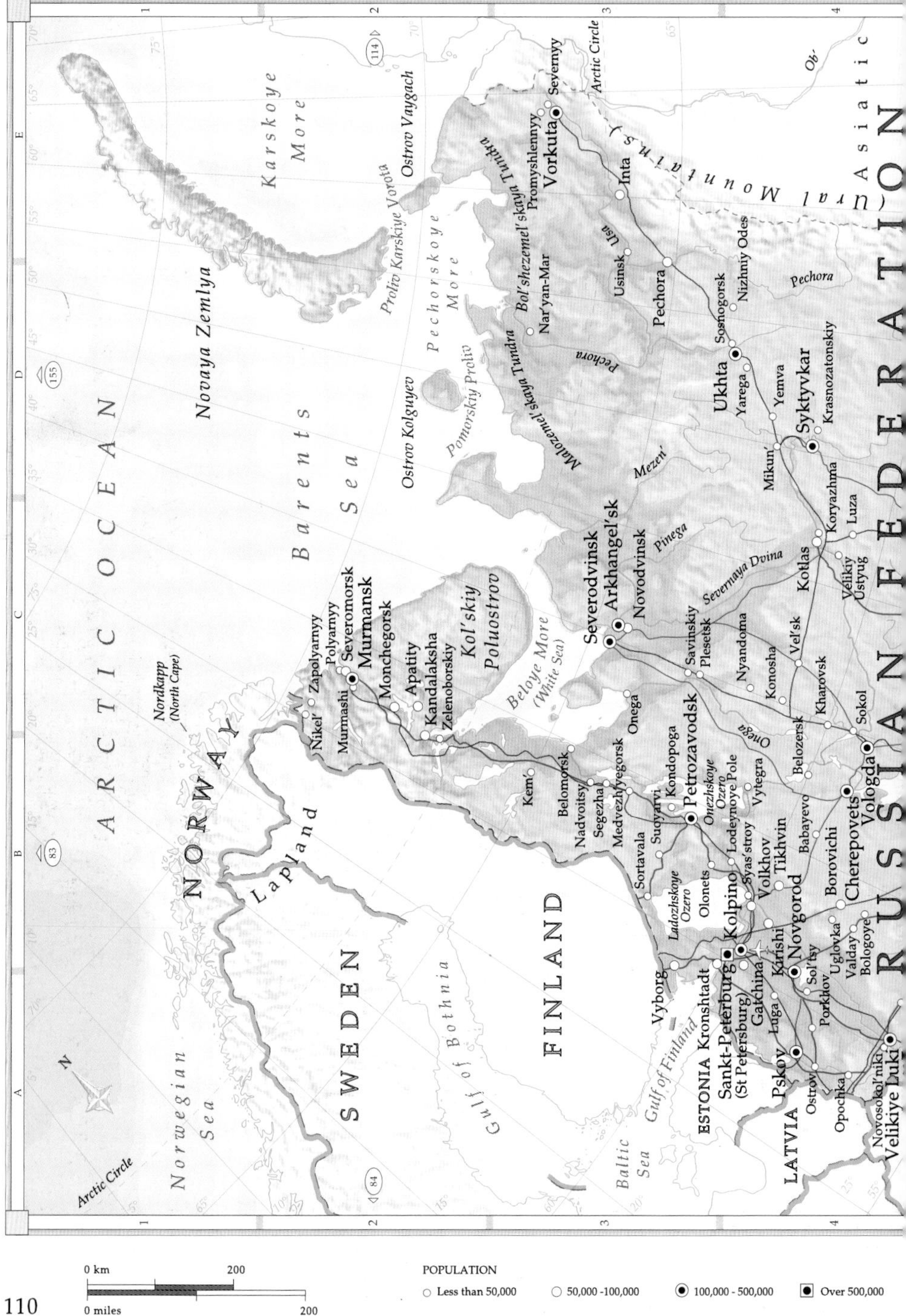

Karskoye More

114

Severnyy

Arctic Circle

Vorkuta

Promyshlennyy

Inta

Novaya Zemlya

Ostrov Vaygach

Prolivy Karskiye Vorota

Bol'shezemel'skaya Tundra

Usinsk

Pechora

Nizhniy Odes

Pechora

155

Ob'

Asiatic

Ostrov Kolguyev

Pomorskiy Proliv

Naryan-Mar

Ukhta

Yarega

Sosnogorsk

Yemva

Krasnozatonskiy

Syktyvkar

Malozemel'skaya Tundra

Pechorskoye More

Mezen'

Mikun'

Koryazhma

Pechora

Barents Sea

Severodvinsk

Arkhangel'sk

Novodvinsk

Pinega

Mezen'

Severnaya Dvina

Vel'sk

Kotlas

Velikiy Ustyug

Luza

ARCTIC OCEAN

Nordkapp
(North Cape)

Kol'skiy Poluostrov

Beloye More
(White Sea)

Onega

Savinskiy

Plesetsk

Nyandoma

Konosha

Kharovsk

Sokol

RUSSIAN FEDERATION

Zapolyarnyy

Polyarnyy

Severomorsk

Murmansk

Monchegorsk

Apatity

Kandalaksha

Zelenoborskiy

Nikel'

Murmashi

Kem'

Onega

NORWAY

Belomorsk

Nadvoitsy

Segezha

Medvezh'yegorsk

Kondopoga

Petrozavodsk

Onezhskoye Ozero

Lodeynoye Pole

Belozersk

Babayevo

Vologda

Cherepovets

155

83

Lapland

Sortavala

Sudyarvi

Onega

Vytegra

Borovichi

SWEDEN

FINLAND

Ladozhskoye Ozero

Olonets

Svyas'stroy

Volkhov

Tikhvin

Valday

Bologoye

Uglovka

Norwegian Sea

Vyborg

Kronshtadt

Sankt-Peterburg
(St Petersburg)

Kolpino

Novgorod

Sol'tsy

Gatchina

Luga

Ostrov

Porkhov

Baltic Sea

Gulf of Bothnia

Gulf of Finland

ESTONIA

Pskov

Opochka

Novosokol'niki

Velikiye Luki

84

Arctic Circle

LATVIA

0 km   200

0 miles   200

POPULATION

○ Less than 50,000   ○ 50,000 -100,000   ◉ 100,000 - 500,000   ■ Over 500,000

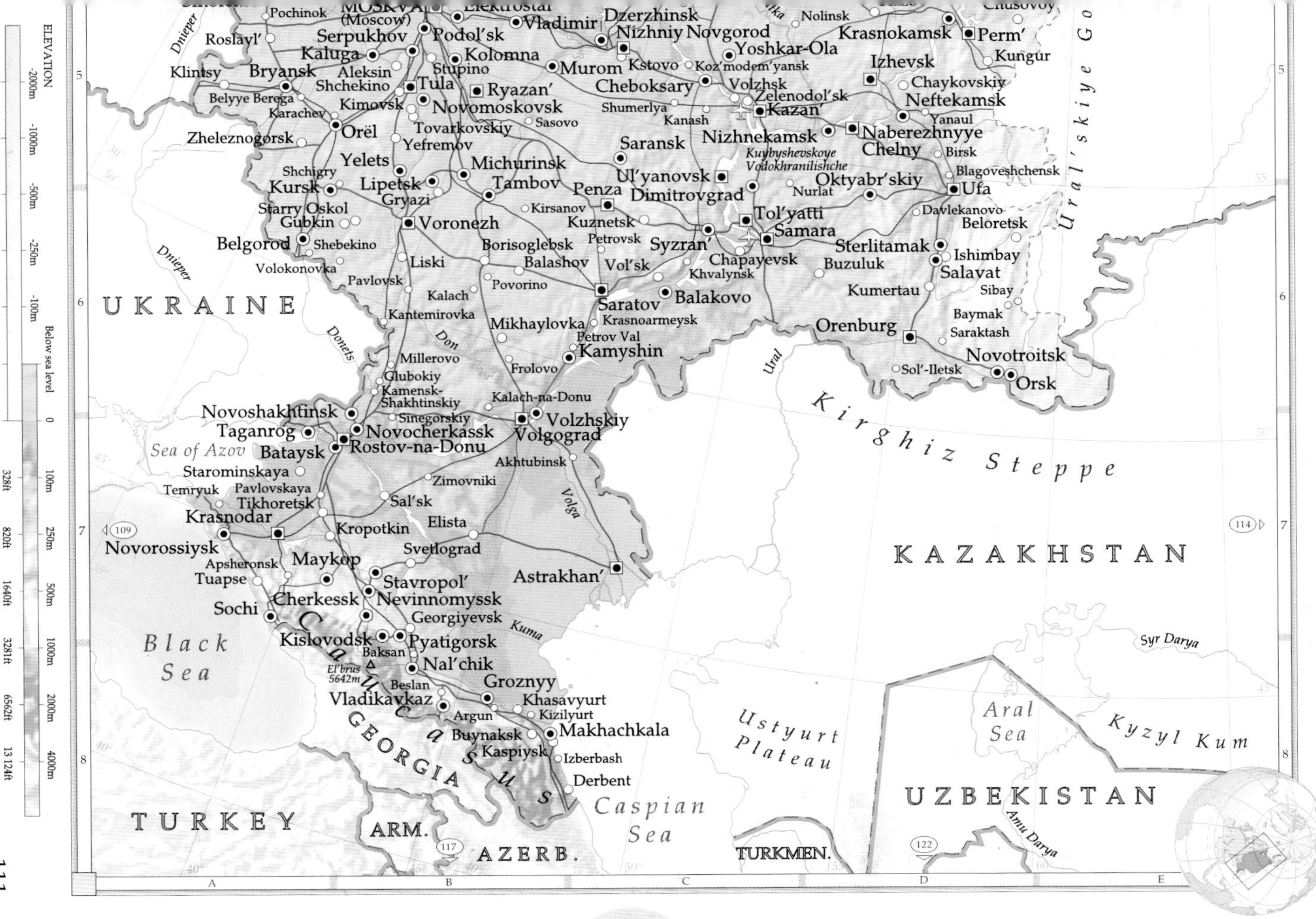

ELEVATION

				Below sea level	0	100m	250m	500m	1000m	2000m	4000m
-2000m	-1000m	-500m	-250m	-100m							
-6562ft	-3281ft	-1640ft	-820ft	-328ft	-164ft/-50m	0	328ft	820ft	1640ft	3281ft	6562ft	13 124ft

NORTH & WEST ASIA

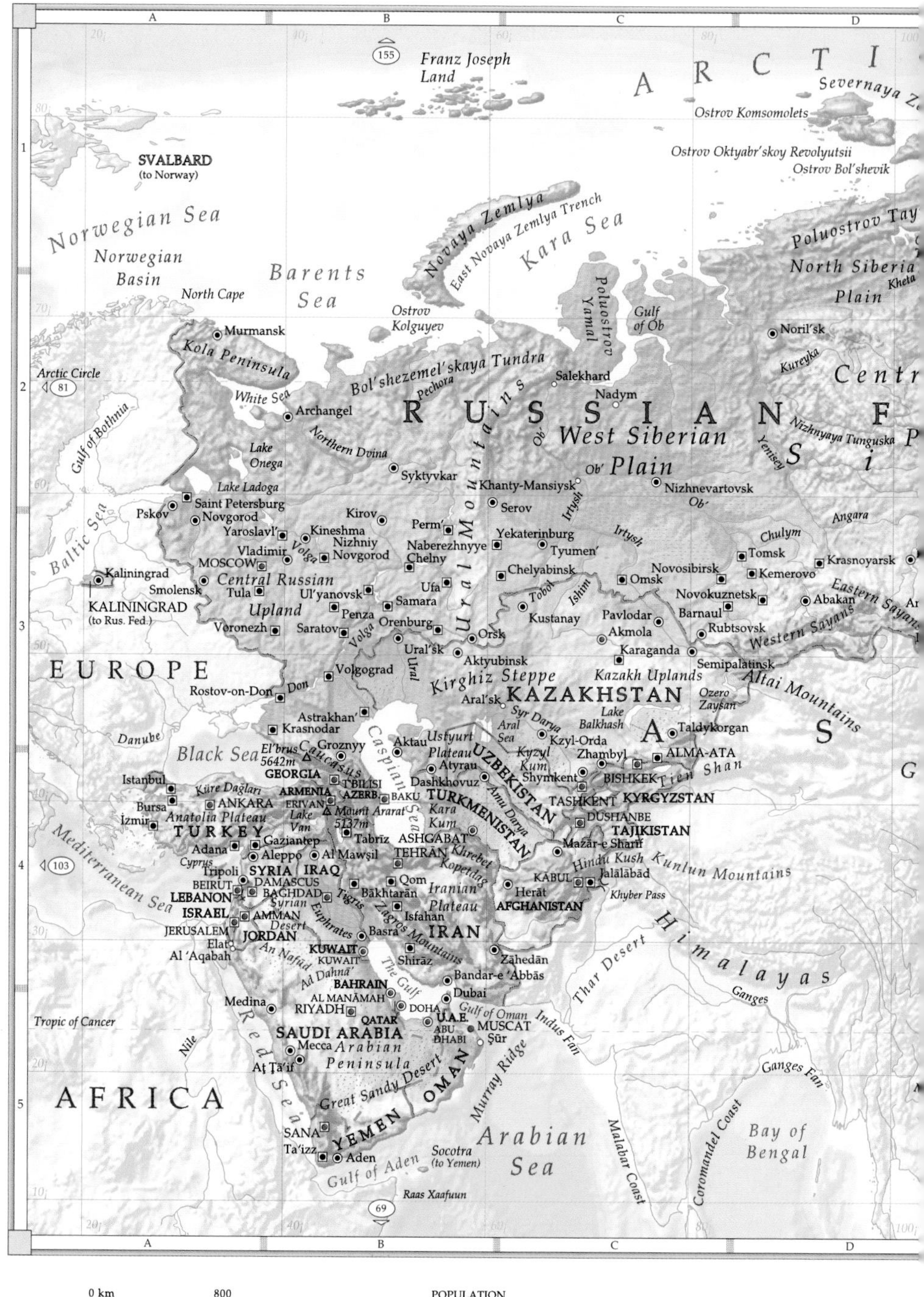

155

Franz Joseph
Land

A R C T I

Severnaya Z.

Ostrov Komsomolets

SVALBARD
(to Norway)

Ostrov Oktyabr'skoy Revolyutsii
Ostrov Bol'shevik

Norwegian Sea

Norwegian
Basin

North Cape

Barents
Sea

Novaya Zemlya

East Novaya Zemlya Trench

Kara Sea

Poluostrov Tay

North Siberia
Plain
Khela

Ostrov
Kolguyev

Gulf
of Ob

poluostrov
Yamal

Murmansk

Kola Peninsula

Arctic Circle 81

White Sea

Archangel

Bol'shezemel'skaya Tundra

Pechora

Salekhard

Nadym

Noril'sk

Kureyka

Centr

Lake
Onega

Northern Dvina

R U S S I A N   F

Ob'

West Siberian

Yenisey

Nizhnyaya Tunguska

Si

P

Lake Ladoga

Syktyvkar

Khanty-Mansiysk

Plain

Ob'

Nizhnevartovsk

Angara

Saint Petersburg
Pskov   Novgorod
Yaroslavl'
Vladimir   Kineshma
MOSCOW   Nizhniy
Novgorod

Kirov

Perm'

Serov

Yekaterinburg

Ob'

Tobol

Tyumen'

Irtysh

Irtysh

Ishim

Chulym

Tomsk

Kemerovo

Krasnoyarsk

Eastern Sayans

Kaliningrad
Smolensk
KALININGRAD
(to Rus. Fed.)

Central Russian
Tula
Upland

Ul'yanovsk

Ufa

Naberezhnyye
Chelny

Chelyabinsk

Samara

Omsk

Novosibirsk

Novokuznetsk

Abakan

Ar

Voronezh

Penza
Saratov

Orenburg

Orsk

Kustanay

Pavlodar
Akmola

Barnaul

Rubtsovsk

Western Sayans

EUROPE

Danube

Rostov-on-Don

Don

Volgograd

Ural

Volga

Ural'sk

Aktyubinsk

Kirghiz Steppe

Karaganda

Kazakh Uplands

Semipalatinsk

Altai Mountains

Ural Mountains

Aral'sk

KAZAKHSTAN

A

S

Black Sea

Astrakhan'
Krasnodar

El'brus
5642m

Groznyy

Aktau

Syr Darya

Aral
Sea

Ustyurt
Plateau

UZBEKISTAN

Atyrau

Kyzyl
Kum

Lake
Balkhash

Taldykorgan

Ozero
Zaysan

Kzyl-Orda

Zhambyl

ALMA-ATA

Tien Shan

G

Istanbul
Bursa
Izmir

Kure Daglari

GEORGIA
T'BILISI

ARMENIA

Caucasus

Caspian Sea

Shymkent

BISHKEK

KYRGYZSTAN

Anatolia Plateau
TURKEY

Lake
Van

ERIVAN
AZERB.

BAKU

Dashkhovuz

Amu Darya

Kara
Kum

TASHKENT

DUSHANBE

TAJIKISTAN

Gaziantep

Mount Ararat
5137m

Tabriz

ASHGABAT

TURKMENISTAN

Mazar-e Sharif

Adana
Cyprus
Tripoli

Aleppo
SYRIA   IRAQ

Al Mawsil

TEHRAN

Qom

Kopet Dag

Herat

KABUL

Hindu Kush

Jalalabad

Kunlun Mountains

BEIRUT
LEBANON
ISRAEL
JERUSALEM

DAMASCUS
BAGHDAD

Bakhtaran

Iranian
Plateau

AFGHANISTAN

Khyber Pass

AMMAN
JORDAN

Tigris

Euphrates

Syrian
Desert

Basra

Isfahan

Zagros Mountains

IRAN

Himalayas

Elat
Al 'Aqabah

KUWAIT
KUWAIT

An Nafud

Shiraz

Zahedan

Thar Desert

Ganges

Ad Dahna'

Bandar-e 'Abbas

BAHRAIN

The Gulf

Dubai

Medina

AL MANAMAH
RIYADH

QATAR

DOHA

UAE

ABU
DHABI

Gulf of Oman

MUSCAT

Sur

Indus Fan

Ganges Fan

Tropic of Cancer

Nile

SAUDI ARABIA
Mecca
At Ta'if

Red Sea

Arabian
Peninsula

OMAN

Murray Ridge

Coromandel Coast

Bay of
Bengal

AFRICA

Great Sandy Desert

Malabar Coast

Arabian
Sea

SANA
Ta'izz
YEMEN
Aden

Socotra
(to Yemen)

Gulf of Aden

Raas Xaafuun

69

0 km   800
0 miles   800

POPULATION

○ Less than 50,000   ◉ 50,000 -100,000   ◉ 100,000 - 500,000   ◼ Over 500,000

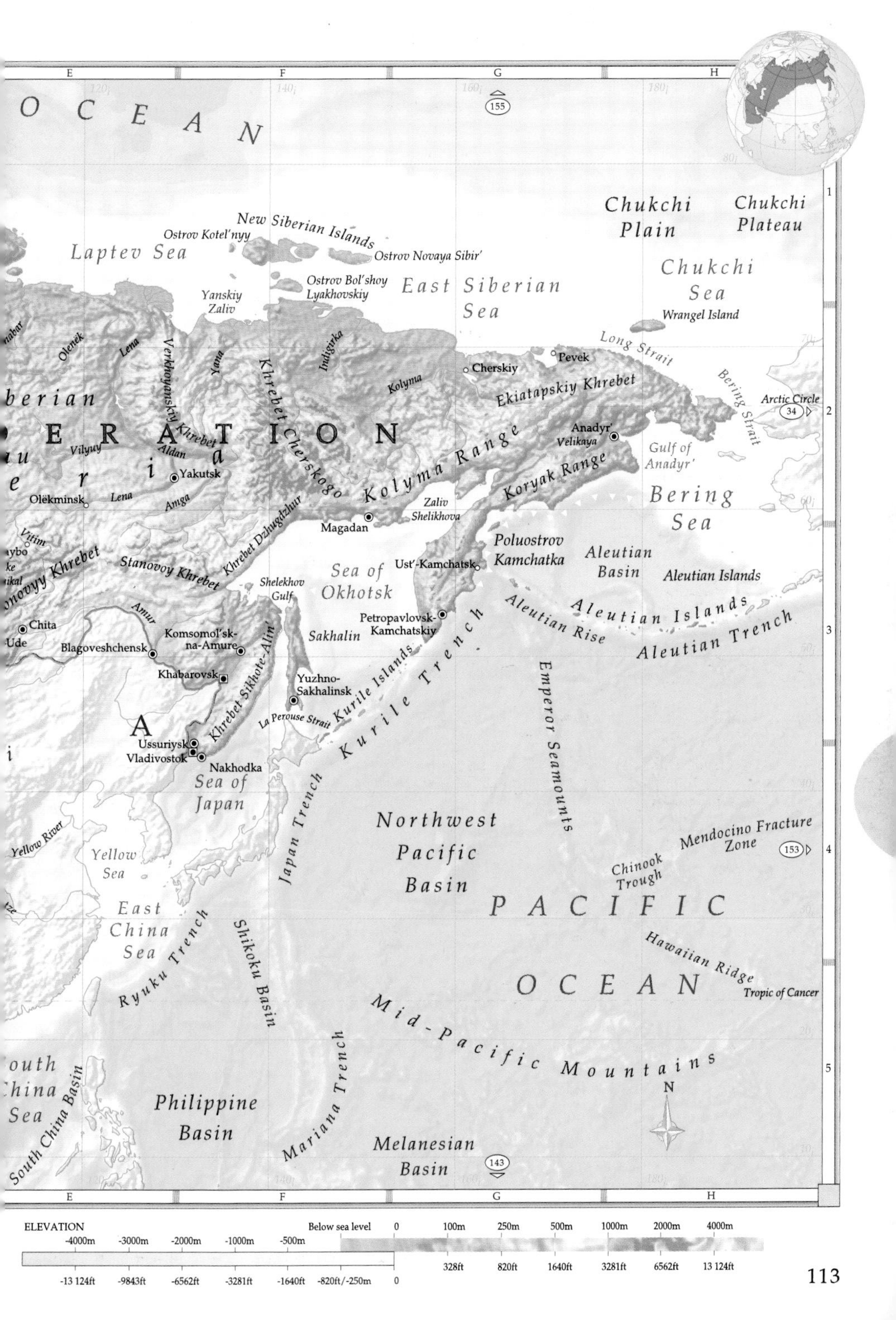

O C E A N

Laptev Sea

New Siberian Islands
Ostrov Kotel'nyy
Ostrov Novaya Sibir'

Yanskiy
Zaliv

Ostrov Bol'shoy
Lyakhovskiy

East Siberian
Sea

Chukchi
Plain

Chukchi
Plateau

Chukchi
Sea

Wrangel Island

Olenek
Lena
Verkhoyanskiy
Khrebet
Yana
Indigirka

Khrebet Cherskogo

Kolyma

Cherskiy
Pevek

Long Strait

Bering Strait

Arctic Circle
34

e r i a n

b e r i a n

E R A T I O N

Vilyuy
Aldan
Yakutsk

Ekiatapskiy Khrebet

Anadyr'
Velikaya

Gulf of
Anadyr'

u
e r i a

Olekminsk
Lena
Amga

Kolyma Range

Zaliv
Shelikhova

Koryak Range

Bering
Sea

Vitim
aybo
ke
ikal
novyy Khrebet

Stanovoy Khrebet

Khrebet Dzhugdzhur

Magadan

Ust'-Kamchatsk

Poluostrov
Kamchatka

Aleutian
Basin

Aleutian Islands

Chita
Ude

Amur
Komsomol'sk-
na-Amure

Shelekhov
Gulf

Sea of
Okhotsk

Petropavlovsk-
Kamchatskiy

Aleutian Rise

Aleutian Islands

Aleutian Trench

Blagoveshchensk

Khabarovsk

Sakhalin

Khrebet Sikhote-Alin'

Yuzhno-
Sakhalinsk

La Perouse Strait

Kurile Islands

Kurile Trench

Emperor Seamounts

A

Ussuriysk
Vladivostok
Nakhodka

Sea of
Japan

Japan Trench

Northwest
Pacific
Basin

Chinook
Trough

Mendocino Fracture
Zone
153

i

Yellow River

Yellow
Sea

East
China
Sea

Ryuku Trench

Shikoku Basin

P A C I F I C

Hawaiian Ridge

Tropic of Cancer

O C E A N

outh
China
Sea

South China Basin

Philippine
Basin

Mariana Trench

Mid-Pacific Mountains

N

Melanesian
Basin
143

155

ELEVATION

-4000m	-3000m	-2000m	-1000m	-500m	Below sea level	0	100m	250m	500m	1000m	2000m	4000m

							328ft	820ft	1640ft	3281ft	6562ft	13 124ft

| -13 124ft | -9843ft | -6562ft | -3281ft | -1640ft | -820ft/-250m | 0 | | | | | | |

RUSSIA & KAZAKHSTAN

NORWAY
DENMARK
SWEDEN
GERMANY
Baltic Sea
KALININGRAD
(to Rus. Fed.)
POLAND
Kaliningrad
LITH.
EST.
LAT.
BELORUSSIA
UKRAINE
Bryansk
Belgorod
Voronezh
Mikhaylovka
Rostov-na-Donu
Krasnodar
Sochi
Stavropol'
El'brus
5642m
Nal'chik
Vladikavkaz
Groznyy
Makhachkala
GEORGIA
ARM.
AZERBAIJAN

SVALBARD
(to Norway)

Arctic Circle
83
Gulf of Bothnia
FINLAND
Nordkapp
(North Cape)
Barents Sea
Murmansk
Olenegorsk
Kandalaksha
Kol'skiy Poluostrov
Severodvinsk
Arkhangel'sk
Belove More
Pskov
Novgorod
Petrozavodsk
Onezhskoye Ozero
Cherepovets
Smolensk
Tver
MOSKVA
(Moscow)
Tula
Ryazan'
Tambov
Penza
Ul'yanovsk
Saratov
Balakovo
Volgograd
Ural'sk
Orenburg
Astrakhan'
Aktyubinsk
Atyrau
Alga
Fort-Shevchenko
Aktau
Novyy Uzen'
Chelkar

Sankt-Peterburg
Ladozhskoye Ozero
Vologda
Yaroslavl'
Kineshma
Kotlas
Vladimir
Nizhniy Novgorod
Kazan'
Kotel'nich
Glazov
Izhevsk
Naberezhnyye
Tol'yatti
Chelny
Samara
Sterlitamak
Magnitogorsk
Orsk
Dzhetygara

Zemlya Frantsa Iosifa
ARCT
Novaya Zemlya
Ostrov Belyy
Dikson
Karskoye More
Ostrov Kolguyev
Nar'yan-Mar
Bol'shezemel'skaya Tundra
Pechora
Vorkuta
Salekhard
Noril'
Igarka
Nadym
Poluostrov Yamal
Obskaya Guba
Zapadno-
Sibirskaya
Ravnina
RUSSIAN
Khanty-Mansiysk
Nizhnevartovsk
Yekaterinburg
Tyumen'
Tobol'sk
Chelyabinsk
Ishim
Rudnyy
Petropavlovsk
Kustanay
Omsk
Tomsk
Novosibirsk
Krasnoya
Kemerov
Barnaul
Novokuznetsk
Aba
Semipalatinsk
Leninogorsk
Zyryanovsk
Gora Belukha
4506m
Altai Mountains
Chulym
Stre

Vologda
Severnaya Dvina
Konosha
Vel'sk
Mezen'
Syktyvkar
Perm'
Serov
Ural'skiye Gory

Black Sea
Sea of Azov
Don
Caucasus
Caspian Sea
TURKMENISTAN
Ustyurt Plateau
Aral Sea
UZBEKISTAN
Kazakhskiy Melkosopochnik
KAZAKHSTAN
Aral'sk
Novokazalinsk
Zhezkazgan
Dzhusaly
Kzyl-Orda
Kyzyl Kum
Sur Darya
Turkestan
Shymkent
Arys'
Kentau
Karatau
Zhambyl
Chu
Kazakhskiy Melkosopochnik
Charsk
Ust'-Kamenogorsk
Balkhash
Ayaguz
Ozero Zaysan
Ozero Balkhash
Lapat
Kokshetau
Atbasar
Shchuchinsk
Akmola
Temirtau
Saran'
Shakhtinsk
Karaganda
Yermak
Kulundinskaya Step'
Alakol'
Charsk
Taldykorgan
Tekeli
ALMATY
(Alma-Ata)
Arys'

IRAN
TURKMENISTAN
TAJIKISTAN
AFGHANISTAN
122
KYRGYZSTAN
Tien Shan
CHINA
Kirgiz Range

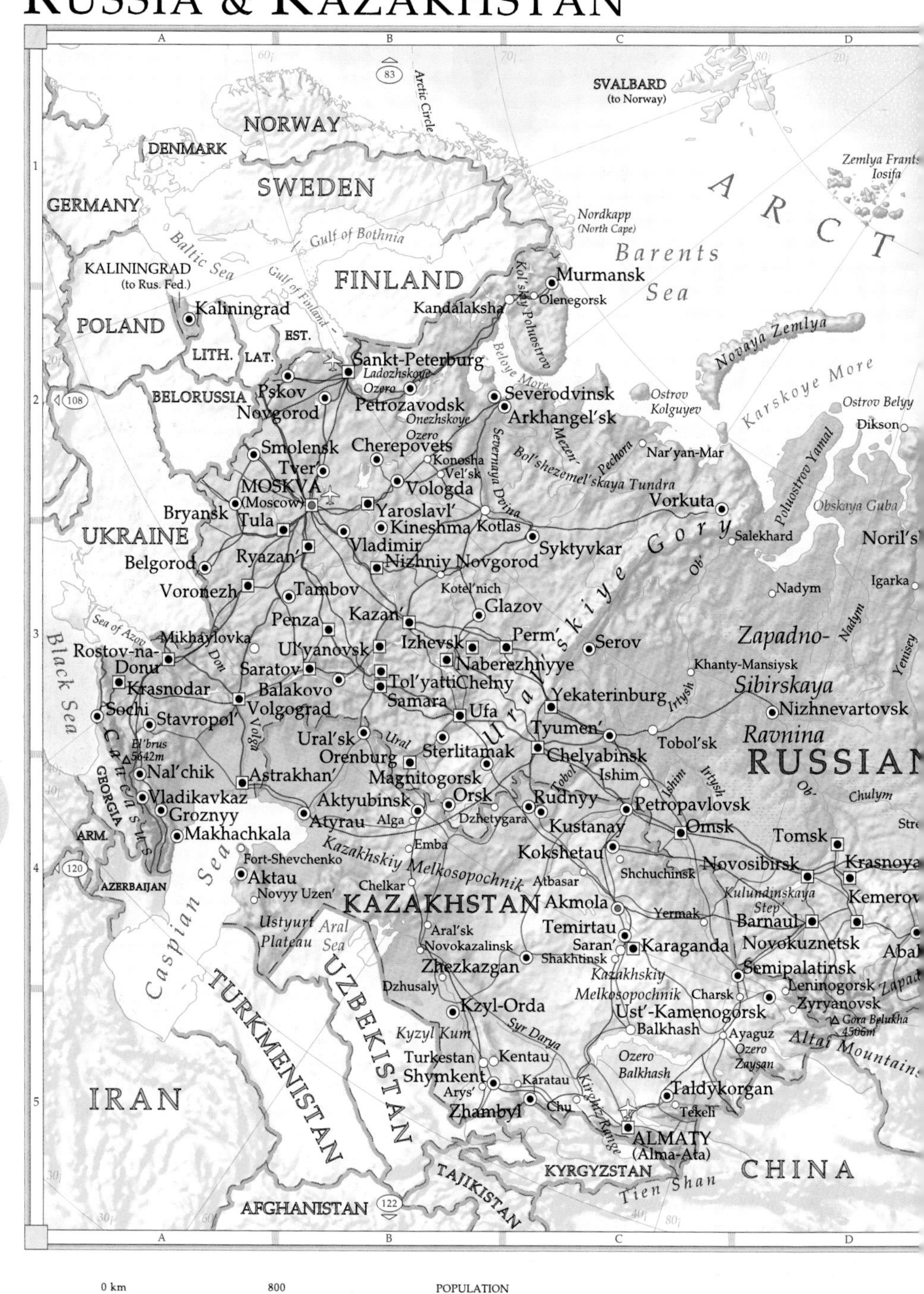

0 km   800
0 miles   800

POPULATION
○ Less than 50,000
◔ 50,000 -100,000
◉ 100,000 - 500,000
◼ Over 500,000

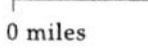

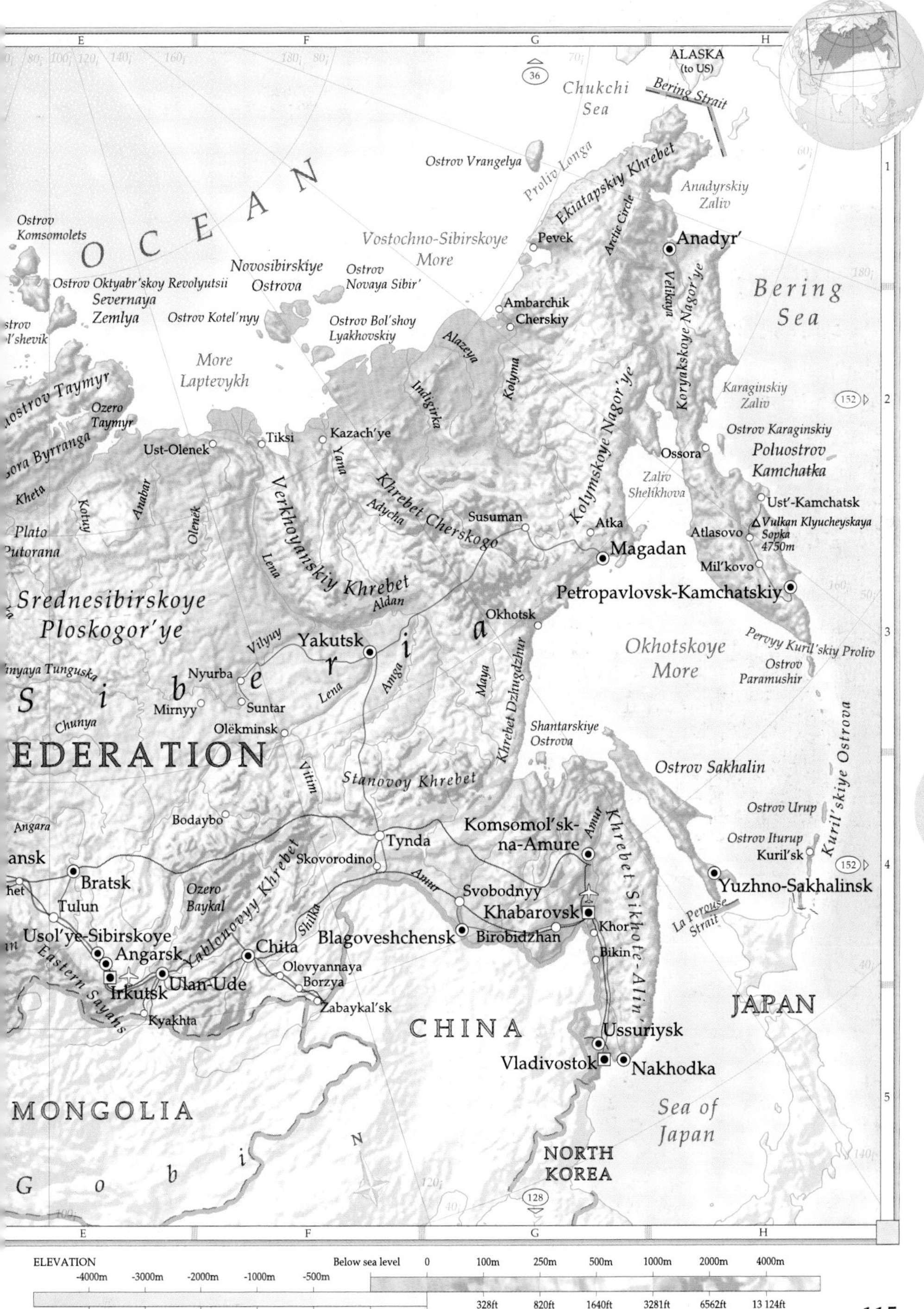

ALASKA
(to US)

Chukchi
Sea

Bering Strait

Ostrov Vrangelya

Proliv Longa

Ekiatapskiy Khrebet

Anadyrskiy
Zaliv

Vostochno-Sibirskoye
More

Pevek

Arctic Circle

Anadyr'

Bering
Sea

Ostrov
Komsomolets

Ostrov Oktyabr'skoy Revolyutsii
Severnaya
Zemlya

Novosibirskiye
Ostrova

Ostrov
Novaya Sibir'

Ambarchik
Cherskiy

Velikaya

Koryakskoye Nagor'ye

strov
l'shevik

Ostrov Kotel'nyy

Ostrov Bol'shoy
Lyakhovskiy

Alazeya

Karaginskiy
Zaliv

152

More
Laptevykh

Kolyma

Kolymskoye Nagor'ye

Ossora

Ostrov Karaginskiy
Poluostrov
Kamchatka

ostrov Taymyr

Ozero
Taymyr

Ust-Olenek

Tiksi

Kazach'ye

Indigirka

Yana

Khrebet Cherskogo

Adycha

Susuman

Zaliv
Shelikhova

Atka

Ust'-Kamchatsk

ora Byrranga

Kheta

Katuy

Anabar

Olenëk

Verkhoyanskiy Khrebet

Atlasovo

Vulkan Klyucheyskaya
Sopka
4750m

Plato
Putorana

Lena

Khrebet

Aldan

Magadan

Mil'kovo

Srednesibirskoye
Ploskogor'ye

imaya Tunguska

Vilyuy

Yakutsk

Lena

Amga

Maya

a

Okhotsk

Petropavlovsk-Kamchatskiy

Okhotskoye
More

Pervyy Kuril'skiy Proliv

Ostrov
Paramushir

S i b

Nyurba

e

r

i

S

Chunya

Mirnyy

Suntar

Olëkminsk

Vitim

Khrebet Dzhugdzhur

Shantarskiye
Ostrova

Ostrov Sakhalin

Ostrov Urup

EDERATION

Angara

Bodaybo

Stanovoy Khrebet

Komsomol'sk-
na-Amure

Ostrov Iturup
Kuril'sk

Kuril'skiye Ostrova

ansk

het

Bratsk
Tulun

Tynda

Skovorodino

Anuy

Svobodnyy

Amur

Khrebet Sikhote-Alin'

152

Yuzhno-Sakhalinsk

Ozero
Baykal

Yablonovyy Khrebet

Shilka

Khabarovsk

La Perouse
Strait

Usol'ye-Sibirskoye
Angarsk

Chita

Blagoveshchensk

Birobidzhan

Khor

JAPAN

Eastern Sayans

Irkutsk
Ulan-Ude

Olovyannaya
Borzya

Bikin

Kyakhta

Zabaykal'sk

CHINA

Ussuriysk

MONGOLIA

N

Vladivostok

Nakhodka

Sea of
Japan

G

o

b

i

NORTH
KOREA

128

ELEVATION

-4000m	-3000m	-2000m	-1000m	-500m	Below sea level 0	100m	250m	500m	1000m	2000m	4000m
-13 124ft	-9843ft	-6562ft	-3281ft	-1640ft	-820ft/-250m 0	328ft	820ft	1640ft	3281ft	6562ft	13 124ft

115

TURKEY & THE CAUCASUS

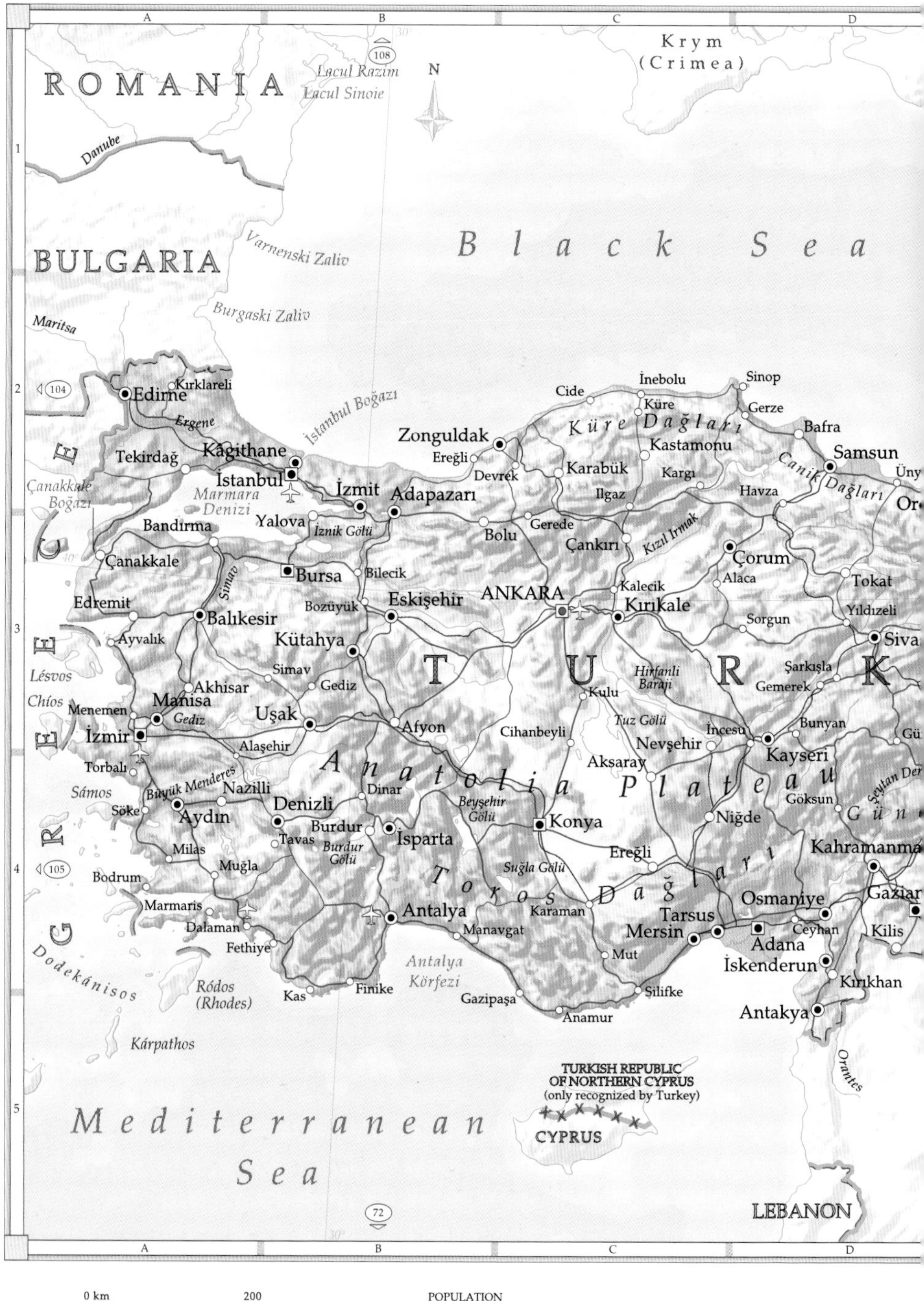

ROMANIA

BULGARIA

Krym
(Crimea)

Black Sea

Lacul Razim
Lacul Sinoie

108

Danube

N

Varnenski Zaliv

Burgaski Zaliv

Maritsa

104

Edirne

Kırklareli

Ergene

Tekirdağ

Kağithane

Istanbul

İzmit

Adapazarı

Zonguldak

Ereğli

Devrek

Karabük

Cide

İnebolu

Küre

Sinop

Gerze

Küre Dağları

Kastamonu

Kargı

Ilgaz

Bafra

Samsun

Üny

Or

Çanakkale
Boğazı

Marmara
Denizi

Yalova

İznik Gölü

Bandırma

Çanakkale

Bursa

Bilecik

Bozüyük

Eskişehir

ANKARA

Bolu

Gerede

Çankırı

Kızıl Irmak

Caniç Dağları

Havza

Çorum

Alaca

Kalecik

Kırıkale

Tokat

Yıldızeli

Edremit

Ayvalık

Balıkesir

Kütahya

Simav

Gediz

TURK

Sorgun

Hirfanlı
Barajı

Kulu

Şarkışla

Gemerek

Siva

K

Lésvos

Chíos

Menemen

İzmir

Akhisar

Manisa

Gediz

Uşak

Alaşehir

Afyon

Cihanbeyli

Tuz Gölü

Nevşehir

İncesu

Bunyan

Kayseri

Gü

Seyhan Der

Torbalı

Sámos

Söke

Büyük Menderes

Nazilli

Aydın

Denizli

Dinar

Beyşehir
Gölü

Aksaray

Niğde

Göksun

Gün

Anatolia Plateau

Milas

Tavas

Burdur
Gölü

Burdur

Isparta

Suğla Gölü

Konya

Ereğli

Karaman

Kahramanma

Muğla

Bodrum

Marmaris

Dalaman

Fethiye

Antalya

Manavgat

Mut

Mersin

Tarsus

Ceyhan

Osmaniye

Adana

İskenderun

Gaziar

Kilis

Kırıkhan

Toros Dağları

Dodekánisos

Ródos
(Rhodes)

Kas

Finike

Antalya
Körfezi

Gazipaşa

Silifke

Anamur

Antakya

Orantes

Kárpathos

Mediterranean
Sea

72

TURKISH REPUBLIC
OF NORTHERN CYPRUS
(only recognized by Turkey)

CYPRUS

LEBANON

0 km   200

0 miles   200

POPULATION

○ Less than 50,000
○ 50,000 -100,000
◉ 100,000 - 500,000
■ Over 500,000

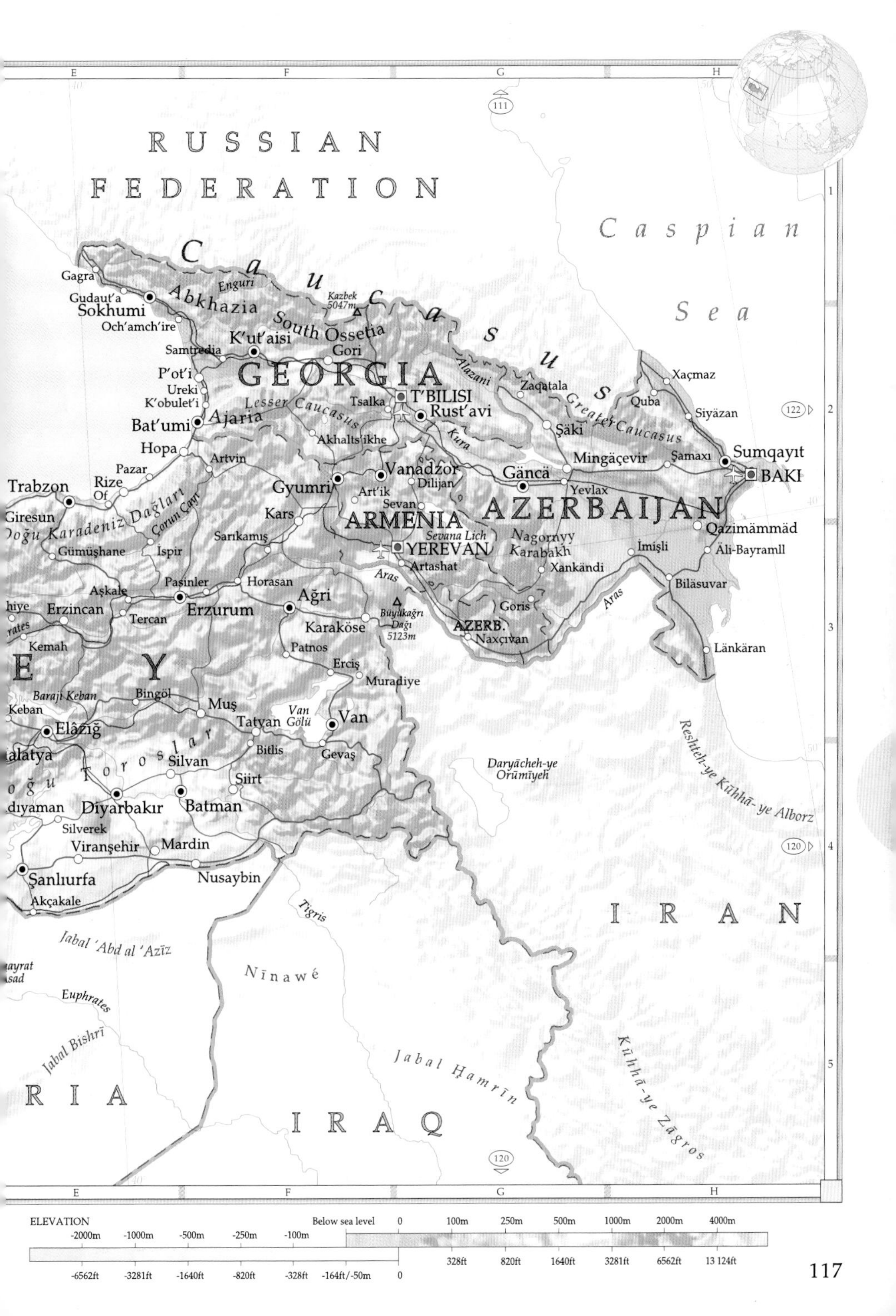

RUSSIAN
FEDERATION

Caspian

Sea

Caucasus

Gagra
Gudaut'a
Sokhumi
Och'amch'ire
Abkhazia
Enguri
Kazbek
5047m
South Ossetia
Samtredia
K'ut'aisi
Gori

Xaçmaz

P'ot'i
Ureki
K'obulet'i
Lesser Caucasus
Tsalka
Alazani
Zaqatala
Quba
Siyäzan

GEORGIA
T'BILISI
Rust'avi
Kura
Säki

Bat'umi
Ajaria
Akhalts'ikhe
Mingäçevir
Şamaxı
Sumqayıt

Hopa
Artvin
Vanadzor
Dilijan
Gäncä
BAKI

Pazar
Rize
Of
Gyumri
Art'ik
Sevan
Yevlax
Qazimämmäd

Trabzon
Daǧlari
Kars
Sarıkamış
ARMENIA
Sevana Lich
YEREVAN
Artashat
Nagornyy
Karabakh
Xankändi
İmişli
Äli-Bayramll

Giresun
Gümüşhane
İspir
Doǧu Karadeniz
Çoruh Çayı
AZERBAIJAN

Biläsuvar

hiye
Aşkale
Paşinler
Horasan
Aras
Goris
Aras

Erzincan
Tercan
Erzurum
Ağrı
Büyükağrı
Daǧı
5123m
AZERB.
Naxçıvan
Länkäran

Kemah
Karaköse
Patnos
Erciş

E
Y
Muradiye

Barajı Keban
Bingöl
Muş
Van
Gölü
Van
Daryācheh-ye
Orūmīyeh

Keban
Elâzığ
Tatyan
Silvan
Bitlis
Gevaş
Reshteh-ye Kūhhā-ye Alborz

alatya
Toroslar
Siirt

o ǧ u
dıyaman
Diyarbakır
Batman

IRAN

Silverek
Viranşehir
Mardin

Şanlıurfa
Akçakale
Nusaybin

Tigris

Jabal 'Abd al 'Azīz

Nīnawé

Kūhhā-ye Zagros

Euphrates

Jabal Bishrī

RIA

IRAQ

Jabal Ḩamrīn

ayrat
asad

ELEVATION

-2000m	-1000m	-500m	-250m	-100m	Below sea level	0	100m	250m	500m	1000m	2000m	4000m
-6562ft	-3281ft	-1640ft	-820ft	-328ft	-164ft/-50m	0	328ft	820ft	1640ft	3281ft	6562ft	13 124ft

117

THE NEAR EAST

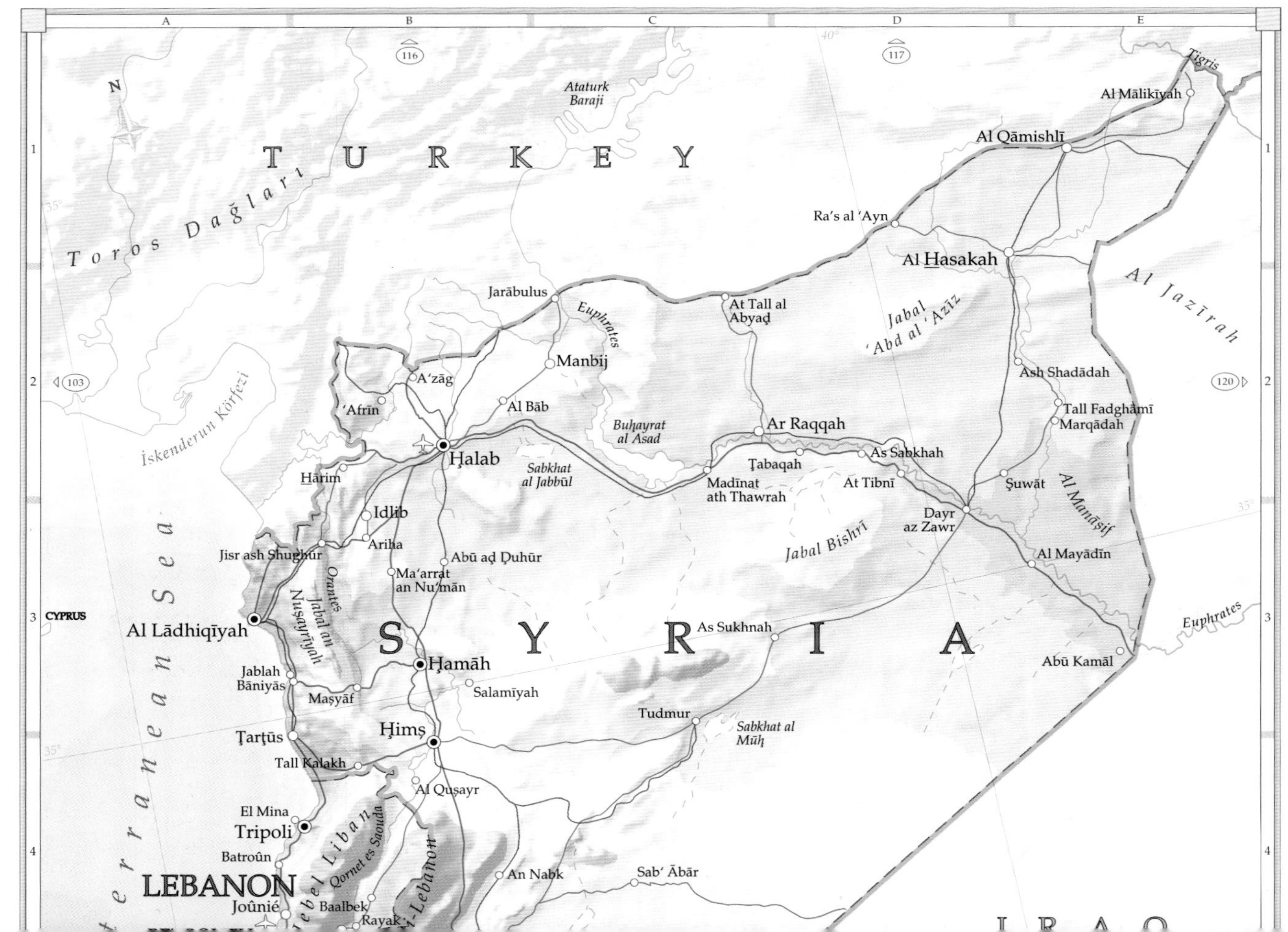

Al Māliklyah
Tigris
Al Qāmishlī
Al Jazīrah
120
Ash Shadādah
Tall Fadghāmī
Marqādah
Euphrates
Al Manāsíf
Abū Kamāl
Şuwār
Al Mayādin
Al Hasakah
IRAQ
Jabal 'Abd al 'Azīz
Ra's al 'Ayn
As Sabkhah
Dayr az Zawr
At Tibnī
At Tall al
Abyad
Ar Raqqah
Tabaqah
Madīnat
ath Thawrah
Jabal Bishrī
Sabkhat al
Mūḥ
As Sukhnah
SYRIA
Buḥayrat
al Asad
Tudmur
Sab' Ābār
Ataturk
Barajı
Euphrates
Manbij
Jarābulus
Al Bāb
Sabkhat
al Jabbūl
Abū aḍ Ẓuhūr
Salamīyah
An Nabk
'A'zāg
Ḥalab
Ma'arrat
an Nu'mān
Ḥamāh
Hims
Al Qusayr
Idlib
'Afrīn
Arīḥā
Massyāf
Jabal Libnān
Anti-Lebanon
'Aynel Qamh es Saoudá
Rayak
Ḥārim
Orontes
Jabal an
Nuṣayrīyah
Tall Kalakh
Baalbek
Jisr ash Shughūr
Jablah
Bāniyās
Ţarţūs
El Mīna
Tripoli
Joūnié
LEBANON
Batroûn
TURKEY
Toros Dağları
İskenderun Körfezi
Al Lādhiqīyah
Mediterranean Sea
N
CYPRUS

0 km   100
0 miles   100

POPULATION
○ Less than 50,000   ○ 50,000 -100,000   ◉ 100,000 - 500,000   ■ Over 500,000

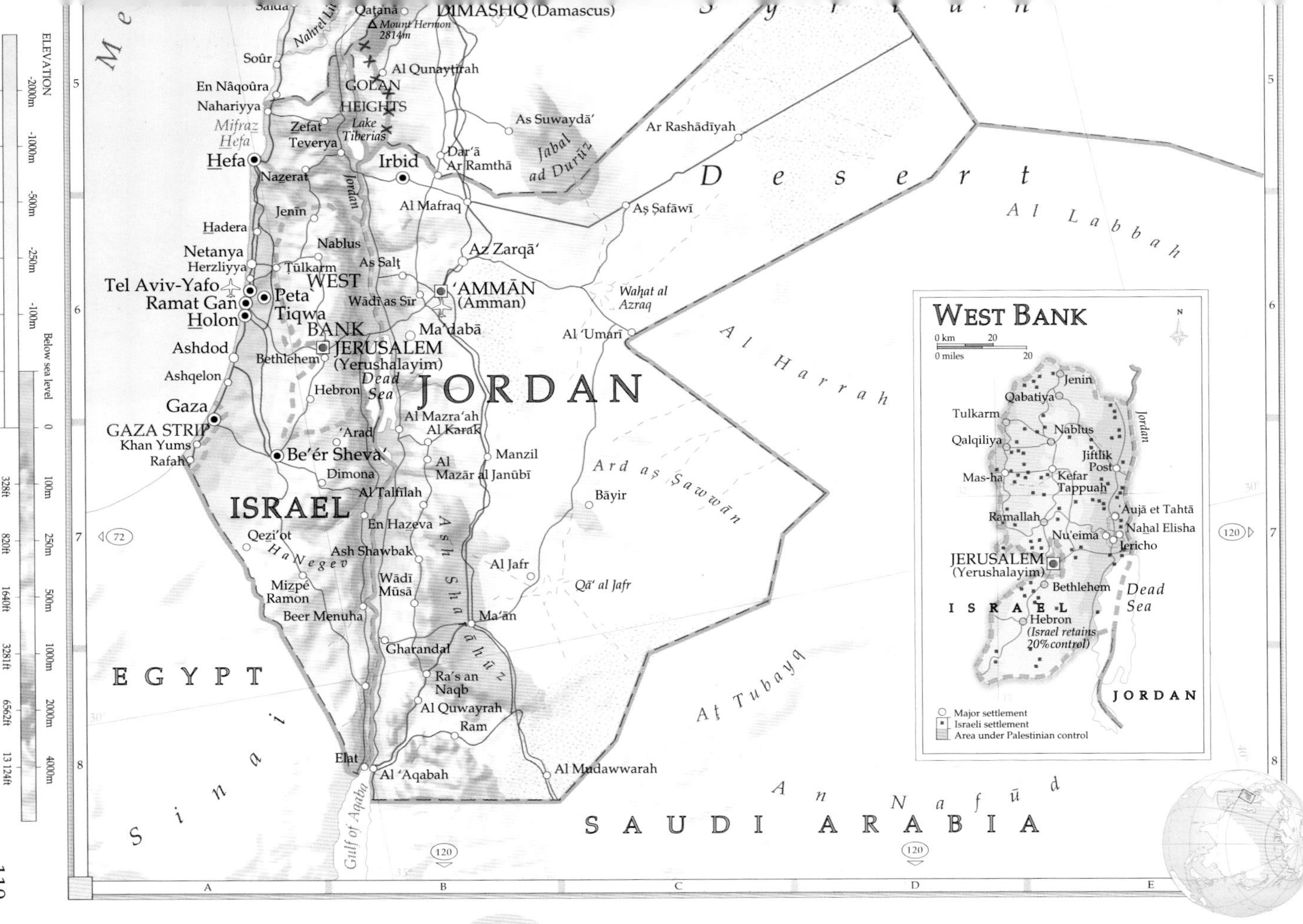

WEST BANK

Jordan

Qabatiya
Jenin
Ṭubas
Nablus
Auja et Taḥtā
Nahal Elisha
Jericho
Jiftlik
Kefar
Tappuaḥ
Nuʿeima
Dead Sea
Tulkarm
Qalqiliya
Mas-ḥa
Ramallah
Bethlehem
JERUSALEM
(Yerushalayim)
Hebron
(Israel retains
20% control)

I S R A E L

J O R D A N

0 km   20
0 miles   20

● Major settlement
■ Israeli settlement
▨ Area under Palestinian control

S y r i a n   D e s e r t

Al Labbah

Al Ḥarrah

Ard aṣ Ṣawwān

An Nafūd

S A U D I   A R A B I A

An Ṭubayq

DIMASHQ (Damascus)

Qaṭanā
Mount Hermon
2814m
Al Qunayṭirah
GOLAN
HEIGHTS
Zefat
Teverya
Lake
Tiberias
Jordan
Nazerat
Jenin

Ar Rashadiyah
Aş Şafāwī
Wāḥat al
Azraq
Al ʿUmarī

As Suwaydāʿ
Jabal ad Durūz

Aş Şafawi

Ar Ramthā
Irbid
Al Mafraq
AMMĀN
(Amman)
Maʿdabā
Az Zarqāʾ

J O R D A N

Bāyir

Qaʿ al Jafr

Al Jafr
Maʿān

Manzil
Al
Al Kerak
Al Mazraʿah
Al Mazār al Janūbī

Ash Sharāh

Ghārandal
Raʾs an
Naqb
Al Qutwayrah
Ram

Al Mudawwarah

Nāʿūr Liṣ
Soûr
En Nāqoûra
Nahariyya
Mifraz
Hefa
Ḥefa

DAMASCUS

Nablus
Ṭulkarm
Peta
Tiqwa
WEST
BANK
Bethlehem
Tel Aviv-Yafo
Ramat Gan
Holon
Hadera
Netanya
Herzliyya
Ashdod
Ashqelon
Gaza
GAZA STRIP
Khan Yunis
Rafaḥ

JERUSALEM
(Yerushalayim)
Hebron
Dead Sea
ʿArad
Dimona
Beʾer Shevaʿ

Jordan

Wādī as Sir
As Salt

Qezʿiot
HaNegev
Mizpe
Ramon
Beer Menuha

En Ḥazeva
Wādī
Mūsā
Ash Shawbak
Al Ṭalfīlah

Gulf of ʿAqaba

Elat
Al ʿAqabah

I S R A E L

E G Y P T

S i n a i

Me

ELEVATION

					Below sea level	0	100m	250m	500m	1000m	2000m	4000m
-2000m	-1000m	-500m	-250m	-100m								
							328ft	820ft	1640ft	3281ft	6562ft	13 124ft
-6562ft	-3281ft	-1640ft	-820ft	-328ft	-164ft/-50m	0						

THE MIDDLE EAST

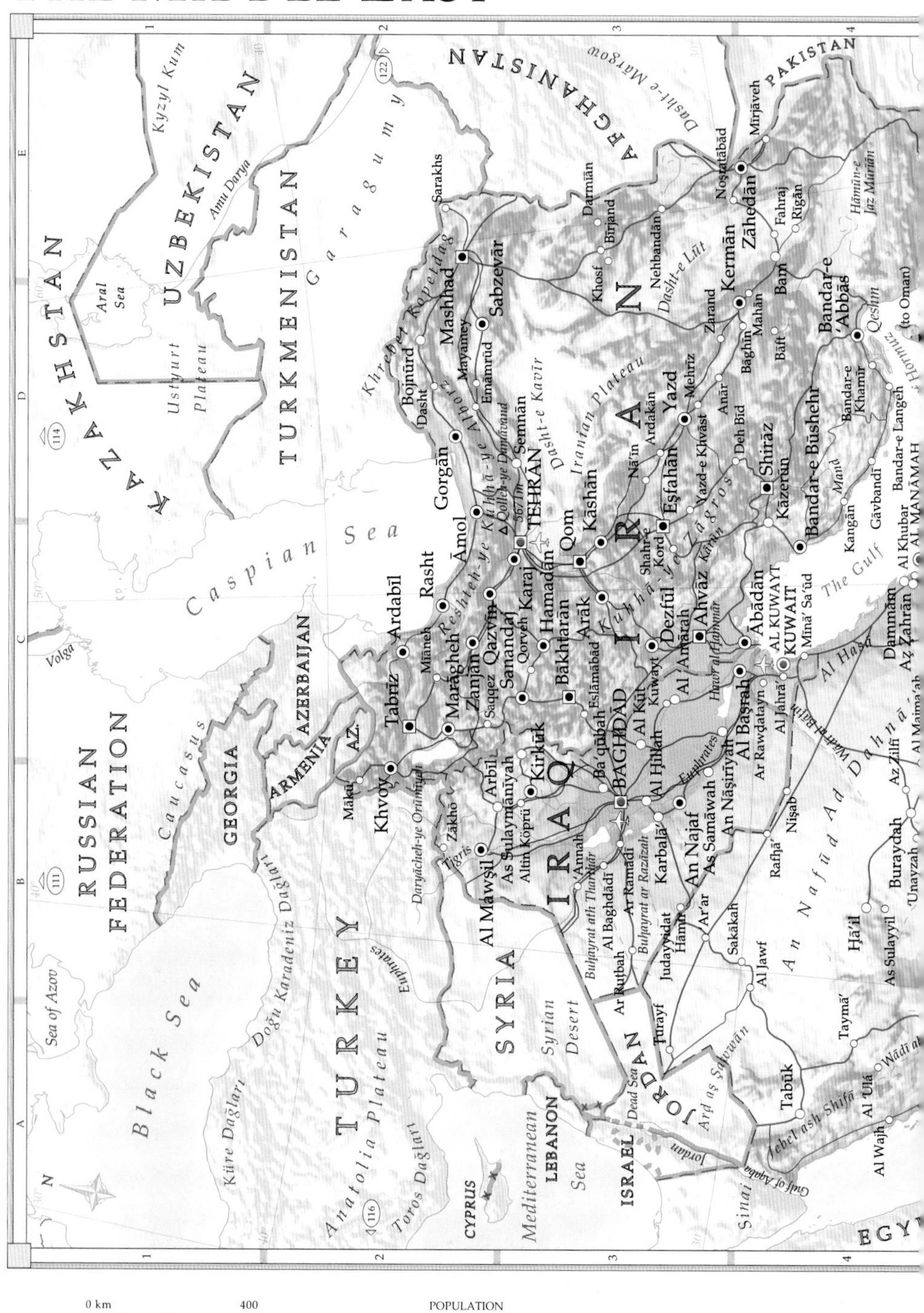

KAZAKHSTAN

Kyzyl Kum

UZBEKISTAN

Aral Sea

Amu Darya

Usthurt Plateau

TURKMENISTAN

Garagumy

122

AFGHANISTAN

Dasht-e Margow

PAKISTAN

Mirjaveh

Mashhad

Sarakhs

Kopet Dag

Klrehrud

Sabzevär

Bojnurd

Dasht

Mayämey

Gorgän

Ämol

Neka

Semnän

Damghän

Khosf

Birjand

Nehbandän

Dasht-e Lut

Kermän

Zähedän

Fahraj

Rigän

Bandar-e 'Abbäs

Qeshm

Hämün-e Jaz Muriän

Rasht

Ardabil

Caspian Sea

Volga

RUSSIAN FEDERATION

Caucasus

GEORGIA

ARMENIA

AZERBAIJAN

AZ.

Makú

Khvoy

Tabriz

Miäneh

Zanjän

Qazvin

Saqqez

Sanandaj

Qorveh

Karaj

TEHRAN

Qom

Kashän

Hamadän

Aräk

Bäkhtarän

Shahr-e Kord

I R A N

Nä'in

Ardakän

Yazd

Mehriz

Yazd-e Khväst

Esfahän

Anär

Zarand

Bäft

Bam

Baghin

Mähän

Deh Bid

Shiräz

Käzerün

Bandar-e Büshehr

Bandar-e Khamir

Bandar-e Langeh

Gävbandi

Kängän

Mand

The Gulf

Al Khubar

Az Zahrän

AL MANAMAH

Dezfül

Ahväz

Abädän

AL KUWAIT

KUWAIT

Mina' Sa'üd

Ad Dammäm

Al Hasä

Iranian Plateau

Dasht-e Kavir

Dasht-e Lut

Zägros

Darya-ye Orümiyeh

Zäkho

Arbil

As Sulaymäniyah

Kirkük

Al Mawsil

Tigris

Euphrates

Ba'qübah

BAGHDAD

Al Küt

Al Hillah

Karbalä'

An Najaf

An Näsiriyah

Al 'Amärah

Al Basrah

Al Jahrä'

Hawr al Hammär

I R A Q

Ar Ramädi

Ar Rutbah

Al Baghdadi

Buhayrat ath Tharthar

Annah

'Änah

Buhayrat ar Razzäzah

As Samäwah

Ar Rawdatayn

Nisäb

SYRIA

Syrian Desert

Judaydat

Hämir

'Ar'ar

Rafhä

Sakäkah

An Nafüd

Az Zulfi

Unayzah

Buraydah

As Sulayyil

Ha'il

Turayf

Al Jawf

Taymä'

Tabük

Taymä'

Al Wajh

Al 'Ulä

Wädi al

JORDAN

'Aqaba

Dead Sea

Jordan

ISRAEL

LEBANON

CYPRUS

Mediterranean Sea

Jabal ash Shifa'

Gulf of Aqaba

Sinai

EGYPT

Black Sea

Sea of Azov

Dnieper

T U R K E Y

Anatolia Plateau

Toros Daglari

Küre Daglari

Doğu Karadeniz Daglari

0 km 400

0 miles 400

POPULATION

○ Less than 50,000   ○ 50,000 -100,000   ◉ 100,000 - 500,000   ■ Over 500,000

120

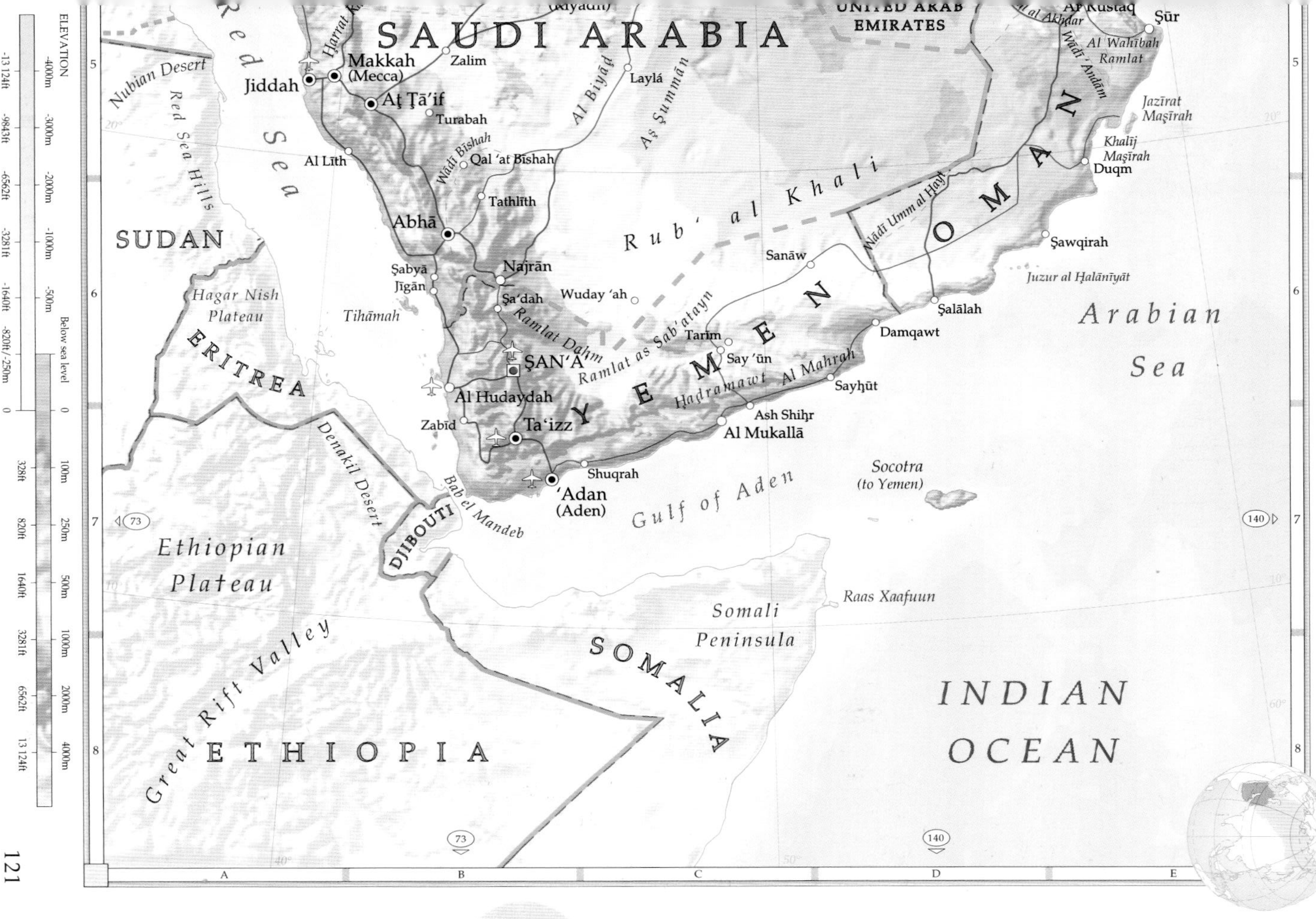

5   6   7   8

140

140

73

E

D

C

B

A

Arabian Sea

INDIAN

OCEAN

OMAN

United Arab
Emirates

Şūr

Al 'Aqabah

Wādī 'Andām

Wādī Halfayn

Jazīrat
Maşīrah

Khalīj
Maşīrah

Duqm

Şawqirah

Juzur al Ḩalāniyāt

Şalālah

Damqawt

Sayḥūt

Sanāw

Sayʼūn

Tarīm

Al Mahrah

Ash Shiḩr

Al Mukallā

*Socotra
(to Yemen)*

Raas Xaafuun

*Somali
Peninsula*

SOMALIA

ETHIOPIA

Rub' al Khali

As Summān

SAUDI ARABIA

Ramlat as Sab'atayn

Layla

Al Biyāḍ

Al Riyadh

Shuqrah

Wudayʼah

SAN'Ā'

'Adan
(Aden)

Ta'izz

Gulf of Aden

Hadramawt

Ramlat Dahm

Najrān

Ṣaʿdah

Qalʻat Bīshah

Tathlith

Al Hudaydah

Zabīd

Bab el Mandeb

YEMEN

DJIBOUTI

Makkah
(Mecca)

At Ṭāʼif

Zalim

Turabah

Wādī Bīshah

Abhā

Sabyā

Jīzān

Ḩarrat

Jiddah

Al Lith

Tihāmah

Denakil Desert

Red Sea Hills

Hagar Nish
Plateau

ERITREA

SUDAN

*Ethiopian
Plateau*

Great Rift Valley

Nubian Desert

Red Sea

ELEVATION

-4000m	-3000m	-2000m	-1000m	-500m	Below sea level	0	100m	250m	500m	1000m	2000m	4000m
-13 124ft	-9843ft	-6562ft	-3281ft	-1640ft	-820ft/-250m	0		328ft	820ft	1640ft	3281ft	6562ft	13 124ft

CENTRAL ASIA

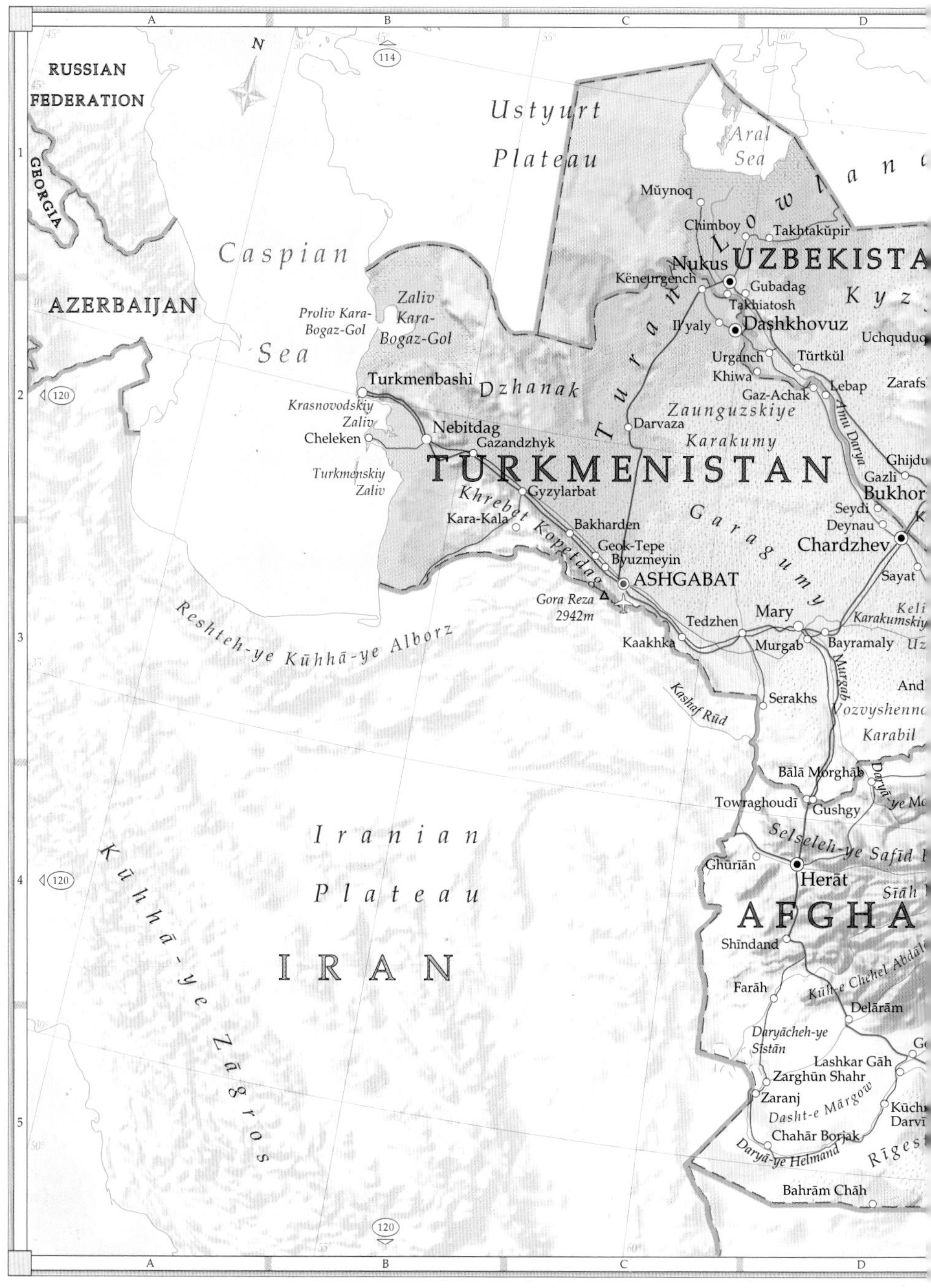

RUSSIAN
FEDERATION

GEORGIA

Caspian

AZERBAIJAN

Sea

114

N

Ustyurt

Plateau

Aral
Sea

Mŭynoq

Chimboy   Takhtakŭpir

Nukus   **UZBEKISTA**

Kŭneŭrgench   Gubadag

Zaliv   Takhiatosh   **K y z**
Kara-   Il'yaly   **Dashkhovuz**
Bogaz-Gol   *Kara-*
Bogaz-Gol   Urganch   Türtkül   Uchquduq

Turkmenbashi   *Dzhanak*   Khiwa   Lebap   Zarafs

Krasnovodskiy   Gaz-Achak
Zaliv   Nebitdag   Darvaza   *Zaunguzskiye*   Ghijdu
Cheleken   Gazandzhyk   *Karakumy*   Gazli

Turkmenskiy   **TURKMENISTAN**   Bukho
Zaliv   Gyzylarbat   Seydi
Khrebet Kopetdag   Deynau   Chardzhev
Kara-Kala   Bakharden   *G a r a g u m y*   Sayat
Geok-Tepe   *Keli*
Byuzmeyin   **ASHGABAT**   *Karakumskiy*

Proliv Kara-

Gora Reza   Tedzhen   Mary   *Uz*
2942m
Kaakhka   Murgab   Bayramaly   And

Reshteh-ye Kŭhhā-ye Alborz   Serakhs   *Vozvyshenno*

Kashaf Rūd   *Karabil*

Bālā Morghāb

Towraghoudī   Gushgy

Iranian   *Selseleh-ye Safīd*

Plateau   Ghūriān   **Herāt**   Sīāh

I R A N   **AFGHA**
Shīndand

Kŭhhā-ye Zāgros   Farāh   Delārām

Daryācheh-ye
Sīstān
Lashkar Gāh   Go
Zarghūn Shahr
Zaranj   *Dasht-e Mārgow*   Kŭch
Chahār Borjak   Darvī
Daryā-ye Helmand   *Rīges*

Bahrām Chāh

120

120

POPULATION

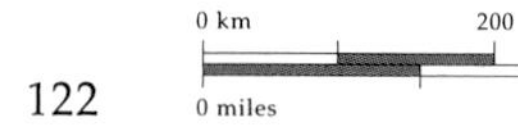

0 km   200

0 miles   200

○ Less than 50,000   ○ 50,000 -100,000   ◉ 100,000 - 500,000   ■ Over 500,000

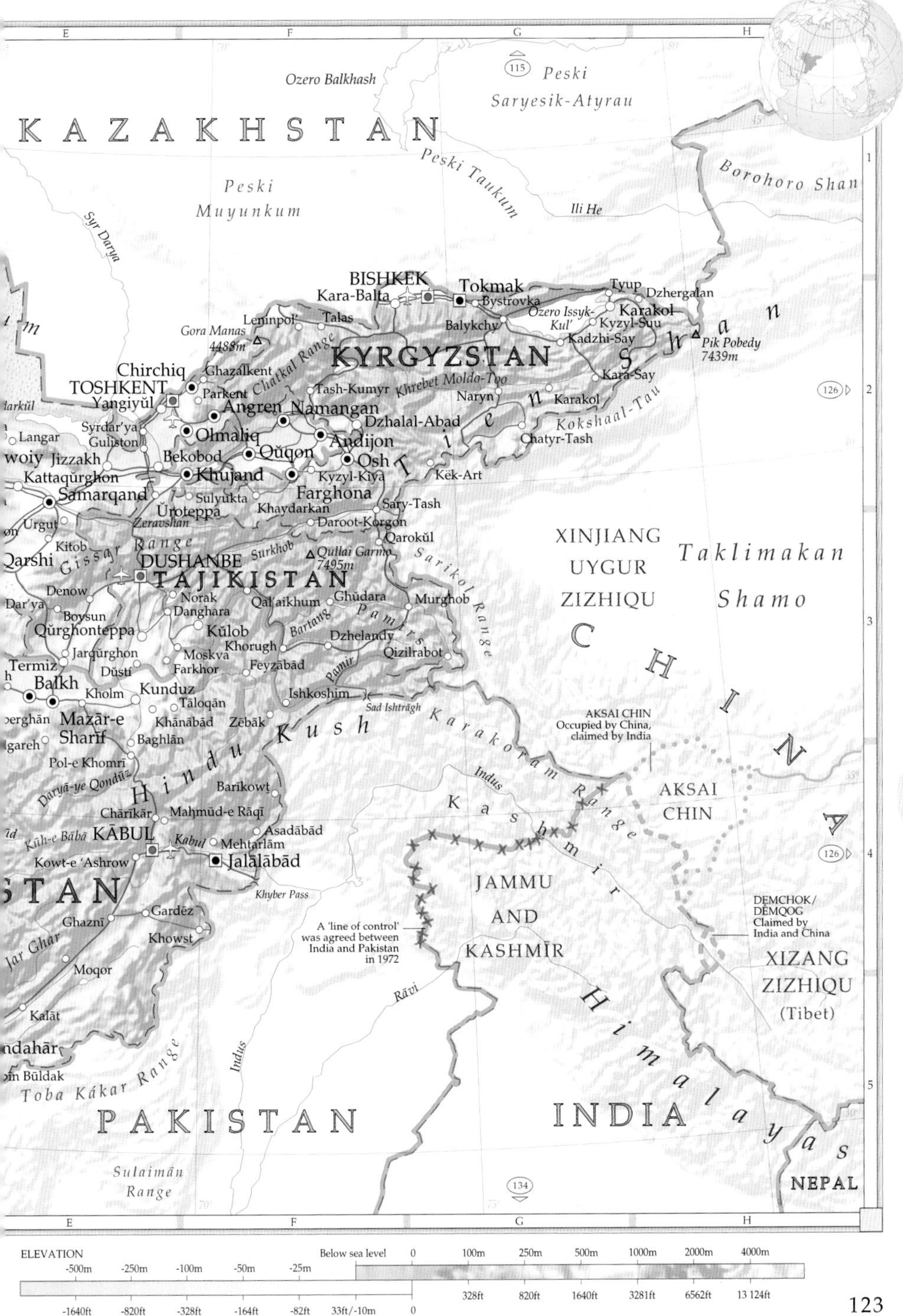

KAZAKHSTAN

Ozero Balkhash

Peski Saryesik-Atyrau

115

Peski Taukum

Syr Darya

Peski Muyunkum

Ili He

Borohoro Shan

126

BISHKEK
Kara-Balta
Tokmak
Bystrovka
Tyup
Dzhergalan
Karakol

Leninpol'
Talas
Balykchy
Ozero Issyk-Kul'
Kyzyl-Suu
Kadzhi-Say

Gora Manas 4488m

KYRGYZSTAN

Pik Pobedy
7439m

Chirchiq
TOSHKENT
Yangiyŭl
Parkent
Ghazalkent
Tash-Kumyr
Khrebet Moldo-Too
Kara-Say
Karakol

Angren
Namangan
Dzhalal-Abad
Naryn

larkŭl
Syrdar'ya
Guliston
Olmaliq
Andijon
Osh
Chatyr-Tash
Kokshaal-Tau

Langar
Jizzakh
Bekobod
Qŭqon
Kék-Art

woiy
Kattaqŭrghon
Khŭjand
Farghona
Kyzyl-Kiya

Samarqand
Ŭroteppa
Sŭlyukta
Khaydarkan
Sary-Tash

Zeravshan
Daroot-Korgon

on
Urgut
Kitob
Range
Surkhob
Qarokŭl

Qarshi
Gissar
DUSHANBE
TAJIKISTAN
Qullai Garmo
7495m
Sarikol Range

Denow
Norak
Ghŭdara
Murghob

XINJIANG
UYGUR
ZIZHIQU

Taklimakan

Boysun
Danghara
Qal'aikhum
Bartang
Dzhelandy

Shamo

Qŭrghonteppa
Kŭlob
Khorugh
Qizilrabot

Jarqŭrghon
Dŭstí
Moskva
Farkhor
Feyzabad
Pamir

C
H
I
N
A

Termiz
Balkh
Farkhor
Ishkoshim

Kholm
Kunduz
Sad Ishtrāgh
Karakoram Range

erghān
Mazār-e
Talogān
Zēbāk

gareh
Sharīf
Khānābād
Baghlān

AKSAI CHIN
Occupied by China,
claimed by India

Pol-e Khomrī

Daryā-ye Qondūz
Barikowt

K
a
s
h
m
i
r

AKSAI
CHIN

Chārīkār
Mahmūd-e Rāqī

Hindu Kush

Kūh-e Bābā
KĀBUL
Kabul
Asadābād
Mehtarlām

126

d
Kowt-e 'Ashrow
Jalālābād

DEMCHOK/
DÊMQOG
Claimed by
India and China

STAN

Gardēz

Khyber Pass

JAMMU
AND
KASHMIR

XIZANG
ZIZHIQU
(Tibet)

Ghazni
Khowst

A 'line of control'
was agreed between
India and Pakistan
in 1972

H
i
m
a
l
a
y
a
s

Moqor

Rāvi

Kalāt

ndahār
om Būldak

Toba Kākar Range

Indus

PAKISTAN

INDIA

NEPAL

Sulaimān Range

134

ELEVATION

					Below sea level	0	100m	250m	500m	1000m	2000m	4000m
-500m	-250m	-100m	-50m	-25m								
							328ft	820ft	1640ft	3281ft	6562ft	13 124ft
-1640ft	-820ft	-328ft	-164ft	-82ft	33ft/-10m	0						

SOUTH & EAST ASIA

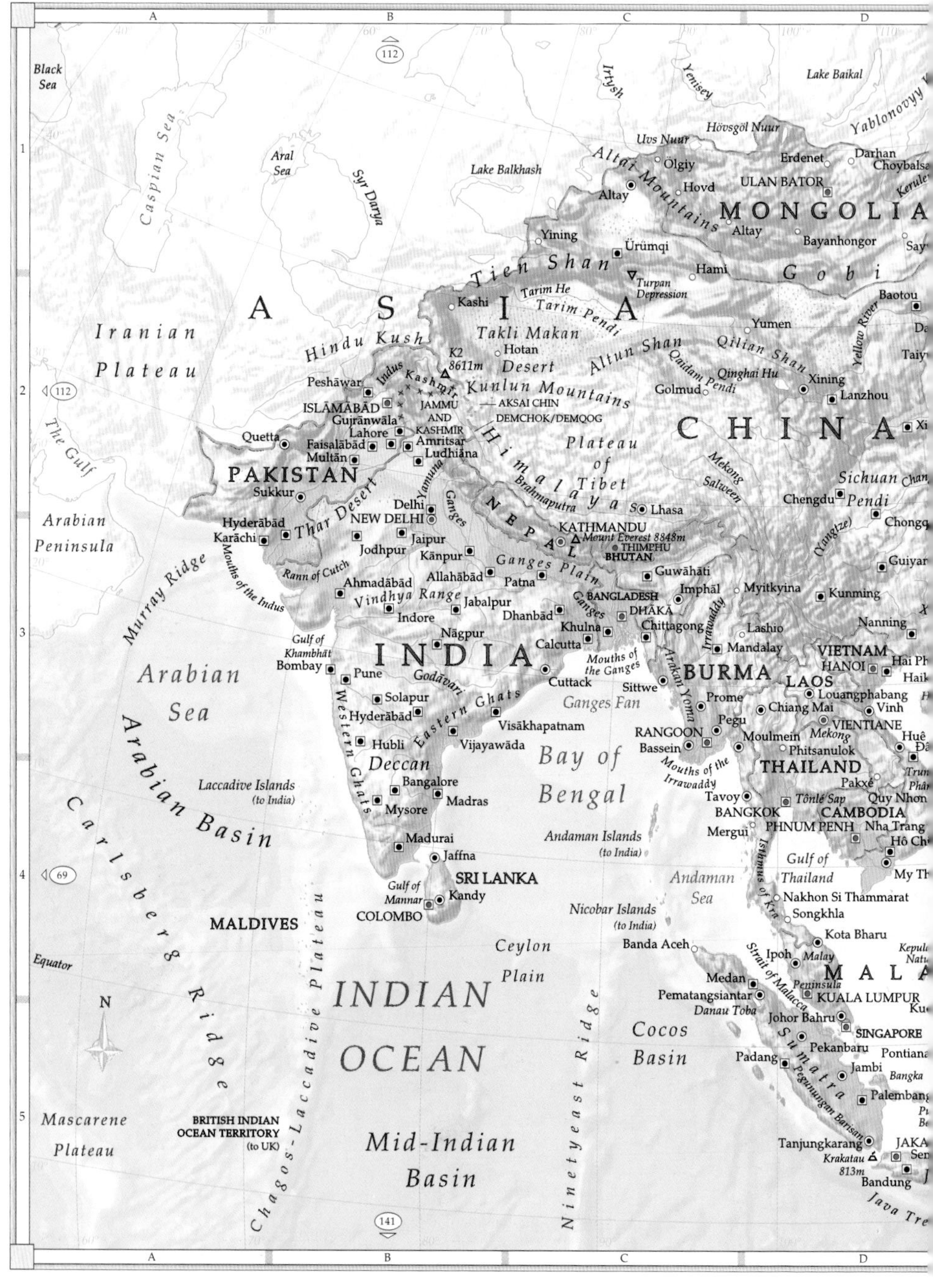

Black Sea

Caspian Sea

Aral Sea

Iranian Plateau

◁ 112

The Gulf

Arabian Peninsula

Syr Darya

Lake Balkhash

Irtysh

Yenisey

Lake Baikal

Uvs Nuur

Hövsgöl Nuur

Olgiy

Altay

Hovd

ULAN BATOR

Erdenet

Darhan

Choybalsan

MONGOLIA

Yining

Ürümqi

Altay

Bayanhongor

Say

Gobi

Hami

Tien Shan

Kashi

Tarim He

Tarim Pendi

Turpan Depression

Baotou

De

A S I A

Yumen

Takli Makan Desert

Hotan

Altun Shan

Qaidam Pendi

Qilian Shan

Qinghai Hu

Taiy

K2 8611m

Kunlun Mountains

Golmud

Xining

Lanzhou

Peshāwar

Hindu Kush

Indus

Kashmir

AKSAI CHIN

DEMCHOK/DEMQOG

Xi

Quetta

ISLĀMĀBĀD

JAMMU AND KASHMIR

Plateau of Tibet

CHINA

Gujrānwāla

Lahore

Amritsar

Ludhiāna

Himalayas

Lhasa

Mekong

Salween

Chengdu

Sichuan Pendi

Chan

Faisalābād

Multān

PAKISTAN

Sukkur

Jhelum

Brahmaputra

Chongq

Hyderābād

Karāchi

Delhi

NEW DELHI

Jaipur

Ganges

NEPAL

KATHMANDU

Mount Everest 8848m

THIMPHU

BHUTAN

Guwāhāti

Guiyar

Jodhpur

Kānpur

Ganges Plain

Patna

Imphāl

Myitkyina

Kunming

Nanning

Thar Desert

Ahmadābād

Allahābād

Jabalpur

Ganges

BANGLADESH

DHĀKA

Lashio

Mandalay

VIETNAM

HANOI

Hai Ph

Rann of Cutch

Vindhya Range

Indore

Dhanbād

Khulna

Chittagong

Irrawaddy

Haik

Mouths of the Indus

Nāgpur

Calcutta

Arakan Yoma

BURMA

LAOS

Louangphabang

Vinh

Gulf of Khambhāt

Bombay

INDIA

Godāvari

Cuttack

Mouths of the Ganges

Prome

Chiang Mai

VIENTIANE

Pune

Solapur

Eastern Ghats

Sittwe

Pegu

Moulmein

Mekong

Huê

Hyderābād

Visākhapatnam

Ganges Fan

RANGOON

THAILAND

Phitsanulok

Đà

Arabian Sea

Hubli

Western Ghats

Vijayawāda

Bay of Bengal

Bassein

Mouths of the Irrawaddy

Pakxé

Trun

Phar

Laccadive Islands (to India)

Deccan

Bangalore

Madras

Tavoy

BANGKOK

Tônlé Sap

CAMBODIA

Quy Nhon

Arabian Basin

Mysore

Madurai

Andaman Islands (to India)

Mergui

PHNUM PENH

Nha Trang

Hô Ch

Jaffna

SRI LANKA

Kandy

Andaman Sea

Gulf of Thailand

My Th

◁ 69

Carlsberg Ridge

Gulf of Mannar

COLOMBO

Nicobar Islands (to India)

Isthmus of Kra

Nakhon Si Thammarat

Songkhla

MALDIVES

Ceylon Plain

Banda Aceh

Kota Bharu

Kepulu Nati

Equator

Chagos-Laccadive Plateau

Medan

Pematangsiantar

Malay Peninsula

Ipoh

KUALA LUMPUR

MALA

Ku

N

Laccadive-Laccadive Plateau

INDIAN OCEAN

Cocos Basin

Danau Toba

Johor Bahru

SINGAPORE

Padang

Pekanbaru

Jambi

Pontiana

Bangka

Mascarene Plateau

BRITISH INDIAN OCEAN TERRITORY (to UK)

Mid-Indian Basin

Ninetyeast Ridge

Sumatra

Pegunungan Barisan

Palemban

Pi

Be

Tanjungkarang

Krakatau 813m

JAKA

Bandung

Java Tre

◁ 141

Java Se

POPULATION

○ Less than 50,000   ○ 50,000 -100,000   ◉ 100,000 - 500,000   ■ Over 500,000

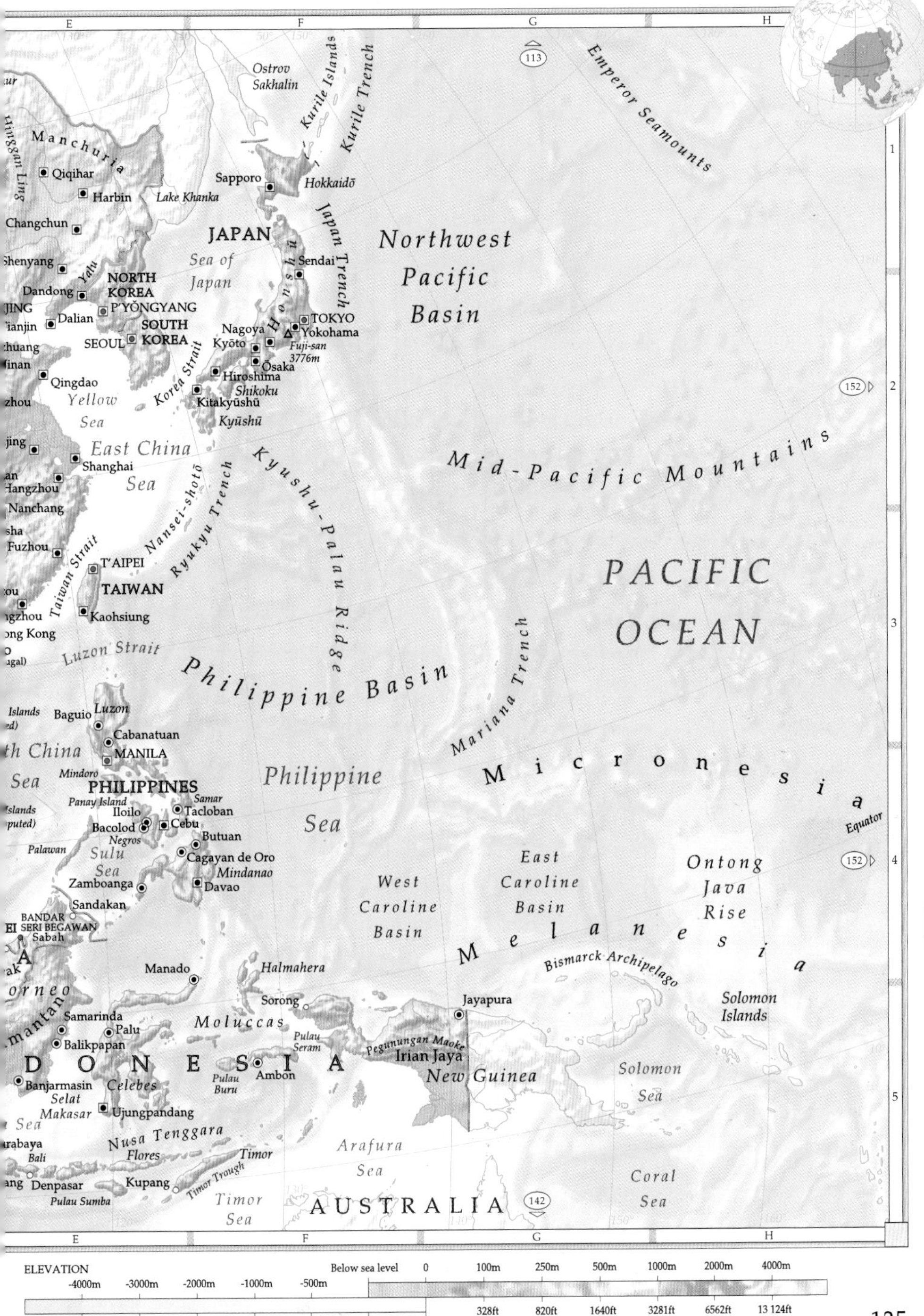

ELEVATION

| | | | | | Below sea level | 0 | 100m | 250m | 500m | 1000m | 2000m | 4000m |

-4000m   -3000m   -2000m   -1000m   -500m

-13 124ft   -9843ft   -6562ft   -3281ft   -1640ft   -820ft/-250m   0   328ft   820ft   1640ft   3281ft   6562ft   13 124ft

WESTERN CHINA & MONGOLIA

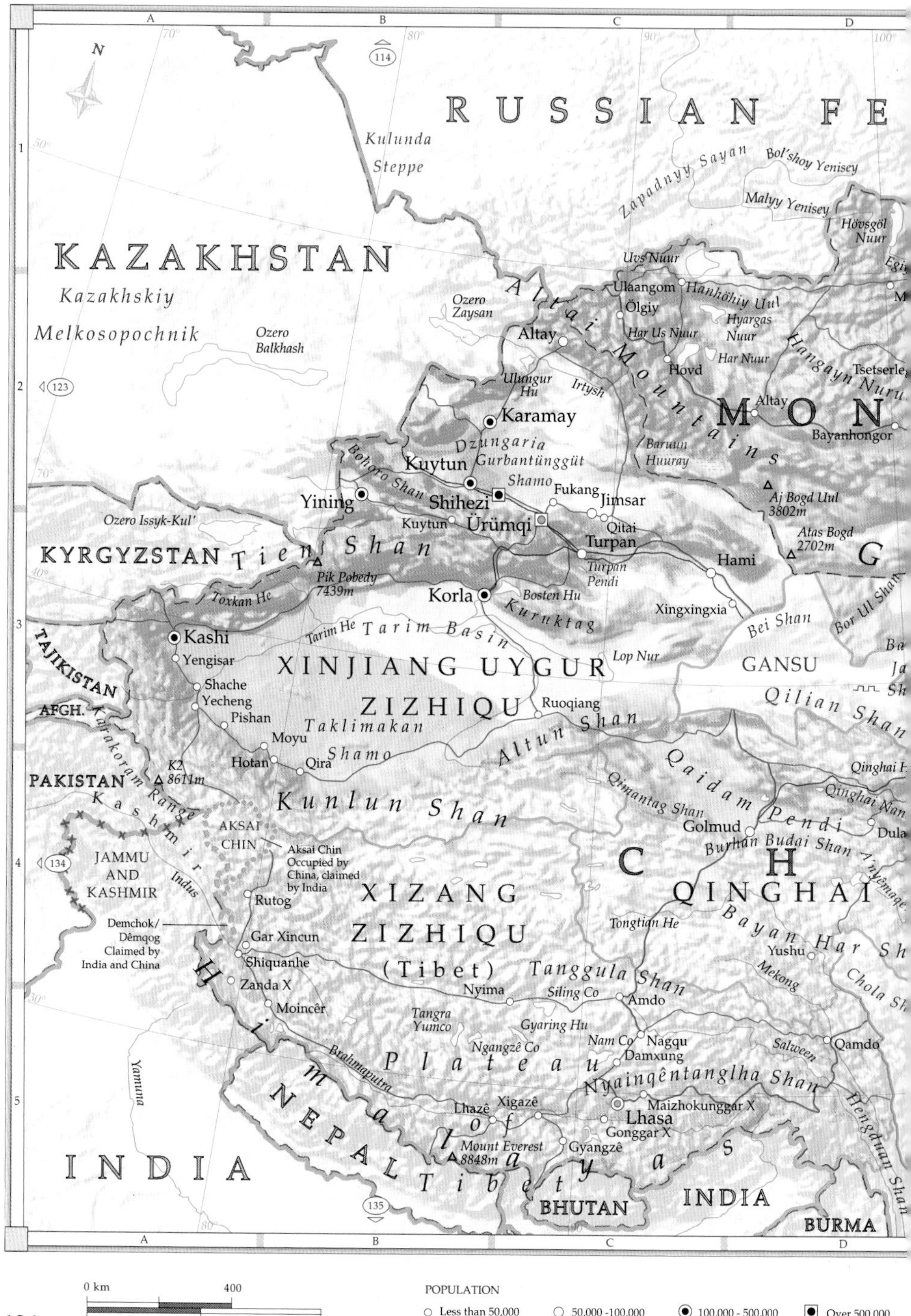

RUSSIAN FE

Kulunda
Steppe

Zapadnyy Sayan

Bol'shoy Yenisey

Malyy Yenisey

*Hövsgöl
Nuur*

KAZAKHSTAN

Kazakhskiy

Melkosopochnik

*Ozero
Balkhash*

*Ozero
Zaysan*

Uvs Nuur

Ulaangom Hanhöhiy Uul

Ölgiy   Hyargas
Nuur

Altay   Har Us Nuur

Hovd   Har Nuur

*Ulungur
Hu*

Irtysh

Karamay

Altay

Dzungaria
Gurbantünggüt

Kuytun *Shamo*

Baruun
Huuray

Fukang

Jimsar

Shihezi

Kuytun   **Ürümqi**

Qitai

Turpan

M O N

Bayanhongor

Aj Bogd Uul
3802m

Atas Bogd
2702m

Behoro Shan

Yining

Ozero Issyk-Kul'

KYRGYZSTAN *Tien Shan*

Pik Pobedy
7439m

Toxkan He

Korla

Bosten Hu

*Turpan
Pendi*

Hami

G

Kuruktag

Xingxingxia

Bei Shan

Bor Ul Sh

Tarim He *Tarim Basin*

Kashi

Yengisar

XINJIANG UYGUR

Lop Nur

GANSU

Ba
Ja
Sh

Qilian Shan

TAJIKISTAN

Shache

Yecheng

ZIZHIQU

Ruoqiang

Altun Shan

AFGH. *Karakoram*

Pishan

Taklimakan

Moyu   *Shamo*

Qinghai I

K2
8611m

Hotan   Qira

PAKISTAN

Kunlun Shan

Qimantag Shan

Golmud

Qaidam Pendi

Qinghai Nan

Dula

Kashmir

AKSAI
CHIN

Aksai Chin
Occupied by
China, claimed
by India

Indus

Rutog

XIZANG

C H

QINGHAI

Burhan Budai Shan *Anyêmaq*

Bayan Har Sh

Yushu

**JAMMU
AND
KASHMIR**

Demchok/
Dêmqog
Claimed by
India and China

Gar Xincun

Shiquanhe

Zanda X

Moincêr

ZIZHIQU

Tongtian He

(Tibet)

Tanggula Shan

Nyima   Siling Co

Amdo

Mekong

Chola Sh

Qamdo

*Tangra
Yumco*

Gyaring Hu

Nam Co Nagqu

Damxung

Yamuna

Brahmaputra

Plateau

Ngangzê Co

Salween

Nyainqêntanglha Shan

Hengduan Shan

INDIA

Himalaya

of

Tibet

Lhazê Xigazê

Mount Everest
8848m

Gyangzê

Lhasa

Gonggar X

Maizhokunggar X

INDIA

NEPAL

BHUTAN

BURMA

0 km   400

0 miles   400

POPULATION

○ Less than 50,000   ○ 50,000 -100,000   ◉ 100,000 - 500,000   ◼ Over 500,000

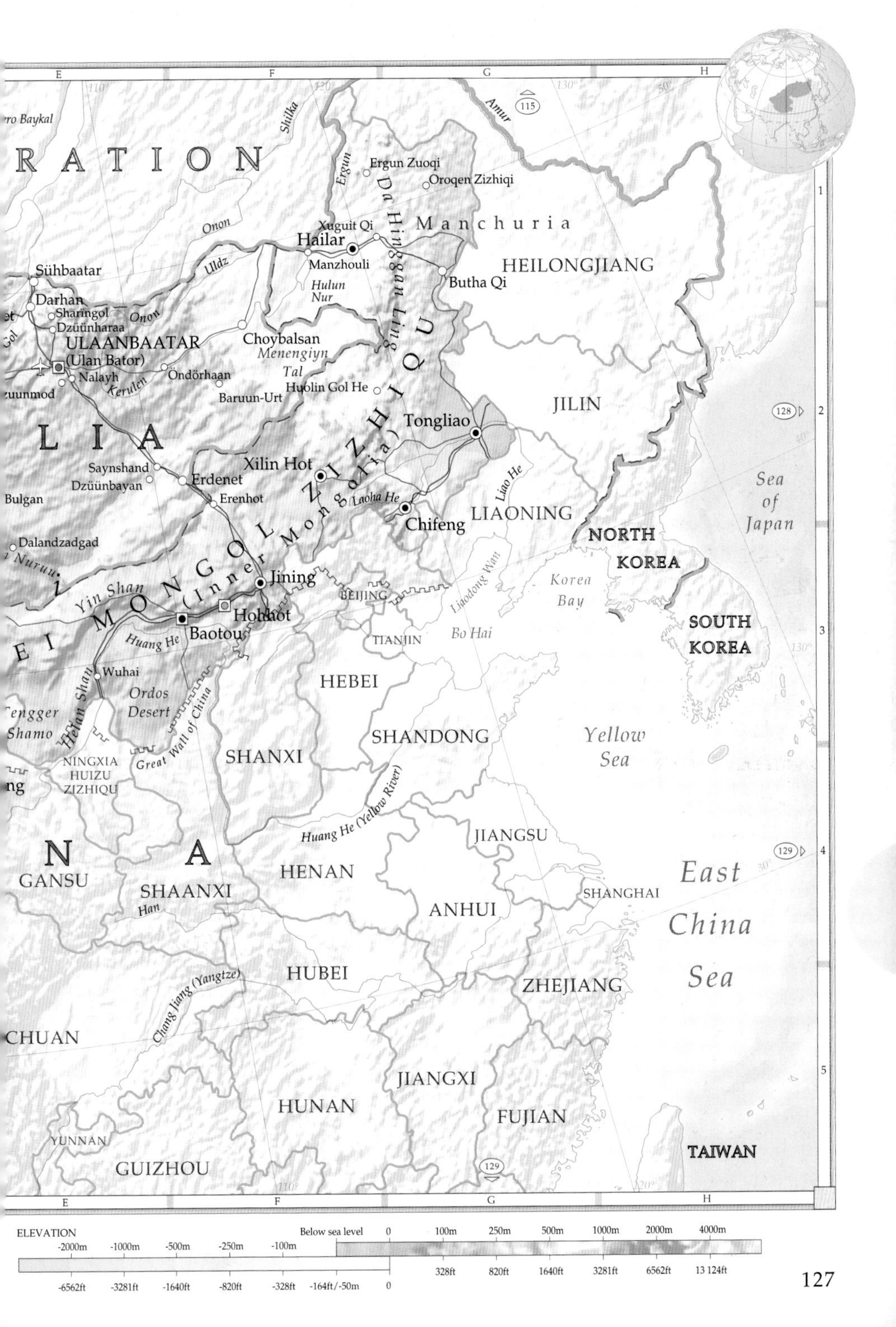

RATION

Ero Baykal

Shilka

Amur

115

Ergun

Ergun Zuoqi

Oroqen Zizhiqi

Onon

Xuguit Qi

Hailar

Da Hinggan Ling

Manchuria

HEILONGJIANG

Sühbaatar

Uldz

Manzhouli

Butha Qi

Darhan

Sharingol

Onon

Hulun
Nur

Dzüünharaa

ULAANBAATAR

Choybalsan

(Ulan Bator)

Nalayh

Ondörhaan

Menengiyn
Tal

Kerulen

Huolin Gol He

JILIN

zuunmod

Baruun-Urt

Tongliao

L I A

Saynshand

Xilin Hot

Mongol Zizhiqu

Liao He

Sea
of
Japan

128

2

Bulgan

Dzüünbayan

Erdenet

Erenhot

Laoha He

Chifeng

LIAONING

Dalandzadgad

Nuruu

Inner

Jining

BEIJING

Korea
Bay

NORTH
KOREA

EI

Yin Shan

MONGOL

Hohhot

Liaodong Wan

SOUTH
KOREA

130

3

Huang He

Baotou

TIANJIN

Bo Hai

Tengger
Shamo

Helan Shan

Wuhai

Ordos
Desert

HEBEI

SHANDONG

Yellow
Sea

ng

NINGXIA
HUIZU
ZIZHIQU

Great Wall of China

SHANXI

N

A

Huang He (Yellow River)

JIANGSU

East
China
Sea

129

4

GANSU

SHAANXI

HENAN

ANHUI

SHANGHAI

Han

30

CHUAN

Chang Jiang (Yangtze)

HUBEI

ZHEJIANG

JIANGXI

5

YUNNAN

GUIZHOU

HUNAN

FUJIAN

129

TAIWAN

ELEVATION

| -2000m | -1000m | -500m | -250m | -100m | Below sea level | 0 | 100m | 250m | 500m | 1000m | 2000m | 4000m |

| -6562ft | -3281ft | -1640ft | -820ft | -328ft | -164ft/-50m | 0 | 328ft | 820ft | 1640ft | 3281ft | 6562ft | 13 124ft |

127

EASTERN CHINA & KOREA

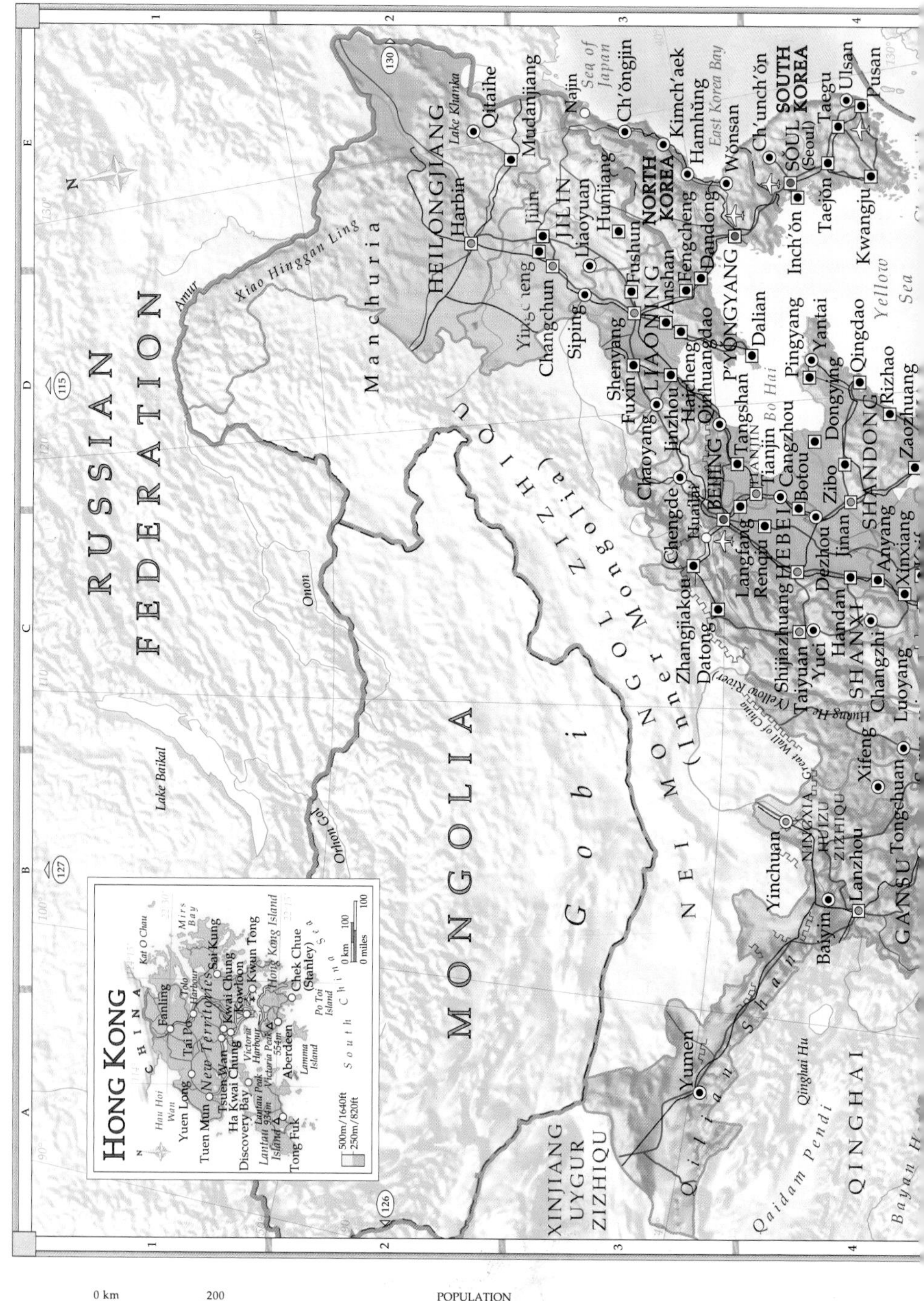

POPULATION

○ Less than 50,000   ◎ 50,000 -100,000   ◉ 100,000 - 500,000   ◼ Over 500,000

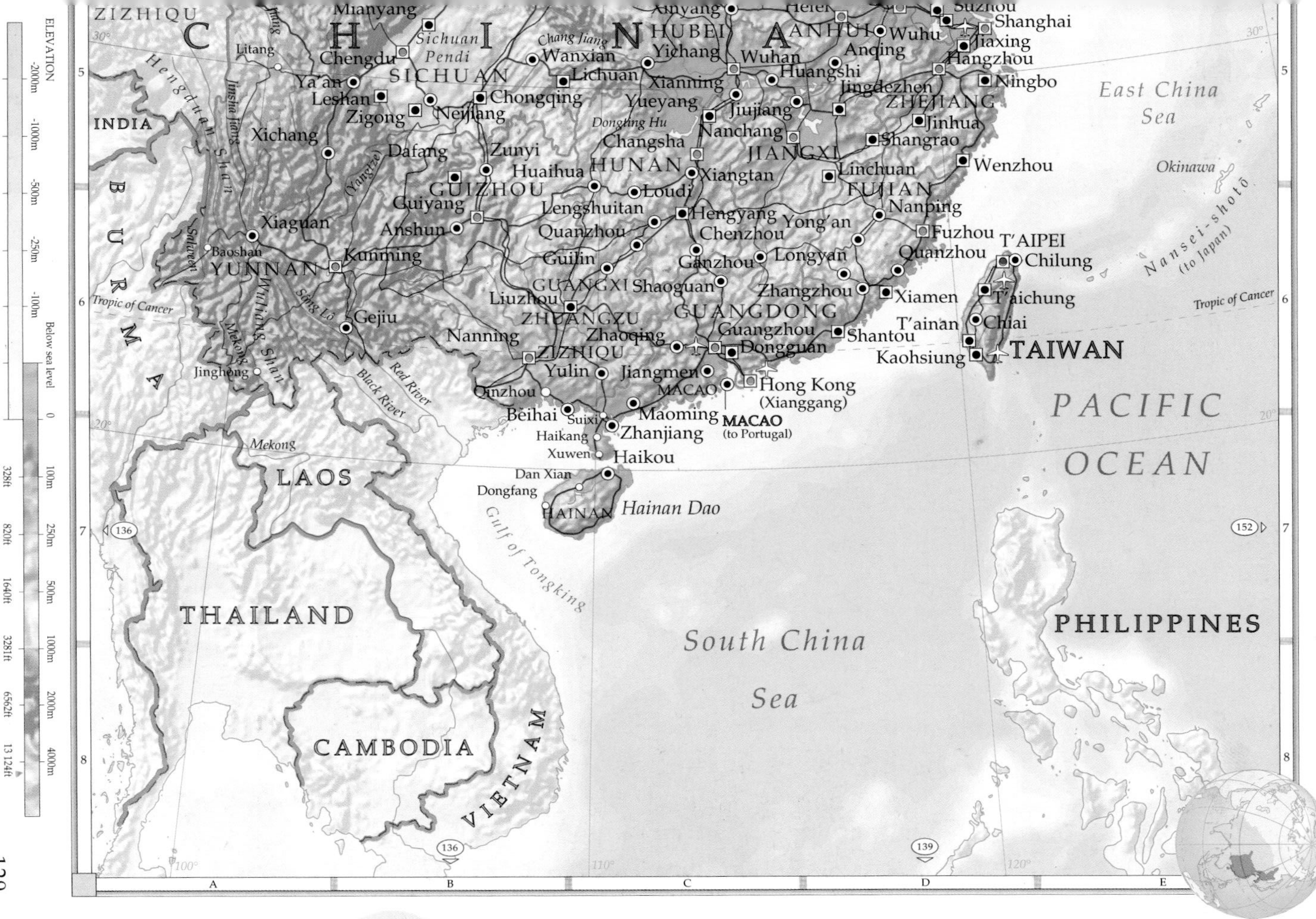

East China Sea

Okinawa

Nansei-shoto (Japan)

Tropic of Cancer

PACIFIC OCEAN

PHILIPPINES

TAIWAN

T'AIPEI
Chilung
Taichung
Chiai
T'ainan
Kaohsiung

Shanghai
Suzhou
Jiaxing
Ningbo
Hangzhou
Wenzhou
ZHEJIANG
Jinhua
Shangrao
Lishui
Linchuan
FUJIAN
Nanping
Fuzhou
Quanzhou
Xiamen
Shantou

ANHUI
Wuhu
Anqing
Huangshi
Jingdezhen
JIANGXI
Nanchang
Yong'an
Longyan
Zhangzhou
GUANGDONG

Wuhan
HUBEI
Yichang
Wanxian
Jiujiang
Changsha
HUNAN
Xiangtan
Hengyang
Yichun
Chenzhou
Zhaoqing
Ganzhou
Guangzhou
Dongguan
Hong Kong (Xianggang)
MACAO (to Portugal)

South China Sea

Chang Jiang
Wuhan
Lichuan
Xianning
Yueyang
Dongting Hu
Huaihua
Lengshuitan
Quanzhou
Guilin
GUANGXI ZHUANGZU
Liuzhou
Shaoguan
Jiangmen
Maoming
Zhanjiang
Haikou
Hainan Dao
HAINAN

Mianyang
Sichuan Pendi
Chengdu
SICHUAN
Zunyi
Dafang
GUIZHOU
Guiyang
Anshun
Kunming
Yulin
Nanning
Beihai
Suxi
Haikang
Xuwen
Dongfang
Dan Xian
Qinzhou
Gulf of Tongking

Ya'an
Leshan
Zigong
Neijiang
Chongqing
Huaihua
YUNNAN
Xiagua
Gejiu
Red River
Black River

VIETNAM
LAOS
THAILAND
CAMBODIA

Jinsha Jiang
Xichang
Baoshan
Jinghong
Song Da
Wuliang Shan
Mekong
Salween
Hengduan Shan
INDIA
BURMA
Tropic of Cancer

ZIZHIQU
XIZHIQU
C H I N A
H E I

ELEVATION

						Below sea level	0	100m	250m	500m	1000m	2000m	4000m
-2000m	-1000m	-500m	-250m	-100m									
								328ft	820ft	1640ft	3281ft	6562ft	13 124ft
-6562ft	-3281ft	-1640ft	-820ft	-328ft	-164ft/-50m	0							

129

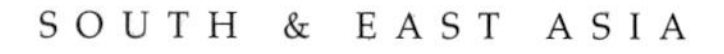

JAPAN

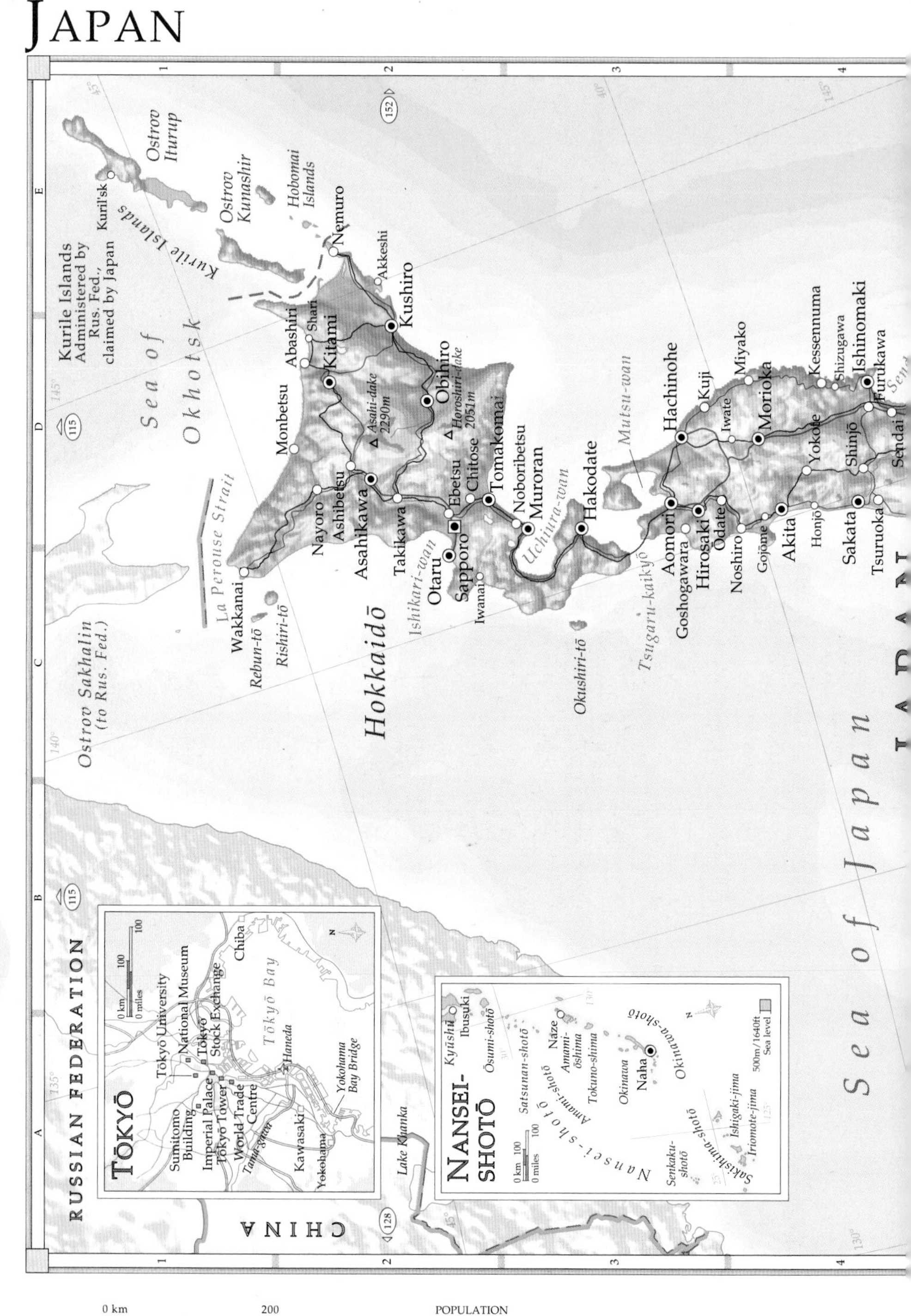

Sea of Okhotsk

Kurile Islands
Administered by
Rus. Fed.,
claimed by Japan

Ostrov Iturup
Ostrov Kunashir
Kuril'sk
Ostrov Sakhalin
(to Rus. Fed.)

Kurile Islands

Hobomai Islands
Nemuro
Akkeshi
Kushiro

Abashiri
Shari
Kitami
△ Asahi-dake 2290m
Obihiro
△ Horoshiri-dake 2051m

Monbetsu
Nayoro
Ashibetsu
Asahikawa
Takikawa
Ebetsu
Chitose
Tomakomai
Noboribetsu
Muroran

Wakkanai
Rishiri-tō
Rebun-tō
Otaru
Iwanai
Sapporo
Uchiura-wan

La Perouse Strait
Ishikari-wan

Hokkaidō

Okushiri-tō

Hakodate
Tsugaru-kaikyō

Mutsu-wan
Hachinohe
Kuji
Iwate
Miyako
Morioka
Yokote
Shinjō
Kessennuma
Shizugawa
Ishinomaki
Furukawa
Sendai

Aomori
Goshogawara
Hirosaki
Odate
Noshiro
Gojome
Honjō
Akita
Sakata
Tsuruoka

Sea of Japan

JAPAN

TŌKYŌ

Chiba
Tōkyō University
National Museum
Tōkyō Stock Exchange
Sumitomo Building
Imperial Palace
Tōkyō Tower
World Trade Centre
Tama-gawa
Haneda
Kawasaki
Yokohama
Yokohama Bay Bridge
Yokosuka
Tōkyō Bay

Lake Kasumi

CHINA

NANSEI-SHOTŌ

Kyūshū
Ibusuki
Ōsumi-shotō
Satsunan-shotō
Amami-shotō
Naze
Amami-ō-shima
Tokuno-shima
Okinawa
Naha
Okinawa-shotō
Tokara-rettō
Ishigaki-jima
Sakishima-shotō
Iriomote-jima
Senkaku-shotō

500m/1640ft
Sea level

CHINA

POPULATION

○ Less than 50,000   ○ 50,000 -100,000   ◉ 100,000 - 500,000   ▣ Over 500,000

0 km   200
0 miles   200

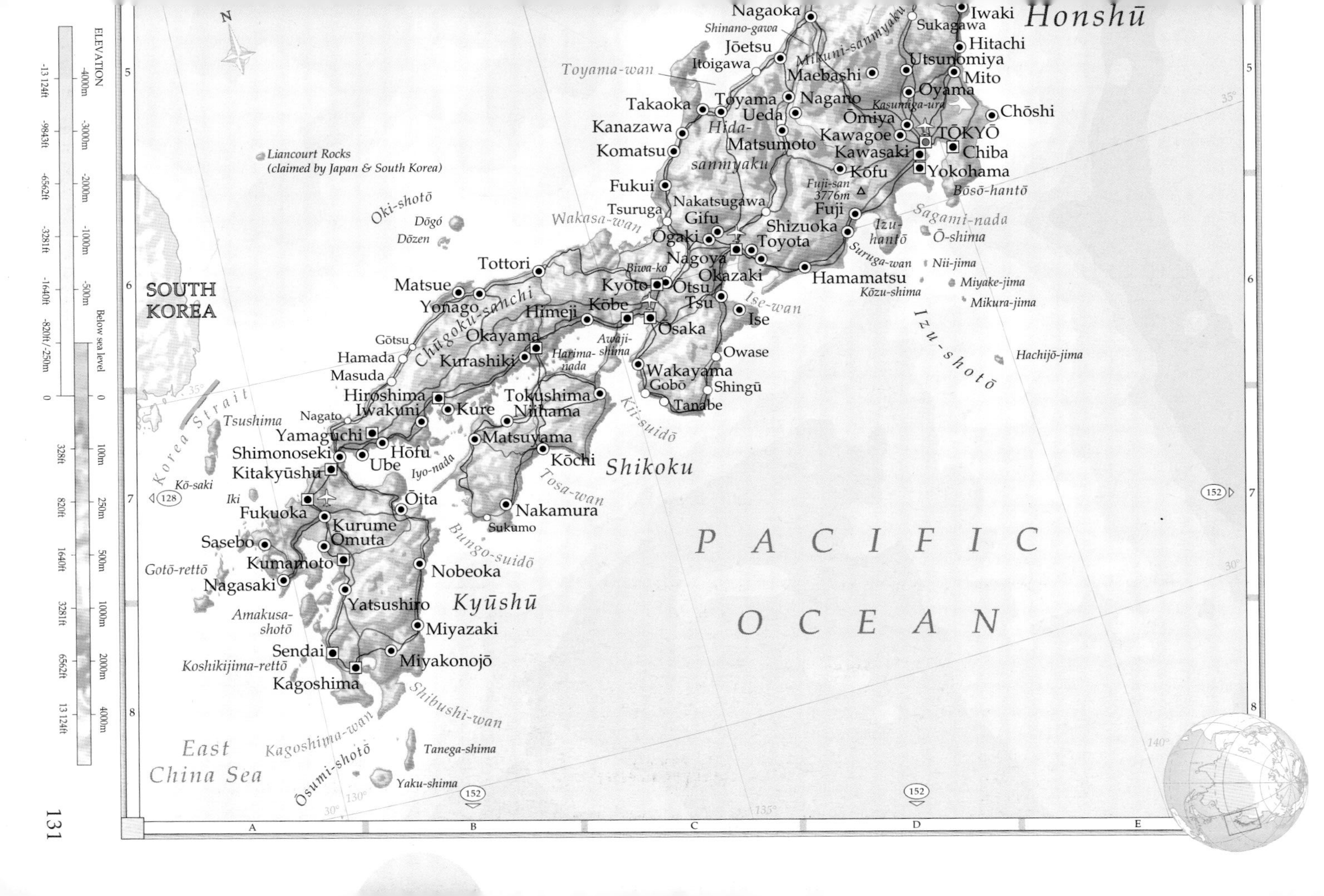

Honshū

PACIFIC OCEAN

Iwaki
Hitachi
Sukagawa
Utsunomiya
Mito
Chōshi
Oyama
TOKYO
Chiba
Yokohama
Bōsō-hantō
Kasumiga-ura
Ōmiya
Kawagoe
Kawasaki
Kōfu
Izu-hantō
Ō-shima
Sagami-nada
Suruga-wan
Nii-jima
Miyake-jima
Mikura-jima
Hachijō-jima
Izu-shotō
Nagano
Maebashi
Matsumoto
Shizuoka
Hamamatsu
Kōzu-shima
Toyota
Fuji
Mikuni-sammyaku
Nagaoka
Jōetsu
Itoigawa
Toyama
Ueda
Fujisan
3776m
Ise-wan
Shinano-gawa
Hida
Owase
Shingū
Takaoka
Kanazawa
Komatsu
Fukui
Tsuruga
Nakatsugawa
Gifu
Ōgaki
Nagoya
Ōtsu
Tsu
Ise
Tanabe
Wakasa-wan
Biwa-ko
Kyōto
Ōsaka
Wakayama
Gobō
Kōbe
Himeji
Awaji-shima
Kii-suidō
PACIFIC OCEAN
Harima-nada
Tottori
Yonago
Okayama
Kurashiki
Kure
Niihama
Tokushima
Matsuyama
Naruto
Kōchi
Shikoku
Nakamura
Tosa-wan
Sukumo
Matsue
Chūgoku-sanchi
Oki-shotō
Dōgo
Dōzen
Gōtsu
Hiroshima
Iwakuni
Hōfu
Iyo-nada
Ōita
Bungo-suidō
Nobeoka
Kyūshū
Miyazaki
Shibushi-wan
Tanega-shima
Yaku-shima
Hamada
Masuda
Nagato
Yamaguchi
Ube
Miyakonojō
Liancourt Rocks
(claimed by Japan & South Korea)
Tsushima
Shimonoseki
Kitakyushu
Fukuoka
Kumamoto
Yatsushiro
Sendai
Kagoshima
Kagoshima-wan
Ōsumi-shotō
East China Sea
Iki
Kō-saki
Sasebo
Nagasaki
Ōmuta
Kurume
Amakusa-shotō
Koshikijima-rettō
Gotō-rettō

Tsugaru

SOUTH KOREA

Korea Strait

152

152

152

128

N

ELEVATION

-4000m	-3000m	-2000m	-1000m	-500m	Below sea level	0	100m	250m	500m	1000m	2000m	4000m
-13 124ft	-9843ft	-6562ft	-3281ft	-1640ft	-820ft/-250m	0	328ft	820ft	1640ft	3281ft	6562ft	13 124ft

SOUTH INDIA & SRI LANKA

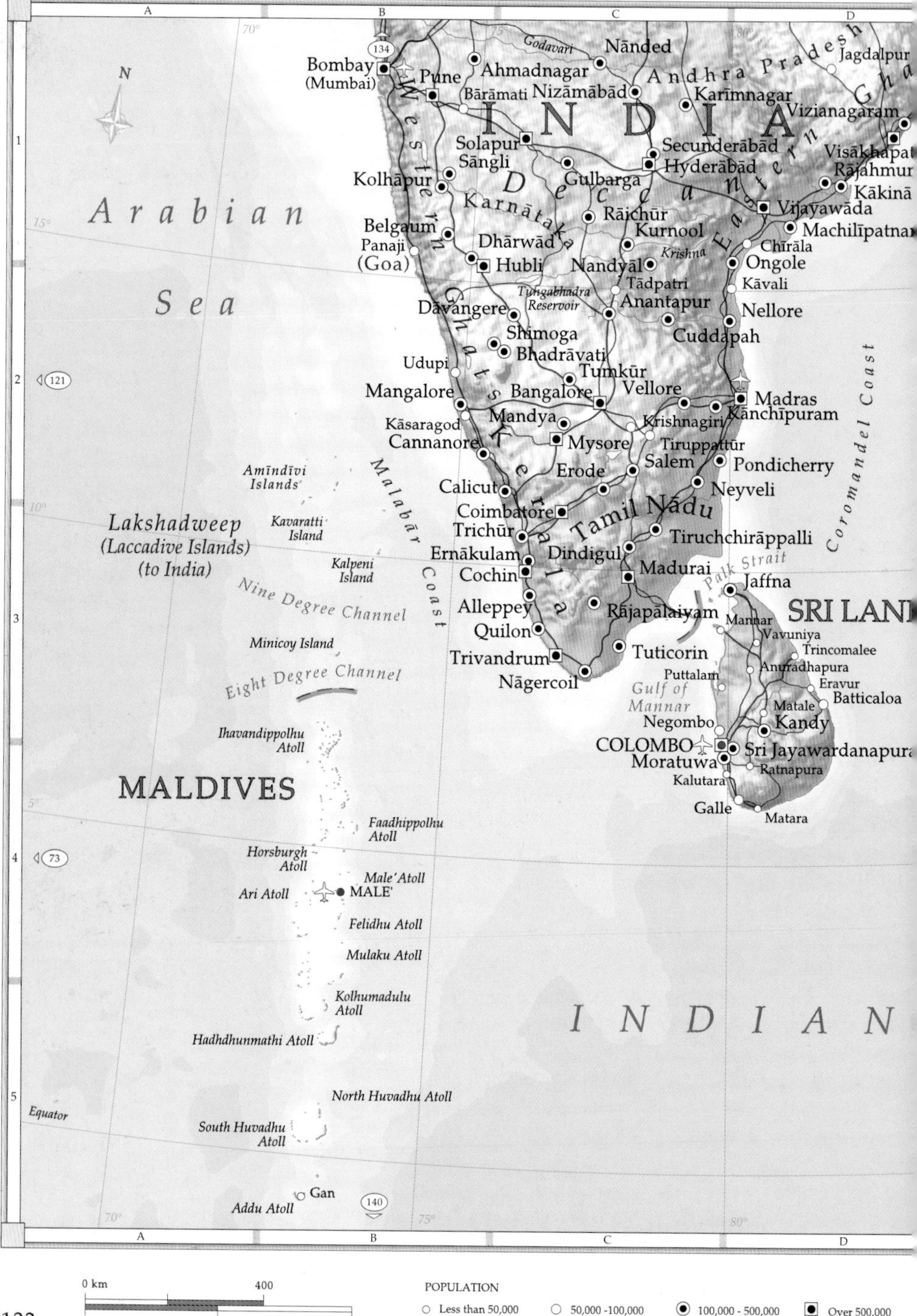

N

A r a b i a n

S e a

Bombay
(Mumbai)
Pune
Ahmadnagar
Bārāmati
Nizāmābād
Nānded
Jagdalpur
Karīmnagar

Andhra Pradesh

I N D I A

Solapur
Sāngli
Secunderābād
Hyderābād
Visākhapa
Rājahmur

Kolhāpur
Gulbarga
Kākinā
Deccan
Eastern Ghats

Karnāta
Rāichūr
Vijayawāda
Belgaum
Kurnool
Machilīpatna
Panaji
(Goa)
Dhārwād
Nandyāl
Krishna
Chīrala
Hubli
Tādpatri
Ongole
Kāvali

Tungabhadra
Reservoir
Anantapur
Nellore
Dāvangere

Shimoga
Cuddapah
Bhadrāvati
Tumkūr

Udupi
Western Ghats

Mangalore
Bangalore
Vellore
Madras
Kāsaragod
Mandya
Krishnagiri
Kānchīpuram
Cannanore
Mysore
Tiruppattūr

Erode
Salem
Pondicherry
Calicut
Neyveli

Coromandel Coast

Coimbatore
Trichūr
Tamil Nādu
Ernākulam
Dindigul
Tiruchchirāppalli
Cochin
Madurai
Jaffna

Malabar Coast

Alleppey
Rājapālaiyam
Mannar
SRI LAN
Quilon

Trivandrum
Tuticorin
Vavuniya
Trincomalee
Anurādhapura
Eravur
Batticaloa
Nāgercoil
Gulf of
Mannar
Puttalam
Matale

Negombo
Kandy
COLOMBO
Sri Jayawardanapura
Moratuwa
Ratnapura
Kalutara
Galle
Matara

Amīndivi
Islands

Lakshadweep
(Laccadive Islands)
(to India)

Kavaratti
Island

Kalpeni
Island

Nine Degree Channel

Minicoy Island

Eight Degree Channel

Ihavandippolhu
Atoll

MALDIVES

Faadhippolhu
Atoll

Horsburgh
Atoll
Male' Atoll
Ari Atoll
MALE'

Felidhu Atoll

Mulaku Atoll

Kolhumadulu
Atoll

Hadhdhunmathi Atoll

North Huvadhu Atoll

Equator

South Huvadhu
Atoll

I N D I A N

Gan
Addu Atoll

0 km	400	
0 miles		400

POPULATION

○ Less than 50,000   ○ 50,000 -100,000   ◉ 100,000 - 500,000   ◼ Over 500,000

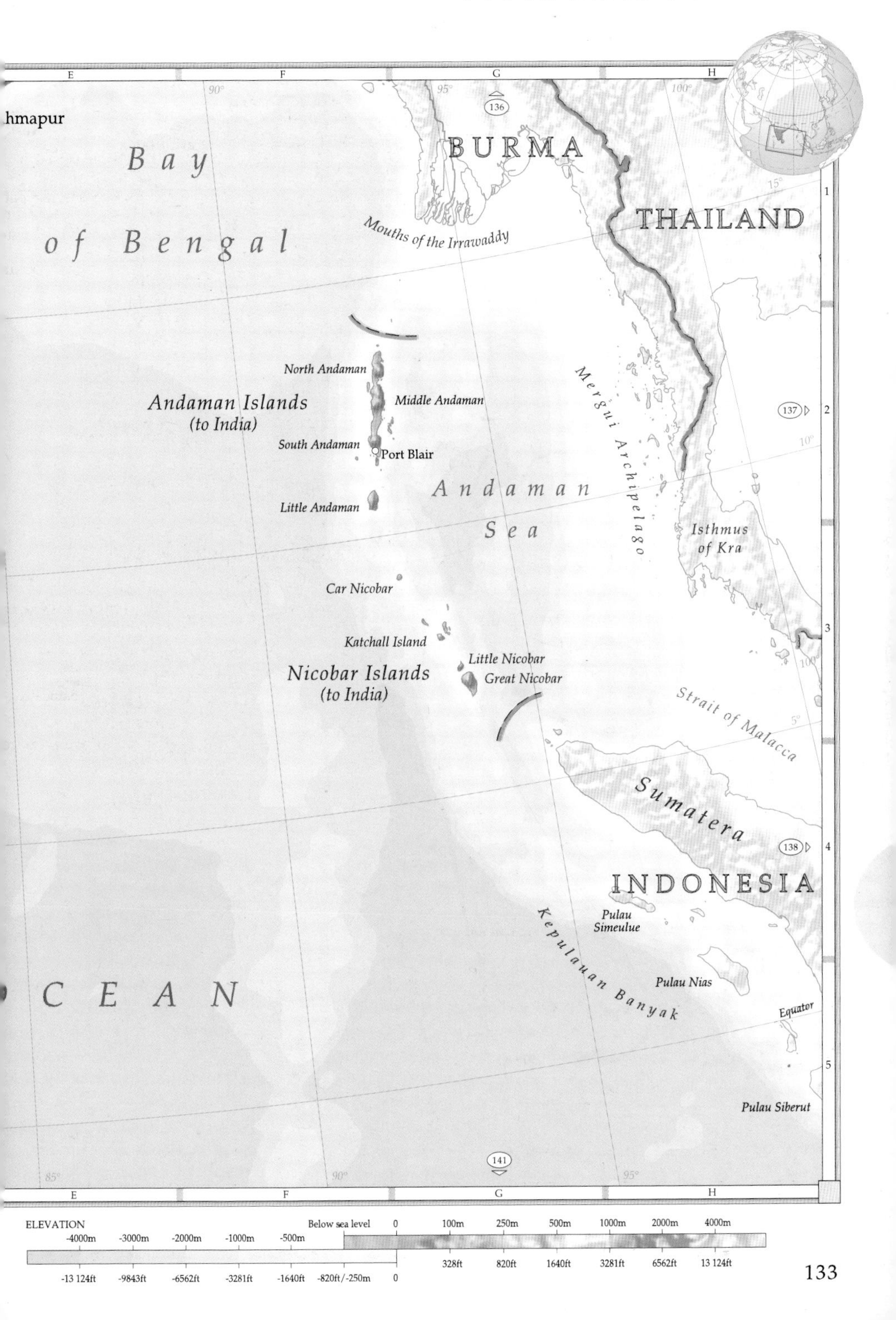

hmapur

Bay

of Bengal

BURMA

THAILAND

Mouths of the Irrawaddy

North Andaman

Andaman Islands
(to India)

Middle Andaman

Mergui Archipelago

South Andaman

Port Blair

A n d a m a n

S e a

Little Andaman

Isthmus
of Kra

Car Nicobar

Katchall Island

Nicobar Islands
(to India)

Little Nicobar
Great Nicobar

Strait of Malacca

Sumatera

INDONESIA

Pulau
Simeulue

Kepulauan Banyak

Pulau Nias

Equator

C E A N

Pulau Siberut

ELEVATION

						Below sea level	0	100m	250m	500m	1000m	2000m	4000m
-4000m	-3000m	-2000m	-1000m	-500m									
								328ft	820ft	1640ft	3281ft	6562ft	13 124ft
-13 124ft	-9843ft	-6562ft	-3281ft	-1640ft	-820ft/-250m	0							

NORTH INDIA, PAKISTAN & BANGLADESH

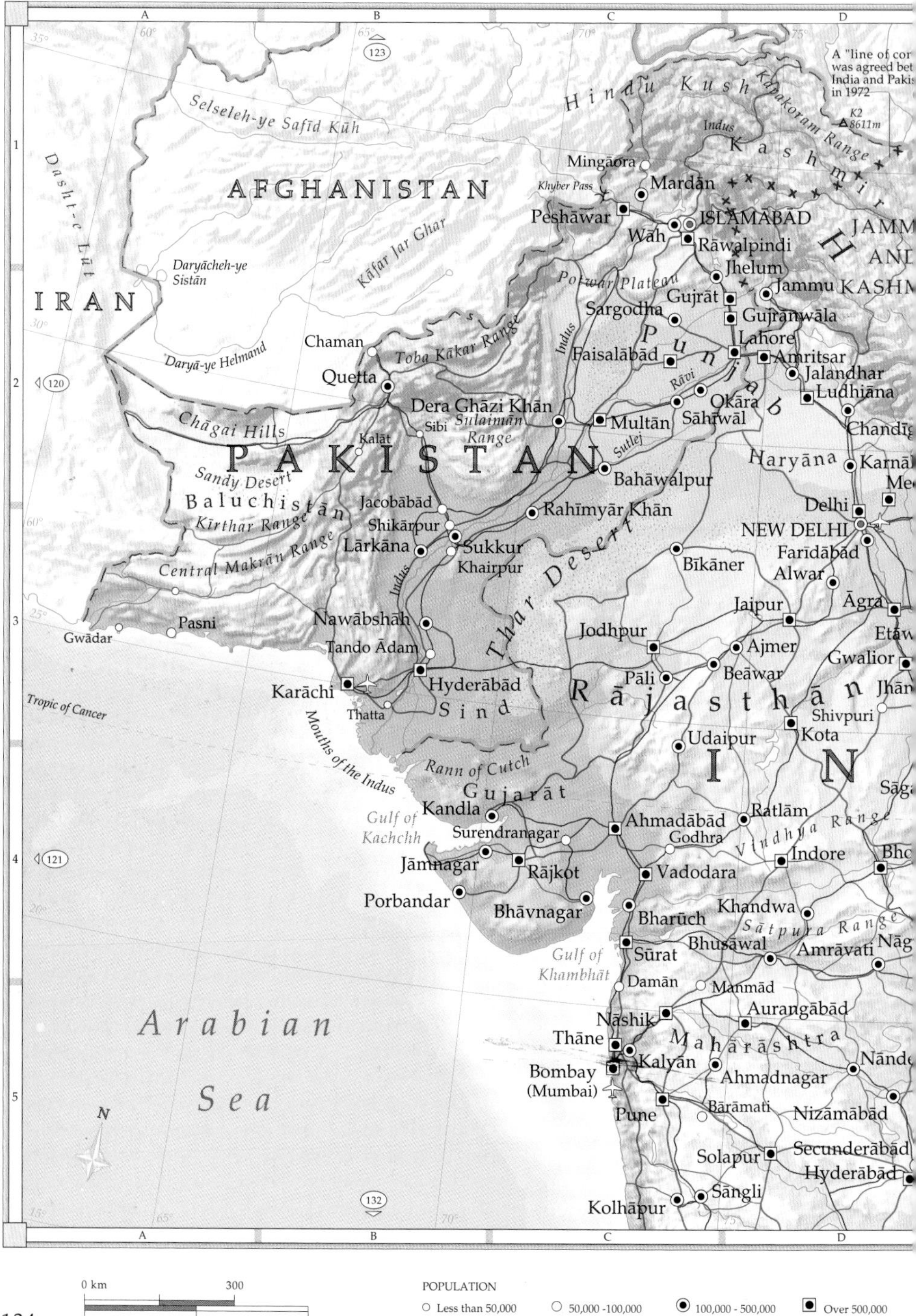

POPULATION

○ Less than 50,000   ○ 50,000 -100,000   ◉ 100,000 - 500,000   ■ Over 500,000

0 km   300

0 miles   300

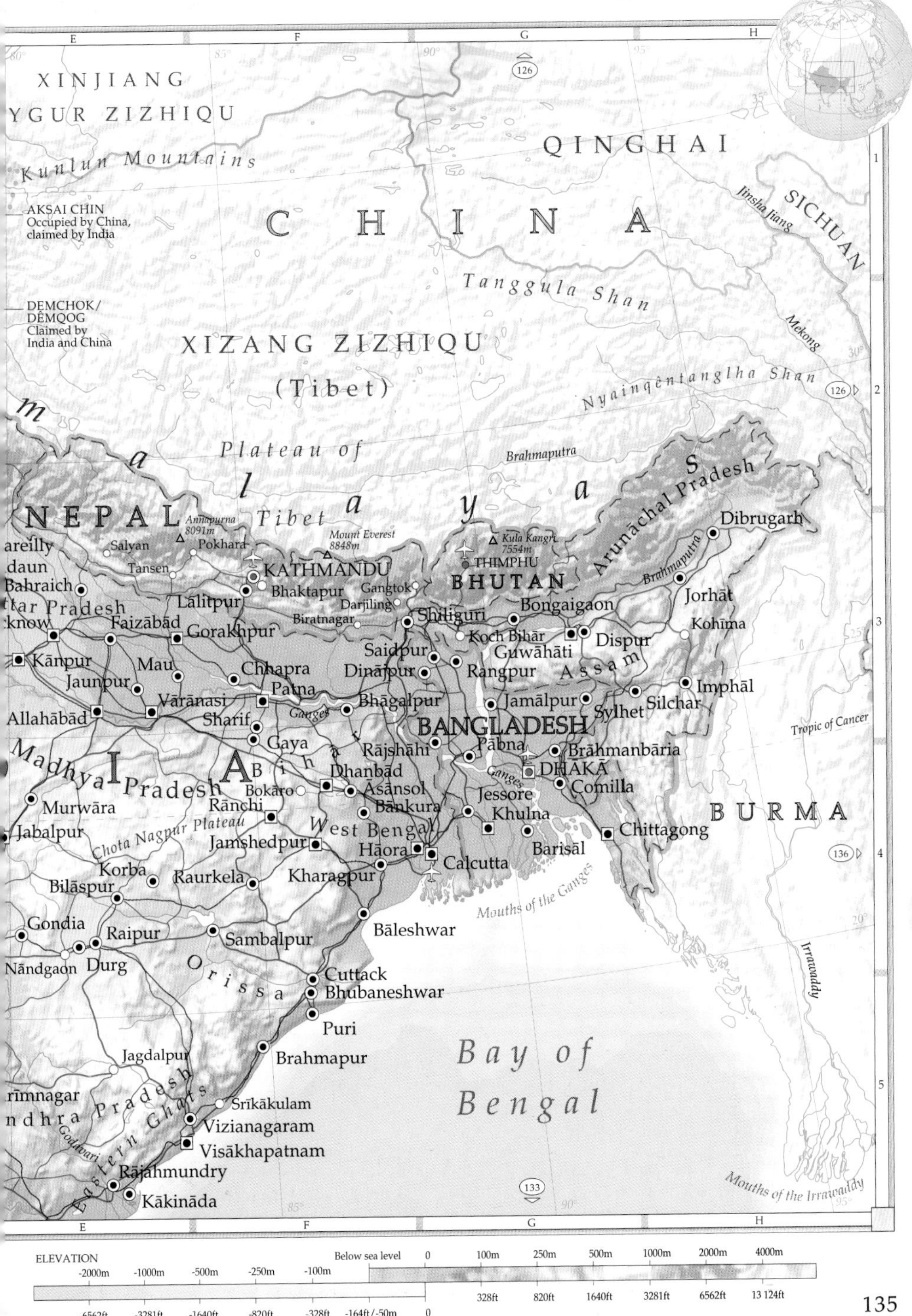

XINJIANG
YGUR ZIZHIQU

Kunlun Mountains

AKSAI CHIN
Occupied by China,
claimed by India

DEMCHOK/
DÊMQOG
Claimed by
India and China

QINGHAI

C H I N A

SICHUAN

Jinsha Jiang

Tanggula Shan

XIZANG ZIZHIQU

(Tibet)

Mekong

Nyainqêntanglha Shan

126

126

m
a
l
Plateau of
a
Tibet
y
a
s

Brahmaputra

Arunāchal Pradesh

NEPAL
Annapurna
8091m
Pokhara

Mount Everest
8848m

Kula Kangri
7554m

THIMPHU

Dibrugarh

Brahmaputra

areilly
Salyan

daun
Tansen

Bahraich
ttar Pradesh

know
Faizābād

Kānpur

Jaunpur

Allahābād

Lālitpur
Gorakhpur

Mau
Chhapra

Vārānasi
Sharif

Patna

Bhaktapur
Gangtok
Darjiling
Biratnagar

Saidpur
Dinājpur

KATHMANDU

BHUTAN

Shiliguri

Koch Bihār
Guwāhāti
Rangpur

Bongaigon

Jorhāt

Dispur

Kohīma

Assam

Imphāl

Silchar

Ganges

Gaya

Bhāgalpur

Jamālpur

Sylhet

Madhya

Pradesh

A

Bokaro

Dhanbād

Rānchi

Murwāra

Jabalpur

Jamshedpur

Korba

Bilāspur

Raurkela

Gondia

Raipur

Nāndgaon
Durg

Sambalpur

Chota Nagpur Plateau

B

Rājshāhi
Āsānsol
Bānkura

West Bengal

Haora

Kharagpur

Orissa

Cuttack
Bhubaneshwar

Sharif

BANGLADESH

Pābna

Ganges

DHAKA

Brāhmanbāria

Comilla

Jessore

Khulna

Barisāl

Calcutta

Chittagong

BURMA

Tropic of Cancer

Bāleshwar

Mouths of the Ganges

136

Irrawaddy

Jagdalpur

Brahmapur

Puri

rīmnagar
ndhra Pradesh

Eastern Ghats

Srīkākulam

Vizianagaram

Visākhapatnam

Godavari

Rājahmundry

Kākināda

B a y   o f
B e n g a l

Mouths of the Irrawaddy

133

135

MAINLAND SOUTHEAST ASIA

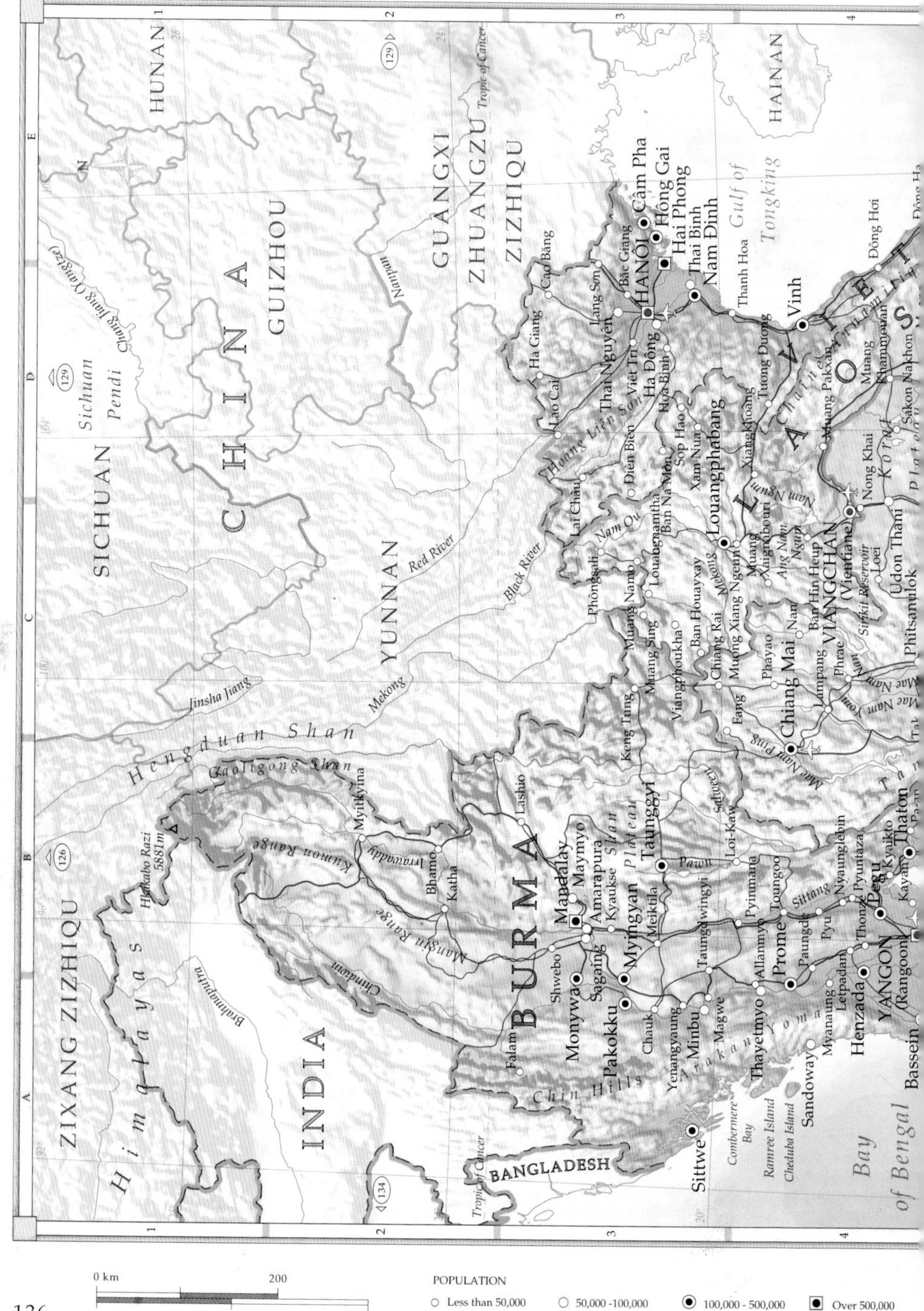

POPULATION

○ Less than 50,000   ○ 50,000 -100,000   ◉ 100,000 - 500,000   ■ Over 500,000

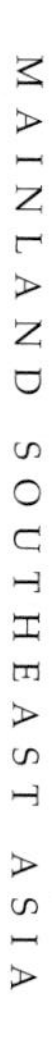

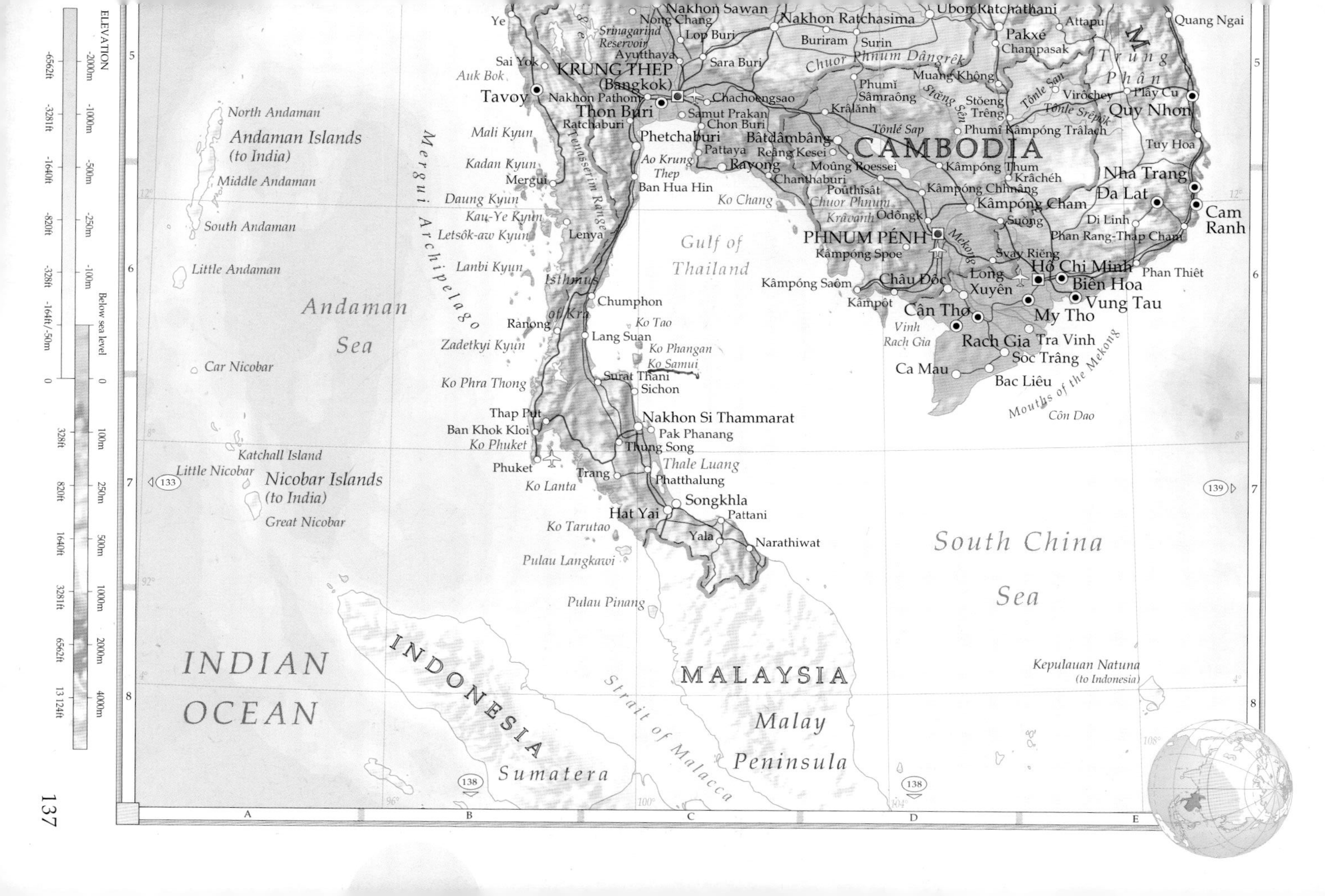
CAMBODIA
MALAYSIA
INDONESIA
South China Sea
Gulf of Thailand
Andaman Sea
INDIAN OCEAN
Strait of Malacca
Malay Peninsula
Mergui Archipelago
Sumatera
Andaman Islands (to India)
Nicobar Islands (to India)
North Andaman
Middle Andaman
South Andaman
Little Andaman
Car Nicobar
Katchall Island
Little Nicobar
Great Nicobar
Kepulauan Natuna (to Indonesia)
Côn Dao
Mouths of the Mekong
Mekong
Tônlé Sap
Vinh Rach Gia
Tenasserim Range
Isthmus of Kra
Chuor Phnum Dângrêk
Chuor Phnum Krâvanh
KRUNG THEP (Bangkok)
PHNUM PÉNH
Hô Chi Minh
Thon Buri
Nakhon Ratchasima
Nakhon Sawan
Ubon Ratchathani
Nakhon Si Thammarat
Songkhla
Hat Yai
Pattani
Narathiwat
Yala
Phatthalung
Surat Thani
Chumphon
Ranong
Phuket
Trang
Tavoy
Mergui
Ye
Sai Yok
Nakhon Pathom
Ratchaburi
Phetchaburi
Pattaya
Rayong
Chanthaburi
Chachoengsao
Samut Prakan
Chon Buri
Bătdâmbâng
Kâmpóng Saôm
Kâmpôt
Kâmpóng Cham
Krâchéh
Pakxé
Champasak
Attapu
Quy Nhon
Nha Trang
Cam Ranh
Đa Lat
Vung Tau
Biên Hoa
My Tho
Cân Thơ
Rach Gia
Long Xuyên
Châu Đốc
Soc Trang
Tra Vinh
Bac Liêu
Ca Mau
Phan Thiêt
Tuy Hoa
Quang Ngai
Buriram
Surin
Sara Buri
Lop Buri
Ayutthaya
Ko Samui
Ko Phangan
Ko Tao
Ko Chang
Ko Phuket
Ko Lanta
Ko Tarutao
Pulau Langkawi
Pulau Pinang
Thale Luang
ELEVATION
Below sea level
-2000m -1000m -500m -250m -100m
-6562ft -3281ft -1640ft -820ft -328ft -164ft/-50m
0 100m 250m 500m 1000m 2000m 4000m
328ft 820ft 1640ft 3281ft 6562ft 13 124ft

MARITIME SOUTHEAST ASIA

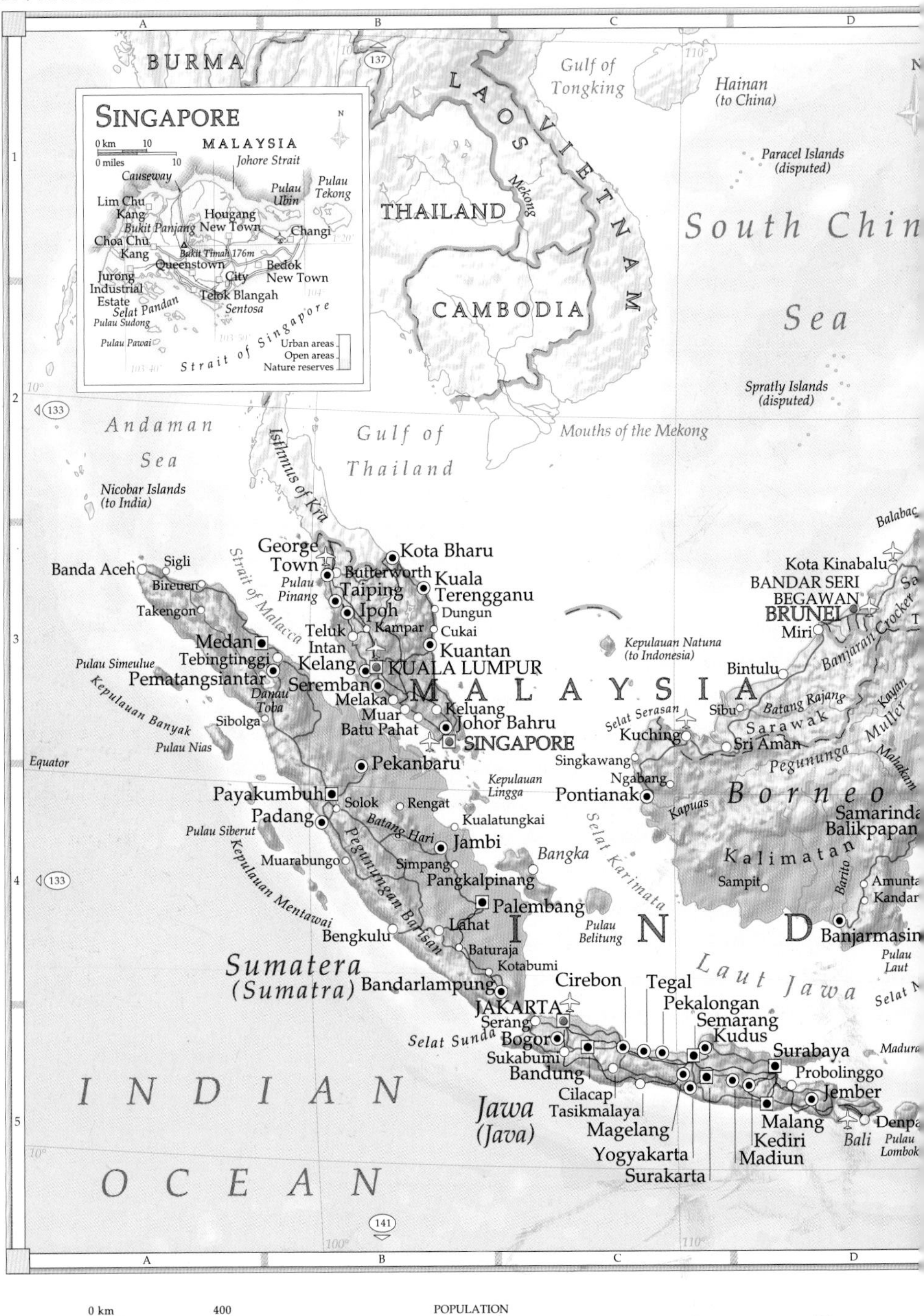

SINGAPORE

0 km   10
0 miles   10

MALAYSIA
Johore Strait

Causeway

Lim Chu Kang
Pulau Ubin
Pulau Tekong

Bukit Panjang New Town
Hougang
Changi

Choa Chu Kang

Bukit Timah 176m

Jurong Industrial Estate
Queenstown
City
Bedok New Town

Telok Blangah

Selat Pandan
Sentosa

Pulau Sudong

Pulau Pawai

Strait of Singapore

Urban areas
Open areas
Nature reserves

BURMA

Gulf of Tongking

Hainan (to China)

LAOS

VIETNAM

THAILAND

Paracel Islands (disputed)

CAMBODIA

South China

Sea

Andaman Sea

Mouths of the Mekong

Gulf of Thailand

Spratly Islands (disputed)

Nicobar Islands (to India)

Isthmus of Kra

Balabac

Banda Aceh
Sigli
Bireuen

George Town
Kota Bharu

Pulau Pinang
Butterworth
Kuala Terengganu

Kota Kinabalu
BANDAR SERI BEGAWAN
BRUNEI

Takengon
Taiping
Ipoh
Dungun

Miri

Teluk
Kampar
Cukai

Kepulauan Natuna (to Indonesia)

Bintulu

Strait of Malacca

Medan
Intan
Kuantan

Banjaran Crocker

Tebingtinggi
Kelang
KUALA LUMPUR

Pematangsiantar
Seremban
M A L A Y S I A

Sibu
Batang Rajang
Sarawak

Pulau Simeulue

Danau Toba
Melaka

Sri Aman
Kayan

Sibolga
Muar
Keluang

Selat Serasan
Kuching

Kepulauan Banyak

Batu Pahat
Johor Bahru

Singkawang

Pegunungan Muller

Pulau Nias

SINGAPORE

B o r n e o

Equator

Pekanbaru

Kepulauan Lingga
Pontianak

Ngabang

Payakumbuh
Solok
Rengat

Kapuas

Samarinda
Balikpapan

Padang
Kualatungkai

Selat Karimata

K a l i m a n t a n

Pulau Siberut

Batang Hari
Jambi

Bangka

Sampit

Amunta Kandar

Muarabungo
Simpang

Pangkalpinang

Bartio

Kepulauan Mentawai

Pesunungan Barisan

Palembang

I
N
D
Banjarmasin

Bengkulu
Lahat
Baturaja

Pulau Belitung

Pulau Laut

Sumatera
(Sumatra)
Bandarlampung

Kotabumi
Cirebon
Tegal

L a u t   J a w a
Selat N

Serang
JAKARTA
Pekalongan
Semarang

Selat Sunda
Bogor
Sukabumi
Kudus

Madura

Bandung
Cilacap
Surabaya

I N D I A N
Jawa
(Java)
Tasikmalaya
Malang
Probolinggo
Jember

Magelang
Kediri
Denpa

O C E A N
Yogyakarta
Madiun
Bali
Pulau Lombok

Surakarta

0 km   400
0 miles   400

POPULATION

○ Less than 50,000   ○ 50,000 -100,000   ◉ 100,000 - 500,000   ■ Over 500,000

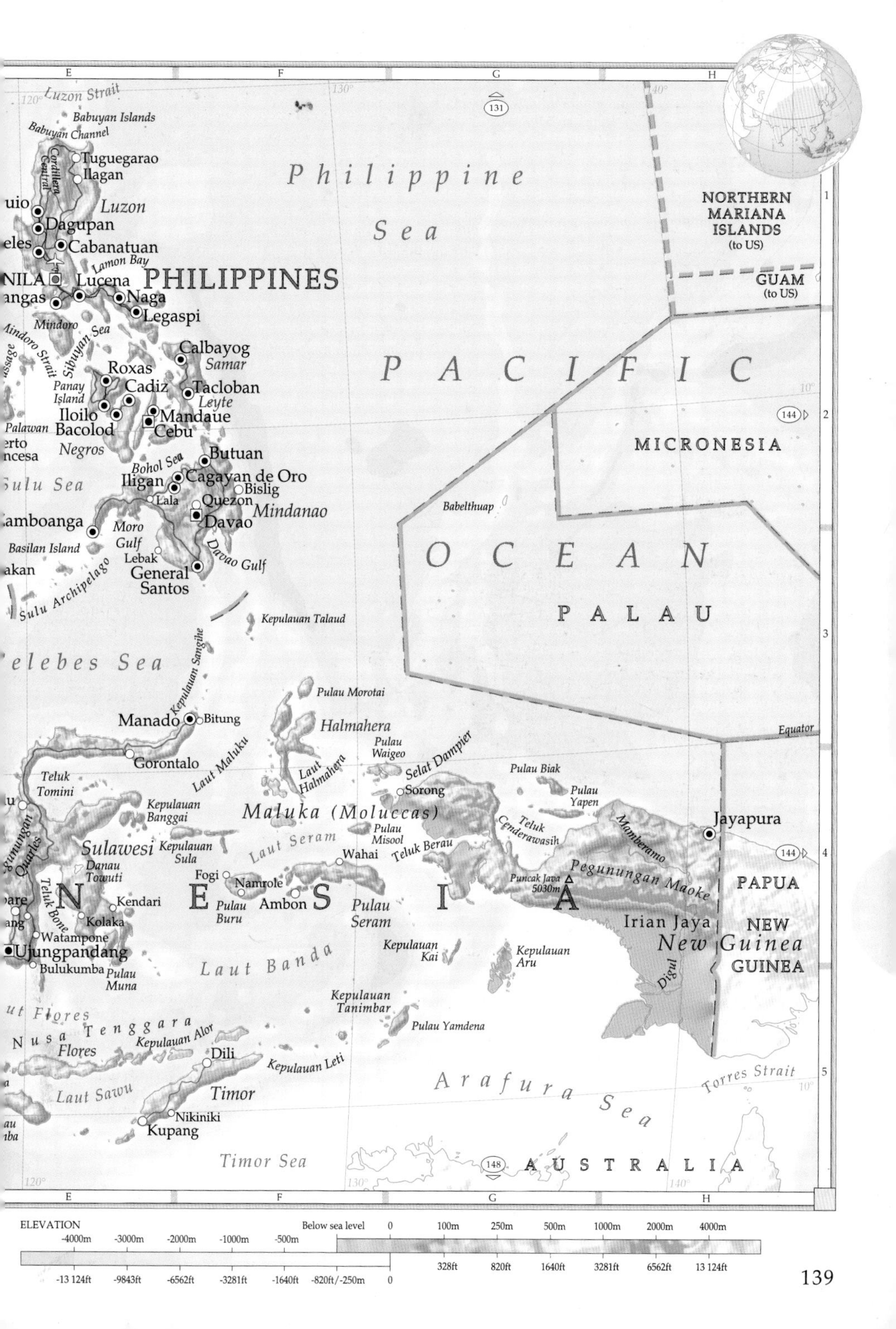

ELEVATION

					Below sea level	0	100m	250m	500m	1000m	2000m	4000m
-4000m	-3000m	-2000m	-1000m	-500m								
							328ft	820ft	1640ft	3281ft	6562ft	13 124ft
-13 124ft	-9843ft	-6562ft	-3281ft	-1640ft	-820ft/-250m	0						

THE INDIAN OCEAN

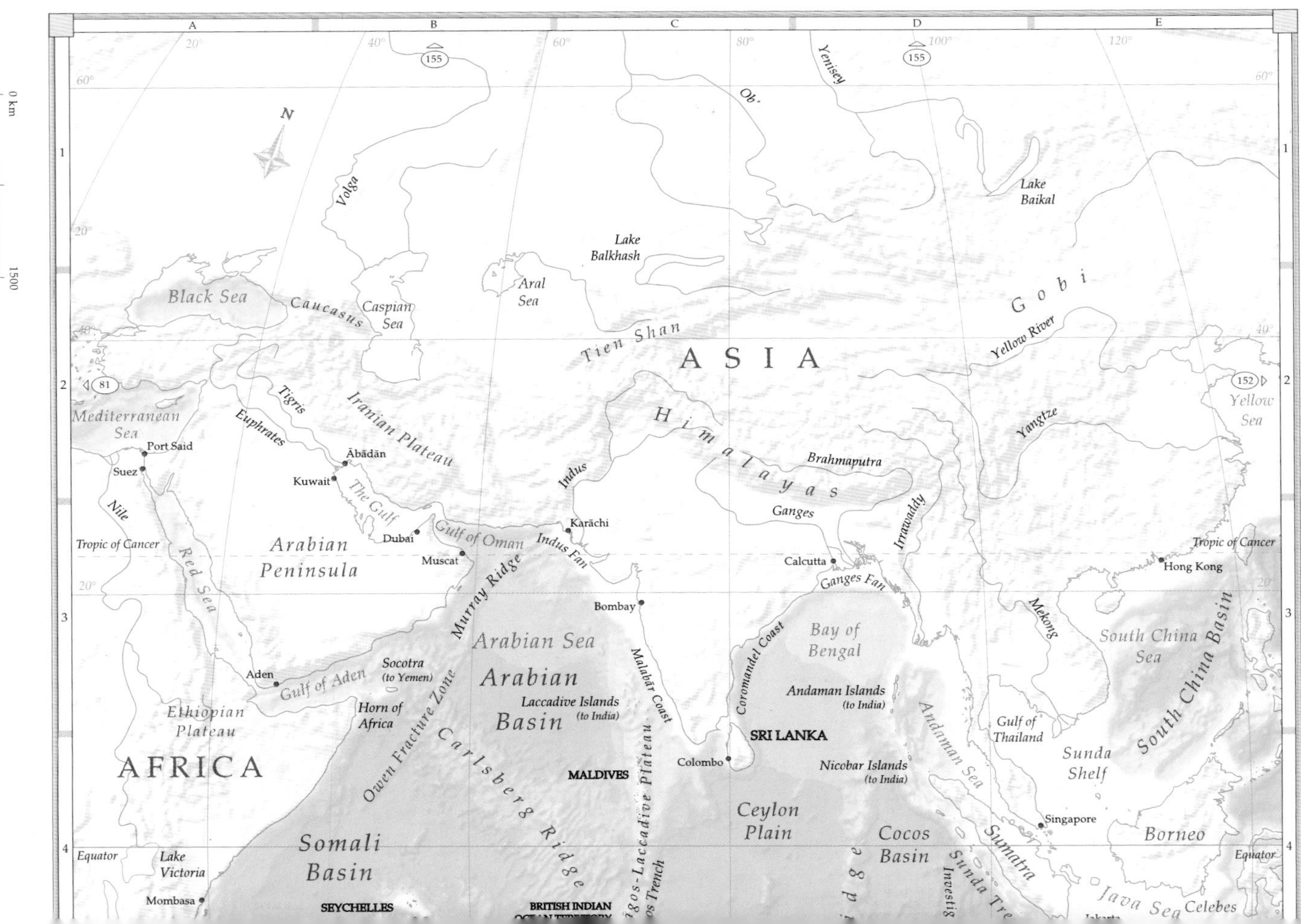

0 km — 1500

0 miles — 1500

• Major ports

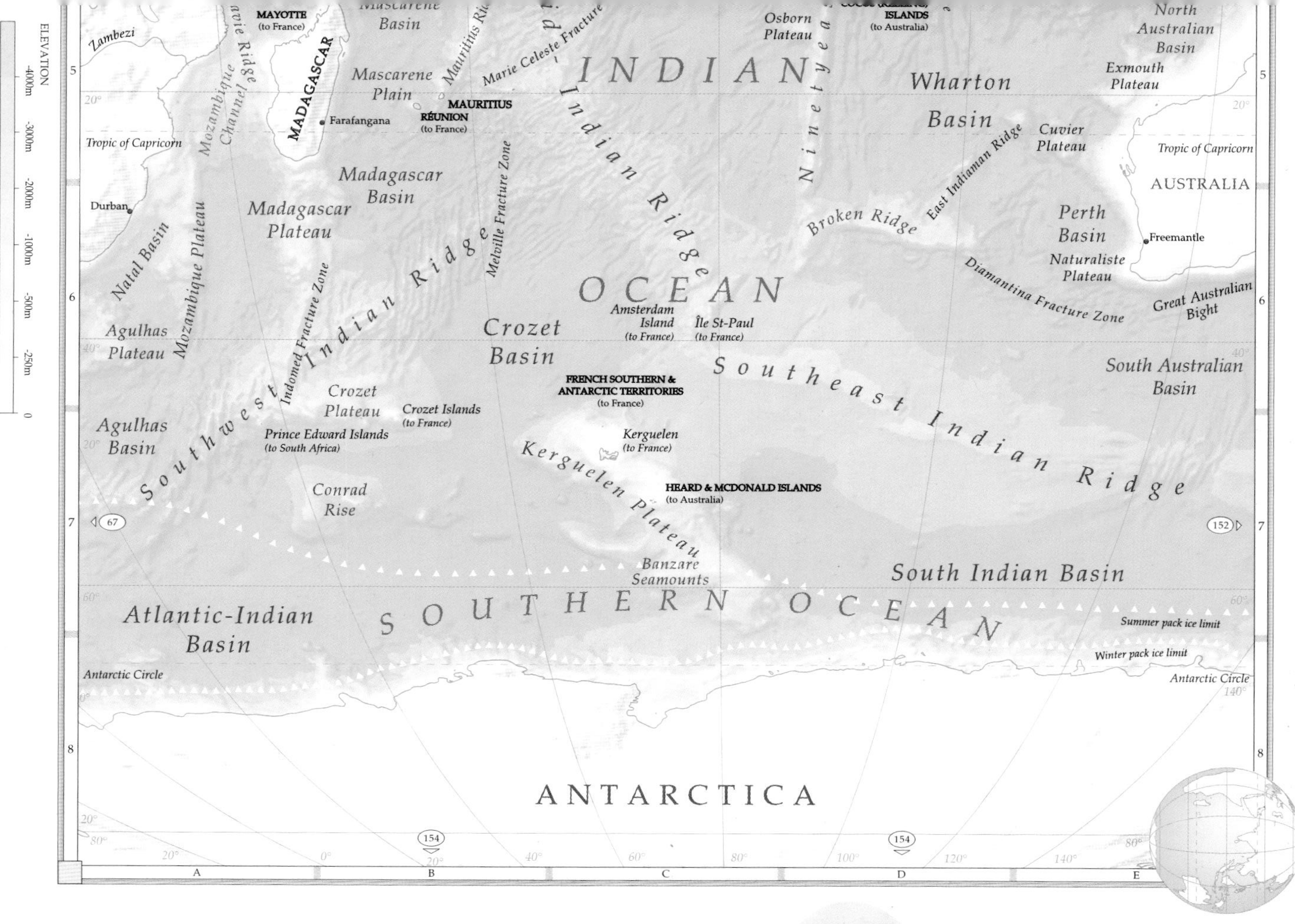

AUSTRALIA

Freemantle

Tropic of Capricorn

North Australian Basin

Exmouth Plateau

Cuvier Plateau

Perth Basin

Great Australian Bight

South Australian Basin

Naturaliste Plateau

Diamantina Fracture Zone

Wharton Basin

East Indiaman Ridge

Broken Ridge

Ninetyeast Ridge

Osborn Plateau

COCOS (KEELING) ISLANDS (to Australia)

INDIAN OCEAN

Mid Indian Ridge

Southeast Indian Ridge

South Indian Basin

Amsterdam Island (to France)

Île St-Paul (to France)

FRENCH SOUTHERN & ANTARCTIC TERRITORIES (to France)

Kerguelen (to France)

HEARD & McDONALD ISLANDS (to Australia)

Kerguelen Plateau

Banzare Seamounts

SOUTHERN OCEAN

ANTARCTICA

Crozet Basin

Melville Fracture Zone

Mid Capelle Fracture

Mauritius Rise

MAURITIUS

RÉUNION (to France)

Mascarene Plain

Mascarene Basin

Madagascar Basin

Madagascar Plateau

Fianarantsoa

MADAGASCAR

MAYOTTE (to France)

vie Ridge

Mozambique Channel

Zambezi

Southwest Indian Ridge

Indomed Fracture Zone

Crozet Plateau

Crozet Islands (to France)

Prince Edward Islands (to South Africa)

Conrad Rise

Atlantic-Indian Basin

Antarctic Circle

Mozambique Plateau

Natal Basin

Agulhas Plateau

Agulhas Basin

Durban

Tropic of Capricorn

Antarctic Circle

Summer pack ice limit

Winter pack ice limit

Antarctic Circle

152

154

154

67

ELEVATION

-4000m	-3000m	-2000m	-1000m	-500m	-250m	0
-13 124ft	-9843ft	-6562ft	-3281ft	-1640ft	-820ft	0

141

AUSTRALASIA & OCEANIA

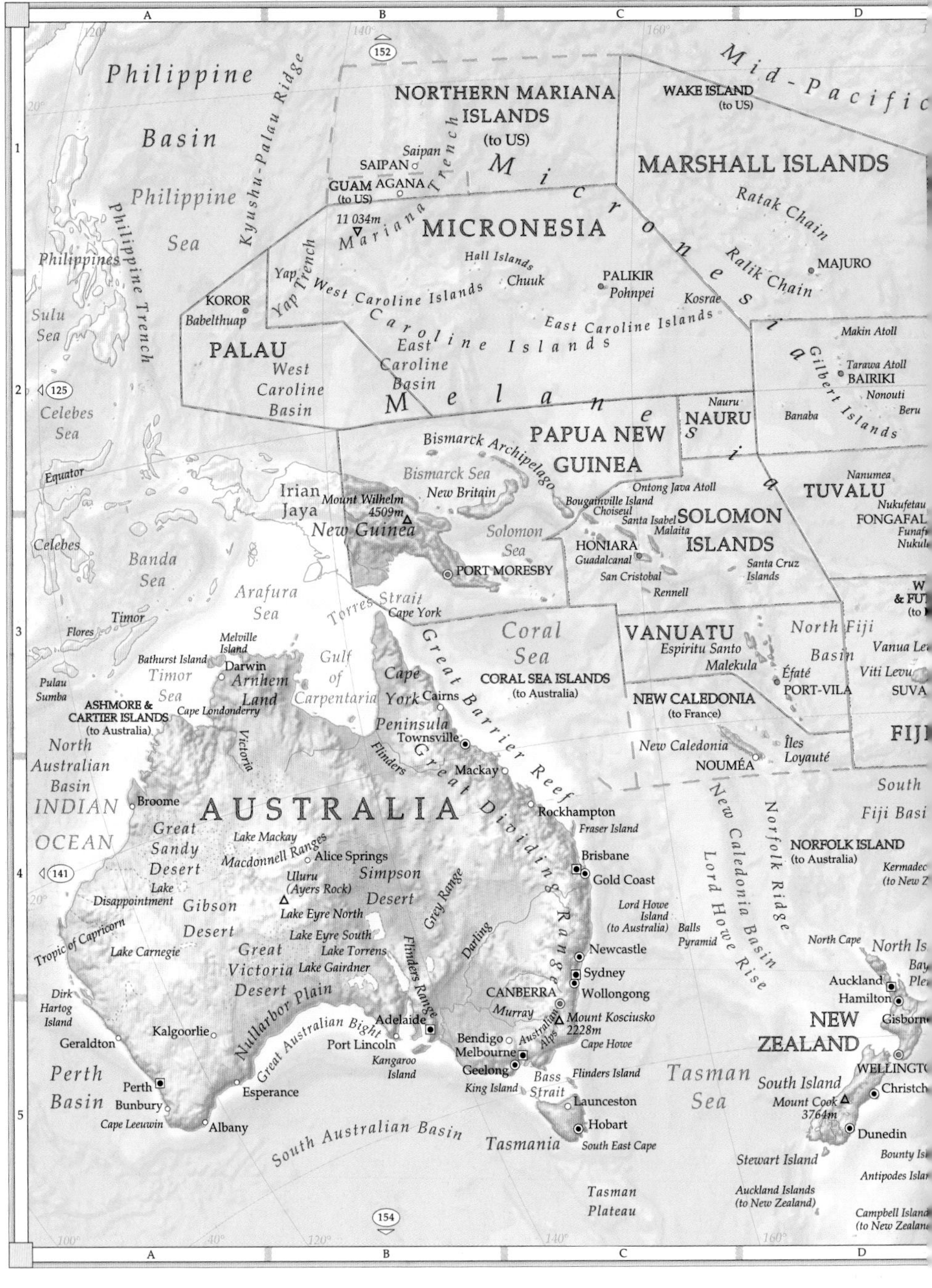

Philippine
Basin
Philippine
Sea
Philippines
Philippine Trench
Kyushu-Palau Ridge
152

NORTHERN MARIANA
ISLANDS
(to US)
Saipan
SAIPAN
GUAM AGANA
(to US)
11 034m
Mariana Trench
West Caroline Islands
Yap Trench
Hall Islands
Chuuk

WAKE ISLAND
(to US)

Mid-Pacific

MARSHALL ISLANDS
Ratak Chain
MAJURO
Ralik Chain

MICRONESIA
PALIKIR
Pohnpei
Kosrae

Sulu
Sea
KOROR
Babelthuap
PALAU
West
Caroline
Basin
East
Caroline
Basin
Caroline Islands
East Caroline Islands

Celebes
Sea
125

Equator

Celebes

Banda
Sea

Timor

Pulau
Sumba

Flores

Bathurst Island
Melville
Island
Darwin
Arnhem
Land
Cape Londonderry
ASHMORE &
CARTIER ISLANDS
(to Australia)

North
Australian
Basin

INDIAN
OCEAN
141

Tropic of Capricorn

Dirk
Hartog
Island
Geraldton

Perth
Basin

Cape Leeuwin

Bismarck Archipelago
Bismarck Sea
New Britain

PAPUA NEW
GUINEA

Irian
Jaya
Mount Wilhelm
4509m
New Guinea

PORT MORESBY

Arafura
Sea
Torres Strait
Cape York

Gulf
of
Carpentaria
Cape
York
Peninsula

AUSTRALIA
Great
Sandy
Desert
Lake Mackay
Macdonnell Ranges
Alice Springs
Uluru
(Ayers Rock)
Simpson
Desert
Gibson
Desert
Lake Eyre North
Great
Victoria Lake Gairdner
Desert
Lake Eyre South
Lake Torrens
Lake Disappointment
Lake Carnegie
Nullarbor Plain

Broome

Kalgoorlie

Perth
Bunbury
Albany
Esperance

Cairns
Townsville
Mackay

Coral
Sea
CORAL SEA ISLANDS
(to Australia)

Great Barrier Reef

Rockhampton
Fraser Island
Brisbane
Gold Coast

Great Dividing Range

Grey Range
Darling
Flinders Ranges
Adelaide
Port Lincoln
Kangaroo
Island
Port Pirie

Bendigo
Melbourne
Geelong

CANBERRA
Murray
Mount Kosciusko
2228m
Cape Howe
Australian Alps

Newcastle
Sydney
Wollongong

Nanumea
Nukufetau
Nukulaelae
TUVALU
FONGAFALE
Funafuti

Makin Atoll
Tarawa Atoll
BAIRIKI
Nonouti
Beru
Gilbert Islands

Nauru
NAURU
Banaba

Micronesia

Melanesia

Ontong Java Atoll
Bougainville Island
Choiseul
Santa Isabel
Malaita
SOLOMON
HONIARA
Guadalcanal
ISLANDS
San Cristobal
Rennell
Santa Cruz
Islands

VANUATU
Espiritu Santo
Malekula
Éfaté
PORT-VILA

NEW CALEDONIA
(to France)
New Caledonia
NOUMÉA

North Fiji
Basin
Vanua Levu
Viti Levu
SUVA
Îles
Loyauté

W
& FUT
(to

FIJI

South
Fiji Basin

NORFOLK ISLAND
(to Australia)
Kermadec
(to New Z

Lord Howe
Island
(to Australia)
Balls
Pyramid

Lord Howe Rise
New Caledonia Basin
Norfolk Ridge
Norfolk Island

North Cape
North Is
Bay
Auckland
Ple
Hamilton

NEW
ZEALAND

Gisborne

Tasman
Sea

WELLINGTON
South Island
Mount Cook
3764m
Christch

Dunedin
Bounty Isl
Antipodes Islan

Flinders Island
Bass
King Island Strait
Launceston
Hobart
Tasmania
South East Cape

Stewart Island

Auckland Islands
(to New Zealand)

Campbell Island
(to New Zealan

Tasman
Plateau
Tasman
Plateau
154

South Australian Basin

Great Australian Bight

Victoria

POPULATION
○ Less than 50,000   ⊙ 50,000 -100,000   ◉ 100,000 - 500,000   ■ Over 500,000

0 km   1000
0 miles   1000

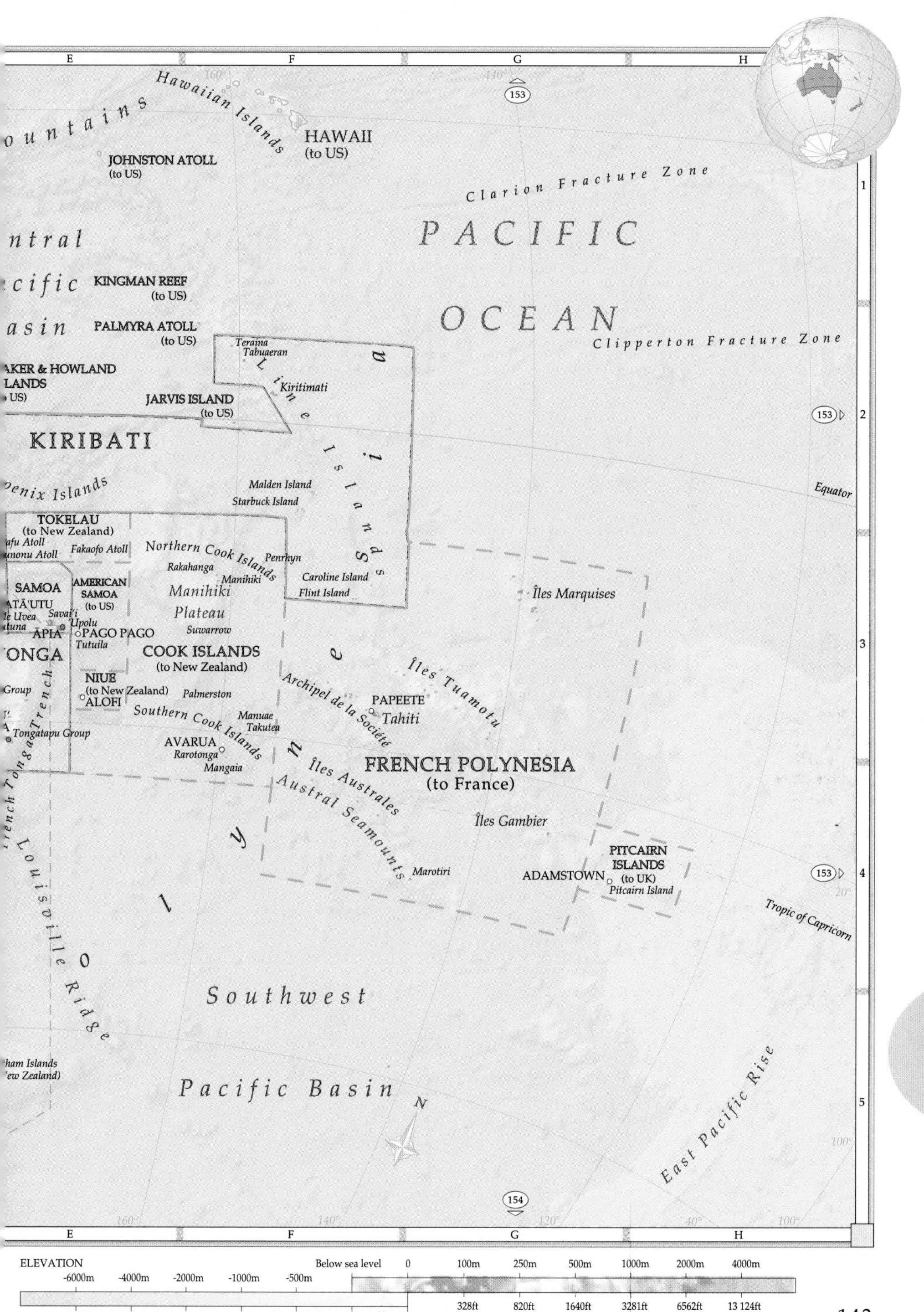

ountains

Hawaiian Islands

HAWAII
(to US)

JOHNSTON ATOLL
(to US)

ntral

cific

asin

KINGMAN REEF
(to US)

PALMYRA ATOLL
(to US)

Clarion Fracture Zone

PACIFIC

OCEAN

Clipperton Fracture Zone

AKER & HOWLAND
LANDS
US)

JARVIS ISLAND
(to US)

Teraina
Tabuaeran

Kiritimati

KIRIBATI

enix Islands

Malden Island
Starbuck Island

Equator

TOKELAU
(to New Zealand)

fu Atoll   Fakaofo Atoll
nonu Atoll

Northern Cook Islands

Rakahanga

Penrhyn

Caroline Island

Flint Island

SAMOA

ATĀ'UTU

Te Uvea   *Savai'i*
tuna   *Upolu*

APIA   *Tutuila*

ONGA

AMERICAN
SAMOA
(to US)

PAGO PAGO

Manihiki

Plateau

Suwarrow

Îles Marquises

COOK ISLANDS
(to New Zealand)

NIUE
(to New Zealand)
ALOFI   *Palmerston*

Group

Southern Cook Islands

Tongatapu Group

Manuae
Takutea

PAPEETE
Tahiti

Archipel de la Société

Îles Tuamotu

AVARUA
Rarotonga
Mangaia

Îles Australes

FRENCH POLYNESIA
(to France)

Austral Seamounts

Îles Gambier

PITCAIRN
ISLANDS
(to UK)

ADAMSTOWN
Pitcairn Island

Marotiri

Tropic of Capricorn

French Tonga Trench

Louisville Ridge

Southwest

ham Islands
ew Zealand)

Pacific Basin

N

East Pacific Rise

E   F   G   H

ELEVATION

| | | | | | Below sea level | 0 | 100m | 250m | 500m | 1000m | 2000m | 4000m |

-6000m   -4000m   -2000m   -1000m   -500m

-19 686ft   -13 124ft   -6562ft   -3281ft   -1640ft   -820ft/-250m   0

328ft   820ft   1640ft   3281ft   6562ft   13 124ft

143

THE SOUTHWEST PACIFIC

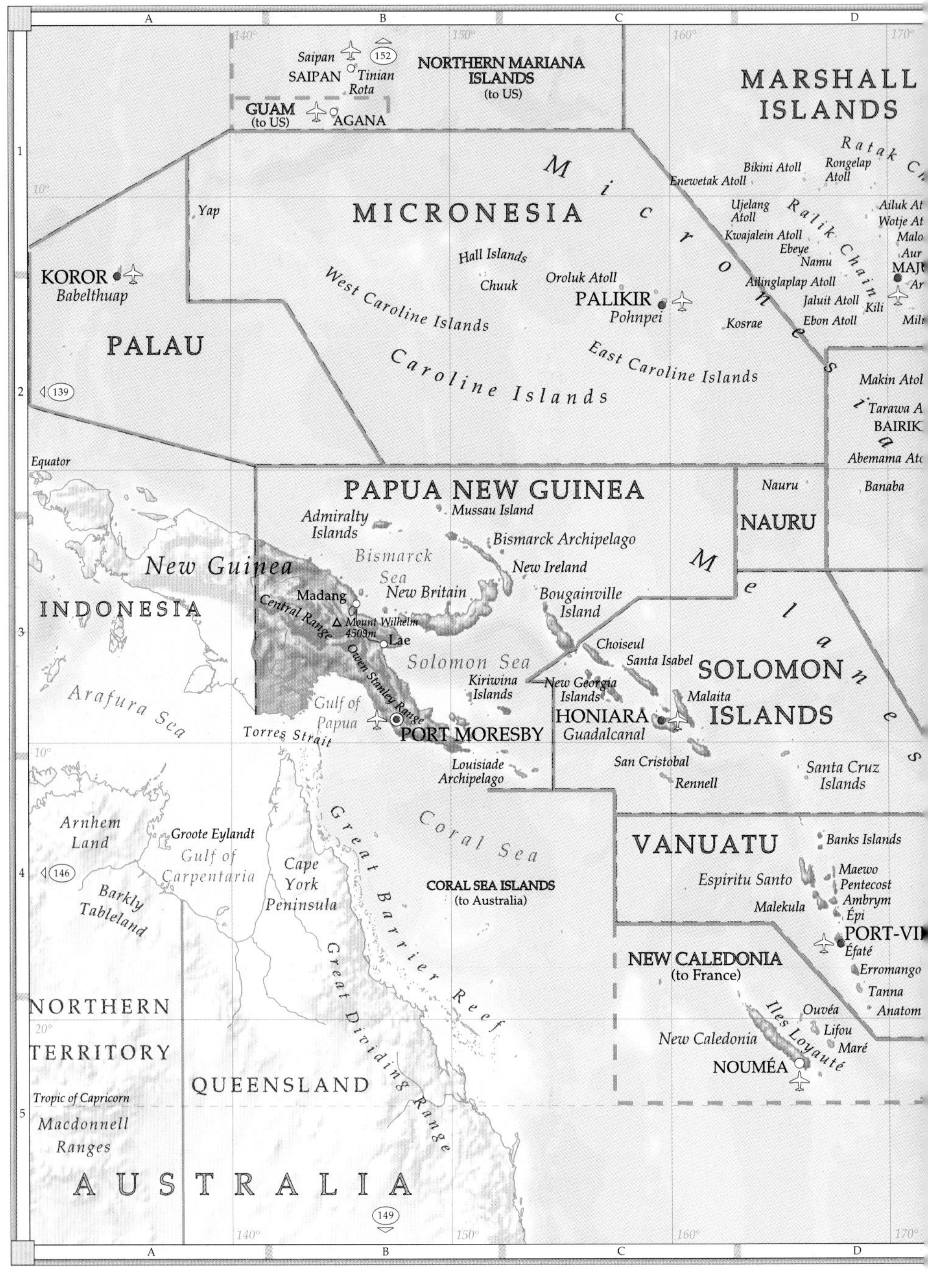

POPULATION

○ Less than 50,000   ○ 50,000 -100,000   ◉ 100,000 - 500,000   ■ Over 500,000

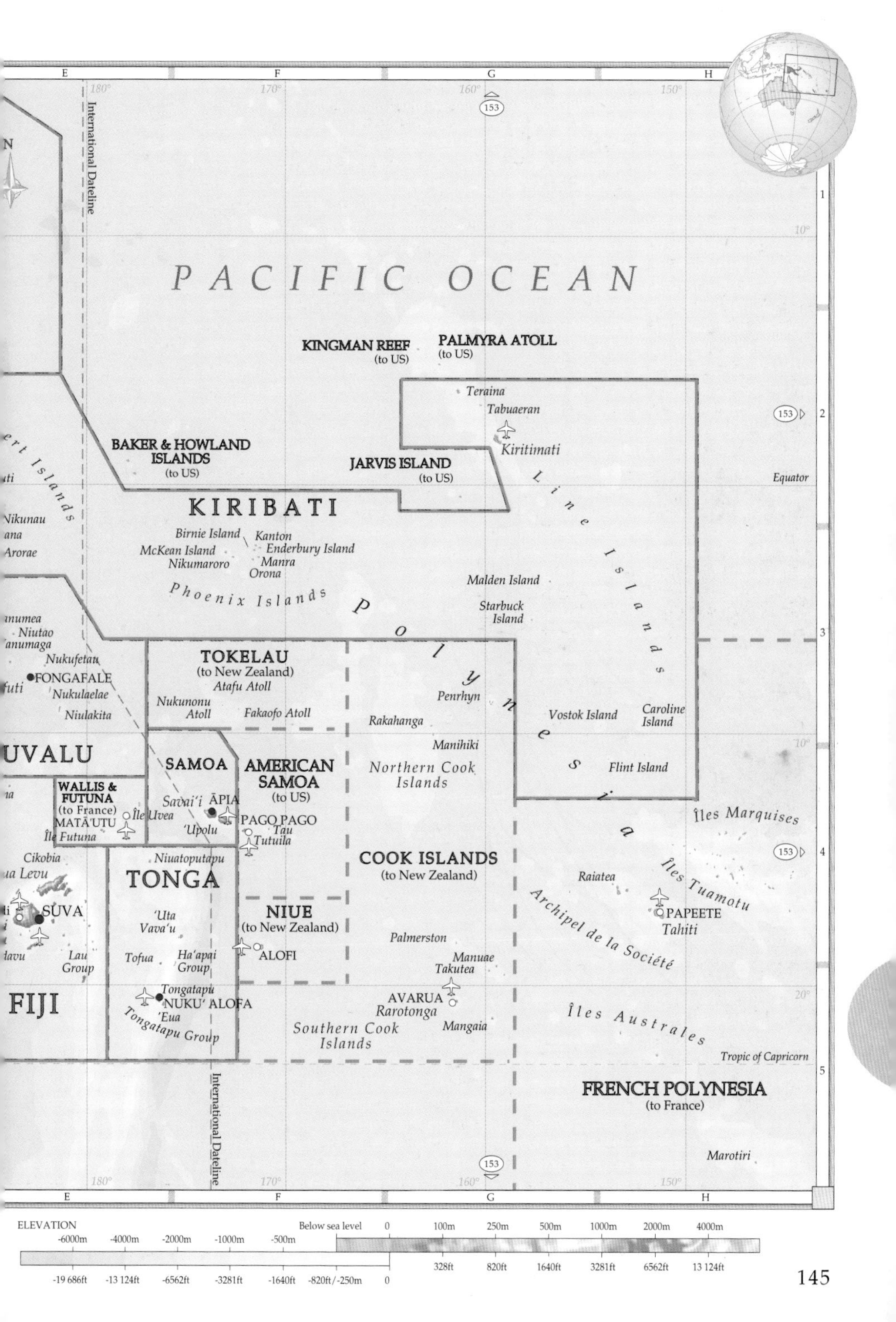

PACIFIC OCEAN

KINGMAN REEF
(to US)

PALMYRA ATOLL
(to US)

Teraina

Tabuaeran

BAKER & HOWLAND
ISLANDS
(to US)

JARVIS ISLAND
(to US)

Kiritimati

L i n e   I s l a n d s

Equator

KIRIBATI

Birnie Island   *Kanton*

McKean Island   *Enderbury Island*

Nikumaroro   *Manra*

Orona

Malden Island

*Starbuck
Island*

P h o e n i x   I s l a n d s

P o l y n e s i a

TOKELAU
(to New Zealand)
Atafu Atoll

Penrhyn

Vostok Island

*Caroline
Island*

*Nukunonu
Atoll*   *Fakaofo Atoll*

Rakahanga

Manihiki

*Northern Cook
Islands*

Flint Island

SAMOA

Savai'i ĀPIA

AMERICAN
SAMOA
(to US)

Upolu   PAGO PAGO
Tau
Tutuila

Îles Marquises

WALLIS &
FUTUNA
(to France)
MATA'UTU   *Île Uvea*
Île Futuna

Niuatoputapu

COOK ISLANDS
(to New Zealand)

Raiatea

Îles Tuamotu

Archipel de la Société

TONGA

'*Uta
Vava'u*

NIUE
(to New Zealand)
ALOFI

Palmerston

*Manuae
Takutea*

PAPEETE
Tahiti

SUVA

Tofua   *Ha'apai
Group*

Tongatapu
NUKU'ALOFA
'*Eua*

*Lau
Group*

AVARUA
Rarotonga

Mangaia

Îles Australes

FIJI

Tongatapu Group

*Southern Cook
Islands*

Tropic of Capricorn

FRENCH POLYNESIA
(to France)

Marotiri

UVALU

UVALU

Nukufetau
•FONGAFALE
Nukulaelae

Niulakita

WALLIS &
FUTUNA

Cikobia
u Levu

Nikunau
ana
Arorae

rt Islands

ti

N

International Dateline

WESTERN AUSTRALIA

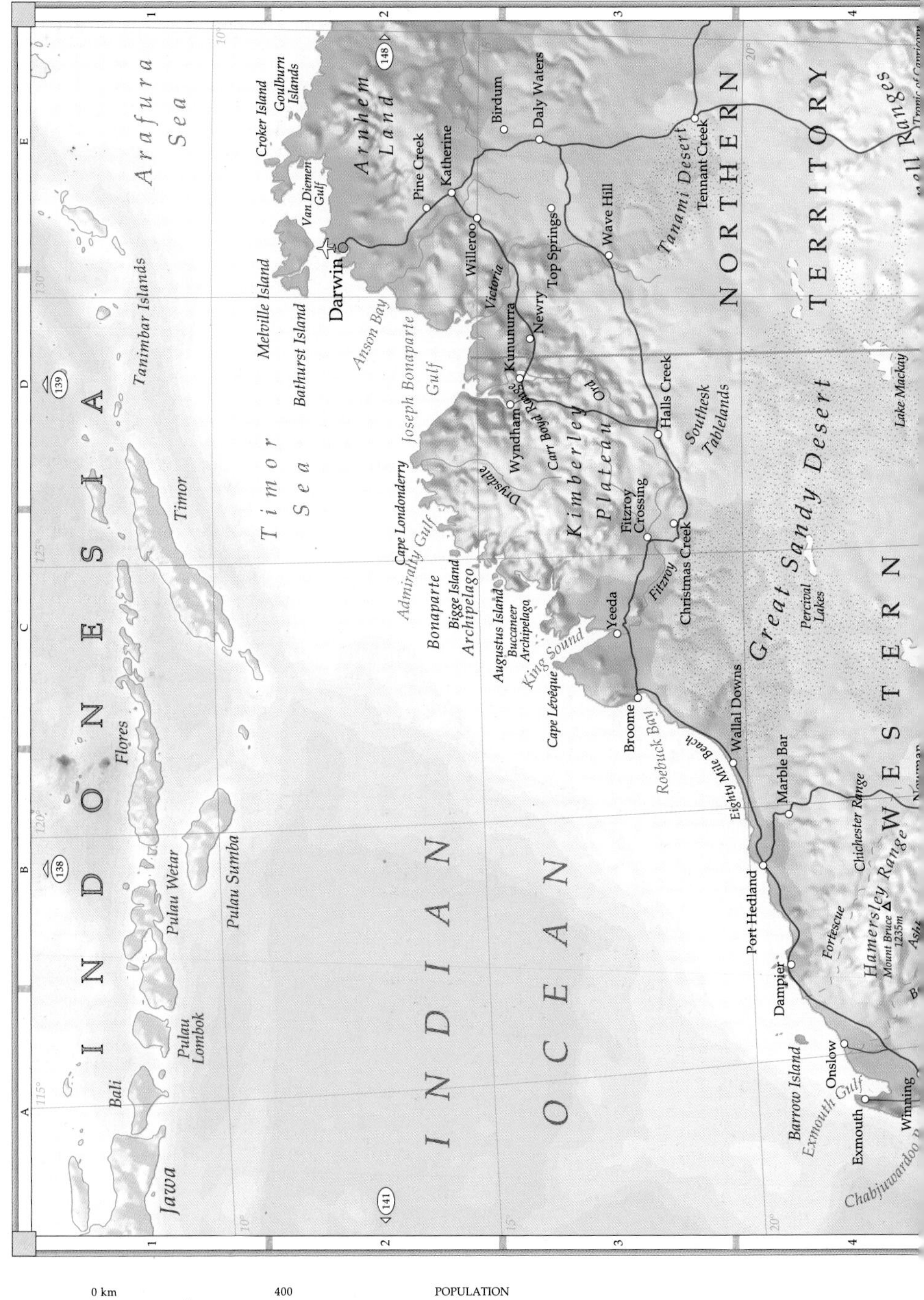

Arafura Sea

Tanimbar Islands

Croker Island
Goulburn Islands

Arnhem Land

Pine Creek
Katherine
Birdum
Daly Waters

Timor Sea

Melville Island
Bathurst Island

Van Diemen Gulf

Darwin

Anson Bay

Willeroo
Victoria
Newry
Top Springs
Wave Hill

Tanami Desert
Tennant Creek

NORTHERN

TERRITORY

Lake Mackay

Timor

INDONESIA

Flores

Pulau Wetar

Pulau Sumba

Pulau Lombok

Bali

Javα

Joseph Bonaparte Gulf

Cape Londonderry
Admiralty Gulf
Bonaparte Archipelago
Bigge Island
Augustus Island
Buccaneer Archipelago
Cape Leveque
King Leveque Sound

Wyndham
Carr Boyd Ranges
Kununurra
Drysdale

Kimberley Plateau
Ord
Halls Creek
Southesk Tablelands
Fitzroy Crossing
Fitzroy
Christmas Creek

Great Sandy Desert

Percival Lakes

WESTERN

Yeeda
Broome
Roebuck Bay
Eighty Mile Beach
Wallal Downs

Marble Bar
Chichester Range
Fortescue
Hamersley Range
Mount Bruce 1235m

Port Hedland
Dampier
Newman

INDIAN

OCEAN

Barrow Island
Onslow
Exmouth Gulf
Exmouth
Winning
Chabjuwardoo

0 km   400

0 miles   400

POPULATION

○ Less than 50,000   ○ 50,000 -100,000   ● 100,000 - 500,000   ■ Over 500,000

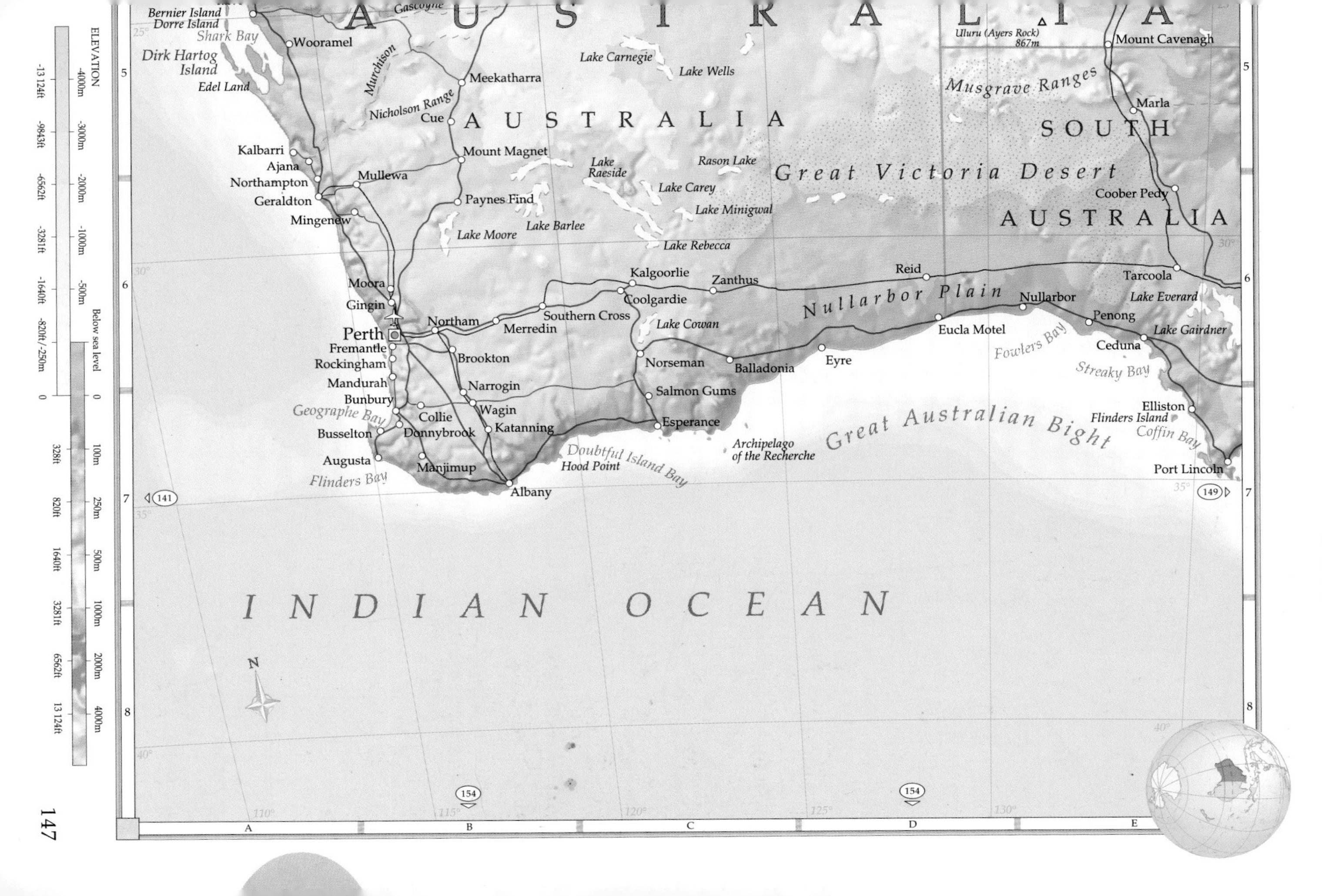

WEST

Bernier Island
Dorre Island
Dirk Hartog Island
Edel Land
Shark Bay

Wooramel
Kalbarri
Ajana
Northampton
Geraldton
Mingenew
Mullewa
Paynes Find
Mount Magnet

Meekatharra
Cue
Nicholson Range
Gascoyne
Murchison

AUSTRALIA
SOUTH
AUSTRALIA

Mount Cavenagh
Marla
Musgrave Ranges
Uluru (Ayers Rock) 867m
Coober Pedy
Great Victoria Desert

Tarcoola
Lake Everard
Penong
Lake Gairdner
Ceduna
Streaky Bay
Fowlers Bay
Elliston
Flinders Island
Coffin Bay
Port Lincoln

AUSTRALIA

Nullarbor
Eucla Motel

Nullarbor Plain

Great Australian Bight

Lake Wells
Lake Carnegie
Rason Lake
Lake Carey
Lake Minigwal
Lake Raeside
Lake Moore
Lake Barlee
Lake Rebecca

Reid

Eyre

Balladonia
Zanthus
Kalgoorlie
Coolgardie
Lake Cowan
Norseman
Salmon Gums
Esperance
Archipelago of the Recherche

Southern Cross
Merredin
Northam
Brookton
Narrogin
Wagin
Katanning
Collie
Donnybrook
Manjimup
Augusta
Busselton
Bunbury
Mandurah
Rockingham
Fremantle
Perth
Gingin
Moora

Doubtful Island Bay
Hood Point
Albany

Geographe Bay
Flinders Bay

INDIAN OCEAN

N

ELEVATION

-4000m	-3000m	-2000m	-1000m	-500m	Below sea level	0	100m	250m	500m	1000m	2000m	4000m
-13 124ft	-9843ft	-6562ft	-3281ft	-1640ft	-820ft/-250m	0	328ft	820ft	1640ft	3281ft	6562ft	13 124ft

EASTERN AUSTRALIA

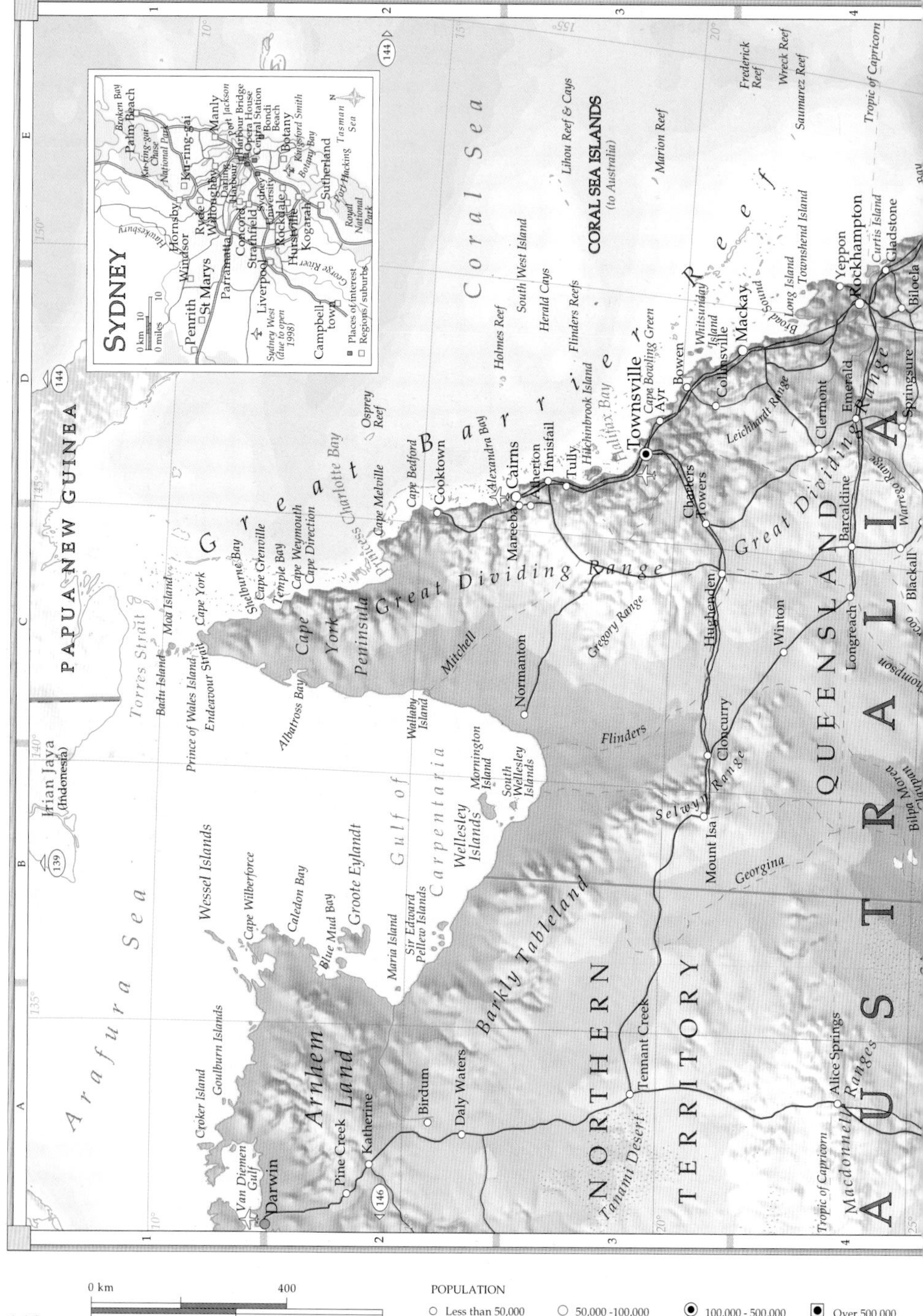

SYDNEY

Broken Bay
Palm Beach
Ku-ring-gai Chase
National Park
Berrowra
Windsor
Hornsby
Manly
Warringah
Sydney Harbour Bridge
Harbour House
Sydney Opera
Central Station
Bondi
Beach
Botany
Rockford Smith
Penrith
St Marys
Parramatta
Concord
Strathfield
Ryde
Bankstown
Liverpool
Sutherland
Hurstville
Kogarah
Campbell Town
Rushcutters
Port Hacking
Royal
National
Park

0 km 10
0 miles 10

Sydney West
(due to open
1998)

■ Places of interest
▨ Regions/suburbs

Tasman
Sea

Kingsway

Creek River

Irian Jaya
(Indonesia)

PAPUA NEW GUINEA

Torres Strait

Batu Island
Prince of Wales Island
Endeavour Strait
Cape York
Maa Island

Shelburne Bay
Cape Grenville
Temple Bay
Cape Weymouth
Cape Direction

Cape
York
Peninsula

Great Dividing Range

Mitchell

Princess Charlotte Bay

Cape Melville

Cape Bedford

Cooktown

Albatross Bay

Wellesby
Island

Normanton

Mitchell

Gregory Range

Flinders

Coral Sea

Holmes Reef

South West Island

Herald Cays

Flinders Reefs

Osprey
Reef

Alexandra Reef
Cairns
Mareeba
Atherton
Innisfail
Tully

Highbrook Island

Halifax Bay

Cape Bowling Green
Ayr

Townsville

Charters
Towers

Hughenden

Winton

Cloncurry

Selwyn Range

Mount Isa

Georgina

Flinders

Lihou Reef & Cays

CORAL SEA ISLANDS
(to Australia)

Marion Reef

Frederick
Reef

Wreck Reef
Saumarez Reef

Tropic of Capricorn

Bowen
Whitsunday
Island
Mackay

Collinsville

Broad
Sound

Long Island
Townshend Island

Yeppon
Rockhampton
Curtis Island
Gladstone

Leichhardt Range

Clermont

Emerald

Barcaldine

Longreach

Blackall

Warrego River

Bilpa

QUEENSLAND

AUSTRALIA

Great Dividing Range

Bulloo

Birdum

Daly Waters

Katherine

Pine Creek

Darwin

Van Diemen
Gulf

Croker Island

Goulburn Islands

Cape Wilberforce

Caledon Bay

Blue Mud Bay

Maria Island

Sir Edward
Pellew Islands

Groote Eylandt

Arnhem
Land

Wessel Islands

Arafura Sea

Gulf of
Carpentaria

Mornington
Island
South
Wellesley
Islands

Wellesley
Islands

Bankly Tableland

NORTHERN

TERRITORY

Tennant Creek

Tanami Desert

Alice Springs

Macdonnell Ranges

Tropic of Capricorn

A U S T R A L I A

0 km 400
0 miles 400

POPULATION

○ Less than 50,000   ○ 50,000 -100,000   ◉ 100,000 - 500,000   ◼ Over 500,000

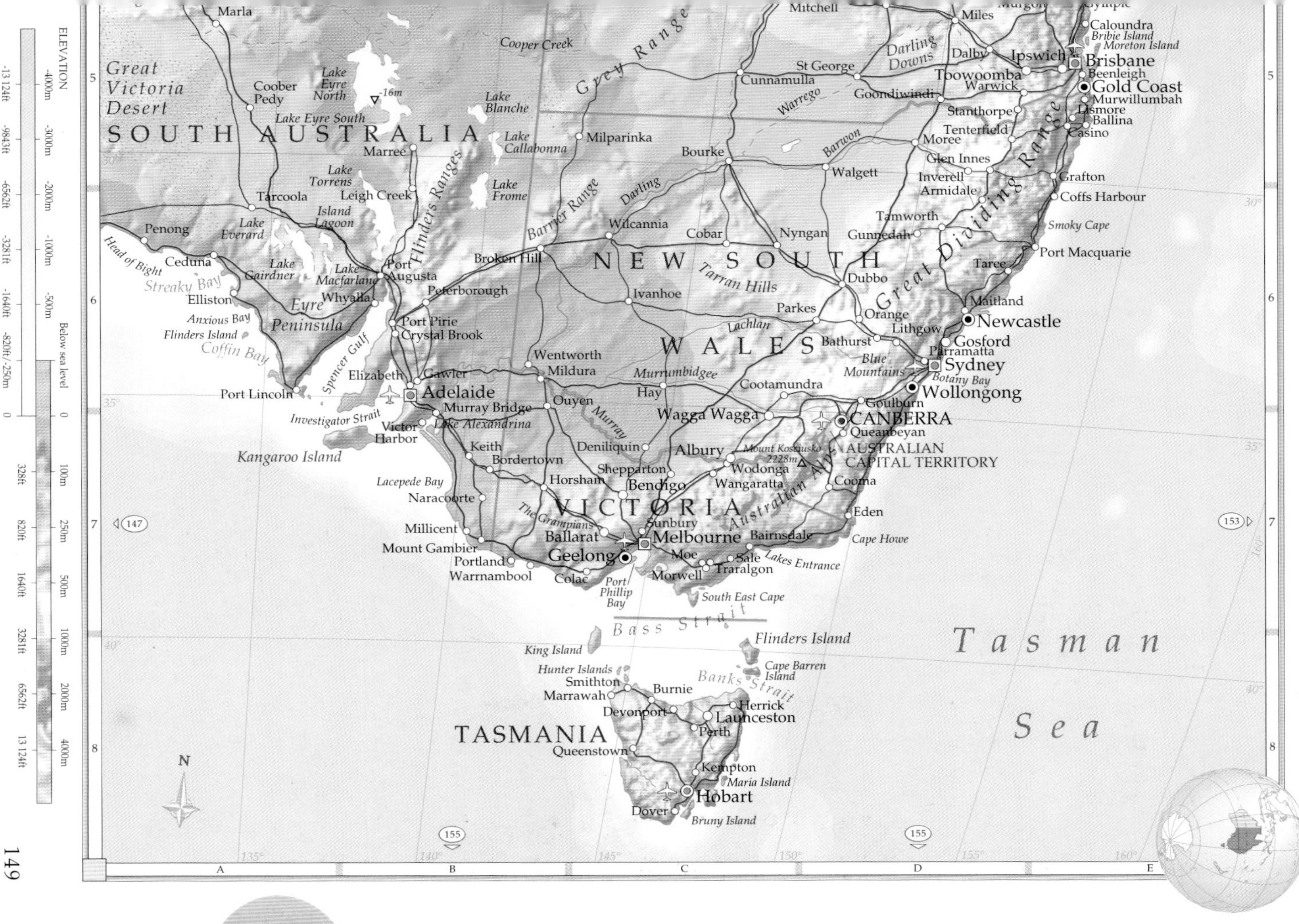

ELEVATION

-4000m	-3000m	-2000m	-1000m	-500m	Below sea level	0	100m	250m	500m	1000m	2000m	4000m

| -13 124ft | -9843ft | -6562ft | -3281ft | -1640ft | -820ft/-250m | 0 | 328ft | 820ft | 1640ft | 3281ft | 6562ft | 13 124ft |

NEW ZEALAND

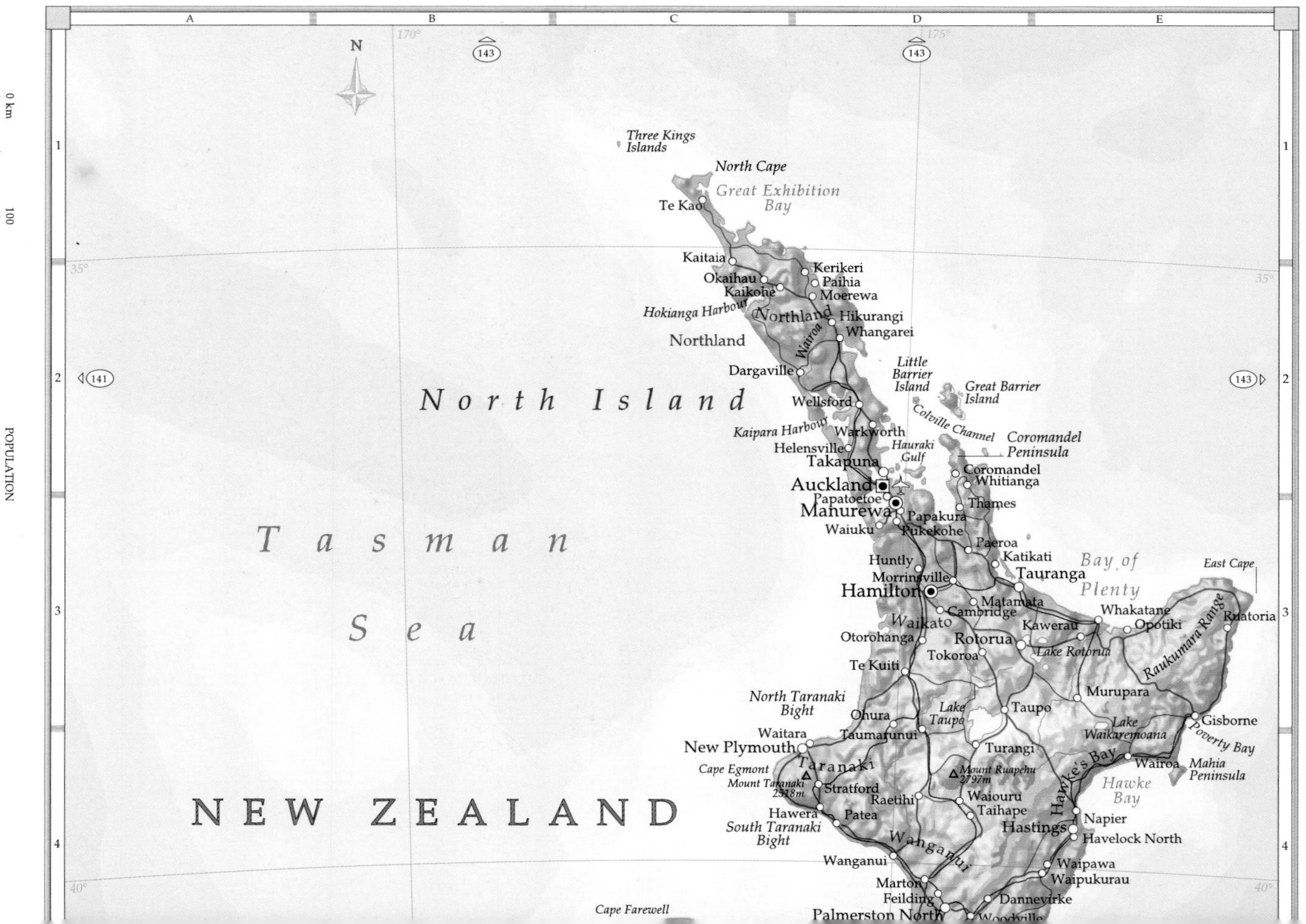

Three Kings Islands

North Cape

Great Exhibition Bay

Te Kao

Kaitaia

Okahau
Kaikohe
Hokianga Harbour
Kerikeri
Paihia
Moerewa
Northland
Northland
Hikurangi
Whangarei

Dargaville

Wairoa

Wellsford
Warkworth
Kaipara Harbour
Helensville
Takapuna
Auckland
Manukau
Mahurewa
Waiuku
Papakura
Pukekohe
Pokeno
Huntly
Morrinsville
Waikato
Otorohanga
Te Kuiti

Hamilton
Cambridge
Matamata

North Taranaki Bight
Waitara
New Plymouth
Cape Egmont
Mount Taranaki
2518 m
Stratford
Hawera
South Taranaki Bight
Patea
Taranaki

North Island

Little Barrier Island
Great Barrier Island
Coromandel Peninsula
Coromandel
Whitianga
Thames
Waihi
Paeroa
Katikati
Tauranga
Kawerau

Bay of Plenty
Whakatane
Opotiki
Murupara
Rotorua
Lake Rotorua
Lake Rotomahana
Tokoroa
Taupo
Lake Taupo
Turangi
Taumarunui
Ohura
Raetihi
Mount Ruapehu
2797 m
Waiouru

Kaimanawa Range
East Cape
Ruatoria
Gisborne
Poverty Bay
Mahia Peninsula
Mahia
Wairoa
Hawke Bay
Napier
Hastings
Havelock North
Waipawa
Waipukurau
Dannevirke
Woodville

Wanganui
Wanganui
Marton
Feilding
Palmerston North

Cape Farewell

Tasman Sea

NEW ZEALAND

0 km   100

0 miles   100

POPULATION

○ Less than 50,000   ○ 50,000 -100,000   ◉ 100,000 - 500,000   ■ Over 500,000

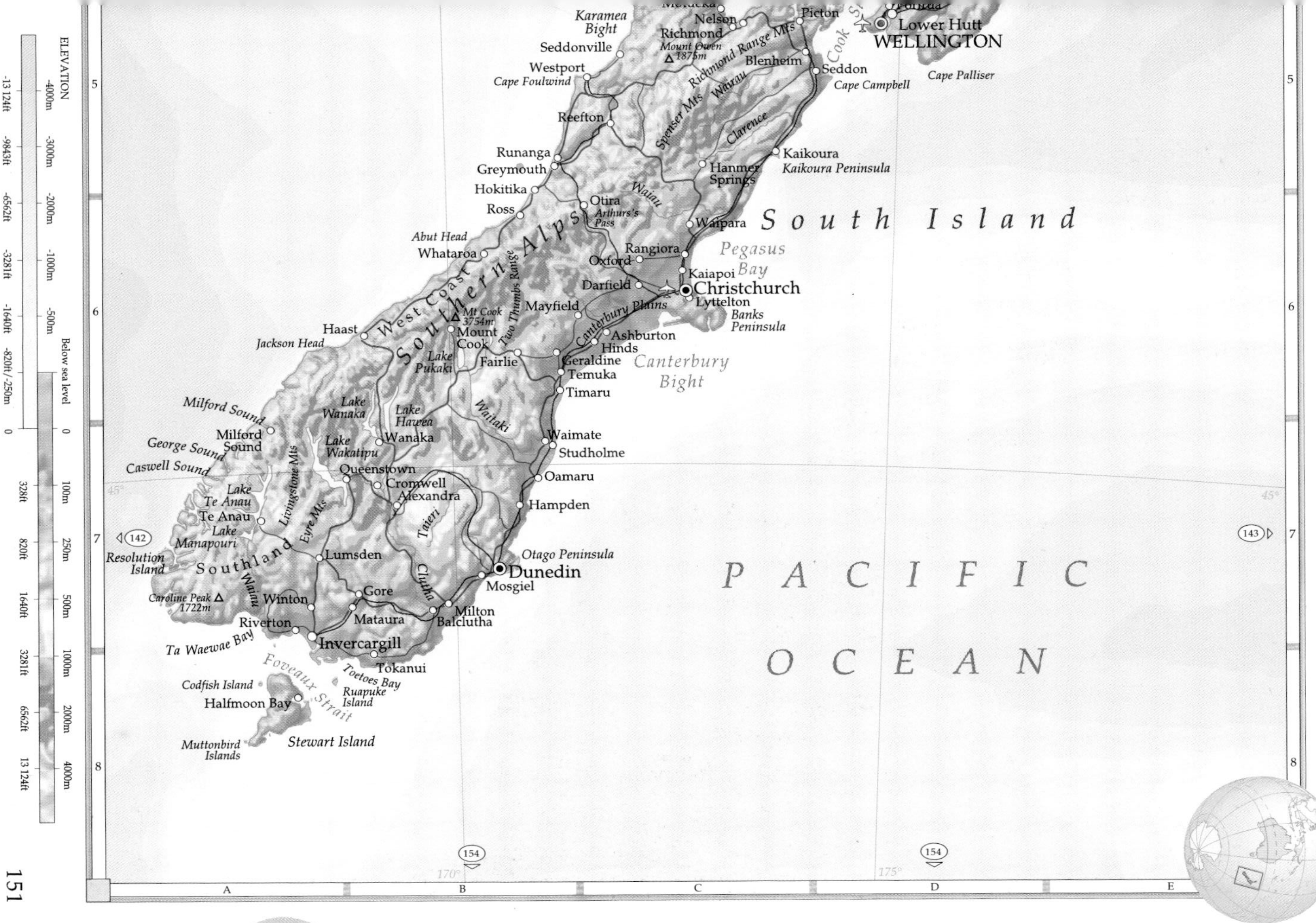

PACIFIC

OCEAN

South Island

Southern Alps

West Coast

Wellington
Lower Hutt
Cape Palliser
Picton
Cape Campbell
Seddon
Blenheim
Nelson
Richmond
Mount Owen 1875m
Spenser Mts
Kaikoura Peninsula
Kaikoura
Waiau
Hanmer Springs
Waipara
Rangiora
Christchurch
Lyttelton
Banks Peninsula
Pegasus Bay
Kaiapoi
Canterbury
Canterbury Plains
Ashburton
Hinds
Rakaia
Geraldine
Temuka
Timaru
Waimate
Studholme
Oamaru
Hampden
Otago Peninsula
Dunedin
Mosgiel
Milton
Balclutha
Clutha
Matauwa
Gore
Tokanui
Totoes Bay
Ruapuke Island
Invercargill
Lumsden
Cromwell
Alexandra
Queenstown
Lake Hawea
Lake Wanaka
Wanaka
Lake Wakatipu
Eyre Mts
Livingstone Mts
Winton
Waiau
Riverton
Ta Waewae Bay
Codfish Island
Halfmoon Bay
Muttonbird Islands
Stewart Island
Foveaux Strait
Lake Te Anau
Lake Manapouri
Te Anau
Cleddau Peak 1722m
Resolution Island
George Sound
Caswell Sound
Milford Sound
Milford
Jackson Head
Haast
Lake Wanaka
Lake Pukaki
Mount Cook 3764m
Cook
Fairlie
Waitaki
Two Thumbs Range
Mayfield
Darfield
Oxford
Otira
Arthur's Pass
Reefton
Greymouth
Hokitika
Ross
Runanga
Abut Head
Whataroa
Westport
Seddonville
Cape Foulwind
Karamea Bight
Cape Campbell
Cook Strait

Karamea Bight

ELEVATION

4000m	-3000m	-2000m	-1000m	-500m		Below sea level	0	100m	250m	500m	1000m	2000m	4000m
-13 124ft	-9843ft	-6562ft	-3281ft	-1640ft		-820ft/-250m	0	328ft	820ft	1640ft	3281ft	6562ft	13 124ft

THE PACIFIC OCEAN

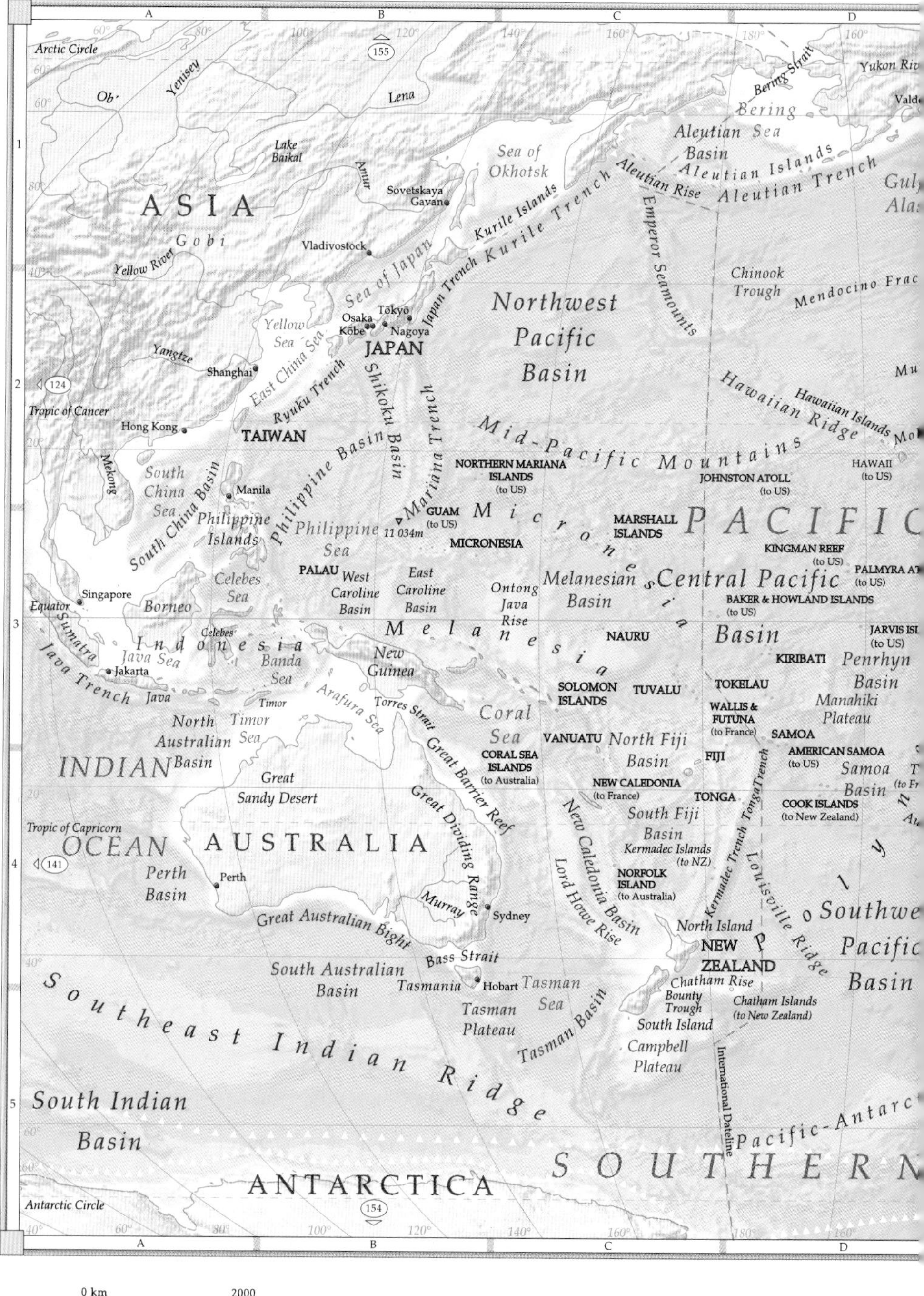

Arctic Circle
155
Yukon Riv
Ob·
Yenisey
Lena
Bering Strait
Valde
Bering
Aleutian Sea
Basin
Lake
Baikal
Sea of
Okhotsk
Aleutian Rise
Aleutian Islands
Gulf
Amur
Sovetskaya
Gavan
Aleutian Trench
Alas
ASIA
Gobi
Emperor Seamounts
Chinook
Trough
Mendocino Frac
Yellow River
Vladivostock
Kurile Islands
Japan Trench
Kurile Trench
Yellow
Sea
Osaka
Kōbe
Tōkyō
Nagoya
Northwest
Pacific
Basin
Yangtze
Shanghai
JAPAN
Mu
Hawaiian Islands
Hawaiian Ridge
Tropic of Cancer
124
East China Sea
Ryuku Trench
Shikoku Basin
Mo
Hong Kong
TAIWAN
Mariana Trench
Mid-Pacific Mountains
HAWAII
(to US)
Mekong
South
China
Sea
Manila
NORTHERN MARIANA
ISLANDS
(to US)
Micronesia
JOHNSTON ATOLL
(to US)
Philippine Basin
Philippine
Islands
Philippine
Sea
GUAM
(to US)
11 034m
MARSHALL
ISLANDS
PACIFIC
South China Basin
Celebes
Sea
PALAU
West
Caroline
Basin
East
Caroline
Basin
MICRONESIA
KINGMAN REEF
(to US)
Singapore
Borneo
Equator
Ontong
Java
Rise
Melanesian
Basin
Central Pacific
BAKER & HOWLAND ISLANDS
(to US)
PALMYRA AT
(to US)
Celebes
Indonesia
Java Sea
Jakarta
Banda
Sea
New
Guinea
Melanesia
NAURU
Basin
JARVIS ISL
(to US)
Java Trench
Java
Sumatra
Timor
Torres Strait
Arafura Sea
KIRIBATI
Penrhyn
Basin
SOLOMON
ISLANDS
TUVALU
TOKELAU
Manahiki
Plateau
North
Australian
Basin
Timor
Sea
Coral
Sea
VANUATU
North Fiji
WALLIS &
FUTUNA
(to France)
SAMOA
INDIAN
Great
Sandy Desert
Great Barrier Reef
CORAL SEA
ISLANDS
(to Australia)
Basin
FIJI
AMERICAN SAMOA
(to US)
Samoa
Basin
T
(to Fr
NEW CALEDONIA
(to France)
TONGA
COOK ISLANDS
(to New Zealand)
Tropic of Capricorn
OCEAN
AUSTRALIA
Great Dividing Range
South Fiji
Basin
Kermadec Islands
(to NZ)
Au
141
Perth
Basin
Perth
New Caledonia Basin
Kermadec Trench
Tonga Trench
NORFOLK
ISLAND
(to Australia)
Louisville Ridge
Southwe
Pacific
Great Australian Bight
Lord Howe Rise
North Island
NEW
ZEALAND
Basin
Murray
Sydney
Bass Strait
South Australian
Basin
Tasmania
Hobart
Tasman
Sea
Tasman
Plateau
Tasman Basin
Chatham Rise
Bounty
Trough
South Island
Chatham Islands
(to New Zealand)
Campbell
Plateau
International Dateline
Southeast Indian Ridge
South Indian
Basin
Pacific-Antarc
SOUTHERN
Antarctic Circle
154
ANTARCTICA

0 km   2000

0 miles   2000

● Major ports

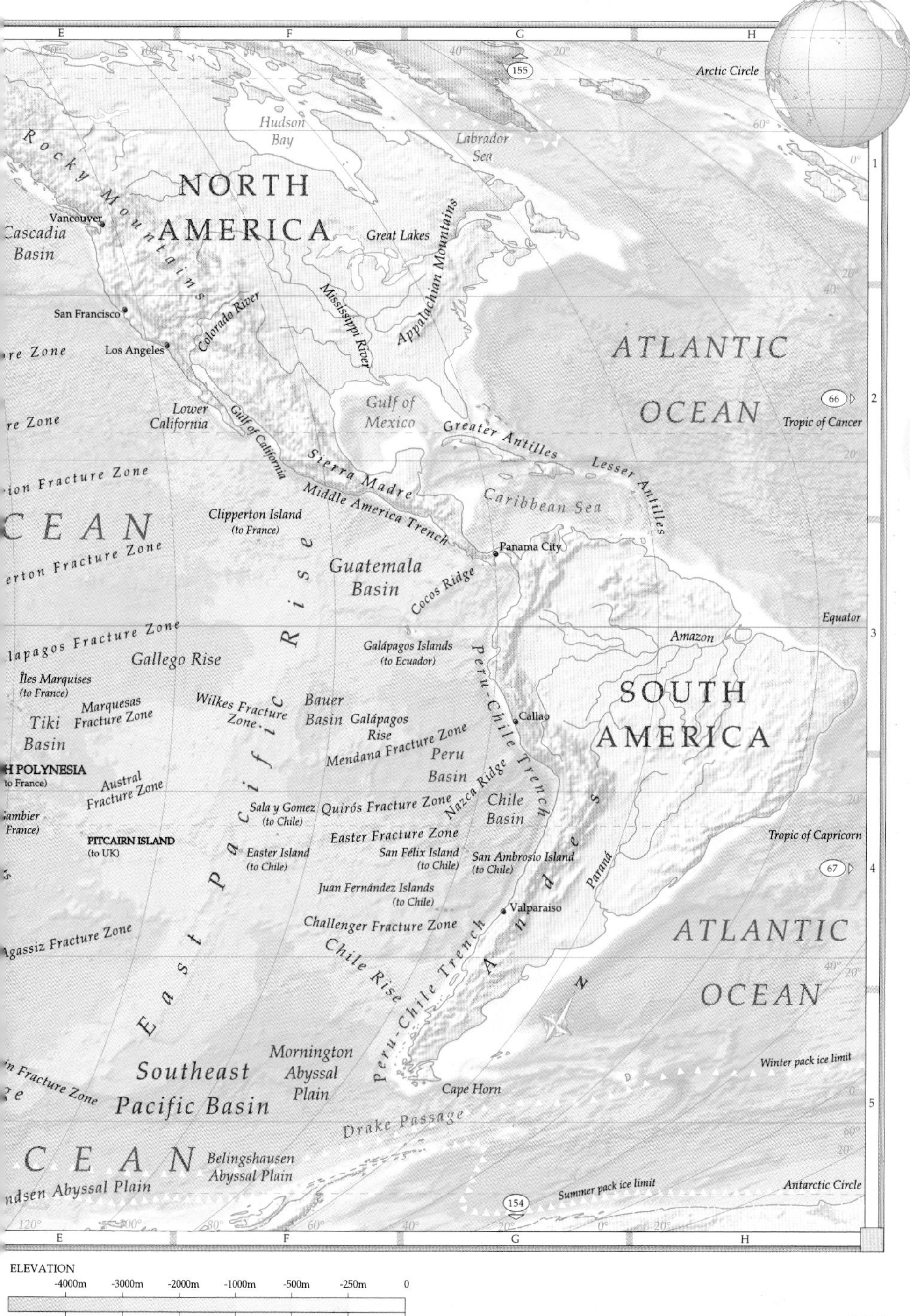

NORTH AMERICA
Hudson Bay
Labrador Sea
Arctic Circle
Rocky Mountains
Vancouver
Cascadia Basin
Great Lakes
Appalachian Mountains
Mississippi River
Colorado River
San Francisco
Los Angeles
Lower California
Gulf of California
Gulf of Mexico
Greater Antilles
Lesser Antilles
Caribbean Sea
Sierra Madre
Middle America Trench
ATLANTIC OCEAN
Tropic of Cancer
Clipperton Island (to France)
Panama City
Guatemala Basin
Cocos Ridge
Equator
Amazon
Galápagos Islands (to Ecuador)
Gallego Rise
Îles Marquises (to France)
Marquesas Fracture Zone
Tiki Basin
Wilkes Fracture Zone
Bauer Basin
Galápagos Rise
Mendana Fracture Zone
Peru Basin
Callao
Peru-Chile Trench
SOUTH AMERICA
Austral Fracture Zone
PITCAIRN ISLAND (to UK)
Sala y Gomez (to Chile)
Quirós Fracture Zone
Nazca Ridge
Chile Basin
Easter Fracture Zone
Easter Island (to Chile)
San Félix Island (to Chile)
San Ambrosio Island (to Chile)
Tropic of Capricorn
Paraná
Juan Fernández Islands (to Chile)
Valparaiso
Challenger Fracture Zone
Agassiz Fracture Zone
Chile Rise
East Pacific Rise
Andes
ATLANTIC OCEAN
Mornington Abyssal Plain
Southeast Pacific Basin
Cape Horn
Winter pack ice limit
Drake Passage
Belingshausen Abyssal Plain
Summer pack ice limit
Antarctic Circle
155
154
66
67
ELEVATION
-4000m -3000m -2000m -1000m -500m -250m 0
-13 124ft -9843ft -6562ft -3281ft -1640ft -820ft 0

ANTARCTICA

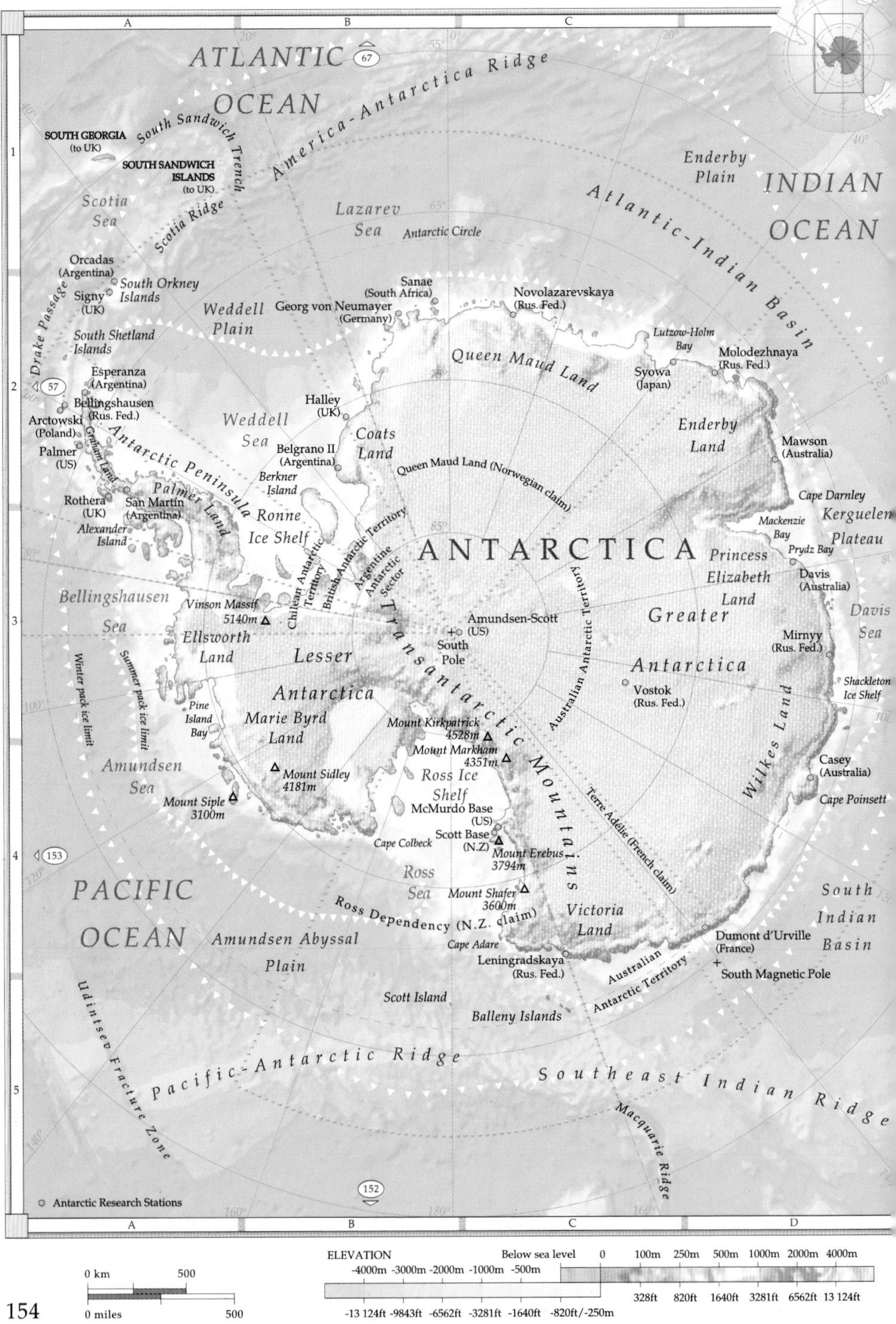

ATLANTIC 67
OCEAN

America-Antarctica Ridge

SOUTH GEORGIA
(to UK)

South Sandwich Trench

SOUTH SANDWICH
ISLANDS
(to UK)

Scotia
Sea

Scotia Ridge

Lazarev
Sea   Antarctic Circle

Enderby
Plain

INDIAN
OCEAN

Atlantic-Indian Basin

Orcadas
(Argentina)   South Orkney
Signy   Islands
(UK)

Weddell
Plain   Georg von Neumayer
(Germany)

Sanae
(South Africa)

Novolazarevskaya
(Rus. Fed.)

Queen Maud Land

Lutzow-Holm
Bay

Syowa
(Japan)

Molodezhnaya
(Rus. Fed.)

South Shetland
Islands

Esperanza
(Argentina)

Bellingshausen
(Rus. Fed.)

Arctowski
(Poland)

Palmer
(US)

Weddell
Sea

Belgrano II
(Argentina)

Berkner
Island

Coats
Land

Queen Maud Land (Norwegian claim)

Enderby
Land

Mawson
(Australia)

Cape Darnley

Drake Passage

57

Antarctic Peninsula

Palmer Land

Rothera   San Martin
(UK)   (Argentina)

Alexander
Island

Ronne
Ice Shelf

Graham Land

Chilean Antarctic Territory
British Antarctic Territory
Argentine Antarctic Sector

ANTARCTICA

Princess
Elizabeth
Land

Mackenzie
Bay   Kerguelen
Plateau

Prydz Bay

Davis
(Australia)

Bellingshausen
Sea

Vinson Massif
5140m ▲

Ellsworth
Land

Lesser
Antarctica

Pine
Island
Bay   Marie Byrd
Land

Amundsen
Sea

Mount Siple ▲
3100m

Mount Sidley ▲
4181m

Amundsen-Scott
(US)
South
Pole

Transantarctic Mountains

Australian Antarctic Territory

Greater
Antarctica

Vostok
(Rus. Fed.)

Mirnyy
(Rus. Fed.)

Davis
Sea

Shackleton
Ice Shelf

Wilkes Land

Casey
(Australia)

Cape Poinsett

Winter pack ice limit
Summer pack ice limit

Mount Kirkpatrick
4528m ▲

Mount Markham
4351m

Ross Ice
Shelf

McMurdo Base
(US)

Scott Base
(N.Z.)

Cape Colbeck

Ross
Sea   Mount Erebus ▲
3794m

Mount Shafer ▲
3600m

PACIFIC

153

OCEAN   Amundsen Abyssal
Plain

Ross Dependency (N.Z. claim)

Cape Adare

Victoria
Land

Leningradskaya
(Rus. Fed.)

Terre Adélie (French claim)

Dumont d'Urville
(France)

South Magnetic Pole

South
Indian
Basin

Scott Island

Balleny Islands

Australian Antarctic Territory

Udintsev Fracture Zone

Pacific-Antarctic Ridge

Southeast Indian Ridge

Macquarie Ridge

152

● Antarctic Research Stations

A   B   C   D

0 km   500
0 miles   500

ELEVATION   Below sea level   0   100m   250m   500m   1000m   2000m   4000m

-4000m -3000m -2000m -1000m -500m

328ft   820ft   1640ft   3281ft   6562ft   13 124ft

-13 124ft -9843ft -6562ft -3281ft -1640ft -820ft/-250m

ARCTIC OCEAN

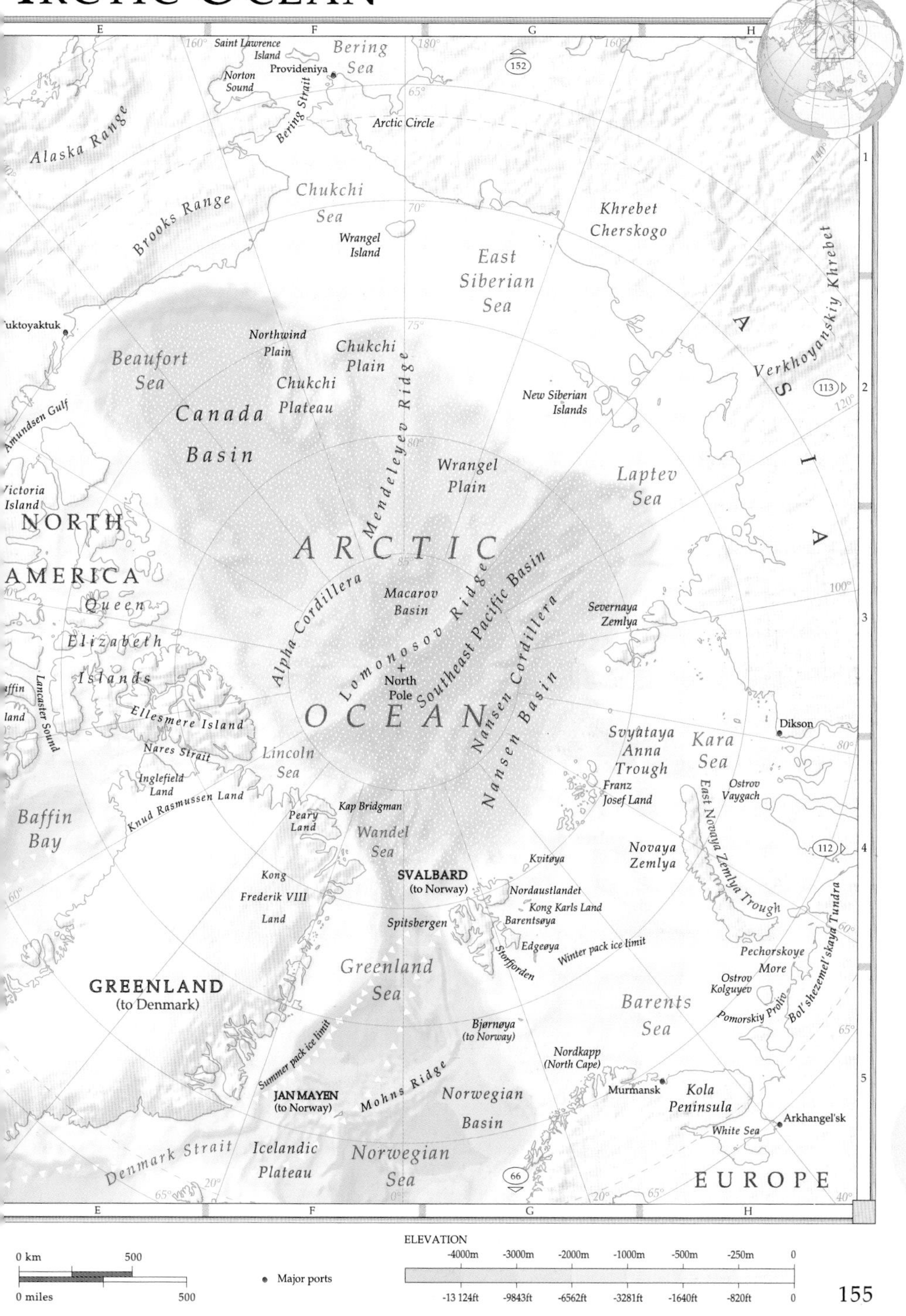

Saint Lawrence Island
Norton Sound
Providenobserv
Bering Sea
160°
180°
152

Bering Strait
Arctic Circle
65°

Alaska Range

Chukchi Sea
Wrangel Island
70°

Khrebet Cherskogo
160°

Brooks Range

East Siberian Sea

Verkhoyanskiy Khrebet

uktoyaktuk

Northwind Plain
Chukchi Plain
75°

New Siberian Islands

113
120°

A S I A

Beaufort Sea
Chukchi Plateau

Mendeleyev Ridge

Canada Basin

Amundsen Gulf

Wrangel Plain

Laptev Sea

100°

ictoria Island

A R C T I C

Alpha Cordillera

Macarov Basin

Lomonosov Ridge

Southeast Pacific Basin

Severnaya Zemlya

NORTH

AMERICA

Queen

North Pole

Nansen Cordillera

Nansen Basin

3

Elizabeth

Islands

O C E A N

Dikson

affin land

Ellesmere Island

Svyataya Anna Trough

Kara Sea

Lancaster Sound

Nares Strait

Lincoln Sea

Franz Josef Land

Ostrov Vaygach

80°

Inglefield Land

Knud Rasmussen Land

Kap Bridgman

Peary Land

East Novaya Zemlya Trough

Baffin Bay

Wandel Sea

Kvitøya

Novaya Zemlya

112
4

60°

Kong Frederik VIII Land

SVALBARD
(to Norway)

Nordaustlandet

Kong Karls Land

Pechorskoye More

Spitsbergen

Barentsøya

Ostrov Kolguyev

Bol'shezemel'skaja Tundra

GREENLAND
(to Denmark)

Edgeøya

Winter pack ice limit

Pomorskiy Proliv

Greenland Sea

Storfjorden

Barents Sea

65°

Bjørnøya
(to Norway)

Nordkapp
(North Cape)

Kola Peninsula

EUROPE

40°

Summer pack ice limit

JAN MAYEN
(to Norway)

Mohns Ridge

Norwegian Basin

Murmansk

White Sea

Arkhangel'sk

Denmark Strait

Icelandic Plateau

Norwegian Sea

66

20°

155

ELEVATION

-4000m   -3000m   -2000m   -1000m   -500m   -250m   0

-13 124ft   -9843ft   -6562ft   -3281ft   -1640ft   -820ft   0

0 km   500

0 miles   500

• Major ports

DESPITE THE RAPID process of decolonization since the Second World War, around 10 million people in 59 territories around the world continue to live under the protection of France, Australia, Denmark, Norway, Portugal, New Zealand, the UK, the USA, or the Netherlands. These remnants of former colonial empires may have persisted for economic, strategic or political reasons and are administered in a variety of ways.

AUSTRALIA

AUSTRALIA'S OVERSEAS TERRITORIES have not been an issue since Papua New Guinea became independent in 1975. Consequently there is no overriding policy towards them. Norfolk Island is inhabited by descendants of the HMS Bounty mutineers and more recent Australian migrants.

ASHMORE & CARTIER ISLANDS
Indian Ocean

STATUS: External territory
CLAIMED: 1978
CAPITAL: Not applicable
POPULATION: None
AREA: 5.2 sq km
(2 sq miles)

CHRISTMAS ISLAND
Indian Ocean

STATUS: External territory
CLAIMED: 1958
CAPITAL: Flying Fish Cove
POPULATION: 2,871
AREA: 134.6 sq km
(52 sq miles)

COCOS ISLANDS
Indian Ocean

STATUS: External territory
CLAIMED: 1955
CAPITAL: No official capital
POPULATION: 555
AREA: 14.24 sq km
(5.5 sq miles)

CORAL SEA ISLANDS
South Pacific

STATUS: External territory
CLAIMED: 1969
CAPITAL: None
POPULATION: 8 (meteorologists)
AREA: Less than 3 sq km
(1.16 sq miles)

HEARD & MCDONALD IS.
Indian Ocean

STATUS: External territory
CLAIMED: 1947
CAPITAL: Not applicable
POPULATION: None
AREA: 417 sq km
(161 sq miles)

NORFOLK ISLAND
South Pacific

STATUS: External territory
CLAIMED: 1913
CAPITAL: Kingston
POPULATION: 2,637
AREA: 34.4 sq km
(13.3 sq miles)

DENMARK

THE FAEROE ISLANDS have been under Danish administration since Queen Margreth I of Denmark inherited Norway in 1380. The Home Rule Act of 1948 gave the Faeroese control over all their internal affairs. Greenland first came under Danish rule in 1380. Today, Denmark remains responsible for the island's foreign affairs and defence.

FAEROE ISLANDS
North Atlantic

STATUS: External territory
CLAIMED: 1380
CAPITAL: Tórshavn
POPULATION: 47,310
AREA: 1,399 sq km
(540 sq miles)

GREENLAND
North Atlantic

STATUS: External territory
CLAIMED: 1380
CAPITAL: Nuuk
POPULATION: 55,385
AREA: 2,175,516 sq km
(840,000 sq miles)

FRANCE

FRANCE HAS DEVELOPED economic ties with its overseas territories, thereby stressing interdependence over independence. Overseas *départements*, officially part of France, have their own governments. Territorial *collectivités* and overseas *territoires* have varying degrees of autonomy.

CLIPPERTON ISLAND
East Pacific

STATUS: Dependency of French Polynesia
CLAIMED: 1930
CAPITAL: Not applicable
POPULATION: None
AREA: 7 sq km
(2.7 sq miles)

FRENCH GUIANA
South America

STATUS: Overseas department
CLAIMED: 1817
CAPITAL: Cayenne
POPULATION: 135,000
AREA: 90,996 sq km
(35,135 sq miles)

FRENCH POLYNESIA
South Pacific

STATUS: Overseas territory
CLAIMED: 1843
CAPITAL: Papeete
POPULATION: 211,000
AREA: 4,165 sq km
(1,608 sq miles)

GUADELOUPE
West Indies

STATUS: Overseas department
CLAIMED: 1635
CAPITAL: Basse-Terre
POPULATION: 413,000
AREA: 1,780 sq km
(687 sq miles)

MARTINIQUE
West Indies
STATUS: Overseas department
CLAIMED: 1635
CAPITAL: Fort-de-France
POPULATION: 371,000
AREA: 1,100 sq km
(425 sq miles)

MAYOTTE
Indian Ocean
STATUS: Territorial collectivity
CLAIMED: 1843
CAPITAL: Mamoudzou
POPULATION: 97,088
AREA: 374 sq km
(144 sq miles)

NEW CALEDONIA
South Pacific
STATUS: Overseas territory
CLAIMED: 1853
CAPITAL: Noumeá
POPULATION: 179,000
AREA: 19,103 sq km
(7,374 sq miles)

RÉUNION
Indian Ocean
STATUS: Overseas department
CLAIMED: 1638
CAPITAL: Denis
POPULATION: 632,000
AREA: 2,512 sq km
(970 sq miles)

ST PIERRE & MIQUELON
North America
STATUS: Territorial collectivity
CLAIMED: 1604
CAPITAL: Saint-Pierre
POPULATION: 6,000
AREA: 242 sq km
(93.4 sq miles)

WALLIS & FUTUNA
South Pacific
STATUS: Overseas territory
CLAIMED: 1842
CAPITAL: Matā'Utu
POPULATION: 14,000
AREA: 274 sq km
(106 sq miles)

NETHERLANDS

THE COUNTRY'S TWO remaining overseas territories were formerly part of the Dutch West Indies. Both are now self-governing, but the Netherlands remains responsible for their defence.

ARUBA
West Indies
STATUS: Autonomous part of the Netherlands
CLAIMED: 1643
CAPITAL: Oranjestad
POPULATION: 69,000
AREA: 194 sq km
(75 sq miles)

NETHERLANDS ANTILLES
West Indies
STATUS: Autonomous part of the Netherlands
CLAIMED: 1816
CAPITAL: Willemstad
POPULATION: 195,000
AREA: 800 sq km
(308 sq miles)

NEW ZEALAND

NEW ZEALAND'S GOVERNMENT has no desire to retain any overseas territories. However, the economic weakness of its dependent territory Tokelau and its freely associated states, Niue and the Cook Islands, has forced New Zealand to remain responsible for their foreign policy and defence.

COOK ISLANDS
South Pacific
STATUS: Associated territory
CLAIMED: 1901
CAPITAL: Avarua
POPULATION: 19,000
AREA: 293 sq km
(113 sq miles)

NIUE
South Pacific
STATUS: Associated territory
CLAIMED: 1901
CAPITAL: Alofi
POPULATION: 2,000
AREA: 264 sq km
(102 sq miles)

TOKELAU
South Pacific
STATUS: Dependent territory
CLAIMED: 1926
CAPITAL: Not applicable
POPULATION: 2,000
AREA: 10.4 sq km
(4 sq miles)

NORWAY

IN 1920, 41 nations signed the Spitsbergen treaty recognizing Norwegian sovereignty over Svalbard. There is a NATO base on Jan Mayen. Bouvet Island is a nature reserve.

BOUVET ISLAND
South Atlantic
STATUS: Dependency
CLAIMED: 1928
CAPITAL: Not applicable
POPULATION: None
AREA: 58 sq km
(22 sq miles)

JAN MAYEN
North Atlantic
STATUS: Dependency
CLAIMED: 1929
CAPITAL: Not applicable
POPULATION: None
AREA: 381 sq km
(147 sq miles)

PETER I ISLAND
Southern Ocean
STATUS: Dependency
CLAIMED: 1931
CAPITAL: Not applicable
POPULATION: None
AREA: 180 sq km
(69 sq miles)

OVERSEAS TERRITORIES & DEPENDENCIES *continued*

NORWAY *continued*

SVALBARD
Arctic Ocean
STATUS: Dependency
CLAIMED: 1920
CAPITAL: Longyearbyen
POPULATION: 3,431
AREA: 62,906 sq km
(24,289 sq miles)

PORTUGAL

AFTER A COUP in 1974, Portugal's overseas possessions were rapidly granted sovereignty. Macao is the only one remaining and it is to become a Special Administrative Region of China in 1999.

MACAO
South China
STATUS: Special territory
CLAIMED: 1557
CAPITAL: Macao
POPULATION: 388,000
AREA: 18 sq km
(7 sq miles)

UNITED KINGDOM

THE UK STILL has the largest number of overseas territories. Locally-governed by a mixture of elected representatives and appointed officials, they all enjoy a large measure of internal self-government, but certain powers, such as foreign affairs and defence, are reserved for Governors of the British Crown.

ANGUILLA
West Indies
STATUS: Dependent territory
CLAIMED: 1650
CAPITAL: The Valley
POPULATION: 8,960
AREA: 96 sq km
(37 sq miles)

ASCENSION
South Atlantic
STATUS: Dependency of St Helena
CLAIMED: 1673
CAPITAL: Not applicable
POPULATION: 1,099
AREA: 88 sq km
(34 sq miles)

BERMUDA
North Atlantic
STATUS: Crown colony
CLAIMED: 1612
CAPITAL: Hamilton
POPULATION: 60,686
AREA: 53 sq km
(20.5 sq miles)

BRITISH INDIAN OCEAN TERRITORY
STATUS: Dependent territory
CLAIMED: 1814
CAPITAL: No official capital
POPULATION: 3,400
AREA: 60 sq km
(23 sq miles)

BRITISH VIRGIN ISLANDS
West Indies
STATUS: Dependent territory
CLAIMED: 1672
CAPITAL: Road Town
POPULATION: 16,644
AREA: 153 sq km
(59 sq miles)

CAYMAN ISLANDS
West Indies
STATUS: Dependent territory
CLAIMED: 1670
CAPITAL: George Town
POPULATION: 25,355
AREA: 259 sq km
(100 sq miles)

FALKLAND ISLANDS
South Atlantic
STATUS: Dependent territory
CLAIMED: 1832
CAPITAL: Stanley
POPULATION: 2,121
AREA: 12,173 sq km
(4,699 sq miles)

GIBRALTAR
Southwest Europe
STATUS: Crown colony
CLAIMED: 1713
CAPITAL: Gibraltar
POPULATION: 28,074
AREA: 6.5 sq km
(2.5 sq miles)

GUERNSEY
Channel Islands
STATUS: Crown dependency
CLAIMED: 1066
CAPITAL: St Peter Port
POPULATION: 58,000
AREA: 65 sq km
(25 sq miles)

ISLE OF MAN
British Isles
STATUS: Crown dependency
CLAIMED: 1765
CAPITAL: Douglas
POPULATION: 71,000
AREA: 572 sq km
(221 sq miles)

JERSEY
Channel Islands
STATUS: Crown dependency
CLAIMED: 1066
CAPITAL: St Helier
POPULATION: 84,082
AREA: 116 sq km
(45 sq miles)

MONTSERRAT
West Indies
STATUS: Dependent territory
CLAIMED: 1632
CAPITAL: Plymouth
POPULATION: 11,000
AREA: 102 sq km
(40 sq miles)

PITCAIRN ISLANDS
South Pacific
STATUS: Dependent territory
CLAIMED: 1887
CAPITAL: Adamstown
POPULATION: 66
AREA: 3.5 sq km (1.35 sq miles)

St Helena
South Atlantic
STATUS: Dependent territory
CLAIMED: 1673
CAPITAL: Jamestown
POPULATION: 6,000
AREA: 122 sq km (47 sq miles)

South Georgia & the Sandwich Islands
South Atlantic
STATUS: Dependent territory
CLAIMED: 1775
POPULATION: No permanent residents
AREA: 3,592 sq km (1,387 sq miles)

Tristan da Cunha
South Atlantic
STATUS: Dependency of St Helena
CLAIMED: 1612
POPULATION: 297
AREA: 98 sq km (38 sq miles)

Turks & Caicos Islands
West Indies
STATUS: Dependent territory
CLAIMED: 1766
CAPITAL: Cockburn Town
POPULATION: 13,000
AREA: 430 sq km (166 sq miles)

UNITED STATES OF AMERICA

AMERICA'S OVERSEAS TERRITORIES have been seen as strategically useful, if expensive, links with its 'backyards'. The US has, in most cases, given the local population a say in deciding their own status. A US Commonwealth territory, such as Puerto Rico has a greater level of independence than that of a US unincorporated or external territory.

American Samoa
South Pacific
STATUS: Unincorporated territory
CLAIMED: 1900
CAPITAL: Pago Pago
POPULATION: 51,000
AREA: 195 sq km (75 sq miles)

Baker & Howland Islands
South Pacific
STATUS: Unincorporated territory
CLAIMED: 1856
CAPITAL: Not applicable
POPULATION: None
AREA: 1.4 sq km (0.54 sq miles)

Guam
West Pacific
STATUS: Unincorporated territory
CLAIMED: 1898
CAPITAL: Agaña
POPULATION: 144,000
AREA: 549 sq km (212 sq miles)

Jarvis Island
South Pacific
STATUS: Unincorporated territory
CLAIMED: 1856
CAPITAL: Not applicable
POPULATION: None
AREA: 4.5 sq km (1.7 sq miles)

Johnston Atoll
Central Pacific
STATUS: Unincorporated territory
CLAIMED: 1858
CAPITAL: Not applicable
POPULATION: 327
AREA: 2.8 sq km (1 sq mile)

Kingman Reef
Central Pacific
STATUS: Administered territory
CLAIMED: 1856
CAPITAL: Not applicable
POPULATION: None
AREA: 1 sq km (0.4 sq miles)

Midway Islands
Central Pacific
STATUS: Administered territory
CLAIMED: 1867
CAPITAL: Not applicable
POPULATION: 453
AREA: 5.2 sq km (2 sq miles)

Navassa Island
West Indies
STATUS: Unincorporated territory
CLAIMED: 1856
CAPITAL: Not applicable
POPULATION: None
AREA: 5.2 sq km (2 sq miles)

Northern Mariana Islands
West Pacific
STATUS: Commonwealth territory
CLAIMED: 1947
CAPITAL: No official capital
POPULATION: 47,000
AREA: 457 sq km (177 sq miles)

Palmyra Atoll
Central Pacific
STATUS: Unincorporated territory
CLAIMED: 1898
CAPITAL: Not applicable
POPULATION: None
AREA: 12 sq km (5 sq miles)

Puerto Rico
West Indies
STATUS: Commonwealth territory
CLAIMED: 1898
CAPITAL: San Juan
POPULATION: 3.6 million
AREA: 8,959 sq km (3,458 sq miles)

Virgin Islands
West Indies
STATUS: Unincorporated territory
CLAIMED: 1917
CAPITAL: Charlotte Amalie
POPULATION: 104,000
AREA: 355 sq km (137 sq miles)

Wake Island
Central Pacific
STATUS: Unincorporated territory
CLAIMED: 1898
CAPITAL: Not applicable
POPULATION: 302
AREA: 6.5 sq km (2.5 sq miles)

GLOSSARY OF GEOGRAPHICAL TERMS

THE GLOSSARY FOLLOWING lists all geographical terms occuring on the maps and in the main-entry names in the Index–Gazetteer. These terms may precede, follow or be run together with the proper elements of the name; where they precede it the term is reversed for indexing purposes – thus Poluostov Yamal is indexed as Yamal, Poluostrov.

A

Å *Danish, Norwegian,* River
Alpen *German,* Alps
Altiplanicie *Spanish,* Plateau
Älv(en) *Swedish,* River
Anse *French,* Bay
Archipiélago *Spanish,* Archipelago
Arcipelago *Italian,* Archipelago
Arquipélago *Portuguese,* Archipelago
Aukštuma *Lithuanian,* Upland

B

Bahía *Spanish,* Bay
Baía *Portuguese,* Bay
Baḥr *Arabic,* River
Baie *French,* Bay
Bandao *Chinese,* Peninsula
Banjaran *Malay,* Mountain range
Batang *Malay,* Stream
-berg *Afrikaans, Norwegian,* Mountain
Birket *Arabic ,* Lake
Boğazı *Turkish,* Lake
Bucht *German,* Bay
Bugten *Danish,* Bay
Buḥayrat *Arabic,* Lake, reservoir
Buḥeiret *Arabic,* Lake
Bukit *Malay,* Mountain
-bukta *Norwegian,* Bay
bukten *Swedish,* Bay
Burnu *Turkish,* Cape, point
Buuraha *Somali,* Mountains

C

Cabo *Portuguese,* Cape
Cap *French,* Cape
Cascada *Portuguese,* Waterfall
Cerro *Spanish,* Mountain
Chaîne *French,* Mountain range
Chau *Cantonese,* Island
Chāy *Turkish,* River
Chhâk *Cambodian,* Bay
Chhu *Tibetan,* River
-chôsuji *Korean,* Reservoir
Chott *Arabic,* Salt lake, depression
Ch'ün-tao *Chinese,* Island group
Cambodian, Mountains
Cordillera *Spanish,* Mountain range
Costa *Spanish,* Coast
Côte *French,* Coast
Cuchilla *Spanish,* Mountains

D

Dağı *Azerbaijani, Turkish,* Mountain
Dağları *Azerbaijani, Turkish,* Mountains
-dake *Japanese,* Peak
Danau *Indonesian,* Lake
Đao *Vietnamese,* Island
Daryā *Persian,* River
Daryācheh *Persian,* Lake
Dasht *Persian,* Plain, desert
Dawḥat *Arabic,* Bay
Dere *Turkish,* Stream
Dili *Azerbaijani,* Spit
-do *Korean,* Island
Dooxo *Somali,* Valley
Düzü *Azerbaijani,* Steppe
-dwīp *Bengali,* Island

E

Embalse *Spanish,* Reservoir
Erg *Arabic,* Dunes
Estany *Catalan,* Lake
Estrecho *Spanish,* Strait
-ey *Icelandic,* Island
Ezero *Bulgarian, Macedonian,* Lake

F

Fjord *Danish,* Fjord
-fjorden *Norwegian,* Fjord
-fjørdhur *Faeroese,* Fjord
Fleuve *French,* River
Fliegu *Maltese,* Channel
-fljór *Icelandic,* River

G

-gang *Korean,* River
Ganga *Nepali, Sinhala,* River
Gaoyuan *Chinese,* Plateau
-gawa *Japanese,* River
Gebel *Arabic,* Mountain

-gebirge *German,* Mountains
Ghubbat *Arabic,* Bay
Gjiri *Albanian,* Bay
Gol *Mongolian,* River
Golfe *French,* Gulf
Golfo *Italian, Spanish,* Gulf
Gora *Russian, Serbian,* Mountain
Gory *Russian,* Mountains
Guba *Russian,* Bay
Gunung *Malay,* Mountain

H

Ḥadd *Arabic,* Spit
-haehyŏp *Korean,* Strait
Haff *German,* Lagoon
Hai *Chinese,* Sea, bay
Ḥammādat *Arabic,* Plateau
Hāmūn *Persian,* Lake
Hawr *Arabic,* Lake
Hāyk' *Amharic,* Lake
He *Chinese,* River
Helodrano *Malagasy,* Bay
-hegység *Hungarian,* Mountain range
Hka *Burmese,* River
-ho *Korean,* Lake
Hô *Korean,* Reservoir
Holot *Hebrew,* Dunes
Hora *Belorussian,* Mountain
Hrada *Belorussian,* Mountains, ridge
Hsi *Chinese,* River
Hu *Chinese,* Lake

I

Île(s) *French,* Island(s)
Ilha(s) *Portuguese,* Island(s)
Ilhéu(s) *Portuguese,* Islet(s)
Irmak *Turkish,* River
Isla(s) *Spanish,* Island(s)
Isola (Isole) *Italian,* Island(s)

J

Jabal *Arabic,* Mountain
Jāl *Arabic,* Ridge
-järvi *Finnish,* Lake
Jazīrat *Arabic,* Island
Jazīreh *Persian,* Island
Jebel *Arabic,* Mountain

Jezero *Serbo-Croatian,* Lake
Jiang *Chinese,* River
-joki *Finnish,* River
-jökull *Icelandic,* Glacier
Juzur *Arabic,* Islands

K

Kaikyō *Japanese,* Strait
-kaise *Lappish,* Mountain
Kali *Nepali,* River
Kalnas *Lithuanian,* Mountain
Kalns *Latvian,* Mountain
Kang *Chinese,* Harbour
Kangri *Tibetan,* Mountain(s)
Kaôh *Cambodian,* Island
Kapp *Norwegian,* Cape
Kavīr *Persian,* Desert
K'edi *Georgian,* Mountain range
Kediet *Arabic,* Mountain
Kepulauan *Indonesian, Malay,* Island group
Khalīg, Khalīj *Arabic,* Gulf
Khawr *Arabic,* Inlet
Khola *Nepali,* River
Khrebet *Russian,* Mountain range
Ko *Thai,* Island
Kolpos *Greek,* Bay
-kopf *German,* Peak
Körfäzi *Azerbaijani,* Bay
Körfezi *Turkish,* Bay
Kõrgustik *Estonian,* Upland
Koshi *Nepali,* River
Kowtal *Persian,* Pass
Kūh(hā) *Persian,* Mountain(s)
-kundo *Korean,* Island group
-kysten *Norwegian,* Coast
Kyun *Burmese,* Island

L

Laaq *Somali,* Watercourse
Lac *French,* Lake
Lacul *Romanian,* Lake
Lago *Italian, Portuguese, Spanish,* Lake
Laguna *Spanish,* Lagoon, Lake

Laht *Estonian*, Bay
Laut *Indonesian*, Sea
Lembalemba *Malagasy*, Plateau
Lerr *Armenian*, Mountain
Lerrnashght'a *Armenian*, Mountain range
Les *Czech*, Forest
Lich *Armenian*, Lake
Liqeni *Albanian*, Lake
Lumi *Albanian*, River
Lyman *Ukrainian*, Estuary

M

Mae Nam *Thai*, River
-mägi *Estonian*, Hill
Maja *Albanian*, Mountain
-man *Korean*, Bay
Marios *Lithuanian*, Lake
-meer *Dutch*, Lake
Melkosopochnik *Russian*, Plain
-meri *Estonian*, Sea
Mifraz *Hebrew*, Bay
Monkhafad *Arabic*, Depression
Mont(s) *French*, Mountain(s)
Monte *Italian*, *Portuguese*, Mountain
More *Russian*, Sea
Mörön *Mongolian*, River

N

Nagor'ye *Russian*, Upland
Nahal *Hebrew*, River
Nahr *Arabic*, River
Nam *Laotian*, River
Nehri *Turkish*, River
Nevado *Spanish*, Mountain (snow-capped)
Nisoi *Greek*, Islands
Nizmennost' *Russian*, Lowland, plain
Nosy *Malagasy*, Island
Nur *Mongolian*, Lake
Nuruu *Mongolian*, Mountains
Nuur *Mongolian*, Lake
Nyzovyna *Ukrainian*, Lowland, plain

O

Ostrov(a) *Russian*, Island(s)
Oued *Arabic*, Watercourse
-oy *Faeroese*, Island
-oy(a) *Norwegian*, Island
Oya *Sinhala*, River
Ozero *Russian*, *Ukrainian*, Lake

P

Passo *Italian*, Pass
Pegunungan *Indonesian*, *Malay*, Mountain range
Pelagos *Greek*, Sea
Penisola *Italian*, Peninsula
Peski *Russian*, Sands
Phanom *Thai*, Mountain
Phou *Laotian*, Mountain
Pic *Catalan*, Peak
Pico *Portuguese*, *Spanish*, Peak
Pik *Russian*, Peak
Planalto *Portuguese*, Plateau
Planina, Planini *Bulgarian, Macedonian, Serbo-Croatian*, Mountain range
Ploskogor'ye *Russian*, Upland
Poluostrov *Russian*, Peninsula
Potamos *Greek*, River
Proliv *Russian*, Strait
Pulau *Indonesian*, *Malay*, Island
Pulu *Malay*, Island
Punta *Portuguese*, *Spanish*, Point

Q

Qā' *Arabic*, Depression
Qolleh *Persian*, Mountain

R

Raas *Somali*, Cape
-rags *Latvian*, Cape
Ramlat *Arabic*, Sands
Ra's *Arabic*, Cape, point, headland
Ravnina *Bulgarian*, *Russian*, Plain
Récif *French*, Reef
Represa (Rep.) *Spanish*, *Portuguese*, Reservoir
-rettō *Japanese*, Island chain
Riacho *Spanish*, Stream
Riban' *Malagasy*, Mountains
Rio *Portuguese*, River
Río *Spanish*, River
Riu *Catalan*, River
Rivier *Dutch*, River
Rivière *French*, River
Rowd *Pashtu*, River
Rūd *Persian*, River
Rudohorie *Slovak*, Mountains
Ruisseau *French*, Stream

S

Sabkhat *Arabic*, Salt marsh
Şaḥrā' *Arabic*, Desert
Samudra *Sinhala*, Reservoir
-san *Japanese, Korean*, Mountain
-sanchi *Japanese*, Mountains
-sanmaek *Korean*, Mountain range
Sarīr *Arabic*, Desert
Sebkha, Sebkhet *Arabic*, Salt marsh, depression
See *German*, Lake
Selat *Indonesian*, Strait
-selkä *Finnish*, Ridge
Selseleh *Persian*, Mountain range
Serra *Portuguese*, Mountain
Serranía *Spanish*, Mountain
Sha'īb *Arabic*, Watercourse
Shamo *Chinese*, Desert
Shan *Chinese*, Mountain(s)
Shan-mo *Chinese*, Mountain range
Shaṭṭ *Arabic*, Distributary
-shima *Japanese*, Island
Shui-tao *Chinese*, Channel
Sierra *Spanish*, Mountains
Son *Vietnamese*, Mountain
Sông *Vietnamese*, River
-spitze *German*, Peak
Štít *Slovak*, Peak
Stoeng *Cambodian*, River
Stretto *Italian*, Strait
Su Anbarı *Azerbaijani*, Reservoir
Sungai *Indonesian*, *Malay*, River
Suu *Turkish*, River

T

Tal *Mongolian*, Plain
Tandavan' *Malagasy*, Mountain range
Tangorombohitr' *Malagasy*, Mountain massif
Tao *Chinese*, Island
Tassili *Berber*, Plateau, mountain
Tau *Russian*, Mountain(s)
Taungdan *Burmese*, Mountain range
Teluk *Indonesian*, *Malay*, Bay

Terara *Amharic*, Mountain
Tog *Somali*, Valley
Tônlé *Cambodian*, Lake
Top *Dutch*, Peak
-tunturi *Finnish*, Mountain
Tur'at *Arabic*, Channel

V

Väin *Estonian*, Strait
-vatn *Icelandic*, Lake
-vesi *Finnish*, Lake
Vinh *Vietnamese*, Bay
Vodokhranilishche (Vdkhr.) *Russian*, Reservoir
Vodoskhovyshche (Vdskh.) *Ukrainian*, Reservoir
Volcán *Spanish*, Volcano
Vozvyshennost' *Russian*, Upland, plateau
Vrh *Macedonian*, Peak
Vysochyna *Ukrainian*, Upland
Vysočina *Czech*, Upland

W

Waadi *Somali*, Watercourse
Wādī *Arabic*, Watercourse
Wāḥat, Wâhat *Arabic*, Oasis
Wald *German*, Forest
Wan *Chinese*, Bay
Wyżyna *Polish*, Upland

X

Xé *Laotian*, River

Y

Yarımadası *Azerbaijani*, Peninsula
Yazovir *Bulgarian*, Reservoir
Yoma *Burmese*, Mountains
Yü *Chinese*, Island

Z

Zaliv *Bulgarian*, *Russian*, Bay
Zatoka *Ukrainian*, Bay
Zemlya *Russian*, Bay

GLOSSARY OF ABBREVIATIONS

THIS GLOSSARY provides a comprehensive guide to the abbreviations used in this Atlas, and in the Index-Gazetteer.

A
abbrev. abbreviation
Afr. Afrikaans
Alb. Albanian
Amh. Amharic
anc. ancient
Ar. Arabic
Arm. Armenian
Az. Azerbaijani

B
Basq. Basque
Bel. Belorussian
Ben. Bengali
Bibl. Biblical
Bret. Breton
Bul. Bulgarian
Bur. Burmese

C
Cam. Cambodian
Cant. Cantonese
Cast. Castilian
Cat. Catalan
Chin. Chinese
Cro. Croat
Cz. Czech

D
Dan. Danish
Dut. Dutch

E
Eng. English
Est. Estonian
est. estimated

F
Faer. Faeroese
Fij. Fijian
Fin. Finnish
Flem. Flemish
Fr. French
Fris. Frisian

G
Geor. Georgian
Ger. German
Gk. Greek
Guj. Gujarati

H
Haw. Hawaiian
Heb. Hebrew
Hind. Hindi
hist. historical
Hung. Hungarian

I
Icel. Icelandic
Ind. Indonesian
Inuit Inuit
Ir. Irish
It. Italian

J
Jap. Japanese

K
Kaz. Kazakh
Kir. Kirghiz
Kor. Korean
Kurd. Kurdish

L
Lao. Laotian
Lapp. Lappish
Lat. Latin

Latv. Latvian
Lith. Lithanian
Lus. Lusatian

M
Mac. Macedonian
Mal. Malay
Malg. Malagasy
Malt. Maltese
Mong. Mongolia

N
Nepali. Nepali
Nor. Norwegian

O
off. offically

P
Pash. Pashtu
Per. Persian
Pol. Polish
Port. Portuguese
prev. previously

R
Rmsch. Romansch
Roman. Romanian
Rus. Russian

S
SCr. Serbian and Croatian
Serb. Serbian
Slvk. Slovak
Slvn. Slovene
Som. Somali
Sp. Spanish
Swa. Swahili
Swe. Swedish

T
Taj. Tajik
Th. Thai
Tib. Tibetan
Turk. Turkish
Turkm. Turkmenistan

U
Uigh. Uighur
Ukr. Ukrainian
Uzb. Uzbek

V
var. variant
Vtn. Vietnamese

W
Wel. Welsh

X
Xh. Xhosa

Y
Yugo. Yugoslavia

Key to country factboxes within the index:

Date of formation
This denotes the country's date of independence or the date when its current borders were established.

Languages
Official language(s) are denoted by an asterisk.

INDEX

A

Aa *see* Gauja
Aachen 94 A 4 *Dut.* Aken,
  Fr. Aix-la-Chapelle; *anc.* Aquae
  Grani, Aquisgranum. W Germany
Aaiún *see* Laâyoune
Aalborg Bugt *see* Ålborg Bugt
Aalen 95 B 6 S Germany
Aalsmeer 86 C 3 C Netherlands
Aalst 87 B 6 *Fr.* Alost. C Belgium
Aalten 86 F 4 E Netherlands
Aalter 87 B 5 NW Belgium
Äänekoski 85 D 5 C Finland
Aar *see* Aare
Aare 95 A 7 *var.* Aar. River,
  W Switzerland
Aarhus *see* Århus
Aasiaat 82 C 3 *var.* Ausiait,
  Dan. Egedesminde. W Greenland
A. nth
Aba 75 G 5 S Nigeria
Aba 77 E 5 NE Congo (Zaire)
Abā as Su'ūd *see* Najrān
Abaco Island *see* Great Abaco
Ābādān 120 C 4 SW Iran
Abagnar Qi *see* Xilin Hot
Abakan 114 D 4
  C Russian Federation
Abancay 60 D 4 SE Peru
Abashiri 130 D 2 *var.* Abasiri.
  Hokkaidō, NE Japan
Abasiri *see* Abashiri
Ābaya Hāyk' 73 C 5 *Eng.* Lake
  Margherita, *It.* Abbaia. Lake,
  SW Ethiopia
Abbatis Villa *see* Abbeville
Abbazia *see* Opatija
Abbeville 90 C 2 *anc.* Abbatis Villa.
  N France
Abbeville 42 B 3 Louisiana, S USA
'Abd al 'Azīz, Jabal 118 D 2
  mountain range, NE Syria
Abéché 76 C 3 *var.* Abécher,
  Abeshr. SE Chad
Abellinum *see* Avellino
Abemama Atoll 144 D 2 *var.*
  Apamama; *prev.* Roger Simpson
  Island. Island, W Kiribati
Abengourou 75 E 5 E Ivory Coast
Aberbrothock *see* Arbroath
Abercorn *see* Mbala
Aberdeen 88 D 3 *anc.* Devana.
  E Scotland, UK
Aberdeen 128 A 2 S Hong Kong
Aberdeen 46 B 2
  Washington, NW USA
Aberdeen 45 E 2
  South Dakota, N USA
Abergwaun *see* Fishguard
Abertawe *see* Swansea
Aberystwyth 89 C 6 W Wales, UK
Abhā 121 B 6 SW Saudi Arabia
Abidavichy 107 D 7
  Rus. Obidovichi. E Belorussia
Abidjan 75 E 5 S Ivory Coast
Abilene 49 F 3 Texas, S USA
Abingdon *see* Pinta, Isla
Abkhazia 117 F 2 region,
  NW Georgia
Åbo *see* Turku
Aboisso 75 E 5 SE Ivory Coast
Abo, Massif d' 76 B 1 mountain
  range, N Chad
Abomey 75 F 5 S Benin
Abou-Déïa 76 C 3 SE Chad
Aboudouhour *see* Abū aḍ Ḍuhūr
Abou Kémal *see* Abū Kamāl
Abrantes 92 B 3 *var.* Abrántes.
  C Portugal

Abrántes *see* Abrantes
Abrashlare *see* Brezovo
Abrolhos Bank 57 E 4 undersea
  bank, W Atlantic Ocean
Abrova 107 B 6 *Rus.* Obrovo.
  SW Belorussia
Abrud 108 B 4 *Hung.* Abrudbánya.
  SW Romania
Abrudbánya *see* Abrud
Abruzzese, Appennino 96 C 4
  mountain range, C Italy
Absaroka Range 44 B 2 mountain
  range, NW USA
Abū aḍ Ḍuhūr 118 B 3 *Fr.*
  Aboudouhour. NW Syria
Abu Dhabi *see* Abū Ẓaby
Abu Hamed 72 C 3 N Sudan
Abuja 75 G 4 country capital,
  C Nigeria
Abū Kamāl 118 E 3
  Fr. Abou Kémal. E Syria
Abuná 61 E 2 *var.* Río Abuná. River,
  Bolivia/Brazil
Abuná, Río *see* Abuná
Abut Head 151 B 6 headland,
  South Island, SW New Zealand
Ābuyē Mēda 73 D 5 mountain,
  C Ethiopia
Abū Ẓaby 121 D 5 *var.* Abū Ẓabī,
  Eng. Abu Dhabi. Country capital,
  C United Arab Emirates
Acalayong 77 A 5
  SW Equatorial Guinea
Acaponeta 50 C 4 C Mexico
Acapulco 51 E 5 *var.* Acapulco de
  Juárez. S Mexico
Acapulco de Juárez *see* Acapulco
Acarai Mountains 59 F 4 *var.*
  Serra Acaraí. Mountain range,
  Brazil/Guyana
Acaraí, Serra *see* Acarai Mountains
Acarigua 58 D 2 N Venezuela
Acay, Abra del 64 C 2 pass,
  N Argentina
Accra 75 E 5 country capital,
  SE Ghana
Achacachi 61 F 4 W Bolivia
Acklins Island 54 D 2 island,
  SE Bahamas
Aconcagua, Cerro 64 B 4 mountain,
  W Argentina
Acora 61 E 4 SE Peru
A Coruña 92 B 1 *Cast.* La Coruña,
  Eng. Corunna; *anc.* Caronium.
  NW Spain
Acre 62 C 2 *off.* Estado do Acre.
  State, W Brazil
Acre 60 D 2 cultural region,
  W Brazil
Acre, Estado do *see* Acre
Açu 63 G 2 NE Brazil
Ada 49 G 2 Oklahoma, C USA
Ada 100 D 3 N Yugoslavia
Ada Bazar *see* Adapazarı
Adáfer 74 D 2 plateau,
  C Mauritania
Adak Island 36 A 3 island, Alaska,
  NW USA
Adamaoua, Massif d' 76 B 4
  Eng. Adamawa Highlands.
  Mountain range, NW Cameroon
Adamawa 68 B 4 province,
  N Cameroon
Adamawa Highlands *see*
  Adamaoua, Massif d'
Adam-jo-Tando *see* Tando Ādam
Adamstown 143 G 4
  dependent territory capital,
  Pitcairn Island,
  SW Pitcairn Islands
'Adan 121 B 7 *Eng.* Aden.
  SW Yemen

Adana 116 D 4 *var.* Seyhan.
S Turkey
Adapazarı 116 B 3 *prev.* Ada Bazar.
NW Turkey
Adare, Cape 154 B 4 headland,
Antarctica
Ad Dahnā' 120 B 4 desert,
E Saudi Arabia
Ad Dakhla 70 A 4 *var.* Dakhla;
prev. Villa Cisneros. W Morocco
Ad Dalanj *see* Dilling
Ad Damazīn *see* Ed Damazin
Ad Dāmūr *see* Damoûr
Ad Dawḥah 120 D 4 *Eng.* Doha.
Country capital, C Qatar
Aḍ Ḍiffah *see* Libyan Plateau
Addis Ababa *see* Ādīs Ābeba
Addu Atoll 132 B 5 island,
S Maldives
Adelaide 149 B 6 South Australia,
S Australia
Aden *see* 'Adan
Aden, Gulf of 121 C 7
var. Badyarada 'Admēd. Gulf,
W Indian Ocean
Adige 96 C 2 *Ger.* Etsch. River,
N Italy
Adirondack Mountains 41 F 2
mountain range, New York,
NE USA
Ādīs Ābeba 73 C 5 *var.* Addis
Ababa. Country capital,
C Ethiopia
Adıyaman 117 E 4 SE Turkey
Adjud 108 C 4 E Romania
Admiralty Gulf 146 C 2 gulf,
E Indian Ocean
Admiralty Islands 144 B 3 island
group, N Papua New Guinea
Adra 93 E 5 S Spain
Adrar 74 C 2 mountainous region,
W Mauritania
Adrar 70 D 3 mountain range,
SE Algeria
Adrian 40 C 3 Michigan, N USA
Adriatic Sea 103 E 2 *Alb.* Deti
Adriatik, *It.* Mare Adriatic, *SCr.*
Jadransko More, *Slvn.* Jadransko
Morje. Sea, N Mediterranean Sea
Adycha 115 F 2 river,
NE Russian Federation
Aegean Sea 103 F 3 *Gk.* Aigaío
Pélagos, Aigaion Pelagos,
Turk. Ege Denizi. Sea,
N Mediterranean Sea
Aegviidu 106 D 2 *Ger.*
Charlottenhof. NW Estonia
Aelok *see* Ailuk Atoll

Afghanistan
122 D 4 *Per.* Dowlat-e Eslāmī-ye
Afghānestān; *prev.* Republic of
Afghanistan. State, C Asia

Official name: Islamic State of
Afghanistan **Date of formation:**
1919 **Capital:** Kābul **Population:**
20.5 million **Total Area:**
652,090 sq km (251,770 sq miles)
Languages: Persian*, Pashtu*
Religions: Sunni Muslim 84%, Shi'a
Muslim 15%, other 1% **Ethnic mix:**
Pashtun 38%, Tajik 25%, Hazara
19%, Uzbek 6%, other 12%
Government: *Mujahideen* coalition
Currency: Afghani = 100 puls

Afmadow 73 D 6 S Somalia
Africa 66 D 4 continent
'Afrīn 118 B 2 NW Syria
Afyon 116 B 3 *prev.* Afyonkarahisar.
W Turkey
Afyonkarahisar *see* Afyon

Agadès *see* Agadez
Agadez 75 G 3 *prev.* Agadès.
C Niger
Agadir 70 B 3 SW Morocco
Agana 144 B 1 *var.* Agaña.
Dependent territory capital,
NW Guam
Agaña *see* Agana
Āgaro 73 C 5 W Ethiopia
Agassiz Fracture Zone 153 E 4
fracture zone, S Pacific Ocean
Agatha *see* Agde
Agathónisi 105 D 6 island,
Dodekánisos, SE Greece
Agde 91 C 6 *anc.* Agatha. S France
Agen 91 B 6 *anc.* Aginnum.
SW France
Agiá 104 B 4 *var.* Ayiá. C Greece
Agía Marína 105 E 6 Leros,
SE Greece
Aginnum *see* Agen
Ágios Nikólaos 105 D 8 *var.* Áyios
Nikólaos. Kríti, SE Greece
Āgra 134 D 3 N India
Ağrı 117 F 3 *var.* Karaköse;
prev. Karakılsse. NE Turkey
Agrigento 97 C 7 *Gk.* Akragas;
prev. Girgenti . SW Italy
Agrínio 105 B 5 *prev.* Agrinion.
W Greece
Agrinion *see* Agrínio
Agriovótano 105 C 5 C Greece
Agropoli 97 D 5 Italy
Aguachica 58 B 2 N Colombia
Aguadulce 53 F 5 S Panama
Agua Prieta 50 B 1 NW Mexico
Aguascalientes 50 D 4 C Mexico
Aguilas 93 E 5 SE Spain
Aguililla 50 D 4 SW Mexico
Agulhas Bank 67 D 6 undersea
bank, SW Indian Ocean
Agulhas Basin 67 E 6 undersea
basin, SW Indian Ocean
Agulhas Plateau 67 E 6 undersea
plateau, SW Indian Ocean
Ahaggar 68 B 3 mountain range,
SE Algeria
Ahlen 94 B 4 W Germany
Ahmadābād 134 C 4
var. Ahmedabad. W India
Ahmadnagar 134 C 5
var. Ahmednagar. W India
Ahmedabad *see* Ahmadābād
Ahmednagar *see* Ahmadnagar
Ahuachapán 52 B 3 W El Salvador
Ahvāz 120 C 3 *var.* Ahwāz;
prev. Nāsiri. SW Iran
Aígina 105 C 6 *var.* Aíyina.
C Greece
Aígio 105 B 5 *prev.* Aíyion. S Greece
Aiken 43 E 2 South Carolina,
SE USA
Ailao Shan 129 A 6 mountain
range, S China
Ailigandí 53 G 4 NE Panama
Ailinglaplap Atoll 144 D 2
var. Aelónlaplap, Ailinglapalap.
Island, S Marshall Islands
Ailuk Atoll 144 D 1 *var.* Aelok.
Island, NE Marshall Islands
Ainaži 106 D 3 *Est.* Heinaste,
Ger. Hainasch. N Latvia
'Aïn Ben Tili 74 D 1 N Mauritania
Aiquile 61 F 4 C Bolivia
Aïr du Azbine *see* Aïr, Massif de l'
Aïr, Massif de l' 75 G 3 *var.* Aïr,
Air du Azbine, Asben. Mountain
range, NC Niger
Aiud 108 B 4 *Ger.* Strassburg,
Hung. Nagyenyed; *prev.* Engeten.
SW Romania

Aix-en-Provence 91 D 6 *var.* Aix;
anc. Aquae Sextiae. SE France
Aizkraukle 106 C 4 S Latvia
Ajaccio 91 E 7 SE France
Ajana 147 A 5 W Australia
Ajaria 117 F 2 region, SW Georgia
Aj Bogd Uul 126 D 2 mountain,
SW Mongolia
Ajdābiyā 71 G 2 *var.* Agedabia,
Ajdābiyah. NE Libya
Ajmer 134 D 3 *var.* Ajmere. N India
Ajmere *see* Ajmer
Akasha 72 B 3 N Sudan
Akçakale 117 E 4 S Turkey
Akchâr 74 C 2 desert,
W Mauritania
Akdar, Jebel *see* Akhḍar al Jabal
Akhalts'ikhe 117 F 2 SW Georgia
Akhḍar, Al Jabal al 121 D 5 *var.*
Jabal al Akhdar. Mountain range,
NW Oman
Akhḍar, Jabal al *see* Akhḍar,
Al Jabal al
Akhisar 116 A 3 W Turkey
Akhmīm 72 B 2 *anc.* Panopolis.
C Egypt
Akhtubinsk 111 C 7
SW Russian Federation
Akhtyrka *see* Okhtyrka
Akimiski Island 38 C 3 island,
Northwest Territories, C Canada
Akita 130 D 4 Honshū, C Japan
Akjoujt 74 C 2 *prev.* Fort-Repoux.
W Mauritania
Akkeshi 130 E 2 Hokkaidō,
NE Japan
Aklavik 36 D 3 North West
Territories, NW Canada
Akmola 114 C 4 *Kaz.* Aqmola;
prev. Akmolinsk, Tselinograd.
N Kazakhstan
Akpatok Island 39 E 1 island,
Northwest Territories,
E Canada
Akron 40 D 4 Ohio, N USA
Akrotiri *see* Akrotírion
Aksai Chin 126 A 4
Chin. Aksayqin. Disputed region,
China/India
Aksaray 116 C 4 C Turkey
Aksay *see* Toxkan He
Aksayqin *see* Aksai Chin
Aktash *see* Oqtosh
Aktau 114 A 4 *Kaz.* Aqtaū;
prev. Shevchenko. W Kazakhstan
Aktsyabrski 107 D 7
Rus. Oktyabr'skiy;
prev. Karpilovka. SE Belorussia
Aktyubinsk 114 B 4 *Kaz.* Aqtöbe.
NW Kazakhstan
Akureyri 83 E 5 N Iceland
Akyab *see* Sittwe
Alabama 42 C 2 *off.* State of
Alabama; *nicknames* Camellia
State, Heart of Dixie, The
Cotton State, Yellowhammer
State. State, S USA
Alabama River 42 C 3 river,
Alabama, S USA
Al Abyār 71 G 2 *var.* Madīnat
al Abyār. NE Libya
Alaca 116 C 3 N Turkey
Alagoas 63 G 2 *off.* Estado de
Alagoas. State, E Brazil
Alagoas, Estado de *see* Alagoas
Alais *see* Alès
Alajuela 53 E 4 C Costa Rica
Alakanuk 36 B 2 Alaska, NW USA
Al 'Alamayn *see* El 'Alamein
Al 'Amārah 120 C 3 *var.* Amara.
E Iraq

Alamosa 44 C 5 Colorado, C USA
Åland 85 C 6 *var.* Aland Islands,
Fin. Ahvenanmaa. Island group,
SW Finland
Aland Sea *see* Ålands hav
Ålands Hav 85 C 6 *var.* Aland Sea.
Strait, C Baltic Sea
Al 'Aqabah 119 B 8 *var.* Akaba,
Aqaba, 'Aqaba; *anc.* Aelana,
Elath. SW Jordan
Alaşehir 116 A 4 W Turkey
Alaska 36 C 3 *off.* State of Alaska;
nicknames Land of the
Midnight Sun, Seward's
Folly, The Last Frontier;
prev. Russian America. State,
NW USA
Alaska, Gulf of 152 D 1 gulf,
NE Pacific Ocean
Alaska Peninsula 36 C 3 peninsula,
Alaska, NW USA
Alaska Range 36 C 3 mountain
range, Alaska, NW USA
Alattio *see* Alta
Alazani 117 G 2 *var.* Qanıx. River,
Azerbaijan/Georgia
Alazeya 115 G 2 river,
NE Russian Federation
Al Bāb 118 B 2 NW Syria
Albacete 93 E 4 C Spain
Al Baghdādī 120 B 3 *var.* Khān
al Baghdādī. SW Iraq
Alba Iulia 108 B 4
Ger. Weissenburg,
Hung. Gyulafehérvár;
prev. Bälgrad, Karlsburg,
Károly-Fehérvár. W Romania
Albania *see* Aubagne

Albania
101 C 6 *Alb.* Republika e
Shqipqërisë, Shqipëria;
prev. People's Socialist Republic
of Albania. Republic,
SE Europe

Official name: Republic of Albania
Date of formation: 1912/1913
Capital: Tiranë **Population:** 3.3
million **Total area:** 28,750 sq km
(11,100 sq miles) **Languages:**
Albanian, Greek **Religions:** Muslim
70%, Greek Orthodox 20%, Roman
Catholic 10% **Ethnic mix:** Albanian
96%, Greek 2%, other (inc.
Macedonian) 2% **Government:**
Multiparty republic **Currency:**
Lek = 100 qindars

Albany 42 D 3 Georgia, SE USA
Albany 38 C 3 river, Ontario,
S Canada
Albany 147 B 7 Western Australia,
SW Australia
Albany 41 F 3 state capital,
New York, NE USA
Albany 46 B 3 Oregon, NW USA
Al Başrah 120 C 4 *Eng.* Basra;
hist. Busra, Bussora. SE Iraq
Albatross Bay 148 C 2 bay,
SE Arafura Sea
Albatross Plateau 35 B 7 undersea
plateau, E Pacific Ocean
Al Batrūn *see* Batroûn
Al Bayḍā' 71 G 2 *var.* Beida.
NE Libya
Albemarle Island *see* Isabela, Isla
Albemarle Sound 43 G 1 inlet,
W Atlantic Ocean
Albergaria-a-Velha 92 B 2
W Portugal
Albert 90 C 3 N France
Alberta 37 E 4 province,
SW Canada

Albert, Lake 77 E 5 *var.* Albert Nyanza, Lac Mobutu Sese Seko. Lake, Congo (Zaire)/Uganda
Albert Lea 45 G 3 Minnesota, N USA
Albertville *see* Kalemie
Albi 91 C 6 *anc.* Albiga. S France
Albiga *see* Albi
Al Biyāḍ 121 C 5 desert, C Saudi Arabia
Ålborg 85 B 7 *var.* Aalborg, Ålborg-Nørresundby; *anc.* Alburgum. N Denmark
Ålborg Bugt 85 B 7 *var.* Aalborg Bugt. Bay, E North Sea
Alborz, Reshteh-ye Kuhhā-ye 120 C 2 *Eng.* Elburz Mountains. Mountain range, N Iran
Albuquerque 48 D 2 New Mexico, SW USA
Albury 149 C 7 New South Wales, SE Australia
Alcácer do Sal 92 B 4 W Portugal
Alcalá de Henares 93 E 3 *Ar.* Alkal'a; *anc.* Complutim, Complutum. C Spain
Alcamo 97 C 7 SW Italy
Alcañiz 93 F 2 NE Spain
Alcántara, Embalse de 92 C 3 reservoir, W Spain
Alcaudete 92 D 4 S Spain
Alcoi *see* Alcoy
Alcoy 93 F 4 *var.* Alcoi. E Spain
Aldabra Group 79 G 2 island group, SW Seychelles
Aldan 115 F 3 river, E Russian Federation
al Dar al Baida *see* Rabat
Alderney 89 D 8 island, N Channel Islands
Aleg 74 C 3 SW Mauritania
Aleksandriya *see* Oleksandriya
Aleksandrovka *see* Oleksandrivka
Aleksin 111 B 5 W Russian Federation
Aleksinac 100 E 4 E Yugoslavia
Alençon 90 B 3 N France
Alenquer 63 E 2 NE Brazil
Aleppo *see* Ḥalab
Alert 37 F 1 Ellesmere Island, Canada
Alès 91 D 6 *prev.* Alais. S France
Aleşd 108 B 3 *Hung.* Élesd. SW Romania
Alessandria 96 B 2 *Fr.* Alexandrie. N Italy
Ålesund 85 A 5 S Norway
Aleutian Basin 152 C 1 undersea basin, SW Pacific Ocean
Aleutian Islands 36 A 3 island group, Alaska, NW USA
Aleutian Range 34 A 2 mountain range, Alaska, NW USA
Aleutian Rise 152 C 1 undersea rise, NW Pacific Ocean
Aleutian Trench 152 D 1 trench, SW Pacific Ocean
Alexander Archipelago 36 C 4 island group, Alaska, NW USA
Alexander City 42 D 2 Alabama, S USA
Alexander Island 154 A 3 island, Antarctica
Alexandra 151 B 7 South Island, SW New Zealand
Alexandra Bay 148 D 2 bay, NE Coral Sea
Alexándreia 104 B 4 *var.* Alexándria. N Greece
Alexandretta *see* İskenderun
Alexandretta, Gulf of *see* İskenderun Körfezi
Alexandria 42 B 3 Louisiana, S USA
Alexandria 41 E 4 Virginia, NE USA
Alexandria 108 C 5 S Romania
Alexandria 45 F 2 Minnesota, N USA
Alexandria 72 B 1 *Ar.* Al Iskandarīyah. N Egypt
Alexándria *see* Alexándreia
Alexandrie *see* Alessandria
Alexandrina, Lake 149 B 7 lake, South Australia, SE Australia
Alexandroúpoli 104 D 3 *var.* Alexandroúpolis, *Turk.* Dedeagaç, Dedeagach. NE Greece
Al Fāshir *see* El Fasher
Alfatar 104 E 1 NE Bulgaria
Alfeiós 105 B 6 *prev.* Alfiós, *anc.* Alpheius, Alpheus. River, S Greece
Alga 114 B 4 *Kaz.* Algha. NW Kazakhstan
Algarve 92 B 4 cultural region, S Portugal
Algeciras 92 C 5 SW Spain
Algeciras, Bahía de *see* Gibraltar, Bay of
Algemesí 93 F 3 E Spain
Alger 70 D 1 *var.* Algiers, Al Jazair, El Djazaïr. Country capital, N Algeria

---

Algeria
70 C 3 NW Africa

Official name: Democratic and Popular Republic of Algeria **Date of formation:** 1962 **Capital:** Algiers **Population:** 27.1 million **Total area:** 2,381,740 sq km (919,590 sq miles) **Languages:** Arabic*, Berber, French **Religions:** Muslim 99%, Christian and Jewish 1% **Ethnic mix:** Arab and Berber 99% European 1% **Government:** Military regime **Currency:** Dinar = 100 centimes

---

Algerian Basin *see* Balearic Plain
Algha *see* Alga
Alghero 97 A 5 W Italy
Algiers *see* Alger
Al Golea *see* El Goléa
Algona 45 F 3 Iowa, C USA
Al Hasā 120 C 4 desert, NE Saudi Arabia
Al Ḫasakah 118 D 1 *var.* Al Hasijah, El Haseke, *Fr.* Hassetché. NE Syria
Al Ḥillah 120 B 3 *var.* Hilla. C Iraq
Al Hudaydah 121 B 6 *Eng.* Hodeida. W Yemen
Al Hufūf 121 C 5 *var.* Hofuf. NE Saudi Arabia
Alíartos 105 C 5 C Greece
Äli-Bayramll 117 H 3 *Rus.* Ali-Bayramly. SE Azerbaijan
Ali-Bayramly *see* Äli-Bayramlı
Alicante 93 F 4 *Cat.* Alacant; *Lat.* Lucentum. SE Spain
Alice 49 G 5 Texas, S USA
Alice Springs 148 A 4 Northern Territory, C Australia
Aliki *see* Alykí
Alindao 76 C 4 S Central African Republic
Aliquippa 40 D 4 Pennsylvania, NE USA
Al Iskandarīyah *see* Alexandria
Alistráti 104 C 3 NE Greece
Alivéri 105 C 5 *var.* Alivérion. Évvoia, C Greece
Alivérion *see* Alivéri
Al Jabal al Akhḍar 71 G 2 *var.* Jebel Akdar. Mountain range, NE Libya
Al Jafr 119 B 7 S Jordan
Al Jaghbūb 71 H 3 NE Libya
Al Jahrā' 120 C 4 *var.* Al Jahrah, Jahra. C Kuwait
Al Jawf 120 B 4 *var.* Jauf. NW Saudi Arabia
Al Karak 119 B 7 *var.* El Kerak, Karak, Kerak; *anc.* Kir Moab, Kir of Moab. W Jordan
Al Khārijah *see* El Khârga
Al-Khobar *see* Al Khubar
Al Khubar 120 C 4 *var.* Al-Khobar. NE Saudi Arabia
Al Khums 71 F 2 *var.* Homs, Khoms, Khums. NW Libya
Alkmaar 86 C 3 NW Netherlands
Al Kufrah 72 A 2 *var.* Kufra Oasis, *It.* Cufra. Oasis, W Libya
Al Kūt 120 C 3 *var.* Kūt al 'Amārah, Kut al Imara. E Iraq
Al Kuwayt 120 C 4 *var.* Kuwait City, Al-Kuwait, *Eng.* Kuwait; *prev.* Qurein. Country capital, E Kuwait
Al Lādhiqīyah 118 A 3 *Eng.* Latakia, *Fr.* Lattaquié; *anc.* Laodicea, Laodicea ad Mare. W Syria
Allahābād 135 E 3 N India
Allanmyo 136 B 4 W Burma
'Allâq, Wâdi el 72 C 3 dry watercourse, Egypt/Sudan
Allegheny Plateau 41 E 3 mountain range, NE USA
Allenstein *see* Olsztyn
Allentown 41 F 4 Pennsylvania, NE USA
Alleppey 132 C 3 *var.* Alappuzha; *prev.* Alleppi. SW India
Alliance 44 D 3 Nebraska, C USA
Al Līth 121 B 5 SW Saudi Arabia
Alma 39 E 4 Québec, SE Canada
Alma-Ata *see* Almaty
Almada 92 B 4 W Portugal
Al Madīnah 121 B 5 *Eng.* Medina. W Saudi Arabia
Al Mafraq 119 B 6 *var.* Mafraq. N Jordan
Al Mahrah 121 C 6 mountain range, E Yemen
Al Majma'ah 120 C 4 C Saudi Arabia
Al Mālikīyah 118 E 1 *var.* Dayrīk, Malkiye, *Fr.* Malkieh. NE Syria
Almalyk *see* Olmaliq
Al Manāmah 120 C 4 *Eng.* Manama. Country capital, N Bahrain
Al Manāṣif 118 E 3 mountain range, E Syria
Almansa 93 E 4 C Spain
Al Marj 71 G 2 *var.* Barka, *It.* Barce. NE Libya
Almaty 114 C 5 *var.* Alma-Ata. Country capital, SE Kazakhstan
Al Mawṣil 120 B 2 *Eng.* Mosul. N Iraq
Al Mayādīn 118 E 3 *var.* Mayadin, *Fr.* Meyadine. E Syria
Al Mazār al Janūbī 119 B 7 *var.* Mazar. W Jordan
Al Mazra'ah 119 B 7 *var.* Al Mazra', Mazra'a. W Jordan
Almelo 86 E 3 E Netherlands
Almendra, Embalse de 92 C 2 reservoir, NW Spain
Almendralejo 92 C 4 W Spain
Almere 86 C 3 *var.* Almere-stad. C Netherlands
Almere-stad *see* Almere
Almería 93 E 5 *Ar.* Al-Mariyya; *anc.* Unci, *Lat.* Portus Magnus. S Spain
Al Mīnā' *see* El Mina
Almirante 53 F 5 NW Panama
Al Mubarraz 120 C 4 E Saudi Arabia
Al Mudawwarah 119 B 8 SW Jordan
Al Mukallā 121 C 7 *var.* Mukalla. SE Yemen
Al Munastīr *see* Monastir
Alofi 145 F 5 dependent territory capital, W Niue
Aloja 106 D 3 N Latvia
Alónnisos 105 C 5 island, Vóreioi Sporádes, E Greece
Álora 92 D 5 S Spain
Alor, Kepulauan 139 E 5 island group, E Indonesia
Alost *see* Aalst
Alpena 40 D 2 Michigan, N USA
Alpha Cordillera 155 F 3 *var.* Alpha Ridge. Seamount range, Arctic Ocean
Alphen *see* Alphen aan den Rijn
Alphen aan den Rijn 86 C 3 *var.* Alphen. C Netherlands
Alpine 49 E 4 Texas, S USA
Alps 80 D 4 *Fr.* Alpes, *Ger.* Alpen, *It.* Alpi. Mountain range, C Europe
Al Qāmishlī 118 E 1 *var.* Kamishli, Qamishly. NE Syria
Al Qaryāt 71 F 3 NW Libya
Al Qaṣrayn *see* Kasserine
Al Qayrawān *see* Kairouan
Al Qunayṭirah 119 B 5 *var.* El Kuneitra, El Quneitra, Kuneitra, Qunaytra. SW Syria
Al Quṣayr 118 B 4 *var.* El Quseir, Quayr, *Fr.* Kousseir. W Syria
Al Quwayrah 119 B 8 *var.* El Quweira. SW Jordan
Alsace 90 E 3 cultural region, NE France
Alsdorf 94 A 4 W Germany
Alta 84 D 2 *Fin.* Alattio. N Norway
Altai Mountains 124 C 1 *var.* Altay Shan. Mountain range, E Asia
AltaY Shan *see* Altai Mountains
Al Ṭafīlah 119 B 7 *var.* Et Tafila, Tafila. W Jordan
Altamaha River 43 E 3 river, Georgia, SE USA
Altamira 63 E 2 NE Brazil
Altamont 46 B 4 Oregon, NW USA
Altamura 97 E 5 *anc.* Lupatia. SE Italy
Altar, Desierto de 50 A 1 desert, Mexico/USA
Altay 126 D 2 W Mongolia
Altay 126 C 2 *Chin.* A-le-t'ai, *Mong.* Sharasume; *prev.* Ch'eng-hua, Chenghwa. NW China
Altin Köprü 120 B 3 *var.* Altun Kupri. Iraq
Alton 40 B 4 Illinois, N USA
Altoona 41 E 4 Pennsylvania, NE USA
Alto Paraná *see* Paraná
Alt-Schwanenburg *see* Gulbene
Altun Kupri *see* Altin Köprü
Altun Shan 126 C 4 *var.* Altyn Tagh. Mountain range, NW China
Altus 49 F 2 Oklahoma, C USA
Altyn Tagh *see* Altun Shan
Alūksne 106 D 3 *Ger.* Marienburg. NE Latvia
Al 'Ulá 120 A 4 NW Saudi Arabia
Al 'Umarī 119 C 6 E Jordan
Alupka 109 F 5 S Ukraine

Al Uqşur *see* Luxor
Alushta 109 F 5 S Ukraine
Alva 49 F 1 Oklahoma, C USA
Alvarado 51 F 4 E Mexico
Alvin 49 H 4 Texas, S USA
Al Wahībah, Ramlat 121 E 5 *var.*
Ramlat Ahl Wahībah, Ramlat
Al Wahaybah, Wahībah Sands.
Desert, N Oman
Al Wajh 120 A 4 NW Saudi Arabia
Alwar 134 D 3 N India
Alykí 104 C 4 *var.* Aliki. Thásos,
N Greece
Alytus 107 B 5 *Pol.* Olita.
S Lithuania
Amadeus, Lake 147 E 5 lake,
South Australia, S Australia
Amadi 73 B 5 SW Sudan
Amadjuak Lake 82 A 2 lake,
N Canada
Amakusa-shotō 131 A 8 island
group, Japan
Åmål 85 B 6 S Sweden
Amami-ōshima 130 A 3 island,
Nansei-shotō, S Japan
Amami-shotō 130 A 3 island group,
Japan
Amantea 97 D 6 SW Italy
Amapá 63 E 1 *off.* Território de
Amapá. State, NE Brazil
Amara *see* Al 'Amārah
Amarapura 136 B 3 C Burma
Amarillo 49 E 2 Texas, S USA
Amay 87 C 6 E Belgium
Amazon 56 C 3 *Sp.* Amazonas.
River, Brazil/Peru
Amazonas 62 D 2 *off.* Estado do
Amazonas. State, N Brazil
Amazonas *see* Amazon
Amazonas, Estado do *see* Amazonas
Amazon Canyons 56 D 2 trough,
C Atlantic Ocean
Amazon Fan 67 B 5 undersea fan,
W Atlantic Ocean
Amazonia 56 B 3 physical region,
N South America
Ambam 77 A 5 S Cameroon
Ambanja 79 G 2 N Madagascar
Ambarchik 115 G 2
NE Russian Federation
Ambato 60 B 1 C Ecuador
Ambérieu-en-Bugey 91 D 5
E France
Amblève 87 D 7 river, E Belgium
Amboasary 79 F 4 S Madagascar
Ambon 139 F 4 *prev.* Amboina,
Amboyna. Pulau Seram,
E Indonesia
Ambositra 79 G 3 C Madagascar
Ambracia *see* Árta
Ambrim *see* Ambrym
Ambriz 78 A 1 NW Angola
Ambrym 144 D 4 *var.* Ambrim.
Island, C Vanuatu
Amchitka Island 36 A 2 island,
Alaska, NW USA
Amdo 126 C 5 W China
Ameland 86 D 1 *Fris.* It Amelân.
Island, N Netherlands
America-Antarctica Ridge 67 C 7
undersea ridge, S Atlantic Ocean
American Falls Reservoir 46 E 4
reservoir, Idaho, NW USA
American Samoa 145 F 4 US
unincorporated territory,
S Pacific Ocean
Americus 42 D 3 Georgia, SE USA
Amersfoort 86 D 3 C Netherlands
Ames 45 F 3 Iowa, C USA
Amfilochía 105 B 5 *var.* Amfilokhía.
C Greece

Amfilokhía *see* Amfilochía
Amga 115 F 3 river,
C Russian Federation
Amherst 39 F 4 Nova Scotia,
SE Canada
Amherst *see* Kyaikkami
Amiens 90 C 3 *anc.* Ambianum,
Samarobriva. N France
Amīndīvi Islands 132 B 2 island
group, Lakshadweep,
SW India
Amirante Bank *see* Amirante Ridge
Amirante Islands 79 G 1
var. Amirantes Group. Island,
C Seychelles
Amirantes Group *see*
Amirante Islands
Amistad, Presa de la *see*
Amistad Reservoir
Amistad Reservoir 49 F 4 *var.* Presa
de la Amistad. Reservoir, Texas,
S Mexico/USA
Amisus *see* Samsun
'Ammān 119 B 6 *var.* Amman;
anc. Philadelphia, *Bibl.* Rabbah
Ammon, Rabbath Ammon.
Country capital, NW Jordan
Amman *see* 'Ammān
Ammassalik 82 D 4 *var.*
Angmagssalik. SE Greenland
Amoentai *see* Amuntai
Āmol 120 D 2 *var.* Amul. N Iran
Amorgós 105 D 6 Amorgós,
SE Greece
Amorgós 105 D 6 island, Kykládes,
SE Greece
Amos 38 D 4 Québec, SE Canada
Amourj 74 D 3 SE Mauritania
Ampato, Nevado 61 E 4 mountain,
S Peru
Amposta 93 F 3 NE Spain
Amraoti *see* Amrāvati
Amrāvati 134 D 4 *prev.* Amraoti.
C India
Amritsar 134 D 2 N India
Amstelveen 86 C 3 C Netherlands
Amsterdam 86 C 3 country capital,
C Netherlands
Amsterdam Island 141 C 6 island,
NE French Southern & Antarctic
Territories
Am Timan 76 C 3 SE Chad
Amu Darya 122 D 2
Rus. Amudar'ya, *Taj.* Dar''yoi
Amu, *Turkm.* Amyderya,
Uzb. Amudaryo; *anc.* Oxus. River,
C Asia
Amu-Dar'ya 123 E 3
SE Turkmenistan
Amul *see* Āmol
Amund Ringnes Island 37 F 2
island, N Canada
Amundsen Abyssal Plain 154 B 4
abyssal plain, S Pacific Ocean
Amundsen Gulf 37 E 3 gulf,
SE Beaufort Sea
Amundsen-Scott 154 B 3 research
station, Antarctica
Amundsen Sea 154 A 4 sea,
S Pacific Ocean
Amuntai 138 D 4 *prev.* Amoentai.
Borneo, C Indonesia
Amur 130 A 1 *Chin.* Heilong Jiang.
River, China/Russian Federation
Amvrosiyevka *see* Amvrosiyivka
Amvrosiyivka 109 H 3
var. Amvrosiyevka. SE Ukraine
Amýntaio 104 B 4 *prev.* Amíndaion.
N Greece
Anabar 115 E 2 river,
N Russian Federation
An Abhainn Mhór *see* Blackwater

Anaco 59 E 2 NE Venezuela
Anaconda 44 B 2
Montana, NW USA
Anacortes 46 B 1
Washington, NW USA
Anadolu Dağları *see* Doğu
Karadeniz Dağları
Anadyr' 115 H 1
NE Russian Federation
Anadyr, Gulf of *see*
Anadyrskiy Zaliv
Anadyrskiy Zaliv 115 H 1
Eng. Gulf of Anadyr. Gulf,
N Bering Sea
Anáfi 105 D 7 *anc.* Anaphe. Island,
Kykládes, SE Greece
Analalava 79 G 2 N Madagascar
Anamur 116 C 5 S Turkey
Anantapur 132 C 2 S India
Anaphe *see* Anáfi
Anápolis 63 F 3 C Brazil
Anār 120 D 3 C Iran
Anatolia *see* Anadolu
Anatolia Plateau 116 C 4 plateau,
C Turkey
Anatom 144 D 5 *var.* Aneityum,
prev. Kéamu. Island, S Vanuatu
Añatuya 64 C 3 N Argentina
An Bhearú *see* Barrow
Anchorage 36 C 3 Alaska, NW USA
Ancona 96 C 3 C Italy
Ancud 65 B 6 *prev.* San Carlos de
Ancud. S Chile
Åndalsnes 85 A 5 S Norway
Andalucía 92 D 4 cultural region,
S Spain
Andaman Islands 133 E 2 island
group, SE India
Andaman Sea 133 G 2 sea,
NE Indian Ocean
'Andām, Wādī 121 E 5 river,
NE Oman
Andenne 87 C 6 SE Belgium
Anderlues 87 B 7 S Belgium
Anderson 40 C 4 Indiana, N USA
Andes 57 B 5 mountain range,
South America
Andhra Pradesh 135 E 5
cultural region, E India
Andhra Pradesh 132 D 1 state,
SE India
Andijon 123 F 2 *Rus.* Andizhan.
E Uzbekistan
Andikíthira *see* Antikýthira
Andipaxi *see* Antípaxoi
Andípsara *see* Antípsara
Ándissa *see* Ántissa
Andizhan *see* Andijon
Andkhvoy 122 D 3 N Afghanistan

Andorra
91 A 7 *Cat.* Valls d'Andorra,
Fr. Vallée d'Andorra. Monarchy,
SW Europe

Official name: Principality of
Andorra **Date of formation:** 1278
Capital: Andorra la Vella
Population: 58,000
Total area: 468 sq km (181 sq miles)
Languages: Catalan*, Spanish
Religions: Roman Catholic 86%,
other 14% **Ethnic mix:** Catalan 61%,
Spanish Castilian 30%, other 9%
Government: Parliamentary
democracy **Currency:** French franc,
Spanish peseta

Andorra la Vella 91 B 7 *var.*
Andorra, *Fr.* Andorre la Vielle,
Sp. Andorra la Vieja. Country
capital, C Andorra

Andover 89 D 7 S England, UK
Andøya 84 C 2 island, C Norway
Andrews 49 E 3 Texas, S USA
Andria 97 E 5 S Italy
An Droichead Nua *see* Newbridge
Andropov *see* Rybinsk
Ándros 105 D 6 Ándros, SE Greece
Ándros 105 D 6 island, Kykládes,
SE Greece
Andros Island 54 C 2 island,
NW Bahamas
Andros Town 54 C 1 NW Bahamas
Angara 112 D 3 river,
C Russian Federation
Angarsk 115 E 4
C Russian Federation
Ånge 85 C 5 C Sweden
Ángel de la Guarda, Isla 50 B 2
island, NW Mexico
Angeles 139 E 1 *off.* Angeles City.
Luzon, N Philippines
Angeles City *see* Angeles
Angel Falls *see* Ángel, Salto
Ángel, Salto 59 E 3 *Eng.* Angel
Falls. Waterfall, E Venezuela
Angerburg *see* Węgorzewo
Ångermanälven 84 C 4 river,
N Sweden
Angermünde 94 D 3 NE Germany
Angers 90 B 4 *anc.* Juliomagus.
NW France
Anglesey 89 C 5 island,
NW England, UK
Anglet 91 A 5 SW France
Angleton 49 H 4 Texas, S USA
Anglia *see* England
Angmagssalik *see* Ammassalik
Ang Nam Ngum 136 C 4 lake,
N Laos

Angola
78 B 2 *prev.* People's Republic of
Angola, Portuguese West Africa.
Republic, S Africa

Official name: Republic of Angola
Date of formation: 1975 **Capital:**
Luanda **Population:** 10.3 million
Total area: 1,246,700 sq km
(481,551 sq miles) **Languages:**
Portuguese* **Religions:** Roman
Catholic/Protestant 64%, traditional
beliefs 34%, other 2% **Ethnic mix:**
Ovimbundu 37%, Kimbundu 25%,
Bakongo 13%, other 25%
Government: Multiparty republic
Currency: Kwanza = 100 lwei

Angola Basin 67 D 5 undersea
basin, E Atlantic Ocean
Angostura *see* Ciudad Bolívar
Angostura, Presa de la 51 G 5
reservoir, SE Mexico
Angoulême 91 B 5 *anc.* Iculisma.
W France
Angoumois 91 B 5 cultural region,
W France
Angra Pequena *see* Lüderitz
Angren 123 F 2 E Uzbekistan
Anguilla 55 G 3 UK dependent
territory, E Caribbean Sea
Anhui 129 C 5 *var.* Anhwei, Wan.
Province, E China
Anina 108 A 4 *Ger.* Steierdorf,
Hung. Stájerlakanina; *prev.*
Ştaierdorf-Anina, Steierdorf-
Anina, Steyerlak-Anina.
SW Romania
Anjou 90 B 4 cultural region,
NW France
Anjouan 79 F 2 *var.* Johanna Island,
Nzwani. Island, Mozambique
Channel/Pacific Ocean

Ankara 116 C 3 *prev.* Angora, *anc.* Ancyra. Country capital, C Turkey
Ankeny 45 F 3 Iowa, C USA
Anklam 94 D 2 NE Germany
An Longfort *see* Longford
An Mhuir Cheilteach *see* Celtic Sea
Annaba 71 E 1 *prev.* Bône. NE Algeria
An Nabk 118 B 4 *var.* El Nebk, Nabk, Nebk, *Fr.* Nébeck. SW Syria
An Nafūd 120 B 4 desert, NW Saudi Arabia
'Annah 120 B 3 *var.* 'Ānah. NW Iraq
An Najaf 120 B 3 *var.* Najaf. S Iraq
Annamitique, Chaîne 136 D 4 mountain range, Laos
Annapolis 41 F 4 state capital, Maryland, NE USA
Annapurna 135 E 3 mountain, C Nepal
An Nāqūrah *see* En Nâqoûra
Ann Arbor 40 C 3 Michigan, N USA
An Nāṣirīyah 120 C 3 *var.* Nasiriya. SE Iraq
Anneciacum *see* Annecy
Annecy 91 D 5 *anc.* Anneciacum. E France
Anniston 42 D 2 Alabama, S USA
Annotto Bay 54 B 5 C Jamaica
An Ómaigh *see* Omagh
Anqing 129 D 5 E China
Ansbach 95 C 6 SE Germany
Anshan 128 D 3 NE China
Anshun 129 B 6 S China
Anson Bay 146 D 2 inlet, W Pacific Ocean
Ansongo 75 E 3 E Mali
An Srath Bán *see* Strabane
Antakya 116 D 5 *anc.* Antioch, Antiochia. S Turkey
Antalaha 79 G 2 NE Madagascar
Antalya 116 B 4 *prev.* Adalia, *anc.* Attaleia, *Bibl.* Attalia. SW Turkey
Antalya Körfezi 116 B 4 *var.* Gulf of Adalia, *Eng.* Gulf of Antalya. Gulf, NE Mediterranean Sea
Antananarivo 79 G 3 *prev.* Tananarive. Country capital, C Madagascar
Antarctica 154 B 3 continent,
Antarctic Peninsula 154 A 2 peninsula, Antarctica
Antequera 92 D 5 *anc.* Anticaria, Antiquaria. S Spain
Antibes 91 E 6 *anc.* Antipolis. SE France
Anticosti, Île d' 39 F 3 *Eng.* Anticosti Island. Island, Québec, E Canada
Antigua 55 G 3 island, S Antigua & Barbuda

Antigua & Barbuda
55 H 3 Commonwealth republic, E Caribbean Sea

Official name: Antigua & Barbuda **Date of formation:** 1981 **Capital:** St John's **Population:** 65,000 **Total area:** 440 sq km (170 sq miles) **Languages:** English*, English Creole **Religions:** Protestant 87%, Roman Catholic 10%, other 3% **Ethnic mix:** Black 98%, other 2% **Government:** Parliamentary democracy **Currency:** E. Caribbean $ = 100 cents

---

Antikýthira 105 C 7 *var.* Andikíthira. Island, S Greece
Anti-Lebanon 118 B 4 *var.* Jebel esh Sharqi, *Ar.* Al Jabal ash Sharqī, *Fr.* Anti-Liban. Mountain range, Lebanon/Syria
Antípaxoi 105 A 5 *var.* Andipaxi. Island, Iónioi Nísoi, W Greece
Antipodes Islands 142 D 5 island group, S New Zealand
Antipolis *see* Antibes
Antípsara 105 D 5 *var.* Andípsara. Island, E Greece
Ántissa 105 D 5 *var.* Ándissa. Lésvos, E Greece
An tIúr *see* Newry
Antivari *see* Bar
Antofagasta 64 B 2 N Chile
Antony 90 C 3 N France
An tSionainn *see* Shannon
Antsirabe 79 G 3 C Madagascar
Antsohihy 79 G 2 N Madagascar
Antwerp *see* Antwerpen
Antwerpen 87 C 5 *Eng.* Antwerp, *Fr.* Anvers. N Belgium
Anuradhapura 132 D 3 C Sri Lanka
Anxious Bay 149 A 6 bay, E Great Australian Bight
Anyang 128 C 4 NE China
A'nyêmaqên Shan 126 D 4 mountain range, C China
Anykščiai 106 C 4 E Lithuania
Anzio 97 C 5 C Italy
Aomori 130 D 3 Honshū, C Japan
Aosta 96 A 1 *anc.* Augusta Praetoria. NW Italy
Aoukâr 74 D 3 *var.* Aouker. Plateau, C Mauritania
Aouk, Bahr 76 C 4 river, Central African Republic/Chad
Aouker *see* Aoukâr
Aozou 76 C 1 N Chad
Apalachee Bay 42 D 3 bay, NE Gulf of Mexico
Apalachicola River 42 D 3 river, Florida, SE USA
Apartadó 58 B 2 NW Colombia
Apatity 110 C 2 NW Russian Federation
Ape 106 D 3 NE Latvia
Apeldoorn 86 D 3 E Netherlands
Apennines *see* Appennino
Āpia 145 F 4 country capital, Savai'i, E Samoa
Apoera 59 G 3 NW Surinam
Apollinopolis Parva *see* Qûṣ
Apostle Islands 40 B 1 island group, Wisconsin, N USA
Appalachian Mountains 35 C 5 mountain range, E USA
Appennino 96 C 3 *Eng.* Apennines. Mountain range, C Italy/ San Marino
Appennino Lucano 97 D 6 mountain range, S Italy
Appingedam 86 E 1 NE Netherlands
Appleton 40 B 2 Wisconsin, N USA
Apple Valley 47 C 7 California, W USA
Apsheronsk 111 A 7 SW Russian Federation
Apure 58 C 2 river, W Venezuela
Apurímac 60 D 3 river, S Peru
Aputiteeq 82 D 4 *var.* Aputitêq. Greenland
Aputitêq *see* Aputiteeq
Aqaba, Gulf of 120 A 4 *var.* Gulf of Elat, Sinus Aelaniticus, *Ar.* Khalīj al 'Aqabah. Gulf, Red Sea/ Indian Ocean
Āqchah 123 E 3 *var.* Āqcheh. N Afghanistan
Āqcheh *see* Āqchah
Aquae Flaviae *see* Chaves
Aquidauana 63 E 4 S Brazil
Aquitaine 91 B 6 cultural region, SW France
Arabian Basin 140 B 3 undersea basin, N Indian Ocean
Arabian Desert 68 D 3 desert, E Egypt
Arabian Peninsula 140 A 3 peninsula, Iraq/Jordan
Arabian Sea 140 B 3 sea, NW Indian Ocean
Aracaju 63 G 3 E Brazil
Araçuai 63 F 3 SE Brazil
Arad 108 A 4 W Romania
'Arad 119 B 7 S Israel
Arafura Sea 152 B 3 sea, W Pacific Ocean
Aragón 93 E 2 cultural region, E Spain
Araguaia, Río 63 E 3 *var.* Araguaya. River, C Brazil
Araguaína 63 F 2 E Brazil
Araguari 63 F 4 SE Brazil
Araguaya *see* Araguaia, Río
Ara Jovis *see* Aranjuez
Arāk 120 C 3 *prev.* Sultānābād. W Iran
Arakan Yoma 136 A 3 mountain range, W Burma
Aral *see* Aral'sk
Aral Sea 122 D 1 *Kaz.* Aral Tengizi, *Rus.* Aral'skoye More, *Uzb.* Orol Dengizi. Inland sea, Kazakhstan/Uzbekistan
Aral'sk 114 B 4 *Kaz.* Aral. SW Kazakhstan
Aranda de Duero 92 D 2 N Spain
Aranđelovac 100 D 4 *prev.* Arandjelovac. C Yugoslavia
Arandjelovac *see* Aranđelovac
Aranjuez 92 D 3 *anc.* Ara Jovis. C Spain
Araouane 75 E 2 N Mali
'Ar'ar 120 B 3 N Saudi Arabia
Ararat, Mount *see* Büyükağri Daği
Aras 117 F 3 *Arm.* Arak's, *Az.* Araz, *Per.* Rūd-e Aras, *Rus.* Araks, *Turk.* Aras Nehri; *prev.* Araxes. River, SW Asia
Arauca 58 C 2 NE Colombia
Arauca 58 D 2 river, Colombia/Venezuela
Arausio *see* Orange
Arbīl 120 B 3 *var.* Erbil, Irbīl, Kurd, Hawlēr; *anc.* Arbela. N Iraq
Arbroath 88 D 4 *anc.* Aberbrothock. E Scotland, UK
Arbuzinka *see* Arbyzynka
Arbyzynka 109 E 3 *Rus.* Arbuzinka. S Ukraine
Arcachon 91 A 5 SW France
Arcata 47 A 5 California, W USA
Archangel *see* Arkhangel'sk
Archidona 92 D 5 S Spain
Arco 96 C 2 N Italy
Arco, Paso del 65 B 5 pass, Argentina
Arctic Bay 37 G 2 Baffin Island, Canada
Arctic Ocean 155 F 3 ocean,
Arctowski 154 A 2 research station, Antarctica
Arda 104 C 3 *var.* Ardhas, *Gk.* Ardas. River, Bulgaria/Greece
Ardabīl 120 C 2 *var.* Ardebil. NW Iran
Ardakān 120 D 3 C Iran
Ard aṣ Ṣawwān 119 C 7 *var.* Ardh es Suwwān. Plain, S Jordan
Ardebil *see* Ardabīl
Ardèche 91 C 5 cultural region, E France
Ardennes 87 D 8 plateau, W Europe
Ardh es Suwwān *see* Arḍ aṣ Ṣawwān
Ardino 104 D 3 S Bulgaria
Ard Mhacha *see* Armagh
Ardmore 49 G 2 Oklahoma, C USA
Arendal 85 A 6 S Norway
Arenys de Mar 93 G 2 NE Spain
Areópoli 105 B 7 *prev.* Areópolis. S Greece
Areópolis *see* Areópoli
Arequipa 61 E 4 SE Peru
Arezzo 96 C 3 *anc.* Arretium. C Italy
Argalastí 105 C 5 C Greece
Argenteuil 90 C 3 N France

Argentina
65 B 5 Republic, S South America

Official name: Argentine Republic **Date of formation:** 1850/1925 **Capital:** Buenos Aires **Population:** 33.5 million **Total area:** 2,766,890 sq km (1,068,296 sq miles) **Languages:** Spanish*, Italian, English, German, French, Indian languages **Religions:** Roman Catholic 90%, Jewish 2%, other 8% **Ethnic mix:** White 85%, other (including *mestizo* and Indian) 15% **Government:** Multiparty republic **Currency:** Peso = 100 centavos

---

Argentina Basin *see* Argentine Basin
Argentina, Republic of *see* Argentina
Argentine Antarctic Sector 154 B 3 Argentine territorial claim, Antarctica
Argentine Basin 67 B 6 *var.* Argentina Basin. Undersea basin, SW Atlantic Ocean
Argentine Rise *see* Falkland Plateau
Argo 72 B 3 N Sudan
Árgos 105 B 6 S Greece
Argostóli 105 A 5 *var.* Argostólion. Kefallinía, W Greece
Argostólion *see* Argostóli
Argun 111 B 8 SW Russian Federation
Århus 85 B 7 *var.* Aarhus. C Denmark
Ari Atoll 132 A 4 island, C Maldives
Arica 64 B 1 *hist.* San Marcos de Arica. N Chile
Aridaía 104 B 3 *var.* Aridhaía. N Greece
Ariha 118 B 3 *var.* Arīhā. W Syria
Arīhā *see* Ariha
Ariminum *see* Rimini
Arinsal 91 A 8 NW Andorra
Arizona 48 B 2 *off.* State of Arizona; *nicknames* Copper State, Grand Canyon State. State, SW USA
Arkansas 42 A 1 *off.* State of Arkansas; nickname Land of Opportunity. State, S USA
Arkansas City 45 F 5 Kansas, C USA
Arkansas River 42 B 2 river, C USA
Arkhangel'sk 110 C 3 *var.* Arcangelo, *Eng.* Archangel. NW Russian Federation
Arkoí 105 E 6 island, Dodekánisos, SE Greece
Arles 91 C 6 *var.* Arles-sur-Rhône; *anc.* Arelas, Arelate. SE France
Arlington 49 G 3 Texas, S USA

Arlington 41 E 4 Virginia, NE USA
Arlon 87 D 8 *Dut.* Aarlen, *Ger.* Arel;
Lat. Orolaunum. SE Belgium
Armagh 89 B 5 *Ir.* Ard Mhacha.
SE Northern Ireland, UK
Armagnac 91 B 6 cultural region,
S France

Armenia
117 F 3 *var.* Ajastan,
Arm. Hayastani Hanrapetut'yun;
prev. Armenian Soviet Socialist
Republic.

Official name: Republic of Armenia
Date of formation: 1991 **Capital:**
Yerevan **Population:** 3.6 million
Total area: 29,000 sq km
(11,505 sq miles) **Languages:**
Armenian*, Azerbaijani, Russian,
Kurdish **Religions:** Armenian
Apostolic 90%, other Christian and
Muslim 10% **Ethnic mix:** Armenian
93%, Azerbaijani 3%, Russian,
Kurdish 4% **Government:** Multiparty
republic **Currency:** Dram = 100 louma

Armenia 58 B 3 W Colombia
Armidale 149 D 6
New South Wales, SE Australia
Armstrong 38 B 3 Ontario,
S Canada
Armyansk *see* Armyans'k
Armyans'k 109 F 4 *Rus.* Armyansk.
S Ukraine
Arnaía 104 C 4 N Greece
Arnaud 82 A 3 river, E Canada
Arnea *see* Arnaía
Arnedo 93 E 2 N Spain
Arnhem 86 D 4 SE Netherlands
Arnhem Land 148 A 2 physical
region, Northern Territory,
N Australia
Arno 96 B 3 river, C Italy
Arno *see* Arno Atoll
Arnold 45 G 5 Missouri, C USA
Arnswalde *see* Choszczno
Arorae 145 E 3 island, W Kiribati
Ar Rahad *see* Er Rahad
Ar Ramādī 120 B 3 *var.* Ramadi,
Rumadiya. SW Iraq
Ar Ramthā 119 B 5 *var.* Ramtha.
N Jordan
Arran, Isle of 88 C 4 island,
SW Scotland, UK
Ar Raqqah 118 C 2 *var.* Rakka;
anc. Nicephorium. N Syria
Arras 90 C 2 *anc.* Nemetocenna.
N France
Ar Rashādīyah 119 C 5 NE Jordan
Ar Rawdatayn 120 C 4 *var.*
Raudhatain. N Kuwait
Arretium *see* Arezzo
Arriaga 51 G 5 SE Mexico
Ar Riyāḍ 121 C 5 *Eng.* Riyadh.
Country capital, C Saudi Arabia
Arroyo Grande 47 B 7 California,
W USA
Ar Rustāq 121 E 5 *var.* Rostak,
Rustaq. N Oman
Ar Ruṭbah 120 B 3 *var.* Rutba.
SW Iraq
Árta 105 A 5 *anc.* Ambracia.
W Greece
Artashat 117 G 3 S Armenia
Artemisa 54 B 2 W Cuba
Artesia 48 D 3 New Mexico,
SW USA
Arthur's Pass 151 C 6 pass,
South Island, New Zealand
Artigas 64 D 3 *prev.* San Eugenio,
San Eugenio del Cuareim.
N Uruguay

Art'ik 117 F 2 W Armenia
Artois 90 C 2 cultural region,
N France
Artsiz *see* Artsyz
Artsyz 108 D 4 *Rus.* Artsiz.
SW Ukraine
Artvin 117 F 2 NE Turkey
Arua 73 B 6 NW Uganda
Aruba 55 E 5 *var.* Oruba. Dutch
autonomous region,
S Caribbean Sea
Aruba 58 C 1 island,
SE Caribbean Sea
Aru, Kepulauan 139 G 4 *Eng.*
Aru Islands; *prev.* Aroe Islands.
Island group, E Indonesia
Arunāchal Pradesh 135 H 3
cultural region, NE India
Arusha 73 C 7 N Tanzania
Arviat 37 G 4 *prev.* Eskimo Point.
North West Territories, C Canada
Arvidsjaur 84 C 4 N Sweden
Arys' 114 B 5 *Kaz.* Arys.
S Kazakhstan
Arys *see* Arys'
Asadābād 123 F 4 *var.* Asadbād;
prev. Chaghasarāy. E Afghanistan
Asad, Buḥayrat al 118 C 2 *Eng.*
Lake Assad. Reservoir, N Syria
Asahi-dake 130 D 2 mountain,
Hokkaidō, NE Japan
Asahikawa 130 D 2 Hokkaidō,
NE Japan
Asamankese 75 E 5 SE Ghana
Āsansol 135 F 4 NE India
Ascension Fracture Zone 67 C 5
fracture zone, C Atlantic Ocean
Ascension Island 69 A 5 island,
E Atlantic Ocean
Ascoli Piceno 96 C 4 *anc.* Asculum
Picenum. C Italy
Asculum Picenum *see* Ascoli Piceno
Ashburton 151 C 6 South Island,
SW New Zealand
Ashburton 146 B 4 river, Western
Australia, W Australia
Ashdod 119 A 6 *anc.* Azotos,
Lat. Azotus. W Israel
Asheville 43 E 1 North Carolina,
SE USA
Ashgabat 122 C 3 *prev.* Ashkhabad,
Poltoratsk. Country capital,
C Turkmenistan
Ashibetsu 130 D 2 *var.* Asibetu.
Hokkaidō, NE Japan
Ashkelon *see* Ashqelon
Ashland 40 D 5 Kentucky, E USA
Ashland 46 B 4 river, Western
Ashmore & Cartier Islands 142 A 3
Australian external territory,
E Indian Ocean
Ashmyany 107 C 5 *Rus.* Oshmyany.
W Belorussia
Ashqelon 119 A 6 *var.* Ashkelon.
C Israel
Ash Shadādah 118 E 2 *var.* Ash
Shaddādah, Jisr ash Shadadi
Shaddādī, Shedadi, Tell Shedadi.
NE Syria
Ash Sharāh 119 B 7 *var.* Esh Sharā.
Mountain range, W Jordan
Ash Shawbak 119 B 7 W Jordan
Ash Shiḥr 121 C 7 SE Yemen
Asia 112 D 3
Asibetu *see* Ashibetsu
Asipovichy 107 D 6 *Pol.*
Mahilyowskaya Voblasts',
Rus. Osipovichi. C Belorussia
Aşkale 117 E 3 NE Turkey
Askersund 85 C 6 C Sweden
Asmara 72 C 4 *Amh.* Āsmara.
Country capital, C Eritrea

Āsmera *see* Asmara
Aspinwall *see* Colón
Assab 72 D 4 *Amh.* Āseb.
SE Eritrea
As Sabkhah 118 D 2 *var.* Sabkha.
NE Syria
Assad, Lake *see* Asad, Buḥayrat al
Aş Şafāwī 119 C 6 N Jordan
As Salamīyah *see* Salamīyah
As Salṭ 119 B 6 *var.* Salt. NW Jordan
Assam 135 G 3 cultural region,
NE India
Assamaka *see* Assamakka
Assamakka 75 F 2 *var.* Assamaka.
NW Niger
As Samāwah 120 B 3 *var.* Samawa.
S Iraq
Assen 86 E 2 NE Netherlands
Assenede 87 B 5 NW Belgium
Assling *see* Jesenice
As Sukhnah 118 D 3 *var.* Sukhne,
Fr. Soukhné. C Syria
As Sulaymānīyah 120 C 3 *var.*
Sulaimaniya, *Kurd.* Slēmānī.
NE Iraq
As Sulayyil 120 B 4 S Saudi Arabia
Aş Şummān 121 C 5 desert,
N Saudi Arabia
As Suwaydā' 119 B 5 *var.*
El Suweida, Es Suweida,
Suweida, *Fr.* Soueida. SW Syria
Asten 87 D 5 SE Netherlands
Asti 96 A 2 *anc.* Asta Colonia, Asta
Pompeia, Hasta Colonia, Hasta
Pompeia. NW Italy
Astigi *see* Ecija
Astorga 92 C 2 *anc.* Asturica
Augusta. N Spain
Astrakhan' 111 C 7
SW Russian Federation
Asturias 92 C 1 cultural region,
NW Spain
Asturias *see* Oviedo
Asturica Augusta *see* Astorga
Astypálaia 105 D 7 *var.* Astipálaia,
It. Stampalia. Island,
Dodekánisos, SE Greece
Asunción 64 D 2 country capital,
S Paraguay
Aswān 72 B 2 *var.* Assouan,
Assuan; *anc.* Syene. SE Egypt
Asyūṭ 72 B 2 *var.* Assiout, Assiut,
Siut; *anc.* Lycopolis. C Egypt
Atacama Desert *see* Atacama,
Desierto de
Atacama, Desierto de 64 B 1 *Eng.*
Atacama Desert. Desert, N Chile
Atafu Atoll 145 F 3 island,
NW Tokelau
Atakora, Chaîne de l' 75 F 4
var. Atakora Mountains.
Mountain range, N Benin
Atakora Mountains *see* Atakora,
Chaîne de l'
Atâr 74 C 2 NW Mauritania
Atas Bogd 126 D 3 mountain,
SW Mongolia
Atascadero 47 B 7 California,
W USA
Atbara 72 C 3 *var.* 'Aṭbārah.
NE Sudan
'Aṭbārah *see* Atbara
Atbasar 114 C 4 N Kazakhstan
Atchison 45 F 4 Kansas, C USA
Ath 87 B 6 *var.* Aat. SW Belgium
Athabasca 37 E 5 Alberta,
SW Canada
Athabasca 37 E 5 *var.* Athabaska.
River, Alberta. SW Canada
Athabasca, Lake 37 F 4 lake,
SW Canada
Athabaska *see* Athabasca

Athens 42 C 1 Alabama, S USA
Athens 42 D 1 Tennessee, S USA
Athens 43 E 2 Georgia, SE USA
Athens 49 G 3 Texas, S USA
Athens 40 D 4 Ohio, N USA
Athens *see* Athína
Atherton 148 D 3 Queensland,
NE Australia
Athína 105 C 6 *Eng.* Athens;
prev. Athinai, *anc.* Athenae.
Country capital, C Greece
Athlone 89 B 6 *Ir.* Baile Átha Luain.
C Ireland
Ath Thawrah *see* Madīnat ath
Thawrah
Ati 76 C 3 C Chad
Atikokan 38 B 4 Ontario, S Canada
Atka 115 G 3 E Russian Federation
Atka Island 36 A 3 island, Alaska,
NW USA
Atlanta 49 H 2 Texas, S USA
Atlanta 35 C 6 state capital,
Georgia, SE USA
Atlantic City 41 F 4 New Jersey,
NE USA
Atlantic-Indian Basin 67 D 8
undersea basin, SW Indian Ocean
Atlantic-Indian Ridge 67 D 7
undersea ridge, SW Indian Ocean
Atlantic Ocean 66 C 4
var. Atlantshaf. Ocean,
Atlantshaf *see* Atlantic Ocean
Atlas Mountains 68 B 2 mountain
range, N Africa
Atlasovo 115 H 3
E Russian Federation
Atlas Saharien 70 D 2 *var.* Saharan
Atlas. Mountain range,
Algeria/Morocco
Atlin 36 D 4 British Columbia,
W Canada
Aṭ Ṭā'if 121 B 5 W Saudi Arabia
Aṭ Tāj 71 H 4 SE Libya
At Tall al Abyaḍ 118 C 2 *var.* Tall al
Abyaḍ, Tell Abyad, *Fr.* Tell Abiad.
N Syria
Attapu 137 E 5 *var.* Attopeu.
SE Laos
Attawapiskat 38 C 3 Ontario,
C Canada
Attawapiskat 38 C 3 river,
S Canada
Attersee 95 D 6 lake, N Austria
At Tibnī 118 D 2 *var.* Tibnī.
NE Syria
Attopeu *see* Samakhixai
Attu Island 36 A 2 island, Alaska,
NW USA
Atuntaqui 60 B 1 N Ecuador
Atyrau 114 B 4 *prev.* Gur'yev.
W Kazakhstan
Aubagne 91 D 6 *anc.* Albania.
SE France
Aubange 87 D 8 SE Belgium
Auburn 42 D 2 Alabama, S USA
Auburn 41 G 2 Maine, NE USA
Auburn 46 B 2 Washington,
NW USA
Auch 91 B 6 *Lat.* Augusta
Auscorum, Elimberrum. S France
Auckland 150 D 2 North Island,
N New Zealand
Auckland Islands 142 D 5 island
group, S New Zealand
Aude 91 C 6 cultural region,
S France
Audenarde *see* Oudenaarde
Audern *see* Audru
Audincourt 90 E 4 E France
Audru 106 D 2 *Ger.* Audern.
SW Estonia

Augila *see* Awjilah
Augsburg 95 C 6 *Fr.* Augsbourg; *anc.* Augusta Vindelicorum. S Germany
Augusta 43 E 2 Georgia, SE USA
Augusta 147 B 7 Western Australia, SW Australia
Augusta 41 G 2 state capital, Maine, NE USA
Augusta Emerita *see* Mérida
Augusta Praetoria *see* Aosta
Augusta Trajana *see* Stara Zagora
Augustobona Tricassium *see* Troyes
Augustodurum *see* Bayeux
Augustów 98 E 2 *Rus.* Avgustov. NE Poland
Augustus Island 146 C 3 island, NW Australia
'Aujā et Tahtā 119 E 7 *var.* Khirbet el 'Aujā et Taḥtā. E West Bank
Auk Bok 137 B 5 *var.* South Island. Island, S Burma
Auob 78 B 4 *var.* Oup. River, E Namibia/South Africa
Aurangābād 134 D 5 W India
Aur Atoll 144 D 1 island, E Marshall Islands
Auray 90 A 4 NW France
Aurelia Aquensis *see* Baden-Baden
Aurelianum *see* Orléans
Aurillac 91 C 5 C France
Aurora 40 B 3 Illinois, N USA
Aurora 45 G 5 Missouri, C USA
Aurora 44 D 4 Colorado, C USA
Aurora 59 F 2 NW Guyana
Aurora *see* Maewo
Aus 78 B 4 SW Namibia
Aussig *see* Ústí nad Labem
Austin 35 C 6 state capital, Texas, S USA
Austin 45 G 3 Minnesota, N USA
Australes, Îles 145 H 5 island group, SW French Polynesia
Austral Fracture Zone 153 E 4 fracture zone, S Pacific Ocean

Australia 142 A 4 Commonwealth republic, Indian Ocean/ Pacific Ocean
Official name: Commonwealth of Australia **Date of formation:** 1901 **Capital:** Canberra **Population:** 17.8 million **Total area:** 7,686,850 sq km (2,967,893 sq miles) **Languages:** English*, Greek, Italian, Malay, Aboriginal languages **Religions:** Protestant 60%, Roman Catholic 26%, other 14% **Ethnic mix:** Caucasian 95%, Asian 4%, Aboriginal, other 1% **Government:** Parliamentary democracy **Currency:** Australian $ = 100 cents

Australian Alps 149 C 7 mountain range, SE Australia
Australian Antarctic Territory 154 C 3 Australian territorial claim, Antarctica
Australian Capital Territory 149 D 7 *prev.* Federal Capital Territory. Territory, SE Australia
Australie, Bassin Nord de l' *see* North Australian Basin
Austral Seamounts 152 D 4 seamount range, S Pacific Ocean
Austrava *see* Ostrov

Austria 95 D 7 *Ger.* Österreich. Republic, C Europe
Official name: Republic of Austria **Date of formation:** 1918/1945 **Capital:** Vienna **Population:** 7.8 million **Total area:** 83,850 sq km (32,375 sq miles) **Languages:** German*, Croatian, Slovene, Hungarian (Magyar) **Religions:** Roman Catholic 85%, Protestant 6%, other 9% **Ethnic mix:** German 99%, other (inc. Hungarian, Slovene, Croat) 1% **Government:** Multiparty republic **Currency:** Schilling = 100 groschen

Ausuitoq *see* Grise Fiord
Auvergne 91 C 5 cultural region, S France
Auxerre 90 C 4 *anc.* Autesiodorum, Autissiodorum. C France
Avaricum *see* Bourges
Avarua 145 G 5 dependent territory capital, Rarotonga, S Cook Islands
Ávdira 104 D 3 NE Greece
Aveiro 92 B 3 *anc.* Talabriga. W Portugal
Avellino 97 D 5 *anc.* Abellinum. S Italy
Avenio *see* Avignon
Aversa 97 D 5 S Italy
Avesta 85 C 6 C Sweden
Aveyron 91 C 6 river, S France
Avezzano 96 C 4 C Italy
Avgustov *see* Augustów
Aviemore 88 C 3 N Scotland, UK
Avignon 91 D 6 *anc.* Avenio. SE France
Ávila 92 D 3 *var.* Avila; *anc.* Abela, Abula, Abyla, Avela. C Spain
Avilés 92 C 1 NW Spain
Avranches 90 B 3 N France
Awaji-shima 131 C 6 island, Japan
Āwash 73 D 5 C Ethiopia
Awbārī 71 F 3 SW Libya
Awjilah 71 G 3 *It.* Augila. NE Libya
Awled Djellal *see* Ouled Djellal
Axel 87 B 5 SW Netherlands
Axel Heiberg Island 37 F 1 *var.* Axel Heiburg. Island, N Canada
Axel Heiburg *see* Axel Heiberg Island
Axiós *see* Vardar
Ayacucho 60 D 4 S Peru
Ayaguz 114 C 5 *Kaz.* Ayaköz; *prev.* Sergiopol. E Kazakhstan
Ayamonte 92 B 5 S Spain
Ayaviri 61 E 4 S Peru
Aydārkŭl 123 E 2 *Rus.* Ozero Aydarkul'. Lake, C Uzbekistan
Aydarkul', Ozero *see* Aydārkŭl
Aydın 116 A 4 *var.* Aïdin; *anc.* Tralles. SW Turkey
Ayers Rock *see* Uluru
Ayeyarwady *see* Irrawaddy
Ayiá *see* Agiá
Ayia Napa *see* Agía Nápa
Ayorou 75 F 3 W Niger
'Ayoûn el 'Atroûs 74 D 3 *var.* Aïoun el Atroûss, Aïoun el Atrous. SE Mauritania
Ayr 88 C 4 SW Scotland, UK
Ayr 148 D 3 Queensland, E Australia
Aytos 104 E 2 E Bulgaria
Ayutthaya 137 C 5 *var.* Phra Nakhon Si Ayutthaya. C Thailand
Ayvalık 116 A 3 NW Turkey
A'zāg 118 B 2 NW Syria
Azahar, Costa del 93 F 3 coastal region, E Spain

Azaouâd 75 E 3 plateau, SW Mali
Azerbaijan 117 G 2 *Az.* Azärbaycan, Azärbaycan Respublikasi; *prev.* Azerbaijan SSR. Republic, SE Asia
Official name: Republic of Azerbaijan **Date of formation:** 1991 **Capital:** Baku **Population:** 7.3 million **Total area:** 86,600 sq km (33,436 sq miles) **Languages:** Azerbaijani*, Russian, Armenian **Religions:** Muslim 83%, Armenian Apostolic, Russian Orthodox 17% **Ethnic mix:** Azerbaijani 83%, Russian 6%, Armenian 6%, other 5% **Government:** Multiparty republic **Currency:** Manat = 100 gopik

Azimabad *see* Patna
Azogues 60 B 2 S Ecuador
Azores 92 A 5 *var.* Açores, Ilhas dos Açores, *Port.* Arquipélago dos Açores. Island group, W Portugal
Azores-Biscay Rise 80 A 3 undersea rise, E Atlantic Ocean
Azoum, Bahr 76 C 3 river, SE Chad
Azov, Sea of 109 G 4 *Rus.* Azovskoye More, *Ukr.* Azovs'ke More. Sea, N Black Sea
Azraq, Waḥat al 119 C 6 oasis, N Jordan
Aztec 48 C 1 New Mexico, SW USA
Azuaga 92 C 4 W Spain
Azuero, Península de 53 F 5 peninsula, S Panama
Azul 65 D 5 E Argentina
Azur, Côte d' 91 C 6 coastal region, SE France
Aẕ Ẕahrān 120 C 4 *Eng.* Dhahran. NE Saudi Arabia
Az Zaqāzīq *see* Zagazig
Az Zarqā' 119 B 6 *var.* Zarqa. NW Jordan
Az Zāwiyah 71 F 2 *var.* Zawia. NW Libya
Az Zilfī 120 B 4 N Saudi Arabia
Æsernia *see* Isernia

B

Baabda 118 A 4 *var.* B'abdā. C Lebanon
Baalbek 118 B 4 *var.* Ba'labakk; *anc.* Heliopolis. E Lebanon
Baar 95 B 7 N Switzerland
Baarle-Nassau 87 C 5 enclave, N Belgium
Baarn 86 C 3 C Netherlands
Babadag 108 D 5 SE Romania
Babahoyo 60 B 2 *prev.* Bodegas. C Ecuador
Babajevo *see* Babayevo
Bābā, Kūh-e 123 E 4 mountain range, C Afghanistan
Babayevo 110 B 4 *var.* Babajevo. NW Russian Federation
B'abdā *see* Baabda
Bab el Mandeb 121 B 7 strait, Arabian Sea/Red Sea
Babelthuap 144 A 2 island, E Palau
Babonneau 55 F 1 N Saint Lucia
Babruysk 107 D 7 *Rus.* Bobruysk. E Belorussia
Babuyan Channel 139 E 1 channel, Philippine Sea/South China Sea
Babuyan Islands 139 E 1 island, N Philippines
Bacabal 63 F 2 E Brazil
Bacău 108 C 4 *Hung.* Bákó. NE Romania

Băc Giang 136 D 3 N Vietnam
Bacheykava 107 D 5 *Rus.* Bocheykovo. N Belorussia
Bačka Palanka 100 D 3 *prev.* Palanka. NW Yugoslavia
Bačka Topola 100 D 3 *Hung.* Topolya; *prev.* Bácstopolya. NW Yugoslavia
Bac Liêu 137 D 6 *var.* Vinh Loi. S Vietnam
Bacolod 139 E 2 *off.* Bacolod City. Negros, C Philippines
Bacolod City *see* Bacolod
Bactra *see* Balkh
Badain Jaran Shamo 126 D 3 desert, N China
Badajoz 92 C 4 *anc.* Pax Augusta. W Spain
Bad Doberan 94 C 2 N Germany
Baden-Baden 95 B 6 *anc.* Aurelia Aquensis. SW Germany
Bad Freienwalde 94 D 3 NE Germany
Bad Hersfeld 94 B 4 C Germany
Bad Homburg *see* Bad Homburg vor der Höhe
Bad Homburg vor der Höhe 95 B 5 *var.* Bad Homburg. W Germany
Bad Ischl 95 D 7 C Austria
Bad Krozingen 95 A 6 SW Germany
Badlands 44 D 2 physical region, North Dakota, N USA
Badu Island 148 C 1 island, Queensland, SW Australia
Bad Vöslau 95 E 6 NE Austria
Badyarada 'Admēd *see* Aden, Gulf of
Bafatá 74 C 4 C Guinea-Bissau
Baffin Bay 82 C 2 bay, NW Atlantic Ocean
Baffin Island 37 G 2 island, Northwest Territories, NE Canada
Bafing 74 C 3 river, NW Africa
Bafoussam 76 A 4 W Cameroon
Bafra 116 D 2 N Turkey
Bāft 120 D 4 S Iran
Bagaces 52 D 4 NW Costa Rica
Bagé 63 E 5 S Brazil
Baghdād 120 B 3 *var.* Bagdad, *Eng.* Baghdad. Country capital, C Iraq
Baghdad *see* Baghdād
Bāghīn 120 D 4 Iran
Baghlān 123 E 4 NE Afghanistan
Bago *see* Pegu
Bagoé 74 D 4 river, Ivory Coast/Mali
Bagrationovsk 106 A 4 *Ger.* Preussisch Eylau. W Russian Federation
Bagrax Hu *see* Bosten Hu
Baguio 139 E 1 *off.* Baguio City. Luzon, N Philippines
Baguio City *see* Baguio
Bagzane, Monts 75 G 3 mountain, N Niger

Bahama Islands *see* Bahamas

Bahamas 54 C 2 Commonwealth republic, N Caribbean Sea
Official name: The Commonwealth of the Bahamas **Date of formation:** 1973 **Capital:** Nassau **Population:** 300,000 **Total area:** 13,880 sq km (5,359 sq miles) **Languages:** English*, English Creole **Religions:** Protestant 76%, Roman Catholic 19%, other 5% **Ethnic mix:** Black 85%, White 15% **Government:** Parliamentary democracy **Currency:** Bahamian $ = 100 cents

Bahamas 35 D 6 *var.* Bahama Islands. Island group, W Atlantic Ocean
Bahariya Oasis 72 B 2 *var.* Wāhat el Bahariya. Oasis, C Egypt
Bahariya, Wāhat el *see* Bahariya Oasis
Bahāwalpur 134 C 2 E Pakistan
Bahia 63 F 3 *off.* Estado da Bahia. State, E Brazil
Bahía Blanca 65 C 5 E Argentina
Bahia, Estado da *see* Bahia
Bahía, Islas de la 52 C 1 *Eng.* Bay Islands. Island group, N Honduras
Bahir Dar 72 C 4 *var.* Bahr Dar, Bahrdar Giyorgis. NW Ethiopia
Bahraich 135 E 3 N India

Bahrain 120 C 4 *Ar.* Al Baḥrayn; *prev.* Bahrein, *anc.* Tylos or Tyros. Monarchy, SW Asia

Official name: State of Bahrain **Date of formation:** 1971 **Capital:** Manama **Population:** 500,000 **Total area:** 680 sq km (263 sq miles) **Languages:** Arabic*, English, Urdu **Religions:** Muslim (Shi'a majority) 85%, Christian 7%, other 8% **Ethnic mix:** Arab 73%, South Asian 14%, Persian 8%, other 5% **Government:** Absolute monarchy (emirate) **Currency:** Dinar = 1,000 fils

Baḥr al Milḥ *see* Razāzah, Buḥayrat ar
Bahrām Chāh 122 D 5 SW Afghanistan
Bahushewsk 107 E 6 *Rus.* Bogushëvsk. NE Belorussia
Baia Mare 108 B 3 *Ger.* Frauenbach, *Hung.* Nagybánya; *prev.* Neustadt. NW Romania
Baia Sprie 108 B 3 *Ger.* Mittelstadt, *Hung.* Felsőbánya. NW Romania
Baïbokoum 76 B 4 SW Chad
Băicoi 108 C 5 SE Romania
Baie-Comeau 39 E 4 Québec, SE Canada
Baikal, Lake *see* Baykal, Ozero
Baile Átha Luain *see* Athlone
Bailén 92 D 4 S Spain
Baile na Mainistreach *see* Newtownabbey
Băileşti 108 B 5 SW Romania
Bailey's Bay 42 A 5 bay, W Atlantic Ocean
Bainbridge 42 D 3 Georgia, SE USA
Bā'ir *see* Bāyir
Baireuth *see* Bayreuth
Bairiki 144 D 2 country capital, Tarawa, W Kiribati
Bairnsdale 149 C 7 Victoria, SE Australia
Baiyin 128 B 4 N China
Baja 99 C 7 S Hungary
Baja California 48 A 5 *Eng.* Lower California. Peninsula, NW Mexico
Baja California 50 A 2 state, NW Mexico
Bajo Boquete *see* Boquete
Bajram Curri 101 C 5 N Albania
Bakala 76 C 4 C Central African Republic
Baker & Howland Islands 145 F 2 US unincorporated territory, C Pacific Ocean
Baker Lake 37 F 3 C Canada

Bakersfield 47 C 7 California, W USA
Bakharden 122 C 3 *Turkm.* Bäherden; *prev.* Bakherden. C Turkmenistan
Bakhchisaray *see* Bakhchysaray
Bakhchysaray 109 F 5 *Rus.* Bakhchisaray. S Ukraine
Bakhmach 109 F 1 N Ukraine
Bākhtarān 120 C 3 *prev.* Kermānshāh, Qahremānshahr. W Iran
Baki 117 H 2 *Eng.* Baku. Country capital, E Azerbaijan
Bákó *see* Bacău
Bakony 99 C 7 *Eng.* Bakony Mountains, *Ger.* Bakonywald. Mountain range, W Hungary
Baksan 111 B 8 SW Russian Federation
Baku *see* Baki
Baku 112 B 4 country capital, E Azerbaijan
Bakwanga *see* Mbuji-Mayi
Balabac, Selat *see* Balabac Strait
Balabac Strait 138 D 3 *var.* Selat Balabac. Strait, W Pacific Ocean
Balaguer 93 F 2 NE Spain
Balakovo 111 C 6 W Russian Federation
Bālā Morghāb 122 D 4 NW Afghanistan
Balao 60 B 2 S Ecuador
Balashov 111 B 6 W Russian Federation
Balasore *see* Bāleshwar
Balaton 99 C 7 *var.* Lake Balaton, *Ger.* Plattensee. Lake, W Hungary
Balbina, Represa 62 D 1 reservoir, NW Brazil
Balboa 53 G 5 C Panama
Balcarce 65 D 5 E Argentina
Balclutha 151 B 7 South Island, SW New Zealand
Baldy Mountain 44 C 1 mountain, Montana, NW USA
Baleares, Islas 93 H 4 *Eng.* Balearic Islands. Island group, E Spain
Balearic Islands *see* Baleares, Islas
Balearic Plain 80 C 5 *var.* Algerian Basin. Undersea basin, E Atlantic Ocean
Baleine, Rivière à la 39 E 2 river, Québec, E Canada
Balen 87 C 5 N Belgium
Bāleshwar 135 F 4 *prev.* Balasore. E India
Bali 138 D 5 island, C Indonesia
Balıkesir 116 A 3 W Turkey
Balikpapan 138 D 4 Borneo, C Indonesia
Balkan Mountains 104 C 2 *Bul./SCr.* Stara Planina. Mountain range, Bulgaria/Yugoslavia
Balkh 123 E 3 *anc.* Bactra. N Afghanistan
Balkhash 114 C 5 *Kaz.* Balqash. SE Kazakhstan
Balkhash, Lake *see* Balkhash, Ozero
Balkhash, Ozero 114 C 5 *Eng.* Lake Balkhash, *Kaz.* Balqash. Lake, SE Kazakhstan
Balladonia 147 C 6 Western Australia, S Australia
Ballarat 149 C 7 Victoria, SE Australia
Balleny Islands 154 B 5 island group, Antarctica
Ballina 149 E 5 New South Wales, SE Australia
Ballinger 49 F 3 Texas, S USA

Balls Pyramid 142 C 4 island, E Australia
Balqash *see* Balkhash
Balş 108 B 5 S Romania
Balsas 63 F 2 E Brazil
Balsas, Río 51 E 5 *var.* Río Mexcala. River, S Mexico
Bal'shavik 107 D 7 *Rus.* Bol'shevik. SE Belorussia
Balta 108 D 3 SW Ukraine
Bălţi 108 D 3 *Rus.* Bel'tsy. N Moldavia
Baltic Sea 66 D 2 *Ger.* Ostee, *Rus.* Baltiskoye More. Sea, NE Atlantic Ocean
Baltimore 41 F 4 Maryland, NE USA
Baluchistān 134 A 3 *var.* Balochistān, Beluchistan. Province, SW Pakistan
Balvi 106 D 4 NE Latvia
Balykchy 123 G 2 *Kir.* Ysyk-Köl; *prev.* Issyk-Kul', Rybach'ye. NE Kyrgyzstan
Balzers 94 E 2 S Liechtenstein
Bam 120 E 4 SE Iran
Bamako 74 D 4 country capital, SW Mali
Bambari 76 C 4 C Central African Republic
Bamberg 95 C 5 SE Germany
Bamenda 76 A 4 W Cameroon
Banaba 144 D 2 *var.* Ocean Island. Island, W Kiribati
Banc St.Lazarus *see* St.Lazarus Bank
Banda Aceh 138 A 3 *var.* Banda Atjeh; *prev.* Koetaradja, Kutaraja. Sumatera, W Indonesia
Banda, Laut 139 F 5 *Eng.* Banda Sea. Sea, W Pacific Ocean
Bandama 74 D 5 *var.* Bandama Fleuve. River, S Ivory Coast
Bandama Blanc 74 D 5 river, C Ivory Coast
Bandama Fleuve *see* Bandama
Bandar-e 'Abbās 120 C 4 *var.* Bandar'Abbās; *prev.* Gombroon. S Iran
Bandar-e Būshehr 120 C 4 *var.* Būshehr, *Eng.* Bushire. S Iran
Bandar-e Khamīr 120 D 4 S Iran
Bandar-e Langeh 120 D 4 *var.* Bandar-e Lengeh, Lingeh. S Iran
Bandarlampung 138 C 4 Sumatera, W Indonesia
Bandar Maharani *see* Muar
Bandar Penggaram *see* Batu Pahat
Bandar Seri Begawan 138 D 3 *prev.* Brunei Town. Country capital, N Brunei
Banda Sea *see* Banda, Laut
Bandırma 116 A 3 *var.* Penderma. NW Turkey
Bandjarmasin *see* Banjarmasin
Bandoeng *see* Bandung
Bandundu 77 C 6 *prev.* Banningville. SW Congo (Zaire)
Bandung 138 C 5 *prev.* Bandoeng. Jawa, C Indonesia
Bangalore 132 C 2 state capital, S India
Bangassou 77 D 5 S Central African Republic
Banggai, Kepulauan 139 E 4 island group, C Indonesia
Banghāzī 71 G 2 *Eng.* Bengazi, Benghazi, *It.* Bengasi. NE Libya
Bangka 138 C 4 island, W Indonesia
Bangkok *see* Krung Thep
Bangkok, Bight of *see* Krung Thep, Ao

Bangladesh 135 F 3 *prev.* East Pakistan. Republic, S Asia

Official name: People's Republic of Bangladesh **Date of formation:** 1971 **Capital:** Dhaka **Population:** 122.2 million **Total Area:** 143,998 sq km (55,598 sq miles) **Languages:** Bangla*, Urdu, Chakma **Religions:** Muslim 83%, Hindu 16%, 1% **Ethnic mix:** Bengali 98%, other 2% **Government:** Multiparty republic **Currency:** Taka = 100 paisa

Bangor 89 C 6 NW Wales, UK
Bangor 89 C 5 *Ir.* Beannchar. E Northern Ireland, UK
Bangor 41 H 2 Maine, NE USA
Bang Pla Soi *see* Chon Buri
Bangui 77 C 5 country capital, SW Central African Republic
Ban Hat Yai *see* Hat Yai
Ban Hin Heup 136 C 4 C Laos
Ban Houayxay 136 C 3 *var.* Ban Houei Sai. NW Laos
Ban Houei Sai *see* Houayxay
Ban Hua Hin 137 C 6 *var.* Hua Hin. C Thailand
Bani 74 D 3 river, S Mali
Banī Suwayf *see* Beni Suef
Bāniyās 118 A 3 *var.* Banias, Baniyas, Paneas. W Syria
Banjak, Kepulauan *see* Banyak, Kepulauan
Banja Luka 101 A 7 NW Bosnia & Herzegovina
Banjarmasin 138 D 4 *prev.* Bandjarmasin. Borneo, C Indonesia
Banjul 74 B 3 *prev.* Bathurst. Country capital, W Gambia
Ban Khok Kloi 137 B 7 S Thailand
Banks, Îles *see* Banks Islands
Banks Island 37 E 2 island, NW Canada
Banks Islands 144 D 4 *Fr.* Îles Banks. Island group, N Vanuatu
Banks Lake 46 C 2 reservoir, Washington, NW USA
Banks Peninsula 151 C 6 peninsula, South Island, C New Zealand
Banks Strait 149 C 8 strait, SW Tasman Sea
Bānkura 135 F 4 NE India
Banmo *see* Bhamo
Ban Na Môn 136 D 3 NE Laos
Banningville *see* Bandundu
Bañolas *see* Banyoles
Ban Pak Phanang *see* Pak Phanang
Banská Bystrica 99 C 6 *Ger.* Neusohl, *Hung.* Besztercebánya. C Slovakia
Bantry Bay 89 A 7 *Ir.* Bá Bheanntraí. Bay, W Atlantic Ocean
Banya 104 E 2 E Bulgaria
Banyak, Kepulauan 138 A 3 *prev.* Kepulauan Banjak. Island group, NW Indonesia
Banyo 76 B 4 W Cameroon
Banyoles 93 G 2 *var.* Bañolas. NE Spain
Banzare Seamounts 141 C 7 seamount range, S Indian Ocean
Baoji 128 B 4 *var.* Pao-chi, Paoki. C China
Baoro 76 C 4 W Central African Republic
Baoshan 129 A 6 *var.* Pao-shan. SW China
Baotou 127 F 3 *var.* Pao-t'ou, Paotow. N China

Ba'qūbah 120 B 3 *var.* Qubba.
C Iraq
Baquerizo Moreno *see*
Puerto Baquerizo Moreno
Bar 101 C 5 *It.* Antivari.
SW Yugoslavia
Baraawe 73 D 6 *It.* Brava. S Somalia
Baraji, Hirfanli 116 C 3 lake,
C Turkey
Baramanni 59 F 2 N Guyana
Bārāmati 134 C 5 W India
Baramita 59 F 2 NW Guyana
Baranavichy 107 B 6 *Pol.*
Baranowicze, *Rus.* Baranovichi.
SW Belorussia

Barbados
55 G 1 Commonwealth republic,
E Caribbean Sea

Official name: Barbados
Date of formation: 1966 **Capital:**
Bridgetown **Population:** 260,000
Total area: 430 sq km (166 sq miles)
Languages: English*, English Creole
Religions: Protestant 94%, Roman
Catholic 5%, other 1%
Ethnic mix: Black 80%, mixed 15%,
White 4%, other 1% **Government:**
Parliamentary democracy
Currency: Barbados $ = 100 cents

Barbados 59 F 1 island,
W Atlantic Ocean
Barbastro 93 F 2 NE Spain
Barbate de Franco 92 C 5 S Spain
Barbuda 55 G 3 island,
N Antigua & Barbuda
Barcaldine 148 C 4 Queensland,
E Australia
Barcelona 93 G 2 *anc.* Barcino,
Barcinona. E Spain
Barcelona 59 E 2 NE Venezuela
Barcoo 148 C 4 river, E Australia
Barcs 99 C 7 SW Hungary
Bardaï 76 C 1 N Chad
Bardejov 99 D 5 *Ger.* Bartfeld,
Hung. Bártfa. NE Slovakia
Bardina, Gora *see* Bardin Seamount
Barduli *see* Barletta
Bareilly 135 E 3 *var.* Bareli.
N India
Bareli *see* Bareilly
Barendrecht 86 C 4
SW Netherlands
Barentin 90 B 3 N France
Barentsburg 83 G 2 W Svalbard
Barentsøya 83 G 2 island,
E Svalbard
Barents Sea 155 H 5 *Nor.* Barents
Havet, *Rus.* Barentsevo More. Sea,
Arctic Ocean
Bari 97 E 5 *var.* Bari delle Puglie;
anc. Barium. S Italy
Barikot *see* Barīkowṭ
Barīkowṭ 123 F 4 *var.* Barikot.
NE Afghanistan
Barillas 52 A 2 *var.* Santa Cruz
Barillas. NW Guatemala
Barinas 58 C 2 W Venezuela
Barisāl 135 G 4 S Bangladesh
Barisan, Pegunungan 138 B 4
mountain range, Sumatera,
W Indonesia
Barito 138 D 4 river, Borneo,
C Indonesia
Barkly Tableland 148 B 3 plateau,
N Australia
Bårlad 108 D 4 *prev.* Bîrlad.
E Romania
Barlavento, Ilhas de 74 A 2 *var.*
Windward Islands. Island group,
N Cape Verde

Bar-le-Duc 90 D 3 *var.*
Bar-sur-Ornain. NE France
Barlee, Lake 147 B 6 lake, Western
Australia, W Australia
Barlee Range 146 B 4 mountain
range, Western Australia,
W Australia
Barletta 97 E 5 *anc.* Barduli. S Italy
Barlinek 98 B 3 *Ger.* Berlinchen.
W Poland
Barmen-Elberfeld *see* Wuppertal
Barmouth 89 C 6 W Wales, UK
Barnaul 114 D 4
C Russian Federation
Barnstaple 89 C 7 SW England, UK
Baroda *see* Vadodara
Baron'ki 107 E 7 *Rus.* Boron'ki.
E Belorussia
Barquisimeto 58 C 2
NW Venezuela
Barra 88 B 3 island, W Wales, UK
Barra de Río Grande 53 E 3
E Nicaragua
Barranca 60 C 3 W Peru
Barrancabermija 58 B 2
N Colombia
Barranquilla 58 B 1 N Colombia
Barreiro 92 B 4 W Portugal
Barrier Range 149 B 6 hill range,
New South Wales, SE Australia
Barrow 89 B 6 *Ir.* An Bhearú. River,
SE Ireland
Barrow 36 D 2 Alaska, NW USA
Barrow-in-Furness 89 C 5
NW England, UK
Barrow Island 146 A 4 island,
W Australia
Barrows 37 F 5 Manitoba, S Canada
Bar-sur-Ornain *see* Bar-le-Duc
Bartang 123 F 3 river,
SE Tajikistan
Bartenstein *see* Bartoszyce
Bartica 59 F 3 N Guyana
Bartlesville 49 G 1 Oklahoma,
C USA
Bartlett 42 C 1 Tennessee, S USA
Bartoszyce 98 D 2 *Ger.* Bartenstein.
N Poland
Baruun Huuray 126 C 2 wetland,
E Mongolia
Baruun-Urt 127 F 2 E Mongolia
Barú, Volcán 53 F 5 *var.* Volcán de
Chiriquí. Volcano, W Panama
Barwon 149 D 5 river, New South
Wales, SE Australia
Barysaw 107 D 6 *Rus.* Borisov.
NE Belorussia
Basarabeasca 108 D 4
Rus. Basarabeasca. SE Moldavia
Basel 95 A 7 *Eng.* Basle, *Fr.* Bâle.
NW Switzerland
Basilan Island 139 E 3 island,
SW Philippines
Basra *see* Al Başrah
Bassano del Grappa 96 C 2 NE Italy
Bassein 136 A 4 *var.* Pathein
SW Burma
Basse-Terre 55 G 4 island,
E Guadeloupe
Basse-Terre 55 G 4 dependent
territory capital, SW Guadeloupe
Basseterre 55 G 3 country capital,
C Saint Kitts & Nevis
Bassikounou 74 D 3 SE Mauritania
Bass, Îlots de *see* Marotiri
Bass Strait 152 B 4 strait,
Indian Ocean/Pacific Ocean
Bassum 94 B 3 NW Germany
Bastia 91 E 7 SE France
Bastogne 87 D 7 SE Belgium
Bastrop 42 B 2 Louisiana, S USA

Bastyn' 107 C 7 *Rus.* Bostyn'.
SW Belorussia
Bata 77 A 5 NW Equatorial Guinea
Batabanó, Golfo de 54 B 2 gulf,
NW Caribbean Sea
Batae Coritanorum *see* Leicester
Batajnica 100 D 3 N Yugoslavia
Batangas 139 E 2 *off.* Batangas City.
Luzon, N Philippines
Batangas City *see* Batangas
Bataysk 111 B 7
SW Russian Federation
Bātdâmbâng 137 D 5 *prev.*
Battambang. NW Cambodia
Batéké, Plateaux 77 B 6 plateau,
S Congo
Bath 89 D 7 *hist.* Akermanceaster,
anc. Aquae Calidae, Aquae Solis.
S England, UK
Bathsheba 55 H 1 E Barbados
Bathurst 39 F 4 New Brunswick,
SE Canada
Bathurst 149 D 6 New South Wales,
SE Australia
Bathurst *see* Banjul
Bathurst Island 37 F 2 island,
N Canada
Bathurst Island 146 D 2 island,
Northern Territory, N Australia
Bāṭin, Wādī al 120 C 4 dry
watercourse, SW Asia
Batman 117 F 4 *var.* Iluh. SE Turkey
Baton Rouge 42 B 3
Louisiana, S USA
Batroûn 118 A 4 *var.* Al Batrūn.
N Lebanon
Battambang *see* Bātdâmbâng
Batticaloa 132 D 3 E Sri Lanka
Battipaglia 97 D 5 S Italy
Bat'umi 117 E 2 W Georgia
Batu Pahat 138 B 3 *prev.* Bandar
Penggaram. W Malaysia
Baturaja 138 B 4 W Indonesia
Bauchi 75 G 4 NE Nigeria
Bauer Basin 153 F 3 undersea
basin, E Pacific Ocean
Baumann, Pic *see* Agou, Mont
Bauru 57 D 5 S Brazil
Bauska 106 C 4 *Ger.* Bauske.
S Latvia
Bauske *see* Bauska
Bautzen 94 D 4 *Lus.* Budyšin.
E Germany
Bawku 75 E 4 N Ghana
Bayamo 54 C 3 E Cuba
Bayan Har Shan 126 D 4 *var.* Bayan
Khar. Mountain range, C China
Bayanhongor 126 D 2 C Mongolia
Bayan Khar *see* Bayan Har Shan
Bay City 49 G 4 Texas, S USA
Bay City 40 C 3 Michigan, N USA
Baydhabo 73 D 6 *var.* Baydhowa,
Isha Baydhabo, *It.* Baidoa.
SW Somalia
Bayern 95 C 6 cultural region,
SE Germany
Bayeux 90 B 3 *anc.* Augustodurum.
N France
Bāyir 119 C 7 *var.* Bā'ir. S Jordan
Bay Islands *see* Bahía, Islas de la
Baykal, Ozero 115 E 4
Eng. Lake Baikal. Lake,
S Russian Federation
Baymak 111 D 6
W Russian Federation
Bayonne 91 A 6 *anc.* Lapurdum.
SW France
Bayram-Ali *see* Bayramaly

Bayramaly 122 D 3 *prev.*
Bayram-Ali. S Turkmenistan
Bayreuth 95 C 5 *var.* Baireuth.
SE Germany
Bayrische Alpen *see* Bavarian Alps
Baysun *see* Boysun
Baza 93 E 4 S Spain
Beagle Channel 65 C 8 channel,
Atlantic Ocean/Pacific Ocean
Béal Feirste *see* Belfast
Beannchar *see* Bangor
Bear Island *see* Bjørnøya
Bear Lake 46 E 4 lake, NW USA
Beas de Segura 93 E 4 S Spain
Beata, Isla 55 E 3 island,
SW Dominican Republic
Beatrice 45 F 4 Nebraska, C USA
Beatton River 37 E 4
British Columbia, W Canada
Beaucaire 91 C 6 S France
Beaufort-Wes *see* Beaufort West
Beaufort West 78 C 5 *Afr.*
Beaufort-Wes. SW South Africa
Beaumont 49 H 4 Texas, S USA
Beaune 90 D 4 C France
Beauvais 90 C 3 *anc.* Bellovacum,
Caesaromagus. N France
Beaver Island 40 C 2 island,
Michigan, N USA
Beaverton 46 B 3 Oregon, NW USA
Beāwar 134 C 3 N India
Bečej 100 D 3 *Ger.* Altbetsche,
Hung. Óbecse, Rácz-Becse; *prev.*
Magyar-Becse, Stari Bečej.
N Yugoslavia
Béchar 70 D 2 *prev.* Colomb-Béchar.
W Algeria
Beckley 40 D 5 West Virginia,
NE USA
Bedford 89 E 6 E England, UK
Bedford, Cape 148 D 2 headland,
Queensland, NE Australia
Bedum 86 E 1 NE Netherlands
Beenleigh 149 E 5 E Australia
Beer Menuha 119 B 7 S Israel
Beernem 87 A 5 NW Belgium
Be'ér Sheva' 119 A 7 *var.* Beersheba,
Ar. Bir es Saba. S Israel
Beesel 87 D 5 SE Netherlands
Beeville 49 G 4 Texas, S USA
Begoml' *see* Byahoml'
Behar *see* Bihār
Beida *see* Al Bayḍā'
Beihai 129 C 6 *var.* Peihai. S China
Beijing 128 D 3 *var.* Pei-ching,
Eng. Peking; *prev.* Pei-p'ing.
Country capital, E China
Beilen 86 E 2 NE Netherlands
Beira 79 E 3 C Mozambique
Bei Shan 126 D 3 mountain range,
C China
Beius 108 B 3 *Hung.* Belényes.
NW Romania
Beja 92 B 4 *anc.* Pax Julia.
SE Portugal
Béjar 92 C 3 N Spain
Békás *see* Bicaz
Békéscsaba 99 D 7 *Rom.*
Bichis-Ciaba. SE Hungary
Bekobod 123 E 2 *Rus.* Bekabad;
prev. Begovat. E Uzbekistan
Bela Crkva 100 E 3
Ger. Weisskirchen, *Hung.*
Fehértemplom. E Yugoslavia
Belarus *see* Belorussia
Belau *see* Palau
Belaya Tserkov' *see* Bila Tserkva
Belchatow *see* Bełchatów
Bełchatów 98 C 4 *var.* Belchatow.
C Poland

Belcher, Îles see Belcher Islands
Belcher Islands 38 C 2
Fr. Îles Belcher. Island group,
Northwest Territories, SE Canada
Beledweyne 73 D 5 *var.* Belet Huen,
It. Belet Uen. C Somalia
Belém 63 F 1 *var.* Pará. N Brazil
Belen 48 D 2 New Mexico, SW USA
Belén 52 D 4 SW Nicaragua
Belényes see Beiuş
Belfast 89 B 5 *Ir.* Béal Feirste.
E Northern Ireland, UK
Belfield 44 D 2 North Dakota,
N USA
Belfort 90 D 4 E France
Belgard see Białogard
Belgaum 132 B 1 W India

Belgium
87 B 6 *Dut.* België, *Fr.* Belgique.
Monarchy, W Europe

Official name: Kingdom of Belgium
Date of formation: 1830 **Capital:**
Brussels **Population:** 10 million
Total area: 33,100 sq km
(12,780 sq miles) **Languages:**
French*, Dutch*, Flemish **Religions:**
Roman Catholic 75%, other 25%
Ethnic mix: Flemish 58%, Walloon
32%, other European 6%, other 4%
Government: Constitutional
monarchy
Currency: Franc = 100 centimes

Belgorod 111 A 6
W Russian Federation
Belgrade see Beograd
Belgrano II 154 B 2 research
station, Antarctica
Beli Manastir 100 C 2
Hung. Pélmonostor;
prev. Monostor. NE Croatia
Bélinga 77 B 5 NE Gabon
Belitung, Pulau 138 C 4 island,
W Indonesia

Belize
52 B 1 *Sp.* Belice; *prev.* Colony of
Belize, British Honduras.
Commonwealth republic, Belize

Official name: Belize **Date of
formation:** 1981 **Capital:** Belmopan
Population: 200,000 **Total area:**
22,960 sq km (8,865 sq miles)
Languages: English*, English
Creole, Spanish **Religions:** Christian
87%, other 13% **Ethnic mix:** *mestizo*
44%, Creole 30%, Indian 11%,
Garifuna 8%, other 7% **Government:**
Parliamentary democracy **Currency:**
Belizean $ =100 cents

Belize 52 B 1 river,
Belize/Guatemala
Belize City 52 C 1 *var.* Belize,
Sp. Belice . NE Belize
Beljak see Villach
Belkofski 36 B 3 Alaska,
NW USA
Belle Île 90 A 4 island, NW France
Belle Isle, Strait of 39 G 3 strait,
Newfoundland and Labrador,
NW Gulf of St.Lawrence
Belleville 40 B 5 Illinois, N USA
Belle Vue 55 F 2 S Saint Lucia
Bellevue 46 B 2 Washington,
NW USA
Bellevue 45 F 4 Nebraska, C USA
Bellingham 46 B 1 Washington,
NW USA
Belling Hausen Mulde see
Southeast Pacific Basin

Bellingshausen 154 A 2 research
station, Antarctica
Bellingshausen Abyssal Plain see
Bellingshausen Plain
Bellingshausen Sea 154 A 3 sea,
SE Pacific Ocean
Bello 58 B 2 W Colombia
Bello Horizonte see Belo Horizonte
Bellville 78 C 5 SW South Africa
Belmopan 52 C 1 country capital,
C Belize
Belogradchik 104 B 1 *var.*
Belogradčik. NW Bulgaria
Belogradčik see Belogradchik
Belo Horizonte 63 F 4 *prev.* Bello
Horizonte. SE Brazil
Belomorsk 110 B 3
NW Russian Federation
Beloretsk 111 D 6
W Russian Federation

Belorussia
107 C 6 *var.* Belarus, *Latv.*
Baltkrievija, *Rus.* Belorusskaya
SSR; *prev.* Belorussian SSR.
Republic, E Europe

Official name: Republic of Belarus
Date of formation: 1991 **Capital:**
Minsk **Population:** 10.3 million
Total area: 207,600 sq km (80,154 sq
miles) **Languages:** Belorussian*,
Russian **Religions:** Russian Orthodox
60%, Roman Catholic 8%, other 32%
Ethnic mix: Belorussian 78%, Russian
13%, Polish 4%, other 5%
Government: Multiparty republic
Currency: Rouble = 100 kopeks

Belorusskaya Gryada see
Byelaruskaya Hrada
Belovár see Bjelovar
Beloye More 110 C 3
Eng. White Sea. Sea,
Arctic Ocean/Barents Sea
Belozersk 110 B 4 *var.* Beloz'orsk.
NW Russian Federation
Beloz'orsk see Belozersk
Belton 49 G 3 Texas, S USA
Bel'tsy see Bălţi
Belynichi see Byalynichy
Belyye Berega 111 A 5
W Russian Federation
Belyy, Ostrov 114 D 2 island,
N Russian Federation
Bemidji 45 F 1 Minnesota, N USA
Bemmel 86 D 4 SE Netherlands
Benavente 92 C 2 N Spain
Bend 46 B 3 Oregon, NW USA
Bendern 94 E 1 NW Liechtenstein
Bendigo 149 C 7 Victoria,
SE Australia
Beneschau see Benešov
Benešov 99 B 5 *Ger.* Beneschau.
W Czech Republic
Benevento 97 D 5 *anc.* Beneventum,
Malventum. S Italy
Bengal, Bay of 133 E 1 bay,
N Indian Ocean
Bengbu 129 D 5 *var.* Peng-pu.
E China
Benghazi see Banghazi
Bengkulu 138 B 4 *prev.* Bengkoeloe,
Benkoelen, Benkulen. Sumatra,
W Indonesia
Benguela 78 B 2 *var.* Benguella.
W Angola
Benguella see Benguela
Beni 77 E 5 E Congo (Zaire)
Beni 61 E 3 river, N Bolivia
Benidorm 93 F 4 SE Spain
Beni-Mellal 70 C 2 C Morocco

Benin
52 F 4 *prev.* Dahomey. Republic,
W Africa

Official name: Republic of Benin
Date of formation: 1960 **Capital:**
Porto-Novo **Population:** 5.1 million
Total area: 112,620 sq km
(43,480 sq miles) **Languages:**
French*, Fon, Bariba, Yoruba, Adja
Religions: Traditional beliefs 70%,
Muslim 15%, Christian 15%
Ethnic mix: Fon 39%, Yoruba 12%,
Adja 10%, other 39%
Government: Multiparty republic
Currency: CFA franc = 100 centimes

Benin, Bight of 75 F 5 bay,
N Gulf of Guinea
Benin City 75 G 5 SW Nigeria
Beni Suef 72 B 2 *var.* Banī Suwayf.
N Egypt
Ben Nevis 88 C 3 mountain,
N Scotland, UK
Bénoué see Benue
Bénoy 76 B 4 S Chad
Benson 48 B 3 Arizona, SW USA
Benton 42 B 2 Arkansas, C USA
Benue 68 A 4 *Fr.* Bénoué. River,
Cameroon/Nigeria
Beograd 100 D 3 *Eng.* Belgrade,
Ger. Belgrad; *anc.* Singidunum.
Country capital, N Yugoslavia
Berat 101 C 6 *var.* Berati, *SCr.*
Beligrad. C Albania
Berau, Teluk 139 G 4 *var.* MacCluer
Gulf. Gulf, W Pacific Ocean
Berbera 72 D 4 NW Somalia
Berbérati 77 B 5
SW Central African Republic
Berck-Plage 90 C 2 N France
Berdichev see Berdychiv
Berdyans'k 109 G 4 *Rus.*
Berdyansk; *prev.* Osipenko.
SE Ukraine
Berdychiv 108 D 2 *Rus.* Berdichev.
N Ukraine
Berehove 108 B 3 *Cz.* Berehovo,
Hung. Beregszász, *Rus.* Beregovo.
W Ukraine
Berettyó 99 D 7 *Rom.* Barcău;
prev. Berătău, Beretău. River,
Hungary/Romania
Berettyóújfalu 99 E 6 E Hungary
Berezhany 108 C 2 *Pol.* Brzeżany
W Ukraine
Berezina see Byerezino
Berezniki 111 D 5
NW Russian Federation
Berga 93 G 2 NE Spain
Bergamo 96 B 2 *anc.* Bergomum.
N Italy
Bergara 93 E 1 N Spain
Bergen 85 A 5 S Norway
Bergen 94 D 2 NE Germany
Bergen 86 C 2 NW Netherlands
Bergen see Mons
Bergerac 91 B 5 SW France
Bergeyk 87 D 5 S Netherlands
Bergomum see Bergamo
Beringen 87 C 5 NE Belgium
Bering Strait see Bering Strait
Bering Sea 152 D 1 sea,
N Pacific Ocean
Bering Strait 152 D 1 *Rus.*
Beringov Proliv. Strait,
N Pacific Ocean
Berja 93 E 5 S Spain
Berkeley 47 B 6 California, W USA
Berkner Island 154 B 2 island,
Antarctica
Berkovitsa 104 C 2 NW Bulgaria

Berlin 94 D 3 country capital,
NE Germany
Berlin 41 G 2 Maine, NE USA
Berlinchen see Barlinek
Bermejo 64 C 2 river, N Argentina
Bermeo 93 E 1 N Spain
Bermuda 35 E 6 *var.* Bermuda
Islands, Bermudas; *prev.* Somers
Islands. UK crown colony,
W Atlantic Ocean
Bermuda Rise 66 B 3 undersea rise,
W Atlantic Ocean
Bern 95 A 7 *Fr.* Berne. Country
capital, W Switzerland
Bernau 94 D 3 NE Germany
Bernburg 94 C 4 C Germany
Berne see Bern
Berner Alpen 95 A 7 *var.* Berner
Oberland, *Eng.* Bernese Oberland.
Mountain range, SW Switzerland
Bernier Island 147 A 5 island,
W Australia
Bernina Pass see Bernina, Passo del
Bernina, Passo del 95 B 7
Eng. Bernina Pass. Pass,
SE Switzerland
Bérnissart 87 B 6 SW Belgium
Berry 90 C 4 cultural region,
C France
Berry Islands 54 C 1 island group,
N Bahamas
Bertoua 77 B 5 C Cameroon
Beru 145 E 2 *var.* Peru. Island,
W Kiribati
Berwick-upon-Tweed 88 D 4
N England, UK
Besançon 90 D 4 *anc.* Besontium,
Vesontio. E France
Beslan 111 B 8
SW Russian Federation
Bessarabka see Basarabeasca
Betanzos 92 B 1 NW Spain
Betanzos 61 F 4 S Bolivia
Bethlehem 78 D 4 C South Africa
Bethlehem 119 E 7 *Ar.* Bayt Laḥm,
Heb. Bet Leḥem. C West Bank
Bético, Sistema 92 D 5 mountain
range, S Spain
Bétou 77 C 5 N Congo
Bette, Pic 71 G 4 *var.* Bîkkū Bittī,
It. Picco Bette. Mountain, S Libya
Beulah 40 C 2 Michigan, N USA
Beveren 87 B 5 N Belgium
Beverley 89 D 5 NE England, UK
Beyrouth 118 A 4 *var.* Bayrūt,
Eng. Beirut; *anc.* Berytus. Country
capital, W Lebanon
Beyşehir Gölü 116 B 4 lake,
C Turkey
Béziers 91 C 6 *anc.* Baeterrae,
Baeterrae Septimanorum,
Julia Beterrae. S France
Bezwada see Vijayawāda
Bhadrāvati 132 C 2 SW India
Bhāgalpur 135 F 3 NE India
Bhaktapur 135 F 3 C Nepal
Bhamo 136 B 2 *var.* Banmo.
N Burma
Bharūch 134 C 4 W India
Bhaunagar see Bhāvnagar
Bhāvnagar 134 C 4 *prev.* Bhaunagar.
W India
Bheanntraí, Bá see Bantry Bay
Bhopāl 134 D 4 state capital,
C India
Bhubaneshwar 135 F 5 *prev.*
Bhubaneswar, Bhuvaneshwar.
State capital, E India
Bhusāval see Bhusāwal
Bhusāwal 134 D 4 *prev.* Bhusaval
C India

Bhutan
135 G 3 *var.* Druk-yul. Monarchy,
S Asia

Official name: Kingdom of Bhutan
Date of formation: 1865 **Capital:**
Thimphu **Population:** 1.7 million
Total Area: 47,000 sq km
(18,147 sq miles) **Languages:**
Dzongkha*, Nepali **Religions:**
Mahayana Buddhist 70%, Hindu 24%,
Muslim 5%, other 1% **Ethnic mix:**
Bhutia 61%, Gurung 15%, Assamese
13%, other 11% **Government:**
Constitutional monarchy
Currency: Ngultrum = 100 chetrum

Biak, Pulau 139 G 4 island,
E Indonesia
Biała Podlaska 98 E 3 E Poland
Białogard 98 B 2 *Ger.* Belgard.
NW Poland
Białystok 98 E 3 *Rus.* Belostok,
Bielostok. E Poland
Bianco, Monte *see* Blanc, Mont
Biarritz 91 A 6 SW France
Bicaz 108 C 4 *Hung.* Békás.
NE Romania
Bichiş-Ciaba *see* Békéscsaba
Biddeford 41 G 2 Maine, NE USA
Bideford 89 C 7 SW England, UK
Biel 95 A 7 *Fr.* Bienne.
W Switzerland
Bielefeld 94 B 4 NW Germany
Bielsko-Biała 99 C 5 *Ger.* Bielitz,
Bielitz-Biala. S Poland
Bielsk Podlaski 98 E 3 E Poland
Biên Hoa 137 E 6 S Vietnam
Bienne *see* Biel
Bienville, Lac 38 D 2 lake, Québec,
C Canada
Bié, Planalto do 69 C 6 *var.* Bié
Plateau. Plateau, C Angola
Bié Plateau *see* Bié, Planalto do
Bigge Island 146 C 2 island,
W Australia
Bighorn Mountains 44 C 2
mountain range,
Wyoming, C USA
Bighorn River 44 C 2
river, NW USA
Bight, Head of 149 A 6 bay,
NE Great Australian Bight
Bight, The 54 C 1 C Bahamas
Bignona 74 B 3 SW Senegal
Bigorra *see* Tarbes
Bigosovo *see* Bihosava
Big Rapids 40 C 2
Michigan, N USA
Big River 37 F 5
Saskatchewan, C Canada
Big Sioux River 45 F 3
river, N USA
Big Spring 49 E 3 Texas, S USA
Bihać 101 A 7
NW Bosnia & Herzegovina
Bihār 135 F 4 *prev.* Behar. State,
N India
Biharamulo 73 B 7 NW Tanzania
Bihosava 105 D 5 *Rus.* Bigosovo.
NW Belorussia
Bijeljina 100 D 3
NE Bosnia & Herzegovina
Bijelo Polje 101 D 5 W Yugoslavia
Bikāner 134 D 3 NW India
Bikin 115 G 4 SE Russian Federation
Bikini Atoll 144 D 1 *var.* Pikinni.
Island, NW Marshall Islands
Bilāspur 135 E 4 C India
Biläsuvar 117 H 3 *Rus.*
Bilyasuvar; *prev.* Pushkino.
SE Azerbaijan

Bila Tserkva 109 E 2 *Rus.* Belaya
Tserkov'. N Ukraine
Bilbao 93 E 1 *Basq.* Bilbo. N Spain
Bilbo *see* Bilbao
Bilecik 116 B 3 NW Turkey
Billings 44 C 2 Montana, NW USA
Biloela 148 D 4 Queensland,
E Australia
Biloku 59 G 4 S Guyana
Biloxi 42 C 3 Mississippi, S USA
Bilpa Morea Claypan 148 B 4 lake,
C Australia
Biltine 76 C 3 E Chad
Bilwi *see* Puerto Cabezas
Bilzen 87 D 6 NE Belgium
Bimini Islands 54 C 1 island group,
W Bahamas
Binche 87 B 7 S Belgium
Bindloe Island *see* Marchena, Isla
Binga, Monte 79 E 3 mountain,
C Mozambique
Bingerville 75 E 5 SE Ivory Coast
Binghamton 41 F 3 New York,
NE USA
Bingöl 117 E 3 E Turkey
Bintulu 138 D 3 Borneo, E Malaysia
Bío Bío 65 B 5 river, C Chile
Bioco, Isla de 77 A 5 *var.* Bioko, *Eng.*
Fernando Po, *Sp.* Fernando Póo;
prev. Macías Nguema Biyogo.
Island, NW Equatorial Guinea
Birāk 71 F 3 *var.* Brak. C Libya
Birao 76 D 3
NE Central African Republic
Biratnagar 135 F 3 E Nepal
Birdum 148 A 2 Northern Territory,
N Australia
Bireuen 138 A 3 W Indonesia
Bīrjand 120 E 3 E Iran
Birkenfeld 95 A 5 SW Germany
Birkenhead 89 C 6
NW England, UK
Bîrlad *see* Bârlad
Birmingham 89 C 6 W England, UK
Birmingham 42 C 2 Alabama,
S USA
Bîr Mogreïn 74 C 1 *var.* Bir
Moghreïn; *prev.* Fort-Trinquet.
N Mauritania
Birnie Island 145 F 3 island,
C Kiribati
Birni-Nkonni *see* Birnin Konni
Birnin Konni 75 F 3 *var.*
Birni-Nkonni. SW Niger
Birobidzhan 115 G 4
SE Russian Federation
Birsen *see* Biržai
Birsk 111 D 5 W Russian Federation
Biržai 106 C 4 *Ger.* Birsen.
NE Lithuania
Bisbee 48 B 3 Arizona, SW USA
Biscay, Bay of 66 D 3 *Fr.* Golfe de
Gascogne, *Sp.* Golfo de Vizcaya.
Bay, NE Atlantic Ocean
Biscay Plain 80 B 4 abyssal plain,
E Atlantic Ocean
Bischheim 90 E 3 NE France
Bischofsburg *see* Biskupiec
Bīshah, Wādī 121 B 5 dry
watercourse, W Saudi Arabia
Bishkek 123 G 2 *var.* Pishpek;
prev. Frunze. Country capital,
N Kyrgyzstan
Bishrī, Jabal 118 D 3 mountain
range, E Syria
Biskra 71 E 2 *var.* Beskra, Biskara.
NE Algeria
Biskupiec 98 D 2 *Ger.* Bischofsburg.
N Poland
Bislig 139 F 2 Mindanao,
S Philippines

Bismarck 45 E 2 state capital,
North Dakota, N USA
Bismarck Archipelago 144 C 3
island group,
NE Papua New Guinea
Bismarck Sea 144 B 3 sea,
SW Pacific Ocean
Bissau 74 B 4 country capital,
W Guinea-Bissau
Bistrița 108 B 3 *Ger.* Bistritz,
Hung. Besztercze; *prev.* Nösen.
N Romania
Bitam 77 B 5 N Gabon
Bitburg 95 A 5 SW Germany
Bitlis 117 F 4 SE Turkey
Bitoeng *see* Bitung
Bitola 101 D 6 *Turk.* Monastir;
prev. Bitolj. S Macedonia
Bitonto 97 E 5 *anc.* Butuntum.
SE Italy
Bitterroot Range 46 D 2
Port. Cadêia Bitterroot. Mountain
range, NW USA
Bitung 139 F 3 *prev.* Bitoeng.
Celebes, C Indonesia
Biu 75 H 4 E Nigeria
Biwa-ko 131 C 6 lake, Honshū,
SW Japan
Biy-Khem *see* Bol'shoy Yenisey
Bizerte 71 E 1 *Ar.* Banzart,
Eng. Bizerta. N Tunisia
Bjelovar 100 B 2 *Hung.* Belovár
N Croatia
Björneborg *see* Pori
Bjørnøya 83 G 3 *Eng.* Bear Island.
Island, N Norway
Blackall 148 C 4 Queensland,
E Australia
Blackfoot 46 E 4 Idaho, NW USA
Black Forest *see* Schwarzwald
Black Hills 44 D 3 mountain range,
N USA
Black Mesa 48 B 1 mountain,
Arizona, SW USA
Black Mountains 48 A 1 mountain
range, Arizona, SW USA
Blackpool 89 C 5 NW England, UK
Black Range 48 C 2 mountain
range, New Mexico, SW USA
Black River 54 A 5 W Jamaica
Black River 136 C 3 *Chin.* Lixian
Jiang, *Fr.* Rivière Noire, *Vtn.* Sông
Đa. River, China/Vietnam
Black Rock Desert 46 C 4 *Port.*
Deserto Black Rock. Desert,
Nevada, W USA
Blacksburg 40 D 5
Virginia, NE USA
Black Sea 81 F 4 *Bul.* Cherno More,
Eng. Euxine Sea, *Rom.* Marea
Neagrã, *Rus.* Chernoye More,
Turk. Karadeniz, *Ukr.* Chorne
More. Sea, NE Mediterranean Sea
Black Sea Lowland *see*
Prychornomors'ka Nyzovyna
Black Volta 75 E 4 *var.* Borongo,
Mouhoun, Moun Hou,
Fr. Volta Noire. River,
NW Africa
Blackwater 89 B 6 *Ir.* An Abhainn
Mhór. River, S Ireland
Blackwell 49 G 1 Oklahoma,
C USA
Blagoevgrad 104 C 3 *prev.* Gorna
Dzhumaya. W Bulgaria
Blagoveshchensk 111 D 5
W Russian Federation
Blagoveshchensk 115 G 4
SE Russian Federation
Blake Plateau 35 D 6 *var.* Blake
Terrace. Undersea plateau,
W Atlantic Ocean

Blake Terrace *see* Blake Plateau
Blanca, Bahía 65 C 5 bay,
SW Atlantic Ocean
Blanca, Costa 93 F 4 physical
region, SE Spain
Blanche, Lake 149 B 5 lake,
South Australia, S Australia
Blanc, Mont 80 C 4 *It.* Monte
Bianco. Mountain, France/Italy
Blanes 93 G 2 NE Spain
Blankenberge 87 A 5 NW Belgium
Blankenheim 95 A 5 W Germany
Blanquilla, Isla 59 E 1 *var.* La
Blanquilla. Island, N Venezuela
Blantyre 79 E 2 *var.* Blantyre-Limbe.
S Malawi
Blantyre-Limbe *see* Blantyre
Blaricum 86 C 3 C Netherlands
Blenheim 151 D 5 South Island,
C New Zealand
Blesae *see* Blois
Blida 70 D 2 *var.* El Boulaïda,
El Boulaïda. N Algeria
Bloemfontein 78 C 4
var. Mangaung. C South Africa
Blois 90 C 4 *anc.* Blesae. C France
Bloomfield 48 C 1 New Mexico,
SW USA
Bloomington 40 C 4
Indiana, N USA
Bloomington 45 F 2
Minnesota, N USA
Bluefields 53 E 3 SE Nicaragua
Blue Mountain Peak 54 B 5
mountain, E Jamaica
Blue Mountains 149 D 6 mountain
range, New South Wales,
SE Australia
Blue Mountains 46 C 3
Port. Montanha Azuis. Mountain
range, NW USA
Blue Mud Bay 148 B 2 bay, Gulf of
Carpentaria/Arafura Sea
Blue Nile 72 C 4 *var.* Bahr el Azraq,
Amh. Abai, Ābay Wenz,
Ar. An Nīl al Azraq. River,
Ethiopia/Sudan
Blumenau 63 F 5 S Brazil
Bo 74 C 4 S Sierra Leone
Boaco 52 D 3 W Nicaragua
Boa Vista 74 A 3 island,
E Cape Verde
Boa Vista 62 D 1 state capital,
NW Brazil
Bobo-Dioulasso 75 E 4
SW Burkina
Bobonong 78 D 3 E Botswana
Bobruysk *see* Babruysk
Bobrynets' 109 E 3 *Rus.* Bobrinets.
C Ukraine
Bocay 52 D 2 N Nicaragua
Bocheykovo *see* Bacheykava
Bocholt 94 A 4 W Germany
Bochum 94 A 4 W Germany
Bocşca 108 A 4 *Ger.* Bokschen,
Hung. Boksánbanyá. SW Romania
Bodaybo 115 F 4
E Russian Federation
Bodega Bay 47 A 6 bay,
E Pacific Ocean
Bodegas *see* Babahoyo
Boden 84 D 3 N Sweden
Bodensee *see* Lake Constance
Bodmin 89 C 7 SW England, UK
Bodø 84 C 3 C Norway
Bodrum 116 A 4 SW Turkey
Boeloekoemba *see* Bulukumba
Boende 77 C 5 C Congo (Zaire)
Boeroe *see* Buru, Pulau
Bogale 137 B 5 S Burma

Bogalusa 42 B 3 Louisiana, S USA
Bogatynia 98 B 4 *Ger.* Reichenau.
SW Poland
Bogendorf *see* Łuków
Bogor 138 C 5 *Dut.* Buitenzorg.
Jawa, C Indonesia
Bogotá 58 B 3 *prev.* Santa Fe, Santa
Fe de Bogotá. Country capital,
C Colombia
Bogushëvsk *see* Bahushewsk
Boguslav *see* Bohuslav
Bo Hai 128 D 4 *var.* Gulf of Chihli.
Gulf, Yellow Sea/Pacific Ocean
Bohemia 99 A 5 *Cz.* Čechy,
Ger. Böhmen. Cultural region,
W Czech Republic
Bohemian Forest 95 C 5 *Cz.* Český
Les, Šumava, *Ger.* Böhmerwald.
Mountain range, C Europe
Bohol Sea 139 E 2 *var.* Mindanao
Sea. Sea, W Pacific Ocean
Bohoro Shan 126 B 2 mountain
range, NW China
Bohuslav 109 E 2 *Rus.* Boguslav.
N Ukraine
Bois Blanc Island 40 C 2 island,
Michigan, N USA
Boise 46 D 3 *var.* Boise City. State
capital, Idaho, NW USA
Boise City *see* Boise
Bois, Lac des *see* Woods, Lake of the
Boizenburg 94 C 3 N Germany
Bojador *see* Boujdour
Bojnûrd 120 D 2 *var.* Bujnurd.
N Iran
Bokáro 135 F 4 N India
Boké 74 C 4 W Guinea
Boknafjorden 85 A 6 fjord,
NE North Sea
Bol 76 B 3 W Chad
Bolesławiec 98 B 4 *Ger.* Bunzlau.
SW Poland
Bolgatanga 75 E 4 N Ghana
Bolgrad *see* Bolhrad
Bolhrad 108 D 4 *Rus.* Bolgrad.
SW Ukraine
Bolívar, Pico 58 C 2 mountain,
W Venezuela

Bolivia
61 F 4 Republic,
W South America

Official name: Republic of Bolivia
Date of formation: 1825/1938
Capital: La Paz **Population:** 7.8
million **Total area:** 1,098,580 sq km
(424,162 sq miles) **Languages:**
Spanish*, Quechua*, Aymará*
Religions: Catholic 95%, other 5%
Ethnic mix: Indian 55%, *mestizo*
27%, White 10%, other 8%
Government: Multiparty republic
Currency: Boliviano = 100 centavos

Bollene 91 D 6 SE France
Bollnäs 85 C 5 C Sweden
Bologna 96 B 3 N Italy
Bolognesi 60 C 2 E Peru
Bologoye 110 B 4
W Russian Federation
Bol'sezemelskaja Tundra *see*
Bol'shezemel'skaya Tundra
Bol'shevik *see* Bal'shavik
Bol'shevik, Ostrov 115 E 2 island,
Severnaya Zemlya,
N Russian Federation
Bol'shezemel'skaya Tundra 110 E 3
var. Bol'sezemelskaja Tundra.
Physical region,
NW Russian Federation
Bol'shoy Lyakhovskiy, Ostrov 115
F 2 island, N Russian Federation

Bolton 89 C 5 *prev.* Bolton-le-Moors.
NW England, UK
Bolton-le-Moors *see* Bolton
Bolu 116 B 3 NW Turkey
Bolungarvík 83 E 4 NW Iceland
Bolyarovo 104 D 3 *prev.* Pashkeni.
SE Bulgaria
Bolzano 96 C 1 *Ger.* Bozen; *anc.*
Bauzanum. N Italy
Boma 77 B 7 W Congo (Zaire)
Bombay 134 C 5 *var.* Mumbai.
State capital, W India
Bomi Hills 74 D 4 hill range,
NW Liberia
Bomu 76 D 4 *var.* M'Bomu,
Mbomou, Mbomu. River, Central
African Republic/Congo (Zaire)
Bonaire 58 D 1 island,
E Netherlands Antilles
Bonanza 52 D 2 NE Nicaragua
Bonaparte Archipelago 146 C 2
island group, NW Australia
Bonda 77 B 6 C Gabon
Bondoukou 75 E 4 E Ivory Coast
Bone *see* Watampone
Bône *see* Annaba
Bone, Teluk 139 E 4 bay,
W Pacific Ocean
Bongaigaon 135 G 3 NE India
Bongo, Massif des 76 D 4
var. Chaîne des Mongos.
Mountain range,
NE Central African Republic
Bongor 76 B 4 SW Chad
Bonifacio 91 E 7 SE France
Bonn 95 A 5 W Germany
Bononia *see* Vidin
Boothia Felix *see* Boothia Peninsula
Boothia, Gulf of 37 F 2 inlet,
Arctic Ocean
Boothia Peninsula 37 F 2
prev. Boothia Felix. Peninsula,
Northwest Territories, NE Canada
Boppard 95 A 5 W Germany
Boquete 53 F 5 *var.* Bajo Boquete.
W Panama
Bor 100 E 4 E Yugoslavia
Bor 73 B 5 S Sudan
Borås 85 B 7 S Sweden
Bordeaux 91 B 5 *anc.* Burdigala.
SW France
Bordertown 149 B 7 South
Australia, S Australia
Borgå *see* Porvoo
Børgefjellet 84 C 4 mountain range,
C Norway
Borger 49 E 1 Texas, S USA
Borger 86 E 2 NE Netherlands
Borgholm 85 C 7 S Sweden
Borgo Maggiore 96 E 1
NW San Marino
Borisoglebsk 111 B 6
W Russian Federation
Borisov *see* Barysaw
Borlänge 85 C 6 C Sweden
Borne 86 E 3 E Netherlands
Borneo 138 C 4 island, SE Asia
Bornholm 85 B 8 *var.* Bornholms
Amt. Island group, E Denmark
Bornholm 94 D 2 island,
E Denmark
Bornholms Amt *see* Bornholm
Boron'ki *see* Baron'ki
Borovan 104 C 2 NW Bulgaria
Borovichi 110 B 4 *var.* Boroviči
Boroviči *see* Borovichi
Borovo 100 D 3 NE Croatia
Borşa 108 C 3 *Hung.* Borsa.
N Romania
Borsa *see* Borşa

Bor Ul Shan 126 D 3 mountain
range, N China
Boryslav 108 B 2 *Pol.* Borysław,
Rus. Borislav. NW Ukraine
Borzya 115 F 5
S Russian Federation
Bosanska Dubica 100 B 3
NW Bosnia & Herzegovina
Bosanska Gradiška 100 C 3
N Bosnia & Herzegovina
Bosanski Brod 100 C 3
N Bosnia & Herzegovina
Bosanski Novi 100 B 3
NW Bosnia & Herzegovina
Bosanski Šamac 100 C 3
N Bosnia & Herzegovina
Boskamp 59 G 3 N Surinam
Boskovice 99 B 5 *Ger.* Boskowitz.
SE Czech Republic
Boskowitz *see* Boskovice
Bosna 101 A 8 river,
N Bosnia & Herzegovina

Bosnia & Herzegovina
100 A 8 Republic, SE Europe

Official name: The Republic of
Bosnia and Herzegovina **Date of
formation:** 1992 **Capital:** Sarajevo
Population: 3.5 million **Total area:**
51,130 sq km (19,741 sq miles)
Languages: Serbian*, Croatian*
Religions: Muslim 40%, Orthodox
Catholic 31%, other 29% **Ethnic mix:**
Bosnian 44%, Serb 31%, Croat 17%,
other 8% **Government:** Multiparty
republic **Currency:** Dinar = 100 para

Bōsō-hantō 131 D 6 peninsula,
Honshū, S Japan
Bossangoa 76 C 4
C Central African Republic
Bossembélé 76 B 4
C Central African Republic
Bossier City 42 A 2 Louisiana,
S USA
Bosten Hu 126 C 3 *var.* Bagrax Hu.
Lake, NW China
Boston 89 D 6 *prev.* St.Botolph's
Town. E England, UK
Boston 41 G 3 state capital,
Massachusetts, NE USA
Boston Mountains 42 B 1 mountain
range, Arkansas, C USA
Bostyn' *see* Bastyn'
Botany Bay 149 D 6 bay,
W Tasman Sea
Boteti 78 C 3 *var.* Botletle. River,
N Botswana
Bothnia, Gulf of 66 D 2
Fin. Pohjanlahti, *Swe.* Bottniska
Viken. Gulf, N Baltic Sea
Botletle *see* Boteti
Botoşani 108 C 3 *Hung.* Botosány.
NE Romania
Botosány *see* Botoşani
Botou 128 D 4 NE China
Botrange 87 D 6 mountain,
E Belgium

Botswana
78 C 3 Republic, S Africa

Official name: Republic of
Botswana **Date of formation:** 1966
Capital: Gaborone **Population:**
1.4 million **Total area:** 581,730 sq km
(224,600 sq miles) **Languages:**
English*, Tswana, Shona, San
Religions: Traditional beliefs 50%,
Christian 50% **Ethnic mix:** Tswana
75%, Shona 12%, San 3%, other 10%
Government: Multiparty republic
Currency: Pula = 100 thebe

Bouar 76 B 4
W Central African Republic
Bou Craa 70 B 3
N Western Sahara
Bougainville Island 144 C 3 island,
NE Papua New Guinea
Bougouni 74 D 4 SW Mali
Boujdour 70 A 3 *var.* Bojador.
W Western Sahara
Boulder 44 B 2 Montana, NW USA
Boulder 44 C 4 Colorado, C USA
Boulogne-sur-Mer 90 B 2 *var.*
Boulogne; *anc.* Bononia,
Gesoriacum, Gessoriacum.
N France
Boûmdeïd 74 C 3 *var.* Boumdeït.
S Mauritania
Boumdeït *see* Boûmdeïd
Boundiali 74 D 4 N Ivory Coast
Bountiful 44 B 4 Utah, C USA
Bounty Basin *see* Bounty Trough
Bounty Islands 142 D 5 island
group, S New Zealand
Bounty Trough 152 C 5 *var.* Bounty
Basin. Trough, S Pacific Ocean
Bourbonnais 90 C 4 cultural region,
C France
Bourgas *see* Burgas
Bourg-en-Bresse 91 D 5 *var.* Bourg,
Bourge-en-Bresse. E France
Bourges 90 C 4 *anc.* Avaricum.
C France
Bourgogne 90 C 4 *Eng.* Burgundy.
Cultural region, E France
Bourke 149 C 5 New South Wales,
SE Australia
Bournemouth 89 D 7 S England, UK
Boutilimit 74 C 3 SW Mauritania
Bowen 148 D 3 Queensland,
NE Australia
Bowling Green 40 D 3 Ohio, N USA
Bowling Green 40 C 5
Kentucky, E USA
Bowling Green, Cape 148 D 3
headland, Queensland,
E Australia
Boxmeer 86 D 4 SE Netherlands
Boyarka 109 E 2 N Ukraine
Boysun 123 E 3 *Rus.* Baysun.
S Uzbekistan
Bozeman 44 B 2 Montana, NW USA
Bozüyük 116 B 3 NW Turkey
Brač 100 B 4 *var.* Brach, *It.* Brazza;
anc. Brattia. Island, S Croatia
Bracara Augusta *see* Braga
Bradenton 43 E 4 Florida, SE USA
Bradford 89 D 5 NW England, UK
Braga 92 B 2 *anc.* Bracara Augusta.
NW Portugal
Bragança 92 C 2 *Eng.* Braganza; *anc.*
Julio Briga. NE Portugal
Brahestad *see* Raahe
Brāhmanbāria 135 G 4
E Bangladesh
Brahmapur 135 F 5 E India
Brahmaputra 124 C 2 *var.* Tsangpo,
Ben. Jamuna, *Chin.* Yarlung
Zangbo Jiang. River, S Asia
Brāila 108 D 4 E Romania
Braine-le-Comte 87 B 6
SW Belgium
Brainerd 45 F 2 Minnesota, N USA
Brak *see* Birāk
Brampton 38 D 5 Ontario, S Canada
Brandberg 78 B 3 mountain,
NW Namibia
Brandenburg 94 C 3 *var.*
Brandenburg an der Havel.
NE Germany
Brandenburg an der Havel *see*
Brandenburg

Brandon 37 F 5 Manitoba, S Canada
Braniewo 98 C 2 *Ger.* Braunsberg. N Poland
Brasília 63 F 3 country capital, C Brazil
Brașov 108 C 4 *Ger.* Kronstadt, *Hung.* Brassó; *prev.* Orașul Stalin. C Romania
Brasstown Bald 42 D 1 mountain, Georgia, SE USA
Bratislava 99 C 6 *Ger.* Pressburg, *Hung.* Pozsony. Country capital, SW Slovakia
Bratsk 115 E 4 C Russian Federation
Braunsberg *see* Braniewo
Braunschweig 94 C 4 *Eng./Fr.* Brunswick. N Germany
Brava 74 A 3 island, SW Cape Verde
Brava *see* Baraawe
Brava, Costa 93 H 2 coastal region, NE Spain
Bravo del Norte *see* Grande, Río
Brawley 47 D 8 California, W USA

Brazil
62 C 2 *var.* Repùblica Federativa do Brasil, *Sp.* Brasil; *prev.* United States of Brazil. Federal republic, NE South America

Official name: Federative Republic of Brazil **Date of formation:** 1822/1929 **Capital:** Brasília **Population:** 164.4 million **Total area:** 8,511,970 sq km (3,286,472 sq miles) **Languages:** Portuguese*, German, Italian **Religions:** Roman Catholic 90%, other 10% **Ethnic mix:** White (Portuguese, Italian, German) 55%, mixed 38%, Black 6%, other 1% **Government:** Multiparty republic **Currency:** Real = 100 centavos

---

Brazil Basin 67 C 5 *var.* Brazilian Basin, Brazil'skaya Kotlovina. Undersea basin, W Atlantic Ocean
Brazilian Highlands 63 F 3 *var.* Planalto Central. Mountain range, E Brazil
Brazos River 49 G 3 river, Texas, S USA
Brazzaville 77 B 6 country capital, S Congo
Brčko 101 B 7 NE Bosnia & Herzegovina
Brecht 87 C 5 N Belgium
Brecon Beacons 89 C 6 mountain range, S Wales, UK
Breda 86 C 4 S Netherlands
Bree 87 D 5 NE Belgium
Bregalnica 101 E 6 river, E Macedonia
Bregovo 104 B 1 NW Bulgaria
Brême *see* Bremen
Bremen 94 B 3 *Fr.* Brême. NW Germany
Bremerhaven 94 B 3 NW Germany
Bremerton 46 B 2 Washington, NW USA
Brenham 49 G 4 Texas, S USA
Brenner Pass 95 C 7 *var.* Col du Brenner, Brenner Sattel, *Ger.* Brennerpass, *It.* Passo del Brennero. Pass, Austria/Italy
Brescia 96 B 2 *anc.* Brixia. N Italy
Breslau *see* Wrocław
Bressanone 96 C 1 *Ger.* Brixen. Italy
Brest 90 A 3 NW France
Brest 107 A 6 *Pol.* Brześć nad Bugiem, *Rus.* Brest-Litovsk; *prev.* Brześć Litewski. SW Belorussia
Bretagne 90 A 3 *Eng.* Brittany; *Lat.* Britannia Minor. Cultural region, NW France
Brezhnev *see* Naberezhnyye Chelny
Brezovo 104 D 2 *prev.* Abrashlare. C Bulgaria
Bria 76 D 4 C Central African Republic
Briançon 91 D 5 *anc.* Brigantio. SE France
Bribie Island 149 E 5 island, Queensland, SE Australia
Bricgstow *see* Bristol
Bridgeport 41 F 3 Connecticut, NE USA
Bridgetown 55 G 2 country capital, SW Barbados
Bridgman, Kap 83 E 1 headland, NE Greenland
Bridlington 89 E 5 NE England, UK
Bridport 89 C 7 SW England, UK
Brig 95 B 7 *Fr.* Brigue, *It.* Briga. SW Switzerland
Brigantio *see* Briançon
Brigham City 44 B 3 Utah, W USA
Brighton 89 E 7 SE England, UK
Brighton 44 D 4 Colorado, C USA
Brindisi 97 E 5 *anc.* Brundisium, Brundusium, SE Italy
Brisbane 149 E 5 state capital, Queensland, E Australia
Bristol 89 D 7 *anc.* Bricgstow. S England, UK
Bristol 43 E 1 Tennessee, S USA
Bristol 40 D 5 Rhode Island, NE USA
Bristol 41 F 3 Connecticut, NE USA
Bristol Bay 36 B 3 bay, SE Bering Sea
Bristol Channel 89 C 7 inlet, Atlantic Ocean/Celtic Sea
British Antarctic Territory 154 B 3 UK territorial claim, Antarctica
British Columbia 36 D 4 *Fr.* Colombie-Britannique. Province, SW Canada
British Indian Ocean Territory 124 B 5 UK dependent territory, C Indian Ocean
British Indian Ocean Territory 140 C 4 *var.* Chagos Islands. Island group, C Indian Ocean
British Isles 66 D 2 island group, NE Atlantic Ocean
British Solomon Islands Protectorate *see* Solomon Islands
British Virgin Islands 55 G 3 *var.* Virgin Islands. UK dependent territory, Caribbean Sea
Brive-la-Gaillarde 91 C 5 *prev.* Brive, *anc.* Briva Curretia. C France
Brixen *see* Bressanone
Brixia *see* Brescia
Brno 99 B 5 *Ger.* Brünn. SE Czech Republic
Broad Sound 148 D 4 sound, SE Coral Sea
Brocēni 106 B 3 SW Latvia
Brockton 41 G 3 Massachusetts, NE USA
Brockville 38 D 5 Ontario, SE Canada
Brodeur Peninsula 37 F 2 peninsula, Baffin Island, NE Canada
Brodnica 98 D 3 *Ger.* Buddenbrock. N Poland
Broek-in-Waterland 86 C 3 C Netherlands
Broken Arrow 49 G 1 Oklahoma, C USA
Broken Hill 149 B 6 New South Wales, SE Australia
Broken Ridge 141 D 6 undersea plateau, S Indian Ocean
Bromberg *see* Bydgoszcz
Brookhaven 42 B 3 Mississippi, S USA
Brookings 45 F 3 South Dakota, N USA
Brooks Range 36 D 2 mountain range, Alaska, NW USA
Brookton 147 B 6 Western Australia, W Australia
Broome 146 C 3 Western Australia, NW Australia
Broomfield 44 C 4 Colorado, C USA
Brovary 109 E 2 N Ukraine
Brownfield 49 E 2 Texas, S USA
Brownsville 49 G 5 Texas, S USA
Brownwood 49 F 3 Texas, S USA
Brozha 107 D 7 E Belorussia
Brozha *see* Brozha
Bruce, Mount 146 B 4 mountain, Western Australia, W Australia
Bruges *see* Brugge
Brugge 87 A 5 *Fr.* Bruges. NW Belgium
Brummen 86 D 4 E Netherlands

Brunei
138 D 3 *Mal.* Negara Brunei Darussalam. Monarchy, Borneo, SE Asia

Official name: The Sultanate of Brunei **Date of formation:** 1984 **Capital:** Bandar Seri Begawan **Population:** 300,000 **Total Area:** 5,770 sq km (2,228 sq miles) **Languages:** Malay*, English, Chinese **Religions:** Muslim 63%, Buddhist 14%, Christian 10%, other 13% **Ethnic mix:** Malay 69%, Chinese 18%, other 13% **Government:** Absolute monarchy **Currency:** Brunei $ = 100 cents

---

Brunei Town *see* Bandar Seri Begawan
Brünn *see* Brno
Brunswick 43 E 3 Georgia, SE USA
Brunswick *see* Braunschweig
Bruny Island 149 C 8 island, Tasmania, SE Australia
Brus Laguna 52 D 2 E Honduras
Brüx *see* Most
Bruxelles 87 C 6 *var.* Brussels, *Dut.* Brussel, *Ger.* Brüssel; *anc.* Broucsella. Country capital, C Belgium
Bryan 49 G 3 Texas, S USA
Bryansk 111 A 5 W Russian Federation
Brzeg 98 C 4 *Ger.* Brieg; *anc.* Civitas Altae Ripae. SW Poland
Brzeżany *see* Berezhany
Bucaramanga 58 B 2 N Colombia
Buccaneer Archipelago 146 C 3 island group, W Australia
Buchanan 74 C 5 *prev.* Grand Bassa. SW Liberia
Buchanan, Lake 49 F 3 reservoir, Texas, S USA
Bucharest *see* Bucharest
Bu Craa *see* Bou Craa
București 108 C 5 *Eng.* Bucharest, *Ger.* Bukarest, Gross Schlatten, *Hung.* Abrudbánya, *Rom.* Bucureti; *prev.* Altenburg, *anc.* Cetatea Damboviței. Country capital, S Romania
Buda-Kashalyova 107 D 7 *Rus.* Buda-Koshelëvo. SE Belorussia
Buda-Koshelëvo *see* Buda-Kashalyova
Budapest 99 D 6 *off.* Budapest Főváros, *SCr.* Budimpešta. Country capital, N Hungary
Budaun 135 E 3 N India
Buddenbrock *see* Brodnica
Budweis *see* České Budějovice
Budyšin *see* Bautzen
Buenaventura 58 A 3 W Colombia
Buena Vista 93 H 5 S Gibraltar
Buena Vista 61 G 4 C Bolivia
Buenos Aires 64 D 4 *hist.* Santa Maria del Buen Aire. Country capital, E Argentina
Buenos Aires 53 E 5 SE Costa Rica
Buenos Aires, Lago 65 B 6 *var.* Lago General Carrera. Lake, Argentina/Chile
Buffalo 41 E 3 New York, NE USA
Buffalo Narrows 37 F 4 Saskatchewan, C Canada
Buff Bay 54 B 5 E Jamaica
Buftea 108 C 5 S Romania
Bug 81 E 3 *Bel.* Zakhodni Buh, *Eng.* Western Bug, *Rus.* Zapadnyy Bug, *Ukr.* Zakhidnyy Buh. River, E Europe
Buga 58 B 3 W Colombia
Bughotu *see* Santa Isabel
Bugojno 100 B 4 C Bosnia & Herzegovina
Buḩayrat ath Tharthār 120 B 3 lake, C Iraq
Buḩeiret Nâșir 72 B 3 *var.* Buíayrat Náir, *Eng.* Lake Nasser. Lake, Egypt/Sudan
Buitenzorg *see* Bogor
Bujalance 92 D 4 S Spain
Bujanovac 101 E 5 SE Yugoslavia
Bujnurd *see* Bojnūrd
Bujumbura 73 B 7 *prev.* Usumbura. Country capital, W Burundi
Bukavu 77 E 6 *prev.* Costermansville. E Congo (Zaire)
Bukhoro 122 D 2 *var.* Bokhara, *Rus.* Bukhara. C Uzbekistan
Bukit Panjang 138 A 1 C Singapore
Bukoba 73 B 6 NW Tanzania
Bülach 95 B 7 NW Switzerland
Bulawayo 78 D 3 *var.* Buluwayo. SW Zimbabwe
Buldur *see* Burdur
Bulgan 127 E 2 N Mongolia

Bulgaria
104 C 2 *var.* Bulgariya, *Bul.* Bŭlgariya; *prev.* People's Republic of Bulgaria. Republic, SE Europe

Official name: Republic of Bulgaria **Date of formation:** 1908/1923 **Capital:** Sofia **Population:** 8.9 million **Total area:** 110,910 sq km (42,822 sq miles) **Languages:** Bulgarian*, Turkish, Macedonian, Romany **Religions:** Christian 85%, Muslim 13%, Jewish 1%, other 1% **Ethnic mix:** Bulgarian 85%, Turkish 9%, Macedonian 3%, Gypsy 3% **Government:** Multiparty republic **Currency:** Lev = 100 stoninki

---

Bulukumba 139 E 5 *prev.* Boeloekoemba. Celebes, C Indonesia
Buluwayo *see* Bulawayo
Bumba 77 D 5 N Congo (Zaire)
Bunbury 147 B 7 Western Australia, SW Australia
Bundaberg 148 D 4 Queensland, E Australia

Bungo-suidō 131 B 7 strait, NW Pacific Ocean
Bunia 77 E 5 NE Congo (Zaire)
Bunyan 116 D 3 C Turkey
Bunzlau *see* Bolesławiec
Buraida *see* Buraydah
Buraydah 120 B 4 *var.* Buraida. N Saudi Arabia
Burdigala *see* Bordeaux
Burdur 116 B 4 *var.* Buldur. SW Turkey
Burē 72 C 4 NW Ethiopia
Burgas 104 E 2 *var.* Bourgas. E Bulgaria
Burgaski Zaliv 104 E 2 gulf, W Black Sea
Burgos 92 D 2 N Spain
Burgundy *see* Bourgogne
Burhan Budai Shan 126 D 4 mountain range, C China
Buriram 137 D 5 *var.* Buri Ram, Puriramya. E Thailand
Burjassot 93 F 3 E Spain
Burkburnett 49 F 2 Texas, S USA
Burke 41 E 4 Virginia, NE USA

Burkina
75 E 3 *prev.* Upper Volta. Republic, NW Africa

Official name: Burkina Faso **Date of formation:** 1960 **Capital:** Ouagadougou **Population:** 9.8 million **Total area:** 274,200 sq km (105,870 sq miles) **Languages:** French*, Mossi, Fulani **Religions:** Traditional beliefs 65%, Muslim 25%, Christian 10% **Ethnic mix:** Mossi 45%, Mande 10%, Fulani 10%, other 35% **Government:** Multiparty republic **Currency:** CFA franc = 100 centimes

Burleson 49 G 3 Texas, S USA
Burlington 41 F 2 Maine, NE USA
Burlington 45 G 4 Iowa, C USA

Burma
136 B 3 *var.* Myanmar. Military dictatorship, SE Asia

Official name: Union of Myanmar **Date of formation:** 1948 **Capital:** Rangoon (Yangon) **Population:** 47.5 million **Total Area:** 676,550 sq km (261,200 sq miles) **Languages:** Burmese*, Karen, Mon **Religions:** Buddhist 89%, Muslim 4%, other 7% **Ethnic mix:** Burman 68%, Shan 9%, Karen 6%, Rakhine 4%, other 13% **Government:** Military regime **Currency:** Kyat = 100 pyas

Burnie 149 C 8 Tasmania, SE Australia
Burnsville 45 F 2 Minnesota, N USA
Burrel 101 D 6 *var.* Burreli. C Albania
Burreli *see* Burrel
Burriana 93 F 3 E Spain
Bursa 116 B 3 *var.* Brussa; *prev.* Brusa, *anc.* Prusa. NW Turkey
Būr Sa'īd *see* Port Said
Burtnieks *see* Burtnieku Ezers
Burtnieku Ezers 106 D 3 *var.* Burtnieks. Lake, N Latvia
Burton 40 C 3 Michigan, N USA

Burundi
73 B 7 *prev.* Kingdom of Burundi, Urundi. Republic, NE Africa

Official name: Republic of Burundi **Date of formation:** 1962 **Capital:** Bujumbura **Population:** 5.8 million **Total area:** 27,830 sq km (10,750 sq miles) **Languages:** Kirundi*, French*, Swahili **Religions:** Christian 68%, traditional beliefs 32% **Ethnic mix:** Hutu 85%, Tutsi 13%, Twa pygmy 1%, other 1% **Government:** Multiparty republic **Currency:** Franc = 100 centimes

Buru, Pulau 139 F 4 *prev.* Boeroe. Island, E Indonesia
Busselton 147 B 7 Western Australia, SW Australia
Busto Arsizio 96 B 2 N Italy
Buta 77 D 5 N Congo (Zaire)
Butembo 77 E 5 NE Congo (Zaire)
Butha Qi 127 G 1 *var.* Zalantun. NE China
Butler 41 E 4 Pennsylvania, NE USA
Bütow *see* Bytów
Butte 44 B 2 Montana, NW USA
Butterworth 138 B 3 W Malaysia
Button Islands 39 E 1 island group, Northwest Territories, NE Canada
Butuan 139 F 2 *off.* Butuan City. Mindanao, S Philippines
Butuan City *see* Butuan
Butuntum *see* Bitonto
Buulobarde 73 D 6 *var.* Buulo Berde. C Somalia
Buulo Berde *see* Buulobarde
Buur Gaabo 73 D 6 S Somalia
Buynaksk 111 B 8 SW Russian Federation
Büyükağrı Dağı 117 G 3 *var.* Aghri Dagh, Agri Dagi, Koh I Noh, Masis, *Eng.* Mount Ararat, Great Ararat. Mountain, E Turkey
Buyuk Menderes 116 A 4 river, SW Turkey
Buzău 108 C 5 SE Romania
Buzuluk 111 D 6 W Russian Federation
Byahoml' 107 D 5 *Rus.* Begoml'. N Belorussia
Byalynichy 107 D 6 *Rus.* Belynichi. E Belorussia
Bydgoszcz 98 C 3 *Ger.* Bromberg. W Poland
Byelaruskaya Hrada 107 B 6 *Rus.* Belorusskaya Gryada. Ridge, N Belorussia
Byerezino 107 D 6 *Rus.* Berezina. River, E Belorussia
Byrranga, Gora 115 E 2 mountain range, N Russian Federation
Bystrovka *see* Kemin
Bystrovka 123 G 2 N Kyrgyzstan
Bytča 99 C 5 NW Slovakia
Bytów 98 C 2 *Ger.* Bütow. NW Poland
Byuzmeyin 122 C 3 *Turkm.* Büzmeyin; *prev.* Bezmein. C Turkmenistan
Byval'ki 107 D 8 SE Belorussia

C

Caála 78 B 2 *var.* Kaala, Robert Williams, *Port.* Vila Robert Williams. C Angola
Caazapá 64 D 3 S Paraguay
Caballo Reservoir 48 C 3 reservoir, New Mexico, SW USA
Cabañaquinta 92 D 1 N Spain
Cabanatuan 139 E 1 *off.* Cabanatuan City. Luzon, N Philippines
Cabanatuan City *see* Cabanatuan
Cabillonum *see* Chalon-sur-Saône
Cabimas 58 C 1 NW Venezuela
Cabinda 77 B 6 *var.* Kabinda. Province, NW Angola
Cabinda 78 A 1 *var.* Kabinda NW Angola
Cabora Bassa, Lake *see* Cahora Bassa, Albufeira de
Caborca 50 B 1 NW Mexico
Cabot Strait 39 G 4 strait Atlantic Ocean/Gulf of St.Lawrence
Cabras, Ilha das 76 E 2 island, E Atlantic Ocean
Cabrera 93 G 3 *anc.* Capraria. E Spain
Čačak 100 D 4 C Yugoslavia
Cáceres 92 C 3 *Ar.* Qazris. W Spain
Cachimbo, Serra do 63 E 2 mountain range, C Brazil
Caconda 78 B 2 C Angola
Čadca 99 C 5 *Hung.* Csaca. N Slovakia
Cadillac 40 C 2 Michigan, N USA
Cadiz 139 E 2 *off.* Cadiz City. Negros, C Philippines
Cádiz 92 C 5 *anc.* Gades, Gadier, Gadir, Gadire. SW Spain
Cadiz City *see* Cadiz
Cádiz, Golfo de 92 B 5 gulf, NE Atlantic Ocean
Cadiz, Gulf of *see* Cádiz, Golfo de
Cadurcum *see* Cahors
Caen 90 B 3 N France
Caerdydd *see* Cardiff
Caer Gybi *see* Holyhead
Caesena *see* Cesena
Cafayate 64 C 2 N Argentina
Cagayan de Oro 139 F 2 *off.* Cagayan de Oro City. Mindanao, S Philippines
Cagayan de Oro City *see* Cagayan de Oro
Cagliari 97 A 6 *anc.* Caralis. W Italy
Caguas 55 F 3 E Puerto Rico
Cahora Bassa, Albufeira de 78 D 2 *var.* Lake Cabora Bassa. Reservoir, NW Mozambique
Cahors 91 B 6 *anc.* Cadurcum. S France
Cahul 108 D 4 *Rus.* Kagul. S Moldavia
Caicos Passage 54 D 2 channel, N Caribbean Sea
Cailungo 96 E 1 N San Marino
Cairns 148 D 3 Queensland, NE Australia
Cairo 72 B 1 *Ar.* Al Qāhirah, El Qâhira. Country capital, N Egypt
Caisleán an Bharraigh *see* Castlebar
Cajamarca 60 B 3 *prev.* Caxamarca. NW Peru
Čajovskij *see* Chaykovskiy
Čakovec 100 B 2 *Ger.* Csakathurn, *Hung.* Csáktornya; *prev. Ger.* Tschakathurn. N Croatia
Calabar 75 G 5 S Nigeria
Calabozo 58 D 2 C Venezuela
Calafat 108 B 5 SW Romania
Calafate *see* El Calafate
Calahorra 93 E 2 N Spain
Calais 90 C 2 N France
Calais 41 H 2 Maine, NE USA
Calama 64 B 2 N Chile
Călăraşi 108 D 3 *var.* Călăras, *Rus.* Kalarash. C Moldavia
Călăraşi 108 C 5 SE Romania
Calatayud 93 E 2 NE Spain
Calbayog 139 F 2 *off.* Calbayog City. Samar, C Philippines
Calbayog City *see* Calbayog
Calcanhar, Cabo 63 G 2 headland, NE Brazil
Calcutta 135 G 4 state capital, NE India
Caldas da Rainha 92 A 3 W Portugal
Caldera 64 B 3 N Chile
Caldwell 46 D 3 Idaho, NW USA
Caledon Bay 148 B 2 bay, Gulf of Carpentaria/Arafura Sea
Caledonia 52 C 1 N Belize
Caleta *see* Catalan Bay
Caleta Olivia 65 B 6 SE Argentina
Calgary 37 E 5 Alberta, SW Canada
Cali 58 A 3 W Colombia
Calicut 132 C 2 *var.* Kozhikode. SW India
Calida, Costa 93 F 5 physical region, SE Spain
California 47 C 7 *off.* State of California; *nicknames* El Dorado, The Golden State. State, W USA
California, Golfo de *see* California, Gulf of
California, Gulf of 153 F 2 *var.* Golfo de California; *prev.* Sea of Cortez. Gulf, E Pacific Ocean
Călimăneşti 108 B 4 SW Romania
Callabonna, Lake 149 B 5 lake, South Australia, S Australia
Callao 60 C 4 W Peru
Callatis *see* Mangalia
Callosa de Segura 93 F 4 E Spain
Calmar *see* Kalmar
Caloundra 149 E 5 Queensland, E Australia
Caltanissetta 97 C 7 SW Italy
Caluula 72 E 4 NE Somalia
Camabatela 78 B 1 NW Angola
Camacupa 78 B 2 *var.* General Machado, *Port.* Vila General Machado. C Angola
Camagüey 54 C 2 *prev.* Puerto Príncipe. C Cuba
Camagüey, Archipiélago de 54 C 2 island group, C Cuba
Camana 61 E 4 *var.* Camaná. SW Peru
Camaná *see* Camana
Camargue 91 D 6 physical region, SE France
Ca Mau 137 D 6 *var.* Quan Long, Quanlong; *prev.* Camau. S Vietnam
Cambay, Gulf of *see* Khambhāt, Gulf of
Camberia *see* Chambéry

Cambodia
137 D 5 *var.* Democratic Kampuchea, Roat Kampuchea, *Cam.* Kampuchea; *prev.* People's Democratic Republic of Kampuchea. Republic, SE Asia

Official name: State of Cambodia **Date of formation:** 1953 **Capital:** Phnom Penh **Population:** 9 million **Total Area:** 181,040 sq km (69,000 sq miles) **Languages:** Khmer*, French **Religions:** Buddhist 88%, Muslim 2%, other 10% **Ethnic mix:** Khmer 94%, Chinese 4%, other 2% **Government:** Constitutional monarchy **Currency:** Riel = 100 sen

Cambrai 90 C 2 *Flem.* Kambryk; *prev.* Cambray, *anc.* Cameracum. N France
Cambrian Mountains 89 C 6 mountain range, C Wales, UK
Cambridge 89 E 6 *Lat.* Cantabrigia. E England, UK
Cambridge 54 A 5 W Jamaica
Cambridge 150 D 3 North Island, N New Zealand

Cambridge Bay 37 F 3 Victoria Island, NW Canada
Cambulo 78 C 1 NE Angola
Camden 42 B 2 South Carolina, SE USA
Cameron 40 A 2 Wisconsin, N USA

Cameroon
76 B 4 *Fr.* Cameroun. Republic, C Africa

Official name: Republic of Cameroon **Date of formation:** 1960 **Capital:** Yaoundé **Population:** 13.6 million **Total area:** 475,440 sq km (183,570 miles) **Languages:** English*, French*, Fang, Bulu **Religions:** Traditional beliefs 51%, Christian 33%, Muslim 16% **Ethnic mix:** Bamileke and Manum 20%, Fang 19%, other 61% **Government:** Multiparty republic **Currency:** CFA franc = 100 centimes

Camiri 61 G 4 S Bolivia
Camocim 63 G 2 E Brazil
Camopi 59 H 3 E French Guiana
Campamento 52 C 2 C Honduras
Campbell, Cape 151 D 5 headland, South Island, SW New Zealand
Campbell Island 142 D 5 island, S New Zealand
Campbell Plateau 152 C 5 undersea plateau, SW Pacific Ocean
Campbell River 36 D 5 Vancouver Island, Canada
Campeche 51 G 4 SE Mexico
Campeche, Bahía de 51 F 4 *Eng.* Bay of Campeche. Bay, S Gulf of Mexico
Campeche, Bay of *see* Campeche, Bahía de
Câm Pha 136 E 3 N Vietnam
Câmpina 108 C 5 *prev.* Cîmpina. SE Romania
Campina Grande 63 G 2 E Brazil
Campinas 63 F 4 S Brazil
Campobasso 97 D 5 S Italy
Campo Criptana *see* Campo de Criptana
Campo de Criptana 93 E 3 *var.* Campo Criptana. C Spain
Campo dos Goitacazes *see* Campos
Campo Grande 63 E 4 state capital, SW Brazil
Campos 63 F 4 *var.* Campo dos Goitacazes. SE Brazil
Câmpulung 108 B 4 *prev.* Câmpulung-Muşcel, Cîmpulung. S Romania
Cam Ranh 137 E 6 SE Vietnam

Canada
34 C 4 Commonwealth republic, N North America

Official name: Canada **Date of formation:** 1867/1949 **Capital:** Ottawa **Population:** 27.8 million **Total area:** 9,976,140 sq km (3,851,788 sq miles) **Languages:** English*, French* Chinese, Italian, German, Inuit **Religions:** Roman Catholic 46%, Protestant 30%, other 24% **Ethnic mix:** British origin 40%, French origin 27%, other 33% **Government:** Parliamentary state **Currency:** Canadian $ = 100 cents

Canada Basin 155 F 2 undersea basin, Arctic Ocean
Canadian River 49 E 2 river, S USA
Çanakkale 116 A 3 *var.* Dardanelli; *prev.* Chanak, Kale Sultanie. W Turkey
Çanakkale Boğazı 116 A 2 *Eng.* Dardanelles. Strait, Marmara Denizi/Mediterranean Sea
Cananea 50 B 1 NW Mexico
Canarias, Islas 70 A 2 autonomous community, SW Spain
Canaries 55 F 1 W Saint Lucia
Canarreos, Archipiélago de los 54 B 2 island group, W Cuba
Canary Basin 66 C 3 *var.* Canaries Basin, Monaco Basin. Undersea basin, E Atlantic Ocean
Canary Islands 70 A 3 island group, SW Spain
Cañas 52 D 4 NW Costa Rica
Canaveral, Cape 43 F 4 headland, Florida, SE USA
Canavieiras 63 G 3 E Brazil
Canberra 149 D 7 country/territory capital, Australian Capital Territory, SE Australia
Cancún 51 H 3 SE Mexico
Cangzhou 128 D 4 NE China
Caniapiscau 39 E 2 river, Québec, E Canada
Caniapiscau, Réservoir de 39 E 2 reservoir, Québec, C Canada
Canik Dağlar 116 D 2 mountain range, N Turkey
Canillo 91 A 8 C Andorra
Çankırı 116 C 3 *var.* Chankiri; *anc.* Gangra, Germanicopolis. N Turkey
Cannanore 132 B 2 *var.* Kananur, Kannur. SW India
Cannes 91 D 6 SE France
Canoas 63 E 5 S Brazil
Canon City 44 D 5 Colorado, C USA
Cantabria 92 D 1 cultural region, N Spain
Cantábrica, Cordillera 92 C 1 mountain range, N Spain
Cantabrigia *see* Cambridge
Cantaura 59 E 2 NE Venezuela
Canterbury 89 E 7 *hist.* Cantwaraburh, *anc.* Durovernum, *Lat.* Cantuaria. SE England, UK
Canterbury Bight 151 C 6 sea area, S Pacific Ocean
Canterbury Plains 151 C 6 plain, South Island, SW New Zealand
Cân Thơ 137 D 6 S Vietnam
Canton *see* Guangzhou
Canton 42 B 2 Mississippi, S USA
Canton 40 D 4 Ohio, N USA
Canyon 49 E 2 Texas, S USA
Cao Băng 136 D 3 *var.* Caobang. N Vietnam
Caobang *see* Cao Băng
Cap-Breton, Île du *see* Cape Breton Island
Cape Barren Island 149 C 8 island, Tasmania, SE Australia
Cape Basin 67 D 6 undersea basin, SW Atlantic Ocean
Cape Breton Island 39 G 4 *Fr.* Île du Cap-Breton. Island, Nova Scotia, SE Canada
Cape Coast 75 E 5 *prev.* Cape Coast Castle. S Ghana
Cape Coast Castle *see* Cape Coast
Cape Coral 43 E 5 Florida, SE USA
Cape Fear River 43 F 2 river, North Carolina, SE USA
Cape Girardeau 45 H 5 Missouri, C USA
Capelle aan den IJssel 86 C 4 SW Netherlands
Cape Palmas *see* Harper
Cape Town 78 B 5 *var.* Ekapa, *Afr.* Kaapstad, Kapstad. SW South Africa

Cape Verde
74 A 2 Port. Ilhas do Cabo Verde, Cabo Verde. Republic, W Africa

Official name: Republic of Cape Verde **Date of formation:** 1975 **Capital:** Praia **Population:** 400,000 **Total area:** 4,030 sq km (1,556 sq miles) **Languages:** Portuguese*, Creole **Religions:** Roman Catholic 98%, Protestant 2% **Ethnic mix:** Creole (*mestiço*) 71%, Black 28%, White 1% **Government:** Multiparty republic **Currency:** Escudo = 100 centavos

Cape Verde Basin 66 C 4 undersea basin, SW Atlantic Ocean
Cape Verde Plain 66 C 4 abyssal plain, E Atlantic Ocean
Cape York Peninsula 148 C 2 peninsula, N Australia
Cap-Haïtien 54 D 3 *var.* Le Cap. N Haiti
Capira 53 G 5 C Panama
Capitán Bado 64 D 2 E Paraguay
Capitán Pablo Lagerenza 64 D 1 *var.* Mayor Pablo Lagerenza. N Paraguay
Capri, Isola di 97 C 5 island, S Italy
Caprivi Strip 78 C 3 *Ger.* Caprivizipfel; *prev.* Caprivi Concession. Cultural region, NE Namibia
Caquetá 58 C 5 *var.* Rio Japurá, Yapurá. River, Brazil/Colombia
C A R *see* Central African Republic
Caracal 108 B 5 S Romania
Caracaraí 62 D 1 W Brazil
Caracas 58 D 1 country capital, N Venezuela
Caracollo 61 F 4 W Bolivia
Caralis *see* Cagliari
Caráquez 60 A 1 *prev.* Bahía de Caráquez. W Ecuador
Caráquez, Bahía de *see* Caráquez
Caraşova 108 A 4 *Hung.* Krassóvár. SW Romania
Caratasca, Laguna de 53 E 2 lagoon, W Caribbean Sea
Carballiño 92 B 1 NW Spain
Carbondale 40 B 5 Illinois, N USA
Carbonia 97 A 6 *var.* Carbonia Centro. S Italy
Carbonia Centro *see* Carbonia
Carcaso *see* Carcassonne
Carcassonne 91 B 6 *anc.* Carcaso. S France
Cárdenas 54 B 2 W Cuba
Cardiff 89 C 7 *Wel.* Caerdydd. SE Wales, UK
Cardigan Bay 89 C 6 bay, SE Irish Sea
Carei 108 B 3 *Ger.* Gross-Karol, Karol, *Hung.* Nagykároly; *prev.* Careii-Mari. NW Romania
Carey, Lake 147 C 6 lake, Western Australia, SW Australia
Cariaco 59 E 1 NE Venezuela
Caribbean Sea 66 B 4 sea, W Atlantic Ocean
Caribou 37 F 4 Manitoba, C Canada
Carlisle 89 C 5 *anc.* Luguvallium, Luguvallum, Caer Luel. NW England, UK
Carlow 89 B 6 *Ir.* Ceatharlach. SE Ireland
Carlsbad 48 D 3 New Mexico, SW USA
Carlsberg Ridge 140 B 4 undersea ridge, NW Indian Ocean
Carlsruhe *see* Karlsruhe
Carmarthen 89 C 6 SW Wales, UK
Carmaux 91 C 6 S France
Carmel 40 C 4 Indiana, N USA
Carmelita 52 B 1 N Guatemala
Carmen 51 G 4 *var.* Ciudad del Carmen. SE Mexico
Carmona 92 D 4 S Spain
Carnavon 147 A 5 Western Australia, W Australia
Carnegie, Lake 147 C 5 salt lake, Western Australia, W Australia
Car Nicobar 133 F 3 island, SW India
Caroço, Ilha 76 E 1 island, E Atlantic Ocean
Carolina 63 F 2 E Brazil
Caroline Island 145 H 3 *prev.* Thornton Island. Island, E Kiribati
Caroline Islands 144 B 2 island group, S Micronesia
Caroline Peak 151 A 7 mountain, South Island, S New Zealand
Caroní 59 E 3 river, E Venezuela
Carora 58 C 2 N Venezuela
Carpathian Mountains 81 E 4 *var.* Carpathians, Cz./Pol. Karpaty, *Ger.* Karpaten. Mountain range, E Europe
Carpaţii Meridionali 108 B 4 *var.* Alpi Transvilvaniei, Carpaţii Sudici, *Eng.* South Carpathians, Transylvanian Alps, *Ger.* Südkarpaten, Transsylvanische Alpen, *Hung.* Déli-Kárpátok, Erdélyi-Havasok. Mountain Range, C Romania
Carpaţii Occidentali 108 B 4 *Eng.* Western Carpathians. Mountain range, W Romania
Carpentaria, Gulf of 148 B 2 gulf, N Arafura Sea
Carpi 96 B 2 N Italy
Carrara 96 B 3 C Italy
Carr Boyd Range 146 D 3 mountain range, N Australia
Čarsk *see* Charsk
Carson City 47 C 5 state capital, Nevada, W USA
Carson Sink 47 C 5 salt flat, Nevada, W USA
Cartagena 93 F 4 *anc.* Carthago Nova. SE Spain
Cartagena 58 B 1 *var.* Cartagena de los Indes. NW Colombia
Cartagena de los Indes *see* Cartagena
Cartago 53 E 4 C Costa Rica
Carthage 45 F 5 Missouri, C USA
Carthago Nova *see* Cartagena
Cartwright 39 G 2 Newfoundland and Labrador, E Canada
Carúpano 59 E 1 NE Venezuela
Carusbur *see* Cherbourg
Caruthersville 45 H 5 Missouri, C USA
Casablanca 70 C 2 *Ar.* Dar-el-Beida. NW Morocco
Casa Grande 48 B 2 Arizona, SW USA
Cascade Range 46 B 4 mountain range, NW USA
Cascadia Basin 153 E 1 undersea basin, NE Pacific Ocean
Cascais 92 B 4 Portugal
Caserta 97 D 5 S Italy
Casey 154 D 4 research station, Antarctica
Casino 149 E 5 New South Wales, SE Australia
Čáslav 99 B 5 *Ger.* Tschaslau. C Czech Republic
Casper 44 C 3 Wyoming, C USA

Caspian Sea 114 A 4 *Az.* Xäzär
Dänizi, *Kaz.* Kaspiy Tengizi,
Per. Daryā-ye Khazar, Baḥr-e
Khazar, *Rus.* Kaspiyskoye More.
Inland sea, Asia/Europe
Cassel *see* Kassel
Casteggio 96 B 2 N Italy
Castelló de la Plana 93 F 3
var. Castellón. E Spain
Castellón *see* Castelló de la Plana
Castelnaudary 91 C 6 S France
Castelo Branco 92 B 3 C Portugal
Castelsarrasin 91 B 6 S France
Castelvetrano 97 C 7 SW Italy
Castilla-La Mancha 93 E 3 cultural
region, NE Spain
Castilla-León 92 C 2 cultural
region, NW Spain
Castlebar 89 A 5 *Ir.* Caisleán an
Bharraigh. W Ireland
Castleford 89 D 5 N England, UK
Castle Harbour 42 B 5 harbour,
E Bermuda
Castricum 86 C 3 W Netherlands
Castries 55 F 1 country capital,
N Saint Lucia
Castro 65 B 6 W Chile
Castrovillari 97 D 6 SW Italy
Castuera 92 C 4 W Spain
Caswell Sound 151 A 7 sound,
S Tasman Sea
Catacamas 52 D 2 C Honduras
Catacaos 60 B 3 NW Peru
Catalan Bay 93 H 4 *var.* Caleta. Bay,
W Mediterranean Sea
Catalan Bay 93 H 4 W E Gibraltar
Catalina 64 B 2 N Chile
Cataluña 93 G 2 cultural region,
N Spain
Catamarca *see* San Fernando del
Valle de Catamarca
Catania 97 D 7 SW Italy
Catanzaro 97 E 6 SW Italy
Catarroja 93 F 3 E Spain
Cat Island 54 C 1 island, C Bahamas
Catskill Mountains 41 F 3
mountain range, New York,
NE USA
Cattaro *see* Kotor
Cauca 58 B 2 river, N Colombia
Caucasia 58 B 2 NW Colombia
Caucasus 117 F 1
Rus. Kavkaz. Mountain range,
Georgia/Russian Federation
Caura 59 E 3 river, E Venezuela
Cavally 74 D 5 *var.* Cavalla, Cavally
Fleuve. River, Ivory
Coast/Liberia
Cave Hill 55 G 2 W Barbdos
Caviana de Fora, Ilha 63 F 1
var. Ilha Caviana. Island, N Brazil
Caviana, Ilha *see*
Caviana de Fora, Ilha
Cawnpore *see* Kānpur
Caxamarca *see* Cajamarca
Caxias do Sul 57 D 5 S Brazil
Caxito 78 B 1 NW Angola
Cayenne 59 H 3 dependent
territory capital,
NE French Guiana
Cayman Brac 54 B 3 island,
E Cayman Islands
Cayman Islands 54 B 3
UK dependent territory,
NW Cayman Islands
Cay Sal 54 B 2 island, SW Bahamas
Cazin 100 B 3
NW Bosnia & Herzegovina
Cazorla 93 E 4 S Spain
Ceará 63 G 2 *off.* Estado do Ceará.
State, C Brazil

Ceará *see* Fortaleza
Ceara Abyssal Plain *see* Ceará Plain
Ceará, Estado do *see* Ceará
Ceará Plain 67 C 5 *var.* Ceara
Abyssal plain,
W Atlantic Ocean
Ceatharlach *see* Carlow
Cébaco, Isla 53 F 5 island,
SW Panama
Cebu 139 E 2 *off.* Cebu City. Cebu,
C Philippines
Cebu City *see* Cebu
Cecina 96 B 3 Italy
Cedar City 44 A 5 Utah, W USA
Cedar Falls 45 G 3 Iowa, C USA
Cedar Rapids 45 G 3 Iowa, C USA
Cedar River 45 E 4 river,
Nebraska, C USA
Cedros, Isla 50 A 2 island,
W Mexico
Ceduna 149 A 6 South Australia,
S Australia
Cefalù 97 C 7 *anc.* Cephaloedium.
SW Italy
Celebes Sea 152 A 3 *Ind.* Laut
Sulawesi. Sea, W Pacific Ocean
Celica 60 B 2 SW Ecuador
Celje 95 E 7 *Ger.* Cilli. C Slovenia
Čelkar *see* Chelkar
Celldömölk 99 C 7 W Hungary
Celle 94 B 3 *var.* Zelle. N Germany
Celovec *see* Klagenfurt
Celtic Sea 89 B 7 *Ir.* An Mhuir
Cheilteach. Sea,
NE Atlantic Ocean
Cenderawasih, Teluk 139 G 4
var. Teluk Cendrawasih. Bay,
W Pacific Ocean
Cenon 91 B 5 SW France

Central African Republic
76 C 4 *var.* République
Centrafricaine, *abbrev.* CAR; *prev.*
Oubangui-Chari, Territoire de
l'Oubangui-Chari, Ubangi-Shari.
Republic, C Africa
Official name: Central African
Republic **Date of formation:** 1960
Capital: Bangui **Population:** 3.3
million **Total area:** 622,980 sq km
(240,530 sq miles) **Languages:**
French*, Sangho, Banda **Religions:**
Christian 50%, traditional beliefs
27%, Muslim 15%, other 8%
Ethnic mix: Baya 34%, Banda 27%,
Mandjia 21%, other 18%
Government: Multiparty republic
Currency: CFA franc = 100 centimes

Central Group *see* Inner Islands
Centralia 46 B 2 Washington,
NW USA
Central Indian Ridge *see*
Mid-Indian Ridge
Central Makrān Range 134 A 3
mountain range, W Pakistan
Central Pacific Basin 152 D 3
undersea basin, C Pacific Ocean
Central Provinces and Berar *see*
Madhya Pradesh
Central Range 144 B 3 mountain
range, New Guinea,
NW Papua New Guinea
Central Russian Upland *see*
Central Russian Upland
Central Siberian Plateau *see*
Srednesibirskoye Ploskogor'ye
Central, Sistema 92 D 3 mountain
range, C Spain
Čepelare *see* Chepelare
Cephaloedium *see* Cefalù
Ceram Sea *see* Seram, Laut

Cereté 58 B 2 NW Colombia
Cerignola 97 D 5 SE Italy
Cernay 90 E 4 NE France
Cerro Chirripó *see*
Chirripó Grande, Cerro
Cerro de Pasco 60 C 3 C Peru
Cervera 93 F 2 NE Spain
Cesena 96 C 3 *anc.* Caesena. N Italy
Cēsis 106 D 3 *Ger.* Wenden.
C Latvia
Česká Republika *see*
Czech Republic
České Budějovice 99 B 5
Ger. Böhmisch-Budweis,
Ger. Budweis. SW Czech Republic
Český Krumlov 99 A 6
var. Böhmisch-Krumau, *Ger.*
Krummau. SW Czech Republic
Cetinje 101 C 5 *It.* Cettigne.
SW Yugoslavia
Cette *see* Sète
Cettigne *see* Cetinje
Ceuta 92 D 5 enclave, Spain
N Africa
Cévennes 91 C 6 mountain range,
S France
Ceyhan 116 D 4 S Turkey
Ceylon Plain 140 C 4 abyssal plain,
N Indian Ocean
Ceyre to the Caribs *see*
Marie-Galante
Chabjuwardoo Bay 146 A 4 bay,
E Indian Ocean
Chachapoyas 60 C 3 NW Peru
Chachevichy 107 D 6 *Rus.*
Chechevichi. E Belorussia
Chachoengsao 137 C 5 *var.*
Chaxerngsao. C Thailand
Chaco *see* Gran Chaco
Chaco Mesa 48 C 1 mountain,
New Mexico, SW USA

Chad
76 C 2 *Fr.* Tchad. Republic,
C Africa
Official name: Republic of Chad
Date of formation: 1960 **Capital:**
N'Djamena **Population:** 6 million
Total area: 1,284,000 sq km
(495,752 sq miles) **Languages:**
French*, Sara, Maba
Religions: Muslim 44%, Christian
33%, traditional beliefs 23% **Ethnic
mix:** Bagirmi, Sara and Kreish 31%,
Sudanic Arab 26%, Teda 7%, other
36% **Government:** Transitional
Currency: CFA franc = 100 centimes

Chad, Lake 76 B 3 *Fr.* Lac Tchad.
Lake, C Africa
Chadron 44 D 3 Nebraska, C USA
Chägai Hills 134 A 2 *var.* Chāh Gay.
Mountain range,
Afghanistan/Pakistan
Chagos Islands *see* British Indian
Ocean Territory
Chagos-Laccadive Plateau 140 C 4
undersea plateau, C Indian Ocean
Chagos Trench 140 C 4 trench,
C Indian Ocean
Chāh Gay *see* Chägai Hills
Chaillu, Massif du 77 B 6
mountain range, C Gabon
Chaîne Côtière *see* Coast Mountains
Chajul 52 B 2 W Guatemala
Chala 60 D 4 SW Peru
Chalatenango 52 C 3 N El Salvador
Chálki 105 E 7 island, Dodekánisos,
SE Greece
Chalkidikí 104 C 4 *var.*
Khalkidhikí; *anc.* Chalcidice.
Peninsula, NE Greece
Challans 90 A 4 NW France

Challapata 61 F 4 SW Bolivia
Challenger Deep *see*
Mariana Trench
Challenger Fracture Zone 153 F 4
fracture zone, SE Pacific Ocean
Châlons-en-Champagne 90 D 3
prev. Châlons-sur-Marne, *hist.*
Arcae Remorum, *anc.* Carolopois.
NE France
Chalon-sur-Saône 90 D 4
anc. Cabillonum. C France
Cha Mai *see* Thung Song
Chaman 134 B 2 SW Pakistan
Chambéry 91 D 5 *anc.* Cambería.
E France
Champagne 90 D 3 cultural region,
N France
Champaign 40 B 4 Illinois, N USA
Champasak 137 D 5 S Laos
Champlain, Lake 41 F 2 lake,
Canada/USA
Champotón 51 G 4 SE Mexico
Chañaral 64 B 3 N Chile
Chanco 64 B 4 C Chile
Chandeleur Islands 42 C 3
island, S USA
Chandīgarh 134 D 2 state capital,
N India
Chandler 48 B 2 Arizona, SW USA
Changane, Rio 78 D 3 river,
S Mozambique
Changchun 128 E 3 *var.*
Ch'ang-ch'un, Ch'angch'un;
prev. Hsinking. Province capital,
NE China
Changi 138 B 1 E Singapore
Chang Jiang 129 C 5 *var.* Yangtze
Kiang, *Eng.* Yangtze. River,
C China
Chang, Ko 137 C 6 island,
C Thailand
Changsha 129 C 5 *var.* Ch'angsha,
Ch'ang-sha. Province capital,
S China
Changzhi 128 C 4 C China
Chaniá 105 C 7 *var.* Khaniá, *Eng.*
Canea; *anc.* Cydonia. SE Greece
Chañi, Nevado de 64 C 2
mountain, N Argentina
Channel Islands 89 C 8 *Fr.* Iles
Normandes. British dependency,
S England, UK
Channel-Port aux Basques 39 G 4
Newfoundland and Labrador,
SE Canada
Channel Tunnel 89 E 7 tunnel,
France/United Kingdom
Chantada 92 C 1 NW Spain
Chanthaburi 137 C 6 *var.*
Chantabun, Chantaburi.
C Thailand
Chanute 45 F 5 Kansas, C USA
Chaoyang 128 D 3 NE China
Chapais 38 D 4 Québec, SE Canada
Chapala 50 D 4 SW Mexico
Chapala, Lago de 50 D 4 lake,
C Mexico
Chapayevsk 111 C 6
W Russian Federation
Chaplynka 109 F 4 S Ukraine
Chapra *see* Chhapra
Chardzhev 122 D 3 *prev.*
Chardzhou, Chardzhui, Leninsk-
Turkmenski, *Turkm.* Chärjew.
E Turkmenistan
Charente 91 B 5 cultural region,
W France
Charhār Borjak 122 D 5
SW Afghanistan
Chari 76 B 3 *var.* Shari. River,
Central African Republic/Chad
Chārīkār 123 E 4 NE Afghanistan

Charity 59 F 2 NW Guyana
Charleroi 87 C 7 S Belgium
Charlesbourg 39 E 4 Québec, SE Canada
Charles Island 38 D 1 island, Northwest Territories, NE Canada
Charleston 43 F 2 South Carolina, SE USA
Charleston 40 B 4 Illinois N USA
Charleston 40 D 5 state capital, West Virginia, NE USA
Charlestown 43 E 1 North Carolina, SE USA
Charleville 149 C 5 Queensland, E Australia
Charleville-Mézières 90 D 3 N France
Charlotte 43 E 1 North Carolina, SE USA
Charlotte Amalie 55 F 3 prev. Saint Thomas. Dependent territory capital, N Virgin Islands (US)
Charlottenhof see Aegviidu
Charlottesville 41 E 5 Virginia, NE USA
Charlotte Town see Roseau
Charlottetown 39 F 4 Prince Edward Island, SE Canada
Charsk 114 D 5 E Kazakhstan
Charters Towers 148 C 3 Queensland, NE Australia
Chartres 90 C 3 anc. Autricum, Civitas Carnutum. C France
Chashniki 107 D 5 N Belorussia
Chashniki see Chashniki
Châteaubriant 90 B 4 NW France
Châteaudun 90 C 4 C France
Châteauroux 90 B 4 prev. Indreville. C France
Château-Thierry 90 D 3 N France
Châtelet 87 C 7 S Belgium
Châtelherault see Châtellerault
Châtellerault 90 B 4 Eng. Châtelherault. W France
Chatham 38 C 5 New Brunswick, SE Canada
Chatham Island see San Cristóbal, Isla
Chatham Island Rise see Chatham Rise
Chatham Islands 152 D 5 island group, E New Zealand
Chatham Rise 152 C 4 var. Chatham Island Rise. Undersea rise, SW Pacific Ocean
Chatkal Range 123 F 2 Rus. Chatkal'skiy Khrebet. Mountain range, Kyrgyzstan/Uzbekistan
Chatkal'skiy Khrebet see Chatkal Range
Chättagām see Chittagong
Chattanooga 42 D 1 Tennessee, S USA
Chatyr-Tash 123 G 2 C Kyrgyzstan
Châu Đôc 137 D 6 var. Chau Phu, Chauphu. SW Vietnam
Chauk 136 A 3 W Burma
Chaumont 90 D 4 prev. Chaumont-en-Bassigny. N France
Chaumont-en-Bassigny see Chaumont
Chausy see Chavusy
Chaves 92 C 2 anc. Aquae Flaviae. N Portugal
Chavusy 107 E 6 Rus. Chausy. E Belorussia
Chaxerngsao see Chachoengsao
Chaykovskiy 111 D 5 var. Čajovskij NW Russian Federation
Cheb 99 A 5 Ger. Eger. W Czech Republic
Cheboksary 111 C 5 W Russian Federation

Cheboygan 40 C 2 Michigan, N USA
Chech, Erg 68 B 3 desert, Algeria/Mali
Checker Hall 55 G 1 N Barbados
Cheduba Island 136 A 4 island, W Burma
Chefchaouen 70 C 2 var. Chaouén, Chaouèn, Chechaouén, Chechaouen, Chechaouèn, Chefchaouèn, Sp. Xauen. N Morocco
Chehel Abdālān, Kūh-e 122 D 4 var. Chalap Dalam, Pash. Chalap Dalan. Mountain range, C Afghanistan
Cheju-do 128 E 4 Jap. Saishū; prev. Quelpart. Island, S South Korea
Cheju Strait 128 E 4 strait, Yellow Sea/Pacific Ocean
Chek Chue 128 B 2 var. Stanley. S Hong Kong
Cheleken 122 B 3 W Turkmenistan
Chelkar 114 B 4 W Kazakhstan
Chełm 98 E 4 Rus. Kholm. SE Poland
Chełmno 98 C 3 Ger. Culm, Kulm. N Poland
Cheltenham 89 D 6 S England, UK
Chelyabinsk 114 C 3 C Russian Federation
Chemnitz 94 D 4 prev. Karl-Marx-Stadt. E Germany
Chengde 128 D 3 var. Jehol. SE China
Chengdu 129 B 5 var. Ch'eng-tu, Chengtu. Province capital, SW China
Chenzhou 129 C 6 SE China
Chepelare 104 C 3 var. Čepelare. S Bulgaria
Chepo 53 G 4 C Panama
Cher 90 C 4 river, C France
Cherbourg 90 B 3 anc. Carusbur. N France
Cherepovets 110 B 4 var. Cerepoveo, Cerepovec. NW Russian Federation
Chergui, Chott ech 70 D 2 salt lake, N Algeria
Cherikov see Cherykaw
Cherkassy see Cherkasy
Cherkasy 109 E 2 Rus. Cherkassy. C Ukraine
Cherkessk 111 B 7 SW Russian Federation
Chernigov see Chernihiv
Chernihiv 109 E 1 Rus. Chernigov. NE Ukraine
Chernivtsi 108 C 3 Ger. Czernowitz, Rom. Cernǎuţi, Rus. Chernovtsy. W Ukraine
Chernomorskoye see Chornomors'ke
Chernyakhovsk 106 A 4 Ger. Insterburg. W Russian Federation
Cherry Hill 41 F 4 New Jersey, NE USA
Cherski see Cherskogo, Khrebet
Cherskogo, Khrebet 115 F 3 var. Cherski. Mountain range, NE Russian Federation
Cherson see Kherson
Chervonohrad see Chervonohrad
Chervonohrad 108 C 2 Rus. Chervonograd. NW Ukraine
Chervyen' 107 D 6 C Belorussia
Cherykaw 107 E 7 Rus. Cherikov. E Belorussia
Chesapeake Bay 41 F 5 bay, W Atlantic Ocean

Chester 89 C 6 Wel. Caerleon; hist. Legaceaster, Lat. Deva, Devana Castra. W England, UK
Chetumal 51 H 4 var. Payo Obispo. SE Mexico
Cheviot Hills 88 D 4 hill range, England/Scotland, UK
Cheyenne 44 D 4 state capital, Wyoming, C USA
Cheyenne River 44 D 3 river, South Dakota, N USA
Chhapra 135 F 3 prev. Chapra. N India
Chiai 129 D 6 var. Chiayi, Kiayi, Jap. Kagi. W Taiwan
Chiang Mai 136 C 4 var. Chiangmai, Chiengmai, Kiangmai. NW Thailand
Chiang Rai 136 C 3 var. Chianpai, Chienrai, Muang Chiang Rai. N Thailand
Chiapa see Chiapa de Cerzo
Chiapa de Cerzo 51 G 5 var. Chiapa. SE Mexico
Chiba 131 D 5 var. Tiba. Honshū, S Japan
Chibougamau 38 D 4 Québec, SE Canada
Chicago 40 B 3 Illinois, N USA
Chicago Heights 40 B 3 Illinois, N USA
Chichester Range 146 B 4 mountain range, W Australia
Chickasha 49 G 2 Oklahoma, C USA
Chiclayo 60 B 3 NW Peru
Chico 65 B 6 var. Argentina
Chico 47 B 5 California, W USA
Chicoutimi 39 E 4 Québec, SE Canada
Chiemsee 95 C 6 lake, SE Germany
Chiesanuova 96 D 2 SW San Marino
Chieti 96 D 4 var. Teate. C Italy
Chifeng 127 G 2 var. Ulanhad. N China
Chigirin see Chyhyryn
Chihli, Gulf of see Bo Hai
Chihuahua 50 C 2 NW Mexico
Childress 49 F 2 Texas, S USA
Chile 64-65 B 6 Republic, S South America

Official name: Republic of Chile
Date of formation: 1818/1929
Capital: Santiago **Population:** 13.8 million **Total area:** 756,950 sq km (292,258 sq miles) **Languages:** Spanish*, Indian languages **Religions:** Roman Catholic 89%, Protestant 11% **Ethnic mix:** White and mestizo 92%, Indian 6%, other 2% **Government:** Multiparty republic **Currency:** Peso = 100 centavos

Chilean Antarctic Territory 154 B 3 Chilean territorial claim, Antarctica
Chile Basin 67 A 5 undersea basin, E Pacific Ocean
Chile Chico 65 B 6 W Chile
Chile, Republic of see Chile
Chile Rise 67 A 6 undersea rise, SE Pacific Ocean
Chilia-Nouǎ see Kiliya
Chililabombwe 78 D 2 C Zambia
Chillán 65 B 5 C Chile
Chillicothe 40 D 4 Ohio, N USA
Chiloé, Isla de 65 A 6 var. Isla Grande de Chiloé. Island, W Chile

Chiloé, Isla Grande de see Chiloé, Isla de
Chilpancingo 51 E 5 var. Chilpancingo de los Bravos. S Mexico
Chilpancingo de los Bravos see Chilpancingo
Chilung 129 D 6 var. Keelung, Jap. Kirun, Kirun'; prev. Sp. Santissima Trinidad. N Taiwan
Chimán 53 G 5 E Panama
Chimbay see Chimboy
Chimborazo 60 B 1 mountain, C Ecuador
Chimbote 60 C 3 W Peru
Chimboy 122 D 1 Rus. Chimbay. NW Uzbekistan
Chimoio 79 E 3 C Mozambique
China 124 D 2 Chin. Chung-hua Jen-min Kung-ho-kuo, Zhonghua Renmin Gonghe Guo; prev. Chinese Empire. Republic, E Asia

Official name: People's Republic of China **Date of formation:** 1949/1950 **Capital:** Beijing **Population:** 1,234.3 million **Total area:** 9,396,960 sq km (3,628,166 sq miles) **Languages:** Mandarin* **Religions:** Confucianist 20%, Buddhist 6%, Taoist 2%, other 72% **Ethnic mix:** Han 93%, Zhaung 1%, Hui 1%, other 5% **Government:** Single-party republic **Currency:** Yuan = 10 jiao = 100 fen

Chinandega 52 C 3 NW Nicaragua
Chincha Alta 60 D 4 SW Peru
Chindwin 136 B 2 river, NW Burma
Chingola 78 D 2 C Zambia
Chinguetti 74 C 2 var. Chinguetti. C Mauritania
Chinguetti see Chinguetti
Chin Hills 136 A 3 mountain range, W Burma
Chinook Trough 152 D 2 trough, N Pacific Ocean
Chioggia 96 C 2 anc. Fossa Claudia. NE Italy
Chíos 105 D 5 var. Hios, Khíos, It. Scio, Turk. Sakiz-Adasi. Chíos, E Greece
Chíos 105 D 5 var. Khíos. Island, E Greece
Chipata 78 D 2 prev. Fort Jameson. E Zambia
Chippewa Falls 40 A 2 Wisconsin, N USA
Chiquimula 52 B 2 SE Guatemala
Chīrāla 132 D 1 E India
Chirchik see Chirchiq
Chirchiq 123 F 2 Rus. Chirchik. E Uzbekistan
Chiriquí, Golfo de 53 F 5 Eng. Chiriquí Gulf. Inlet, E Pacific Ocean
Chiriquí Gulf see Chiriquí, Golfo de
Chiriquí, Laguna de 53 F 5 inlet, E Pacific Ocean
Chiriquí, Volcán de see Barú, Volcán
Chirripó Grande, Cerro 53 E 4 var. Cerro Chirrripó. Mountain, SE Costa Rica
Chisec 52 B 2 C Guatemala
Chisholm 45 F 1 Minnesota, N USA
Chişinǎu 108 D 4 Rus. Kishinev. C Moldavia
Chita 115 F 4 C Russian Federation
Chitangwiza see Chitungwiza
Chitina 36 D 3 Alaska, NW USA

Chitose 130 D 2 *var.* Titose.
Hokkaidō, NE Japan
Chitré 53 F 5 S Panama
Chittagong 135 G 4 *Ben.*
Chāttagām. SE Bangladesh
Chitungwiza 78 D 3 *prev.*
Chitangwiza. NE Zimbabwe
Chkalov *see* Orenburg
Chlef 70 D 2 *var.* Ech Cheleff,
Ech Cheliff; *prev.* Al-Asnam, El
Asnam, Orléansville. NW Algeria
Choa Chu Kang 138 A 1
W Singapore
Chocolate Mountains 47 D 8
mountain range, California,
W USA
Chodzież 98 C 3 NW Poland
Choele Choel 65 C 5 C Argentina
Choiseul 55 F 2 SW Saint Lucia
Choiseul 144 C 3 *var.* Lauru. Island,
NW Solomon Islands
Ch'ok'ē 72 C 4 *var.* Choke
Mountains. Mountain range,
NW Ethiopia
Choke Mountains *see* Ch'ok'ē
Cholet 90 B 4 NW France
Choluteca 52 C 3 S Honduras
Choma 78 D 2 S Zambia
Chomutov 98 A 4 *Ger.* Komotau.
NW Czech Republic
Chon Buri 137 C 5 *prev.* Bang Pla
Soi. C Thailand
Chone 60 A 1 W Ecuador
Ch'ŏngjin 128 E 3 NE North Korea
Chongqing 129 B 5 *var.* Ch'ung-
ching, Ch'ung-ch'ing, Chungking,
Pahsien, Tchongking, Yuzhou.
SW China
Chonos, Archipiélago de los 65 A 7
island group, S Chile
Chornomors'ke 109 E 5 *Rus.*
Chernomorskoye. S Ukraine
Chortkiv 108 C 2 *Rus.* Chortkov.
W Ukraine
Chortkov *see* Chortkiv
Chorum *see* Çorum
Chorzów 99 C 5 *Ger.* Königshütte;
prev. Królewska Huta. S Poland
Chōshi 131 D 5 *var.* Tyōsi. Honshū,
S Japan
Choszczno 98 B 3 *Ger.* Arnswalde.
W Poland
Chota Nagpur Plateau 135 E 4
plateau, C India
Choybalsan 127 F 2 E Mongolia
Christchurch 151 C 6 South Island,
C New Zealand
Christiana 54 B 5 C Jamaica
Christiansand *see* Kristiansand
Christmas Creek 146 C 3
NW Australia
Christmas Island 141 D 5
Australian external territory,
E Indian Ocean
Christmas Island *see* Kiritimati
Chu 114 C 5 *Kaz.* Shū.
SE Kazakhstan
Chubut 65 B 6 *river*, SE Argentina
Chūgoku-sanchi 131 B 6 mountain
range, Honshū, SW Japan
Chuí 64 E 4 *var.* Chuy E Uruguay
Chukchi Plain 155 F 2 abyssal
plain, Arctic Ocean
Chukchi Plateau 155 F 2 undersea
plateau, Arctic Ocean
Chukchi Sea 36 C 1
Rus. Chukotskoye More. Sea,
Arctic Ocean
Chukotskoye More *see* Chukchi Sea
Chula Vista 47 C 8
California, W USA
Chulucanas 60 B 2 NW Peru

Chulym 114 D 4 *river*,
C Russian Federation
Chumphon 137 C 6 *var.* Jumporn.
S Thailand
Ch'unch'ŏn 128 E 4 *Jap.* Shunsen
N South Korea
Chunya 115 E 3 *river*,
C Russian Federation
Chuor Phnum Dângrêk 137 D 5
var. Phanom Dang Raek,
Phanom Dong Rak, *Fr.* Chaîne
des Dangrek. Mountain range,
Cambodia/Thailand
Chuquicamata 64 B 2 N Chile
Chur 95 B 7 *Fr.* Coire, *It.* Coira,
Rmsch. Cuera, Quera; *anc.* Curia
Rhaetorum. E Switzerland
Churchill 37 G 4 Manitoba,
C Canada
Churchill 39 F 2 river, E Canada
Chuska Mountains 48 C 1
mountain range, SW USA
Chusovoy 111 D 5 *var.* Čusovoj
NW Russian Federation
Chuuk 144 B 2 *var.* Hogoley
Islands. Island group,
C Micronesia
Chyhyryn 109 E 3 *Rus.* Chigirin.
N Ukraine
Ciadîr-Lunga 108 D 4 *var.* Ceadâr-
Lunga, *Rus.* Chadyr-Lunga.
S Moldavia
Cide 116 C 2 N Turkey
Ciechanów 98 D 3 *prev.* Zichenau.
C Poland
Ciego de Ávila 54 C 2 C Cuba
Ciénaga 58 B 1 N Colombia
Cienfuegos 54 B 2 C Cuba
Cieza 93 E 4 SE Spain
Cihanbeyli 116 C 3 C Turkey
Cikobia 145 E 4 *prev.* Thikombia.
Island, N Fiji
Cilacap 138 C 5 *prev.* Tjilatjap. Jawa,
C Indonesia
Cill Airne *see* Killarney
Cill Chainnigh *see* Kilkenny
Cilli *see* Celje
Cîmpina *see* Câmpina
Cincinnati 40 C 4 Ohio, N USA
Ciney 87 C 7 SE Belgium
Cintra *see* Sintra
Cipolletti 65 B 5 C Argentina
Cirebon 138 C 4 *prev.* Tjirebon.
Jawa, C Indonesia
Cirò Marina 97 E 6 Italy
Cisnădie 108 B 4 *Ger.* Heltau,
Hung. Nagydisznód. SW Romania
Citharista *see* la Ciotat
Citlaltépetl 35 C 7 mountain,
S Mexico
Citrus Heights 47 B 5 California,
W USA
City of Manila *see* Manila
Ciudad Acuña 50 D 2 *var.* Villa
Acuña. NE Mexico
Ciudad Bolívar 59 E 2 *prev.*
Angostura. E Venezuela
Ciudad Camargo 50 D 2 N Mexico
Ciudad Cortés *see* Cortés
Ciudad Darío 52 D 3 *var.* Dario.
W Nicaragua
Ciudad de Dolores Hidalgo *see*
Dolores Hidalgo
Ciudad del Carmen *see* Carmen
Ciudad del Este 64 E 2 *prev.* Cuidad
Presidente Stroessner, Presidente
Stroessner, Puerto Presidente
Stroessner. SE Paraguay
Ciudad Delicias *see* Delicias
Ciudad Guayana 59 E 2 *prev.* San
Tomé de Guayana, Santo Tomé de
Guayana. NE Venezuela

Ciudad Guzmán 50 D 4 SW Mexico
Ciudad Hidalgo 51 G 5 SE Mexico
Ciudad Juárez 50 C 1 N Mexico
Ciudad Lerdo 50 D 3 C Mexico
Ciudad Madero 51 E 3 *var.* Villa
Cecilia. C Mexico
Ciudad Mante 51 E 3 C Mexico
Ciudad Miguel Alemán 51 E 2
C Mexico
Ciudad Obregón 50 B 2 NW Mexico
Ciudad Ojeda 58 C 1
NW Venezuela
Ciudad Porfirio Díaz *see*
Piedras Negras
Ciudad Real 92 D 4 C Spain
Ciudad-Rodrigo 92 C 3 N Spain
Ciudad Trujillo *see* Santo Domingo
Ciudad Valles 51 E 4 C Mexico
Ciudad Victoria 51 E 3 C Mexico
Ciutadella *see* Ciutadella de
Menorca
Ciutadella de Menorca 93 G 3
var. Ciutadella. E Spain
Civitanova Marche 96 D 4 C Italy
Civitas Eburovicum *see* Évreux
Civitavecchia 96 C 4 *anc.* Centum
Cellae, Trajani Portus. C Italy
Claremore 49 G 1 Oklahoma,
C USA
Clarence 151 C 5 *river*, South
Island, C New Zealand
Clarence Town 54 D 2 C Bahamas
Clarinda 45 F 4 Iowa, C USA
Clarion Fracture Zone 153 E 2
fracture zone, NE Pacific Ocean
Clarión, Isla 50 A 5 island,
W Mexico
Clark Fork 44 A 1 *river*, NW USA
Clark Hill Lake 43 E 2 *var.* J.Storm
Thurmond Reservoir. Reservoir,
SE USA
Clarksburg 40 D 4
West Virginia, NE USA
Clarksdale 42 B 2
Mississippi, S USA
Clarksville 42 C 1
Tennessee, S USA
Clearwater 43 E 4 Florida, SE USA
Clearwater Mountains 46 D 2
mountain range, Idaho, NW USA
Clearwater River 46 D 2 *river*,
Idaho, NW USA
Cleburne 49 G 3 Texas, S USA
Clermont 148 D 4 Queensland,
E Australia
Clermont-Ferrand 91 C 5 C France
Cleveland 42 D 1 Tennessee, S USA
Cleveland 42 B 2
Mississippi, S USA
Cleveland 40 D 3 Ohio, N USA
Clifton 48 C 2 Arizona, SW USA
Clinton 42 B 3 Mississippi, S USA
Clinton 49 F 1 Oklahoma, C USA
Clipperton Fracture Zone 153 E 3
fracture zone, E Pacific Ocean
Clipperton Island 153 F 3 island,
E Pacific Ocean
Cloncurry 148 B 3 Queensland,
C Australia
Clonmel 89 A 6 *Ir.* Cluain Meala.
S Ireland
Cloppenburg 94 B 3 NW Germany
Cloquet 45 F 2 Minnesota, N USA
Cloud Peak 44 C 3 mountain,
Wyoming, C USA
Clovis 49 E 2 New Mexico, SW USA
Clovis 47 C 6 California, W USA
Cluain Meala *see* Clonmel
Cluj-Napoca 108 B 3 *Ger.*
Klausenburg, *Hung.* Kolozsvár;
prev. Cluj. NW Romania

Clutha 151 B 7 *river*, South Island,
SW New Zealand
Clyde 88 C 4 *river*, C Scotland, UK
Coari 62 D 2 N Brazil
Coast Mountains 36 D 4 *Fr.* Chaîne
Côtière. Mountain range,
Canada/USA
Coast Ranges 46 A 4 mountain
range, W USA
Coats Island 38 C 1 island,
Northwest Territories, NE Canada
Coats Land 154 B 2 physical region,
Antarctica
Coatzacoalcos 51 F 4
var. Quetzalcoalco; *prev.* Puerto
México. E Mexico
Cobán 52 B 2 C Guatemala
Cobar 149 C 6 New South Wales,
SE Australia
Cobija 61 E 3 NW Bolivia
Coburg 95 C 5 SE Germany
Coca *see* Puerto Francisco de
Orellana
Cocanada *see* Kākināda
Cochabamba 61 F 4 *hist.* Oropeza.
C Bolivia
Cochin 132 C 3 *var.* Kochi.
SW India
Cochrane 37 C 5 Ontario, S Canada
Cochrane 38 C 4 Ontario, S Canada
Cockburn Town 55 E 2 dependent
territory capital, E Turks &
Caicos Islands
Cockpit Country, The 54 A 4
physical region, NW Jamaica
Coco 52 D 2 *var.* Río Wanki,
Segoviao Wangkí. River,
Honduras/Nicaragua
Cocobeach 77 A 5 NW Gabon
Coconino Plateau 48 B 1 plain,
Arizona, SW USA
Cocos (Keeling) Islands 141 D 5
Australian external territory,
E Indian Ocean
Cocos Basin 140 D 4 undersea
basin, E Indian Ocean
Cocos Island Ridge *see* Cocos Ridge
Cocos Ridge 153 G 4 *var.* Cocos
Island Ridge. Undersea ridge,
E Pacific Ocean
Cod, Cape 41 G 3 headland,
Massachusetts, NE USA
Codfish Island 151 A 8 island,
South Island, SW New Zealand
Cod Island 39 F 1 island,
Newfoundland and Labrador,
E Canada
Codlea 108 C 4 *Ger.* Zeiden, *Hung.*
Feketehalom. C Romania
Cody 44 C 2 Wyoming, C USA
Coeur d'Alene 46 C 2 Idaho,
NW USA
Coevorden 86 E 2 NE Netherlands
Coffin Bay 149 A 6 South Australia,
S Australia
Coffs Harbour 149 E 6 New South
Wales, SE Australia
Cognac 91 B 5 *anc.* Compniacum.
W France
Coiba, Isla de 53 F 5 island,
SW Panama
Coihaique 65 B 6 *var.* Coyhaique.
S Chile
Coimbatore 132 C 3 S India
Coimbra 92 B 3 *anc.* Conimbria,
Conimbriga. W Portugal
Coín 92 D 5 S Spain
Coirib, Loch *see* Corrib, Lough
Colac 149 B 7 Victoria, SE Australia
Colbeck, Cape 154 B 4 headland,
Antarctica
Colby 45 E 4 Kansas, C USA

Colchester 89 E 6 *hist.* Colneceaster, *anc.* Camulodunum.

Coleman 49 F 3 Texas, S USA

Coleraine 88 B 4 *Ir.* Cúil Raithin. N Northern Ireland, UK

Colesberg 78 C 5 C South Africa

Coles, Punta 61 E 5 headland, S Peru

Colima 50 D 4 S Mexico

Coll 88 B 3 island, W Scotland, UK

College Station 49 G 3 Texas, S USA

Collie 147 B 7 Western Australia, W Australia

Collinsville 148 D 3 Queensland, E Australia

Collinsville 40 B 4 Illinois, N USA

Collipo *see* Leiria

Colmar 90 E 4 *Ger.* Kolmar. NE France

Colomb-Béchar *see* Béchar

Colombia
58 B 3 . Republic, N South America

Official name: Republic of Colombia
Date of formation: 1819/1922
Capital: Bogotá **Population:** 34 million **Total area:** 1,138,910 sq km (439,733 sq miles) **Languages:** Spanish*, Indian languages, English Creole **Religions:** Roman Catholic 95%, other 5% **Ethnic mix:** *mestizo* 58%, White 20%, mixed 14%, other 8% **Government:** Multiparty republic **Currency:** Peso = 100 centavos

Colombian Basin 66 A 4 undersea basin, W Atlantic Ocean

Colombie-Britannique *see* British Columbia

Colombo 132 C 4 country capital, W Sri Lanka

Colón 53 G 4 *prev.* Aspinwall. C Panama

Colón, Archipiélago de *see* Galapagos Islands

Colonia *see* Kolonia

Colorado 65 B 5 river, E Argentina

Colorado 35 B 5 *var.* Río Colorado. River, Mexico/USA

Colorado 44 C 4 *off.* State of Colorado; *nicknames* Centennial State, Silver State. State, C USA

Colorado City 49 F 3 Texas, S USA

Colorado, Río *see* Colorado

Colorado Springs 44 D 5 Colorado, C USA

Columbia 43 E 2 state capital, South Carolina, SE USA

Columbia 42 C 1 Tennessee, S USA

Columbia 41 F 4 Maryland, NE USA

Columbia 45 G 4 Missouri, C USA

Columbia Plateau 46 C 3 plateau, NW USA

Columbia River 46 B 2 river, NW USA

Columbine 44 C 4 Colorado, C USA

Columbus 42 D 2 Georgia, SE USA

Columbus 42 C 2 Mississippi, S USA

Columbus 40 D 4 state capital, Ohio, N USA

Columbus 45 E 4 Nebraska, C USA

Colville Channel 150 D 2 channel, Bay of Plenty/Hauraki Gulf

Comacchio 96 C 3 *var.* Commachio; *anc.* Comactium. N Italy

Comalcalco 51 G 4 SE Mexico

Coma Pedrosa, Pic Alt de la *see* Coma Pedrosa, Pic de

Coma Pedrosa, Pic de 91 A 7 *var.* Pic Alt de la Coma Pedrosa. Mountain, NW Andorra

Comarapa 61 G 4 C Bolivia

Comarnic 108 C 4 SE Romania

Comayagua 52 C 2 W Honduras

Combermere Bay 136 A 4 bay, Bay of Bengal/Indian Ocean

Comilla 135 G 4 *Ben.* Kumillā. E Bangladesh

Comino *see* Comino

Comitán 51 G 5 *var.* Comitán de Domínguez. SE Mexico

Comitán de Domínguez *see* Comitán

Commissioner's Point 42 A 5 headland, W Bermuda

Como 96 B 2 *anc.* Comum. N Italy

Comodoro Rivadavia 65 B 6 SE Argentina

Como, Lago di 96 B 2 *var.* Lario, *Eng.* Lake Como, *Ger.* Comer See. Lake, N Italy

Comoros
79 F 2 *Fr.* République Fédérale Islamique des Comores. Republic, Indian Ocean

Official name: Federal Islamic Republic of the Comoros
Date of formation: 1975 **Capital:** Moroni **Population:** 600,000 **Total area:** 2,230 sq km (861 sq miles) **Languages:** Arabic*, French* **Religions:** Muslim 86%, Roman Catholic 14% **Ethnic mix:** Comorian 96%, Makua 2%, other 2% **Government:** Islamic republic **Currency:** Franc = 100 centimes

Compiègne 90 C 3 N France

Compniacum *see* Cognac

Comrat 108 D 4 *Rus.* Komrat. S Moldova

Comum *see* Como

Conakry 74 C 4 country capital, SW Guinea

Conca *see* Cuenca

Concarneau 90 A 3 NW France

Concepción 65 B 5 C Chile

Concepción 64 D 2 *var.* Villa Concepción. C Paraguay

Concepción 61 G 3 E Bolivia

Concepción *see* La Concepción

Concepción de la Vega *see* La Vega

Conchos, Río 50 C 2 river, NW Mexico

Concord 41 G 3 state capital, New Hampshire, NE USA

Concordia 64 D 4 E Argentina

Concordia 45 E 4 Kansas USA

Condate *see* St-Claude

Condega 52 D 3 NW Nicaragua

Congo
77 B 5 *Fr.* Moyen-Congo; *prev.* Middle Congo. Republic, C Africa

Official name: The Republic of the Congo **Date of formation:** 1960 **Capital:** Brazzaville **Population:** 2.4 million **Total area:** 342,000 sq km (132,040 sq miles) **Languages:** French*, Kongo **Religions:** Roman Catholic 50%, traditional beliefs 48%, other 2% **Ethnic mix:** Bakongo 48%, Teke 17%, Mboshi 17%, other 18% **Government:** Multiparty republic **Currency:** CFA franc = 100 centimes

Congo (Zaire)
77 D 6 *prev.* Zaire, Belgian Congo, Congo (Kinshasa). Republic, C Africa

Official name: Democratic Republic of the Congo **Date of formation:** 1960 **Capital:** Kinshasa **Population:** 41.2 million **Total area:** 2,345,410 sq km (905,563 sq miles) **Languages:** French*, Kiswahili, Tshiluba **Religions:** Christian 70%, traditional beliefs 20%, Muslim 10% **Ethnic mix:** Bantu 23%, Hamitic 23%, other 54% **Government:** Transitional **Currency:** Congolese franc

Congo 77 C 6 *var.* Kongo, *Fr.* Zaire. River, C Africa

Congo *see* Zaire

Congo Basin 77 C 6 basin, W Congo (Zaire)

Congo Cone *see* Congo Fan

Coni *see* Cuneo

Conjeeveram *see* Kānchīpuram

Connaught 89 A 5 cultural region, W Ireland

Connecticut 41 G 3 *off.* State of Connecticut; *nicknames* Blue Law State, Constitution State, Land of Steady Habits, Nutmeg State. State, NE USA

Connersville 40 C 4 Indiana, N USA

Conrad Rise 141 B 7 undersea rise, SW Indian Ocean

Conroe 49 H 3 Texas, S USA

Consentia *see* Cosenza

Consolación del Sur 54 A 2 W Cuba

Con Son *see* Côn Đao

Con Son Island 137 E 7 Island, S Vietnam

Constance, Lake 95 B 6 *Ger.* Bodensee. Lake, Germany/Switzerland

Constanţa 108 D 5 *var.* Küstendje, *Eng.* Constanza, *Ger.* Konstanza, *Turk.* Küstence. SE Romania

Constantia *see* Coutances

Constantine 71 E 2 *var.* Qacentina, *Ar.* Qoussantina. NE Algeria

Conway 43 F 2 South Carolina, SE USA

Coober Pedy 149 A 5 South Australia, S Australia

Cook Islands 145 F 4 territory in free association with New Zealand (defence, UN), S Pacific Ocean

Cook, Mount 151 B 6 *prev.* Aoraki, Aorangi. Mountain, South Island, SW New Zealand

Cook Strait 151 D 5 *var.* Raukawa. Channel, Pacific Ocean/ Tasman Sea

Cooktown 148 D 2 Queensland, NE Australia

Coolgardie 147 C 6 Western Australia, W Australia

Cooma 149 D 7 New South Wales, SE Australia

Coomassie *see* Kumasi

Coon Rapids 45 F 2 Minnesota, N USA

Cooper Creek 149 B 5 *var.* Barcoo, Cooper's Creek. River, S Australia

Coos Bay 46 A 3 Oregon, NW USA

Cootamundra 149 C 6 New South Wales, SE Australia

Copacabana 61 E 4 W Bolivia

Copenhagen *see* København

Copiapó 64 B 3 *hist.* San Francisco de Selva . N Chile

Copiapó 57 B 5 N Chile

Copperas Cove 49 G 3 Texas, S USA

Coppermine 37 E 3 *var.* Qurlurtuuq. Northwest Territories, NW Canada

Coquilhatville *see* Mbandaka

Coquimbo 64 B 3 N Chile

Corabia 108 B 5 S Romania

Coral Harbour 37 G 3 Southampton Island, NE Canada

Coral Sea 148 B 4 sea, W Pacific Ocean

Coral Sea Islands 148 E 3 Australian external territory. NE Australia

Corcaigh *see* Cork

Corcovado, Golfo 65 B 6 gulf, SE Pacific Ocean

Cordele 42 D 3 Georgia, SE USA

Cordillera Central 55 E 3 mountain range, C Dominican Republic

Cordillera Central 58 B 3 mountain range, W Colombia

Cordillera Central 139 E 1 mountain range, Luzon, N Philippines

Cordillera Occidental 58 B 3 mountain range, W Colombia

Cordillera Occidental 61 F 5 mountain range, Bolivia/Chile

Cordillera Occidental 60 D 4 mountain range, W Peru

Cordillera Oriental 61 F 4 mountain range, Bolivia

Córdoba 92 D 4 *var.* Cordoba, *Eng.* Cordova; *anc.* Corduba. SW Spain

Córdoba 64 C 4 C Argentina

Córdoba 51 F 4 E Mexico

Cordova 36 C 3 Alaska, NW USA

Córdova 60 D 4 SW Peru

Corfu *see* Kérkyra

Coria 92 C 3 W Spain

Corinth 42 C 1 Mississippi, S USA

Corinto 52 C 3 NW Nicaragua

Cork 89 A 6 *Ir.* Corcaigh. S Ireland

Corner Brook 39 G 3 Newfoundland and Labrador, E Canada

Corn Islands *see* Maíz, Islas del

Cornwallis Island 37 F 2 island, N Canada

Coro 58 C 1 *prev.* Santa Ana de Coro. NW Venezuela

Corocoro 61 F 4 W Bolivia

Coromandel 150 D 2 North Island, N New Zealand

Coromandel Coast 132 D 2 physical region, E India

Coromandel Peninsula 150 D 2 peninsula, North Island, N New Zealand

Coronado, Bahía de 53 E 5 inlet, E Pacific Ocean

Coronel Dorrego 65 C 5 E Argentina

Coronel Oviedo 64 D 2 SE Paraguay

Corozal 52 C 1 N Belize

Corozo Pando 58 D 2 C Venezuela

Corpus Christi 49 G 5 Texas, S USA

Corpus Christi Bay 49 G 5 bay, NW Gulf of Mexico

Corrib, Lough 89 A 5 *Ir.* Loch Coirib. Lake, W Ireland

Corrientes 64 D 3 NE Argentina

Corse 91 E 7 *Eng.* Corsica. Island, SE France

Corsica *see* Corse

Corsicana 49 G 3 Texas, S USA

Cortegana 92 C 4 S Spain

Cortés 53 E 5 *var.* Ciudad Cortés. SE Costa Rica

Cortina d'Ampezzo 96 C 1 NE Italy

Coruche 92 B 3 C Portugal

Çorum 116 D 3 *var.* Chorum. N Turkey

Çorun Çayı 117 E 3 river, NE Turkey

Corvallis 46 B 3 Oregon, NW USA
Corvo 92 A 5 *var.* Ilha do Corvo. Island, W Portugal
Corvo, Ilha do *see* Corvo
Cosenza 97 D 6 *anc.* Consentia. SW Italy
Cosne-Cours-sur-Loire 90 C 4 *var.* Cosne-sur-Loire; *anc.* Condate. C France
Costa Dorada *see* Daurada, Costa

Costa Rica
53 E 4 Republic, C Central America

Official name: Republic of Costa Rica **Date of formation:** 1821/1838 **Capital:** San José **Population:** 3.3 million **Total area:** 51,100 sq km (19,730 miles) **Languages:** Spanish*, English Creole, Bribri, Cabecar **Religions:** Catholic 95%, other 5% **Ethnic mix:** White/*mestizo* (Euro-Indian) 96%, Black 2%, Indian 2% **Government:** Multiparty republic **Currency:** Colón = 100 centimos

Costermansville *see* Bukavu
Cotagaita 61 G 5 S Bolivia
Côte d'Ivoire *see* Ivory Coast
Côte d'Or 90 D 4 cultural region, E France
Cotonou 75 F 5 *var.* Kotonu. S Benin
Cotswold Hills 89 D 6 *var.* Cotswolds. Hill range, S England, UK
Cotswolds *see* Cotswold Hills
Cottbus 94 D 4 *prev.* Kottbus. E Germany
Cottica 59 H 3 E Surinam
Cotyora *see* Ordu
Couentrey *see* Coventry
Couëron 90 B 4 France
Council Bluffs 45 F 4 Iowa, C USA
Courantyne River 59 G 4 *var.* Corantijn Rivier, Corentyne River. River, Guyana/Surinam
Courland Lagoon 106 A 4 *Ger.* Kurisches Haff, *Rus.* Kurskiy Zaliv. Lagoon, SE Baltic Sea
Courtrai *see* Kortrijk
Coutances 90 B 3 *anc.* Constantia. N France
Couvin 87 C 7 S Belgium
Coventry 89 D 6 *anc.* Couentrey. C England, UK
Covilhã 92 C 3 E Portugal
Cowan, Lake 147 C 6 lake, Western Australia, SW Australia
Coyhaique *see* Coihaique
Cozumel, Isla 51 H 3 island, SE Mexico
Cradock 78 C 5 S South Africa
Craig 44 C 4 Colorado, C USA
Craiova 108 B 5 SW Romania
Cranbrook 37 E 5 Alberta. SW Canada
Crawley 89 E 7 SE England, UK
Cremona 96 B 2 N Italy
Cres 100 A 3 *It.* Cherso; *anc.* Crexa. Island, W Croatia
Creston 45 F 4 Iowa, C USA
Crestview 42 D 3 Florida, SE USA
Crete *see* Kriti
Créteil 90 C 3 N France
Creuse 90 B 4 river, C France
Crewe 89 C 6 W England, UK
Crikvenica 100 A 2 *It.* Cirquenizza; *prev.* Crikvenica, Crjkvenica. NW Croatia
Crimea *see* Krym
Cristóbal 53 G 4 C Panama

Cristóbal Colón, Pico 58 B 1 mountain, N Colombia
Cristuru Secuiesc 108 C 4 *Ger.* Kreutz, *Hung.* Székelykeresztúr; *prev.* Cristur, Cristuru Săcuiesc, Sitaş Cristuru Szitás-Keresztúr, Szitás-Keresztúr. C Romania
Crna Gora *see* Montenegro
Crna Reka 101 E 6 river, S Macedonia

Croatia
100 B 2 *Ger.* Kroatien, *SCr.* Hrvatska. Republic, SE Europe

Official name: Republic of Croatia **Date of formation:** 1991 **Capital:** Zagreb **Population:** 4.9 million **Total area:** 56,540 sq km (21,830 sq miles) **Languages:** Croatian*, Serbian **Religions:** Roman Catholic 77%, Orthodox Catholic 11%, Protestant 1%, Muslim 1%, other 10% **Ethnic mix:** Croat 80%, Serb 12%, Hungarian, Slovenian, other 8% **Government:** Multiparty republic **Currency:** Kuna = 100 para

Crocker, Banjaran 138 D 3 *var.* Crocker Range. Mountain range, Borneo, E Malaysia
Crocker Range *see* Crocker, Banjaran
Crocodile *see* Limpopo
Croker Island 146 E 2 island, N Australia
Cromwell 151 B 7 South Island, SW New Zealand
Crooked Island 54 D 2 island, SE Bahamas
Crooked Island Passage 54 D 2 channel, N Caribbean Sea
Crookston 45 F 1 Minnesota, N USA
Crotone 97 E 6 *var.* Cotrone; *anc.* Crotona, Croton. SW Italy
Croydon 89 E 7 SE England, UK
Crozet Basin 141 B 6 undersea basin, S Indian Ocean
Crozet Islands 141 B 7 island group, W French Southern & Antarctic Territories
Crozet Plateau 141 B 6 *var.* Crozet Plateaus. Undersea plateau, SW Plateau
Crozet Plateaus *see* Crozet Plateau
Crystal Brook 149 B 6 South Australia, S Australia
Csaca *see* Čadca
Csorna 99 C 6 NW Hungary
Csurgó 99 C 7 SW Hungary
Cuamba 79 E 2 *prev.* Nova Freixo. N Mozambique
Cuando *see* Kwando
Cuango 77 C 7 NW Angola
Cuango *see* Kwango
Cuanza 69 C 5 *var.* Kwanza. River, C Angola
Cuauhtémoc 50 C 2 N Mexico
Cuautla 51 E 4 S Mexico

Cuba
54 B 2 Republic, N Caribbean Sea

Official name: Republic of Cuba **Date of formation:** 1902 **Capital:** Havana **Population:** 10.9 million **Total area:** 110,860 sq km (42,803 sq miles) **Languages:** Spanish*, English, French, Chinese **Religions:** Roman Catholic 85%, other 15% **Ethnic mix:** White 66%, Afro-European 22%, other 12% **Government:** Socialist republic **Currency:** Peso = 100 centavos

Cubal 78 B 2 W Angola
Cubango 78 B 2 *var.* Kuvango. *Port.* Vila Artur de Paiva, Vila da Ponte. C Angola
Cubango 78 B 2 *var.* Kavango, Kavengo, Kubango, Okavanggo, Okavango. River, S Africa
Cúcuta 58 C 2 *var.* San José de Cúcuta. N Colombia
Cuddapah 132 C 2 S India
Cue 147 B 5 Western Australia, W Australia
Cuenca 93 E 3 *anc.* Conca. C Spain
Cuenca 60 B 2 S Ecuador
Cuernavaca 51 E 4 S Mexico
Cuiabá 63 E 3 *prev.* Cuyabá. State capital, SW Brazil
Cuijck 86 D 4 SE Netherlands
Cúil Raithin *see* Coleraine
Cuito 78 B 2 *var.* Kwito. River, SE Angola
Cukai 138 B 3 *var.* Chukai, Kemaman. W Malaysia
Culiacán 50 C 3 *var.* Culiacán Rosales, Culiacán-Rosales. C Mexico
Cullera 93 F 3 E Spain
Cullman 42 C 2 Alabama, S USA
Culpepper Island *see* Darwin, Isla
Cumaná 59 E 1 NE Venezuela
Cumbal, Nevada de 58 A 4 mountain, SW Colombia
Cumberland 41 E 4 Maryland, NE USA
Cumberland Plateau 42 D 1 hill range, Alabama, S USA
Cumberland River 43 E 1 river, S USA
Cunene 78 A 3 *var.* Kunene. River, Angola/Namibia
Cuneo 96 A 2 *Fr.* Coni. NW Italy
Cunnamulla 149 C 5 Queensland, E Australia
Cuprija 100 D 4 C Yugoslavia
Curaçao 55 E 5 island, C Netherlands Antilles
Curicó 64 B 4 C Chile
Curitiba 63 F 4 *prev.* Curytiba. State capital, S Brazil
Curtea de Argeş 108 B 4 *var.* Curtea-de-Arges. S Romania
Curtea-de-Arges *see* Curtea de Argeş
Curtici 108 A 4 *Ger.* Kurtitsch, *Hung.* Kürtös. W Romania
Curtis Island 148 E 4 island, Queensland, SE Australia
Curuguaty 64 E 2 E Paraguay
Curytiba *see* Curitiba
Cusco 60 D 4 *var.* Cuzco. C Peru
Čusovoj *see* Chusovoy
Cusset 91 C 5 C France
Cutch, Rann of 134 B 4 *var.* Rann of Kachh, Rann of Kutch. Wetland, India/Pakistan
Cuttack 135 F 5 E India
Cuvier Plateau 141 E 5 undersea plateau, E Indian Ocean
Cuxhaven 94 B 2 NW Germany
Cuyabá *see* Cuiabá
Cuyuni 59 F 2 *var.* Río Cuyuni. River, Guyana/Venezuela
Cuyuni, Río *see* Cuyuni River
Cuzco *see* Cusco
Čvrsnica 100 C 4 mountain range, SW Bosnia & Herzegovina
Cyclades *see* Kykládes
Cymru *see* Wales

Cyprus
103 H4 Gk. Kypros, Turk. Kibris, Kibris Cumhuriyeti. Republic, SW Asia

Official name: Republic of Cyprus **Date of formation:** 1960/1983 **Capital:** Nicosia **Population:** 700,000 **Total area:** 9,251 sq km (3,572 sq miles) **Languages:** Greek*, Turkish, other **Religions:** Greek Orthodox 77%, Muslim 18%, other 5% **Ethnic mix:** Greek 77%, Turkish 18%, other (mainly British) 5% **Government:** Multiparty republic **Currency:** Cypriot £/Turkish lira

Cyprus
103 H4 Gk. Kypros, Turk. Kibris, Kibris. Island, NE Mediterranean Sea

Czech Republic
99 B 5 *Cz.* Česká Republika. Republic, C Europe

Official name: Czech Republic **Date of formation:** 1993 **Capital:** Prague **Population:** 10.4 million **Total area:** 78,370 sq km (30,260 sq miles) **Languages:** Czech*, Slovak, Romany **Religions:** Roman Catholic 44%, Protestant 6%, other Christian 12%, other 38% **Ethnic mix:** Czech 85%, Moravian 13%, other 2% **Government:** Multiparty republic **Currency:** Koruna = 100 halura

Częstochowa 98 C 4 *Ger.* Czenstochau, Tschenstochau, *Rus.* Czenstokhov. S Poland
Człuchów 98 C 3 *Ger.* Schlochau. NW Poland

D

Dabajuro 58 C 1 NW Venezuela
Dabeiba 58 B 2 NW Colombia
Dąbrowa Tarnowska 99 D 5 SE Poland
Dabryn' 107 C 8 *Rus.* Dobryn'. SE Belorussia
Dacca *see* Dhākā
Dadanawa 59 F 4 SW Guyana
Dafang 129 B 5 E China
Dagana 74 B 3 N Senegal
Dagda 106 D 4 SE Latvia
Dagupan 139 E 1 *off.* Dagupan City. Luzon, N Philippines
Dagupan City *see* Dagupan
Da Hinggan Ling 127 G 1 *Eng.* Great Khingan Range. Mountain range, NE China
Dahm, Ramlat 121 B 6 desert, NW Yemen
Daimiel 92 D 3 C Spain
Daimoniá 105 B 7 S Greece
Daingin, Bá an *see* Dingle Bay
Dakar 74 B 3 country capital, W Senegal
Dakhla Oasis 72 B 2 *var.* Wāhat el Dākhla. Oasis, C Egypt
Dakoro 75 G 3 S Niger
Đakovica 101 D 5 *var.* Djakovica, *Alb.* Gjakovë. SW Yugoslavia
Đakovo 100 C 3 *var.* Djakovo, *Hung.* Diakovár. E Croatia
Dakshin *see* Deccan
Dalaman 116 A 4 Turkey
Dalandzadgad 127 E 3 S Mongolia
Dalarna 85 C 5 *prev. Eng.* Dalecarlia. Cultural region, C Sweden

Đa Lat 137 E 6 S Vietnam
Dalby 149 D 5 Queensland,
   E Australia
Dalecarlia *see* Dalarna
Dale City 41 E 4 Virginia, NE USA
Dalhart 49 E 1 New Mexico,
   SW USA
Dalian 128 D 4 *var.* Dairen,
   Dalien, Jay Dairen, Lüda,Ta-lien,
   Rus. Dalny. NE China
Dallas 49 G 3 Texas, S USA
Dalmacija 100 B 4 *Eng.* Dalmatia,
   Ger. Dalmatien, *It.* Dalmazia.
   Cultural region S Croatia
Dalton 42 D 1 Georgia, SE USA
Daly Waters 148 A 2 Northern
   Territory, N Australia
Damachava 107 A 6
   var. Damachova, *Pol.* Domaczewo,
   Rus. Domachëvo. SW Belorussia
Damān 134 C 5 *Port.* Damão.
   W India
Damão *see* Damān
Damara 76 C 4
   S Central African Republic
Damascus *see* Damascus
Damietta *see* Dumyât
Dammām 120 C 4 *var.* Ad
   Dammān. NE Saudi Arabia
Damoûr 119 A 5 *var.* Ad Dāmūr.
   W Lebanon
Dampier 146 B 4 Western Australia,
   W Australia
Dampier, Selat 139 G 4 strait,
   W Pacific Ocean
Damqawt 121 D 6 *var.* Damqut.
   E Yemen
Damqut *see* Damqawt
Damxung 126 C 5 W China
Danané 74 D 5 W Ivory Coast
Đà Nâng 137 E 5 *prev.* Tourane.
   C Vietnam
Danborg *see* Daneborg
Danbury 41 F 3 Connecticut,
   NE USA
Dandong 128 E 3 *var.* Tan-tung;
   prev. An-tung. NE China
Daneborg 83 E 3 *var.* Danborg.
   E Greenland
Dangara *see* Danghara
Danghara 123 E 3 *Rus.* Dangara.
   SW Tajikistan
Dangriga 52 C 1 *prev.* Stann Creek.
   E Belize
Danlí 52 D 3 S Honduras
Danmark Havn 83 E 2 E Greenland
Danmarksstraedet *see*
   Denmark Strait
Dannenberg 94 C 3 N Germany
Dannevirke 150 D 4 North Island,
   C New Zealand
Danube 81 E 4 *Bul.* Dunav, *Cz.*
   Dunaj, *Ger.* Donau, *Hung.* Duna,
   Rom. Dunărea. River, C Europe
Danube, Mouths of the 108 D 5
   Rom. Delta Dunării. Delta,
   Romania/Ukraine
Danubian Plain *see*
   Dunavska Ravnina
Danum *see* Doncaster
Danville 41 E 5 Virginia, NE USA
Danville 40 B 4 Illinois, N USA
Dan Xian 129 C 7 *var.* Danxian,
   Nada. Hainan Dao, S China
Danzig, Gulf of 98 C 2 *var.* Gulf
   of Gdańsk, *Ger.* Danziger Bucht,
   Pol. Zakota Gdańska, *Rus.*
   Gdan'skaya Bukhta. Gulf,
   S Baltic Sea
Daqm *see* Duqm
Dar'ā 119 B 5 *var.* Der'a, *Fr.* Déraa.
   SW Syria

Darabani 108 C 3 NW Romania
Daraut-Kurgan *see* Daroot-Korgon
Darbënai 106 B 3 NW Lithuania
Dardanelles *see* Çanakkale Boğazı
Dar-el-Beida *see* Casablanca
Dar es Salaam 73 D 7 E Tanzania
Darfield 151 C 6 South Island,
   C New Zealand
Darfur 72 A 4 *var.* Darfur Massif.
   Mountain range, W Sudan
Darfur Massif *see* Darfur
Dargaville 150 D 2 North Island,
   N New Zealand
Darhan 127 E 2 N Mongolia
Darién, Golfo del *see* Darien,
   Gulf of
Darien, Gulf of 53 H 4
   Sp. Golfo del Darién. Gulf,
   SE Caribbean Sea
Darién, Serranía del 53 H 5
   mountain range,
   Colombia/Panama
Dario *see* Ciudad Darío
Dariorigum *see* Vannes
Darjeeling *see* Darjiling
Darjiling 135 F 3 *prev.* Darjeeling.
   NE India
Darling 145 C 6 river,
   New South Wales, SE Australia
Darling Downs 149 D 5 hill range,
   Queensland, SE Australia
Darlington 89 D 5 N England, UK
Darmian 120 E 3 E Iran
Darmstadt 95 B 5 SW Germany
Darnah 71 G 2 *var.* Dérna. NE Libya
Darnley, Cape 154 D 3 headland,
   Antarctica
Daroca 93 E 2 NE Spain
Daroot-Korgon 123 F 3 *var.*
   Daraut-Kurgan. SW Kyrgyzstan
Dartmoor 89 C 7 heathland,
   SW England, UK
Dartmouth 39 F 4 Nova Scotia,
   SE Canada
Darvaza 122 C 2 *Turkm.* Derweze.
   C Turkmenistan
Darwin 148 A 2 *prev.* Palmerston,
   Port Darwin. Territory capital,
   Northern Territory, N Australia
Darwin, Isla 60 A 4 *var.* Culpepper
   Island. Island, Galapagos Islands,
   E Pacific Ocean
Dashkawka 107 D 6
   Rus. Dashkovka. E Belorussia
Dashkhovuz 122 C 2
   Turkm. Dashhowuz; *prev.* Tashauz.
   N Turkmenistan
Dashkovka *see* Dashkawka
Dasht 120 D 2 N Iran
Datong 128 C 3 *var.* Tatung,
   Ta-t'ung. N China
Daugavpils 106 D 4 *Ger.* Dünaburg;
   prev. Rus. Dvinsk. SE Latvia
Daung Kyun 137 B 6 island,
   S Burma
Dauphiné 91 D 5 cultural region,
   E France
Daurada, Costa 93 G 2 *var.* Costa
   Dorada. Coastal region, E Spain
Dävangere 132 C 2 W India
Davao 139 F 2 *off.* Davao City.
   Mindanao, S Philippines
Davao City *see* Davao
Davao Gulf 139 F 3 gulf,
   W Pacific Ocean
Davenport 45 G 3 Iowa, C USA
David 53 F 5 W Panama
Davie Ridge 141 A 5 undersea
   ridge, W Indian Ocean
Davis 154 D 3 research station,
   Antarctica
Davis 47 B 6 California, W USA

Davis Mountains 48 D 3 mountain
   range, Texas, S USA
Davis Sea 154 D 3 sea,
   S Indian Ocean
Davis Strait 82 B 3 strait, Baffin
   Bay/Labrador Sea
Davlekanovo 111 D 6
   W Russian Federation
Dawei *see* Tavoy
Dawra 70 B 3 *var.* Daora, Daoura.
   NW Western Sahara
Dax 91 B 6 *var.* Ax; *anc.* Aquae
   Augustae, Aquae Tarbelicae.
   SW France
Dayr az Zawr 118 D 3 *var.* Deir ez
   Zor. E Syria
Dayton 40 C 4 Ohio, N USA
Daytona Beach 43 E 4
   Florida, SE USA
De Aar 78 C 5 C South Africa
Dead Sea 119 E 7 *var.* Bahret Lut,
   Lacus Asphaltites, *Ar.* Al Baḥr al
   Mayyit, Baḥrat Lūt, *Heb.* Yam
   HaMelaḥ. Salt lake, Israel/Jordan
Deán Funes 64 C 3 C Argentina
Death Valley 47 D 6 valley,
   California, W USA
Debar 101 D 6 *var.* Dibra,
   Turk. Debre. W Macedonia
De Bildt *see* De Bilt
De Bilt 86 C 3 *var.* De Bildt.
   C Netherlands
Debrecen 99 D 6 *Ger.* Debreczin,
   Rom. Debreţin; *prev.* Debreczen.
   E Hungary
Decatur 42 C 2 Alabama, S USA
Decatur 40 B 4 Illinois, N USA
Deccan 132 C 1 *Hind.* Dakshin.
   Plateau, C India
Děčín 98 A 4 *Ger.* Tetschen.
   NW Czech Republic
Dedemsvaart 86 E 3 E Netherlands
Dee 88 C 3 river, E Scotland, UK
Deering 36 C 2 Alaska, NW USA
De Funiak Springs 42 D 3 Florida,
   SE USA
Deggendorf 95 D 6 SE Germany
Deh Bīd 120 D 4 C Iran
Deinze 87 B 6 NW Belgium
Deir ez Zor *see* Dayr az Zawr
Deirgeirt, Loch *see* Derg, Lough
Dej 108 B 3 *Hung.* Dés; *prev.* Deés.
   NW Romania
De Jouwer *see* Joure
Dékoa 76 C 4
   C Central African Republic
De Land 43 E 4 Florida, SE USA
Delano 47 C 7 California, W USA
Delārām 122 D 5 SW Afghanistan
Delaware 41 F 4 *off.* State of
   Delaware; *nicknames* Blue Hen
   State, Diamond State, First State.
   State, E USA
Delaware 40 D 4 Ohio, N USA
Delaware Bay 41 F 5 bay,
   W Atlantic Ocean
Delft 86 C 4 W Netherlands
Delfzijl 86 E 1 NE Netherlands
Delgo 72 B 3 N Sudan
Delhi 134 D 3 *var.* Dehli, *Hind.* Dilli;
   hist. Shahjahanabad. N India
Delicias 50 C 2 *var.* Ciudad
   Delicias. N Mexico
Delmenhorst 94 B 3 NW Germany
Del Rio 49 F 4 Texas, S USA
Demba 77 D 6 S Congo (Zaire)
Dembia 76 D 4
   SE Central African Republic
Demchok 126 A 4 *var.*
   Dêmqog. Disputed region,
   China/India

Deming 48 C 3 New Mexico,
   SW USA
Demmin 94 D 2 NE Germany
Dêmqog 126 A 4 *var.* Demchok.
   Disputed region, China/India
Denali *see* McKinley, Mount
Denau *see* Denow
Dender 87 B 6 *Fr.* Dendre. River,
   W Belgium
Dendre *see* Dender
Denekamp 86 E 3 E Netherlands
Den Ham 86 E 3 E Netherlands
Den Helder 86 C 2
   NW Netherlands
Denia 93 F 4 E Spain
Deniliquin 149 C 7
   New South Wales, SE Australia
Denison 49 G 2 Texas, S USA
Denison 45 F 3 Iowa, C USA
Denizli 116 B 4 SW Turkey

Denmark
   85 A 7 *Dan.* Danmark,
   anc. Hafnia. Monarchy, N Europe

Official name: Kingdom of
Denmark **Date of formation:**
AD 960/1953 **Capital:** Copenhagen
Population: 5.2 million
Total area: 43,069 sq km
(16,629 sq miles) **Languages:**
Danish* **Religions:** Evangelical
Lutheran 91% other Christian 9%
Ethnic mix: Danish 96%, Faeroese
and Inuit 1%, other 3% **Government:**
Constitutional monarchy
Currency: Krone = 100 øre

Denmark Strait 82 D 4
   var. Danmarksstraedet. Strait,
   N Atlantic Ocean
Dennery 55 F 1 E Saint Lucia
Denow 123 E 3 *Rus.* Denau.
   S Uzbekistan
Denpasar 138 D 5 *prev.* Paloe. Bali,
   C Indonesia
Denton 49 G 2 Texas, S USA
Denver 44 D 4 state capital,
   Colorado, C USA
Dera Ghāzi Khān 134 C 2 *var.* Dera
   Ghāzikhān. C Pakistan
Dera Ghāzikhān *see* Dera Ghāzi
   Khān
Đeravica 101 D 5 mountain,
   SW Yugoslavia
Derbent 111 C 8
   SW Russian Federation
Derby 89 D 6 C England, UK
Dergachi *see* Derhachi
Derg, Lough 89 A 6 *Ir.* Loch
   Deirgeirt. Lake, W Ireland
Derhachi 109 G 2 *Rus.* Dergachi.
   E Ukraine
De Ridder 42 A 3 Louisiana,
   S USA
Dérna *see* Darnah
Dertosa *see* Tortosa
Derventa 100 C 3
   N Bosnia & Herzegovina
Derweze *see* Darvaza
Deschutes River 46 B 3 river,
   Oregon, NW USA
Desē 72 D 4 *var.* Desse, *It.* Dessie.
   N Ethiopia
Deseado 65 B 7 river, S Argentina
Desertas, Ilhas 70 A 2 island group,
   Madeira, E Atlantic Ocean
Des Moines 45 F 4 state capital,
   Iowa, C USA
Desna 109 E 1 river,
   Russian Federation/Ukraine
Dessau 94 C 4 E Germany
Destêrro *see* Florianópolis

Detroit 40 D 3 Michigan, N USA
Detroit Lakes 45 F 2
 Minnesota, N USA
Deurne 87 D 5 SE Netherlands
Deutsch-Eylau *see* Iława
Deutsch Krone *see* Wałcz
Deva 108 B 4 *Ger.* Diemrich,
 Hung. Déva. W Romania
Devana *see* Aberdeen
Deventer 86 D 3 E Netherlands
Devils Lake 45 E 1 Missouri, C USA
Devoll *see* Devollit, Lumi i
Devollit, Lumi i 101 D 6 *var.*
 Devoll. River, SE Albania
Devon Island 37 F 2 *prev.* North
 Devon Island. Island, NE Canada
Devonport 149 C 8 Tasmania,
 SE Australia
Devrek 116 C 2 N Turkey
Dexter 45 G 5 Missouri, C USA
Deynau 122 D 3 *var.* Dyanev,
 Turkm. Dänew. NE Turkmenistan
Dezfūl 120 C 3 *var.* Dizful. SW Iran
Dezhou 128 D 4 NE China
Dhahran *see* Aẕ Ẕahrān
Dhākā 135 G 4 *prev.* Dacca. Country
 capital, C Bangladesh
Dhanbād 135 F 4 NE India
Dhārwād 132 B 1 *prev.* Dharwar.
 SW India
Dhíkti Ori *see* Díkti
Dhomokós *see* Domokós
Dhráma *see* Dráma
Dhrepanon, Akra *see* Drépano, Ákra
Dhún na nGall, Bá *see* Donegal Bay
Diamantina, Chapada 63 F 3
 mountain range, E Brazil
Diamantina Fracture Zone 141 E 6
 fracture zone, E Indian Ocean
D'Iberville 42 C 3
 Mississippi, S USA
Dibio *see* Dijon
Dibrugarh 135 H 3 NE India
Dickinson 44 D 2 North Dakota,
 N USA
Didymóteicho 104 D 3 *var.*
 Dhidhimótikhon, Didimotiho.
 NE Greece
Diedenhofen *see* Thionville
Diekirch 87 D 8 C Luxembourg
Diên Biên 136 D 3 *var.* Bien Bien,
 Dien Bien Phu. NW Vietnam
Diepenbeek 87 D 6 NE Belgium
Diepholz 94 B 3 NW Germany
Dieppe 90 C 2 N France
Dieren 86 D 4 E Netherlands
Differdange 87 D 8
 SW Luxembourg
Digby 39 F 5 Nova Scotia,
 SE Canada
Digne 91 D 6 *var.* Digne-les-Bains.
 SE France
Digne-les-Bains *see* Digne
Digoel *see* Digul, Sungai
Digoin 90 C 4 C France
Digul 139 H 5 *prev.* Digoel. River,
 New Guinea, E Indonesia
Dijon 90 D 4 *anc.* Dibio. C France
Dikhil 72 D 4 SW Djibouti
Dikson 114 D 2
 N Russian Federation
Díkti 105 D 8 *var.* Dhíkti Ori.
 Mountain range, Kríti, SE Greece
Dili 139 F 5 *var.* Dilli, Dilly. Timor,
 C Indonesia
Dilia 75 G 3 *var.* Dillia. River,
 SE Niger
Dilijan 117 G 2 *Rus.* Dilizhan.
 NE Armenia
Di Linh 137 E 6 S Vietnam
Dilizhan *see* Dilijan

Dillia *see* Dilia
Dilling 72 B 4 *var.* Ad Dalanj.
 C Sudan
Dillon 44 B 2 Montana, NW USA
Dilolo 77 D 8 S Congo (Zaire)
Dimashq 119 B 5 *var.* Ash Shām,
 Esh Sham, *Eng.* Damascus,
 Fr. Damas, *It.* Damasco.
 Country capital, SW Syria
Dimitrovgrad 111 C 6
 W Russian Federation
Dimitrovgrad 104 D 3 S Bulgaria
Dimitrovo *see* Pernik
Dimlang 75 G 4 *var.* Vogel Peak.
 Mountain, E Nigeria
Dimona 119 A 7 S Israel
Dimovo 104 B 1 NW Bulgaria
Dinājpur 135 G 3 NW Bangladesh
Dinan 90 A 3 NW France
Dinant 87 C 7 S Belgium
Dinar 116 B 4 SW Turkey
Dinara *see* Dinaric Alps
Dinaric Alps 100 C 4 *var.* Dinara.
 Mountain range, Bosnia &
 Herzegovina/Croatia
Dindigul 132 C 3 SE India
Dingle Bay 89 A 6 *Ir.* Bá an
 Daingin. Inlet, NE Atlantic Ocean
Dinguiraye 74 C 4 N Guinea
Diourbel 74 B 3 W Senegal
Direction, Cape 148 C 2 headland,
 Queensland, NE Australia
Dirē Dawa 73 D 5 E Ethiopia
Dirk Hartog Island 147 A 5 island,
 W Australia
Dirra 72 A 4 Sudan
Dirschau *see* Tczew
Disappointment, Lake 146 C 4
 salt lake, Western Australia,
 W Australia
Discovery Bay 128 A 1 *Cant.*
 Tai Pak Wan. W Hong Kong
Dispur 135 G 3 NE India
Divinópolis 63 F 4 SE Brazil
Divo 74 D 5 S Ivory Coast
Diyarbakır 117 E 4 *var.* Diarbekr;
 anc. Amida. SE Turkey
Dizful *see* Dezfūl
Djambala 77 B 6 C Congo
Djambi *see* Hari, Batang
Djanet 71 E 4 *prev.* Fort Charlet.
 SE Algeria
Djelfa 70 D 2 *var.* El Djelfa.
 N Algeria
Djéma 76 D 4
 E Central African Republic
Djember *see* Jember
Djérem 75 H 5 river, C Cameroon
Djibouti 72 D 4 *var.* Jibuti. Country
 capital, E Djibouti

Djibouti
 72 D 4 *var.* Jibuti; *prev.* French
 Somaliland, French Territory
 of the Afars and Issas, *Fr.* Côte
 Française des Somalis,
 Territoire Français des Afars et
 des Issas. Republic,
 NE Africa

Official name: Republic of Djibouti
Date of formation: 1977
Capital: Djibouti **Population:**
500,000 **Total area:** 23,200 sq km
(8,958 sq miles) **Languages:**
Arabic*, French*, Somali :
Religions: Christian 87%, other 13%
Ethnic mix: Issa 35%, Afar 20%,
Gadaboursis and Isaaks 28%,
other 17% **Government:**
Single-party republic
Currency: Franc = 100 centimes

Djiguéni 74 D 3 SE Mauritania
Djisr el Choghour *see*
 Jisr ash Shughūr
Djourab, Erg du 76 C 2 desert,
 N Chad
Djúpivogur 83 E 5 SE Iceland
Dneprodzerzhinskoye
 Vodokhranilishche *see*
 Dniprodzerzhyns'ke
 Vodoskhovyshche
Dneprorudnoye *see* Dniprorudne
Dnieper 81 F 4 *Bel.* Dnyapro,
 Rus. Dnepr, *Ukr.* Dnipro. River,
 W Europe
Dnieper Lowland 109 F 2
 Bel. Prydnyaprowskaya Nizina,
 Ukr. Prydniprovs'ka Nyzovyna.
 Lowlands, Belorussia/Ukraine
Dniester 108 D 3 *var.* Tyras, *Rom.*
 Nistru, *Rus.* Dnestr, *Ukr.* Dnister.
 River, Moldavia/Ukraine
Dniprodzerzhyns'k 109 F 3
 Rus. Dneprodzerzhinsk;
 prev. Kamenskoye. C Ukraine
Dniprodzerzhyns'ke
 Vodoskhovyshche 109 F 3
 Rus. Dneprodzerzhinskoye
 Vodokhranilishche. Reservoir,
 NE Ukraine
Dnipropetrovs'k 109 F 3 *Rus.*
 Dnepropetrovsk; *prev.*
 Yekaterinoslav. E Ukraine
Dniprorudne 109 F 3
 Rus. Dneprorudnoye. SE Ukraine
Doba 76 C 4 S Chad
Döbeln 94 D 4 E Germany
Doboj 100 C 3
 N Bosnia & Herzegovina
Dobre Miasto 98 D 2
 Ger. Guttstadt. N Poland
Dobrich 104 E 2 *var.* Dobrič,
 Rom. Bazargic; *prev.* Tolbukhin.
 NE Bulgaria
Dobrush 107 D 8 SE Belorussia
Dobryn' *see* Dabryn'
Dodecanese *see* Dodekánisos
Dodekánisos 105 D 6 *var.* Nóties
 Sporádes, *Eng.* Dodecanese; *prev.*
 Dhodhekánisos. Island group,
 SE Greece
Dodge City 45 E 5 Kansas, C USA
Dodoma 73 C 7 country capital,
 C Tanzania
Dogana 96 E 1 NE San Marino
Dōgo 131 B 6 island, Oki-shotō,
 W Japan
Dogondoutchi 75 F 3 SW Niger
Dogrular *see* Pravda
Doğu Karadeniz Dağları 117 E 3
 var. Anadolu Daēları. Mountain
 range, NE Turkey
Doha *see* Ad Dawḥah
Dokkum 86 D 1 N Netherlands
Dokuchayevs'k 109 G 3 *var.*
 Dokuchayevsk. SE Ukraine
Dokuchayevsk *see* Dokuchayevs'k
Doldrums Fracture Zone 66 C 4
 fracture zone, W Atlantic Ocean
Dôle 90 D 4 E France
Dolina *see* Dolyna
Dolinskaya *see* Dolyns'ka
Dolisie 77 B 6 *prev.* Loubomo.
 S Congo
Dolomitiche, Alpi 96 C 1
 var. Dolomiti, *Eng.* Dolomites.
 Mountain range, NE Italy
Dolores 64 D 4 W Uruguay
Dolores 64 D 4 E Argentina
Dolores 52 B 3 N Guatemala
Dolores Hidalgo 51 E 4
 var. Ciudad de Dolores Hidalgo.
 C Mexico

Dolyna 108 B 2 *Rus.* Dolina.
 W Ukraine
Dolyns'ka 109 F 3 *Rus.* Dolinskaya.
 S Ukraine
Dombås 85 B 5 S Norway
Domesnes, Cape *see* Kolkasrags
Domeyko 64 B 3 N Chile

Dominica
 55 H 4 Republic, E Caribbean Sea

Official name: Commonwealth of
Dominica **Date of formation:** 1978
Capital: Roseau **Population:** 72,000
Total area: 750 sq km (290 sq miles)
Languages: English*, French Creole,
Carib, Cocoy **Religions:** Roman
Catholic 77%, Protestant 15%, other
8% **Ethnic mix:** Black 98%, Indian 2%
Government: Multiparty republic
Currency: E. Caribbean $ = 100 cents

Dominican Republic
 55 E 3 Republic, N Caribbean Sea

Official name: Dominican Republic
Date of formation: 1865 **Capital:**
Santo Domingo **Population:**
7.6 million **Total area:** 48,730 sq km
(18,815 sq miles) **Languages:**
Spanish*, French Creole
Religions: Roman Catholic 95%,
other 5% **Ethnic mix:** Afro-European
73%, White 16%, Black 11%
Government: Multiparty republic
Currency: Peso = 100 centavos

Domokós 105 B 5 *var.* Dhomokós.
 C Greece
Don 81 F 3 *var.* Duna, Tanais. River,
 SW Russian Federation
Donauwörth 95 C 6 S Germany
Don Benito 92 C 4 W Spain
Doncaster 89 D 5 *anc.* Danum.
 N England, UK
Dondo 78 B 1 NW Angola
Donegal 89 A 5 *Ir.* Dún na nGall.
 NW Ireland
Donegal Bay 89 A 5 *Ir.* Bá Dhún na
 nGall. Bay, E Atlantic Ocean
Donets 109 G 2 river,
 Russian Federation/Ukraine
Donets'k 109 G 3 *Rus.* Donetsk;
 prev. Stalino. E Ukraine
Dongfang 129 B 7 Hainan Dao,
 S China
Dongguan 129 C 6 SW China
Đông Ha 136 E 4 C Vietnam
Dong Hai *see* East China Sea
Đông Hới 136 E 4 C Vietnam
Dongola 72 B 3 *var.* Donqola,
 Dunqula. N Sudan
Dongou 77 C 5 NE Congo
Dongting Hu 129 C 5 *var.*
 Tung-t'ing Hu. Lake, SE China
Dongying 128 D 4 NE China
Donnybrook 147 B 7 SW Australia
Donostia-San Sebastián 93 E 1
 N Spain
Door Peninsula 40 C 2 peninsula,
 Wisconsin, N USA
Dooxo Nugaaleed 73 E 5 *var.* Nogal
 Valley. Valley, E Somalia
Dordogne 91 B 5 cultural region,
 SW France
Dordogne 91 B 5 river, W France
Dordrecht 86 C 4 *var.* Dordt, Dort.
 SW Netherlands
Doré Lake 37 F 5 Saskatchewan,
 C Canada
Dorohoi 108 C 3 NE Romania
Dorotea 84 C 4 N Sweden
Dorre Island 147 A 5 island,
 W Australia

Dortmund 94 A 4 W Germany
Dos Hermanas 92 C 5 S Spain
Dospat 104 C 3 SW Bulgaria
Dothan 42 D 3 Alabama, S USA
Dotnuva 106 B 4 C Lithuania
Douai 90 C 2 *prev.* Douay,
anc. Duacum. N France
Douala 77 A 5 *var.* Duala.
W Cameroon
Doubtful Island Bay 147 C 7 bay,
SE Indian Ocean
Douglas 89 C 5 dependent territory
capital, E Isle of Man, British Isles
Douglas 43 E 3 Georgia, SE USA
Douglas 48 C 3 Arizona, SW USA
Douglas 44 C 3 Wyoming, C USA
Douma *see* Dūmā
Douro 92 B 2 *Sp.* Duero. River,
Portugal/Spain
Douro, Rio *see* Duero
Dover 89 E 7 *Fr.* Douvres; *Lat.*
Dubris Portus. SE England, UK
Dover 149 C 8 Tasmania,
SE Australia
Dover 41 G 3
New Hampshire, NE USA
Dover 41 F 4 state capital,
Delaware, NE USA
Dover, Strait of 90 C 2 *var.* Straits of
Dover, *Fr.* Pas de Calais. Channel,
NE Atlantic Ocean
Dovrefjell 85 B 5 mountain range,
S Norway
Downpatrick 89 C 5 *Ir.* Dún
Pádraig. SE Northern Ireland, UK
Dōzen 131 B 6 island, Oki-shotō,
W Japan
Drachten 86 D 2 N Netherlands
Drăgăşani 108 B 5 SW Romania
Dragoman 104 B 2 W Bulgaria
Dragon's Mouth, The 59 F 1 strait,
W Atlantic Ocean
Dra, Hamada du 70 C 3 *var.*
Hammada du Drâa, Haut Plateau
du Dra. Plateau, W Algeria
Drahichyn 107 B 6 *Pol.* Drohiczyn
Poleski, *Rus.* Drogichin.
SW Belorussia
Drakensberg 78 D 5 mountain
range, Lesotho/South Africa
Drake Passage 153 F 5 passage,
Atlantic Ocean/Pacific Ocean
Dralfa 104 D 2 N Bulgaria
Dráma 104 C 3 *var.* Dhráma.
NE Greece
Dramburg *see* Drawsko Pomorskie
Drammen 85 B 6 S Norway
Drava 100 C 3 *var.* Drau,
Eng. Drave, *Hung.* Dráva. River,
C Europe
Drawsko Pomorskie 98 B 3
Ger. Dramburg. NW Poland
Drépano, Akra 104 C 4 *var.* Akra
Dhrepanon. Headland, N Greece
Drepanum *see* Trapani
Dresden 94 D 4 E Germany
Drina 100 D 4 river, Bosnia &
Herzegovina/Yugoslavia
Drini i Zi 101 D 5 *var.* Black Drin,
Alb. Lumi i Drinit të Zi, *SCr.* Crni
Drim. River, Albania/Macedonia
Drissa 107 D 5 *Bel.* Drysa. River,
Belorussia/Russian Federation
Drobeta-Turnu Severin 108 B 5
prev. Turnu Severin. SW Romania
Drogheda 89 B 5 *Ir.* Droichead
Átha. NE Ireland
Drohobych 108 B 2 *Pol.* Drohobycz,
Rus. Drogobych. NW Ukraine
Droichead Átha *see* Drogheda
Drôme 91 D 6 cultural region,
SE France

Dronning Maud Land *see*
Queen Maud Land
Drug *see* Durg
Drummond Island 40 D 2 island,
Michigan, N USA
Drummondville 39 E 4 Québec,
SE Canada
Druskienniki *see* Druskininkai
Druskininkai 107 B 5 *Pol.*
Druskienniki. S Lithuania
Dryden 38 B 3 Ontario, C Canada
Drysa *see* Drissa
Drysdale 146 D 3 river, N Australia
Duala *see* Douala
Dubai *see* Dubayy
Dubăsari 108 D 3 *Rus.* Dubossary.
NE Moldavia
Dubawnt 37 F 4 river, Northwest
Territories, C Canada
Dubayy 120 D 4 *Eng.* Dubai.
NE United Arab Emirates
Dubbo 149 D 6 New South Wales,
SE Australia
Dublin 89 B 6 *Ir.* Baile Átha Cliath;
anc. Eblana. Country capital,
E Ireland
Dublin 43 E 2 Georgia, SE USA
Dubno 108 C 2 NW Ukraine
Dubossary *see* Dubăsari
Dubrovnik 101 A 8 *It.* Ragusa.
SE Croatia
Dubuque 45 G 3 Iowa, C USA
Dudelange 87 D 8 *var.* Forge du
Sud, *Ger.* Dudelingen.
S Luxembourg
Duero 92 D 2 *Port.* Rio Douro.
River, Portugal/Spain
Duero *see* Douro
Duesseldorf *see* Düsseldorf
Duffel 87 C 5 C Belgium
Dufour Spitze 95 A 8 *var.* Punta
Dufour, *It.* Pizzo Dufour.
Mountain, Italy/Switzerland
Dugi Otok 100 A 3 *var.* Isola
Grossa, *It.* Isola Lunga. Island,
W Croatia
Duisburg 94 A 4 *prev.*
Duisburg-Hamborn. W Germany
Duisburg-Hamborn *see* Duisburg
Duitama 58 B 3 C Colombia
Duiven 86 D 4 E Netherlands
Duk Faiwil 73 B 5 Sudan
Dulan Xian 126 D 4 C China
Dulce, Golfo 53 E 5 gulf,
E Pacific Ocean
Dulce, Golfo *see* Izabal, Lago de
Dülmen 94 A 4 W Germany
Dulovo 104 E 1 NE Bulgaria
Duluth 45 G 2 Minnesota, N USA
Dūmā 119 B 5 *Fr.* Douma. SW Syria
Dumas 49 E 1 Texas, S USA
Dumfries 88 C 4 S Scotland, UK
Dumont d'Urville 154 D 4 research
station, Antarctica
Dumyât 72 B 1 *Eng.* Damietta.
N Egypt
Dunării, Delta *see* Danube,
Mouths of the
Dunaújváros 99 C 7 *prev.*
Dunapentele, Sztálinváros.
C Hungary
Dunavska Ravnina 104 C 2 *Eng.*
Danubian Plain. Plain, N Bulgaria
Duncan 49 G 2 Oklahoma, C USA
Dundalk 89 B 5 *Ir.* Dún Dealgan.
NE Ireland
Dundalk 41 F 4 Maryland, NE USA
Dún Dealgan *see* Dundalk
Dundee 88 C 4 E Scotland, UK
Dundee 78 D 4 E South Africa

Dunedin 151 B 7 South Island,
SW New Zealand
Dunfermline 88 C 4
C Scotland, UK
Dungu 77 E 5 NE Congo (Zaire)
Dungun 138 B 3 *var.* Kuala
Dungun. W Malaysia
Dunholme *see* Durham
Dunkerque 90 C 2 *Eng.* Dunkirk,
Flem. Duinekerke; *prev.*
Dunquerque. N France
Dún Laoghaire 89 B 6
Eng. Dunleary; *prev.* Kingstown.
E Ireland
Dún na nGall *see* Donegal
Dupnitsa 104 C 2 *prev.* Stanke
Dimitrov, Marek. W Bulgaria
Duqm 121 E 5 *var.* Daqm. E Oman
Durance 91 D 6 river, SE France
Durango 50 D 3 *var.* Victoria de
Durango. W Mexico
Durango 44 C 5 Colorado, C USA
Durankulak 104 E 1 *Rom.* Răcari;
prev. Blatnitsa, Duranulac.
NE Bulgaria
Durant 49 G 2 Oklahoma, C USA
Durban 78 D 5 *var.* Port Natal.
E South Africa
Durbe 106 B 3 *Ger.* Durben.
W Latvia
Durben *see* Durbe
Durg 135 E 4 *prev.* Drug. C India
Durham 89 D 5 *hist.* Dunholme.
N England, UK
Durham 43 F 1
North Carolina, SE USA
Durrës 101 C 6 *var.* Durrësi, Dursi,
It. Durazzo, *SCr.* Drač, *Turk.* Draç,
W Albania
Durūz, Jabal ad 119 C 5 mountain ,
SW Syria
Dushanbe 123 E 3 *var.* Dyushambe,
Taj. Stalinobod; *prev.* Stalinabad.
Country capital,
W Tajikistan
Düsseldorf 94 A 4 *var.* Duessedorf.
W Germany
Dusti *see* Dŭstí
Dŭstí 123 E 3 *Rus.* Dusti.
SW Tajikistan
Dutch Harbor 36 B 3 Unalaska
Island, Alaska, USA
Dutch West Indies *see*
Netherlands Antilles
Dyersburg 42 C 1 Tennessee, S USA
Dzerzhinsk 111 C 5
W Russian Federation
Dzhalal-Abad 123 F 2
Kir. Jalal-Abad. W Kyrgyzstan
Dzhanak 122 C 2 physical region,
W Turkmenistan
Dzhankoy 109 F 4 S Ukraine
Dzharkurgan *see* Jarqŭrghon
Dzhelandy 123 F 3 SE Tajikistan
Dzhergalan 123 H 2 *Kir.* Jyrgalan.
NE Kyrgyzstan
Dzhetygara 114 B 4 *Kaz.* Zhetiqara.
NW Kazakhstan
Dzhizak *see* Jizzakh
Dzhugdzhur, Khrebet 115 G 3
mountain range,
E Russian Federation
Dzhusaly 114 B 4 *Kaz.* Zholsaly.
SW Kazakhstan
Działdowo 98 D 3 C Poland
Dzungaria 126 C 2 *var.* Sungaria,
Zungaria. Physical region,
W China
Dzüünbayan 127 E 2 SE Mongolia
Dzüünharaa 127 E 2 N Mongolia
Dzuunmod 127 E 2 C Mongolia

E

Eagle Lake 47 B 5 lake,
California, W USA
Eagle Pass 49 F 4 Texas, S USA
Easley 43 E 1
South Carolina, SE USA
East Antarctica *see*
Greater Antarctica
East Australian Basin *see*
Tasman Basin
Eastbourne 89 E 7 SE England, UK
East Cape 150 E 3 region, North
Island, New Zealand
East Caroline Basin 152 B 3
undersea basin, SW Pacific Ocean
East Caroline Islands 144 C 2
island group, E Micronesia
East China Sea 152 B 2 *Chin.* Dong
Hai. Sea, NW Pacific Ocean
Easter Fracture Zone 153 F 4
fracture zone, E Pacific Ocean
Easter Island 153 F 4 island,
E Pacific Ocean
Eastern Ghats 124 B 3 mountain
range, SE India
Eastern Sayans 115 E 4
Mong. Dzüün Soyoni Nuruu,
Rus. Vostochnyy Sayan. Mountain
range, Mongolia/
Russian Federation
Eastern Sierra Madre *see*
Madre Oriental, Sierra
East Falkland 65 D 8 *var.* Soledad.
Island, E Falkland Islands
East Frisian Islands *see*
Ostfriesische Inseln
East Grand Forks 45 F 1 Minnesota,
N USA
East Indiaman Ridge 141 D 5
undersea ridge, E Indian Ocean
East Kilbride 88 C 4 S Scotland, UK
East Korea Bay 128 E 3 bay,
Sea of Japan/Pacific Ocean
Eastleigh 89 D 7 S England, UK
East London 78 D 5 *Afr.* Oos-
Londen; *prev.* EMonti, Port Rex.
S South Africa
Eastmain 38 D 3 river, Québec,
C Canada
East Novaya Zemlya Trough 155
H 4 *var.* Novaya Zemlya Trough.
Trough, Arctic Ocean
East Pacific Rise 153 F 4 undersea
rise, E Pacific Ocean
East Saint Louis 40 B 4
Illinois, N USA
East Siberian Sea *see* Vostochno-
Sibirskoye More
Eau Claire 40 A 2
Wisconsin, N USA
Ébano 51 E 3 C Mexico
Ebensee 95 D 6 N Austria
Eberswalde-Finow 94 D 3
E Germany
Ebetsu 130 D 2 *var.* Ebetu.
Hokkaidō, NE Japan
Ebetu *see* Ebetsu
Ebeye 144 D 1 island,
C Marshall Islands
Ebolowa 77 A 5 S Cameroon
Ebon Atoll 144 D 2 *var.* Epoon.
Island, S Marshall Islands
Ébrié, Lagune 74 D 5 lake,
SW Ivory Coast
Ebro 93 E 2 river, NE Spain
Ecbatana *see* Hamadān
Echo Bay 37 E 3 Northwest
Territories, C Canada
Echt 87 D 5 SE Netherlands
Ecija 92 D 4 *anc.* Astigi. SW Spain
Eckengraf *see* Viesīte

Ecuador
60 A 2 Republic,
NW South America

Official name: Republic of Ecuador
Date of formation: 1830/1942
Capital: Quito **Population:** 11.3
million **Total area:** 283,560 sq km
(109,483 sq miles) **Languages:**
Spanish*, Quechua*, eight other
Indian languages **Religions:** Roman
Catholic 95%, other 5% **Ethnic mix:**
mestizo (Euro-Indian) 55%, Indian
25%, Black 10%, White 10%
Government: Multiparty republic
Currency: Sucre = 100 centavos

Edd *see* Ed
Ed Da'ein 72 A 4 W Sudan
Ed Damazin 72 C 4 *var.*
Ad Damazīn. E Sudan
Ed Damer 72 C 3 *var.* Ad Damar,
Ad Dāmir. NE Sudan
Ed Debba 72 B 3 N Sudan
Ede 75 F 5 SW Nigeria
Ede 86 D 4 C Netherlands
Edéa 77 A 5 SW Cameroon
Edel Land 147 A 5 headland,
Western Australia, W Australia
Eden 43 F 1 North Carolina, SE USA
Eden 149 D 7 New South Wales,
SE Australia
Edfu *see* Idfu
Edgeøya 83 G 2 island, S Svalbard
Edinburg 49 G 5 Texas, S USA
Edinburgh 88 C 4 SE Scotland, UK
Edingen *See* Enghien
Edirne 116 A 2 *var.* Adrianopolis,
Hadrianopolis. NW Turkey
Edmonds 46 B 2 Washington,
NW USA
Edmonton 37 E 5 province capital,
Alberta, SW Canada
Edmundston 39 E 4 New
Brunswick, SE Canada
Edna 49 G 4 Texas, S USA
Edolo 96 B 1 N Italy
Edremit 116 A 3 NW Turkey
Edward, Lake 77 E 6 *var.* Albert
Edward Nyanza, Edward Nyanza,
Lac Idi Amin, Lake Rutanzige.
Lake, Congo (Zaire)/Uganda
Eeklo 87 B 5 *var.* Eekloo.
NW Belgium
Eekloo *see* Eeklo
Eems *see* Ems
Eersel 87 D 5 S Netherlands
Êťaté 144 D 4 *Fr.* Vaté; *prev.*
Sandwich Islands. Island group,
C Vanuatu
Effingham 40 B 4 Illinois, N USA
Eforie Sud 108 D 5 E Romania
Efstrátios, Ágios 104 D 4 *var.* Ayios
Evstratios. Island, E Greece
Egadi, Isole 97 B 7 island group,
S Italy
Eger 99 D 6 *Ger.* Erlau. NE Hungary
Eger *see* Cheb
Éghezèe 87 C 6 C Belgium
Egiyn Gol 126 D 2 *var.* Egiyn Gul.
River, N Mongolia
Egiyn Gul *see* Egiyn Gol
Egmont *see* Taranaki, Mount
Egmont, Cape 150 C 4 headland,
North Island, C New Zealand

Egypt
72 B 2 *Ar.* Jumhūrīyah Mişr al
'Arabīyah; *prev.* United Arab
Republic, *anc.* Aegyptus.
Republic, NE Africa

Official name: Arab Republic of

Egypt Date of formation: 1936/1982
Capital: Cairo **Population:** 64.2
million **Total area:** 1,001,450 sq km
(386,660 sq miles) **Languages:**
Arabic*, French, English **Religions:**
Muslim 94%, other 6% **Ethnic mix:**
Eastern Hamitic 90%, other 10%
Government: Multiparty republic
Currency: Pound = 100 piastres

Eibar 93 E 1 N Spain
Eibergen 86 E 3 E Netherlands
Eidfjord 85 A 5 S Norway
Eifel 95 A 5 plateau, W Germany
Eigg 88 B 3 island, W Scotland, UK
Eight Degree Channel 132 B 3
channel, N Indian Ocean
Eighty Miles Beach 146 B 3 beach,
Western Australia, W Australia
Eijsden 87 D 6 SE Netherlands
Eindhoven 87 D 5 S Netherlands
Eisenhüttenstadt 94 D 4 E Germany
Eisleben 94 C 4 C Germany
Eivissa 93 G 3 *var.* Iviza, *Cast.* Ibiza;
anc. Ebusus. Island, E Spain
Eivissa 93 G 4 *var.* Iviza, *Cast.* Ibiza;
anc. Ebusus. E Spain
Ejea de los Caballeros 93 F 2
NE Spain
Ekiatapskiy Khrebet 115 G 1
mountain range,
NE Russian Federation
El' Alamein 72 B 1 *var.*
Al 'Alamayn. N Egypt
Elat 119 B 8 *var.* Eilat, Elath.
S Israel
Elâzığ 117 E 3 *var.* Elâziz. E Turkey
Elâziz *see* Elâzığ
Elba, Isola d' 96 B 4 island, C Italy
Elbasan 101 D 6 *var.* Elbasani.
C Albania
Elbasani *see* Elbasan
Elbe 94 C 3 *Cz.* Labe. River,
Czech Republic/Germany
Elbert, Mount 44 C 4 mountain,
Colorado, C USA
Elbląg 98 D 2 *var.* Elblag,
Ger. Elbing. N Poland
El'brus 111 B 8 *var.* Gora El'brus.
Mountain, SW Russian Federation
El'brus, Gora *see* El'brus
El Burgo de Osma 93 E 2 C Spain
Elburz Mountains *see* Alborz,
Reshteh-ye Kūhhā-ye
El Calafate 65 B 7 *var.* Calafate.
S Argentina
El Callao 59 F 2 E Venezuela
El Campo 49 G 4 Texas, S USA
El Carmen de Bolívar 58 B 2
NW Colombia
El Centro 47 D 8 California, W USA
Elche 93 F 4 *var.* Elx- Elche;
anc. Ilici, *Lat.* Illicis. E Spain
Elda 93 F 4 E Spain
El Djelfa *see* Djelfa
El Dorado 50 C 3 C Mexico
El Dorado 45 F 5 Kansas, C USA
El Dorado 59 F 2 E Venezuela
Eldorado 64 E 3 NE Argentina
Eldoret 73 C 6 W Kenya
Elektrostal' 111 B 5
W Russian Federation
Elephant Butte Reservoir 48 C 2
reservoir, New Mexico, SW USA
Élesd *see* Aleşd
Eleuthera Island 54 C 1 island,
N Bahamas
El Fasher 72 A 4 *var.* Al Fāshir.
W Sudan
Elgin 88 C 3 UK
Elgin 40 B 3 Illinois, N USA

El Giza 72 B 1 *var.* Al Jīzah, Gîza,
Gizeh. N Egypt
El Goléa 70 D 3 *var.* Al Golea.
C Algeria
El Hank 68 A 3 desert ,
Mali/ Mauritania
El Hank 74 D 1 cliff, S Mauritania
El Hasaheisa 72 C 4 *var.*
Al Hasahisa, Al Ḩuşayḩişah,
Hasaheisa. C Sudan
Élisabethville *see* Lubumbashi
Elista 111 B 7
SW Russian Federation
Elizabeth 149 B 6 South Australia,
S Australia
Elizabeth City 43 G 1
North Carolina, SE USA
Elizabethtown 40 C 5
Kentucky, E USA
El-Jadida 70 C 2 *prev.* Mazagan.
W Morocco
Elk 98 E 2 *Ger.* Lyck. NE Poland
Elk City 49 F 1 Oklahoma, C USA
Elkford 37 E 5 Alberta, SW Canada
El Khârga 72 B 2 *var.* Al Khārijah.
C Egypt
Elkhart 40 C 3 Indiana, N USA
Elk River 45 F 2 Minnesota, N USA
Ellef Ringnes Island 37 F 1 island,
N Canada
Ellen, Mount 44 B 5 mountain,
Utah, W USA
Ellensburg 46 B 2 Washington,
NW USA
Ellesmere Island 37 F 1 island,
N Canada
Ellice Islands, The *See* Tuvalu
Elliston 149 A 6 South Australia,
S Australia
Ellsworth Land 154 A 3 physical
region, Antarctica
El Mina 118 B 4 *var.* Al Mīnā'.
N Lebanon
El Minya 72 B 2 *var.* Al Minyā,
Minya. C Egypt
Elmira 41 E 3 New York, NE USA
El Mreyyé 74 D 2 desert,
E Mauritania
Elmshorn 94 B 3 N Germany
El Muglad 72 B 4 C Sudan
El Obeid 72 B 4 *var.* Al Obayyid,
Al Ubayyiḍ. C Sudan
El Oued 71 E 2 *var.* Al Oued,
El Ouâdi, El Wad. NE Algeria
Eloy 48 B 3 Arizona, SW USA
El Paso 48 D 3 Texas, SW USA
El Porvenir 53 G 4 N Panama
El Progreso 52 C 2 NW Honduras
El Puerto de Santa María 92 B 5
S Spain
El Quweira 92 B 5 *var.* Al Quwayrah
El Rama 53 E 3 SE Nicaragua
El Real 53 H 5 *var.* El Real de Santa
María. SE Panama
El Real de Santa María *see* El Real
El Reno 49 F 1 Oklahoma, C USA

El Salvador
52 B 3 Republic,
W Central America

Official name: Republic of
El Salvador **Date of formation:**
1856/1838 **Capital:** San Salvador
Population: 5.4 million **Total area:**
21,040 sq km (8,124 sq miles)
Languages: Spanish*, Nahua
Religions: Roman Catholic 75%,
other 25% **Ethnic mix:** *mestizo* (Euro-
Indian) 89%, Indian 10%, White 1%
Government: Multiparty republic
Currency: Colón = 100 centavos

El Serrat 91 A 7 N Andorra
Elst 86 D 4 E Netherlands
Eltanin Fracture Zone 153 E 5
fracture zone, SE Pacific
El Tigre 59 E 2 NE Colombia
Elva 106 D 3 *Ger.* Elwa. SE Estonia
Elvas 92 C 4 C Portugal
El Vendrell 93 G 2 NE Spain
El Vigía 58 C 2 NW Venezuela
Elwa *see* Elva
Elwell, Lake 44 B 1 reservoir,
Montana, NW USA
El Yopal *see* Yopal
Emajõgi 106 D 3 *Ger.* Embach.
River, SE Estonia
Emámrúd 120 D 2 *prev.* Shāhrūd.
N Iran
Emba 114 B 4 *Kaz.* Embi.
W Kazakhstan
Embach *see* Emajõgi
Embi *see* Emba
Emden 94 A 3 NW Germany
Emerald 148 D 4 Queensland,
E Australia
Emerald Isle *see* Montserrat
Emi Koussi 68 C 3 mountain, N Chad
Emmaste 106 C 2 Hiiumaa,
W Estonia
Emmeloord 86 D 2 N Netherlands
Emmen 86 E 2 NE Netherlands
Emmendingen 95 A 6 SW Germany
Empalme 50 B 2 NW Mexico
Emperor Seamounts 152 C 1
seamount range, NW Pacific Ocean
Emporia 45 F 5 Kansas, C USA
Ems 94 A 3 *Dut.* Eems. River,
Germany
Encamp 91 A 8 C Andorra
Encarnación 64 D 3 S Paraguay
Encinitas 47 C 8 California, W USA
Encs 99 D 6 NE Hungary
Endeavour 55 G 1 NW Barbados
Endeavour Strait 148 C 1 strait,
Arafura Sea/Coral Sea
Enderbury Island 145 F 3 island,
C Kiribati
Enderby Land 154 D 2 physical
region, Antarctica
Enderby Plain 154 D 1 abyssal
plain, S Indian Ocean
Endersdorf *see* Jędrzejów
Enewetak Atoll 144 C 1
var. Ánewetak, Eniwetok. Island,
W Marshall Islands
Enghien 87 B 6 *Dut.* Edingen.
SW Belgium
England 89 D 6 *Lat.* Anglia.
National region, UK
Englewood 44 D 4 Colorado, C USA
English Channel 90 B 2 *var.*
The Channel, *Fr.* la Manche.
Channel, NE Atlantic Ocean
Engure 106 C 3 W Latvia
Engures Ezers 106 C 3 lake,
NW Latvia
Enguri 117 F 1 *Rus.* Inguri. River,
NW Georgia
En Hazeva 119 B 7 S Israel
Enid 49 F 1 Oklahoma, C USA
En Nâqoûra 119 A 5 *var.* An
Nāqūrah. SW Lebanon
Ennedi 76 D 2 plateau, E Chad
Ennis 89 A 6 *Ir.* Inis. W Ireland
Ennis 49 G 3 Texas, S USA
Enniskillen 89 A 5 *var.* Inniskilling,
Ir. Inis Ceithleann. S Northern
Ireland, UK
Enns 95 D 6 river, C Austria
Enschede 86 E 3 E Netherlands
Ensenada 50 A 1 NW Mexico
Ensley 42 C 3 Florida, SE USA

Entebbe 73 B 6 S Uganda
Entre Vientos 65 B 8 Chile
Entroncamento 92 B 3 C Portugal
Enugu 75 G 5 S Nigeria
Eolie, Isole 97 D 6 *var.* Isole Lipari, *Eng.* Lipari Islands, Aeolian Islands. Island group, S Italy
Epanomí 104 B 4 N Greece
Epéna 77 C 5 NE Congo
Épi 144 D 4 island, C Vanuatu
Épinal 90 D 4 NE France
Epoon *see* Ebon Atoll

Equatorial Guinea
77 A 5 Guinea. Republic, C Africa

Official name: Republic of Equatorial Guinea **Date of formation:** 1968 **Capital:** Malabo **Population:** 400,000 **Total area:** 28,050 sq km (10,830 sq miles) **Languages:** Spanish*, Fang **Religions:** Christian 89%, other 11% **Ethnic mix:** Fang 72%, Bubi 14%, Duala 3%, other 11% **Government:** Multiparty republic **Currency:** CFA franc = 100 centimes

Eravur 132 D 3 E Sri Lanka
Erciş 117 F 3 E Turkey
Erdenet 127 F 2 SE Mongolia
Erdenet 127 E 2 C Mongolia
Erdi 76 D 2 plateau, NE Chad
Erdi Ma 76 D 2 desert, NE Chad
Erebus, Mount 154 C 4 mountain, Antarctica
Ereğli 116 B 2 NW Turkey
Ereğli 116 C 4 S Turkey
Erenhot 127 F 2 *var.* Erlian. NE China
Erfurt 94 C 4 C Germany
Ergene 116 A 2 *var.* Ergene Irmaĕı. River, NW Turkey
Ergene Irmağı *see* Ergene
Erg Iguid 70 C 3 *var.* Erg Iguîdi. Desert , Algeria / Mauritania
Erg Iguîdi *see* Erg Iguid
Erguig, Bahr 76 C 3 river, SW Chad
Ergun 127 F 1 river, N China
Ergun Zuoqi 127 F 1 N China
Erie 41 E 3 Pennsylvania, NE USA
Érié, Lac *see* Erie, Lake
Erie, Lake 40 D 3 *Fr.* Lac Érié. Lake, Canada/USA

Eritrea
72 C 4 Transitional government, NE Africa

Official name: State of Eritrea **Date of formation:** 1993 **Capital:** Asmara **Population:** 3.5 million **Total area:** 93,680 sq km (36,170 sq miles) **Languages:** Tigrinya*, Arabic*, Tigre **Religions:** Coptic Christian 45%, Muslim 45%, other 10% **Ethnic mix:** Nine main Ethnic groups **Government:** Provisional military government **Currency:** Ethiopian birr = 100 cents

Erivan *see* Yerevan
Erlangen 95 C 5 S Germany
Erlau *see* Eger
Erlian *see* Erenhot
Ermelo 86 D 3 C Netherlands
Ermióni 105 C 6 S Greece
Ermoúpoli 105 D 6 *var.* Hermoupolis; *prev.* Ermoúpolis. Kykládes, SE Greece
Ernākulam 132 C 3 SW India
Erode 132 C 2 SE India
Erquelinnes 87 B 7 S Belgium
Er-Rachidia 70 C 2 *var.* al Raudia, Ksar al Soule. E Morocco
Er Rahad 72 B 4 *var.* Ar Rahad. C Sudan
Erromango 144 D 4 island, S Vanuatu
Erzerum *see* Erzurum
Erzgebirge 95 D 5 *var.* Krušné Hory, *Eng.* Ore Mountains. Mountain range, Czech Republic/Germany
Erzincan 117 E 3 *var.* Erzinjan. E Turkey
Erzinjan *see* Erzincan
Erzurum 117 E 3 *prev.* Erzerum. NE Turkey
Esbjerg 85 A 7 W Denmark
Esbo *see* Espoo
Escaldes 91 A 8 C Andorra
Escanabar 40 C 2 Michigan, N USA
Escárcega 51 G 4 SE Mexico
Esch-sur-Alzette 87 D 8 S Luxembourg
Escondido 47 C 8 California, W USA
Escuinapa 50 C 4 *var.* Escuinapa de Hidalgo. C Mexico
Escuinapa de Hidalgo *see* Escuinapa
Escuintla 51 G 5 SE Mexico
Escuintla 52 B 3 S Guatemala
Eşfahān 120 D 3 *Eng.* Isfahan; *anc.* Aspadana. C Iran
Esil *see* Ishim
Eskimo Point *see* Arviat
Eskişehir 116 B 3 *var.* Eskishehr. W Turkey
Eskishehr *see* Eskişehir
Esla, Embalse de 92 C 2 *var.* Embalse de Elsa. Reservoir, NW Spain
Eslāmābād 120 C 3 *var.* Eslāmābād-e Gharb; *prev.* Shāhābād, Harunabad. W Iran
Esmeraldas 60 A 1 N Ecuador
Esna *see* Isna
Espanola 48 D 1 New Mexico, SW USA
Esperance 147 C 7 Western Australia, SW Australia
Esperanza 50 B 2 NW Mexico
Esperanza 154 A 2 research station, Antarctica
Esperanza 60 D 3 E Peru
Espinal 58 B 3 C Colombia
Espinhaço, Serra do 63 F 3 mountain range, SE Brazil
Espírito Santo 63 G 4 *off.* Estado do Espírito Santo. State, SE Brazil
Espírito Santo, Estado do *see* Espírito Santo
Espiritu Santo 144 C 4 *var.* Santo. Island, W Vanuatu
Espoo 85 D 6 *Swe.* Esbo. S Finland
Esquel 65 B 6 SW Argentina
Essaouira 70 B 2 *prev.* Mogador. W Morocco
Es Semara *see* Smara
Essen 94 A 4 *var.* Essen an der Ruhr. W Germany
Essen 87 C 5 N Belgium
Essen an der Ruhr *see* Essen
Essequibo 56 C 2 river, C Guyana
Estacado, Llano 49 E 2 plain, SW USA
Estados, Isla de los 65 C 8 prev *Eng.* Staten Island. Island, S Argentina
Estância 63 G 3 E Brazil
Estelí 52 D 3 NW Nicaragua
Estella 93 E 1 N Spain
Estepona 92 D 5 S Spain
Estevan 37 F 5 Saskatchewan, S Canada

Estonia
106 D 2 *Est.* Eesti Vabariik, *Ger.* Estland, *Latv.* Igaunija; *prev.* Estonian SSR, *Rus.* Estonskaya SSR. Republic, E Europe

Official name: Republic of Estonia **Date of formation:** 1991 **Capital:** Tallinn **Population:** 1.6 million **Total area:** 45,125 sq km (17,423 sq miles) **Languages:** Estonian*, Russian **Religions:** Evangelical Lutheran 98%, Eastern Orthodox, Baptist 2% **Ethnic mix:** Estonian 62%, Russian 30%, Ukrainian 3%, other 5% **Government:** Multiparty republic **Currency:** Kroon = 100 cents

Estrela, Serra da 92 C 3 mountain range, C Portugal
Estremoz 92 B 4 C Portugal
Esztergom 99 C 6 *Ger.* Gran; *anc.* Strigonium. N Hungary
Etāwah 134 D 3 N India

Ethiopia
73 C 5 *var.* Abyssinia; *prev.* People's Democratic Republic of Ethiopia. Republic, NE Africa

Official name: Undetermined **Date of formation:** 1903/1993 **Capital:** Addis Ababa **Population:** 56.7 million **Total area:** 1,128,221 sq km (435,605 sq miles) **Languages:** Amharic*, English, Arabic **Religions:** Muslim 43%, Christian 37%, traditional beliefs, other 20%, **Ethnic mix:** Oromo 40%, Amhara and Tigrean 32%, other 28% **Government:** Multiparty republic **Currency:** Birr = 100 cents

Ethiopian Highlands *see* Ethiopian Plateau
Ethiopian Plateau 73 C 5 *var.* Ethiopian Highlands. Plateau, N Ethiopia
Etna, Monte 97 C 7 *Eng.* Mount Etna. Volcano, SW Italy
Etna, Mount *see* Etna, Monte
Etosha Pan 78 B 3 salt lake, N Namibia
Etoumbi 77 B 5 NW Congo
Etsch *see* Adige
Ettelbrück 87 D 8 C Luxembourg
'Eua 145 E 5 *prev.* Middleburg Island. Island, S Tonga
Euboea *see* Évvoia
Eucla 147 D 6 Western Australia, S Australia
Euclid 40 D 3 Ohio, N USA
Eufaula 42 D 3 Alabama, S USA
Eufaula Lake 49 G 1 *var.* Eufaula Reservoir. Reservoir, Oklahoma, C USA
Eufaula Reservoir *see* Eufaula Lake
Eugene 46 B 3 Oregon, NW USA
Eunice 42 B 3 Louisiana, S USA
Eupen 87 D 6 E Belgium
Euphrates 120 C 3 *var.* Firat Nehri, Al-Furat. River, SW Asia
Eureka 37 F 1 Ellesmere Island, Canada
Eureka 47 A 5 California, W USA
Eureka 44 A 1 Montana, NW USA
Europa Point 93 H 5 headland, S Gibraltar
Europe 66 E 3 continent
Euskirchen 95 A 5 W Germany
Eutin 94 C 2 N Germany
Evansdale 45 G 3 Iowa, C USA
Evanston 40 B 3 Illinois, N USA
Evanston 44 B 4 Wyoming, C USA
Evansville 40 B 5 Indiana, N USA
Eveleth 45 G 1 Minnesota, N USA
Everard, Lake 149 A 6 salt lake, S Australia
Everest, Mount 124 C 3 *Chin.* Qomolangma Feng, *Nep.* Sagarmatha. Mountain, China/Nepal
Everett 46 B 2 Washington, NW USA
Everglades, The 43 E 5 wetland, Florida, SE USA
Evje 85 A 6 S Norway
Évora 92 B 4 *Lat.* Liberalitas Julia, *anc.* Ebora. C Portugal
Évreux 90 C 3 *anc.* Civitas Eburovicum. N France
Évry 90 C 3 N France
Evstratios, Ayios *see* Efstrátios, Ágios
Évvoia 105 C 5 *Lat.* Euboea. Island, Kykládes, C Greece
Ewarton 54 B 5 C Jamaica
Excelsior Springs 45 F 4 Missouri, C USA
Exe 89 C 7 river, SW England, UK
Exeter 89 C 7 *anc.* Isca Damnoniorum. SW England, UK
Exmoor 89 C 7 heathland, SW England, UK
Exmouth 89 C 7 SW England, UK
Exmouth 146 A 4 Western Australia, W Australia
Exmouth Gulf 146 A 4 gulf, W Indian Ocean
Exmouth Plateau 141 E 5 undersea plateau, E Indian Ocean
Extremadura 92 C 3 cultural region, W Spain
Exuma Cayes 54 C 1 island group, C Bahamas
Eyre 147 D 6 Western Australia, W Australia
Eyre Mountains 151 A 7 mountain range, South Island, SW New Zealand
Eyre North, Lake 149 B 5 salt lake, S Australia
Eyre Peninsula 149 A 6 peninsula, S Australia
Eyre South, Lake 149 B 5 salt lake, S Australia
Ezequiel Ramos Mexía, Embalse 65 B 5 lake, C Argentina

F

Faadhippolhu Atoll 132 B 4 *var.* Fadiffolu, Lhaviyani Atoll. Island, N Maldives
Fabens 48 D 3 Texas, S USA
Fada 76 C 2 E Chad
Fada-Ngourma 75 E 4 E Burkina
Fadghāmī *see* Tall Fadghāmī
Faenza 96 C 3 *anc.* Faventia. N Italy
Faeroe-Iceland Ridge 80 C 1 undersea ridge, NW Norwegian Sea
Faeroe Islands 83 F 5 *Dan.* Færøerne, *Faer.* Føroyar. Danish external territory, N Atlantic Ocean
Faeroe Islands 66 D 2 island group, NE Atlantic Ocean
Faetano 96 E 2 E San Marino
Făgăraş 108 C 4 *Ger.* Fogarasch, *Hung.* Fogaras. C Romania
Fagibina, Lake *see* Faguibine, Lac
Fagne 87 C 7 hill range, S Belgium
Faguibine, Lac 75 E 3 *var.* Lake Fagibina. Lake, NW Mali
Fahlun *see* Falun

Fahraj 120 E 4 SE Iran
Faial 92 A 5 *var.* Ilha do Faial.
  Island, W Portugal
Faial, Ilha do *see* Faial
Faifo *see* Hôi An
Fairbanks 36 C 3 Alaska, NW USA
Fairfield 47 B 6 California, W USA
Fair Isle 88 D 2 island,
  NE Scotland, UK
Fairlie 151 B 6 South Island,
  SW New Zealand
Fairmont 45 F 3 Minnesota, N USA
Faisalābād 134 C 2 *prev.* Lyallpur.
  NE Pakistan
Faizābād 135 E 3 N India
Fakaofo Atoll 145 F 3 island,
  SE Tokelau
Falam 136 A 3 NW Burma
Falconara Marittima 96 C 3 C Italy
Falkland Islands 65 C 7 island
  group, SW Atlantic Ocean
Falkland Plateau 57 D 7 *var.*
  Argentine Rise. Undersea plateau,
  SW Atlantic Ocean
Fallbrook 47 C 8 California, W USA
Falmouth 89 C 8 SW England, UK
Falmouth 54 A 4 W Jamaica
Fălticeni 108 C 3 *Hung.* Falticsén.
  NE Romania
Falticsén *see* Fălticeni
Falun 85 C 5 *var.* Fahlun.
  C Sweden
Famenne 87 C 7 physical region,
  SE Belgium
Fang 136 C 3 N Thailand
Fanling 128 A 1 N Hong Kong
Fanning Island *see* Tabuaeran
Fano 96 C 3 *anc.* Fanum Fortunae,
  Colonia Julia Fanestris. C Italy
Farafangana 79 G 4 SE Madagascar
Farafra Oasis 72 B 2 *var.* Wāhat el
  Farāfra. Oasis, C Egypt
Farāfra, Wāhat el *see* Farafra Oasis
Farāh 122 D 4 *var.* Farah, Fararud.
  W Afghanistan
Faranah 74 C 4 S Guinea
Farewell, Cape 150 C 4 headland,
  South Island, C New Zealand
Farghona 123 F 2 *Rus.* Fergana;
  prev. Novyy Margilan .
  E Uzbekistan
Fargo 45 F 2 North Dakota, N USA
Faribault 45 F 3 Minnesota, N USA
Farīdābād 134 D 3 N India
Farkhor 123 E 3 *Rus.* Parkhar.
  SW Tajikistan
Farmington 48 C 1
  New Mexico, SW USA
Farmington 45 G 5
  Missouri, C USA
Faro 92 B 5 S Portugal
Farquhar Group 79 G 2 island
  group, S Seychelles
Fastiv 109 E 2 *Rus.* Fastov.
  NW Ukraine
Fastov *see* Fastiv
Fauske 84 C 3 C Norway
Faventia *see* Faenza
Faxa Bay *see* Faxaflói
Faxaflói 83 E 5 *Eng.* Faxa Bay. Bay,
  N Atlantic Ocean
Faya 76 C 2 *prev.* Faya-Largeau,
  Largeau. N Chad
Fayetteville 42 A 1
  Arkansas, SE USA
Fayetteville 43 F 1
  North Carolina, SE USA
Fazzān 71 F 4 *Eng.* Fezzan.
  Cultural region, W Libya
Færingehavn 82 B 4 *var.*
  Kangerluarsoruseq. S Greenland

Fdérik 74 C 2 *var.* Fdérick, Fderik,
  Fr. Fort Gouraud. NW Mauritania
Fear, Cape 43 F 2 headland,
  North Carolina, SE USA
Fécamp 90 B 3 N France
Fédala *see* Mohammedia
Federal Capital Territory *see*
  Australian Capital Territory
Fehérgyarmat 99 E 6 E Hungary
Fehmarn 94 C 2 island, N Germany
Feijó 62 C 2 W Brazil
Feilding 150 D 4 North Island,
  C New Zealand
Feira *see* Feira de Santana
Feira de Santana 63 G 3 *var.* Feira.
  E Brazil
Felanitx 93 H 3 *anc.* Canati,
  Felaniche. E Spain
Feldkirchen in Kärnten 95 D 7
  Slvn. Trg. S Austria
Félegyháza *see* Kiskunfélegyháza
Felidhu Atoll 132 B 4 island,
  C Maldives
Felipe Carrillo Puerto 51 H 4
  SE Mexico
Felixstowe 89 E 6 E England, UK
Fellin *see* Viljandi
Femerbælt 94 C 2 *Dan.* Femer Bælt,
  Ger. Fehmarnbelt. Channel,
  SW Baltic Sea
Femunden 85 B 5 lake, S Norway
Fénérive *see* Fenoarivo Atsinanana
Fengcheng 128 D 3 *var.* Feng-cheng,
  Jap. Fenghwangcheng.
  NE China
Fenoarivo Atsinanana 79 G 3 *prev.*
  Fénérive. NE Madagascar
Fens, The 89 F 6 wetland,
  E England, UK
Feodosiya 109 G 5 *var.* Kefe, *It.*
  Kaffa; *anc.* Theodosia. S Ukraine
Féres 104 D 3 NE Greece
Fergus Falls 45 F 2
  Minnesota, N USA
Ferizaj *see* Uroševac
Fernandina, Isla 60 A 5
  var. Narborough Island. Island,
  Galapagos Islands, E Pacific Ocean
Fernando de la Mora 64 D 2
  S Paraguay
Fernando de Noronha 63 H 2
  island, E Brazil
Ferrara 96 C 2 *anc.* Forum Alieni.
  N Italy
Ferrol 92 B 1 *var.* El Ferrol; *prev.*
  El Ferrol del Caudillo. NW Spain
Fertő *see* Neusiedler See
Fès 70 C 2 *Eng.* Fez, *prev.* Morocco
Fethiye 116 B 4 SW Turkey
Fetlar 88 D 1 island,
  NE Scotland, UK
Feyzābād 123 F 3 *var.* Faizabad,
  Faizābād, Feyzābād, Fyzabad.
  NE Afghanistan
Fez *see* Fès
Fezzan *see* Fazzān
Fianarantsoa 79 F 3 C Madagascar
Fianga 76 B 4 SW Chad
Fier 101 C 6 *var.* Fieri, SW Albania
Fieri *see* Fier
Figeac 91 C 5 S France
Figig *see* Figuig
Figueira da Foz 92 B 3 W Portugal
Figueres 93 G 2 E Spain
Figuig 70 D 2 *var.* Figig. E Morocco

Fiji
  145 E 5 *Fij.* Viti. Republic,
  SW Pacific Ocean

Official name: Sovereign
Democratic Republic of Fiji **Date of**
formation: 1970 **Capital:** Suva
Population: 700,000 **Total Area:**
18,270 sq km (7,054 sq miles)
Languages: English*, Fijian, Hindu,
Urdu, Tamil, Telugu **Religions:**
Christian 52%, Hindu 8%, Muslim
8%, other 2% **Ethnic mix:** Native
Fijian 49%, Indo-Fijian 46%, other
5% **Government:** Multiparty
republic **Currency:** Fiji $ = 100 cents

Filadelfia 52 D 4 W Costa Rica
Filiaşi 108 B 5 SW Romania
Filipstad 85 B 6 C Sweden
Finale Ligure 96 A 3 Italy
Findlay 40 D 4 Ohio, N USA
Finike 116 B 4 SW Turkey

Finland
  84 D 4 *Fin.* Suomen Tasavalta,
  Suomi. Republic, N Europe

Official name: Republic of Finland
Date of formation: 1917/1920
Capital: Helsinki **Population:** 5
million **Total Area:** 338,130 sq km
(130,552 sq miles) **Languages:**
Finnish*, Swedish, Lappish
Religions: Evangelical Lutheran
89%, Greek Orthodox 1%, other 10%
Ethnic mix: Finnish 93%, Swedish
6%, other (inc. Sami)1%
Government: Multiparty republic
Currency: Markka = 100 pennia

Finland, Gulf of 85 E 6 *Est.*
  Soome Laht, *Fin.* Suomenlahti,
  Ger. Finnischer Meerbusen, *Rus.*
  Finskiy Zaliv, *Swe.* Finska Viken.
  Gulf, Atlantic Ocean/Baltic Sea
Finnmarksvidda 84 D 2 physical
  region, N Norway
Finsterwalde 94 D 4 E Germany
Fiorina 96 E 1 NE San Marino
Firenze 96 C 3 *Eng.* Florence;
  anc. Florentia. C Italy
Fischbacher Alpen 95 E 7 mountain
  range, E Austria
Fischhausen *see* Primorsk
Fish 78 B 4 *var.* Vis. River, S Namibia
Fishguard 89 B 6 *Wel.* Abergwaun.
  SW Wales, UK
Fiskenæsset *see* Qeqertarsuatsiaat
Fisterra, Cabo 92 B 1 headland,
  NW Spain
Fitzgerald 43 E 3 Georgia, SE USA
Fitzroy 146 C 3 river, Western
  Australia, N Australia
Fitzroy Crossing 146 C 3 Western
  Australia, NW Australia
Flagstaff 48 B 2 Arizona, SW USA
Flanders 87 A 6 *Dut.* Vlaanderen,
  Fr. Flandre. Cultural region,
  Belgium/France
Flathead Lake 44 B 1 lake,
  Montana, NW USA
Flatts Village 42 B 5 *var.* The Flatts
  Village. C Bermuda
Flensburg 94 B 2 N Germany
Flinders 148 C 3 river,
  N Australia
Flinders 149 B 7 bay,
  SE Indian Ocean
Flinders Island 149 C 8 island,
  Tasmania, SE Australia
Flinders Island 149 A 6 island,
  South Australia, S Australia
Flinders Ranges 149 B 6 mountain
  range, S Australia
Flinders Reefs 148 D 3 reef,
  W Coral Sea
Flin Flon 37 F 5 Manitoba,
  C Canada
Flint 40 D 3 Michigan, N USA

Flint Island 145 H 4 island,
  E Kiribati
Florence 43 F 2
  South Carolina, SE USA
Florencia 58 B 4 S Colombia
Flores 92 A 5 island, W Portugal
Flores 52 B 1 N Guatemala
Flores 139 E 5 island, Nusa
  Tenggara, C Indonesia
Flores, Laut 139 E 5 *Eng.* Flores Sea.
  Sea, W Pacific Ocean
Flores Sea *see* Flores, Laut
Floriano 63 F 2 E Brazil
Florianópolis 63 F 5 *prev.* Destêrro.
  State capital, S Brazil
Florida 43 E 4 *off.* State of Florida;
  nicknames Peninsular State,
  Sunshine State. State, SE USA
Florida 64 D 4 S Uruguay
Florida Bay 43 E 5 bay,
  E Gulf of Mexico
Florida Keys 43 E 5 island, Florida,
  SE USA
Florida Negra 65 C 7 SE Argentina-
Florida, Straits of 43 F 5 strait,
  W Atlantic Ocean
Flórina 104 B 4 *var.* Phlórina.
  N Greece
Florissant 45 G 4 Missouri, C USA
Floúda, Ákra 105 D 7 headland,
  Astypálaia, SE Greece
Flylän *see* Vlieland
Foča 100 C 4
  SE Bosnia & Herzegovina
Focşani 108 C 4 E Romania
Foggia 97 D 5 SE Italy
Fogi 139 F 4 E Indonesia
Fogo 74 A 3 island, SW Cape Verde
Foix 91 B 6 S France `
Folégandros 105 C 7 island,
  Kykládes, SE Greece
Foleyet 38 C 4 Ontario, S Canada
Foligno 96 C 4 C Italy
Folkestone 89 E 7 SE England, UK
Folsom 47 B 5 California, W USA
Fond-du-Lac 37 F 4 Saskatchewan,
  C Canada
Fongafale 145 E 3 *var.* Funafuti.
  Country capital, Funafuti,
  C Tuvalu
Fonseca, Golfo de *see* Fonseca,
  Gulf of
Fonseca, Gulf of 52 C 3 *Sp.* Golfo
  de Fonseca. Gulf, E Pacific Ocean
Fontainebleau 90 C 3 N France
Fontenay-le-Comte 90 A 4
  NW France
Fonyód 99 C 7 W Hungary
Forchheim 95 C 5 SE Germany
Forel, Mount 82 D 4 mountain,
  SE Greenland
Forfar 88 C 3 NE Scotland, UK
Forlì 96 C 3 *anc.* Forum Livii.
  N Italy
Formentera 93 G 4 *anc.* Ophiusa,
  Lat. Frumentum. Island, E Spain
Formosa 64 D 3 NE Argentina
Formosa Bay 73 D 7 *var.* Ungama
  Bay. Bay, NW Indian Ocean
Formosa, Serra 63 E 3 mountain
  range, C Brazil
Fort Albany 38 C 3 Ontario,
  C Canada
Fortaleza 63 G 2 *prev.* Ceará. State
  capital, NE Brazil
Fortaleza 61 F 2 N Bolivia
Fort-Archambault *see* Sarh
Fort Charlet *see* Djanet
Fort-Chimo *see* Kuujjuaq
Fort Collins 44 D 4 Colorado, C USA
Fort-Crampel *see* Kaga Bandoro**

Fort-de-France 55 H 4 *prev.* Fort-Royal. Dependent territory capital, W Martinique
Fort Dodge 45 F 3 Iowa, C USA
Fortescue 146 B 4 river, W Australia
Fort-Foureau *see* Kousséri
Fort Frances 38 B 4 Ontario, S Canada
Fort Good Hope 37 E 3 *var.* Good Hope. Northwest Territories, W Canada
Forth 88 C 4 river, S Scotland, UK
Forth, Firth of 88 D 4 estuary, NW North Sea
Fortín General Diaz 64 D 2 W Paraguay
Fort Jameson *see* Chipata
Fort Lauderdale 43 F 5 Florida, SE USA
Fort Liard 37 E 4 *var.* Liard. Northwest Territories, W Canada
Fort Madison 45 G 4 Iowa, C USA
Fort McMurray 37 F 4 Alberta, C Canada
Fort McPherson 36 D 3 *var.* McPherson. Northwest Territories, NW Canada
Fort Morgan 44 D 4 Colorado, C USA
Fort Myers 43 E 5 Florida, SE USA
Fort Nelson 37 E 4 British Columbia, W Canada
Fort Peck Lake 44 C 1 reservoir, Montana, NW USA
Fort Pierce 43 F 4 Florida, SE USA
Fort Providence 37 E 4 *var.* Providence. Northwest Territories, W Canada
Fort-Repoux *see* Akjoujt
Fort Rosebery *see* Mansa
Fort-Rousset *see* Owando
Fort-Royal *see* Fort-de-France
Fort St.John 37 E 5 British Columbia, W Canada
Fort Scott 45 F 5 Kansas, C USA
Fort Severn 38 C 2 Ontario, C Canada
Fort-Shevchenko 114 A 4 W Kazakhstan
Fort-Sibut *see* Sibut
Fort Simpson 37 E 4 *var.* Simpson. Northwest Territories, W Canada
Fort Smith 37 E 4 Northwest Territories, W Canada
Fort Smith 42 A 1 Arkansas, C USA
Fort Stockton 49 E 3 Texas, S USA
Fort Vermilion 37 E 4 Alberta, W Canada
Fort Walton Beach 42 D 3 Florida, SE USA
Fort Wayne 40 C 4 Indiana, N USA
Fort William 88 B 3 W Scotland, UK
Fort Worth 49 G 3 Texas, S USA
Fort Yukon 36 D 3 Alaska, NW USA
Forum Alieni *see* Ferrara
Forum Livii *see* Forlì
Fossa Claudia *see* Chioggia
Fougamou 77 A 6 C Gabon
Fougères 90 B 3 NW France
Foulwind, Cape 151 B 5 headland, South Island, C New Zealand
Foumban 76 A 4 NW Cameroon
Fouta Djallon 68 A 4 *var.* Futa Jallon. Mountain range, W Guinea
Foveaux Strait 151 A 8 strait, S Pacific Ocean
Fowlers Bay 147 E 6 bay, Great Australian Bight/Indian Ocean
Foxe Basin 82 B 2 undersea basin, NE Hudson Bay

Fox Mine 37 F 4 Manitoba, C Canada
Fraga 93 F 2 NE Spain

France 90 B 4 It./Sp. Francia; *prev.* Gaul, Gaule, *Lat.* Gallia. Republic, W Europe
Official name: The French Republic **Date of formation:** 1685/1920 **Capital:** Paris **Population:** 57.4 million **Total area:** 551,500 sq km (212,930 sq miles) **Languages:** French*, Provençal, Breton, Catalan, Basque **Religions:** Roman Catholic 90%, Protestant 2%, Jewish 1%, other 7% **Ethnic mix:** French 92%, North African 3%, other 5% **Government:** Multiparty republic **Currency:** Franc = 100 centimes

Franceville 77 B 6 *var.* Massoukou, Masuku. E Gabon
Franche-Comté 90 D 4 cultural region, E France
Francis Case, Lake 45 E 3 reservoir, South Dakota, N USA
Francisco Beltrão 63 E 5 S Brazil
Francistown 78 D 3 NE Botswana
Frankfort 40 C 5 state capital, Kentucky, E USA
Frankfurt *see* Słubice
Frankfurt am Main 95 B 5 *var.* Frankfurt, *Fr.* Francfort; *prev. Eng.* Frankfort on the Main. SW Germany
Frankfurt an der Oder 94 D 3 E Germany
Fränkische Alb 95 C 6 *var.* Frankenalb, *Eng.* Franconian Jura. Mountain range, S Germany
Franklin 42 C 1 Tennessee, S USA
Franklin D.Roosevelt Lake 46 C 1 reservoir, Washington, NW USA
Frantsa-Iosifa, Zemlya 114 D 1 *Eng.* Franz Josef Land. Island group, N Russian Federation
Franz Josef Land *see* Frantsa-Iosifa, Zemlya
Fraserburgh 88 D 3 NE Scotland, UK
Fraser Island 148 E 4 *var.* Great Sandy Island island, E Australia
Frauenburg *see* Saldus
Frederick Reef 148 E 4 reef, W Coral Sea
Fredericksburg 41 E 5 Virginia, NE USA
Fredericton 39 F 4 New Brunswick, SE Canada
Frederiksdal *see* Narsaq Kujalleq
Fredrikshald *see* Halden
Fredrikstad 85 B 6 S Norway
Freeport 54 C 1 N Bahamas
Freeport 49 H 4 Texas, S USA
Freetown 74 C 4 country capital, W Sierra Leone
Freiburg im Breisgau 95 A 6 *var.* Freiburg, *Fr.* Fribourg-en-Brisgau. SW Germany
Fremantle 147 B 6 Western Australia, SW Australia
Fremont 47 B 6 California, W USA
Fremont 45 F 4 Nebraska, C USA
French Guiana 59 H 3 *var.* Guiana, Guyane. French overseas department, NE South America
French Polynesia 145 G 5 French overseas territory, S Pacific Ocean
French Southern & Antarctic Territories 141 C 6 *Fr.* Terres Australes et Antarctiques Françaises. French overseas territory, S Indian Ocean

Fresnillo 50 D 3 *var.* Fresnillo de Gonzales Echeverria, Fresnillo de González Echeverría. C Mexico
Fresno 47 C 6 California, W USA
Freyming-Merlebach 90 E 3 NE France
Frías 64 C 3 N Argentina
Friedek-Mistek *see* Frýdek-Místek
Friedrichshafen 95 B 7 S Germany
Frobisher Bay *see* Iqaluit
Frohavet 84 B 4 sound, SE Norwegian Sea
Frolovo 111 B 6 SW Russian Federation
Frome, Lake 149 B 6 salt lake, S Australia
Frontera 51 G 4 SE Mexico
Frontignan 91 C 6 S France
Frostviken *see* Kvarnbergsvattnet
Frøya 84 A 4 island, W Norway
Frutal 63 F 4 SE Brazil
Frýdek-Místek 99 C 5 *Ger.* Friedek-Mistek. SE Czech Republic
Fuengirola 92 D 5 S Spain
Fuerte Olimpo 64 D 2 *var.* Olimpo. NE Paraguay
Fuerteventura 70 B 3 island, Islas Canarias, SW Spain
Fuji 131 D 6 *var.* Huzi. Honshū, S Japan
Fujian 129 D 6 *var.* Fu-chien, Fuhkien, Fukien, Min. Province, SE China
Fuji-san 131 D 6 *var.* Fujiyama, Mount Fuji. Mountain, Honshū, SE Japan
Fukang 126 C 2 W China
Fukui 131 C 6 *var.* Hukui. Honshū, SW Japan
Fukuoka 131 A 7 *var.* Hukuoka; *hist.* Najima. Kyūshū, SW Japan
Fukushima 130 D 4 *var.* Hukusima. Honshū, C Japan
Fulda 95 B 5 C Germany
Funafuti 145 E 3 island, C Tuvalu
Funafuti *see* Fongafale
Funchal 70 A 2 Madeira, SW Portugal
Fundy, Bay of 39 F 5 inlet, NW Atlantic Ocean
Fünen *see* Fyn
Fung Wong Shan *see* Lantau Peak
Furnes *see* Veurne
Fürth 95 C 5 S Germany
Furukawa 130 D 4 *var.* Hurukawa. Honshū, C Japan
Fushun 128 D 3 *var.* Fou-shan, Fu-shun. NE China
Füssen 95 C 7 S Germany
Futa Jallon *see* Fouta Djallon
Futog 100 D 3 N Yugoslavia
Futuna, Île 145 E 4 island, N Wallis & Futuna
Fuxin 128 D 3 *var.* Fou-hsin, Fu-hsin, Fusin. NE China
Fuzhou 129 D 6 *var.* Foochow, Fu-chou. Province capital, SE China
Fyn 85 B 8 *Ger.* Fünen. Island, C Denmark

G

Gaafu Alifu Atoll *see* North Huvadhu Atoll
Gaafu Dhaalu Atoll *see* South Huvadhu Atoll
Gaalkacyo 73 E 5 *var.* Galka'yo', *It.* Galcaio. C Somalia
Gabela 78 B 2 W Angola
Gaberones *see* Gaborone

Gabès 71 E 2 *var.* Qābis. E Tunisia
Gabès, Golfe de 71 F 2 *Ar.* Khalīj Qābis. Gulf, S Mediterranean Sea

Gabon 77 B 6 Republic, C Africa
Official name: The Gabonese Republic **Date of formation:** 1960 **Capital:** Libreville **Population:** 1.3 million **Total area:** 267,670 sq km (103,347 sq miles) **Languages:** French*, Fang **Religions:** Roman Catholic, other Christian 96%, Muslim 2%, other 2% **Ethnic mix:** Fang 36%, Mpongwe 15%, Mbete 14%, other 35% **Government:** Multiparty republic **Currency:** CFA franc = 100 centimes

Gaborone 78 C 4 *prev.* Gaberones. Country capital, S Botswana
Gabrovo 104 D 2 C Bulgaria
Gadsden 42 D 2 Alabama, S USA
Gaeta 97 C 5 Italy
Gaeta, Golfo di 97 C 5 *var.* Gulf of Gaeta Gulf, E Tyrrhenian Sea
Gaeta, Gulf of *see* Gaeta, Golfo di
Gafsa 71 E 2 *var.* Qafşah. W Tunisia
Gagnoa 74 D 5 C Ivory Coast
Gagra 117 E 1 NW Georgia
Gaillac 91 C 6 *var.* Gaillac-sur-Tarn. S France
Gaillac-sur-Tarn *see* Gaillac
Gaillimh *see* Galway
Gaillimhe, Cuan na *see* Galway Bay
Gailtaler Alpen 95 D 7 mountain range, S Austria
Gainesville 42 D 2 Georgia, SE USA
Gainesville 43 E 3 Florida, SE USA
Gainesville 49 G 2 Texas, S USA
Gairdner, Lake 149 A 6 salt lake, S Australia
Gaiziņ *see* Gaiziņa Kalns
Gaiziņa Kalns 106 D 4 *var.* Gaiziņ. Mountain, E Latvia
Galán, Cerro 64 B 2 mountain, N Argentina
Galanta 99 C 6 *Hung.* Galánta. SW Slovakia
Galánta *see* Galanta
Galapagos Fracture Zone 153 E 3 fracture zone, C Pacific Ocean
Galapagos Islands 153 G 3 *var.* Archipiélago de Colón. island group, E Pacific Ocean
Galapagos Rise 153 F 3 undersea rise, E Pacific Ocean
Galashiels 88 D 4 SE Scotland, UK
Galaţi 108 D 5 *Ger.* Galatz. E Romania
Galatz *see* Galaţi
Galesburg 40 B 4 Illinois, N USA
Galibi 59 H 3 NE Surinam
Galicia 92 B 1 cultural region, NW Spain
Galiuro Mountains 48 B 3 mountain range, Arizona, SW USA
Gallatin 42 D 1 Tennessee, S USA
Galle 132 D 4 *prev.* Point de Galle. SW Sri Lanka
Gallego Rise 153 F 3 undersea rise, E Pacific Ocean
Gallipoli 97 E 6 SW Italy
Gällivare 84 D 3 N Sweden
Gallup 48 C 1 New Mexico, SW USA
Galveston 49 H 4 Texas, S USA
Galveston Bay 49 H 4 bay, N Gulf of Mexico
Galway 89 A 6 *Ir.* Gaillimh. W Ireland
Galway Bay 89 A 6 *Ir.* Cuan na Gaillimhe. Bay, NE Atlantic Ocean

Gámas see Kaamanen
Gambell 36 B 2 Saint Lawrence Island, Alaska, USA
Gambia 74 C 3 river, Gambia/Senegal

Gambia
74 B 3 Republic, W Africa

Official name: Republic of The Gambia Date of formation: 1965 Capital: Banjul Population: 900,000 Total area: 11,300 sq km (4,363 sq miles) Languages: English* Religions: Muslim 85%, Christian 9%, traditional beliefs 6% Ethnic mix: Mandinka 41%, Fulani 14%, Wolof 13%, other 32% Government: Military regime Currency: Dalasi = 100 butut

Gambier, Îles 153 E 4 island group, E French Polynesia
Gamboma 77 B 6 E Congo
Gan 132 B 5 C Maldives
Gäncä 117 G 2 *Rus.* Gyandzha; *prev.* Kirovabad, Yelisavetpol. W Azerbaijan
Gandajika 77 D 7 S Congo (Zaire)
Gander 39 G 3 Newfoundland and Labrador, SE Canada
Gandía 93 F 4 E Spain
Ganges 135 G 4 *Ben.* Padma. River, Bangladesh/India
Ganges Cone see Ganges Fan
Ganges Fan 140 D 3 *var.* Ganges Cone. Undersea fan, N Indian Ocean
Ganges, Mouths of the 135 G 4 delta, Bangladesh/India
Ganges Plain 124 C 3 plain, India/Pakistan
Gangtok 135 G 3 NE India
Gansu 128 B 4 *var.* Gan,Kansu. Province, C China
Ganzhou 129 C 6 S China
Gao 75 E 3 E Mali
Gaoligong Shan 136 B 1 mountain range, Burma/China
Gaoual 74 C 4 N Guinea
Gap 91 D 6 *anc.* Vapincum. SE France
Garabogazköl Bogazy see Kara-Bogaz-Gol, Proliv
Garachiné 53 G 5 SE Panama
Garagum Kanaly see Karakumskiy Kanal
Garagumy 122 C 3 *var.* Black Sand Desert, Qara Qum, *Eng.* Kara Kum, *Turkm.* Garagum; *prev.* Peski Karakumy. Desert, C Turkmenistan
Gara Khitrino 104 D 2 NE Bulgaria
Gárassavon see Kaaresuvanto
Garbsen 94 B 3 N Germany
Garda, Lago di 96 C 2 *var.* Benaco, *Eng.* Lake Garda, *Ger.* Gardasee. Lake, NE Italy
Garden City 45 E 5 Kansas, C USA
Gardēz 123 E 4 *var.* Gardayz, Gardez, Gordiaz. E Afghanistan
Garegegasnjárga see Karigasniemi
Gargždai 106 B 3 W Lithuania
Garissa 73 D 7 E Kenya
Garland 49 G 2 Texas, S USA
Garmo, Qullai 123 F 3 *Eng.* Communism Peak, *Rus.* Kommunizma Pik; *prev.* Stalin Peak. Mountain, E Tajikistan
Garoe see Garoowe
Garonne 91 B 5 *anc.* Garumna. River, S France
Garoowe 73 E 5 *var.* Garoe. N Somalia

Garoua 76 B 4 *var.* Garua. N Cameroon
Garrygala see Kara-Kala
Garsen 73 D 6 SE Kenya
Garua see Garoua
Garumna see Garonne
Garwolin 98 D 4 E Poland
Gar Xincun 126 A 4 *var.* Gar. W China
Gary 40 B 3 Indiana, N USA
Garzón 58 B 4 S Colombia
Gascogne 91 B 6 *Eng.* Gascony. Cultural region, S France
Gascogne, Golfe de see Gascony, Gulf of
Gascony see Gascogne
Gascony, Gulf of 91 A 6 *var.* Golfe de Gascogne. Inlet, NE Atlantic Ocean
Gascoyne 147 B 5 river, W Australia
Gaspé, Péninsule de 39 F 4 *var.* Péninsule de la Gaspésie. Peninsula, Québec, SE Canada
Gaspésie, Péninsule de la see Gaspé, Péninsule de
Gastoúni 105 B 6 S Greece
Gatchina 110 B 4 *var.* Gatčina. NW Russian Federation
Gatčina see Gatchina
Gatineau 38 D 4 Québec, SE Canada
Gatooma see Kadoma
Gatún, Lago 53 F 5 reservoir, C Panama
Gauhāti see Guwāhāti
Gauja 106 D 3 *Ger.* Aa. River, Latvia/Estonia
Gävbandī 120 D 4 S Iran
Gavere 87 B 6 NW Belgium
Gävle 85 C 5 *var.* Gäfle; *prev.* Gefle. C Sweden
Gawler 149 B 6 South Australia, S Australia
Gaya 135 F 4 N India
Gaya see Kyjov
Gaysin see Haysyn
Gaza 119 A 6 *Ar.* Ghazzah, *Heb.* 'Azza. NE Gaza Strip
Gaz-Achak 122 D 2 Turkm.
Gazojak see Turkmenistan
Gazalkent see Ghazalkent
Gazandzhyk 122 B 2 Turkm. Gazanjyk; *prev.* Kazandzhik. W Turkmenistan
Gaza Strip 119 A 7 *Ar.* Qita Ghazzah. Disputed region, SW Asia
Gaziantep 116 D 4 *var.* Gazi Antep; *prev.* Aintab, Antep. S Turkey
Gazipaşa 116 C 5 S Turkey
Gazli 122 D 2 C Uzbekistan
Gazojak see Gaz-Achak
Gdańsk 98 C 2 *Fr.* Dantzig, *Ger.* Danzig.
Gdingen see Gdynia
Gdynia 98 C 2 *Ger.* Gdingen. N Poland
Gedaref 72 C 4 *var.* Al Qaḍārif, El Gedaref. E Sudan
Gediz 116 A 3 river, W Turkey
Gediz 116 B 3 W Turkey
Geel 87 C 5 *var.* Gheel. N Belgium
Geelong 149 C 7 Victoria, SE Australia
Geilo 85 A 5 S Norway
Gejiu 129 B 6 *var.* Kochiu. S China
Gela 97 C 7 *prev.* Terranova di Sicilia. SW Italy

Geldermalsen 86 C 4 C Netherlands
Geleen 87 D 6 SE Netherlands
Gelib see Jilib
Gelinsoor see Gellinsoor
Gellinsoor 73 E 5 *var.* Gelinsoor. C Somalia
Gembloux 87 C 6 C Belgium
Gemena 77 C 5 NW Congo (Zaire)
Gemerek 116 D 3 Turkey
Gemona del Friuli 96 D 2 NE Italy
Genck see Genk
General Alvear 64 B 4 W Argentina
General Carrera, Lago see Buenos Aires, Lago
General Eugenio A.Garay 64 C 1 NW Paraguay
General José F.Uriburu see Zárate
General Santos 139 F 3 *off.* General Santos City. Mindanao, S Philippines
General Santos City see General Santos
Geneva, Lake 95 A 7 *var.* le Léman, *Fr.* Lac Léman, Lac de Genève, *Ger.* Genfer See. Lake, France/Switzerland
Genève 95 A 8 *Eng.* Geneva, *Ger.* Genf, *It.* Ginevra. SW Switzerland
Genichesk see Heniches'k
Genk 87 D 6 *var.* Genck. NE Belgium
Gennep 86 D 4 SE Netherlands
Genoa see Genova
Genoa, Gulf of see Genova, Golfo di
Genova 96 A 2 *Eng.* Genoa, *Fr.* Gênes, *anc.* Genua. NW Italy
Genova, Golfo di 96 A 3 *Eng.* Gulf of Genoa. Gulf, N Ligurian Sea
Genovesa, Isla 60 B 5 *var.* Tower Island. Island, Galapagos Islands, E Pacific Ocean
Gent 87 B 5 *Eng.* Ghent, *Fr.* Gand. NW Belgium
Geographe Bay 147 A 7 bay, E Indian Ocean
Geok-Tepe 122 C 3 *var.* Gëkdepe, *Turkm.* Gökdepe. C Turkmenistan
George 78 C 5 S South Africa
George, Lake 43 E 4 lake, Florida, SE USA
Georges Bank 35 D 5 undersea bank, W Atlantic Ocean
George Sound 151 A 7 sound, S Tasman Sea
George Town 54 C 2 C Bahamas
George Town 54 B 3 *var.* Georgetown. Dependent territory capital, SW Cayman Islands
George Town 138 B 3 *var.* Penang, Pinang. Pulau Pinang, W Malaysia
Georgetown 43 F 2 South Carolina, SE USA
Georgetown 59 G 2 country capital, N Guyana
Georgetown see George Town
Georgia 42 D 2 *off.* State of Georgia; *nicknames* Empire State of the South, Peach State. State, SE USA

Georgia
117 F 2 *Geor.* Sak'art'velo, *Rus.* Gruzinskaya SSR, Gruziya; *prev.* Georgian SSR. Republic, SW Asia

Official name: Republic of Georgia Date of formation: 1991 Capital: Tbilisi Population 5.5 million Total area: 69,700 sq km (26,911 sq miles) Languages: Georgian*, Russian Religions: Georgian Orthodox 70%, Russian Orthodox 10%, other 20%

Ethnic mix: Georgian 69%, Armenian 9%, Russian 6%, Azerbaijani 5%, other 11% Government: Republic Currency: Coupons

Georgian Bay 38 C 5 lake bay, Ontario, S Canada
Georgina 148 B 4 river, C Australia
Georgiu-Dezh see Liski
Georgiyevsk 111 B 7 SW Russian Federation
Georg von Neumayer 154 B 2 research station, Antarctica
Gera 94 C 4 E Germany
Geráki 105 B 6 S Greece
Geral de Goiás, Serra 63 F 3 mountain range, E Brazil
Geraldine 151 B 6 South Island, SW New Zealand
Geraldton 147 A 5 Western Australia, W Australia
Gerdauen see Zheleznodoroznyy
Gerede 116 C 2 N Turkey
Gereshk 122 D 5 SW Afghanistan
Gering 44 D 4 Nebraska, C USA
Gerlachovský Štít 99 D 5 *var.* Gerlachovka, *Ger.* Gerlsdorfer Spitze, *Hung.* Gerlachfalvi Csúcs; *prev.* Stalinov Štít, *Ger.* Franz-Josef Spitze, *Hung.* Ferencz-Jósef Csúcs. Mountain, N Slovakia

Germany
94 B 4 *Ger.* Deutschland. Federal republic, W Europe

Official name: Federal Republic of Germany Date of formation: 1871/1990 Capital: Berlin Population: 80.6 million Total area: 356,910 sq km (137,800 sq miles) Languages: German*, Sorbian Religions: Protestant 45%, Roman Catholic 37%, other 18% Ethnic mix: German 92%, other 8% Government: Multiparty republic Currency: Deutsche Mark = 100 pfennigs

Geroliménas 105 B 7 S Greece
Gerpinnes 87 C 7 S Belgium
Gerze 116 D 2 N Turkey
Getafe 92 D 3 C Spain
Gevaş 117 F 4 SE Turkey
Gevgelija 101 E 6 *var.* Devđelija, Djevdjelija, *Turk.* Gevgeli. SE Macedonia

Ghana
75 E 5 Republic, W Africa

Official name: Republic of Ghana Date of formation: 1957 Capital: Accra Population: 16.4 million Total area: 238,540 sq km (92,100 sq miles) Languages: English,* Akan, Mossi Religions: Traditional beliefs 38%, Muslim 30%, Christian 24%, other 8% Ethnic mix: Akan 52%, Mossi 15%, Ewe 12%, Ga 8%, other 13% Government: Multiparty republic Currency: Cedi = 100 pesewas

Ghanzi 78 C 3 *var.* Khanzi. W Botswana
Gharandal 119 B 7 SW Jordan
Gharvān see Gharyān
Gharyān 71 F 2 *var.* Gharvān. NW Libya
Ghawdex 97 C 8 *var.* Gozo. Island, NW Malta
Ghazalkent 123 F 2 *Rus.* Gazalkent. E Uzbekistan
Ghaznī 123 E 4 *var.* Ghazni. E Afghanistan

Ghazni *see* Ghaznī
Gheel *see* Geel
Gheorgheni 108 C 4 *Ger.* Niklasmarkt, *Hung.* Gyergyószentmiklós; *prev.* Gheorghieni, Sîn-Miclăuş. C Romania
Gherla 108 B 3 *Ger.* Neuschliss, *Hung.* Szamosújvár; *prev. Ger.* Armenierstadt. NW Romania
Ghijduwon 122 D 2 *Rus.* Gizhduvan. C Uzbekistan
Ghŭdara 123 F 3 *var.* Gudara, *Rus.* Kudara. SE Tajikistan
Ghūrīān 122 D 4 W Afghanistan
Giannitsá 104 B 4 *var.* Yiannitsá. N Greece
Gibeon 78 B 4 S Namibia
Gibraltar 93 G 4 UK dependent territory, S Gibraltar
Gibraltar, Bay of 93 G 5 *var.* Bahía de Algeciras. Bay, NE Atlantic Ocean
Gibraltar Harbour 93 H 4 W Gibraltar
Gibraltar, Strait of 92 C 5 *Fr.* Détroit de Gibraltar, *Sp.* Estrecho de Gibraltar Strait, Atlantic Ocean/ Mediterranean Sea
Gibson Desert 147 C 5 desert, Western Australia, W Australia
Giedraičiai 107 C 5 E Lithuania
Giessen 95 B 5 W Germany
Gifu 131 C 6 *var.* Gihu. Honshū, SW Japan
Giganta, Sierra de la 50 B 3 mountain range, W Mexico
Gihu *see* Gifu
Gijón 92 D 1 NW Spain
Gila River 48 A 2 river, Arizona, SW USA
Gilbert Islands 145 E 2 island group, W Kiribati
Gilf Kebir Plateau 72 A 2 *Ar.* Haḍabat al Jilf al Kab ir. Plateau, SW Egypt
Gillette 44 D 3 Wyoming, C USA
Gilroy 47 B 6 California, W USA
Gimie, Mount 55 F 1 mountain, C Saint Lucia
Gingin 147 B 6 Western Australia, SW Australia
Gipeswic *see* Ipswich
Girardot 58 B 3 C Colombia
Giresun 117 E 2 *var.* Kerasunt; *anc.* Cerasus, Pharnacia. NE Turkey
Girona 93 G 2 *var.* Gerona; *anc.* Gerunda. E Spain
Gisborne 150 E 3 North Island, NE New Zealand
Gissar Range 123 E 3 *Rus.* Gissarskiy Khrebet. Mountain range, Tajikistan/Uzbekistan
Gissarskiy Khrebet *see* Gissar Range
Giulianova 96 D 4 C Italy
Giurgiu 108 C 5 S Romania
Gizhduvan *see* Ghijduwon
Gjirokastër 101 C 7 *var.* Gjirokastra, *It.* Argirocastro, *Gk.* Argyrokastron; *prev.* Gjinokastër, Gjirokastra. S Albania
Gjoa Haven 37 F 3 King William Island, Canada
Gjøvik 85 B 5 S Norway
Glace Bay 39 G 4 Nova Scotia, SE Canada
Gladstone 148 E 4 Queensland, E Australia
Glåma 85 B 5 river, E Norway
Glasgow 88 C 4 C Scotland, UK
Glass Mountains 49 E 4 mountain range, Texas, S USA
Glazov 111 D 5 NW Russian Federation
Gleiwitz *see* Gliwice
Glendale 48 B 2 Arizona, SW USA
Glendale 47 C 7 California, W USA
Glendive 44 D 2 Montana, NW USA
Glen Innes 149 D 5 New South Wales, SE Australia
Glina 100 B 3 NE Croatia
Glittertind 85 A 5 mountain, S Norway
Gliwice 99 C 5 *Ger.* Gleiwitz. S Poland
Globino *see* Hlobyne
Głogów 98 B 4 *Ger.* Glogau, Glogow. W Poland
Glommen *see* Glomma
Gloucester 89 C 6 *hist.* Caer Glou, *Lat.* Glevum. W England, UK
Gloversville 41 F 3 New York, NE USA
Głowno 98 D 4 *var.* Główno. C Poland
Główno *see* Głowno
Glubokiy 111 B 6 SW Russian Federation
Glubokoye *see* Hlybokaye
Glukhov *see* Hlukhiv
Gnesen *see* Gniezno
Gniezno 98 C 3 *Ger.* Gnesen. C Poland
Gnjilane 101 E 5 *var.* Gilani, *Alb.* Gjilan. S Yugoslavia
Goa 132 B 2 *var.* Old Goa, *Port.* Goa Velha. State, India
Gobabis 78 B 3 E Namibia
Gobi 124 D 1 desert, China/Mongolia
Gobō 131 C 7 Honshū, SW Japan
Godavari 135 E 5 river, S India
Godhra 134 C 4 W India
Göding *see* Hodonín
Godoy Cruz 64 B 4 W Argentina
Goeree 86 B 4 island, SW Netherlands
Goettingen *see* Göttingen
Gogebic Range 40 B 1 hill range, N USA
Goiânia 63 F 3 *prev.* Goyania. State capital, C Brazil
Goiás 63 E 3 *off.* Estado de Goiás; *prev.* Goiaz or Goyaz. State, C Brazil
Gojōme 130 D 4 Honshū, NW Japan
Göksun 116 D 4 C Turkey
Gol 85 A 5 S Norway
Golan Heights 119 B 5 *Ar.* Al Jawlān, *Heb.* HaGolan. Mountain range, SW Syria
Golaya Pristan *see* Hola Prystan'
Gołdap 98 E 2 *Ger.* Goldap. NE Poland
Goldap *see* Gołdap
Gold Coast 75 E 5 coastal region, S Ghana
Gold Coast 149 E 5 Queensland, E Australia
Golden Bay 150 C 4 bay, South Island, E Tasman Sea
Goldingen *see* Kuldīga
Goldsboro 43 F 1 North Carolina, SE USA
Goleniów 98 B 3 *Ger.* Gollnow. NW Poland
Gollnow *see* Goleniów
Golmud 126 D 4 *var.* Ge'e'mu, Golmo, *Chin.* Ko-erh-mu. C China
Golovanevsk *see* Holovanivs'k
Goma 77 E 6 NE Congo (Zaire)
Gomel' *see* Homyel'
Gomera 70 A 3 island, Islas Canarias, SW Spain
Gómez Palacio 50 D 3 C Mexico
Gonaïves 54 D 3 *var.* Les Gonaïves. N Haiti
Gonâve, Île de la 54 D 3 island, C Haiti
Gondar *see* Gonder
Gonder 72 C 4 *var.* Gondar. NW Ethiopia
Gondia 135 E 4 C India
Gonggar X 126 C 5 W China
Gongola 75 G 4 river, E Nigeria
Gónnoi 104 B 4 *var.* Gónnos; *prev.* Derelí. C Greece
Good Hope *see* Fort Good Hope
Good Hope, Cape of 78 C 5 *Afr.* Kaap die Goeie Hoop; *var.* Kaap de Goede Hoop. Headland, SW South Africa
Goodland 44 D 4 Kansas, C USA
Goondiwindi 149 D 5 Queensland, E Australia
Goor 86 E 3 E Netherlands
Goose Creek 43 F 2 South Carolina, SE USA
Goose Green 65 D 7 E Falkland Islands
Goose Lake 46 B 4 *var.* Lago dos Gansos. Lake, W USA
Göppingen 95 B 6 SW Germany
Gorakhpur 135 E 3 N India
Gorany *see* Harany
Goražde 101 A 8 SE Bosnia & Herzegovina
Gorbovichi *see* Harbavichy
Gore 151 B 7 South Island, SW New Zealand
Gorē 73 C 5 W Ethiopia
Goré 76 C 4 S Chad
Gorgān 120 D 2 *var.* Astarabad, Astrabad, Gurgan; *prev.* Asterābād, *anc.* Hyrcania. N Iran
Gori 117 F 2 C Georgia
Gorinchem 86 C 4 *var.* Gorkum. C Netherlands
Goris 117 G 3 SE Armenia
Gorki *see* Horki
Gor'kiy *see* Nizhniy Novgorod
Gorkum *see* Gorinchem
Görlitz 94 D 4 E Germany
Görlitz *see* Zgorzelec
Gorna Dzhumaya *see* Blagoevgrad
Gornji Milanovac 100 D 4 C Yugoslavia
Gorodets *see* Haradzyets
Gorodishche *see* Horodyshche
Gorodnya *see* Horodnya
Gorodok *see* Haradok
Gorontalo 139 E 4 Celebes, C Indonesia
Gorssel 86 D 3 E Netherlands
Gorzów Wielkopolski 98 B 3 *Ger.* Landsberg, Landsberg an der Warthe. W Poland
Gosford 149 D 6 New South Wales, SE Australia
Goshogawara 130 D 3 *var.* Gosyogawara. Honshū, C Japan
Gospić 100 A 3 C Croatia
Gostivar 101 D 6 W Macedonia
Gosyogawara *see* Goshogawara
Götaland 85 B 6 cultural region, S Sweden
Göteborg 85 B 7 *Eng.* Gothenburg. S Sweden
Gotel Mountains 75 G 5 mountain range, E Nigeria
Gotha 94 C 4 C Germany
Gothenburg *see* Göteborg
Gotland 85 C 6 island, SE Sweden
Gotō-rettō 131 A 7 island group, Japan
Gotska Sandön 85 C 6 island, SE Sweden
Gōtsu 131 B 6 *var.* Gôtu. Honshū, SW Japan
Göttingen 94 B 4 *var.* Goettingen. C Germany
Gottschee *see* Kočevje
Gottwaldov *see* Zlín
Gôtu *see* Gōtsu
Gouda 86 C 4 C Netherlands
Gough Fracture Zone 67 C 6 fracture zone, S Atlantic Ocean
Gough Island 69 B 8 island, S Atlantic Ocean
Gouin, Réservoir 38 D 4 reservoir, Québec, SE Canada
Goulburn 149 D 7 New South Wales, SE Australia
Goulburn Islands 148 A 1 island group, Northern Territory, N Australia
Goundam 75 E 3 NW Mali
Gouré 75 G 3 SE Niger
Goverla, Gora *see* Hoverla, Hora
Governador Valadares 63 F 4 SE Brazil
Govĭ Altayn Nuru 127 E 3 mountain range, S Mongolia
Goya 64 D 3 NE Argentina
Goyania *see* Goiânia
Goz Beïda 76 D 3 SE Chad
Gozo *see* Gozo
Gračanica 100 C 3 NE Bosnia & Herzegovina
Graciosa 92 A 5 *var.* Ilha Graciosa. Island, W Portugal
Graciosa, Ilha *see* Graciosa
Gradačac 100 C 3 N Bosnia & Herzegovina
Gradaús, Serra dos 63 E 3 mountain range, C Brazil
Grafton 149 E 6 New South Wales, SE Australia
Grafton 45 E 1 North Dakota, N USA
Graham Land 154 A 2 physical region, Antarctica
Grain Coast 74 C 5 coastal region, S Liberia
Grajewo 98 E 2 NE Poland
Grampian Mountains 88 C 3 mountain range, C Scotland, UK
Grampians, The 149 B 7 mountain range, Victoria, SE Australia
Granada 92 D 5 S Spain
Granada 52 D 3 SW Nicaragua
Gran Canaria 70 A 3 *var.* Grand Canary. Island, Islas Canarias, SW Spain
Gran Chaco 61 G 4 *var.* Chaco. Physical region, W South America
Grand Bahama Island 54 C 1 island, N Bahamas
Grand Banks of Newfoundland 66 B 3 undersea basin, NW Atlantic Ocean
Grand Bassa *see* Buchanan
Grand Canary *see* Gran Canaria
Grand Canyon 48 B 1 valley, Arizona, SW USA
Grand Cayman 54 B 3 island, SW Cayman Islands
Grande, Bahía 65 C 7 bay, SW Atlantic Ocean
Grande Comore 79 F 2 *var.* Njazidja, Great Comoro. Island, NW Comoros

Grande Deux, Réservoir la 38 D 3 reservoir, Québec, E Canada
Grande Prairie 37 E 5 Alberta, W Canada
Grand Erg de Bilma 75 H 3 desert, NE Niger
Grand Erg Occidental 70 D 3 desert, W Algeria
Grand Erg Oriental 71 E 3 desert, Algeria/Tunisia
Grande, Rio 49 F 5 *var.* Río Bravo, Río Bravo del Norte. River, Mexico/USA
Grande Rivière 55 F 1 C Saint Lucia
Grande Terre 55 G 3 island, E Guadeloupe
Grand Falls 39 G 3 New Brunswick, SE Canada
Grand Forks 45 E 1 North Dakota, N USA
Grandichi *see* Hrandzichy
Grand Island 45 E 4 Nebraska, C USA
Grand Junction 44 C 4 Colorado, C USA
Grand Lac de l'Ours *see* Great Bear Lake
Grand Lac des Esclaves *see* Great Slave Lake
Grand Paradis *see* Gran Paradiso
Grand Rapids 40 C 3 Michigan, N USA
Grand Rapids 45 F 1 Minnesota, N USA
Grand Ronde River 46 C 3 river, NW USA
Grand-Santi 59 H 3 W French Guiana
Gran Malvina *see* West Falkland
Granollers 93 G 2 *var.* Granollérs. NE Spain
Granollérs *see* Granollers
Gran Paradiso 96 A 2 *Fr.* Grand Paradis. Mountain, NW Italy
Gran Santiago *see* Santiago
Grantley Adams 55 H 2 international airport, SE Barbados
Grants 48 C 2 New Mexico, SW USA
Grants Pass 46 B 4 Oregon, NW USA
Granville 90 B 3 N France
Gratz *see* Graz
Graulhet 91 C 6 S France
Grave 86 D 4 SE Netherlands
Grayling 36 C 2 Alaska, NW USA
Graz 95 E 7 *prev.* Gratz. SE Austria
Great Abaco 54 C 1 *var.* Abaco Island. Island, N Bahamas
Great Australian Bight 152 B 4 bight, E Indian Ocean
Great Barrier Island 150 D 2 island, North Island, N New Zealand
Great Barrier Reef 148 D 2 reef W Pacific Ocean
Great Basin 47 C 5 basin, Nevada, W USA
Great Bear Lake 37 E 3 *Fr.* Grand Lac de l'Ours. Lake, Northwest Territories, NW Canada
Great Bend 45 E 5 Kansas, C USA
Great Dividing Range 148 C 2 mountain range, E Australia
Greater Antarctica 154 C 3 *var.* East Antarctica. Physical region, Antarctica
Greater Antilles 54 D 3 island group, N West Caribbean Sea
Greater Caucasus 117 G 2 *Az.* Ba Qafqaz Silsiläsi, *Geor.* Kavkasioni, *Rus.* Bol'shoy Kavkaz. Mountain range, N Azerbaijan / Georgia / Russian Federation

Great Exhibition Bay 150 C 1 inlet, S Pacific Ocean
Great Exuma Island 54 C 2 island, C Bahamas
Great Falls 44 B 1 Montana, NW USA
Great Grimsby *see* Grimsby
Great Hungarian Plain 99 D 7 *var.* Great Alföld, Plain of Hungary, *Hung.* Alföld. Plain, SE Europe
Great Inagua 54 D 2 *var.* Inagua Islands. Island, S Bahamas
Great Karoo 78 C 5 *var.* Great Karroo, High Veld, *Afr.* Groot Karoo, Hoë Karoo. Physical region, S South Africa
Great Khingan Range *see* Da Hinggan Ling
Great Lake *see* Tônlé Sap
Great Nicobar 133 G 3 island, SE India
Great Plains 45 E 3 physical region, C Canada/USA
Great Rift Valley 69 D 5 *var.* Rift Valley, Depression. Africa/Asia
Great Ruaha 73 C 7 river, S Tanzania
Great Saint Bernard Pass 95 A 8 *Fr.* Col du Grand-Saint-Bernard, *It.* Passo di Gran San Bernardo. Pass, Italy/Switzerland
Great Salt Desert *see* Kavīr, Dasht-e
Great Salt Lake 44 B 3 salt lake, Utah, W USA
Great Salt Lake Desert 44 A 4 plain, Utah, W USA
Great Sand Sea 72 A 2 desert, Egypt/Libya
Great Sandy Desert 146 C 4 desert, Western Australia, W Australia
Great Sandy Desert 112 B 5 desert, SW Asia
Great Sandy Island *see* Fraser Island
Great Slave Lake 37 E 4 *Fr.* Grand Lac des Esclaves. Lake, Northwest Territories, NW Canada
Great Sound 42 A 5 bay, W Atlantic Ocean
Great Victoria Desert 142 A 4 desert, Western Australia, W Australia
Great Wall of China 127 E 4 ancient monument, C China
Great Yarmouth 89 E 6 *var.* Yarmouth. E England, UK
Grebenka *see* Hrebinka
Gredos, Sierra de 92 D 3 mountain range, C Spain

Greece
105 A 5 *Gk.* Ellás; *anc.* Hellas. Republic, SE Europe
Official name: Hellenic Republic **Date of formation:** 1830/1947 **Capital:** Athens **Population:** 10.2 million **Total area:** 131,990 sq km (50,961 sq miles) **Languages:** Greek*, Turkish, Albanian, Macedonian **Religions:** Greek Orthodox 98%, Muslim 1%, other 1% **Ethnic mix:** Greek 98%, other 2% **Government:** Multiparty republic **Currency:** Drachma = 100 lepta

Greeley 44 D 4 Colorado, C USA
Green Bay 40 B 2 N USA
Green Bay 40 B 2 lake bay, Wisconsin, N USA
Greeneville 43 E 1 Tennessee, S USA
Greenland 82 D 3 *Dan.* Grønland, *Inuit* Kalaallit Nunaat. Danish external territory, Arctic Ocean/ Atlantic Ocean

Greenland Sea 83 F 2 sea, Arctic Ocean
Green Mountains 41 G 3 mountain range, Vermont, NE USA
Greenock 88 C 4 SW Scotland, UK
Green River 40 C 5 river, Kentucky, E USA
Green River 44 B 4 river, C USA
Greensboro 43 F 1 North Carolina, SE USA
Greenville 43 F 1 North Carolina, SE USA
Greenville 42 B 2 Arkansas, C USA
Greenville 42 D 3 Alabama, S USA
Greenville 43 E 1 South Carolina, SE USA
Greenville 49 G 2 Texas, S USA
Greenwood 42 B 2 Mississippi, S USA
Greenwood 43 E 2 South Carolina, SE USA
Gregory Range 148 C 3 mountain range, Queensland, E Australia
Greifswald 94 D 2 NE Germany
Grenada 42 C 2 Mississippi, S USA

Grenada
55 G 5 Commonwealth republic, E Caribbean Sea
Official name: Grenada **Date of formation:** 1974 **Capital:** St George's **Population:** 91,000 **Total area:** 340 sq km (131 sq miles) **Languages:** English*, English Creole **Religions:** Roman Catholic 68%, Protestant 32% **Ethnic mix:** Black 84%, Afro-European 13%, South Asian 3% **Government:** Parliamentary democracy **Currency:** E. Caribbean $ = 100 cents

Grenadines, The 55 H 5 island group, E Caribbean Sea
Grenoble 91 D 5 *anc.* Cularo, Gratianopolis. E France
Grenville, Cape 148 C 2 headland, Queensland, NE Australia
Gresham 46 B 3 Oregon, NW USA
Grevelingen 86 B 4 estuary, S North Sea
Grevená 104 B 4 N Greece
Greymouth 151 B 5 South Island, C New Zealand
Grey Range 149 C 5 mountain range, E Australia
Greytown *see* San Juan del Norte
Grimari 76 C 4 C Central African Republic
Grimsby 89 E 5 *prev.* Great Grimsby; *hist.* Great Grimsby. E England, UK
Grise Fiord 37 F 2 *var.* Ausuitoq. Ellesmere Island, N Canada
Grobin *see* Grobiņa
Grobiņa 106 B 3 *Ger.* Grobin. W Latvia
Grodno *see* Hrodna
Groesbeek 86 D 4 SE Netherlands
Grójec 98 D 4 C Poland
Groningen 86 E 1 NE Netherlands
Groote Eylandt 148 B 2 island, N Australia
Grootfontein 78 B 3 N Namibia
Groot Karasberge 78 B 4 mountain range, S Namibia
Gros Islet 55 F 1 N Saint Lucia
Grosser Sund *see* Suur Väin
Grosseto 96 B 4 N W Italy
Grossglockner 95 D 7 mountain, W Austria
Grosskanizsa *see* Nagykanizsa
Groznyy 111 B 8 SW Russian Federation

Grudziądz 98 C 3 *var.* Grudziädz, *Ger.* Graudenz. N Poland
Grums 85 B 6 C Sweden
Grünau 78 B 4 S Namibia
Gryazi 111 B 6 W Russian Federation
Gryfice 98 B 2 *Ger.* Greifenberg, Greifenberg in Pommern. NW Poland
Guabito 53 E 4 NW Panama
Guadalajara 93 E 3 *Ar.* Wad Al-Hajarah; *anc.* Arriaca. C Spain
Guadalajara 50 D 4 C Mexico
Guadalcanal 144 C 3 island, C Solomon Islands
Guadalquivir 92 D 4 river, W Spain
Guadalupe 50 D 3 C Mexico
Guadalupe Mountains 48 D 3 mountain range, SW USA
Guadeloupe 55 H 3 French overseas department, E Caribbean Sea
Guadiana 92 C 4 river, Portugal/Spain
Guadix 93 E 5 S Spain
Guaico 55 H 5 C Trinidad & Tobago
Guaimaca 52 C 2 C Honduras
Guajira, Península de la 58 C 1 peninsula, N Colombia
Gualaco 52 D 2 C Honduras
Gualán 52 B 2 C Guatemala
Gualaquiza 60 B 2 E Ecuador
Gualdicciolo 96 D 1 NW San Marino
Gualeguaychú 64 D 4 E Argentina
Guam 144 A 1 US unincorporated territory, W Pacific Ocean
Guamúchil 50 C 3 C Mexico
Guanabacoa 54 B 2 W Cuba
Guanare 58 C 2 N Venezuela
Guanare 58 D 2 river, NW Venezuela
Guangdong 129 C 6 *var.* Kuang-tung, Kwangtung, Yue. Province, SE China
Guangxi Zhuangzu Zizhiqu 129 B 6 *var.* Guangxi, Gui, Kuang-hsi, Kwangsi, *Eng.* Kwangsi Chuang Autonomous Region. Autonomous region, S China
Guangyuan 129 B 5 *var.* Kuang-yuan, Kwangyuan. SW China
Guangzhou 129 C 6 *var.* Kuang-chou, Kwangchow, *Eng.* Canton. Province capital, SE China
Guantánamo 54 D 3 SE Cuba
Guantanamo Bay 54 D 3 US military base, E Cuba
Guaporé 61 F 3 *var.* Río Iténez. River, Bolivia/Brazil
Guarda 92 C 3 E Portugal
Guarumal 53 F 5 S Panama
Guasave 50 C 3 C Mexico

Guatemala
52 A 2 Republic, NW Central America
Official name: Republic of Guatemala **Date of formation:** 1838 **Capital:** Guatemala City **Population:** 10 million **Total area:** 108,890 sq km (42,043 sq miles) **Languages:** Spanish*, Quiché, Mam, Kekchi **Religions:** Christian 99%, other 1% **Ethnic mix:** Indian 55%, *ladino* (Euro-Indian, White) 45% **Government:** Multiparty republic **Currency:** Quetzal = 100 centavos

Guatemala Basin 153 F 3 undersea basin, E Pacific Ocean
Guatemala City *see* Guatemala, Ciudad de

Guatemala, Ciudad de 52 B 2 *Eng.*
Guatemala City; *prev.* Santiago de
los Caballeros. Country capital,
C Guatemala
Guatemala, Republic of *see*
Guatemala
Guaviare 58 C 3 river, E Colombia
Guayana, Macizo de las *see*
Guiana Highlands
Guayaquil 60 B 2 *var.* Santiago de
Guayaquil. SW Ecuador
Guayaquil, Gulf of 60 A 2 gulf,
E Pacific Ocean
Guayaramerín 61 F 2 N Bolivia
Guaymas 50 B 2 NW Mexico
Gubadag 122 D 2 *Turkm.* Tel'man;
prev. Tel'mansk. N Turkmenistan
Gubakha 111 D 5 *var.* Gubachaj,
Gubaha. NW Russian Federation
Guben 94 D 4 *var.* Wilhelm-Pieck-
Stadt. E Germany
Gubkin 111 B 6 W Russian Federation
Gudaut'a 117 E 1 NW Georgia
Guelta Zemmur 70 B 3
E Western Sahara
Guéret 91 C 5 C France
Guerguerat 70 A 4 SW Western Sahara
Guernsey 89 D 8 island,
W Channel Islands
Guerrero Negro 50 A 2 NW Mexico
Guiana Basin 66 B 4 undersea
basin, W Atlantic Ocean
Guiana Highlands 56 C 2 *var.*
Macizo de las Guayana. Mountain
range, N South America
Guidder *see* Guider
Guider 76 B 4 *var.* Guidder.
N Cameroon
Guidimouni 75 G 3 S Niger
Guildford 89 D 7 SE England, UK
Guilin 129 C 6 *var.* Kuei-lin,
Kweilin. E China
Guimarães *see* Guimarães
Guimarães 92 B 2 *var.* Guimaráes.
N Portugal

Guinea
74 C 4 *var.* Guinée; *prev.* French
Guinea, People's Revolutionary
Republic of Guinea. Republic,
W Africa

Official name: Republic of Guinea
Date of formation: 1958 **Capital:**
Conakry **Population:** 6.3 million
Total area: 245,860 sq km (94,926 sq
miles) **Languages:** French*, Fulani,
Malinke, Susu **Religions:** Muslim
85%, Christian 8%, traditional
beliefs 7% **Ethnic mix:** Fulani 40%,
Malinke 25%, Susu 12%, other 23%
Government: Multiparty republic
Currency: Franc = 100 centimes

Guinea Basin 67 D 5 undersea
basin, E Atlantic Ocean

Guinea-Bissau
74 B 4 *Fr.* Guinée-Bissau, *Port.*
Guiné-Bissau; *prev.* Portuguese
Guinea. Republic, W Africa

Official name: Republic of Guinea-
Bissau **Date of formation:** 1974
Capital: Bissau **Population:**
1 million **Total area:** 36,120 sq km
(13,940 sq miles) **Languages:**
Portuguese*, local languages
Religions: Traditional beliefs 54%,
Muslim 38%, Christian 8% **Ethnic
mix:** Balante 27%, Fulani 22%,
Malinke 12%, other 39%
Government: Multiparty republic
Currency: Peso = 100 centavos

Guinea, Gulf of 69 B 5 *Fr.* Golfe de
Guinée. Inlet, E Atlantic Ocean
Guinée, Golfe de *see* Guinea,Gulf of
Güiria 59 E 1 NE Venezuela
Guiyang 129 B 6 *var.* Kuei-Yang,
Kuei-yang, Kueyang, Kweiyang;
prev. Kweichu. Province capital,
S China
Guizhou 129 B 6 *var.* Kuei-chou,
Kweichow, Qian. Province,
S China
Gujarāt 134 C 4 *var.* Gujerat. State,
W India
Gujerat *see* Gujarāt
Gujrānwāla 134 D 2 NE Pakistan
Gujrāt 134 C 2 E Pakistan
Gulbarga 132 C 1 C India
Gulbene 106 D 3 *Ger.* Alt-
Schwanenburg. NE Latvia
Gulf, The 120 C 4 *var.* Persian Gulf,
Ar. Khalīj al 'Arabī, *Per.* Khalīj-e
Fars. Gulf, W Arabian Sea
Gulistan *see* Guliston
Guliston 123 E 2 *Rus.* Gulistan.
E Uzbekistan
Gulkana 36 D 3 Alaska, NW USA
Gulu 73 B 6 N Uganda
Gulyantsi 104 C 1 NW Bulgaria
Guma *see* Pishan
Gumbinnen *see* Gusev
Gümüşhane 117 E 3 *var.*
Gumushkhane, Gümüşane.
NE Turkey
Güney Doğu Toroslar 117 E 4
mountain range, SE Turkey
Gunnedah 149 D 6 New South
Wales, SE Australia
Gunnison 44 C 5
Colorado, C USA
Gurbantünggüt Shamo 126 C 2
desert, NW China
Guri, Embalse de 59 E 2 reservoir,
E Venezuela
Gurktaler Alpen 95 D 7 mountain
range, S Austria
Gürün 116 D 3 C Turkey
Gur'yev *see* Atyrau
Gusau 75 G 4 N Nigeria
Gusev 106 B 4 *Ger.* Gumbinnen.
W Russian Federation
Gushgy 122 D 4 *prev.* Kushka.
S Turkmenistan
Gustavus 36 D 4 Alaska, NW USA
Güstrow 94 C 3 NE Germany
Gütersloh 94 B 4 W Germany
Guthrie 49 G 1 Oklahoma, C USA
Gutland 87 D 8 physical region,
S Luxembourg
Guttstadt *see* Dobre Miasto
Guwāhāti 135 G 3 *prev.* Gauhāti.
NE India

Guyana
59 F 3 *prev.* British Guiana.
Republic, N South America

Official name: Cooperative
Republic of Guyana **Date of
formation:** 1966 **Capital:**
Georgetown **Population:** 800,000
Total area: 214,970 sq km
(83,000 sq miles) **Languages:**
English*, English Creole, other
Religions: Christian 57%, Hindu
33%, Muslim 9%, other 1%
Ethnic mix: South Asian 51%, Black
and mixed 43%, other 6%
Government: Multiparty republic
Currency: Guyana $ =100 cents

Guymon 49 E 1 Oklahoma, C USA
Gvardeysk 106 A 4 *Ger.* Tapaiu.
W Russian Federation

Gwādar 134 A 3 *var.* Gwadur.
SW Pakistan
Gwadur *see* Gwādar
Gwalior 134 D 3 C India
Gwanda 78 D 3 SW Zimbabwe
Gwy *see* Wye
Gyangzê 126 C 5 W China
Gyaring Hu 126 C 5 lake, C China
Gympie 149 E 5 Queensland,
E Australia
Gyomaendrőd 99 D 7 SE Hungary
Gyöngyös 99 D 6 NE Hungary
Győr 99 C 6 *Ger.* Raab;
Lat. Arrabona. NW Hungary
Gýtheio 105 B 6 *prev.* Yíthion.
S Greece
Gyumri 117 F 2 *var.* Giumri,
Rus. Kumayri; *prev.* Leninakan,
Aleksandropol'. W Armenia
Gyzylarbat 122 C 2 *prev.* Kizyl-
Arvat. W Turkmenistan

H

Haabai *see* Ha'apai Group
Haacht 87 C 6 C Belgium
Haaksbergen 86 E 3 E Netherlands
Ha'apai Group 145 F 5 *var.* Haabai.
Island group, C Tonga
Haapsalu 106 D 2 *Ger.* Hapsal.
W Estonia
Haarlem 86 C 3 *prev.* Harlem.
W Netherlands
Haast 151 B 6 South Island,
SW New Zealand
Habomai Islands 130 E 2 island
group, SE Russian Federation
Hachijō-jima 131 E 2 *var.* Hatizyô
Zima. Island, Izu-shotō, E Japan
Hachinohe 130 D 3 Honshū,
C Japan
Hadejia 75 G 4 N Nigeria
Hadejia 75 G 4 river, N Nigeria
Hadera 119 A 6 C Israel
Hadhdhunmati Atoll 132 A 5
var. Haddummati Atoll, Laamu
Atoll. Island, S Maldives
Hadhramaut *see* Ḩaḑramawt
Ha Đông 136 D 3 *var.* Hadong.
N Vietnam
Hadong *see* Ha Đông
Ḩaḑramawt 121 C 6 *Eng.*
Hadhramaut. Mountain range,
S Yemen
Hafren *see* Severn
Hagerstown 41 E 4 Maryland,
NE USA
Ha Giang 136 D 3 NW Vietnam
Hagondange 90 D 3 NE France
Haguenau 90 E 3 NE France
Haicheng 128 D 3 NE China
Haidarabad *see* Hyderābād
Haifa, Bay of *see* Ḩefa, Mifraz
Haikang 129 C 7 *var.* Leizhou.
S China
Haikou 129 C 7 *var.* Hai-k'ou,
Hoihow, *Fr.* Hoï-Hao. Hainan
Dao, S China
Ḩā'il 120 B 4 NW Saudi Arabia
Hailar 127 F 1 *var.* Hai-la-erh; *prev.*
Hulun. N China
Hailuoto 84 D 4 *Swe.* Karlö. Island,
W Finland
Hainan 129 B 7 *var.* Qiong.
Province, S China
Hainan Dao 129 C 7 island, S China
Haines 36 D 4 Alaska, NW USA
Hainichen 94 D 4 E Germany
Hai Phong 136 E 3 *var.* Haifong,
Haiphong. N Vietnam

Haiti
54 D 3 Republic, N Haiti

Official name: Republic of Haiti
Date of formation: 1804 **Capital:**
Port-au-Prince **Population:** 6.9
million **Total area:** 27,750 sq km
(10,714 sq miles) **Languages:**
French*, French Creole, English
Religions: Roman Catholic 80%,
Protestant 16%, Voodoo 4% **Ethnic
mix:** Black 95%, Afro-European 5%
Government: Multiparty republic
Currency: Gourde = 100 centimes

Hajdúhadház 99 E 6 E Hungary
Hakodate 130 D 3 Hokkaidō,
NE Japan
Hakosberge 78 B 4 mountain range,
C Namibia
Ha Kwai Chung 128 A 1
W Hong Kong
Hal *see* Halle
Ḩalab 118 B 2 *Eng.* Aleppo,
Fr. Alep; *anc.* Beroea. NW Syria
Ḩalānīyāt, Juzur al 121 D 6 *var.*
Jazā'ir Bin Ghalfān, *Eng.* Kuria
Muria Islands. Island group,
S Oman
Halberstadt 94 C 4 C Germany
Halden 85 B 6 *prev.* Fredrikshald.
S Norway
Halfmoon Bay 151 A 8 *var.* Oban.
South Island, SW New Zealand
Halifax 39 F 4 Nova Scotia,
SE Canada
Halifax Bay 148 D 3 bay,
W Pacific Ocean
Halle 94 C 4 *var.* Halle an der Saale.
C Germany
Halle 87 B 6 *Fr.* Hal. C Belgium
Halle an der Saale *see* Halle
Halle-Neustadt 94 C 4 C Germany
Halley 154 B 2 research station,
Antarctica
Hall Islands 144 B 1 island group,
C Micronesia
Halls Creek 146 D 3 Western
Australia, NW Australia
Halmahera 139 F 3 *prev.* Djailolo,
Gilolo, Jailolo. Island, E Indonesia
Halmahera, Laut 139 F 4 sea,
W Pacific Ocean
Halmstad 85 B 7 S Sweden
Hälsingborg *see* Helsingborg
Hamada 131 B 6 Honshū, SW Japan
Hamadān 120 C 3 *anc.* Ecbatana.
W Iran
Ḩamāh 118 B 3 *var.* Hama; *anc.*
Epiphania, *Bibl.* Hamath. W Syria
Hamamatsu 131 D 6 *var.*
Hamamatu. Honshū, S Japan
Hamamatu *see* Hamamatsu
Hamar 85 B 5 *prev.* Storhammer.
S Norway
Hamburg 94 B 3 N Germany
Ḩamḑ, Wādī al 120 A 4 dry
watercourse, W Saudi Arabia
Hämeenlinna 85 D 5 *Swe.*
Tavastehus. SW Finland
Hamersley Range 146 B 4
mountain range, Western
Australia, W Australia
Hamhŭng 128 E 3 C North Korea
Hami 126 C 3 *var.* Ha-mi, *Uigh.*
Kumul, Qomul. NW China
Hamilton 58 C 4 S Scotland, UK
Hamilton 42 A 5 dependent
territory capital, C Bermuda
Hamilton 150 D 3 North Island,
N New Zealand
Hamilton 38 D 5 Ontario,
S Canada

Hamm 94 B 3 *var.* Hamm in Westfalen. W Germany

Ḥammāmāt, Khalīj al *see* Hammamet, Golfe de

Ḥammār, Hawr al 120 C 3 lake, SE Iraq

Hamm in Westfalen *see* Hamm

Hampden 151 B 7 South Island, SW New Zealand

Hampton 41 F 5 Virginia, NE USA

Handan 128 C 4 *var.* Han-tan. NE China

HaNegev 119 A 7 *Eng.* Negev. Desert, S Israel

Hanford 47 C 7 California, W USA

Hangayn Nuruu 126 D 2 mountain range, W Mongolia

Hangö *see* Hanko

Hangzhou 129 D 5 *var.* Hang-chou, Hangchow. Province capital, E China

Hanhöhiy Uul 126 C 2 mountain range, NW Mongolia

Hanko 85 D 6 *Swe.* Hangö. SW Finland

Hanmer Springs 151 C 5 South Island, C New Zealand

Hanna 37 E 5 Alberta, SW Canada

Hannibal 45 G 4 Missouri, C USA

Hannover 94 B 3 *Eng.* Hanover. NW Germany

Hanöbukten 85 B 7 bay, SW Baltic Sea

Ha Nôi 136 D 3 *var.* Ha Noi, Ha noi, *Eng.* Hanoi, *Fr.* Ha noi. Country capital, N Vietnam

Hanover *see* Hannover

Han-tan *see* Handan

Hantsavichy 107 B 6 *Pol.* Hancewicze, *Rus.* Gantsevichi. SW Belorussia

Hanzhong 129 B 5 C China

Hāora 135 G 4 *prev.* Howrah. NE India

Hapsal *see* Haapsalu

Haradok 107 E 5 *Rus.* Gorodok. N Belorussia

Haradzyets 107 B 6 *Rus.* Gorodets. SW Belorussia

Haramachi 131 D 5 Honshū, E Japan

Harany 107 D 5 *Rus.* Gorany. N Belorussia

Hārar 73 D 5 Ethiopia

Harare 78 D 3 *prev.* Salisbury. Country capital, NE Zimbabwe

Harbavichy 107 E 6 *Rus.* Gorbovichi. E Belorussia

Harbel 74 C 5 W Liberia

Harbin 128 E 2 *var.* Haerbin, Ha-erh-pin, Kharbin; *prev.* Haerhpin, Pinkiang, Pingkiang. Province capital, NE China

Hardanger-fjorden 85 A 5 fjord, E Norwegian Sea

Hardangervidda 85 A 6 mountain range, S Norway

Hardenberg 86 E 3 E Netherlands

Hardy 42 B 1 Arkansas, C USA

Harelbeke 87 A 6 *var.* Harlebeke. W Belgium

Harem *see* Ḩārim

Haren 86 E 2 NE Netherlands

Hargeisa *see* Hargeysa

Hargeysa 73 D 5 *var.* Hargeisa. NW Somalia

Hariana *see* Haryāna

Hari, Batang 138 B 4 *prev.* Djambi. River, Sumatera, W Indonesia

Ḩārim 118 B 2 *var.* Harem. W Syria

Harima-nada 131 B 6 sea, NW Pacific Ocean

Harīrūd 123 E 4 river, C Asia

Harlan 45 F 3 Iowa, C USA

Harlebeke *see* Harelbeke

Harlem *see* Haarlem

Harlingen 49 G 5 Texas, S USA

Harlingen 86 D 2 *Fris.* Harns. N Netherlands

Harlow 89 E 6 SE England, UK

Harmanli *see* Kharmanli

Harney Lake 46 C 4 lake, Oregon, NW USA

Härnösand 85 C 5 *var.* Hernösand. C Sweden

Harns *see* Harlingen

Har Nuur 126 C 2 lake, NW Mongolia

Harper 74 D 5 *var.* Cape Palmas. NE Liberia

Ḩarrat Rahaṭ 121 B 5 lavaflow, W Saudi Arabia

Harris 88 B 3 physical region, NW Scotland, UK

Harrisburg 41 E 4 state capital, Pennsylvania, NE USA

Harrison 42 B 1 Arkansas, C USA

Harrisonburg 41 E 5 Virginia, NE USA

Harrison, Cape 39 F 2 headland, Newfoundland and Labrador, E Canada

Harrogate 89 D 5 N England, UK

Hârşova 108 D 5 *prev.* Hîrsova. SE Romania

Harstad 84 C 2 N Norway

Hartford 41 G 3 state capital, Connecticut, NE USA

Hartlepool 89 D 5 N England, UK

Har Us Nuur 126 C 2 lake, NW Mongolia

Harwich 89 E 6 E England, UK

Haryāna 134 D 2 *var.* Hariana. State, N India

Haskovo *see* Khaskovo

Hasselt 87 D 6 NE Belgium

Hastings 89 E 7 SE England, UK

Hastings 55 G 2 SW Barbados

Hastings 150 E 4 North Island, NE New Zealand

Hastings 45 E 4 Nebraska, C USA

Haṭeg 108 B 4 *Ger.* Wallenthal, *Hung.* Hátszeg; *prev. Ger.* Hatzeg, Hötzing. SW Romania

Hattem 86 D 3 E Netherlands

Hatteras, Cape 43 G 1 headland, North Carolina, SE USA

Hattiesburg 42 C 3 Mississippi, S USA

Hat Yai 137 C 7 *var.* Ban Hat Yai. S Thailand

Haugesund 85 A 6 S Norway

Hau Hoi Wan 128 A 1 bay, NW Hong Kong

Haukeligrend 85 A 6 S Norway

Haukivesi 85 E 5 lake, SE Finland

Hauraki Gulf 150 D 2 gulf, S Pacific Ocean

Haut Atlas 70 C 3 *Eng.* High Atlas. Mountain range, C Morocco

Hautes Fagnes 87 D 6 *Ger.* Hohes Venn. Mountain range, E Belgium

Hauts Plateaux 70 D 2 *var.* Hauts-Plateaux. Plateau, Algeria/Morocco

Hauts-Plateaux *see* Hauts Plateaux

Hauzenberg 95 D 6 SE Germany

Havana 53 D 6 country capital, NW Cuba

Havana *see* La Habana

Havant 89 D 7 S England, UK

Havelock 43 F 1 North Carolina, SE USA

Havelock North 150 E 4 North Island, NE New Zealand

Haverfordwest 89 B 6 SW Wales, UK

Havířov 99 C 5 E Czech Republic

Havre 44 C 1 Montana, C USA

Havre-St-Pierre 39 F 3 Québec, E Canada

Havza 116 D 2 N Turkey

Hawaii 47 A 8 *off.* state of Hawaii; *nicknames* Aloha State, Paradise of the Pacific. State, W USA

Hawaii 47 B 8 *Haw.* Hawai'i. Island, W USA

Hawaiian Islands 152 D 2 *var.* The Hawaiian Islands; *prev.* The Sandwich Islands. Island group, C Pacific Ocean

Hawaiian Ridge 152 D 2 undersea ridge, N Pacific Ocean

Hawea, Lake 151 B 6 lake, South Island, SW New Zealand

Hawera 150 D 4 North Island, C New Zealand

Hawick 88 D 4 S Scotland, UK

Hawke Bay 150 E 4 bay, S Pacific Ocean

Hawke's Bay 150 E 4 cultural region, North Island, N New Zealand

Hay 149 C 6 New South Wales, SE Australia

Hay River 37 E 4 Northwest Territories, W Canada

Hays 45 E 5 Kansas, C USA

Haysyn 108 D 3 *Rus.* Gaysin. C Ukraine

Heard & McDonald Islands 141 C 7 Australian external territory, S Indian Ocean

Hearst 38 C 4 Ontario, S Canada

Hebei 128 C 4 *var.* Hopeh, Hopei, Ji; *prev.* Chihli. Province, NE China

Hebron 39 F 1 Newfoundland and Labrador, NE Canada

Hebron 119 E 7 *var.* Al Khalil, El Khalil, *Heb.* Hevron; *anc.* Kiriath-Arba. S West Bank

Heemskerk 86 C 3 W Netherlands

Heerde 86 D 3 E Netherlands

Heerenveen 86 D 2 *Fris.* It Hearrenfean. N Netherlands

Heerhugowaard 86 C 2 NW Netherlands

Heerlen 87 D 6 SE Netherlands

Hefa 119 A 5 *var.* Haifa; *hist.* Caiffa, Caiphas, *anc.* Sycaminum. N Israel

Hefa, Mifraz 119 A 5 *Eng.* Bay of Haifa. Bay, E Mediterranean Sea

Hefei 129 D 5 *var.* Hofei; *hist.* Luchow. E China

Heide 94 B 2 N Germany

Heidelberg 95 B 5 SW Germany

Heidenheim *see* Heidenheim an der Brenz

Heidenheim an der Brenz 95 B 6 *var.* Heidenheim. S Germany

Heilbronn 95 B 6 SW Germany

Heiligenbeil *see* Mamonovo

Heilong Jiang *see* Amur

Heilongjiang 128 D 2 *var.* Hei, Hei-lung-chiang, Heilungkiang. Province, NE China

Heiloo 86 C 3 NW Netherlands

Heilsberg *see* Lidzbark Warmiński

Heimdal 84 B 4 S Norway

Helan Shan 127 E 3 mountain range, N China

Helena 44 B 2 state capital, Montana, NW USA

Helensville 150 D 2 North Island, N New Zealand

Helgoländer Bucht 94 A 2 *var.* Helgoland Bay, Heligoland Bight. Bay, SE North Sea

Hellevoetsluis 86 B 4 SW Netherlands

Hellín 93 E 4 C Spain

Helmand, Daryā-ye 122 D 5 *var.* Hirmand Rūd-e. River, Afghanistan/Iran

Helmond 87 D 5 S Netherlands

Helsingborg 85 B 7 *prev.* Hälsingborg. S Sweden

Helsingfors *see* Helsinki

Helsinki 85 D 5 *Swe.* Helsingfors. Country capital, S Finland

Henan 129 C 5 *var.* Honan, Yu. Province, C China

Henderson 43 F 1 North Carolina, SE USA

Henderson 49 H 3 Texas, S USA

Henderson 40 B 5 Kentucky, E USA

Henderson 47 D 7 Nevada, W USA

Hendersonville 43 E 1 North Carolina, SE USA

Hendū Kosh *see* Hindu Kush

Hengduan Shan 126 D 5 mountain range, SW China

Hengelo 86 E 3 E Netherlands

Hengyang 129 C 6 *var.* Hengnan, Heng-yang; *prev.* Hengchow. S China

Heniches'k 109 F 4 *Rus.* Genichesk. S Ukraine

Hennebont 90 A 3 NW France

Hentiesbaai 78 B 3 W Namibia

Henzada 136 B 4 SW Burma

Herald Cays 148 D 3 island, E Australia

Herât 122 D 4 *var.* Herat; *anc.* Aria. W Afghanistan

Herchmer 37 G 4 Manitoba, C Canada

Heredia 53 E 4 C Costa Rica

Hereford 49 E 2 Texas, S USA

Herford 94 B 4 NW Germany

Héristal *see* Herstal

Herk-de-Stad 87 C 6 NE Belgium

Hermansverk 85 A 5 S Norway

Hermiston 46 C 2 Oregon, NW USA

Hermon, Mount 119 B 5 *Ar.* Jabal ash Shaykh. Mountain, SW Syria

Hermosillo 50 B 2 NW Mexico

Hernösand *see* Härnösand

Herrera del Duque 92 D 3 W Spain

Herrick 149 C 8 Tasmania, SE Australia

Herselt 87 C 5 C Belgium

Herstal 87 D 6 *Fr.* Héristal. E Belgium

Hervey Bay 148 E 4 bay, SE Coral Sea

Herzliyya 119 A 5 *var.* Hertseliya, Herzeliyya. C Israel

Hessen 95 B 5 cultural region, C Germany

Heydekrug *see* Šilutė

Hialeah 43 F 5 Florida, SE USA

Hibbing 45 F 1 Minnesota, N USA

Hidalgo del Parral 50 C 2 *var.* Parral. N Mexico

Hida-sanmyaku 131 C 5 mountain range, Honshū, S Japan

Hierro 70 A 3 *var.* Ferro. Island, Islas Canarias, SW Spain

High Atlas *see* Haut Atlas

High Point 43 F 1 North Carolina, SE USA

Hiiumaa 106 C 2 *Ger.* Dagden, *Swe.* Dagö. Island, W Estonia
Hikurangi 150 D 2 North Island, N New Zealand
Hildesheim 94 B 4 N Germany
Hilla *see* Al Ḥillah
Hillaby, Mount 55 G 1 mountain, N Barbados
Hill Bank 52 C 1 N Belize
Hillegom 86 C 3 W Netherlands
Hilo 47 B 8 Hawaii, W USA
Hilton Head Island 43 E 2 South Carolina, SE USA
Hilversum 86 C 3 C Netherlands
Himalayas 124 C 2 *var.* Himalaya, *Chin.* Himalaya Shan. Mountain range, S Asia
Himeji 131 C 6 *var.* Himezi. Honshū, SW Japan
Himezi *see* Himeji
Ḥimṣ 118 B 4 *var.* Homs; *anc.* Emesa. C Syria
Hînceşti 108 D 4 *var.* Hânceşti; *prev.* Kotovsk. C Moldavia
Hinds 151 C 6 South Island, SW New Zealand
Hindu Kush 123 F 4 *Per.* Hendū Kosh. Mountain range, Afghanistan/Pakistan
Hinesville 43 E 3 Georgia, SE USA
Hinson Bay 42 A 5 bay, W Atlantic Ocean
Hīrmand Rūd-e *see* Helmand, Daryā-ye
Hirosaki 130 D 3 Honshū, C Japan
Hiroshima 131 B 7 *var.* Hirosima. Honshū, SW Japan
Hirosima *see* Hiroshima
Hirson 90 D 3 N France
Hîrşova *see* Hârşova
Hitachi 131 D 5 *var.* Hitati. Honshū, S Japan
Hitati *see* Hitachi
Hitchinbrook Island 148 D 3 island, Queensland, NE Australia
Hitra 84 A 4 *prev.* Hitteren. Island, S Norway
Hitteren *see* Hitra
Hjälmaren 85 C 6 *Eng.* Lake Hjalmar. Lake, C Sweden
Hjalmar, Lake *see* Hjälmaren
Hjørring 85 B 7 N Denmark
Hkakabo Razi 136 B 1 mountain, Burma/China
Hlobyne 109 F 2 *Rus.* Globino. NE Ukraine
Hlukhiv 109 F 1 *Rus.* Glukhov. NE Ukraine
Hlybokaye 107 D 5 *Rus.* Glubokoye, N Belorussia
Hoa Binh 136 D 3 N Vietnam
Hoang Liên Son 136 D 3 mountain range, N Vietnam
Hobart 149 C 8 *prev.* Hobart Town, Hobarton. State capital, Tasmania, SE Australia
Hobbs 49 E 3 New Mexico, SW USA
Hobro 85 A 7 N Denmark
Hô Chi Minh 137 E 6 *var.* Ho Chi Minh, Ho Chi Minh City, Thanh Pho-Ho Chi Minh, Thanh Pho Ho Chi Minh, *prev.* Saigon, Sai Gon. S Vietnam
Hodeida *see* Al Ḥudaydah
Hódmezővásárhely 99 D 7 SE Hungary
Hodonín 99 B 6 *Ger.* Göding. SE Czech Republic
Hof 95 C 5 SE Germany
Höfu 131 B 7 Honshū, SW Japan
Hofuf *see* Al Hufūf
Hohenems 95 B 7 W Austria

Hohenstadt *see* Zábřeh
Hohes Venn *see* Hautes Fagnes
Hohe Tauern 95 C 7 mountain range, W Austria
Hohhot 127 F 3 *var.* Huhehot, Huhohaot'e, *Mong.* Kukukhoto; *prev.* Kweisui, Kwesui. N China
Hôi An 137 E 5 *prev.* Faifo. C Vietnam
Hokianga Harbour 150 C 2 harbour, North Island, N New Zealand
Hokitika 151 B 5 South Island, SW New Zealand
Hokkaidō 130 C 2 territory, Hokkaidō, NE Japan
Hola Prystan' 109 E 4 *Rus.* Golaya Pristan. S Ukraine
Holbrook 48 B 2 Arizona, SW USA
Holetown 55 G 1 *prev.* Jamestown. W Barbados
Holguín 54 C 2 SE Cuba
Hollabrunn 95 E 6 NE Austria
Holland 40 C 3 Michigan, N USA
Hollywood 43 F 5 Florida, SE USA
Holman 37 E 3 Victoria Island, Canada
Holmes Reef 148 D 3 Reef, W Coral Sea
Holmsund 84 D 4 N Sweden
Holon 119 A 6 C Israel
Holovanivs'k 109 E 3 *Rus.* Golovanevsk. C Ukraine
Holstebro 85 A 7 W Denmark
Holyhead 89 C 6 *Wel.* Caer Gybi. NW Wales, UK
Holyoke 41 G 3 Massachusetts, NE USA
Hombori Tondo 75 E 3 mountain, E Mali
Homestead 43 F 5 Florida, SE USA
Homonsova, Khrebet *see* Lomonosov Ridge
Homr, Dar el 72 B 4 physical region, C Sudan
Homyel' 107 D 7 *Rus.* Gomel'. SE Belorussia
Hondo 49 F 4 Texas, S USA

Honduras 52 C 2 Republic, N Central America

Official name: Republic of Honduras **Date of formation:** 1838 **Capital:** Tegucigalpa **Population:** 5.6 million **Total area:** 112,090 sq km (43,278 sq miles) **Languages:** Spanish*, English Creole, Garifuna, Indian languages **Religions:** Roman Catholic 97%, other 3% **Ethnic mix:** mestizo 90%, Indian 7%, Garifuna (Black Carib) 2%, White 1% **Government:** Multiparty republic **Currency:** Lempira = 100 centavos

Honduras, Gulf of 52 C 2 *Sp.* Golfo de Honduras. Gulf, W Caribbean Sea
Honduras, Republic of *see* Honduras
Hønefoss 85 B 6 S Norway
Hông Gai 136 E 3 *var.* Hon Gai, Hongay. N Vietnam
Hong Kong (official name Xianggang) 129 C 6 former UK dependent territory, S. China
Hong Kong Island 128 B 2 island, S Hong Kong
Honiara 144 C 3 country capital, C Solomon Islands
Honjō 130 D 4 *var.* Honzyô. Honshū, C Japan

Honolulu 47 A 8 state capital, Hawaii, W USA
Honshū, 131 E 5 *var.* Hondo, Honsyû. Island, Japan
Honzyô *see* Honjō
Hood Point 147 B 7 headland, Western Australia, W Australia
Hoogeveen 86 E 2 NE Netherlands
Hoogezand-Sappemeer 86 E 2 NE Netherlands
Hoorn 86 C 2 NW Netherlands
Hopa 117 F 2 NE Turkey
Hope 36 C 3 Alaska, NW USA
Hopedale 39 F 2 Newfoundland and Labrador, NE Canada
Hopewell 41 E 5 Virginia, NE USA
Hopkinsville 40 B 5 Kentucky, S USA
Horasan 117 F 3 NE Turkey
Horki 107 E 6 *Rus.* Gorki. E Belorussia
Horlivka 109 G 3 *Rom.* Adâncata, *Rus.* Gorlovka. E Ukraine
Hormuz, Strait of 120 D 4 *var.* Strait of Ormuz; *Per.* Tangeh-ye Hormoz. Strait, Arabian Sea/Gulf, The
Hornepayne 38 C 4 Ontario, S Canada
Hornos, Cabo de 65 C 8 *Eng.* Cape Horn. Headland, S Chile
Horodnya 109 E 1 *Rus.* Gorodnya. NE Ukraine
Horodok 108 B 2 *Pol.* Gródek Jagiello'nski, *Rus.* Gorodok, Gorodok Yagellonoil. NW Ukraine
Horodyshche 109 E 2 *Rus.* Gorodishche. C Ukraine
Horoshiri-dake 130 D 2 *var.* Horosiri Dake. Mountain, Hokkaidō, NE Japan
Horosiri Dake *see* Horoshiri-dake
Horsburgh Atoll 132 B 4 island, N Maldives
Horseshoe Bay 42 A 5 bay, W Atlantic Ocean
Horsham 149 B 7 Victoria, SE Australia
Horst 87 D 5 SE Netherlands
Horten 85 B 6 S Norway
Hospitalet *see* L'Hospitalet de Llobregat
Hotan 126 B 4 *var.* Khotan, Chin. Ho-t'ien. NW China
Hoting 84 C 4 C Sweden
Hot Springs 42 B 1 Arkansas, C USA
Hougang New Town 138 A 1 N Singapore
Houghton Lake 40 C 2 lake, Michigan, N USA
Houilles 91 B 6 France
Houston 49 H 4 Texas, S USA
Hovd 126 C 2 *var.* Khovd. W Mongolia
Hove 89 D 7 S England, UK
Hoverla, Hora 108 B 3 *Rus.* Gora Goverla. Mountain, W Ukraine
Hovsgol, Lake *see* Hövsgöl Nuur
Hövsgöl Nuur 126 D 1 *var.* Lake Hovsgol. Lake, N Mongolia
Howe, Cape 149 D 7 headland, SE Australia
Howrah *see* Hāora
Hoy 88 C 2 island, N Scotland, UK
Hoyerswerda 94 D 4 E Germany
Hradec Králové 99 B 5 *Ger.* Königgrätz. NE Czech Republic
Hrandzichy 107 B 5 *Rus.* Grandichi. W Belorussia
Hranice 99 C 5 *Ger.* Mährisch-Weisskirchen. E Czech Republic

Hrasnica 100 C 4 SE Bosnia & Herzegovina
Hrebinka 109 E 2 *Rus.* Grebenka. NE Ukraine
Hrodna 107 B 5 *Pol.* Grodno. W Belorussia
Huacho 60 C 4 W Peru
Hua Hin *see* Ban Hua Hin
Huaihua 129 C 6 C China
Huailai 128 C 3 NE China
Huainan 129 D 5 *var.* Huai-nan, Hwainan. E China
Huajuapan 51 E 5 *var.* Huajuapan de León. SE Mexico
Huajuapan de León *see* Huajuapan
Hualapai Mountains 48 A 2 mountain range, Arizona, SW USA
Huallaga 60 C 2 river, N Peru
Huambo 78 B 2 *Port.* Nova Lisboa. C Angola
Huancavelica 60 D 4 SW Peru
Huancayo 60 D 4 C Peru
Huang He (Yellow River) 128 C 4 *var.* Yellow River. River, C China
Huangshi 129 C 5 *var.* Huang-shih, Hwangshih. E China
Huanta 60 D 4 C Peru
Huánuco 60 C 3 C Peru
Huanuni 61 F 4 W Bolivia
Huaral 60 C 4 W Peru
Huarás *see* Huaraz
Huaraz 60 C 3 *var.* Huarás. W Peru
Huarmey 60 C 3 W Peru
Huatabampo 50 B 2 NW Mexico
Hubei 129 C 5 *var.* E, Hupei. Province, C China
Hubli 132 B 2 SW India
Huddersfield 89 D 5 N England, UK
Hudiksvall 85 C 5 C Sweden
Hudson Bay 38 C 1 inlet, NW Atlantic Ocean
Hudson, Détroit d' *see* Hudson Strait
Hudson Strait 38 D 1 *Fr.* Détroit d'Hudson. Strait, Atlantic Ocean/Hudson Bay
Huê 136 E 4 C Vietnam
Huehuetenango 52 A 2 W Guatemala
Huelva 92 C 5 *anc.* Onuba. SW Spain
Huesca 93 F 2 *anc.* Osca. NE Spain
Huéscar 93 E 4 S Spain
Hughenden 148 C 3 NE Australia
Hugo 49 G 2 Oklahoma, C USA
Huíla Plateau 78 B 2 plateau, S Angola
Huixtla 51 G 5 SE Mexico
Hukui *see* Fukui
Hukusima *see* Fukushima
Hull 38 D 4 Québec, SE Canada
Hull *see* Kingston upon Hull
Hull Island *see* Orona
Hulst 87 B 5 SW Netherlands
Hulun Nur 127 F 1 *var.* Hu-lun Ch'ih; *prev.* Dalai Nor. Lake, NE China
Humaitá 62 D 2 N Brazil
Humboldt 42 C 1 Tennessee, S USA
Humboldt River 47 C 5 river, Nevada, W USA
Humpolec 99 B 5 *Ger.* Gumpolds, Humpoletz. C Czech Republic
Hunan 129 C 5 *var.* Xiang. Province, S China
Hunedoara 108 B 4 *Ger.* Eisenmarkt, *Hung.* Vajdahunyad. SW Romania
Hünfeld 95 B 5 C Germany

Hungary
99 D 6 *Ger.* Ungarn, *Hung.* Magyarország, *Rom.* Ungaria, *SCr.* Mađarska, *Ukr.* Uhorshchyna; *prev.* Hungarian People's Republic. Republic, C Europe

Official name: Republic of Hungary **Date of formation:** 1918/1945 **Capital:** Budapest **Population:** 10.5 million **Total area:** 93,030 sq km (35,919 sq miles) **Languages:** Hungarian (Magyar)*, German, Slovak **Religions:** Roman Catholic 68%, Protestant 25%, other 7% **Ethnic mix:** Hungarian (Magyar) 90%, German 2%, other 8% **Government:** Multiparty republic **Currency:** Forint = 100 filler

Hunjiang 128 E 3 NE China
Hunter Islands 149 B 8 island group, Tasmania, NW Australia
Huntington 40 D 5 West Virginia, NE USA
Huntington Beach 47 C 8 California, W USA
Huntly 150 D 3 North Island, N New Zealand
Huntsville 42 D 1 Alabama, S USA
Huntsville 38 D 5 Ontario, S Canada
Huntsville 49 G 3 Texas, S USA
Huolin Gol He 127 F 2 NE China
Hurghada 72 C 2 *var.* Al Ghurdaqah, Ghurdaqah. E Egypt
Huri Hills 73 C 5 mountain range, NW Kenya
Huron 45 E 3 South Dakota, N USA
Huron, Lake 40 D 2 lake, Canada/USA
Hurukawa *see* Furukawa
Húsavík 83 E 4 NE Iceland
Husum 94 B 2 N Germany
Hutchinson 45 E 5 Kansas, C USA
Huy 87 C 6 *Dut.* Hoei, Hoey. E Belgium
Hvannadalshnúkur 83 E 5 mountain, S Iceland
Hvar 100 B 4 *It.* Lesina; *anc.* Pharus. Island, S Croatia
Hwange 78 D 3 *prev.* Wankie. W Zimbabwe
Hyargas Nuur 126 D 2 lake, W Mongolia
Hyderābād 134 D 5 *var.* Haidarabad. C India
Hyderābād 134 B 3 *var.* Haidarabad. SE Pakistan
Hyères 91 D 6 SE France
Hyères, Îles d' 91 D 6 island group, S France
Hyvinge *see* Hyvinkää
Hyvinkää 85 D 5 *Swe.* Hyvinge. S Finland

I

Ialomiţa 108 C 5 river, SE Romania
Iaşi 108 D 4 *Ger.* Jassy. NE Romania
Ibadan 75 F 5 SW Nigeria
Ibagué 58 B 3 C Colombia
Ibar 100 D 4 *Alb.* Ibër. River, C Yugoslavia
Ibarra 60 B 1 *var.* San Miguel de Ibarra. N Ecuador
Ibër *see* Ibar
Iberian Basin 66 C 3 undersea basin, E Atlantic Ocean
Iberian Peninsula 68 B 2 physical region, Portugal/Spain
Ibérico, Sistema 93 E 2 *var.* Cordillera Ibérica, *Eng.* Iberian Mountains. Mountain range, NE Spain
Ibiza *see* Eivissa
Ibusuki 130 B 2 Kyūshū, SW Japan
Ica 60 D 4 SW Peru
Içá *see* Putumayo

Iceland
83 E 4 *Dan.* Island, *Icel.* Ísland. Republic, NW Europe

Official name: Republic of Iceland **Date of formation:** 1944 **Capital:** Reykjavik **Population:** 300,000 **Total area:** 103,000 sq km (39,770 sq miles) **Languages:** Icelandic*, English **Religions:** Evangelical Lutheran 96%, other Christian 3%, other 1% **Ethnic mix:** Icelandic (Norwegian-Celtic descent) 98%, other 2% **Government:** Constitutional republic **Currency:** Krona = 100 aurar

Iceland Basin 66 C 2 undersea basin, N Atlantic Ocean
Icelandic Plateau 155 F 5 *var.* Iceland Plateau. Undersea plateau, Arctic Ocean/Atlantic Ocean
Iculisma *see* Angoulême
Idabel 49 H 2 Oklahoma, C USA
Idaho 46 D 3 *off.* State of Idaho; *nicknames* Gem State, Gem of the Mountains. State, NW USA
Idaho Falls 46 E 3 Idaho, NW USA
Idensalmi *see* Iisalmi
Idfu 72 B 2 *var.* Edfu. SE Egypt
Idlib 118 B 3 NW Syria
Idre 85 B 5 C Sweden
Iecava 106 C 3 S Latvia
Ieper 87 A 6 *Fr.* Ypres. W Belgium
Ierápetra 105 D 8 Kríti, SE Greece
Ierisós *see* Ierissós
Ierissós 104 C 4 *var.* Ierisós. N Greece
Iferouâne 75 G 2 N Niger
Ifôghas, Adrar des 75 F 2 *var.* Adrar des Iforas. Mountain range, NE Mali
Iforas, Adrar des *see* Adrar des Ifôghas
Igarka 114 D 3 N Russian Federation
Iglesias 97 A 5 W Italy
Igloolik 37 G 3 Northwest Territories, N Canada
Ignace 38 B 4 Ontario, S Canada
Igoumenítsa 104 A 4 W Greece
Iguala 51 E 5 *var.* Iguala de la Independencia. S Mexico
Iguala de la Independencia *see* Iguala
Ihavandiffulu Atoll *see* Ihavandippolhu Atoll
Ihavandippolhu Atoll 132 B 4 *var.* Ihavandiffulu Atoll. Island, N Maldives
Ihosy 79 F 4 S Madagascar
Iisalmi 84 E 4 *var.* Idensalmi. C Finland
Ijâfene 74 D 2 desert, Mauritania
IJssel 86 D 3 *var.* Yssel. River, Germany/Netherlands
IJsselmeer 86 C 2 *prev.* Zuider Zee. Lake, N Netherlands
IJsselmuiden 86 D 3 E Netherlands
Ijzer 87 A 6 river, W Belgium
Ikaría 105 D 6 *var.* Kariot, Nicaria, Nikaria; *anc.* Icaria. Island, SE Greece
Iki 131 A 7 island, Japan
Ilagan 139 E 1 Luzon, N Philippines
Iława 98 D 3 *Ger.* Deutsch-Eylau. N Poland
Ilebo 77 C 6 *prev.* Port-Francqui. W Congo (Zaire)
Île-de-France 90 C 3 cultural region, N France
Ilfracombe 89 C 7 SW England, UK
Ilgaz 116 C 2 Turkey
Ílhavo 92 B 3 W Portugal
Iliamna Lake 36 C 3 lake, Alaska, NW USA
Il'ichevsk *see* Illichivs'k
Iligan 139 F 2 *off.* Iligan City. Mindanao, S Philippines
Iligan City *see* Iligan
Illapel 64 B 4 C Chile
Illichivs'k 109 E 4 *Rus.* Il'ichevsk. SW Ukraine
Illinois 40 B 4 *off.* State of Illinois; *nicknames* Prairie State, Sucker State. State, C USA
Illinois River 40 B 4 river, Illinois, N USA
Illuro *see* Mataró
Ilo 61 E 4 SW Peru
Iloilo 139 E 2 *off.* Iloilo City. Panay Island, C Philippines
Iloilo City *see* Iloilo
Ilorin 75 F 4 W Nigeria
Iluh *see* Batman
Ilulissat 82 C 3 *Dan.* Jakobshavn. W Greenland
Il'yaly 122 C 2 *var.* Yylanly. N Turkmenistan
Imatra 85 E 5 SE Finland
Imishli *see* İmişli
İmişli 117 H 3 *Rus.* Imishli. C Azerbaijan
Imola 96 C 3 N Italy
Imperatriz 63 F 2 NE Brazil
Imperia 96 A 3 NW Italy
Impfondo 77 C 5 NE Congo
Imphāl 135 H 3 NE India
Inagua Islands *see* Great Inagua/Little Inagua
I-n-Amenas 71 E 3 *var.* In Aménas, In Amnas. E Algeria
Inarijärvi 84 D 2 *Lapp.* Aanaarjävri, *Swe.* Enareträsk. Lake, N Finland
Inawashiro-ko 131 D 5 *var.* Inawasiro Ko. Lake, Honshū, C Japan
Inawasiro Ko *see* Inawashiro-ko
İncesu 116 D 3 C Turkey
Inch'ŏn 128 E 4 *off.* Inch'ŏn-kwangyŏksi, *Jap.* Jinsen; *prev.* Chemulpo. NW South Korea
Independence 45 F 4 Missouri, C USA
Independence Fjord 83 E 1 fjord, W Wandell Sea
Independence Island *see* Malden Island
Independence Mountains 46 D 4 mountain range, Nevada, W USA

India
124 B 3 *var.* Indian Union, Union of India, *Hind.* Bhārat. Republic, S Asia

Official name: Republic of India **Date of formation:** 1947/1961 **Capital:** New Delhi **Population:** 953 million **Total Area:** 3,287,590 sq km (1,269,338 sq miles) **Languages:** Hindi*, English* **Religions:** Hindu 83%, Muslim 11%, Christian 2%, Sikh 2%, other 2% **Ethnic mix:** Indo-Aryan 72%, Dravidian 25%, Mongoloid and other 3% **Government:** Multiparty republic **Currency:** Rupee = 100 paisa

Indiana 40 B 4 *off.* State of Indiana; nickname Hoosier State. State, C USA
Indianapolis 40 C 4 state captal, Indiana, N USA
Indian Church 52 C 1 N Belize
Indian Ocean 141 C 5 ocean,
Indianola 45 F 4 Iowa, C USA
Indigirka 115 G 2 river, NE Russian Federation
Indija 100 D 3 *var.* Inđija, *Hung.* India. N Yugoslavia
Indio 47 D 8 California, W USA
Indomed Fracture Zone 141 A 6 fracture zone, SW Indian Ocean

Indonesia
138 C 4 *Ind.* Republik Indonesia; *prev.* Dutch East Indies, Netherlands East Indies, United States of Indonesia. Republic, SE Asia

Official name: Republic of Indonesia **Date of formation:** 1949/1963 **Capital:** Jakarta **Population:** 200.6 million **Total Area:** 1,904,570 sq km (735,555 sq miles) **Languages:** Bahasa Indonesia*, 250 (est.) languages or dialects **Religions:** Muslim 87%, Christian 10%, Hindu 2%, Buddhist 1% **Ethnic mix:** Javanese 45%, Sundanese 14%, Madurese 8%, other 33% **Government:** Multiparty republic **Currency:** Rupiah = 100 sen

Indonesian Borneo *see* Kalimantan
Indore 134 D 4 C India
Indreville *see* Châteauroux
Indus 134 C 2 *Chin.* Yindu He; *prev.* Yin-tu Ho. River, S Asia
Indus Cone *see* Indus Fan
Indus Fan 140 B 3 *var.* Indus Cone. Undersea fan, N Indian Ocean
Indus, Mouths of the 134 B 4 delta, S Pakistan
İnebolu 116 C 2 N Turkey
Ineu 108 A 4 *Hung.* Borosjenő; *prev.* Inâu. W Romania
Infiernillo, Presa del 51 E 4 reservoir, S Mexico
Inglefield Land 82 D 1 physical region, NW Greenland
Ingolstadt 95 C 6 S Germany
Ingulets *see* Inhulets'
Inguri *see* Enguri
Inhambane 79 E 4 SE Mozambique
Inhulets' 109 F 3 *Rus.* Ingulets. E Ukraine
Inis *see* Ennis
Inn 95 C 6 river, C Europe
Inner Hebrides 88 B 4 island group, W Scotland, UK
Inner Islands 79 H 1 *var.* Central Group. Island group, Seychelles
Innisfail 148 D 3 Queensland, NE Australia
Innsbruch *see* Innsbruck
Innsbruck 95 C 7 *var.* Innsbruch. W Austria
Inowrocław 98 C 3 *Ger.* Hohensalza; *prev.* Inowrazlaw. C Poland
I-n-Salah 70 D 3 *var.* In Salah. C Algeria
In Salah *see* I-n-Salah
Insterburg *see* Chernyakhovsk
Inta 110 E 3 NW Russian Federation
Interamna *see* Teramo

Interamna Nahars *see* Terni
International Falls 45 F 1
Minnesota, N USA
Inukjuak 38 D 2 *var.* Inoucdjouac;
prev. Port Harrison. Québec,
NE Canada
Inuuvik *see* Inuvik
Inuvik 37 E 3 *var.* Inuuvik.
Northwest Territories,
NW Canada
Invercargill 151 A 7 South Island,
SW New Zealand
Inverell 149 D 6 New South Wales,
SE Australia
Inverness 88 C 3 N Scotland, UK
Investigator Ridge 140 D 4
undersea ridge, E Indian Ocean
Investigator Strait 149 A 7 strait,
SE Indian Ocean
Inyangani 78 D 3 mountain,
NE Zimbabwe
Ioánnina 104 A 4 *var.* Janina,
Yannina. W Greece
Iola 45 F 5 Kansas, C USA
Ionia Basin *see* Ionian Basin
Ionian Basin 80 D 5 *var.*
Ionia Basin. Undersea basin,
C Mediterranean Sea
Ionian Islands *see* Iónioi Nísoi
Ionian Sea 103 E 3 *Gk.* Iónio
Pélagos, *It.* Mar Ionio. Sea,
C Mediterranean Sea
Iónioi Nísoi 105 A 5 *Eng.* Ionian
Islands. Island group, W Greece
Íos 105 D 7 Íos, SE Greece
Íos 105 D 7 *var.* Nio. Island,
Kykládes, SE Greece
Iowa 45 F 3 *off.* State of Iowa;
nickname Hawkeye State.
State, C USA
Iowa City 45 G 3 Iowa, C USA
Iowa Falls 45 G 3 Iowa, C USA
Ipel' 99 D 6 *var.* Ipoly, *Ger.* Eipel.
River, Hungary/Slovakia
Ipiales 58 A 4 SW Colombia
Ipirá 63 G 3 E Brazil
Ipoh 138 B 3 W Malaysia
Ippy 76 C 4
C Central African Republic
Ipswich 89 E 6 *hist.* Gipeswic.
E England, UK
Ipswich 149 E 5 Queensland,
E Australia
Iqaluit 37 H 3 *prev.* Frobisher Bay.
Baffin Island, NE Canada
Iquique 64 B 1 N Chile
Iquitos 60 C 1 N Peru
Irákleio 105 D 8 *var.* Herakleion,
Eng. Candia; *prev.* Iráklion.
Kriti, SE Greece

Iran
120 C 3 *prev.* Persia.
Republic, SW Asia

Official name: Islamic Republic of
Iran **Date of formation:** 1906
Capital: Tehran **Population:** 68.7
million **Total area:** 1,648,000 sq km
(636,293 sq miles) **Languages:** Farsi
(Persian)*, Azerbaijani, Kurdish
Religions: Shi'a Muslim 95%, Sunni
Muslim 4%, other 1% **Ethnic mix:**
Persian 52%, Azerbaijani 24%,
Kurdish 9%, other 15%
Government: Islamic Republic
Currency: Rial = 100 dinars

Iranian Plateau 120 D 3 *var.*
Plateau of Iran. Plateau, C Iran
Iran, Plateau of *see*
Iranian Plateau
Irapuato 51 E 4 C Mexico

Iraq
120 B 3 *Ar.* 'Irāq. Republic,
SW Asia

Official name: Republic of Iraq
Date of formation: 1932/1981
Capital: Baghdad **Population:** 21
million **Total area:** 438,320 sq km
(169,235 sq miles) **Languages:**
Arabic*, Kurdish, Turkish, Farsi
(Persian) **Religions:** Shi'a Muslim
63%, Sunni Muslim 34%, other 3%
Ethnic mix: Arab 79%, Kurdish 16%,
Persian 3%, Turkish 2%
Government: Single-party republic
Currency: Dinar = 1,000 fils

Irbid 119 B 5 NW Jordan

Ireland, Republic of
89 B 5 *Ir.* Ireland, *Ir.* Éire.
Republic, NW Europe

Official name: Republic of Ireland
Date of formation: 1921/1922
Capital: Dublin **Population:** 3.5
million **Total area:** 70,280 sq km
(27,155 sq miles) **Languages:**
English*, Irish Gaelic* **Religions:**
Roman Catholic 95%, Protestant 5%,
other 2% **Ethnic mix:** Irish 95%,
other 5% **Government:** Multiparty
republic **Currency:** Irish pound =
100 pence

Irian Jaya 139 H 4 cultural region,
E Indonesia
Iringa 73 C 7 C Tanzania
Iriomote-jima 130 A 4 island,
Sakishima-shotō, SW Japan
Iriona 52 D 2 NE Honduras
Irish Sea 89 C 5 *Ir.* Muir Éireann.
Sea, NE Atlantic Ocean
Irkutsk 115 E 4 C Russian Federation
Iroise 90 A 3 sea, NW France
Irrawaddy 136 B 2 *var.*
Ayeyarwady. River, C Burma
Irrawaddy, Mouths of the 137 A 5
delta area, SW Burma
Irtysh 114 C 4 *var.* Irtish, *Kaz.* Ertis.
River, C Asia
Irún 93 E 1 N Spain
Irving 49 G 2 Texas, S USA
Isabela, Isla 60 A 5 *var.* Albemarle
Island. Island, W Ecuador
Isaccea 108 D 5 E Romania
Isachsen 37 F 1 Ellef Ringnes
Island, N Canada
Isbarta *see* Isparta
Isca Damnoniorum *see* Exeter
Ischia, Isola d' 97 C 5 island, S Italy
Ise 131 C 6 Honshū, SW Japan
Iseghem *see* Izegem
Isère 91 D 5 river, E France
Isernia 97 D 5 *var.* Æsernia. S Italy
Ise-wan 131 C 6 bay,
NW Pacific Ocean
Isfahan *see* Isfahan
Isherton 59 F 4 S Guyana
Ishigaki-jima 130 A 4 *var.* Isigaki
Zima. Island, Sakishima-shotō,
SW Japan
Ishikari-wan 130 C 2 bay,
NE Sea of Japan
Ishim 114 C 4 C Russian Federation
Ishim 114 C 4 *Kaz.* Esil. River,
Kazakhstan/Russian Federation
Ishimbay 111 D 6
W Russian Federation
Ishinomaki 130 D 4 *var.* Isinomaki.
Honshū, C Japan
Ishkashim *see* Ishkoshim
Ishkoshim 123 F 3 *Rus.* Ishkashim.
S Tajikistan

Isinomaki *see* Ishinomaki
Isiro 77 E 5 NE Congo (Zaire)
Iskăr *see* Iskŭr
İskenderun 116 D 4 *Eng.*
Alexandretta. S Turkey
Iskŭr 104 C 2 *var.* Iskăr. River,
NW Bulgaria
Iskŭr, Yazovir 104 C 2 *prev.* Stalin,
Yazovir. Reservoir, W Bulgaria
Isla Cristina 92 C 5 S Spain
Isla de León *see* San Fernando
Islāmābād 134 C 1 country capital,
NE Pakistan
Island Lagoon 149 B 6 lake,
South Australia, S Australia
Islay 88 B 4 island,
SW Scotland, UK
Isle 91 B 5 river, W France
Ismailia *see* Ismâ'ilîya
Ismâ'ilîya 72 B 1 *var.* Ismailia.
N Egypt
Isna 72 B 2 *var.* Esna. SE Egypt
Isoka 78 D 1 NE Zambia
İsparta 116 B 4 *var.* Isbarta.
SW Turkey
İspir 117 E 3 NE Turkey

Israel
119 A 7 *var.* Medinat Israel,
Heb. Yisrael, Yisra'el. Republic,
SW Asia

Official name: State of Israel
Date of formation: 1948/1982
Capital: Jerusalem **Population**
5.4 million **Total area:** 20,700 sq km
(7,992 sq miles) **Languages:**
Hebrew*, Arabic, Yiddish
Religions: Jewish 83%, Muslim 13%,
Christian 2%, other 2% **Ethnic mix:**
Jewish 83%, Arab 17%
Government: Multiparty republic
Currency: New shekel = 100 agorot

Issoire 91 C 5 C France
Issyk-Kul', Ozero 123 G 2 *var.* Issiq
Köl, *Kir.* Ysyk-Köl. Lake,
E Kyrgyzstan
İstanbul 116 B 2 *Bul.* Tsarigrad, *Eng.*
Istanbul; *prev.* Constantinople,
anc. Byzantium. NW Turkey
Istanbul *see* Istanbul
İstanbul Boğazı 116 B 2 *var.*
Bosporus Thracius, *Eng.*
Bosporus, *Turk.* Karadeniz Boğazi.
Strait, Sea of Marmara/Black Sea
Istra 96 D 2 *Eng.* Istria. Peninsula,
Slovenia/Yugoslavia
Istra 100 A 2 *Eng.* Istria, *Ger.* Istrien.
Cultural region, NW Croatia
Istria *see* Istra
Itabuna 63 G 3 E Brazil
Itagüí 58 B 3 W Colombia
Itaituba 63 E 2 NE Brazil

Italy
96 C 3 *It.* Italia, Replica
Italiana. Republic, S Europe

Official name: Italian Republic
Date of formation: 1871/1954
Capital: Rome **Population:** 57.8
million **Total area:** 301,270 sq km
(116,320 sq miles) **Languages:**
Italian*, French,
Rhaeto-Romanic, Sardinian **Religions:**
Roman Catholic 98%, other 2%
Ethnic mix: Italian 98%, other 2%
Government: Multiparty republic
Currency: Lira = 100 centesimi

It Amelân *see* Ameland
Iténez, Río *see* Guaporé
Ithaca 41 F 3 New York, NE USA

It Hearrenfean *see* Heerenveen
Itoigawa 131 C 5 Honshū, C Japan
Ittoqqortoormiit 83 E 4
var. Itseqqortoormiit,
Dan. Scoresbysund, *Eng.* Scoresby
Sound. SE Greenland
Iturup, Ostrov 115 H 4 island,
Kuril'skiye Ostrova,
SE Russian Federation
Itzehoe 94 B 2 N Germany
Ivalo 84 D 2 *Lapp.* Avvil, Avveel.
N Finland
Ivanava 107 B 7 *var.* Janów Poleski,
Pol. Janów, *Rus.* Ivanovo.
SW Belorussia
Ivangrad 101 D 5 *var.* Berane
C Yugoslavia
Ivanhoe 149 C 6 New South Wales,
SE Australia
Ivano-Frankivs'k 108 C 2
Ger. Stanislau, *Pol.* Stanisławów,
Rus. Ivano-Frankovsk;
prev. Stanislav. W Ukraine
Ivanovo 111 C 5
W Russian Federation
Ivatsevichy 107 B 6 *Pol.*
Iwacewicze, *Rus.* Ivantsevichi,
Ivatsevichi. SW Belorussia
Ivigtut *see* Ivittuut
Ivittuut 82 B 4 *var.* Ivigtut.
SW Greenland
Ivory Coast 74 D 5 *Fr.* Côte
d'Ivoire. Coastal region,
S Ivory Coast

Ivory Coast
74 D 4 *Fr.* République de la Côte
d'Ivoire, Côte d'Ivoire. Republic,
NW Africa

Official name: Republic of the Ivory
Coast **Date of formation:** 1960
Capital: Yamoussoukro **Population:**
13.4 million **Total area:** 322,463 sq
km (124,503 sq miles) **Languages:**
French*, Akran **Religions:**
Traditional beliefs 63%, Muslim
25%, Christian 12% **Ethnic mix:**
Baoule 23%, Bété 18%, Kru 17%,
Malinke 15%, other 27%
Government: Multiparty republic
Currency: CFA franc = 100 centimes

Ivujivik 38 D 1 Québec, NE Canada
Iwaki 131 D 5 Honshū, N Japan
Iwakuni 131 B 7 Honshū, SW Japan
Iwanai 130 C 2 Hokkaidō,
NE Japan
Iwate 130 D 4 Honshū, N Japan
Ixtapa 51 E 5 S Mexico
Ixtepec 51 F 5 SE Mexico
Iyo-nada 131 B 7 sea,
NW Pacific Ocean
Izabal, Lago de 52 B 2 *prev.* Golfo
Dulce. Lake, E Guatemala
Izberbash 111 B 8
SW Russian Federation
Izegem 87 A 6 *prev.* Iseghem.
W Belgium
Izhevsk 111 D 5 *prev.* Ustinov.
NW Russian Federation
Izmail *see* Izmayil
Izmayil 108 D 4 *Rus.* Izmail.
SW Ukraine
İzmir 116 A 3 *prev.* Smyrna.
W Turkey
İzmit 116 B 3 *var.* Ismid;
anc. Astacus. NW Turkey
İznik Gölü 116 B 3 lake,
NW Turkey
Izúcar de Matamoros *see*
Matamoros
Izu-hantō 131 D 6 peninsula,
Honshū, S Japan

Izu-shotō 131 D 6 island group, Japan
Izvor 104 B 2 W Bulgaria
Izyaslav 108 C 2 W Ukraine
Izyum 109 G 2 E Ukraine

J

Jabalpur 135 E 4 *prev.* Jubbulpore. C India
Jabbūl, Sabkhat al 118 C 2 salt flat, NW Syria
Jablah 118 B 3 *var.* Jeble, *Fr.* Djéblé. W Syria
Jaca 93 F 1 NE Spain
Jacaltenango 52 A 2 W Guatemala
Jackson 42 B 2 Mississippi, S USA
Jackson 42 C 1 Alabama, S USA
Jackson 42 C 3 Tennessee, S USA
Jackson 45 H 5 Missouri, C USA
Jackson Head 151 A 6 headland, South Island, SW New Zealand
Jacksonville 43 E 3 Florida, SE USA
Jacksonville 43 F 1 North Carolina, SE USA
Jacksonville 42 B 1 Arkansas, SE USA
Jacksonville 49 H 3 Texas, S USA
Jacksonville 40 B 4 Illinois, N USA
Jacksonville Beach 43 E 3 Florida, SE USA
Jacmel 54 D 3 *var.* Jaquemel. S Haiti
Jacob *see* Nkayi
Jacobābād 134 B 3 SE Pakistan
Jadotville *see* Likasi
Jādū 71 F 2 NW Libya
Jaén 92 D 4 SW Spain
Jaén 60 B 3 N Peru
Jaffna 132 D 3 N Sri Lanka
Jagdalpur 135 E 5 C India
Jagodina *see* Svetozarevo
Jaipur 134 D 3 *prev.* Jeypore. State capital, N India
Jajce 100 B 3 W Bosnia & Herzegovina
Jakarta 138 C 5 *Dut.* Batavia; *prev.* Djakarta. Country capital, Jawa, C Indonesia
Jakobshavn *see* Ilulissat
Jakobstad 84 D 4 *Fin.* Pietarsaari. W Finland
Jakobstadt *see* Jēkabpils
Jalal-Abad *see* Dzhalal-Abad
Jalālābād 123 F 4 *var.* Jalalabad, Jelalabad. E Afghanistan
Jalandhar 134 D 2 *prev.* Jullundur. N India
Jalapa 52 D 3 NW Nicaragua
Jalpa 50 D 4 C Mexico
Jaluit Atoll 144 D 2 *var.* Jalwoj. Island, S Marshall Islands
Jālwōj *see* Jaluit Atoll
Jamaame 73 D 6 *It.* Giamame; *prev.* Margherita. S Somalia

Jamaica
54 A 4 Commonwealth republic, N Caribbean Sea

Official name: Jamaica **Date of formation:** 1962 **Capital:** Kingston **Population:** 2.5 million **Total area:** 10,990 sq km (4,243 sq miles) **Languages:** English*, English Creole, other **Religions:** Christian 60%, other 40% **Ethnic mix:** Black 75%, mixed 15%, South Asian 5%, other 5% **Government:** Parliamentary democracy **Currency:** Jamaican $ = 100 cents

Jamaica Channel 54 D 3 channel, N Caribbean Sea
Jamālpur 135 G 3 N Bangladesh
Jambi 138 B 4 *var.* Telanaipura; *prev.* Djambi. Sumatera, W Indonesia
Jamdena *see* Yamdena, Pulau
James Bay 38 C 3 bay, S Hudson Bay
James River 45 E 3 river, N USA
Jamestown 41 E 3 New York, NE USA
Jamestown 45 E 2 North Dakota, N USA
Jamestown *see* Holetown
Jammerbugten 85 A 7 bay, E North Sea
Jammu 134 D 2 *prev.* Jummoo. State capital, NW India
Jammu and Kashmir 134 D 1 *var.* Jammu-Kashmir, Kashmir. State, NW India
Jammu and Kashmir *see* Kashmir
Jāmnagar 134 C 4 *prev.* Navanagar. W India
Jamshedpur 135 F 4 NE India
Janaúba 63 F 3 SE Brazil
Janesville 40 B 3 Wisconsin, N USA
Janischken *see* Joniškis
Jankovac *see* Jánoshalma
Jan Mayen 83 F 4 Norwegian territory, N Norwegian Sea
Jánoshalma 99 D 7 *SCr.* Jankovac. S Hungary

Japan
130 C 4 *var.* Nippon, *Jap.* Nihon. Monarchy, E Asia

Official name: Japan **Date of formation:** 1868/1945 **Capital:** Tokyo **Population:** 125 million **Total Area:** 377,800 sq km (145,869 sq miles) **Languages:** Japanese*, Korean, Chinese **Religions:** Shinto and Buddhist 76%, Buddhist 16%, other 8% **Ethnic mix:** Japanese 99.4%, other 0.6% **Government:** Constitutional monarchy **Currency:** Yen = 100 sen

Japan, Sea of 130 B 4 *Rus.* Yaponskoye More. Sea, SW Pacific Ocean
Japan Trench 152 B 2 trench, NW Pacific Ocean
Japen *see* Yapen, Pulau
Japiim 62 C 2 *var.* Máncio Lima. W Brazil
Japurá, Rio 62 C 1 *var.* Rio Caquetá, Yapurá. River, Brazil/Colombia
Jaqué 53 G 5 SE Panama
Jaquemel *see* Jacmel
Jarābulus 118 C 2 *var.* Jarablos, Jerablus, *Fr.* Djérablous. N Syria
Jaransk *see* Yaransk
Jardines de la Reina, Archipiélago de los 54 B 2 island, group C Cuba
Jarega *see* Yarega
Jarīd, Shatt al *see* Jerid, Chott el
Jarocin 98 C 4 C Poland
Jaroslavl *see* Yaroslavl'
Jarosław 99 E 5 *Ger.* Jaroslau, *Rus.* Yaroslav. SE Poland
Jarqŭrghon 123 E 3 *Rus.* Dzharkurgan. S Uzbekistan
Jarvis Island 145 F 2 US unincorporated territory, C Pacific Ocean
Jasło 99 D 5 SE Poland
Jasper 42 C 2 Alabama, S USA

Jassy *see* Iaşi
Jastrzębie-Zdrój 99 C 5 *var.* Jastrzebie Zdrój, Jastrzebie-Zdrój. S Poland
Jataí 63 E 3 C Brazil
Jauf *see* Al Jawf
Jaunpiebalga 106 D 3 NE Latvia
Jaunpur 135 E 3 N India
Java *see* Jawa
Javari 60 D 2 *var.* Yavari. River, Brazil/ Peru
Javari *see* Yavarí
Java Sea *see* Jawa, Laut
Java Trench 141 E 5 trench, E Indian Ocean
Jawa 138 C 5 *Eng.* Java; *prev.* Djawa. Island, C Indonesia
Jawa, Laut 138 D 4 *Eng.* Java Sea. Sea, W Pacific Ocean
Jawhar 73 D 6 *var.* Jowhar, *It.* Giohar. S Somalia
Jaya, Puncak 139 G 4 *prev.* Puntjak Carstensz, Puntjak Sukarno. Mountain, New Guinea, E Indonesia
Jayapura 139 H 4 *var.* Djajapura, *Dut.* Hollandia; *prev.* Kotabaru, Sukarnapura. New Guinea, E Indonesia
Jaz Murian, Hamun-e 120 E 4 lake, SE Iran
Jebba 75 F 4 W Nigeria
Jebel ash Shifā 120 A 4 desert, NW Saudi Arabia
Jedda *see* Jiddah
Jędrzejów 98 D 4 *Ger.* Endersdorf. S Poland
Jefferson City 45 G 5 state capital, Missouri, C USA
Jega 75 F 4 NW Nigeria
Jehol *see* Chengde
Jēkabpils 106 D 4 *Ger.* Jakobstadt. S Latvia
Jelenia Góra 98 B 4 *Ger.* Hirschberg, Hirschberg im Riesengebirge, Hirschberg in Riesengebirge, Hirschberg in Schlesien. SW Poland
Jelgava 106 C 3 *Ger.* Mitau. C Latvia
Jemappes 87 B 7 S Belgium
Jember 138 D 5 *prev.* Djember. Jawa, C Indonesia
Jena 94 C 4 C Germany
Jenīn 119 E 6 N Israel
Jequitinhonha 56 E 4 river, E Brazil
Jerada 70 D 2 NE Morocco
Jerba, Île de 71 F 2 *var.* Djerba, Jazīrat Jarbah. Island, E Tunisia
Jérémie 54 D 3 SW Haiti
Jerez de la Frontera 92 C 5 *var.* Jerez; *prev.* Xeres. SW Spain
Jerez de los Caballeros 92 C 4 W Spain
Jericho 119 E 7 *Ar.* Arīḩā, *Heb.* Yeriho. E West Bank
Jerid, Chott el 71 E 2 lake, W Tunisia
Jersey 89 D 8 island, S Channel Islands
Jersey City 41 F 4 New Jersey, NE USA
Jerusalem 119 B 6 *var.* Al Quds ash Sharīf, *Ar.* Al Quds, *Heb.* Yerushalayim; *anc.* Hierosolyma. Country capital, NE Israel
Jesenice 95 D 7 *Ger.* Assling. NW Slovenia
Jesselton *see* Kota Kinabalu
Jessore 135 G 4 W Bangladesh
Jesús María 64 C 3 C Argentina
Jeypore *see* Jaipur
Jhānsi 134 D 3 N India
Jhelum 134 C 2 NE Pakistan

Jiangmen 129 C 6 SE China
Jiangsu 128 D 4 *var.* Chiang-su, Kiangsu, Su. Province, E China
Jiangxi 129 C 5 var.Chiang-hsi, Gan, Kiangsi. Province, SE China
Jiaxing 129 D 5 E China
Jibuti *see* Djibouti
Jiddah 121 A 5 *Eng.* Jedda. W Saudi Arabia
Jiftlik Post 119 E 7 E West Bank
Jīgān 121 B 6 *var.* Qīzān. SW Saudi Arabia
Jihlava 99 B 5 *Ger.* Iglau, *Pol.* Iglawa. S Czech Republic
Jilf al Kabīr, Haḍabat al *see* Gilf Kebir Plateau
Jilib 73 D 6 *It.* Gelib. S Somalia
Jilin 128 E 3 *var.* Chi-lin, Girin, Kirin; *prev.* Yunki, Yungki. NE China
Jilin 128 E 3 *var.* Chi-lin, Girin, Kirin, Ji. Province, NE China
Jill, Kediet ej 74 C 2 *var.* Kédia d'Idjil, Kediet Ijill. Mountain, NW Mauritania
Jīma 73 C 5 *var.* Jimma, *It.* Gimma. SW Ethiopia
Jimbolia 108 A 4 *Ger.* Hatzfeld, *Hung.* Zsombolya. W Romania
Jiménez 50 D 2 N Mexico
Jimsar 126 C 3 W China
Jinan 128 D 4 *var.* Chinan, Chi-nan, Tsinan. Province capital, E China
Jingdezhen 129 D 5 E China
Jinghong 129 A 6 S China
Jinhua 129 D 5 E China
Jining 127 F 3 N China
Jinja 73 C 5 S Uganda
Jinotega 52 D 3 NW Nicaragua
Jinotepe 52 D 3 SW Nicaragua
Jinsha 129 A 5 river, SW China
Jinzhou 128 D 3 *var.* Chin-chou, Chinchow; *prev.* Chinhsien. NE China
Ji-Paraná 62 D 3 W Brazil
Jisr ash Shughūr 118 B 3 *Fr.* Djisr el Choghour. NW Syria
Jiu 108 B 5 *Ger.* Schil, Schyl, *Hung.* Zsil, Zsily. River, S Romania
Jiujiang 129 D 5 E China
Jiulong *see* Kowloon
Jizl, Wādī al 120 A 4 dry watercourse, W Saudi Arabia
Jizzakh 123 E 2 *Rus.* Dzhizak. C Uzbekistan
João Pessoa 63 G 2 *prev.* Paraíba. State capital, E Brazil
Joazeiro *see* Juazeiro
Jodhpur 134 C 3 NW India
Joensuu 84 E 4 SE Finland
Jõetsu 131 C 5 *var.* Zyôetu. Honshū, C Japan
Johannesburg 78 D 4 *var.* Egoli, Erautini, Gauteng, *abbrev.* Jo'burg. NE South Africa
Johannisburg *see* Pisz
John Day River 46 B 3 river, Oregon, NW USA
John H.Kerr Reservoir 43 F 1 *var.* Buggs Island Lake, Kerr Lake. Reservoir, SE USA
Johnson City 41 F 3 New York, NE USA
Johor Bahru 138 B 3 *var.* Johor Baharu, Johore Bahru. W Malaysia
Johore Strait 138 A 1 *Mal.* Selat Johor. Strait, Indian Ocean/ Pacific Ocean
Joinvile *see* Joinville

Joinville 63 F 5 *var.* Joinvile. S Brazil
Jojutla 51 E 4 *var.* Jojutla de Juárez. S Mexico
Jojutla de Juárez *see* Jojutla
Jokkmokk 84 C 3 N Sweden
Joliet 40 B 3 Illinois, N USA
Jonava 106 B 4 *Ger.* Janow, *Pol.* Janów. C Lithuania
Jonesboro 42 B 1 Louisiana, S USA
Joniškis 106 C 4 *Ger.* Janischken. N Lithuania
Jönköping 85 B 7 S Sweden
Jonquière 39 E 4 Québec, SE Canada
Joplin 45 F 5 Missouri, C USA
Jordan 119 B 6 *Ar.* Al Mamlaka al Urduniya al Hashemiyah, Al Urdunn; *prev.* Transjordan. Monarchy, SW Asia

Official name: Hashemite Kingdom of Jordan **Date of formation:** 1946/1976 **Capital:** Amman **Population:** 4.4 million **Total area:** 89,210 sq km (34,440 sq miles) **Languages:** Arabic*, Armenian **Religions:** Muslim 95%, Christian 5% **Ethnic mix:** Arab 98%, (Palestinian 49%), Armenian 1%, Circassian 1% **Government:** Constitutional monarchy **Currency:** Dinar = 1,000 fils

Jorhāt 135 H 3 NE India
Jos 75 G 4 C Nigeria
Joseph Bonaparte Gulf 146 D 2 gulf, S Timor Sea
Jos Plateau 75 G 4 plateau, C Nigeria
Jotunheimen 85 A 5 mountain range, S Norway
Joûnié 118 A 4 *var.* Junīyah. W Lebanon
Joure 86 D 2 *Fris.* De Jouwer. N Netherlands
Joutseno 85 E 5 SE Finland
J. Storm Thurmond Reservoir *see* Clark Hill Lake
Juan Aldama 50 D 3 C Mexico
Juan de Fuca, Strait of 46 A 1 strait, Canada/USA
Juan Fernández Islands 153 G 4 *Eng.* Juan Fernandez Islands. Island group, SE Pacific Ocean
Juazeiro 63 G 2 *prev.* Joazeiro. E Brazil
Juazeiro do Norte 63 G 2 E Brazil
Juba 73 B 5 *var.* Jūbā. S Sudan
Jūbā *see* Juba
Jubbulpore *see* Jabalpur
Jucar *see* Júcar
Júcar 93 E 3 *var.* Jucar. River, C Spain
Juchitán 51 F 5 *var.* Juchitán de Zaragosa. SE Mexico
Juchitán de Zaragosa *see* Juchitán
Judayyidat Hāmir 120 B 3 S Iraq
Judenburg 95 D 7 C Austria
Juigalpa 52 D 3 S Nicaragua
Juiz de Fora 63 F 4 SE Brazil
Jujuy *see* San Salvador de Jujuy
Juliaca 61 E 4 SE Peru
Juliana Top 59 G 3 mountain, C Surinam
Julianehåb *see* Qaqortoq
Juliomagus *see* Angers
Jullundur *see* Jalandhar
Jumba 73 D 6 S Somalia
Jumilla 93 F 4 SE Spain
Jummoo *see* Jammu
Jumna *see* Yamuna
Jumporn *see* Chumphon
Junction City 45 F 4 Kansas, C USA
Juneau 36 D 4 state capital, Alaska, NW USA
Jungfrau 95 A 7 mountain, S Switzerland
Junín 64 C 4 E Argentina
Junīyah *see* Joûnié
Jura 88 B 4 island, SW Scotland, UK
Jura 95 A 7 *var.* Jura Mountains. Mountain range, France/Switzerland
Jura Mountains *see* Jura
Jurbarkas 106 B 4 *Ger.* Georgenburg, Jurburg. W Lithuania
Jūrmala 106 C 3 C Latvia
Juruá 62 C 2 *var.* Río Yuruá. River, Brazil/Peru
Jutiapa 52 B 2 S Guatemala
Juticalpa 52 D 2 C Honduras
Jutland *see* Jylland
Juvavum *see* Salzburg
Juventud, Isla de la 54 A 2 *var.* Isla de Pinos, *Eng.* Isle of Youth; *prev.* The Isle of the Pines. Island, W Cuba
Jwaneng 78 C 4 SE Botswana
Jylland 85 A 7 *Eng.* Jutland. Peninsula, W Denmark
Jyrgalan *see* Dzhergalan
Jyväskylä 85 D 5 C Finland

K

K2 134 D 1 *Chin.* Qogir Feng, *Eng.* Mount Godwin Austen. Mountain, China/Pakistan
Kaafu Atoll *see* Male' Atoll
Kaaimanston 59 G 3 N Surinam
Kaakhka 122 C 3 *var.* Kaka. S Turkmenistan
Kaamanen 84 D 2 *Lapp.* Gámas. N Finland
Kaambooni 73 D 6 S Somalia
Kaaresuvanto 84 D 2 *Lapp.* Gárassavon. N Finland
Kabale 73 B 6 SW Uganda
Kabinda 77 D 7 SE Congo (Zaire)
Kabinda *see* Cabinda
Kabul 123 F 4 *var.* Daryā-ye Kābul. River, Afghanistan/Pakistan
Kābul 123 E 4 *var.* Kabul, *Per.* Kābol. Country capital, E Afghanistan
Kābul, Daryā-ye *see* Kabul
Kabwe 78 D 2 C Zambia
Kachchh, Gulf of 134 B 4 *var.* Gulf of Cutch, Gulf of Kutch. Gulf, N Arabian Sea
Kadan Kyun 137 B 6 *prev.* King Island. Island, S Burma
Kadavu 145 E 4 *prev.* Kandavu. Island, S Fiji
Kadoma 78 D 3 *prev.* Gatooma. C Zimbabwe
Kadugli 72 B 4 S Sudan
Kaduna 75 G 4 C Nigeria
Kadzhi-Say 123 G 2 *Kir.* Kajisay. NE Kyrgyzstan
Kaédi 74 C 3 S Mauritania
Kāfar Jar Ghar 123 E 5 mountain range, C Afghanistan
Kafue 78 C 2 river, C Zambia
Kafue 78 D 2 SE Zambia
Kaga Bandoro 76 C 4 *prev.* Fort-Crampel. C Central African Republic
Kagan *see* Kogon
Kâğıthane 116 B 2 Turkey
Kagoshima 131 A 8 *var.* Kagosima. Kyūshū, SW Japan
Kagoshima-wan 131 A 8 bay, NW Pacific Ocean
Kagosima *see* Kagoshima
Kagul *see* Cahul
Kahramanmaraş 116 D 4 *var.* Kahraman Maraş, Maraş, Marash. S Turkey
Kaiapoi 151 C 6 South Island, C New Zealand
Kaifeng 128 C 4 C China
Kai, Kepulauan 139 G 4 *prev.* Kei Islands. Island group, Maluka, E Indonesia
Kaikohe 150 C 2 North Island, N New Zealand
Kaikoura 151 C 5 South Island, C New Zealand
Kaikoura Peninsula 151 C 5 peninsula, South Island, C New Zealand
Kainji Lake *see* Kainji Reservoir
Kainji Reservoir 75 F 4 *var.* Kainji Lake. Reservoir, W Nigeria
Kaipara Harbour 150 C 2 harbour, North Island, N New Zealand
Kairouan 71 E 2 *var.* Al Qayrawān. E Tunisia
Kaiserslautern 95 A 5 SW Germany
Kaišiadorys 107 B 5 S Lithuania
Kaitaia 150 C 2 North Island, N New Zealand
Kajaani 84 E 4 *Swe.* Kajana. C Finland
Kajan *see* Kayan, Sungai
Kajana *see* Kajaani
Kajisay *see* Kadzhi-Say
Kaka *see* Kaakhka
Kake 36 D 4 Alaska, NW USA
Kakhovka 109 F 4 S Ukraine
Kakhovs'ka Vodoskhovyshche 109 F 4 *Rus.* Kakhovskoye Vodokhranilishche. Reservoir, SE Ukraine
Kakhovskoye Vodokhranilishche *see* Kakhovs'ka Vodoskhovyshche
Kākināda 132 D 1 *prev.* Cocanada. E India
Ka-Krem *see* Malyy Yenisey
Kakshaal-Too, Khrebet *see* Kokshaal-Tau
Kaktovik 36 D 2 Alaska, NW USA
Kalach 111 B 6 W Russian Federation
Kalach-na-Donu 111 B 6 SW Russian Federation
Kalahari Desert 78 C 4 desert, S Africa
Kalaikhum *see* Qal'aikhum
Kalámai *see* Kalámata
Kalamariá 104 C 4 N Greece
Kalámata 105 B 6 *prev.* Kalámai. S Greece
Kalamazoo 40 C 3 Michigan, N USA
Kalambaka *see* Kalampáka
Kálamos 105 C 5 C Greece
Kalampáka 104 B 4 C Greece
Kalanchak 109 F 4 S Ukraine
Kalasin 136 D 4 *var.* Muang Kalasin. NE Thailand
Kalāt 134 B 2 *var.* Kelat, Khelat. SW Pakistan
Kalāt 123 E 5 *Per.* Qalāt. S Afghanistan
Kalbarri 147 A 5 Western Australia, W Australia
Kalecik 116 C 3 N Turkey
Kalemie 77 E 7 *prev.* Albertville. SE Congo (Zaire)
Kalgoorlie 147 C 6 SW Australia
Kalima 77 D 6 E Congo (Zaire)
Kalimantan 138 D 4 *Eng.* Indonesian Borneo. Geopolitical region, Borneo, C Indonesia
Kálimnos 105 D 6 island, W Greece
Kalinin *see* Tver'
Kaliningrad 106 A 4 Russian Federation
Kaliningrad 106 A 4 enclave, W Russian Federation
Kalinkavichy 107 C 7 *Rus.* Kalinkovichi. SE Belorussia
Kalinkovichi *see* Kalinkavichy
Kalispell 44 B 1 Montana, NW USA
Kalisz 98 C 4 *Ger.* Kalisch, *Rus.* Kalish; *anc.* Calisia. C Poland
Kalix 84 D 4 N Sweden
Kalixälven 84 D 3 river, N Sweden
Kallaste 106 E 3 *Ger.* Krasnogor. SE Estonia
Kallavesi 85 E 5 lake, SE Finland
Kalloní 105 D 5 Lésvos, E Greece
Kalmar 85 C 7 *var.* Calmar. S Sweden
Kalmthout 87 C 5 N Belgium
Kalpáki 104 A 4 W Greece
Kalpeni Island 132 B 3 island, Lakshadweep, SW India
Kaltdorf *see* Pruszków
Kaluga 111 B 5 W Russian Federation
Kalush 108 C 2 *Pol.* Kałusz. W Ukraine
Kałusz *see* Kalush
Kalutara 132 D 4 SW Sri Lanka
Kalvarija 107 B 5 *Pol.* Kalwaria. S Lithuania
Kalwaria *see* Kalvarija
Kalyān 134 C 5 W India
Kama 110 D 4 river, Russian Federation
Kamarang 59 F 3 W Guyana
Kamchatka *see* Kamchatka, Poluostrov
Kamchatka, Poluostrov 115 H 2 *Eng.* Kamchatka. Peninsula, NE Russian Federation
Kamchiya 104 D 2 river, E Bulgaria
Kamenets-Podol'skiy *see* Kam"yanets'-Podil's'kyy
Kamenka Dneprovskaya *see* Kam"yanka-Dniprovs'ka
Kamensk-Shakhtinskiy 111 B 6 SW Russian Federation
Kamina 77 D 7 S Congo (Zaire)
Kamloops 37 E 5 British Columbia, SW Canada
Kampala 73 B 6 country capital, S Uganda
Kampar 138 B 3 W Malaysia
Kâmpóng Cham 137 D 6 *prev.* Kompong Cham. S Cambodia
Kâmpóng Chhnăng 137 D 6 *prev.* Kompong. C Cambodia
Kâmpóng Saôm 137 D 6 *prev.* Kompong Som, Sihanoukville. SW Cambodia
Kâmpóng Spoe 137 D 6 *prev.* Kompong Speu. S Cambodia
Kâmpóng Thum 137 D 6 *prev.* Kompong Thom. C Cambodia
Kâmpôt 137 D 6 S Cambodia
Kam"yanets'-Podil's'kyy 108 C 3 *Rus.* Kamenets-Podol'skiy. W Ukraine
Kam"yanka-Dniprovs'ka 109 F 3 *Rus.* Kamenka Dneprovskaya. SE Ukraine
Kamyshin 111 C 6 SW Russian Federation
Kananga 77 D 7 *prev.* Luluabourg. S Congo (Zaire)

Kanash 111 C 5
  W Russian Federation
Kanazawa 131 C 5 Honshū,
  SW Japan
Kānchīpuram 132 C 2 *prev.*
  Conjeeveram. SE India
Kandahār 123 E 5 *var.* Qandahār.
  S Afghanistan
Kandalaksha 110 C 2 *var.*
  Kandalak3a, *Fin.* Kantalahti.
  NW Russian Federation
Kandangan 138 D 4 Borneo,
  C Indonesia
Kandau *see* Kandava
Kandava 106 C 3 *Ger.* Kandau.
  W Latvia
Kandavu *see* Kadavu
Kandla 134 C 4 W India
Kandy 132 D 3 C Sri Lanka
Kane Fracture Zone 66 B 4 fracture
  zone, NW Atlantic Ocean
Kaneohe 47 A 8 *Haw.* Kāne'ohe.
  Hawaii, W USA
Kāne'ohe *see* Kaneohe
Kanestron, Akra *see* Palioúri, Ákra
Kanëv *see* Kaniv
Kanevskoye Vodokhranilishche *see*
  Kanivs'ke Vodoskhovyshche
Kangaatsiaq 82 C 3 *var.* Kangatsiak,
  Kangâtsiaq. W Greenland
Kangān 120 D 4 S Iran
Kangaroo Island 149 A 7 island,
  S Australia
Kangerluarsoruseq *see* Færingehavn
Kangerlussuaq 82 C 3 *Dan.* Søndre
  Strømfjord. SW Greenland
Kangertittivaq 83 E 4 *Dan.* Scoresby
  Sund. Inlet, N Atlantic Ocean
Kaniv 109 E 2 *Rus.* Kanëv.
  C Ukraine
Kanivs'ke Vodoskhovyshche 109
  E 2 *Rus.* Kanevskoye
  Vodokhranilishche. Reservoir,
  C Ukraine
Kanjiža 100 D 2 *Ger.* Altkanischa,
  Hung. Magyarkanizsa, Ókanizsa;
  prev. Stara Kanjiža. N Yugoslavia
Kankaanpää 85 D 5 SW Finland
Kankakee 40 B 4 Illinois, N USA
Kankan 74 D 4 E Guinea
Kano 75 G 4 N Nigeria
Kānpur 135 E 3 *Eng.* Cawnpore.
  N India
Kansas 45 E 5 *off.* State of Kansas;
  nicknames Jayhawker State,
  Sunflower State. State, C USA
Kansas City 45 F 4 Kansas, C USA
Kansas City 45 F 4 Missouri,
  C USA
Kansas River 45 F 5 River, Kansas,
  C USA
Kansk 115 E 4 S Russian Federation
Kántanos 105 C 8 Kríti, SE Greece
Kantemirovka 111 B 6
  W Russian Federation
Kantipur *see* Kathmandu
Kanton 145 F 3 *var.* Abariringa,
  Canton Island; *prev.* Mary Island.
  Island, C Kiribati
Kanye 78 C 4 SE Botswana
Kaohsiung 129 D 6 *var.* Gaoxiong,
  Jap. Takao, Takow. SW Taiwan
Kaolack 74 B 3 *var.* Kaolak.
  W Senegal
Kaolak *see* Kaolack
Kaoma 78 C 2 W Zambia
Kapelle 87 B 5 SW Netherlands
Kapellen 87 C 5 N Belgium
Kapka, Massif du 76 D 2 mountain
  range, E Chad
Kapoeas *see* Kapuas, Sungai
Kaposvár 99 C 7 SW Hungary

Kappeln 94 B 2 N Germany
Kaptsevichy 107 C 7
  Rus. Koptsevichi. SE Belorussia
Kapuas 138 C 4 *prev.* Kapoeas.
  River, Borneo, C Indonesia
Kapuskasing 38 C 4 Ontario,
  S Canada
Kapyl' 107 C 6 *Rus.* Kopyl'.
  C Belorussia
Kara-Balta 123 F 2 N Kyrgyzstan
Karabil', Vozvyshennost' 122 D 3
  mountain range, S Turkmenistan
Kara-Bogaz-Gol, Proliv 122 B 2
  Turkm. Garabogazköl Bogazy.
  Strait, E Caspian Sea
Kara-Bogaz-Gol, Zaliv 122 B 2 bay,
  E Caspian Sea
Karabük 116 C 2 N Turkey
Karachev 111 B 5
  W Russian Federation
Karāchi 134 B 3 province capital,
  SE Pakistan
Karácsonkő *see* Piţra-Neamt
Karaganda 114 C 4 *Kaz.*
  Qaraghandy. C Kazakhstan
Karaginskiy, Ostrov 115 H 2 island,
  E Russian Federation
Karaginskiy Zaliv 115 H 2 bay,
  W Bering Sea
Karaj 120 C 3 N Iran
Kara-Kala 122 C 3 *var.* Garrygala.
  W Turkmenistan
Karakax *see* Moyu
Karakol 123 G 2 *var.* Karakolka.
  NE Kyrgyzstan
Karakol 123 G 2 *prev.* Przheval'sk.
  NE Kyrgyzstan
Karakolka *see* Karakol
Karakoram Range 134 D 1
  mountain range, India/Pakistan
Karaköse 117 F 3 N Turkey
Karakul' *see* Qarokūl
Kara Kum *see* Garagumy
Karakumskiy Kanal 122 D 3
  Turkm. Garagum Kanaly. Canal,
  C Turkmenistan
Karaman 116 C 4 S Turkey
Karamay 126 B 2 *var.* Karamai,
  Kelamayi, *Chin.* K'o-la-ma-i.
  NW China
Karamea Bight 151 C 5 bight,
  South Island, E Tasman Sea
Karapelit 104 E 1 *Rom.* Stejarul.
  NE Bulgaria
Kara-Say 123 G 2 NE Kyrgyzstan
Karasburg 78 B 4 S Namibia
Kara Sea *see* Karskoye More
Karatau 114 C 5 *Kaz.* Qarataū.
  S Kazakhstan
Karavanke *see* Karawanken
Karavás 105 B 7 Kýthira, S Greece
Karbalā' 120 B 4 *var.* Kerbala,
  Kerbela. S Iraq
Kardhítsa *see* Kardítsa
Kardítsa 105 B 5 *var.* Kardhítsa.
  C Greece
Kärdla 106 C 2 *Ger.* Kertel.
  Hiiumaa, W Estonia
Kargı 116 C 2 N Turkey
Kargilik *see* Yecheng
Kariba 78 D 3 N Zimbabwe
Kariba, Lake 78 D 3 reservoir,
  Zambia/Zimbabwe
Karibib 78 B 3 C Namibia
Karies *see* Karyés
Karigasniemi 84 D 2 *Lapp.*
  Garegegasnjárga. N Finland
Karimata 138 C 4 strait,
  Java Sea/South China Sea
Karīmnagar 135 E 5 C India
Karin 72 D 4 N Somalia

Káristos *see* Kárystos
Karkinits'ka Zatoka 109 F 4
  Rus. Karkinitskiy Zaliv. Gulf,
  N Black Sea
Karkinitskiy Zaliv *see*
  Karkinits'ka Zatoka
Karl-Marx-Stadt *see* Chemnitz
Karló *see* Hailuoto
Karlovac 100 B 2 *Ger.* Karlstadt,
  Hung. Károlyváros. C Croatia
Karlovy Vary 99 A 5 *Ger.* Karlsbad;
  prev. Eng. Carlsbad.
  W Czech Republic
Karlskrona 85 C 7 S Sweden
Karlsruhe 95 B 6 *var.* Carlsruhe.
  SW Germany
Karlstad 85 B 6 C Sweden
Karnāl 134 D 2 N India
Karnātaka 132 C 1 *var.* Kanara; *prev.*
  Maisur, Mysore. State, W India
Karnobat 104 E 2 E Bulgaria
Karnul *see* Kurnool
Kárpathos 105 E 7 Kárpathos,
  SE Greece
Kárpathos 105 E 7 *It.* Scarpanto;
  anc. Carpathos, Carpathus. Island,
  Dodekánisos, SE Greece
Karpenísi 105 B 5 *prev.*
  Karpenísion. C Greece
Karpenísion *see* Karpenísi
Kars 117 F 3 *var.* Qars. NE Turkey
Kārsava 106 D 4 *Ger.* Karsau;
  prev. Rus. Korsovka. E Latvia
Karskoye More 114 D 2
  Eng. Kara Sea. Sea, Arctic Ocean
Kārūn 120 C 3 *var.* Rúd-e Kárún.
  River, SW Iran
Kārūn, Rūd-e *see* Kārūn
Karyés 104 C 4 *var.* Karies.
  N Greece
Kárystos 105 C 6 *var.* Káristos.
  Évvoia, C Greece
Kas 116 B 5 SW Turkey
Kasai 77 C 6 *var.* Cassai, Kassai.
  River, Angola/Congo (Zaire)
Kasaji 77 D 7 S Congo (Zaire)
Kasama 78 D 1 N Zambia
Kasan *see* Koson
Kasane 78 C 3 NE Botswana
Kāsaragod 132 B 2 SW India
Kāshān 120 C 3 C Iran
Kashi 126 A 3 *Chin.* Kaxgar, K'o-
  shih, *Uigh.* Kashgar. NW China
Kashmir 134 D 1 cultural region,
  N India
Kaskaskia River 40 B 5 river,
  Illinois, N USA
Kasongo 77 D 6 E Congo (Zaire)
Kásos 105 F 7 island, S Greece
Kaspiysk 111 B 8
  SW Russian Federation
Kassala 72 C 4 E Sudan
Kassel 94 B 4 *prev.* Cassel.
  C Germany
Kasserine 71 E 2 *var.* Al Qaşrayn.
  W Tunisia
Kastamonu 116 C 2 *var.* Castamoni,
  Kastamuni. N Turkey
Kastaneá 104 B 4 N Greece
Kastélli 105 C 7 Kríti, SE Greece
Kastoría 104 B 4 N Greece
Kástro 105 C 6 Sífnos, SE Greece
Kastsyukovichy 107 E 7
  Rus. Kostyukovichi. E Belorussia
Kastsyukowka 107 D 7
  Rus. Kostyukovka. SE Belorussia
Kasulu 73 B 7 W Tanzania
Kasumiga-ura 131 D 5 lake,
  Honshū, S Japan
Katalla 36 C 3 Alaska, NW USA
Katana *see* Qaţanā

Katanning 147 B 7 Western
  Australia, W Australia
Katchall Island 133 F 3 island,
  SW India
Kateríni 104 B 4 N Greece
Katha 136 B 2 N Burma
Katherina, Gebel 72 C 2
  var. Jabal Katrínah, *Eng.* Mount
  Catherine. Mountain, NE Egypt
Katherine 148 A 2 Northern
  Territory, N Australia
Kathmandu 135 F 3 *prev.* Kantipur.
  Country capital, C Nepal
Katikati 150 D 3 North Island,
  NE New Zealand
Katima Mulilo 78 C 3 NE Namibia
Katiola 74 D 4 C Ivory Coast
Káto Achaía 105 B 6
  var. Káto Akhaía. S Greece
Káto Akhaía *see* Káto Achaía
Kat O Chau 128 B 1 island,
  NE Hong Kong
Katoúna 105 B 5 C Greece
Katowice 99 C 5 *Ger.* Kattowitz.
  S Poland
Katsina 75 G 4 N Nigeria
Kattakurgan *see* Kattaqürghon
Kattaqürghon 123 E 2
  Rus. Kattakurgan. C Uzbekistan
Kattavía 105 E 7 Ródos, SE Greece
Kattegat 85 B 7 *Dan.* Kattegatt.
  Strait, E North Sea
Kattegatt *see* Kattegat
Kattowitz *see* Katowice
Kauai 47 A 7 *Haw.* Kaua'i. Island,
  Hawaii, W USA
Kaua'i *see* Kauai
Kaufbeuren 95 C 6 S Germany
Kaunas 106 B 4 *Ger.* Kauen,
  Pol. Kowno; *prev. Rus.* Kovno.
  C Lithuania
Kauno Marios 106 B 4 reservoir,
  S Lithuania
Kau-Ye Kyun 137 B 6
  var. Sir Charles Forbes Island.
  Island, S Burma
Kavadar *see* Kavadarci
Kavadarci 101 E 6 *Turk.* Kavadar.
  C Macedonia
Kavajë 101 C 6 *It.* Cavaia, Kavaja.
  W Albania
Kavakli *see* Topolovgrad
Kaválla 104 C 3 *prev.* Kaválla.
  NE Greece
Kávali 132 D 2 E India
Kaválla *see* Kavála
Kavaratti Island 132 B 3 island,
  Lakshadweep, SW India
Kavarna 104 E 2 NE Bulgaria
Kavír, Dasht-e 120 D 3 *var.*
  Dasht-e-Kavir. Salt lake,
  N Iran
Kavkaz *see* Caucasus
Kawagoe 131 D 5 Honshū, S Japan
Kawasaki 131 D 5 Honshū,
  S Japan
Kawerau 150 E 3 North Island,
  NE New Zealand
Kaya 75 E 4 C Burkina
Kayan 136 B 4 S Burma
Kayan 138 D 3 *prev.* Kajan. River,
  Borneo, C Indonesia
Kayes 74 C 3 W Mali
Kayseri 116 D 3 *var.* Kaisaria;
  anc. Caesarea Mazaca, Mazaca.
  C Turkey
Kazach'ye 115 F 2
  N Russian Federation
Kazakhskiy Melkosopochnik
  114 B 4 *Eng.* Kazakh Uplands,
  Kirghiz Steppe, *Kaz.* Saryarqa.
  Physical region, C Kazakhstan

Kazakhstan
114 B 4 Qazaqstan Respublikasy,
var. Kazakstan, *Kaz.* Qazaqstan;
prev. Kazakh Soviet Socialist
Republic, *Rus.* Kazakhskaya SSR.
Republic, C Asia

Official name: Republic of
Kazakhstan **Date of formation:** 1991
Capital: Almaty **Population:** 17.2
million **Total Area:** 2,717,300 sq km
(1,049,150 sq miles) **Languages:**
Kazakh*, Russian **Religions:**
Muslim 47%, other 53% (mostly
Russian Orthodox, Lutheran) **Ethnic
mix:** Kazakh 40%, Russian 38%,
Ukrainian 6%, other 16%
Government: Multiparty republic
Currency: Tenge = 100 tein

Kazakh Uplands *see* Kazakhskiy
Melkosopochnik
Kazan' 111 D 5
W Russian Federation
Kazan' 111 D 5 international
airport, W Russian Federation
Kazanlŭk 104 D 2 *var.* Kazanlāk;
prev. Kazanlik. C Bulgaria
Kazatin *see* Kozyatyn
Kazbek 117 F 2 *Geor.* Mqinvartsveri.
Mountain, Armenia/Georgia
Kāzerūn 120 D 4 S Iran
Kazi Magomed *see* Qazimämmäd
Kazvin *see* Qazvīn
Kéa 105 C 6 Kéa, SE Greece
Kéa 105 C 6 *prev.* Kéos, *anc.* Ceos.
Island, Kykládes, SE Greece
Kearney 45 E 4 Nebraska, C USA
Keban 117 E 3 Turkey
Keban, Baraji 117 E 3 lake,
C Turkey
Kebkabiya 72 A 4 W Sudan
Kebnekaise 84 C 3 mountain,
N Sweden
Kecskemét 99 D 7 C Hungary
Kediri 138 D 5 Jawa, C Indonesia
Keetmanshoop 78 B 4 S Namibia
Keewatin 38 A 3 Ontario, S Canada
Kefallinía 105 A 5 *var.* Kefallonía.
Island, Iónioi Nísoi, W Greece
Kefallonía *see* Kefallinía
Kefar Tappuaḥ 119 E 7
C West Bank
Kegel *see* Keila
Kehl 95 A 6 SW Germany
Kei Islands *see* Kai, Kepulauan
Keila 106 D 2 *Ger.* Kegel.
NW Estonia
Keïta 75 F 3 C Niger
Keitele 84 D 4 lake, C Finland
Keith 149 B 7 South Australia,
S Australia
Keizer 46 B 3 Oregon, NW USA
Kēk-Art 123 G 2 *prev.* Alaykel',
Alay-Kuu. SW Kyrgyzstan
Kékes 99 D 6 mountain,
N Hungary
Kelang 138 B 3 *var.* Kelang; *prev.*
Port Swettenham. W Malaysia
Kelifskiy Uzboy 122 D 3 wetland,
E Turkmenistan
Kelmė 106 B 4 C Lithuania
Kélo 76 B 4 SW Chad
Kelowna 37 E 5 British Columbia,
SW Canada
Kelso 46 B 2 Washington, NW USA
Keltsy *see* Kielce
Keluang 138 B 3 *var.* Kluang.
W Malaysia
Kem' 110 B 3
NW Russian Federation
Kemah 117 E 3 E Turkey

Kemerovo 114 D 4
prev. Shcheglovsk.
C Russian Federation
Kemi 84 D 3 NW Finland
Kemijärvi 84 D 3 *Swe.* Kemiträsk.
N Finland
Kemijoki 84 D 3 river, NW Finland
Kemiö *see* Kimito
Kemiträsk *see* Kemijärvi
Kempele 84 D 4 C Finland
Kempten 95 C 7 S Germany
Kempton 149 C 8 Tasmania,
SE Australia
Kendal 89 C 5 NW England, UK
Kendall 43 F 5 Florida, SE USA
Kendari 139 E 4 Celebes,
C Indonesia
Kenedy 49 G 4 Texas, S USA
Kenema 74 C 4 SE Sierra Leone
Këneurgench 122 C 2
Turkm. Köneürgench; *prev.*
Kunya-Urgench. N Turkmenistan
Kenge 77 C 6 SW Congo (Zaire)
Keng Tung 136 C 3 *var.* Kentung.
SE Burma
Kénitra 70 C 2 *prev.* Port-Lyautey.
NW Morocco
Kennebec River 41 G 2 river,
Maine, NE USA
Kenner 42 B 3 Louisiana, S USA
Kennett 45 H 5 Missouri, C USA
Kennewick 46 C 2 Washington,
NW USA
Kenora 38 A 3 Ontario, S Canada
Kenosha 40 B 3 Wisconsin, N USA
Kent 46 B 2 Washington, NW USA
Kentau 114 B 5 S Kazakhstan
Kentucky 40 C 5 *off.*
Commonwealth of Kentucky;
nickname Bluegrass State. State,
C USA
Kentucky Lake 40 B 5 reservoir,
E USA
Kentung *see* Keng Tung

Kenya
73 C 6 Republic, NE Africa

Official name: Republic of Kenya
Date of formation: 1963
Capital: Nairobi **Population:** 29.1
million **Total area:** 580,370 sq km
(224,081 sq miles) **Languages:**
Swahili*, English, Kikuyu, Luo,
Kamba **Religions:** Christian 66%,
traditional beliefs 26%, other 8%
Ethnic mix: Kikuyu 21%, Luhya
14%, Kamba 11%, other 54%
Government: Multiparty republic
Currency: Shilling = 100 cents

Kenya, Mount *see* Kirinyaga
Keokuk 45 G 4 Iowa, C USA
Kępno 98 C 4 C Poland
Kerala 132 C 2 state, S India
Keratea *see* Keratéa
Keratéa 105 C 6 *var.* Keratea.
C Greece
Kerch 109 G 5 *Rus.* Kerch'.
SE Ukraine
Kerch' *see* Kerch
Kerch Strait 109 G 4 *var.* Bosporus
Cimmerius, Enikale Strait,
Rus. Kerchenskiy Proliv,
Ukr. Kerchens'ka Protska. Strait,
Sea of Azov/Black Sea
Keremitlik *see* Lyulyakovo
Kerguelen 141 C 7 island,
C French Southern &
Antarctic Territories
Kerguelen Plateau 141 C 7
undersea plateau, S Indian Ocean
Kerí 105 A 6 Zákynthos, W Greece

Kerikeri 150 D 2 North Island,
N New Zealand
Kerki 123 E 3 E Turkmenistan
Kerkrade 87 D 6 SE Netherlands
Kérkyra 104 A 4 *var.* Kérkira,
Eng. Corfu. Island, Iónioi Nísoi,
W Greece
Kérkyra 104 A 4 *var.* Kérkira,
Eng. Corfu. Kérkyra, W Greece
Kermadec Islands 152 C 4 island
group, NE New Zealand
Kermadec Trench 152 D 4 trench,
S Pacific Ocean
Kermān 120 D 4 *var.* Kirman;
anc. Carmana. C Iran
Kerrville 49 F 4 Texas, S USA
Kertel *see* Kärdla
Kerulen 127 E 2 *Chin.* Herlen He,
Mong. Herlen Gol. River,
China/Mongolia
Kessennuma 130 D 4 Honshū,
C Japan
Keszthely 99 C 7 SW Hungary
Ketchikan 36 D 4 Alaska,
NW USA
Kettering 89 D 6 C England, UK
Kettering 40 C 4 Ohio, N USA
Keupriya *see* Primorsko
Keuruu 85 D 5 C Finland
Keweenaw Peninsula 40 B 1
headland, Michigan, N USA
Key Largo 54 B 2 island, W Cuba
Key West 43 E 5 Florida, SE USA
Khabarovsk 115 G 4
SE Russian Federation
Khachmas *see* Xaçmaz
Khairpur 134 B 3 SE Pakistan
Khambhāt, Gulf of 134 C 4
Eng. Gulf of Cambay. Gulf,
NE Arabian Sea
Khānābād 123 E 3 NE Afghanistan
Khān al Baghdādī *see* Al Baghdādī
Khandwa 134 D 4 C India
Khanh Hung *see* Soc Trăng
Khanka, Lake 123 E 2 *var.*
Hsing-K'ai Hu, Lake Hanka,
Chin. Xingkai Hu, *Rus.* Ozero
Khanka. Lake, China/
Russian Federation
Khanty-Mansiysk 114 C 3
prev. Ostyako-Voguls'k.
C Russian Federation
Khan Yums 119 A 7 S Israel
Khanzi *see* Ghanzi
Kharagpur 135 F 4 NE India
Khar'kov 109 G 2 *Rus.* Khar'kov.
NE Ukraine
Khar'kov *see* Kharkiv
Kharmanli 104 D 3 *var.* Harmanli.
S Bulgaria
Kharovsk 110 C 4 *var.* Charovsk,
Harovsk. NW Russian Federation
Khartoum 72 B 4 *var.* Al Kharṭūm,
Khartum. Country capital,
C Sudan
Khasavyurt 111 B 8
SW Russian Federation
Khashm el Girba 72 C 4 E Sudan
Khaskovo 104 D 3 *var.* Haskovo.
S Bulgaria
Khaybar, Kowtal-e *see* Khyber Pass
Khaydarkan 123 F 2 *var.*
Khaydarken. SW Kyrgyzstan
Khaydarken *see* Khaydarkan
Kherson 109 E 4 *var.* Cherson.
S Ukraine
Kheta 115 E 2 river,
N Russian Federation
Khíos *see* Chíos
Khiva *see* Khiwa
Khiwa 122 D 2 *Rus.* Khiva.
W Uzbekistan

Khmel 'nyts'kyy 108 C 2
Rus. Khmel'nitskiy;
prev. Proskurov. W Ukraine
Khodasy 107 E 7 *Rus.* Khodosy.
E Belorussia
Khodoriv 108 C 2 *Pol.* Chodorów,
Rus. Khodorov. NW Ukraine
Khodosy *see* Khodasy
Kholm 123 E 3 *var.* Tashqurghan,
Pash. Khulm. N Afghanistan
Kholm *see* Chełm
Khong Sedone *see* Muang
Khôngxédôn
Khon Kaen 136 D 4 *var.* Muang
Khon Kaen. N Thailand
Khor 115 G 4 SE Russian Federation
Khorugh 123 F 3 *var.* Horog,
Rus. Khorog. S Tajikistan
Kho Sawai Plateau *see*
Korat Plateau
Khosf 120 E 3 E Iran
Khouribga 70 C 2 C Morocco
Khovd *see* Hovd
Khowst 123 F 4 E Afghanistan
Khoyniki 107 D 8 SE Belorussia
Khujand 123 F 2 *var.* Khodzhent,
Khojend, *Rus.* Khudzhand,
Taj. Leninobod; *prev.* Leninabad.
N Tajikistan
Khulna 135 G 4 SW Bangladesh
Khust 108 B 3 *var.* Husté, *Cz.* Chust,
Hung. Huszt. W Ukraine
Khvalynsk 111 C 6
W Russian Federation
Khvoy 120 C 2 *var.* Khoi, Khoy.
NW Iran
Khyber Pass 123 F 4 *var.* Kowtal-e
Khaybar. Pass, Afghanistan/
Pakistan
Kiáto 105 B 6 *prev.* Kiáton. S Greece
Kiáton *see* Kiáto
Kibangou 77 B 6 SW Congo
Kibombo 77 D 6 E Congo (Zaire)
Kičevo 101 D 6 SW Macedonia
Kidderminster 89 C 6
W England, UK
Kiel 94 B 2 N Germany
Kielce 98 D 4 *Rus.* Keltsy.
SE Poland
Kieler Bucht 94 C 2 bay,
W Baltic Sea
Kiev *see* Kyyiv
Kiffa 74 C 3 S Mauritania
Kigali 73 B 6 country capital,
C Rwanda
Kigoma 73 B 7 W Tanzania
Kihnu 106 C 2 *var.* Kihnu Saar,
Ger. Kühnö. Island, SW Estonia
Kihti *see* Skiftet
Kii-suidō 131 C 7 strait,
NW Pacific Ocean
Kikinda 100 D 3 *Ger.* Grosskikinda,
Hung. Nagykikinda; *prev.* Velika
Kikinda. NE Yugoslavia
Kikwit 77 C 6 W Congo (Zaire)
Kili 144 D 2 Island,
S Marshall Islands
Kilien Mountains *see* Qilian Shan
Kilimanjaro 73 C 7 *var.* Vhuru
Peak. Mountain, NE Tanzania
Kilingi-Nõmme 106 D 3
Ger. Kurkund. SW Estonia
Kilis 116 D 4 S Turkey
Kiliya 108 D 4 *Rom.* Chilia-Nouă.
SW Ukraine
Kilkenny 89 B 6 *Ir.* Cill Chainnigh.
S Ireland
Kilkís 104 B 3 N Greece
Killarney 89 A 6 *Ir.* Cill Airne.
SW Ireland
Killeen 49 G 3 Texas, S USA

Kilmarnock 88 C 4
SW Scotland, UK
Kimberley 78 C 4 C South Africa
Kimberley Plateau 146 D 3 plateau,
Western Australia,
NW Australia
Kimch'aek 128 E 3 *prev.* Sŏngjin.
E North Korea
Kími *see* Kými
Kimito 85 D 6 *Swe.* Kemiö.
Island,
SW Finland
Kimovsk 111 B 5
W Russian Federation
Kindersley 37 F 5 Saskatchewan,
S Canada
Kindia 74 C 4 SW Guinea
Kindley Field Airport 42 B 5
international airport,
E Bermuda
Kindu 77 D 6 *prev.* Kindu-Port-
Empain. C Congo (Zaire)
Kindu-Port-Empain *see* Kindu
Kineshma 111 C 5 *var.* Kinešma.
W Russian Federation
Kinešma *see* Kineshma
King Charles Islands *see*
Kong Karls Land
King Christian IX Land *see*
Kong Christian IX Land
King Christian X Land *see*
Kong Christian X Land
King Frederik VI Coast 82 C 4 *see*
Kong Frederik VI Kyst.
King Frederik VIII Land 83 E 2 *see*
Kong Frederik VIII Land.
King Frederik IX Land 82 C 3 *see*
Kong Frederik IX Land.
King I *see* Kadan Kyun
King Island 149 B 8 island,
Tasmania, SE Australia
Kingman 48 A 2 Arizona, SW USA
Kingman Reef 145 G 2 reef,
NE Australia
King's Lynn 89 E 6 *var.* Bishop's
Lynn, Kings Lynn, Lynn, Lynn
Regis. E England, UK
King Sound 146 C 3 inlet,
Indian Ocean/Timor Sea
Kingsport 43 E 1 Tennessee, S USA
Kingston 54 B 5 country capital,
SE Jamaica
Kingston 38 D 5 Ontario,
SE Canada
Kingston 41 F 3 New York,
NE USA
Kingston upon Hull 89 E 5
var. Hull. NE England, UK
Kingstown 55 H 4 country capital,
N Saint Vincent & the Grenadines
Kingsville 49 G 5 Texas, S USA
King William Island 37 F 3 island,
N Canada
Kinrooi 87 D 5 NE Belgium
Kinshasa 77 B 6 *prev.* Léopoldville.
Country capital, W Congo (Zaire)
Kinston 43 F 1 North Carolina,
SE USA
Kintyre 88 B 4 peninsula,
NE Scotland, UK
Kinyeti 73 B 5 mountain, S Sudan
Kiparissía *see* Kyparissía
Kipili 73 B 7 W Tanzania
Kipushi 77 E 8 SE Congo (Zaire)
Kirghiz Range 114 C 5
Rus. Kirgizskiy Khrebet;
prev. Alexander Range. Mountain
range, Kazakhstan/Kyrgyzstan
Kirghiz Steppe *see* Kazakhskiy
Melkosopochnik
Kırıkale 116 C 3 C Turkey
Kırıkhan 116 D 4 S Turkey

Kiribati
145 F 2 Republic, C Pacific Ocean

Official name: Republic of Kiribati
Date of formation: 1979 **Capital:**
Bairiki **Population:** 7,500 **Total Area:**
710 sq km (274 sq miles) **Languages:**
English*, Kiribati **Religions:** Roman
Catholic 53%, Protestant 40%, other
Christian 4%, other 3% **Ethnic mix:**
I-Kiribati 98%, other 2%
Government: Multiparty republic
Currency: Australian $ = 100 cents

Kiribati, Republic of *see* Kiribati
Kirinyaga 73 C 6 *prev.* Mount
Kenya. Volcano, C Kenya
Kirishi 110 B 4 *var.* Kirisi.
NW Russian Federation
Kirisi *see* Kirishi
Kiritimati 145 G 2 *prev.* Christmas
Island. Island, E Kiribati
Kiriwina Islands 144 C 3 *var.*
Trobriand Islands. Island group,
S Papua New Guinea
Kirkenes 84 E 2 *var.* Kirkkoniemi.
N Norway
Kirk-Kilissa *see* Kırklareli
Kirkkoniemi *see* Kirkenes
Kirkland Lake 38 D 4 Ontario,
S Canada
Kırklareli 116 A 2 *prev.* Kirk-Kilissa.
NW Turkey
Kirkpatrick, Mount 154 C 3
mountain, Antarctica
Kirksville 45 G 4 Missouri, C USA
Kirkūk 120 B 3 *var.* Karkūk,
Kerkuk. N Iraq
Kirkwall 88 C 2 island authority
area capital, NE Scotland, UK
Kirkwood 45 G 5 Missouri, C USA
Kirov 110 C 4 *prev.* Vyatka.
NW Russian Federation
Kirovakan *see* Vanadzor
Kirovo-Cepeck *see* Kirovo-Chepetsk
Kirovo-Chepetsk 111 D 5
var. Kirovo-Cepeck.
NW Russian Federation
Kirovohrad 109 E 3
Rus. Kirovograd; *prev.*
Kirovo,Yelizavetgrad,
Zinov'yevsk. C Ukraine
Kirsanov 111 B 6
W Russian Federation
Kīrthar Range 134 A 3 mountain
range, S Pakistan
Kiruna 84 C 3 N Sweden
Kisangani 77 E 5 *prev.* Stanleyville.
NE Congo (Zaire)
Kishinev *see* Chişinău
Kiskörei-víztároló 99 D 6 reservoir,
E Hungary
Kiskunfélegyháza 99 D 7
var. Félegyháza. C Hungary
Kislovodsk 111 B 7
SW Russian Federation
Kismaayo 73 D 6 *var.* Chisimayu,
Kismayu, *It.* Chisimaio. S Somalia
Kismayu *see* Kismaayo
Kissidougou 74 C 4 S Guinea
Kissimmee 43 E 4 Florida, SE USA
Kistna *see* Krishna
Kisumu 73 C 6 *prev.* Port Florence.
W Kenya
Kisvárda 99 E 6 *Ger.* Kleinwardein.
E Hungary
Kita 74 D 3 W Mali
Kitab *see* Kitob
Kitakyūshū 131 A 7 *var.*
Kitakyûsyû. Kyūshū, SW Japan
Kitakyûsyû *see* Kitakyūshū
Kitami 130 D 2 Hokkaidō,
NE Japan
Koch Bihār 135 G 3 NE India

Kitchener 38 C 5 Ontario, S Canada
Kitimat 36 D 5 British Columbia,
SW Canada
Kitinen 84 D 3 river, N Finland
Kitob 123 E 3 *Rus.* Kitab.
S Uzbekistan
Kitwe 78 D 2 *var.* Kitwe-Nkana.
C Zambia
Kitwe-Nkana *see* Kitwe
Kitzbühler Alpen 95 D 7 mountain
range, W Austria
Kivalina 36 C 2 Alaska, NW USA
Kivalo 84 D 3 ridge, C Finland
Kivertsi 108 C 1 *Pol.* Kiwerce,
Rus. Kivertsy. NW Ukraine
Kivu, Lac *see* Kivu, Lake
Kivu, Lake 77 E 6 *Fr.* Lac Kivu.
Lake, Congo (Zaire)/Rwanda
Kiyevskoye Vodokhranilishche *see*
Kyyivs'ke Vodoskhovyshche
Kizel 111 D 5 NW Russian Federation
Kızıl Irmak 116 C 3 river, C Turkey
Kizilyurt 111 B 8
SW Russian Federation
Kizyl-Arvat *see* Gyzylarbat
Kjølen *see* Kölen
Kladno 99 A 5 NW Czech Republic
Klagenfurt 95 D 7 *Slvn.* Celovec.
S Austria
Klaipėda 106 B 3 *Ger.* Memel.
NW Lithuania
Klamath Falls 46 B 4 Oregon,
NW USA
Klamath Mountains 46 B 4
mountain range, W USA
Klarälven 85 B 6 river,
Norway/Sweden
Klatovy 99 A 5 *Ger.* Klattau.
SW Czech Republic
Klattau *see* Klatovy
Klazienaveen 86 E 2
NE Netherlands
Kleinwardein *see* Kisvárda
Kleisoúra 105 A 5 W Greece
Klerksdorp 78 D 4 N South Africa
Klimavichy 107 E 7 *Rus.*
Klimovichi. E Belorussia
Klimovichi *see* Klimavichy
Klintsy 111 A 5
W Russian Federation
Klisura 104 C 2 C Bulgaria
Ključ 100 B 3
NW Bosnia & Herzegovina
Klobuck 98 C 4 S Poland
Klondike 36 D 3 river, Yukon
Territory, W Canada
Kluang *see* Keluang
Kluczbork 98 C 4 *Ger.* Kreuzburg,
Kreuzburg in Oberschlesien.
SW Poland
Knin 100 B 4 S Croatia
Knjaževac 100 E 4 E Yugoslavia
Knokke-Heist 87 A 5 NW Belgium
Knoxville 42 D 1 Tennessee, S USA
Knud Rasmussen Land 82 D 1
physical region, N Greenland
Kōbe 131 C 6 Honshū, SW Japan
København 85 B 7
Eng. Copenhagen; *anc.* Hafnia.
Country capital, E Denmark
Kobenni 74 D 3 S Mauritania
Koblenz 95 A 5 *Fr.* Coblence;
prev. Coblenz, *anc.* Confluentes.
W Germany
Kobryn 107 A 6 *Pol.* Kobryn,
Rus. Kobrin. SW Belorussia
K'obulet'i 117 F 2 W Georgia
Kočani 101 E 6 NE Macedonia
Kočevje 95 E 8 *Ger.* Gottschee.
S Slovenia

Kōchi 131 B 7 *var.* Kôti. Shikoku,
SW Japan
Kochi *see* Cochin
Kochiu *see* Gejiu
Kodiak 36 C 3 Kodiak Island,
Alaska, USA
Kodiak Island 36 C 3 island,
Alaska, NW USA
Koedoes *see* Kudus
Koepang *see* Kupang
Kofa Mountains 48 A 2 mountain
range, Arizona, SW USA
Kōfu 131 D 5 *var.* Kôhu. Honshū,
S Japan
Kogon 122 D 2 *Rus.* Kagan .
C Uzbekistan
Kohīma 135 H 3 *var.* Kohima.
NE India
Kohima *see* Kohīma
Kohtla-Järve 106 E 2 NE Estonia
Kokkola 84 D 4 *Swe.* Karleby; *prev.*
Swe. Gamlakarleby. W Finland
Kokrines 36 C 3 Alaska, NW USA
Kokshaal-Tau 123 G 2 *Rus.* Khrebet
Kakshaal-Too. Mountain range,
China/Kyrgyzstan
Kokshetau 114 C 4 *Kaz.* Kökshetaü;
prev. Kokchetav. N Kazakhstan
Koksijde 87 A 5 W Belgium
Kokstad 78 D 5 E South Africa
Kolaka 139 E 4 Celebes, C Indonesia
Kola Peninsula *see*
Kol'skiy Poluostrov
Kolari 84 D 3 NW Finland
Kolárovo 99 C 6 *Ger.* Gutta, *Hung.*
Gúta; *prev.* Guta. SW Slovakia
Kolberg *see* Kołobrzeg
Kolda 74 B 3 S Senegal
Kolding 85 A 7 C Denmark
Kôle *see* Kili Island
Kolguyev, Ostrov 110 D 2 island,
NW Russian Federation
Kolhāpur 132 B 1 SW India
Kolhumadulu Atoll 132 B 5
var. Kolumadulu Atoll, Thaa
Atoll. Island, S Maldives
Kolín *see* Kolín
Kolín 99 B 5 *Ger.* Kolin.
C Czech Republic
Kolka 106 C 2 NW Latvia
Kolkasrags 106 C 2 *prev. Eng.* Cape
Domesnes. Headland, NW Latvia
Kolmar *see* Colmar
Köln 94 A 5 *var.* Koeln,
Eng./Fr. Cologne; *prev.* Cöln,
anc. Colonia Agrippina, Oppidum
Ubiorum. W Germany
Koło 98 C 3 C Poland
Kołobrzeg 98 B 2 *Ger.* Kolberg.
NW Poland
Kolokani 74 D 3 W Mali
Kolomea *see* Kolomyya
Kolomna 111 B 5
W Russian Federation
Kolomyya 108 B 3 *Ger.* Kolomea.
W Ukraine
Kolpa 100 A 2 *Ger.* Kulpa, *SCr.*
Kupa. River, Croatia/Slovenia
Kolpino 110 B 4
NW Russian Federation
Kol'skiy Poluostrov 110 C 2
Eng. Kola Peninsula. Peninsula,
NW Russian Federation
Kolwezi 77 D 7 S Congo (Zaire)
Kolyma 115 G 2 river,
NE Russian Federation
Kolyma Range 113 G 2 mountain
range, NE Russian Federation
Kolymskoye Nagor'ye 115 G 2
var. Khrebet Kolymskiy, *Eng.*
Kolyma Range. Mountain range,
NE Russian Federation

Komatsu 131 C 5 *var.* Komatu.
Honshū, SW Japan
Komatu *see* Komatsu
Komoé 75 E 4 *var.* Komoé Fleuve.
River, E Ivory Coast
Komoé Fleuve *see* Komoé
Komotau *see* Chomutov
Komotiní 104 D 3 *var.* Gümüljina,
Turk. Gümülcine. NE Greece
Kompong *see* Kâmpóng Chhnăng
Kompong Cham *see*
Kâmpóng Cham
Kompong Speu *see* Kâmpóng Spoe
Kompong Thom *see*
Kâmpóng Thum
Komrat *see* Comrat
Komsomolets, Ostrov 115 E 1
island, Severnaya Zemlya,
N Russian Federation
Komsomol'sk-na-Amure 115 G 4
SE Russian Federation
Kondolovo 104 E 3 SE Bulgaria
Kondopoga 110 B 3
NW Russian Federation
Kong Christian IX Land 82 D 4
Eng. King Christian IX Land.
Physical region, SE Greenland
Kong Christian X Land 83 E 3
Eng. King Christian X Land.
Physical region, E Greenland
Kong Frederik VI Kyst 82 C 4
Eng. King Frederik VI Coast.
Physical region, SE Greenland
Kong Frederik VIII Land 83 E 2
Eng. King Frederik VIII Land.
Physical region, NE Greenland
Kong Frederik IX Land 82 C 3
Eng. King Frederik IX Land.
Physical region, SW Greenland
Kong Karls Land 83 G 2
Eng. King Charles Islands.
Island group, SE Svalbard
Kongor 73 B 5 SE Sudan
Kongsberg 85 B 6 S Norway
Königgrätz *see* Hradec Králové
Konin 98 C 3 *Ger.* Kuhnau.
C Poland
Konispol 101 C 7 *var.* Konispoli.
S Albania
Kónitsa 104 A 4 W Greece
Konjic 100 C 4
S Bosnia & Herzegovina
Konoša *see* Konosha
Konosha 110 C 4 *var.* Konoša.
NW Russian Federation
Konotop 109 F 1 NE Ukraine
Konstantinovka *see* Kostyantynivka
Konstanz 95 B 7 *var.* Constanz,
Eng. Constance; *hist.* Kostnitz,
anc. Constantia. S Germany
Konya 116 C 4 *var.* Konieh; *prev.*
Konia, *anc.* Iconium. C Turkey
Kôohu *see* Kôfu
Kôotió *see* Kôĺchi
Kopaonik 101 D 5 mountain range,
C Yugoslavia
Koper 95 D 8 *It.* Capodistria,
prev. Kopar. SW Slovenia
Kopetdag, Khrebet 122 C 3
Turkm. Kopetdag Gershi, *Per.*
Koppeh Dāgh. Mountain range,
Iran/Turkmenistan
Koprivnica 100 C 2 *Ger.*
Kopreinitz, *Hung.* Kaproncza.
N Croatia
Köprülü *see* Veles
Koptsevichi *see* Kaptsevichy
Kopyl' *see* Kapyl'
Korat Plateau 136 D 4 plateau,
NE Thailand
Korba 135 E 4 N India

Korçë 101 D 7 *var.* Korça;
Gk. Korytsa, *It.* Corriza;
prev. Koritsa. SE Albania
Korčula 100 B 4 *It.* Curzola; *anc.*
Corcyra Nigra. Island, S Croatia
Korea Strait 131 A 7 *Jap.* Chōsen-
kaikyŏ, *Kor.* Taehan-haehyŏp .
Strait, East China Sea/
Sea of Japan
Korhogo 74 D 4 N Ivory Coast
Korinthiakós Kólpos 105 B 5 *Eng.*
Gulf of Corinth; *anc.* Corinthiacus
Sinus. Gulf, E Ionian Sea
Kórinthos 105 B 6 *Eng.* Corinth;
anc. Corinthus. S Greece
Kōriyama 131 D 5 Honshū, C Japan
Korjazma *see* Koryazhma
Korla 126 B 3 *Chin.* K'u-erh-lo.
NW China
Körmend 99 B 7 W Hungary
Koróni 105 B 6 S Greece
Koror 144 A 2 country capital,
Babelthuap, C Palau
Korosten' 108 D 1 NW Ukraine
Koro Toro 76 C 2 N Chad
Kortrijk 87 A 6 *Fr.* Courtrai.
W Belgium
Koryak Range *see* Koryakskoye
Nagor'ye
Koryakskoye Nagor'ye 115 H 2 *var.*
Koryakskiy Khrebet, *Eng.* Koryak
Range. Mountain range,
NE Russian Federation
Koryazhma 110 C 4 *var.* Korjazma.
NW Russian Federation
Kos 105 E 6 Kos, SE Greece
Kos 105 E 6 *It.* Coo; *anc.* Cos.
Island, Dodekánisos, SE Greece
Kō-saki 131 A 7 headland,
Tsushima, SW Japan
Kościerzyna 98 C 2 NW Poland
Kosciusko, Mount 149 C 7
mountain, New South Wales,
SE Australia
Koshikijima-rettō 131 A 8 *var.*
Kosikizima Rettô. Island group,
Japan
Košice 99 D 6 *Ger.* Kaschau, *Hung.*
Kassa. E Slovakia
Kosikizima Rettô *see* Koshikijima-
rettō
Köslin *see* Koszalin
Koson 123 E 3 *Rus.* Kasan.
S Uzbekistan
Kosovo 101 E 5 *prev.* Autonomous
Province of Kosovo and Metohija.
Cultural region, S Yugoslavia
Kosovo Polje 101 D 5 S Yugoslavia
Kosovska Mitrovica 101 D 5
Alb. Mitrovicë; *prev.* Mitrovica,
Titova Mitrovica. S Yugoslavia
Kosrae 144 D 2 *prev.* Kusaie. Island,
E Micronesia
Kostenets 104 C 2 *var.* Kostenec;
prev. Georgi Dimitrov. W Bulgaria
Kostroma 110 C 4
NW Russian Federation
Kostyantynivka 109 G 3
Rus. Konstantinovka. SE Ukraine
Kostyukovichi *see* Kastsyukovichy
Kostyukovka *see* Kastsyukowka
Koszalin 98 B 2 *Ger.* Köslin.
NW Poland
Kota 134 D 3 *prev.* Kotah. N India
Kota Bharu 138 B 3 *var.* Kota
Baharu, Kota Bahru. W Malaysia
Kotabaru *see* Kotabumi
Kotabumi 138 B 4 *var.* Kotaboemi.
W Indonesia
Kotah *see* Kota
Kota Kinabalu 138 D 3 *prev.*
Jesselton. Borneo, E Malaysia

Kota Kota *see* Nkhotakota
Kotelnič *see* Kotel'nich
Kotel'nich 114 B 3 *var.* Kotelnič.
NW Russian Federation
Kotel'nyy, Ostrov 115 F 2 island,
Novosibirskiye Ostrova,
N Russian Federation
Kotka 85 E 5 S Finland
Kotlas 110 C 4
NW Russian Federation
Kotonu *see* Cotonou
Kotor 101 C 5 *It.* Cattaro.
SW Yugoslavia
Kotovs'k 108 D 3 *Rus.* Kotovsk.
SW Ukraine
Kotovsk *see* Kotovs'k
Kottbus *see* Cottbus
Kotto 76 D 4 river, Central African
Republic/Congo (Zaire)
Kotuy 115 E 2 river,
N Russian Federation
Koudougou 75 E 4 C Burkina
Koulamoutou 77 B 6 C Gabon
Koulikoro 74 D 4 SW Mali
Koumra 76 C 4 S Chad
Kourou 59 H 3 N French Guiana
Kousséri 76 B 3 *prev.* Fort-Foureau.
NE Cameroon
Kouvola 85 E 5 S Finland
Kovel' 108 C 1 *Pol.* Kowel.
NW Ukraine
Kowel *see* Kovel'
Kowloon 128 A 1 *Chin.* Jiulong.
SW Hong Kong
Kowt-e 'Ashrow 123 E 4
E Afghanistan
Kozáni 104 B 4 N Greece
Kozara 100 B 3 mountain range,
NW Bosnia & Herzegovina
Kozhikode *see* Calicut
Koz'modem'yansk 111 C 5
W Russian Federation
Kōzu-shima 131 D 6 island, Izu-
shotō, E Japan
Kozyaty 108 D 2 *Rus.* Kazatin.
C Ukraine
Kpalimé 75 E 5 *var.* Palimé.
SW Togo
Krácheh 137 D 6 *prev.* Kratie.
E Cambodia
Kragujevac 100 D 4 C Yugoslavia
Krainburg *see* Kranj
Kra, Isthmus of 137 B 6 isthmus,
Malaysia/Thailand
Krakatau 124 D 5 volcano,
C Indonesia
Kraków 99 D 5 *Eng.* Cracow,
Ger. Krakau; *anc.* Cracovia.
S Poland
Králǎnh 137 D 5 NW Cambodia
Kraljevo 100 D 4 *prev.* Rankovićevo.
C Yugoslavia
Kramators'k 109 G 3
Rus. Kramatorsk. SE Ukraine
Kramatorsk *see* Kramators'k
Kramfors 85 C 5 C Sweden
Kranéa 104 B 4 N Greece
Kranj 95 D 7 *Ger.* Krainburg.
NW Slovenia
Krāslava 106 D 4 SE Latvia
Krasnaye 107 C 5 *Rus.* Krasnoye.
C Belorussia
Krasnoarmeysk 111 C 6
W Russian Federation
Krasnodar 111 A 7 *prev.*
Yekaterinodar. Kray capital,
SW Russian Federation
Krasnodon 109 H 3 E Ukraine
Krasnogor *see* Kallaste
Krasnogvardeyskoye *see*
Krasnohvardiys'ke

Krasnohvardiys'ke 109 F 4 *Rus.*
Krasnogvardeyskoye. S Ukraine
Krasnokamsk 111 D 5
W Russian Federation
Krasnoperekops'k 109 F 4
Rus. Krasnoperekopsk. S Ukraine
Krasnoperekopsk *see*
Krasnoperekops'k
Krasnostav *see* Krasnystaw
Krasnovodsk *see* Turkmenbashi
Krasnovodskiy Zaliv 122 B 2
Turkm. Krasnowodsk Aylagy.
Gulf, E Caspian Sea
Krasnowodsk Aylagy *see*
Krasnovodskiy Zaliv
Krasnoyarsk 114 D 4
C Russian Federation
Krasnoye *see* Krasnaye
Krasnozatonskiy 110 D 4 *var.*
Krasnozatonski, Krasnozatonskij.
NW Russian Federation
Krasnystaw 98 E 4 *Rus.* Krasnostav.
SE Poland
Krasnyy Luch 109 H 3
prev. Krindachevka. E Ukraine
Krassóvár *see* Carașova
Kratie *see* Krácheh
Krâvanh, Chuôr Phnum 137 D 6
Eng. Cardamom Mountains,
Fr. Chaîne des Cardamomes.
Mountain range, SW Cambodia
Krefeld 94 A 4 W Germany
Kremenchug *see* Kremenchuk
Kremenchuk 109 F 3 *Rus.*
Kremenchug. C Ukraine
Kremenchuts'ke Vodoskhovyshche
109 F 2 *Eng.* Kremenchuk
Reservoir, *Rus.* Kremenchugskoye
Vodokhranilishche. Reservoir,
C Ukraine
Kremenets' 108 C 2 *Pol.*
Krzemieniec, *Rus.* Kremenets.
W Ukraine
Kremennaya *see* Kreminna
Kreminna 109 H 2 *Rus.*
Kremennaya. E Ukraine
Kresena *see* Kresna
Kresna 104 C 3 *var.* Kresena.
SW Bulgaria
Kretinga 106 B 3 *Ger.* Krottingen.
NW Lithuania
Kreuz *see* Risti
Krichëv *see* Krychaw
Krindachevka *see* Krasnyy Luch
Krishna 132 C 1 *prev.* Kistna. River,
C India
Krishnagiri 132 C 2 SE India
Kristiansand 85 A 6 *var.*
Christiansand. S Norway
Kristianstad 85 B 7 S Sweden
Kristiansund 84 A 4 *var.*
Christiansund. S Norway
Kríti 105 D 8 *Eng.* Crete. Island,
SE Greece
Krivoy Rog *see* Kryvyy Rih
Krivyje Ozero *see* Kryve Ozero
Križevci 100 B 2 *Ger.* Kreuz,
Hung. Körös. NE Croatia
Krk 100 A 2 *It.* Veglia; *anc.* Curieta.
Island, NW Croatia
Krolevets' 109 F 1 *Rus.* Krolevets.
NE Ukraine
Krolevets *see* Krolevets'
Kronach 95 C 5 E Germany
Kronshtadt 110 B 4 *var.* Kronštadt.
NW Russian Federation
Kronštadt *see* Kronshtadt
Kroonstad 78 D 4 C South Africa
Kropotkin 111 B 7
SW Russian Federation
Krosno 99 E 5 *Ger.* Krossen.
SE Poland

Krosno Odrzańskie 98 B 3 *Ger.* Crossen, Kreisstadt. W Poland
Krossen *see* Krosno
Krottingen *see* Kretinga
Krško 95 E 8 *Ger.* Gurkfeld; *prev.* Videm-Krško. E Slovenia
Krugloye *see* Kruhlaye
Kruhlaye 107 D 6 *Rus.* Krugloye. E Belorussia
Krujë 101 D 6 *var.* Kruja, *It.* Croia. C Albania
Krung Thep 137 C 5 *var.* Krung Thep Mahanakhon, *Eng.* Bangkok. Country capital, C Thailand
Krung Thep, Ao 137 C 5 bay, South China Sea/Pacific Ocean
Krupki 107 D 6 C Belorussia
Kruševac 100 D 4 C Yugoslavia
Krychaw 107 E 7 *Rus.* Krichëv. E Belorussia
Krym 109 F 5 *var.* Crimea. Cultural region, S Ukraine
Kryms'ki Hory 109 F 5 mountain range, S Ukraine
Kryve Ozero 109 E 3 *Rus.* Krivyje Ozero. SW Ukraine
Kryvyy Rih 109 F 3 *Rus.* Krivoy Rog. SE Ukraine
Ksar-el-Kebir 70 C 2 *var.* Alcázar, Ksar al Kabir, Ksar el Kebir, Ksar-el-Kébir, *Ar.* Al-Kasr al-Kebir, Al-Qsar al-Kbir, *Sp.* Alcazarquivir. NW Morocco
Kstovo 111 C 5 W Russian Federation
Kuala Dungun *see* Dungun
Kuala Lumpur 138 B 3 country capital, W Malaysia
Kuala Terengganu 138 B 3 *var.* Kuala Trengganu. W Malaysia
Kuala Trengganu *see* Kuala Terengganu
Kualatungkai 138 B 4 W Indonesia
Kuantan 138 B 3 W Malaysia
Kuba *see* Quba
Kuching 138 C 3 *prev.* Sarawak. Borneo, E Malaysia
Kūchnay Darvīshān 122 D 5 S Afghanistan
Kuçovë 101 C 6 *var.* Kuçova; *prev.* Qyteti Stalin. C Albania
Kudus 138 C 5 *prev.* Koedoes. Jawa, C Indonesia
K'u-erh-lo *see* Korla
Kufra Oasis *see* Al Kufrah
Kuhmo 84 E 4 E Finland
Kuhnau *see* Konin
Kuito 78 B 2 *Port.* Silva Porto. C Angola
Kuji 130 D 3 *var.* Kuzi. Japan
Kula Kangri 135 G 3 mountain, Bhutan/China
Kuldīga 106 B 3 *Ger.* Goldingen. W Latvia
Kullorsuaq 82 C 2 *var.* Kuvdlorssuak, Kuvdlorssuaq. NW Greenland
Kŭlob 123 F 3 *Rus.* Kulyab. SW Tajikistan
Kulu 116 C 3 W Turkey
Kulundinskaya Step' 114 D 4 physical region, S Russian Federation
Kulyab *see* Kŭlob
Kuma 111 B 7 river, SW Russian Federation
Kumaka 59 F 3 SE Guyana
Kumamoto 131 A 7 Kyūshū, SW Japan
Kumanova *see* Kumanovo
Kumanovo 101 E 5 *Turk.* Kumanova. N Macedonia
Kumasi 75 E 5 *prev.* Coomassie. C Ghana
Kumba 77 A 5 W Cameroon
Kumertau 111 D 6 W Russian Federation
Kumillā *see* Comilla
Kumo 75 G 4 E Nigeria
Kumon Range 136 B 2 mountain range, N Burma
Kunashir, Ostrov 130 E 1 *var.* Kunashiri. Island, Kurile Islands, SE Russian Federation
Kunda 106 E 2 NE Estonia
Kunduz 123 E 3 *var.* Kondoz, Kundūz, Qondūz, *Per.* Kondūz. NE Afghanistan
Kunene *see* Cunene
Kungsbacka 85 B 7 S Sweden
Kungur 111 D 5 NW Russian Federation
Kunlun Mountains *see* Kunlun Shan
Kunlun Shan 126 B 4 *var.* Kunlun Mountains. Mountain range, China/India
Kunming 129 B 6 *var.* K'un-ming; *prev.* Yunnan. Province capital, SW China
Kununurra 146 D 3 Western Australia, N Australia
Kuopio 84 E 4 C Finland
Kupang 139 E 5 *prev.* Koepang. Timor, C Indonesia
Kup"yans'k 109 G 2 *Rus.* Kupyansk. E Ukraine
Kupyansk *see* Kup"yans'k
Kura 117 G 2 *Az.* Kür, *Geor.* Mtkvari, *Turk.* Kura Nehri. River, SW Asia
Kurashiki 131 B 6 *var.* Kurasiki. Honshū, SW Japan
Kurasiki *see* Kurashiki
Kŭrdzhali 104 D 3 *var.* Kărdžali, Kirdzhali. S Bulgaria
Kure 131 B 7 Honshū, SW Japan
Küre 116 C 2 Turkey
Küre Dağları 116 C 2 mountain range, N Turkey
Kuressaare 106 C 2 *Ger.* Arensburg; *prev.* Kingissepp. Saaremaa, W Estonia
Kureyka 115 E 3 river, C Russian Federation
Kurgan-Tyube *see* Qŭrghonteppa
Kuria Muria Bay *see* Ḩalānīyāt, Khalʿij al
Kurile Islands *see* Kuril'skiye Ostrova
Kurile-Kamchatka Depression *see* Kurile Trench
Kurile Trench 152 C 1 *var.* Kurile-Kamchatka Depression. Trench, NW Pacific Ocean
Kuril'sk 115 H 4 Kuril'skiye Ostrova, SE Russian Federation
Kuril'skiye Ostrova 115 H 4 *Eng.* Kurile Islands. Island group, E Russian Federation
Kurkund *see* Kilingi-Nõmme
Kurnool 132 C 1 *var.* Karnul. S India
Kursk 111 B 6 W Russian Federation
Kuršumlija 101 D 5 SE Yugoslavia
Kuruktag 126 C 3 mountain range, NW China
Kurume 131 A 7 Kyūshū, SW Japan
Kurupukari 59 F 3 C Guyana
Kurzeme 106 B 3 *Eng.* Courland, *Ger.* Kurland. Cultural region, W Latvia
Kusaie *see* Kosrae
Kushiro 130 D 2 *var.* Kusiro. Hokkaidō, NE Japan
Kushka *see* Gushgy
Kusiro *see* Kushiro
Kuskokwim Mountains 36 C 3 mountain range, Alaska, NW USA
Kustanay 114 C 4 *Kaz.* Qostanay. N Kazakhstan
Kütahya 116 B 3 *prev.* Kutaia. W Turkey
Kutaia *see* Kütahya
K'ut'aisi 117 F 2 W Georgia
Kutina 100 B 3 NE Croatia
Kutno 98 D 3 C Poland
Kuujjuaq 39 E 2 *prev.* Fort-Chimo. Québec, E Canada
Kuujjuarapik 38 D 2 Québec, C Canada
Kuusamo 84 E 3 E Finland

Kuwait
120 C 4 *var.* Dawlat al Kuwait, Koweit, Kuweit. Monarchy, SW Asia

Official name: State of Kuwait **Date of formation:** 1961/1981 **Capital:** Kuwait City **Population:** 1.8 million **Total area:** 17,820 sq km (6,880 sq miles) **Languages:** Arabic*, English **Religions:** Muslim 92%, Christian 6%, other 2% **Ethnic mix:** Arab 85%, South Asian 9%, Persian 4%, other 2% **Government:** Constitutional monarchy **Currency:** Dinar = 1,000 fils

Kuwajleen *see* Kwajalein Atoll
Kuwayt 120 C 3 E Iraq
Kuybyshev *see* Samara
Kuybyshevskoye Vodokhranilishche 111 C 5 *var.* Kuibyshev, *Eng.* Kuybyshev Reservoir. Reservoir, W Russian Federation
Kuytun 126 B 3 NW China
Kuytun 126 B 2 NW China
Kuzi *see* Kuji
Kuznetsk 111 C 6 W Russian Federation
Kvaløya 84 C 2 island, N Norway
Kvarnbergs-vattnet 84 B 4 *var.* Frostviken. Lake, N Sweden
Kvarner 100 A 3 *var.* Carnaro, *It.* Quarnero. Gulf, Adriatic Sea/Mediterranean Sea
Kvitøya 83 G 1 island, NE Svalbard
Kwai Chung 128 A 1 C Hong Kong
Kwajalein Atoll 144 D 1 *var.* Kuwajleen. Island, C Marshall Islands
Kwando *see* Cuando
Kwando 78 C 2 *var.* Cuando. River, S Africa
Kwangju 128 E 4 *off.* Kwangju-kwangyŏksi, *var.* Kwangchu, *Jap.* Kōshū. SW South Korea
Kwango 77 C 7 *Port.* Cuango. River, Angola/Congo (Zaire)
Kwango *see* Cuango
Kwanza *see* Cuanza
Kwekwe 78 D 3 *prev.* Que Que. C Zimbabwe
Kwidzyń 98 C 2 *Ger.* Marienwerder. N Poland
Kwigillingok 36 B 3 Alaska, NW USA
Kwilu 78 B 1 river, W Congo (Zaire)
Kwito *see* Cuito
Kwun Tong 128 B 1 SE Hong Kong
Kyabé 76 C 4 S Chad
Kyaikkami 137 B 5 *prev.* Amherst. SE Burma
Kyaiklat 136 B 4 S Burma
Kyaikto 136 B 4 S Burma
Kyakhta 115 E 5 S Russian Federation
Kyaukse 136 B 3 C Burma
Kyjov 99 C 5 *Ger.* Gaya. SE Czech Republic
Kykládes 105 D 6 *var.* Kikládhes, *Eng.* Cyclades. Island group, SE Greece
Kými 105 C 5 *prev.* Kími. Évvoia, C Greece
Kyōto 131 C 6 Honshū, SW Japan
Kyparissía 105 B 6 *var.* Kiparissía. S Greece
Kyrá Panagía 105 C 5 island, Vóreioi Sporádes, E Greece

Kyrgyzstan
123 F 2 *var.* Kirghizia; *prev.* Kirghiz SSR, Kirgizskaya SSR, Republic of Kyrgyzstan. Republic, C Asia

Official name: Kyrgyz Republic **Date of formation:** 1991 **Capital:** Bishkek **Population:** 4.6 million **Total Area:** 198,500 sq km (76,640 sq miles) **Languages:** Kirghiz*, Russian, Uzbek **Religions:** Muslim 65%, other (mostly Russian Orthodox) 35% **Ethnic mix:** Kirghiz 52%, Russian 21%, Uzbek 13%, other (mostly Kazakh and Tajik) 14% **Government:** Multiparty republic **Currency:** Som = 100 teen

Kýthira 105 B 7 *var.* Kíthira, *It.* Cerigo; *Lat.* Cythera. Kýthira, S Greece
Kýthira 105 C 7 *var.* Kíthira, *It.* Cerigo; *Lat.* Cythera. Island, S Greece
Kýthnos 105 C 6 Kýthnos, SE Greece
Kýthnos 105 C 6 *var.* Kíthnos, Thermiá, *It.* Termia; *anc.* Cythnos. Island, Kykládes, SE Greece
Kythréa *see* Değirmenlik
Kyūshū 131 B 8 *var.* Kyûsyû. Island, Japan
Kyustendil 104 B 2 *var.* Kjustendil; *anc.* Pautalia. W Bulgaria
Kyusyu-Palau Ridge *see* Kyushu-Palau Ridge
Kyyiv 109 E 2 *Eng.* Kiev, *Rus.* Kiyev. Country capital, N Ukraine
Kyyivs'ke Vodoskhovyshche 109 E 1 *Rus.* Kiyevskoye Vodokhranilishche. Reservoir, N Ukraine
Kyzyl-Kiya 123 F 2 *Kir.* Kyzyl-Kyya. SW Kyrgyzstan
Kyzyl Kum 122 D 2 *var.* Kizil Kum, Qizil Qum, *Uzb.* Qizilqum. Desert, Kazakhstan/Uzbekistan
Kyzyl-Kyya *see* Kyzyl-Kiya
Kyzylrabot *see* Qizilrabot
Kyzyl-Suu 123 G 2 *prev.* Pokrovka. NE KyKazakhstan/Uzbekistanrgyzstan
Ky\`usy\`u *see* Kyūshū
Kzyl-Orda 114 B 5 *var.* Qizil Orda, *Kaz.* Qyzylorda; *prev.* Perovsk. S Kazakhstan

L

Laaland *see* Lolland
La Algaba 92 C 4 S Spain
Laarne 87 B 5 NW Belgium
La Asunción 59 E 1 NE Venezuela

Laâyoune 70 A 3 *var.* Aaiún. Country capital, NW Western Sahara
La Baie 39 E 4 Québec, SE Canada
la Baule-Escoublac 90 A 4 NW France
Labe *see* Elbe
Labé 74 C 4 NW Guinea
La Blanquilla *see* Blanquilla, Isla
Laborca *see* Laborec
Laborec 99 E 5 *Hung.* Laborca. River, E Slovakia
Labrador 39 F 2 physical region, Newfoundland and Labrador, SW Canada
Labrador Basin 66 B 2 undersea basin, NW Atlantic Ocean
Labrador Sea 39 G 1 sea, NW Atlantic Ocean
Labutta 137 A 5 SW Burma
Laç 101 C 6 *var.* Laci. C Albania
La Calera 64 B 4 C Chile
La Carolina 92 D 4 S Spain
Laccadive Islands 132 A 3 island group, SW India
La Ceiba 52 D 2 N Honduras
Lacepede Bay 149 B 7 bay, E Indian Ocean
Lacey 46 B 2 Washington, NW USA
Lachanás 104 C 3 N Greece
La Chaux-de-Fonds 95 A 7 W Switzerland
Lachlan 149 C 6 river, SE Australia
Laci *see* Laç
la Ciotat 91 D 6 *anc.* Citharista. SE France
Lacobriga *see* Lagos
La Concepción 53 E 5 *var.* Concepción. W Panama
La Concepción 58 C 1 NW Venezuela
Laconia 41 G 2 New Hampshire, NE USA
La Croix Maingot 55 F 1 NW Saint Lucia
La Cruz 52 D 4 NW Costa Rica
Ladozhskoye Ozero 110 B 3 *var.* Laa Tokka, *Eng.* Lake Ladoga, *Fin.* Laatokka. Lake, NW Russian Federation
Lae 144 B 3 New Guinea, W Papua New Guinea
La Esperanza 52 C 2 SW Honduras
Lafayette 42 B 3 Louisiana, S USA
Lafayette 40 C 4 Indiana, N USA
La Fé 54 A 2 W Cuba
Lafia 75 G 4 C Nigeria
la Flèche 90 B 4 NW France
Laghouat 70 D 2 N Algeria
Lagos 92 B 5 *anc.* Lacobriga. S Portugal
Lagos 75 F 5 SW Nigeria
Lagos de Moreno 50 D 4 SW Mexico
La Grande 46 C 3 Oregon, NW USA
La Grange 42 D 2 Georgia, SE USA
Lagunas 64 B 1 N Chile
Lagunillas 61 G 4 SE Bolivia
La Habana 54 B 2 *var.* Havana. Country capital, W Cuba
Lahat 138 B 4 Sumatera, W Indonesia
Laholm 85 B 7 S Sweden
Lahore 134 D 2 province capital, NE Pakistan
Lahr 95 A 6 S Germany
Lahti 85 E 5 *Swe.* Lahtis. S Finland
Lahtis *see* Lahti
Laï 76 B 4 *prev.* Behagle, De Behagle. S Chad
Lai Châu 136 D 3 NW Vietnam
Laila *see* Laylá
La Junta 44 D 5 Colorado, C USA
Lake Charles 42 A 3 Louisiana, S USA
Lake City 43 E 3 South Carolina, SE USA
Lake District 89 C 5 physical region, NW England, UK
Lake Havasu City 48 A 2 Arizona, SW USA
Lake Jackson 49 H 4 Texas, S USA
Lakeland 43 E 4 Florida, SE USA
Lakes Entrance 149 D 7 inlet, W Tasman Sea
Lakeside 47 D 8 California, W USA
Lakewood 44 C 4 Colorado, C USA
Lake Worth 43 F 5 Florida, SE USA
Lakhnau *see* Lucknow
Lakonikós Kólpos 105 B 7 gulf, C Mediterranean Sea
Lakselv 84 D 2 N Norway
Lakshadweep 132 A 3 *prev.* the Laccadive, Minicoy and Amindivi Islands. Union territory, SW India
Lala 139 E 2 SW Philippines
La Laguna 70 A 3 Tenerife, SW Spain
La Libertad 52 B 1 N Guatemala
La Libertad 60 A 2 W Ecuador
La Ligua 64 B 4 C Chile
Lalín 92 C 1 NW Spain
Lalitpur 135 F 3 C Nepal
La Louvière 87 B 6 S Belgium
La Maçana *see* La Massana
La Maddalena 96 A 4 W Italy
Lamar 44 D 5 Iowa, C USA
La Massana 91 A 8 *var.* la Maçana. W Andorra
Lambaré 64 D 2 S Paraguay
Lambaréné 77 A 6 W Gabon
Lamego 92 C 2 N Portugal
Lamesa 49 E 3 Texas, S USA
Lamezia 97 D 6 SE Italy
Lamía 105 B 5 C Greece
Lamma Island 128 A 2 *Cant.* Pok Liu Chau. Island, S Hong Kong
Lamon Bay 139 E 1 bay, SW Philippine Sea
Lamoni 45 F 4 Wyoming, C USA
La Mosquitia 53 E 3 *var.* Miskito Coast, *Eng.* Mosquito Coast. Coastal region, E Nicaragua
Lampang 136 C 4 *var.* Muang Lampang. NW Thailand
Lámpeia 105 B 6 S Greece
Lanbi Kyun 137 B 6 *prev.* Sullivan Island. Island, S Burma
Lancaster 89 C 5 NW England, UK
Lancaster 40 D 4 Ohio, N USA
Lancaster 47 C 7 California, W USA
Lancaster Sound 37 F 2 channel, Arctic Ocean/Baffin Bay
Landen 87 C 6 C Belgium
Lander 44 C 3 Wyoming, C USA
Landerneau 90 A 3 NW France
Landes 91 B 5 cultural region, SW France
Landsberg am Lech 95 C 6 S Germany
Land's End 89 B 8 headland, SW England, UK
Landshut 95 C 6 SE Germany
Langar 123 E 2 *Rus.* Lyangar. C Uzbekistan
Langfang 128 D 4 NE China
Langres 90 D 4 N France
Lang Sơn 136 D 3 *var.* Langson. N Vietnam
Langson *see* Lang Sơn
Lang Suan 137 C 6 Thailand
Languedoc 91 C 6 cultural region, S France
Länkäran 117 H 3 *Rus.* Lenkoran'. S Azerbaijan
Lansing 40 C 3 state capital, Michigan, N USA
Lanta, Ko 137 B 7 island, S Thailand
Lantau Island 128 A 2 *Cant.* Tai Yue Shan. Island, SW Hong Kong
Lantau Peak 128 A 1 *Cant.* Fung Wong Shan. Mountain, Lantau Island, W Hong Kong
Lantung, Gulf of *see* Liaodong Wan
Lanzarote 70 B 3 island, Islas Canarias, SW Spain
Lanzhou 128 B 4 *var.* Lan-chou, Lanchow, Lan-chow; *prev.* Kaolan. Province capital, C China
Lao Cai 136 D 3 NW Vietnam
Laoet *see* Laut, Pulau
Laoha He 127 F 2 river, NE China
Laon 90 D 3 *var.* la Laon; *anc.* Laudunum. N France
Lao People's Democratic Republic *see* Laos
La Orchila, Isla 58 D 1 island, N Venezuela
La Oroya 60 C 3 C Peru

Laos
136 C 4 . Republic, SE Asia

Official name: Lao People's Democratic Republic **Date of formation:** 1953 **Capital:** Vientiane **Population:** 4.6 million **Total Area:** 236,800 sq km (91, 428 sq miles) **Languages:** Lao*, Miao, Yao **Religions:** Buddhist 85%, Christian 2%, other 13% **Ethnic mix:** Lao Loum 56%, Lao Theung 34%, Lao Soung 10% **Government:** Single-party republic **Currency:** Kip = 100 cents

La Palma 53 G 5 SE Panama
La Palma 70 A 3 island, Islas Canarias, SW Spain
La Paz 50 B 3 NW Mexico
La Paz 61 F 4 *var.* La Paz de Ayacucho. Country capital, W Bolivia
La Paz, Bahía de 50 B 3 bay, Golfo de California/Pacific Ocean
La Paz de Ayacucho *see* La Paz
La Perouse Strait 130 C 1 *Jap.* Sōya-kaikyō, *Rus.* Proliv Laperuza. Strait, Sea of Japan/Sea of Okhotsk
Lápithos *see* Lapta
Lapland 84 D 2 *Fin.* Lappi, *Swe.* Lappland. Cultural region, N Europe
La Plata 64 D 4 E Argentina
Lappeenranta 85 E 5 *Swe.* Villmanstrand. SE Finland
Lappo *see* Lapua
Laptev Sea *see* Laptevykh, More
Laptevykh, More 115 F 2 *Eng.* Laptev Sea. Sea, Arctic Ocean
Lapua 85 D 5 *Swe.* Lappo. W Finland
La Puebla *see* Sa Pobla
Lapurdum *see* Bayonne
Łapy 98 E 3 E Poland
La Quiaca 64 C 2 N Argentina
L'Aquila 96 C 4 *var.* Aquila, Aquila degli Abruzzi. C Italy
Laracha 92 B 1 NW Spain
Larache 70 C 2 *var.* al Araïch, El Araïch, *Ar.* Al-Araish; *prev.* El Araïche, *anc.* Lixus. NW Morocco
Laramie 44 C 4 Wyoming, C USA
Laramie Mountains 44 C 3 mountain range, Wyoming, C USA
Laredo 93 E 1 N Spain
Laredo 49 F 5 Texas, S USA
La Réunion *see* Réunion
Largo 43 E 4 Florida, SE USA
La Rioja 93 E 2 cultural region, N Spain
La Rioja 64 C 3 NW Argentina
Lárisa 104 B 4 *var.* Larissa. C Greece
Larissa *see* Lárisa
Lārkāna 134 B 3 *var.* Larkhana. SE Pakistan
Larkhana *see* Lārkāna
la Rochelle 90 A 4 *anc.* Rupella. W France
la Roche-sur-Yon 90 A 4 *prev.* Bourbon Vendée, Napoléon-Vendée. NW France
La Roda 93 E 3 C Spain
La Romana 55 E 3 E Dominican Republic
La Sarre 38 D 4 Québec, SE Canada
Las Cabezas de San Juan 92 C 5 S Spain
Las Cruces 48 D 3 New Mexico, SW USA
La See d'Urgel 93 F 2 *var.* La Seu d'Urgell, Seo de Urgel. NE Spain
La Serena 64 B 3 N Chile
la Seyne-sur-Mer 91 D 6 SE France
Lashio 136 B 3 NE Burma
Lashkar Gāh 122 D 5 *var.* Lashkar Gah, Lash-Kar-Gar'. S Afghanistan
La Sila 97 E 6 mountain range, SW Italy
La Sirena 52 D 3 E Nicaragua
Łask 98 C 4 C Poland
Las Lomitas 64 D 2 N Argentina
La Solana 93 E 4 C Spain
Las Palmas 70 A 3 *var.* Las Palmas de Gran Canaria. Regional capital, Gran Canaria, SW Spain
Las Petas 61 H 3 NE Bolivia
La Spezia 96 B 3 NW Italy
Las Piedras 61 E 3 E Peru
Las Tablas 53 G 5 S Panama
Las Tunas 54 C 2 *var.* Victoria de las Tunas. E Cuba
Las Vegas 47 D 7 Nevada, W USA
Las Yaras 61 E 4 S Peru
Latacunga 60 B 1 C Ecuador
la Teste 91 A 5 SW France
Latgale 106 D 4 *Eng.* Latgallia. Cultural region, SE Latvia
Latgallia *see* Latgale
Latina 97 C 5 *prev.* Littoria. C Italy
La Tortuga, Isla 59 E 1 *var.* Isla Tortuga. Island, N Venezuela
La Tuque 39 E 4 Québec, SE Canada

Latvia
106 C 3 *Ger.* Lettland, *Latv.* Latvija, Latvijas Republika, *Rus.* Latviyskaya SSR; *prev.* Latvian SSR. Republic, NE Europe

Official name: Republic of Latvia **Date of formation:** 1991 **Capital:** Riga **Population:** 2.7 million **Total area:** 64,589 sq km (24,938 sq miles) **Languages:** Latvian*, Russian **Religions:** Evangelical Lutheran 85%, other Christian 15% **Ethnic mix:** Latvian 52%, Russian 34%, Belorussian 5%, other 9% **Government:** Multiparty republic **Currency:** Lats = 100 santimi

Lau Group 145 E 4 island group, E Fiji
Launceston 149 C 8 Tasmania, SE Australia
La Unión 93 F 4 SE Spain
La Unión 65 B 5 C Chile
La Unión 52 C 2 C Honduras
La Unión 60 C 3 C Peru
Laurel 42 C 3 Mississippi, S USA
Laurel 44 C 2 Montana, NW USA
Laurentian Highlands 39 E 3 *var.* Laurentian Mountains, *Fr.* Les Laurentides. Plateau, Canada/USA
Lauria 97 D 6 S Italy
Laurinburg 43 F 1 North Carolina, SE USA
Lauru *see* Choiseul
Lausanne 95 A 7 *It.* Losanna SW Switzerland
Laut, Pulau 138 D 4 *prev.* Laoet. Island, C Indonesia
Laval 90 B 3 NW France
Laval 38 D 4 Québec, SE Canada
La Vega 55 E 3 *var.* Concepción de la Vega. C Dominican Republic
La Vila Jojosa *see* Villajoyosa
Lávrio 105 C 6 *prev.* Lávrion. C Greece
Lávrion *see* Lávrio
Lawrence 41 G 3 Massachusetts, NE USA
Lawrenceburg 42 C 1 Tennessee, S USA
Lawton 49 F 2 Oklahoma, C USA
Laylá 121 C 5 *var.* Laila. C Saudi Arabia
Lazarev Sea 154 B 1 sea, S Atlantic Ocean
Lázaro Cárdenas 50 D 5 SW Mexico
Læsø 85 B 7 island, N Denmark
League City 49 H 4 Texas, S USA
Leal *see* Lihula
Leamhcán *see* Lucan
Leamington 38 C 5 Ontario, S Canada
Lebak 139 E 3 Mindanao, S Philippines
Lebanon 42 D 1 Tennessee, S USA
Lebanon 41 G 2 Kentucky, NE USA
Lebanon 46 B 3 Oregon, NW USA
Lebanon 45 G 5 Missouri, C USA

Lebanon
118 A 4 *Ar.* Al Lubnān, *Fr.* Liban. Republic, SW Asia

Official name: Republic of Lebanon **Date of formation:** 1944 **Capital:** Beirut **Population:** 2.9 million **Total area:** 10,400 sq km (4,015 sq miles) **Languages:** Arabic*, French, Armenian, Assyrian **Religions:** Muslim (mainly Sunni) 57%, Christian (mainly Maronite) 43% **Ethnic mix:** Arab 93% (Lebanese 83%, Palestinian 10%), other 7% **Government:** Multiparty republic **Currency:** Pound = 100 piastres

---

Lebap 122 D 2 NE Turkmenistan
Lebedin *see* Lebedyn
Lebedyn 109 F 2 *Rus.* Lebedin. NE Ukraine
Lebel-sur-Quévillon 38 D 4 Québec, SE Canada
Lębork 98 C 2 *var.* Lębórk, *Ger.* Lauenburg, Lauenburg in Pommern. NW Poland
Lebrija 92 C 5 S Spain
Lebu 65 A 5 C Chile
le Cannet 91 D 6 SE France
Le Cap *see* Cap-Haïtien
Lecce 97 E 6 SE Italy
Lechainá 105 B 6 *var.* Lekhainá. S Greece
Ledo Salinarius *see* Lons-le-Saunier
Leduc 37 E 5 Alberta, SW Canada
Leech Lake 45 F 2 lake, Minnesota, N USA
Leeds 89 D 5 N England, UK
Leek 86 E 2 NE Netherlands
Leer 94 A 3 NW Germany
Leesburg 43 E 4 Florida, SE USA
Leeuwarden 86 D 1 *Fris.* Ljouwert. N Netherlands
Leeuwin, Cape 142 A 5 headland, Western Australia, SW Australia
Leeward Islands 55 G 3 *var.* Society Islands. Island group, E Caribbean Sea
Leeward Islands *see* Sotavento, Ilhas de
Lefkáda 105 A 5 *prev.* Levkás. Lefkáda, W Greece
Lefkáda 105 A 5 *It.* Santa Maura; *prev.* Levkás, *anc.* Leucas. Island, Iónioi Nísoi, W Greece
Lefká Óri 105 C 7 mountain range, Kríti, SE Greece
Lefkímmi 105 A 5 *var.* Levkímmi. Kérkyra, W Greece
Legaspi 139 E 2 *off.* Legaspi City. Luzon, N Philippines
Legaspi City *see* Legaspi
Leghorn *see* Livorno
Legnica 98 B 4 *Ger.* Liegnitz. W Poland
le Havre 90 B 3 *Eng.* Havre; *prev.* le Havre-de-Grâce. N France
Lehčevo *see* Lekhchevo
Leicester 89 D 6 *Lat.* Batae Coritanorum. C England, UK
Leichhardt Range 148 D 4 mountain range, Queensland, NE Australia
Leiden 86 C 3 *prev.* Leyden, *anc.* Lugdunum Batavorum. W Netherlands
Leie 87 B 6 *Fr.* Lys. River, Belgium/France
Leigh Creek 149 B 6 South Australia, S Australia
Leinster 89 B 6 cultural region, E Ireland
Leipsoi 105 E 6 island, Dodekánisos, SE Greece
Leipzig 94 C 4 *Pol.* Lipsk; hist. *Eng.* Leipsic, *anc.* Lipsia. E Germany
Leiria 92 B 3 *anc.* Collipo. W Portugal
Leirvik 85 A 6 S Norway
Leizhou *see* Haikang
Lek 86 C 4 river, SW Netherlands
Lekhchevo 104 C 2 *var.* Lehčevo. NW Bulgaria
Leksand 85 C 5 C Sweden
Lel'chitsy *see* Lyel'chytsy
Lelystad 86 D 3 C Netherlands
le Mans 90 B 3 NW France
le Maroni Fleuve *see* Marowijne Rivier
Lemnos *see* Límnos
Lena 115 F 3 river, E Russian Federation
Lengshuitan 129 C 6 E China
Lenine 109 G 5 *Rus.* Lenino. S Ukraine
Leningradskaya 154 C 4 research station, Antarctica
Lenino *see* Lenine
Leninogorsk 114 D 5 *Kaz.* Lenīngor. E Kazakhstan
Leninpol' 123 F 2 NW Kyrgyzstan
Lenkoran' *see* Lenkeran
Lenti 99 B 7 SW Hungary
Lentia *see* Linz
Lenya 137 B 6 S Burma
Leoben 95 E 7 C Austria
León 92 D 1 NW Spain
León 51 E 4 *var.* León de los Aldamas. C Mexico
León 52 C 3 NW Nicaragua
León de los Aldamas *see* León
Leonídi 105 B 6 S Greece
Léopold II, Lac *see* Mai-Ndombe, Lac
Léopoldville *see* Kinshasa
Lepe 92 C 4 S Spain
Lepel' *see* Lyepyel'
Lepontine Alps 95 B 7 *Fr.* Alpes Lépontiennes, *It.* Alpi Lepontine. Mountain range, Italy/Switzerland
le Portel 90 C 2 N France
le Puy 91 C 5 *prev.* le Puy-en-Velay, *hist.* Anicium, Podium Anicensis. C France
Léré 76 B 4 SW Chad
Lérida *see* Lleida
Lerma 92 D 2 N Spain
Léros 105 D 6 island, Dodekánisos, SE Greece
Lerwick 88 D 1 island authority area capital, NE Scotland, UK
Lesbos *see* Lésvos
Les Cayes 54 D 3 *var.* Cayes. SW Haiti
Les Gonaïves *see* Gonaïves
Leshan 129 B 5 C China
les Herbiers 90 B 4 NW France
Leskovac 101 E 5 SE Yugoslavia

Lesotho
78 D 4 *prev.* Basutoland. Monarchy, S Africa

Official name: Kingdom of Lesotho **Date of formation:** 1966 **Capital:** Maseru **Population:** 1.9 million **Total area:** 30,350 sq km (11,718 sq miles) **Languages:** English*, Sesotho*, Zulu **Religions:** Christian 93%, other 7% **Ethnic mix:** Basotho 99%, other 1% **Government:** Constitutional monarchy **Currency:** Loti = 100 lisente

---

les Sables-d'Olonne 90 A 4 NW France
Lesser Antarctica 154 B 3 *var.* West Antarctica. Physical region, Antarctica
Lesser Antilles 55 E 5 island group, SE Caribbean Sea
Lesser Caucasus 117 F 2 *Rus.* Malyy Kavkaz. Mountain range, SW Asia
Lesser Khingan Range *see* Xiao Hinggan Ling
Lesser Sunda Islands *see* Nusa Tenggara
Lésvos 105 D 5 *anc.* Lesbos. Island, E Greece
Leszno 98 B 4 *Ger.* Lissa. W Poland
Lethbridge 37 E 5 Alberta, SW Canada
Lethem 59 F 3 S Guyana
Leticia 58 C 3 S Colombia
Leti, Kepulauan 139 F 5 island group, E Indonesia
Letpadan 136 B 4 SW Burma
Letsôk-aw Kyun 137 B 6 *var.* Letsutan Island; *prev.* Domel Island. Island, S Burma
Leuven 87 C 6 *Fr.* Louvain, *Ger.* Löwen. C Belgium
Leuze *see* Leuze-en-Hainaut
Leuze-en-Hainaut 87 B 6 *var.* Leuze. SW Belgium
Levanger 84 B 4 C Norway
Levelland 49 E 2 Texas, S USA
Lévêque, Cape 146 C 3 headland, Western Australia, W Australia
Leverkusen 94 A 4 W Germany
Levice 99 C 6 *var.* Lewentz, *Ger.* Lewenz, *Hung.* Léva. SW Slovakia
Levin 150 D 4 North Island, C New Zealand
Levkás *see* Lefkáda
Levkímmi *see* Lefkímmi
Lewis, Isle of 88 B 3 island, NW Scotland, UK
Lewis Range 44 B 1 mountain range, NW USA
Lewis Smith Lake 42 C 2 reservoir, Alabama, S USA
Lewiston 41 G 2 Maine, NE USA
Lewiston 46 C 2 Idaho, NW USA
Lewistown 44 C 1 Montana, NW USA
Lexington 40 C 5 Kentucky, E USA
Lexington 45 E 4 Nebraska, C USA
Leyte 139 F 2 island, Visayan Islands, C Philippines
Leżajsk 99 E 5 SE Poland
Lezhë 101 C 6 *var.* Lezha; *prev.* Lesh, Leshi. NW Albania
Lhasa 126 C 5 *var.* La-sa, Lassa. W China
Lhazê 126 C 5 SW China
L'Hospitalet de Llobregat 93 G 2 *var.* Hospitalet. NE Spain
Liancourt Rocks 131 A 5 island group, Japan/South Korea
Lianyungang 128 D 4 *var.* Xinpu. E China
Liaoning 128 D 3 *var.* Liao, Shengking; *hist.* Fengtien, Shenking. Province, NE China
Liao-yang *see* Liaoyang
Liaoyuan 128 E 3 *var.* Shuang-liao, *Jap.* Chengchiatun. NE China
Liard *see* Fort Liard
Liban, Jebel 118 B 4 *var.* Jabal al Gharbt, *Ar.* Jabal Lubnán, *Eng.* Mount Lebanon. Mountain range, C Lebanon
Libau *see* Liepāja
Libby 44 A 1 Montana, NW USA
Liberal 45 E 5 Kansas, C USA
Liberec 98 B 4 *Ger.* Reichenberg. N Czech Republic

Liberia
75 D 5 Republic, W Africa

Official name: Republic of Liberia **Date of formation:** 1847/1907 **Capital:** Monrovia **Population:** 2.8 million **Total area:** 111,370 sq km (43,000 sq miles) **Languages:** English*, Kpelle, Bassa Vai **Religions:** Traditional beliefs 70%, Muslim 20%, Christian 10% **Ethnic mix:** Kpelle 20%, Bassa 14%, Americo-Liberians 5%, other 61% **Government:** Transitional **Currency:** Liberian $ = 100 cents

---

Liberia 52 D 4 NW Costa Rica
Libourne 91 B 5 SW France
Libreville 77 A 5 country capital, NW Gabon

Libya
71 F 3 *Ar.* Al Jamāhīrīyah al 'Arabīyah al Lībīyah ash Sha'bīyah al Ishtirākīyah; *prev.* Libyan Arab Republic. Islamic state, N Africa

Official name: The Great Socialist People's Libyan Arab *Jamahiriya* **Date of formation:** 1951 **Capital:** Tripoli **Population:** 5.5 million **Total area:** 1,759,540 sq km (679,358 sq miles) **Languages:** Arabic*, Tuareg **Religions:** Muslim 97%, other 3% **Ethnic mix:** Arab and Berber 97%, other 3% **Government:** Socialist *jamahiriya* (state of the masses) **Currency:** Dinar = 1,000 dirhams

Libyan Desert 68 C 3 *var.* Libian Desert, *Ar.* Aş Şahrā' al Lībīyah. Desert, NE Africa

Libyan Plateau 68 C 2 plateau, Egypt/Libya

Lichtenfels 95 C 5 SE Germany

Lichtenvoorde 86 E 4 E Netherlands

Lichuan 129 C 5 C China

Lida 107 B 5 W Belorussia

Lidköping 85 B 6 S Sweden

Lidoríki 105 B 5 *prev.* Lidhorikíon, Lidokhorikíon. C Greece

Lidzbark Warmiński 98 D 2 *Ger.* Heilsberg. N Poland

Liechtenstein 94 D 1 Monarchy, C Europe

Official name: Principality of Liechtenstein **Date of formation:** 1719 **Capital:** Vaduz **Population:** 29,000 **Total area:** 160 sq km (62 sq miles) **Languages:** German*, Alemannish **Religions:** Roman Catholic 87%, Protestant 8%, other 5% **Ethnic mix:** Liechtensteiner 63%, Swiss 15%, German 9%, other 13% **Government:** Constitutional monarchy **Currency:** Swiss franc = 100 centimes

Liechtenstein, Principality of *see* Liechtenstein

Liège 87 D 6 *Dut.* Luik, *Ger.* Lüttich. E Belgium

Liegnitz *see* Legnica

Lienz 95 D 7 W Austria

Liepāja 106 B 3 *Ger.* Libau. W Latvia

Lievenhof *see* Līvāni

Liezen 95 D 7 C Austria

Liffey 89 B 6 river, E Ireland

Lifou 144 D 5 island, E New Caledonia

Liger *see* Loire

Ligure, Appennino 96 A 2 *Eng.* Ligurian Mountains. Mountain range, NW Italy

Ligurian Mountains *see* Ligure, Appennino

Ligurian Sea 102 D 2 *Fr.* Mer Ligurienne, *It.* Mar Ligure. Sea, N Mediterranean Sea

Lihou Reef & Cays 148 E 3 reef, C Coral Sea

Lihue 47 A 8 *Haw.* Līhu'e. Hawaii, W USA

Līhu'e *see* Lihue

Lihula 106 D 2 *Ger.* Leal. W Estonia

Likasi 77 D 8 *prev.* Jadotville. SE Congo (Zaire)

Liknes 85 A 6 S Norway

Lille 90 C 2 *var.* l'Isle, *Dut.* Rijssel, *Flem.* Ryssel; *prev.* Lisle, *anc.* Insula. N France

Lillehammer 85 B 5 S Norway

Lillestrøm 85 B 6 S Norway

Lilongwe 79 E 2 country capital, W Malawi

Lilybaeum *see* Marsala

Lima 60 C 4 country capital, W Peru

Limanowa 99 D 5 S Poland

Limassol *see* Lemesós

Lim Chu Kang 138 A 1 NW Singapore

Limerick 89 A 6 *Ir.* Luimneach. SW Ireland

Limín Vathéos *see* Sámos

Límnos 104 D 4 *anc.* Lemnos. Island, E Greece

Limoges 91 C 5 *anc.* Augustoritum Lemovicensium, Lemovices. C France

Limón 53 E 4 *var.* Puerto Limón. E Costa Rica

Limón 52 D 2 NE Honduras

Limousin 91 C 5 cultural region, C France

Limoux 91 C 6 S France

Limpopo 78 D 3 *var.* Crocodile. River, S Africa

Linares 92 D 4 S Spain

Linares 64 B 4 C Chile

Linares 51 E 3 NE Mexico

Linchuan 129 D 5 E China

Lincoln 89 D 6 *anc.* Lindum, Lindum Colonia. E England, UK

Lincoln 45 F 4 state capital, Nebraska, C USA

Lincoln Sea 83 E 1 sea, Arctic Ocean

Linden 59 G 3 E Guyana

Líndhos *see* Líndos

Lindi 73 D 8 SE Tanzania

Líndos 105 E 7 *var.* Líndhos. Ródos, SE Greece

Line Islands 145 H 3 island group, E Kiribati

Lingen 94 A 3 *var.* Lingen an der Ems. NW Germany

Lingen an der Ems *see* Lingen

Lingga, Kepulauan 138 B 4 island group, W Indonesia

Linköping 85 C 6 S Sweden

Linz 95 D 6 *anc.* Lentia. N Austria

Lion, Golfe du 91 C 7 *Eng.* Gulf of Lion, Gulf of Lions; *anc.* Sinus Gallicus. Inlet, NW Mediterranean Sea

Liozno *see* Lyozna

Lipari, Isola 97 D 7 island, S Italy

Lipetsk 111 B 5 W Russian Federation

Lipova 108 A 4 *Hung.* Lippa. W Romania

Lipovets *see* Lypovets'

Lippa *see* Lipova

Lippstadt 94 B 4 W Germany

Lira 73 B 6 N Uganda

Lisala 77 C 5 N Congo (Zaire)

Lisboa 92 B 4 *var.* Lisbon; *anc.* Felicitas Julia, Olisipo. Country capital, W Portugal

Lisbon *see* Lisboa

Lisichansk *see* Lysychans'k

Lisieux 90 B 3 *anc.* Noviomagus. N France

Liski 111 B 6 *prev.* Georgiu-Dezh. W Russian Federation

Lismore 149 E 5 New South Wales, SE Australia

Lissa *see* Leszno

Lisse 86 C 3 W Netherlands

Litang 129 A 5 C China

Litani, Nahrel 119 B 5 *var.* Nahr al Litant. River, C Lebanon

Litant, Nahr al *see* Litani, Nahrel

Lithgow 149 D 6 New South Wales, SE Australia

Lithuania 106 B 4 *Ger.* Litauen, *Lith.* Lietuva, *Pol.* Litwa, *Rus.* Litva, Litovskaya SSR; *prev.* Lithuanian SSR. Republic, NE Europe

Official name: Republic of Lithuania **Date of formation:** 1991 **Capital:** Vilnius **Population:** 3.8 million **Total area:** 65,200 sq km (25,174 sq miles) **Languages:** Lithuanian*, Russian **Religions:** Roman Catholic 87%, Russian Orthodox 10%, other 3% **Ethnic mix:** Lithuanian 80%, Russian 9%, Polish 8%, other 3% **Government:** Multiparty republic **Currency:** Litas = 100 centas

Litóchoro 104 B 4 *var.* Litókhoron. N Greece

Little Alföld 99 C 6 *Ger.* Kleines Ungarisches Tiefland, *Hung.* Kisalföld, *Slvk.* Podunajská Rovina. Plain, Hungary/Slovakia

Little Andaman 133 F 2 island, SW India

Little Barrier Island 150 D 2 island, North Island, N New Zealand

Little Bay 93 H 5 bay, NE Atlantic Ocean

Little Cayman 54 B 3 island, E Cayman Islands

Little Falls 45 F 2 Minnesota, N USA

Littlefield 49 E 2 Texas, S USA

Little Fort 37 E 5 British Columbia, SW Canada

Little Inagua 54 D 2 *var.* Inagua Islands. Island, S Bahamas

Little Minch, The 88 B 3 strait, NE Atlantic Ocean

Little Missouri River 44 D 2 river, NW USA

Little Nicobar 133 G 3 island, SW India

Little Rock 42 B 1 state capital, Arkansas, C USA

Little St.Bernard Pass 96 A 2 *Fr.* Col du Petit St-Bernard, *It.* Colle di Piccolo San Bernardo. Pass, France/Italy

Little Sound 42 A 5 bay, W Atlantic Ocean

Littleton 44 C 4 Colorado, C USA

Littoria *see* Latina

Liuzhou 129 C 6 *var.* Liu-chou, Liuchow. S China

Livanátes 105 C 5 *prev.* Livanátai. C Greece

Līvāni 106 D 4 *Ger.* Lievenhof. SE Latvia

Liverpool 89 C 5 NW England, UK

Liverpool 39 F 5 Nova Scotia, SE Canada

Livingston 44 B 2 Montana, NW USA

Livingstone 78 C 3 *var.* Maramba. S Zambia

Livingstone Mountains 151 A 7 mountain range, South Island, SW New Zealand

Livingston, Lake 49 H 3 reservoir, Texas, S USA

Livno 100 B 4 SW Bosnia & Herzegovina

Livojoki 84 D 4 river, C Finland

Livonia *see* Vidzeme

Livorno 96 C 3 *Eng.* Leghorn. C Italy

Lixoúri 105 A 5 *prev.* Lixoúrion. Iónioi Nísoi, W Greece

Lixoúrion *see* Lixoúri

Ljouwert *see* Leeuwarden

Ljubljana 95 D 8 *Ger.* Laibach, *It.* Lubiana; *anc.* Aemona, Emona. Country capital, C Slovenia

Ljungby 85 B 7 S Sweden

Ljusdal 85 C 5 C Sweden

Ljusnan 85 C 5 river, C Sweden

Llallagua 61 F 4 SW Bolivia

Llanelli 89 C 7 *prev.* Llanelly. S Wales, UK

Llanelly *see* Llanelli

Llanes 92 D 1 N Spain

Llanos 58 D 2 physical region, Colombia/Venezuela

Lleida 93 F 2 *var.* Lérida; *anc.* Ilerda. NE Spain

Lluchmayor *see* Llucmajor

Llucmajor 93 G 3 *var.* Lluchmayor. E Spain

Lobatse 78 C 4 *var.* Lobatsi. SE Botswana

Lobatsi *see* Lobatse

Löbau 94 D 4 E Germany

Lobito 78 B 2 W Angola

Lobositz *see* Lovosice

Loburi *see* Lop Buri

Lochem 86 E 3 E Netherlands

Loch Garman *see* Wexford

Lockport 41 E 3 New York, NE USA

Lodeynoye Pole 110 B 4 *var.* Lodejnoje Pole, Lodeinoje Polje. NW Russian Federation

Lodi 47 B 6 California, W USA

Lodja 77 D 6 C Congo (Zaire)

Lodz *see* Łódź

Łódź 98 D 4 *Rus.* Lodz. C Poland

Loei 134 C 4 *var.* Loey, Muang Loei. N Thailand

Lofoten 84 B 3 *var.* Lofoten Islands. Island group, C Norway

Lofoten Islands *see* Lofoten

Logan 44 B 3 Utah, W USA

Logan, Mount 36 D 3 mountain, Yukon Territory, W Canada

Logansport 40 C 4 Indiana, N USA

Logroño 93 E 2 *anc.* Vareia, *Lat.* Juliobriga. N Spain

Loibl Pass 95 D 7 *Ger.* Loiblpass, *Slvn.* Ljubelj. Pass, Austria/Slovenia

Loi-Kaw 136 B 4 E Burma

Loire 90 B 4 *var.* Liger. River, C France

Loita Hills 73 C 6 hill range, SW Kenya

Loja 60 B 2 S Ecuador

Lokitaung 73 C 5 NW Kenya

Lokoja 75 G 5 C Nigeria

Loksa 106 E 2 *Ger.* Loxa. NW Estonia

Lolland 85 A 8 *prev.* Laaland. Island, S Denmark

Lom 75 H 5 river, Cameroon/ Central African Republic

Lom 104 C 2 *prev.* Lom-Palanka. NW Bulgaria

Loma Mansa *see* Bintimani

Lomami 77 D 6 river, C Congo (Zaire)

Lomas de Zamora 64 D 4 E Argentina

Lombok, Pulau 138 D 5 island, C Indonesia

Lomé 75 F 5 country capital, S Togo

Lommel 87 D 5 N Belgium

Lomond, Loch 88 C 4 lake, W Scotland, UK

Lomonsov Ridge 155 F 3 *var.* Harris Ridge, *Rus.* Khrebet Lomonsova. Undersea ridge, Arctic Ocean

Lom-Palanka *see* Lom
Lompoc 47 B 7 California, W USA
Lom Sak 136 C 4 *var.* Muang Lom Sak. N Thailand
Łomża 98 D 3 *Rus.* Lomzha. NE Poland
Lomzha *see* Łomża
Loncoche 65 B 5 C Chile
London 89 E 7 *anc.* Augusta, *Lat.* Londinium. Country capital, SE England, UK
London 38 C 5 Ontario, S Canada
Londonderry 88 A 4 *var.* Derry, *Ir.* Doire. N Northern Ireland, UK
Londonderry, Cape 146 C 2 headland, Western Australia, W Australia
Londrina 63 E 4 S Brazil
Longa, Proliv 115 G 1 *Eng.* Long Strait. Strait, Chukchi Sea/East Siberian Sea
Long Bay 43 F 2 bay, NW Atlantic Ocean
Long Beach 47 C 8 California, W USA
Longford 89 B 5 *Ir.* An Longfort. C Ireland
Long Island 54 D 2 island, C Bahamas
Long Island 148 D 4 island, Queensland, E Australia
Long Island 41 G 4 island, New York, NE USA
Long Island Sound 41 G 3 sound, W Atlantic Ocean
Longlac 38 C 4 Ontario, S Canada
Longmont 44 C 4 Colorado, C USA
Longreach 148 C 4 Queensland, E Australia
Long Strait *see* Longa, Proliv
Longview 49 H 3 Texas, S USA
Longview 46 B 2 Washington, NW USA
Long Xuyên 137 D 6 *var.* Longxuyen. SW Vietnam
Longxuyen *see* Long Xuyên
Longyan 129 D 6 SE China
Longyearbyen 83 G 2 dependent territory capital, W Svalbard
Lons-le-Saunier 90 D 4 *anc.* Ledo Salinarius. E France
Lop Buri 137 C 5 *var.* Loburi. C Thailand
Lop Nur 126 C 3 *var.* Lob Nor, Lop Nor, Lo-pu Po. Lake, NW China
Loppersum 86 E 1 NE Netherlands
Lorain 40 D 3 Ohio, N USA
Lorca 93 E 4 *Ar.* Lurka; *anc.* Eliocroca, *Lat.* Illur co. S Spain
Lord Howe Island 142 C 4 island, E Australia
Lord Howe Rise 152 C 4 undersea rise, SW Pacific Ocean
Loreto 50 B 3 W Mexico
Lorient 90 A 4 *prev.* l'Orient. NW France
l'Orient *see* Lorient
Lorn, Firth of 88 B 4 inlet, NE Atlantic Ocean
Lörrach 95 A 7 S Germany
Lorraine 90 D 3 cultural region, NE France
Los Alamos 48 D 1 New Mexico, SW USA
Los Amates 52 B 2 E Guatemala
Los Angeles 47 C 8 California, W USA
Los Ángeles 65 B 5 C Chile
Losanna *see* Lausanne
Los Banos 47 B 6 California, W USA
Losinj 100 A 3 *var.* Lošinj, *Ger.* Lussin, *It.* Lussino. Island, W Croatia
Loslau *see* Wodzisław Śląski
Los Mochis 50 C 3 C Mexico
Lô, Sông 128 A 1 *var.* Panlong Jiang. River, China/Vietnam
Los Roques, Islas 58 D 1 island group, N Venezuela
Los Testigos 59 E 1 island, NE Venezuela
Lost River Range 46 D 3 mountain range, Idaho, NW USA
Lot 91 B 5 cultural region, SW France
Lot 91 B 5 river, S France
Lotagipi Swamp 73 C 5 wetland, Kenya/Sudan
Loualaba *see* Lualaba
Louangnamtha 136 C 3 *var.* Luong Nam Tha. N Laos
Louangphabang 136 C 3 *var.* Louangphrabang, Luang Prabang. C Laos
Loubomo *see* Dolisie
Loudéac 90 A 3 NW France
Loudi 129 C 6 E China
Louga 74 B 3 NW Senegal
Louisiade Archipelago 144 C 4 island group, SE Papua New Guinea
Louisiana 42 A 2 *off.* State of Louisiana; *nicknames* Creole State, Pelican State. State, S USA
Louisville 40 C 5 Kentucky, E USA
Louisville Ridge 152 D 4 undersea ridge, SW Pacific Ocean
Lourdes 91 B 6 S France
Lourenço Marques *see* Maputo
Louth 89 E 5 E England, UK
Loutrá 104 C 4 N Greece
Louvain-la Neuve 87 C 6 C Belgium
Louviers 90 C 3 N France
Loveč *see* Lovech
Lovech 104 C 2 *var.* Loveč. NW Bulgaria
Loveland 44 C 4 Colorado, C USA
Lovosice 98 A 4 *Ger.* Lobositz. NW Czech Republic
Lóvua 78 C 1 NE Angola
Lowell 41 G 3 Massachusetts, NE USA
Lower California *see* Baja California
Lower Hutt 151 D 5 North Island, C New Zealand
Lower Lough Erne 89 A 5 lake, SW Northern Ireland, UK
Lower Red Lake 45 F 1 Lake, Minnesota, USA
Lower Tunguska *see* Nizhnyaya Tunguska
Lowestoft 89 E 6 E England, UK
Loxa *see* Loksa
Loyauté, Îles 144 D 5 island group, S New Caledonia
Loyev *see* Loyew
Loyew 107 D 8 *Rus.* Loyev. SE Belorussia
Loznica 100 D 3 W Yugoslavia
Lualaba 77 D 7 *Fr.* Loualaba. River, SE Congo (Zaire)
Luanda 78 A 1 *var.* Loanda, Paulo de Loanda, *Port.* São. Country capital, NW Angola
Luang, Thale 137 C 7 lagoon, South China Sea/Pacific Ocean
Luanshya 78 D 2 C Zambia
Luarca 92 C 1 N Spain
Lubaczów 99 E 5 *var.* Lúbaczów. SE Poland
Lubań 98 B 4 *Ger.* Kosten. SW Poland
Lubānas Ezers *see* Lubāns
Lubango 78 B 2 *Port.* Sá da Bandeira. SW Angola
Lubāns 106 D 4 *var.* Lubānas Ezers. Lake, E Latvia
Lubao 77 D 6 C Congo (Zaire)
Lübben 94 D 4 E Germany
Lübbenau 94 D 4 E Germany
Lubbock 49 E 2 Texas, S USA
Lübeck 94 C 2 N Germany
Lubelska, Wyżyna 98 E 4 plateau, SE Poland
Lüben *see* Lubin
Lubin 98 B 4 *Ger.* Lüben. W Poland
Lublin 98 E 4 *Rus.* Lyublin. E Poland
Lubliniec 98 C 4 S Poland
Lubny 109 F 2 NE Ukraine
Lubsko 98 B 4 *Ger.* Sommerfeld. W Poland
Lubumbashi 77 E 8 *prev.* Élisabethville. SE Congo (Zaire)
Lubutu 77 D 6 E Congo (Zaire)
Luca 61 F 5 SW Bolivia
Luca *see* Lucca
Lucan 89 B 5 *Ir.* Leamhcán. E Ireland
Lucanian Mountains *see* Lucano, Appennino
Lucano, Appennino 97 D 6 *Eng.* Lucanian Mountains. Mountain range, S Italy
Lucapa 78 C 1 *var.* Lukapa. NE Angola
Lucca 96 B 3 *anc.* Luca. C Italy
Lucea 54 A 4 W Jamaica
Lucedale 42 C 3 Mississippi, S USA
Lucena 92 D 4 S Spain
Lucena 139 E 1 *off.* Lucena City. Luzon, N Philippines
Lucena City *see* Lucena
Lučenec 99 D 6 *Ger.* Losontz, *Hung.* Losonc. S Slovakia
Lucerne, Lake of *see* Vierwaldstätter See
Lucknow 135 E 3 *var.* Lakhnau. State capital, N India
Lüderitz 78 B 4 *prev.* Angra Pequena. SW Namibia
Ludhiāna 134 D 2 N India
Ludsan *see* Ludza
Luduş 108 B 4 *Ger.* Ludasch, *Hung.* Marosludas. C Romania
Ludvika 85 C 6 C Sweden
Ludwiglust 94 C 3 N Germany
Ludwigsburg 95 B 6 SW Germany
Lüdwigsfelde 94 D 4 NE Germany
Ludwigshafen 95 B 5 W Germany
Ludza 106 D 4 *Ger.* Ludsan. E Latvia
Luebo 77 C 6 SW Congo (Zaire)
Luena 78 C 2 *var.* Lwena, *Port.* Luso. E Angola
Lufira 77 E 7 river, SE Congo (Zaire)
Lufkin 49 H 3 Texas, S USA
Luga 110 A 4 NW Russian Federation
Lugenda, Rio 79 E 2 river, N Mozambique
Lugh Ganana *see* Luuq
Lugo 92 C 1 *anc.* Lugus Augusti. NW Spain
Lugoj 108 A 4 *Ger.* Lugosch, *Hung.* Lugos. W Romania
Lugus Augusti *see* Lugo
Luhans'k 109 H 3 *Rus.* Lugansk; *prev.* Voroshilovgrad. E Ukraine
Luimneach *see* Limerick
Lukapa *see* Lucapa
Lukenie 77 D 6 river, C Congo (Zaire)
Lukovit 104 C 2 NW Bulgaria
Łuków 98 E 4 *Ger.* Bogendorf. E Poland
Lukuga 77 E 7 river, SE Congo (Zaire)
Luleå 84 D 4 N Sweden
Luleälven 84 C 3 river, N Sweden
Lulonga 77 C 5 river, NW Congo (Zaire)
Luluabourg *see* Kananga
Lumberton 43 F 1 North Carolina, SE USA
Lumbo 79 F 2 NE Mozambique
Lumi i Vjosës 104 A 4 *var.* Vijosa, Vijosë, *Gk.* Aóos. River, Albania/Greece
Lumsden 151 A 7 South Island, SW New Zealand
Lund 85 B 7 S Sweden
Lüneburg 94 B 3 N Germany
Lungué-Bungo *see* Lungwebungu
Lungwebungu 78 C 2 *var.* Lungué-Bungo. River, Angola/Zambia
Luninyets 107 B 7 *Pol.* Łuniniec, *Rus.* Luninets. SW Belorussia
Lunteren 86 D 4 C Netherlands
Luong Nam Tha *see* Louangnamtha
Luoyang 128 C 4 *var.* Honan, Lo-yang. C China
Lupatia *see* Altamura
Lúrio 79 F 2 NE Mozambique
Lúrio, Rio 79 E 2 river, NE Mozambique
Lusaka 78 D 2 country capital, SE Zambia
Lushnja *see* Lushnjë
Lushnjë 101 C 6 *var.* Lushnja. C Albania
Lūt, Dasht-e 120 D 3 *var.* Kavīr-e Lūt. Desert, E Iran
Lūt, Kavīr-e *see* Lūt, Dasht-e
Luton 89 D 6 S England, UK
Łutselk'e 37 F 4 *prev.* Snowdrift. Northwest Territories, C Canada
Luts'k 108 C 1 *Pol.* Łuck, *Rus.* Lutsk. NW Ukraine
Lutzow-Holm Bay 154 C 2 *var.* Lützow Holmbukta. Bay, Atlantic Ocean/Indian Ocean
Lützow Holmbukta *see* Lutzow-Holm Bay
Luuq 73 D 6 *It.* Lugh Ganana. SW Somalia
Luvua 77 E 7 river, SE Congo (Zaire)
Luxembourg 87 D 8 country capital, S Luxembourg

Luxembourg
87 D 8 *var.* Lëtzebuerg, Luxemburg. Monarchy, W Europe

Official name: Grand Duchy of Luxembourg **Date of formation:** 1890 **Capital:** Luxembourg **Population:** 400,000 **Total area:** 2,586 sq km (998 sq miles) **Languages:** Letzeburgish*, French, Portuguese, Italian **Religions:** Roman Catholic 97%, other 3% **Ethnic mix:** Luxemburger 72%, Portuguese 9%, Italian 5%, other 14% **Government:** Constitutional monarchy **Currency:** Franc = 100 centimes

---

Luxor 72 B 2 *Ar.* Al Uqşur. E Egypt
Luza 110 C 4 NW Russian Federation
Luzern 95 B 7 *Fr.* Lucerne, *It.* Lucerna. C Switzerland

Luzon 139 E 1 island, N Philippines
Luzon Strait 139 E 1 strait, W Pacific Ocean
L'viv 108 B 2 *Ger.* Lemberg, *Pol.* Lwów, *Rus.* L'vov. W Ukraine
Lyakhavichy 107 D 6 *Rus.* Lyakhovichi. SW Belorussia
Lyakhovichi *see* Lyakhavichy
Lyallpur *see* Faisalābād
Lyangar *see* Langar
Lyck *see* Ełk
Lycksele 84 C 4 N Sweden
Lyel'chytsy 107 C 7 *Rus.* Lel'chitsy. SE Belorussia
Lyepyel' 107 D 5 *Rus.* Lepel'. N Belorussia
Lyme Bay 89 D 7 bay, Atlantic Ocean/English Channel
Lynchburg 41 E 5 Virginia, NE USA
Lynn 41 G 3 Massachusetts, NE USA
Lyon 91 D 5 *Eng.* Lyons; *anc.* Lugdunum. E France
Lyozna 107 E 6 *Rus.* Liozno. NE Belorussia
Lypovets' 108 D 2 *Rus.* Lipovets. C Ukraine
Lys *see* Leie
Lysychans'k 109 H 3 *Rus.* Lisichansk. E Ukraine
Lyttelton 151 C 6 South Island, C New Zealand
Lyublin *see* Lublin
Lyubotin *see* Lyubotyn
Lyubotyn 109 G 2 *Rus.* Lyubotin. E Ukraine
Lyulyakovo 104 E 2 *prev.* Keremitlik. E Bulgaria
Lyusina 107 C 6 *Rus.* Lyusino. SW Belorussia
Lyusino *see* Lyusina

M

Ma'ān 119 B 7 SW Jordan
Maardu 106 D 2 *Ger.* Maart. NW Estonia
Maarmorilik 82 C 3 *var.* Mârmorilik. W Greenland
Ma'arrat an Nu'mān 118 B 3 *var.* Ma'aret-en-Nu'man, *Fr.* Maarret enn Naamâne. NW Syria
Maart *see* Maardu
Maas *see* Meuse
Maaseik 87 D 5 *prev.* Maeseyck. NE Belgium
Maastricht 87 D 6 *var.* Maestricht; *anc.* Traieclum ad Mosam, Traiectum Tungorum. SE Netherlands
Macao 129 C 7 *var.* Macau, *Chin.* Aomen, *Port.* Mação. Portuguese territory, E Asia
Macao 129 C 6 *var.* Macau, Mação. Territory capital, N Macao
Macará 60 B 2 S Ecuador
Macarov Basin 155 G 3 undersea basin, Arctic Ocean
Macarsca *see* Makarska
Macău *see* Makó
MacCluer Gulf *see* Berau, Teluk
Macdonnell Ranges 142 A 4 mountain range, Northern Territory, C Australia

---

Macedonia
101 D 6 *abbrev.* FYR Macedonia, *Mac.* Makedonija. Republic, SE Europe

Official name: Former Yugoslav Republic of Macedonia **Date of formation:** 1991 **Capital:** Skopje **Population:** 1.9 million **Total area:** 25,715 sq km (9,929 sq miles) **Languages:** Macedonian, Albanian Turkish (*no official language*) **Religions:** Christian 80%, Muslim 20% **Ethnic mix:** Macedonian 67%, Albanian 20%, Turkish 4%, other 9% **Government:** Multiparty republic **Currency:** Denar = 100 deni

---

Maceió 63 G 3 state capital, E Brazil
Macfarlane, Lake 149 B 6 *var.* Lake Mcfarlane. Lake, South Australia, S Australia
Machachi 60 B 1 C Ecuador
Machakos 73 C 6 S Kenya
Machala 60 B 2 SW Ecuador
Machanga 79 E 3 E Mozambique
Machattie, Lake 148 B 4 lake, C Australia
Machilīpatnam 132 D 1 *var.* Bandar, Masulipatnam. E India
Machiques 58 C 2 NW Venezuela
Măcin 108 D 5 SE Romania
Mackay 148 D 4 Queensland, NE Australia
Mackay, Lake 146 D 4 salt lake, C Australia
Mackenzie 37 E 3 river, Northwest Territories, NW Canada
Mackenzie Bay 154 D 3 bay, C Indian Ocean
Mackenzie Mountains 36 D 3 mountain range, Northwest Territories, NW Canada
Macleod, Lake 146 A 4 lake, W Australia
Macomb 40 A 4 Illinois, N USA
Macomer 97 A 5 W Italy
Macon 42 D 2 Georgia, SE USA
Macon 45 G 4 Missouri, C USA
Mâcon 91 D 5 *anc.* Matisco, Matisco Ædourum. C France
Macquarie Ridge 154 C 5 undersea ridge, SW Pacific Ocean
Macuspana 51 G 4 SE Mexico
Ma'dabā 119 B 6 *var.* Mādabā, Madeba; *anc.* Medeba. NW Jordan

---

Madagascar
79 F 3 *Malg.* Madagasikara; *prev.* Malagasy Republic. Republic, E Africa

Official name: Democratic Republic of Madagascar **Date of formation:** 1960 **Capital:** Antananarivo **Population:** 13.3 million **Total area:** 587,040 sq km (226,660 sq miles) **Languages:** Malagasy*, French* **Religions:** Traditional beliefs 52%, Christian 41%, Muslim 7% **Ethnic mix:** Merina 26%, Betsimisaraka 15%, Betsileo 12%, other 47% **Government:** Multiparty republic **Currency:** Franc = 100 centimes

---

Madagascar Basin 141 B 5 undersea basin, W Indian Ocean
Madagascar Plateau 141 A 6 *var.* Madagascar Ridge, Madagascar Rise, Madagaskarskiy Khrebet. Undersea plateau, W Indian Ocean
Madang 144 B 3 New Guinea, N Papua New Guinea
Madanīyīn *see* Médenine
Made 86 C 4 S Netherlands
Madeira 62 D 2 *var.* Río Madera. River, Bolivia/Brazil
Madeira 70 A 2 Portuguese autonomous region, E Atlantic Ocean
Madeira 70 A 2 *var.* Ilha de Madeira. Island, E Atlantic Ocean
Madeira, Ilha de *see* Madeira
Madeleine, Îles de la 39 F 4 *Eng.* Magdalen Islands. Island group, Québec, E Canada
Madera 47 C 6 California, W USA
Madera, Río *see* Madeira
Madhya Pradesh 135 E 4 *prev.* Central Provinces and Berar. State, C India
Madīnat al Abyār *see* Al Abyār
Madīnat ath Thawrah 118 C 2 *var.* Ath Thawrah. N Syria
Madioen *see* Madiun
Madison 40 B 3 state capital, Wisconsin, N USA
Madison 45 F 3 South Dakota, N USA
Madiun 138 D 5 *prev.* Madioen. Jawa, C Indonesia
Madoera *see* Madura, Pulau
Madona 106 D 4 *Ger.* Modohn. E Latvia
Madras 132 D 2 S India
Madras *see* Tamil Nādu
Madre de Dios 61 E 3 river, Bolivia/Peru
Madre del Sur, Sierra 51 E 5 mountain range, S Mexico
Madre, Laguna 49 G 5 lake, Texas, S USA
Madre, Laguna 51 F 3 lagoon, NW Gulf of Mexico
Madre Occidental, Sierra 50 C 2 *var.* Western Sierra Madre. Mountain range, C Mexico
Madre Oriental, Sierra 51 E 3 *var.* Eastern Sierra Madre. Mountain range, C Mexico
Madrid 92 D 3 country capital, C Spain
Madura 138 D 5 *prev.* Madoera. Island, C Indonesia
Madurai 132 C 3 *prev.* Madura, Mathurai. S India
Maebashi 131 D 5 *var.* Maebasi, Mayebashi. Honshū, S Japan
Maeikiai 106 B 3 NW Lithuania
Mae Nam Nan 136 C 4 river, S Thailand
Mae Nam Yom 136 C 4 river, S Thailand
Maeseyck *see* Maaseik
Maewo 144 D 4 *prev.* Aurora. Island, C Vanuatu
Mafraq *see* Al Mafraq
Magadan 115 G 3 NE Russian Federation
Magallanes *see* Punta Arenas
Magallanes, Estrecho de *see* Magellan, Strait of
Magangué 58 B 2 N Colombia
Magdalena 50 B 2 NW Mexico
Magdalena 61 F 3 N Bolivia
Magdalena, Isla 50 B 3 island, W Mexico
Magdalen Islands *see* Madeleine, Îles de la
Magdeburg 94 C 4 C Germany
Magdelena 58 B 2 river, C Colombia
Magelang 138 C 5 Jawa, C Indonesia
Magellan, Strait of 65 C 8 *Sp.* Estrecho de Magallanes. Strait, Atlantic Ocean/Pacific Ocean
Magerøy *see* Magerøya
Magerøya 84 D 1 *var.* Magerøy. Island, N Norway
Maggiore, Lago *see* Maggiore, Lake
Maggiore, Lake 96 B 1 *It.* Lago Maggiore. Lake, Italy/Switzerland
Maglaj 100 C 3 N Bosnia & Herzegovina
Maglie 97 E 6 SE Italy
Magna 44 B 4 Utah, W USA
Magnitogorsk 114 B 4 C Russian Federation
Magṭa' Laḥjar 74 C 3 *var.* Magta' Lahjar, Magtá Lahjar, Magta Lahjar. SW Mauritania
Magway *see* Magwe
Magwe 136 A 3 *var.* Magway. W Burma
Mahajanga 79 G 3 *var.* Majunga. N Madagascar
Mahakam, 138 D 4 *var.* Koetai, Kutai. River, Borneo, C Indonesia
Mahalapye 78 D 3 *var.* Mahalatswe. SE Botswana
Mahalatswe *see* Mahalapye
Mahān 120 D 4 E Iran
Mahārāshtra 134 D 5 state, W India
Mahé 79 H 1 island, NE Seychelles
Mahia Peninsula 150 E 4 peninsula, North Island, E New Zealand
Mahilyow 107 E 6 *Rus.* Mogilëv. E Belorussia
Mahmūd-e 'Erāqī *see* Maḥmūd-e Rāqī
Maḥmūd-e Rāqī 123 E 4 *var.* Mahmūd-e 'Erāqī. NE Afghanistan
Mahón 93 H 3 *Cat.* Maó, *Eng.* Port Mahon; *anc.* Portus Magonis. E Spain
Mährisch-Weisskirchen *see* Hranice
Maicao 58 C 1 N Colombia
Maidstone 89 E 7 SE England, UK
Maiduguri 75 H 4 NE Nigeria
Main 95 B 5 river, C Germany
Mai-Ndombe, Lac 77 C 6 *prev.* Lac Léopold II. Lake, W Congo (Zaire)
Maine 90 B 3 cultural region, NW France
Maine 41 G 2 *off.* State of Maine; *nicknames* Lumber State, Pine Tree State. State, NE USA
Maine, Gulf of 41 H 2 gulf, NW Atlantic Ocean
Mainland 88 D 2 island, NE Scotland, UK
Mainland 88 D 1 island NE Scotland, UK
Mainz 95 B 5 *Fr.* Mayence. SW Germany
Maio 74 A 3 *var.* Mayo. Island, SE Cape Verde
Maisur *see* Mysore
Maitland 149 D 6 New South Wales, SE Australia
Maizhokunggar X 126 C 5 W China
Maíz, Islas del 53 E 3 *var.* Corn Islands. Island group, SE Nicaragua
Majunga *see* Mahajanga
Majuro 142 D 2 *var.* D-U-D Municipality. Country capital, SE Marshall Islands
Makale *see* Mek'elē
Makarikari Pans *see* Makgadikgadi
Makarska 100 B 4 *It.* Macarsca. SE Croatia
Makasar, Selat 138 D 4 *Eng.* Makassar Strait. Strait, Celebes Sea/Java Sea
Makassar Strait *see* Makasar, Selat
Makeni 74 C 4 C Sierra Leone
Makgadikgadi 78 C 3 *var.* Makarikari Pans. Salt lake, NE Botswana
Makhachkala 111 B 8 *prev.* Petrovsk-Port. SW Russian Federation
Makin Atoll 144 D 2 *prev.* Pitt Island. Island, W Kiribati

Makira see San Cristobal
Makiyivka 109 G 3 *Rus.*
Makeyevka; *prev.* Dmitriyevsk.
E Ukraine
Makkah 121 A 5 *Eng.* Mecca.
W Saudi Arabia
Makkovik 39 F 2 Newfoundland
and Labrador, NE Canada
Makó 99 D 7 *Rom.* Macău.
SE Hungary
Makoua 77 B 5 C Congo
Makran Coast 120 E 4 physical
region, SE Iran
Makrany 107 A 6 *Rus.* Mokrany.
SW Belorussia
Mākū 120 B 2 NW Iran
Makurdi 75 G 5 C Nigeria
Mala see Malaita
Malabār Coast 132 B 3 physical
region, SW India
Malabo 77 A 5 *prev.* Santa Isabel.
Country capital,
NW Equatorial Guinea
Malaca see Málaga
Malacca see Melaka
Malacca, Strait of 138 A 3 strait,
Indian Ocean/Pacific Ocean
Malacka see Malacky
Malacky 99 C 6 *Hung.* Malacka.
W Slovakia
Maladzyechna 107 C 5 *Pol.*
Molodeczno, *Rus.* Molodechno.
C Belorussia
Málaga 92 D 5 *anc.* Malaca. S Spain
Malagarasi River 73 B 7 river,
SW Tanzania
Malaita 144 C 3 *var.* Mala. Island,
N Solomon Islands
Malakal 73 B 5 S Sudan
Malambo 58 B 1 N Colombia
Malang 138 D 5 Jawa, C Indonesia
Malange see Malanje
Malanje 78 B 1 *var.* Malange.
NW Angola
Mälaren 85 C 6 lake, C Sweden
Malatya 117 E 4 *anc.* Melitene.
SE Turkey
Mala Vyska 109 E 3
Rus. Malaya Viska. S Ukraine

Malawi
79 E 1 *prev.* Nyasaland,
Nyasaland Protectorate. Republic,
S Africa

Official name: Republic of Malawi
Date of formation: 1964 **Capital:**
Lilongwe **Population:** 10.7 million
Total area: 118,480 sq km
(45,745 sq miles) **Languages:** English*
Chewa **Religions:** Christian 66%,
traditional beliefs 18%,
other 16% **Ethnic mix:** Maravi 55%,
Lomwe 17%, Yao 13%, other 15%
Government: Multiparty republic
Currency: Kwacha = 100 tambala

Malaya Viska see Mala Vyska

Malaysia
138 B 3 *var.* Federation of
Malaysia; *prev.* the separate
territories of Federation of
Malaya, Sarawak and Sabah
(NorthBorneo) and Singapore.
Monarchy, SE Asia

Official name: Malaysia **Date of**
formation: 1957/1965 **Capital:**
Kuala Lumpur **Population:** 20.6
million **Total Area:** 329,750 sq km
(127,317 sq miles) **Languages:** Malay*,
Chinese, Tamil **Religions:** Muslim
53%, Buddhist and Confucianist

30%, other 17% **Ethnic mix:** Malay
and aborigine 60%, Chinese 30%,
Indian 8%, other 2% **Government:**
Federal constitutional monarchy
Currency: Ringgit = 100 cents

Malbork 98 C 2 *Ger.* Marienburg,
Marienburg in Westpreussen.
N Poland
Malchin 94 C 3 N Germany
Malden 45 H 5 Missouri, C USA
Malden Island 145 G 3 *prev.*
Independence Island. Island,
E Kiribati

Maldives
132 A 4 Republic, Indian Ocean

Official name: Republic of Maldives
Date of formation: 1965
Capital: Male' **Population:** 200,000
Total Area: 300 sq km (116 sq miles)
Languages: Dhivehi (Maldivian)*,
Sinhala, Tamil **Religions:** Sunni
Muslim 100% **Ethnic mix:** Maldavian
99%, Sinhalese and other South
Asian 1% **Government:** Republic
Currency: Rufiyaa - 100 laari

Male' 132 B 4 country capital,
C Maldives
Male' Atoll 132 B 4 *var.* Kaafu
Atoll. Island, C Maldives
Malekula 144 D 4 *var.* Malakula;
prev. Mallicolo. Island, W Vanuatu
Malesína 105 C 5 E Greece
Malheur Lake 46 C 3 lake,
Oregon, NW USA
Malheur River 46 C 4 river,
Oregon, NW USA

Mali
75 E 2 . *Fr.* République du Mali;
prev. Sudanese Republic, French
Sudan. Republic, W Africa

Official name: Republic of Mali
Date of formation: 1960 **Capital:**
Bamako **Population:** 10.1 million
Total area: 1,240,190 sq km
(478,837 sq miles) **Languages:**
French*, Bambara, Fulani, Senufo
Religions: Muslim 80%, traditional
beliefs 18%, Christian 2% **Ethnic**
mix: Bambara 31%, Fulani 13%,
Senufo 12%, other 44%
Government: Multiparty republic
Currency: CFA franc = 100 centimes

Malik, Wadi al see Milk, Wadi el
Mali Kyun 137 B 5 *var.* Tavoy
Island. Island, S Burma
Malin see Malyn
Malindi 73 D 7 SE Kenya
Malko Tŭrnovo 104 E 3
SE Bulgaria
Mallaig 88 C 3 W Scotland, UK
Mallawī 72 B 2 C Egypt
Mallorca 93 H 3 *Eng.* Majorca; *anc.*
Baleares Major. Island, E Spain
Malmberget 84 C 3 N Sweden
Malmédy 87 D 7 E Belgium
Malmö 85 B 7 S Sweden
Malmyž see Malmyzh
Maloelap 144 D 1 *var.* Maoeap.
Island, E Marshall Islands
Maloelap see Maloelap Atoll
Małopolska 98 D 4 plateau,
S Poland
Malozemel'skaya Tundra see
Malozemel'skaya Tundra
Malozemel'skaya Tundra 110 D 3
var. Malozemel'skaja Tundra.
Physical region,
NW Russian Federation

Malta
97 C 8 Republic, Mediterranean

Official name: Republic of Malta
Date of formation: 1964 **Capital:**
Valletta **Population:** 400,000
Total area: 320 sq km (124 sq miles)
Languages: Maltese*, English
Religions: Roman Catholic 98%,
other (mostly Anglican) 2%
Ethnic mix: Maltese (mixed Arab,
Sicilian, Norman, Spanish, Italian,
English) 98%, other 2%
Government: Multiparty republic
Currency: Lira = 100 cents

Malta 97 C 8 island, S Europe
Malta 106 D 4 SE Latvia
Malta 44 C 1 Montana, NW USA
Malta, Canale di see Malta Channel
Malta Channel 97 C 8 *It.* Canale di
Malta. Channel,
C Mediterranean Sea
Malta, Republic of see Malta
Maluka 139 F 4 *Eng.* Moluccas,
Dut. Molukken; *prev.* Spice
Islands. Island group, E Indonesia
Maluku, Laut 139 F 4 *Eng.* Molucca
Sea. Sea, W Pacific Ocean
Malung 85 B 5 C Sweden
Malyn 108 D 2 *Rus.* Malin.
N Ukraine
Malyy Kavkaz see Lesser Caucasus
Mamberamo 139 H 4 river,
New Guinea, E Indonesia
Mamonovo 106 A 4
Ger. Heiligenbeil.
W Russian Federation
Mamoré 61 F 3 river, Bolivia/Brazil
Mamou 74 C 4 W Guinea
Mamoudzou 79 F 2 dependent
territory capital, N Mayotte
Mamuno 78 C 3 W Botswana
Manacor 93 H 3 E Spain
Manado 139 F 3 *prev.* Menado.
Celebes, C Indonesia
Managua 52 D 3 country capital,
W Nicaragua
Managua, Lago de 52 C 3 *var.*
Xolotlán. Lake, W Nicaragua
Manahiki Plateau 152 D 3
undersea plateau,
SW Pacific Ocean
Manakara 79 G 4 SE Madagascar
Manama see Al Manāmah
Mananjary 79 G 3 SE Madagascar
Manáos see Manaus
Manapouri, Lake 151 A 7 lake,
South Island, SW New Zealand
Manar see Mannar
Manas, Gora 123 F 2 mountain,
Kyrgyzstan/Uzbekistan
Manaus 62 D 2 *prev.* Manáos. State
capital, NW Brazil
Manavgat 116 A 4 SW Turkey
Manbij 118 C 2 *var.* Mambij,
Fr. Membidj. N Syria
Manchester 89 D 5 *Lat.*
Mancunium. N England, UK
Manchester 41 G 3 New
Hampshire, NE USA
Man-chou-li see Manzhouli
Manchuria 128 D 2 cultural region,
NE China
Máncio Lima see Japiim
Máncora 60 B 2 NE Peru
Mancunium see Manchester
Mand 120 D 4 *var.* Rūd-e Mand.
River, S Iran
Mandalay 136 B 3 N Burma
Mandan 45 E 2
North Dakota, N USA

Mandara Mountains 75 H 4
mountain range, E Nigeria
Mandaue 139 E 2 *off.* Mandaue City.
Cebu, C Philippines
Mandaue City see Mandaue
Mandeville 54 B 5 C Jamaica
Mándra 105 C 6 C Greece
Mand, Rūd-e see Mand
Mandurah 147 B 6 Western
Australia, SW Australia
Mandya 132 C 2 C India
Manfredonia 97 D 5 SE Italy
Mangai 77 C 6 W Congo (Zaire)
Mangaia 145 G 5 island group,
S Cook Islands
Mangalia 108 D 5 *anc.* Callatis.
SE Romania
Mangalmé 76 C 3 SE Chad
Mangalore 132 B 2 W India
Mangaung see Bloemfontein
Mangin Range 136 B 2 mountain
range, C Burma
Mango see Sansanné-Mango
Mangoky 79 F 3 river,
SW Madagascar
Manhattan 45 F 4 Kansas, C USA
Manicouagan, Réservoir 39 E 3
lake, Québec, E Canada
Manihiki 145 G 4 island,
N Cook Islands
Maniitsoq 82 C 3 *var.* Manîtsoq,
Dan. Sukkertoppen.
SW Greenland
Manila 139 E 1 *off.* City of Manila.
Country capital, Luzon,
N Philippines
Manisa 116 A 3 *var.* Manissa;
prev. Saruhan, *anc.* Magnesia.
W Turkey
Man, Isle of 89 C 5 British
dependency, W England, UK
Manistee River 40 C 2 river,
Michigan, N USA
Manitoba 37 F 5 province,
S Canada
Manitoulin Island 38 C 5 island,
Ontario, S Canada
Manitowoc 40 B 2
Wisconsin, N USA
Manizales 58 B 3 W Colombia
Manjimup 147 B 7 Western
Australia, SW Australia
Mankato 45 F 3 Minnesota, N USA
Manlleu 93 G 2 NE Spain
Manmād 134 C 5 W India
Mannar 132 C 3 *var.* Manar.
NW Sri Lanka
Mannar, Gulf of 132 C 3 gulf,
N Indian Ocean
Mannheim 95 B 5 SW Germany
Manono 77 E 7 SE Congo (Zaire)
Manosque 91 D 6 SE France
Manra 145 F 3 *prev.* Sydney Island.
Island, C Kiribati
Mansa 78 D 2 *prev.* Fort Rosebery.
N Zambia
Mansel Island 38 C 1 island,
Northwest Territories, NE Canada
Mansfield 40 D 4 Ohio, N USA
Manta 60 A 2 W Ecuador
Manteca 47 B 6 California, W USA
Mantova 96 B 2 *Eng.* Mantua,
Fr. Mantoue. NW Italy
Manuae 145 G 5 island,
S Cook Islands
Manukau see Manurewa
Manurewa 150 D 3 *var.* Manukau.
North Island, N New Zealand
Manzanares 93 E 4 C Spain
Manzanillo 54 C 3 E Cuba
Manzanillo 50 D 4 SW Mexico

Manzano Mountains 48 D 2
mountain range, New Mexico,
SW USA
Manzhouli 127 F 1
var. Man-chou-li. N China
Manzil 119 B 7 W Jordan
Mao 76 B 3 W Chad
Maoke, Pegunungan 139 H 4
Dut. Sneeuw-gebergte, *Eng.* Snow
Mountains. Mountain range,
New Guinea, E Indonesia
Maoming 129 C 6 S China
Maputo 78 D 4 *prev.* Lourenço
Marques. Country capital,
S Mozambique
Maputo, Baía de 79 E 4 *var.* Baía de
Lourenço Marques, *Eng.* Delagoa
Bay. Bay, W Indian Ocean
Marabá 63 F 2 NE Brazil
Maracaibo 58 C 1 NW Venezuela
Maracaibo, Lago de 58 C 2
var. Lake Maracaibo. Lagoon,
NW Venezuela
Maracaibo, Lake *see*
Maracaibo, Lago de
Maracay 58 D 1 N Venezuela
Maradi 75 G 3 S Niger
Maragha *see* Marāgheh
Marāgheh 120 C 2 *var.* Maragha.
NW Iran
Marajó, Baía de 63 F 1 bay,
W Atlantic Ocean
Marajó, Ilha de 63 E 1 island,
N Brazil
Maramba *see* Livingstone
Maranhão 63 F 2 *off.* Estado do
Maranhão. State, E Brazil
Maranhão, Estado do *see* Maranhão
Marañón 60 C 2 river, N Peru
Marathon 38 C 4 Ontario, S Canada
Marathón *see* Marathónas
Marathónas 105 C 5 *prev.*
Marathón. C Greece
Marbella 92 D 5 S Spain
Marble Bar 146 B 4 Western
Australia, W Australia
Marburg *see* Maribor
Marburg an der Lahn 94 B 4 hist.
Eng. Marburg . W Germany
March *see* Morava
Marche 91 C 5 cultural region,
C France
Marche-en-Famenne 87 D 7
SE Belgium
Marchena, Isla 60 B 5 *var.* Bindloe
Island. Island, Galapagos Islands,
E Pacific Ocean
Marchfield 55 H 2 SE Barbados
Mar Chiquita, Laguna 64 C 3 lake,
C Argentina
Marcona 60 D 4 SW Peru
Marcounda *see* Markounda
Mardān 134 C 1 N Pakistan
Mar del Plata 65 D 5 E Argentina
Mardin 117 E 4 SE Turkey
Maré 144 D 5 island,
E New Caledonia
Mareeba 148 C 3 Queensland,
NE Australia
Marganets *see* Marhanets'
Margarita, Isla de 59 E 1 island,
N Venezuela
Margate 89 E 7 *prev.* Mergate.
SE England, UK
Marghita 108 B 3 *Hung.* Margitta.
NW Romania
Margitta *see* Marghita
Mārgow, Dasht-e 122 D 5 desert,
SW Afghanistan
Marhanets' 109 F 3 *Rus.* Marganets.
E Ukraine

Maria Cleofas, Isla 50 C 4 island,
C Mexico
Maria Island 149 C 8 island,
Tasmania, SE Australia
Maria Island 148 B 2 island,
Northern Territory, NE Australia
Maria Madre, Isla 50 C 4 island,
C Mexico
Maria Magdalena, Isla 50 C 4
island, C Mexico
Marianao 54 B 2 NW Cuba
Mariana Trench 152 B 2
var. Challenger Deep. Trench,
W Pacific Ocean
Mariánské Lázně 99 A 5 *Ger.*
Marienbad. W Czech Republic
Marías, Islas 50 C 4 island group,
C Mexico
Marias River 44 C 1 river,
Montana, NW USA
Maribor 95 E 7 *Ger.* Marburg.
NE Slovenia
Maridi 73 B 5 SW Sudan
Marie Byrd Land 154 B 3 physical
region, Antarctica
Marie Celeste Fracture Zone 141
C 5 fracture zone,
C Indian Ocean
Marie Galante 55 H 4 *var.* Ceyre to
the Caribs. Island, SE Guadeloupe
Marienbad *see* Mariánské Lázně
Marienburg *see* Alūksne
Marienhausen *see* Viļšļaka
Mariental 78 B 4 SW Namibia
Marienwerder *see* Kwidzyń
Mariestad 85 B 6 S Sweden
Marília 63 E 4 S Brazil
Marín 92 B 2 NW Spain
Marina 47 B 6 California, W USA
Mar'ina Gorka *see* Mar"ina Horka
Mar"ina Horka 107 C 6 *Rus.*
Mar'ina Gorka. C Belorussia
Maringá 63 E 4 S Brazil
Marion 40 C 4 Indiana, N USA
Marion 40 D 4 Ohio, N USA
Marion 45 G 3 Iowa, C USA
Marion, Lake 43 E 2 reservoir,
South Carolina, SE USA
Marion Reef 148 E 3 reef,
C Coral Sea
Mariscal Estigarribia 64 D 2
NW Paraguay
Marisule Estate 55 F 1 N Saint Lucia
Maritsa 104 D 3 *var.* Marica,
Gk. Évros, *Turk.* Meriç; *anc.*
Hebrus. River, SE Europe
Maritzburg *see* Pietermaritzburg
Mariupol' 109 G 4 *prev.* Zhdanov.
SE Ukraine
Marka 73 D 6 *var.* Merca. S Somalia
Markham, Mount 154 C 4
mountain, Antarctica
Markounda 76 C 4 *var.* Marcounda.
NW Central African Republic
Marktredwitz 95 C 5 E Germany
Marla 149 A 5 South Australia,
S Australia
Marmanda *see* Marmande
Marmande 91 B 5 *anc.* Marmanda.
SW France
Marmara Denizi 116 A 2
Eng. Sea of Marmara. Sea,
NE Mediterranean Sea
Marmara, Sea of *see* Marmara
Denizi
Marmaris 116 A 4 SW Turkey
Mârmorilik *see* Maarmorilik
Marne 90 D 3 river, N France
Marne 90 D 3 cultural region,
N France
Maro 76 C 4 S Chad

Maroantsetra 79 G 3
NE Madagascar
Maromme 90 C 3 N France
Maroni 59 H 3 *Dut.* Marowijne.
River, French Guiana/Surinam
Marotiri 145 H 5 *var.* Îlots de Bass.
Island group, SE French Polynesia
Maroua 76 B 3 N Cameroon
Marowijne 59 G 3 *var.* le Maroni
Fleuve. River, French
Guiana/Surinam
Marqādah 118 E 2 NE Syria
Marquesas Fracture Zone 153 E 3
fracture zone, E Pacific Ocean
Marquesas Islands *see*
Marquises, Îles
Marquesas Keys 43 E 5 island,
Florida, SE USA
Marquette 40 C 1 Michigan, N USA
Marquises, Îles 145 H 4 *Eng.*
Marquesas Islands. Island group,
N French Polynesia
Marrakech 70 C 2 *var.* Marakesh,
Eng. Marrakesh; *prev.* Morocco.
W Morocco
Marrakesh *see* Marrakech
Marrawah 149 B 8 Tasmania,
SE Australia
Marree 149 B 5 South Australia,
S Australia
Marsala 97 B 7 *anc.* Lilybaeum.
SW Italy
Marsberg 94 B 4 W Germany
Marseille 91 D 6 *Eng.* Marseilles;
anc. Massilia. SE France
Marshall 49 H 3 Texas, S USA
Marshall 45 F 2 Minnesota, N USA

Marshall Islands
144 D 1. Republic,
C Pacific Ocean

Official name: Republic of the
Marshall Islands **Date of formation:**
1986 **Capital:** Majuro **Population:**
48,000 **Total Area:** 181 sq km
(70 sq miles) **Languages:** English*,
Marshallese* **Religions:** Protestant
80%, Roman Catholic 15%, other 5%
Ethnic mix: Marshallese 90%, other
Pacific Islanders 10% **Government:**
Republic **Currency:** US $ = 100 cents

Marsh Harbour 54 C 1 W Bahamas
Marsh Island 42 A 3 island, S USA
Martaban 136 B 4 *var.* Moktama.
SE Burma
Martigues 91 D 6 SE France
Martin 99 C 5 *Ger.* Sankt Martin,
Hung. Turócszentmárton;
prev. Svätý Martin, Turčiansky.
NW Slovakia
Martinique 55 G 4 French overseas
department, E Caribbean Sea
Martinique Passage 55 G 4 *var.*
Dominica Channel, Martinique
Channel. Channel, Atlantic
Ocean/Caribbean Sea
Martinsville 41 E 5 Virginia,
NE USA
Marton 150 D 4 North Island,
C New Zealand
Martos 92 D 4 S Spain
Marungu 77 E 7 mountain range,
SE Congo (Zaire)
Mary 122 D 3 *prev.* Merv.
S Turkmenistan
Maryborough 149 E 5 Queensland,
E Australia
Maryland 41 F 5 *off.* State of
Maryland; *nicknames* America in
Miniature, Cockade State, Free
State, Old Line State. State, E USA
Maryville 42 D 1 Tennessee, S USA

Maryville 45 F 4 Missouri, C USA
Masai Steppe 73 C 8 grassland,
NW Tanzania
Masaka 73 B 6 SW Uganda
Masasi 73 C 8 SE Tanzania
Masaya 52 D 3 W Nicaragua
Mascarene Basin 141 B 5 undersea
basin, W Indian Ocean
Mascarene Islands 79 H 4 island
group, W Madagascar
Mascarene Plain 141 B 5 abyssal
plain, W Indian Ocean
Mascarene Plateau 140 B 4
undersea plateau,
W Indian Ocean
Maseru 78 D 4 country capital,
W Lesotho
Mas-ha 119 D 7 W West Bank
Mashhad 120 E 2 *var.* Meshed.
NE Iran
Maṣīrah, Jazīrat 121 E 5 *var.* Masíra.
Island, E Oman
Maṣīrah, Khalīj 121 E 5 *var.*
Gulf of Masira. Gulf, E Oman
Masindi 73 B 6 W Uganda
Masíra, Gulf of *see* Maṣīrah, Khalīj
Mason City 45 G 3 Iowa, C USA
Masqaṭ 121 E 5 *var.* Maskat,
Eng. Muscat. Country capital,
NE Oman
Massa 96 B 3 C Italy
Massachusetts 41 G 3
off. Commonwealth of
Massachusetts; *nicknames* Bay
State, Old Bay State, Old Colony
State. State, NE USA
Massawa 72 C 4 *Amh.* Mits'iwa.
E Eritrea
Massenya 76 B 3 SW Chad
Massif Central 91 C 5 plateau,
C France
Mastanli *see* Momchilgrad
Masterton 151 D 5 North Island,
C New Zealand
Masty 107 B 5 *Rus.* Mosty.
W Belorussia
Masuda 131 B 6 Honshū,
SW Japan
Masvingo 78 D 3 *prev.* Victoria, Fort
Victoria, Nyanda. SE Zimbabwe
Maṣyāf 118 B 3 *Fr.* Misiaf. W Syria
Matadi 77 B 7 W Congo (Zaire)
Matagalpa 52 D 3 C Nicaragua
Matagorda Bay 49 H 4 bay, Texas,
S Gulf of Mexico
Matale 132 D 3 S Sri Lanka
Matam 74 C 3 NE Senegal
Matamata 150 D 3 North Island,
N New Zealand
Matamoros 51 E 2 *var.* Izúcar de
Matamoros. S Mexico
Matamoros 50 D 3 NE Mexico
Matane 39 E 4 Québec, SE Canada
Matanzas 54 B 2 NW Cuba
Matara 132 D 4 S Sri Lanka
Mataró 93 G 2 *anc.* Illuro. E Spain
Mataura 151 B 7 South Island,
SW New Zealand
Mata Uta *see* Matä'utu
Matá'utu 145 E 4 *var.* Mata Uta.
Dependent territory capital,
S Wallis & Futuna
Matera 97 E 5 S Italy
Matías Romero 51 G 5 SE Mexico
Mato Grosso 63 E 3 *off.* Estado de
Mato Grosso; *prev.* Matto Grosso.
State, W Brazil
Mato Grosso do Sul 63 E 4
off. Estado de Mato Grosso do Sul.
State, S Brazil
Mato Grosso do Sul, Estado de *see*
Mato Grosso do Sul

Matosinhos 92 B 2
prev. Matozinhos. NW Portugal
Matozinhos *see* Matosinhos
Mătrăşeşti 108 C 4 E Romania
Matsue 131 B 6 *var.* Matsuye,
Matue. Honshū, SW Japan
Matsumoto 131 C 5 *var.* Matumoto.
Honshū, S Japan
Matsuyama 131 B 7 *var.* Matuyama.
Shikoku, SW Japan
Matthews Ridge 59 F 2 N Guyana
Matthew Town 54 D 2 S Bahamas
Matumoto *see* Matsumoto
Maturín 59 E 2 NE Venezuela
Matuyama *see* Matsuyama
Mau 135 E 3 *var.* Maunāth Bhanjan.
N India
Maui 47 B 8 island, Hawaii, W USA
Maun 78 C 3 C Botswana
Maunāth Bhanjan *see* Mau
Mauren 94 E 1 NE Liechtenstein

Mauritania
74 C 2 *Ar.* Múrítáníyah. Republic,
W Africa

Official name: Islamic Republic of
Mauritania **Date of formation:** 1960
Capital: Nouakchott **Population:**
2.2 million **Total area:** 1,025,520 sq km
(395,953 sq miles) **Language:**
French*, Hassaniyah Arabic, Wolof
Religions: Muslim 100%
Ethnic mix: Maure 80%, Wolof 7%,
Tukulor 5%, other 8%
Government: Multiparty republic
Currency: Ouguiya = 5 khoums

Mauritius
79 H 3 *Fr.* Maurice. Republic,
E Africa

Official name: Mauritius **Date of
formation:** 1968 **Capital:** Port Louis
Population: 1.1 million **Total area:**
1,860 sq km (718 sq miles)
Languages: English*, French Creole,
Hindi **Religions:** Hindu 52%, Roman
Catholic, 26%, Muslim 17%,
other 5% **Ethnic mix:** Creole 55%,
South Asian 40%, Chinese 3%,
other 2% **Government:** Multiparty
republic **Currency:** Rupee = 100 cents

Mauritius Ridge 141 B 5 undersea
ridge, W Indian Ocean
Mawson 154 D 2 research station,
Antarctica
Maya 115 G 3 river,
E Russian Federation
Mayaguana 54 D 2 island,
SE Bahamas
Mayaguana Passage 54 D 2
channel, N Caribbean Sea
Mayagüez 55 F 3 W Puerto Rico
Mayamey 120 D 2 N Iran
Maya Mountains 52 B 1
Sp. Montañas Mayas. Mountain
range, Belize/Guatemala
Maych'ew 72 D 4 *var.* Mai Chio,
It. Mai Ceu. N Ethiopia
Mayence *see* Mainz
Mayfield 151 C 6 South Island,
SW New Zealand
Maykop 111 B 7
SW Russian Federation
Maymyo 136 B 3 N Burma
Mayo *see* Maio
Mayor Pablo Lagerenza *see* Capitán
Pablo Lagerenza
Mayotte 79 F 2 French territorial
collectivity, E Africa
May Pen 54 B 5 C Jamaica
Mazabuka 78 D 2 S Zambia

Mazagan *see* El-Jadida
Mazar *see* Al Mazār al Janūbī
Mazār-e Sharīf 123 E 3
var. Mazar-i-Sharif, Mazār-i
Sharif. N Afghanistan
Mazatlán 50 C 3 C Mexico
Mazirbe 106 C 2 NW Latvia
Mazury 98 D 3 physical region,
NE Poland
Mazyr 107 C 7 *Rus.* Mozyr'.
SE Belorussia
Mbabane 78 D 4 country capital,
NW Swaziland
M'Baiki *see* Mbaïki
Mbaïki 77 C 5 *var.* M'Baiki.
SW Central African Republic
Mbala 78 D 1 *prev.* Abercorn.
NE Zambia
Mbale 73 C 6 E Uganda
Mbandaka 77 C 5 *prev.*
Coquilhatville. NW Congo (Zaire)
M'Banza Congo 78 B 1 *var.* Mbanza
Congo; *prev.* São Salvador do
Congo, São Salvador. NW Angola
Mbanza-Ngungu 77 B 6
W Congo (Zaire)
Mbarara 73 B 6 SW Uganda
Mbé 76 B 4 N Cameroon
Mbeya 73 C 8 SW Tanzania
Mbomou 77 C 5 *var.* Bomu,
M'Bomu, Mbomu. River,
Central African Republic/
Congo (Zaire)
Mbour 74 B 3 W Senegal
Mbuji-Mayi 77 D 7 *prev.*
Bakwanga. S Congo (Zaire)
McAdam 39 F 4 New Brunswick,
SE Canada
McAlester 49 G 2
Oklahoma, C USA
McAllen 49 G 5 Texas, S USA
McClintock Channel 37 F 2
channel, Arctic Ocean
McComb 42 B 3 Mississippi, S USA
McCook 45 E 4 Nebraska, C USA
Mcfarlane, Lake *see* Macfarlane,
Lake
McKean Island 145 E 3 island,
C Kiribati
McKinley, Mount 36 C 3
var. Denali. Mountain,
Alaska, NW USA
McKinley Park 36 D 3
Alaska, NW USA
McMinnville 46 B 3
Oregon, NW USA
McMurdo Base 154 C 4 research
station, Antarctica
McPherson 45 F 5 Kansas, C USA
McPherson *see* Fort McPherson
Mead, Lake 48 A 1 reservoir,
W USA
Meander River 37 E 4 Alberta,
W Canada
Mecca *see* Makkah
Mechelen 87 C 5 *Eng.* Mechlin,
Fr. Malines. C Belgium
Mecheria 70 D 2 *var.* Mechriyya.
NW Algeria
Mechriyya *see* Mecheria
Mecklenburg 94 C 3 cultural
region, N Germany
Mecklenburger Bucht 94 C 2 bay,
SW Baltic Sea
Mecsek 99 C 7 mountain range,
SW Hungary
Medan 138 B 3 Sumatera,
E Indonesia
Medellín 58 B 3 NW Colombia
Médenine 71 F 2 *var.* Madanīyīn.
SE Tunisia
Medeshamstede *see* Peterborough

Medford 46 B 4 Oregon, NW USA
Medgidia 108 D 5 SE Romania
Mediaş 108 B 4 *Ger.* Mediasch,
Hung. Medgyes. C Romania
Medicine Hat 37 F 5 Alberta,
SW Canada
Medina *see* Al Madīnah
Medinaceli 93 E 2 N Spain
Medina del Campo 92 C 2 N Spain
Mediolanum *see* Saintes
Mediterranean Sea 102 D 3
Fr. Mer Méditerranée. Sea,
E Atlantic Ocean
Méditerranée, Mer *see*
Mediterranean Sea
Médoc 91 B 5 cultural region,
SW France
Medvezh'yegorsk 110 B 3 *var.*
Medvežiegorsk, Medvezjegorsk.
NW Russian Federation
Meekatharra 147 B 5 Western
Australia, W Australia
Meemu Atoll *see* Mulaku Atoll
Meerssen 87 D 6 *var.* Mersen.
SE Netherlands
Meerut 134 D 2 N India
Mehrīz 120 D 3 C Iran
Mehtarlām 123 F 4 *var.* Mehtar
Lām, Meterlam, Methariam,
Metharlam. E Afghanistan
Meiktila 136 B 3 C Burma
Mejerda 71 E 2 *var.* Oued Medjerda,
Wādī Majardah. River,
Algeria/Tunisia
Mejillones 64 B 2 N Chile
Mek'elē 72 C 4 *var.* Makale.
N Ethiopia
Mékhé 74 B 3 NW Senegal
Mekong 124 D 3 *var.* Lan-ts'ang
Chiang, *Cam.* Mékôngk,
Chin. Lancang Jiang, *Lao.* Mènam
Khong, *Th.* Mae Nam Khong,
Tib. Dza Chu, *Vtn.* Sông Tiên
Giang. River, E Asia
Mekong, Mouths of the 137 E 7
delta, S Vietnam
Melaka 138 B 3 *var.* Malacca.
W Malaysia
Melanesia 144 D 3 island group,
SW Pacific Ocean
Melanesian Basin 152 C 3 undersea
basin, W Pacific Ocean
Melbourne 43 E 4 Florida, SE USA
Melbourne 149 C 7 state capital,
Victoria, SE Australia
Melchor, Isla 65 A 6 island,
S Chile
Melghir, Chott 71 E 2 *var.* Chott
Melrhir. Salt lake, E Algeria
Melilla 68 B 2 *anc.* Rusaddir,
Russadir. Spain, North Africa
Melilla 70 C 2 enclave, Spain
N Africa
Melita 37 F 5 Manitoba, S Canada
Melitene *see* Malatya
Melitopol' 109 G 4 SE Ukraine
Melle 87 B 5 NW Belgium
Mellerud 85 B 6 S Sweden
Mellizo Sur, Cerro 65 B 7
mountain, S Chile
Melo 64 E 4 NE Uruguay
Melodunum *see* Melun
Melun 90 C 3 *anc.* Melodunum.
N France
Melville, Cape 148 C 2 headland,
Queensland, NE Australia
Melville Fracture Zone 141 B 6
fracture zone, C Indian Ocean
Melville Island 37 F 2 island,
NW Canada
Melville Island 146 D 2 island,
N Australia

Melville, Lake 39 F 2 lake,
Newfoundland and Labrador,
E Canada
Melville Peninsula 37 G 3
peninsula, Northwest Territories,
NE Canada
Melville Sound *see* Viscount
Melville Sound
Memel *see* Klaipėda
Memmingen 95 B 6 S Germany
Memphis 42 C 1 Tennessee, S USA
Menaam *see* Menaldum
Menado *see* Manado
Ménaka 75 F 3 E Mali
Menaldum 86 D 1 *Fris.* Menaam.
N Netherlands
Mendaña Fracture Zone 153 F 4
fracture zone, E Pacific Ocean
Mende 91 C 6 *anc.* Mimatum.
S France
Mendeleyev Ridge 155 F 2
undersea ridge, Arctic Ocean
Mendocino Fracture Zone 152 D 2
fracture zone, NE Pacific Ocean
Mendoza 64 B 4 W Argentina
Menemen 116 A 3 W Turkey
Menengiyn Tal 127 F 2 plain,
E Mongolia
Menomonie 40 A 2
Wisconsin, N USA
Menongue 78 B 2 *var.* Vila Serpa
Pinto, *Port.* Serpa Pinto.
C Angola
Menorca 93 H 3 *Eng.* Minorca; *anc.*
Balearis Minor. Island, E Spain
Mentawai, Kepulauan 138 B 4
island group, W Indonesia
Meppel 86 D 2 NE Netherlands
Meran *see* Merano
Merano 96 C 1 *Ger.* Meran. N Italy
Merca *see* Marka
Mercedes 64 D 3 E Argentina
Mercedes 64 D 4 W Uruguay
Mercedes 64 C 4 NE Argentina
Meredith, Lake 49 E 1 reservoir,
Texas, S USA
Merefa 109 G 2 E Ukraine
Mergate *see* Margate
Mergui 137 B 6 SE Burma
Mergui Archipelago 137 B 6
island group, S Burma
Mérida 92 C 4 *anc.* Augusta
Emerita. W Spain
Mérida 51 H 3 SW Mexico
Mérida 58 C 2 W Venezuela
Mérida, Cordillera de 58 C 2
var. Sierra Nevada de Mérida.
Mountain range,
W Venezuela
Meridian 42 C 2
Mississippi, S USA
Mérignac 91 A 5 SW France
Merkinė 107 B 5 S Lithuania
Merkulovichi *see* Myerkulavichy
Merredin 147 B 6 Western
Australia, SW Australia
Mersen *see* Meerssen
Mersey 89 D 6 river,
NW England, UK
Mersin 116 C 4 S Turkey
Mērsrags 106 C 3 NW Latvia
Meru 73 C 6 C Kenya
Merv *see* Mary
Merzig 95 A 5 SW Germany
Mesa 48 B 2 Arizona, SW USA
Meseritz *see* Międzyrzecz
Meshed *see* Mashhad
Messalo, Rio 79 E 2 *var.* Mualo.
River, NE Mozambique
Messina 97 D 7 *var.* Messana,
Messene; *anc.* Zancle. SW Italy

Messina 78 D 3 NE South Africa
Messina, Strait of *see* Messina,
  Stretto di
Messina, Stretto di 97 D 7
  Eng. Strait of Messina. Strait,
  C Mediterranean Sea
Messíni 105 B 6 S Greece
Mestghanem *see* Mostaganem
Mestre 96 C 2 NE Italy
Meta 58 C 3 river,
  Colombia/Venezuela
Metairie 42 B 3 Louisiana USA
Metan 64 C 2 N Argentina
Metapán 52 B 2 NW El Salvador
Metković 100 B 4 SE Croatia
Métsovo 104 B 4 *prev.* Métsovon.
  C Greece
Métsovon *see* Métsovo
Metz 90 D 3 *anc.* Divodurum
  Mediomatricum, Mediomatrica,
  Metis. NE France
Meuse 86 D 4 *Dut.* Maas. River,
  W Europe
Mexcala, Río *see* Balsas, Río
Mexicali 50 A 1 NW Mexico
Mexicana, Altiplanicie 49 E 5
  Eng. Mexican Plateau, Plateau of
  Mexico. Plateau, N Mexico

Mexico
  50 C 3 *var.* Méjico, México,
  Sp. Estados Unidos Mexicanos.
  Federal republic,
  S North America

Official name: United Mexican States
Date of formation: 1836/1867
Capital: Mexico City **Population:**
95.5 million **Total area:** 1,958,200 sq
km (756,061 sq miles) **Languages:**
Spanish*, Mayan dialects **Religions:**
Roman Catholic 89%, Protestant 6%,
other 5% **Ethnic mix:** *mestizo* 60%,
Indian 30%, White 6%, other 9%
Government: Multiparty republic
Currency: Peso = 100 centavos

Mexico 45 G 4 Missouri, C USA
México 51 E 4 *var.* Ciudad de
  México, *Eng.* Mexico City.
  Country capital, C Mexico
Mexico Basin 35 C 6
  var. Sigsbee Deep. Undersea
  basin, N Gulf of Mexico
Mexico City *see* Mexico
México, Golfo de *see* Mexico, Gulf of
Mexico, Gulf of 66 A 4 *Sp.* Golfo de
  México. Gulf, W Atlantic Ocean
Mezen' 110 D 3 river,
  NW Russian Federation
Mezőtúr 99 D 7 E Hungary
Miahuatlán 51 F 5 *var.* Miahuatlán
  de Porfirio Díaz. SE Mexico
Miahuatlán de Porfirio Díaz *see*
  Miahuatlán
Miami 43 F 5 Florida, SE USA
Miami 49 G 1 Oklahoma, C USA
Miami Beach 43 F 5 Florida, SE USA
Miāneh 120 C 2 *var.* Miyáneh.
  NW Iran
Mianyang 129 B 5 C China
Miastko 98 C 2 *Ger.* Rummelsburg
  in Pommern. NW Poland
Michalovce 99 E 6 *Ger.*
  Grossmichel, *Hung.* Nagymihály.
  E Slovakia
Michigan 40 C 2 *off.* State of
  Michigan; *nicknames* Great Lakes
  State, Lake State, Wolverine State.
  State, N USA
Michigan, Lake 40 C 3 lake, N USA
Michurinsk 111 B 5
  W Russian Federation

Micoud 55 F 2 SE Saint Lucia
Micronesia 144 C 1 island group,
  W Pacific Ocean

Micronesia
  144 B 1 Federation,
  W Pacific Ocean

Official name: Federated States of
Micronesia **Date of formation:** 1986
Capital: Kolonia **Population:**
101,000 **Total Area:** 2,900 sq km
(1,120 sq miles) **Languages:**
English*, Trukese, Pohnpeian,
Mortlockese **Religions:** Catholic
50%, Protestant 48%, other 2%
Ethnic mix: Micronesian 99%, other
1% **Government:** Republic
Currency: US $ = 100 cents

Micronesia, Federated States of *see*
  Micronesia
Mid-Atlantic Ridge 67 C 5
  var. Mid-Atlantic Cordillera, Mid-
  Atlantic Rise, Mid-Atlantic Swell.
  Undersea ridge, C Atlantic Ocean
Middelburg 87 B 5 SW Netherlands
Middelharnis 86 B 4
  SW Netherlands
Middelkerke 87 A 5 W Belgium
Middle America Trench 153 F 3
  trench, E Pacific Ocean
Middle Andaman 133 G 2 island,
  SE India
Middle Atlas *see* Moyen Atlas
Middlesboro 40 C 5
  Kentucky, E USA
Middlesbrough 89 D 5
  N England, UK
Middletown 41 F 4
  New Jersey, NE USA
Middletown 41 F 3
  Connecticut, NE USA
Mid-Indian Basin 140 C 4 undersea
  basin, C Indian Ocean
Mid-Indian Ridge 141 C 5
  var. Central Indian Ridge.
  Undersea ridge, C Indian Ocean
Midland 38 D 5 Ontario, S Canada
Midland 49 E 3 Texas, S USA
Midland 40 C 3 Michigan, N USA
Mid-Pacific Mountains 152 C 2 *var.*
  Mid-Pacific Seamounts. Seamount
  range, NW Pacific Ocean
Mid-Pacific Seamounts *see*
  Mid-Pacific Mountains
Miechów 99 D 5 S Poland
Międzyrzec Podlaski 98 E 3 E Poland
Międzyrzecz 98 B 3 *Ger.* Meseritz.
  W Poland
Mielec 99 D 5 SE Poland
Miercurea-Ciuc 108 C 4 *Ger.*
  Szeklerburg, *Hung.* Csíkszereda.
  C Romania
Mieres 92 D 1 NW Spain
Mī'ēso 73 D 5 *var.* Meheso, Miesso.
  C Ethiopia
Miguel Asua 50 D 3 *var.* Miguel
  Auza. C Mexico
Miguel Auza *see* Miguel Asua
Mijdrecht 86 C 3 C Netherlands
Mikashevichy 107 C 7 *Pol.*
  Mikaszewicze, *Rus.* Mikashevichi.
  SW Belorussia
Mikhaylovka 111 B 6
  SW Russian Federation
Míkonos *see* Mýkonos
Mikre 104 C 2 C Bulgaria
Mikun' 110 D 4
  NW Russian Federation
Mikuni-sanmyaku 131 D 5
  mountain range, Honshū,
  N Japan

Mikura-jima 131 D 6 island,
  Izu-shotō, E Japan
Milagro 60 B 2 SW Ecuador
Milan *see* Milano
Milange 79 E 2 NE Mozambique
Milano 96 B 2 *Eng.* Milan,
  Ger. Mailand; *anc.* Mediolanum.
  N Italy
Milas 116 A 4 SW Turkey
Milashavichy 107 C 7
  Rus. Milashevichi. SE Belorussia
Milashevichi *see* Milashavichy
Mildura 149 B 6 Victoria,
  SE Australia
Mile *see* Mili Atoll
Miles 149 D 5 Queensland,
  E Australia
Miles City 44 C 2 Montana,
  NW USA
Milford *see* Milford Haven
Milford Haven 89 B 7 *prev.* Milford.
  SW Wales, UK
Milford Sound 151 A 7
  South Island, SW New Zealand
Milford Sound 151 A 7 sound,
  E Tasman Sea
Mili Atoll 144 D 2 *var.* Mile. Island,
  SE Marshall Islands
Mil'kovo 115 H 3
  E Russian Federation
Milk River 37 E 5 Alberta,
  SW Canada
Milk River 44 C 1 river, NW USA
Milk, Wadi el 72 B 4 *var.* Wadi al
  Malik. River, C Sudan
Milledgeville 43 E 2 Georgia,
  SE USA
Mille Lacs Lake 45 F 2 lake,
  Minnesota, N USA
Millerovo 111 B 6
  SW Russian Federation
Millet 55 F 1 C Saint Lucia
Millicent 149 B 7 South Australia,
  S Australia
Millwood Lake 42 A 2 reservoir,
  Arkansas, C USA
Milo 74 D 4 river, E Guinea
Mílos 105 C 6 Mílos, SE Greece
Mílos 105 C 7 island, Kykládes,
  SE Greece
Milparinka 149 C 5
  New South Wales, SE Australia
Milton 151 B 7 South Island,
  SW New Zealand
Milton Keynes 89 D 6
  SE England, UK
Milwaukee 40 B 3
  Wisconsin, N USA
Mimatum *see* Mende
Mīnā' Sa'ūd 120 C 4 *var.* Mīnā'
  Su'ūd. SE Kuwait
Minas Gerais 63 F 3 *off.* Estado de
  Minas Gerais. State, SE Brazil
Minas Gerais, Estado de *see*
  Minas Gerais
Minatitlán 51 F 4 E Mexico
Minbu 136 A 3 W Burma
Minch, The 88 B 2 *var.* North
  Minch. Strait, NE Atlantic Ocean
Mindanao 139 F 2 island,
  S Philippines
Mindanao Sea *see* Bohol Sea
Mindelheim 95 C 6 S Germany
Mindelo 74 A 2 *var.* Mindello;
  prev. Porto Grande. N Cape Verde
Minden 94 B 4 *anc.* Minthun.
  NW Germany
Mindoro 139 E 2 island,
  N Philippines
Mindoro Strait 139 E 2 strait,
  South China Sea/Sulu Sea
Mineral Wells 49 G 3 Texas, S USA

Mingäçevir 117 G 2
  Rus. Mingechaur, Mingechevir
  C Azerbaijan
Mingan 39 F 3 Québec, E Canada
Mingāora 134 C 1 *var.* Mingora,
  Mongora. N Pakistan
Mingenew 147 B 6 W Australia
Minho 92 B 2 *Sp.* Miño. River,
  Portugal/Spain
Minho *see* Miño
Minicoy Island 132 A 3 island,
  Lakshadweep, SW India
Minigwal, Lake 147 C 6 lake,
  C Australia
Minneapolis 45 F 2 Minnesota,
  N USA
Minnesota 45 F 2 *off.* State of
  Minnesota; *nicknames* Gopher
  State, New England of the West,
  North Star State. State, N USA
Miño 92 B 2 *var.* Mino, Minius, *Port.*
  Minho. River, Portugal/Spain
Minot 44 D 1 North Dakota, N USA
Minsk 107 C 6 country capital,
  C Belorussia
Minskaya Wzvyshsha 107 C 6
  mountain range, E Belorussia
Minthun *see* Minden
Minto, Lac 38 D 2 lake, Québec,
  C Canada
Miranda de Ebro 93 E 1 N Spain
Mirgorod *see* Myrhorod
Miri 138 D 3 Borneo, E Malaysia
Mirim Lagoon 63 E 5 *var.* Lake
  Mirim, *Port.* Lagoa Mirim,
  Sp. Laguna Merín. Lagoon,
  SW Atlantic Ocean
Mírina *see* Mýrina
Mirjāveh 120 E 4 SE Iran
Mirnyy 115 F 3
  C Russian Federation
Mirnyy 154 D 3 research station,
  Antarctica
Mirs Bay 128 B 1 bay,
  NE Hong Kong
Mirtóo Pelagos 105 C 6
  Eng. Mirtoan Sea; *anc.* Myrtoum
  Mare. Sea, SW Aegean Sea
Misiaf *see* Maşyāf
Miskitos, Cayos 53 E 2 island
  group, NE Nicaragua
Miskolc 99 D 6 NE Hungary
Misool, Pulau 139 G 4 island,
  E Indonesia
Mişrātah 71 F 2 *var.* Misurata.
  NW Libya
Mission 49 G 5 Texas, S USA
Mississippi 42 B 2 *off.* State of
  Mississippi; *nicknames* Bayou
  State, Magnolia State. State,
  SE USA
Mississippi Delta 35 C 6 delta,
  Mississippi, S USA
Mississippi River 35 C 6 river,
  C USA
Mississippi River Delta 42 C 4
  river delta, Louisiana, S USA
Missoula 44 A 1
  Montana, NW USA
Missouri 45 G 5 *off.* State of
  Missouri; *nicknames* Bullion State,
  Show Me State. State, C USA
Missouri City 49 H 4 Texas, S USA
Missouri River 45 F 4 river, N USA
Mistassini 38 D 3 lake, river,
  Québec, SE Canada
Mistelbach an der Zaya 95 E 6
  NE Austria
Misti, Volcán 61 E 4 mountain,
  S Peru
Misurata *see* Mişrātah
Mitau *see* Jelgava

Mitchell 148 C 2 river, NE Australia
Mitchell 149 D 5 Queensland, E Australia
Mitchell 45 E 3 South Dakota, N USA
Mi Tho *see* My Tho
Mito 131 D 5 Honshū, S Japan
Mitú 58 C 4 SE Colombia
Mitumba, Monts 77 E 7 *var.* Chaîne des Mitumba, Mitumba Range. Mountain range, E Congo (Zaire)
Miyake-jima 131 D 6 island, Sakishima-shotō, SW Japan
Miyako 130 D 4 Honshū, C Japan
Miyakonojō 131 B 8 *var.* Miyakonzyō. Kyūshū, SW Japan
Miyakonzyō *see* Miyakonojō
Miyāneh *see* Mīāneh
Miyazaki 131 B 8 Kyūshū, SW Japan
Mizija 104 C 1 NW Bulgaria
Mizil 108 C 5 SE Romania
Mizpé Ramon 119 A 7 S Israel
Mjøsa 85 B 5 *var.* Mjøsen. Lake, S Norway
Mjøsen *see* Mjøsa
Mladenovac 100 D 4 Yugoslavia
Mława 98 D 3 C Poland
Mljet 101 B 5 *It.* Meleda; *anc.* Melita. Island, S Croatia
Mmabatho 78 C 4 N South Africa
Moab 44 B 5 Utah, W USA
Moa Island 148 C 1 island, Queensland, NW Australia
Moanda 77 B 6 *var.* Mouanda SE Gabon
Moba 77 E 7 E Congo (Zaire)
Mobay *see* Montego Bay
Mobaye 77 C 5 S Central African Republic
Moberly 45 G 4 Missouri, C USA
Mobile 42 C 3 Alabama, S USA
Mobile Bay 42 C 3 bay, N Gulf of Mexico
Moçambique 79 F 2 NE Mozambique
Mochudi 78 C 4 SE Botswana
Mocímboa da Praia 79 F 2 *var.* Vila de Mocímboa da Praia. N Mozambique
Môco 78 B 2 *var.* Morro de Môco. Mountain, W Angola
Mocoa 58 A 4 SW Colombia
Môco, Morro de *see* Môco
Mocuba 79 E 3 NE Mozambique
Modena 96 B 3 *anc.* Mutina. N Italy
Modesto 47 B 6 California, W USA
Modica 97 C 8 *anc.* Motyca. SW Italy
Modohn *see* Madona
Modriča 100 C 3 N Bosnia & Herzegovina
Moe 149 C 7 Victoria, SE Australia
Möen *see* Møn
Moena *see* Muna, Pulau
Moerewa 150 D 2 North Island, N New Zealand
Moero, Lac *see* Mweru, Lake
Moeskroen *see* Mouscron
Mogadishu *see* Muqdisho
Mogador *see* Essaouira
Mogilëv *see* Mahilyow
Mogilev-Podol'skiy *see* Mohyliv-Podil's'kyy
Mogilno 98 C 3 C Poland
Moguer 92 C 4 S Spain
Mohammedia 70 C 2 *prev.* Fédala. NW Morocco
Mohave, Lake 47 D 7 lake, W USA

Mohawk Mountains 48 A 3 mountain range, Arizona, SW USA
Mohéli 79 F 2 island, S Comoros
Mohns Ridge 155 F 5 undersea ridge, Arctic Ocean
Moho 61 E 4 SW Peru
Mohoro 73 C 7 E Tanzania
Mohyliv-Podil's'kyy 108 C 3 *Rus.* Mogilev-Podol'skiy. C Ukraine
Moi 85 A 6 S Norway
Moincêr 126 B 5 SW China
Moíres 105 D 8 Kríti, SE Greece
Mõisaküla 106 D 3 *Ger.* Moisekūll. S Estonia
Moisekūll *see* Mõisaküla
Mo i Rana 84 C 3 C Norway
Moissac 91 B 6 S France
Mojácar 93 E 5 S Spain
Mojave Desert 47 D 7 plain, California, W USA
Mokrany *see* Makrany
Moktama *see* Martaban
Mol 87 C 5 *prev.* Moll. N Belgium

Moldavia 108 D 3 *var.* Moldova, *Rus.* Moldavskaya SSR; *prev.* Moldavian SSR. Republic, E Europe

Official name: Republic of Moldova **Date of formation:** 1991 **Capital:** Chişinău **Population:** 4.4 million **Languages:** Moldavian*, Ukrainian **Religions:** Romanian Orthodox 98%, Jewish 2%, other 1% **Ethnic mix:** Moldavian (Romanian) 65%, Ukrainian 14%, Russian 13%, other 8% **Government:** Multiparty republic **Currency:** Leu = 100 bani

Molde 85 A 5 S Norway
Moldotau, Khrebet *see* Moldo-Too, Khrebet
Moldo-Too, Khrebet 123 G 2 *prev.* Khrebet Moldotau. Mountain range, C Kyrgyzstan
Moldova *see* Moldavia
Moldova Nouă 108 A 4 *Ger.* Neumoldowa, *Hung.* Újmoldova. W Romania
Molfetta 97 E 5 SE Italy
Moline 40 B 3 Illinois, N USA
Moll *see* Mol
Mollendo 61 E 4 S Peru
Mölndal 85 B 7 S Sweden
Molochans'k 108 C 3 *Rus.* Molochansk. SE Ukraine
Molochansk *see* Molochans'k
Molodezhnaya 154 D 2 research station, Antarctica
Molokai 47 B 8 *Haw.* Moloka'i. Island, Hawaii, W USA
Moloka'i *see* Molokai
Molokai Fracture Zone 153 E 2 fracture zone, NE Pacific Ocean
Molopo 78 C 4 river, Botswana/South Africa
Mólos 105 B 5 C Greece
Molotov *see* Perm'
Moluccas *see* Moluccas
Molucca Sea *see* Maluku, Laut
Mombasa 73 D 7 SE Kenya
Momchilgrad 104 D 3 *prev.* Mastanli. S Bulgaria
Møn 85 B 8 *var.* Möen. Island, SE Denmark
Monaco 91 B 7 *var.* Monaco-Ville; *anc.* Monoecus. Country capital, C Monaco

Monaco 91 B 7 Monarchy, W Europe

Official name: Principality of Monaco **Date of formation:** 1861 **Capital:** Monaco **Population:** 28,000 **Total area:** 1.95 sq km (0.75 sq miles) **Languages:** French*, Italian **Religions:** Roman Catholic 95%, other 5% **Ethnic mix:** French 47%, Monégasque 17%, Italian 16%, other 20% **Government:** Constitutional monarchy **Currency:** French franc = 100 centimes

Monaco, Principality of *see* Monaco
Monahans 49 E 3 Texas, S USA
Mona, Isla 55 F 3 island, W Puerto Rico
Mona Passage 55 F 3 channel, N Caribbean Sea
Monastir 71 F 2 *var.* Al Munastīr. NE Tunisia
Monbetsu 130 D 2 *var.* Mombetsu, Monbetu. Hokkaidō, NE Japan
Moncalieri 96 A 2 NW Italy
Mončegorsk *see* Monchegorsk
Monchegorsk 110 C 2 *var.* Mončegorsk. NW Russian Federation
Monclova 50 D 2 NE Mexico
Moncton 39 F 4 New Brunswick, SE Canada
Mondovì 96 A 2 NW Italy
Mondsee 95 D 6 lake, N Austria
Monfalcone 96 D 2 NE Italy
Monforte 92 C 1 NW Spain
Mongo 76 C 3 C Chad

Mongolia 126 C 2 *Mong.* Mongol Uls. Republic, Mongolia

Official name: Mongolia **Date of formation:** 1924 **Capital:** Ulan Bator **Population:** 2.4 million **Total Area:** 1,565,000 sq km (604,247 sq miles) **Languages:** Khalkha Mongol*, Turkic, Russian, Chinese **Religions:** Predominantly Tibetan Buddhist, with a Muslim minority **Ethnic mix:** Khalkha Mongol 90%, Kazakh 4%, Chinese 2%, other 4% **Government:** Multiparty republic **Currency:** Tughrik = 100 möngös

Mongos, Chaîne des *see* Bongo, Massif des
Mongu 78 C 2 W Zambia
Monkey Bay 79 E 2 SE Malawi
Monkey River *see* Monkey River Town
Monkey River Town 52 C 2 *var.* Monkey River. SE Belize
Mono Lake 47 C 6 lake, California, W USA
Monóvar 93 F 4 E Spain
Monroe 42 B 2 Louisiana, S USA
Monroe 43 E 1 North Carolina, SE USA
Monrovia 74 C 5 country capital, W Liberia
Mons 87 B 6 *Dut.* Bergen. S Belgium
Monselice 96 C 2 N Italy
Montana 44 B 1 off. State of Montana; *nicknames* Mountain State, Treasure State. State, NW USA
Montana 104 C 2 *prev.* Ferdinand, Mikhaylovgrad. NW Bulgaria
Montañas Mayas *see* Maya Mountains
Montargis 90 C 4 C France
Montauban 91 B 6 S France
Montbéliard 90 D 4 E France

Montcalm, Lake *see* Dogai Coring
Mont Cenis, Col du 91 E 5 pass, E France
Mont-de-Marsan 91 A 6 SW France
Monteagudo 61 G 4 S Bolivia
Monte Alegre 63 E 2 N Brazil
Monte-Carlo 91 C 8 *var.* Monte Carlo. NE Monaco
Monte Carlo *see* Monte-Carlo
Monte Caseros 64 D 3 E Argentina
Monte Cristi 55 E 3 *var.* San Fernando de Monte Cristi. NW Dominican Republic
Montegiardino 96 E 2 SE San Marino
Montego Bay 54 A 4 *var.* Mobay. W Jamaica
Montélimar 91 C 6 *anc.* Acunum Acusio, Montilium Adhemari. E France
Montemorelos 51 E 3 NE Mexico
Montenegro 101 C 5 *Serb.* Crna Gora. Constituent republic of Yugoslavia, Yugoslavia. *See also* Yugoslavia
Monte Patria 64 B 3 N Chile
Monterey 47 B 6 California, W USA
Monterey *see* Monterrey
Monterey Bay 47 A 6 bay, E Pacific Ocean
Montería 58 B 2 NW Colombia
Montero 61 G 4 C Bolivia
Monterrey 51 E 3 *var.* Monterey. NE Mexico
Montes Claros 63 F 3 SE Brazil
Montevideo 64 D 4 country capital, S Uruguay
Montevideo 45 F 2 Minnesota, N USA
Montgenèvre, Col de 91 E 5 pass, France/Italy
Montgomery 42 D 2 state capital, Alabama, S USA
Montgomery *see* Sāhīwāl
Monthey 95 A 8 SW Switzerland
Montluçon 90 C 4 C France
Montmagny 39 E 4 Québec, SE Canada
Monto 148 D 4 Queensland, E Australia
Montoro 92 D 4 S Spain
Montpelier 41 G 2 state capital, Vermont, NE USA
Montpellier 91 C 6 S France
Montreal *see* Montréal
Montréal 39 E 4 *Eng.* Montreal. Québec, SE Canada
Montrose 88 D 3 E Scotland, UK
Montrose 44 C 5 Colorado, C USA
Montserrat 55 G 3 *var.* Emerald Isle. UK dependent territory, E Caribbean Sea
Monturaqui 64 B 2 NE Chile
Monywa 136 B 3 NW Burma
Monza 96 B 2 N Italy
Monze 78 D 2 S Zambia
Monzón 93 F 2 NE Spain
Moora 147 B 6 Western Australia, SW Australia
Moore 49 G 1 Oklahoma, C USA
Moore, Lake 147 B 6 lake, Western Australia, W Australia
Moorhead 45 F 2 North Dakota, N USA
Moosehead Lake 41 G 1 lake, Maine, NE USA
Moosonee 38 C 3 Ontario, SE Canada
Mopti 75 E 3 C Mali
Moqor 123 E 4 SE Afghanistan
Moquegua 61 E 4 SE Peru

Mora 85 C 5 C Sweden
Morales 52 C 2 E Guatemala
Morant Bay 54 B 5 E Jamaica
Moratalla 93 E 4 SE Spain
Moratuwa 132 D 4 SW Sri Lanka
Morava 99 C 5 *var.* March. River,
C Europe
Morava 101 E 5 *var.* March.
C Europe
Moravia 99 B 5 *Cz.* Morava,
Ger. Mähren. Cultural region,
E Czech Republic
Morawhanna 59 F 2 N Guyana
Moray Firth 88 C 3 inlet,
NW North Sea
Moreau River 44 D 2 river,
South Dakota, N USA
Moree 149 D 5 New South Wales,
SE Australia
Morelia 51 E 4 S Mexico
Morena, Sierra 92 C 4 mountain
range, SW Spain
Moreni 108 C 5 S Romania
Moreno 61 E 2 N Bolivia
Moreton Island 149 E 5 island,
Queensland, SE Australia
Morgan City 42 B 3
Louisiana, S USA
Morghāb, Daryā-ye 122 D 4 *var.*
Murgap Deryasy, *Rus.* Murgab.
River, Afghanistan/Turkmenistan
Morioka 130 D 4 Honshū, C Japan
Morlaix 90 A 3 NW France
Mornington Abyssal Plain 153 F 5
abyssal plain, SE Pacific Ocean
Mornington Island 148 B 2 island,
Queensland, NW Australia

Morocco
70 C 2 *Ar.* Al Mamlakah.
Monarchy, NW Africa
Official name: Kingdom of Morocco
Date of formation: 1956
Capital: Rabat **Population:** 27 million
Total area: 698,670 sq km
(269,757 sq miles) **Languages:**
Arabic*, Berber, French **Religions:**
Muslim 99%, other 1%
Ethnic mix: Arab and Berber 99%,
European 1% **Government:**
Constitutional monarchy
Currency: Dirham =100 centimes

Morococha 60 C 4 W Peru
Morogoro 73 C 7 E Tanzania
Moro Gulf 139 E 3 gulf,
N Celebes Sea
Morón 54 C 2 C Cuba
Morón 64 D 4 E Argentina
Mörön 126 D 2 N Mongolia
Morondava 79 F 3 W Madagascar
Moroni 79 F 2 country capital,
N Comoros
Morotai, Pulau 139 F 3 island,
E Indonesia
Morrinsville 150 D 3 North Island,
N New Zealand
Morris 45 F 2 Minnesota, N USA
Morristown 43 E 1
Tennessee, S USA
Mors 85 A 7 island, NW Denmark
Morvan 90 D 4 physical region,
C France
Morwell 149 C 7 Victoria,
SE Australia
Moscow 46 D 2 Idaho, NW USA
Moscow *see* Moskva
Mosel 95 A 5 *Fr.* Moselle. River,
W Europe
Moselle *see* Mosel
Mosgiel 151 B 7 South Island,
SW New Zealand

Moshi 73 C 7 NE Tanzania
Mosjøen 84 B 3 C Norway
Moskva 111 B 5 *Eng.* Moscow.
Country capital,
W Russian Federation
Moskva 123 E 3 *Rus.* Moskovskiy;
prev. Chubek. SW Tajikistan
Mosonmagyaróvár 99 C 6 *Ger.*
Wieselburg-Ungarisch-Altenburg;
prev. Moson and Magyaróvár,
Ger. Wieselburg and Ungarisch-
Altenburg. NW Hungary
Mosquito Coast *see* La Mosquitia
Mosquito Gulf *see* Mosquitos,
Golfo de los
Mosquitos, Golfo de los 53 F 5
Eng. Mosquito Gulf. Gulf,
S Caribbean Sea
Moss 85 B 6 S Norway
Mosselbaai 78 C 5 *var.* Mosselbai,
Eng. Mossel Bay.
SW South Africa
Mossendjo 77 B 6 SW Congo
Mossoró 63 G 2 NE Brazil
Most 98 A 4 *Ger.* Brüx.
NW Czech Republic
Mostaganem 70 D 2
var. Mestghanem. NW Algeria
Mostar 100 C 4
S Bosnia & Herzegovina
Mosty *see* Masty
Mosul *see* Al Mawşil
Mota del Cuervo 93 E 3 C Spain
Motril 92 D 5 S Spain
Motru 108 B 5 SW Romania
Motueka 151 C 5 South Island,
C New Zealand
Motul 51 H 3 *var.* Motul de Felipe
Carrillo Puerto. SE Mexico
Motul de Felipe Carrillo Puerto *see*
Motul
Motyca *see* Modica
Mouanda *see* Moanda
Mouila 77 A 6 C Gabon
Mould Bay 37 E 2
Prince Patrick Island, N Canada
Moulins 90 C 4 C France
Moulmein 136 B 4 *var.* Maulmain,
Mawlamyine. SE Burma
Moultrie, Lake 43 F 2 reservoir,
South Carolina, SE USA
Moundou 76 B 4 SW Chad
Moŭng Roessei 137 D 5
W Cambodia
Mount Cavenagh 147 E 5
C Australia
Mount Cook 151 B 6 South Island,
SW New Zealand
Mount Desert Island 41 H 2 island,
Maine, NE USA
Mount Friendship 55 G 2
SW Barbados
Mount Gambier 149 B 7
South Australia, S Australia
Mount Isa 148 B 3 Queensland,
C Australia
Mount Magnet 147 B 5
Western Australia, W Australia
Mount Pleasant 40 C 3
Michigan, N USA
Mount Pleasant 45 G 4 Iowa, C USA
Mount Vernon 40 B 5
Illinois, N USA
Mount Vernon 46 B 1
Washington, NW USA
Mouscron 87 A 6 *Dut.* Moeskroen.
W Belgium
Moussoro 76 C 3 W Chad
Moyen Atlas 70 C 2
Eng. Middle Atlas. Mountain
range, N Morocco
Moyobamba 60 C 2 NW Peru

Moyu 126 B 4 *var.* Karakax.
NW China
Moyynqum *see* Muyunkum, Peski

Mozambique
79 E 3 *off.* Republic of
Mozambique; *prev.* People's
Republic of Mozambique,
Portuguese East Africa. Republic,
S Africa
Official name: Republic of
Mozambique **Date of formation:**
1975 **Capital:** Maputo
Population: 15.3 million **Total area:**
801,590 sq km (309,493 sq miles)
Languages: Portuguese* **Religions:**
Traditional beliefs 60%, Christian
30%, Muslim 10% **Ethnic mix:**
Makua-Lomwe 47%, Tsonga 23%,
Malawi 12%, other 18%
Government: Multiparty republic
Currency: Metical = 100 centavos

Mozambique Basin *see* Natal Basin
Mozambique Channel 69 E 6
Fr. Canal de Mozambique,
Mal. Lakandranon' i Mozambika,
Port. Canal de Moçambique.
Channel, W Indian Ocean
Mozambique Plateau 67 E 6
var. Mozambique Rise. Undersea
plateau, SW Indian Ocean
Mozambique Rise *see*
Mozambique Plateau
Mozambique Scarp *see*
Mozambique Escarpment
Mozyr' *see* Mazyr
Mpama 77 B 6 river, C Congo
Mpika 78 D 2 NE Zambia
Mqinvartsveri *see* Kazbek
Mrągowo 98 D 2 *var.* Mragowo,
Ger. Sensburg. NE Poland
M'Sila 71 E 2 *var.* Msila. N Algeria
Msila *see* M'Sila
Mtwara 73 D 8 SE Tanzania
Mualo *see* Messalo, Rio
Muang Kalasin *see* Kalasin
Muang Khammouan 136 D 4
var. Thakhek. S Laos
Muang Khanthabuli *see*
Khanthabouli
Muang Không 137 D 5 S Laos
Muang Khôngxédôn 137 D 5
var. Khong Sedone. S Laos
Muang Khon Kaen *see* Khon Kaen
Muang Lampang *see* Lampang
Muang Lom Sak *see* Lom Sak
Muang Namo 136 C 3 N Laos
Muang Nan *see* Nan
Muang Pakxan 136 D 4
var. Pak Sane. C Laos
Muang Phalan 136 D 4 *var.* Muang
Phalane. S Laos
Muang Phalane *see* Muang Phalan
Muang Phayao *see* Phayao
Muang Sing 136 C 3 NW Laos
Muang Xaignabouri 136 C 4
var. Sayaboury. W Laos
Muar 138 B 3 *var.* Bandar Maharani.
W Malaysia
Muarabungo 138 B 4 Sumatera,
W Indonesia
Muchinga Escarpment 78 D 2
mountain range, NE Zambia
Mucojo 79 F 2 N Mozambique
Mudanjiang 128 E 3
var. Mu-tan-chiang. NE China
Mudon 137 B 5 SE Burma
Mufulira 78 D 2 C Zambia
Mughla *see* Muğla
Muğla 116 A 4 *var.* Mughla.
SW Turkey

Müḩ, Sabkhat al 118 C 3 lake,
C Syria
Muir Éireann *see* Irish Sea
Muisne 60 A 1 NW Ecuador
Mukacheve 108 B 3 *Cz.* Mukačevo,
Hung. Munkács, *Rus.* Mukachevo.
W Ukraine
Mukalla *see* Al Mukallā
Mula 93 E 4 SE Spain
Mulaku Atoll 132 B 4 *var.* Meemu
Atoll. Island, C Maldives
Muleshoe 49 E 2 Texas, S USA
Mulhacén 93 E 5 mountain, S Spain
Mülhausen *see* Mulhouse
Mulhouse 90 E 4 *Ger.* Mülhausen.
NE France
Müller-gerbergte *see*
Muller, Pegunungan
Muller, Pegunungan 138 D 4
Dut. Müller-gerbergte. Mountain
range, Borneo, Indonesia
Mullewa 147 B 6 W Australia
Müllheim 95 A 6 SW Germany
Mull, Isle of 88 B 4 island,
W Scotland, UK
Mulongo 77 D 7 SE Congo (Zaire)
Multān 134 C 2 E Pakistan
Mumbai *see* Bombay
Mumbwa 78 D 2 C Zambia
Muna, Pulau 139 E 5
prev. Moena. Island, C Indonesia
München 95 C 5 E Germany
München 95 C 6 *var.* Muenchen,
Eng. Munich, *It.* Monaco.
SE Germany
Muncie 40 C 4 Indiana, N USA
Mu Nggava *see* Rennell
Munich *see* München
Munster 89 A 6 cultural region,
S Ireland
Munster 94 A 4 NW Germany
Muong Xiang Ngeun 136 C 4
var. Xieng Ngeun. C Laos
Muonio 84 D 3 N Finland
Muonionjoki 84 D 3
var. Muoniojoki, *Swe.* Muoniöälv.
River, Finland/Sweden
Muqdisho 73 D 6 *Eng.* Mogadishu,
It. Mogadiscio. Country capital,
S Somalia
Mur 95 E 7 *SCr.* Mura. River,
C Europe
Mura *see* Mur
Muradiye 117 F 3 E Turkey
Murapara *see* Murupara
Murata 96 E 2 S San Marino
Murchison 147 B 5 river, Western
Australia, W Australia
Murcia 93 E 4 cultural region,
SE Spain
Murcia 93 F 4 SE Spain
Mureş 108 A 4 *var.* Maros, Mureşul,
Ger. Marosch, Mieresch. River,
Hungary/Romania
Murfreesboro 42 D 1
Tennessee, S USA
Murgab 122 D 3 *var.* Murghab,
Pash. Daryā-ye Morghāb,
Turkm. Murgap Deryasy. River,
Afghanistan/Turkmenistan
Murgab *see* Murghob
Murghob 123 G 3 *Rus.* Murgab.
SE Tajikistan
Murgon 149 D 5 Queensland,
E Australia
Müritz 94 C 3 *var.* Müritzee. Lake,
NE Germany
Müritzee *see* Müritz
Murmansk 110 C 2
NW Russian Federation
Murmashi 110 C 2 *var.* Murmaši.
NW Russian Federation

Murmaši *see* Murmashi
Murom 111 B 5 W Russian Federation
Muroran 130 D 3 Hokkaidō, NE Japan
Muros 92 B 1 NW Spain
Murray 149 C 7 river, SE Australia
Murray Bridge 149 B 7 South Australia, SE Australia
Murray Fracture Zone 153 E 2 fracture zone, NE Pacific Ocean
Murray, Lake 43 E 2 reservoir, South Carolina, SE USA
Murray Range *see* Murray Ridge
Murray Ridge 140 B 3 *var.* Murray Range. Undersea ridge, N Indian Ocean
Murrumbidgee 149 C 6 river, SE Australia
Murska Sobota 95 E 7 *Ger.* Olsnitz. NE Slovenia
Murupara 150 E 3 *var.* Murapara. North Island, NE New Zealand
Murwāra 135 E 4 N India
Murwillumbah 149 E 5 New South Wales, SE Australia
Mürzzuschlag 95 E 7 E Austria
Muş 117 F 3 *var.* Mush. E Turkey
Musala 104 C 3 mountain, W Bulgaria
Muscat *see* Masqaṭ
Muscatine 45 G 4 Iowa, C USA
Musgrave Ranges 147 D 5 mountain range, South Australia, S Australia
Mush *see* Muş
Muskegon 40 C 3 Michigan, N USA
Muskogean *see* Tallahassee
Muskogee 49 G 1 Oklahoma, C USA
Musoma 73 C 6 N Tanzania
Mussau Island 144 B 3 island, NE Papua New Guinea
Mustafa-Pasha *see* Svilengrad
Musters, Lago 65 B 6 lake, S Argentina
Mut 116 C 4 S Turkey
Mu-tan-chiang *see* Mudanjiang
Mutare 78 D 3 *var.* Mutari; *prev.* Umtali. E Zimbabwe
Mutina *see* Modena
Mutsu-wan 130 D 3 bay, NW Pacific Ocean
Muttonbird Islands 151 A 8 island group, South Island, SW New Zealand
Mu Us Shamo *see* Ordos Desert
Muy Muy 52 D 3 C Nicaragua
Muynak *see* Mŭynoq
Mŭynoq 122 C 1 *Rus.* Muynak. NW Uzbekistan
Mužlja 100 D 3 *Hung.* Felsőmuzslya; *prev.* Gornja Mužlja. NE Yugoslavia
Mvolo 73 B 5 Sudan
Mwanza 73 C 7 NW Tanzania
Mweka 77 C 6 C Congo (Zaire)
Mwene-Ditu 77 D 7 S Congo (Zaire)
Mweru, Lake 78 D 1 *var.* Lac Moero. Lake, Congo (Zaire)/Zambia
Myadzel 107 C 5 *Pol.* Miadzioł Nowy, *Rus.* Myadel'. N Belorussia
Myanaung 136 B 4 SW Burma
Myaungmya 136 A 4 SW Burma
Myerkulavichy 107 D 7 *Rus.* Merkulovichi. SE Belorussia
Myingyan 136 B 3 C Burma
Myitkyina 136 B 2 N Burma
Mykolayiv 109 E 4 *Rus.* Nikolayev. S Ukraine
Mýkonos 105 D 6 *var.* Míkonos. Island, Kykládes, SE Greece
Myrhorod 109 F 2 *Rus.* Mirgorod. NE Ukraine
Mýrina 104 D 4 *var.* Mírina. Límnos, SE Greece
Myrtle Beach 43 F 2 South Carolina, SE USA
Mýrtos 105 D 8 Kríti, SE Greece
Myślibórz 98 B 3 W Poland
Mysore 132 C 2 *var.* Maisur W India
My Tho 137 E 6 *var.* Mi Tho. S Vietnam
Mytilíni 105 D 5 *var.* Mitilíni; *anc.* Mytilene. Lésvos, E Greece
Mytishchi 111 B 5 W Russian Federation
Mzuzu 79 E 2 N Malawi

N

Naberezhnyye Chelny 111 D 5 *prev.* Brezhnev. W Russian Federation
Nablus 119 E 7 *var.* Nābulus, *Heb.* Shekhem; *anc.* Neapolis, *Bibl.* Shechem. N West Bank
Nacala 79 F 2 NE Mozambique
Nacogdoches 49 H 3 Texas, S USA
Nadi 145 E 4 *prev.* Nandi. Viti Levu, W Fiji
Nadvirna 108 B 3 *Pol.* Nadwóma, *Rus.* Nadvornaya. W Ukraine
Nadvoicy *see* Nadvoitsy
Nadvoitsy 110 B 3 *var.* Nadvoicy. NW Russian Federation
Nadym 114 D 3 N Russian Federation
Nadym 114 D 3 river, C Russian Federation
Náfpaktos 105 B 5 *var.* Návpaktos. C Greece
Náfplio 105 B 6 *prev.* Návplion. S Greece
Naga 139 E 1 *off.* Naga City; *prev.* Nueva Caceres. Luzon, N Philippines
Nagano 131 D 5 Honshū, S Japan
Nagaoka 131 D 5 Honshū, C Japan
Nagasaki 131 A 7 Kyūshū, SW Japan
Nagato 131 A 7 Honshū, SW Japan
Nāgercoil 132 C 3 SE India
Nagornyy Karabakh 117 G 3 *var.* Avtonomnaya Oblast Nagorno- Karabakhskaya, *Arm.* Lerrnayin Gharabakh, *Az.* Dağliq Quarabaĝ. Former autonomous region, SW Azerbaijan
Nagoya 131 C 6 Honshū, SW Japan
Nāgpur 134 D 4 C India
Nagqu 126 C 5 *Chin.* Na-Ch'ii; *prev.* Hei-ho. W China
Nagykálló 99 E 6 E Hungary
Nagykanizsa 99 B 7 *Ger.* Grosskanizsa. SW Hungary
Nagykőrös 99 D 7 C Hungary
Nagysurány *see* Šurany
Nagyszalonta *see* Salonta
Nagytapolcsány *see* Topoľčany
Nahal Elisha 119 E 7 E West Bank
Nahariya *see* Nahariyya
Nahariyya 119 A 5 *var.* Nahariya. N Israel
Nahuel Huapi, Lago 65 B 5 lake, W Argentina
Nain 39 F 2 Newfoundland and Labrador, NE Canada
Nā'īn 120 D 3 C Iran
Nairobi 73 C 6 country capital, S Kenya
Najaf *see* An Najaf
Najin 128 E 3 NE North Korea
Najrān 121 B 6 *var.* Abā as Su'ūd. S Saudi Arabia
Nakamura 131 B 7 Shikoku, SW Japan
Nakatsugawa 131 C 6 *var.* Nakatugawa. Honshū, SW Japan
Nakatugawa *see* Nakatsugawa
Nakhichevan' *see* Naxçıvan
Nakhodka 115 G 5 SE Russian Federation
Nakhon Pathom 137 C 5 *var.* Nagara Pathom, Nakorn Pathom. C Thailand
Nakhon Ratchasima 137 C 5 *var.* Khorat, Korat. E Thailand
Nakhon Sawan 137 C 5 *var.* Muang Nakhon Sawan, Nagara Svarga. W Thailand
Nakhon Si Thammarat 137 C 7 *var.* Nagara Sridharmaraj, Nakhon Sithamnaraj. S Thailand
Nakina 38 C 3 British Columbia, W Canada
Nakuru 73 C 6 W Kenya
Nalayh 127 E 2 C Mongolia
Nal'chik 111 B 8 SW Russian Federation
Nālūt 71 F 2 NW Libya
Namangan 123 F 2 E Uzbekistan
Nam Co 126 C 5 lake, W China
Nam Đinh 136 D 3 N Vietnam
Namen *see* Namur
Namib Desert 78 B 3 desert, W Namibia
Namibe 78 A 2 *Port.* Moçâmedes, Mossâmedes. SW Angola

Namibia
78 B 3 *Afr.* Suidwes-Afrika, *Eng.* South West Africa, *Ger.* Deutsch-Südwestafrika; *prev.* German Southwest Africa, South-West Africa. Republic, S Africa

Official name: Republic of Namibia **Date of formation:** 1990/1994 **Capital:** Windhoek **Population:** 1.6 million **Total area:** 824,290 sq km (318,260 sq miles) **Languages:** English*, Afrikaans, Ovambo **Religions:** Christian 90%, other 10% **Ethnic mix:** Ovambo 50%, Kavango 9%, Herero 7%, Damara 7%, other 27% **Government:** Multiparty republic **Currency:** Rand = 100 cents

---

Nam Ngum 136 D 4 river, C Laos
Namo *see* Namu Atoll
Nam Ou 136 C 3 river, N Laos
Nampa 46 D 3 Idaho, NW USA
Nampula 79 E 2 NE Mozambique
Namrole 139 F 4 E Indonesia
Namsos 84 B 4 C Norway
Namu 36 D 5 British Columbia, SW Canada
Namu 144 D 2 island, C Marshall Islands
Namur 87 C 6 *Dut.* Namen. SE Belgium
Nan 136 C 4 *var.* Muang Nan. N Thailand
Nanaimo 36 D 5 Vancouver Island, SW Canada
Nanchang 129 C 5 *var.* Nan-ch'ang, Nanch'ang-hsien. Province capital, SE China
Nancy 90 D 3 NE France
Nandaime 52 D 4 SW Nicaragua
Nānded 134 D 5 C India
Nandi *see* Nadi
Nandyāl 132 C 2 E India
Naniwa *see* Ōsaka
Nanjing 129 D 5 *var.* Nan-ching, Nanking; *prev.* Chian-ning, Chianning, Kiang-ning. Province capital, E China
Nanning 129 B 6 *var.* Nan-ning; *prev.* Yung-ning. Autonomous region capital, S China
Nanortalik 82 C 5 S Greenland
Nanping 129 D 6 *var.* Nan-p'ing; *prev.* Yenping. E China
Nansei-shotō 130 A 2 *var.* Ryukyu Islands. Island group, Japan
Nansei Syotō Trench *see* Ryukyu Trench
Nansen Basin 155 G 4 undersea basin, Arctic Ocean
Nansen Cordillera 155 G 3 seamount range, Arctic Ocean
Nansha Qundao *see* Spratly Islands
Nanterre 90 C 3 N France
Nantes 90 A 4 *Bret.* Naoned; *anc.* Condivincum, Namnetes. NW France
Nantucket Island 41 G 3 island, Massachusetts, NE USA
Nanumaga 145 E 3 *var.* Nanumanga. Island, NW Tuvalu
Nanumanga *see* Nanumaga
Nanumea 145 E 3 island, NW Tuvalu
Nanyang 129 C 5 *var.* Nan-yang. C China
Nan-yang *see* Nanyang
Napa 47 B 6 California, W USA
Napier 150 E 4 North Island, N New Zealand
Naples 43 E 5 Florida, SE USA
Naples *see* Napoli
Napo 60 C 1 river, Ecuador/Peru
Napoli 97 D 5 *Eng.* Naples, *Ger.* Neapel; *anc.* Neapolis. S Italy
Naracoorte 149 B 7 South Australia, S Australia
Naradhivas *see* Narathiwat
Narathiwat 137 C 7 *var.* Naradhivas. S Thailand
Narbo Martius *see* Narbonne
Narbonne 91 C 6 *anc.* Narbo Martius. S France
Narborough Island *see* Fernandina, Isla
Nares Abyssal Plain *see* Nares Plain
Nares Plain 35 E 6 *var.* Nares Abyssal Plain. Abyssal plain, NW Atlantic Ocean
Nares Strait 82 D 1 *Dan.* Nares Stræde. Strait, S Lincoln Sea
Nares Stræde *see* Nares Strait
Narew 98 E 3 river, E Poland
Narova *see* Narva
Narovlya *see* Narowlya
Narowlya 107 C 8 *Rus.* Narovlya. SE Belorussia
Närpes 85 D 5 *Fin.* Närpiö. W Finland
Närpiö *see* Närpes
Narrogin 147 B 7 SW Australia
Narsaq 82 C 4 *var.* Narssaq. SW Greenland
Narsaq Kujallea 82 C 5 *Dan.* Frederiksdal. S Greenland
Narssaq *see* Narsaq
Narva 106 E 2 NE Estonia
Narva 106 E 2 *prev.* Narova. River, Estonia/Russian Federation
Narva Bay 106 E 2 *Est.* Narva Laht, *Ger.* Narwa-Bucht. *Rus.* Narvskiy Zaliv. Bay, E Baltic Sea
Narva Reservoir 106 E 2 *Est.* Narva Veehoidla, *Rus.* Narvskoye Vodokhranilishche. Reservoir, Estonia/Russian Federation

Narvik 84 C 3 C Norway
Nar'yan-Mar 110 D 3 *var.* Narjan-Mar, Nar'jan-Mar; *prev.* Dzerzhinskiy, Beloshchel'ye. NW Russian Federation
Naryn 123 G 2 C Kyrgyzstan
Năsăud 108 B 3 *Ger.* Nussdorf, *Hung.* Naszód. N Romania
Nāshik 134 C 5 *prev.* Nāsik. W India
Nashua 41 G 3 New Hampshire, NE USA
Nashville 42 C 1 state capital, Tennessee, S USA
Näsijärvi 85 D 5 lake, SW Finland
Nāsik *see* Nāshik
Nasiriya *see* An Nāşirīyah
Nassau 54 C 1 country capital, C Bahamas
Nasser, Lake 68 D 3 lake, Egypt/Sudan
Nata 78 C 3 NE Botswana
Natal 63 G 2 state capital, E Brazil
Natal Basin 141 A 6 *var.* Mozambique Basin. Undersea basin, SW Indian Ocean
Natchitoches 42 A 3 Louisiana, S USA
National City 47 C 8 California, W USA
Natitingou 75 F 4 NW Benin
Natuna, Kepulauan 138 C 3 island group, W Indonesia
Naturaliste Plateau 141 E 6 undersea plateau, E Indian Ocean
Naujamiestis 106 C 4 C Lithuania
Nauru 144 D 2 Island, W Pacific Ocean

Nauru
144 D 3 *prev.* Pleasant Island. Republic, W Pacific Ocean

Official name: Republic of Nauru **Date of formation:** 1968 **Capital:** No offical Capital **Population:** 10,000 **Total Area:** 21.2 sq km (8.2 sq miles) **Languages:** Nauruan*, English **Religions:** Christian 95%, other 5% **Ethnic mix:** Nauruan 58%, other Pacific Islanders 26%, Chinese 8%, European 8% **Government:** Parliamentary democracy **Currency:** Australian $ = 100 cents

Nauta 60 C 2 N Peru
Navahrudak 107 C 6 *Pol.* Nowogródek, *Rus.* Novogrudok. W Belorussia
Navanagar *see* Jāmnagar
Navapolatsk 107 D 5 *Rus.* Novopolotsk. N Belorussia
Navarra 93 E 2 cultural region, N Spain
Navassa Island 54 D 3 US unincorporated territory, N Caribbean Sea
Navoi *see* Nawoiy
Navojoa 50 B 2 NW Mexico
Navolat 50 C 3 *var.* Navolato. C Mexico
Navolato *see* Navolat
Návpaktos *see* Náfpaktos
Návplion *see* Náfplio
Nawabashah *see* Nawābshāh
Nawābshāh 134 B 3 *var.* Nawabashah. S Pakistan
Nawoiy 123 E 2 *Rus.* Navoi. C Uzbekistan
Naxçıvan 117 G 3 *Rus.* Nakhichevan'. SW Azerbaijan
Naxos *see* Náxos
Náxos 105 D 6 *var.* Naxos. Náxos, SE Greece
Náxos 105 D 6 island, Kykládes, SE Greece
Nayoro 130 D 2 Hokkaidō, NE Japan
Nazca 60 D 4 S Peru
Nazca Ridge 57 A 5 undersea ridge, E Pacific Ocean
Naze 130 B 3 Nansei-shotō, S Japan
Nazerat 119 A 5 *Ar.* En Nazira, *Eng.* Nazareth. N Israel
Nazilli 116 A 4 SW Turkey
Nazrēt 73 C 5 *var.* Adama, Hadama. C Ethiopia
N'Dalatando 78 B 1 *var.* Salazar, *Port.* Vila Salazar. NW Angola
Ndélé 76 C 4 N Central African Republic
Ndendé 77 A 6 S Gabon
Ndindi 77 A 6 S Gabon
Ndjamena 76 B 3 *var.* N'Djamena, *prev.* Fort-Lamy. Country capital, W Chad
Ndjolé 77 A 5 C Gabon
Ndola 78 D 2 C Zambia
Neagh, Lough 89 B 5 lake, E Northern Ireland, UK
Néa Moudanía 104 C 4 *var.* Néa Moudhaniá. N Greece
Néa Moudhaniá *see* Néa Moudanía
Neápoli 104 B 4 *prev.* Neápolis. N Greece
Neápoli 105 C 7 SE Greece
Neápoli 105 D 8 Kríti, SE Greece
Neápolis *see* Neápoli
Néa Zíchni 104 C 3 *var.* Néa Zíkhni; *prev.* Néa Zíkhna. NE Greece
Nebaj 52 B 2 W Guatemala
Nebitdag 122 B 2 W Turkmenistan
Neblina, Pico da 62 D 1 mountain, NW Brazil
Nebraska 44 D 4 *off.* State of Nebraska; *nicknames* Blackwater State, Cornhusker State, Tree Planters State. State, C USA
Nebraska City 45 F 4 Nebraska, C USA
Neches River 49 H 3 river, Texas, S USA
Neckar 95 B 6 river, SW Germany
Necochea 65 D 5 E Argentina
Necocli 58 A 2 NW Colombia
Nederland 49 H 4 Texas, S USA
Nederweert 87 D 5 SE Netherlands
Neede 86 E 3 E Netherlands
Neerpelt 87 D 5 NE Belgium
Neftekamsk 111 D 5 W Russian Federation
Neftezavodsk *see* Seydi
Negēlē 73 D 5 *var.* Negelli, *It.* Neghelli. S Ethiopia
Negev *see* HaNegev
Negomane 79 E 2 *var.* Negomano. N Mozambique
Negomano *see* Negomane
Negombo 132 C 3 SW Sri Lanka
Negotin 100 E 4 E Yugoslavia
Negra, Punta 60 A 3 headland, NW Peru
Negreşti-Oaş 108 B 3 *Hung.* Avasfelsőfalu; *prev.* Negreşti. NE Romania
Negro, Río 65 C 5 river, Brazil/Uruguay
Negro, Río 62 D 1 river, N South America
Negros 139 E 2 island, Visayan Islands, C Philippines
Nehbandān 120 E 3 E Iran
Neijiang 129 B 5 C China
Nei Mongol Zizhiqu 127 F 3 *var.* Nei Mongol, *Eng.* Inner Mongolian Autonomous Region, Inner Mongolia; *prev.* Nei Monggol Zizhiqu. Autonomous region, N China
Neiva 58 B 3 S Colombia
Nellore 132 D 2 E India
Nelson 151 C 5 South Island, C New Zealand
Neman 106 B 4 *Bel.* Nyoman, *Ger.* Memel, *Lith.* Nemunas, *Pol.* Niemen. River, NE Europe
Neman 106 B 4 *Ger.* Ragnit. W Russian Federation
Neméa 105 B 6 S Greece
Nemetocenna *see* Arras
Nemours 90 C 4 N France
Nemuro 130 E 2 Hokkaidō, NE Japan
Neochóri 105 B 5 C Greece

Nepal
135 E 3 . Monarchy, S Asia

Official name: Kingdom of Nepal **Date of formation:** 1769 **Capital:** Kathmandu **Population:** 21.1 million **Total Area:** 140,800 sq km (54,363 sq miles) **Languages:** Nepali*, Maithilli **Religions:** Hindu 90%, Buddhist 5%, Muslim 3%, other 2% **Ethnic mix:** Nepalese 58%, Bihari 19%, Tamang 6%, other 17% **Government:** Constitutional monarchy **Currency:** Rupee = 100 paisa

Nepean 38 D 5 Ontario, SE Canada
Nereta 106 C 4 S Latvia
Neretava 100 C 4 river, Bosnia & Herzegovina/Croatia
Neringa 106 A 3 *Ger.* Nidden; *prev.* Nida. SW Lithuania
Neris 107 C 5 *Bel.* Viliya, *Pol.* Wilia; *prev. Pol.* Wilja. River, Belorussia/Lithuania
Nerva 92 C 4 S Spain
Neskaupstadhur 83 E 5 E Iceland
Ness, Loch 88 C 3 lake, N Scotland, UK
Néstos 104 C 3 *Bul.* Mesta, *Turk.* Kara Su. River, Bulgaria/Greece
Netanya 119 A 6 *var.* Natanya, Nathanya. C Israel

Netherlands
86 C 3 *var.* Holland, *Dut.* Koninkrijk der Nederlanden, Nederland. Monarchy, W Europe

Official name: Kingdom of the Netherlands **Date of formation:** 1815/1890 **Capitals:** Amsterdam, The Hague **Population:** 15.3 million **Total area:** 37,330 sq km (14,410 sq miles) **Languages:** Dutch*, Frisian **Religions:** Roman Catholic 36%, Protestant 27%, other 37% **Ethnic mix:** Dutch 96%, other 4% **Government:** Constitutional monarchy **Currency:** Guilder = 100 cents

Netherlands Antilles 55 F 5 *prev.* Dutch West Indies. Autonomous region of Netherlands, S Caribbean Sea
Nettilling Lake 82 A 2 lake, N Canada
Netze *see* Noteć
Neu Amerika *see* Pulawy
Neubrandenburg 94 D 3 NE Germany
Neuchâtel, Lac de 95 A 7 *Ger.* Neuenburger See. Lake, W Switzerland
Neuenburger See *see* Neuchâtel, Lac de
Neufchâteau 87 D 8 SE Belgium
Neukuhren *see* Pionerskiy
Neumünster 94 B 2 N Germany
Neunkirchen 95 A 5 SW Germany
Neunkirchen 95 E 6 *var.* Neunkirchen am Steinfeld E Austria
Neunkirchen am Steinfeld *see* Neunkirchen
Neuquén 65 B 5 SE Argentina
Neuruppin 94 C 3 NE Germany
Neu Sandec *see* Nowy Sącz
Neusiedler See 95 E 6 *Hung.* Fertő. Lake, Austria/Hungary
Neustadt an der Weinstrasse 95 B 5 *prev.* Neustadt an der Haardt; *hist.* Niewenstat, *anc.* Nova Civitas. SW Germany
Neustettin *see* Szczecinek
Neustrelitz 94 D 3 NE Germany
Neu-Ulm 95 B 6 S Germany
Neuwied 95 A 5 W Germany
Neuzen *see* Terneuzen
Nevada 47 C 5 *off.* State of Nevada; *nicknames* Battle Born State, Sagebrush State, Silver State. State, W USA
Nevada, Sierra 92 D 5 mountain range, S Spain
Nevers 90 C 4 *anc.* Noviodunum. C France
Nevinnomyssk 111 B 7 SW Russian Federation
Nevşehir 116 C 3 *var.* Nevshehr. C Turkey
Nevshehr *see* Nevşehir
Newala 73 D 8 SE Tanzania
New Albany 42 C 2 Mississippi, S USA
New Albany 40 C 5 Indiana, N USA
New Amsterdam 59 G 3 E Guyana
Newark 41 F 4 New Jersey, N USA
Newark 40 D 4 Ohio, NE USA
New Bedford 41 G 3 Massachusetts, NE USA
Newberg 46 B 3 Oregon, NW USA
New Bern 43 F 1 North Carolina, SE USA
New Braunfels 49 G 4 Texas, S USA
Newbridge 89 B 6 *Ir.* An Droichead Nua. C Ireland
New Britain 41 G 3 Connecticut, NE USA
New Britain 144 B 3 island, E Papua New Guinea
New Brunswick 39 F 4 *Fr.* Nouveau-Brunswick. Province, SE Canada
New Caledonia 144 C 4 *var.* Kanaky, *Fr.* Nouvelle-Calédonie. French overseas territory, S Pacific Ocean
New Caledonia 144 C 5 island, S New Caledonia
New Caledonia Basin 152 C 4 undersea basin, W Pacific Ocean
Newcastle 149 D 6 New South Wales, SE Australia
Newcastle upon Tyne 88 D 4 *var.* Newcastle; *hist.* Monkchester, *Lat.* Pons Aelii. N England, UK
New Delhi 134 D 3 country capital, N India
Newfoundland 39 G 3 *Fr.* Terre-Neuve. Island, Newfoundland and Labrador, SE Canada

Newfoundland & Labrador 39 F 2
 Fr. Terre Neuve. Province,
 E Canada
Newfoundland Basin 66 B 3
 undersea basin,
 NW Atlantic Ocean
New Georgia Islands 144 C 3
 island group, NW Solomon Islands
New Glasgow 39 F 4
 Nova Scotia, SE Canada
New Guinea 144 A 3 *Dut.*
 Nieuw Guinea, *Ind.* Irian. Island,
 Indonesia/Papua New Guinea
New Hampshire 41 F 2 *off.* State of
 New Hampshire; nickname
 Granite State. State, NE USA
New Haven 41 G 3
 Connecticut, NE USA
New Iberia 42 B 3 Louisiana, S USA
New Ireland 144 C 3 island,
 NE Papua New Guinea
New Jersey 41 F 4 *off.* State of New
 Jersey; nickname Garden State.
 State, E USA
Newman 146 B 4 Western
 Australia, W Australia
Newmarket 89 E 6 E England, UK
New Mexico 48 C 2 *off.* State of
 New Mexico; nicknames Land
 of Enchantment, Sunshine State.
 State, SW USA
New Orleans 42 B 3
 Louisiana, S USA
New Plymouth 150 D 4
 North Island, C New Zealand
Newport 89 D 7 S England, UK
Newport 89 D 7 SE Wales, UK
Newport 42 B 1 Arkansas, C USA
Newport 40 C 4 Kentucky, E USA
Newport 41 G 2 Maine, NE USA
Newport News 41 F 5
 Virginia, NE USA
New Providence 54 C 1 island,
 N Bahamas
Newquay 89 B 7 SW England, UK
Newry 89 B 5 *Ir.* An tÍur.
 SE Northern Ireland, UK
Newry 146 D 3 N Australia
New Sarum *see* Salisbury
New Siberian Islands *see*
 Novosibirskiye Ostrova
New Smyrna Beach 43 E 4
 Florida, SE USA
New South Wales 149 C 6 state,
 SE Australia
New Territories 128 A 1
 geopolitical region, N Hong Kong
Newton 45 F 5 Iowa, C USA
Newton 45 G 3 Kansas, C USA
Newtownabbey 89 B 5
 Ir. Baile na Mainistreach.
 E Northern Ireland, UK
New Ulm 45 F 3 Minnesota, N USA
New York 41 F 3 New York,
 NE USA
New York 41 E 3 state, NE USA

New Zealand
 150 A 4 Commonwealth republic,
 SW Pacific Ocean

Official name: The Dominion of
New Zealand **Date of formation:**
1947 **Capital:** Wellington
Population: 3.5 million **Total Area:**
268,680 sq km (103,730 sq miles)
Languages: English*, Maori
Religions: Protestant 62%, Roman
Catholic 18%, other 20% **Ethnic mix:**
European 88%, Maori 9%,
other 3% **Government:**
Constitutional monarchy
Currency: NZ $ = 100 cents

Neyveli 132 C 2 SE India
Nezhin *see* Nizhyn
Ngabang 138 C 4 Borneo,
 C Indonesia
Ngangzê Co 126 B 5 lake, W China
N'Gaoundéré *see* Ngaoundéré
Ngaoundéré 76 B 4 *var.*
 N'Gaoundéré. N Cameroon
N'Giva 78 B 3 *var.* Ondjiva,
 Port. Vila Pereira de Eça. S Angola
Ngo 77 B 6 SE Congo
Ngoko 77 B 5 river,
 Cameroon/Congo
Ngorongoro Crater 69 D 5 crater,
 N Tanzania
Ngourti 75 H 3 E Niger
N'Guigmi *see* Nguigmi
Nguigmi 75 H 3 *var.* N'Guigmi.
 SE Niger
Nguru 75 G 4 NE Nigeria
Nha Trang 137 E 6 SE Vietnam
Niagara Falls 38 D 5 Ontario,
 S Canada
Niagara Falls 41 E 3 New York,
 NE USA
Niagara Falls 35 D 5 waterfall,
 Canada/USA
Niamey 75 F 3 country capital,
 SW Niger
Niangay, Lac 75 E 3 lake, E Mali
Nia-Nia 77 D 5 NE Congo (Zaire)
Nias, Pulau 138 A 3 island,
 W Indonesia

Nicaragua
 52 D 3 Republic, C Central
 America

Official name: Republic of
Nicaragua **Date of formation:** 1838
Capital: Managua **Population:** 4.1
million **Total area:** 130,000 sq km
(50,193 sq miles) **Languages:**
Spanish*, English Creole, Miskito
Religions: Roman Catholic 95%,
other 5% **Ethnic mix:** *mestizo* 69%,
White 17%, Black 9%, Indian 5%
Government: Multiparty republic
Currency: Córdoba = 100 pence

Nicaragua, Lago de 52 D 4 *var.*
 Cocibolca, Gran Lago, *Eng.* Lake
 Nicaragua. Lake, S Nicaragua
Nicaragua, Lake *see* Nicaragua,
 Lago de
Nicaragua, Republic of *see*
 Nicaragua
Nice 91 D 6 *It.* Nizza; *anc.* Nicaea.
 SE France
Nicholas II Land *see*
 Severnaya Zemlya
Nicholls Town 54 C 1
 NW Bahamas
Nicholson Range 147 B 5 mountain
 range, W Australia
Nicobar Islands 133 F 3 island
 group, SE India
Nicoya 52 D 4 W Costa Rica
Nicoya, Golfo de 52 D 5 gulf,
 E Pacific Ocean
Nicoya, Península de 52 D 4
 peninsula, NW Costa Rica
Nidzica 98 D 3 *Ger.* Niedenburg.
 N Poland
Niedenburg *see* Nidzica
Niedere Tauern 95 D 7 mountain
 range, C Austria
Nieuw Amsterdam 59 G 3
 NE Surinam
Nieuw-Bergen 86 D 4
 SE Netherlands
Nieuwegein 86 C 4 C Netherlands
Nieuw Nickerie 59 G 3 NW Surinam

Niğde 116 C 4 C Turkey
Niger 75 F 4 river, W Africa

Niger
 75 F 3 Republic, W Africa

Official name: Republic of Niger
Date of formation: 1960 **Capital:**
Niamey **Population:** 8.5 million
(489,188 sq miles) **Languages:**
French*, Hausa, Djerma, Fulani
Religions: Muslim 85%, traditional
beliefs 14%, Christian 1% **Ethnic mix:**
Hausa 56%, Djerma 22%, Fulani 9%,
other 13% **Government:** Multiparty
republic **Currency:** CFA franc =
100 centimes

Nigeria
 75 F 4 Nigeria. Federal republic,
 W Africa

Official name: Federal Republic of
Nigeria **Date of formation:** 1960
Capital: Abuja **Population:** 115
million **Total area:** 923,770 sq km
(356,668 sq miles) **Languages:**
English*, Hausa, Yoruba, Ibo
Religions: Muslim 50%, Christian
40%, traditional beliefs 10%
Ethnic mix: Hausa 21%, Yoruba
20%, Ibo 17%, Fulani 9%, other 33%
Government: Military regime
Currency: Naira = 100 kobo

Niger, Mouths of the 75 G 5 delta,
 S Nigeria
Niigata 131 D 5 Honshū, C Japan
Niihama 131 B 7 Japan
Niihau 47 A 7 island,
 Hawaii, USA
Nii-jima 131 D 6 island,
 Izu-shotō, E Japan
Nijkerk 86 D 3 C Netherlands
Nijlen 87 C 5 N Belgium
Nijmegen 86 D 4 *Ger.* Nimwegen;
 anc. Noviomagus. SE Netherlands
Nikel' 110 C 2
 NW Russian Federation
Nīkiniki 139 E 5 Timor, S Indonesia
Nikólaos, Ágios *see* Ágios Nikólaos
Nikolayev *see* Mykolayiv
Nikopol' 109 F 3 SE Ukraine
Nikšić 101 C 5 SW Yugoslavia
Nikumaroro 145 F 3 *prev.* Gardner
 Island, Kemins Island. Island,
 C Kiribati
Nikunau 145 E 3 *var.* Nukunau;
 prev. Byron Island. Island,
 W Kiribati
Nile 72 B 1 *Ar.* Nahr an Nīl. River,
 NE Africa
Nile Delta 72 B 1 delta, N Egypt
Nimba, Mount 74 D 4 mountain,
 W Africa
Nîmes 91 C 6 *anc.* Nemausus,
 Nismes. S France
Nīnawē 117 F 5 N Iraq
Nine Degree Channel 132 B 3
 channel, N Indian Ocean
Ninetyeast Ridge 141 D 5 undersea
 ridge, E Indian Ocean
Ningbo 129 D 5 *var.* Ning-po, Yin-
 hsien; *prev.* Ninghsien. E China
Ningxia Huizu Zizhiqu 128 B 4
 autonomous region, N China
Nio *see* Íos
Niobrara River 45 E 3 river, C USA
Nioro 74 D 3 *var.* Nioro du Sahel.
 W Mali
Nioro du Sahel *see* Nioro
Niort 90 B 4 W France

Nipigon 38 B 4 Ontario, S Canada
Nipigon, Lake 38 B 3 lake, Ontario,
 S Canada
Niš 101 E 5 *Eng.* Nish, *Ger.* Nisch;
 anc. Naissus. SE Yugoslavia
Nişab 120 B 4 N Saudi Arabia
Nisibin *see* Nusaybin
Nisiros *see* Nísyros
Nisko 98 E 4 SE Poland
Nissan Islands *see* Green Islands
Nissum Bredning 85 A 7 inlet,
 E North Sea
Nísyros 105 E 7 *var.* Nisiros. Island,
 Dodekánisos, SE Greece
Nitra 99 C 6 *Ger.* Neutra,
 Hung. Nyitra. River, W Slovakia
Nitra 99 C 6 *Ger.* Neutra,
 Hung. Nyitra. W Slovakia
Niuatoputapu 145 E 4 *var.*
 Niuatobutabu; *prev.* Keppel
 Island. Island, N Tonga
Niue 145 F 4 self-governing
 territory, S Pacific Ocean
Niulakita 145 E 3 *var.* Nurakita.
 Island, S Tuvalu
Niutao 145 E 3 island, NW Tuvalu
Nivernais 90 C 4 cultural region,
 C France
Nizāmābād 134 D 5 C India
Nizhnegorskiy *see* Nyzhn'ohirs'kyy
Nizhnekamsk 111 C 5
 W Russian Federation
Nizhnevartovsk 114 D 3
 C Russian Federation
Nizhniy Novgorod 111 C 5 *prev.*
 Gor'kiy. W Russian Federation
Nizhniy Odes 110 D 4
 var. Nižni Odes, Nižnij Odes.
 NW Russian Federation
Nizhnyaya Tunguska 115 E 3
 Eng. Lower Tunguska. River,
 C Russian Federation
Nizhyn 109 E 1 *Rus.* Nezhin.
 NE Ukraine
Njombe 73 C 8 S Tanzania
Nkayi 77 B 6 *prev.* Jacob. S Congo
Nkhotakota 79 E 2 *var.* Kota Kota.
 C Malawi
N'Kongsamba *see* Nkongsamba
Nkongsamba 76 A 4
 var. N'Kongsamba. W Cameroon
Nobeoka 131 B 7 Kyūshū,
 SW Japan
Noboribetsu 130 D 3 *var.*
 Noboribetu. Hokkaidō, NE Japan
Noboribetu *see* Noboribetsu
Nogales 48 B 3 Arizona, SW USA
Nogales 50 B 1 NW Mexico
Nogal Valley *see* Dooxo Nugaaleed
Nokia 85 D 5 SW Finland
Nokou 76 B 3 SW Chad
Nola 77 B 5
 SW Central African Republic
Nolinsk 111 D 5
 NW Russian Federation
Nong Chang 137 C 5 W Thailand
Nong Khai 136 D 4 *var.* Mi Chai,
 Nongkaya. NE Thailand
Nonouti 145 E 2 *prev.* Sydenham
 Island. Island, W Kiribati
Noord-Beveland 86 B 4 *var.* North
 Beveland. Island, SW Netherlands
Noordoewer 78 B 4 S Namibia
Noordwijk aan Zee 86 C 3
 W Netherlands
Nora 85 C 6 C Sweden
Norak 123 E 3 *Rus.* Nurek.
 W Tajikistan
Nord 83 F 1 N Greenland
Nordaustlandet 83 G 1 island,
 NE Svalbard

Norden 94 A 3 NW Germany
Norderstedt 94 B 3 N Germany
Nordfriesische Inseln 94 B 2
var. North Frisian Islands.
Island group, N Germany
Nordhausen 94 C 4 C Germany
Nordhorn 94 A 3 NW Germany
Nordkapp 84 D 1 *Eng.* North Cape.
Headland, N Norway
Nord-Ouest, Territoires du *see*
Northwest Territories
Norfolk 41 F 5 Virginia, NE USA
Norfolk 45 F 3 Nebraska, C USA
Norfolk Ridge 142 D 4 undersea
ridge, W Pacific Ocean
Noril'sk 114 D 3
N Russian Federation
Normal 40 B 4 Illinois, N USA
Norman 49 G 2 Oklahoma, C USA
Normandes, Iles *see*
Channel Islands
Normandie 90 B 3 *Eng.* Normandy.
Cultural region, N France
Normandy *see* Normandie
Normanton 148 C 3 Queensland,
NE Australia
Norquay 37 F 5 Saskatchewan,
S Canada
Norrköping 85 C 6 S Sweden
Norrtälje 85 C 6 S Sweden
Norseman 147 C 6 Western
Australia, SW Australia
North Albanian Alps 101 D 5
Alb. Bjeshkët e Namuna,
SCr. Prokletije. Mountain range,
Albania/Yugoslavia
Northallerton 89 D 5 N England, UK
Northam 147 B 6 Western Australia,
SW Australia
North America 66 A 3 continent
North American Basin 66 B 3
undersea basin, W Atlantic Ocean
Northampton 89 D 6 C England, UK
Northampton 147 A 6 W Australia
North Andaman 133 F 2 island,
E India
North Australian Basin 152 A 3
Fr. Bassin Nord de l' Australie.
Undersea basin,
E Indian Ocean
North Bay 38 D 4 Ontario, S Canada
North Beveland *see* Noord-Beveland
North Cape 150 C 1 headland,
North Island, N New Zealand
North Cape *see* Nordkapp
North Carolina 43 E 1 *off.* State of
North Carolina; *nicknames*
Old North State, Tar Heel State,
Turpentine State. State, SE USA
North Charleston 43 F 2
South Carolina, SE USA
North Dakota 45 E 1 *off.* State of
North Dakota; *nicknames*
Flickertail State, Peace Garden
State, Sioux State. State, N USA
North Devon Island *see*
Devon Island
Northeim 94 B 4 C Germany
Northern Cook Islands 145 G 4
island group, N Cook Islands
Northern Dvina *see*
Severnaya Dvina
Northern Ireland 88 B 4
var. the Six Counties.
Political division, UK
Northern Mariana Islands 144 C 1
US commonwealth territory,
W Pacific Ocean
Northern Territory 148 A 3
territory, N Australia
Northfield 45 G 2
Minnesota, N USA

North Fiji Basin 152 C 3 undersea
basin, SW Pacific Ocean
North Frisian Islands *see*
Nordfriesische Inseln
North German Plain *see*
Norddeutsches Tiefland
North Huvadhu Atoll 132 B 5
var. Gaafu Alifu Atoll. Island,
S Maldives
North Island 150 B 2 island,
North Island, N New Zealand

North Korea
128 E 3 *Kor.* Chosŏn-minjujuŭi-
inmin-kanghwaguk. Republic,
E Asia

Official name: Democratic People's
Republic of Korea **Date of**
formation: 1948 **Capital:** Pyongyang
Population: 23.1 million **Total Area:**
120,540 sq km (46,540 sq miles)
Languages: Korean*, Chinese
Religions: Traditional beliefs 16%,
Ch'ondogyo 14%, Buddhist 2%,
non-religious 68% **Ethnic mix:**
Korean 99%, other 1% **Government:**
Single-party republic
Currency: Won = 100 chon

North Las Vegas 47 D 7
Nevada, W USA
North Little Rock 42 B 1
Arkansas, C USA
North Minch *see* Minch, The
North Mole 93 H 4 harbour wall,
N Gibraltar
North Platte 45 E 4
Nebraska, C USA
North Platte River 44 D 4
river, N USA
North Pole 155 F 3 pole,
Arctic Ocean
North Saskatchewan 37 F 5 river,
S Canada
North Scotia Ridge *see*
South Georgia Ridge
North Sea 66 D 2 *var.* Mare
Germanicum, *Dan.* Nordsøen,
Dut. Noordzee, *Fr.* Mer du Nord,
Ger. Nordsee, *Nor.* Nordsjøen;
prev. German Ocean. Sea,
NE Atlantic Ocean
North Siberian Plain 112 D 2 plain,
N Russian Federation
North Taranaki Bight 150 D 3
bight, E Tasman Sea
North Uist 88 B 3 island,
NW Scotland, UK
Northwest Atlantic Mid-Ocean
Canyon 66 B 2 trough,
NW Atlantic Ocean
North West Highlands 88 C 3
mountain range,
NW Scotland, UK
Northwest Pacific Basin 152 C 2
undersea basin,
NW Pacific Ocean
Northwest Providence 54 C 1
channel, N Caribbean Sea
Northwest Territories 37 E 3
Fr. Territoires du Nord-Ouest.
Territory, NW Canada
Northwind Plain 155 F 2 abyssal
plain, Arctic Ocean
Norton Sound 36 C 2 inlet,
N Bering Sea

Norway
85 A 5 *Nor.* Norge. Monarchy,
N Europe

Official name: Kingdom of Norway
Date of formation: 1905/1930
Capital: Oslo **Population:** 4.3

million **Total area:** 323,900 sq km
(125,060 sq miles) **Languages:**
Norwegian (*Bokmal* and *Nynorsk*)*,
Lappish, Finnish **Religions:**
Evangelical Lutheran 88%,
other Christian 12%
Ethnic mix: Norwegian 95%, Lapp
1%,other 4% **Government:**
Constitutional monarchy
Currency: Krone = 100 øre

Norwegian Basin 66 D 2 undersea
basin, NE Atlantic Ocean
Norwegian Sea 66 D 2 *var.* Norske
Havet, Norskehavet. Sea,
NE Atlantic Ocean
Norwich 89 E 6 E England, UK
Noshiro 130 D 4 *var.* Nosiro; *prev.*
Noshirominato. Honshū, C Japan
Nosivka 109 E 1 *Rus.* Nosovka.
NE Ukraine
Nosop 78 C 4 *var.* Nossob, Nossop.
River, Botswana/Namibia
Nosovka *see* Nosivka
Noşratābād 120 E 3 E Iran
Notabile *see* Mdina
Noteć 98 C 3 *Ger.* Netze. River,
NW Poland
Nottingham 89 D 6 C England, UK
Nouâdhibou 74 B 2 *prev.* Port-
Étienne. W Mauritania
Nouakchott 74 B 2 country capital,
SW Mauritania
Nouméa 144 D 5 dependent
territory capital, S New Caledonia
Nouveau-Brunswick *see*
New Brunswick
Nouvelle Écosse *see* Nova Scotia
Nova Freixo *see* Cuamba
Nova Gorica 95 D 8 W Slovenia
Nova Gradiška 100 C 3
Ger. Neugradisk, *Hung.*
Újgradiska. NE Croatia
Nova Iguaçu 63 F 4 SE Brazil
Nova Kakhovka 109 F 4 *Rus.*
Novaya Kakhovka.
SE Ukraine
Nova Lisboa *see* Huambo
Novara 96 A 2 *anc.* Novaria.
NW Italy
Novaria *see* Novara
Nova Scotia 39 F 4 *Fr.* Nouvelle
Écosse. Province, SE Canada
Nova Scotia 35 E 5 physical region,
E Canada
Novaya Kakhovka *see*
Nova Kakhovka
Novaya Sibir', Ostrov 115 F 1
island, Novosibirskiye Ostrova,
N Russian Federation
Novaya Zemlya 110 D 1 island
group, N Russian Federation
Novgorod 110 B 4
W Russian Federation
Novi Iskăr *see* Novi Iskŭr
Novi Iskŭr 104 C 2 *var.* Novi Iskăr.
W Bulgaria
Noviodunum *see* Nevers
Noviomagus *see* Lisieux
Novi Pazar 101 D 5 *Turk.* Yenipazar.
C Yugoslavia
Novi Sad 100 D 3 *Ger.* Neusatz,
Hung. Újvidék. N Yugoslavia
Novoaleksejevka *see*
Novoaleksejevka
Novoazovs'k 109 H 4
Rus. Novoazovsk. E Ukraine
Novoazovsk *see* Novoazovs'k
Novocherkassk 111 B 6
SW Russian Federation
Novodvinsk 110 C 3
NW Russian Federation

Novograd-Volynskiy *see*
Novohrad-Volyns'kyy
Novohrad-Volyns'kyy 108 D 2 *Rus.*
Novograd-Volynskiy. N Ukraine
Novokazalinsk 114 B 4 *Kaz.*
Zhangaqazaly. SW Kazakhstan
Novokuznetsk 114 D 4 *prev.*
Stalinsk. C Russian Federation
Novolazarevskaya 154 C 2 research
station, Antarctica
Novo Mesto 95 E 8 *Ger.*
Rudolfswert; *prev. Ger.* Neustadtl.
SE Slovenia
Novomoskovsk 111 B 5
W Russian Federation
Novomoskovs'k 109 F 3
Rus. Novomoskovsk. C Ukraine
Novomoskovsk *see* Novomoskovs'k
Novopolotsk *see* Navapolatsk
Novoradomsk *see* Radomsko
Novorossiysk 111 A 7
SW Russian Federation
Novoshakhtinsk 111 B 7
SW Russian Federation
Novosibirsk 114 D 4
C Russian Federation
Novosibirskiye Ostrova 115 F 1
Eng. New Siberian Islands. Island
group, N Russian Federation
Novosokol'niki 110 A 4
W Russian Federation
Novotroitsk 111 D 6
W Russian Federation
Novotroitskoye *see* Novotroyits'ke
Novotroyits'ke 109 F 4
Rus. Novotroitskoye. S Ukraine
Novovolyns'k 108 C 1
Rus. Novovolynsk. NW Ukraine
Novovolynsk *see* Novovolyns'k
Novy Dvor 107 B 6
Rus. Novyy Dvor. W Belorussia
Novyy Bug *see* Novyy Buh
Novyy Buh 109 E 3
Rus. Novyy Bug. S Ukraine
Novyy Dvor *see* Novy Dvor
Novyy Uzen' 114 A 4
Kaz. Zhangaözen. W Kazakhstan
Nowogard 98 B 3 *var.* Nowógard,
Ger. Naugard. NW Poland
Nowy Dwór Mazowiecki 98 D 3
C Poland
Nowy Sącz 99 D 5 *Ger.* Neu Sandec.
S Poland
Nowy Tomyśl 98 B 3
var. Nowy Tomysl. W Poland
Nowy Tomysl *see* Nowy Tomyśl
Noyon 90 C 3 N France
Nsanje 79 E 3 S Malawi
Nsawam 75 E 5 SE Ghana
Ntomba, Lac 77 C 6 *var.* Lac Tumba.
Lake, NW Congo (Zaire)
Nubian Desert 72 C 3 desert,
NE Sudan
Nu'eima 119 E 7 E West Bank
Nueva Gerona 54 B 2 S Cuba
Nueva Rosita 50 D 2 NE Mexico
Nuevitas 54 C 2 E Cuba
Nuevo, Bajo 53 F 1 reef,
NW Colombia
Nuevo Casas Grandes 50 C 1
N Mexico
Nuevo, Golfo 65 C 6 gulf,
SW Atlantic Ocean
Nuevo Laredo 51 E 2 NE Mexico
Nŭgătšiaq *see* Nuugaatsiaq
Nui 145 E 3 island, W Tuvalu
Nuku' alofa 145 E 5 country
capital, Tongatapu, S Tonga
Nukufetau 145 E 3 island,
C Tuvalu
Nukulaelae 145 E 3 *var.* Nukulailai.
Island, E Tuvalu

Nukulailai *see* Nukulaelae Atoll
Nukunonu Atoll 145 F 3 island,
  C Tokelau
Nukus 122 C 2 W Uzbekistan
Nullarbor 147 E 6 South Australia,
  S Australia
Nullarbor Plain 147 D 6 plateau,
  S Australia
Nuneaton 89 D 6 C England, UK
Nunivak Island 36 B 2 island,
  Alaska, NW USA
Nunspeet 86 D 3 E Netherlands
Nuoro 97 A 5 W Italy
Nuquí 58 A 3 W Colombia
Nurakita *see* Niulakita
Nurata *see* Nurota
Nurek *see* Norak
Nuremberg *see* Nürnberg
Nurlat 111 C 6
  W Russian Federation
Nurmes 84 E 4 E Finland
Nürnberg 95 C 5 *Eng.* Nuremberg.
  S Germany
Nurota 123 E 2 *Rus.* Nurata.
  C Uzbekistan
Nusa Tenggara 139 E 5 *Eng.* Lesser
  Sunda Islands. Island group,
  C Indonesia
Nusaybin 117 F 4 *var.* Nisibin.
  SE Turkey
Nuşayrīyah, Jabal an 118 B 3
  mountain range, W Syria
Nuugaatsiaq 82 C 3 *var.* Nûgâtsiaq.
  W Greenland
Nuuk 82 B 4 *var.* Nûk, *Dan.*
  Godthåb, Godthaab. Dependent
  territory capital, SW Greenland
Nuussuaq 82 C 2 *var.* Nûgssuaq,
  Dan. Kraulshavn. W Greenland
Nyainqêntanglha Shan 126 C 5
  mountain range, W China
Nyala 72 A 4 W Sudan
Nyamapanda 78 D 3 NE Zimbabwe
Nyamlell 73 B 5 SW Sudan
Nyamtumbo 73 C 8 S Tanzania
Nyandoma 110 C 4 *var.*
  Njandoma, N'andoma.
  NW Russian Federation
Nyantakara 73 B 7 NW Tanzania
Nyasa, Lake 79 E 2 *var.* Lake
  Malawi, *Port.* Lago Niassa;
  prev. Lago Nyassa. Lake, S Africa
Nyasvizh 107 C 6 *Pol.* Nieśwież,
  Rus. Nesvizh. C Belorussia
Nyaunglebin 136 B 4 S Burma
Nyeboe Land 83 E 1 physical
  region, NW Greenland
Nyeri 73 C 6 C Kenya
Nyima 126 C 5 W China
Nyíregyháza 99 E 6 NE Hungary
Nykøbing 85 B 8 SE Denmark
Nyköping 85 C 6 S Sweden
Nylstroom 78 D 4 NE South Africa
Nyngan 149 C 6 New South Wales,
  SE Australia
Nyurba 115 F 3 E Russian Federation
Nyzhn'ohirs'kyy 109 F 5
  Rus. Nizhnegorskiy. S Ukraine
Nzega 73 C 7 NW Tanzania
Nzérékoré 74 C 5 SE Guinea

O

Oahu 47 A 8 *Haw.* O'ahu. Island,
  Hawaii, W USA
O'ahu *see* Oahu
Oak Harbor 46 B 1
  Washington, NW USA
Oakland 47 B 6 California, W USA
Oamaru 151 B 7 South Island,
  SW New Zealand

Oaxaca 51 F 5 *var.* Oaxaca de
  Juárez; *prev.* Antequera.
  SE Mexico
Ob' 114 C 3 river,
  C Russian Federation
Obal' 107 D 5 *Rus.* Obol'.
  N Belorussia
Oban 88 B 4 W Scotland, UK
Oban *see* Halfmoon Bay
Obando *see* Puerto Inírida
Oban Hills 75 G 5 hill range,
  Cameroon/Nigeria
Obdorsk *see* Salekhard
Obeliai 106 C 4 NE Lithuania
Oberhollabrunn *see* Tulln
Ob, Gulf of *see* Obskaya Guba
Obidovichi *see* Abidavichy
Obihiro 130 D 2 Hokkaidō,
  NE Japan
Obo 76 D 4
  E Central African Republic
Obock 72 D 4 E Djibouti
Obol' *see* Obal'
Oborniki 98 B 3 W Poland
Obrovo *see* Abrova
Obskaya Guba 114 D 2 *Eng.*
  Gulf of Ob. Gulf, S Kara Sea
Ocala 43 E 4 Florida, SE USA
Ocaña 92 D 3 C Spain
Ocaña 58 B 2 N Colombia
Ocean Falls 36 D 5 British
  Columbia, SW Canada
Ocean Island *see* Banaba
Oceanside 47 C 8
  California, W USA
Ochakiv 109 E 4 *Rus.*
  Ochakov. S Ukraine
Ochakov *see* Ochakiv
Ochamchira *see* Och'amch'ire
Och'amch'ire 117 E 2
  Rus. Ochamchira W Georgia
Ocho Rios 54 B 4 C Jamaica
Ocozocuautla 51 G 5 SE Mexico
October Revolution Island *see*
  Oktyabr'skoy Revolyutsii, Ostrov
Ocú 53 F 5 S Panama
Ōdate 130 D 3 Honshū, C Japan
Odenburg *see* Sopron
Odenpäh *see* Otepää
Odense 85 B 7 C Denmark
Oder 80 D 3 *Cz./Pol.* Odra. River,
  C Europe
Oderhaff 94 D 3 *var.* Stettiner Haff,
  Zalew Szczeciński. Bay,
  S Baltic Sea
Odesa 109 E 4 *Rus.* Odessa.
  SW Ukraine
Odessa 49 E 3 Texas, S USA
Odessa *see* Odesa
Odienné 74 D 4 NW Ivory Coast
Ôdôngk 137 D 6 S Cambodia
Odoorn 86 E 2 NE Netherlands
Odra *see* Oder
Oeiras 92 B 4 W Portugal
Of 117 E 2 NE Turkey
Ofanto 97 D 5 river, S Italy
Offenbach 95 B 5 *var.* Offenbach am
  Main. W Germany
Offenbach am Main *see* Offenbach
Offenburg 95 B 6 SW Germany
Ōgaki 131 C 6 Honshū, SW Japan
Ogallala 44 D 4 Nebraska, C USA
Ogbomosho 75 F 4 W Nigeria
Ogden 44 B 4 Utah, W USA
Ogulin 100 B 3 NW Croatia
Ohio 40 C 4 *off.* State of Ohio;
  nickname Buckeye State. State,
  NE USA
Ohio River 40 D 4 river, N USA
Ohlau *see* Oława

Ohrid 101 D 6 *Turk.* Ochrida, Ohri.
  SW Macedonia
Ohrid, Lake 101 D 6 *var.* Lake
  Ochrida, *Alb.* Liqeni i Ohrit,
  Mac. Ohridsko Ezero. Lake,
  Albania/Macedonia
Ohura 150 D 3 North Island,
  C New Zealand
Oildale 47 C 7 California, W USA
Oirschot 87 C 5 S Netherlands
Oise 90 C 3 river, N France
Oistins 55 G 2 S Barbados
Ōita 131 B 7 Kyūshū, SW Japan
Ojinaga 50 D 2 N Mexico
Ojos del Salado, Nevado 64 B 3
  mountain, N Chile
Okaihau 150 C 2 North Island,
  N New Zealand
Okāra 134 C 2 E Pakistan
Okavango 78 C 3 *var.* Cubango,
  Kavango, Kavengo, Kubango,
  Okavanggo. River, S Africa
Okavango Delta 78 C 3 wetland,
  N Botswana
Okayama 131 B 6 Honshū,
  SW Japan
Okazaki 131 C 6 Honshū, C Japan
Okeechobee, Lake 43 E 4 lake,
  Florida, SE USA
Okhotsk 115 G 3
  SE Russian Federation
Okhotsk, Sea of 152 C 1 sea,
  NW Pacific Ocean
Okhtyrka 109 F 2 *Rus.* Akhtyrka.
  NE Ukraine
Okinawa 130 A 3 island, Japan
Okinawa-shotō 130 A 3 island
  group, Nansei-shotō, S Japan
Oki-shotō 131 B 6 *var.* Oki-guntō.
  Island group, SW Japan
Oklahoma 49 G 2 *off.* State of
  Oklahoma; nickname Sooner
  State. State, C USA
Oklahoma City 49 G 1 state capital,
  Oklahoma, C USA
Okmulgee 49 G 1 Oklahoma, C USA
Oktyabr'skiy 111 D 6
  W Russian Federation
Oktyabr'skoy Revolyutsii, Ostrov
  115 E 2 *Eng.* October Revolution
  Island. Island, Severnaya Zemlya,
  N Russian Federation
Okulovka *see* Uglovka
Okushiri-tō 130 C 3 *var.* Okusiri Tô.
  Island, Japan
Okusiri Tô *see* Okushiri-tō
Öland 85 C 7 island, S Sweden
Olavarría 65 D 5 E Argentina
Oława 98 C 4 *Ger.* Ohlau. SW Poland
Olbia 97 A 5 *prev.* Terranova
  Pausania. W Italy
Oldebroek 86 D 3 E Netherlands
Oldenburg 94 C 2 N Germany
Oldenburg 94 B 3 N Germany
Oldenzaal 86 E 3 E Netherlands
Old Harbour 54 B 5 C Jamaica
Olean 41 E 3 New York, NE USA
Olëkminsk 115 F 3
  C Russian Federation
Oleksandrivka 109 E 3
  Rus. Aleksandrovka. C Ukraine
Oleksandriya 109 E 3
  Rus. Aleksandriya. C Ukraine
Olenegorsk 114 C 2
  NW Russian Federation
Olenëk 115 F 3 river,
  C Russian Federation
Olenyok *see* Olenëk
Oléron, Île d' 91 A 5 island,
  W France
Olevs'k 108 D 1 *Rus.* Olevsk.
  N Ukraine

Olevsk *see* Olevs'k
Ölgiy 126 C 2 W Mongolia
Olhão 92 B 5 S Portugal
Olimpo *see* Fuerte Olimpo
Olita *see* Alytus
Oliva 93 F 4 E Spain
Olivet 90 C 4 C France
Olmaliq 123 F 2 *Rus.* Almalyk.
  E Uzbekistan
Olomouc 99 C 5 *Ger.* Olmütz,
  Pol. Ołomuniec. E Czech Republic
Olonec *see* Olonets
Olonets 110 B 3 *var.* Olonec.
  NW Russian Federation
Olovyannaya 115 F 4
  S Russian Federation
Olpe 94 B 4 W Germany
Olshanka *see* Vil'shanka
Olsnitz *see* Murska Sobota
Olsztyn 98 D 2 *Ger.* Allenstein.
  N Poland
Olt 108 B 5 *var.* Oltul, *Ger.* Alt.
  River, S Romania
Oltenita 108 C 5 S Romania
Olvera 92 C 5 S Spain
Ol'viopol' *see* Pervomays'k
Olympia 46 B 2 state capital,
  Washington, NW USA
Olympic Mountains 46 B 2
  mountain range, Washington,
  NW USA
Ólympos 104 B 4 *var.* Ólimbos,
  Eng. Mount Olympus. Mountain,
  N Greece
Omagh 89 B 5 *Ir.* An Ómaigh.
  C Northern Ireland, UK
Omaha 45 F 4 Nebraska, C USA

Oman
  121 D 6 *Ar.* Saltanat 'Umān;
  prev. Muscat and Oman, Sultanat
  Masqat wah Oman. Monarchy,
  SW Asia

Official name: Sultanate of Oman
Date of formation: 1650/1951
Capital: Muscat **Population:** 1.7
million **Total area:** 212,460 sq km
(82,030 sq miles) **Languages:** Arab*,
Baluchi **Religions:** Ibadi Muslim
75%, other Muslim 11%, Hindu 14%
Ethnic mix: Arab 75%, Baluchi 15%
Government: Monarchy with
Consultative Council
Currency: Rial = 1,000 baizas

Oman, Gulf of 120 E 4 *Ar.* Khalīj
  'Umān. Gulf, W Arabian Sea
Omboué 77 A 6 W Gabon
Omdurman 72 B 4
  var. Umm Durmān. C Sudan
Ometepe, Isla de 52 D 4 island,
  S Nicaragua
Ōmiya 131 D 5 Honshū, SE Japan
Ommen 86 E 3 E Netherlands
Omsk 114 C 4 C Russian Federation
Ōmuta 131 A 7 Kyūshū, SW Japan
Onda 93 F 3 E Spain
Ondangua *see* Ondangwa
Ondangwa 78 B 3 *var.* Ondangua.
  N Namibia
Öndörhaan 127 E 2 E Mongolia
Onega 110 C 3
  NW Russian Federation
Onega 110 C 4 river,
  NW Russian Federation
Onega, Lake *see* Onezhskoye Ozero
Onex 95 A 8 SW Switzerland
Onezhskoye Ozero 110 B 3
  Eng. Lake Onega. Lake,
  NW Russian Federation
Ongole 132 D 2 E India
Onitsha 75 G 5 S Nigeria

Onon 127 E 2 river, N Mongolia
Onslow 146 A 4 Western Australia, W Australia
Onslow Bay 43 G 2 bay, NW Atlantic Ocean
Ontario 38 B 3 province, S Canada
Ontario, Lake 41 E 3 lake, Canada/USA
Onteniente see Ontinyent
Ontinyent 93 F 4 var. Onteniente. E Spain
Ontong Java Rise 152 C 3 undersea rise, W Pacific Ocean
Onuba see Huelva
Oodeypore see Udaipur
Oostakker 87 B 5 NW Belgium
Oostburg 87 B 5 SW Netherlands
Oostende 87 A 5 Eng. Ostend, Fr. Ostende. NW Belgium
Oosterbeek 86 D 4 SE Netherlands
Oosterhout 86 C 4 S Netherlands
Opatija 100 A 2 It. Abbazia. NW Croatia
Opava 99 C 5 Ger. Troppau. E Czech Republic
Opelousas 42 B 3 Louisiana, S USA
Opmeer 86 C 2 NW Netherlands
Opochka 110 A 4 var. Opočka. W Russian Federation
Opočka see Opochka
Opole 98 C 4 Ger. Oppeln. SW Poland
Opotiki 150 E 3 North Island, NE New Zealand
Oppeln see Opole
Oqtosh 123 E 2 Rus. Aktash. C Uzbekistan
Oradea 108 A 3 prev. Oradea Mare, Ger. Grosswardein, Hung. Nagyvárad. NW Romania
Orahovac 101 D 5 Alb. Rahovec. S Yugoslavia
Oral see Ural'sk
Oran 70 D 2 var. Ouahran, Wahran. NW Algeria
Orange 91 D 6 anc. Arausio. SE France
Orange 49 H 4 Texas, S USA
Orange 149 D 6 New South Wales, SE Australia
Orangeburg 43 E 2 South Carolina, SE USA
Orange Cone see Orange Fan
Orange Fan 67 D 6 var. Orange Cone. Undersea fan, SW Indian Ocean
Orange River 78 B 4 Afr. Oranjerivier. River, S Africa
Orange Walk 52 C 1 N Belize
Oranienburg 94 D 3 NE Germany
Oranjemund 78 B 4 var. Orangemund; prev. Orange Mouth. SW Namibia
Oranjerivier see Orange River
Oranjestad 55 E 5 dependent territory capital, W Aruba
Orantes 118 B 3 var. Ononte, Orontes, Ar. Nahr al 'Aşī, Nahr al 'Āşī Oronte, Nahr el Aassi. River, SW Asia
Orany see Varėna
Orašje 100 C 3 N Bosnia & Herzegovina
Oravita 108 A 4 Ger. Orawitsa, Hung. Oravicabanyá. W Romania
Orbetello 96 B 4 W Italy
Orcadas 154 A 2 research station, Antarctica
Orchard Homes 44 B 1 Montana, NW USA
Ord 146 D 3 river, N Australia
Ordino 91 A 8 NW Andorra

Ordos Desert 127 E 3 Chin. Mu Us Shamo. Desert, N China
Ordu 116 D 2 anc. Cotyora. N Turkey
Ordzhonikidze 109 F 3 E Ukraine
Orealla 59 G 3 E Guyana
Örebro 85 C 6 C Sweden
Oregon 40 D 3 Ohio, N USA
Oregon 46 B 3 off. State of Oregon; nicknames Beaver State, Sunset State, Valentine State, Webfoot State. State, NW USA
Oregon City 46 B 3 Oregon, NW USA
Orekhov see Orikhiv
Orël 111 B 5 W Russian Federation
Orem 44 B 4 Utah, W USA
Orenburg 111 D 6 prev. Chkalov. W Russian Federation
Orestiáda 104 D 3 prev. Orestiás NE Greece
Orestiás see Orestiáda
Orhei 108 D 3 var. Orheiu, Rus. Orgeyev. N Moldavia
Orhon Gol 127 E 2 river, N Mongolia
Oriental, Cordillera 58 B 3 mountain range, C Colombia
Oriental, Cordillera 61 F 4 mountain range, C Bolivia
Oriental, Cordillera 60 D 3 mountain range, C Peru
Orihuela 93 F 4 E Spain
Orikhiv 109 G 3 Rus. Orekhov. SE Ukraine
Orillia 38 D 5 Ontario, S Canada
Orinoco 58 D 3 river, Colombia/Venezuela
Orissa 135 F 5 state, NE India
Orissaar see Orissaare
Orissaare 106 C 2 Ger. Orissaar. Saaremaa, W Estonia
Oristano 97 A 5 W Italy
Orito 58 A 4 SW Colombia
Orkney Islands 88 C 2 var. Orkneys, Orkney. Island group, NE Scotland, UK
Orlando 43 E 4 Florida, SE USA
Orléanais 90 C 4 cultural region, C France
Orléans 90 C 4 anc. Aurelianum. C France
Orlya 107 B 6 W Belorussia
Örnsköldsvik 84 C 4 C Sweden
Oroluk Atoll 144 C 2 island, C Micronesia
Oromocto 39 F 4 New Brunswick, SE Canada
Orona 145 F 3 prev. Hull Island. Island, C Kiribati
Oropeza see Cochabamba
Oroqen Zizhiqi 127 G 1 N China
Orsha 107 E 6 NE Belorussia
Orsk 111 D 6 W Russian Federation
Orşova 108 A 5 Ger. Orschowa, Hung. Orsova. W Romania
Ortelsburg see Szczytno
Orthez 91 B 6 SW France
Ortona 96 D 4 C Italy
Oruba see Aruba
Orūmīyeh, Daryācheh-ye 120 B 2 var. Matianus, Sha Hi, Urumi Yeh, Eng. Lake Urmia; prev. Daryācheh-ye Rezā'īyeh. Lake, NW Iran
Oruro 61 F 4 W Bolivia
Ōsaka 131 C 6 hist. Naniwa. Honshū, SW Japan
Osa, Península de 53 E 5 peninsula, S Costa Rica

Osborn Plateau 141 D 5 undersea plateau, E Indian Ocean
Osca see Huesca
Osh 123 F 2 SW Kyrgyzstan
Oshawa 38 D 5 Ontario, SE Canada
Oshikango 78 B 3 N Namibia
Ō-shima 131 D 6 island, E Japan
Oshmyany see Ashmyany
Osijek 100 C 3 Ger. Esseg, Hung, Eszék; prev. Osiek, Osjek. E Croatia
Oskaloosa 45 G 4 Iowa, C USA
Oskarshamn 85 C 7 S Sweden
Öskemen see Ust'-Kamenogorsk
Oskil see Oskol
Oskol 109 G 2 Ukr. Oskil. River, Russian Federation/Ukraine
Oslo 85 B 6 prev. Christiania, Kristiania. Country capital, S Norway
Osmaniye 116 D 4 S Turkey
Osnabrück 94 B 4 NW Germany
Osogovski Planini 104 B 3 var. Osogovske Planine, Mac. Osogovski Planini. Mountain range, Bulgaria/Macedonia
Osorno 65 B 5 C Chile
Osprey Reef 148 D 2 reef, NW Coral Sea
Oss 86 D 4 S Netherlands
Ossabaw Island 43 E 3 island, SE USA
Ossa, Serra d' 92 C 4 mountain range, SE Portugal
Ossora 115 H 2 E Russian Federation
Oster 109 E 1 N Ukraine
Östermyra see Seinäjoki
Östersund 84 C 4 C Sweden
Ostfriesische Inseln 94 A 3 Eng. East Frisian Islands. Island group, NW Germany
Ostiglia 96 C 2 N Italy
Ostrava 99 C 5 E Czech Republic
Ostróda 98 D 2 Ger. Osterode, Osterode in Ostpreussen. N Poland
Ostrołęka 98 D 3 Ger. Wiesenhof, Rus. Ostrolenka. NE Poland
Ostrov 110 A 4 Latv. Austrava. W Russian Federation
Ostrowiec Świętokrzyski 98 D 4 var. Ostrowiec, Ostrowiec Świętokrzyski, Rus. Ostrovets. SE Poland
Ostrów Mazowiecka 98 D 3 var. Ostrów Mazowiecki. NE Poland
Ostrów Mazowiecki see Ostrów Mazowiecka
Ostrów Wielkopolski 98 C 4 var. Ostrów, Ger. Ostrowo. C Poland
Ostyako-Voguls'k see Khanty-Mansiysk
Osum see Osumit, Lumi i
Ōsumi-shotō 131 A 8 island group, Nansei-shotō, S Japan
Osumit, Lumi i 101 D 7 var. Osum. River, SE Albania
Osuna 92 D 5 S Spain
Oswego 41 F 3 New York, NE USA
Otago Peninsula 151 B 7 peninsula, South Island, SW New Zealand
Otaki 150 D 4 North Island, C New Zealand
Otaru 130 C 2 Hokkaidō, NE Japan
Otavalo 60 B 1 N Ecuador
Otavi 78 B 3 N Namibia
Oţelu Roşu 108 A 4 Ger. Ferdinandsberg, Hung. Nándorhgy. SW Romania
Otepää 106 D 3 Ger. Odenpäh. SE Estonia

Otira 151 C 6 South Island, C New Zealand
Otjiwarongo 78 B 3 N Namibia
Otorohanga 150 D 3 North Island, N New Zealand
Otra 85 A 6 river, S Norway
Otranto, Canale d' see Otranto, Strait of
Otranto, Strait of 103 E 3 It. Canale d'Otranto. Strait, Adriatic Sea/Ionian Sea
Otrokovice 99 C 5 Ger. Otrokowitz. SE Czech Republic
Otrokowitz see Otrokovice
Ōtsu 131 C 6 var. Ōtu. Honshū, SW Japan
Ottawa 38 D 5 country capital, Ontario, SE Canada
Ottawa 40 B 3 Illinois, N USA
Ottawa 45 F 5 Kansas, C USA
Ottawa Islands 38 C 1 island group, Northwest Territories, C Canada
Ottignies 87 C 6 C Belgium
Ottobrunn 95 C 6 SE Germany
Ottumwa 45 G 4 Iowa, C USA
Otu see Ōtsu
Ouachita Mountains 42 A 1 mountain range, S USA
Ouachita River 42 B 2 river, Arkansas, C USA
Ouâd Nâga 74 B 2 SW Mauritania
Ouagadougou 75 E 4 var. Wagadugu. Country capital, C Burkina
Ouahigouya 75 E 3 NW Burkina
Oualata see Oualâta
Oualâta 74 D 3 var. Oualata. SE Mauritania
Ouanary 59 H 3 E French Guiana
Ouanda Djallé 76 D 4 NE Central African Republic
Ouarâne 74 D 2 physical region, C Mauritania
Ouargla 71 E 2 var. Wargla. NE Algeria
Ouarzazate 70 C 3 S Morocco
Oubangui see Ubangi
Oudenaarde 87 B 6 Fr. Audenarde. SW Belgium
Ouessant, Île d' 90 A 3 Eng. Ushant. Island, NW France
Ouésso 77 B 5 NW Congo
Oujda 70 D 2 Ar. Ujda, Oudjda. NE Morocco
Oujeft 74 C 2 C Mauritania
Ouled Djellal 71 E 2 var. Awled Djellal. N Algeria
Oulu 84 D 4 Swe. Uleåborg. C Finland
Oulujärvi 84 D 4 Swe. Uleträsk. Lake, C Finland
Oulujoki 84 D 4 Swe. Uleälv. River, C Finland
Ounasjoki 84 D 3 river, N Finland
Ounianga Kébir 76 C 2 N Chad
Oup see Auob
Oupeye 87 D 6 E Belgium
Our 87 D 7 river, NW Europe
Ourense 92 C 2 Cast. Orense; Lat. Aurium. NW Spain
Ourique 92 B 4 S Portugal
Ourthe 87 D 7 river, E Belgium
Ouse 89 D 5 river, N England, UK
Outaouais see Ottawa
Outer Hebrides 88 B 2 var. Western Isles. Island group, NW Scotland, UK
Outer Islands 79 G 1 island group, SW Seychelles
Outes 92 B 1 NW Spain

Outreau 90 C 2 N France
Ouvéa 144 D 5 island,
NE New Caledonia
Ouyen 149 B 6 Victoria,
SE Australia
Ovalle 64 B 3 N Chile
Ovar 92 B 2 W Portugal
Overflakkee 86 B 4 island,
SW Netherlands
Overijse 87 C 6 C Belgium
Oviedo 92 D 1 *anc.* Asturias.
NW Spain
Ovilava *see* Wels
Ovruch 108 D 1 N Ukraine
Owando 77 B 6 *prev.* Fort-Rousset.
C Congo
Owase 131 C 6 Honshū, SW Japan
Owatonna 45 F 3
Minnesota, N USA
Owen Fracture Zone 140 B 4
fracture zone, NW Indian Ocean
Owen, Mount 151 C 5 mountain,
South Island, C New Zealand
Owensboro 40 B 5 Kentucky, E USA
Owen Stanley Range 144 B 3
mountain range,
S Papua New Guinea
Owerri 75 G 5 S Nigeria
Owo 75 F 5 SW Nigeria
Owyhee River 46 C 4 river,
NW USA
Oxford 89 D 6 *Lat.* Oxonia.
S England, UK
Oxford 151 C 6 South Island,
C New Zealand
Oxford 40 C 4 Ohio, N USA
Oxkutzcab 51 H 4 SE Mexico
Oxnard 47 C 7
California, W USA
Oxonia *see* Oxford
Oyama 131 D 5 Honshū, S Japan
Oyem 77 B 5 N Gabon
Oyo 75 F 5 W Nigeria
Oyo 77 B 6 C Congo
Ozark 42 D 3 Alabama, S USA
Ozark Plateau 45 G 5 plain,
Missouri, C USA
Ozarks, Lake of the 45 G 5
Fr. Lac des Bois. Reservoir,
Missouri, C USA
Ózd 99 D 6 NE Hungary
Ozieri 97 A 5 W Italy

P

Paamiut 82 B 4 *var.* Påmiut, *Dan.*
Frederikshåb. SW Greenland
Pa-an 136 B 4 SE Burma
Pābna 135 G 4 W Bangladesh
Pacaraima, Serra 59 F 3 *var.*
Pakaraima Mountains. Mountain
range, N South America
Pachuca 51 E 4 *var.* Pachuca
de Soto. C Mexico
Pachuca de Soto *see* Pachuca
Pacific-Antarctic Ridge 152 D 5
undersea ridge, S Pacific Ocean
Pacific Ocean 152 D 3 ocean
Padang 138 B 4 Sumatera,
W Indonesia
Paderborn 94 B 4 NW Germany
Padma *see* Ganges
Padova 96 C 2 *Eng.* Padua;
anc. Patavium. NE Italy
Padre Island 49 G 5 island, Texas,
S USA
Paducah 40 B 5 Kentucky, E USA
Paeroa 150 D 3 North Island,
N New Zealand
Pag 100 A 3 *It.* Pago. Island,
C Croatia

Page 48 B 1 Arizona, SW USA
Pago *see* Pag
Pago Pago 145 F 4 dependent
territory capital,
W American Samoa
Pahiatua 150 D 4 North Island,
C New Zealand
Paide 106 D 2 *Ger.* Weissenstein.
N Estonia
Paihia 150 D 2 North Island,
N New Zealand
Päijänne 85 E 5 lake, S Finland
Paine, Cerro 65 B 7 mountain,
S Chile
Painted Desert 48 B 1 plain,
Arizona, SW USA
Paisley 88 C 4 W Scotland, UK
País Valenciano 93 F 3 cultural
region, NE Spain
País Vasco 93 E 1 cultural region,
N Spain
Paita 60 B 3 NW Peru
Pakanbaru *see* Pekanbaru

Pakistan
134 A 2 *var.* Islami Jamhuriya e
Pakistan. Republic, S Asia

Official name: Islamic Republic of
Pakistan **Date of formation:**
1947/1972 **Capital:** Islamabad
Population: 144.5 million **Total Area:**
796,100 sq km (307,374 sq miles)
Languages: Urdu*, Punjabi
Religions: Sunni Muslim 77%, Shi'a
Muslim 20%, Hindu 2%,
Christian 1% **Ethnic mix:** Punjabi
56%, Sindhi 13%, Pashtun 8%,
other 23% **Government:**
Multiparty republic
Currency: Rupee = 100 paisa

Pakokku 136 A 3 W Burma
Pak Phanang 137 C 7 *var.* Ban Pak
Phanang. S Thailand
Pakruojis 106 C 4 N Lithuania
Paks 99 C 7 S Hungary
Paksé *see* Pakxé
Pakxé 137 D 5 *var.* Paksé. S Laos
Palafrugell 93 G 2 NE Spain
Palagruža 101 B 5 *It.* Pelagosa.
Island, SW Croatia
Palaiá Epídavros 105 C 6
S Greece
Palamós 93 G 2 NE Spain
Palamuse 106 E 2 *Ger.* Sankt-
Bartholomäi. E Estonia
Palanka *see* Bačka Palanka
Palapye 78 D 3 SE Botswana
Palatka 43 E 3 Florida, SE USA

Palau
144 A 2 *var.* Belau. Republic,
W Pacific Ocean

Official name: Republic of Palau
Date of formation: 1994 **Capital:**
Koror **Population:** 16,000 **Total
Area:** 497 sq km (192 sq miles)
Languages: Palauan*, English
Religions: Christian 70%, traditional
beliefs 30% **Ethnic mix:** Palauan 99%,
other 1% **Government:** Multiparty
republic **Currency:** US $ = 100 cents

Palawan 139 E 2 island,
W Philippines
Palawan Passage 139 E 2 passage,
SE South China Sea
Paldiski 106 D 2 *prev.* Baltiski,
Ger. Baltischport; *prev. Eng.* Baltic
Port. NW Estonia
Palembang 138 B 4 Sumatera,
W Indonesia

Palencia 92 D 2 *anc.* Palantia,
Pallantia. NW Spain
Palermo 97 C 7 *Fr.* Palerme; *anc.*
Panormus, Panhormus. SW Italy
Palestine 49 G 3 Texas, S USA
Pāli 134 C 3 N India
Palimé *see* Kpalimé
Palioúri, Ákra 104 C 4 *var.* Akra
Kanestron. Headland, N Greece
Palk Strait 132 D 3 strait,
N Indian Ocean
Palliser, Cape 151 D 5 headland,
North Island, C New Zealand
Palma 93 G 3 *var.* Palma de
Mallorca. E Spain
Palma de Mallorca *see* Palma
Palmar Sur 53 E 5 SE Costa Rica
Palma Soriano 54 C 3 E Cuba
Palmdale 47 C 7 California, W USA
Palmer 154 A 2 research station,
Antarctica
Palmer Land 154 A 3 physical
region, Antarctica
Palmerston 145 G 4 island,
S Cook Islands
Palmerston North 150 D 4
North Island, C New Zealand
Palmi 97 D 7 SW Italy
Palmira 58 B 3 W Colombia
Palm Springs 47 D 8
California, W USA
Palmyra Atoll 145 G 2
US unincorporated territory,
C Pacific Ocean
Palo Alto 47 B 6 California, W USA
Paloe *see* Denpasar
Paloe *see* Palu
Palu 139 E 4 *prev.* Paloe. Celebes,
C Indonesia
Pamiers 91 B 6 S France
Pamir 123 F 3 *var.* Daryā-ye Pāmīr.
River, Afghanistan/Tajikistan
Pāmīr, Daryā-ye *see* Pamirs
Pamirs 123 F 3 *Pash.* Daryā-ye
Pāmīr, *Rus.* Pamir, *Taj.* Daryoi
Pomir. Mountain range,
C Asia
Pamlico Sound 43 G 1 bay,
NW Atlantic Ocean
Pampa 49 F 1 Texas, S USA
Pampa Aullagas, Lago *see* Poopó,
Lago
Pampas 64 C 4 plain, C Argentina
Pamplona 93 E 1 *Basq.* Iruñea;
prev. Pampeluna, *anc.* Pompaelo.
N Spain
Pamplona 58 C 2 N Colombia
Panaji 132 B 1 *var.* New Goa,
Pangim, Panjim. State capital,
W India

Panama
53 G 5 Republic,
SE Central America

Official name: Republic of Panama
Date of formation: 1903/1914
Capital: Panama City **Population:**
2.6 million **Total area:** 77,080 sq km
(29,761 sq miles) **Languages:** Spanish*,
English Creole, Indian languages
Religions: Roman Catholic 93%,
other 7% **Ethnic mix:** *mestizo* 70%,
Black 14%, White 10%, Indian 6%
Government: Multiparty republic
Currency: Balboa = 100 centesimos

Panamá 53 G 5 *var.* Ciudad de
Panamá, *Eng.* Panama City.
Country capital, C Panama
Panamá, Bahía de 53 G 5 bay,
W Pacific Ocean

Panama Basin 56 A 2 undersea
basin, E Pacific Ocean
Panama Canal 53 F 4 canal,
E Panama
Panama City 42 D 3 Florida, SE USA
Panama City 35 D 7 country
capital, C Panama
Panama City *see* Panamá
Panamá, Golfo de 53 G 5 *var.* Gulf
of Panama. Gulf, E Pacific Ocean
Panama, Gulf of *see* Panamá,
Golfo de
Panama, Isthmus of *see* Panama,
Isthmus of
Panamá, Istmo de 53 G 4 *Eng.*
Isthmus of Panama; *prev.* Isthmus
of Darien. Isthmus, E Panama
Panama, Republic of *see* Panama
Panay Island 139 E 2 island,
C Philippines
Pančevo 100 D 3 *Ger.* Pantschowa,
Hung. Pancsova. NE Yugoslavia
Pandan, Selat 138 A 2 strait,
Indian Ocean/Pacific Ocean
Panevėžys 106 C 4 C Lithuania
Pangkalpinang 138 C 4 Bangka,
W Indonesia
Panlong Jiang *see* Lô, Sông
Panopolis *see* Akhmîm
Pánormos 105 C 7 Kríti, SE Greece
Pantanal 63 E 4 *var.* Pantanalmato-
Grossense. Wetland, SW Brazil
Pantanalmato-Grossense *see*
Pantanal
Pantelleria, Isola di 97 B 7 island,
SW Italy
Pánuco 51 E 3 E Mexico
Pao-shan *see* Baoshan
Papagayo, Golfo de 52 D 4 gulf,
E Pacific Ocean
Papakura 150 D 3 North Island,
N New Zealand
Papantla 51 F 4 *var.* Papantla de
Olarte. E Mexico
Papantla de Olarte *see* Papantla
Papatoetoe 150 D 3 North Island,
N New Zealand
Papeete 145 H 4 dependent
territory capital, Tahiti,
W French Polynesia
Paphos *see* Páfos
Papilė 106 B 3 NW Lithuania
Papillion 45 F 4 Nebraska, C USA
Papua, Gulf of 144 B 3 gulf,
S Papua New Guinea

Papua New Guinea
144 B 3 *prev.* Territory of
Papua and New Guinea.
Commonwealth republic,
Indian Ocean/Pacific Ocean

Official name: The Independent
State of Papua New Guinea **Date of
formation:** 1975 **Capital:** Port
Moresby **Population:** 4.1 million
Total Area: 462, 840 sq km
(178,700 sq miles) **Languages:** Pidgin
English*, Motu*, 750 (est.) native
languages **Religions:** Christian 66%,
other 34% **Ethnic mix:** Papuan 85%,
other 15% **Government:**
Parliamentary democracy
Currency: Kina = 100 toea

Papuk 100 C 3 mountain range,
NE Croatia
Pará 63 E 2 *off.* Estado do Pará.
State, NE Brazil
Pará *see* Belém
Paracas, Bahía de 60 C 4 bay,
E Pacific Ocean
Paracel Islands 138 D 1 disputed
territory, N South China Sea

Paraćin 100 E 4 C Yugoslavia
Pará, Estado do *see* Pará
Paragua 59 E 3 river, SE Venezuela

Paraguay
64 D 2 country, S South America

Official name: Republic of
Paraguay Date of formation:
1811/1935 Capital: Asunción
Population: 4.5 million Total area:
406,750 sq km (157,046 sq miles)
density: 11 people per sq km
Languages: Spanish*, Guaraní
Religions: Roman
Catholic 90%, other 10% Ethnic mix:
mestizo (Euro-Indian) 95%, White
3%, Indian 2% Government:
Multiparty republic
Currency: Guaraní = 100 centimos

Paraguay 64 D 2 *Port.* Rio Paraguai.
River, S South America
Paraíba 63 G 2 *off.* Estado da
Paraíba; *var.* Parahiba, Parahyba.
State, E Brazil
Paraíba *see* João Pessoa
Parakou 75 F 4 C Benin
Paramaribo 59 G 3 country capital,
N Surinam
Paramushir, Ostrov 115 H 3 island,
E Russian Federation
Paraná 64 E 3 *var.* Alto Paraná.
River, S South America
Paraná 64 D 4 E Argentina
Paraná 63 E 4 *off.* Estado do Paraná.
State, S Brazil
Paraná, Estado do *see* Paraná
Paranéstio 104 C 3 NE Greece
Paraparaumu 151 D 5 North Island,
C New Zealand
Parchim 94 C 3 N Germany
Parczew 98 E 4 E Poland
Pardubice 99 B 5 *Ger.* Pardubitz.
C Czech Republic
Pardubitz *see* Pardubice
Parechcha 107 B 5 *Pol.* Porzecze,
Rus. Porech'ye. W Belorussia
Parecis, Chapada dos 62 D 3 *var.*
Serra dos Parecis. Mountain
range, W Brazil
Parecis, Serra dos *see* Parecis,
Chapada dos
Parenzo *see* Poreč
Parepare 139 E 4 Celebes,
C Indonesia
Párga 105 A 5 W Greece
Paria, Golfo de *see* Paria, Gulf of
Paria, Gulf of 59 E 1 *var.* Golfo de
Paria. Gulf, W Atlantic Ocean
Parika 59 F 2 NE Guyana
Paris 90 C 3 *anc.* Lutetia, Lutetia
Parisiorum, Parisii. Country
capital, N France
Paris 42 C 1 Tennessee, S USA
Paris 49 G 2 Texas, S USA
Parkent 123 F 2 E Uzbekistan
Parkersburg 40 D 4 West Virginia,
NE USA
Parkes 149 C 6 New South Wales,
SE Australia
Parkhar *see* Farkhor
Parma 96 B 2 N Italy
Parnahyba *see* Parnaíba
Parnaíba 63 G 2 *var.* Parnahyba.
E Brazil
Pärnu 106 D 2 *Ger.* Pernau,
Latv. Pērnava; *prev. Rus.* Pernov.
SW Estonia
Pärnu 106 D 2 river, SW Estonia
Ger. Pernau. River, SW Estonia
Pärnu-Jaagupi 106 D 2 *Ger.* Sankt-
Jakobi. SW Estonia

Pärnu Laht 106 D 2 *Ger.* Pernauer
Bucht. Bay, Baltic Sea/
Gulf of Riga
Páros 105 D 6 Páros, SE Greece
Páros 105 D 6 island, Kykládes,
SE Greece
Parral 64 B 4 C Chile
Parral *see* Hidalgo del Parral
Parramatta 149 D 6
New South Wales, SE Australia
Parras 50 D 3 *var.* Parras de la
Fuente. NE Mexico
Parras de la Fuente *see* Parras
Parsons 45 F 5 Kansas, C USA
Pasadena 49 H 4 Texas, S USA
Pasadena 47 C 7 California, W USA
Paşcani 108 C 3 *Hung.* Páskán.
NE Romania
Pasco 46 C 2 Washington, NW USA
Pasewalk 94 D 3 NE Germany
Pashkeni *see* Bolyarovo
Pasłęk 98 D 2 *Ger.* Preußisch
Holland. N Poland
Pasinler 117 F 3 NE Turkey
Páskán *see* Paşcani
Pasni 134 A 3 SW Pakistan
Paso de Indios 65 B 6 S Argentina
Paso de los Vientos *see*
Windward Passage
Passarowitz *see* Požarevac
Passau 95 D 6 SE Germany
Passo Fundo 63 E 5 S Brazil
Pastavy 107 C 5 *Pol.* Postawy,
Rus. Postawy. NW Belorussia
Pastaza 60 B 2 river, Ecuador/Peru
Pasto 58 A 4 SW Colombia
Pasvalys 106 C 4 N Lithuania
Patagonia 65 B 7 physical region,
Argentina/Chile
Patani *see* Pattani
Patea 150 D 4 North Island,
C New Zealand
Paterson 41 F 4 New Jersey,
NE USA
Pathein *see* Bassein
Pátmos 105 D 6 island,
Dodekánisos, SE Greece
Patna 135 F 3 *var.* Azimabad.
State capital, N India
Patnos 117 F 3 E Turkey
Patos, Lagoa dos 63 E 5 lagoon,
SW Atlantic Ocean
Pátra 105 B 5 *Eng.* Patras;
prev. Pátrai. S Greece
Patras *see* Pátra
Pattani 137 C 7 *var.* Patani.
S Thailand
Pattaya 137 C 5 C Thailand
Patuca 52 D 2 river, E Honduras
Pau 91 B 6 SW France
Paulatuk 37 E 3 Northwest
Territories, NW Canada
Paungde 136 B 4 SW Burma
Pavia 96 B 2 *anc.* Ticinum. N Italy
Pāvilosta 106 B 3 W Latvia
Pavlikeni 104 D 2 N Bulgaria
Pavlodar 112 C 3 NE Kazakhstan
Pavlograd *see* Pavlohrad
Pavlohrad 109 G 3 *Rus.* Pavlograd.
E Ukraine
Pavlovsk 111 B 6
W Russian Federation
Pavlovskaya 111 A 7
SW Russian Federation
Pawai, Pulau 138 A 2 island,
SW Singapore
Pawn 136 B 3 river, C Burma
Pax Augusta *see* Badajoz
Paxí 105 A 5 island, Iónioi Nísoi,
W Greece
Pax Julia *see* Beja

Payakumbuh 138 B 4 Sumatera,
W Indonesia
Paynes Find 147 B 6 W Australia
Payo Obispo *see* Chetumal
Paysandú 64 D 4 NW Uruguay
Pazar 117 E 2 NE Turkey
Pazardzhik 104 C 3 *var.* Pazardžik;
prev. Tatar Pazardzhik.
SW Bulgaria
Pearl Islands *see* Perlas,
Archipiélago de las
Pearl Lagoon *see* Perlas, Laguna de
Pearl River 42 B 3 river, S USA
Pearsall 49 F 4 Texas, S USA
Peary Land 83 E 1 physical region,
Greenland
Peć 101 D 5 *Alb.* Pejë, *Turk.* Ipek.
C Yugoslavia
Pechora 110 E 3 *var.* Pečora.
NW Russian Federation
Pechora 110 D 3 *var.* Pečora. River,
NW Russian Federation
Pechorskoye More 110 D 2 sea,
Arctic Ocean/Barents Sea
Pečora *see* Pechora
Pecos 49 E 3 Texas, S USA
Pecos Plains 49 E 3 plain,
Texas, S USA
Pecos River 49 E 3 river,
SW USA
Pécs 99 C 7 *Ger.* Fünfkirchen;
Lat. Sopianae. SW Hungary
Pedra Lume 74 A 3 NE Cape Verde
Pedro Cays 54 C 3 island group,
S Jamaica
Pedro Juan Caballero 64 D 2
E Paraguay
Peer 87 D 5 NE Belgium
Pegasus Bay 151 C 6 bay,
S Pacific Ocean
Pegu 136 B 4 *var.* Bago. S Burma
Pehuajó 64 C 4 E Argentina
Peihai *see* Beihai
Peine 94 B 4 C Germany
Peiraiás 105 C 6 *prev.* Piraiévs,
Eng. Piraeus. C Greece
Pekalongan 138 C 5 Jawa,
C Indonesia
Pekanbaru 138 B 4 *var.* Pakanbaru.
Sumatera, W Indonesia
Pekin 40 B 4 Illinois, N USA
Peking *see* Beijing
Pelagie, Isole 97 B 8 island group,
SW Italy
Pelagosa *see* Palagruža
Pelly Bay 37 F 3 Northwest
Territories, N Canada
Pelopónnisos 105 B 6
var. Morea, *Eng.* Peloponnese;
anc. Peloponnesus. Peninsula,
S Greece
Pematangsiantar 138 B 3 Sumatera,
W Indonesia
Pemba 73 D 7 island, E Tanzania
Pemba 79 F 2 *prev.* Port Amelia,
Porto Amélia. NE Mozambique
Pembroke 38 D 4 Ontario,
SE Canada
Penderma *see* Bandırma
Pendleton 46 C 3 Oregon, NW USA
Pend Oreille, Lake 46 D 1 lake,
Idaho, NW USA
Peng-pu *see* Bengbu
Peniche 92 B 3 W Portugal
Penn Hills 41 E 4 Pennsylvania,
NE USA
Pennine Alps 95 A 8 *Fr.* Alpes
Pennines, *It.* Alpi Pennine; *Lat.*
Alpes Penninae. Mountain range,
Italy/Switzerland
Pennine Chain *see* Pennines

Pennines 89 D 5 *var.* Pennine
Chain. Mountain range,
NW England, UK
Pennsylvania 41 E 4 *off.*
Commonwealth of Pennsylvania;
nickname Keystone State. State,
NE USA
Penobscot River 41 H 1 river,
Maine, NE USA
Penong 147 E 6 South Australia,
S Australia
Penonomé 53 F 5 C Panama
Penrhyn 145 G 3 island,
N Cook Islands
Penrhyn Basin 152 D 3 undersea
basin, C Pacific Ocean
Penrith 89 D 5 NW England, UK
Pensacola 42 C 3 Florida, SE USA
Pentecost 144 D 4 *Fr.* Pentecôte.
Island, C Vanuatu
Pentecôte *see* Pentecost
Penza 111 C 6
W Russian Federation
Penzance 89 B 8 SW England, UK
Peoria 40 B 4 Illinois, N USA
Perchtoldsdorf 95 E 6 NE Austria
Percival Lakes 146 C 4 lake,
Western Australia, NW Australia
Pereira 58 B 3 W Colombia
Peremyshl *see* Przemyśl
Pergamino 64 D 4 E Argentina
Périgueux 91 B 5 *anc.* Vesuna.
SW France
Perito Moreno 65 B 6 S Argentina
Perlas, Archipiélago de las 53 G 5
Eng. Pearl Islands. Island group,
SE Panama
Perlas, Laguna de 53 E 3
var. Pearl Lagoon. Lagoon,
W Caribbean Sea
Perleberg 94 C 3 N Germany
Perlepe *see* Prilep
Perm' 111 D 5 *prev.* Molotov.
NW Russian Federation
Pernambuco 63 G 2 *off.* Estado de
Pernambuco. State, E Brazil
Pernambuco *see* Recife
Pernambuco Abyssal Plain *see*
Pernambuco Plain
Pernambuco, Estado de *see*
Pernambuco
Pernambuco Plain 67 C 5
var. Pernambuco Abyssal Plain.
Abyssal plain, E Atlantic Ocean
Pernauer Bucht *see* Pärnu Laht
Pernik 104 C 2 *prev.* Dimitrovo.
W Bulgaria
Perote 51 F 4 E Mexico
Perpignan 91 C 7 S France
Perryton 49 F 1 Texas, S USA
Perryville 45 H 5
Missouri, C USA
Persian Gulf *see* Gulf, The
Perth 88 C 4 E Scotland, UK
Perth 38 D 5 Ontario, SE Canada
Perth 149 C 8 Tasmania,
SE Australia
Perth 147 B 6 state capital,
Western Australia, SW Australia
Perth Basin 141 E 6 undersea basin,
SE Indian Ocean
Peru *see* Beru

Peru
60 C 3 Republic,
W South America

Official name: Republic of Peru
Date of formation: 1824/1942
Capital: Lima Population: 22.9
million Total area: 1,285,220 sq km
(496,223 sq miles) Languages:
Spanish*, Quechua*, Aymará*

Religions: Roman Catholic 95%, other 5% **Ethnic mix:** Indian 45%, *mestizo* 37%, White 15%, other 3% **Government:** Multiparty republic **Currency:** New sol = 100 centimos

Peru Basin 56 A 4 undersea basin, E Pacific Ocean
Peru-Chile Trench 56 A 4 trench, E Pacific Ocean
Perugia 96 C 4 *Fr.* Pérouse; *anc.* Perusia. C Italy
Peru, Republic of *see* Peru
Péruwelz 87 B 6 SW Belgium
Pervomays'k 109 E 3 *prev.* Ol'viopol'. S Ukraine
Pervyy Kuril'skiy Proliv 115 H 3 strait, Pacific Ocean/ Sea of Okhotsk
Pesaro 96 C 3 *anc.* Pisaurum C Italy
Pescara 96 D 4 *anc.* Aternum, Ostia Aterni. C Italy
Peshāwar 134 C 1 N Pakistan
Peshkopi 101 D 6 *var.* Peshkopia, Peshkopija. NE Albania
Pessac 91 B 5 SW France
Pétange 87 D 8 SW Luxembourg
Peta` Tiqwa 119 A 6 *var.* Petach-Tikva, Petah Tiqva. C Israel
Peterborough 89 E 6 *prev.* Medeshamstede. E England, UK
Peterborough 38 D 5 Ontario, SE Canada
Peterborough 149 B 6 South Australia, S Australia
Peterhead 88 D 3 NE Scotland, UK
Petersburg 41 E 5 Virginia, NE USA
Peters Mine 59 F 3 *var.* Peter's Mine. N Guyana
Peter's Mine *see* Peters Mine
Peto 51 H 4 SE Mexico
Petra *see* Wādī Mūsá
Petrich 104 C 3 SW Bulgaria
Petrikov *see* Pyetrykaw
Petrinja 100 B 3 C Croatia
Petropavl *see* Petropavlovsk
Petropavlovsk 114 C 4 *Kaz.* Petropavl. N Kazakhstan
Petropavlovsk-Kamchatskiy 115 H 3 NE Russian Federation
Petroşani 108 B 4 *var.* Petroşeni, *Ger.* Petroschen, *Hung.* Petrozsény. W Romania
Petroskoi *see* Petrozavodsk
Petrovsk 111 C 6 W Russian Federation
Petrovsk-Port *see* Makhachkala
Petrov Val 111 C 6 SW Russian Federation
Petrozavodsk 110 B 3 *Fin.* Petroskoi. NW Russian Federation
Pevek 115 G 1 NE Russian Federation
Pezinok 99 C 6 *Ger.* Bösing, *Hung.* Bazin. SW Slovakia
Pforzheim 95 B 6 SW Germany
Pfungstadt 95 B 5 W Germany
Phangan, Ko 137 C 6 island, S Thailand
Phan Rang-Thap Cham 137 E 6 *var.* Phan Rang, Phanrang, Phan Rang Thap Cham. SE Vietnam
Phan Thiêt 137 E 6 S Vietnam
Phatthalung 137 C 7 *var.* Padalung, Patalung. S Thailand
Phayao 136 C 4 *var.* Muang Phayao. N Thailand
Phenix City 42 D 2 Alabama, S USA
Phetchaburi 137 C 5 *var.* Bejraburi, Petchaburi, Phet Buri. C Thailand
Philadelphia 41 F 4 Pennsylvania, NE USA
Philippeville *see* Skikda
Philippine Basin 152 B 2 undersea basin, W Pacific Ocean

Philippines
139 F 1 *off.* Republic of the Philippines. Republic, SE Asia

Official name: Republic of the Philippines **Date of formation:** 1946 **Capital:** Manila **Population:** 66.5 million **Total Area:** 300,000 sq km (115,831 sq miles) **Languages:** Pilipino*, English **Religions:** Roman Catholic 83%, Protestant 9%, Muslim 5%, other 3% **Ethnic mix:** Filipino 96%, Chinese 2%, other 2% **Government:** Multiparty republic **Currency:** Peso = 100 centavos

Philippine Sea 152 B 3 sea, W Pacific Ocean
Philippines, Republic of the *see* Philippines
Philippine Trench 142 A 1 trench, W Pacific Ocean
Phitsanulok 136 C 4 *var.* Bisnulok, Muang Phitsanulok, Pitsanulok. N Thailand
Phlórina *see* Flórina
Phnom Penh *see* Phnum Penh
Phnum Penh 137 D 6 *var.* Phnom Penh. Country capital, S Cambodia
Phoenix 48 B 2 state capital, Arizona, SW USA
Phoenix Islands 145 F 3 island group, C Kiribati
Phôngsali 136 C 3 *var.* Phong Saly. N Laos
Phong Saly *see* Phôngsali
Phrae 136 C 4 *var.* Muang Phrae, Prae. N Thailand
Phra Nakhon Si Ayutthaya *see* Ayutthaya
Phra Thong, Ko 137 B 7 island, S Thailand
Phuket 137 B 7 *var.* Bhuket, Puket, *Mal.* Ujung Salang; *prev.* Junkseylon, Salang. S Thailand
Phuket, Ko 137 B 7 island, S Thailand
Phumĭ Kâmpóng Trâlach 137 D 5 C Cambodia
Phumĭ Sâmraông 137 D 5 NW Cambodia
Phu Vinh *see* Tra Vinh
Piacenza 96 B 2 *Fr.* Paisance; *anc.* Placentia. N Italy
Piatra-Neamţ 108 C 3 *Hung.* Karácsonkő. NE Romania
Piauí 63 F 2 *off.* Estado do Piauí; *prev.* Piauhy. State, E Brazil
Picardie 90 C 3 *Eng.* Picardy. Cultural region, N France
Picardy *see* Picardie
Picayune 42 C 3 Mississippi, S USA
Pichilemu 64 B 4 C Chile
Pichincha 60 B 1 NE Ecuador
Pico 92 A 5 *var.* Ilha do Pico. Island, W Portugal
Pico, Ilha do *see* Pico
Picos 63 G 2 E Brazil
Picsi 60 B 3 W Peru
Picton 151 C 5 South Island, C New Zealand
Piedras Negras 51 E 2 *var.* Ciudad Porfirio Díaz. NE Mexico
Pielinen 84 E 4 *var.* Pielisjärvi. Lake, E Finland
Pielisjärvi *see* Pielinen
Pierre 45 E 3 state capital, South Dakota, N USA
Piešt'any 99 C 6 *Ger.* Pistyan, *Hung.* Pöstyén. W Slovakia
Pietarsaari *see* Jakobstad
Pietermaritzburg 78 D 4 *var.* Maritzburg. E South Africa
Pietersburg 78 D 4 NE South Africa
Pigs, Bay of 54 B 2 *Sp.* Bahía de Cochinos. Bay, N Caribbean Sea
Pijijiapán 51 G 5 SE Mexico
Pikes Peak 44 C 5 mountain, Colorado, C USA
Pikine 74 B 3 *var.* Pikini Bougou. W Senegal
Pikini Bougou *see* Pikine
Pikinni *see* Bikini Atoll
Piła 98 C 3 *Ger.* Schneidemühl. NW Poland
Pilar 64 D 3 *var.* Villa del Pilar. S Paraguay
Pilar 63 G 3 W Brazil
Pilcomayo 64 C 2 river, S South America
Pilos *see* Pýlos
Pinang, Pulau 138 B 3 *var.* Penang, Pinang; *prev.* Prince of Wales Island. Island, W Malaysia
Pinar del Río 54 A 2 W Cuba
Píndos 104 A 4 *var.* Píndhos Óros, *Eng.* Pindus Mountains; *prev.* Píndhos. Mountain range, C Greece
Pindus Mountains *see* Píndos
Pine Bluff 42 B 2 Arkansas USA
Pine Creek 148 A 2 Northern Territory, N Australia
Pine Dock 37 G 5 Manitoba, S Canada
Pinega 110 C 3 river, NW Russian Federation
Pineiós 104 B 4 *var.* Piniós; *anc.* Peneius. River, C Greece
Pine Island Bay 154 A 3 bay, S Pacific Ocean
Pines, Lake O' the 49 H 2 reservoir, Texas, S USA
Pingdingshan 128 C 4 C China
Ping, Mae Nam 136 B 4 river, NW Thailand
Pingyang 128 D 4 E China
Pínnes, Ákra 104 C 4 headland, N Greece
Pinotepa Nacional 51 F 5 *var.* Santiago Pinotepa Nacional. SE Mexico
Pinsk 107 B 7 *Pol.* Pińsk. SW Belorussia
Pińsk *see* Pinsk
Pinta, Isla 60 A 5 *var.* Abingdon. Island, Galapagos Islands, E Pacific Ocean
Piombino 96 B 3 C Italy
Pionerskiy 106 A 4 *Ger.* Neukuhren. W Russian Federation
Piotrków Trybunalski 98 D 4 *Ger.* Petrikau, *Rus.* Petrokov. C Poland
Piraeus *see* Peiraías
Pírgos *see* Pýrgos
Piripiri 63 G 2 E Brazil
Pirna 94 D 4 E Germany
Pirot 101 E 5 E Yugoslavia
Piryatin *see* Pyryatyn
Pisa 96 B 3 *var.* Pisae. C Italy
Pisae *see* Pisa
Pisaurum *see* Pesaro
Pisco 60 D 4 SW Peru
Písek 99 A 5 SW Czech Republic
Pishan 126 A 3 *var.* Guma. NW China
Pistoia 96 B 3 *anc.* Pistoria, Pistoriæ. C Italy
Pisz 98 D 3 *Ger.* Johannisburg. NE Poland
Pita 74 C 4 NW Guinea
Pitalito 58 B 4 S Colombia
Pitcairn Islands 143 H 4 UK dependent territory, S Pacific Ocean
Piteå 84 D 4 N Sweden
Piteşti 108 B 5 S Romania
Pitt Island *see* Makin
Pittsburg 45 F 5 Kansas, C USA
Pittsburgh 41 E 4 Pennsylvania, NE USA
Pittsfield 41 F 3 New York, NE USA
Pituffik 82 C 1 *var.* Uummannaq; *prev.* Dundas. NW Greenland
Piura 60 B 3 NW Peru
Pivdennyy Buh 109 E 3 *Rus.* Yuzhnyy Bug. River, S Ukraine
Placetas 54 B 2 C Cuba
Plainview 49 E 2 Texas, S USA
Planeta Rica 58 B 2 NW Colombia
Planken 94 E 1 C Liechtenstein
Plano 49 G 2 Texas, S USA
Plasencia 92 C 3 W Spain
Plata, Rio de la 64 D 4 estuary, SW Atlantic Ocean
Platinum 36 B 3 Alaska, NW USA
Platte River 45 E 4 river, Nebraska, C USA
Plattsburgh 41 F 2 Vermont, NE USA
Plauen 95 C 5 *var.* Plauen im Vogtland. E Germany
Plauen im Vogtland *see* Plauen
Pļaviņas 106 D 4 *Ger.* Stockmannshof. S Latvia
Plây Cu 137 E 5 *var.* Pleiku. S Vietnam
Pleiku *see* Plây Cu
Plenty, Bay of 150 E 3 inlet, SW Pacific Ocean
Plérin 90 A 3 NW France
Pleseck *see* Plesetsk
Plesetsk 110 C 3 *var.* Pleseck. NW Russian Federation
Pleshchenitsy *see* Plyeshchanitsy
Pleszew 98 C 4 C Poland
Pleven 104 C 2 *prev.* Plevna. N Bulgaria
Plevna *see* Pleven
Pljevlja 100 C 4 *prev.* Plevlja, Plevlje. N Yugoslavia
Ploče 100 B 4 *It.* Plocce; *prev.* Kardeljevo. SE Croatia
Płock 98 D 3 *Ger.* Plozk. C Poland
Plöcken Pass 95 C 7 *Ger.* Plöckenpass, *It.* Passo di Monte Croce Carnico. Pass, SW Austria
Ploeşti *see* Ploieşti
Ploieşti 108 C 5 *prev.* Ploeşti. SE Romania
Plomári 105 D 5 *prev.* Plomárion. Lésvos, E Greece
Plomárion *see* Plomári
Plön 94 C 2 N Germany
Płońsk 98 D 3 C Poland
Plovdiv 104 C 3 *prev.* Eumolpias, *anc.* Evmolpia, Philippopolis, *Lat.* Trimontium. C Bulgaria
Plozk *see* Płock
Plungė 106 B 3 W Lithuania
Plyeshchanitsy 107 D 6 *Rus.* Pleshchenitsy. N Belorussia
Plymouth 89 C 7 SW England, UK
Plymouth 55 G 3 dependent territory capital, SW Montserrat
Plzeň 99 A 5 *Ger.* Pilsen, *Pol.* Pilzno. W Czech Republic

Po 96 A 2 river, N Italy
Pobedy, Pik 132 H 2 *var.* Pobeda Peak, *Chin.* Tomur Feng. Mountain, China/Kyrgyzstan
Po, Bocche del *see* Po, Foci del
Pocatello 46 E 4 Idaho, NW USA
Pochinok 111 A 5 W Russian Federation
Pocking 95 D 6 SE Germany
Poděbrady 99 B 5 *Ger.* Podiebrad. C Czech Republic
Podgorica 101 C 5 *prev.* Titograd. Country capital, SW Yugoslavia
Podiebrad *see* Poděbrady
Podil's'ka Vysochyna 108 D 3 *Rus.* Podol'skaya Vozvyshennost'. Mountain range, SW Ukraine
Podol'sk 111 B 5 W Russian Federation
Podol'skaya Vozvyshennost' *see* Podil's'ka Vysochyna
Podravska Slatina 100 C 2 *Hung.* Szlatina; *prev.* Slatina. NE Croatia
Podujevo 101 D 5 C Yugoslavia
Po, Foci del 96 C 2 *var.* Bocche del Po. River, Italy
Pogradec 101 D 6 *var.* Pogradeci. SE Albania
Pogradeci *see* Pogradec
Pohnpei 144 C 2 *prev.* Ponape Ascension Island. Island, E Micronesia
Pohnpei 144 C 2 island group, E Micronesia
Poinsett, Cape 154 D 4 headland, Antarctica
Point Au Fer Island 42 B 4 island, S USA
Point de Galle *see* Galle
Pointe-à-Pitre 55 G 3 C Guadeloupe
Pointe-Noire 77 A 6 S Congo
Point Lay 36 C 2 Alaska, NW USA
Poitiers 90 B 4 *prev.* Poictiers, *anc.* Limonum. W France
Poitou 90 B 4 cultural region, W France
Pokhara 135 F 3 C Nepal
Pok Liu Chau *see* Lamma Island
Pokrovka *see* Kyzyl-Suu
Pokrovs'ke 109 G 3 *Rus.* Pokrovskoye. E Ukraine
Pokrovskoye *see* Pokrovs'ke
Pola de Lena 92 C 1 N Spain

Poland
98 C 4 *var.* Polish Republic, Polska Rzeczpospolita Ludowa, Rzeczpospolita Polska, *Pol.* Polska; *prev.* The Polish People's Republic. Republic, C Europe

Official name: Republic of Poland **Date of formation:** 1918/1945 **Capital:** Warsaw **Population:** 38.5 million **Total area:** 312,680 sq km (120,720 sq miles) **Languages:** Polish*, German **Religions:** Roman Catholic 95%, other Christian 5% **Ethnic mix:** Polish 98%, other 2% **Government:** Multiparty republic **Currency:** Zloty = 100 groszy

Polatsk 107 D 5 *Rus.* Polotsk. N Belorussia
Pol-e Khomrī 123 E 4 *var.* Pul-i-Khumri. NE Afghanistan
Polikraište *see* Polikrayshte
Polikrayshte 104 D 2 *var.* Polikraište. N Bulgaria
Pollença 93 G 3 *var.* Pollensa. E Spain
Pollensa *see* Pollença
Pologi *see* Polohy
Polohy 109 G 3 *Rus.* Pologi. SE Ukraine
Polonne 108 D 2 *Rus.* Polonnoye. NW Ukraine
Polonnoye *see* Polonne
Polotsk *see* Polatsk
Polsko Kosovo 104 D 2 N Bulgaria
Poltava 109 F 2 NE Ukraine
Põlva 106 E 3 *Ger.* Pölwe. SE Estonia
Pölwe *see* Põlva
Polyarnyy 110 C 2 *var.* Pol'arnyj, Poljarny. NW Russian Federation
Polýkastro 104 B 3 *prev.* Políkastron. N Greece
Polynesia 145 G 3 island group, SW Pacific Ocean
Pomeranian Bay 94 D 2 *Ger.* Pommersche Bucht, *Pol.* Zatoka Pomorska. Bay, S Baltic Sea
Pommern 94 D 2 cultural region, NE Germany
Pompano Beach 43 F 5 Florida, SE USA
Ponape Ascension Island *see* Pohnpei
Ponca City 49 G 1 Oklahoma, C USA
Ponce 55 F 3 S Puerto Rico
Pondicherry 132 D 2 *var.* Puduchcheri. SE India
Ponferrada 92 C 1 NW Spain
Poniatowa 98 E 4 E Poland
Pons Vetus *see* Pontevedra
Ponta Delgada 92 A 5 W Portugal
Ponta Grossa 63 E 4 S Brazil
Pontarlier 90 D 4 E France
Pontchartrain, Lake 42 C 3 lake, Louisiana USA
Ponteareas 92 B 2 NW Spain
Ponte da Barca 92 B 2 N Portugal
Pontevedra 92 B 1 *anc.* Pons Vetus. NW Spain
Pontiac 40 D 3 Michigan, N USA
Pontianak 138 C 4 Borneo, C Indonesia
Pontivy 90 A 3 NW France
Pontoise 90 C 3 *anc.* Briva Isarae, Cergy-Pontoise, Pontisarae. N France
Ponton 37 F 5 Manitoba, C Canada
Ponziane, Isole 97 C 5 island, C Italy
Poole 89 D 7 S England, UK
Poona *see* Pune
Poopó, Lago 61 F 4 *var.* Lago Pampa Aullagas. Lake, W Bolivia
Popayán 58 A 4 SW Colombia
Poperinge 87 A 6 W Belgium
Poplar Bluff 45 G 5 Missouri, C USA
Popocatépetl 51 E 4 volcano, S Mexico
Poprad 99 D 5 *Ger.* Popper, *Hung.* Poprád. River, Poland/Slovakia
Poprad 99 D 5 *Ger.* Deutschendorf, *Hung.* Poprád. NE Slovakia
Porbandar 134 B 4 W India
Pordenone 96 C 2 *anc.* Portenau. NE Italy
Poreč 100 A 2 *It.* Parenzo. NW Croatia
Pori 85 D 5 *Swe.* Björneborg. SW Finland
Porirua 151 D 5 North Island, C New Zealand
Porkhov 110 A 4 W Russian Federation
Porlamar 59 E 1 NE Venezuela
Póros 105 C 6 S Greece
Póros 105 A 5 Kefallinía, W Greece
Porsangen 84 D 2 fjord, NE Norway
Porsgrunn 85 B 6 S Norway
Portachuelo 61 G 4 C Bolivia
Portadown 89 B 5 *Ir.* Port An Dúnáin. SE Northern Ireland, UK
Portalegre 92 C 3 *anc.* Ammaia, Amoea. E Portugal
Port Alexander 36 D 4 Alaska, NW USA
Port Alfred 78 D 5 S South Africa
Port An Dúnáin *see* Portadown
Port Angeles 46 B 1 Washington, NW USA
Port Antonio 54 B 5 NE Jamaica
Port Augusta 149 B 6 South Australia, S Australia
Port-au-Prince 54 D 3 country capital, C Haiti
Port Blair 133 F 2 SE India
Port d'Envalira 91 B 8 W Andorra
Port Elizabeth 78 C 5 S South Africa
Portenau *see* Pordenone
Porterville 47 C 7 California, W USA
Port-Étienne *see* Nouâdhibou
Port Florence *see* Kisumu
Port-Francqui *see* Ilebo
Port-Gentil 77 A 6 W Gabon
Port Harcourt 75 G 5 S Nigeria
Port Hardy 36 D 5 Vancouver Island, SW Canada
Port Hedland 146 B 4 Western Australia, W Australia
Port Huron 40 D 3 Michigan, N USA
Portimão 92 B 5 *var.* Vila Nova de Portimão. S Portugal
Port Láirge *see* Waterford
Portland 49 G 5 Texas, S USA
Portland 149 B 7 Victoria, SE Australia
Portland 41 G 2 Maine, NE USA
Portland 46 B 3 Oregon, NW USA
Portland Bight 54 B 5 bay, N Caribbean Sea
Port Laoise 89 B 6 *var.* Portlaoise, *Ir.* Portlaoighise; *prev.* Maryborough. C Ireland
Port Lavaca 49 G 4 Texas, S USA
Port Lincoln 149 A 6 South Australia, S Australia
Port Louis 79 H 3 country capital, NW Mauritius
Port-Lyautey *see* Kénitra
Port Macquarie 149 E 6 New South Wales, SE Australia
Portmore 54 B 5 C Jamaica
Port Moresby 144 B 3 country capital, New Guinea, SW Papua New Guinea
Port Natal *see* Durban
Porto 92 B 2 *Eng.* Oporto; *anc.* Portus Cale. NW Portugal
Porto Alegre 63 E 5 *var.* Pôrto Alegre. State capital, S Brazil
Porto Alegre 76 E 2 S Sao Tome & Principe
Pôrto Alegre *see* Porto Alegre
Porto Alexandre *see* Tombua
Portobelo 53 G 4 *var.* Porto Bello, Puerto Bello. N Panama
Portoferraio 96 B 4 W Italy
Port-of-Spain 55 H 5 country capital, C Trinidad & Tobago
Portogruaro 96 C 2 NE Italy
Porto-Novo 75 F 5 country capital, S Benin
Porto Santo 70 A 2 *var.* Ilha do Porto Santo. Island, Madeira, Portugal
Porto Torres 97 A 5 W Italy
Porto Velho 62 D 2 *var.* Velho. State capital, W Brazil
Portoviejo 60 A 2 *var.* Puertoviejo. W Ecuador
Port Phillip Bay 149 C 7 bay, SW Tasman Sea
Port Pirie 149 B 6 South Australia, S Australia
Port Said 72 B 1 *Ar.* Būr Saʿīd. N Egypt
Portsmouth 89 D 7 S England, UK
Portsmouth 40 D 4 Ohio, N USA
Portsmouth 41 G 3 New Hampshire, NE USA
Port Stanley *see* Stanley
Port Sudan 72 C 3 NE Sudan
Port Talbot 89 C 7 S Wales, UK

Portugal
92 B 3 Republic, W Europe

Official name: Republic of Portugal **Date of formation:** 1140/1640 **Capital:** Lisbon **Population:** 9.9 million **Total area:** 92,390 sq km (35,670 sq miles) **Languages:** Portuguese* **Religions:** Roman Catholic 97%, Protestant 1%, other 2% **Ethnic mix:** Portuguese 98%, African 1%, other 1% **Government:** Multiparty republic **Currency:** Escudo = 100 centavos

Port-Vila 144 D 4 *var.* Vila. Country capital, Éfaté, C Vanuatu
Porvenir 65 B 8 S Chile
Porvenir 61 E 3 NW Bolivia
Porvoo 85 E 5 *Swe.* Borgå. S Finland
Posadas 64 D 3 NE Argentina
Posterholt 87 D 5 SE Netherlands
Postojna 95 D 8 *Ger.* Adelsberg, *It.* Postumia. SW Slovenia
Potamós 105 C 7 Andikithira, S Greece
Potentia *see* Potenza
Potenza 97 D 5 *anc.* Potentia. S Italy
P'ot'i 117 F 2 W Georgia
Potiskum 75 G 4 NE Nigeria
Po Toi Island 128 A 2 island, S Hong Kong
Potosí 61 F 4 S Bolivia
Potsdam 94 D 3 NE Germany
Potwar Plateau 134 C 2 plateau, NE Pakistan
Poûthĭsât 137 D 6 *prev.* Pursat. W Cambodia
Po Valley 96 B 2 *It.* Valle del Po. Valley, N Italy
Považská Bystrica 99 C 5 *Ger.* Waagbistritz, *Hung.* Vágbeszterce. NW Slovakia
Poverty Bay 150 E 4 bay, SW Pacific Ocean
Póvoa de Varzim 92 B 2 NW Portugal
Povorino 111 B 6 W Russian Federation
Povungnituk *see* Puvirnituq
Poway 47 C 8 California, W USA
Powder River 44 D 2 river, Montana, NW USA
Powell 44 C 2 Wyoming, C USA
Powell, Lake 44 B 5 lake, Utah, W USA
Požarevac 100 E 4 *Ger.* Passarowitz. E Yugoslavia
Poza Rica 51 F 4 *var.* Poza Rica de Hidalgo. E Mexico
Poza Rica de Hidalgo *see* Poza Rica
Požega 100 D 4 C Yugoslavia

Poznań 98 B 3 *Ger.* Posen, Posnania. W Poland
Pozoblanco 92 D 4 S Spain
Pozzallo 97 C 8 SW Italy
Prachatice 99 A 5 *Ger.* Prachatitz. SW Czech Republic
Prachatitz *see* Prachatice
Prague *see* Praha
Praha 99 B 5 *Eng.* Prague, *Ger.* Prag, *Pol.* Praga. Country capital, NW Czech Republic
Praia 74 A 3 country capital, S Cape Verde
Praslin 55 F 1 E Saint Lucia
Prato 96 B 3 C Italy
Pratt 45 E 5 Kansas, C USA
Prattville 42 D 2 Alabama, S USA
Pravia 92 C 1 N Spain
Preny *see* Prienai
Prenzlau 94 D 3 NE Germany
Prerau *see* Přerov
Přerov 99 C 5 *Ger.* Prerau. E Czech Republic
Prescott 48 B 2 Arizona USA
Preševo 101 D 5 S Yugoslavia
Presidente Epitácio 63 E 4 S Brazil
Presidente Prudente 57 D 5 S Brazil
Prešov 99 D 5 *var.* Preschau, *Ger.* Eperies, *Hung.* Eperjes. NE Slovakia
Prespa, Lake 101 D 7 *var.* Limni Prespa, Prespansko Jezero, *Alb.* Liqen i Prespës, *Gk.* Límni Megáli Préspa, *Mac.* Prespansko Ezero. Lake, SE Europe
Preston 89 C 5 NW England, UK
Prestwick 88 C 4 SW Scotland, UK
Pretoria 78 D 4 *var.* Epitoli, Tshwane. Country capital, NE South Africa
Preussisch Eylau *see* Bagrationovsk
Preussisch-Stargard *see* Starogard Gdański
Preußisch Holland *see* Pasłęk
Préveza 105 A 5 W Greece
Pribilof Islands 36 A 3 island group, Alaska, NW USA
Priboj 100 D 4 W Yugoslavia
Price 44 B 4 Utah, W USA
Prichard 42 C 3 Alabama, S USA
Pridneprovskaya Vozvyshennost' *see* Prydniprovs'ka Vysochnya
Priekulė 106 B 3 *Ger.* Prökuls. W Lithuania
Prienai 107 B 5 *Pol.* Preny. S Lithuania
Prieska 78 C 5 C South Africa
Prijedor 100 B 3 NW Bosnia & Herzegovina
Prijepolje 100 D 4 W Yugoslavia
Prilep 101 D 6 *Turk.* Perlepe. S Macedonia
Priluki *see* Pryluky
Primorsk 106 A 4 *Ger.* Fischhausen. W Russian Federation
Primorsko 104 E 2 *prev.* Keupriya. SE Bulgaria
Prince Albert 37 F 5 Saskatchewan, S Canada
Prince-Édouard, Île-du *see* Prince Edward Island
Prince Edward Island 39 F 4 *Fr.* Île-du Prince-Édouard. Province, SE Canada
Prince Edward Islands 69 E 8 island group, S South Africa
Prince George 37 E 5 British Columbia, SW Canada
Prince of Wales Island 37 F 2 island, NW Canada
Prince of Wales Island 148 B 1 island, Queensland, N Australia
Prince Patrick Island 37 E 2 island, NW Canada
Prince Rupert 36 D 4 British Columbia, SW Canada
Princess Charlotte Bay 148 C 2 bay, W Coral Sea
Princess Elizabeth Land 154 D 3 physical region, Antarctica
Príncipe 76 E 1 *var.* Príncipe Island, *Eng.* Prince's Island. Island, N Sao Tome & Principe
Prinzapolka 53 E 3 NE Nicaragua
Pripet 107 C 7 *Bel.* Prypyats', *Ukr.* Prypyat'. River, Belorussia/Ukraine
Pripet Marshes 107 B 7 wetland, Belorussia/Ukraine
Prishtinë *see* Priština
Priština 101 D 5 *Alb.* Prishtinë. C Yugoslavia
Privas 91 C 5 E France
Prizren 101 D 5 *Alb.* Prizreni. S Yugoslavia
Prizreni *see* Prizren
Probolinggo 138 D 5 Jawa, C Indonesia
Probstberg *see* Wyszków
Progreso 51 H 3 SE Mexico
Prökuls *see* Priekulė
Prokuplje 101 E 5 C Yugoslavia
Prome 136 B 4 *var.* Pyè. SW Burma
Promyshlennyy 110 E 3 *var.* Promšlennyj, Promyšlenny. NW Russian Federation
Prostějov 99 C 5 *Ger.* Prossnitz, *Pol.* Prosciejów. SE Czech Republic
Provence 91 D 6 cultural region, SE France
Providence 41 G 3 state capital, Rhode Island, NE USA
Providence *see* Fort Providence
Providencia, Isla de 53 F 3 island, Colombia
Provo 44 B 4 Utah, W USA
Provost 37 E 5 Alberta, SW Canada
Prudhoe Bay 36 D 2 Alaska, NW USA
Pruszków 98 D 3 *Ger.* Kaltdorf. C Poland
Prut 108 D 4 *Ger.* Pruth. River, E Europe
Pruth *see* Prut
Pružana *see* Pruzhany
Pruzhany 107 B 6 *Pol.* Pruzana. SW Belorussia
Prychornomors'ka Nyzovyna 109 E 4 *Eng.* Black Sea Lowland. Physical region, S Ukraine
Prydniprovs'ka Vysochnya 109 G 3 *Rus.* Pridneprovskaya Vozvyshennost'. Mountain range, NW Ukraine
Prydz Bay 154 D 3 bay, S Indian Ocean
Pryluky 109 E 2 *Rus.* Priluki. NE Ukraine
Prymors'k 109 G 4 *Rus.* Primorsk; *prev.* Primorskoye. SE Ukraine
Przemyśl 99 E 5 *Rus.* Peremyshl. SE Poland
Przheval'sk *see* Karakol
Psará 105 D 5 island, E Greece
Pskov 110 A 4 *Ger.* Pleskau, *Latv.* Pleskava. W Russian Federation
Pskov, Lake 106 E 3 *Est.* Pihkva Järv, *Ger.* Pleskauer See, *Rus.* Pskovskoye Ozero. Lake, Estonia/Russian Federation
Ptich' *see* Ptsich
Ptsich 107 C 7 *Rus.* Ptich'. River, SE Belorussia
Ptsich 107 C 7 *Rus.* Ptich'. SE Belorussia
Ptuj 95 E 7 *Ger.* Pettau; *anc.* Poetovio. NE Slovenia
Pucallpa 60 C 3 C Peru
Puck 98 C 2 N Poland
Pudasjärvi 84 E 4 C Finland
Puduchcheri *see* Pondicherry
Puebla 51 F 4 *var.* Puebla de Zaragoza. S Mexico
Puebla de Zaragoza *see* Puebla
Pueblo 44 D 5 Colorado, C USA
Puerto Acosta 61 E 4 W Bolivia
Puerto Aisén 65 B 6 S Chile
Puerto Arturo 61 G 3 N Bolivia
Puerto Ayacucho 58 D 3 SW Venezuela
Puerto Bahía Negra 64 D 1 N Paraguay
Puerto Baquerizo Moreno 60 B 5 *var.* Baquerizo Moreno. Galapagos Islands, E Pacific Ocean
Puerto Barrios 52 C 2 E Guatemala
Puerto Berrío 58 B 2 C Colombia
Puerto Cabello 58 D 1 N Venezuela
Puerto Cabezas 53 E 2 *var.* Bilwi. NE Nicaragua
Puerto Carreño 58 D 3 NE Colombia
Puerto Casado 64 D 2 C Paraguay
Puerto Cortés 52 C 2 NW Honduras
Puerto Cumarebo 58 C 1 N Venezuela
Puerto Deseado 65 C 7 SE Argentina
Puerto Escondido 51 F 5 W Mexico
Puerto Francisco de Orellana 60 B 1 *var.* Coca. N Ecuador
Puerto Inírida 58 D 3 *var.* Obando. E Colombia
Puerto La Cruz 59 E 1 NE Venezuela
Puerto Lempira 53 E 2 E Honduras
Puerto Limón *see* Limón
Puertollano 92 D 4 SW Spain
Puerto López 58 C 1 N Colombia
Puerto Maldonado 61 E 3 E Peru
Puerto Montt 65 B 5 C Chile
Puerto Natales 65 B 7 S Chile
Puerto Nuevo 58 C 3 N Colombia
Puerto Obaldía 53 H 5 NE Panama
Puerto Plata 55 E 3 *var.* San Felipe de Puerto Plata. N Dominican Republic
Puerto Portillo 60 D 3 E Peru
Puerto Princesa 139 E 2 *off.* Puerto Princesa City. Palawan, W Philippines
Puerto Princesa City *see* Puerto Princesa
Puerto Príncipe *see* Camagüey
Puerto Rico 55 F 3 *off.* Commonwealth of Puerto Rico; *prev.* Porto Rico. US commonwealth territory, N Caribbean Sea
Puerto Rico Trench 66 B 4 trench, W Atlantic Ocean
Puerto San José *see* San José
Puerto San Julián 65 B 7 *var.* San Julián. SE Argentina
Puerto Suárez 61 H 4 E Bolivia
Puerto Supe 60 C 3 W Peru
Puerto Vallarta 50 D 4 SW Mexico
Puerto Varas 65 B 5 C Chile
Puerto Viejo 53 E 4 NE Costa Rica
Puertoviejo *see* Portoviejo
Puerto Williams 65 C 8 S Chile
Puget Sound 46 B 1 inlet, E Pacific Ocean
Pukaki, Lake 151 B 6 lake, South Island, SW New Zealand
Pukekohe 150 D 3 North Island, N New Zealand
Pukhavichy 107 D 6 *Rus.* Pukhovichi. C Belorussia
Pukhovichi *see* Pukhavichy
Pula 100 A 3 *It.* Pola; *prev.* Pulj. NW Croatia
Puławy 98 E 4 *Ger.* Neu Amerika. E Poland
Pul-i-Khumri *see* Pol-e Khomrī
Pullman 46 C 2 Washington, NW USA
Pułtusk 98 D 3 C Poland
Puná, Isla 60 A 2 island, SW Ecuador
Pune 134 C 5 *prev.* Poona. W India
Punjab 134 C 2 *prev.* Western Punjab, West Punjab. Province, E Pakistan
Puno 61 E 4 SE Peru
Punta Alta 65 C 5 E Argentina
Punta Arenas 65 B 8 *prev.* Magallanes . S Chile
Punta Gorda 53 E 4 SE Nicaragua
Punta Gorda 52 C 2 SE Belize
Puntarenas 52 D 4 W Costa Rica
Punto Fijo 58 C 1 N Venezuela
Pupuya, Nevado 61 E 4 mountain, W Bolivia
Puri 135 F 5 *var.* Jagannath. E India
Purmerend 86 C 3 C Netherlands
Pursat *see* Poŭthĭsăt
Purus 62 C 2 *var.* Río Purús. River, Brazil/Peru
Purús, Río *see* Purus
Pusan 128 E 4 *off.* Pusan-kwangyŏksi, *var.* Busan, *Jap.* Fusan. SE South Korea
Püspökladány 99 D 6 E Hungary
Putorana Mountains *see* Putorana, Plato
Putorana, Plato 115 E 3 *var.* Putorana Mountains. Mountain range, N Russian Federation
Puttalam 132 C 3 W Sri Lanka
Puttgarden 94 C 2 N Germany
Putumayo 58 B 5 *var.* Içá. River, N South America
Putumayo, Río *see* Içá
Puurmani 106 D 2 *Ger.* Talkhof. E Estonia
Puvirnituq 38 D 1 *prev.* Povungnituk. Québec, NE Canada
Puyallup 46 B 2 Washington, NW USA
Pyatigorsk 111 B 7 SW Russian Federation
Pyatikhatki *see* P"yatykhatky
P"yatykhatky 109 F 3 *Rus.* Pyatikhatki. C Ukraine
Pyè *see* Prome
Pyetrykaw 107 C 7 *Rus.* Petrikov. SE Belorussia
Pyinmana 136 B 4 C Burma
Pýlos 105 B 6 S Greece
P'yŏngyang 128 D 4 *Eng.* Pyongyang. Country capital, SW North Korea
Pyramiden 83 G 2 W Svalbard
Pyramid Lake 47 C 5 lake, Nevada, W USA
Pyrenees 93 F 1 *Fr.* Pyrénées, *Sp.* Pirineos; *anc.* Pyrenaei Montes. Mountain range, SW Europe
Pýrgos 105 B 6 *var.* Pírgos. S Greece
Pyritz *see* Pyrzyce

Pyryatyn 109 F 2 *Rus.* Piryatin. NE Ukraine
Pyrzyce 98 B 3 *Ger.* Pyritz. NW Poland
Pyu 136 B 4 S Burma
Pyuntaza 136 B 4 S Burma

Q

Qā' al Jafr 119 C 7 lake, S Jordan
Qaanaaq 82 D 1 *var.* Qânâq, *Dan.* Thule. N Greenland
Qabatiya 119 E 6 N West Bank
Qābis *see* Gabès
Qābis, Khalīj *see* Gabès, Golfe de
Qafṣah *see* Gafsa
Qaidam Pendi 126 C 4 basin, C China
Qal'aikhum 123 F 3 *Rus.* Kalaikhum. S Tajikistan
Qalāt *see* Kalāt
Qal 'at Bīshah 121 B 5 SW Saudi Arabia
Qalqiliya 119 D 7 *var.* Qalqiliya. W West Bank
Qamdo 126 D 5 S China
Qandahār *see* Kandahār
Qanıx *see* Alazani
Qaqortoq 82 C 5 *Dan.* Julianehåb. SW Greenland
Qaraghandy *see* Karaganda
Qarataū *see* Karatau
Qarokŭl 123 F 3 *Rus.* Karakul'. E Tajikistan
Qars *see* Kars
Qarshi 123 E 3 *Rus.* Karshi; *prev.* Bek-Budi. S Uzbekistan
Qasigiannguit 82 C 3 *var.* Qasigianguit, *Dan.* Christianshåb. W Greenland
Qaṭanā 119 B 5 *var.* Katana. SW Syria

Qatar
120 D 4 *Ar.* Dawlat Qaṭar. Monarchy, Qatar

Official name: State of Qatar **Date of formation:** 1971 **Capital:** Doha **Population:** 500,000 **Total area:** 11,000 sq km (4,247 sq miles) **Languages:** Arabic*, Farsi (Persian), Urdu, Hindi, English **Religions:** Sunni Muslim 86%, Hindu 10%, Christian 4% **Ethnic mix:** Arab 40%, South Asian 35%, Persian 12%, other 13% **Government:** Absolute monarchy **Currency:** Riyal = 100 dirhams

Qattara Depression *see* **Qaṭṭâra, Monkhafad el**
Qaṭṭâra, Monkhafad el 72 B 1 *var.* Munkhafaḑ al Qaḑḑárah, *Eng.* Qattara Depression. Desert, NW Egypt
Qazimämmäd 117 H 3 *Rus.* Kazi Magomed. SE Azerbaijan
Qazris *see* Cáceres
Qazvīn 120 C 2 *var.* Kazvin. NW Iran
Qena 72 B 2 *var.* Qinā; *anc.* Caene, Caenepolis. E Egypt
Qeqertarsuaq 82 C 3 *var.* Qeqertarssuaq, *Dan.* Godhavn. W Greenland
Qeqertarsuaq 82 C 3 island, W Greenland
Qeqertarsuatsiaat 82 B 4 *Dan.* Fiskenæsset. S Greenland
Qeshm 120 D 4 *var.* Jazīreh-ye Qeshm, Qeshm Island. Island, S Iran
Qeẕi'ot 119 A 7 S Israel
Qilian Shan 128 A 3 *var.* Kilien Mountains. Mountain range, N China
Qimantag Shan 126 C 4 mountain range, C China
Qimusseriarsuaq 82 C 2 *Dan.* Melville Bugt, *Eng.* Melville Bay. Bay, E Baffin Bay
Qingdao 128 D 4 *var.* Ching-Tao, Ch'ing-tao, Tsingtao, Tsintao, *Ger.* Tsingtau. E China
Qinghai 126 D 4 *var.* Chinghai, Koko Nor, Qing, Tsinghai. Province, C China
Qinghai Hu 126 D 4 *var.* Ch'ing Hai, Tsing Hai, *Mong.* Koko *Nor.* Lake, C China
Qinghai Nanshan 126 D 4 mountain range, N China
Qinhuangdao 128 D 3 NE China
Qinzhou 129 B 6 SE China
Qiong *see* Hainan
Qiqihar 125 E 1 *var.* Ch'i-ch'i-ha-erh,Tsitsihar; *prev.* Lungkiang. NE China
Qira 126 B 4 NW China
Qita Ghazzah *see* Gaza Strip
Qitai 126 C 3 NW China
Qitaihe 128 E 2 NE China
Qīzān *see* Jīzān
Qizilrabot 123 G 3 *Rus.* Kyzylrabot. SE Tajikistan
Qolleh-ye Damāvand 120 D 3 mountain, N Iran
Qom 120 C 3 *var.* Kum, Qum. N Iran
Qondūz, Daryā-ye 123 E 4 river, NE Afghanistan
Qornet es Saouda 118 B 4 mountain, NE Lebanon
Qorveh 120 C 3 *var.* Qerveh, Qurveh. W Iran
Quang Ngai 137 E 5 *var.* Quangngai, Quang Nghia. E Vietnam
Quanzhou 129 C 6 S China
Quanzhou 129 D 6 *var.* Ch'uan-chou, Tsinkiang; *prev.* Chin-chiang. SE China
Quarles, Pegunungan 139 E 4 mountain range, Celebes, W Indonesia
Quartu Sant' Elena 97 A 6 W Italy
Quba 117 H 2 *Rus.* Kuba. N Azerbaijan
Qubba *see* Ba'qūbah
Queanbeyan 149 D 7 New South Wales, SE Australia
Quebec *see* Québec
Québec 38 D 3 *var.* Quebec. Province, Québec, SE Canada
Queen Charlotte 36 C 5 Queen Charlotte Islands, SW Canada
Queen Charlotte Islands 36 D 5 *Fr.* Îles de la Reine-Charlotte. Island group, SW Canada
Queen Charlotte Sound 36 D 5 bay, NE Pacific Ocean
Queen Elizabeth Islands 37 F 2 *Fr.* Îles de la Reine-Élisabeth. Island group, N Canada
Queen Maud Land 154 C 2 *var.* Dronning Maud Land. Physical region, Antarctica
Queensland 148 B 4 state, N Australia
Queenstown 151 B 7 South Island, SW New Zealand
Queenstown 149 B 8 Tasmania, SE Australia
Queenstown 78 D 5 S South Africa
Queenstown 138 A 1 S Singapore
Quelimane 79 E 3 *var.* Kilimane, Kilmain, Quilimane. NE Mozambique
Quepos 53 E 5 S Costa Rica
Que Que *see* Kwekwe
Querétaro 51 E 4 C Mexico
Quesada 53 E 4 *var.* Ciudad Quesada, San Carlos. N Costa Rica
Quetta 134 B 2 province capital, SW Pakistan
Quetzaltenango *see* Quezaltenango
Quezaltenango 52 A 2 *var.* Quetzaltenango. W Guatemala
Quezon 139 F 2 *off.* Quezon City. C Philippines
Quezon City *see* Quezon
Quibdó 58 B 3 W Colombia
Quilon 132 C 3 *var.* Kolam, Kollam. SW India
Quimper 90 A 3 *anc.* Quimper Corentin. NW France
Quimper Corentin *see* Quimper
Quimperlé 90 A 3 NW France
Quincy 40 A 4 Illinois, N USA
Quirós Fracture Zone 153 F 4 fracture zone, E Pacific Ocean
Quissico 79 E 4 S Mozambique
Quito 60 B 1 country capital, N Ecuador
Qŭqon 123 F 2 *var.* Khokand, *Rus.* Kokand. E Uzbekistan
Qŭrghonteppa 123 E 3 *Rus.* Kurgan-Tyube. SW Tajikistan
Qurlurtuuq *see* Coppermine
Qûs 72 B 2 *anc.* Apollinopolis Parva. E Egypt
Quy Nhơn 137 E 5 *var.* Qui Nhon, Quinhon. SE Vietnam

R

Raab *see* Rába
Raahe 84 D 4 *Swe.* Brahestad. W Finland
Raalte 86 D 3 E Netherlands
Raamsdonksveer 86 C 4 S Netherlands
Raasiku 106 D 2 *Ger.* Rasik. NW Estonia
Raas Xaafuun 72 E 4 *var.* Ras Hafun. Headland, NE Somalia
Rabat 70 C 2 *var.* al Dar al Baida. Country capital, NW Morocco
Rabat *see* Victoria
Rabinal 52 B 2 C Guatemala
Rabka 99 D 5 S Poland
Rabyānah, Ramlat 71 G 3 *var.* Rebiana Sand Sea, Ṣaḥrā' Rabyānah. Desert, SE Libya
Race, Cape 39 H 4 headland, Newfoundland and Labrador, E Canada
Rach Gia 137 D 6 SW Vietnam
Rach Gia, Vinh 137 D 6 bay, South China Sea / Pacific Ocean
Racine 40 B 3 Wisconsin, N USA
Rădăuţi 108 C 3 *Ger.* Radautz, *Hung.* Rádóc. N Romania
Radom 98 D 4 C Poland
Radomsko 98 C 4 *Rus.* Novoradomsk. C Poland
Radomyshl' 108 D 2 N Ukraine
Radoviš 101 E 6 *prev.* Radovište. E Macedonia
Radovište *see* Radoviš
Radviliškis 106 C 4 N Lithuania
Radzyń Podlaski 98 E 4 E Poland
Rae-Edzo 37 E 4 Northwest Territories, NW Canada
Raeside, Lake 147 C 5 lake, C Australia
Raetihi 150 D 4 North Island, C New Zealand
Rafaela 64 C 3 E Argentina
Rafah 119 A 7 S Israel
Rafḩā' 120 B 4 N Saudi Arabia
Ragged Island Range 54 C 2 island group, S Bahamas
Ragnit *see* Neman
Ragusa 97 C 7 SW Italy
Ragusa *see* Dubrovnik
Rahachow 107 D 7 *Rus.* Rogachëv. SE Belorussia
Rahaeng *see* Tak
Rahīmyār Khān 134 C 3 SE Pakistan
Rahovec *see* Orahovac
Raiatea 145 G 4 island, W French Polynesia
Rāichūr 132 C 1 C India
Rainy Lake 38 B 4 lake, Ontario, S Canada
Raipur 135 E 4 C India
Rājahmundry 135 E 5 E India
Rajang *see* Rajang, Batang
Rajang, Batang 138 D 3 *var.* Rajang. River, Borneo, E Malaysia
Rājapālaiyam 132 C 3 SE India
Rājasthān 134 C 3 state, NW India
Rājkot 134 C 4 W India
Rāj Nāndgaon 135 E 4 C India
Rājshāhi 135 G 4 *prev.* Rampur Boalia. W Bangladesh
Rakahanga 145 F 3 island, N Cook Islands
Rakke 106 E 2 NE Estonia
Rakvere 106 E 2 *Ger.* Wesenberg. N Estonia
Raleigh 43 F 1 state capital, North Carolina, SE USA
Raleigh Bay 43 G 1 bay, NW Atlantic Ocean
Ralik Chain 144 D 1 island group, W Marshall Islands
Ram 119 B 8 SW Jordan
Ramallah 119 E 7 C West Bank
Ramat Gan 119 A 6 C Israel
Râmnicu Sărat 108 C 4 *prev.* Râmnicul-Sărat, Rîmnicu-Sărat. E Romania
Râmnicu Vîlcea 108 B 4 *prev.* Rîmnicu Vîlcea. C Romania
Ramotswa 78 C 4 SE Botswana
Rampur Boalia *see* Rājshāhi
Ramree Island 136 A 4 island, W Burma
Ramtha *see* Ar Ramthā
Rancagua 64 B 4 C Chile
Rānchi 135 F 4 N India
Randers 85 B 7 C Denmark
Rangiora 151 C 6 South Island, C New Zealand
Rangoon *see* Yangon
Rangpur 135 G 3 N Bangladesh
Rankin Inlet 37 G 3 Northwest Territories, C Canada
Rankovićevo *see* Kraljevo
Ranong 137 B 6 SW Thailand
Rantoul 40 B 4 Illinois, N USA
Rapid City 44 D 3 South Dakota, N USA
Räpina 106 E 3 *Ger.* Rappin. SE Estonia
Rapla 106 D 2 *Ger.* Rappel. NW Estonia
Rappel *see* Rapla
Rappin *see* Räpina
Rarotonga 145 F 5 island, S Cook Islands

Ras al'Ain *see* Ra's al 'Ayn
Ra's al 'Ayn 118 D 1 *var.* Ras al'Ain. N Syria
Ra's an Naqb 119 B 8 S Jordan
Raseiniai 106 B 4 C Lithuania
Ras Hafun *see* Raas Xaafuun
Rasht 120 C 2 *var.* Resht. NW Iran
Rasik *see* Raasiku
Râşnov 108 C 4 *Hung.* Barcarozsnyó; *prev.* Rîşnov, *Hung.* Rozsnyó. C Romania
Rason Lake 147 C 5 lake, C Australia
Ratak Chain 144 D 1 island group, E Marshall Islands
Ratan 85 C 5 C Sweden
Rat Buri *see* Ratchaburi
Ratchaburi 137 C 5 *var.* Rat Buri. C Thailand
Ratlām 134 D 4 *prev.* Rutlam. C India
Ratnapura 132 D 4 S Sri Lanka
Raton 48 D 1 New Mexico, SW USA
Rättvik 85 C 5 C Sweden
Raudhatain *see* Ar Rawḑatayn
Raufarhöfn 83 E 4 NE Iceland
Raukawa *see* Cook Strait
Rauma 85 D 5 *Swe.* Raumo. SW Finland
Raumo *see* Rauma
Raurkela 135 F 4 *prev.* Rourkela. E India
Ravenna 96 C 3 N Italy
Rāvi 134 C 2 river, India/Pakistan
Rāwalpindi 134 C 1 NE Pakistan
Rawa Mazowiecka 98 D 4 C Poland
Rawicz 98 C 4 *Ger.* Rawitsch. W Poland
Rawitsch *see* Rawicz
Rawlins 44 C 3 Wyoming, C USA
Rawson 65 C 6 SE Argentina
Rayak 118 B 4 *var.* Rayaq, Riyāq. E Lebanon
Rayong 137 C 6 C Thailand
Razāzah, Buḩayrat ar 120 B 3 *var.* Baḩr al Milḩ. Lake, C Iraq
Razdolnoye *see* Rozdol'ne
Razelm, Lacul *see* Razim, Lacul
Razgrad 104 D 2 NE Bulgaria
Razim, Lacul 108 D 5 *prev.* Lacul Razelm. Lagoon, W Black Sea
Rāznas Ezers 106 D 4 lake, SE Latvia
Reading 89 D 7 S England, UK
Reading 41 F 4 Pennysylvania, NE USA
Realicó 64 C 4 C Argentina
Reâng Kesei 137 D 5 W Cambodia
Rebecca, Lake 147 C 6 lake, Western Australia, C Australia
Rebun-tō 130 C 1 island, Japan
Recherche, Archipelago of the 147 C 7 island group, SW Australia
Rechitsa *see* Rechytsa
Rechytsa 107 D 7 *Rus.* Rechitsa. SW Belorussia
Recife 63 G 2 *prev.* Pernambuco. State capital, E Brazil
Recklinghausen 94 A 4 W Germany
Recogne 87 D 7 SE Belgium
Reconquista 64 D 3 NE Argentina
Red Bluff Lake 49 E 3 lake, SW USA
Red Deer 37 E 5 Alberta, SW Canada
Redding 47 B 5 California, W USA
Redon 90 B 4 NW France
Red River 136 C 2 *var.* Yijan Chiang. River, China/Vietnam
Red River 35 C 6 river, S USA
Red River 45 E 1 river, Canada/USA
Red Sea 140 A 3 *var.* Sinus Arabious. Sea, NW Indian Ocean
Red Sea Hills 72 C 3 hill range, NE Sudan
Red Wing 45 G 2 Minnesota, N USA
Reedley 47 C 6 California, W USA
Reefton 151 C 5 South Island, C New Zealand
Reese River 47 C 5 river, Nevada, W USA
Refahiye 117 E 3 C Turkey
Regensburg 95 C 6 *Eng.* Ratisbon, *Fr.* Ratisbonne; *hist.* Ratisbona, *anc.* Castra Regina, Reginum. SE Germany
Regenstauf 95 C 6 SE Germany
Reggane 70 D 3 C Algeria
Reggio di Calabria 97 D 7 *var.* Reggio Calabria, *Gk.* Rhegion; *anc.* Regium, Rhegium. SW Italy
Reggio nell' Emilia 96 B 2 *var.* Reggio Emilia, *abbrev.* Reggio; *anc.* Regium Lepidum. N Italy
Reghin 108 C 4 *Ger.* Sächsisch-Reen, *Hung.* Szászrégen; *prev.* Reghinul Săsesc, *Ger.* Sächsisch-Regen. C Romania
Regina 37 F 5 province capital, Saskatchewan, S Canada
Registan *see* Rīgestān
Rehoboth 78 B 4 C Namibia
Reichenau *see* Bogatynia
Reichenberg *see* Liberec
Reid 147 D 6 Western Australia, S Australia
Reikjavik *see* Reykjavík
Ré, Île de 90 A 4 island, W France
Reims 90 D 3 *Eng.* Rheims; *anc.* Durocortorum, Remi. N France
Reindeer Lake 34 C 4 lake, C Canada
Reine-Charlotte, Îles de la *see* Queen Charlotte Islands
Reine-Élisabeth, Îles de la *see* Queen Elizabeth Islands
Reinosa 92 D 1 N Spain
Reliance 37 F 4 Northwest Territories, C Canada
Rendina *see* Rentína
Rendsburg 94 B 2 N Germany
Rengat 138 B 4 Sumatera, W Indonesia
Reni 108 D 4 SW Ukraine
Rennell 144 C 4 *var.* Mu Nggava. Island, S Solomon Islands
Rennes 90 B 3 *Bret.* Roazon; *anc.* Condate. NW France
Reno 47 C 5 Nevada, W USA
Renqiu 128 C 4 NE China
Rentína 105 B 5 *var.* Rendina. C Greece
Repulse Bay 37 G 3 Northwest Territories, NE Canada
Resht *see* Rasht
Resistencia 64 D 3 NE Argentina
Reşiţa 108 A 4 *Ger.* Reschitza, *Hung.* Resicabánya. W Romania
Resolute 37 F 2 Cornwallis Island, N Canada
Resolution Island 151 A 7 island, South Island, SW New Zealand
Resolution Island 39 E 1 island, Northwest Territories, NE Canada
Réunion 79 H 4 *off.* La Réunion. French overseas department, E Africa
Reus 93 F 2 E Spain
Reutlingen 95 B 6 S Germany
Reuver 87 D 5 SE Netherlands
Revillagigedo Islands *see* Revillagigedo, Islas
Revillagigedo, Islas 50 B 5 *Eng.* Revillagigedo Islands. Island group, SW Mexico
Rexburg 46 E 3 Idaho, NW USA
Reyes 61 F 3 NW Bolivia
Rey, Isla del 53 G 5 island, SE Panama
Reykjanes Basin 66 C 2 undersea basin, N Atlantic Ocean
Reykjavík 83 E 5 *var.* Reikjavik. Country capital, W Iceland
Reynosa 51 E 2 C Mexico
Reza, Gora 122 C 3 *var.* Gora Riza. Mountain, SW Turkmenistan
Rezé 90 B 4 NW France
Rēzekne 106 D 4 *Ger.* Rositten; *prev. Rus.* Rezhitsa. SE Latvia
Rezovo 104 E 3 *Turk.* Rezve. SE Bulgaria
Rezve *see* Rezovo
Rhätikon 95 B 7 mountain range, C Europe
Rheine 94 A 4 *var.* Rheine in Westfalen. NW Germany
Rheine in Westfalen *see* Rheine
Rheinisches Schiefergebirge 95 A 5 *var.* Rhine State Uplands, *Eng.* Rhenish Slate Mountains. Mountain range, W Germany
Rhine 80 D 4 *Dut.* Rijn, *Fr.* Rhin, *Ger.* Rhein. River, W Europe
Rhinelander 40 B 2 Wisconsin, N USA
Rho 96 B 2 N Italy
Rhode Island 41 G 3 *off.* State of Rhode Island and Providence Plantations; *nicknames* Little Rhody, Ocean State. State, NE USA
Rhodes *see* Ródos
Rhodope Mountains 104 C 3 *var.* Rodhópi Óri, *Bul.* Rhodope Planina, Rodopi, *Gk.* Orosirá Rodhópis, *Turk.* Dospad Dagh. Mountain range, Bulgaria/Greece
Rhondda 89 C 7 S Wales, UK
Rhône 80 C 4 river, France/Switzerland
Rhum 88 B 3 *var.* Rum. Island, W Scotland, UK
Ribble 89 D 5 river, NW England, UK
Ribeira 92 B 1 NW Spain
Ribeirão Preto 63 F 4 S Brazil
Riberalta 61 E 2 N Bolivia
Rîbniţa 108 D 3 *var.* Râbniţa, *Rus.* Rybnitsa. NE Moldavia
Richard Toll 74 B 3 N Senegal
Richfield 44 B 4 Utah, W USA
Richland 46 C 2 Washington, NW USA
Richmond 151 C 5 North Island, C New Zealand
Richmond 41 E 5 state capital, Virginia, NE USA
Richmond 40 C 5 Kentucky, E USA
Richmond Range 151 C 5 mountain range, North Island, C New Zealand
Ricomagus *see* Riom
Ridgecrest 47 C 7 California, W USA
Ried *see* Ried im Innkreis
Ried im Innkreis 95 D 6 *var.* Ried. NW Austria
Riemst 87 D 6 NE Belgium
Riesa 94 D 4 E Germany
Rift Valley *see* Great Rift Valley
Riga *see* Rīga
Rīga 106 C 3 *var.* Rīga, *Eng.* Riga. Country capital, C Latvia
Riga, Gulf of 106 C 3 *Est.* Liivi Laht, *Ger.* Rigaer Bucht, *Latv.* Rīgas Jūras Līcis, *Rus.* Rizhskiy Zaliv; *prev.* Riia Laht. Gulf, E Baltic Sea
Rīgān 120 E 4 SE Iran
Rīgestān 122 D 5 *var.* Registan. Physical region, S Afghanistan
Riihimäki 85 D 5 S Finland
Rijeka 100 A 2 *Ger.* Sankt Veit am Flaum, *It.* Fiume, *Slvn.* Reka; *anc.* Tarsatica. NW Croatia
Rijssen 86 E 3 E Netherlands
Rimah, Wādī ar 120 B 4 *var.* Wādī ar Rummah. Dry watercourse, C Saudi Arabia
Rimini 96 C 3 *anc.* Ariminum. N Italy
Rîmnicu Vîlcea *see* Râmnicu Vâlcea
Rimouski 39 E 4 Québec, SE Canada
Rincón del Bonete, Lago Artificial de *see* Río Negro, Embalse del
Ringebu 85 B 5 S Norway
Ringen *see* Rõngu
Ringkøbing Fjord 85 A 7 fjord, E North Sea
Ringsaker 85 B 5 S Norway
Ringvassøy 84 C 2 island, N Norway
Rio *see* Rio de Janeiro
Riobamba 60 B 1 C Ecuador
Río Bravo 51 E 2 C Mexico
Río Cuarto 64 C 4 C Argentina
Rio de Janeiro 63 F 4 *var.* Rio. State capital, SE Brazil
Río Gallegos 65 B 7 *var.* Gallegos, Puerto Gallegos. S Argentina
Rio Grande 63 E 5 *var.* São Pedro do Rio Grande do Sul. S Brazil
Rio Grande do Norte 63 G 2 *off.* Estado do Rio Grande do Norte. State, E Brazil
Rio Grande do Norte, Estado do *see* Rio Grande do Norte
Rio Grande do Sul 63 E 5 *off.* Estado do Rio Grande do Sul. State, S Brazil
Rio Grande do Sul, Estado do *see* Rio Grande do Sul
Rio Grande Plateau *see* Rio Grande Rise
Rio Grande Rise 57 E 5 *var.* Rio Grande Plateau. Undersea plateau, SW Atlantic Ocean
Riohacha 58 C 1 N Colombia
Riom 91 C 5 *anc.* Ricomagus. C France
Río Negro, Embalse del 64 D 4 *var.* Lago Artificial de Rincón del Bonete. Reservoir, C Uruguay
Rio Rancho Estates 48 D 2 New Mexico, SW USA
Río Santa Cruz 65 B 7 S Argentina
Rioverde *see* Río Verde
Río Verde 51 E 4 *var.* Rioverde. C Mexico
Ripoll 93 G 2 NE Spain
Rishiri-tō 130 C 2 *var.* Risiri Tô. Island, NE Japan
Risiri Tô *see* Rishiri-tō
Risti 106 D 2 *Ger.* Kreuz. W Estonia
Rivas 52 D 4 SW Nicaragua
Rivera 64 D 3 N Uruguay
River Falls 40 A 2 Wisconsin, N USA
Riverside 47 C 8 California, W USA

Riverton 151 A 7 South Island, SW New Zealand
Riverton 44 C 3 Wyoming, C USA
Riviera Beach 43 F 4 Florida, SE USA
Rivière-du-Loup 39 E 4 Québec, SE Canada
Rivne 108 C 1 *Pol.* Równe, *Rus.* Rovno. NW Ukraine
Rivoli 96 A 2 NW Italy
Rixheim 90 E 4 E France
Riyadh *see* Ar Riyāḑ
Riza, Gora *see* Reza, Gora
Rize 117 E 2 NE Turkey
Rizhao 128 D 4 E China
Rkîz, Lac 74 B 3 lake, SW Mauritania
Road Town 55 F 3 dependent territory capital, C British Virgin Islands
Roanne 91 D 5 *anc.* Rodunma. E France
Roanoke 41 E 5 Virginia, NE USA
Roanoke Rapids 43 F 1 North Carolina, SE USA
Roanoke River 43 F 1 river, E USA
Roatán 52 C 2 *var.* Coxen Hole, Coxin Hole. N Honduras
Robinson Ranges 147 B 5 mountain range, Western Australia, W Australia
Robson, Mount 37 E 5 mountain, Alberta, SW Canada
Robstown 49 G 5 Texas, S USA
Roca Partida, Isla 50 B 5 island, W Mexico
Rocas, Atol das 63 H 2 island, E Brazil
Rochefort 91 B 5 *var.* Rochefort sur Mer. W France
Rochefort 87 C 7 SE Belgium
Rochefort sur Mer *see* Rochefort
Rochester 41 E 3 New York, NE USA
Rochester 41 G 2 New Hampshire, NE USA
Rochester 45 G 3 Minnesota, N USA
Rockall Bank 66 C 2 undersea bank, N Atlantic Ocean
Rockford 40 B 3 Illinois, N USA
Rockhampton 148 D 4 Queensland, E Australia
Rock Hill 43 E 1 South Carolina, SE USA
Rockingham 147 B 6 Western Australia, SW Australia
Rock Island 40 B 3 Illinois, N USA
Rock Sound 54 C 1 C Bahamas
Rock Springs 44 B 3 Wyoming, C USA
Rockstone 59 F 3 C Guyana
Rocky Mountains 34 B 4 *var.* Rockies, *Fr.* Montagnes Rocheuses. Mountain range, NW USA
Roden 86 E 2 NE Netherlands
Rodez 91 C 6 *anc.* Segodunum. S France
Ródos 105 E 7 *var.* Ródhos, *Eng.* Rhodes, *It.* Rodi. Ródos, SE Greece
Ródos 105 E 7 *var.* Ródhos, *Eng.* Rhodes, *It.* Rodi; *anc.* Rhodos. Island, Dodekánisos, SE Greece
Rodunma *see* Roanne
Roebuck Bay 146 B 3 bay, E Indian Ocean
Roermond 87 D 5 SE Netherlands
Roeselare 87 A 6 *Fr.* Roulers; *prev.* Rousselaere. W Belgium
Rogachëv *see* Rahachow
Rogers 42 A 1 Arkansas, C USA
Roggeveld Berge 78 C 5 mountain range, S South Africa
Roi Et 137 D 5 *var.* Muang Roi Et, Roi Ed. NE Thailand
Roja 106 C 2 NW Latvia
Rokiškis 106 C 4 NE Lithuania
Rokycany 99 A 5 *Ger.* Rokytzan. W Czech Republic
Rokytzan *see* Rokycany
Rôlas, Ilha das 76 E 2 island, S Sao Tome & Principe
Rolla 45 G 5 Missouri, C USA
Röm *see* Rømø
Roma 96 C 4 *Eng.* Rome. Country capital, C Italy
Roma 149 D 5 Queensland, E Australia
Roman 108 C 4 *Hung.* Románvásár. NE Romania
Roman 104 C 2 NW Bulgaria

Romania
108 B 4 *Bul.* Rumŭniya, *Ger.* Rumänien, *Hung.* Románia, *Rom.* România, *SCr.* Rumunjska, *Ukr.* Romuniya; *prev.* Republica Socialistă România, Roumania, Rumania, Socialist Republic of Romania, *Rom.* Romînia. Republic, SE Europe

Official name: Romania **Date of formation:** 1947 **Capital:** Bucharest **Population:** 23.4 million **Total area:** 237,500 sq km (91,700 sq miles) **Languages:** Romanian*, Hungarian **Religions:** Romanian Orthodox 70%, Roman Catholic 6%, Protestant 6%, other 18% **Ethnic mix:** Romanian 89%, Hungarian 8%, other (inc. Gypsy) 3% **Government:** Multiparty republic **Currency:** Leu = 100 bani

---

Románvásár *see* Roman
Rome 42 D 2 Georgia, SE USA
Rome *see* Roma
Romny 109 F 2 NE Ukraine
Rømø 85 A 7 *Ger.* Röm. Island, SW Denmark
Ronda 92 D 5 S Spain
Rondônia 62 D 3 *off.* Território de Rondônia. State, W Brazil
Rondonópolis 63 E 3 W Brazil
Rongelap Atoll 144 D 1 *var.* Rónlap. Island, NW Marshall Islands
Rõngu 106 D 3 *Ger.* Ringen. SE Estonia
Rōnļap *see* Rongelap Atoll
Rønne 85 B 8 E Denmark
Ronne Ice Shelf 154 B 3 ice shelf, Antarctica
Roosendaal 87 C 5 S Netherlands
Roraima 62 D 1 *off.* Território de Roraima; *prev.* Território de Rio Branco. State, N Brazil
Roraima, Mount 59 F 3 mountain, N South America
Røros 85 B 5 S Norway
Rosa, Lake 54 D 2 lake, S Bahamas
Rosario 64 D 4 E Argentina
Rosario 64 D 2 C Paraguay
Rosario *see* Rosarito
Rosarito 50 A 1 *var.* Rosario. NW Mexico
Roscianum *see* Rossano
Roscommon 40 C 2 Michigan, N USA
Roseau 55 G 4 *prev.* Charlotte Town. Country capital, SW Dominica
Roseburg 46 B 4 Oregon, NW USA
Rosenberg 49 G 4 Texas, S USA
Rosengarten 94 B 3 N Germany
Rosenheim 95 C 6 S Germany
Rosia 93 H 5 W Gibraltar
Rosia Bay 93 H 5 bay, NE Atlantic Ocean
Roșiori de Vede 108 B 5 S Romania
Roslavl' 111 A 5 W Russian Federation
Rosmalen 86 D 4 S Netherlands
Ross 151 B 6 South Island, SW New Zealand
Rossano 97 E 6 *anc.* Roscianum. SW Italy
Ross Dependency 154 B 4 dependent territory of New Zealand, Antarctica
Ross Ice Shelf 154 B 4 ice shelf, Antarctica
Rosso 74 B 3 SW Mauritania
Ross Sea 154 B 4 sea, S Pacific Ocean
Rostock 94 C 2 NE Germany
Rostov-na-Donu 111 B 7 *var.* Rostov, *Eng.* Rostov-on-Don. SW Russian Federation
Rostov-on-Don *see* Rostov-na-Donu
Roswell 48 D 2 New Mexico, SW USA
Rota 144 B 1 island, S Northern Mariana Islands
Rotcher Island *see* Tamana
Rothera 154 A 3 research station, Antarctica
Rotomagus *see* Rouen
Rotorua 150 D 3 North Island, NE New Zealand
Rotorua, Lake 150 E 3 lake, North Island, NE New Zealand
Rotterdam 86 C 4 SW Netherlands
Rottweil 95 B 6 S Germany
Rotuma 145 E 4 island, NW Fiji
Roubaix 90 D 2 N France
Rouen 90 C 3 *anc.* Rotomagus. N France
Round Rock 49 G 3 Texas, S USA
Rourkela *see* Raurkela
Roussillon 91 C 7 cultural region, S France
Rouyn-Noranda 38 D 4 Québec, SE Canada
Rovaniemen mlk 84 D 3 N Finland
Rovigno *see* Rovinj
Rovigo 96 C 2 NE Italy
Rovinj 100 A 2 *It.* Rovigno. NW Croatia
Rovuma 69 D 5 *var.* Ruvuma. River, Mozambique/Tanzania
Roxas 139 E 2 Panay Island, C Philippines
Royale, Isle 40 B 1 island, Michigan, N USA
Royan 91 B 5 W France
Rozdol'ne 109 F 4 *Rus.* Razdolnoye. S Ukraine
Rožňava 99 D 6 *Ger.* Rosenau, *Hung.* Rozsnyó. E Slovakia
Ruacana 78 B 3 NW Namibia
Ruapehu, Mount 150 D 4 mountain, North Island, C New Zealand
Ruapuke Island 151 B 8 island, South Island, SW New Zealand
Ruatoria 150 E 3 North Island, NE New Zealand
Rub' al Khali 121 C 6 *Eng.* Empty Quarter, Great Sandy Desert. Desert, SW Asia
Rubezhnoye *see* Rubizhne
Rubizhne 109 H 2 *Rus.* Rubezhnoye. E Ukraine
Ruby Mountains 47 D 5 mountain range, Nevada, W USA
Rucava 106 B 3 SW Latvia
Rudensk *see* Rudzyensk
Rūdiškės 107 B 5 S Lithuania
Rudnik 104 E 2 E Bulgaria
Rudny *see* Rudnyy
Rudnyy 114 C 4 *var.* Rudny. N Kazakhstan
Rudolf, Lake 68 D 4 *var.* Lake Turkana. Lake, N Kenya
Rudzyensk 107 C 6 *Rus.* Rudensk. C Belorussia
Rufino 64 C 4 C Argentina
Rugāji 106 D 4 E Latvia
Ruggell 94 E 1 N Liechtenstein
Ruhnu 106 C 2 *var.* Ruhnu Saar, *Swe.* Runö. Island, SW Estonia
Rūjiena 106 D 3 *Est.* Ruhja, *Ger.* Rujen. N Latvia
Rukwa, Lake 73 B 7 lake, SE Tanzania
Rum *see* Rhum
Ruma 100 D 3 N Yugoslavia
Rumbek 73 B 5 S Sudan
Rum Cay 54 D 2 island, C Bahamas
Rumia 98 C 2 N Poland
Rummah, Wādī ar *see* Rimah, Wādī ar
Rummelsburg in Pommern *see* Miastko
Runanga 151 B 5 South Island, C New Zealand
Runaway Bay 54 B 4 C Jamaica
Rundu 78 C 3 *var.* Runtu. NE Namibia
Runtu *see* Rundu
Ruoqiang 126 C 3 *var.* Jo-ch'iang, Ruoqiaang, *Uigh.* Charkhlik, Charkhliq, Qarkilik. NW China
Rupea 108 C 4 *Ger.* Reps, *Hung.* Kőhalom; *prev.* Cohalm. C Romania
Rupel 87 C 5 river, N Belgium
Rupella *see* la Rochelle
Rupert, Rivière de 38 D 3 river, Québec, C Canada
Ruse 104 D 1 *var.* Ruschuk, Rustchuk, *Turk.* Rusçuk. N Bulgaria

---

Russian Federation
110 B 4 *var.* Russia, *Latv.* Krievija, *Rus.* Rossiyskaya Federatsiya. Republic, Asia/Europe

Official name: Russian Federation **Date of formation:** 1991 **Capital:** Moscow **Population:** 149.2 million **Total area:** 17,075,400 sq km (6,592,800 sq miles) **Languages:** Russian* **Religions:** Russian Orthodox 80%, other (inc. Jewish, Muslim) 20% **Ethnic mix:** Russian 80%, Tartar 4%, Ukrainian 3%, other 13% **Government:** Multiparty republic **Currency:** Rouble = 100 kopeks

---

Rust'avi 117 G 2 SE Georgia
Rutba *see* Ar Ruţbah
Rutlam *see* Ratlām
Rutland 41 G 2 Vermont, NE USA
Rutog 126 A 4 *var.* Rutok. W China
Rutok *see* Rutog
Ruvuma *see* Rovuma, Rio
Ruwenzori 77 E 5 mountain range, Congo (Zaire)/Uganda
Ruzhany 107 B 6 SW Belorussia
Ružomberok 99 D 5 *Ger.* Rosenberg, *Hung.* Rózsahegy. N Slovakia

Rwanda
73 B 6 *prev.* Ruanda. Republic,
NE Africa

Official name: Republic of Rwanda
Date of formation: 1962 **Capital:**
Kigali **Population:** 7.5 million **Total
area:** 26,340 sq km (10,170 sq miles)
Languages: Kinyarwanda*, French*,
Kiswahili **Religions:** Christian 74%,
traditional beliefs 25%, other 1%
Ethnic mix: Hutu 90%, Tutsi 9%,
Twa pygmy 1% **Government:**
Multiparty republic **Currency:**
Franc = 100 centimes

Ryazan' 111 B 5
W Russian Federation
Rybinsk 110 B 4 *prev.* Andropov.
W Russian Federation
Rybnik 99 C 5 S Poland
Ryki 98 E 4 E Poland
Rypin 98 D 3 C Poland
Rysy 99 D 5 mountain, S Poland
Ryukyu Islands *see* Nansei-shotō
Ryukyu Trench 152 B 2 *var.* Nansei
Syotō Trench. Trench,
NW Pacific Ocean
Rzeszów 99 E 5 SE Poland
Ržev *see* Rzhev
Rzhev 110 B 4 *var.* Ržev.
W Russian Federation

S

Saalfeld 95 C 5 *var.* Saalfeld an der
Saale. C Germany
Saalfeld an der Saale *see* Saalfeld
Saarbrücken 95 A 6 *Fr.* Sarrebruck.
SW Germany
Sääre 106 C 2 *var.* Sjar. Saaremaa,
W Estonia
Saaremaa 106 C 2 *Ger.* Oesel, Ösel;
prev. Saare. Island, W Estonia
Saariselkä 84 D 2 *Lapp.* Suoločielgi.
N Finland
Sab' Ābār 118 C 4 *var.* Sab'a Biyar,
Sa'b Bi'ār. C Syria
Šabac 100 D 3 W Yugoslavia
Sabadell 93 G 2 E Spain
Sabah 138 D 3 cultural region,
Borneo, E Malaysia
Sabanalarga 58 B 1 N Colombia
Sabaneta 58 C 1 N Venezuela
Sab'atayn, Ramlat as 121 C 6
desert, C Yemen
Sabaya 61 F 5 S Bolivia
Sabḥā 71 F 3 C Libya
Sabi *see* Save, Rio
Sabinas 50 D 2 NE Mexico
Sabinas Hidalgo 51 E 2 NE Mexico
Sabine Lake 49 H 4 lake, SW USA
Sabine River 49 H 3 river, SW USA
Sabkha *see* As Sabkhah
Sable, Cape 39 F 5 headland,
Newfoundland and Labrador,
SE Canada
Sable Island 39 G 4 island,
Nova Scotia, SE Canada
Sabzawar *see* Sabzevār
Sabzevār 120 D 2 *var.* Sabzawar.
NE Iran
Săcele 108 C 4 *Hung.* Négyfalu;
prev. Sieben Dörfer, *Hung.*
Hétfalu. C Romania
Sachsen 94 D 4 *Eng.* Saxony, *Fr.*
Saxe. Cultural region, E Germany
Sachs Harbour 37 E 2 Banks Island,
NW Canada
Sächsische Saale 94 C 4 river,
C Germany

Sacramento 47 B 6 state capital,
California, W USA
Sacramento Mountains 48 D 2
mountain range, New Mexico,
SW USA
Sacramento River 47 B 5 river,
California, W USA
Sacramento Valley 47 B 5 valley,
California, W USA
Sá da Bandeira *see* Lubango
Şa'dah 121 B 6 NW Yemen
Sad Ishtrāgh 123 F 3 pass,
Afghanistan/Pakistan
Sado 131 C 5 *var.* Sadoga-shima.
Island, N Japan
Sadoga-shima *see* Sado
Şafāqis *see* Sfax
Säffle 85 B 6 C Sweden
Safford 48 C 3 Arizona, SW USA
Safi 70 B 2 W Morocco
Safīd Kūh, Selseleh-ye 122 D 4
mountain range, NW Afghanistan
Sagaing 136 B 3 C Burma
Sagami-nada 131 D 6 inlet,
NW Pacific Ocean
Sāgar 134 D 4 *prev.* Saugor. C India
Saginaw 40 C 3 Michigan, N USA
Saginaw Bay 40 D 2 lake bay,
Michigan, N USA
Sagua la Grande 54 B 2 C Cuba
Sagunto 93 F 3 *var.* Sagunt,
Ar. Murviedro; *anc.* Saguntum.
E Spain
Sahara 68 B 3 desert, Algeria/Libya
Sahara el Gharbīya 72 B 2
var. Aşşahrā' al Gharbīyah,
Eng. Western Desert.
C Egypt
Saharan Atlas *see* Atlas Saharien
Sahel 74 D 3 physical region,
N Africa
Sāhīwāl 134 C 2 *prev.* Montgomery.
E Pakistan
Sahtinsk *see* Shakhtinsk
Saïda 119 A 5 *var.* Şaydā, Sayida;
anc. Sidon. W Lebanon
Saidpur 135 G 3 *var.* Syedpur.
NW Bangladesh
Sai Kung 128 B 1 E Hong Kong
Saimaa 85 E 5 lake, SE Finland
St.Anthony 39 G 3 Newfoundland
and Labrador, SE Canada
St.Catharines 38 D 5 Ontario,
S Canada
St.George's 55 H 5 *country Capital*,
SW Grenada
St.John 39 F 4 New Brunswick,
SE Canada
St.John's 39 H 3 *province capital*,
Newfoundland and Labrador,
E Canada
St.Lawrence 39 E 4 *Fr.* Fleuve
St-Laurent. River, Canada/USA
St.Patricks 55 H 2 S Barbados
St Albans 89 E 7 *anc.* Verulamium.
SE England, UK
Saint Albans 40 D 5 West Virginia,
NE USA
St Andrews 88 D 4 E Scotland, UK
St.Ann's Bay 54 B 4 C Jamaica
Saint Augustine 43 E 3 Florida,
SE USA
St Austell 89 C 7 SW England, UK
St.Botolph's Town *see* Boston
Saint Catherines Island 43 E 3
island, SE USA
Saint Clair, Lake 40 D 3 lake,
Canada/USA
Saint Cloud 45 F 2
Minnesota, N USA
St Croix 55 G 3 island,
S Virgin Islands (US)

Saint Croix River 40 A 2 river,
N USA
St David's Island 42 B 5 island,
E Bermuda
Saintes 91 B 5 *anc.* Mediolanum.
W France
St George 42 B 4 N Bermuda
St George 149 D 5 Queensland,
E Australia
Saint George 44 A 5 Utah, W USA
Saint George's Channel 89 B 6
channel, Celtic Sea/Irish Sea
St George's Island 42 B 4 island,
E Bermuda
St.Gotthard Pass *see* San Gottardo,
Passo del
St Helena 67 D 5 island,
E Atlantic Ocean
St.Helena Bay 78 B 5 bay,
SW South Africa
Saint Helena Sound 43 F 2 bay,
NW Atlantic Ocean
Saint Helens, Mount 34 B 4
volcano, Washington, NW USA
St Helier 89 D 8 *dependent
territory capital*,
S Jersey, Channel Islands
St.Iago de la Vega *see* Spanish Town
Saint Joe River 46 D 2 river,
N USA
St John's 55 G 3 *country capital*,
S Antigua & Barbuda
St Kilda 88 A 3 island,
NW Scotland, UK

Saint Kitts & Nevis
55 G 3 *var.* Saint Christopher-
Nevis. Commonwealth republic,
E Caribbean Sea

Official name: Federation of Saint
Christopher and Nevis **Date of
formation:** 1983 **Capital:** Basseterre
Population: 44,000 **Total area:**
360 sq km (139 sq miles) **Languages:**
English*, English Creole **Religions:**
Protestant 85%, Roman Catholic
10%, other Christian 5% **Ethnic mix:**
Black 95%, mixed 5% **Government:**
Parliamentary democracy
Currency: E. Caribbean $ = 100 cents

St.Lawrence, Gulf of 39 F 3 gulf,
NW Atlantic Ocean
Saint Lawrence Island 36 C 2
island, Alaska, NW USA
St.Lawrence Seaway 41 F 2
waterway, NW Atlantic Ocean
St Louis 45 G 5 Missouri, C USA

Saint Lucia
55 E 1 Commonwealth republic,
E Caribbean Sea

Official name: Saint Lucia **Date of
formation:** 1979 **Capital:** Castries
Population: 156,000 **Total area:**
620 sq km (239 sq miles)
Languages: English*, French Creole,
Hindi, Urdu **Religions:** Roman
Catholic 90%, other 10% **Ethnic mix:**
Black 90%, Afro-European 6%,
South Asian 4% **Government:**
Parliamentary democracy
Currency: E. Caribbean $ = 100 cents

St Lucia Channel 55 H 4 channel,
E Caribbean Sea
St.Margareth's Bay *see*
St.Margareth's Bay
Saint Martin *see* Sint Maarten
St.Matthew's Island *see*
Zadetkyi Kyun
Saint Nicholas *see* São Nicolau
Saint-Nicolas *see* Sint-Niklaas

Saint Paul 45 F 2 *state capital*,
Minnesota, N USA
St.Paul Island *see* St-Paul, Île
St Peter Port 89 D 8 *dependent
territory capital*, C Guernsey,
Channel Islands
Saint Petersburg 43 E 4 Florida,
SE USA
Saint Petersburg *see* Sankt-Peterburg
St Pierre 39 G 4 *dependent
territory capital*,
Saint Pierre & Miquelon
Saint Simon Island 43 E 3 island,
SE USA
Saint Thomas *see* Charlotte Amalie
Saint Thomas *see* São Tomé
Saint Vincent 55 G 4 island,
N Saint Vincent & the Grenadines
Saint Vincent *see* São Vicente

Saint Vincent & the Grenadines
55 H 4 Commonwealth republic,
E Caribbean Sea

Official name: St Vincent and the
Grenadines **Date of formation:** 1979
Capital: Kingstown **Population:**
109,000 **Total area:** 340 sq km
(131 sq miles) **Languages:** English*,
English Creole **Religions:** Protestant
62% Roman Catholic 19%,
other 19% **Ethnic mix:** Black 82%,
mixed 14%, White 3%, South
Asian 1% **Government:**
Parliamentary democracy
Currency: E. Caribbean $ = 100 cents

Saint Vincent, Cape *see*
São Vicente, Cabo de
Saint Vincent Passage 55 H 4
channel, E Caribbean Sea
Saipan 144 B 1 island,
S Northern Mariana Islands
Sai Yok 137 B 5 C Thailand
Sajama, Nevado 61 F 4 mountain,
W Bolivia
Sajószentpéter 99 D 6 NE Hungary
Sakākah 120 B 4
NW Saudi Arabia
Sakakawea, Lake 44 D 2 reservoir,
North Dakota, N USA
Sakata 130 D 4 Honshū, C Japan
Sakhalin *see* Sakhalin, Ostrov
Sakhalin, Ostrov 115 H 4
var. Sakhalin. Island,
SE Russian Federation
Saki *see* Saky
Şāki 117 C 2 *Rus.* Sheki;
prev. Nukha. NW Azerbaijan
Sakishima-shotō 130 A 3
var. Sakisima Syotō. Island group,
Nansei-shotō, S Japan
Sakon Nakhon 136 D 4 *var.* Muang
Sakon Nakhon, Sakhon Nakhon.
NE Thailand
Saky 109 F 5 *Rus.* Saki. S Ukraine
Sal 74 A 3 island, NE Cape Verde
Sala 85 C 6 C Sweden
Salacgrīva 106 C 3 *Est.* Salatsi.
N Latvia
Sala Consilina 97 D 5 S Italy
Salado 64 C 3 river, C Argentina
Şalālah 121 D 6 SW Oman
Salamá 52 B 2 C Guatemala
Salamanca 92 D 2 *anc.* Helmantica,
Salmantica. NW Spain
Salamanca 64 B 3 C Chile
Salamīyah 118 B 3
var. As Salamīyah. W Syria
Salantai 106 B 3 NW Lithuania
Salatsi *see* Salacgrīva
Salavan 137 E 5 *var.* Saravan,
Saravane. SE Laos

Salavat 111 D 6
W Russian Federation
Sala y Gomez 153 F 4 *island,*
E Pacific Ocean
Šalčininkai 107 C 5 SE Lithuania
Saldus 106 B 3 *Ger.* Frauenburg.
W Latvia
Sale 149 C 7 Victoria, SE Australia
Salé 70 C 2 NW Morocco
Salekhard 114 D 3 *prev.* Obdorsk.
N Russian Federation
Salem 46 B 3 state capital,
Oregon, NW USA
Salem 132 C 2 SE India
Salentina, Penisola 97 E 6
peninsula, S Italy
Salerno 97 D 5 *anc.* Salernum.
S Italy
Salerno, Golfo di 97 D 5 *Eng.* Gulf
of Salerno. Gulf, E Tyrrhenian Sea
Salerno, Gulf of *see* Salerno, Golfo di
Salernum *see* Salerno
Salihorsk 107 C 7 *Rus.* Soligorsk.
S Belorussia
Salima 79 E 2 C Malawi
Salina 45 E 5 Kansas, C USA
Salina Cruz 51 F 5 SE Mexico
Salinas 47 B 6
California, W USA
Salinas de Santiago 61 G 4
E Bolivia
Salinas Grandes 64 C 3 wetland,
C Argentina
Salisbury 89 D 7 *var.* New Sarum.
S England, UK
Salisbury *see* Harare
Sallisaw 49 H 1
Oklahoma, C USA
Sallūm, Khalīj as *see* Salūm, Gulf of
Sallyana *see* Salyan
Salmon Gums 147 C 7
SW Australia
Salmon River 46 D 3 river, Idaho,
NW USA
Salmon River Mountains 46 D 3
mountain range, Idaho,
NW USA
Salo 85 D 6 SW Finland
Salon-de-Provence 91 D 6
SE France
Salonta 108 A 3 *Hung.*
Nagyszalonta. NW Romania
Sal'sk 111 B 7
SW Russian Federation
Salt *see* As Salţ
Salta 64 C 2 NW Argentina
Saltash 89 C 7 SE England, UK
Saltillo 51 E 3 NE Mexico
Salt Lake City 44 B 4 state capital,
Utah, W USA
Salto 64 D 4 NW Uruguay
Salton Sea 47 D 8 *var.* Mar de
Salton. Lake, California,
W USA
Salvador 63 G 3 *prev.* São Salvador.
State capital, E Brazil
Salvador, Lake 42 B 3 lake,
Louisiana, S USA
Salween 136 B 3 *var.* Nu Jiang,
Bur. Thanlwin, *Chin.* Nu Chiang.
River, SE Asia
Salyan 135 E 3 *var.* Sallyana.
W Nepal
Salzburg 95 D 6 *anc.* Juvavum.
N Austria
Salzgitter 94 B 4 *prev.* Watenstedt-
Salzgitter. C Germany
Salzwedel 94 C 3 N Germany
Samar 139 F 2 island, Visayan
Islands, C Philippines
Samara 111 C 6 *prev.* Kuybyshev.
W Russian Federation

Samarang *see* Semarang
Samarinda 138 D 4 Borneo,
C Indonesia
Samarkand *see* Samarqand
Samarqand 123 E 2
Rus. Samarkand. C Uzbekistan
Samawa *see* As Samāwah
Şamaxı 117 H 2 *Rus.* Shemakha.
C Azerbaijan
Sambalpur 135 F 4 E India
Sambava 79 G 2 NE Madagascar
Sambir 108 B 2 *Rus.* Sambor.
NW Ukraine
Sambor *see* Sambir
Sambre 87 B 7 *river,*
Belgium/France
Samfya 78 D 2 N Zambia
Saminatal 94 E 2 valley,
Austria/Liechtenstein
Samnān *see* Semnān
Sam Neua *see* Xam Nua

Samoa
145 F 4 *Sam.* Smoa-i-Sisifo;
prev. Western Samoa. Monarchy,
S Pacific Ocean

Official name: Independent State of
Samoa **Date of formation:** 1962
Capital: Apia
Population: 162,000 **Total Area:**
2,840 sq km (1,027 sq miles)
Languages: Samoan*, English
Religions: Protestant 74%, Roman
Catholic 26% **Ethnic mix:** Samoan
93%, other 7% **Government:**
Parliamentary state
Currency: Tala = 100 sene

Samoa Basin 152 D 4 undersea
basin, W Pacific Ocean
Samobor 100 B 2 N Croatia
Sámos 105 E 6 *prev.* Limín Vathéos.
Sámos, SE Greece
Sámos 105 D 6 island, SE Greece
Samothrace *see* Samothráki
Samothráki 104 D 4 Samothráki,
NE Greece
Samothráki 104 D 4 *anc.*
Samothrace. Island, NE Greece
Sampit 138 D 4 C Indonesia
Samsun 116 D 2 *anc.* Amisus.
N Turkey
Samtredia 117 F 2 W Georgia
Samui, Ko 137 C 6 *island,*
S Thailand
Samut Prakan 137 C 5 *var.* Muang
Samut Prakan, Paknam.
C Thailand
San 99 E 5 *river,* SE Poland
San 74 D 3 C Mali
Sana 100 B 3 *river,*
NW Bosnia & Herzegovina
Şan'ā' 121 B 6 *Eng.* Sana. Country
capital, W Yemen
Sana *see* Şan'ā'
Saña 60 B 3 NW Peru
Sanae 154 B 2 research station,
Antarctica
San Ambrosio Island 153 G 4
var. Isla San Ambrosio. Island,
SE Pacific Ocean
San Ambrosio, Isla *see*
San Ambrosio Island
Sanandaj 120 C 3 *prev.* Sinneh.
W Iran
San Andrés, Isla de 53 F 3 *island,*
Colombia
San Andrés Tuxtla 51 F 4
var. Tuxtla. E Mexico
San Angelo 49 F 3 Texas, S USA
San Antonio 64 B 4 C Chile
San Antonio 49 F 4 Texas, S USA

San Antonio 52 B 2 S Belize
San Antonio Bay 49 H 4 bay, Texas,
S Gulf of Mexico
San Antonio Oeste 65 C 5
E Argentina
San Antonio River 49 G 4 *river,*
Texas, S USA
Sanāw 121 D 6 *var.* Sanaw.
NE Yemen
Sanaw *see* Sanāw
San Benedicto, Isla 50 B 5 *island,*
W Mexico
San Benito 49 G 5 Texas, S USA
San Benito 52 B 1 N Guatemala
San Bernardino 47 C 7
California, W USA
San Blas 50 C 3 C Mexico
San Blas, Cordillera de 53 G 4
mountain range, NE Panama
San Carlos de Ancud *see* Ancud
San Carlos de Bariloche 65 B 5
SW Argentina
San Carlos del Zulia 58 C 2
W Venezuela
San Carlos Reservoir 48 B 2
reservoir, Arizona, SW USA
San Clemente Island 47 C 8 *island,*
California, W USA
San Cristobal 144 C 4 *var.* Makira.
Island, SE Solomon Islands
San Cristóbal 58 C 2 W Venezuela
San Cristóbal *see* San Cristóbal de
Las Casas
San Cristóbal de Las Casas 51 G 5
var. San Cristóbal. SE Mexico
San Cristóbal, Isla 60 B 5
var. Chatham Island, San
Galapagos Islands, E Pacific Ocean
Sancti Spíritus 54 B 2 C Cuba
Sandakan 139 E 3 Borneo,
E Malaysia
Sandanski 104 C 3 *prev.* Sveti
Vrach. SW Bulgaria
Sand Hills 44 D 3 mountain range,
Nebraska, C USA
Sandia 48 D 2 New Mexico,
SW USA
San Diego 47 C 8 California,
W USA
Sandnes 85 A 6 S Norway
Sandomierz 98 D 4 *Rus.* Sandomir.
SE Poland
Sandomir *see* Sandomierz
Sandoway 136 A 4 W Burma
Sand Springs 49 G 1 Oklahoma,
C USA
Sandvika 85 B 6 S Norway
Sandviken 85 C 5 C Sweden
Sandy Bay 93 H 5 bay,
W Mediterranean Sea
Sandy City 44 B 4 Utah, W USA
Sandy Desert 134 A 2 physical
region, W Pakistan
Sandy Lake 38 B 3 lake, Ontario,
C Canada
Sandy Springs 42 D 2
Georgia, SE USA
San Esteban 52 D 2 C Honduras
San Felipe 58 D 1 NW Venezuela
San Felipe de Puerto Plata *see*
Puerto Plata
San Félix Island 153 G 4
Eng. San Felix Island. Island,
SE Pacific Ocean
San Fernando 92 C 5
prev. Isla de León. S Spain
San Fernando 55 H 5
S Trinidad & Tobago
San Fernando 64 B 4 C Chile
San Fernando 58 D 2 *var.*
San Fernando de Apure.
C Venezuela

San Fernando de Apure *see*
San Fernando
**San Fernando del Valle de
Catamarca** 64 C 3 *var.* Catamarca.
NW Argentina
San Fernando de Monte Cristi *see*
Monte Cristi
San Francisco 64 C 4 C Argentina
San Francisco 47 A 6 California,
W USA
San Francisco Bay 47 A 6 bay,
California, W Pacific Ocean
San Francisco del Oro 50 C 2
N Mexico
San Francisco de Macorís 55 E 3
C Dominican Republic
San Francisco de Selva *see* Copiapó
San Fructuoso *see* Tacuarembó
Sanger 47 C 6 California, W USA
Sangihe, Kepulauan 139 F 3 island
group, C Indonesia
Sāngli 132 B 1 W India
Sangmélima 77 B 5 S Cameroon
San Gottardo, Passo del 95 B 7
Eng. St.Gotthard Pass. Pass,
S Switzerland
Sangre de Cristo Mountains 44 D 5
mountain range, C USA
San Ignacio 52 B 1 *prev.* Cayo,
El Cayo. W Belize
San Ignacio 61 F 3 N Bolivia
San Joaquin Valley 47 B 6 valley,
California, W USA
San Jorge, Golfo 65 C 6
var. Gulf of San Jorge. Gulf,
SW Atlantic Ocean
San Jorge, Gulf of *see* San Jorge,
Golfo
San Jose 47 B 6 *Port.* San José.
California, W USA
San José 52 B 3 *var.* Puerto San José.
S Guatemala
San José 53 E 4 country capital
C Costa Rica
San José 61 G 4 *var.* San José de
Chiquitos. E Bolivia
San José *see* San José del Guaviare
San José de Chiquitos *see* San José
San José de Cúcuta *see* Cúcuta
San José del Guaviare 58 C 4
var. San José. S Colombia
San Juan 55 F 3 dependent territory
capital, NE Puerto Rico
San Juan 64 B 4 W Argentina
San Juan 53 E 4 river, Costa
Rica/Nicaragua
San Juan *see* San Juan de los Morros
San Juan Bautista 64 D 3
S Paraguay
San Juan Bautista *see* Villahermosa
San Juan Bautista Tuxtepec *see*
Tuxtepec
San Juan de Alicante 93 F 4
E Spain
San Juan del Norte 53 E 4
var. Greytown. SE Nicaragua
San Juan del Norte, Bahía de 53 E 4
bay, W Caribbean Sea
San Juan de los Morros 58 D 2
var. San Juan. N Venezuela
San Juan del Río 51 E 4 C Mexico
San Juanito, Isla 50 C 4 *island,*
C Mexico
San Juan Mountains 44 C 5
mountain range, Colorado,
C USA
San Juan River 44 B 5 river, C USA
San Julián *see* Puerto San Julián
Sankt-Bartholomäi *see* Palamuse
Sankt Gallen 95 B 7 *var.* St.Gallen,
Eng. Saint Gall, *Fr.* St-Gall.
NE Switzerland

Sankt-Jakobi see Pärnu-Jaagupi
Sankt-Peterburg 110 B 4
  prev. Leningrad, Petrograd,
  Eng. Saint Petersburg, *Fin.* Pietari.
  NW Russian Federation
Sankt Pölten 95 E 6 N Austria
Sankuru 77 D 7 river,
  C Congo (Zaire)
San Lázaro 64 D 2 NE Paraguay
Şanlıurfa 117 E 4 *prev.* Sanli Urfa,
  Urfa, *anc.* Edessa. S Turkey
San Lorenzo 61 G 5 S Bolivia
San Lorenzo 60 A 1 N Ecuador
San Lorenzo, Isla 60 C 4 island,
  W Peru
Sanlúcar de Barrameda 92 C 5
  S Spain
San Luis 64 C 4 C Argentina
San Luis 50 A 1 *var.* San Luis Río
  Colorado. NW Mexico
San Luis 52 B 2 NE Guatemala
San Luis Obispo 47 B 7
  California, W USA
San Luis Potosí 51 E 3 C Mexico
San Luis Río Colorado see San Luis
San Marcos 49 G 4 Texas, S USA
San Marcos 52 A 2 W Guatemala
San Marcos 60 C 3 W Peru
San Marcos de Arica see Arica
San Marino 96 E 1 country capital,
  C San Marino

San Marino
  96 D 1 Marino. Republic,
  S Europe

Official name: Republic of San
Marino **Date of formation:** AD
301/1862 **Capital:** San Marino
Population: 23,000 **Total area:** 61 sq
km (24 sq miles) **Languages:** Italian*
Religions: Roman Catholic 96%,
Protestant 2%, other 2%
Ethnic mix: Sammarinese 95%,
Italian 4%, other 1% **Government:**
Multiparty republic
Currency: Italian lira = 100 centesimi

San Martín 154 A 3 research
  station, Antarctica
San Mateo 47 B 6
  California, W USA
San Mateo 59 E 2 NE Venezuela
San Matías 61 H 3 E Bolivia
San Matías, Golfo 65 C 6 gulf,
  SW Atlantic Ocean
Sanmenxia 128 C 4 *var.* Shan Xian.
  C China
San Miguel 52 C 3 SE El Salvador
San Miguel 61 G 3 river,
  Colombia/Ecuador
San Miguel de Allende 51 E 4
  C Mexico
San Miguel de Ibarra see Ibarra
San Miguel de Tucumán 64 C 3
  var. Tucumán. N Argentina
San Miguelito 53 G 4 C Panama
Sannär see Sennar
San Nicolás, Bahía 60 D 4 bay,
  E Pacific Ocean
San Nicolas Island 47 C 8 island,
  California, W USA
Sânnicolau Mare 108 A 4
  var. Sânnicolaul-Mare,
  Hung. Nagyszentmiklós;
  prev. Sânmiclăus Mare, Sinnicolau
  Mare. W Romania
Sanok 99 E 5 SE Poland
San Pablo 61 F 5 S Bolivia
San Pedro 50 D 3 *var.* San Pedro de
  las Colonias. NE Mexico
San Pedro 52 C 1 NE Belize
San-Pédro 74 D 5 S Ivory Coast

San Pedro de las Colonias see
  San Pedro
San Pedro de Lloc 60 B 3 NW Peru
San Pedro Mártir, Sierra 50 A 1
  mountain range, NW Mexico
San Pedro Sula 52 C 2
  NW Honduras
San Rafael 64 B 4 W Argentina
San Rafael Mountains 47 B 7
  mountain range,
  California, W USA
San Ramón de la Nueva Orán 64
  C 2 N Argentina
San Remo 96 A 3 NW Italy
San Salvador 54 D 1 *prev.* Watlings
  I. Island, E Bahamas
San Salvador 52 B 3 country
  capital, SW El Salvador
San Salvador de Jujuy 64 C 2
  var. Jujuy. N Argentina
Sansanné-Mango 75 E 4
  var. Mango. N Togo
Sansepolcro 96 C 3 C, Italy
San Severo 97 D 5 SE Italy
Santa 60 C 3 W Peru
Santa Ana 52 B 3 NW El Salvador
Santa Ana 47 C 8 California, W USA
Santa Ana 61 F 3 N Bolivia
Santa Ana de Coro see Coro
Santa Barbara 50 C 2 N Mexico
Santa Barbara 47 C 7
  California, W USA
Santa Catalina, Gulf of 47 B 8 gulf,
  W USA
Santa Catalina Island 47 C 8 island,
  California, W USA
Santa Catarina 63 E 5 *off.* Estado de
  Santa Catarina. State, S Brazil
Santa Catarina, Estado de see
  Santa Catarina
Santa Clara 54 B 2 C Cuba
Santa Clara 47 B 6
  California, W USA
Santa Comba 92 B 1 NW Spain
Santa Cruz 65 B 7 river,
  S Argentina
Santa Cruz 47 B 6
  California, W USA
Santa Cruz 76 E 2 *var.* São João. São
  Tomé, SE Sao Tome & Príncipe
Santa Cruz 61 G 4 *var.* Santa Cruz
  de la Sierra. C Bolivia
Santa Cruz Barillas see Barillas
Santa Cruz de la Sierra see
  Santa Cruz
Santa Cruz del Quiché 52 B 2
  W Guatemala
Santa Cruz de Tenerife 70 A 3
  regional capital, Tenerife,
  SW Spain
Santa Cruz, Isla 60 B 5 *var.*
  Indefatigable Island, Isla Chávez.
  Island, Galapagos Islands,
  E Pacific Ocean
Santa Cruz Islands 144 D 4 island
  group, E Solomon Islands
Santa Elena 64 D 3 NE Argentina
Santa Elena 52 B 1 W Belize
Santa Fe 64 D 4 NE Argentina
Santa Fe 48 D 1 state capital,
  New Mexico, SW USA
Santa Inês 63 F 2 NE Brazil
Santa Isabel 144 C 3 *var.* Bughotu.
  Island, N Solomon Islands
Santa Isabel see Malabo
Santa Lucia Range 47 B 6 mountain
  range, California, W USA
Santa Margarita, Isla 50 B 3 island,
  W Mexico
Santa Maria 92 A 5 island,
  W Portugal
Santa Maria 63 E 5 S Brazil

Santa Maria 47 B 7
  California, W USA
Santa Maria del Buen Aire see
  Buenos Aires
Santa María del Orinoco 58 D 2
  C Venezuela
Santa María, Isla 60 A 5
  var. Charles Island, Isla Floreana.
  Island, Galapagos Islands,
  E Pacific Ocean
Santa Marta 58 B 1 N Colombia
Santana 76 E 2 São Tomé,
  C Sao Tome & Príncipe
Santander 92 D 1 N Spain
Santanilla, Islas 53 E 1
  Eng. Swan Islands. Island,
  NE Honduras
Santarém 92 B 3 *anc.* Scalabis.
  W Portugal
Santarém 63 E 2 N Brazil
Santa Rosa 65 C 5 C Argentina
Santa Rosa 47 B 6
  California, W USA
Santa Rosa see Santa Rosa de Copán
Santa Rosa de Copán 52 C 2
  var. Santa Rosa. W Honduras
Santa Rosa Island 47 B 8 island,
  California, W USA
Sant Carles de la Ràpida see Sant
  Carles de la Ràpita
Sant Carles de la Ràpita 93 F 3
  var. Sant Carles de la Rápida.
  NE Spain
Santiago 92 B 1 *var.* Santiago de
  Compostela, *Eng.* Compostella;
  anc. Campus Stellae.
  NW Spain
Santiago 55 E 3 *var.* Santiago de los
  Caballeros.
  N Dominican Republic
Santiago 64 B 4 *var.* Gran Santiago.
  Country capital, C Chile
Santiago 74 A 3 *var.* São Tiago.
  Island, S Cape Verde
Santiago 53 F 5 S Panama
Santiago 60 B 2 river, N Peru
Santiago see Santiago de Cuba
Santiago de Cuba 54 C 3
  var. Santiago. E Cuba
Santiago de Guayaquil see
  Guayaquil
Santiago del Estero 64 C 3
  C Argentina
Santiago de los Caballeros see
  Santiago
Santiago, Isla 60 A 5 *var.* Isla San
  Salvador, James Island. Island,
  Galapagos Islands,
  E Pacific Ocean
Santiago Mountains 49 E 4
  mountain range, Texas, S USA
Santiago Pinotepa Nacional see
  Pinotepa Nacional
Sant Julià de Lòria 91 A 8
  SW Andorra
Santo see Espiritu Santo
Santo André 63 F 4 S Brazil
Santo Antão 74 A 2 island,
  N Cape Verde
Santo António 76 E 1
  var. São António Príncipe,
  N Sao Tome & Príncipe
Santo Domingo 55 E 3 *prev.* Ciudad
  Trujillo. Country capital,
  SE Dominican Republic
Santo Domingo de Los Colorados
  60 B 1 NW Ecuador
Santo Domingo Tehuantepec see
  Tehuantepec
San, Tônle 137 E 5 *var.* San, Sé.
  River, Cambodia/Vietnam
Santos 63 F 4 S Brazil

Santos Plateau 57 D 5 undersea
  plateau, SW Atlantic Ocean
Santo Tomé 64 D 3 NE Argentina
San Valentín, Cerro 65 B 7
  mountain, S Chile
San Vicente 52 C 3 C El Salvador
São António see Santo António
São Francisco 63 F 3 river,
  E Brazil
Sao Hill 73 C 7 S Tanzania
São João see Santa Cruz
São João da Madeira 92 B 2
  W Portugal
São Jorge 92 A 5 island, W Portugal
São Luís 63 F 2 state capital,
  NE Brazil
São Marcos, Baía de 63 F 1 bay,
  W Atlantic Ocean
Saona, Isla 55 E 3 island,
  SE Dominican Republic
Saône 91 D 5 river, E France
São Nicolau 74 A 3 *Eng.* Saint
  Nicholas. Island, N Cape Verde
São Paulo 63 F 4 state capital,
  S Brazil
São Paulo 63 E 4 *off.* Estado de São
  Paulo. State, S Brazil
São Paulo, Estado de see São Paulo
São Pedro do Rio Grande do Sul see
  Rio Grande
São Salvador see Salvador
São Tiago see Santiago
São Tomé 76 E 2 *Eng.* Saint
  Thomas. Island,
  S Sao Tome & Príncipe
São Tomé 76 E 2 country capital,
  S São Tome & Príncipe

Sao Tome & Príncipe
  76 D 1 of Sao Tome and Principe,
  Port. São Tomé e Príncipe.
  Republic, C Africa

Official name: Democratic Republic
of Sao Tome and Principe **Date of
formation:** 1975 **Capital:** São Tomé
Population: 121,000 **Total area:**
964 sq km (372 sq miles) **Languages:**
Portuguese*, Portuguese Creole
Religions: Roman Catholic 90%,
other Christian 10%
Ethnic mix: Black 90%, Portuguese
and Creole 10%
Government: Multiparty republic
Currency: Dobra = 100 centimos

São Tomé, Pico de 76 E 2
  mountain, São Tomé,
  S Sao Tome & Príncipe
São Vicente 74 A 3 *Eng.* Saint
  Vincent. Island, N Cape Verde
São Vicente, Cabo de 92 B 5
  Eng. Cape Saint Vincent.
  Headland, SW Portugal
Sápai see Sápes
Sapele 75 F 5 S Nigeria
Sápes 104 D 3 *var.* Sápai. NE Greece
Sa Pobla 93 G 3 *var.* La Puebla.
  E Spain
Sapporo 130 D 2 Hokkaidō,
  NE Japan
Sapri 97 D 6 Italy
Sapulpa 49 G 1 Oklahoma, C USA
Saqqez 120 C 2 *var.* Saghez, Sakiz,
  Saqqiz. NW Iran
Sara Buri 137 C 5 *var.* Saraburi.
  C Thailand
Saraburi see Sara Buri
Saragt see Serakhs
Saraguro 60 B 2 S Ecuador
Sarajevo 101 A 8 country capital,
  SE Bosnia & Herzegovina
Sarakhs 120 E 2 NE Iran

Saraktash 111 D 6
  W Russian Federation
Saran' 114 C 4 *Kaz.* Saran.
  C Kazakhstan
Saran *see* Saran'
Sarandë 101 C 7 *var.* Saranda,
  It. Porto Edda; *prev.* Santi
  Quaranta. S Albania
Saransk 111 C 5
  W Russian Federation
Sarasota 43 E 4 Florida, SE USA
Saratov 111 C 6
  W Russian Federation
Sarawak 138 D 3 cultural region,
  Borneo, E Malaysia
Sarawak *see* Kuching
Sardegna 97 A 5 *Eng.* Sardinia.
  Island, W Italy
Sardinia *see* Sardegna
Sar-e Pol *see* Sar-e Pol-e Žahāb
Sargasso Sea 66 B 4 sea,
  N Atlantic Ocean
Sargodha 134 C 2 NE Pakistan
Sarh 76 C 4 *prev.* Fort-Archambault.
  S Chad
Saría 105 E 7 island, Dodekánisos,
  SE Greece
Sarıkamış 117 F 3 NE Turkey
Sarikol Range 123 G 3 mountain
  range, China/Tajikistan
Sark 89 D 8 *Fr.* Sercq. Island ,
  C Channel Islands
Şarkışla 116 D 3 C Turkey
Sarmiento 65 B 6 S Argentina
Sarnia 38 C 5 Ontario, S Canada
Sarny 108 C 1 NW Ukraine
Sarochyna 107 D 5 *Rus.* Sorochino.
  N Belorussia
Sarpsborg 85 B 6 S Norway
Sarrebruck *see* Saarbrücken
Sartène 91 E 7 SE France
Sarthe 90 B 4 cultural region,
  NW France
Sárti 104 C 4 N Greece
Sary-Tash 123 F 3 SW Kyrgyzstan
Sasebo 131 A 7 Kyūshū, SW Japan
Saskatchewan 37 F 5 province,
  SW Canada
Saskatchewan 37 F 5 river, C Canada
Saskatoon 37 F 5 Saskatchewan,
  S Canada
Sasovo 111 B 5
  W Russian Federation
Sassandra 74 D 5 S Ivory Coast
Sassandra 74 D 5 *var.* Ibo,
  Sassandra Fleuve. River,
  S Ivory Coast
Sassari 97 A 5 W Italy
Sassenheim 86 C 3 W Netherlands
Sassnitz 94 D 2 NE Germany
Sátoraljaújhely 99 E 6 NE Hungary
Sātpura Range 134 D 4 mountain
  range, C India
Satsunan-shotō 130 A 3
  var. Satunan Syotô. Island group,
  Nansei-shotō, S Japan
Sattanen 84 D 3 NE Finland
Satu Mare 108 B 3 *Ger.* Sathmar,
  Hung. Szatmárrnémeti.
  NW Romania
Sauceda Mountains 48 B 3 mountain
  range, Arizona, SW USA

Saudi Arabia
  121 B 5 *Ar.* Al 'Arabīyah as
  Su'ūdīyah, Al Mamlakah al
  'Arabīyah as Su'ūdīyah.
  Monarchy, SW Asia

Official name: Kingdom of Saudi
Arabia **Date of formation:**
1932/1981 **Capital:** Riyadh

Population: 16.5 million **Total area:**
2,149,690 sq km (829,995 sq miles)
Languages: Arabic* **Religions:**
Sunni Muslim 85%, Shi'a Muslim
14%, Christian 1% **Ethnic mix:** Arab
90%, Yemeni 8%, other Arab 1%,
other 1% **Government:** Absolute
monarchy **Currency:** Riyal = 100
malalah

Sauer *see* Sûre
Saugor *see* Sāgar
Saulkrasti 106 C 3 C Latvia
Sault Ste.Marie 38 C 4 Ontario,
  S Canada
Sault Ste Marie 40 C 2
  Michigan, N USA
Saumarez Reef 148 E 4 reef,
  S Coral Sea
Saumur 90 B 4 NW France
Saurimo 78 C 1 *var.* Henrique de
  Carvalho, *Port.* Vila Henrique de
  Carvalho. NE Angola
Sava 100 B 3 river, SE Europe
Sava 107 E 6 E Belorussia
Savá 52 D 2 N Honduras
Savai'i 145 E 4 island, NW Samoa
Savannah 43 E 2 Georgia, SE USA
Savannah River 43 E 2 river,
  SE USA
Savannakhét 136 D 4 S Laos
Savanna-La-Mar 54 A 5 W Jamaica
Save, Rio 79 E 3 *var.* Sabi. River,
  Mozambique/Zimbabwe
Saverne 90 E 3 *var.* Zabern;
  anc. Tres Tabernae. NE France
Savigliano 96 A 2 NW Italy
Savigsivik *see* Savissivik
Savinski *see* Savinskiy
Savinskiy 110 C 3 *var.* Savinski.
  NW Russian Federation
Savissivik 82 D 1 *var.* Savigsivik.
  NW Greenland
Savoie 91 D 5 cultural region,
  SE France
Savona 96 A 2 NW Italy
Sävsjö 85 B 7 S Sweden
Savu Sea *see* Sawu, Laut
Sawakin *see* Suakin
Şawqirah 121 E 6 *var.* Suqrah.
  S Oman
Sawu, Laut 139 E 5 *Eng.* Savu Sea.
  Sea, E Indian Ocean
Sayaboury *see* Xaignabouli
Sayat 122 D 3 E Turkmenistan
Sayaxché 52 B 2 N Guatemala
Sayhūt 121 D 6 E Yemen
Saylac 72 D 4 *var.* Zeila.
  NW Somalia
Saynshand 127 E 2 S Mongolia
Say 'ūn 121 C 6 *var.* Saywūn.
  C Yemen
Saywūn *see* Say 'ūn
Scalabis *see* Santarém
Scandinavia 66 D 2 geophysical
  region, NW Europe
Scania *see* Skåne
Scarborough 89 D 5
  NE England, UK
Scarborough 38 D 5 Ontario,
  S Canada
Schaan 94 E 1 W Liechtenstein
Schaerbeek 87 C 6 C Belgium
Schaffhausen 95 B 7 *Fr.*
  Schaffhouse. N Switzerland
Schaffhouse *see* Schaffhausen
Schagen 86 C 2 NW Netherlands
Schaulen *see* Šiauliai
Schaumburg 40 B 3 Illinois, N USA
Schebschi Mountains *see*
  Shebshi Mountains

Scheessel 94 B 3 NW Germany
Schefferville 39 E 2 Québec,
  E Canada
Scheldt 87 B 5 *Dut.* Schelde,
  Fr. Escaut. River, W Europe
Schell Creek Range 47 D 5
  mountain range, Nevada, W USA
Schenectady 41 F 3 New York,
  NE USA
Scherrebek *see* Skærbæk
Schertz 49 G 4 Texas, S USA
Schiedam 86 C 4 SW Netherlands
Schiermonnikoog 86 D 1
  Fris. Skiermûntseach. Island,
  N Netherlands
Schijndel 86 D 4 S Netherlands
Schivelbein *see* Świdwin
Schleswig 94 B 2 N Germany
Schleswig-Holstein 94 B 2 cultural
  region, N Germany
Schlettstadt *see* Sélestat
Schlochau *see* Człuchów
Schneekoppe *see* Sněžka
Schneidemühl *see* Piła
Schönebeck 94 C 4 C Germany
Schönlanke *see* Trzcianka
Schooten *see* Schoten
Schoten 87 C 5 *var.* Schooten.
  N Belgium
Schouwen 86 B 4 island,
  SW Netherlands
Schwäbische Alb 95 B 6 *var.*
  Schwabenalb, *Eng.* Swabian Jura.
  Mountain range, S Germany
Schwandorf 95 C 5 SE Germany
Schwarzwald 95 B 6 *Eng.* Black
  Forest. Mountain range,
  SW Germany
Schwaz 95 C 7 W Austria
Schweidnitz *see* Świdnica
Schweinfurt 95 B 5 SE Germany
Schwerin 94 C 3 N Germany
Schwertberg *see* Świecie
Schwiebus *see* Świebodzin
Scilly, Isles of 89 B 8 island group,
  SW England, UK
Scoresby Sund *see* Kangertittivaq
Scotia Ridge 154 A 1 undersea
  ridge, S Atlantic Ocean
Scotia Sea 67 B 7 sea,
  SW Atlantic Ocean
Scotland 88 C 3 national region, UK
Scott Base 154 C 4 research station,
  Antarctica
Scott Island 154 B 5 island,
  Antarctica
Scottsbluff 44 D 3 Nebraska, C USA
Scottsdale 48 B 2 Arizona, SW USA
Scranton 41 F 3 Pennysylvania,
  NE USA
Scrobesbyrig' *see* Shrewsbury
Scutari, Lake 101 C 5 *Alb.* Liqeni i
  Shkodrës; *SCr.* Skadarsko Jezero.
  Lake, Albania/Yugoslavia
Seaside 47 B 6 California, W USA
Seattle 46 B 2 Washington, NW USA
Sébaco 52 D 3 W Nicaragua
Sebago Lake 41 G 2 lake, Maine,
  NE USA
Sebastían Vizcaíno, Bahía 50 A 2
  bay, E Pacific Ocean
Sebastopol *see* Sevastopol'
Sebenico *see* Šibenik
Sebta *see* Ceuta
Sechura, Bahía de 60 A 3 bay,
  W Pacific Ocean
Secunderābād 132 C 1
  var. Sikandarabad. C India
Sedan 90 D 3 N France
Seddon 151 D 5 South Island,
  C New Zealand

Seddonville 151 C 5 South Island,
  C New Zealand
Sédhiou 74 B 4 SW Senegal
Sedona 48 B 2 Arizona, SW USA
Seesen 94 B 4 C Germany
Segeža *see* Segezha
Segezha 110 B 3 *var.* Segeža.
  NW Russian Federation
Segodunum *see* Rodez
Ségou 74 D 3 *var.* Segu. C Mali
Segovia 92 D 2 C Spain
Segu *see* Ségou
Séguédine 75 H 2 NE Niger
Seguin 49 G 4 Texas, S USA
Segura 93 E 4 river, S Spain
Seinäjoki 85 D 5 *Swe.* Östermyra.
  W Finland
Seine 90 C 3 river, N France
Seine, Baie de la 90 B 3 bay,
  E English Channel
Sekondi *see* Sekondi-Takoradi
Sekondi-Takoradi 75 E 5
  var. Sekondi. S Ghana
Sélestat 90 E 4 *Ger.* Schlettstadt.
  NE France
Seleucia *see* Silifke
Selfoss 83 E 5 SW Iceland
Sélibaby *see* Sélibabi
Selibi Phikwe 78 D 3 E Botswana
Selima Oasis 72 B 3 oasis, N Sudan
Selma 47 C 6 California, W USA
Selway River 46 D 2 river, Idaho,
  NW USA
Selwyn Range 148 B 3 mountain
  range, Queensland, NW Australia
Selzaete *see* Zelzate
Semarang 138 C 5 *var.* Samarang.
  Jawa, C Indonesia
Sembé 77 B 5 NW Congo
Semendria *see* Smederevo
Semey *see* Semipalatinsk
Semezhevo *see* Syemyezhava
Seminole 49 E 3 Texas, S USA
Seminole, Lake 42 D 3 reservoir,
  SE USA
Semipalatinsk 114 D 4 *Kaz.* Semey.
  E Kazakhstan
Semna 72 B 3 N Sudan
Semnān 120 D 3 *var.* Samnān.
  N Iran
Semois 87 C 8 river, SE Belgium
Senatobia 42 C 2 Mississippi,
  S USA
Sendai 130 D 4 Honshū, C Japan
Sendai 131 A 8 Kyūshū, SW Japan
Sendai-wan 130 D 4 bay,
  NW Pacific Ocean
Senec 99 C 6 *Ger.* Wartberg,
  Hung. Szenc; *prev.* Szempcz.
  W Slovakia
Senegal 74 C 3 *Fr.* Sénégal. River,
  W Africa

Senegal
  74 B 3 *Fr.* Sénégal. Republic,
  W Africa

Official name: Republic of Senegal
Date of formation: 1960 **Capital:**
Dakar **Population:** 7.9 million **Total
area:** 196,720 sq km (75,950 sq miles)
Languages: French*, Wolof, Fulani
Religions: Muslim 92%, traditional
beliefs 6%, Christian 2% **Ethnic mix:**
Wolof 46%, Fulani 25%, Serer 16%,
other 13% **Government:** Multiparty
republic **Currency:**
CFA franc = 100 centimes

Senftenberg 94 D 4 E Germany
Sengkang 139 E 4 *var.* Singkang.
  Celebes, C Indonesia

Senica 99 C 6 *Ger.* Senitz, *Hung.* Szenice. W Slovakia
Seniça *see* Sjenica
Senj 100 A 3 *Ger.* Zengg, *It.* Segna; *anc.* Senia. NW Croatia
Senja 84 C 2 *prev.* Senjen. Island, N Norway
Senjen *see* Senja
Senkaku-shotō 130 A 3 island group, Nansei-shotō, S Japan
Senlis 90 C 3 N France
Sennar 72 C 4 *var.* Sannār. C Sudan
Sens 90 C 4 *anc.* Agendicum, Senones. C France
Sên, Stœng 137 D 5 river, N Cambodia
Senta 100 D 2 *Hung.* Zenta. N Yugoslavia
Sentosa 138 A 2 island, S Singapore
Sept-Îles 39 E 3 Québec, SE Canada
Seraing 87 D 6 E Belgium
Serakhs 122 D 3 *var.* Saragt. S Turkmenistan
Seram, Laut 139 F 4 *Eng.* Ceram Sea. Sea, W Pacific Ocean
Seram, Pulau 139 F 4 *var.* Serang, *Eng.* Ceram. Island, Maluka, E Indonesia
Serang 138 C 5 Jawa, C Indonesia
Serasan, Selat 138 C 3 strait, W Pacific Ocean
Serbia 100 D 4 *Ger.* Serbien, *Serb.* Srbija. Constituent republic of Yugoslavia, Yugoslavia. *See also* Yugoslavia
Sercq *see* Sark
Serdo 72 D 4 N Ethiopia
Seremban 138 B 3 W Malaysia
Serenje 78 D 2 E Zambia
Sérifos 105 C 6 *anc.* Seriphos. Island, Kykládes, SE Greece
Seriphos *see* Sérifos
Serov 114 C 3 C Russian Federation
Serowe 78 D 3 SE Botswana
Serpent's Mouth, The 59 F 2 *Sp.* Boca de la Serpiente. Strait, W Atlantic Ocean
Serpiente, Boca de la *see* Serpent's Mouth, The
Serpukhov 111 B 5 W Russian Federation
Serravalle 96 E 1 N San Marino
Sérres 104 C 3 *var.* Seres; *prev.* Sérrai. NE Greece
Sesto San Giovanni 96 B 2 N Italy
Sesvete 100 B 2 N Croatia
Sète 91 C 6 *prev.* Cette. S France
Sétif 71 J 2 *var.* Stif. N Algeria
Setté Cama 77 A 6 SW Gabon
Setúbal 92 B 4 *Eng.* Saint Ubes, Saint Yves. W Portugal
Setúbal, Baía de 92 B 4 bay, NE Atlantic Ocean
Seul, Lac 38 B 3 lake, Ontario, S Canada
Sevan 117 G 2 C Armenia
Sevana Lich 117 G 3 *Eng.* Lake Sevan, *Rus.* Ozero Sevan. Lake, E Armenia
Sevastopol' 109 F 5 *Eng.* Sebastopol. S Ukraine
Severn 89 D 7 *Wel.* Hafren. River, England/Wales, UK
Severn 38 B 2 river, Ontario, S Canada
Severnaya Dvina 110 C 4 *var.* Northern Dvina. River, NW Russian Federation
Severnaya Zemlya 115 E 2 *var.* Nicholas II Land, North Land. Island group, N Russian Federation

Severnyy 110 E 3 *var.* Severny, Severnyj. NW Russian Federation
Severodonetsk *see* Syeverodonets'k
Severodvinsk 110 C 3 *prev.* Molotov, Sudostroy. NW Russian Federation
Severomorsk 110 C 2 NW Russian Federation
Sevier Lake 44 A 4 lake, Utah, W USA
Sevier River 44 B 5 river, W USA
Sevilla 92 C 5 *Eng.* Seville; *anc.* Hispalis, SW Spain
Seville *see* Sevilla
Sevlievo 104 D 2 C Bulgaria

Seychelles
79 G 1 E Africa
Official name: Republic of the Seychelles **Date of formation:** 1976 **Capital:** Victoria **Population:** 69,000 **Total area:** 280 sq km (108 sq miles) **Languages:** Creole*, French, English **Religions:** Roman Catholic 90%, other 10% **Ethnic mix:** Seychellois (mixed African, South Asian and European) 95%, Chinese and South Asian 5% **Government:** Multiparty republic **Currency:** Rupee = 100 cents

Seydhisfjördhur 83 E 5 E Iceland
Seydi 122 D 2 *prev.* Neftezavodsk. E Turkmenistan
Seyhan *see* Adana
Şeytan Deresi 116 D 4 river, NW Turkey
Sfákia 105 C 8 Kríti, SE Greece
Sfântu Gheorghe 108 C 4 *Ger.* Sankt-Georgen, *Hung.* Sepsiszentgyörgy; *prev.* Şepsi-Sângeorz, Sfintu Gheorghe. C Romania
Sfax 71 F 2 *var.* Şafāqis. E Tunisia
's-Gravenhage 86 B 4 *var.* Den Haag, *Eng.* The Hague, *Fr.* La Haye. Seat of government, W Netherlands
's-Gravenzande 86 B 4 W Netherlands
Shaanxi 129 B 5 *var.* Shaan, Shan-hsi, Shenshi, Shensi. Province, C China
Shabani *see* Zvishavane
Shache 126 A 3 *var.* Yarkant. NW China
Shackleton Ice Shelf 154 D 3 ice shelf, Antarctica
Shafer, Mount 154 C 4 mountain, Antarctica
Shahr-e Kord 120 C 3 *var.* Shahr Kord. C Iran
Shahr Kord *see* Shahr-e Kord
Shakawe 78 C 3 NW Botswana
Shakhtinsk 114 C 4 C Kazakhstan
Shaluli Shan 129 A 5 mountain range, S China
Shandī *see* Shendi
Shandong 128 C 4 *var.* Lu, Shantung. Province, E China
Shanghai 129 D 5 *var.* Shang-hai. E China
Shang-hai *see* Shanghai
Shangrao 129 D 5 E China
Shannon 89 A 6 C Ireland
Shannon 89 A 6 *Ir.* An tSionainn. River, W Ireland
Shan Plateau 136 B 3 plateau, C Burma
Shantar Islands *see* Shantarskiye Ostrova

Shantarskiye Ostrova 115 G 3 *Eng.* Shantar Islands. Island group, SE Russian Federation
Shantou 129 D 6 *var.* Shan-t'ou, Swatow. SE China
Shanxi 128 C 4 *var.* Jin, Shan-hsi, Shansi. Province, NE China
Shan Xian *see* Sanmenxia
Shaoguan 129 C 6 *var.* Shao-kuan, *Cant.* Kukong; *prev.* Ch'u-chiang. SE China
Shaqrā' 120 C 4 C Saudi Arabia
Shaqrā *see* Shuqrah
Shari *see* Chari
Shari 130 D 2 Hokkaidō, NE Japan
Sharif 135 F 3 N India
Sharīngol 127 E 2 N Mongolia
Shark Bay 147 A 5 bay, E Indian Ocean
Sharqī, Jazīrat ash *see* Chergui, Île
Shashe 78 D 3 *var.* Shashi. River, Botswana/Zimbabwe
Shashi *see* Shashe
Shasta Lake 47 B 5 reservoir, California, W USA
Shawnee 49 G 1 Oklahoma, C USA
Shaykh, Jabal ash *see* Hermon, Mount
Shchadryn 107 D 7 *Rus.* Shchedrin. SE Belorussia
Shchedrin *see* Shchadryn
Shcheglovsk *see* Kemerovo
Shchekino 111 B 5 W Russian Federation
Shchigry 111 B 5 W Russian Federation
Shchors 109 E 1 N Ukraine
Shchuchinsk 114 C 4 *prev.* Shchuchye. N Kazakhstan
Shchuchyn 107 B 5 *Pol.* Szczuczyn Nowogródzki, *Rus.* Shchuchin. W Belorussia
Shebekino 111 A 6 W Russian Federation
Shebeli 73 D 5 *Amh.* Wabē Shebelē Wenz, *It.* Scebeli, *Som.* Webi Shabeelle. River, Ethiopia/Somalia
Sheberghān 123 E 3 *var.* Shibargan, Shibarghān, Shiberghan, Shibirghān. N Afghanistan
Sheboygan 40 B 3 Wisconsin, N USA
Shebshi Mountains 75 H 4 *var.* Schebschi Mountains. Mountain range, E Nigeria
Sheffield 89 D 6 N England, UK
Shelburne 39 F 5 Ontario, S Canada
Shelburne Bay 148 C 1 bay, NW Coral Sea
Shelby 44 B 1 Montana, NW USA
Shelbyville, Lake 40 B 4 reservoir, Illinois, N USA
Sheldon 45 F 3 Iowa, C USA
Shelekhov Gulf *see* Shelikhova, Zaliv
Shelikhova, Zaliv 115 H 2 *Eng.* Shelekhov Gulf. Gulf, N Sea of Okhotsk
Shemakha *see* Şamaxı
Shendi 72 C 3 *var.* Shandī. NE Sudan
Shenyang 128 D 3 *Chin.* Shen-yang, *Eng.* Mukden, Mukden; *prev.* Fengtien. Province capital, NE China
Shepetivka 108 D 2 *Rus.* Shepetovka. NW Ukraine
Shepetovka *see* Shepetivka
Shepparton 149 C 7 Victoria, SE Australia

Sherbrooke 39 E 4 Québec, SE Canada
Shereik 72 C 3 N Sudan
Shergui, Shatt al- *see* Ech Chergui, Chott
Sheridan 44 C 2 Wyoming, C USA
Sherman 49 G 2 Texas, S USA
's-Hertogenbosch 86 D 4 *Fr.* Bois-le-Duc, *Ger.* Herzogenbusch. S Netherlands
Shetland Islands 88 D 1 island group, NE Scotland, UK
Shibushi-wan 131 B 8 bay, NW Pacific Ocean
Shihezi 126 C 2 NW China
Shiichi *see* Shyichy
Shijiazhuang 128 C 4 *var.* Shih-chia-chuang, Shihkiachwang; *prev.* Shihmen. Province capital, NE China
Shikārpur 134 B 3 S Pakistan
Shikoku 131 C 7 *var.* Sikoku. Island, Japan
Shikoku Basin 152 B 2 *var.* Sikoku Basin. Undersea basin, NE Pacific Ocean
Shiliguri 135 F 3 *prev.* Siliguri. NE India
Shilka 115 F 4 river, C Russian Federation
Shimbir Berris *see* Shimbiris
Shimbiris 72 E 4 *var.* Shimbir Berris. Mountain, N Somalia
Shimoga 132 C 2 W India
Shimonoseki 131 A 7 *var.* Simonoseki; *hist.* Akamagaseki, Bakan. Honshū, SW Japan
Shinano-gawa 131 C 5 *var.* Sinano Gawa. River, Honshū, C Japan
Shīndand 122 D 4 W Afghanistan
Shingū 131 C 7 *var.* Singū. Honshū, SW Japan
Shinjō 130 D 4 *var.* Sinzyô. Honshū, C Japan
Shinyanga 73 C 7 NW Tanzania
Shiprock 48 C 1 New Mexico, SW USA
Shiquanhe 126 A 4 W China
Shīrāz 120 D 4 *var.* Shīrāz. S Iran
Shīrāz *see* Shīrāz
Shishchitsy *see* Shyshchytsy
Shivpuri 134 D 3 C India
Shizugawa 130 D 4 Honshū, NE Japan
Shizuoka 131 D 6 *var.* Sizuoka. Honshū, S Japan
Shklov *see* Shklow
Shklow 107 E 6 *Rus.* Shklov. E Belorussia
Shkodër 101 C 5 *var.* Shkodra, *It.* Scutari, *SCr.* Skadar. NW Albania
Shkumbinit, Lumi i 101 D 6 *var.* Shkumbî, Shkumbin. River, C Albania
Shoal Lake 37 F 5 Manitoba, S Canada
Sholāpur *see* Solapur
Shostka 109 F 1 NE Ukraine
Show Low 48 B 2 Arizona, SW USA
Shpola 109 E 3 N Ukraine
Shreveport 42 A 2 Louisiana, S USA
Shrewsbury 89 C 6 *hist.* Scrobesbyrig'. W England, UK
Shūlgareh 123 E 3 N Afghanistan
Shumagin Islands 36 B 3 island group, Alaska, NW USA
Shumen 104 D 2 NE Bulgaria
Shumerlya 111 C 5 W Russian Federation
Shumilina 107 E 5 *Rus.* Shumilino. NE Belorussia

Shumilino *see* Shumilina
Shunsen *see* Ch'unch'ŏn
Shuqrah 121 C 7 *var.* Shaqrā. SW Yemen
Shwebo 136 B 3 N Burma
Shyichy 107 C 7 *Rus.* Shiichi. SE Belorussia
Shymkent 114 B 5 *var.* Čimkent; *prev.* Chimkent. S Kazakhstan
Shyshchytsy 107 C 6 *Rus.* Shishchitsy. C Belorussia
Sīāh Kūh 122 D 4 mountain range, Afghanistan/Iran
Šiauliai 106 B 4 *Ger.* Schaulen. N Lithuania
Siazan' *see* Siyäzän
Sibay 111 D 6 W Russian Federation
Šibenik 100 A 4 *It.* Sebenico. S Croatia
Siberia 115 E 3 *var.* Sibir'. Physical region, C Russian Federation
Siberoet *see* Siberut, Pulau
Siberut, Pulau 138 A 4 *prev.* Siberoet. Island, Kepulauan Mentawai, W Indonesia
Sibi 134 B 2 SW Pakistan
Sibiu 108 B 4 *Ger.* Hermannstadt, *Hung.* Nagyszeben. C Romania
Sibolga 138 B 3 Sumatera, N Indonesia
Sibu 138 D 3 Borneo, E Malaysia
Sibut 76 C 4 *prev.* Fort-Sibut. S Central African Republic
Sibuyan Sea 139 E 2 sea, W Pacific Ocean
Sichon 137 C 7 *var.* Ban Sichon, Si Chon. S Thailand
Sichuan 129 B 5 *var.* Chuan, Ssu-ch'uan, Szechuan, Szechwan. Province, C China
Sichuan Pendi 129 B 5 depression, C China
Sicilia 97 C 7 *Eng.* Sicily; anc.Trinacria. Island, S Italy
Sicilian Channel *see* Sicily, Strait of
Sicily *see* Sicilia
Sicuani 61 E 4 S Peru
Sidári 104 A 4 Kérkyra, W Greece
Siderno 97 D 7 SW Italy
Sidhirókastron *see* Sidirókastro
Sîdi Barrâni 72 A 1 NW Egypt
Sidi Bel Abbès 70 D 2 *var.* Sidi bel Abbès, Sidi-Bel-Abbès. NW Algeria
Sidirókastro 104 C 3 *prev.* Sidhirókastron. NE Greece
Sidley, Mount 154 B 4 mountain, Antarctica
Sidney 40 C 4 Ohio, N USA
Sidney 44 D 1 Nebraska, C USA
Sidney 44 D 4 Missouri, C USA
Siedlce 98 E 3 *Ger.* Sedlez, *Rus.* Sesdlets. E Poland
Siegen 94 B 4 W Germany
Siemiatycze 98 E 3 E Poland
Siena 96 C 3 *Fr.* Sienne; *anc.* Saena Julia. C Italy
Sieradz 98 C 4 C Poland
Sierpc 98 D 3 C Poland
Sierra de Soconusco *see* Sierra Madre

Sierra Leone
74 C 4 Leone. Republic, W Africa

Official name: Republic of Sierra Leone **Date of formation:** 1961 **Capital:** Freetown **Population:** 4.5 million **Total area:** 71,740 sq km (27,699 sq miles) **Languages:** English*, Krio (Creole) **Religions:** Traditional beliefs 52%, Muslim 40%, Christian 8% **Ethnic mix:** Mende 34%, Temne 31%, Limba 9%, Kono 5%, other 21% **Government:** Military regime **Currency:** Leone = 100 cents

---

Sierra Leone Basin 66 C 4 undersea basin, E Atlantic Ocean
Sierra Leone Rise 66 C 4 *var.* Sierra Leone Ridge, Sierra Leone Schwelle. Undersea rise, E Atlantic Ocean
Sierra Madre 52 A 2 *var.* Sierra de Soconusco. Mountain range, Guatemala/Mexico
Sierra Nevada 47 C 6 mountain range, California, W USA
Sierra Nevada de Mérida *see* Mérida, Cordillera de
Sierra Vieja 48 D 4 mountain range, Texas, S USA
Sierra Vista 48 B 3 Arizona, SW USA
Sífnos 105 C 6 *anc.* Siphnos. Island, Kykládes, SE Greece
Sigli 138 A 3 W Indonesia
Siglufjördhur 83 E 4 N Iceland
Signy 154 A 2 research station, Antarctica
Sigsbee Deep *see* Mexico Basin
Siguatepeque 52 C 2 W Honduras
Siguiri 74 D 4 NE Guinea
Siilinjärvi 84 E 4 C Finland
Siirt 117 F 4 *var.* Sert; *anc.* Tigranocerta. SE Turkey
Sikainana *see* Stewart Island
Sikandarabad *see* Secunderābād
Sikasso 74 D 4 S Mali
Sikeston 45 H 5 Iowa, C USA
Sikhote-Alin', Khrebet 115 G 4 mountain range, SE Russian Federation
Siklós 99 C 7 SW Hungary
Sikoku *see* Shikoku
Sikoku Basin *see* Shikoku Basin
Šilalė 106 B 4 W Lithuania
Silchar 135 G 3 NE India
Silifke 116 C 4 *anc.* Seleucia. S Turkey
Siliguri *see* Shiliguri
Siling Co 126 C 5 lake, W China
Silistra 104 E 1 *var.* Silistria; *anc.* Durostorum. NE Bulgaria
Sillamäe 106 E 2 *Ger.* Sillamäggi. NE Estonia
Sillamäggi *see* Sillamäe
Silsbee 49 H 3 Texas, S USA
Šilutė 106 B 4 *Ger.* Heydekrug. W Lithuania
Silvan 117 E 4 SE Turkey
Silva Porto *see* Kuito
Silverek 117 E 4 SE Turkey
Simanichy 107 C 7 *Rus.* Simonichi. SE Belorussia
Simav 116 B 3 W Turkey
Simav 116 A 3 river, NW Turkey
Simbirsk *see* Ul'yanovsk
Simeto 97 C 7 river, SW Italy
Simeulue, Pulau 138 A 3 island, NW Indonesia
Simferopol' 109 F 5 S Ukraine
Simitli 104 C 3 SW Bulgaria
Şimleu Silvaniei 108 B 3 *Hung.* Szilágysomlyo; *prev.* Şimlâul Silvaniei, Şimleul Silvaniei. NW Romania
Simonichi *see* Simanichy
Simpang 138 B 4 W Indonesia
Simpelveld 87 D 6 SE Netherlands
Simplon Pass 95 B 8 pass, S Switzerland
Simplon Tunnel 95 B 8 tunnel, Italy/Switzerland
Simpson *see* Fort Simpson
Simpson Desert 148 B 4 desert, C Australia
Sīnā' *see* Sinai
Sinai 72 C 2 *Ar.* Shibh Jazīrat Sīnā', Sīnā'. Physical region, NE Egypt
Sinaia 108 C 4 SE Romania
Sinano Gawa *see* Shinano-gawa
Sincelejo 58 B 2 NW Colombia
Sind 134 B 3 *var.* Sindh. Province, SE Pakistan
Sindelfingen 95 B 6 SW Germany
Sindh *see* Sind
Sindi 106 D 2 *Ger.* Zintenhof. SW Estonia
Sinegorskiy 111 B 7 SW Russian Federation
Sinel'nikovo *see* Synel'nykove
Sines 92 B 4 S Portugal

Singapore
138 A 1 Singapore. Republic, SE Asia

Official name: Republic of Singapore **Date of formation:** 1965 **Capital:** Singapore City **Population:** 2.8 million **Total Area:** 620 sq km (239 sq miles) **Languages:** Malay*, Chinese **Religions:** Buddhist 30%, Christian 20%, Muslim 17%, other 33% **Ethnic mix:** Chinese 76%, Malay 15%, South Asian 7%, other 2% **Government:** Multiparty democracy **Currency:** Singapore $ = 100 cents

---

Singapore, Republic of *see* Singapore
Singapore, Strait of 138 A 2 strait, W Pacific Ocean
Singen 95 B 7 S Germany
Singida 73 C 7 C Tanzania
Singkang *see* Sengkang
Singkawang 138 C 4 Borneo, C Indonesia
Singû *see* Shingū
Siniscola 97 A 5 W Italy
Sinj 100 B 4 SE Croatia
Sinnamarie *see* Sinnamary
Sinnamary 59 H 3 *var.* Sinnamarie. N French Guiana
Sinneh *see* Sanandaj
Sinoe, Lacul *see* Sinoie, Lacul
Sinoie, Lacul 108 D 5 *prev.* Lacul Sinoe. Lagoon, W Black Sea
Sinop 116 D 2 *anc.* Sinope. N Turkey
Sinope *see* Sinop
Sinsheim 95 B 6 SW Germany
Sint Maarten 55 G 3 *Eng:* Saint Martin. Island, N Netherlands Antilles
Sint-Michielsgestel 86 D 4 S Netherlands
Sint-Niklaas 87 B 5 *Fr.* Saint-Nicolas. N Belgium
Sint-Pieters-Leeuw 87 B 6 C Belgium
Sintra 92 B 4 *prev.* Cintra. W Portugal
Sinujiif 73 E 5 NE Somalia
Sinus Arabious *see* Red Sea
Sinzyô *see* Shinjō
Siorapaluk 82 D 1 NW Greenland
Sioux City 45 F 3 South Dakota, N USA
Sioux Falls 45 F 3 South Dakota, N USA
Siphnos *see* Sífnos
Siping 128 D 3 *var.* Ssu-p'ing, Szeping; *prev.* Ssu-p'ing-chieh NE China
Siple, Mount 154 A 4 mountain, Antarctica
Siquirres 53 E 4 E Costa Rica
Siracusa 97 D 7 *Eng.* Syracuse. SW Italy
Sir Charles Forbes Island *see* Kau-Ye Kyun
Sir Edward Pellew Islands 148 B 2 island group, Northern Territory, NE Australia
Siret 108 C 3 *var.* Siretul, *Ger.* Sereth, *Rus.* Seret, *Ukr.* Siret. River, Romania/Ukraine
Sirikit Reservoir 136 C 4 lake, N Thailand
Sirna *see* Sýrna
Sirte, Gulf of 103 E 4 *var.* Khalīj Surt, *Eng.* Gulf of Sidra, Gulf of Sirti, Sidra. Gulf, S Mediterranean Sea
Sisak 100 B 3 *var.* Siscia, *Ger.* Sissek, *Hung.* Sziszek; *anc.* Segestica. C Croatia
Sisimiut 82 C 3 *var.* Holsteinborg, Holsteinsborg, Holstenborg, Holstensborg. W Greenland
Sīstān, Daryācheh-ye 122 D 5 *var.* Daryācheh-ye Hāmūn, Hāmūn-e flāberī. Lake, E Iran
Siteía 105 D 8 *var.* Sitía. Kríti, SE Greece
Sitges 93 G 2 NE Spain
Sitía *see* Siteía
Sittang 136 B 4 *var.* Sittoung. River, C Burma
Sittard 87 D 5 SE Netherlands
Sittoung *see* Sittang
Sittwe 136 A 3 *var.* Akyab. W Burma
Siuna 52 D 3 NE Nicaragua
Sivas 116 D 3 *anc.* Sebaste, Sebastia. C Turkey
Siwa Oasis 72 A 2 oasis, NW Egypt
Six Counties, The *see* Northern Ireland
Six-Fours-les-Plages 91 D 6 SE France
Siyäzän 117 H 2 *Rus.* Siazan'. NE Azerbaijan
Sizuoka *see* Shizuoka
Sjar *see* Sääre
Sjælland 85 B 8 *Eng.* Zealand, *Ger.* Seeland. Island, E Denmark
Sjenica 101 D 5 *Turk.* Seniça. SW Yugoslavia
Skagerrak 85 A 6 *var.* Skagerak, Skag-e-rak. Channel, Baltic Sea /North Sea
Skagit River 46 B 1 river, Washington, NW USA
Skalka 84 C 3 lake, N Sweden
Skåne 85 B 7 *prev. Eng.* Scania. Cultural region, S Sweden
Skaudvilė 106 B 4 SW Lithuania
Skegness 89 E 6 E England, UK
Skeleton Coast 78 A 3 physical region, NW Namibia
Skellefteå 84 D 4 N Sweden
Skellefteälven 84 C 4 river, N Sweden
Ski 85 B 6 S Norway
Skíathos 105 C 5 Vóreioi Sporádes, E Greece
Skidal' 107 B 5 *Rus.* Skidel'. W Belorussia
Skidel' *see* Skidal'
Skiermûntseach *see* Schiermonnikoog
Skíros *see* Skýros

Skópelos 105 C 5 Vóreioi Sporádes, E Greece
Skopje 101 D 6 *var.* Üsküb, *Turk.* Üsküp; *prev.* Skoplje, *anc.* Scupi. Country capital, N Macedonia
Skovorodino 115 F 4 SE Russian Federation
Skrīveri 106 C 4 S Latvia
Skuodas 106 B 3 *Ger.* Schoden, *Pol.* Szkudy. NW Lithuania
Skye, Isle of 88 B 3 island, W Scotland, UK
Skylge *see* Terschelling
Skýros 105 C 5 *var.* Skíros. Skýros, E Greece
Skýros 105 C 5 *var.* Skíros; *anc.* Scyros. Island, Vóreioi Sporádes, E Greece
Slagelse 85 B 7 E Denmark
Slatina 108 B 4 S Romania
Slave Coast 75 F 5 coastal region, W Africa
Slavgorod *see* Slawharad
Slavonska Požega 100 C 3 *Ger.* Poschega, *Hung.* Pozsega; *prev.* Požega. NE Croatia
Slavonski Brod 100 C 3 *Ger.* Brod, *Hung.* Bród; *prev.* Brod, Brod na savi. NE Croatia
Slavuta 108 C 2 NW Ukraine
Slavyansk *see* Slov"yans'k
Slawharad 107 E 7 *Rus.* Slavgorod. E Belorussia
Sławno 98 B 2 NW Poland
Sléibhte Chill Mhantáin *see* Wicklow Mountains
Sligeach *see* Sligo
Sligo 89 A 5 *Ir.* Sligeach. NW Ireland
Sliven 104 D 2 *var.* Slivno. E Bulgaria
Slivnitsa 104 C 2 W Bulgaria
Slivno *see* Sliven
Slobozia 108 D 5 SE Romania
Slonim 107 B 6 *Pol.* Słonim, *Rus.* Slonim. W Belorussia

Slovakia 99 D 6 *Ger.* Slowakei, *Hung.* Szlovákia, *Slvk.* Slovensko. Republic, C Europe
Official name: Slovak Republic
Date of formation: 1993 **Capital:** Bratislava **Population:** 5.3 million
Total area: 49,500 sq km (19,100 sq miles) **Languages:** Slovak*, Hungarian (Magyar), Czech **Religions:** Roman Catholic 80%, Protestant 12%, other 8%
Ethnic mix: Slovak 85%, Hungarian 9%, Czech 1%, other (inc. Gypsy) 5% **Government:** Multiparty republic
Currency: Koruna = 100 halierov

Slovenia 95 D 8 *Ger.* Slowenien, *Slvn.* Slovenija. Republic, C Europe
Official name: Republic of Slovenia
Date of formation: 1991 **Capital:** Ljubljana **Population:** 2 million
Total area: 20,250 sq km (7,820 sq miles) **Languages:** Slovene*, Serbian, Croatian **Religions:** Roman Catholic 96%, Muslim 1%, other 3% **Ethnic mix:** Slovene 92%, Croat 3%, Serb 1%, other 4% **Government:** Multiparty republic
Currency: Tolar = 100 stotins

Slovenské Rudohorie 99 D 6 *var.* Ungarisches Erzgebirge, *Eng.* Slovak Ore Mountains, *Ger.* Slowakisches Erzgebirge. Mountain range, C Slovakia

Slov"yans'k 109 G 3 *Rus.* Slavyansk. E Ukraine
Słubice 98 B 3 *Ger.* Frankfurt. W Poland
Sluch 108 D 1 river, NW Ukraine
Słupsk 98 C 2 *Ger.* Stolp. NW Poland
Slutsk 107 C 6 S Belorussia
Småland 85 B 7 cultural region, S Sweden
Smallwood Reservoir 39 F 2 lake, Newfoundland and Labrador, S Canada
Smara 70 B 3 N Western Sahara
Smarhon' 107 C 5 *Pol.* Smorgonie, *Rus.* Smorgon'. W Belorussia
Smederevo 100 E 4 *Ger.* Semendria. N Yugoslavia
Smela *see* Smila
Smila 109 E 2 *Rus.* Smela. C Ukraine
Smilten *see* Smiltene
Smiltene 106 D 3 *Ger.* Smilten. N Latvia
Smithton 149 C 8 Tasmania, SE Australia
Smoky Cape 149 E 6 headland, New South Wales, SE Australia
Smøla 84 A 4 island, W Norway
Smolensk 111 A 5 W Russian Federation
Smyrna *see* İzmir
Snake River 46 C 3 river, NW USA
Snake River Plain 46 D 4 plain, Idaho, NW USA
Sneek 86 D 2 N Netherlands
Sněžka 98 B 4 *Ger.* Schneekoppe. Mountain, N Czech Republic
Sniečkus *see* Visaginas
Snina 99 E 5 *Hung.* Szinna. E Slovakia
Snowdonia 89 C 6 mountain range, N Wales, UK
Snowdrift *see* Łutselk'e
Snyder 49 F 3 Texas, S USA
Sobradinho, Barragem de *see* Sobradinho, Represa de
Sobradinho, Represa de 63 F 2 *var.* Barragem de Sobradinho. Reservoir, E Brazil
Socabaya 61 E 4 SE Peru
Sochi 111 A 7 SW Russian Federation
Société, Archipel de la 145 G 4 *var.* Îles de la Société, *Eng.* Society Islands. Island group, W French Polynesia
Society Islands *see* Leeward Islands
Socorro 50 B 5 island, W Mexico
Socotra 121 D 7 *var.* Sokotra. Island, SE Yemen
Soc Trăng 137 D 6 *var.* Khanh Hung. S Vietnam
Socuéllamos 93 E 3 C Spain
Sodankylä 84 D 3 N Finland
Söderhamn 85 C 5 C Sweden
Södertälje 85 C 6 C Sweden
Sodiri 72 B 4 *var.* Sawdiri, Sodari. C Sudan
Soekaboemi *see* Sukabumi
Sofia *see* Sofiya
Sofiya 104 C 2 *var.* Sofija, Sophia, *Eng.* Sofia; *Lat.* Serdica . Country capital, W Bulgaria
Sogamoso 58 D 3 C Colombia
Sognefjorden 85 A 5 fjord, NE North Sea
Sohâg 72 B 2 *var.* Sawhâj, Suliag. C Egypt
Sohar *see* Şuḩār
Sokal' 108 C 2 *Rus.* Sokal. NW Ukraine

Sokal *see* Sokal'
Söke 116 A 4 SW Turkey
Sokhumi 117 E 1 *Rus.* Sukhumi. NW Georgia
Sokodé 75 F 4 C Togo
Sokol 110 C 4 NW Russian Federation
Sokółka 98 E 3 W Hungary
Sokolov 99 A 5 *Ger.* Falkenau an der Eger; *prev.* Falknov nad Ohří. W Czech Republic
Sokoto 75 F 4 State capital NW Nigeria
Sokotra *see* Socotra
Solapur 132 C 1 *prev.* Sholāpur. SW India
Solca 108 C 3 *Ger.* Solka. N Romania
Sol, Costa del 92 D 5 coastal region, S Spain
Soldeu 91 B 8 NE Andorra
Solec Kujawski 98 C 3 W Poland
Soledad 58 B 1 N Colombia
Soledad *see* East Falkland
Soligorsk *see* Salihorsk
Solikamsk 110 D 4 NW Russian Federation
Sol'-Iletsk 111 D 6 W Russian Federation
Solin 100 B 4 *It.* Salona; *anc.* Salonae. S Croatia
Solingen 94 A 4 W Germany
Solka *see* Solca
Sollentuna 85 C 6 C Sweden
Solok 138 B 4 W Indonesia

Solomon Islands 144 D 3 *prev.* British Solomon Islands Protectorate. Commonwealth republic, SW Pacific Ocean
Official name: Solomon Islands
Date of formation: 1978
Capital: Honiara **Population:** 400,000 **Total Area:** 289,000 sq km (111,583 sq miles) **Languages:** English*, 87 (est.) native languages **Religions:** Christian 91%, other 9% **Ethnic mix:** Melanesian 94%, other 6% **Government:** Parliamentary democracy
Currency: Solomon Is $ = 100 cents

Solomon Sea 144 B 3 sea, SW Pacific Ocean
Soltau 94 B 3 NW Germany
Sol'tsy 110 A 4 *var.* Solcy,Sol'cy. W Russian Federation
Solwezi 78 D 2 NW Zambia
Sōma 130 D 4 Honshū, C Japan

Somalia 73 E 5 *Som.* Jamuuriyada Demuqraadiga Soomaaliyeed, *Soomaaliya; prev.* Italian Somaliland, Somaliland Protectorate. Republic, NE Africa
Official name: Somali Democratic Republic **Date of formation:** 1960
Capital: Mogadishu **Population:** 9.5 million **Total area:** 637,660 sq km (246,200 sq miles) **Languages:** Somali,* Arabic **Religions:** Sunni Muslim 99%, other (inc. Christian) 1% **Ethnic mix:** Somali 98%, Bantu, Arab and other 2%
Government: Transitional
Currency: Shilling = 100 cents

Somali Basin 140 B 4 undersea basin, W Indian Ocean
Somali Peninsula 68 C 4 coastal feature, NE Somalia

Sombor 100 D 3 *Hung.* Zombor. NW Yugoslavia
Someren 87 D 5 SE Netherlands
Somerset 42 A 3 *var.* Somerset Village. W Bermuda
Somerset 40 C 5 Massachusetts, NE USA
Somerset Island 37 F 2 island, NW Canada
Somerset Island 42 A 5 island, W Bermuda
Somerset Village *see* Somerset
Somerton 48 A 3 Arizona, SW USA
Somerville Lake 49 G 3 reservoir, Texas, S USA
Somes 108 B 3 *var.* Someşul, Szamos, *Ger.* Samosch, Somesch. River, Hungary/Romania
Somme 90 C 2 river, N France
Sommerfeld *see* Lubsko
Somotillo 52 C 3 NW Nicaragua
Somoto 52 D 3 NW Nicaragua
Sonaguera 52 D 2 N Honduras
Søndre Strømfjord *see* Kangerlussuaq
Songea 73 C 8 S Tanzania
Sŏngjin *see* Kimch'aek
Songkhla 137 C 7 *var.* Songkla, *Mal.* Singora. S Thailand
Sông Srepok *see* Srêpôk, Tônle
Sonsonate 52 B 3 W El Salvador
Sop Hao 136 D 3 NE Laos
Sopot 98 C 2 *Ger.* Zoppot. N Poland
Sopron 99 B 6 *Ger.* Ödenburg. NW Hungary
Sorgues 91 D 6 SE France
Sorgun 116 D 3 C Turkey
Soria 93 E 2 N Spain
Soroca 108 D 3 *Rus.* Soroki. N Moldavia
Sorocaba 57 D 5 S Brazil
Sorochino *see* Sarochyna
Soroki *see* Soroca
Sorong 139 G 4 New Guinea, E Indonesia
Søröy *see* Sørøya
Sørøya 84 C 2 *var.* Sørøy. Island, N Norway
Sortavala 110 B 3 NW Russian Federation
Sosnogorsk 110 D 4 NW Russian Federation
Sotavento, Ilhas de 74 A 3 *var.* Leeward Islands. Island group, S Cape Verde
Sotkamo 84 E 4 C Finland
Souanké 77 B 5 NW Congo
Soufli 104 D 3 *prev.* Souflion. NE Greece
Souflion *see* Soufli
Soufrière 55 F 2 W Saint Lucia
Sŏul 128 E 4 *off.* Sŏul-t'ŭkpyŏlsi, *Eng.* Seoul, *Jap.* Keijō; *prev.* Kyŏngsŏng; Country capital, NW South Korea
Soûr 119 A 5 *var.* Şūr; *anc.* Tyre. SW Lebanon
Souris River 45 E 1 river, Canada/USA
Sourpi 105 B 5 C Greece
Sousse 71 F 2 *var.* Sūsah. NE Tunisia

South Africa 78 C 4 Africa, *Afr.* Suid-Afrika. Republic, S Africa
Official name: Republic of South Africa **Date of formation:** 1910/1934 **Capitals:** Pretoria, Cape Town, Bloemfontein **Population:** 37.4 million **Total area:** 1,221,040 sq km

(471,443 sq miles) **Languages:**
Afrikaans*, English, 11 African
languages **Religions:** Protestant
55%, Roman Catholic 9%, Hindu
1%, Muslim 1%, other 34%
Ethnic mix: Black 75%, White 14%,
mixed 9%, South Asian 2%
Government: Multiparty republic
Currency: Rand = 100 cents

South America 67 B 5 continent
Southampton 89 D 7 *hist.* Hamwih,
Lat. Clausentum. S England, UK
Southampton Island 37 G 3 island,
NE Canada
South Andaman 133 F 2 island,
SE India
South Australia 149 A 5 state,
S Australia
South Australian Basin 152 B 4
undersea basin, SW Indian Ocean
South Bend 40 C 3 Indiana, N USA
South Beveland *see* Zuid-Beveland
South Carolina 43 E 2 *off.* State of
South Carolina; nickname
Palmetto State. State, SE USA
South China Basin 152 A 3
undersea basin, E Pacific Ocean
South China Sea 152 A 2 *Chin.* Nan
Hai, *Ind.* Laut Cina Selatan, *Vtn.*
Biển fông. Sea, E Pacific Ocean
South Dakota 45 E 2 *off.* State of
South Dakota; nicknames Coyote
State, Sunshine State. State,
N USA
South East Cape 149 C 7 headland,
Victoria, S Australia
Southeast Indian Ridge 141 D 6
undersea ridge, S Indian Ocean
Southeast Pacific Basin 153 F 5
var. Belling Hausen Mulde.
Undersea basin,
SE Pacific Ocean
Southend-on-Sea 89 E 6
SE England, UK
Southern Alps 151 B 6 mountain
range, South Island,
SW New Zealand
Southern Cook Islands 145 F 5
island group, S Cook Islands
Southern Cross 147 B 6 Western
Australia, SW Australia
Southern Ocean 152 C 5 ocean
Southern Uplands 88 C 4 mountain
range, S Scotland, UK
Southesk Tablelands 146 D 3 plain,
NW Australia
South Fiji Basin 152 C 4 undersea
basin, S Pacific Ocean
South Georgia 154 A 1 island,
SW Atlantic Ocean
South Georgia Ridge 57 C 8
var. North Scotia Ridge.
Undersea ridge,
SW Atlantic Ocean
South Huvadhu Atoll 132 B 5
var. Gaafu Dhaalu Atoll. Island,
S Maldives
South Indian Basin 141 D 7
undersea basin, S Indian Ocean
South Indian Lake 37 F 4
Manitoba, C Canada
South Indian Lake 38 A 2 lake,
Manitoba, C Canada
South Island 151 C 6 island,
South Island, S New Zealand
South Island *see* Auk Bok

South Korea
128 E 4 *Kor.* Taehan Min'guk.
Republic, E Asia

Official name: Republic of Korea
Date of formation: 1948 **Capital:**

Seoul **Population:** 44.5 million **Total
Area:** 99,020 sq km (38,232 sq miles)
Languages: Korean*, Chinese
Religions: Mahayana Buddhist 47%,
Protestant 38%, Roman Catholic
11%, Confucianist 3%, other 1%
Ethnic mix: Korean 99.9% other
0.1% **Government:** Multiparty
republic **Currency:** Won = 100 chon

South Lake Tahoe 47 C 5
California, W USA
South Magnetic Pole 154 D 5 pole,
Antarctica
South Orkney Islands 154 A 2
island group, Antarctica
South Ossetia 117 F 2 region,
C Georgia
South Pacific Basin *see*
Southwest Pacific Basin
South Platte River 44 D 4 river,
C USA
South Pole 154 B 3 pole, Antarctica
South Portland 41 G 2 Maine,
NE USA
South Sandwich Islands 154 A 1
island group, S Atlantic Ocean
South Sandwich Trench 154 A 1
trench, SW Atlantic Ocean
South Shetland Islands 154 A 2
island group, Antarctica
South Shields 88 D 4 N England, UK
South Sioux City 45 F 3
Nebraska, C USA
South Taranaki Bight 150 C 4
bight, E Tasman Sea
South Tasmania Plateau *see*
Tasman Plateau
South Uist 88 B 3 island,
W Scotland, UK
South Wellesley Islands 148 B 3
island group, Northern Territory,
N Australia
Southwest Indian Ocean Ridge *see*
Southwest Indian Ridge
Southwest Indian Ridge 141 A 6
var. Southwest Indian Ocean
Ridge. Undersea ridge,
SW Indian Ocean
South West Island 148 D 3 island,
E Australia
Southwest Pacific Basin 152 D 4
var. South Pacific Basin. Undersea
basin, SE Pacific Ocean
Soweto 78 D 4 NE South Africa

Spain
92-93 0 *Sp.* España; *anc.* Hispania,
Iberia, *Lat.* Hispana. Monarchy,
SW Europe

Official name: Kingdom of Spain
Date of formation: 1492/1713
Capital: Madrid **Population:** 39.2
million **Total area:** 504,780 sq km
(194,900 sq miles) **Languages:**
Castilian Spanish*, Catalan*,
Galician*, Basque*
Religions: Roman Catholic 99%,
other 1% **Ethnic mix:** Castilian
Spanish 72%, Catalan 16%, Galician
7%, other 5% **Government:**
Constitutional monarchy
Currency: Peseta = 100 céntimos

Spalato *see* Split
Spaldings 54 B 5 C Jamaica
Spanish Town 54 B 5 *hist.* St.Iago
de la Vega. C Jamaica
Spanish Wells 54 C 1 C Bahamas
Sparks 47 C 5 Nevada, W USA
Sparta *see* Spárti
Spartanburg 43 E 1
South Carolina, SE USA

Spárti 105 B 6 *Eng.* Sparta. S Greece
Spearfish 44 D 3
South Dakota, N USA
Speightstown 55 G 1 W Barbados
Spencer 45 F 3 Iowa, C USA
Spencer Gulf 149 B 6 gulf,
E Indian Ocean
Spenser Mountains 151 C 5
mountain range, South Island,
C New Zealand
Spey 88 C 3 river, NE Scotland, UK
Spijkenisse 86 B 4 SW Netherlands
Spíli 105 C 8 Kríti, SE Greece
Spīn Būldak 123 E 5 S Afghanistan
Spitsbergen 83 G 2 island,
NW Svalbard
Split 101 A 8 *It.* Spalato. S Croatia
Spogi 106 D 4 SE Lithuania
Spokane 46 C 2 Washington,
NW USA
Spratly Islands 125 E 4 island
group, S South China Sea
Spratly Islands 138 D 2
Chin. Nansha Qundao. Disputed
territory, C South China Sea
Spree 94 D 4 river, E Germany
Springfield 40 C 4 Ohio, NE USA
Springfield 41 G 3 state capital,
Illinois, N USA
Springfield 46 B 3 Oregon, NW USA
Springfield 45 G 5 Missouri, C USA
Spring Garden 59 F 2 NE Guyana
Spring Hill 43 E 4 Florida, SE USA
Springsure 148 D 4 Queensland,
E Australia
Sprottau *see* Szprotawa
Srbobran 100 D 3
var. Bácsszenttamás,
Hung. Szenttamás. N Yugoslavia
Srebrenica 100 C 4
E Bosnia & Herzegovina
Sredets 104 E 2 *var.* Sredec;
prev. Syulemeshlii. C Bulgaria
Srednesibirskoye Ploskogor'ye 115
E 3 *var.* Central Siberian Uplands,
Eng. Central Siberian Plateau.
Mountain range,
C Russian Federation
Sremska Mitrovica 100 D 3
Ger. Mitrowitz; *prev.* Mitrovica.
NW Yugoslavia
Srêpôk, Tônle 137 E 5
var. Sông Srepok. River,
Cambodia/Vietnam
Sri Aman 138 C 3 *var.* Bandar Sri
Aman, Simanggang. Borneo,
E Malaysia
Sri Jayawardanapura 132 D 4
W Sri Lanka
Srīkākulam 135 F 5 E India

Sri Lanka
132 D 3 Republic of Sri Lanka;
prev. Ceylon. Republic, S Asia

Official name: Democratic Socialist
Republic of Sri Lanka **Date of
formation:** 1948 **Capital:** Colombo
Population:17.9 million **Total Area:**
65,610 sq km (25,332 sq miles)
Languages: Sinhala*, Tamil, English
Religions: Buddhist 70%, Hindu
15%, Christian 8%, Muslim 7%
Ethnic mix: Sinhalese 74%, Tamil
18%, other 8% **Government:**
Multiparty republic
Currency: Rupee = 100 cents

Srinagarind Reservoir 137 C 5 lake,
W Thailand
Stabroek 87 C 5 N Belgium
Stade 94 B 3 NW Germany
Stadskanaal 86 E 2 NE Netherlands

Stafford 89 D 6 W England, UK
Staicele 106 D 3 N Latvia
Stakhanov 109 H 3 E Ukraine
Stalinsk *see* Novokuznetsk
Stalinski Zaliv *see* Varnenski Zaliv
Stalowa Wola 98 E 4 SE Poland
Stamford 41 F 3
Connecticut, NE USA
Stanley 65 D 7 *var.* Port Stanley.
Dependent territory capital,
E Falkland Islands
Stanley *see* Chek Chue
Stanleyville *see* Kisangani
Stann Creek *see* Dangriga
Stanovoy Khrebet 115 F 4
mountain range,
E Russian Federation
Stanthorpe 149 D 5 Queensland,
SE Australia
Staphorst 86 D 3 E Netherlands
Starachowice 98 D 4 SE Poland
Stara Pazova 100 D 3 *Ger.* Altpasua,
Hung. Ópazova. N Yugoslavia
Stara Planina *see* Balkan Mountains
Stara Zagora 104 D 2 *Lat.* Augusta
Trajana. C Bulgaria
Starbuck Island 145 G 3
prev. Volunteer Island. Island,
E Kiribati
Stargard in Pommern *see* Stargard
Szczeciński
Stargard Szczeciński 98 B 3
Ger. Stargard in Pommern.
NW Poland
Starobel'sk *see* Starobil's'k
Starobil's'k 109 H 2
Rus. Starobel'sk. E Ukraine
Starobin *see* Starobyn
Starobyn 107 C 7 *Rus.* Starobin.
S Belorussia
Starogard Gdański 98 C 2
Ger. Preussisch-Stargard.
N Poland
Starokonstantinov *see*
Starokostyantyniv
Starokostyantyniv 108 D 2 *Rus.*
Starokonstantinov. NW Ukraine
Starominskaya 111 A 7
SW Russian Federation
Starry Oskol 111 B 6
W Russian Federation
Staryya Darohi 107 C 7
Rus. Staryye Dorogi. S Belorussia
Staryye Dorogi *see* Staryya Darohi
Staten Island *see* Estados, Isla de los
State of Eritrea *see* Eritrea
Statesboro 43 E 2 Georgia, SE USA
Staunton 41 E 5 Virginia, NE USA
Stavanger 85 A 6 S Norway
St-Avertin 90 B 4 W France
Stavropol' 111 B 7
prev. Voroshilovsk.
SW Russian Federation
Stavropol' *see* Tol'yatti
St-Brieuc 90 A 3 NW France
St-Chamond 91 D 5 E France
St-Claude 91 D 5 *anc.* Condate.
E France
St-Denis 90 C 3 N France
St-Denis 79 H 4 dependent
territory capital, N Réunion
St-Dié 90 E 4 NE France
Steamboat Springs 44 C 4
Colorado, C USA
Steenwijk 86 D 2 N Netherlands
St-Egrève 91 D 5 E France
Steier *see* Steyr
Steinkjer 84 B 4 C Norway
Stejarul *see* Karapelit
Stendal 94 C 3 C Germany
Stephenville 49 G 3 Texas, S USA

Sterling 40 B 3 Illinois, N USA
Sterling 44 D 4 Colorado, C USA
Sterling Heights 40 D 3
  Michigan, N USA
Sterlitamak 111 D 6
  W Russian Federation
St-Étienne 91 C 5 E France
Stettin *see* Szczecin
Stevenage 89 E 6 SE England, UK
Stevens Point 40 B 2
  Wisconsin, N USA
Stewart 36 D 4 British Columbia,
  W Canada
Stewart Island 151 A 8 *var.*
  Sikainana. Island, South Island,
  S New Zealand
Steyr 95 D 6 *var.* Steier. N Austria
St-Flour 91 C 5 C France
St-Gaudens 91 B 6 S France
St-Georges 39 E 4 Québec,
  SE Canada
St-Georges 59 H 3 E French Guiana
Stif *see* Sétif
Stillwater 49 G 1 Oklahoma,
  C USA
Štip 101 E 6 E Macedonia
Stirling 88 C 4 S Scotland, UK
St-Jean-de-Luz 91 A 6 SW France
St-Jean, Lac 39 E 4 lake, Québec,
  SE Canada
Stjørdal 84 B 4 C Norway
St-Laurent *see* St-Laurent-du-Maroni
St-Laurent-du-Maroni 59 H 3 *var.*
  St-Laurent. NW French Guiana
St-Lô 90 B 3 *anc.* Briovera, Laudus.
  N France
St-Louis 90 E 4 NE France
St-Louis 74 B 3 NW Senegal
St-Malo 90 B 3 NW France
St-Malo, Golfe de 90 B 3 inlet,
  C English Channel
St-Max 90 D 3 NE France
St-Nazaire 90 A 4 NW France
Stockach 95 B 6 S Germany
Stockholm 85 C 6 country capital,
  C Sweden
Stockmannshof *see* Pļaviņas
Stockton 47 B 6 California, W USA
Stœng Trêng 137 D 5 *prev.* Stung
  Treng. N Cambodia
Stoke *see* Stoke-on-Trent
Stoke-on-Trent 89 C 6 *var.* Stoke.
  W England, UK
Stolp *see* Słupsk
Stolpmünde *see* Ustka
St-Omer 90 C 2 N France
Stómio 104 B 4 C Greece
Storebælt 85 B 7 *var.* Store Bælt,
  Storebelt, *Eng.* Great Belt.
  Channel, Baltic Sea/North Sea
Støren 85 B 5 S Norway
Storfjorden 83 G 2 fjord, Barents
  Sea/Norwegian Sea
Storhammer *see* Hamar
Stornoway 88 B 3 island authority
  area capital, NW Scotland, UK
Storsjön 85 B 5 lake, C Sweden
Storuman 84 C 4 lake, N Sweden
Storuman 84 C 4 N Sweden
Stowbtsy 107 C 6 *Pol.* Stolbce, *Rus.*
  Stolbtsy. C Belorussia
St-Paul, Île 141 C 6 *var.* St.Paul
  Island. Island, NE French
  Southern & Antarctic Territories
St-Pierre & Miquelon 39 G 4
  Fr. Îles St-Pierre et Miquelon.
  French Territorial Collectivity,
  NW Atlantic Ocean
St-Pierre et Miquelon, Îles *see*
  St-Pierre and Miquelon
St-Quentin 90 D 3 N France

Strabane 89 B 5 *Ir.* An Srath Bán.
  C Northern Ireland, UK
Strakonice 99 A 5 *Ger.* Strakonitz.
  SW Czech Republic
Strakonitz *see* Strakonice
Stralsund 94 D 2 NE Germany
Stranraer 89 B 5 SW Scotland, UK
Strasbourg 90 E 3 *Ger.* Strassburg;
  anc. Argentoratum. NE France
Strǎşeni 108 D 4 *var.* Strasheny.
  C Moldavia
Strasheny *see* Strǎşeni
Stratford 150 D 4 North Island,
  C New Zealand
Straubing 95 C 6 SE Germany
Streaky Bay 149 A 6 bay,
  SE Indian Ocean
Strehaia 108 B 5 SW Romania
Strelka 114 D 4
  C Russian Federation
Strofília *see* Strofyliá
Strofyliá 105 C 5 *var.* Strofília.
  Évvoia, C Greece
Stromboli, Isola 97 D 6 island,
  S Italy
Stromeferry 88 B 3
  NW Scotland, UK
Strömstad 85 B 6 S Sweden
Strömsund 84 C 4 C Sweden
Struga 101 D 6 SW Macedonia
Struma 104 C 3 *Gk.* Strymónas.
  River, Bulgaria/Greece
Strumica 101 E 6 E Macedonia
Strumyani 104 C 3 SW Bulgaria
Stryy 108 B 2 NW Ukraine
Studholme 151 B 7 South Island,
  SW New Zealand
Stung Treng *see* Stœng Trêng
Stupino 111 B 5
  W Russian Federation
Sturgis 44 D 3
  South Dakota, N USA
Stuttgart 95 B 6 SW Germany
Stykkishólmur 83 E 5 W Iceland
Styr 108 C 1 river, NW Ukraine
Suakin 72 C 3 *var.* Sawakin.
  NE Sudan
Subačius 106 C 4 NE Lithuania
Subotica 100 D 2 *Ger.* Maria-
  Theresiopel, *Hung.* Szabadka.
  N Yugoslavia
Suceava 108 C 3 *Ger.* Suczawa,
  Hung. Szucsava. NE Romania
Sucre 61 F 4 *hist.* Chuquisaca,
  La Plata. Country capital,
  S Bolivia
Sudan 74 C 4 physical region,
  W Africa

Sudan
  72 A 4 *Ar.* Jamhuryat es-Sudan,
  Jumhuriyat as-Sudan; *prev.*
  Anglo-Egyptian *Sudan.* Republic,
  NE Africa

Official name: Republic of Sudan
Date of formation: 1956 **Capital:**
Khartoum **Population:** 27.4 million
Total area: 2,505,815 sq km
(967,493 sq miles) **Languages:**
Arabic*, other **Religions:** Muslim
70%, traditional beliefs 20%,
Christian 5%, other 5%
Government: Military regime
Currency: Pound = 100 piastres

Sudbury 38 C 4 Ontario, S Canada
Sudd 73 B 5 wetland, S Sudan
Suddie 59 F 2 NE Guyana
Sudeten 99 C 5 *var.* Sudetes,
  Sudetic Mountains, Cz./Pol.
  Sudety. Mountain range, Czech
  Republic/Poland

Sudong, Pulau 138 A 2 island,
  SW Singapore
Sueca 93 F 3 E Spain
Sue Wood Bay 42 B 5 bay,
  W Atlantic Ocean
Suez 72 B 1 *Ar.* As Suways,
  El Suweis. NE Egypt
Suez Canal 72 C 1 *Ar.* Qanāt as
  Suways. Canal, NE Egypt
Suez, Gulf of 72 B 1 *Ar.* Khalīj as
  Suways. Gulf, NW Red Sea
Suffolk 41 F 5 Virginia, NE USA
Suğla Gölü 116 C 4 lake,
  SW Turkey
Sühbaatar 127 E 1 N Mongolia
Suhl 95 C 5 C Germany
Şuḩār 121 D 5 *var.* Sohar. N Oman
Suixi 129 C 7 S China
Sukabumi 138 C 5 *prev.*
  Soekaboemi. Jawa, C Indonesia
Sukagawa 131 D 5 Honshū,
  C Japan
Sukhumi *see* Sokhumi
Sukkur 134 B 3 SE Pakistan
Sukumo 131 B 7 Shikoku,
  SW Japan
Sulaimān Range 134 C 2 mountain
  range, C Pakistan
Sula, Kepulauan 139 F 4 *prev.*
  Soela, Xulla Islands. Island group,
  E Indonesia
Sulawesi 139 E 4 island,
  C Indonesia
Sulawesi, Laut *see* Celebes Sea
Sullana 60 B 2 NW Peru
Sullivan Island *see* Lanbi Kyun
Sulphur 42 A 3 Louisiana, S USA
Sulphur Springs 49 G 2
  Texas, S USA
Sultānābād *see* Arāk
Sulu Archipelago 139 E 3 island
  group, SW Philippines
Sülüktü *see* Sulyukta
Sulu, Laut *see* Sulu Sea
Sulu Sea 139 E 2 *var.* Laut Sulu.
  Sea, W Pacific Ocean
Sulyukta 123 F 2 *Kir.* Sülüktü.
  SW Kyrgyzstan
Sulz am Neckar *see* Sulz
Sulz am Neckar 95 B 6 *var.* Sulz.
  SW Germany
Sumatera 138 A 4 *Eng.* Sumatra.
  Island, W Indonesia
Sumatera *see* Sumatra
Sumba, Pulau 139 E 5 *Eng.*
  Sandalwood Island; *prev.* Soemba.
  Island, Nusa Tenggara,
  C Indonesia
Sumba, Selat 138 D 5 strait, Indian
  Ocean/Savu Sea
Sumbawanga 73 B 7 W Tanzania
Sumbay 61 E 4 SE Peru
Sumbe 78 B 2 *var.* N'Gunza, *Port.*
  Novo Redondo. W Angola
Šumen *see* Shumen
Sumgait *see* Sumqayıt
Summer Lake 46 B 4 lake, Oregon,
  NW USA
Sumqayıt 117 H 2 *Rus.* Sumgait.
  E Azerbaijan
Sumy 109 F 1 NE Ukraine
Suna 73 C 5 S Sudan
Sunbury 149 C 7 Victoria,
  SE Australia
Sun City 48 B 2 Arizona, SW USA
Sunda, Selat 138 B 5 strait, Indian
  Ocean/Pacific Ocean
Sunda Shelf 140 E 4 continental
  shelf, W Pacific Ocean
Sunda Trench 140 D 4 trench,
  NE Indian Ocean

Sunderland 88 D 4 *var.* Wearmouth.
  N England, UK
Sundsvall 85 C 5 C Sweden
Sunne 85 B 6 C Sweden
Sunnyside 46 C 2
  Washington, NW USA
Sunnyvale 47 B 6
  California, W USA
Suntar 115 F 3 E Russian Federation
Sunyani 75 E 5 W Ghana
Suoločielgi *see* Saariselkä
Suomussalmi 84 E 4 E Finland
Suŏng 137 D 6 SE Cambodia
Suoyarvi 110 B 3
  NW Russian Federation
Supérieur, Lac *see* Superior, Lake
Superior 40 A 1 Wisconsin, N USA
Superior, Lake 40 B 1 *Fr.* Lac
  Supérieur. Lake, Canada/USA
Suqrah *see* Şawqirah
Şūr 121 E 5 NE Oman
Surabaya 138 D 5 *prev.* Soerabaja,
  Surabaja. Jawa, C Indonesia
Surakarta 138 C 5 *Eng.* Solo; *prev.*
  Soerakarta. Jawa, C Indonesia
Šurany 99 C 6 *Hung.* Nagysurány.
  SW Slovakia
Sūrat 134 C 4 W India
Suratdhani *see* Surat Thani
Surat Thani 137 C 7 *var.*
  Suratdhani. S Thailand
Surazh 107 E 5 NE Belorussia
Surdulica 101 E 5 SE Yugoslavia
Sûre 87 D 7 *var.* Sauer. River,
  W Europe
Surendranagar 134 C 4 W India
Surin 137 D 5 E Thailand

Surinam
  59 G 3 *var.* Suriname; *prev.* Dutch
  Guiana, Netherlands Guiana.
  Republic, NE South America

Official name: Republic of Surinam
Date of formation: 1975 **Capital:**
Paramaribo **Population:** 400,000
Total area: 163,270 sq km
(63,039 sq miles) **Languages:**
Dutch*, Pidgin English (Taki-Taki),
Hindi, Javanese, Carib **Religions:**
Christian 48%, Hindu 27%, Muslim
20%, other 5% **Ethnic mix:** South
Asian 37%, Creole 31%, Javanese
15%, other 17% **Government:**
Multiparty republic
Currency: Guilder = 100 cents

Surkhob 123 F 3 river,
  C Tajikistan
Surt 71 G 2 *var.* Sidra,
  Sirte. N Libya
Surtsey 83 E 5 island, S Iceland
Suruga-wan 131 D 6 bay,
  NW Pacific Ocean
Susa 96 A 2 NW Italy
Sūsah *see* Sousse
Susitna 36 C 3 Alaska, NW USA
Susteren 87 D 5 SE Netherlands
Susuman 115 G 3
  E Russian Federation
Sutlej 134 C 2 river, India/Pakistan
Suur Munamägi 106 D 3 *var.*
  Munamägi, *Ger.* Eier-Berg.
  Mountain, SE Estonia
Suur Väin 106 C 2 *Ger.* Grosser
  Sund. Strait, E Baltic Sea
Suva 145 E 4 country capital,
  Viti Levu, W Fiji
Suwałki 98 E 2 *Lith.* Suvalkai,
  Rus. Suvalki. NE Poland
Suwannee River 43 E 3 river,
  SE USA
Şuwāt 118 D 2 E Syria

Suways, Khalīj as see Suez, Gulf of
Suways, Qanāt as see Suez Canal
Suzhou 129 D 5 var. Soochow,
Su-chou, Suchow; prev. Wuhsien.
E China
Svalbard 83 G 2 Norwegian
dependency, Arctic Ocean
Svartisen 84 C 3 glacier, C Norway
Svay Riêng 137 D 6 SE Cambodia
Sveg 85 C 5 C Sweden
Svenstavik 85 C 5 C Sweden
Sverdlovsk see Yekaterinburg
Sveti Vrach see Sandanski
Svetlogorsk see Svyetlahorsk
Svetlograd 111 B 7
SW Russian Federation
Svetlovodsk see Svitlovods'k
Svetozarevo 100 E 4 var. Jagodina.
C Yugoslavia
Svilengrad 104 D 3 prev. Mustafa-
Pasha. SE Bulgaria
Svisloch' see Svislach
Svitlovods'k 109 E 2
Rus. Svetlovodsk. C Ukraine
Svobodnyy 115 G 4
SE Russian Federation
Svyataya Anna Trough 155 H 4
trough, Arctic Ocean
Svyetlahorsk 107 D 7 Rus.
Svetlogorsk. SE Belorussia
Swakopmund 78 B 3 W Namibia
Swan Islands see Santanilla, Islas
Swansea 89 C 7 Wel. Abertawe.
S Wales, UK
Swarzędz 98 C 3 W Poland

Swaziland
78 D 4 S Monarchy, S Africa

Official name: Kingdom of
Swaziland **Date of formation:** 1968
Capital: Mbabane **Population:**
800,000 **Total area:** 17,360 sq km
(6,703 sq miles) **Languages:** Siswati*,
English*, Zulu:**Religions:** Christian
60%, traditional beliefs 40%
Ethnic mix: Swazi 95%, other 5%
Government: Executive monarchy
Currency: Lilangeni = 100 cents

Sweden
84 B 4 Swe. Sverige. Monarchy,
N Europe

Official name: Kingdom of Sweden
Date of formation: 1809/1905
Capital: Stockholm **Population:** 8.7
million **Total area:** 449,960 sq km
(173,730 sq miles) **Languages:**
Swedish*, Finnish, Lappish
Religions: Evangelical Lutheran
94%, Roman Catholic 2%, other 4%
Ethnic mix: Swedish 87%, Finnish
and Lapp 1%, other European 12%
Government: Constitutional
monarchy **Currency:** Krona = 100 öre

Sweetwater 49 F 3 Texas, S USA
Świdnica 98 B 4 Ger. Schweidnitz.
SW Poland
Świdwin 98 B 2 Ger. Schivelbein.
NW Poland
Świebodzice 98 B 4 Ger. Freiburg in
Schlesien, Swiebodzice.
SW Poland
Świebodzin 98 B 3 Ger. Schwiebus.
W Poland
Świecie 98 C 3 Ger. Schwertberg.
N Poland
Swindon 89 D 7 S England, UK
Swinemünde see Świnoujście
Świnoujście 98 A 2
Ger. Swinemünde. NW Poland

Switzerland
95 A 7 Fr. La Suisse,
Ger. Schweiz, It. Svizzera;
anc. Helvetica. Federal republic,
C Europe

Official name: Swiss Confederation
Date of formation: 1815 **Capital:**
Bern **Population:** 6.9 million **Total
area:** 41,290 sq km (15,940 sq miles)
Languages: German*, French*,
Italian* **Religions:** Roman Catholic
48%, Protestant 44%, other 8%
Ethnic mix: German 65%, French
18%, Italian 10%, other 7%
Government: Federal republic
Currency: Franc = 100 centimes

Syas'stroy 110 B 4 var.
S'as'stroj, Sjasstroj.
NW Russian Federation
Sydenham Island see Nonouti
Sydney 39 G 4 Nova Scotia,
SE Canada
Sydney 149 D 6 state capital,
New South Wales, SE Australia
Sydney Island see Manra
Sydney Mines 39 G 4 Nova Scotia,
SE Canada
Syedpur see Saidpur
Syemyezhava 107 C 6
Rus. Semezhevo. C Belorussia
Syeverodonets'k 109 H 3
Rus. Severodonetsk. E Ukraine
Syktyvkar 110 E 4 prev. Ust'-
Sysol'sk. NW Russian Federation
Sylacauga 42 D 2 Alabama, S USA
Sylhet 135 G 3 NE Bangladesh
Synel'nykove 109 G 3 var.
Sinel'nikovo. E Ukraine
Syowa 154 C 2 research station,
Antarctica
Syracuse 41 F 3 New York,
NE USA
Syracuse see Siracusa
Syr Darya 114 C 5 var. Sai Hun,
Sir Darya, Syrdarya,
Kaz. Syrdariya, Rus. Syrdar'ya,
Uzb. Sirdaryo; anc. Jaxartes. River,
C Asia
Syrdar'ya 123 E 2 E Uzbekistan

Syria
118 B 3 var. Siria, Syrie, Ar. Al-
Jumhūrīyah al-'Arabīyah as-
Sūrīyah, Jumhuriya al-Arabya as-
Suriya, Sūrīya. Republic, SW Asia

Official name: Syrian Arab
Republic **Date of formation:** 1946
Capital: Damascus **Population:** 13.8
million **Total area:** 185,180 sq km
(71,500 sq miles) **Languages:**
Arabic*, French, Kurdish, Armenian
Religions: Sunni Muslim 74%, other
Muslim 16%, Christian 10%
Ethnic mix: Arab 90%, other 10%
Government: Single-party republic
Currency: Pound = 100 piastres

Syriam 136 B 4 S Burma
Syrian Desert 119 D 5
Ar. Ådiyat ash Sham, Al Hamad,
Bādiyat ash Shām. Desert,
SW Asia
Sýrna 105 E 7 var. Sirna. Island,
Dodekánisos, SE Greece
Syvash, Zatoka 109 F 4 Rus. Zaliv
Syvash. Inlet, W Sea of Azov
Syzran' 111 C 6
W Russian Federation
Szamotuły 98 B 3 W Poland
Szczecin 98 B 3 Eng./Ger. Stettin.
NW Poland

Szczecinek 98 C 2 Ger. Neustettin.
NW Poland
Szczytno 98 D 3 Ger. Ortelsburg.
NE Poland
Szeged 99 D 7 Ger. Szegedin,
Rom. Seghedin. SE Hungary
Székesfehérvár 99 C 7
Ger. Stuhlweissenberg;
anc. Alba Regia. W Hungary
Szekszárd 99 C 7 S Hungary
Szinna see Snina
Szolnok 99 D 7 C Hungary
Szombathely 99 B 6
Ger. Steinamanger; anc. Sabaria,
Savaria. W Hungary
Szprotawa 98 B 4 Ger. Sprottau.
W Poland

T

Ţabaqah 118 D 2 N Syria
Tabasará, Serranía de 53 F 5
mountain range, W Panama
Tábor 99 B 5 SW Czech Republic
Tabora 73 B 7 W Tanzania
Tabrīz 120 C 2 var. Tauris, Tebriz.
NW Iran
Tabuaeran 145 G 2 prev. Fanning
Island. Island, E Kiribati
Tabūk 120 A 4 NW Saudi Arabia
Täby 85 C 6 C Sweden
Tachau see Tachov
Tachov 99 A 5 Ger. Tachau.
W Czech Republic
Tacloban 139 F 2 off. Tacloban City.
Leyte, C Philippines
Tacloban City see Tacloban
Tacna 61 E 4 SE Peru
Tacoma 46 B 2 Washington,
NW USA
Tacuarembó 64 D 4
prev. San Fructuoso. N Uruguay
Tademaït, Plateau du 70 D 3
plateau, C Algeria
Tādpatri 132 C 2 E India
Taegu 128 E 4 off. Taegu-
kwangyŏksi, var. Daegu,
Jap. Taikyū. SE South Korea
Taejŏn 128 E 4 off. Taejŏn-
kwangyŏksi, Jap. Taiden.
C South Korea
Tafí Viejo 64 C 3 NW Argentina
Taganrog 111 A 7
SW Russian Federation
Taganrog, Gulf of 109 G 4
Rus. Taganrogskiy Zaliv,
Ukr. Tahanroz'ka Zatoka. Gulf,
Black Sea/Sea of Azov
Taguatinga 63 F 3 C Brazil
Tagus 92 C 3 Port. Rio Tejo, Sp.
Río Tajo. River, Portugal/Spain
Tahat 71 E 4 mountain, SE Algeria
Tahiti 145 H 4 island,
W French Polynesia
Tahlequah 49 G 1
Oklahoma, C USA
Tahoe, Lake 47 B 5 lake, W USA
Tahoua 75 F 3 W Niger
T'aichung 129 D 6 Jap. Taichou,
Taichū; prev. Taiwan. W Taiwan
Taieri 151 B 7 river, South Island,
SW New Zealand
Taihape 150 D 4 North Island,
C New Zealand
T'ainan 129 D 6 Jap. Tainan;
prev. Dainan. SW Taiwan
Tai Pak Wan see Discovery Bay
T'aipei 129 D 6 Jap. Taihoku;
prev. Daihoku. Country capital,
N Taiwan
Taiping 138 B 3 W Malaysia
Tai Po 128 A 1 N Hong Kong

Taiwan
129 D 6 var. Formosa, Formo'sa.
Republic, E Asia

Official name: Republic of China
(Taiwan) **Date of formation:** 1949
Capital: Taipei **Population:** 20.8
million **Total Area:** 36,179 sq km
(13,969 sq miles) **Languages:**
Mandarin* **Religions:** Buddhist,
Confucianist, Taoist 93%, other 7%
Ethnic mix: Taiwanese 84%,
mainland Chinese 14%, other 2%
Government: Multiparty republic
Currency: New Taiwan $ = 100 cents

Taiwan Strait 125 E 3 var. Formosa
Strait, Chin. T'aiwan Haihsia,
Taiwan Haixia. Strait, East China
Sea/South China Sea
Taiyuan 128 C 4 var. T'ai-yuan,
T'ai-yüan; prev. Yangku. Province
capital, N China
Tai Yue Shan see Lantau Island
Ta'izz 121 B 7 SW Yemen

Tajikistan
123 E 3 Rus. Tadzhikistan, Taj.
Jumhurii Tojikiston; prev. Tajik
SSR. Republic, C Asia

Official name: Republic of
Tajikistan **Date of formation:** 1991
Capital: Dushanbe **Population:** 5.7
million **Total Area:** 143,100 sq km
(55,251 sq miles) **Languages:** Tajik*,
Uzbek, Russian **Religions:**
Sunni Muslim 85%, Shi'a Muslim
5%, other 10% **Ethnic mix:** Tajik
62%, Uzbek 24%, Russian 4%, Tartar
2%, other 8% **Government:**
Single-party republic
Currency: Tajik rouble = 100 kopeks

Tak 136 C 4 var. Rahaeng.
W Thailand
Takaoka 131 C 5 Honshū, SW Japan
Takapuna 150 D 2 North Island,
N New Zealand
Takengon 138 A 3 W Indonesia
Takhiatash see Takhiatosh
Takhiatosh 122 C 2 Rus. Takhiatash.
W Uzbekistan
Takhtaküpir 122 D 1 Rus.
Takhtakupyr. W Uzbekistan
Takhtakupyr see Takhtaküpir
Takikawa 130 D 2 Hokkaidō,
NE Japan
Takli Makan Desert see Taklimakan
Shamo
Taklimakan Shamo 126 B 3
Eng. Takli Makan Desert. Desert,
NW China
Takutea 145 G 5 island,
S Cook Islands
Talabriga see Aveiro
Talachyn 107 D 6 Rus. Tolochin.
NE Belorussia
Talamanca, Cordillera de 53 E 5
mountain range, C Costa Rica
Talara 60 B 2 NW Peru
Talas 123 F 2 NW Kyrgyzstan
Talaud, Kepulauan 139 F 3 island
group, E Indonesia
Talavera de la Reina 92 D 3
anc. Caesarobriga, Talabriga.
C Spain
Talca 64 B 4 C Chile
Talcahuano 65 B 5 C Chile
Taldykorgan 114 C 5
Kaz. Taldyqorghan; prev.
Taldy-Kurgan. SE Kazakhstan
Taliq-an see Tāloqān
Tal'ka 107 D 6 C Belorussia

Talkhof *see* Puurmani
Tallahassee 42 D 3
prev. Muskogean. State capital,
Florida, SE USA
Tall Fadghāmī 118 E 2
var. Fadghāmī. NE Syria
Tallinn 106 D 2 *Ger.* Reval,
Rus. Tallin; *prev.* Revel. Country
capital, NW Estonia
Tall Kalakh 118 B 4 *var.*
Tell Kalakh. W Syria
Tallulah 42 B 2 Louisiana, S USA
Tal′ne 109 E 3 *Rus.* Tal′noye.
C Ukraine
Tal′noye *see* Tal′ne
Tāloqān 123 E 3 *var.* Taliq-an.
NE Afghanistan
Talsen *see* Talsi
Talsi 106 C 3 *Ger.* Talsen.
NW Latvia
Taltal 64 B 2 N Chile
Talvik 84 D 2 N Norway
Tamale 75 E 4 C Ghana
Tamana 145 E 3 *prev.* Rotcher
Island. Island, W Kiribati
Tamanrasset 71 E 4 *var.*
Tamenghest. S Algeria
Tamar 89 C 7 river,
SW England, UK
Tamatave *see* Toamasina
Tamazunchale 51 E 4 C Mexico
Tambacounda 74 C 3 SE Senegal
Tambo 148 C 4 Queensland,
C Australia
Tambov 111 B 6
W Russian Federation
Tambura 73 B 5 SW Sudan
Tamchaket *see* Tâmchekket
Tâmchekket 74 C 3 *var.* Tamchaket.
S Mauritania
Tamenghest *see* Tamanrasset
Tamiahua, Laguna de 51 F 4 coastal
lagoon, SW Gulf of Mexico
Tam Ky 137 E 5 E Vietnam
Tammerfors *see* Tampere
Tampa 43 E 4 Florida, SE USA
Tampa Bay 43 E 4 bay, Florida,
SE Gulf of Mexico
Tampere 85 D 5 *Swe.* Tammerfors.
SW Finland
Tampico 51 E 3 C Mexico
Tamshiyacu 60 C 1 N Peru
Tamworth 149 D 6 New South
Wales, SE Australia
Tana 84 D 2 *var.* Tenojoki,
Fin. Teno, *Lapp.* Dealnu. River,
Finland/Norway
Tana 84 D 2 N Norway
Tanabe 131 C 7 Honshū,
SW Japan
Tanaga Island 36 A 3 island,
Alaska, NW USA
T′ana Häyk′ 72 C 4 *var.* Lake Tana.
Lake, NW Ethiopia
Tana, Lake *see* T′ana Häyk′
Tanami Desert 146 E 3 desert,
Northern Territory, N Australia
Tananarive *see* Antananarivo
Ţăndărei 108 D 5 SE Romania
Tandil 65 D 5 E Argentina
Tando Ādam 134 B 3 *var.* Adam-jo-
Tando. S Pakistan
Tanega-shima 131 B 8 island,
Ōsumi-shotō, SW Japan
Tanen Taunggyi *see* Tane Range
Tane Range 136 B 4 *Bur.* Tanen
Taunggyi. Mountain range,
N Thailand
Tanezrouft 70 D 4 desert,
Algeria/Mali
Tanga 73 C 7 E Tanzania

Tanganyika, Lake 73 B 7 lake,
NE Africa
Tanger 70 C 2 *var.* Tangier, Tangiers,
Fr./Ger. Tanger, *Sp.* Tánger;
anc. Tingis. NW Morocco
Tanggula Shan 126 C 4 *var.* Dangla,
Tangla Range. Mountain range,
W China
Tangier *see* Tanger
Tangiers *see* Tanger
Tangra Yumco 126 B 5 *var.* Tangro
Tso. Lake, W China
Tangro Tso *see* Tangra Yumco
Tangshan 128 D 3 *var.* T′angshan,
T′ang-shan. NE China
Tanimbar, Kepulauan 139 G 5
island group, Maluku,
E Indonesia
Tanna 144 D 5 island, S Vanuatu
Tansen 135 E 3 C Nepal
Tan-Tan 70 B 3 SW Morocco

Tanzania
73 C 7 Swa.Jamhuri ya
Muungano wa Tanzania;
prev. German East Africa,
Tanganyika and Zanzibar.
Republic, NE Africa

Official name: United Republic of
Tanzania **Date of formation:** 1964
Capital: Dodoma **Population:** 28.8
million **Total area:** 945,090 sq km
(364,900 sq miles) **Languages:**
English*, Swahili* **Religions:**
Traditional beliefs 42%, Muslim
31%, Christian 27% **Ethnic mix:** 120
Ethnic Bantu groups 99%, other 1%
Government: Single-party republic
Currency: Shilling = 100 cents

Tao, Ko 137 C 6 island, C Thailand
Taoudenit *see* Taoudenni
Taoudenni 75 E 2 *var.* Taoudenit.
N Mali
Tapa 106 E 2 *Ger.* Taps.
NE Estonia
Tapachula 51 G 5 SE Mexico
Tapaiu *see* Gvardeysk
Tapajós 63 E 2 *var.* Tapajóz. River,
NW Brazil
Tapajóz *see* Tapajós
Taps *see* Tapa
Ţarābulus 71 F 2 *var.* Ţarābulus al
Gharb; *Eng.* Tripoli. Country
capital, NW Libya
Taraclia 108 D 4 *Rus.* Tarakilya.
S Moldavia
Tarakilya *see* Taraclia
Taranaki, Mount 150 D 4 *var.*
Egmont. Mountain, North Island,
C New Zealand
Tarancón 93 E 3 C Spain
Taranto 97 E 5 *var.* Tarentum.
SE Italy
Taranto, Golfo di 97 E 6 *Eng.* Gulf
of Taranto. Gulf, N Ionian Sea
Taranto, Gulf of *see* Taranto, Golfo di
Tarapoto 60 C 2 N Peru
Tarare 91 D 5 E France
Tarascon 91 D 6 SE France
Tarawa Atoll 144 D 2 island,
W Kiribati
Tarazona 93 E 2 NE Spain
Tarbes 91 B 6 *anc.* Bigorra.
S France
Tarcoola 149 A 6 South Australia,
S Australia
Taree 149 D 6 New South Wales,
SE Australia
Tarentum *see* Taranto
Târgoviște 108 C 5 *prev.* Tîrgoviște.
S Romania

Targu Jui 108 B 4 *prev.* Tîrgu Jiu.
W Romania
Târgu Mureş 108 B 4
Ger. Neumarkt, *Hung.*
Marosvásárhely; *prev.* Oşorhei,
Tîrgu Mures. C Romania
Târgu-Neamţ 108 C 3 *var.* Tárgul-
Neamt; *prev.* Tîrgu-Neamt.
NE Romania
Târgu Ocna 108 C 4 *Hung.*
Aknavásár; *prev.* Tîrgu Ocna.
E Romania
Târgu Secuiesc 108 C 4
Ger. Neumarkt, Szekler
Neumarkt, *Hung.* Kezdivásárhely;
prev. Chezdi-Oşorheiu, Tárgul-
Săcuiesc, Tîrgu Secuiesc.
E Romania
Tarija 61 G 5 S Bolivia
Tarīm 121 C 6 C Yemen
Tarim Basin 126 B 3 *var.* Tarim
Pendi. Basin, NW China
Tarim He 126 B 3 river, NW China
Tarim Pendi *see* Tarim Basin
Tarma 60 C 3 C Peru
Tarn 91 C 6 cultural region, S France
Tarn 91 C 6 river, S France
Tárnäveni 108 B 4 *Ger.* Marteskirch,
Martinskirch, *Hung.*
Dicsőszentmárton; *prev.*
Sînmartin, Tîrnăveni. C Romania
Tarnobrzeg 98 D 4 SE Poland
Tarnów 99 D 5 SE Poland
Taroom 149 D 5 Queensland,
SE Australia
Tarraco *see* Tarragona
Tarragona 93 G 2 *anc.* Tarraco.
E Spain
Tarran Hills 149 C 6 hill range,
New South Wales, C Australia
Tarrasa *see* Terrassa
Tarrega *see* Tàrrega
Tàrrega 93 F 2 *var.* Tarrega.
NE Spain
Tarsus 116 C 4 S Turkey
Tartu 106 E 3 *Ger.* Dorpat; *prev.*
Rus. Yurev, Yuryev. SE Estonia
Ţarţūs 118 B 4 *Fr.* Tartouss;
anc. Tortosa. W Syria
Tarutao, Ko 137 C 7 island,
S Thailand
Tarvisio 96 D 2 NE Italy
Tarvisium *see* Treviso
Tashkent *see* Toshkent
Tash-Kömür *see* Tash-Kumyr
Tash-Kumyr 123 F 2
Kir. Tash-Kömür. W Kyrgyzstan
Tasikmalaja *see* Tasikmalaya
Tasikmalaya 138 C 5 *prev.*
Tasikmalaja. Jawa, Indonesia
Tasiusaq 82 C 2 *var.* Tasiusak,
Tasiussaq. W Greenland
Tasman Basin 152 C 5 *var.* East
Australian Basin. Undersea basin,
SW Pacific Ocean
Tasman Bay 151 C 5 inlet,
E Tasman Sea
Tasmania 149 B 8
prev. Van Diemen's Land. State,
SE Australia
Tasman Plateau 142 C 5
var. South Tasmania Plateau.
Undersea plateau, S Tasman Sea
Tasman Sea 152 C 5 sea,
SW Pacific Ocean
Tassili N′Ajjer 71 E 4 *var.* Hamada
du Tinghert. Plateau, E Algeria
Tatabánya 99 C 6 NW Hungary
Tathlīth 121 B 6 S Saudi Arabia
Tatra Mountains 99 D 5 *Ger.* Tatra,
Hung. Tátra, *Pol./Slvk.* Tatry.
Mountain range, Poland/Slovakia

Tatvan 117 F 3 SE Turkey
Tau 145 F 4 *var.* Ta′ú. Island,
E American Samoa
Taumarunui 150 D 4 North Island,
C New Zealand
Taungdwingyi 136 B 3 W Burma
Taunggyi 136 B 3 C Burma
Taunton 89 C 7 SW England, UK
Taupo 150 D 3 North Island,
N New Zealand
Taupo, Lake 150 D 3 lake,
North Island, N New Zealand
Tauragė 106 B 4 *Ger.* Tauroggen.
SW Lithuania
Tauranga 150 D 3 North Island,
NE New Zealand
Tauroggen *see* Tauragė
Taurus Mountains *see* Toros Dağları
Tavas 116 B 4 SW Turkey
Tavastehus *see* Hämeenlinna
Tavira 92 C 5 SE Portugal
Tavoy 137 B 5 *var.* Dawei. SE Burma
Tavoy Island *see* Mali Kyun
Ta Waewae Bay 151 A 7 bay,
S Pacific Ocean
Tawakoni, Lake 49 G 2 reservoir,
Texas, S USA
Tawau 138 D 3 Borneo, E Malaysia
Ţawkar *see* Tokar
Tawzar *see* Tozeur
Taxco 51 E 4 *var.* Taxco de Alarcón.
S Mexico
Taxco de Alarcón *see* Taxco
Tay 88 C 3 river, C Scotalnd, UK
Taylor 49 G 3 Texas, S USA
Taymā′ 120 A 4 NW Saudi Arabia
Taymyr, Ozero 115 E 2 lake,
N Russian Federation
Taymyr, Poluostrov 115 E 2
peninsula, N Russian Federation
Tayshet 115 E 4
S Russian Federation
T′bilisi 117 G 2 *Eng.* Tiflis. Country
capital, SE Georgia
Tchad, Lac *see* Chad, Lake
Tchien *see* Zwedru
Tczew 98 C 2 *Ger.* Dirschau.
N Poland
Te Anau 151 A 7 South Island,
SW New Zealand
Te Anau, Lake 151 A 7 lake,
South Island, SW New Zealand
Teapa 51 G 5 SE Mexico
Teate *see* Chieti
Tebingtinggi 138 B 3 Sumatera,
N Indonesia
Teboe Top 59 G 3 SE Surinam
Techirghiol 108 D 5 E Romania
Tecomán 50 D 4 SW Mexico
Tecpan 51 E 5 *var.* Tecpan de
Galeana. S Mexico
Tecpan de Galeana *see* Tecpan
Tecuci 108 D 4 E Romania
Tedzhen 122 D 3 *Turkm.* Tejen.
S Turkmenistan
Tees 89 D 5 river, N England, UK
Tefé 62 D 2 N Brazil
Tegal 138 C 4 Jawa, C Indonesia
Tegelen 87 D 5 SE Netherlands
Tegucigalpa 52 C 3 country capital,
SW Honduras
Tehama *see* Tihāmah
Teheran *see* Tehrān
Tehrān 120 C 3 *var.* Teheran.
Country capital, N Iran
Tehuacán 51 F 4 S Mexico
Tehuantepec 51 F 5 *var.* Santo
Domingo Tehuantepec. SE Mexico
Tehuantepec, Golfo de 51 G 5
var. Gulf of Tehuantepec. Gulf,
E Pacific Ocean

Tehuantepec, Gulf of *see* Tehuantepec, Golfo de
Tehuantepec, Isthmus of *see* Tehuantepec, Istmo de
Tehuantepec, Istmo de 51 F 5 *var.* Isthmus of Tehuantepec. Isthmus, SE Mexico
Tejen *see* Tedzhen
Te Kao 150 C 1 North Island, N New Zealand
Tekax 51 H 4 *var.* Tekax de Álvaro Obregón. SE Mexico
Tekax de Álvaro Obregón *see* Tekax
Tekeli 114 C 5 SE Kazakhstan
Tekirdağ 116 A 2 *It.* Rodosto; *anc.* Bisanthe, Raidestos, Rhaedestus. NW Turkey
Tekong, Pulau 138 B 1 island, E Singapore
Te Kuiti 150 D 3 North Island, N New Zealand
Tela 52 C 2 NW Honduras
Tel Aviv-Jaffa *see* Tel Aviv-Yafo
Tel Aviv-Yafo 119 A 6 *var.* Tel Aviv-Jaffa. C Israel
Telish 104 C 2 *var.* Teliš; *prev.* Azizie. NW Bulgaria
Tell Atlas *see* Atlas Tellien
Tell Kalakh *see* Tall Kalakh
Telschen *see* Telšiai
Telšiai 106 B 3 *Ger.* Telschen. NW Lithuania
Teluk Intan 138 B 3 *var.* Telok Anson, Telok Intan, Teluk Anson. W Malaysia
Tema 75 E 5 SE Ghana
Temerin 100 D 3 N Yugoslavia
Temirtau 114 C 4 *prev.* Samarkandski, Samarkandskoye. C Kazakhstan
Tempe 48 B 2 Arizona, SW USA
Tempio Pausania 97 A 5 W Italy
Temple 49 G 3 Texas, S USA
Temple Bay 148 C 2 bay, NW Coral Sea
Temryuk 111 A 7 SW Russian Federation
Temuco 65 B 5 C Chile
Temuka 151 B 6 South Island, SW New Zealand
Téna Kourou 74 D 4 mountain, SW Burkina
Tenasserim Range 137 C 6 mountain range, S Burma
Ténenkou 74 D 3 C Mali
Ténéré 75 G 2 desert, Algeria/Niger
Ténéré du Tafassâsset 75 G 2 desert, N Niger
Tenerife 70 A 3 island, Islas Canarias, SW Spain
Tengger Shamo 127 E 3 desert, N China
Tengréla 74 D 4 *var.* Tingréla. N Ivory Coast
Tenkodogo 75 E 4 S Burkina
Tennant Creek 148 A 3 Northern Territory, C Australia
Tennessee 42 C 1 *off.* State of Tennessee; nickname Volunteer State. State, SE USA
Tenos *see* Tínos
Tenterfield 149 D 5 New South Wales, SE Australia
Ten Thousand Islands 43 E 5 island, Florida, SE USA
Tepelenë 101 C 7 *var.* Tepelena, *It.* Tepeleni. S Albania
Tepic 50 D 4 C Mexico
Teplice 98 A 4 *Ger.* Teplitz; *prev.* Teplice-Šanov, Teplitz-Schönau. NW Czech Republic
Tequila 50 D 4 SW Mexico
Teraina 145 G 2 *prev.* Washington Island. Island, E Kiribati
Teramo 96 D 4 *anc.* Interamna. C Italy
Tercan 117 E 3 NE Turkey
Terceira 92 A 5 *var.* Ilha Terceira. Island, W Portugal
Terceira, Ilha *see* Terceira
Terekhovka *see* Tsyerakhowka
Teresina 63 F 2 *var.* Therezina. State capital, NE Brazil
Termez *see* Termiz
Términos, Laguna de 51 G 4 lagoon, SE Gulf of Mexico
Termiz 123 E 3 *Rus.* Termez. S Uzbekistan
Termoli 96 D 4 C Italy
Terneuzen 87 B 5 *var.* Neuzen. SW Netherlands
Terni 96 C 4 *anc.* Interamna Nahars. C Italy
Ternopil' 108 C 2 *Pol.* Tarnopol, *Rus.* Ternopol'. W Ukraine
Terrace Bay 38 B 4 Ontario, S Canada
Terracina 97 C 5 W Italy
Terranova di Sicilia *see* Gela
Terranova Pausania *see* Olbia
Terrassa 93 G 2 *Cast.* Tarrasa. E Spain
Terre Adélie 154 C 4 French dependent territory, Antarctica
Terre Neuve *see* Newfoundland and Labrador
Terre-Neuve *see* Newfoundland
Terschelling 86 C 1 *Fris.* Skylge. Island, N Netherlands
Teruel 93 F 3 *anc.* Turba. E Spain
Tervel 104 E 1 *prev.* Kurtbunar, *Rom.* Curtbunar. NE Bulgaria
Tervueren *see* Tervuren
Tervuren 87 C 6 *var.* Tervueren. C Belgium
Teseney 72 C 4 *var.* Tessenei. W Eritrea
Tessalit 75 E 2 NE Mali
Tessaoua 75 G 3 S Niger
Tessenderlo 87 C 5 NE Belgium
Tessenei *see* Teseney
Tete 79 E 2 NW Mozambique
Teterow 94 C 3 NE Germany
Tetouan 70 C 2 *var.* Tétouan, Tetuán. N Morocco
Tetovo 101 D 6 *Alb.* Tetova, Tetovë, *Turk.* Kalkandelen. NW Macedonia
Tetschen *see* Děčín
Tevere 96 C 4 *Eng.* Tiber. River, C Italy
Teverya 119 B 5 *var.* Tiberias. N Israel
Texarkana 42 A 2 Arkansas, C USA
Texarkana 49 H 2 Texas, S USA
Texas 49 G 3 *off.* State of Texas; *nickname* Lone Star State. State, S USA
Texas City 49 H 4 Texas, S USA
Texel 86 C 2 island, NW Netherlands
Texoma, Lake 49 G 2 reservoir, SW USA
Teziutlán 51 F 4 S Mexico
Thai Binh 136 D 3 N Vietnam

Thailand
137 C 5 *Th.* Prathet Thai; *prev.* Siam. Monarchy, SE Asia

Official name: Kingdom of Thailand **Date of formation:** 1882/1887 **Capital:** Bangkok **Population:** 56.9 million **Total Area:** 513,120 sq km (198,116 sq miles) **Languages:** Thai*, Chinese, Malay **Religions:** Buddhist 95%, Muslim 4%, other 1% **Ethnic mix:** Thai 75%, Chinese 14%, Malay 4%, other 7% **Government:** Constitutional monarchy **Currency:** Baht = 100 stangs

---

Thailand, Gulf of 137 C 6 *var.* Gulf of Siam, *Th.* Ao Thai, *Vtn.* Vinh Thai Lan. Gulf, Pacific Ocean/South China Sea
Thai Nguyên 136 D 3 N Vietnam
Thakhek *see* Thakhèk
Thames 89 D 7 river, S England, UK
Thames 150 D 3 North Island, N New Zealand
Thāna *see* Thāne
Thāne 134 C 5 *prev.* Thāna. W India
Thanh Hoa 136 D 4 N Vietnam
Thap Put 137 B 7 S Thailand
Thar Desert 134 C 3 *var.* Great Indian Desert, Indian Desert. Desert, India/Pakistan
Thásos 104 C 4 Thásos, E Greece
Thásos 104 C 4 island, E Greece
Thaton 136 B 4 SE Burma
Thatta 134 B 3 SE Pakistan
Thayetmyo 136 A 4 W Burma
The Dalles 46 B 3 Oregon, NW USA
The Flatts Village *see* Flatts Village
The Hague *see* 's-Gravenhage
The Pas 37 F 5 Manitoba, C Canada
Therezina *see* Teresina
Thérma 105 D 6 Ikaría, SE Greece
Thermaïkós Kólpos 104 B 4 *Eng.* Thermaic Gulf; *anc.* Thermaicus Sinus. Gulf, NW Aegean Sea
Thérmo 105 B 5 C Greece
The Rock 93 H 4 E Gibraltar
Thessaloníki 104 B 4 *Eng.* Salonica, Salonika, *SCr.* Solun, *Turk.* Selânik. N Greece
The Valley 55 G 3 dependent territory capital, E Anguilla
The Village 49 G 1 Oklahoma, C USA
The Woodlands 49 H 4 Texas, S USA
Thiamis *see* Thýamis
Thief River Falls 45 F 1 Minnesota, N USA
Thiers 91 C 5 C France
Thiès 74 B 3 W Senegal
Thikombia *see* Cikobia
Thimphu 135 G 3 *var.* Thimbu; *prev.* Tashi Chho Dzong. Country capital, W Bhutan
Thionville 90 D 3 *Ger.* Diedenhofen. NE France
Thíra 105 D 7 Thíra, SE Greece
Thíra 105 D 7 *prev.* Santorin, Santoríni, *anc.* Thera. Island, Kykládes, SE Greece
Thiruvanathapuram *see* Trivandrum
Tholen 86 B 4 island, SW Netherlands
Thomasville 42 D 3 Georgia, SE USA
Thompson 37 G 5 Manitoba, C Canada
Thompson 148 C 4 river, E Australia
Thon Buri 137 C 5 C Thailand
Thonon-les-Bains 91 D 5 E France
Thonze 136 B 4 SW Burma
Thorlákshöfn 83 E 5 SW Iceland
Thorn *see* Toruń
Thornton Island *see* Caroline Island
Thorshavn *see* Tórshavn
Thouars 90 B 4 W France
Thoune *see* Thun
Thracian Sea 104 D 4 *Gk.* Thrakikó Pélagos; *anc.* Thracium Mare. Sea, N Aegean Sea
Thrakikó Pélagos *see* Thracian Sea
Three Kings Island 150 C 1 island, North Island, N New Zealand
Thrissur *see* Trichūr
Thuin 87 B 7 S Belgium
Thun 95 A 7 *Fr.* Thoune. W Switzerland
Thunder Bay 38 B 4 Ontario, S Canada
Thuner See 95 A 7 lake, C Switzerland
Thung Song 137 C 7 *var.* Cha Mai. S Thailand
Thüringer Wald 95 C 5 *Eng.* Thuringian Forest. Mountain range, C Germany
Thuringian Forest *see* Thüringer Wald
Thurso 88 C 2 N Scotland, UK
Thýamis 104 A 4 *var.* Thiamis. River, W Greece
Tianjin 128 D 4 NE China
Tianshui 128 B 4 C China
Tiba *see* Chiba
Tiber *see* Tevere
Tiber *see* Tivoli
Tiberias *see* Teverya
Tiberias, Lake 119 B 5 *var.* Chinnereth, Sea of Bahr Tabariya, Sea of Galilee, *Ar.* Bahrat Tabariya, *Heb.* Yam Kinneret. Lake, N Israel
Tibesti 76 C 2 *var.* Tibesti Massif, *Ar.* Tībistī. Mountain range, N Africa
Tibet, Plateau of 126 C 5 plateau, S Asia
Tibnī *see* At Tibnī
Tiburón, Isla 50 B 2 *var.* Isla del Tiburón. Island, NW Mexico
Tiburón, Isla del *see* Tiburón, Isla
Tichau *see* Tychy
Tîchît 74 D 2 *var.* Tichitt. C Mauritania
Tichitt *see* Tîchît
Tichvin *see* Tikhvin
Ticinum *see* Pavia
Ticul 51 H 4 SE Mexico
Tiel 86 C 4 C Netherlands
Tienen 87 C 6 *var.* Thienen, *Fr.* Tirlemont. C Belgium
Tien Shan 123 G 2 *Chin.* Thian Shan, Tian Shan, T'ien Shan, *Rus.* Tyan Shan , Tyan'-Shan'. Mountain range, China/Kyrgyzstan
Tierp 85 C 6 C Sweden
Tierra del Fuego 65 B 8 island, Argentina/Chile
Tiflis *see* T'bilisi
Tifton 43 E 3 Georgia, SE USA
Tighina 108 D 4 *Rus.* Bendery; *prev.* Bender. E Moldavia
Tigris 120 B 2 *Ar.* Dijlah, *Turk.* Dicle. River, Iraq/Turkey
Tihāmah 121 B 6 *var.* Tehama. Plain, Saudi Arabia/Yemen
Tijuana 50 A 1 NW Mexico
Tikhoretsk 111 A 7 SW Russian Federation
Tikhvin 110 B 4 *var.* Tichvin. NW Russian Federation
Tiki Basin 153 E 3 undersea basin, S Pacific Ocean
Tiksi 115 F 2 N Russian Federation
Tilburg 86 C 4 S Netherlands

Tillabéri 75 F 3 *var.* Tillabéry.
   W Niger
Tillabéry *see* Tillabéri
Tílos 105 E 7 island, Dodekánisos,
   SE Greece
Timah, Bukit 138 B 1 hill,
   C Singapore
Timaru 151 B 6 South Island,
   SW New Zealand
Timbedgha 74 D 3 *var.* Timbédra.
   SE Mauritania
Timbédra *see* Timbedgha
Timbuktu *see* Tombouctou
Timétrine 75 E 2 mountain range,
   C Mali
Timis 108 A 4 river, W Romania
Timisoara 108 A 4 *Ger.*
   Temeschwar, Temeswar,
   Hung. Temesvár; *prev.*
   Temeschberg. W Romania
Timmins 38 C 4 Ontario, S Canada
Timor 139 F 5 island, Nusa
   Tenggara, C Indonesia
Timor Sea 152 A 3 sea,
   E Indian Ocean
Timor Trench *see* Timor Trough
Timor Trough 125 F 5 *var.* Timor
   Trench. Trough, N Timor Sea
Timrå 85 C 5 C Sweden
Tindouf 70 C 3 W Algeria
Tineo 92 C 1 N Spain
Tinghert, Hamada du *see* Tassili
   N'Ajjer
Tingo María 60 C 3 C Peru
Tingréla *see* Tingréla
Tinhosa Grande 76 E 2 island,
   C Sao Tome & Principe
Tinhosa Pequena 76 E 1 island,
   C Sao Tome & Principe
Tinian 144 B 1 island,
   S Northern Mariana Islands
Tínos 105 D 6 Tínos, SE Greece
Tínos 105 D 6 *anc.* Tenos. Island,
   Kykládes, SE Greece
Tinrhert, Hamada de 71 E 3
   var. Plateau du Tinghert. Plateau,
   W Algeria
Tipitapa 52 D 3 W Nicaragua
Tirana *see* Tiranë
Tiranë 101 D 6 *var.* Tirana. Country
   capital, C Albania
Tirasberge 78 B 4 mountain range,
   SW Namibia
Tiraspol 108 D 4 *Rus.* Tiraspol'.
   E Moldavia
Tiraspol' *see* Tiraspol
Tiree 88 B 3 island, W Scotland, UK ·
Tîrgovişte *see* Târgovişte
Tîrgu Jiu *see* Targu Jui
Tírnavos *see* Týrnavos
Tirol 95 C 7 *var.* Tyrol, *It.* Tirolo.
   Cultural region, W Austria
Tirreno, Mare *see* Tyrrhenian Sea
Tiruchchiráppalli 132 C 3
   prev. Trichinopoly. SE India
Tiruntán 60 C 3 C Peru
Tiruppattūr 132 C 2 SE India
Tisza 81 E 4 *var.* Tisa, Tysa,
   Rus. Tissa. River, E Europe
Tiszakécske 99 D 7 Hungary
Tit 70 D 3 C Algeria
Titano, Monte 96 E 1 mountain,
   C San Marino
Titicaca, Lake 61 E 4 lake,
   Bolivia/Peru
Titograd *see* Podgorica
Titose *see* Chitose
Titovo Užice *see* Užice
Titov Veles 101 E 6 C Macedonia
Titu 108 C 5 S Romania
Titule 77 D 5 N Congo (Zaire)

Tiverton 89 C 7 SW England, UK
Tivoli 96 C 4 *anc.* Tiber. C Italy
Tizimín 51 H 3 SE Mexico
Tizi Ouzou 71 E 1 *var.* Tizi-Ouzou.
   N Algeria
Tizi-Ouzou *see* Tizi Ouzou
Tiznit 70 B 3 SW Morocco
Tjilatjap *see* Cilacap
Tjirebon *see* Cirebon
Tlaquepaque 50 D 4 C Mexico
Tlaxcala 51 E 4 *var.* Tlascala,
   Tlaxcala de Xicohténcatl. C Mexico
Tlemcen 70 D 2 *var.* Tilimsen,
   Tlemsen. NW Algeria
Tmassah 71 G 3 C Libya
Toamasina 79 G 3 *var.* Tamatave.
   E Madagascar
Toba, Danau 138 B 3 lake,
   Sumatera, W Indonesia
Tobago 55 H 5 island,
   NE Trinidad & Tobago
Toba Kākar Range 134 B 2
   mountain range, NW Pakistan
Tobol 114 C 4 *Kaz.* Tobyl.
   River, Kazakhstan/
   Russian Federation
Tobol'sk 114 C 3
   C Russian Federation
Tobyl *see* Tobol
Tocantins 63 F 3 river, N Brazil
Tocoa 52 D 2 N Honduras
Tocopilla 64 B 2 N Chile
Todi 96 C 4 C Italy
Todos os Santos, Baía de 63 G 3
   bay, W Atlantic Ocean
Toetoes Bay 151 B 8 bay,
   SW Pacific Ocean
Tofua 145 E 5 island, C Tonga

Togo
   75 E 4 *prev.* French Togoland.
   Republic, W Africa

Official name: Togolese Republic
Date of formation: 1960 **Capital:**
Lomé **Population:** 3.9 million **Total
area:** 56,790 sq km (21,927 sq miles)
Languages: French*, Ewe, Kabye,
Gurma **Religions:** Traditional beliefs
70%, Christian 20%, Muslim 10%
Ethnic mix: Ewe 43%, Kabye 26%,
Gurma 16%, other 15%
Government: Multiparty republic
Currency: CFA franc = 100 centimes

Toiyabe Range 47 C 5 mountain
   range, Nevada, W USA
Tokanui 151 B 8 South Island,
   SW New Zealand
Tokar 72 C 3 *var.* Ţawkar. NE Sudan
Tokat 116 D 3 N Turkey
Tokelau 145 F 3 New Zealand
   overseas territory, S Pacific Ocean
Tőketerebes *see* Trebišov
Tokio *see* Tōkyō
Tokmak 109 G 4 *var.* Velykyy
   Tokmak. SE Ukraine
Tokmak 123 G 2 *Kir.* Tokmok.
   N Kyrgyzstan
Tokmok *see* Tokmak
Tokoroa 150 D 3 North Island,
   N New Zealand
Tokuno-shima 130 A 3 island,
   Amami-shotō, SW Japan
Tokushima 131 C 7 *var.* Tokusima.
   Shikoku, SW Japan
Tokusima *see* Tokushima
Tōkyō 131 D 5 country capital,
   Honshū, S Japan
Tōkyō Bay 130 A 1 bay,
   NW Pacific Ocean
Toledo 92 D 3 *anc.* Toletum.
   C Spain

Toledo 40 D 3 Ohio, N USA
Toledo 61 F 4 W Bolivia
Toledo Bend Reservoir 49 H 3
   reservoir, SW USA
Toletum *see* Toledo
Toliara 79 F 4 *var.* Toliary;
   prev. Tuléar. SW Madagascar
Tolmin 95 D 8 *Ger.* Tolmein,
   It. Tolmino. W Slovenia
Tolna 99 C 7 *Ger.* Tolnau. S Hungary
Tolnau *see* Tolna
Tolochin *see* Talachyn
Tolo Harbour 128 B 1
   NE Hong Kong
Tolosa 93 E 1 N Spain
Tolosa *see* Toulouse
Toluca 51 E 4 *var.* Toluca de Lerdo.
   S Mexico
Toluca de Lerdo *see* Toluca
Tol'yatti 111 C 6 *prev.* Stavropol'.
   W Russian Federation
Tomakomai 130 D 2 Hokkaidō,
   NE Japan
Tomar 92 B 3 W Portugal
Tomaschow *see* Tomaszów Lubelski
Tomaszów Lubelski 98 E 4
   Ger. Tomaschow. SE Poland
Tomaszów Mazowiecki 98 D 4
   var. Tomaszów Mazowiecka;
   prev. Tomaszów, *Ger.* Tomaschow.
   C Poland
Tombigbee River 42 C 3 river,
   SE USA
Tombouctou 75 E 3 *Eng.* Timbuktu.
   N Mali
Tombua 78 A 2 *Port.* Porto
   Alexandre. SW Angola
Tomelloso 93 E 3 C Spain
Tomini, Teluk 139 E 4 *prev.* Teluk
   Gorontalo. Bay, N Molucca Sea
Tomsk 114 D 4
   C Russian Federation
Tonezh *see* Tonyezh

Tonga
   145 E 4 *var.* Friendly Islands.
   Monarchy, S Pacific Ocean

Official name: Kingdom of Tonga
Date of formation: 1970 **Capital:**
Nuku'alofa **Population:** 101,000
Total Area: 750 sq km (290 sq miles)
Languages: Tongan*, English
Religions: Protestant 82
Roman Catholic 18% **Ethnic mix:**
Tongan 98% other 2% **Government:**
Constitutional monarchy
Currency: Pa'anga = 100 seniti

Tongatapu 145 E 5 island, S Tonga
Tongatapu Group 145 E 5 island
   group, S Tonga
Tonga Trench 152 D 4 trench,
   S Pacific Ocean
Tongchuan 128 C 4 C China
Tongeren 87 D 6 *Fr.* Tongres.
   NE Belgium
Tong Fuk 128 A 2 SW Hong Kong
Tongking, Gulf of 136 E 4 *Chin.*
   Beibu Wan, *Vtn.* Vinh Bắc Bô.
   Gulf, Pacific Ocean/
   South China Sea
Tongliao 127 G 2 N China
Tongres *see* Tongeren
Tongtian He 126 C 4 river, C China
Tonj 73 B 5 SW Sudan
Tônlé Sap 137 D 5 *Eng.* Great Lake.
   Lake, W Cambodia
Tonyezh 107 C 7 *Rus.* Tonezh.
   SE Belorussia
Tooele 44 B 4 Utah, W USA
Toowoomba 149 E 5 Queensland,
   E Australia

Topeka 45 F 4 state capital,
   Kansas, C USA
Topliţa 108 C 3 *Ger.* Töplitz,
   Hung. Maroshévíz; *prev.* Oláh-
   Toplicza, Toplicza, Topliţa
   Română. C Romania
Topol'čany 99 C 6 *Hung.*
   Nagytapolcsány. W Slovakia
Topolovgrad 104 D 3 *prev.* Kavakli.
   SE Bulgaria
Top Springs 146 E 3 Northern
   Territory, N Australia
Torbalı 116 A 4 W Turkey
Torez 109 H 3 SE Ukraine
Torgau 94 D 4 E Germany
Torhout 87 A 5 W Belgium
Torino 96 A 2 *Eng.* Turin.
   NW Italy
Torneå *see* Tornio
Torneträsk 84 C 3 lake, N Sweden
Tornio 84 D 3 *Swe.* Torneå.
   NW Finland
Tornionjoki 84 D 3 *var.* Torniojoki,
   Swe. Torneälven. River,
   Finland/Sweden
Toro 92 D 2 N Spain
Toronto 38 D 5 province capital,
   Ontario, S Canada
Toropec *see* Toropets
Toropets 110 A 4 *var.* Toropec.
   W Russian Federation
Toros Dağları 116 C 4 *Eng.* Taurus
   Mountains. Mountain range,
   S Turkey
Torquay 89 C 7 SW England, UK
Torre, Alto da 92 C 3 mountain,
   C Portugal
Torre del Greco 97 D 5 S Italy
Torrejón de Ardoz 93 E 3 C Spain
Torrejón, Embalse de 92 C 3
   reservoir, W Spain
Torrelavega 92 D 1 N Spain
Torrens, Lake 149 B 5 salt lake,
   South Australia, S Australia
Torrente 93 F 3 *var.* Torrent, Torrent
   de l'Horta. E Spain
Torreón 50 D 3 C Mexico
Torres Strait 148 C 1 strait,
   Queensland, Arafura Sea/
   Coral Sea
Torres Vedras 92 A 3 W Portugal
Torrington 44 D 3
   Wyoming, C USA
Tórshavn 83 F 5 *Dan.* Thorshavn.
   Dependent territory capital,
   N Faeroe Islands
Tortosa 93 F 2 *anc.* Dertosa. E Spain
Tortue, Montagne 59 H 3 mountain
   range, C French Guiana
Tortuga, Isla *see* La Tortuga, Isla
Toruń 98 C 3 *Ger.* Thorn. C Poland
Tõrva 106 D 3 *Ger.* Tõrwa. S Estonia
Tõrwa *see* Tõrva
Torzhok 110 B 4 *var.* Toržok.
   W Russian Federation
Toržok *see* Torzhok
Tosa-wan 131 B 7 bay,
   NW Pacific Ocean
Toscano, Archipelago 96 B 4
   Eng. Tuscan Archipelago. Island
   group, C Italy
Toshkent 123 E 2 *Rus.* Tashkent.
   Country capital, E Uzbekistan
Totana 93 E 4 SE Spain
Totness 59 G 3 N Surinam
Tottori 131 B 6 Honshū, SW Japan
Touba 74 B 3 W Senegal
Touboro 76 B 4 NE Cameroon
Touggourt 71 E 2 NE Algeria
Toukoto 74 C 3 W Mali
Toul 90 D 3 NE France

Toulon 91 D 6 *anc.* Telo Martius, Tilio Martius. SE France
Toulouse 91 B 6 *anc.* Tolosa. S France
Toungoo 136 B 4 S Burma
Touraine 90 B 4 cultural region, C France
Tourane *see* Đă Nâng
Tourcoing 90 D 2 N France
Tournai 87 B 6 *var.* Tournay, *Dut.* Doornik; *anc.* Tornacum. SW Belgium
Tournavista 60 C 3 C Peru
Tours 90 B 4 *anc.* Caesarodunum, Turoni. C France
Tovarkovskiy 111 B 5 W Russian Federation
Tower Island *see* Genovesa, Isla
Townshend Island 148 D 4 island, Queensland, E Australia
Townsville 148 D 3 Queensland, NE Australia
Towoeti Meer *see* Towuti, Danau
Towraghoudī 122 D 4 NW Afghanistan
Towson 41 F 4 Maryland, NE USA
Towuti, Danau 139 E 4 *Dut.* Towoeti Meer. Lake, Celebes, C Indonesia
Toxkan He 126 A 3 *var.* Aksay. River, China/Kyrgyzstan
Toyama 131 C 5 Honshū, SW Japan
Toyama-wan 131 B 5 bay, E Sea of Japan
Toyota 131 C 6 Honshū, SW Japan
Tozeur 71 E 2 *var.* Tawzar. W Tunisia
Trabzon 117 E 2 *Eng.* Trebizond; *anc.* Trapezus. NE Turkey
Traiskirchen 95 E 6 NE Austria
Trajectum ad Rhenum *see* Utrecht
Trakai 107 C 5 *Ger.* Traken, *Pol.* Troki. SE Lithuania
Tralee 89 A 6 *Ir.* Trá Lí. SW Ireland
Trá Lí *see* Tralee
Trang 137 C 7 S Thailand
Transantarctic Mountains 154 C 3 mountain range, Antarctica
Transylvania 108 B 4 *Eng.* Ardeal, Transilvania, *Ger.* Siebenbürgen, *Hung.* Erdély. Cultural Region, NW Romania
Trapani 97 B 7 *anc.* Drepanum. SW Italy
Traralgon 149 C 7 Victoria, SE Australia
Trasimeno, Lago 96 B 3 *Eng.* Lake of Perugia, *Ger.* Trasimenischersee. Lake, C Italy
Traù *see* Trogir
Traunsee 95 D 6 *var.* Gmundner See, *Eng.* Lake Traun. Lake, N Austria
Traunstein 95 C 6 SE Germany
Traverse City 40 C 2 Michigan, N USA
Tra Vinh 137 E 6 *var.* Phu Vinh. S Vietnam
Travis, Lake 49 F 4 reservoir, Texas, S USA
Travnik 100 C 4 C Bosnia & Herzegovina
Trbovlje 95 E 8 *Ger.* Trifail. C Slovenia
Třebíč 99 B 5 *Ger.* Trebitsch. S Czech Republic
Trebinje 101 C 5 S Bosnia & Herzegovina
Trebišov 99 E 6 *Hung.* Tőketerebes. E Slovakia
Trebitsch *see* Třebíč
Trebnitz *see* Trzebnica
Trélazé 90 B 4 NW France
Trelew 65 C 6 SE Argentina
Tremelo 87 C 6 C Belgium
Trenčín 99 C 6 *Ger.* Trentschin, *Hung.* Trencsén. W Slovakia
Trenque Lauquen 64 C 4 E Argentina
Trento 96 C 2 *Eng.* Trent, *Ger.* Trient; anc.Tridentum. N Italy
Trenton 41 F 4 state capital, New Jersey, NE USA
Tres Arroyos 65 D 5 E Argentina
Treskavica 100 C 4 mountain range, SE Bosnia & Herzegovina
Treviso 96 C 2 *anc.* Tarvisium. NE Italy
Trg *see* Feldkirchen in Kärnten
Trichinopoly *see* Tiruchchirāppalli
Trichūr 132 C 3 *var.* Thrissur. SW India
Trier 95 A 5 *Eng.* Treves, *Fr.* Trèves; *anc.* Augusta Treverorum. SW Germany
Triesen 94 E 2 SW Liechtenstein
Triesenberg 94 E 2 SW Liechtenstein
Trieste 96 D 2 *Slvn.* Trst. NE Italy
Trifail *see* Trbovlje
Tríkala 104 B 4 *prev.* Trikkala. C Greece
Trikkala *see* Tríkala
Trincomalee 132 D 3 *var.* Trinkomali. NE Sri Lanka
Trinidad 55 H 5 island, C Trinidad & Tobago
Trinidad 64 D 4 SW Uruguay
Trinidad 44 D 5 Colorado, C USA
Trinidad 61 F 3 N Bolivia

Trinidad & Tobago
55 H 5 & Tobago. Republic, SE Caribbean Sea

Official name: Republic of Trinidad and Tobago **Date of formation:** 1962 **Capital:** Port-of-Spain **Population:** 1.3 million **Total area:** 5,130 sq km (1,981 sq miles) **Languages:** English* **Religions:** Christian 58%, Hindu 30%, Muslim 8%, other 4% **Ethnic mix:** Black 43%, South Asian 40%, mixed 14%, other 3% **Government:** Multiparty republic **Currency:** Trin. & Tob. $ = 100 cents

---

Trinité, Montagnes de la 59 H 3 mountain range, C French Guiana
Trinity River 49 G 3 river, Texas, S USA
Trinkomali *see* Trincomalee
Tripoli 118 B 4 *var.* Ţarābulus, Ţarābulus ash Shām, Trâblous; *anc.* Tripolis. N Lebanon
Tripoli *see* Ţarābulus
Trípoli 105 B 6 *prev.* Trípolis. S Greece
Trípolis *see* Trípoli
Tristan da Cunha 69 A 7 *var.* Tristan da Cunha Islands. Island group, S Atlantic Ocena
Tristan da Cunha 67 C 6 island, S Atlantic Ocean
Tristan da Cunha Islands *see* Tristan da Cunha
Trivandrum 132 C 3 *var.* Thiruvanathapuram. State capital, SW India
Trnava 99 C 6 *Ger.* Tyrnau, *Hung.* Nagyszombat. W Slovakia
Trobriand Islands *see* Kiriwina Islands
Trogir 100 B 4 *It.* Traù. S Croatia
Troglav 100 B 4 mountain, Bosnia & Herzegovina/Croatia
Troía Peninsula 92 B 4 peninsula, W Portugal
Troisdorf 95 A 5 W Germany
Trois-Rivières 39 E 4 Québec, SE Canada
Trojan *see* Troyan
Trollhättan 85 B 6 S Sweden
Tromsø 84 C 2 *Fin.* Tromssa. N Norway
Tromssa *see* Tromsø
Trondheim 84 B 4 *Ger.* Drontheim; *prev.* Nidaros, Trondhjem. S Norway
Trondheimsfjorden 84 A 4 fjord, E North Sea
Troodos Mountains *see* Troódos
Troppau *see* Opava
Troy 42 D 3 Alabama, S USA
Troy 41 F 3 New York, NE USA
Troyan 104 C 2 *var.* Trojan. C Bulgaria
Troyes 90 D 4 *anc.* Augustobona Tricassium. N France
Trst *see* Trieste
Trstenik 100 D 4 C Yugoslavia
Trujillo 92 C 3 W Spain
Trujillo 52 D 2 NE Honduras
Trujillo 60 B 3 NW Peru
Trŭn 104 B 2 W Bulgaria
Trung Phân 137 E 5 physical region, S Vietnam
Truro 89 C 7 SW England, UK
Truro 39 F 4 Nova Scotia, SE Canada
Trzcianka 98 B 3 *Ger.* Schönlanke. NW Poland
Trzebnica 98 C 4 *Ger.* Trebnitz. SW Poland
Ţsafjördhur 83 E 4 NW Iceland
Tsalka 117 F 2 SE Georgia
Tsaochuang *see* Zaozhuang
Tsarevo 104 E 2 *var.* Mičurin; *prev.* Michurin. SE Bulgaria
Tschaslau *see* Čáslav
Tsetserleg 126 D 2 W Mongolia
Tshela 77 B 6 W Congo (Zaire)
Tshikapa 77 C 7 SW Congo (Zaire)
Tshuapa 77 D 6 river, C Congo (Zaire)
Tsodilo Hills 78 C 3 mountain range, NW Botswana
Tsu 131 C 6 *var.* Tu. Honshū, SW Japan
Tsuen Wan 128 A 1 W Hong Kong
Tsugaru-kaikyō 130 C 3 strait, Pacific Ocean/Sea of Japan
Tsumeb 78 B 3 N Namibia
Tsuruga 131 C 6 *var.* Turuga. Honshū, SW Japan
Tsuruoka 130 D 4 *var.* Turuoka. Honshū, C Japan
Tsushima 131 A 7 *var.* Tsushima-tō, Tusima. Island group, SW Japan
Tsyerakhowka 107 D 8 *Rus.* Terekhovka. SE Belorussia
Tsyurupinsk *see* Tsyurupyns'k
Tsyurupyns'k 109 F 4 *Rus.* Tsyurupinsk. S Ukraine
Tu *see* Tsu
Tuamotu, Îles 145 H 4 *var.* Tuamotu Islands. Island group, N French Polynesia
Tuamotu Islands *see* Tuamotu, Îles
Tuapi 53 E 2 NE Nicaragua
Tuapse 111 A 7 SW Russian Federation
Tuba City 48 B 1 Arizona, SW USA
Tubbergen 86 E 3 E Netherlands
Tubeke *see* Tubize
Tubize 87 B 6 *Dut.* Tubeke. C Belgium
Tubmanburg 74 C 5 county capital, NW Liberia
Tucker's Town 42 B 5 E Bermuda
Tuckum *see* Tukums
Tucson 48 B 3 Arizona, SW USA
Tucumán *see* San Miguel de Tucumán
Tucupita 59 E 2 NE Venezuela
Tucuruí 63 F 2 NE Brazil
Tucuruí, Represa de 63 F 2 reservoir, NE Brazil
Tudela 93 E 2 *Basq.* Tutera; *anc.* Tutela. N Spain
Tudmur 118 C 3 *var.* Tadmur, Tamar, *Gk.* Palmyra; *Bibl.* Tadmor. C Syria
Tuen Mun 128 A 1 W Hong Kong
Tuguegarao 139 E 1 Luzon, N Philippines
Tuktoyaktuk 37 E 3 Northwestern Territories, NW Canada
Tukums 106 C 3 *Ger.* Tuckum. W Latvia
Tula 111 B 5 W Russian Federation
Tulancingo 51 E 4 C Mexico
Tulare 47 C 7 California, W USA
Tulcán 60 B 1 N Ecuador
Tulcea 108 D 5 E Romania
Tul'chin *see* Tul'chyn
Tul'chyn 108 D 3 *Rus.* Tul'chin. C Ukraine
Tulia 49 E 2 Texas, S USA
Tulkarm 119 D 7 NW West Bank
Tullahoma 42 D 1 Tennessee, S USA
Tulle 91 C 5 *anc.* Tutela. C France
Tulln 95 E 6 *var.* Oberhollabrunn. NE Austria
Tully 148 D 3 Queensland, NE Australia
Tulsa 49 G 1 Oklahoma, C USA
Tuluá 58 B 3 W Colombia
Tulun 115 E 4 S Russian Federation
Tumaco 58 A 4 SW Colombia
Tumba, Lac *see* Ntomba, Lac
Tumbes 60 B 2 NW Peru
Tumkūr 132 C 2 W India
Tumuc-Humac Mountains 63 E 1 *var.* Serra Tumucumaque, *Port.* Serra Tumuc-Humac. Mountain range, N South America
Tunca Nehri *see* Tundzha
Tunduru 73 C 8 S Tanzania
Tundzha 104 D 3 *Turk.* Tunca Nehri. River, Bulgaria/Turkey
Tungabhadra Reservoir 132 C 2 lake, S India
Tungsten 37 E 4 Northwestern Territories, W Canada
Tung-t'ing Hu *see* Dongting Hu
Tunis 71 E 1 *var.* Tūnis. Country capital, NE Tunisia

Tunisia
71 E 2 *Ar.* Al Jumhūrīyah at Tūnisīyah, *Fr.* République Tunisienne. Republic, N Africa

Official name: Republic of Tunisia **Date of formation:** 1956 **Capital:** Tunis **Population:** 8.6 million **Total area:** 163,610 sq km (63,170 sq miles) **Languages :** Arabic*, French **Religions:** Muslim 98%, Christian 1%, other 1% **Ethnic mix:** Arab and Berber 98%, European 1%, other 1% **Government:** Multiparty republic **Currency:** Dinar = 1,000 millimes

---

Tūnis, Khalīj *see* Tunis, Golfe de
Tunja 58 B 3 C Colombia
Tuong Buong *see* Tương Đương

Tương Đương 136 D 4
var. Tuong Buong. N Vietnam
Túp *see* Tyup
Tupelo 42 C 2 Mississippi, S USA
Tupiza 61 G 5 S Bolivia
Turabah 121 B 5 W Saudi Arabia
Turangi 150 D 4 North Island,
N New Zealand
Turan Lowland 122 C 2
var. Turan Plain, *Rus.* Turanskaya
Nizmennost'. Plain, C Asia ·
Ţurayf 120 A 3
NW Saudi Arabia
Turba *see* Teruel
Turda 108 B 4 *Ger.* Thorenburg,
Hung. Torda. NW Romania
Turin *see* Torino
Turkana, Lake 73 C 6 *Eng.* Lake
Rudolf. Lake, E Africa
Turkestan 114 B 5 *Kaz.* Türkistan.
S Kazakhstan

Turkey
116 B 3 *Turk.* Türkiye
Cumhuriyeti. Republic, SW Asia

Official name: Republic of Turkey
Date of formation: 1923/1939
Capital: Ankara **Population:** 63.1
million **Total area:** 779,450 sq km
(300,950 sq miles) **Languages:**
Turkish*, Kurdish, Arabic **Religions:**
Muslim 99%, other 1% **Ethnic mix:**
Turkish 80%, Kurdish 17%, other 3%
Government: Multiparty republic
Currency: Turkish lira = 100 krural

**Turkish Republic of Northern
Cyprus** 116 C 5 country, SW Asia
Türkistan *see* Turkestan
Türkmen Aylagy *see*
Turkmenskiy Zaliv
Turkmenbashi 122 B 2 *prev.*
Krasnovodsk. W Turkmenistan

Turkmenistan
122 B 2 *prev.* Turkmenskaya
Soviet Socialist Republic.
Republic, C Asia

Official name: Republic of
Turkmenistan **Date of formation:**
1991 **Capital:** Ashgabat **Total Area:** 488,100 sq km
(188,455 sq miles) **Languages:**
Turkmen*, Russian, Uzbek **Religions:**
Muslim 85%, Eastern Orthodox 10%,
other 5% **Ethnic mix:** Turkmen 72%,
Russian 9%, Uzbek 9%, other 10%
Government: Single-party republic
Currency: Manat = 100 tenge

Turkmenskiy Zaliv 122 B 2
Türkm. Türkmen Aylagy. Inlet,
S Caspian Sea
Turks & Caicos Islands 55 E 2 UK
dependent territory,
N Caribbean Sea
Turku 85 D 6 *Swe.* Åbo. SW Finland
Turlock 47 B 6 California, W USA
Turnau *see* Turnov
Turnhout 87 C 5 N Belgium
Turnov 98 B 4 *Ger.* Turnau.
N Czech Republic
Turnu Măgurele 108 B 5 *var.*
Turnu-Măgurele. S Romania
Turnu Severin *see*
Drobeta-Turnu Severin
Turpan 126 C 3 *var.* Turfan.
NW China
Turpan Depression 124 C 2
depression, NW China
Turpan Pendi 126 C 3 *Eng.* Turpan
Depression. Depression depth,
NW China

Türtkül 122 D 2
prev. Petroaleksandrovsk,
Rus. Turtkul'. W Uzbekistan
Turuga *see* Tsuruga
Turuoka *see* Tsuruoka
Tuscaloosa 42 C 2 Alabama, S USA
Tuscan Archipelago *see* Toscano,
Archipelago
Tutela *see* Tulle
Tuticorin 132 C 3 SE India
Tutrakan 104 D 1 NE Bulgaria
Tutuila 145 F 4 Island,
W American Samoa

Tuvalu
145 E 4 *prev.* The Ellice Islands.
Commonwealth republic,
C Pacific Ocean

Official name: Tuvalu **Date of
formation:** 1978 **Capital:**
Fongafale **Population:** 9,000
Total Area: 26 sq km (10 sq miles)
Languages: Tuvaluan*, Kiribati
Religions: Protestant 97%, other 3%
Ethnic mix: Tuvaluan 95% other 5%
Government: Constitutional
monarchy **Currency:** Australian $ =
100 cents

Tuxpan 50 D 4 C Mexico
Tuxpan 51 F 4 *var.* Tuxpán de
Rodríguez Cano. E Mexico
Tuxpán de Rodríguez Cano *see*
Tuxpán
Tuxtepec 51 F 4 *var.* San Juan
Bautista Tuxtepec. S Mexico
Tuxtla 51 G 5 *var.* Tuxtla Gutiérrez.
SE Mexico
Tuxtla *see* San Andrés Tuxtla
Tuxtla Gutiérrez *see* Tuxtla
Tuy Hoa 137 E 5 SE Vietnam
Tuz Gölü 116 C 3 lake, C Turkey
Tuzla 100 C 3
NE Bosnia & Herzegovina
Tuz, Lake *see* Tuz Gölü
Tver' 110 B 4 *prev.* Kalinin.
W Russian Federation
Twante 136 B 4 S Burma
Twin Falls 46 D 4 Idaho, NW USA
Two Thumbs Range 151 B 6
mountain range, South Island,
SW New Zealand
Tychy 99 C 5 *Ger.* Tichau. S Poland
Tyler 49 H 3 Texas, S USA
Tynda 115 F 4
SE Russian Federation
Tyne 88 D 4 river, N England, UK
Tyôsi *see* Chōshi
Týrnavos 104 B 4 *var.* Tírnavos.
C Greece
Tyrrhenian Sea 97 B 6 *It.* Mare
Tirreno. Sea, C Mediterranean Sea
Tyumen' 114 C 3
C Russian Federation
Tyup 123 G 2 *Kir.* Tüp.
NE Kyrgyzstan
Tywyn 89 C 6 W Wales, UK
Tzekung *see* Zigong

U

Uaco Cungo 78 B 2 *var.* Waku
Kungo, *Port.* Santa Comba.
C Angola
UAE *see* United Arab Emirates
Uaupés, Rio *see* Vaupés, Río
Ubangi 77 C 5 *Fr.* Oubangui. River,
C Africa
Ube 131 B 7 Honshū, SW Japan
Ubeda 93 E 4 S Spain
Uberaba 63 F 4 SE Brazil

Uberlândia 63 F 4 SE Brazil
Ubin, Pulau 138 B 1 island,
NE Singapore
Ubon Ratchathani 137 D 5
var. Muang Ubon, Ubol
Rajadhani, Ubol Ratchathani,
Udon Ratchathani. E Thailand
Ubrique 92 C 5 S Spain
Ubsu-Nur, Ozero *see* Uvs Nuur
Ucayali 60 D 3 river, C Peru
Uchiura-wan 130 D 3 bay,
NW Pacific Ocean
Uchkuduk *see* Uchquduq
Uchquduq 122 D 2 *Rus.* Uchkuduk.
N Uzbekistan
Udaipur 134 C 4 *prev.* Oodeypore.
C India
Uddevalla 85 B 6 S Sweden
Udine 96 D 2 *anc.* Utina. NE Italy
Udintsev Fracture Zone 154 A 5
fracture zone, SE Pacific Ocean
Udipi *see* Udupi
Udon Thani 136 D 4 *var.* Ban Mak
Khaeng, Udorndhani. N Thailand
Udupi 132 B 2 *var.* Udipi. SW India
Ueckermünde 94 D 3 NE Germany
Ueda 131 C 5 *var.* Uyeda. Honshū,
S Japan
Uele 77 D 5 *var.* Welle. River,
N Congo (Zaire)
Uelzen 94 C 3 N Germany
Ufa 111 D 6 W Russian Federation
Ugāle 106 C 3 NW Latvia

Uganda
73 C 6 Republic, NE Africa

Official name: Republic of Uganda
Date of formation: 1962 **Capital:**
Kampala **Population:** 19.2 million
Total area: 235,880 sq km
(91,073 sq miles) **Languages:**
English*, Luganda, Nkole, Chiga
Religions: Christian 66%, traditional
beliefs 18%, Muslim 16% **Ethnic
mix:** Buganda 18%, Banyoro 14%,
Teso 9%, other 59% **Government:**
Multiparty republic **Currency:**
Shilling = 100 cents

Uglovka 110 B 4 *var.* Okulovka.
W Russian Federation
Uíge 78 B 1 *Port.* Carmona, Vila
Marechal Carmona. NW Angola
Uinta Mountains 44 B 4 mountain
range, Utah, W USA
Uitenhage 78 C 5 S South Africa
Uithoorn 86 C 3 C Netherlands
Ujelang Atoll 144 C 1 *var.* Wujlán.
Island, W Marshall Islands
Ujungpandang 139 E 4
var. Macassar, Makassar; *prev.*
Makasar. Celebes, C Indonesia
UK 89 B 5 *off.* UK of Great Britain
and Northern Ireland. Monarchy,
NW Europe
Ukhta 110 D 4 *var.* Uchta, Uhta.
NW Russian Federation
Ukiah 47 B 5 California, W USA
Ukmergė 106 C 4 *Pol.* Wiłkomierz.
C Lithuania

Ukraine
108 C 2 *Rus.* Ukraina, *Ukr.*
Ukrayina; *prev.* Ukrainian Soviet
Socialist Republic, Ukrainskaya
S.S.R. Republic, E Europe

Official name: Ukraine **Date of
formation:** 1991 **Capital:** Kiev
Population: 52.2 million **Total area:**
603,700 sq km (223,090 sq miles)
Languages: Ukrainian*, Russian,
Tartar **Religions:** mostly Ukrainian

Orthodox, with Roman Catholic,
Protestant and Jewish minorities
Ethnic mix: Ukrainian 73%, Russian
22%, other (inc. Tartar) 5%
Government: Multiparty republic
Currency: Karbovanets (coupons)

Ulaanbaatar 127 E 2 *Eng.* Ulan
Bator. Country capital,
C Mongolia
Ulaangom 126 C 2 NW Mongolia
Ulan Bator *see* Ulaanbaatar
Ulanhad *see* Chifeng
Ulan-Ude 115 E 4
prev. Verkhneudinsk.'
C Russian Federation
Uldz 127 F 1 river, NE Mongolia
Uleåborg *see* Oulu
Uleålv *see* Oulujoki
Uleträsk *see* Oulujärvi
Ulft 86 E 4 E Netherlands
Ullapool 88 B 3 N Scotland, UK
Ulm 95 B 6 S Germany
Ulsan 128 E 4 *Jap.* Urusan.
SE South Korea
Ulster 89 B 5 cultural region,
N Ireland
Ulungur Hu 126 C 2 lake,
NW China
Uluru 146 E 5 *var.* Ayers Rock.
Rock, Northern Territory,
C Australia
Ulyanivka 109 E 3 *Rus.* Ul'yanovka.
C Ukraine
Ul'yanovka *see* Ulyanivka
Ul'yanovsk 111 C 5 *prev.* Simbirsk.
W Russian Federation
Uman' 109 E 3 *Rus.* Uman.
C Ukraine
Uman *see* Uman'
Umán 51 G 3 SE Mexico
'Umān, Khalīj *see* Oman, Gulf of
Umbrian-Machigian Mountains *see*
Umbro-Marchigiano, Appennino
Umbro-Marchigiano, Appennino
96 C 4 *Eng.* Umbrian-Machigian
Mountains. Mountain range,
C Italy
Umeå 84 D 4 N Sweden
Umeälven 84 C 4 river, N Sweden
Umiat 36 D 2 Alaska, NW USA
Umm al Ḩayt, Wādī 121 D 6 *var.*
Wādī Amiliayt. River, SW Oman
Umm Durmān *see* Omdurman
Umm Ruwaba 72 B 4 *var.* Umm
Ruwābah, Um Ruwāba. C Sudan
Umnak Island 36 A 3 island,
Alaska, NW USA
Umtata 78 D 5 SE South Africa
Una 100 B 3 river,
Bosnia & Herzegovina / Croatia
Unalaska Island 36 A 3 island,
Alaska, NW USA
'Unayzah 120 B 4 C Saudi Arabia
Uncompahgre Peak 44 C 5
mountain, Colorado, C USA
Ungama Bay *see* Formosa Bay
Ungava Bay 39 E 1 bay,
W Labrador Sea
Ungava, Péninsule d' 38 D 1
peninsula, Québec, SE Canada
Ungeny *see* Ungheni
Ungheni 108 D 3 *Rus.* Ungeny.
W Moldavia
Unguja *see* Zanzibar
Üngüz Angyrsyndaky Garagum *see*
Zaunguzskiye Karakumy
Unimak Island 36 B 3 island,
Alaska, NW USA
Union 43 E 1
South Carolina, SE USA
Union City 42 C 1 Tennessee, S USA

United Arab Emirates
121 E 5 *Ar.* Al Imārāt al
'Arabīyahal Muttaḥidah, *abbrev.*
UAE; *prev.* Trucial States.
Federation, SW Asia

Official name: United Arab
Emirates **Date of formation:** 1971
Capital: Abu Dhabi **Population:** 1.7
million **Total area:** 83,600 sq km
(32,278 sq miles) **Languages:**
Arabic*, Farsi (Persian), Urdu, Hindi
Religions: Sunni Muslim 77%, Shi'a
Muslim 19%, other 4% **Ethnic mix:**
South Asian 50%, Emirian 19%,
other Arab 23%, other 8%
Government: Federation of monarchs
Currency: Dirham = 100 fils

UnitedKingdom
89 B 5 Monarchy, NW Europe

Official name: United Kingdom of
Great Britain and Northern Ireland
Date of formation: 1801/1922
Capital: London **Population:** 57.8
million **Total area:** 244,880 sq km
(94,550 sq miles) **Languages:**
English* **Religions:** Protestant 52%,
Roman Catholic 9%, Muslim 3%,
other 36% **Ethnic mix:** English 81%,
Scottish 10%, Welsh 2%,
other 7% **Government:**
Constitutional monarchy
Currency: Pound sterling = 100 pence

United States of America
var. America, The States
abbrev. USA, U.S, U.S.A.
Federal Republic, North America

Official name: United States of
America **Date of formation:**
1787/1959 **Capital:** Washington DC
Population: 265.8 million **Total area:**
9,372,610 sq km (3,681,760 sq miles)
Languages: English*, Spanish
Religions: Protestant 56%, Roman
Catholic 28%, Jewish 2%, other 14%
Ethnic mix: White (inc. Hispanic)
83%, Black 13%, other 4%
Government: Multiparty republic
Currency: US $ = 100 cents

Unst 88 D 1 island,
NE Scotland, UK
Ünye 116 D 2 W Turkey
Upala 52 D 4 NW Costa Rica
Upata 59 E 2 E Venezuela
Upemba, Lake 77 D 7 lake,
SE Congo (Zaire)
Upernavik 82 C 2 *var.* Upernivik.
W Greenland
Upernivik *see* Upernavik
Upington 78 C 4 W South Africa
'**Upolu** 145 F 4 island, SE Samoa
Upper Darby 41 F 4 Pennsylvania,
NE USA
Upper Klamath Lake 46 B 4 lake,
Oregon, NW USA
Upper Lough Erne 89 B 5 lake,
S Northern Ireland, UK
Upper Red Lake 45 F 1 lake,
Minnesota, N USA
Uppsala 85 C 6 C Sweden
Ural 114 B 3 *Kaz.* Zayyq. River, ,
Kazakhstan/Russian Federation
Ural Mountains *see* Ural'skiye Gory
Ural'sk 114 B 3 *Kaz.* Oral.
NW Kazakhstan
Ural'skiye Gory 114 C 3
var. Ural'skiy Khrebet, *Eng.* Ural
Mountains. Mountain range,
Kazakhstan/Russian Federation
Uraricoera 62 D 1 N Brazil
Ura-Tyube *see* Ŭroteppa

Urbandale 45 F 4 Iowa, C USA
Ureki 117 F 2 W Georgia
Uren' 111 C 5 W Russian Federation
Urganch 122 D 2 *Rus.* Urgench;
prev. Novo-Urgench.
W Uzbekistan
Urgut 123 E 3 C Uzbekistan
Uroševac 101 D 5 *Alb.* Ferizaj.
S Yugoslavia
Ŭroteppa 123 E 2 *Rus.* Ura-Tyube.
NW Tajikistan
Uruapan 51 E 4 *var.* Uruapan del
Progreso. SW Mexico
Uruapan del Progreso *see* Uruapan
Uruguai, Rio *see* Uruguay

Uruguay
64 D 4 *off.* Oriental Republic of
Uruguay; *prev.* La Banda Oriental.
Republic, S South America

Official name: Republic of Uruguay
Date of formation: 1828/1909
Capital: Montevideo **Population:** 3.1
million **Total area:** 177,410 sq km
(68,498 sq miles) **Languages:**
Spanish*, other **Religions:** Roman
Catholic 77%, Protestant 3%, Jewish
2%, other 18% **Ethnic mix:** White
88%, *mestizo* (Euro-Indian) 8%, Black
4% **Government:** Multiparty republic
Currency: Peso = 100 centesimos

Uruguay 64 D 3 river, NE Uruguay
Urumaco 58 C 1 NW Venezuela
Ürümqi 126 C 3 *var.* Tihwa,
Urumchi, Urumqi, Urumtsi, Wu-
lu-k'o-mu-shi, Wu-lu-mu-ch'i;
prev. Ti-hua. NW China
Urup, Ostrov 115 H 4 island,
Kuril'skaya Ostrova,
SE Russian Federation
Urusan *see* Ulsan
Urziceni 108 C 5 SE Romania
Usa 110 E 3 river,
NW Russian Federation
Uşak 116 B 3 *prev.* Ushak. W Turkey
Ushak *see* Uşak
Ushant *see* Ouessant, Île d'
Ushuaia 65 B 8 S Argentina
Usinsk 110 E 3 NW Russian
Federation
Usmas Ezers 106 B 3 lake,
NW Latvia
Usol'ye-Sibirskoye 115 E 4
C Russian Federation
Ussel 91 C 5 C France
Ussuriysk 115 G 5 *prev.* Nikol'sk,
Nikol'sk-Ussuriyskiy, Voroshilov.
SE Russian Federation
Ustica, Isola d' 97 B 6 island, S Italy
Ústí nad Labem 98 A 4 *Ger.* Aussig.
N Czech Republic
Ustinov *see* Izhevsk
Ustka 98 B 2 *Ger.* Stolpmünde.
NW Poland
Ust'-Kamchatsk 115 H 2
NE Russian Federation
Ust'-Kamenogorsk 114 D 5
Kaz. Öskemen. E Kazakhstan
Ust'-Olenëk 115 F 2
N Russian Federation
Ust'-Sysol'sk *see* Syktyvkar
Ustyurt Plateau 122 C 1
var. Ust Urt, *Uzb.* Ustyurt Platosi.
Plateau, Kazakhstan/Uzbekistan
Usulután 52 C 3 SE El Salvador
Usumacinta 52 A 1 river,
Guatemala/Mexico
Usumbura *see* Bujumbura
Utah 44 B 4 *off.* State of Utah;
nicknames Beehive State,
Mormon State. State, W USA

Utah Lake 44 B 4 lake, Utah, W USA
'**Uta Vava'u** 145 F 4 island, C Tonga
Utena 106 C 4 E Lithuania
Utica 41 F 3 New York, NE USA
Utina *see* Udine
Utrecht 86 C 3 *Lat.* Trajectum ad
Rhenum. C Netherlands
Utsunomiya 131 D 5 *var.*
Utunomiya. Honshū, S Japan
Uttar Pradesh 135 E 3 *prev.* United
Provinces, United Provices of
Agra and Oudh. State, N India
Utunomiya *see* Utsunomiya
Uulu 106 D 2 SW Estonia
Uummannaq 82 C 3 *var.* Umanak,
Umanaq. Greenland
Uummannarsuaq 82 B 5
var. Nunap Isua, *Dan.* Kap
Farvel, *Eng.* Cape Farewell.
Headland, S Greenland
Uvalde 49 F 4 Texas, S USA
Uvarovichy 107 D 7
Rus. Uvarovichi. SE Belorussia
Uvarovichi *see* Uvarovichy
Uvea, Île 145 E 4 island,
S Wallis & Futuna
Uvs Nuur 126 C 1 *var.* Ozero
Ubsu-Nur. Lake, Mongolia/
Russian Federation
Uyeda *see* Ueda
Uyuni 61 F 5 W Bolivia

Uzbekistan
122 C 1 Republic, C Asia

Official name: Republic of
Uzbekistan **Date of formation:** 1991
Capital: Tashkent **Population:** 21.9
million **Total area:** 1,138,910 sq km
(439,733 sq miles) **Languages:**
Uzbek*, Russian **Religions:** Muslim
88%, other (mostly Eastern
Orthodox) 12% **Ethnic mix:** Uzbek
71%, Russian 8%, Tajik 5%, Kazakh
4%, other 12% **Government:**
Single-party republic
Currency: Sum = 100 teen

Uzhhorod 108 B 2 *Rus.* Uzhgorod;
prev. Ungvár. W Ukraine
Užice 100 D 4 *prev.* Titovo Užice.
W Yugoslavia

V

Vaal 78 D 4 river, C South Africa
Vaals 87 D 6 SE Netherlands
Vaasa 84 D 4 *Swe.* Vasa; *prev.*
Nikolainkaupunki. W Finland
Vaassen 86 D 3 E Netherlands
Vác 99 C 6 *Ger.* Waitzen. N Hungary
Vacaville 47 B 6 California, W USA
Vadodara 134 C 4 *prev.* Baroda
W India
Vaduz 94 E 2 country capital,
W Liechtenstein
Váh 99 C 5 *Ger.* Waag,
Hung. Vág. River, W Slovakia
Väinameri 106 C 2 *Ger.* Moon-
Sund; *prev.* Muhu Väin. Sea,
E Baltic Sea
Vainode 106 B 3 SW Latvia
Valdaj *see* Valday
Valday 110 B 4 *var.* Valdaj.
W Russian Federation
Valdecañas, Embalse de 92 D 3
reservoir, W Spain
Valdepeñas 93 E 3 C Spain
Valdés, Península 65 C 6 peninsula,
SE Argentina
Valdez 36 C 3 Alaska, NW USA
Valdivia 65 B 5 C Chile
Val-d'Or 38 D 4 Québec, SE Canada

Valdosta 43 E 3 Georgia, SE USA
Valence 91 D 5 *anc.* Valentia,
Valentia Julia, Ventia. E France
Valencia 93 F 3 E Spain
Valencia 58 D 2 N Venezuela
Valencia, Golfo de 93 G 3
var. Gulf of Valencia. Gulf,
W Mediterranean Sea
Valencia, Gulf of *see* Valencia,
Golfo de
Valenciennes 90 D 2 N France
Valera 58 C 2 NW Venezuela
Valetta *see* Valletta
Valga 106 D 3 *Ger.* Walk, *Latv.*
Valka. S Estonia
Valira 91 A 8 river, Andorra/Spain
Valjevo 100 D 4 W Yugoslavia
Valjok 84 D 2 N Norway
Valka 106 D 3 *Ger.* Walk. N Latvia
Valkenswaard 87 D 5 S Netherlands
Valladolid 92 D 2 NW Spain
Valladolid 51 H 3 SE Mexico
Vall d'Uxó 93 F 3 E Spain
Valle de La Pascua 58 D 2
N Venezuela
Valle del Po *see* Po Valley
Valledupar 58 B 1 N Colombia
Vallejo 47 B 6 California, W USA
Vallenar 64 B 3 N Chile
Valletta 80 D 5 *prev.* Valetta.
Country capital, E Malta
Valley City 45 E 2 North Dakota,
N USA
Valls 93 F 2 NE Spain
Valmiera 106 D 3 *Est.* Volmari,
Ger. Wolmar. N Latvia
Valona Bay *see* Vlorës, Gjiri i
Valozhyn 107 C 5 *Pol.* Wołożyn,
Rus. Volozhin. C Belorussia
Valparaíso 40 C 3 Indiana, N USA
Valparaíso 64 B 4 C Chile
Valverde del Camino 92 B 4 S Spain
Van 117 F 3 E Turkey
Vanadzor 117 F 2 *prev.* Kirovakan.
N Armenia
Vancouver 37 E 5 British Columbia,
SW Canada
Vancouver 46 B 2
Washington, NW USA
Vancouver Island 36 D 5 island,
SW Canada
Vanda *see* Vantaa
Van Diemen Gulf 146 E 2 gulf,
SW Arafura Sea
Van Diemen's Land *see* Tasmania
Vänern 85 B 6 *Eng.* Lake Vaner;
prev. Lake Väner. S Sweden
Vangaindrano 79 G 4 S Madagascar
Van Gölü 117 F 3 *var.* Thospitis,
Eng. Lake Van. Salt lake, E Turkey
Van, Lake *see* Van Gölü
Vannes 90 A 4 *anc.* Dariorigum.
NW France
Vantaa 85 D 6 *Swe.* Vanda.
S Finland
Vanua Levu 145 E 4 island, N Fiji

Vanuatu
144 C 4 *prev.* New Hebrides.
Republic, S Pacific Ocean

Official name: Republic of Vanuatu
Date of formation: 1980 **Capital:**
Port-Vila **Population:** 155,000 **Total
Area:** 12,190 sq km (4,706 sq miles)
Languages: Bislama*, English*,
French* **Religions:** Protestant 77%,
Roman Catholic 15%, traditional
beliefs 8% **Ethnic mix:** Ni-Vanuatu
98%, other 2% **Government:**
Multiparty republic
Currency: Vatu - 100 centimes

Vapincum *see* Gap
Varakļani 106 D 4 C Latvia
Vārānasi 135 E 3 *prev.* Banaras, Benares, *hist.* Kasi. N India
Varangerfjorden 84 E 2 fjord, SW Barents Sea
Varangerhalvøya 84 E 1 peninsula, N Norway
Varaždin 100 B 2 *Ger.* Warasdin, *Hung.* Varasd. N Croatia
Varberg 85 B 7 S Sweden
Vardar 101 E 6 *Gk.* Axiós. River, Greece/Macedonia
Varde 85 A 7 W Denmark
Varėna 107 B 5 *Pol.* Orany. S Lithuania
Varese 96 B 2 N Italy
Vârful Moldoveanu 108 B 4 *var.* Moldoveanul; *prev.* Vîrful Moldoveanu. Mountain, C Romania
Varkaus 85 E 5 C Finland
Varna 104 E 2 *prev.* Stalin, *anc.* Odessus. NE Bulgaria
Varnenski Zaliv 104 E 2 *prev.* Stalinski Zaliv. Bay, NW Black Sea
Vasilikí 105 A 5 Kríti, SE Greece
Vasilishki 107 B 5 *Pol.* Wasiliszki. W Belorussia
Vasil'kov *see* Vasyl'kiv
Vaslui 108 D 4 C Romania
Västerås 85 C 6 C Sweden
Vasyl'kiv 109 E 2 *var.* Vasil'kov. N Ukraine

Vatican City
97 A 7 Papal state, S Europe

Official name: Vatican City State **Date of formation:** 1929 **Capital:** Not applicable **Population:** 1,000 **Total area:** 0.44 sq km (0.17 sq miles) **Languages:** Italian*, Latin* **Religions:** Roman Catholic 100% **Ethnic mix:** Italian 90%, Swiss 10% (including the Swiss Guard, which is responsible for papal security) **Government:** Papal Commission **Currency:** Italian lira = 100 centesimi

Vatican City State *see* Vatican City
Vatnajökull 83 E 5 glacier, SE Iceland
Vättern 85 B 6 *Eng.* Lake Vatter; *prev.* Lake Vetter. Lake, S Sweden
Vaupés 58 C 4 *var.* Rio Uaupés. River, Brazil/Colombia
Vava'u Group 143 E 3 island group, N Tonga
Vavuniya 132 D 3 N Sri Lanka
Vawkavysk 107 B 6 *Pol.* Wołkowysk, *Rus.* Volkovysk. W Belorussia
Växjö 85 C 7 *var.* Vexiö. S Sweden
Vaygach, Ostrov 110 E 2 Island, NW Russian Federation
Veendam 86 E 2 NE Netherlands
Veenendaal 86 D 4 C Netherlands
Vega 84 B 4 island, C Norway
Veisiejai 107 B 5 S Lithuania
Vejer de la Frontera 92 C 5 S Spain
Veldhoven 87 D 5 S Netherlands
Velebit 100 A 3 mountain range, C Croatia
Velenje 95 E 7 *Ger.* Wöllan. N Slovenia
Velho *see* Porto Velho
Velika Gorica 100 B 2 N Croatia
Velika Morava 100 E 4 *var.* Glavn'a Morava, Morava, *Ger.* Grosse Morava. River, C Yugoslavia
Velika Plana 100 D 4 C Yugoslavia
Velikaya 115 H 2 river, NE Russian Federation
Velike-Luki *see* Velikiye Luki
Velikij Ust'ug *see* Velikiy Ustyug
Velikiye Luki 110 A 4 *var.* Velike-Luki. W Russian Federation
Velikiy Ustyug 110 C 4 *var.* Velikij Ust'ug. NW Russian Federation
Veliko Tŭrnovo 104 D 2 *var.* Veliko Tărnovo; *prev.* Tirnovo, Trnovo, Tŭrnovo. N Bulgaria
Velingrad 104 C 3 SW Bulgaria
Vel'ký Krtíš 99 D 6 S Slovakia
Vellore 132 C 2 SE India
Velsen *see* Velsen-Noord
Velsen-Noord 86 C 3 *var.* Velsen. W Netherlands
Vel'sk 110 C 4 *var.* Velsk. NW Russian Federation
Velsk *see* Vel'sk
Velvendos *see* Velvendós
Velvendós 104 B 4 *var.* Velvendos. N Greece
Velykyy Tokmak *see* Tokmak
Vendée 90 B 4 cultural region, W France
Vendôme 90 B 4 C France
Venezia 96 C 2 *Eng.* Venice, *Fr.* Venise, *Ger.* Venedig; anc.Venetia. NE Italy

Venezuela
58 D 2 *prev.* Estados Unidos de Venezuela, United States of Venezuela. Republic, N South America

Official name: Republic of Venezuela **Date of formation:** 1830/1929 **Capital:** Caracas **Population:** 20.6 million **Total area:** 912,050 sq km (352,143 sq miles) **Languages:** Spanish*, Indian languages **Religions:** Roman Catholic 96%, Protestant 2%, other 2% **Ethnic mix:** *mestizo* 67%, White 21%, Black 10%, Indian 2% **Government:** Multiparty republic **Currency:** Bolívar = 100 centimos

Venezuela, Golfo de 58 C 1 *Eng.* Gulf of Maracaibo, Gulf of Venezuela. Gulf, E Caribbean Sea
Venezuelan Basin 66 B 4 undersea basin, W Atlantic Ocean
Venice 43 E 4 Florida, SE USA
Venice 42 C 4 Louisiana, S USA
Venice *see* Venezia
Venice, Gulf of 96 D 2 *It.* Golfo di Venezia, *Slvn.* Beneški Zaliv. Gulf, N Adriatic Sea
Venlo 87 D 5 *prev.* Venloo. SE Netherlands
Venloo *see* Venlo
Venta 106 B 3 *Ger.* Windau. River, Latvia/Lithuania
Ventimiglia 96 A 3 NW Italy
Ventspils 106 B 2 *Ger.* Windau. NW Latvia
Ventura 47 C 7 California, W USA
Vera 64 D 3 NE Argentina
Veracruz 51 F 4 *var.* Veracruz Llave. E Mexico
Veracruz Llave *see* Veracruz
Vercellae *see* Vercelli
Vercelli 96 A 2 *anc.* Vercellae. NW Italy
Verdalsøra 84 B 4 C Norway
Verde, Costa 92 D 1 coastal region, N Spain
Verden 94 B 3 NW Germany
Verkhnedvinsk *see* Vyerkhnyadzvinsk
Verkhneudinsk *see* Ulan-Ude
Verkhoyanskiy Khrebet 115 F 3 mountain range, E Russian Federation
Vermillion 45 F 3 South Dakota, N USA
Vermont 41 F 2 *off.* State of Vermont; nickname Green Mountain State. State, NE USA
Vernal 44 B 4 Utah, W USA
Vernon 49 F 2 Texas, S USA
Vero Beach 43 F 4 Florida, SE USA
Véroia 104 B 4 *var.* Veria, Vérroia, *Turk.* Karaferiye. N Greece
Verona 96 B 2 NE Italy
Versailles 90 C 3 N France
Verulamium *see* St Albans
Verviers 87 D 6 E Belgium
Veselinovo 104 E 2 E Bulgaria
Vesoul 90 D 4 *anc.* Vesulium, Vesulum. E France
Vesterålen 84 B 2 island group, N Norway
Vestfjorden 84 C 3 fjord, E Norwegian Sea
Vestmannaeyjar 83 E 5 S Iceland
Vesuna *see* Périgueux
Vesuvio 97 D 5 *Eng.* Vesuvius. Volcano, S Italy
Vesuvius *see* Vesuvio
Veszprém 99 C 7 *Ger.* Veszprim. W Hungary
Veszprim *see* Veszprém
Vetrino 104 E 2 NE Bulgaria
Vetrino *see* Vyetryna
Veurne 87 A 5 *var.* Furnes. W Belgium
Vexiö *see* Växjö
Vhuru Peak *see* Kilimanjaro
Viacha 61 F 4 W Bolivia
Viana do Castelo 92 B 2 *var.* Viana de Castelo; *anc.* Velobriga. NW Portugal
Vianden 87 D 7 NE Luxembourg
Vianen 86 C 4 C Netherlands
Viangchan 136 D 4 *Eng./Fr.* Vientiane. Country capital, C Laos
Viangphoukha 136 C 3 *var.* Vieng Pou Kha. NW Laos
Viareggio 96 B 3 C Italy
Viborg 85 A 7 NW Denmark
Vic 93 G 2 *var.* Vich; *anc.* Ausa, Vicus Ausonensis. NE Spain
Vicentia *see* Vicenza
Vicenza 96 C 2 *anc.* Vicentia. NE Italy
Vichy 91 C 5 C France
Victor Harbor 149 B 7 South Australia, S Australia
Victoria 36 D 5 province capital, Vancouver Island, SW Canada
Victoria 65 B 5 C Chile
Victoria 49 G 4 Texas, S USA
Victoria 149 B 7 state, SE Australia
Victoria 146 D 3 river, Western Australia, N Australia
Victoria 79 H 1 country capital, NE Seychelles
Victoria de Durango *see* Durango
Victoria de las Tunas *see* Las Tunas
Victoria Falls 78 C 3 W Zimbabwe
Victoria Falls 78 C 3 waterfall, Zambia/Zimbabwe
Victoria Harbour 128 A 1 harbour, S Hong Kong
Victoria Island 37 F 3 island, NW Canada
Victoria, Lake 73 B 6 *var.* Victoria Nyanza. Lake, NE Africa
Victoria Land 154 C 4 physical region, Antarctica
Victoria Nyanza *see* Victoria, Lake
Victoria Peak 128 A 2 mountain, S Hong Kong
Victorville 47 C 7 California, W USA
Vicus Elbii *see* Viterbo
Vidalia 43 E 2 Georgia, SE USA
Vidin 104 B 1 *anc.* Bononia. NW Bulgaria
Vidzeme 106 C 3 *Eng.* Livonia. Cultural region, NE Latvia
Vidzy 107 C 5 NW Belorussia
Viedma 65 C 5 E Argentina
Vieng Pou Kha *see* Viangphoukha
Vienna *see* Vienne
Vienna *see* Wien
Vienne 91 D 5 *anc.* Vienna. E France
Vienne 91 B 5 river, W France
Vientiane *see* Viangchan
Vierwaldstätter See 95 B 7 *Eng.* Lake of Lucerne. Lake, C Switzerland
Vierzon 90 C 4 C France
Viesíte 106 C 4 *var.* Viesīte, *Ger.* Eckengraf. S Latvia

Vietnam
136 D 4 *Vtn.* Công Hoa Xa Hôi Chu Nghia Viêt Nam, Công Hôa Xã Hôi Chu Nghĩa Viêt Nam. Republic, SE Asia

Official name: Socialist Republic of Viet-Nam **Date of formation:** 1976 **Capital:** Hanoi **Population:** 76.2 million **Total Area:** 329,560 sq km (127,243 sq miles) **Languages:** Vietnamese* **Religions:** Buddhist 55%, Roman Catholic 7%, Muslim 1%, other 37% **Ethnic mix:** Vietnamese 88%, Chinese 4%, Thai 2%, other 6% **Government:** Single-party republic **Currency:** Dong = 10 hao = 100 xu

Viêt Tri 136 D 3 *var.* Vietri. N Vietnam
Vieux Fort 55 F 2 S Saint Lucia
Vigo 92 B 2 NW Spain
Viipuri *see* Vyborg
Vijayawāda 132 D 1 *prev.* Bezwada. SE India
Vila *see* Port-Vila
Vila de Mocímboa da Praia *see* Mocímboa da Praia
Vila do Conde 92 B 2 NW Portugal
Vila do Zumbo 78 D 2 *prev.* Vila do Zumbu, Zumbo . NW Mozambique
Vilafranca del Penedès 93 F 2 *var.* Villafranca del Panadés. NE Spain
Viļaka 106 D 4 *Ger.* Marienhausen. NE Latvia
Vilalba 92 C 1 NW Spain
Vila Nova de Gaia 92 B 2 NW Portugal
Vila Nova de Portimão *see* Portimão
Vila Real 92 B 2 *var.* Vila Rial. N Portugal
Vila-real de los Infantes 93 F 3 *var.* Villarreal. E Spain
Vila Rial *see* Vila Real
Vilhelmina 84 C 4 N Sweden
Vilhena 62 D 3 W Brazil
Vília 105 C 5 C Greece
Viljandi 106 D 2 *Ger.* Fellin. S Estonia
Vilkaviškis 106 B 4 *Pol.* Wyłkowyszki. SW Lithuania

Villa Acuña *see* Ciudad Acuña
Villacarrillo 93 E 4 S Spain
Villa Cecilia *see* Ciudad Madero
Villach 95 D 7 *Slvn.* Beljak. S Austria
Villacidro 97 A 5 W Italy
Villa Concepción *see* Concepción
Villa del Pilar *see* Pilar
Villafranca de los Barros 92 C 4 W Spain
Villafranca del Panadés *see* Vilafranca del Penedès
Villahermosa 51 G 4 *prev.* San Juan Bautista. SE Mexico
Villajoyosa 93 F 4 *var.* La Vila Jojosa. E Spain
Villalcampo, Embalse de 92 C 2 reservoir, NW Spain
Villa María 64 C 4 C Argentina
Villa Martín 61 F 5 SW Bolivia
Villanueva 50 D 4 C Mexico
Villanueva de la Serena 92 C 4 W Spain
Villanueva de los Infantes 93 E 4 C Spain
Villa Ojo de Agua 64 C 3 Argentina
Villarreal *see* Vila-real de los Infantes
Villarrica 64 D 2 SE Paraguay
Villavicencio 58 B 3 C Colombia
Villaviciosa 92 D 1 N Spain
Villazón 61 G 5 S Bolivia
Villena 93 E 4 E Spain
Villeneuve d'Ascq 90 D 2 NE France
Villeurbanne 91 D 5 E France
Villingen-Schwenningen 95 B 6 S Germany
Villmanstrand *see* Lappeenranta
Vilnius 107 C 5 *Ger.* Wilna, *Pol.* Wilno; *prev. Rus.* Vilna. Country capital, SE Lithuania
Vil'shanka 109 E 3 *Rus.* Olshanka. C Ukraine
Vilvoorde 87 C 6 *Fr.* Vilvorde. C Belgium
Vilvorde *see* Vilvoorde
Vilyeyka 107 C 5 *Pol.* Wilejka, *Rus.* Vileyka. NW Belorussia
Vilyuy 115 F 3 river, C Russian Federation
Viña del Mar 64 B 4 C Chile
Vinaròs 93 F 3 E Spain
Vincennes 40 B 4 Indiana, N USA
Vindhya Mountains *see* Vindhya Range
Vindhya Range 134 D 4 *var.* Vindhya Mountains. Mountain range, N India
Vineland 41 F 4 Delaware, NE USA
Vinh 136 D 4 NE Vietnam
Vinh Loi *see* Bac Liêu
Vinishte 104 B 2 *var.* Vinište. NW Bulgaria
Vinište *see* Vinishte
Vinita 49 G 1 Oklahoma, C USA
Vinkovci 100 C 3 *Ger.* Winkowitz, *Hung.* Vinkovcze. E Croatia
Vinnitsa *see* Vinnytsya
Vinnytsya 108 D 2 *Rus.* Vinnitsa. C Ukraine
Vinson Massif 154 B 3 mountain, Antarctica
Viranşehir 117 E 4 SE Turkey
Virginia 41 E 5 *off.* Commonwealth of Virginia; *nicknames* Old Dominion, Mother of Presidents, Mother of States. State, E USA
Virginia 45 G 1 Minnesota, N USA
Virginia Beach 41 F 5 Virginia, NE USA
Virgin Islands 55 F 3 *var.* Virgin Islands of the United States; *prev.* Danish West Indies. US unincorporated territory, E Caribbean Sea
Virgin Islands *see* British Virgin Islands
Virôchey 137 E 5 NE Cambodia
Virovitica 100 C 2 *Ger.* Virovititz, *Hung.* Verőcze; *prev. Ger.* Werowitz. NE Croatia
Virton 87 D 8 SE Belgium
Virtsu 106 D 2 *Ger.* Werder. W Estonia
Vis 100 B 4 *It.* Lissa; *anc.* Issa. Island, S Croatia
Vis *see* Fish
Visaginas 106 C 4 *prev.* Sniečkus. E Lithuania
Visākhapatnam 132 D 1 SE India
Visalia 47 C 7 California, W USA
Visby 85 C 7 *Ger.* Wisby. SE Sweden
Viscount Melville Sound 37 F 2 *prev.* Melville Sound. Sound, Arctic Ocean
Visé 87 D 6 E Belgium
Viseu 92 C 3 *prev.* Vizeu. N Portugal
Vişeu de Sus 108 B 3 *var.* Vişeul de Sus, *Ger.* Oberwischau, *Hung.* Felsővisó. N Romania
Visoko 100 C 4 C Bosnia & Herzegovina
Vista 47 C 8 California, W USA
Vistula *see* Wisła
Vistula Lagoon 98 C 2 *Ger.* Frisches Haff, *Pol.* Zalew Wiślany, *Rus.* Vislinskiy Zaliv. Lagoon, S Baltic Sea
Vitebsk *see* Vitsyebsk
Viterbo 96 C 4 *anc.* Vicus Elbii. C Italy
Viti Levu 145 E 4 island, C Fiji
Vitim 115 F 4 river, C Russian Federation
Vitória 63 G 4 state capital, SE Brazil
Vitória da Conquista 63 G 3 E Brazil
Vitoria-Gasteiz 93 E 1 *var.* Vitoria, *Eng.* Vittoria. N Spain
Vitré 90 B 3 NW France
Vitsyebsk 107 E 5 *Rus.* Vitebsk. NE Belorussia
Vittoria 97 C 7 SW Italy
Vizeu *see* Viseu
Vizianagaram 132 D 1 *var.* Vizianagram. E India
Vizianagram *see* Vizianagaram
Vjosës, Lumi i 101 C 7 *var.* Vijosa, Vijosë, *Gk.* Aóos. River, Albania/ Greece
Vlaardingen 86 C 4 SW Netherlands
Vladikavkaz 111 B 8 *prev.* Dzaudzhikau, Ordzhonikidze. SW Russian Federation
Vladimir 111 B 5 W Russian Federation
Vladivostok 115 G 5 SE Russian Federation
Vlagtwedde 86 E 2 NE Netherlands
Vlasotince 101 E 5 SE Yugoslavia
Vlieland 86 C 1 *Fris.* Flylân. Island, N Netherlands
Vlijmen 86 C 4 S Netherlands
Vlissingen 87 B 5 *Eng.* Flushing, *Fr.* Flessingue. SW Netherlands
Vlodava *see* Włodawa
Vlorë 101 C 7 *It.* Valona, Vlora; *prev.* Vlonë. SW Albania
Vlorës, Gjiri i 101 C 6 *var.* Valona Bay. S Adriatic Sea
Vlotslavsk *see* Włocławek
Vöcklabruck 95 D 6 NW Austria
Vogel Peak *see* Dimlang
Voiron 91 D 5 E France
Vojvodina 100 D 3 *Ger.* Wojwodina. Cultural region, N Yugoslavia
Volga 111 C 7 river, W Russian Federation
Volgograd 111 B 7 *prev.* Stalingrad, Tsaritsyn. SW Russian Federation
Volkhov 110 B 4 *var.* Volchov, Volnov, NW Russian Federation
Volnovakha 109 G 3 SE Ukraine
Volodymyr-Volyns'kyy 108 C 1 *Pol.* Włodzimierz, *Rus.* Vladimir-Volynskiy. NW Ukraine
Vologda 110 B 4 W Russian Federation
Volokonovka 111 A 6 W Russian Federation
Vólos 105 B 5 C Greece
Vol'sk 111 C 6 W Russian Federation
Volta 75 E 4 river, SE Ghana
Volta, Lake 75 E 4 reservoir, SE Ghana
Volturno 97 D 5 river, S Italy
Volunteer Island *see* Starbuck Island
Volzhsk 111 C 5 W Russian Federation
Volzhskiy 111 B 6 SW Russian Federation
Võnnu 106 E 3 *Ger.* Wendau. SE Estonia
Voorst 86 D 3 E Netherlands
Voranava 107 C 5 *Pol.* Werenów, *Rus.* Voronovo. W Belorussia
Vorderrhein 95 B 7 river, SE Switzerland
Vóreioi Sporádes 105 C 5 *var.* Vórioi Sporádhes, *Eng.* Northern Sporades. Island group, E Greece
Vorkuta 110 E 3 NW Russian Federation
Vormsi 106 D 2 *var.* Vormsi Saar, *Ger.* Worms, *Swe.* Ormsö. Island, W Estonia
Voronezh 111 B 6 W Russian Federation
Voroshilovsk *see* Stavropol'
Vorskla 109 F 2 river, C Ukraine
Võrtsjärv 106 D 3 *Ger.* Wirz-See. Lake, SE Estonia
Võru 106 D 3 *Ger.* Werro. SE Estonia
Vosges 90 E 4 mountain range, NE France
Vostochno-Sibirskoye More 115 G 1 *Eng.* East Siberian Sea. Sea, Arctic Ocean
Vostok 154 C 3 research station, Antarctica
Vostok Island 145 G 3 *var.* Vostock Island; *prev.* Stavers Island. Island, E Kiribati
Voznesens'k 109 E 3 *Rus.* Voznesensk. S Ukraine
Voznesensk *see* Voznesens'k
Vraca *see* Vratsa
Vrangelya, Ostrov 115 G 1 *Eng.* Wrangel Island. Island, NE Russian Federation
Vranje 101 E 5 SE Yugoslavia
Vranov nad Topľou 99 E 5 *var.* Vranov, *Hung.* Varannó. E Slovakia
Vratsa 104 C 2 *var.* Vraca. NW Bulgaria
Vrbas 100 C 3 river, N Bosnia & Herzegovina
Vrbas 100 D 3 N Yugoslavia
Vršac 100 E 3 *Ger.* Werschetz, *Hung.* Versecz. NE Yugoslavia
Vsetín 99 C 5 *Ger.* Wsetin. E Czech Republic
Vučitrn 101 D 5 C Yugoslavia
Vukovar 100 D 3 *Hung.* Vukovár. E Croatia
Vukovár *see* Vukovar
Vulcan 37 E 5 Alberta, SW Canada
Vulcan 108 B 4 *Ger.* Wulkan, *Hung.* Zsilyvajdevulkán; *prev.* Crivadia Vulcanului, Vaidei, *Hung.* Sily-Vajdej, Vajdej. W Romania
Vulcano, Isola 97 C 7 island, S Italy
Vung Tau 137 E 6 *prev. Fr.* Cap Saint-Jacques, *Eng.* Cape Saint Jacques. S Vietnam
Vyatka 111 C 5 *var.* V'atka, Viatka. River, NW Russian Federation
Vyatka *see* Kirov
Vyborg 110 B 3 *Fin.* Viipuri. NW Russian Federation
Vyerkhnyadzvinsk 107 D 5 *Rus.* Verkhnedvinsk. N Belorussia
Vyetryna 107 D 5 *Rus.* Vetrino. N Belorussia
Vynohradiv 108 B 3 *Cz.* Sevluš, *Hung.* Nagyszöllös, *Rus.* Vinogradov; *prev.* Sevlyush. W Ukraine
Vytegra 110 B 4 NW Russian Federation

W

Wa 75 E 4 NW Ghana
Waal 86 D 4 river, S Netherlands
Wabash River 40 B 5 river, NE USA
Waco 49 G 3 Texas, S USA
Waddān 71 F 3 NW Libya
Waddeneilanden 86 C 1 *Eng.* West Frisian Islands. Island group, N Netherlands
Waddenzee 86 C 2 *var.* Wadden Zee, *Eng.* Wadden Sea. Sea, E North Sea
Waddington, Mount 36 D 5 mountain, SW Canada
Wādī as Sīr 119 B 6 *var.* Wadi es Sir. NW Jordan
Wadi es Sir *see* Wādī as Sīr
Wadi Halfa 72 B 3 *var.* Wādī Ḩalfā'. N Sudan
Wādī Ḩalfā' *see* Wadi Halfa
Wādī Mūsā 119 B 7 *var.* Petra. S Jordan
Wad Madanī *see* Wad Medani
Wad Medani 72 C 4 *var.* Wad Madanī. C Sudan
Wagadugu *see* Ouagadougou
Wagga Wagga 149 C 7 New South Wales, SE Australia
Wagin 147 B 7 Western Australia, SW Australia
Wāh 134 C 1 NE Pakistan
Wahai 139 F 4 Pulau Seram, E Indonesia
Wahiawa 47 A 8 *Haw.* Wahiawā. Hawaii, W USA
Wahiawā *see* Wahiawa
Wahpeton 45 F 2 North Dakota, N USA
Waiau 151 C 5 river, South Island, New Zealand
Waigeo, Pulau 139 G 4 island, Maluka, E Indonesia
Waikaremoana, Lake 150 E 4 lake, North Island, E New Zealand
Wailuku 47 B 8 Hawaii, W USA
Waimate 151 B 7 South Island, SW New Zealand

Waiouru 150 D 4 North Island,
C New Zealand
Waipara 151 C 6 South Island,
C New Zealand
Waipawa 150 E 4 North Island,
NE New Zealand
Waipukurau 150 E 4 North Island,
NE New Zealand
Wairau 151 C 5 river, South Island,
C New Zealand
Wairoa 150 D 2 river, North Island,
N New Zealand
Wairoa 150 E 4 North Island,
NE New Zealand
Waitaki 151 B 7 river, South Island,
SW New Zealand
Waitara 150 D 4 North Island,
C New Zealand
Waitzen *see* Vác
Waiuku 150 D 3 North Island,
N New Zealand
Wakasa-wan 131 C 6 bay,
SE Sea of Japan
Wakatipu, Lake 151 A 7 lake,
South Island, SW New Zealand
Wakayama 131 C 6 Honshū,
SW Japan
Wake Island 142 D 1 US
unincorporated territory,
W Pacific Ocean
Wakkanai 130 C 1 Hokkaidō,
NE Japan
Wałbrzych 98 B 4 *Ger.* Waldenburg,
Waldenburg in Schlesien.
SW Poland
Walcourt 87 C 7 S Belgium
Wałcz 98 B 3 *Ger.* Deutsch Krone.
NW Poland
Wales 89 C 6 *Wel.* Cymru.
National region, UK
Wales 36 C 2 Alaska, NW USA
Walgett 149 D 5 New South Wales,
SE Australia
Walk *see* Valka
Walker Lake 47 C 6 lake, Nevada,
W USA
Wallaby Island 148 C 2 island,
Queensland, N Australia
Wallachia 108 B 5 *var.* Walachia,
Ger. Walachei, *Rom.* Valachia.
Cultural region, S Romania
Wallal Downs 146 B 3 W Australia
Walla Walla 46 C 2
Washington, NW USA
Wallis & Futuna 145 F 4
Fr. Territoire de Wallis et Futuna.
French overseas territory,
S Pacific Ocean
Wallis et Futuna, Territoire de *see*
Wallis and Futuna
Walnut Ridge 42 B 1
Arkansas, C USA
Walvisbaai *see* Walvis Bay
Walvis Bay 78 B 4 *Afr.* Walvisbaai.
W Namibia
Walvis Bay 78 B 4 bay,
W Atlantic Ocean
Walvish Ridge *see* Walvis Ridge
Walvis Ridge 67 D 6 *var.* Walvish
Ridge. Undersea ridge,
E Atlantic Ocean
Wanaka 151 B 7 South Island,
SW New Zealand
Wanaka, Lake 151 B 6 lake,
South Island, SW New Zealand
Wandel Sea 83 F 1 sea,
Arctic Ocean
Wanganui 150 D 4 North Island,
C New Zealand
Wangaratta 149 C 7 Victoria,
SE Australia
Wankie *see* Hwange

Wanlaweyn 73 D 6 *var.* Wanle
Weyn, *It.* Uanle Uen. SW Somalia
Wanxian 129 B 5 C China
Warburg 94 B 4 W Germany
Ware 37 E 4 British Columbia,
W Canada
Waremme 87 C 6 E Belgium
Waren 94 C 3 NE Germany
Wargla *see* Ouargla
Warnemünde 94 C 2 NE Germany
Warnes 61 G 4 C Bolivia
Warrego 149 D 5 river,
New South Wales/Queensland,
E Australia
Warrego Range 148 D 4 mountain
range, E Australia
Warren 40 D 4 Ohio, N USA
Warren 40 D 3 Michigan, N USA
Warri 75 F 5 S Nigeria
Warrnambool 149 B 7 Victoria,
SE Australia
Warsaw *see* Warszawa
Warszawa 98 D 3 *Eng.* Warsaw,
Ger. Warschau, *Rus.* Varshava.
Country capital, C Poland
Warta 98 C 4 *Ger.* Warthe. River,
W Poland
Warthe *see* Warta
Warwick 149 D 5 Queensland,
E Australia
Washington 40 D 4 Pennsylvania,
NE USA
Washington 46 B 2 *off.* State of
Washington; *nicknames* Chinook
State, Evergreen State. State,
NW USA
Washington D.C. 41 E 4 country
capital, District of Columbia,
NE USA
Washington Island *see* Teraina
Washington Land 82 D 1 physical
region, NW Greenland
Wash, The 89 E 6 inlet,
SW North Sea
Waspam 53 E 2 *var.* Waspán.
NE Nicaragua
Waspán *see* Waspam
Watampone 139 E 4 *var.* Bone.
Sulawesi, C Indonesia
Watenstedt-Salzgitter *see* Salzgitter
Waterbury 41 G 3
Connecticut, NE USA
Waterford 89 B 6 *Ir.* Port Láirge.
S Ireland
Waterloo 45 G 3 Iowa, C USA
Watertown 41 F 2 New York,
NE USA
Watertown 45 E 2
South Dakota, N USA
Waterville 41 G 2 Maine, NE USA
Watford 89 E 7 SE England, UK
Watlings Island *see* San Salvador
Watsa 77 E 5 NE Congo (Zaire)
Watsonville 47 B 6
California, W USA
Wau 73 B 5 *var.* Wáw. S Sudan
Waukegan 40 B 3 Illinois, N USA
Waukesha 40 B 3 Wisconsin, N USA
Wausau 40 B 2 Wisconsin, N USA
Wave Hill 146 E 3 N Australia
Waverly 45 G 3 Iowa, C USA
Wavre 87 C 6 C Belgium
Wáw *see* Wau
Wawa 38 C 4 Ontario, S Canada
Waycross 43 E 3 Georgia, SE USA
Wearmouth *see* Sunderland
Weatherford 49 F 1
Oklahoma, C USA
Webster City 45 F 3 Iowa, C USA
Weddell Plain 154 A 2 abyssal
plain, SW Atlantic Ocean

Weddell Sea 154 B 2 sea,
SW Atlantic Ocean
Weener 94 A 3 NW Germany
Weert 87 D 5 SE Netherlands
Weesp 86 C 3 C Netherlands
Węgorzewo 98 D 2 *Ger.* Angerburg.
NE Poland
Weimar 94 C 4 C Germany
Weissenburg 95 C 6 SE Germany
Weissenstein *see* Paide
Wejherowo 98 C 2 NW Poland
Welchman Hall 55 G 1 C Barbados
Weldiya 72 C 4 *var.* Waldia,
It. Valdia. N Ethiopia
Welkom 78 D 4 C South Africa
Welle *see* Uele
Wellesley Islands 148 B 2 island
group, N Australia
Wellington 151 D 5 country capital,
North Island, C New Zealand
Wellington 45 F 5 Kansas, C USA
Wellington *see* Wellington, Isla
Wellington, Isla 65 B 7
var. Wellington. Island, S Chile
Wellsford 150 D 2 North Island,
N New Zealand
Wells, Lake 147 C 5 lake, Western
Australia, C Australia
Wels 95 D 6 *anc.* Ovilava. N Austria
Wemmel 87 B 6 C Belgium
Wenatchee 46 C 2 Washington,
NW USA
Wenchi 75 E 4 W Ghana
Wen-chou *see* Wenzhou
Wendau *see* Võnnu
Wenden *see* Cēsis
Wenmen Island *see* Wolf, Isla
Wentworth 149 B 6 New South
Wales, SE Australia
Wenzhou 129 D 5 *var.* Wen-chou.
E China
Werda 78 C 4 S Botswana
Werder *see* Virtsu
Werkendam 86 C 4 S Netherlands
Werro *see* Võru
Wesenberg *see* Rakvere
Wessel Islands 148 B 1 island
group, N Australia
West Antarctica *see*
Lesser Antarctica
West Australian Basin *see* Wharton
Basin
West Bank 119 D 6 disputed region,
SW Asia
West Bend 40 B 3
Wisconsin, N USA
West Bengal 135 F 4 state, NE India
West Caroline Basin 152 B 3
undersea basin, SW Pacific Ocean
West Caroline Islands 144 B 2
island group, C Micronesia
West Des Moines 45 F 4
Iowa, C USA
Westerland 94 B 2 N Germany
Western Australia 146 C 4 state,
W Australia
Western Carpathians *see*
Carpaţii Occidentali
Western Dvina 106 D 4
Bel. Dzvina, *Ger.* Düna,
Latv. Daugava, *Rus.* Zapadnaya
Dvina. River, Asia/Europe
Western Ghats 132 B 1 mountain
range, SW India
Western Isles *see* Outer Hebrides
Western Punjab *see* Punjab
Western Sahara 70 B 4 territory of
NW Africa, occupied by Morocco
from 1976
Western Samoa *see* Samoa
Western Sayans *see* Zapadnyy Sayan

Western Sierra Madre *see*
Madre Occidental, Sierra
Westerschelde 87 B 5 *Eng.* Western
Scheldt; *prev.* Honte. Channel,
S North Sea
Westerville 40 C 4 Ohio, N USA
West European Basin 66 C 3
undersea basin,
N Atlantic Ocean
Westfalen 94 A 4 cultural region,
W Germany
West Falkland 65 C 7 *var.*
Gran Malvina. Island,
W Falkland Islands
West Fargo 45 F 2
North Dakota, N USA
West Frisian Islands *see*
Waddeneilanden
West Indies 66 A 4 island group,
W Atlantic Ocean
Westliche Morava *see*
Zapadna Morava
Weston-super-Mare 89 D 7
SW England, UK
West Palm Beach 43 F 5
Florida, SE USA
Westport 151 C 5 South Island,
C New Zealand
West Punjab *see* Punjab
West Siberian Plain *see* Zapadno-
Sibirskaya Ravnina
West Virginia 40 D 4 *off.*
State of West Virginia;
nickname Mountain State.
State, E USA
Wetar, Pulau 138 D 5 island,
E Indonesia
Wetzlar 95 B 5 W Germany
Wevok 36 C 2 *var.* Wewuk.
Alaska, NW USA
Wewuk *see* Wevok
Wexford 89 B 6 *Ir.* Loch Garman.
SE Ireland
Weyburn 37 F 5 Saskatchewan,
S Canada
Weymouth 89 D 7 S England, UK
Weymouth 41 G 3
Massachusetts, NE USA
Weymouth, Cape 148 C 2 headland,
Queensland, NE Australia
Wezep 86 D 3 E Netherlands
Whakatane 150 E 3 North Island,
NE New Zealand
Whale Cove 37 G 4 Northwest
Territories, C Canada
Whangarei 150 D 2 North Island,
N New Zealand
Wharton Basin 141 D 5 *var.* West
Australian Basin. Undersea basin,
E Indian Ocean
Whataroa 151 B 6 South Island,
SW New Zealand
Wheatland 44 D 3
Wyoming, C USA
Wheeling 40 D 4
West Virginia, NE USA
Whitby 89 D 5 N England, UK
Whitefish 44 B 1 Montana,
NW USA
Whitehaven 89 C 5
NW England, UK
Whitehorse 36 D 4 territory capital,
Yukon Territory, W Canada
White Lake 42 A 3 lake,
Louisiana, S USA
White Mountains 41 G 2
mountain range, NE USA
White Nile 72 B 4 *Ar.* Al Baḥr
al Abyaḍ, An Nil al Abyaḍ,
Bahr el Jebel. River, SE Sudan
White River 44 D 3 river,
South Dakota, N USA

White Sea *see* Beloye More
White Volta 75 E 4 *var.* Nakambé, *Fr.* Volta Blanche. River, Burkina/Ghana
Whitewater Bay 43 E 5 bay, Florida, SE Gulf of Mexico
Whitianga 150 D 2 North Island, N New Zealand
Whitney, Mount 47 C 6 mountain, California, W USA
Whitsunday Island 148 D 3 island, Queensland, E Australia
Whyalla 149 A 6 South Australia, S Australia
Wichita 45 F 5 Kansas, C USA
Wichita Falls 49 F 2 Texas, S USA
Wichita River 49 F 2 river, Texas, S USA
Wicklow Mountains 89 B 6 *Ir.* Sléibhte Chill Mhantáin. Mountain range, E Ireland
Wiehl 94 A 4 W Germany
Wieliczka 99 D 5 S Poland
Wieluń 98 C 4 C Poland
Wien 95 E 6 *Eng.* Vienna, *Hung.* Bécs, *Slvk.* Vídeŏ, *Slvn.* Dunaj; *anc.* Vindobna, Vindobona. Country capital, NE Austria
Wiener Neustadt 95 E 6 E Austria
Wierden 86 E 3 E Netherlands
Wiesbaden 95 B 5 W Germany
Wight, Isle of 89 D 7 island, S England, UK
Wigorna Ceaster *see* Worcester
Wijchen 86 D 4 SE Netherlands
Wijk bij Duurstede 86 D 4 C Netherlands
Wilberforce, Cape 148 B 1 headland, Northern Territory, N Australia
Wilcannia 149 C 6 New South Wales, SE Australia
Wilhelm, Mount 144 B 3 mountain, New Guinea, C Papua New Guinea
Wilhelm-Pieck-Stadt *see* Guben
Wilhelmshaven 94 B 3 NW Germany
Wilkes Barre 41 F 3 Pennsylvania, NE USA
Wilkes Fracture Zone 153 F 3 fracture zone, E Pacific Ocean
Wilkes Land 154 D 4 physical region, Antarctica
Wilkes Rise *see* Wilkes Guyot
Wiłkomierz *see* Ukmergė
Willebroek 87 C 5 C Belgium
Willemstad 55 E 5 dependent territory capital, C Netherlands Antilles
Willeroo 146 E 2 N Australia
Williston 44 D 1 North Dakota, N USA
Wilmington 43 F 2 North Carolina, SE USA
Wilmington 41 F 4 Delaware, NE USA
Wilrijk 87 C 5 N Belgium
Winchester 89 D 7 *hist.* Wintanceaster, *Lat.* Venta Belgarum. S England, UK
Winchester 41 E 4 Virginia, NE USA
Windau *see* Venta
Windau *see* Ventspils
Windhoek 78 B 3 *Ger.* Windhuk. Country capital, C Namibia
Windhuk *see* Windhoek
Windsor 89 D 7 S England, UK
Windsor 38 C 5 Ontario, S Canada
Windsor 41 G 3 Connecticut, NE USA
Windward Islands 55 H 4 island group, SE Caribbean Sea
Windward Islands *see* Barlavento, Ilhas de
Windward Passage 54 D 3 *Sp.* Paso de los Vientos. Channel, N Caribbean Sea
Winisk 38 C 2 river, Ontario, S Canada
Winisk 38 C 2 Ontario, C Canada
Winnebago, Lake 40 B 2 lake, Wisconsin, N USA
Winning 146 A 4 W Australia
Winnipeg 37 G 5 province capital, Manitoba, S Canada
Winnipeg, Lake 37 G 5 lake, Manitoba, C Canada
Winnipesaukee, Lake 41 G 2 lake, New Hampshire, NE USA
Winona 45 G 3 Minnesota, N USA
Winschoten 86 E 2 NE Netherlands
Winsen 94 B 3 N Germany
Winslow 48 B 2 Arizona, SW USA
Winston Salem 43 E 1 North Carolina, SE USA
Winsum 86 D 1 NE Netherlands
Winter Haven 43 E 4 Florida, SE USA
Winterswijk 86 E 4 E Netherlands
Winterthur 95 B 7 NE Switzerland
Winton 151 A 7 South Island, SW New Zealand
Winton 148 C 4 Queensland, E Australia
Wirz-See *see* Võrtsjärv
Wisby *see* Visby
Wisconsin 40 A 2 *off.* State of Wisconsin; nickname Badger State. State, N USA
Wisconsin Rapids 40 B 2 Wisconsin, N USA
Wisconsin River 40 B 3 river, Wisconsin, N USA
Wisła 98 D 4 *Eng.* Vistula, *Ger.* Weichsel. River, C Poland
Wismar 94 C 2 N Germany
Wittenberge 94 C 3 N Germany
Wittlich 95 A 5 SW Germany
Wittstock 94 C 3 NE Germany
W.J.van Blommesteinmeer 59 G 3 reservoir, E Surinam
Władysławowo 98 C 2 N Poland
Włocławek 98 C 3 *Ger./Rus.* Vlotslavsk. C Poland
Włodawa 98 E 4 *Rus.* Vlodava. SE Poland
Wodonga 149 C 7 Victoria, SE Australia
Wodzisław Śląski 99 C 5 *Ger.* Loslau. S Poland
Wōjjā *see* Wotje Atoll
Wojwodina *see* Vojvodina
Woking 89 E 7 SE England, UK
Wolf, Isla 60 A 4 *var.* Wenmen Island. Island, Galapagos Islands, E Pacific Ocean
Wolfsburg 94 C 3 N Germany
Wolgast 94 D 2 NE Germany
Wöllan *see* Velenje
Wollaston Lake 37 F 4 Saskatchewan, C Canada
Wollongong 149 D 6 New South Wales, SE Australia
Wolvega 86 D 2 *Fris.* Wolvegea. N Netherlands
Wolvegea *see* Wolvega
Wolverhampton 89 C 6 W England, UK
Wonowon 37 E 4 British Columbia, W Canada
Wônsan 128 E 3 SE North Korea
Woodburn 46 B 3 Oregon, NW USA
Woodland 47 B 5 California, W USA
Woodruff 40 B 2 Wisconsin, N USA
Woods, Lake of the 38 B 3 *Fr.* Lac des Bois. Lake, Canada/USA
Woodville 150 D 4 North Island, C New Zealand
Woodward 49 F 1 Oklahoma, C USA
Wooramel 147 A 5 W Australia
Worb 95 A 7 C Switzerland
Worcester 89 D 6 *hist.* Wigorna Ceaster. W England, UK
Worcester 41 G 3 Massachusetts, NE USA
Worcester 78 C 5 SW South Africa
Workington 89 C 5 NW England, UK
Worland 44 C 3 Wyoming, C USA
Worms 95 B 5 *anc.* Augusta Vangionum, Borbetomagus, Wormatia. SW Germany
Worthington 45 F 3 Minnesota, N USA
Wotje Atoll 144 D 1 *var.* Wōjjā. Island, E Marshall Islands
Woudrichem 86 C 4 S Netherlands
Wrangel Island *see* Vrangelya, Ostrov
Wrangel Plain 155 G 2 abyssal plain, Arctic Ocean
Wreck Reef 148 F 4 reef, W Coral Sea
Wrocław 98 C 4 *Eng./Ger.* Breslau. SW Poland
Września 98 C 3 C Poland
Wsetin *see* Vsetín
Wuday 'ah 121 C 6 S Saudi Arabia
Wuhai 127 E 3 N China
Wuhan 129 C 5 *var.* Han-kou, Han-k'ou, Hanyang, Wuchang, Wu-han; *prev.* Hankow. Province capital, C China
Wuhu 129 D 5 *var.* Wu-na-mu. E China
Wujlān *see* Ujelang Atoll
Wukari 75 G 5 E Nigeria
Wuliang Shan 129 A 6 mountain range, S China
Wu-na-mu *see* Wuhu
Wuppertal 94 A 4 *prev.* Barmen-Elberfeld. W Germany
Würzburg 95 B 5 SW Germany
Wuxi 129 D 5 *var.* Wuhsi, Wu-hsi, Wusih. E China
Wye 89 C 6 *Wel.* Gwy. River, England/Wales, UK
Wyłkowyszki *see* Vilkaviškis
Wyndham 146 D 3 Western Australia, W Australia
Wyoming 40 C 3 Michigan, N USA
Wyoming 44 B 3 *off.* State of Wyoming; nickname Equality State. State, C USA
Wyszków 98 D 3 *Ger.* Probstberg. NE Poland

X

Xaçmaz 117 H 2 *Rus.* Khachmas. N Azerbaijan
Xai-Xai 79 E 4 *prev.* João Belo, Vila de João *Bel.* S Mozambique
Xam Nua 136 D 3 *var.* Sam Neua. NE Laos
Xankändi 117 G 3 *Rus.* Khankendi; *prev.* Stepanakert. SW Azerbaijan
Xánthi 104 C 3 NE Greece
Xátiva 93 F 4 *var.* Jativa; *anc.* Setabis. E Spain
Xiaguan 129 A 6 S China
Xiamen 129 D 6 *var.* Hsia-men; *prev.* Amoy. SE China
Xi'an 128 C 4 *var.* Changan, Hsi-an Sian, Sian, Signan, Siking,Singan, Xian. Province capital, C China
Xiang *see* Hunan
Xianggang *see* Hong Kong
Xiangkhoang 136 D 4 *var.* Xieng Khouang. E Laos
Xiangtan 129 C 5 *var.* Hsiang-t'an, Siangtan. S China
Xianning 129 C 5 E China
Xiao Hinggan Ling 128 E 2 *Eng.* Lesser Khingan Range. Mountain range, NE China
Xichang 129 B 5 C China
Xieng Khouang *see* Pèk
Xieng Ngeun *see* Muong Xiang Ngeun
Xifeng 128 B 4 N China
Xigazê 126 C 5 *var.* Jih-k'a-tse, Shigatse, Xigaze. W China
Xi Jiang 124 D 3 *var.* Hsi Chiang, *Eng.* West River. River, S China
Xilin Hot 127 F 2 *var.* Abagnar Qi. NE China
Xilokastro *see* Xylókastro
Xingu 63 E 2 river, C Brazil
Xingxingxia 126 D 3 C China
Xining 127 E 4 *var.* Hsining, Hsi-ning, Sining. C China
Xinjiang Uygur Zizhiqu 126 B 3 *var.* Sinkiang, Sinkiang Uighur, Sinkiang Uighur Autonomous Region, Xin, Xinjiang. Autonomous region, NW China
Xinpu *see* Lianyungang
Xinxiang 128 C 4 NE China
Xinyang 129 C 5 *var.* Hsin-yang, Sinyang. C China
Xinzo de Limia 92 C 2 NW Spain
Xizang Zizhiqu 126 B 4 *var.* Thibet, Xizang, *Chin.* Sitsang, *Eng.* Tibet. Autonomous region, W China
Xolotlán *see* Managua, Lago de
Xuguit Qi 127 F 1 *var.* Yakeshi. N China
Xuwen 129 C 7 S China
Xuzhou 128 D 4 *var.* Hsu-chou, Suchow, Tongshan; *prev.* T'ung-shan. E China
Xylókastro 105 B 6 *var.* Xilokastro. S Greece

Y

Ya'an 129 B 5 *var.* Yaan. C China
Yaan *see* Ya'an
Yabēlo 73 C 5 S Ethiopia
Yablis 53 E 2 NE Nicaragua
Yablonovyy Khrebet 115 F 4 mountain range, C Russian Federation
Yafran 71 F 2 NW Libya
Yaghan Basin 67 B 7 undersea basin, SE Pacific Ocean
Yagotin *see* Yahotyn
Yahotyn 109 E 2 *Rus.* Yagotin. N Ukraine
Yahualica 50 D 4 SW Mexico
Yakeshi *see* Xuguit Qi
Yakima 46 B 2 Washington, NW USA
Yakima River 46 B 2 river, Washington, NW USA
Yakoruda 104 C 3 SW Bulgaria
Yaku-shima 131 B 8 island, **Ōsumi-shotō, SW Japan**
Yakutat 36 C 4 Alaska, NW USA

Yakutsk 115 F 3 E Russian Federation
Yakymivka 109 F 4 SE Ukraine
Yala 137 C 7 S Thailand
Yalizava 107 D 6 *Rus.* Yelizovo. E Belorussia
Yalong Jiang 129 A 5 river, C China
Yalova 116 B 3 NW Turkey
Yalpug, Ozero *see* Yalpuh, Ozero
Yalpuh, Ozero 108 D 4 *Rus.* Ozero Yalpug. Lake, SW Ukraine
Yalta 109 F 5 S Ukraine
Yalu 125 E 2 *Chin.* Yalu Jiang, *Jap.* Oryokko, *Kor.* Amnok-kang. River, China/North Korea
Yamaguchi 131 B 7 *var.* Yamaguti. Honshū, SW Japan
Yamaguti *see* Yamaguchi
Yamal, Poluostrov 114 D 2 peninsula, N Russian Federation
Yambio 73 B 5 *var.* Yambiyo. S Sudan
Yambiyo *see* Yambio
Yambol 104 D 2 *var.* Jambol, *Turk.* Yanboli. E Bulgaria
Yamdena, Pulau 139 G 5 *prev.* Jamdena. Island, Kepulauan Tanimbar, E Indonesia
Yamoussoukro 74 D 5 country capital, C Ivory Coast
Yana 115 F 2 river, N Russian Federation
Yanaul 111 D 5 W Russian Federation
Yanbu' al Baḩr 121 A 5 W Saudi Arabia
Yangambi 77 D 5 N Congo (Zaire)
Yangchow *see* Yangzhou
Yangiyŭl 123 E 2 *Rus.* Yangiyul'. E Uzbekistan
Yangiyul' *see* Yangiyŭl
Yangon 136 B 4 *var.* Rangoon. Country capital, S Burma
Yangtze 129 B 5 *var.* Chang Jiang, Yangtze Kiang. River, C China
Yangzhou 129 D 5 *var.* Yangchow. NE China
Yankton 45 E 3 South Dakota, N USA
Yantai 128 D 4 *var.* Yan-t'ai; *prev.* Chefoo, Chih-fu. E China
Yaoundé 77 B 5 *var.* Yaunde. Country capital, S Cameroon
Yap 144 A 1 state, W Micronesia
Yapanskoye More *see* Japan, Sea of
Yapen, Pulau 139 G 4 *prev.* Japen. Island, E Indonesia
Yap Trough *see* Yap Trench
Yaqui, Río 50 B 2 river, NW Mexico
Yaransk 111 C 5 *var.* Jaransk. NW Russian Federation
Yarega 110 D 4 *var.* Jarega. NW Russian Federation
Yarkant *see* Shache
Yarmouth 39 F 5 Nova Scotia, SE Canada
Yarmouth *see* Great Yarmouth
Yaroslavl' 110 B 4 *var.* Jaroslavl. W Russian Federation
Yarumal 58 B 2 NW Colombia
Yasyel'da 107 B 7 river, SW Belorussia
Yatsushiro 131 A 7 *var.* Yatusiro. Kyūshū, SW Japan
Yatusiro *see* Yatsushiro
Yaunde *see* Yaoundé
Yavarí 56 B 3 *var.* Javari. River, C Brazil
Yavarí *see* Javari
Yaviza 53 H 5 SE Panama
Yavoriv 108 B 2 *Pol.* Jaworów, *Rus.* Yavorov. NW Ukraine
Yazd 120 D 3 *var.* Yezd. C Iran
Yazd-e Khvāst 120 D 3 C Iran
Yazoo City 42 B 2 Mississippi, S USA
Yding Skovhøj 85 A 7 hill, C Denmark
Ýdra 105 C 6 *var.* Ídhra. S Greece
Ye 137 B 5 SE Burma
Yecheng 126 A 3 *var.* Kargilik. NW China
Yeeda 146 C 3 NW Australia
Yefremov 111 B 5 W Russian Federation
Yei 73 B 5 S Sudan
Yekaterinburg 114 C 3 *prev.* Sverdlovsk. C Russian Federation
Yekaterinodar *see* Krasnodar
Yelets 111 B 5 W Russian Federation
Yelizovo *see* Yalizava
Yell 88 D 1 island, NE Scotland, UK
Yellowknife 37 E 4 territory capital, Northwest Territories, W Canada
Yellow River 124 D 2 river, C China
Yellow River *see* Huang He
Yellow Sea 128 D 4 *Chin.* Huang Hai, *Kor.* Hwang-Hae. Sea, NW Pacific Ocean
Yellowstone River 44 C 2 river, NW USA
Yel'sk 107 C 8 SE Belorussia
Yelwa 75 F 4 W Nigeria
Yemassee 43 E 2 South Carolina, SE USA

Yemen
121 C 7 *Ar.* Al Jumhuriyah al Yamaniyah, Al Yaman. Republic, SW Asia

Official name: Republic of Yemen **Date of formation:** 1990 **Capital:** Sana **Population:** 13 million **Total area:** 527,970 sq km (203,849 sq miles) **Languages:** Arabic* **Religions:** Sunni Muslim 55%, Shi'a Muslim 42%, other 3% **Ethnic mix:** Arab 95%, Afro-Arab 3%, South Asian, African, European 2% **Government:** Multi-party republic **Currency:** Rial (North), Dinar (South) - both are legal currency

---

Yemva 110 D 4 *var.* Železnodorožny, Zeleznodorožnyj; *prev.* Zheleznodorozhnyy. NW Russian Federation
Yenakiyeve 109 G 3 *Rus.* Yenakiyevo; *prev.* Ordzhonikidze, Rykovo. E Ukraine
Yenangyaung 136 A 3 W Burma
Yendi 75 E 4 NE Ghana
Yengisar 126 A 3 NW China
Yenipazar *see* Novi Pazar
Yenisey 114 D 3 river, Mongolia/Russian Federation
Yeovil 89 D 7 S England, UK
Yeppon 148 D 4 Queensland, E Australia
Yerevan 117 G 3 *var.* Erevan, *Eng.* Erivan. Country capital, C Armenia
Yermak 114 C 4 *Kaz.* Ermak. NE Kazakhstan
Yerushalayim *see* Jerusalem
Yeu, Île d' 90 A 4 island, NW France
Yevlakh *see* Yevlax
Yevlax 117 G 2 *Rus.* Yevlakh. C Azerbaijan
Yevpatoriya 109 F 5 S Ukraine
Yezd *see* Yazd
Yezerishche *see* Yezyaryshcha
Yezyaryshcha 107 E 5 *Rus.* Yezerishche. NE Belorussia
Yiannitsá *see* Giannitsá
Yichang 129 C 5 C China
Yıldızeli 116 D 3 N Turkey
Yinchuan 128 B 4 *var.* Yinch'uan, Yin-ch'uan, Yinchwan. Autonomous region capital N China
Yingcheng 128 E 3 C China
Yining 126 B 2 *var.* I-ning, *Uigh.* Gulja, Kuldja. NW China
Yin Shan 127 E 3 mountain range, N China
Yof 74 B 3 W Senegal
Yogyakarta 138 C 5 *prev.* Djokjakarta, Jogjakarta, Jokyakarta. Jawa, C Indonesia
Yokohama 131 D 5 Honshū, S Japan
Yokote 130 D 4 Honshū, C Japan
Yola 75 H 4 E Nigeria
Yonago 131 B 6 Honshū, SW Japan
Yong'an 129 D 6 *var.* Yongan. SE China
Yongan *see* Yong'an
Yonkers 41 F 4 New York, NE USA
Yonne 90 C 4 river, C France
Yopal 58 C 3 *var.* El Yopal. C Colombia
York 89 D 5 *anc.* Eboracum, Eburacum. N England, UK
York 45 E 4 Nebraska, C USA
York, Cape 148 C 1 headland, Queensland, NE Australia
Yorkton 37 F 5 Saskatchewan, S Canada
Yoro 52 C 2 C Honduras
Yoshkar-Ola 111 C 5 W Russian Federation
Youngstown 40 D 4 Ohio, N USA
Ypres *see* Ieper
Yssel *see* IJssel
Yuba City 47 B 5 California, W USA
Yucatán, Canal de *see* Yucatan Channel
Yucatan Channel 54 A 2 *Sp.* Canal de Yucatán. Channel Caribbean Sea/Gulf of Mexico
Yucatan Peninsula *see* Yucatán, Península de
Yucatán, Península de 51 H 4 *Eng.* Yucatan Peninsula. Peninsula, Guatemala/Mexico
Yuci 128 C 4 NE China
Yuen Long 128 A 1 NW Hong Kong
Yueyang 129 C 5 S China

Yugoslavia
100 D 4 *SCr.* Jugoslavija, Savezna Republika Jugoslavija. Federal republic, SE Europe. See also Serbia, Montenegro

Official name: Federal Republic of Yugoslavia **Date of formation:** 1992 **Capital:** Belgrade **Population:** 10.6 million **Total area:** 102,173 sq km (39,449 sq miles) **Languages:** Serbian*, Croatian* **Religions:** Orthodox Catholic 65%, Muslim 19%, other 16% **Ethnic mix:** Serb 63%, Albanian 14%, Montenegrin 6%, other 17% **Government:** Multiparty republic **Currency:** Dinar = 100 para

---

Yukhavichy 107 D 5 *Rus.* Yukhovichi. N Belorussia
Yukhovichi *see* Yukhavichy
Yukon River 36 D 3 river, Canada/USA
Yukon Territory 36 D 3 *var.* Yukon, *Fr.* Territoire du Yukon. Territory, NW Canada
Yulin 129 C 6 S China
Yuma 48 A 2 Arizona, SW USA
Yumen 128 A 3 *var.* Lao-chün-miao, Laojunmiao, Yümen, Yu-men. N China
Yunjinghong *see* Jinghong
Yunnan 129 A 6 *var.* Yun, Yünna, Yun-nan. Province, SW China
Yuruá, Río *see* Juruá
Yushu 126 D 4 C China
Yuty 64 D 3 S Paraguay
Yuzhno-Sakhalinsk 115 H 4 *Jap.* Toyohara; *prev.* Vladimirovka. Ostrov Sakhalin, SE Russian Federation
Yuzhnyy Bug *see* Pivdennyy Buh
Yylanly *see* Il'yaly

Z

Zaandam *see* Zaanstad
Zaanstad 86 C 3 *prev.* Zaandam. C Netherlands
Zabaykal'sk 115 F 5 S Russian Federation
Zabīd 121 B 7 W Yemen
Ząbkowice Śląskie 98 C 4 *var.* Ząbkowice, *Ger.* Frankenstein, Frankenstein in Schlesien. SW Poland
Zábřeh 99 B 5 *Ger.* Hohenstadt. E Czech Republic
Zacapa 52 B 2 E Guatemala
Zacatecas 50 D 3 C Mexico
Zacatepec 51 E 4 S Mexico
Zacháro 105 B 6 *var.* Zakháro. S Greece
Zadar 100 A 3 *It.* Zara; *anc.* Iader. W Croatia
Zadetkyi Kyun 137 B 6 island, S Burma
Zafra 92 C 4 W Spain
Zagazig 72 B 1 *var.* Az Zaqāzīq. N Egypt
Zagreb 100 B 2 *Ger.* Agram, *Hung.* Zágráb. Country capital, N Croatia
Zāgros, Kuhhā-ye 120 C 3 *Eng.* Zagros Mountains. Mountain range, W Iran
Zagros Mountains *see* Zāgros, Kūhhā-ye
Zāhedān 120 E 4 *var.* Zahidan; *prev.* Duzdab. SE Iran
Zaḩlah *see* Zahlé
Zahlé 118 B 4 *var.* Zaḩlah. C Lebanon
Záhony 99 E 6 NE Hungary
Zaire 78 C 1 *prev.* Congo. Province, NW Angola
Zaire *see* Congo (Zaire)
Zaječar 100 E 4 E Yugoslavia
Zakataly *see* Zaqatala
Zākhō 120 B 2 *var.* Zākhū. N Iraq
Zākhū *see* Zākhō
Zákynthos 105 A 6 *var.* Zákinthos, *It.* Zante. Island, W Greece
Zalantun *see* Butha Qi
Zalău 108 B 3 *Ger.* Waltenberg, *Hung.* Zilah; *prev.* Zillenmarkt. NW Romania
Zalim 121 B 5 W Saudi Arabia
Zaliv Syvash *see* Syvash, Zatoka
'Załni Pjašaci *see* Zlatni Pyasŭtsi
Zambesi Canyon *see* Zambezi Canyon

Zambezi 78 D 2 *var.* Zambesi, *Port.* Zambeze. River, S Africa
Zambezi 78 C 2 W Zambia

Zambia
78 C 2 *prev.* Northern Rhodesia. Republic, S Africa

Official name: Republic of Zambia **Date of formation:** 1964 **Capital:** Lusaka **Population:** 8.9 million **Total area:** 752,610 sq km (290,563 sq miles) **Languages:** English*, Bemba, Tonga, Nyanja **Religions:** Christian 63%, 50%, traditional beliefs 35%, other 2% **Ethnic mix:** Bemba 36%, Maravi 18%, Tonga 15%, other 31% **Government:** Multiparty republic **Currency:** Kwacha = 100 ngweee

Zamboanga 139 E 3 *off.* Zamboanga City. Mindanao, S Philippines
Zamboanga City *see* Zamboanga
Zambrów 98 E 3 E Poland
Zamora 92 D 2 NW Spain
Zamora de Hidalgo 50 D 4 SW Mexico
Zamość 98 E 4 *Rus.* Zamostye. SE Poland
Zamostye *see* Zamość
Zanda X 126 A 4 W China
Zanjān 120 C 2 *var.* Zenjan, Zinjan. NW Iran
Zanthus 147 C 6 S Australia
Zanzibar 73 D 7 *Swa.* Unguja. Island, E Tanzania
Zanzibar 73 D 7 E Tanzania
Zaozhuang 128 D 4 *var.* Tsaochuang. E China
Zapadna Morava 100 D 4 *Ger.* Westliche Morava. River, C Yugoslavia
Zapadnaya Dvina 110 A 4 W Russian Federation
Zapadno-Sibirskaya Ravnina 114 D 3 *Eng.* West Siberian Plain. Plain, Kazakhstan/ Russian Federation
Zapadnyy Sayan 114 D 4 *Eng.* Western Sayans. Mountain range, C Russian Federation
Zapala 65 B 5 W Argentina
Zapiola Ridge 67 B 6 undersea ridge, SW Atlantic Ocean
Zapolyarnyy 110 C 2 *var.* Zapol'arnyj, Zapoljarny. NW Russian Federation
Zaporizhzhya 109 G 3 *Rus.* Zaporozh'ye; *prev.* Aleksandrovsk. SE Ukraine
Zapotiltic 50 D 4 SW Mexico
Zaqatala 117 G 2 *Rus.* Zakataly. NW Azerbaijan
Zara 116 D 3 C Turkey
Zarafshan *see* Zarafshon
Zarafshon 122 D 2 *Rus.* Zarafshan. N Uzbekistan
Zarafshon *see* Zeravshan
Zaragoza 93 F 2 *Eng.* Saragossa; *anc.* Caesaraugusta, Salduba NE Spain
Zarand 120 D 3 C Iran
Zaranj 122 D 5 SW Afghanistan
Zarasai 106 C 4 E Lithuania
Zárate 64 D 4 *prev.* General José F.Uriburu. E Argentina
Zarautz 93 E 1 *var.* Zarauz. N Spain
Zarauz *see* Zarautz
Zaraza 59 E 2 N Venezuela
Zarghūn Shahr 122 D 5 SE Afghanistan
Zaria 75 G 4 C Nigeria
Zarós 105 D 8 Kríti, SE Greece
Zarqa *see* Az Zarqā'
Żary 98 B 4 *Ger.* Sorau, Sorau in der Niederlausitz. W Poland
Zaunguzskiye Karakumy 122 C 2 *Turkm.* Üngüz Angyrsyndak Garagum. Desert, N Turkmenistan
Zavertse *see* Zawiercie
Zavet 104 D 1 NE Bulgaria
Zavidovići 100 C 3 N Bosnia & Herzegovina
Zawiercie 98 C 4 *Rus.* Zavertse. S Poland
Zaysan Köl *see* Zaysan, Ozero
Zaysan, Ozero 114 D 5 *Kaz.* Zaysan Köl. Lake, E Kazakhstan
Zayyq *see* Ural
Zbarazh 108 C 2 W Ukraine
Zduńska Wola 98 C 4 C Poland
Zēbāk 123 F 3 NE Afghanistan
Zeebrugge 87 A 5 NW Belgium
Zeewolde 86 D 3 C Netherlands
Zefat 119 B 5 *var.* Safed, *Ar.* Safad. N Israel
Zeila *see* Saylac
Zeist 86 C 4 C Netherlands
Zele 87 B 5 NW Belgium
Zelenoborski *see* Zelenoborskiy
Zelenoborskiy 110 C 2 *var.* Zelenoborski. NW Russian Federation
Zelenodol'sk 111 C 5 W Russian Federation
Zelenograd 111 B 5 W Russian Federation
Zelenogradsk 106 A 4 *var.* Kranz, *Ger.* Cranz. W Russian Federation
Železnodorožny *see* Yemva
Zelle *see* Celle
Zel'va 107 B 6 *Pol.* Zelwa. W Belorussia
Zelwa *see* Zel'va
Zelzate 87 B 5 *var.* Selzaete. NW Belgium
Žemaičių Aukštumas 106 B 3 physical region, W Lithuania
Zemst 87 C 6 C Belgium
Zemun 100 D 3 N Yugoslavia
Zenica 100 C 4 C Bosnia & Herzegovina
Zenta *see* Senta
Žepa 100 C 4 SE Bosnia & Herzegovina
Zeravshan 123 E 3 Taj./Uzb. Zarafshon. River, Tajikistan/Uzbekistan
Zevenaar 86 D 4 SE Netherlands
Zevenbergen 86 C 4 S Netherlands
Zgierz 98 C 4 *Ger.* Neuhof, *Rus.* Zgerzh. C Poland
Zgorzelec 98 B 4 *Ger.* Görlitz. SW Poland
Zhabinka 107 A 6 *Pol.* Żabinka. SW Belorussia
Zhambyl 114 C 5 *prev.* Aulie Ataprev, Auliye-Ata, Džambul, Dzhambul. S Kazakhstan
Zhangaözen *see* Novyy Uzen'
Zhangaqazaly *see* Novokazalinsk
Zhangjiakou 128 C 3 *var.* Changkiakow, Zhang-chia-k'ou, *Eng.* Kalgan; *prev.* Wanchuan. NE China
Zhangzhou 129 D 6 SE China
Zhanjiang 129 C 7 *var.* Chanchiang, Chan-chiang, *Cant.* Tsamkong, *Fr.* Fort-Bayard. S China
Zhaoqing 129 C 6 SE China
Zhdanov *see* Mariupol'
Zhejiang 129 D 5 *var.* Che-chiang, Chekiang, Zhe. Province, E China
Zheleznodoroznyy 106 A 4 *Ger.* Gerdauen. W Russian Federation
Zheleznogorsk 111 A 5 W Russian Federation
Zhëltyye Vody *see* Zhovti Vody
Zhengzhou 128 C 4 *var.* Ch'eng-chou, Chengchow; *prev.* Chenghsien. Province capital, C China
Zhezkazgan 114 C 4 *var.* Džezkazgan, *Kaz.* Zhezqazghan; *prev.* Dzhezkazgan. C Kazakhstan
Zhitkovichi *see* Zhytkavichy
Zhitomir *see* Zhytomyr
Zhmerinka *see* Zhmerynka
Zhmerynka 108 D 2 *Rus.* Zhmerinka. C Ukraine
Zhodino *see* Zhodzina
Zhodzina 107 D 6 *Rus.* Zhodino. C Belorussia
Zhovkva 108 C 2 *Pol.* Żółkiew, Rus.Zholkev, Zholkva; *prev.* Nesterov. NW Ukraine
Zhovti Vody 109 F 3 *Rus.* Zhëltyye Vody. C Ukraine
Zhovtneve 109 E 4 *Rus.* Zhovtnevoye. S Ukraine
Zhovtnevoye *see* Zhovtneve
Zhydachiv 108 C 2 *Pol.* Żydaczów, *Rus.* Zhidachov. NW Ukraine
Zhytkavichy 107 C 7 *Rus.* Zhitkovichi. SE Belorussia
Zhytomyr 108 D 2 *Rus.* Zhitomir. NW Ukraine
Zibo 128 D 4 *var.* Chang-tien, Zhangdian. E China
Zichenau *see* Ciechanów
Zielona Góra 98 B 4 *Ger.* Grünberg, Grünberg in Schlesien, Grüneberg. W Poland
Zierikzee 86 B 4 SW Netherlands
Zigong 129 B 5 *var.* Tzekung. SW China
Ziguinchor 74 B 4 SW Senegal
Žilina 99 C 5 *Ger.* Sillein, *Hung.* Zsolna. NW Slovakia
Zillertaler Alpen 95 C 7 *Eng.* Zillertal Alps, *It.* Alpi Aurine. Mountain range, Austria/Italy

Zimbabwe
78 D 3 *prev.* Rhodesia. Republic, S Africa

Official name: Republic of Zimbabwe **Date of formation:** 1980 **Capital:** Harare **Population:** 10.9 million **Total area:** 390,580 sq km (150,800 sq miles) **Languages:** English*, Shona, Ndebele **Religions:** Syncretic (Christian and traditional beliefs) 50%, Christian 26%, traditional beliefs 24% **Ethnic mix:** Shona 71%, Ndebele 16%, other 11%, White, Asian 2% **Government:** Multiparty republic **Currency:** Zimbabwe $ = 100 cents

Zimnicea 108 C 5 S Romania
Zimovniki 111 B 7 SW Russian Federation
Zinder 75 G 3 S Niger
Zintenhof *see* Sindi
Zipaquirá 58 B 3 C Colombia
Zittau 94 D 4 E Germany
Zlatni Pyasŭtsi 104 E 2 *var.* `Załni Pjašaci. NE Bulgaria
Zlín 99 C 5 *prev.* Gottwaldov. SE Czech Republic
Złotów 98 C 3 NW Poland
Znaim *see* Znojmo
Znamenka *see* Znam"yanka
Znam"yanka 109 E 3 *Rus.* Znamenka. C Ukraine
Żnin 98 C 3 W Poland
Znojmo 99 B 5 *Ger.* Znaim. S Czech Republic
Zoetermeer 86 C 4 W Netherlands
Zolochev *see* Zolochiv
Zolochiv 108 C 2 *Pol.* Złoczów, *Rus.* Zolochev. W Ukraine
Zolochiv 109 G 2 *Rus.* Zolochev. E Ukraine
Zolote 109 H 3 *Rus.* Zolotoye. E Ukraine
Zolotonosha 109 E 2 C Ukraine
Zolotoye *see* Zolote
Zomba 79 E 2 S Malawi
Zombor *see* Sombor
Zongo 77 C 5 N Congo (Zaire)
Zonguldak 116 C 2 NW Turkey
Zonhoven 87 D 6 NE Belgium
Zoppot *see* Sopot
Żory 99 C 5 *var.* Zory, *Ger.* Sohrau. S Poland
Zouar 76 C 1 N Chad
Zouérat 74 C 2 *var.* Zouérate, Zouîrât. N Mauritania
Zrenjanin 100 D 3 *Ger.* Grossbetschkerek, *Hung.* Nagybecskerek; *prev.* Petrovgrad, Veliki Bečkerek. N Yugoslavia
Zsupanya *see* Županja
Zugspitze 95 C 7 mountain, S Germany
Zuid-Beveland 87 B 5 *var.* South Beveland. Island, SW Netherlands
Zuider Zee *see* IJsselmeer
Zuidhorn 86 E 1 NE Netherlands
Zuidlaren 86 E 2 NE Netherlands
Zujevka *see* Zuyevka
Zula 72 D 4 E Eritrea
Zumbo *see* Vila do Zumbo
Zundert 87 C 5 S Netherlands
Zunyi 129 B 5 E China
Županja 100 C 3 *Hung.* Zsupanya. E Croatia
Zürich 95 B 7 *Eng./Fr.* Zurich, *It.* Zurigo. N Switzerland
Zurich, Lake *see* Zürichsee
Zürichsee 95 B 7 *Eng.* Lake Zurich. Lake, NE Switzerland
Zutphen 86 D 3 E Netherlands
Zuwārah 71 F 2 NW Libya
Zuyevka 111 D 5 *var.* Zujevka. NW Russian Federation
Zvenigorodka *see* Zvenyhorodka
Zvenyhorodka 109 E 2 *Rus.* Zvenigorodka. C Ukraine
Zvishavane 78 D 3 *prev.* Shabani. S Zimbabwe
Zvolen 99 C 6 *Ger.* Altsohl, *Hung.* Zólyom. C Slovakia
Zvornik 100 C 4 E Bosnia & Herzegovina
Zwedru 74 D 5 *var.* Tchien. E Liberia
Zwettl 95 E 6 N Austria
Zwevegem 87 A 6 W Belgium
Zwickau 95 C 5 E Germany
Zwiesel 95 D 6 SE Germany
Zwolle 86 D 3 E Netherlands
Zyôetu *see* Jōetsu
Zyryanovsk 114 D 5 E Kazakhstan

MAP FINDER

NORTH & WEST ASIA 112-113

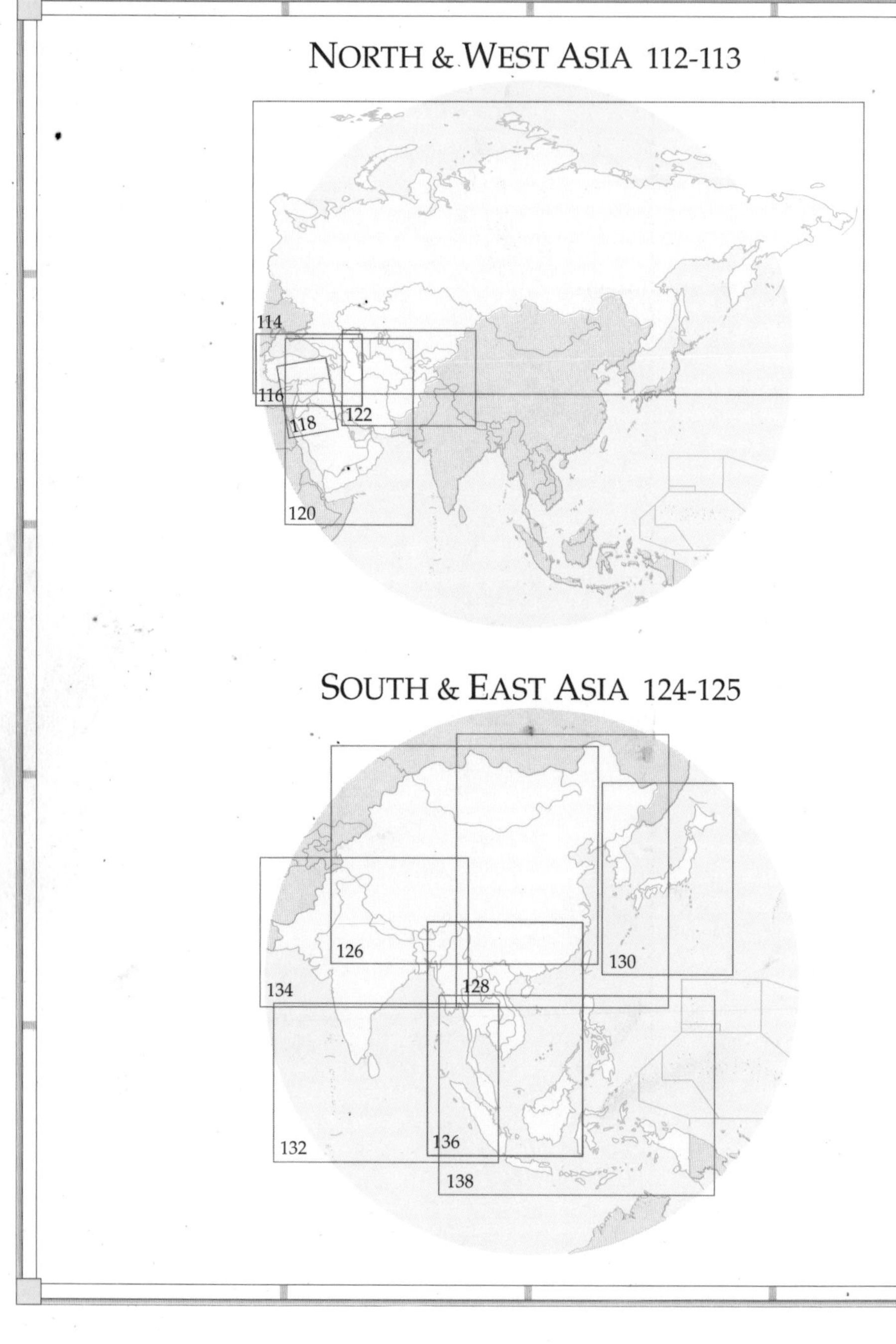

114
116
118
122
120

SOUTH & EAST ASIA 124-125

126
130
134
128
132
136
138